TENNESSEE WILLIAMS: A TRIBUTE

TennesseeWilliams:A Tribute

EDITED BY JAC THARPE

UNIVERSITY PRESS OF MISSISSIPPI

JACKSON

1977

Copyright © 1977 by the
University Press of Mississippi
Manufactured in the United States of America
Printed by Heritage Printers, Inc., Charlotte, North Carolina

THIS VOLUME IS AUTHORIZED
AND SPONSORED BY
THE UNIVERSITY OF SOUTHERN MISSISSIPPI

Library of Congress Cataloging in Publication Data
Main entry under title:

Tennessee Williams : a tribute.

"Authorized and sponsored by the University of
Southern Mississippi, Hattiesburg."
    Bibliography: p.
    Includes index.
    1. Williams, Tennessee, 1911–   —Criticism and
interpretation—Addresses, essays, lectures. I. Tharpe,
Jac. II. Mississippi. University of Southern
Mississippi, Hattiesburg.
PS3545.I5365Z847   812'.5'4   76–52971
ISBN 0–87805–032–9

To
AUBREY K. LUCAS
President, University of Southern Mississippi
for encouragement
both personal and professional

Acknowledgments

for excerpts from Jacob H. Adler, *"Night of the Iguana,* A New Tennessee Williams?" *Ramparts* I (November 1962). Reprinted by permission of *Ramparts.*

for excerpts from Tennessee Williams, *The Glass Menagerie.* Copyright 1945, Random House. Reprinted by permission.

for excerpts from Eugene O'Neill, *Nine Plays by Eugene O'Neill.* Copyright 1932, Random House. Reprinted by permission.

for excerpts from Karl S. Guthke, *Modern Tragicomedy.* Copyright © 1966, Random House, Reprinted by permission.

for excerpts from T. S. Eliot, *Murder in the Cathedral.* Copyright 1935, © 1963. Reprinted by permission of Harcourt Brace Jovanovich, Inc.

for excerpts from Dylan Thomas, *The Poems of Dylan Thomas.* Copyright 1952. Reprinted by permission of New Directions Publishing Corporation.

for excerpts from *Reflections in a Golden Eye* by Carson McCullers, Introduction by Tennessee Williams. Copyright 1941 by Carson Smith Mc-Cullers. Reprinted by permission of New Directions Publishing Corporation for the author.

for excerpts from St.–John Perse, *Anabasis,* trans. by T. S. Eliot, copyright © 1938, 1949 Harcourt Brace Jovanovich. Reprinted by permission.

for excerpts from T. S. Eliot, "Burnt Norton" in *Four Quartets.* Copyright © Harcourt Brace Jovanovich. Reprinted by permission.

for excerpts from "Sailing to Byzantium" from *Collected Poems of William Butler Yeats.* Copyright 1928 by Macmillan Publishing Co., Inc., renewed 1956 by Georgie Yeats.

Contents

ix

Assessment   813

Preface

THE editor is grateful to the many who wrote essays for this collection. The administration of the University of Southern Mississippi has given its usual generous support. William D. Mc-Cain, President Emeritus of the University, at once approved the project, and President Aubrey K. Lucas added his support immediately. Charles W. Moorman, Vice President for Academic Affairs, recommended the work to both presidents. J. Barney McKee, Director of the University Press of Mississippi, has been consistently helpful and congenial, as have the members of the local Press committee. Wallace Kay of the Honors College has not only granted but also anticipated the editor's numerous requests for help and time.

Among publishers, New Directions has been exemplary in ready cooperation, especially Else Albrecht-Carrié. The permissions department of Random House has been pleasantly responsive to requests for permission to quote from *The Glass Menagerie.*

Bill Barnes, of International Creative Management, extended two or three busy days to reply to telephone calls in arranging for permission to quote from unpublished Williams manuscripts at the University of Texas.

The original plan was to issue a short volume with a minimum of paraphernalia—and that primarily to prevent frustration for the graduate or undergraduate student unfamiliar with the major secondary documents. Both the scope of the material and the publication of volume five of *The Theatre of Tennessee Williams* have gradually made documentation complex and difficult, unfortunately increasing chances for confusion and error. Uniform citation of the first four volumes of *The Theatre* at first simplified much of the documentation, requiring in addition a list of only those works by Williams issued by New Directions in separate, uncollected editions—the poetry, the short stories, most of the short plays and some of the later plays. Both *Confessional*, for example, and the later expansion published as *Small Craft Warnings*, were easily documented, since *Confessional* appeared in *Dragon Country* and *Small Craft Warnings* was published by itself, both volumes still in print.

Some essays were prepared before publication of volume five in April 1976, which contains a third version of *Out Cry* (still in print under that title), published again as *The Two-Character Play* (also still in print with that title), reentitled *The Two-Character Play*. Volume five has a considerably less revised version of *Kingdom of Earth* (now otherwise out of print). Where possible, editing and revision of paraphernalia have adapted to this recent publication, and citations are generally to the five volumes of *The Theatre of Tennessee Williams*, published by New Directions. The volume number is given in the first of a series of quotations and usually dropped from quotations following. Citations from earlier versions of recent plays and from other works by Williams are noted in the text.

The Theatre is inconsistent in use of typeface as well as typography. These matters and a few obvious errors or inconsistencies (use of hyphens, for example) in the collected edition of the plays are silently conformed. Williams' own frequent use of ellipsis points generally accounts for apparent inconsistencies in editing, though ellipsis points have occasionally been used in an attempt at clarity and of course to indicate omissions. To reduce costs of typesetting, italic used in stage directions is uniformly avoided, and parentheses are used instead of brackets. To reduce clutter, even lines of dialogue run into the text have but one set of quotation marks. In general, quotations from either Williams or other sources, when appearing in the same paragraph, are identified only at the last quotation. When citation is clear from the text, the page number may be dropped. Hyphens are intentionally cut wherever possible, not at the expense of clarity, one hopes, and foreign words are not usually italicized.

Since many essays cite the most familiar secondary material on Williams and since a proliferation of repetitive notes adds useless expense to production costs while also increasing the chance for error, citation has been simplified where possible. The bibliography is designed therefore only to supplement abbreviated internal references. A bibliography on Williams would have been a project in itself.

The content of the volume reflects the interests and opinions of the contributors. The editor has encouraged and coordinated but otherwise intruded only in writing the brief introductions to sections of the book. Nothing was rejected by a preconception about studies of Tennessee Williams. A proposed section on Williams and American drama was dropped for lack of material, as was a section dealing with Williams' influence on younger playwrights abroad.

Publication of this collection of studies coincides with a renewal of interest in the work of Tennessee Williams. Professor Gene Phillips, Loyola University of Chicago, is preparing a volume on Williams and the film. Professor Stephen S. Stanton, The University of Michigan, has prepared *Tennessee Williams: A Collection of Critical Essays* for the Spectrum Books series published by Prentice-Hall. By its size alone, *this* huge volume shows appreciation for all of Tennessee Williams' decades of survival.

J. T.

Honors College
University of Southern Mississippi
Hattiesburg, 1977

TENNESSEE WILLIAMS: A TRIBUTE

Introductory

Peggy W. Prenshaw attempts to locate Tennessee Williams within the broad context of what critics have gradually designated as Southern Literature, a body of work somehow distinguished from American Literature yet peculiarly expressive of the American Experience. Within this paradox is the paradoxical world of Williams, an artist strongly aware of the dichotomy between Cavalier and Puritan as well as that between frontier and genteel. One significant result for Williams is an ambivalence toward the past and especially the southern past. Within this setting, an ambivalence toward both sexuality and the role of the artist has produced characters memorable for their struggles. Yet, these figures are frequently entrapped within the artist's paradoxical view and are therefore unable either to reconcile opposing forces in themselves or achieve a vision—aesthetic or religious—encouraging transcendence.

Jacob Adler's essay is the only one in this volume that reprints published material—a combination and revision of the widely known article that first appeared in the *South: Modern Southern Literature in Its Cultural Setting* (edited by Louis D. Rubin and Robert D. Jacobs) and an article on *The Night of the Iguana* published in *Ramparts* (see bibliography). The essay deals with *Summer and Smoke* and several other plays in a juxtaposition of the concepts of culture and power. The discussion of *The Night of the Iguana* suggests the limitations of Williams' achievement. These first two essays are complementary, and both should be compared with the essays in ASSESSMENT, the last section of the collection, and with that by Norman Fedder at the end of TECHNIQUES.

Esther Jackson, whose *Broken World of Tennessee Williams* is one of the most significant studies of the playwright's work, finds in Williams a developing poetic theory based upon the American adaptations of German philosophizing. She also traces the development of Williams' concerns in his dramaturgy—themes and disposition—providing an overview that suggests lines for further investigation beyond the provincial. She feels that Williams' drama reflects and possibly anticipates the changing times. The brief concluding section concisely summarizes the main points of the essay. The notes genuinely supplement the text, with references to Whitman and his German sources.

The Paradoxical Southern World
of Tennessee Williams

PEGGY W. PRENSHAW

IN HIS STUDY of the writers of the twentieth-century South, Hugh Holman has remarked that however one approaches the "southern riddle," he will find at its heart a "union of opposites, a condition of instability, a paradox."[1] Holman, like most critics of southern literature, finds the southern writer's apprehension and engagement of cultural paradox one of the chief causes of the literary renaissance. One thinks here of Faulkner's phrase in his Nobel Prize acceptance speech to explain the subject of his works, "the problems of the human heart in conflict with itself," or Allen Tate's well-known account in "The New Provincialism" of the backward glance that writers took just after World War I, a glance that gave a consciousness of the past separated from, but paradoxically fused with, the present. The cultural paradoxes that shaped the literary imagination of William Faulkner, Robert Penn Warren, Tennessee Williams, and a host of other southern writers have been intricately probed and formulated in such characters as Quentin Compson, Jack Burden, Blanche DuBois. Their South embodies the complex union of opposites cataloged by Holman: "Calm grace and raw hatred. Polished manners and violence. An intense individualism and intense group pressures toward conformity. A reverence to the point of idolatry of self-determining action and a caste and class structure

5

presupposing an aristocratic hierarchy. . . . A region breeding both Thomas Jefferson and John C. Calhoun" (p. 1).

Characters of twentieth-century southern literature yearn for freedom from the past, from suffocating family responsibilities, old mistakes and corruptions, illusions, compromises, mendacity. Americans all, they harbor to some degree the strong impulse to escape history, assert their innocence and declare independence from entanglements that would thwart their individualism. But they finally cannot act on this impulse because as Southerners they sense that self-proclaimed pure motives, magnificent vitality and millenialist faith do not constitute a destiny of liberty and the pursuit of happiness. They have a knowledge "carried to the heart," as the narrator says in Tate's "Ode to the Confederate Dead": confederacies lose, mansions decay, riches turn to rags. More important than their knowing the irony of southern history, however, but perhaps largely because of it, most of the southern protagonists ultimately perceive, or at least portray, the ancient tragic vision of the inescapable consequence of being human. To resist fate, to refuse the responsibility of acting in a time and place to answer another's need, to dismiss compassion, moderation and self-denial and deny the validity of the community's claim—this is to risk an awful freedom that sweeps away the old guideposts for measuring and directing oneself, the old sources of wisdom and contentment. To persist in such radical innocence is a fatal, self-defeating prospect in the view of Faulkner and the Fugitive-Agrarians, who regard an existential freedom as a product of modernity leading rather to solipsism and despair than to exhilarating truth. But alas, even these traditionalists among the writers of the twentieth-century South suggest that the achievement of the classical/Christian vision comes only fitfully. And a character like Quentin Compson of *The Sound and the Fury* not only lives the paradoxes but understands he is doing so. For him *knowing*, not *performing*, his duty is the problem. At the conclusion of *All the King's Men*, Jack Burden moves "out of history into history and the awful responsibility of time," but the question remains whether any clearly defined community exists in which he can enact his moral vision. The young visitor in John Crowe Ransom's "Old Mansion" honors the meaning and the claim for attention symbolized by an aging southern manor resembling Belle Reve. But turned away at the door, he realizes he will never enter the mansion. Even as he stands at its door, he sees—"Emphatically, the old house crumbled."

The dialectic—or exploration of paradox—that formed the core of the southern literary imagination between the world wars was, as Tate has remarked, a fortunate turn in southern letters away from the rhetoric of the nineteenth century with its melodrama and sentimentality. Another Southerner, Cleanth Brooks, has in fact identified paradox as "the language appropriate and inevitable to poetry,"[2] meaning, of course, a language of tension and ambiguity that evokes the complexity of experience in a concrete image. It was perhaps fortuitous that southern writers should share a cultural temper that characteristically values the concrete, particular and anecdotal over the abstract, general and philosophical. One might have expected that such a milieu would have led to a theatrical flowering, since of all the literary arts the theater is preeminently concrete, dependent on dialectic realized in dramatic conflict. Something like the Irish theater might have emerged, but the agrarian South had no comparable theatrical tradition. In fact, only two southern playwrights have established themselves as important writers—Lillian Hellman and Tennessee Williams—and only Williams bids now for a major reputation. Accounts of Tennessee Williams' life leading up to his first Broadway production, that of *The Glass Menagerie* in 1945, have appeared in numerous newspaper and magazine interviews, autobiographical essays, notes to plays, and most recently in the *Memoirs*. In many respects his early years were marked by exactly the cultural paradoxes that Holman describes. His mother, Edwina Dakin Williams, embodied the genteel tradition of the South, a tradition compounded of grace, sensitivity, a love of the beautiful, and, above all else, decorum. The strong religious element characteristic of southern gentility came not only from his mother but also from his beloved Dakin grandparents with whom he lived for his first eight years. His grandfather, who during this time was the Episcopal rector in Columbus, Mississippi, is remembered by Williams for his dignity; his grandmother ("Grand") for her kind loyalty through the years. Williams writes that "all that is not the worst of me surely comes from Grand, except my Williams anger and endurance, if those be virtues. Whatever I have of gentleness in my nature . . . comes from the heart of Grand, as does the ineluctable grace and purity of heart that belong to the other Rose in my life, my sister" (*Memoirs*, pp. 110–11).

The Glass Menagerie, drawn so closely from Williams' own experience, implies much of the charm and virtues of the genteel tradition, but at the same time it exposes the tradition's propensity for artificiality, pretentiousness, and a fragile otherworldliness that is mercilessly—if innocently—exploitative. In the play and in Williams' family, one finds an excessive concern for appearance and a pressure for conformity fused with an aristocratic elitism and romanticized individualism. Williams reports that when Laurette Taylor opened the play in Chicago as Amanda Wingfield, she asked Mrs. Williams, who came backstage after the production, "Well . . . how did you like yourself?" (*Memoirs*, p. 85).

In *Menagerie*, the Wingfield father is absent—he is the telephone man who has fallen in love with long distance. In the Williams family during the playwright's youth, his father Cornelius Coffin (C. C.) was also absent much of the time—he was a traveling salesman, the prototype of Charlie Colton in *The Last of My Solid Gold Watches*. But more important, his way of life—a slam-bang lustiness —counterpointed the genteel tradition, even, one might say, deserted it. Descended from a long line of East Tennessee settlers, he took pride in his eminent ancestors but finally was more loyal to their frontier robustness than to the eminence so much valued by his wife. A successful Mississippi drummer and later an executive in a St. Louis shoe company, he was gregarious, hard-drinking, profane—a sensualist and materialist with sure roots in the old frontier South and in the new. During the family's flush times in St. Louis, however, he suffered "a remarkable misadventure during an all-night poker party" that sounds like a Mike Fink story. Williams describes the incident in the *Memoirs*. "Somebody in the poker game had called Dad a 'son of a bitch' and my father, being of legitimate and distinguished lineage in East Tennessee, had knocked the bastard down and the bastard had scrambled back up and had bit off my father's ear, or at least he had bit off most of the external part of it, and 'C.C.' had been hospitalized for plastic surgery" (p. 8). Later (in *Memoirs*) Williams identifies the poker game and the subsequent "decline and fall of 'Big Daddy'" (p. 36) as the turn in the family's fortunes, specifically as the cause of Rose's loss of a potential husband and the beginning of her mysterious stomach trouble.

By Williams' own account and the evidence of repeated thematic motifs in his work, the conflict between the parents was irresolvable, lifelong, and irresistible as a shaping force on his imagination. Despite the detrimental psychological effect of the difficult early years— and we have much evidence that Williams' childhood was difficult— it was a productive coincidence that the contrarieties of experience, and especially the southern experience, should have been so fully and simply focused in his family. Largely as a result of this influence, I judge, an influence of manifold substantiation, by the way, arising as it did from every level of the playwright's experience—from parents, community, the whole region—Tennessee Williams has perceived and portrayed in his work a world of singular paradox. His characters and themes are built upon paradox. The exciting, sometimes brilliant, characters may oppose one another's values, both of which are arguable and tenable, but they are most affecting when they embody the opposition within themselves. Unlike the classical protagonists of flawed but admirable stature, the Williams protagonist, like most heroes of modern drama, derives from no fixed moral context. His challenge is not, however, the summoning of courage to live in the face of absolute uncertainty and loneliness, but rather in reconciling ancient claims of body and soul, the tensions of which dispose one to lonely separateness.

Perhaps the most striking feature of Williams' world view is his ambivalence of belief—in this he is less like William Faulkner than like Quentin Compson, and surely very different, at least in his early works, from the European Existentialists. He can neither disbelieve nor believe that life has significance, nor can he quite achieve either a classical detachment or a modern irony to deal with the conundrum. There are few Vladimirs or Estragons in the Williams canon and little of an unsparing irony that pities but finally repudiates the vision of Blanche or Alma or Kilroy. Rather, strangers build momentary communities; tenderness like "violets in the mountains" breaks the rocks (II, 527). Nonetheless, Williams and his characters speak repeatedly of life as solitary confinement within one's own skin. He says in his introduction to Carson McCullers' *Reflections in a Golden Eye* that the modern artist is afflicted with a sense of ineffable dread—reminiscent of Kierkegaard, though he does not make the explicit connection. But then he goes on, paradoxically, to explain the dread as "a kind of spiritual intuition of something almost too incredible and shocking to talk about, which underlies the whole so-called thing. It is . . . *mystery*" (p. xv). He might be getting at what Kurtz discovered in the jungle or even what Ahab suspected behind the whiteness of the whale, but the words he chooses suggest rather a Manichean vision, that of an unseeable Force that mercilessly destines man to entrapment by his dual impulses for good and evil.

Although Williams is a contemporary writer who understands and writes much about the modern affliction of meaninglessness, he is in many ways an old-fashioned moralist. He vacillates between opposing dogmas, however, never quite convinced of either Cavalier sensuality or Puritan transcendence. Arthur Ganz, calling him a "desperate moralist," writes: "Williams is passionately committed to the great Romantic dictum inherent in his neo-Lawrentian point of view, that the natural equals the good, that the great natural instincts that well up out of the subconscious depths of men—and particularly the sexual instinct, whatever form it may take—are to be trusted absolutely. But Williams is too strong a moralist, far too permeated with a sense of sin, to be able to accept such an idea with equanimity. However pathetic he may make the martyred homosexual, however seemingly innocent the wandering love-giver, the moral strength that led Williams to punish the guilty Blanche impels him to condemn Brick and Chance."[3]

The uneasy union of opposites characterizes all of Williams' work. When the tensions are perfectly balanced, the equilibrium is intellectually stimulating and aesthetically pleasing. But more often than not the center waffles, mainly, it seems, because Williams lacks the detachment necessary for a controlling vision. Despite the confused action of many of the plays, however, the brilliance of such characters as the Wingfields, Blanche and Stanley, Alma, the Pollitts, Hannah Jelkes and Lawrence Shannon commands attention. With varying intensity they and other Williams characters embody Williams' paradoxical view of life. Three paradoxes appear consistently: the effect of the past on the present, especially that of the southern past, the consequence of human sexuality, and the role of the artist.

As noted, Williams came to write of the southern myth of the plantation aristocracy out of his own experience as a Southerner. In his early *Battle of Angels* (1940), which years later was revised as *Orpheus Descending*, he creates in Sandra (Cassandra) Whiteside a decadent southern belle who can neither regain the assurance and power of her family's past nor give up the effort. Like Faulkner's Temple Drake she represents womanhood defiled, and like Temple of *Requiem for a Nun* she prophesies that the tensions between the old ideal of southern womanhood and the combined actualities of the moment and of the flesh at last exhaust the will. Her moral paralysis anticipates that of Brick Pollitt and Lawrence Shannon. She says to Val Xavier, whose name incidentally is a version of a Williams family name, Sevier, that they both are "things whose license has been revoked in the civilized world." She speaks of her own neuroticism, the result of blood "gone bad from too much interbreeding" (I, 45), and says that she has a guillotine inside her own body. She wears dark glasses to conceal eyes that hold disgusting secrets, but they seem only to enhance her fragile loneliness.

In Sandra, Williams exposes the desiccation of the old tradition. He also pinpoints its source, much as Faulkner does in *Go Down, Moses*. When the later generation is undistracted by plantation building and the ego trip of dynasty making, it finds it is caretaking a corrupt way of life, one that fiercely possesses the land and dispossesses the black laborers who work it. It finds it really has no ethical tradition to guide it, and so is faced with deriving one. Carol Cutrere, Sandra's counterpart in *Orpheus Descending*, explains to Val, who represents a kind of savior figure, her youthful effort to right the injustice she has seen. She was, she says, a "Christ-bitten reformer" who "wrote letters of protest about the gradual massacre of the colored majority in the county" (III, 251). She had put up free clinics with the money inherited from her mother and had protested the execution of Willie McGee—"he was sent to the chair for having improper relations with a white whore." Then she concludes: "I walked barefoot in this burlap sack to deliver a personal protest to the governor of the state. Oh, I suppose it was partly exhibitionism on my part, but it wasn't completely exhibitionism;

there was something else in it, too. You know how far I got? Six miles out of town—hooted, jeered at, even spit on!—every step of the way—and then arrested! Guess what for? Lewd vagrancy! Uh-huh, that was the charge, 'lewd vagrancy,' because they said that potato sack I had on was not a respectable garment. . . . Well, all that was a pretty long time ago, and now I'm not a reformer any more. I'm just a 'lewd vagrant'" (III, 252).

Predictably, she does not find absolution and renewal in her effort to reform the world and so takes refuge in a self-pitying and indulgent sensualism. She is like a Flannery O'Connor character searching for the far country but cut off by pride. Her confession to Val is that of the weary sinner who cannot feel guilt. Accordingly, she concludes that all the past has to teach her is "Live, live, . . . just live" (p. 252), but Williams shows that the simple lesson is clearly inadequate for Carol.

When Williams comes in the same play to portray an alternative to Carol's self-destructiveness, he creates Lady Torrance (Myra in *Battle of Angels*), who is rescued by Val from the barrenness and death represented by her dying husband. With heavy-handed symbolism, Williams suggests in her a Madonna figure—she is like a barren fig tree that at last puts forth fruit, or a Christmas tree hung with ornaments. In an ecstatic annunciation scene she cries out: "I've won, I've won, Mr. Death, I'm going to bear!" (p. 338). But shortly afterward she and Val die at the hands of her husband and a mob of angry townspeople. The potential saviors, Val and Lady, presumably are prevented from enacting their roles of renewal only because of the murderous intolerance of others. But ironically, their solutions, despite an overlay of religious hopefulness, are exactly the same as Carol's—live, procreate. In *Battle of Angels* Sandra says to Myra in the last act: "You've learned what I've learned, that there's nothing on earth . . . but catch at whatever comes near you with both your hands, until your fingers are broken!" (I, 100).

Like Sandra (Carol), Blanche, Alma (*Summer and Smoke* and *Eccentricities of a Nightingale*) and even Laura of *Glass Menagerie* represent the last of the southern ladies. Mothlike, sensitive, and fragile in a way that is ultimately self-destructive, they are portrayed as romantic idealists undone by a graceless and callous age. It is a view echoed by Williams in the *Memoirs*: "Nowadays is, indeed, lit by lightning, a plague has stricken the moths, and Blanche has been 'put away'" (p. 125). The crux of the paradox in the portrait of these characters is their innocence and moral purity. We are to understand that they are betrayed by the mortality that attaches to the flesh and to tradition alike but that salvation lies in a natural and healthful gratification of the flesh. Furthermore, the fastidious discrimination that raises them above the vulgar mass is at once a mark of quality and a harmful pretention. Williams ventures a similar portrait of his sister Rose, whom he exalts, as he does Laura, for her inescapable "difference." On the other hand, he locates the "true seat of Rose's affliction" as that of "a very normal—but highly sexed—girl who was tearing herself apart mentally and physically by those repressions imposed upon her by Miss Edwina's monolithic Puritanism" (*Memoirs*, p. 119). The morbid paradox is that disease is beautiful.

In *Summer and Smoke* when Alma comes to her senses and at last releases her subdued doppelgänger, she realizes her delicacy has "suffocated in smoke from something on fire inside her" (II, 243). To have clung to it would have meant dying "empty-handed," as the Alma of "The Yellow Bird" assuredly did not. But what Alma has at the end of the play is a stranger she has picked up. Her enormous dream is gone, and in its place she has a transitory affair that will be all of "Eternity" she is to know. She has searched for substance to fulfill her dream—or to replace the genteel hollowness of her life— and ends up feeling like a "water-lily on a Chinese lagoon" (p. 255). Jacob H. Adler, who regards *Summer and Smoke* as Williams' most revealing play about the South, calls it "an allegory of the Southern dilemma."[4] He sees Alma as the soul of the South, "daughter of a desiccated religion and of the sort of dementia that causes retreat into childhood" (p. 357). Retreating into the past produces a superficial grace but "a grotesque and childish ugliness" beneath the pleasant surface. The young doctor, John Buchanan, suggests a thoroughly contemporary South, cut off from its past. The violent murder of John's father, says Adler, is the result of these tensions and shows the failure of the South to know itself. "Thus Williams depicts a stale, poetico-idealistic culture, refusing to face reality, yet still partly beautiful; and unable to achieve, or to attract, power, until reality is faced" (p. 358). Adler concludes that the play is ironic in its juxtaposition of culture and power, although he views its ultimate statement as that of a cautious hope for compromise, which he interprets as more desirable than either sterility or violence.

An even more deeply ingrained irony in the portrait of Alma bears directly on Williams' paradoxical view of southern history and the effects of the past on the present. Alma's ancestry is at once Cavalier and Puritan—her mother wears a plumed hat; her father is a preacher. Alma cultivates social graces, romanticizes sex, and in a manner dictated by her genteel code immediately sets out to satisfy her desire for John. The forthright pursuit of self-satisfaction that John urges on her is already present, implicit in her nature. At the same time she admires Gothic cathedrals, has faith in a transcendent principle behind existence, and shows self-righteous assertiveness. Culture and power inhere in both traditions that have produced Alma—and the South. At the end of the play she has not so much tempered beautiful illusion with mundane reality as she has shown herself ignorant of any historical perspective. Although it is uncertain that Williams intended or even recognized the irony of Alma's final action, her decision to take what gratification this earth has to offer—giving little thought to the consequences—is a playback of the South's history. All that is lacking is for her to devise a new myth and ritual to justify her different circumstance.

Another level of the Alma paradox is her dual link with Edenic innocence and civilization's corruption. She sings "The Voice That Breathed O'er Eden" with an effeteness, a moral naïveté, that dissociates her from the ugly world. But her glory is civilization's hard-won humanism—in *Eccentricities of a Nightingale* she dreams of making Glorious Hill, Mississippi, an Athens of the Delta! The realization that innocence, moral purity, is irrecoverable is nowhere implied in Alma's actions. Such a realization would have forestalled her effort to dump her past and start over, and thus to sacrifice the accumulated wisdom of history in hopes of a new main chance. It is John Buchanan, like Hannah Jelkes of *Night of the Iguana*, who discovers what the most insightful of the Faulkner and Warren heroes discover: that a stoic acceptance of the burdens of the past is man's only chance for freedom and for the connectedness that can allay loneliness. In short, they understand the impossibility of commuting between Eden and Athens. This knowledge eludes most

Williams characters from Cassandra Whiteside to Moise. They confuse "savage" and "aristocrat," viewing both as sensualists, which they both may well be, but they then impute to the sensualism an innocence controverted by history. They misunderstand that the nature of the freedom available before and after the Fall is of two radically different kinds. Thus Williams has Val Xavier grow up in a primeval swamp (Eden), discover the ecstasy of sex and the painful agony of separateness, and then with this knowledge ironically achieve a renewed innocence. Even Blanche goes to her end dressed in Della Robbia (Madonna) blue.

Thomas Porter has analyzed A Streetcar Named Desire for the paradoxes contained in the myth of the Old South as it is represented in Blanche.[5] He finds in her characterization an admiration of the tradition perfectly balanced by a rejection of it. The divisions of value and personality that operate within Blanche cause her madness and dissolution. They are divisions that obsessively engage Williams, appearing as we have seen in Cassandra, Laura, Alma and existing in some degree in many other characters—Amanda, Mrs. Stone, Brick Shannon, or more recently, Violet of Small Craft Warnings. Audiences and critics debate whether Blanche's demise is a victory or a defeat, depending largely on their view of Stanley, but in either case they view it as the inevitable passing of an old order. In one important respect, however, Stanley does not really represent an opposition to Blanche. The expense of will that built Belle Reve and the profligacy that lost it are in fact reborn in Stanley's vitality and assertiveness. He has a frontier rawness, to be sure, but that in time can be polished. What is lost on Stanley and to a large degree on Blanche herself is the tragic lesson of Belle Reve: the past has inescapable consequences for the present. Though Blanche tries, she cannot escape her past, either through nights with soldiers at the Flamingo Hotel or in a new start with Mitch. Blanche is most admirable when she turns backward—in her account of her selfless devotion to her dying relatives and in her self-condemnation for her cruelty to her young husband. Past prides—her own and that of a long family line—taint her life, but she earns her dignity in dealing with them (which is a confronting of her reality). Sadly, she does not recognize her moral strength, devalues it, and tries to recover her youth and innocence when she joins Stella. The ambiguities of *Streetcar* make it impossible to determine whether the playwright sees Blanche's crucial flaw as her pretentions and illusions (which would oppose her to Stanley), or sees and wants us to see her failure of moral courage. If the latter, the position of Stanley and Stella is implicitly condemned; if the former, the "Southern myth" is trivialized and made meaningless. But in either case, Blanche DuBois is an immensely human, absorbing character.

In *Cat on a Hot Tin Roof* the grandeur of the plantation myth obviously suffers, but its foundations are more clearly shown than in *Streetcar*. Big Daddy's lusty aggressiveness could be that of any captain of industry. He is the crude but eloquent spokesman for the sensual life, a southern planter whose strength is power, not culture. Like an early settler he has built the plantation out of his magnificent will and "twenty-eight thousand acres of the richest land this side of the valley Nile" (III, 110) and has furnished it with boxcars of "stuff" from Europe's "big auction." Unlike Faulkner's Thomas Sutpen his design is not so much fulfilment of a cultural ideal as gratification of his raw appetite for power and pleasure. He is the spiritual progenitor of daughter-in-law Maggie, who is the sexual life force that can save husband Brick from "moral paralysis," a term Williams uses in a note of explanation about revisions he made in the play. Maggie admires Big Daddy because, she says, he "*is* what he *is*, and he makes no bones about it. He hasn't turned gentleman farmer, he's still a Mississippi redneck, as much of a redneck as he must have been when he was just overseer here" (p. 53). Although she comes from a "well-connected" family, she was poor and knows better than anyone that the elegant refinements of the plantation life depend upon having money.

Brick's despair over discovering his culpability in his friend Skipper's death comes from his feeling of guilt. Obviously, he is foolish to condemn himself for his sexuality, but if one is to consider him in some moral framework, then I judge Brick to be quite right in feeling responsible for his actions, sexual and otherwise. The thematic paradox in this play revolves not around the contemporary replay of the old plantation South—it is unambiguously exposed. What is ironic is that Big Daddy's vitality, untempered by moral compunction, is represented in Maggie as a saving grace, her success to be proved if she can get Brick to bed. The fusion of the natural and the ethical, the sensual and the materialistic, neutralizes the play's moral impulse. But as in *Menagerie* and *Streetcar*, the characters are compelling on the stage, indeed perhaps because they so fully express our culture's tensions, our contradictory yearning for both innocence and material success.

Williams has not often created characters who successfully resolve or learn to live with these tensions. John Buchanan in *Summer and Smoke* reaches an accommodation, but the effect of his moral progress is blunted in his secondary role to Alma. In the earlier characters, particularly in Tom Wingfield and Stella Kowalski, Williams explores the possibility for reconciliation of memory and desire. In *The Glass Menagerie*, which he calls a memory play, Tom searches the farthest reaches of the past's hold on him in his effort to free himself of it. At the end of the play he realizes the futility of his effort to put his family behind, but the knowledge forms no basis for action. In his concluding speech Tom reveals the ceaseless flight that has marked the years since he left home: "I descended the steps of this fire escape for a last time and followed, from then on, in my father's footsteps, attempting to find in motion what was lost in space" (I, 236–37). This perspective on the past is ultimately nostalgic and sentimental. It impels him to painful recollection, but it does not produce the weary and humble acceptance of one who has experienced tragedy. In fact, the play is a good example of the point Kierkegaard makes in his study of ancient and modern drama in *Either/Or*: that in classical tragedy, with its concept of fate, the sorrow is deeper and the pain less, whereas in the modern, the pain is greater and the sorrow less. In the recent *Out Cry*, which in some respects is like a sequel to *Glass Menagerie*, Williams creates an inversion of Tom's strategy of escape in the character of Felice, who never leaves the home that "has turned into a prison" (p. 55). Trapped inside their *Two-Character Play*, he and his sister Clare are as haplessly bound to their destined end as are Rosencrantz and Guildenstern.

Stella Kowalski, more emphatically even than Tom Wingfield, isolates herself from her family and the Belle Reve tradition. In her, as he had done with Myra Torrance, Williams tries to figure a spiritual rejuvenation in a pregnancy. But the fusion glosses the difficulty of redemption, whether ethical or religious.

Perhaps it is with Hannah Jelkes in *Night of the Iguana* that Williams most successfully resolves the problem of the burdensome legacy of the past, the "old order." Like that of John Buchanan, her role is secondary in the play, and we do not see her painful passage from innocence to knowledge except through her reflections. But as Shannon's mentor, she reveals how fully she understands that the past constrains an individual's action, even though the past turns out to be morally ambiguous and tainted with selfishness. In the earlier short story Hannah's background is southern and she is very much a southern lady, a product like Alma of the Puritan and the Cavalier strains. In her, as in so many of his characters, Williams sketches the same portrait of the divided southern mind that historian W. J. Cash has described: "The official moral philosophy of the South moved steadily toward the position of that of the Massachusetts Bay Colony . . . and this . . . coincidentally with the growth of that curious hedonism which was its antithesis. The two streams could and would flow forward side by side, and with a minimum of conflict." Cash goes on to say that the Southerner "succeeded in uniting the two incompatible tendencies in a single person, without ever allowing them to come into open and decisive contention" (pp. 59–60).

Precisely these forces come finally into open conflict in Williams' plays, however, forming in fact the chief contention of most of his work. In *Night of the Iguana* Hannah's internal conflicts have largely taken place before the action begins, but as a veteran who stood her ground and stayed for the battle, she can tutor Shannon in the art of fighting "spooks" and "blue devils," a way of remembrance and endurance. She accepts responsibility for her grandfather, though doing so is a costly sacrifice of independence. She supports herself, making whatever adjustments and compromises are necessary. Her unsparing demands on herself—her self-denial—produce in her a boundless capacity for tenderness and compassion toward others. A not quite emancipated Puritan, she understands and lives by the paradox that to win her freedom she must give up the self. By contrast, Shannon has spent years in a wearying rebellion against the restraints on him—against God, the bishops, the tour company he works for, the ladies on the bus, even the easygoing widow Maxine. Hannah helps him to cut free from his struggle by showing him that the ties to the past and to others cannot be repudiated. Shannon asks: "You mean that I'm stuck here for good? Winding up with the . . . inconsolable widow?" Hannah replies: "We all wind up with something or with someone, and if it's someone instead of just something, we're lucky, perhaps . . . unusually lucky" (IV, 365). She accepts limitations on her freedom and self-gratification more readily than on her delicate but tested idealism, and her acceptance delivers her from moral paralysis and disgust with life. To her own cri de coeur, she turns a pitiless deaf ear; it is a price very few of Williams' characters are able or willing to pay. For Hannah the result is an honorable humanism, which she expresses in the much-quoted line: "Nothing human disgusts me unless it's unkind, violent" (pp. 363–4). Although not many will choose her way, it at least reveals a valid and morally consistent solution to the plight expressed in Esmeralda's prayer in *Camino Real*: "God bless all con men and hustlers and pitch-men who hawk their hearts on the street, all two-time losers who're likely to lose once more, the courtesan who made the mistake of love, . . . the poet who wandered far from his heart's green country. . . . look down with a smile tonight on the last cavaliers, the ones with the rusty armor and soiled white plumes, and . . . oh, sometime and somewhere, let there be something to mean the word *honor* again!" (II, 585–86).

To consider Williams' paradoxical vision of sexuality is really to look only more deeply into his view of the past. In the stories and the plays sex is the repeated metaphor of the ecstatic life fully lived in the present moment, freed of all inheritances—secular or sacred. It thus has the positive and negative attributes of giving man pleasure and delight with little sacrifice of freedom, but of offering no means of transcending the amoral and mortal. Sexuality is transformed into salvation when it is seen as the only fulfilment this life has to offer. Chance Wayne expresses the view early in *Sweet Bird of Youth* to Alexandra del Lago, the aging movie queen: "the great difference between people in this world is not between the rich and the poor or the good and the evil, [but] . . . between the ones that had or have pleasure in love and those that haven't" (IV, 50). But to those sick of this world—its grossness and mutability—sexuality is the unmistakable symptom of rot. By the end of *Sweet Bird* Chance has come to pronounce the limits of the flesh: "Princess, the age of some people can only be calculated by the level of . . . rot in them. And by that measure I'm ancient" (p. 122).

In *Memoirs*, Williams expresses the pleasure and revulsion that have marked his attitude toward sex throughout the plays. For example, he writes of "the deviant satyriasis" which "happily afflicted" him (p. 53) during his early years in New York. An interesting reverse of the stereotyped Puritan (whose piety masks lust), Williams' satyriasis is betrayed by his judgmental streak: "Being a sensual creature—and why do I keep saying creature instead of man?—I will go on doing what I am doing while waiting" (p. 249).

Two early one-acts, *The Purification* and *Auto-Da-Fé*, illustrate very well self-condemnation and guilt that attach to sexuality, especially if anything is thought perverse or abnormal about it. In the first play, a verse drama in the manner of Lorca, Rosalio—son and brother—"purifies" himself in a ritual suicide for the violation of his sister. His love for her had made a normal life impossible, and it ultimately brought on her murder by her husband. Although he feels intense guilt for his actions, Rosalio is nonetheless portrayed as blameless—the innocent victim of "sangre mala." His mother defends him: "His ways are derived of me./I also rode on horseback through the mountains/in August" (p. 39). Similarly, in *Auto-Da-Fé*, Eloi atones for the sinfulness he recognizes in his obsession with some "indecent pictures" he has discovered in his job as a postal clerk. Unable to bring himself to report or burn the pictures, he locks himself in a burning house, thus cleansing the "infection" he has exposed. Realistically, the sin is nothing more than a sexual desire that he labels lust because of the prudish influence of his mother. But in Williams' symbolism Eloi, like Rosalio, serves as scapegoat for the world's corruption by the flesh, and his auto-da-fé is an act of faith and redemption.

To counteract the self-destructive consequences of shame and penance, Williams in some of his works takes the tack of D. H. Lawrence and makes a religion of sex. In *Battle of Angels*, with a heavy overlay of Christian symbolism, Val Xavier becomes the savior who restores to health and hope the frigid, barren and dying. The passion of the flesh and the Passion of Christ merge, and even poor Vee Talbot, the religious fanatic and primitive artist, translates her sexual desire for Val into a mystical anointment. In distorting her carnal impulse by perceiving it as spiritual, she is like a Flannery O'Connor freak in reverse. Of course, the consummate spokesman for the religion of sex is Serafina of *The Rose Tattoo*. To the priest Father De Leo she describes the pure relationship she had with husband Rosario Delle Rose: "I give him the glory. To me the big bed was beautiful like a religion" (II, 342). When she conceives, a rose matching her husband's tattoo appears on her breast as Annunciation. Although Rosario's death stills her passion for a time, the play's action concentrates on the arrival of Alvaro, who returns her to the world of the loving.

Such attainment of grace through sex is hard for Williams to maintain dramatically, though, for it nullifies one of his most affecting conflicts. Furthermore, the insistent religious metaphor paradoxically leads almost inevitably back to the Christian premise of the subjugation of body to spirit. Hence the reflective and sensitive characters never convincingly escape into natural joy. In fact, Williams is most successful in portraying worry-free sex when he spoofs the subject slightly in the comic *Baby Doll*. A perfect innocent, Baby Doll Meighan is, as husband Archie calls her, a U. W. (Useless Woman), except for one thing—her irresistible sexuality. When Vacarro, the operator of the new gin, takes up residence on the front porch, the "faunlike" lover and the nymph commence a breathless chase that leaves Archie and compunction far behind. The whole episode reminds one of a Eula Varner escaping the mechanistic Flem Snopes.

In the case of some characters, a tolerable sense of sinfulness for the acts of the flesh yields a kind of voluptuous suffering—an observation with which Hannah Jelkes needles Shannon: "Who wouldn't like to suffer and atone for the sins of himself and the world if it could be done in a hammock with ropes instead of nails?" (IV, 344). For most of the Williams characters of an artistic and philosophical (or religious) turn of mind, however, the "happy affliction" of carnality is the product of neither will nor chance, and is the source of neither remorse nor delight—but all of these at once. In *Eccentricities of a Nightingale* Williams parodies the Eden story in a serious little allegory of man's earthly circumstance. Alma's Aunt Albertine—wearing a plumed hat—had run away from the rectory with a bigamist, a mechanical genius named Schwarzkopf. They traveled about happily with a display of mechanical marvels, chief of which was Schwarzkopf's beloved masterpiece, a mechanical bird-girl who "smiled and nodded, lifted her arms as if to embrace a lover" (II, 87). Then suddenly one winter they made the mistake of mortgaging the Musée Mécanique to buy a snake. They had heard "Big snakes pay good," but the snake swallowed a blanket and died; and, rather than lose the museum to creditors, Schwarzkopf destroyed it and himself in flames. Albertine, grasping one of his buttons, was dragged from the building alive. " 'Some people,' she said, 'don't even die empty-handed!' " (p. 87).

The museum had been a blissful Eden but bloodless and soulless, and so, in wanting more, they "bought" the snake of phallic power and mortality. The loss of the warm, carefree nest sent one into fatal grief for what was irrecoverable, the other into gratitude for the little reminder of their original joy. Only in a fantasy such as the story "The Yellow Bird" does Williams manage to make the rewards of the sexual life commensurate with its delight. By contrast, in the realistic "Hello from Bertha," the aging prostitute dies "empty-handed" with only her few pathetic memories of her former lover, Charlie.

The fear, the near-fatal grief, that so many of the characters have for their incompleteness, their mortality or waning creative vitality, expresses itself in flight from the thoughtful to the sexual life. To Mrs. Stone the handsome young Romans arrest the "enormous drifting of time and existence" (p. 145). Alexandra del Lago and Flora Goforth can forget they are aging in body and in artistic power, if they can have the "distraction" of lovemaking. But such characters as Chance Wayne and Sebastian Venable, who live in the full paradox of their sexual natures, contending with the strain between desire and guilt, tire at last and yearn to be freed. Williams obviously attempts to represent in them what he describes in the foreword to *Sweet Bird* as the only chance man has to "rise above his moral condition, imposed upon him at birth and long before birth, by the nature of his breed"—the "willingness to know it, to face its existence in him" (IV, 6).

When Chance comes finally to say at the end of the play, "Something's got to mean something" (p. 121), he is like Joanna Burden

in *Light in August* who decides after her orgiastic affair with Joe
Christmas that it is "time to pray." Chance's surrender to Boss
Finley's gang is his auto-da-fé. Similarly, Sebastian in *Suddenly Last
Summer* at last renounces his corruption in an act of self-sacrifice.
In recounting his story after his death, Catharine gives it the co-
herence and inevitability of a morality play.

Sebastian for years viewed the world as mercilessly naturalistic,
imaged in the scene of the Galapagos turtles that were prey to
ravenous birds. His "Poem of Summer," a hymn to such a world, ag-
grandizes—and mitigates—it by transforming the violence and pain
into poetic metaphor. Traveling each year with his mother Violet,
who helps him turn his gaze "out, not in," he keeps up his poetic
pretensions and homosexual affairs until fear and revulsion overtake
him. He sees in cousin Catharine the moral discrimination so lacking in Violet: Catharine condemns her violator and judges the ugliness and corruption that surround her. Thus on his last journey he
takes Catharine, not Violet, to Cabeza de Lobo and exposes the
degradation so long masked by youth and graceful refinement: "Suddenly, last summer Cousin Sebastian changed to the afternoons and
the [public] beach" (III, 410). Although Catharine regards herself
as having tried to save him from completing some "terrible image"
of himself, she actually enables him to do so. That summer, for the
first time, Sebastian "attempted to correct a human situation" (p.
419), and having introduced judgment into his world, he inevitably
has to judge himself. Catharine describes with horror how at last he
climbed the steep street and delivered himself to a "band of naked
children," who like a flock of birds pursued and devoured him.

In his most reflective characters Williams creates a model of man's
body-and-soul dilemma that suggests an aerialist suspended perilously on an unsteady wire. Alternately it is jerked taut from the
physical and spiritual poles, each of which holds a perch that offers
both island of refuge and hostile territory. In *Period of Adjustment*
Ralph says that "if you took the human heart out of the human body
and put a pair of legs on it and told it to walk a straight line, it
couldn't do it. It could never pass the drunk test" (IV, 241). Lovers
of life are thus like the lovers in John Crowe Ransom's "The Equili-
brists," who burn "with fierce love always to come near" until "honor

[beats] them back and [keeps] them clear." Employing a paradoxical image that Williams too has frequently used, Ransom writes: "Their flames were not more radiant than their ice."

Williams' strategy for escaping the "torture of equilibrium" is like that of the narrator of the poem, through the detachment of art. But rarely, if ever, do even the artists in Williams' works escape the paradox; thus, they never arrive at the ironic stance of the poem's narrator, who smiles pityingly at the intense lovers and chides them for their simple dialectic. In the recent novel, *Moise and the World of Reason*, for example, the narrator describes a "beautiful blonde acrobat" who "performed a metaphor" between two tall buildings, but he interprets the act with no trace of irony as a dramatic death dare.

Most often in Williams' work, art functions ideally in a direct way to release the artist from his animal passions and mortality and to offer a chance for victory over anarchy and time (the "sailing to Byzantium" theme). Interestingly, for both the playwright and his characters the attitude toward art is decidedly modern and chiefly therapeutic—what art can do for the artist. But the problem here is that viewing art as an extension of the artist, either for what he is or what he needs, leads solipsistically back to the mortal and flawed being that the artist seeks to transcend. Thus the artistic creation is constantly endangered by the "personal lyricism" that Williams talks so much about. At the most extreme, art simply distracts the artist from his self-destructiveness, as in Sebastian's case, and the distraction, or creation, is extremely tenuous, "as thin and fine as the web of a spider," says Violet (III, 408). In both his expository and his dramatic writings, Williams implies that the "poet's vocation" is the road to truth, but at the same time he refutes the conviction, suspicious that art is simply the "truth" of an illusionist —or theatrical showman. The young writer of "The Lady of Larkspur Lotion," or even Tom Wingfield, casts a magical web over experience, transforming the ordinary and ugly, and even painful, into a thing of beauty. But undermining their transformations of life into art is their (and their creator's) lurking doubt that the vision is wholly truthful or that it is sufficiently beautiful to outlast mortality.

Thus in Williams' world the artist's defeat of time is uncertain, probably illusory. Alexandra del Lago escapes the "withering country" of time only to the extent that her art is admired. (A has-been-who-never-was, like Chance Wayne, never has a hope of salvation through art.) Alexandra is like Sabbatha, one of the eight mortal ladies possessed, whose slipping talent and prestige constantly threaten her hope of victory, which is even further threatened by her medium, that of acting. In the *Memoirs*, Williams writes that his goal in writing has been to "capture the constantly evanescent quality of existence" (p. 84), but as an artist he seems to subvert his goal and whatever satisfactions it might bring by his introspective focus on "evanescence" and the paradox it holds for the artist. To the writer-narrator, Moise says, "Evanescent, you're evanescent by nature. Infinitely variable as the snake of the Nile . . ." (p. 170). Williams' view that such a nature gives the writer the knowledge and empathy necessary to the creation of art and at the same time the flaw that makes his creation specious is the worrisome paradox, I suspect, that has eroded his artistic power. His latest works reveal clearly the entrapment in self-consciousness.

In the earlier works the role of the artist is like that of Byron in *Camino Real*. He is aware of his limitations but is not paralyzed by them in his goal to translate *"noise into music, chaos into—order"* (II, 507). What the artist, and even a scientist like John Buchanan, sees when he looks outward is part anarchy and part order, but as long as his gaze is outward, he can reconcile these opposites in an artistic creation. When like Sebastian he looks inward, he apparently must forget his art and tend to his soul or make of his art a dialogue of the self. *Out Cry* illustrates such a dialogue, with characters reminiscent of Roderick and Madeline Usher. The doppelgänger symbol of the cripplingly divided nature of the human psyche is more overt than Poe's, however, and the action even more static. Sister Clare's attempt to escape the playhouse, which is like an "empty vault," carries little of the shock of Madeline's return from the grave, and only a muffled revelation of the play's subject: the destructiveness of radical self-consciousness and the futility of escape.

Philosophical rather than dramatic, the play is among Williams' closest approaches to the European drama. Unfortunately, it is so far refined from the outward world of particularity that the characters lack substance and appeal. Even the question of the murder-suicide of the parents never creates suspense because the knowing is impossible and inconsequential. The epistemological motif of an illusion locked within an illusion, as old as Narcissus, has long intrigued writers, especially modern ones. But when a relentless preoccupation with the universal circumstance overwhelms the preoccupation with the particular, which has not often happened to southern writers, including Williams, the result is a thin, anemic art. And of the character, or artist, who is trapped inside his own image, one can never know whether he has defeated time or is frozen in timelessness.

At the beginning of this essay, I suggested that Williams' disposition to see the world in paradoxical terms and to embody the paradoxes in memorably concrete and human characters aligned him closely with the writers of the modern South. That some of his plays, especially the later ones, show a declining concern with the society that surrounds the characters and a consequent declining vitality bears out an observation that Lewis Simpson has made in a recent study of southern literature. He writes that the southern literary renaissance seems to have occurred in two stages: the first roughly from 1920 to 1950, and the second perhaps still not completed. In the earlier period the writers sought to understand the full meaning of the past, to go beyond the romanticized, pastoral view that had for so long paralyzed the South's will to face up to its present. Of course, Williams' career begins in this period, and we see in such plays as *Glass Menagerie, Streetcar* and *Summer and Smoke* his preoccupation with the effects of the past and the great difficulty of penetrating the illusions to get at the truth about it. Although his view of history is far less complex than that of a Faulkner or Warren—or Chekhov—he shows a similar historical impulse. The second stage of Williams' career coincides interestingly with the second period Simpson describes. In it, the writers record their failure to gain an understanding of the past and suggest that they have lost trust in the power of their own vision—"suggest, moreover, that the process of the destruction of memory and history within the literary mind symbolized by Poe in 'The Fall of the House of Usher' cannot be halted; that inauguration of any attempt to establish a new literary covenant with the past is futile and that the only meaningful covenant for the latter-day writer is one with the self on terms generally defined as existential."[6]

Perhaps the ultimate paradox of Williams' Southern-ness is that he is caught between two Souths of the literary imagination. (Even *Out Cry* is set in the "deep Southern town" of New Bethesda, the end of the line for Clare and Felice.) Even so, the "southern matter" of his work, invigorated by his own ambivalence and tense effort to reconcile the oppositions within the tradition, has furnished the source of his most affecting characters. They loom unforgettably, even when they are appallingly self-ignorant, in their embodiments of the "heart in conflict with itself."

The sexual-spiritual duality of man has, like the southern matter, formed a chief strain of ambiguity and conflict in Williams' works. The ancient body and soul struggle shows no waning in its power to obsess and little susceptibility to resolution in his "sensual-romantic" vision. Nonetheless, he tries to create in some characters a capacity for innocent sexuality, untainted by Puritan repressions (Baby Doll, Rosa delle Rose, Alma of "Yellow Bird"), or a heightened, mystical sexuality that can be a saving grace (Lady Torrance, Serafina, Maggie). But the most serious protagonists, those who count most in Williams' world, suffer the division that Leona describes of Violet in *Small Craft Warnings*: "Her mind floats on a cloud and her body floats on water. And her dirty fingernail hands reach out to hold onto something she hopes can hold her together. . . . Oh, my God, she's at it again, she got a hand under the table" (V, 284).

Williams expresses the dilemma in dialogue, of course, but he also represents it in a cluster of images which he draws on repeatedly. To simplify greatly, the color blue serves as a metaphor of spirituality, roses of carnality, and birds as a fusion of the two impulses. Blanche wears "Madonna blue"; Myra Torrance in her reborn state buys a dream of "ecstasy blue"; Elena in *The Purification* is the "blue" girl. Rosalio, Rose Comfort, Rosa delle Rose, Rosario, and a host of other roses, human and floral, are linked with sexuality or earthliness and occur throughout the works. And the yellow bird named Bobo is only one of many otherworldly messengers who bear enigmatic or paradoxical meaning for anxious mortals. Similarly, Williams' combination of realism and Expressionism serves as apt theatrical metaphor for the conflict of body and spirit. Flannery O'Connor once remarked that the writer whose world view is deterministic will produce tragic naturalism, whereas the writer who believes that life is essentially mysterious will use concrete detail in a more drastic way, the way of distortion.[7] I suspect that Williams' alternation between the two outlooks accounts in part for his continual alternation between the realistic and expressionistic modes.

Insofar as his vision is directed to this world, he sees transcendence of the self as available only through art: "all we have to do is remember that if we're not artists, we're nothing" (p. 22), says Felice in *Out Cry*. Characters from the plays and the fiction, as well as the playwright himself, according to his account in the *Memoirs*, engage life with "Blue Jay" notebook always at hand. Sebastian's poem, nevertheless, goes unfinished, and Nonno at age ninety-seven barely manages to complete his poem before he dies. The uncertainties and fragmentation that plague existence also threaten art, and even the artist's truth. With neither art nor God to depend upon, the yearning of the heart for transcendence can never be assuaged. "For me," Williams writes in *Memoirs*, "what is there but to feel beneath me the steadily rising current of mortality and to summon from my blood whatever courage is native to it[?]" (p. 249). In Williams' plays the paradoxes of this life provoke in the characters their bitterest frustrations, and their quandaries are those of their creator. Lacking the resources to encompass paradox in some larger perspective, Williams is frequently trapped inside, and the result is melodrama, inadvertent comedy or intellectual myopia. But the view from inside can also be charged with all the danger that goes with personal risk. When this view is transmuted on the stage into an evocative Laura or Amanda, Blanche, Alma, Maggie, or Big Daddy, we are likely to be held in our seats, transfixed in blood and glands, if not in brain. In their compelling pathos, they resemble, finally, the birds in Wallace Stevens' "Sunday Morning" in making "Ambiguous undulations as they sink,/Downward to darkness, on extended wings."

Notes to Peggy W. Prenshaw, "The
Paradoxical Southern World of Tennessee Williams"

1. C. Hugh Holman, *The Roots of Southern Writing* (Athens: University of Georgia Press, 1972), p. 1.

2. Cleanth Brooks, *The Well Wrought Urn* (New York: Harvest-Harcourt, Brace, & World, 1947), p. 3.

3. Arthur Ganz, "The Desperate Morality of the Plays of Tennessee Williams," in

American Drama and its Critics: A Collection of Critical Essays, ed. Alan S. Downer (Chicago: University of Chicago Press, 1965), pp. 216–17.

4. Jacob H. Adler, "The Rose and the Fox: Notes on the Southern Drama," in *South: Modern Southern Literature in Its Cultural Setting*, ed. Louis D. Rubin and Robert D. Jacobs (Garden City, N.Y.: Dolphin-Doubleday, 1961), p. 353.

5. Thomas E. Porter, *Myth and Modern American Drama* (Detroit: Wayne State University Press, 1969), pp. 153–176.

6. Lewis P. Simpson, *The Dispossessed Garden: Pastoral and History in Southern Literature* (Athens: University of Georgia Press, 1975), p. 71.

7. Flannery O'Connor, *Mystery and Manners* (New York: Farrar, Straus, & Giroux, 1962), pp. 41–42.

Tennessee Williams' South:
The Culture and the Power

JACOB H. ADLER

O F ALL WILLIAMS' plays which say things about the South, *Summer and Smoke* says the most. Yet on the face of it *Summer and Smoke* need not have been set in the South at all. The situation that it develops, of the oversensual boy and the over-spiritual girl, could have spun itself out almost anywhere. Williams does not even provide, as he does in other plays—notably for Amanda in *The Glass Menagerie*—an appropriate accent or rhythm of speech. No blacks appear, and the only visible class differences are based on morality (patently loose women are outcast), as they might be in any small midwestern town. The minister is a minister from anywhere, the doctor a doctor from anywhere, the Fourth of July celebration—itself a surprise since other writers might have used a southern Memorial Day—has much the same flavor, and occurs in about the same year, as the one in the Connecticut of O'Neill's *Ah, Wilderness!*

Nor is Alma's predicament, on the face of it, related closely to the South, as that of Blanche in *A Streetcar Named Desire* so unmistakably is. One thing that Alma represents, the soul which must find its body, is of universal application—as much so, and in much the same way, as the New England village of Thornton Wilder's *Our Town*. That majority of Broadway critics who dismissed Alma as

30

just another neurotic southern female were wrong. Neither her plight, that of the repressed smalltown minister's daughter, nor her story is obviously southern; and in one sense the play's locale is Mississippi only because that is a region Williams knows.

Yet Alma Winemiller is beyond question southern. Even in the recent past, if not today, there were southern women so like her as to make a Southerner's hackles rise in recognition as he reads her lines: the overelaborate vocabulary, the overgreat expectations from others, the living of life as though it were a work of fiction, the insulation from the world. The genteel code was stronger in the South, and lasted longer, and caused perhaps more pain.

But for a dramatist who in some of his other plays could create so completely circumstantial a South, and such completely circumstantial Southerners, this is a curious, and not even generally recognizable, minimum; and it leads to another and related question: Why did Williams choose to lay this story, alone among his plays, in a rather distant past? Now the past affects the present in all of Williams' major plays, just as it does in Faulkner's novels. Yet once, and once only, in his novels Faulkner goes back to that past and creates, in *Absalom, Absalom!*, a story not at all typical of the South either as we know it or as we remember it—Sutpen is out of Greek tragedy, not out of the South—and of that story makes an allegory of the southern dilemma. And this is what Williams does in *Summer and Smoke.* For this atypical story is unmistakably an allegory, an allegory of body and soul; and if it has meaning in terms of all mankind, as Sutpen does, it may also, like Sutpen, have a special meaning for the South. The South, Williams seems unmistakably to say, has experienced the greatest difficulty in bringing into harmony, into integration, its body and its soul.

Let us then explore the use of the past and of the allegorical form and content of *Summer and Smoke*, to see how they illuminate the play and the South. The time of the setting is important to the play as both drama and allegory. First, the time makes Alma more believable. An audience might not easily suspend disbelief in so thoroughgoing a prudery as Alma's if the play took place in the present; or, at the very least, Williams would have had to expend much effort in explaining how that prudery came to be. If Williams was to concentrate, as he apparently wished to, on the allegory, he had to gain audience acceptance of Alma by a minimum of means: the South, a preacher's daughter, the past before World War I.

Similarly, the past can manage with slight local color; but Williams had to choose his past with care. Give an audience the antebellum South, or the Civil War South, or the Reconstruction South, and it will expect all the elaborate apparatus, part real, part mythical, with which it has become familiar. But the South of the turn of the century? And, moreover, a middle-class South, neither aristocratic nor poor-white nor black? A forgotten world, from which all needless detail can be stripped away; an island, lost in space and time, which is what allegory seems to require. (Sutpen's Hundred is another such island, though in the rich texture of a novel it can be surrounded, in both space and time, by the familiar waters of reality. *Everyman* may also come to mind, and *Pilgrim's Progress*, and *Penguin Island*.)

Moreover, Williams uses various devices to universalize the past, devices which he may have derived in part from Faulkner and from such bits in *Our Town* as the address on the envelope which begins with Grover's Corners and ends with the Mind of God. The sets are reduced to the barest essentials of reality without abandoning it altogether as Wilder does; but to the extent that the sets are recognizable, they are Gothic (the houses), classical (the statue), and scientific (the anatomy chart), thus covering almost the whole spread of Western cultural history. The Gothic and the classical are, it is true, not unsuitable to the South's historical and architectural past; but they also suggest further reaches of time. And the genuine Gothic is underlined in Alma's talk of the spirituality of Gothic cathedrals, the genuine classical in Williams' description of John as "a Promethean figure" with "the fresh and shining look of an epic hero"; while Gothic tale and Greek tragedy may both be recalled in the sudden and dreadful death of John's father through the unwitting responsibility of both hero and heroine. And over all, besides the statue of Eternity, there is the sky, in Williams as it was in Wilder, with the wheeling constellations and the inevitable round of years.

Williams' allegory is an allegory both of the South and of all mankind. It is therefore not only timely (the past as a comment on the present) but timeless; and timelessness is a quality which fits poorly with the actuality of the now. Wilder, in *Our Town*, achieves it through the past plus fantasy; Williams achieves it through the past plus allegory. The statue of Eternity may brood over the past, and by implication over the present; for it to brood directly over the present would be far less believable. Hence the use of the past helps Williams in various ways: it assists belief; it helps strip away the details useful to realism but detrimental to allegory; and it directly assists the allegory, both southern and universal.

Summer and Smoke takes the form of an allegorical ritual, a modern psychological version of the medieval dialogue between body and soul. The set itself—the two matching houses, the statue between and above them, and the sky over all—is formal and suggestive of ritual. The opening scene of John and Alma in childhood provides almost all the thematic movements of the ritual: Alma loves John but can approach him only through cultural assistance (handkerchiefs to wipe his nose). John is embarrassed by Alma's efforts, but is also attracted and makes minor efforts to please her (washes his face). His principal methods of approach, however, are the violent (throws a stone) and the physical (forces a kiss). He even sneers at the meaning of Alma's name (soul), and he is unmoved, while Alma is greatly moved, at the discovery that the statue is named Eternity.

The play develops these themes by use of increasingly complex approaches and withdrawals. John crosses to Alma's house—and is repelled by the pseudo-culture of her literary club. Alma crosses to John's house—and is offered the reality of science (astronomical distances), the comfort of science (sleeping pills), and a drive in the country. The scene under the bower at the lake, which is the climax of act one, is a long series of approaches and withdrawals, of attractions and repulsions, a sort of ideational minuet. John proposes a cockfight; Alma is repelled. John praises sensual satisfaction as the only good in life; Alma counters with Gothic cathedrals. Alma quotes an idealistic epigram; John tells her it is by Oscar Wilde. John kisses Alma; and Alma is attracted, but John, finding he still feels impelled to call her *Miss* Alma, withdraws. Alma suggests he would want a lady as the mother of his children; John suggests that marriage must be founded in sexual harmony, and "ladies" are often cold. John suggests an immediate bed; Alma, violently repelled, goes home in a taxi.

The ritualistic dance, however, is not repetitive but developmental; and eventually the two change places (and John and Nellie give Alma a handkerchief), so that Alma, near the play's end, can make a comparison with another ritual: they are "like two people exchanging a call on each other at the same time, and each one finding the other one gone out, the door locked against him and no one to answer the bell!" (II, 247). And the ritual pattern is further emphasized by the alternation of scenes in the two houses; by the play's beginning and ending under the statue of Eternity; by Alma's characteristic pose of someone prepared to take communion; by John's going to Alma for spiritual consolation and making with her a tableau of "a stone Pietà"; and by the statue of Eternity's being a fountain, from which Alma and others periodically drink. Still other specific rituals occur; and as is natural in a world where body and soul never achieve complete integration, almost all of them are flawed or parodied or specifically evil. There are, for example, the faintly satirized Fourth of July celebration; the club meeting, a burlesqued ritual of modern culture; the scene in the bower, a mock ritual of courtship; the much-mentioned ritual of the cockfight; the orgiastic ritual of Rosa's dance; the ritual of a funeral (mocked by John) off in the background. John's summer life has a grossly sexual rhythm which repels even him, and his consequent mention of castration is a reminder of further rituals. John and Alma both go through a period of suffering, from which they emerge more nearly whole. And there is the ritualistic change of the season itself, and the movement of the stars.

Thus in its use of the past and its ritualism, *Summer and Smoke* minimizes realism for the sake of allegory. But the universal allegory is present only in general terms: souls are crippled without bodies; bodies are violent without souls; each without the other takes part in seriously flawed rituals; and mutual awareness of the lack, if achieved, may come too late for complete integration. Yet the *details* of the play, which will not fit into the universal allegory, fit very well into an allegory of the South; and that allegory therefore requires further scrutiny.

That it *is* an allegory of the South is made immediately clear by the name of the town: Glorious Hill. To represent the whole world, a town might better be called something like Grover's Corners. But the South could have been said to consider itself a Glorious Hill, its past glories continuing under the aspect of Eternity. Alma, the soul of the South, is the daughter of religion, and hence of tradition and truth, but in the person of her father, religion has become a religion of appearances only. Alma herself does some good (she helps Nellie, the daughter of the town prostitute) but refuses to face basic problems. Her principal characteristics, as soul, are prudery and affectation and a dry-as-dust, attenuated culture which lingers out of the romantic past.

But Alma is also the daughter of a psychotic mother—the daughter, then, of a desiccated religion and of the sort of dementia that causes retreat into childhood. This is not true of the soul in the universal sense, but it can very well be how Williams saw the soul of the South: in retreating to the past, hence avoiding responsibility and reality, it achieved a grotesque and childish ugliness. So Alma has trouble with her mother: that is, she has difficulty in keeping this aspect of her inheritance repressed. One scene is actually a physical battle between mother and daughter; and again and again Alma must employ tactics that seem unworthy of her to keep her mother in bounds. Clearly, too, while Alma is still capable of redemption, the danger exists that she will follow her mother; her neuroticism is pronounced, and her crisis is a dangerous one. Thus Williams says (1) that this aspect of the southern soul was slightly grotesque, pleasant on the surface (Alma) but very ugly underneath (her mother); and (2) that the South's soul was still redeemable in this respect, though the danger of an irrevocable retreat remained. So long as the soul of the South refused to face reality, it had no future; Mrs. Winemiller is as futureless as the day before yesterday, and Alma, so long as she secludes herself, is squired only by an effeminate, mother-fixated boy.

It is appropriate that John is the son of a doctor, but it is at least equally interesting that he is motherless. The prologue points out that he does not use a handkerchief—that is, he is cut off from the cultural advantages that a mother would give. It also points out that the spectacle of his dying mother repelled him violently—that is, he is cut off from certain aspects of his past. And so with the South: its body strong and attractive but dangerous and purposeless ("the excess of his power has not yet found a channel," says Williams of John. "If it remains without one, it will burn him up," II, 132), because it is severed from its soul. And John dissipates his physical inheritance to the benefit of outsiders (Rosa and her father), and becomes involved in violence.

For the central violence of the play, however—the murder of John's father—all are responsible. The violence is committed by an outsider, but it happens only because the South does not know itself: the soul, Alma, is ignorant of the physical violence she is tampering with when she telephones John's father; the body, John, has not been taught to recognize the evil that can lie in the depths of the soul. The responsibility for violence in the South lay everywhere—in the outsider, but also in the divided South itself: the sterile remnants of the cultural past, cut off from the present reality; the gaudy grimness of the present reality, cut off from the cultural past.

But the violence results in genuine crises for both John and Alma; and both effect compromises. John becomes successful and self-sacrificial as a doctor, has glimmerings of understanding about man's nonphysical nature, but, remaining physically powerless with Alma, marries a young and flighty but well-meaning girl. Alma sheds her affectations and her repressions, renounces idealism (the statue's "body is stone and her blood is mineral water," II, 237), tries by the frankest of means to win John, and, failing, picks up a young, eager, reasonably attractive boy. Thus Williams depicts a stale, poetico-idealistic culture refusing to face reality yet still partly beautiful; and unable to achieve, or to attract, power until reality is faced. And he warns that waiting too long to come to terms with reality can result, when reality *is* faced in a complete denial of the ideal, in a failure to attract genuine power, and in a comparatively trivial fulfilment. On the other hand, the South's genuine power, both intellectual and physical, is dissipated because it can find no valid ideal, or is psychologically cut off from pursuing such an ideal, if found. And all this happens in Glorious Hill under the wings of the Angel of Eternity! This is pessimistic and ironic; and *Summer and Smoke* is a pessimistic, ironic sort of allegory and play. "Too little and too late," it says, as we watch the beauty of life evaporate in the vapidity of an effeminate and quibbling literary club, while the force of life is equally wasted in the remote and unreal cockfights and assignations of the appropriately named Moon Lake.

Yet the picture is not entirely pessimistic; the compromise unions are better than no unions at all. By the end of the play, Alma has faced reality sufficiently to become much better integrated. The partners whom Alma and John have found are immature, to be sure, but with at least *some* potential. And Alma, in a final gesture, seems to come to terms with Eternity. The awful heat of summer ends as the smoke of the battle of the psyche dissipates. (And if summer is light and smoke dark, who is to say that the race question does not underlie the imagery?) What is seen in the South in the final cool clarity may be compromise, but compromise (Williams says) is at any rate the better truth in this world—better than sterility and violence. For any other truth, one must turn to the Glorious Hill of Eternity.

Here, then, is Williams' full interpretation of the southern predicament as he saw it in the forties, presented through allegory. *Summer and Smoke* is much better than most of its early critics made it out to be, and it is profoundly interesting as Williams' most complete interpretation of the South; but this is not to say that the play is as successful *dramatically* as his other major productions. Probably allegory is inherently less dramatic than many other dramatic methods; certainly for audiences accustomed to realism it is as infrequent as it is risky.

Williams' other plays about the South use other means. Like *Summer and Smoke*, all to some extent juxtapose the physical and violent with the cultural and ideal. But the result is a wider variety of methods than is usually recognized; and if changes are rung on more or less the same theme, this is also what Faulkner does, and the result in both cases is a wide panorama of life in and about the South.

Before looking at Williams' other plays about the South from this perspective, however, one further point must be made: the regular symbol of power in Williams is sex. But in the full-length plays at least, vital power, with potential for achievement, involves strong sexuality but not promiscuity, loss of control, or abnormality. Thus Stanley and Stella, strongly sexed and in perfect union, have potential for the future; Blanche, the promiscuous, does not. Stanley's rape of Blanche, to say the least of it, is presented as a misuse of power. In *Summer and Smoke*, John gains in meaningful power when he gives up promiscuity. Even in the Big Daddy of *Cat on a Hot Tin Roof*, whose power derives from money and who represents money to almost all who surround him, sexuality is prominent; there is the latent suggestion that without the sexuality the drive which resulted in tremendous aggrandizement could not have existed; and in Brick the achievement of normal sexuality is the sine qua non of his inheriting his father's wealth. Not that Williams' treatment of sex is always successful or consistent. At its worst, it is obvious, over-done, and needlessly vulgar, though vulgarity is not always needless, in Williams, any more than in Chaucer. At its best his treatment of sex declares in believable dramatic terms that promiscuity and prud-ery are alike signs of neurosis, hence signs of limited power; that abnormal sexuality (for example, homosexuality in *Streetcar*, *Cat*, and *Suddenly Last Summer*) has evil effects; that strong sexual drive without promiscuity is a sign of vitality and strength; and that, be-yond the sex-power equation, any union involving love or even kind-ness is a symbol for success in humanity's ceaseless effort to destroy loneliness.

To a certain extent autobiographical, *The Glass Menagerie* is less subject to large interpretations than many of the other plays; and since Williams feels more than usual affection for his characters, he searches for devices which will soften the portraits that artistic honesty requires him to present. Hence the narrator presenting the play as memory; hence the mood music, the scrim, the beauty of Laura, the underlying nobility of Amanda, the unexpected kindness and understanding of the gentleman caller; hence, indeed, the glass menagerie itself. Critics pointed out as early as 1945 that Williams owes a debt to Chekhov. And certainly in *The Glass Menagerie* the combination of impressionism of effect and realism of detail, the compassion and objectivity, the development by conflict of mood and temperament, the comedy achieved through pathos, the portrait of hopeless inheritors of a lost tradition—all derive from Chekhov.

The most interesting comparison, for present purposes, is the treatment of the central symbol in Williams and in Chekhov. The sea gull in Chekhov's play is titular, it represents a young girl, it is brought forward again and again, it is unnecessary to the plot, yet it is used developmentally, not merely allowed to exist as static. In contrast, the anatomy chart in *Summer and Smoke*, being allegorical not symbolic, is not really used and never changes; yet it is necessary in a way that the sea gull is not. But the glass menagerie, like the sea gull, represents a young girl: like Laura, it is fragile, beautiful, useless. Highly appropriate to both Laura and the mood, it is unnecessary to the story, yet it is brought forward again and again; and, through the breaking of the unicorn's horn, it is a *developed* symbol to which something really happens that gives it a new meaning. Yet to make the menagerie signify anything beyond Laura is as difficult as making the play mean anything beyond the characters portrayed.

This difficulty is not surprising if the play is autobiographical. Still, some sort of meaning emerges from the dichotomy of the physical-violent and the cultural-ideal. Rather oddly, both Tom and Amanda combine in themselves the opposites: each has both culture (Tom writes poetry) and the potential for power; but culture and power are wasted in them because mother and son alike are cut off from their cultural past and unable to accept the cultural (or lack of cultural) present. In Amanda, the case is hopeless because she is too much tied to the past; yet she in a sense can live in the world of the present as Tom cannot. If the case is not hopeless in Tom, he must find fulfilment in escape from both past and present in some indefinable future; but he seems unlikely to do so, since his violent break from his family leaves him with guilt feelings. (May we say, then, that Williams felt the South could not find itself by becoming something other than the South?) Crippled mentally and physically, Laura has neither the culture nor the power. Both lie latent in her, but they can be awakened only by an outsider (Tom and Amanda, the inheritors of the lost past, are helpless) who recognizes the beauty and potential underneath the grotesqueness of deformity. Since few outsiders would be sufficiently unattached and perceptive both to see the potential and to act upon it, her chances are slim. If all this seems farfetched, the intellectual content of the play is slight; and certainly in an autobiographical, impressionistic play the intellectual content is not likely to be primary. Yet the pattern I have described is similar enough to other patterns in Williams' plays to make it persuasive. And it gains in persuasiveness, since at the one moment when the glass menagerie is used developmentally, it is used to show an unreal creature become real—a creature (a horse) of genuine beauty and power.

In *A Streetcar Named Desire* the contrast between culture and power is at its sharpest; and appropriately, this is a violently naturalistic play. Mood music appears again, and, as usual in Williams, a great deal derives from Chekhov; yet the effect is of the clearest, harshest reality. What is primary is story and people as they are, as they inevitably are; what is secondary is Blanche and the others as representative of the culture-power dichotomy and the southern dilemma; what is tertiary (an aspect not present in *The Glass Menagerie*) is Blanche as representative of the sensitive individual lost in the complex, impersonal modern world.

The symbols in *Streetcar* therefore grow out of the reality, not the reality out of the symbols. Whether or not this is the "best" method, it is certainly the method modern audiences prefer; and the method may explain why *Streetcar* received the greatest acclaim of Williams' first three important plays. It is true that to get to Stella's slum apartment, Blanche has had to transfer from Desire to Cemeteries and arrive at Elysian Fields (where she is alien), but once stated—more as a theme than a symbol—this imagery rarely intrudes on the play. In contrast with a somewhat artificial symbol, like glass animals, the typical symbol in *Streetcar*, such as the overhead naked light bulb which Blanche covers with a Chinese lantern, grows naturally out of the environment and situation. When Mitch pulls the lantern from the light and thrusts the brilliant bulb in Blanche's face, reality becomes symbol in an exact reversal of the crisis in *The Glass Menagerie*, where the act of breaking the unicorn's horn makes symbol for a moment become reality.

Given greater reality and larger scope than *Summer and Smoke* or *The Glass Menagerie*, the culture-power conflict in *Streetcar* is especially complex. Blanche, the representative of the cultural and ideal, is as sexually immoral as the earlier John, the representative of power in *Summer and Smoke*. As representative of the Old South, Blanche dissipates her power, but for the opposite of John's reasons; far from failing to recognize her cultural (and personal) past, she is inextricably bound to it. Caught in a neurotic limbo, she combines in herself the irreconcilable opposites of John's exaggerated physical urges and Alma's culture, pretense, and affectation. (The critics who said Blanche was Alma in a later stage of development were wrong; Alma in the end shed her affectations and came to terms at least partly with her ideals.) In John, recognition of the ideal brings self-control; in Alma, recognition of the real brings release from repression and prudery; but in Blanche, who is involved with both real and ideal and cannot reconcile them, nymphomania and prudery, love of the past and hatred of the past, genuine culture and pretentious fakery exist at the same time. And thus Blanche represents one way the South could take: unable to face the contrast between the romantic past and the realistic present, Blanche violently betrays her code while desperately pretending to maintain it. That way inevitably lies Cemeteries.

Another way, as everyone has noticed, is Stella's. Like Tom in *Menagerie*, Stella attempts to get away from the past by denying it utterly. But she is more successful than Tom; indeed, she lives in Elysian Fields. (For that matter, Stella, unlike Blanche, is not particularly southern in outward manifestations at all; she is a *person*, unbound to geography—as of course many Southerners are.) True, she is wedded to a man who represents not only power but violence, not only violence, but the very special violence rape; but out of the match one is apparently supposed to see a future in which—perhaps —a new culture can be born. Stanley is by no means all bad, his strength is not all directionless, his love for Stella is pathetically real. The child of immigrants, he is the new, untamed pioneer, who brings to the South, Williams seems to be saying, a power more exuberant than destructive, a sort of power the South may have lost. This is apparently Williams' attitude toward foreigners in *The Rose Tattoo* and *Baby Doll* as well as *Streetcar*. Curiously, it is not the attitude in *Summer and Smoke*, where the foreigners prey on the South and deplete its native strength, nor in *Orpheus Descending*, where the foreigners are themselves victims of southern violence. At any rate, in *Streetcar*, the possibility for physical power representing the South lies in Harold Mitchell, the only prominent southern male in the play, and a man definitely interested in sex and marriage. But he is deceived, as Stanley is not for a moment, by Blanche's cultural pretenses; and his potential for power is limited by his being psychologically tied to his mother, and by his inability to accept in marriage anything short of the unsullied innocence his mother would expect;

a man, then, tied to a dead culture and a dead past. Blanche's husband was also psychologically bound and hence not fully masculine; and so Williams seems to say that only a less than complete man can be attracted by the past that Blanche represents. Yet Blanche has in her something of a genuine culture and beauty which Stella has abandoned and which Stanley cannot see; and, as with the aristocrats in *The Cherry Orchard*, we must regret its passing, even as we recognize the decadence and futility and even degradation which make its passing both necessary and inevitable.

The Rose Tattoo, on the other hand, presents a group not tied to the Old South at all, a colony of Sicilian immigrants on the Gulf Coast. If *The Rose Tattoo* has to do with the South, it must be by contrast, for its characters are in the South only by chance, and, except for the lush tropical atmosphere, which could be, and in Williams has been, achieved in other places, the story it has to tell has almost no southern connections. Yet here, interestingly, is *another* southern race, bred to both culture and violence. Underlying a tremendously foreign exterior, Serafina, the mother in the play, has characteristics quite familiar to the South: religion and superstition, honor and courage, awe of rank, and high standards for her child; and, when reality becomes unbearable, a tendency to violence or to an almost psychotic withdrawal. Yet she has about her a lushness beyond any southern lushness, emphasized almost to the point of nausea by the constant symbol of the rose; and she has a power of fertility, hence a share in the real future, which many of Williams' other plays say much of the South has lost. As with Stanley Kowalski, then, we find *too much* power, an overflowing of it, too little direction, yet an overwhelming reality and an overwhelming demand for genuine fulfilment.

This is a wildly exuberant comedy, and it is probably unfair to seek very elaborate meaning. Yet something must be done with the rose symbol, the constant reiteration of which has been, with much justice, a principal criticism of the play; and within the context of this essay a reason for its presence can be educed. The roses cluster around Serafina, while Rosa's only direct connection with them is her name. Of all the flamboyant qualities that Serafina shares with the South, the only quality which (according to Williams) the

South does not share with *her* is the one quality unmistakably inherited by Rosa: that overwhelming sexuality which—clearly, from Serafina's joy at conception—is Shaw's life force. Otherwise, her environment has made Rosa not Sicilian, not southern, but American. And she is apparently to marry a Southerner who, like Stella in *Streetcar*, seems simply American too. Thus in one respect *The Rose Tattoo* is *Streetcar* in reverse—therefore a comedy, because the more picturesque and violent portions of the foreign inheritance are left to the older generation. This argument is not absolutely to defend the symbol of the rose in *The Rose Tattoo*, which appears in every form from tattoos to the color of a shirt to the scent of hair oil. Doubtless the symbol is overstressed and overstrained. But at least the roses are appropriate both to Serafina's Mediterranean exuberance and to the underlying meaning of the play.

Cat on a Hot Tin Roof differs from all the earlier plays in that its major characters are in origin neither aristocratic nor middle-class nor foreign. Big Daddy and Big Mama command a degree of respect, but they obviously lack culture in the context in which it is used in this essay, and their two children give little hope for the future regarding culture—or even regarding power. Indeed, in this play even fertility is not necessarily a sign of power. Brick's brother Gooper, with his apparently endless stream of children, is the epitome of the crass and the personally weak, of sex uncontrolled; and if he gains financial power it will be only by default, with no reason to expect any result other than its being misused, with no gain in either culture or power either for his own descendants or for the South. Brick, on the other hand, has the capacity for acquiring culture, which is typical throughout history in a class rising from low to middle through the acquisition of money. But fear and disillusionment have cost him both the capacity for culture and the capacity for power, in a state of limbo. Repelled by the sex act and possibly fearful of homosexuality, he must for these reasons find a way to return to normal sexuality: to achieve the power of reproduction; to gain financial power from his father, which depends on his having offspring; and to recover that self-confidence which would make cultural growth possible. Finally, there is Maggie, a southern girl of cultured background who deliberately sheds her culture to fight for the power she wants in this ferociously acquisitive family. And, as compared to the previous southern plays, the action occurs in a highly stylized presentation moving close to the expressionistic.

What is to be made of all this? The central representative of power, Big Daddy, has, as things stand in the play, one worthless and one badly confused son—the power may have been wasted—and his own power will soon go through death by cancer. The other most capable representative of power, Maggie, will, as the play was originally written, gain power only by force, not by love, if she gains it at all. Everyone—including a repulsive member of the ministry—is lost in a world not just where power is wasted and culture inadequate, but in a world of insufficient love, love which might make both the power and the culture come to fruition. The very uncommonness of the dialogue between father and son in act two emphasizes the usual paucity of love, or inability to express it. Maggie, as cat on a hot tin roof, seems to need sex more than love, and power more than either. *Cat on a Hot Tin Roof* is about sex and money and culture and power; but except that it may say that the way out of the southern dilemma is not through financial acquisitiveness, it is perhaps less a play about the South than a play resembling, both in content and in nonrealistic form, Williams' immediately previous play, *Camino Real*. The unreal world of *Camino* is filled with people like Brick who have lost courage, people incapable of love (or even sex: Kilroy's heart condition precludes intercourse), a world from which the only escape is through recovery of courage, recovery of purpose, discovery of the kind of love that means capacity for self-sacrifice. If *Cat on a Hot Tin Roof* succeeded where *Camino Real* essentially failed, the reason may be not that *Cat* is the better play but that Americans usually dislike pure expressionism, dislike all plays with whose characters they cannot relate. And Williams, whatever his intentions might have been, created in *Cat* three lusty, determined, fighting, *real* human beings, Big Daddy, Big Mama, and Maggie the Cat, filled with grotesque virtues, faults, and fears, with whom it is impossible not to sympathize.

In Williams' next three plays, all laid in the South, the pattern as well as the quality goes askew. One, *Suddenly Last Summer*, has its good points. The other two, *Orpheus Descending* (a revision of the early *Battle of Angels*) and *Sweet Bird of Youth*, are more seriously flawed. And all three reveal questionable attitudes and motifs which one might have foreseen from earlier, better plays. Thus Sebastian, in *Suddenly Last Summer*, is a homosexual like Blanche's husband; and both are dead. But Blanche's husband's death was a psychologically likely event; Sebastian's was grisly and Gothic, and one must decide both whether it works dramatically and whether it has sufficient meaning to justify both its horror and its improbability. In the other two plays central male characters are at the same time sexual athletes and both proud and ashamed of their athleticism. One of them ends up dead through a lynching by blowtorch, and the other ends up castrated. Now John in *Summer and Smoke* is promiscuous, comes to be ashamed of it, and even mentions castration; but John recovers, achieves a healthy monogamy, and is a basically decent person with whom it is possible to sympathize. Brick in *Cat* is as badly confused about sex as Chance in *Sweet Bird*; but while Brick is not the most effective character in *Cat*, at least the second act makes it possible to understand him and pity him. And promiscuity results in a death in *Summer and Smoke*, but it is much more believable and organic than the death in *Orpheus Descending*.

To the extent that *Suddenly Last Summer* is successful, it is successful because it is a cold Gothic structure in which no demand is made upon the audience to expend sympathy: a record of a horrible world of no faith except in money and science, of no love, of sterility amidst luxuriance, where the only God is that of Gloucester in *Lear* who kills men for sport, and the only courage is the neurotic courage of desperation. Among Williams' plays with claim to quality, it seems to represent the nadir of hope. Not only in the South but everywhere, apparently, people are tyrants or victims, the devouring or the devoured. There is no hint of any meaningful future. Culture is meaningless, and power has either a quality of madness or that sort of scientific objectivity which turns human beings into specimens for the microscope.

To discuss both *Orpheus* and *Sweet Bird* at any length seems superfluous, since they are bad, and bad in similar ways. Even the symbolism, the stylization does not work. In *Orpheus*, one cannot sympathize with a self-pitying prudish libertine like Val, nor with a woman as stupid as Lady; and the symbols of Orpheus, birds, confectionery, snakeskin jacket, and various aspects of the Passion seem cold and dead. If *Sweet Bird* is a better play, it is better almost entirely for the flamboyant character of Alexandra del Lago, one of Williams' gallery of splendid female creations who deserves what most of the others get, and she does not: a good play to be in.

Sweet Bird can be exciting on the stage, but its excitement is largely spurious, and its problems are multifold. The view is intensely gloomy. If power in Williams is associated with sex and fertility, as it is, then here we have a man who is to be castrated, a woman who has had a hysterectomy, a man who is impotent, or very near it, and a woman for whom sex means nothing but a temporary release from panic, like hashish or a pill. Whatever power exists is only the power of mindless violence, coercion, and the crassest use of money to gain degraded or nefarious ends. Whatever culture once existed has been dissipated through fear and misuse, and a consequent collapse into drugs and sexual degradation. The people we are asked to take an interest in are monsters—monsters with some shreds of human feeling left, but monsters nonetheless. The two central characters even call themselves so.

If that is how Williams sees the South, then all right. It is how he sees the South in *Suddenly Last Summer* and his filmscript *Baby Doll*, too. But there are three problems. First, it is not how he sees the South in his major plays. Second, *Sweet Bird* differs from *Suddenly Last Summer* and *Baby Doll* in that the latter two are clear, cold visions, the one Gothic, the other semicomic, whereas in *Sweet Bird* we are asked not to view objectively but to sympathize. And finally, the two central characters in the play are, respectively, bereft of southern characteristics (Chance) or not southern in any conceivable sense at all.

Now a play does not have to be "about" the South, even if it is laid there. In one respect, *Sweet Bird* does indeed concern the South, and the pattern traced in this essay. Williams seems to be trying to show that the South's culture and power alike have fallen prey to the Boss Finleys, the corrupt, pseudo-savior, rabble-rousing politicians; and that if so the future looks grim. But this accounts for only a minor portion of the material in the play. And the play as a whole has to be about something. It cannot confuse the material of *Light in August* with the material of *True Romances* with the material of farce with the material of a Hollywood columnist, and have much chance of coming to any valid insights or conclusions. The very stage directions make the confusion obvious. As sometimes in O'Neill, they demonstrate that the action and dialogue alone cannot achieve what the playwright wants, or make plain what it *is* he wants, and that he hopes some mysterious communicative power in actors and directors will do the job instead.

Williams does tell us, at the very end, through Chance, that the play has a theme: it is about what time does to us all. But time does not do to us all what it does to everyone in this play. In Williams' own earlier plays, time does not always destroy or degrade or corrupt or dehumanize. Big Daddy will die, as we all must; but he will die with dignity. Serafina regains her joy in living. John is redeemed. Kilroy and Casanova and others in *Camino Real* become not worse but better, and succeed in escaping from limbo. *Menagerie* shows at the end what is best in Amanda after showing earlier what is worst. Even Blanche is given the chance at the end to go off comforted. And Williams' next play but one after *Sweet Bird*, *The Night of the Iguana*, shows two persons who have never succumbed to time at all, and never will, and two more who are saved from destruction. The theme in *Sweet Bird* is not only invalid—and I have not explored the whole range of its invalidity; whether time does the destroying is dubious—but it is also a denial of the attitude in Williams' better plays.

But *Sweet Bird* looks backward and forward in certain of its other aspects, and the similarities and differences are again revealing. Thus when Chance comes forward and makes his curtain speech to the audience, asking for their sympathy as he waits, quite unnecessarily, to be castrated, he recalls Tom Wingfield who comes forward at the end of *The Glass Menagerie* to comment on his condition. Some have reacted negatively to the technique: Tom has deserted his family, and his guilt feelings are no atonement. But at a minimum the effect in *Menagerie* works. What Tom has done is believable; he has run away from entrapment. One can blame him for it, but one can also understand the conflict of feelings within him; and there behind the scrim are Laura and Amanda, making clear precisely what wrong Tom has committed. Moreover Tom does not ask for sympathy, as Chance, even while he denies it, does. A wanderer like the Ancient Mariner, Tom has compelled us to listen to his story; a story, apparently, in which he is fairer to the people he has hurt than he is to himself. But no need to labor the point. The method in *Menagerie* works. In *Sweet Bird* it does not.

Sweet Bird looks backward also in its use of the material of the Crucifixion. Williams' treatment of this theme in *Suddenly Last Summer*, *Orpheus*, and *Sweet Bird* may also, like Chance's castration, be related to *Light in August*. But Faulkner makes the parallel work, and Williams does not. Here, in *Sweet Bird*, he seems to be trying to contrast the merely rhetorical religiosity of Boss Finley with genuine sacrifice. On Easter Sunday, Chance Wayne, guilty of real sexual (and other) evil and seeing no possibility of living otherwise, will sacrifice his capacity for evil to avoid hurting himself and others further. But this is not sacrifice, it is masochism; not sacrifice, but self-deception; not sacrifice, but that most unchristian of emotions, despair. And in asking us to recognize ourselves in him, Chance is not really asking us to recognize our own capacity for evil (which would be legitimate) but attempting to justify his own.

The Crucifixion parallel also foreshadows events in *The Night of the Iguana*, as do Chance's panic, his tendency to nervous breakdown, his sexual destructiveness, his self-pity. But *Iguana*, as we shall presently see, handles these matters differently and better.

In summary, then, *Sweet Bird of Youth* lacks meaningful intellectual content, meaningful emotional content. It falls, like *Orpheus Descending*, into that category of Williams' plays where we are asked to sympathize with fallen characters and where, unlike that epitome of fallen characters, Blanche, the sympathy is both undeserved and ungrantable.

Williams' next play, *Period of Adjustment*, is not bad, merely trivial. Its being laid in Memphis has nothing significant to do with its content, and it contributes nothing to this study.

On the other hand, his next play, *The Night of the Iguana*, requires careful consideration, not because it is about the South, but, paradoxically, because it is not. Its central female character, Hannah, is so completely the opposite of Blanche that it seems impossible not to consider the contrast intentional. Blanche is Williams' most prominent and unmistakable representative of the South. Hannah is about as nonsouthern as one can get in terms of how Americans are pigeonholed: she is quite gratuitously, unless for the contrast, from

Nantucket. Blanche ends as a psychotic. Hannah has verged on nervous breakdowns, but has managed to draw back (and always will) out of sheer determination and sense of responsibility. Blanche is repelled by vulgarity; Hannah finds nothing repulsive except cruelty which is alien to her (and Blanche can be cruel), and can use vulgarity herself as a weapon when she must. Blanche is both promiscuous and prudish; Hannah is a virgin without being unsexed. Both have met sexual aberration; Blanche has reacted with horror, Hannah with sympathetic understanding. Blanche has impossible ideals that she cannot begin to live up to; Hannah lives by a realistic but difficult code—and succeeds in being believable because she is not the model of perfection Blanche would like to be; because she knows she does not have all the answers; and because she has not found God (except in human faces) but is only seeking him. Blanche has been tied to sick and elderly relations and has reacted with bitterness and repulsion. Hannah has had for many years sole responsibility for her frail grandfather and takes her circumstances completely in stride, with love and a sense of humor. In a difficult situation, Blanche covers light bulbs with lanterns. In a difficult situation, Hannah can light a match in the wind. Here, for the first time, is a central character who has *not* fallen, who is neither neurotic nor depraved, and who has resolved the problem of sex through virginity without prudery, intolerance, or psychological instability.

And there are other new departures. Maxine, another in a long series of sex-hungry, more or less grotesque women, at least knows the difference between sex and love and has a genuine concern for others (though she tries to hide it); her loneliness and insecurity are made believable, partly because they are concealed under so brassy an exterior. Shannon starts out as no more admirable than Williams' earlier ministers, no more admirable than the line of sexually destructive young men who preceded him. But unlike Sebastian, Val, and Chance, he ends the play alive and whole; and he ends it in a state of genuine sacrifice (at least in the Broadway version, where he walks out with the iguana's rope around his neck), with the probability of being henceforth sexually beneficial rather than destructive. Shannon's predecessors can never recover from their internal conflicts; Shannon apparently will, and has acquired, moreover, the possibility of gaining genuine faith. Yet the Crucifixion parallels from the previous plays are specifically repudiated: when Shannon is tied in the hammock, Hannah tells him he is enjoying it: "Isn't that a comparatively comfortable, almost voluptuous kind of crucifixion to suffer for the guilt of the world, Mr. Shannon?" (IV, 344). And when he finally breaks free from the ropes, "Yes, I never doubted that you could get loose, Mr. Shannon" (IV, 351). A more complete repudiation of the behavior of Chance in *Sweet Bird* would be hard to imagine; and Chance's readiness to be destroyed, which we are supposed to accept, also contrasts with Shannon's attempt at suicide by drowning (something Chance had also threatened), which those around him rightly prevent by tying him in the hammock, and which he presently comes to abandon. Also, in contrast to many earlier plays, the tying in the hammock is almost the only instance of violence, and it is violence to save, not to destroy.

The play seemed like a new beginning. In its conclusion, no sympathy is demanded which is not justified; and Hannah herself asks for none at all. Shock-value material, prominent in earlier plays and sometimes justifiable, sometimes not, is reduced to a minimum: no rape, cannibalism, lynching, castration. Hannah and Shannon tell each other shocking stories from their pasts, but the stories are entirely justified as representing their views of life; to her, nothing human considered alien; to him, until she puts him on the road to recovery, the world a place where starving men and women pick through manure for bits of undigested food.

Moreover the symbols, after a long hiatus, work, and there is almost no stylization—real rain falls through real holes in a real roof. I have mentioned the symbol of the match in the wind. But there is also the iguana itself, grotesque as the night and the situation are grotesque, which is freed, as Shannon probably is, from the likelihood of torture and violence. Even the Nazi Germans in the play seem valid thematically. More than in any of his earlier plays, Williams here explores the whole gamut of guilt and responsibility. And he here shows us that only the utterly guileless (a man of ninety-seven who creates a fine poem, thanks God for it, and dies) or the utterly callous (the Germans) can be carefree. The rest of us must carry our burdens. The symbols may not work for everyone, and the grandfather and the Germans tremble on the respective brinks of absurdity and incredibility. But the symbols are a decided improvement, and the characters are in general believable human beings who not only gain but deserve our interest.

But the play takes place in Mexico, not the South—the first of Williams' full-length plays except *Camino Real* to concern neither the South nor Southerners. Yet it is here, and not in the southern plays, that the culture-power conflict is resolved, in Hannah, who is whole, who is an artist, who loves her grandfather and his poetry, and who will, come what may, survive. Indeed, while many other characters in Williams have survival power, she is the only one to show that mankind may, as Faulkner said in his Nobel Prize address, not merely survive but prevail. It is as though Williams had not only regained but increased his faith in the human race which seemed so totally lost in *Suddenly Last Summer* and *Sweet Bird*, and had, moreover, gained a new ability to display it without resorting to an unreal world like that of *Camino Real*. But in the display he takes his eyes off the South, and indeed in the contrast with Blanche seems specifically to repudiate it. Whether it was accident, whether it meant he felt more optimistic about mankind in general than about the land of his ancestors—who knows? Either way, *The Night of the Iguana* seemed like a new beginning.

When I first read *Iguana*, and saw it during its Broadway run, I wrote an article, "*Night of the Iguana*: a New Tennessee Williams?" (see bibliography). Sadly, ever since, I have been more and more thankful for the question mark. The vision, for whatever reason, did not hold; and while Williams has the right to whatever vision he sees, he has clearly written best when his vision is at least partly affirmative. Only two plays since *Iguana*, other than the egregious revision of *Summer and Smoke* into *The Eccentricities of a Nightingale*, are laid in the South: the equally egregious *Seven Descents of Myrtle* (*Kingdom of Earth*) and the play-within-the-play in the minor *Out Cry*. Obviously, there are bits and pieces in any Williams play which communicate effectively. But on the whole, since *Iguana*, all the worst of Williams, regarding shock value, characters undeserving of sympathy, unsuccessful symbols, ineffective stylization—in a word, decadence—becomes dominant. To trace a pattern through plays like these seems pointless. Better to remember Williams at his best, as in *Menagerie*, *Streetcar*, and *Cat*, as he dealt in a variety of vital ways with the problems of culture and power (and of course many other things) through vivid characters in artistic structures that worked. In *Summer and Smoke* he explored the southern dilemma most fully, in *Streetcar* most poignantly; and in both with a degree of hope. That hope dwindles into the coldness of *Suddenly Last Summer*, the emptiness of *Sweet Bird*. Faith, as dead as the ministers variously portrayed, bursts forth again in *Night of the Iguana*, and a minister is apparently saved. In that play, not only a portion of the earth has hope for the future; mankind does. But after *Night of the Iguana*, alas, comes not the dawn but the darkness.

Tennessee Williams:
Poetic Consciousness in Crisis

ESTHER M. JACKSON

for you must learn, even you, what we have learned,
that some things are marked by their nature to be not
    completed
but only longed for and sought for a while and abandoned.
(from "Orpheus Descending," *Winter of Cities*, p. 28)

I

ANY SERIOUS REVIEW of the history of the American drama in the twentieth century must assign to Tennessee Williams a position of significance, both as a practicing playwright and as a dramatic theorist. Not only has Williams' idea of form been a primary factor in determining the course of the American drama in the last half of the twentieth century; it has had a significant effect on the interpretation of reality in our time.[1] Like Eugene O'Neill, Williams has given dramatic form to those factors which distinguish the condition of man in the New World from those of his European, African and Asian ancestors.

Although Williams shares with O'Neill some perceptions of the nature of human destiny in the New World, he differs from the earlier playwright in the focus of his dramatic inquiry. O'Neill's world, while drawn in terms of the particulars of American experience, is intended to be received as universal. The dramatic world of Tennessee Williams is, by design if not by inference, more limited.[2] It is the symbolization of a personal vision of reality, the concretization of the singular imagination of a poet. The dramas which Williams has shaped throughout his career have in common with poetry their identity as transformations of consciousness; that is, as concretizations of moments of insight.

53

Tennessee Williams can be described as a dramatist in the Romantic tradition; however, his concept of form differs in some ways from those which have evolved out of European experience. Following the examples of American writers such as Walt Whitman, he has set the Romantic quest in a new imaginative environment—in the consciousness of a "New World" protagonist.[3] Like that of Walt Whitman—and his mentor Ralph Waldo Emerson—Williams' brand of Romanticism is synthetic; it represents an accommodation of artistic and intellectual traditions inherited from the European past to ideas of form generated by American life. But there is a second sense in which Williams' "Romanticism" is synthetic. Plays such as A *Streetcar Named Desire* (1947) embody forms and contents adapted from the traditions of poetry, fiction, and the prose essay, as well as from the artifacts of popular culture. To this time, Williams remains the most successful of the American dramatists in translating events, attitudes, values, and ideas expressive of the American imagination into a popular symbolism; that is, into an accessible stage language.

One of the major challenges of Williams' career as a dramatist has been that of devising an American theatrical language. For the idea of form which he has developed has required a vocabulary capable of interpreting states of consciousness for an essentially nonliterary public. The theatrical language which he developed in the early years of his career conformed in some ways to the notions set forth by theorists in the postromantic tradition of existentialism.[4] In plays such as The Purification (published 1945), he sought to give "concrete identity" to moments of intuition.

During the late thirties and forties, Williams developed a high level of skill in the translation of the faculties of poetic consciousness—emotion, memory, thought, and fantasy—into the language of theater; not merely into written words, but also into character, gesture, action, speech, costume, setting, light, music, sound and filmic effects. In these early plays, his protagonists assume the persona of the poet, recording the flow of experience and interpreting the manner in which consciousness can confer on life itself the aesthetic properties of order, meaning, harmony, beauty, and light.[5]

Plays such as The Purification show how Williams attempted to engage the spectator in this poetic process.[6] Here, the spectator is urged to share in both the discovery of hidden meanings in life and the reordering of the universe of human experience. The instrument of the poetic transformation of the world of conscious experience is imagery. Through such theatrical images—set forth in titles such as *This Property is Condemned, Portrait of a Girl in Glass,* and *27 Wagons Full of Cotton*—Williams invites the spectator to share his efforts to synthesize fragments of knowable experience within an enriching and ennobling totality.

II

Now Orpheus, crawl, O shamefaced fugitive, crawl
back under the crumbling broken wall of yourself,
for you are not stars, sky-set in the shape of a lyre,
but the dust of those who have been dismembered by Furies!
(*Winter of Cities,* p. 28)

The one-act plays which Tennessee Williams composed during the early years of his career—like the poetry and fiction written in this period—can be described as images of "felt" experience.[7] The dramatist writes that he became increasingly concerned about the subjectivity of these works. In a second phase of his career, he sought to translate instants of poetic insight into more objective forms. *The Glass Menagerie* (1945) is an example of such an attempt to objectify poetic vision. The play is composed of a series of remembered moments. These poetic instants are organized within a framework symbolic of the structure of consciousness. In the "Production Notes," Williams comments on the tension between subjective (textural) and objective (structural) modalities within consciousness: "In an episodic play, such as this, the basic structure or narrative line may be obscured from the audience; the effect may seem fragmentary rather than architectural. . . . The legend or image upon the screen will strengthen the effect of what is merely allusion in the writing and allow the primary point to be made more simply and lightly than if the entire responsibility were on the spoken lines. Aside from this structural value, I think the screen will have a definite emotional appeal, less definable but just as important."

In this work, Williams symbolizes the continuity of conscious experience by means of a mechanism borrowed from the French novelist Marcel Proust. *The Glass Menagerie* is a phantom of the memory; that is, a vision "recollected in tranquility":

> The play is memory. . . . In memory everything seems to happen to music. That explains the fiddle in the wings.
> I am the narrator of the play, and also a character in it. The other characters are my mother, Amanda, my sister, Laura, and a gentleman caller who appears in the final scenes. He is the most realistic character in the play, being an emissary from a world of reality that we were somehow set apart from. But since I have a poet's weakness for symbols, I am using this character also as a symbol; he is the long delayed but always expected something that we live for (I, 145).

The playwright has described the images created for this work as "plastic." In the "Production Notes," he observes, "Everyone should know nowadays the unimportance of the photographic in art: that truth, life, or reality is an organic thing which the poetic imagination can represent or suggest, in essence, only through transformation, through changing into other forms than those which were merely present in appearance.

"These remarks are not meant as a preface only to this particular play. They have to do with a conception of a new, plastic theatre which must take the place of the exhausted theatre of realistic conventions if the theatre is to resume vitality as a part of our culture" (I, 131).

Williams' notion of imagery is itself synthetic. It recalls some principles drawn from the Imagists and Symbolists of the late nineteenth and early twentieth centuries and anticipates others which would be developed by the Structuralists of the fifties and sixties. For in *The Glass Menagerie*, the playwright attempts to represent both the texture and the structure of poetic vision; that is, to reveal the tension between dynamic and static planes of meaning within human consciousness. In "The Timeless World of the Play," he writes that the drama—of all the arts—is best suited to the interpretation of this relationship: "If the world of a play did not offer us this occasion to view its characters under that special condition of a *world without time*, then, indeed, the characters and occurrences of drama would become equally pointless, equally trivial, as corresponding meetings and happenings in life. . . . In a play, time is arrested in the sense of being confined. By a sort of legerdemain, events are made to remain *events*, rather than being reduced so quickly to mere *occurrences*" (II, 260–61).

III

It may happen that image and form, experience and
structure, inflame one another like lightning. . . .
(Wigman, "*The Language of Dance*," p. 13)

From the beginning of his career as a dramatist, Tennessee Williams was to use the stage as the model of human consciousness, equating poetic vision to more conventional modes of human understanding. Whereas the primary intent of his early works appears to have been linguistic—that is, directed toward encoding levels of conscious reality, that of a second phase of Williams' career can be described as "epistemological." *A Streetcar Named Desire, Summer and Smoke* (1948), and *Camino Real* (1953) are concerned with the problem of knowing; that is, with the verification of the truth of insight. In "Person to Person," the playwright describes the motive for this second phase of his development: "The fact that I want you to observe what I do for your possible pleasure and to give you knowledge of things that I feel I may know better than you . . . is not enough excuse for a personal lyricism that has not yet mastered its necessary trick of rising above the singular to the plural concern, from personal to general import. But for years and years now, which may have passed like a dream because of this obsession, I have been trying to learn how to perform this trick and make it truthful, and sometimes I feel that I am able to do it" (III, 4–5).[8]

The late forties and early fifties saw Tennessee Williams turn from his preoccupation with "imaging" reality to an interest in the verification of meaning. He was to add to his notion of *imagery* as primordial language the idea of *symbol* as the abstraction of truth.[9] The meaning of that distinction can be understood by comparing the playwright's comments on *The Glass Menagerie* with his observations about *Camino Real* (1953). Of *Camino Real*, he writes, "More than any other work that I have done, this play has seemed to me like the construction of another world, a separate existence. Of course, it is nothing more nor less than my conception of the time and world that I live in, and its people are mostly archetypes of certain basic attitudes and qualities with those mutations that would occur if they had continued along the road to this hypothetical terminal point in it" (II, 419).

In the preface to *Camino Real,* Williams describes imagery as the representation of primal truths; that is, as the form of vision: "We all have in our conscious and unconscious minds a great vocabulary of images, and I think all human communication is based on these images as are our dreams; and a symbol in a play has only one legitimate purpose which is to say a thing more directly and simply and beautifully than it could be said in words" (II, 421).

The playwright observes that the form of *Camino Real* is also characterized by a tension between vision and structure. In his introductory essay, Williams describes this tension as symbolic of the conflict between freedom and form in reality, as in the poetic consciousness: "My desire was to give these audiences my own sense of something wild and unrestricted that ran like water in the mountains, or clouds changing shape in a gale, or the continually dissolving and transforming images of a dream. This sort of freedom is not chaos nor anarchy. On the contrary, it is the result of painstaking design, and in this work I have given more conscious attention to form and construction than I have in any work before. Freedom is not achieved simply by working freely" (II, 420).

The poetic figures created to interpret the action in *Camino Real* differ in an important way from those used in *The Glass Menagerie.* These are not "natural" images surfacing from a naive consciousness. Rather, they are configurations which have been subjected to the process of intellection. Williams recognizes the distinction between his earlier imagery and these poetic constructions. He describes these later figures as "symbols": "I hate writing that is a parade of images for the sake of images; I hate it so much that I close a book in disgust when it keeps on saying one thing is like another; I even get disgusted with poems that make nothing but comparisons between one thing and another. But I repeat that symbols, when used respectfully, are the purest language of plays. Sometimes it would take page after tedious page of exposition to put across an idea that can be said with an object or a gesture on the lighted stage" (II, 421–22).

The playwright's distinction between the *imagery* of *The Glass Menagerie* and the *symbolism* of *Camino Real* is appropriate. For in this later work, he has undertaken a function which goes beyond that apparent in the earlier work. In *Camino Real*, Williams uses symbols not merely to verify the truth of poetic vision, but as a way of transforming reality. The poet Byron, in *Camino Real*, speaks of the power of symbols to purify human experience:

> But a poet's vocation, which used to be my vocation, is to influence the heart in a gentler fashion than you have made your mark on that loaf of bread. He ought to purify it and lift it above its ordinary level. For what is the heart but a sort of—
>
> .   .   .   .
>
> —A sort of—*instrument!*—that translates *noise* into *music*, chaos into —*order* . . .
>
> .   .   .   .
>
> —*a mysterious order!* (II, 507).

IV

> He thought of belief and the gradual loss of belief
> and the piecing together of something like it again.
> ("Mornings on Bourbon Street," *Winter of Cities*, p. 115)

Camino Real marks a major transition in Williams' progression as a dramatist. It foreshadows his development of the dominant theme of his drama in the fifties; that is, the relationship of his poetic protagonist to the world outside himself. The playwright acknowledges this modification of his essentially Romantic intent. In the "Afterword" to *Camino Real*, he comments on his growing concern about the social implications of poetic vision: "My own creed as a playwright is fairly close to that expressed by the painter in Shaw's play *The Doctor's Dilemma*: 'I believe in Michelangelo, Velasquez and Rembrandt; in the might of design, the mystery of color, the redemption of all things by beauty everlasting and the message of art that has made these hands blessed. Amen.' . . . I feel, as the painter did, that the message lies in those abstract beauties of form and color and line, to which I would add light and motion" (II, 421–22).

In the plays of the fifties and early sixties, Williams shifts his

ground of action from the inner consciousness to the world outside
the self.[10] *The Rose Tattoo* (1951), *Cat on a Hot Tin Roof* (1955),
Orpheus Descending (1957), *Suddenly Last Summer* (1958), *Sweet
Bird of Youth* (1959), *Period of Adjustment* (1960), and *Night of
the Iguana* (1962) take place in a universe of which society is the
material form.

A number of themes emerge through the pattern of these middle
dramas. One of these, a motif developed by Eugene O'Neill, treats
the impact of society on the search for selfhood. Another involves
the degree to which contemporary American society is itself the expression of moral ideas. But the dominant motif in these works appears to go beyond these conventional Romantic themes. For in
these middle works, Williams moves from the phenomenological,
linguistic, and epistemological preoccupations of his earlier dramas
to the formulation of a social ethic.

The theme of moral responsibility does indeed appear in earlier
works: in stories such as *One Arm*, short plays such as *The Purification*, and in long works such as *A Streetcar Named Desire*. However,
in these earlier works, the playwright is concerned primarily with the
defense of a personal ethic; that is, with the attempt of the poet-
protagonist to protect his vision of truth against the "corrupting"
influence of society. In the works of the fifties, a different vision of
the relationship between the poet and society emerges. Plays such
as *Sweet Bird of Youth* are not so much studies of societal constraints
on the individual's search for truth as explorations of the nature of
the protagonist's responsibility for his moral condition and that of
the world in which he lives. In these middle dramas, Williams attributes both the failures of the individual and those of society
to the inadequacy of the ethical principles which govern their
interdependence.[11]

The primary theme of these "social plays" is foreshadowed in
Camino Real by Lord Byron, who describes his relationship to the
world in which he lives:

—That was my vocation once upon a time, before it was obscured by
vulgar plaudits!—Little by little it was lost among gondolas and palaz-
zos!—masked balls, glittering salons, huge shadowy courts and torch-lit
entrances!

.   .   .   .

Oh, I wrote many cantos in Venice and Constantinople and in Raven-
na and Rome, on all of those Latin and Levantine excursions that my
twisted foot led me into—but I wonder about them a little. They seem
to improve as the wine in the bottle—dwindles . . . *There is a passion
for declivity in this world!* (II, 507–8).

Williams, like O'Neill, traces moral crises to an essentially aesthetic cause; that is, to the inability of modern man to reconcile
personal ideals to societal conditions. But although they have similar
views of moral crisis, Williams' protagonists seem to possess a higher
level of social consciousness than do O'Neill's heroic figures. While
O'Neill's moral heroes seek redemption in a world beyond society,
the protagonists of Williams' social plays hope for reconciliation *in*
and *with* the world outside the self.[12]

The dramatic progression traced in the social plays of the fifties
can be described as "tragic." For the efforts of these protagonists
to use moral freedom to create a practical ethic fail. It is important
to observe, however, that such efforts fail, not primarily because of a
hostile society, but because of fundamental problems within the
characters themselves. Williams has written of the power of the
drama to interpret this tragic theme: "Yet plays in the tragic tradition offer us a view of certain moral values in violent juxtaposition.
Because we do not participate, except as spectators, we can view
them clearly, within the limits of our emotional equipment. These
people on the stage do not return our looks. We do not have to answer
their questions nor make any sign of being in company with them,
nor do we have to compete with their virtues nor resist their offenses.
All at once, for this reason, we are able to *see* them!" (II, 262).

Perhaps the most evident of the alterations in form which characterize the plays of the fifties are those related to dramatic structure. *Cat on a Hot Tin Roof*, for example, is clearly not restricted to
the interpretation of inner states of consciousness. Like other works
written in this period, it is constructed so as to direct the attention
of the spectator to actions in the world of events; that is, to the unfolding of moral crises which have tragic implications for both the
individual and society.

It can be argued that the social dramas which Williams wrote in
the fifties are variations on the forms shaped by the European masters of the nineteenth century; that is, by Henrik Ibsen, August

Strindberg, and Anton Chekhov.[13] Like these Romantic-realists, Williams has used the drama to reveal the relationship of man's interior life to both his existence in society and his destiny in the moral universe. But if Williams, in this instance, has adapted forms created for the theater of nineteenth-century Europe, he has clothed them in materials drawn from American experience. Whereas the structural forms of these social tragedies are modeled after the examples of European dramatists, their textural forms are derived from American sources.

Following Walt Whitman, Williams has attempted to interpret the distinctive quality of life in the New World; particularly, to symbolize those changes in consciousness which have attended the establishment of a social order grounded in the principle of moral freedom.[14] In the early phases of his career as a playwright, Williams appeared to regard his dramas as celebrations of that principle of freedom. In the preface to 27 Wagons Full of Cotton, he wrote in Whitmanesque terms of art as the exploration of the tension between freedom and form in the democratic consciousness: "In my opinion art is a kind of anarchy, and the theater is a province of art. . . . I must modify that statement about art and anarchy. Art is only anarchy in juxtaposition with organized society. It runs counter to the sort of orderliness on which organized society apparently must be based. It is a benevolent anarchy: it must be that and if it is true art, it is. It is benevolent in the sense of constructing something which is missing, and what it constructs may be merely criticism of things as they exist."[15]

But if Tennessee Williams inherited his concept of moral freedom from Walt Whitman, his views of other aspects of reality would come to differ significantly from those set forth by the nineteenth-century poet. Whitman's concept of freedom was based on his firm belief in a principle of law governing the universe—a "planned Idea."[16] Major alterations in the texture of Williams' world-view were to result from his inability to confirm the existence of such a principle—in society, in the moral universe, or, indeed, in man himself. It was to be the apparent failure of the playwright's "knightly quest," the growing frustration of his search for an ethical principle capable of reconciling the conflict between freedom and law in human experience which was to become the dominant motif of the prose, fiction, and drama of the sixties and seventies.

V

Turn again, turn again, turn once again;
the freaks of the cosmic circus are men.
("Carousel Tune," *Winter of Cities*, p. 95)

Perhaps the most striking characteristic of the works of the sixties and seventies is the change in the setting against which dramatic actions are set. Whereas the plays of the fifties and early sixties take place in society, those of the late sixties and seventies are set in a highly ambiguous environment. In plays such as *Out Cry* (1973), Williams seems to have abandoned the exploration of the interaction between the individual and society, in order to consider the problem of human destiny in a universe of theological definition.[17]

In these late plays, Williams' symbolic hierarchy has, to all intents and purposes, been reversed. Whereas plays such as *Camino Real* employ theological figures to interpret sexual energies repressed in the recesses of the consciousness, these late works use sexual language to mask theological themes. In plays such as *The Seven Descents of Myrtle* (1968), later called *Kingdom of Earth*, sexuality is the symbol of the illusion of living; the mask disguising the dominant principle in existence—death.[18]

In the short story "Happy August the Tenth," one of two women companions sets forth this theme in explicit language: "Yesterday evening, Horne, you looked out at the city from the balcony and you said, My God, what a lot of big tombstones, a necropolis with brilliant illumination, the biggest tombstones in the world's biggest necropolis. I repeated this remark to Dr. Schreiber and told him it had upset me terribly. He said, 'You are living with, you are sharing your life with, a very sick person. To see great architecture in a great city and call it tombstones in a necropolis is a symptom of a deep psychic disturbance'" (*Eight Mortal Ladies*, p. 6).

Each of the protagonists who inhabit this universe of recent definition is the victim of a fatal disease. In some instances, as in *The Milk Train Doesn't Stop Here Anymore*, *The Mutilated*, and *The*

Seven Descents of Myrtle, this sickness is given a specific description. In others, as in *In the Bar of a Tokyo Hotel, Small Craft Warnings,* and *Out Cry,* the exact nature of the illness remains undisclosed. Actually, images of the dead and dying appear throughout the body of Williams' poetry, fiction, and drama. In works such as *A Streetcar Named Desire,* however, such visions of death are transitory. The poet-spectator, in these earlier works, awakes from the dream of death to join in the celebration of life. It can be argued that visions of death become increasingly apparent in the dramas of the fifties. However, the actual change of setting from the world of the living to this universe of the dead and dying takes place in *The Night of the Iguana* (1962). The contour of a purgatorial landscape emerges in succeeding works; in *The Milk Train Doesn't Stop Here Anymore* (1963), *The Mutilated* and *The Gnädiges Fräulein* (both 1966), *The Seven Descents of Myrtle* (1968), *In the Bar of a Tokyo Hotel* (1969), *Small Craft Warnings* (1972), and *Out Cry* (1973).

Not only are these works characterized by distortions of the symbolic forms developed in earlier works, but the uncertain progression toward light which is the motive of plays such as *The Glass Menagerie* appears all but abandoned.[19] Instead, "Orpheus" is seen "descending into final darkness."[20] That descent is the theme of *The Milk Train Doesn't Stop Here Anymore.*[21] Here, the playwright uses as an epigraph lines from William Butler Yeats's "Sailing to Byzantium":

> Consume my heart away, sick with desire
> And fastened to a dying animal
> It knows not what it is; and gather me
> Into the artifice of eternity.

Williams describes this allegorical play as a "fairy tale" and suggests that it should be produced in the manner of the Kabuki theater of Japan: "I have added to the cast a pair of stage assistants that function in a way that's between the Kabuki Theatre of Japan and the chorus of Greek theatre. My excuse, or reason, is that I think the play will come off better the further it is removed from conventional theatre, since it's been rightly described as an allegory and as a 'sophisticated fairy tale' " (V, 3).

Perhaps the most detailed description of this theological universe appears in the recent novel *Moise and the World of Reason* (1975). This work—like Imamu Amiri Baraka's *The System of Dante's Hell* (1965)—is an account of a poet's desperate search for meaning in the underground of the city.[22] In this novel, as in its Dantean models, the symbolic journey into darkness is undertaken by several figures— masques of a single poetic identity.

The title of the novel is used in an ironic manner. For the painter Moise, the black ice-skater of the narrator's memory, the failed play- wright, and the observing self (the writer "I") exist in a world devoid of reason. It is Moise who describes this universe: "I think I lived in something more like your world once, I mean a world of reason, but things became more and more untenable and I began to leave the room of that world and to retire into this one. I don't know how long ago" (p. 26).

The characters who inhabit this world have been all but divested of the humanity purchased with suffering by the protagonists of earlier works. They have lost their capacities to act, feel, create, know, and, ultimately, to be. They are victims of destructive forces which have their expression both within the individual and the world outside the self. The universe which Williams depicts in these works is absurd. In the closing lines of the novel, the narrator com- ments on the uncertainty of human destiny in this universe without reason: "It isn't yet dark in the room but dim and dimmer and all that I hear now are the footsteps of a giant being, as hushed as they are gigantic, footsteps of the Great Unknown One approaching our world of reason or unreason, you name it as you conceive it. And now

The last Blue Jay is completed" (p. 190).

In 1973, Williams wrote that he regarded *Out Cry* as the most mature work of this recent period.[23] In this drama, the playwright used the stage as the symbol of a universe characterized by absurdity. Like Hamlet, Felice and Clare attempt to make the stage the "mirror of conscience," the instrument of meaning. In this symbolic setting, they hope to bring the disordered facets of their common existence into some kind of harmony.

This work has developed through a number of stage versions. An early script, *The Two-Character Play*, was mounted in 1967, at the Hampstead Theatre Club, London. A revised script, with the title

Out Cry, was produced in Chicago, in 1971. It was "reworked" for a 1973 production on Broadway. In 1975, Williams reclaimed the title *The Two-Character Play* for a third version, which was given an Off Broadway production. (This version appears in volume five of *The Theatre*.)

In all these versions, the playwright has used the same general plot. Abandoned by their company in a state theater in an unnamed country, two actors, a brother and sister, substitute for their scheduled production a two-character play, an autobiographical drama. A crisis develops when Felice and Clare discover they are unable to discern the boundaries between past and present. Their sense of crisis accelerates as the two actors attempt vainly to distinguish between fiction and fact, illusion and reality. Members of the audience, bewildered, leave. Finding that they have been locked within the cold, darkening theater, Felice and Clare seek a means of escape. Failing to discover a way out of the place in which they have been imprisoned, the actors seek to append a resolution to both fictional and actual lines of action.

Certain differences in the contexts of meaning distinguish *The Two-Character Play* from *Out Cry*. In *The Two-Character Play*, Williams focuses the spectator's attention on the roots of suffering in human actions. In this work, he attributes Felice's and Clare's dilemma both to their own ungovernable passions and to the tragic legacy of their parents' murder-suicide. In *Out Cry*, however, he treats human suffering as a symptom of a more comprehensive problem. In this work, the playwright makes the isolation of Felice and Clare in the cold and darkened theater a symbol of the destiny of mankind in a cruel and unfeeling universe.

In both plays, death is projected as the ultimate solution to both actual and fictional dilemma. However, this solution is given two somewhat different interpretations. In *The Two-Character Play* the projected deaths of Felice and Clare are motivated psychologically:

(He [Felice] moves a few steps toward the revolver, then picks it up and slowly, with effort points it at CLARE. FELICE tries very hard to pull the trigger: he cannot. Slowly he lowers his arm, and drops the revolver to the floor. There is a pause. FELICE raises his eyes to watch the light fade from the face of his sister as it is fading from his: in both their faces is a tender admission of defeat. They reach out their hands to one another, and the light lingers a moment on their hands lifting toward each other. As they slowly embrace, there is total dark in which:) THE CURTAIN FALLS (V, 370).

In *Out Cry*, death is interpreted as a mode of transcendence, the only access to meaning:

> (She crosses to the sofa: lifts the pillow beneath which the revolver is concealed: gasps and drops the pillow back: looks toward Felice.)
> FELICE: Hurry, it won't hold!
> (She crosses to him and touches his hand.)
> CLARE:—Magic is a habit.
> (They look slowly up at the sunflower projections.)
> FELICE:—Magic is the habit of our existence. . .
> (The lights fade, and they accept its fading, as a death, somehow transcended.) CURTAIN (pp. 71–2).

Both *The Two-Character Play* and *Out Cry* can be described as theological dramas, visions of human destiny. In both versions of the play, Williams seems to abandon the philosophic optimism of the plays of the forties and fifties, adopting instead a kind of pessimism not unlike that apparent in the works of other American dramatists of the sixties and seventies.

It is perhaps his use of this essentially absurdist vision of reality which has rendered both versions of this late play so difficult to interpret in performance. Perhaps the most disappointing aspect of this work, for many critics and spectators, is the diminution of the quality of light which characterized Williams' resolutions of moral crises in earlier works. Whereas in works such as *The Glass Menagerie*, the playwright held out hope that drama itself offered a way of bringing human experience into harmony with universal law, he appears to suggest in works such as *Out Cry* that all efforts to achieve man's reconciliation with the universe, or indeed, with himself are doomed to failure.

In an essay called "Too Personal," Williams acknowledges that the luminous vision of early works such as *The Glass Menagerie* has, in *Out Cry*, dimmed. To the charge that the problem lies in his failure—in works such as *Out Cry*—to objectify his personal vision, the playwright has responded, "My answer is: 'What else can . . . [the poet] do?'—I mean the very root-necessity of all creative work is to express those things most involved in his experience. Otherwise, is the work, however well executed, not a manufactured, a synthetic thing? . . . So far I have spoken only in defense of the personal kind of writing. Now I assure you that I know it can be overdone. It is the responsibility of the writer to put his experience as a being into work that refines it and elevates it and that makes of it an essence that a wide audience can somehow manage to feel in themselves: 'This is true' " (V, 219–20).

VI

> I don't suppose that he will be able to build these
>   fires much longer
> as part of himself must burn like a match struck to
>   light them.
>   ("Part of a Hero," *Winter of Cities*, p. 58)

A review of the work of Tennessee Williams, published over the past thirty years or more, would seem to lead to the conclusion that the body of his poetry, fiction, and drama represents a pattern of variations on a single idea of form. For Williams, form is the concretion of stages in the progression of the poetic consciousness; the imitation of crises which have their immediate point of origin in the protagonist's soul.

Williams' career as a dramatist has been devoted to an attempt to give consciousness concrete form. In the first period of his career as a playwright, that consciousness assumed a lyrical shape, corresponding in many ways to the forms devised by dramatists in the tradition of European Romanticism. But if Williams followed European writers in seeking to interpret the contour of the poetic imagination, his symbolic forms were to assume an expressive identity which is American.

As a young writer, Williams shared with Walt Whitman an interest in creating an art for a democratic people. The visions of reality interpreted in his early fiction, prose, and drama reflect much of the nineteenth-century optimism of Whitman and Emerson. During the late forties and fifties, Williams' poetic consciousness assumed a more social quality, not only interpreting themes drawn from the American past, but integrating within its images and symbols, scientific, political, social, and ethical ideas. In the sixties and seventies, the dramatist was to turn his attention to the problem of revealing the theological universe in which contemporary man has his existence.

Throughout all phases of his career as a writer, Tennessee Williams has sought to record the progression of a singularly poetic consciousness, as it attempts to confer meaning on a changing reality. In the early stages of his career, the artist interpreted this attempt as an essentially personal endeavor. In the fifties, he turned his attention outward—to the relationship between the individual and society.[24] In these middle plays, he sought to interpret contemporary humanity's search for a social ethic. The drama, fiction, and prose of the middle-to-late sixties and seventies have had, as a dominant theme, theological crisis; that is, man's seeming connivance with a hostile universe to achieve his own destruction.

A variety of factors has apparently served to intensify the despairing vision of experience which came to characterize the playwright's sensibility in the sixties. Undoubtedly, one of these has been a mounting sense of crisis in society. Whereas Williams' early works were created in a relatively confident era of American history, his later works reflect the anxieties which came to pervade much of the public mind in the sixties. But a more personal factor is involved in this change, one which relates to alterations in the playwright's perception of the moral universe in which man pursues his destiny. The dying Whitman could speak with nostalgic tenderness of possibilities inherent in experience; Williams, by the middle of the sixties, had come to interpret human existence in profoundly pessimistic terms. If the Williams protagonist went forth in the forties, like Whitman's "child" from the Adamic garden, he had come in the sixties to envision himself as the symbol of "fallen" humanity.[25]

Despite his apparent difficulties in reconciling form and content in these later works, Tennessee Williams remains one of the most important figures in the American theater of the twentieth century. Both short works, such as *This Property Is Condemned,* and long plays, such as *The Glass Menagerie, A Streetcar Named Desire* and *Cat on a Hot Tin Roof,* have earned critical and popular acclaim throughout the world, for the effectiveness of their symbolizations of the interior lives of contemporary men and women. Wider acceptance for more complex works, such as *Summer and Smoke* and *Camino Real*, is developing, as audiences become familiar with their forms and contents. Williams' importance is not, however, limited to his success as a practicing playwright. The concept of imitation interpreted in his poetry, fiction, films, and dramas has had a significant influence on the evolution of new modes of interpretation throughout the entire pattern of the American arts.

It is difficult to assess the "future history"[26] of works written in the most recent period of Tennessee Williams' career. Certainly, these late works have not found the critical or popular acceptance accorded his work during the forties, fifties, and early sixties. It may be that later decades will find these recent dramas, like the late plays of Shakespeare, not merely indications of the decline of the artist's powers of creation, but rather the record of a new stage in the unceasing progression of a poetic consciousness; the symbolization of hidden realities of profound meaning as yet to be recognized by society.

Notes to Esther M. Jackson, "Tennessee Williams:
Poetic Consciousness in Crisis"

1. A more comprehensive discussion of some of the materials in this essay is included in my earlier study, *The Broken World of Tennessee Williams*.

2. Williams' concept of form as the imitation of consciousness is indebted to the theories of the German idealists. See, for example, Immanuel Kant's discussion of the relationship of form to imaginative processes, in *The Critique of Judgment*, trans. J. H. Bernard, *Selections from Kant*, ed. Theodore Meyer Greene (New York: Charles Scribner's Sons, 1929), pp. 426–30.

Many aspects of Williams' notion of consciousness are, like those of Walt Whitman, adapted from the theories of Hegel. See, for example, the discussion of consciousness in Georg W. F. Hegel, *The Phenomenology of the Spirit*, trans. James B. Baillie, rev. Carl J. Friedrich, in *The Philosophy of Hegel*, ed. Carl J. Friedrich (New York: Modern Library, 1953), pp. 399–457.

In his emphasis on consciousness as the ground of reality, Williams is closely aligned with the tradition of European Romanticism. See, for example, Richard Wagner, *Opera and Drama*, trans. Edwin Evans, 2 vols. (London: William Reeves, 1913), I, 317–96.

3. See Walt Whitman's theory of art for common men, *Democratic Vistas*, in *Prose Works*, ed. Floyd Stovall, 2 vols. (New York: New York University Press, 1963–65), II, 361–426.

Whitman discusses the need for a language for the American people in a number of essays. See, for example, *American National Literature*, in *Prose Works*, II, 667–8.

4. The notion of form as the concretion of an instant of truth appears in the works of religiously oriented thinkers such as Henri Bergson and Martin Buber and in those of secular existentialists such as Maurice Merleau-Ponty. See Henri Bergson's *Laughter*, trans. Cloudesley Brereton and Fred Rothwell (New York: The Macmillan Com-

pany, 1911), pp. 150–57. See also Martin Buber, "Drama and Theater," in *Martin Buber and the Theater*, ed. Maurice Friedman (New York: Funk and Wagnalls, 1969), pp. 83–7.

"Concrete form" is one of Merleau-Ponty's concepts. See *The Phenomenology of Perception*, trans. Colin Smith (New York: Humanities Press, 1962), pp. 126–7. It is a concept suggested by Walt Whitman. See his notes on a "New Poetry," in *Prose Works*, II, 519–21.

5. This concept of form as the concretion of vision informs Williams' early poetry, fiction and drama. See *American Blues: Five Short Plays* (New York: Dramatists Play Service, 1948). Examples of his early poetry appear in *Five Young American Poets* (New York: New Directions, 1944). For examples of his early fiction, see *One Arm and Other Stories* (New York: New Directions, 1948).

6. Williams' concepts of images, symbols, and metaphors as modes of "salvation" are adapted, in part, from the theories of Walt Whitman and from those of his disciple, Hart Crane. See Crane's discussion of the metaphysical uses of poetry, in *Collected Poems of Hart Crane* (New York: Liveright, 1933), Appendix B, p. 177.

7. "Felt experience" is Susanne K. Langer's language. See *Feeling and Form* (New York: Charles Scribner's Sons, 1953). In this connection, see Williams, *This Property Is Condemned*, in *27 Wagons Full of Cotton*.

8. Fiction written in this period also seems to reflect changes in Williams' view of the protagonist's relationship to society. See, for example, "Three Players of a Summer Game," in *Hard Candy: A Book of Stories*. This story provided the plot and character outlines which Williams developed in *Cat on a Hot Tin Roof*.

9. For interesting insights into the problem of giving theatrical form to Williams' poetic vision, see *Kazan on Kazan* (a series of taped interviews with the director Elia Kazan), ed. Michael Ciment (New York: The Viking Press, 1974), pp. 66–82.

10. For a discussion of the progression of Williams' poetic consciousness, see Robert B. Heilman, "Tennessee Williams: Approaches to Tragedy," *The Southern Review*, n. s. I, nos. 3–4 (October 1965), pp. 770–90.

11. For a discussion of Williams' interpretations of society, see Jackson, *Broken World*, pp. 43–67, 129–55.

12. Whereas Williams borrowed many of the organizing mechanisms which he employed in *The Glass Menagerie* from arts and letters, he was to find the principal validating structures for his social plays in the sciences and social sciences. While the works of nineteenth-century scientists such as Charles Darwin provided the playwright with symbols for the verification of his perceptions of the world outside the self, he was to find support for his concept of interior life in the psychological treatises of Sigmund Freud and Carl Gustav Jung. Both thinkers derived from artists such as Goethe and Schiller, as well as from philosophers such as Kant and Hegel, a primary interest in the revelation, identification, and interpretation of crises within the consciousness. While Freud sought to interpret the nature of conflict in the individual consciousness, Jung turned his attention to the interpretation of crisis in the collective mind. Significantly, for Williams, each directed his attention to the interpretation of the ethical relationship between the individual and society.

13. Francis Fergusson observes that these nineteenth-century dramatists extended the form of the well-made play with interpretations of the interior lives of their protagonists. Plays such as *The Lady from the Sea* (1888), *Miss Julie* (1888), and *The Seagull* (1896) have patterns of exposition which fuse Romantic and realistic techniques in much the same manner as do these "social plays" of Williams. See *The Idea of a Theater* (Princeton: Princeton University Press, 1949), pp. 156–58.

14. For a useful discussion of consciousness, see W. T. Stace, *The Philosophy of Hegel* (New York: Dover Publications, 1955), originally published in 1923. Stace's discussion of Hegel's concept of the progression from lyrical to ethical considerations, in the individual consciousness as well as in society, is especially useful in interpreting

changes in the poetic vision of Tennessee Williams. See Part IV, "The Philosophy of Spirit," pp. 321–404.

15. "Something Wild . . . ," introduction to 27 *Wagons Full of Cotton*, pp. vii–viii, xi. The tone of this essay is more political than are those of later discussions of form published by Williams. Here, Williams claims that art is the expression, if not the instrument, of political, social, and intellectual freedom. He invokes not the names of European artists such as Dante, Baudelaire, Proust and Yeats, but those of American thinkers such as Thomas Paine, Thomas Jefferson, and Abraham Lincoln.

16. See Whitman, *Democratic Vistas*, p. 381. Whitman saw no irreconcilable conflict between the idea of freedom and the idea of eternal law. He believed nature to be the primary expression of that creative interaction between freedom and form which is the basis of life.

17. On theological perspectives in the drama of Williams, see John J. Fritscher, "Some Attitudes and a Posture: Religious Metaphor and Ritual in Tennessee Williams' Query of the American God," *Modern Drama* 13: 201–15.

See also Sister M. Carol Blitgen, BVM, "Tennessee Williams, Modern Idolator," in *Renascence* 22: 192–7.

18. A number of critics and scholars have discussed the death imagery which recurs throughout Williams' work. See, for example, Robert Hauptman, "The Pathological Vision—Three Studies: Jean Genet, Louis-Ferdinand Céline, Tennessee Williams," Ph.D. diss., Ohio State University, 1971.

19. More detailed pictures of this universe appear in the fiction of this period. See, for example, *The Knightly Quest: A Novella and Four Short Stories*.

20. For a discussion of earlier and less consistent treatments of this theme, see Jackson, pp. 68–87.

21. See Alvin Goldfarb's analysis of the plays of this later period, in "Selected Late Plays of Tennessee Williams," M. A. thesis, Hunter College of the City University of New York, 1974.

22. See Imamu Amiri Baraka (LeRoi Jones), *The System of Dante's Hell* (New York: Grove Press, 1965).

23. Tennessee Williams, "A Dispensable Foreword," introductory note for *Out Cry*, p. 3.

24. See Jim Gaines, "A Talk about Life and Style with Tennessee Williams," *Saturday Review*, April 29, 1972, pp. 25–9.

25. For a discussion of Williams' search for truth, see Robert Skloot, "Submitting Self to Flame: The Artist's Quest in Tennessee Williams, 1935–1954," *Educational Theatre Journal* 24: 2 (May 1973), 199–206.

26. This is Whitman's term. It appears in both his poetry and his prose. See, for example, "To a Historian," from "Inscriptions," *Leaves of Grass*, ed. Harold W. Blodgett and Sculley Bradley (New York: New York University Press, 1965), p. 4.

Plays

A Streetcar Named Desire . . .

If the essays submitted for this collection are accurate indication, *A Streetcar Named Desire* is the most intriguing of Williams' plays. Leonard Quirino's close reading and detailed analysis of the play will demand an extra appreciation even from those other essayists who write respectfully of it. The title draws on the language of fortune tellers but refers, as the author says, to "two very ordinary symbols—the cards of destiny and the voyage of experience."

Normand Berlin sees *Streetcar* as designed to, as he says, "keep the sides balanced" between Blanche and Stanley. He finds that theme and symbolism contribute to this conclusion. Britton Harwood points out what others imply—that the discussion of *Streetcar* continues in part because its genre is difficult of definition. His opening remarks may be compared with those of Leonard Quirino. John Roderick feels that difficulties with *Streetcar* are resolved if the play is interpreted as a deliberate—and successful—effort at tragicomedy and not as a failure at tragedy.

Alan Ehrlich studies technique, the results of the obtrusion of a stranger within an established order. Williams uses the technique often—in *Kingdom of Earth, Orpheus Descending* and *The Rose Tattoo*, with variants in other plays.

Bert Cardullo reinterprets *Streetcar* with the intent of clarifying Stanley's role and thereby the roles of Blanche and Stella. The lengthy note five is in effect an essay on the role of the baby—a subject that might be studied throughout Williams' work. (The idea comes from Ulrich Petermann of Munich, Germany, who unfortunately was unable to contribute to the collection.)

The essay by Vivienne Dickson is a fascinating study of the playwright at work. An examination of the fragments and early drafts of *Streetcar* shows how this intriguing play evolved.

. . . and Other Plays

In writing about *Battle of Angels* and the revision entitled *Orpheus Descending*, David Matthew concentrates on the figure of the artist. He considers the artist in these plays as a sacrificial figure, even a version of Dionysus, and as the hero on a quest. The treatment here of Williams' multilayered use of myth is expanded in Judith Thompson's essay (in TECHNIQUES), and Diane Turner in this section uses myth in studying *Camino Real*. George Niesen's essay (in THEMES) elaborates on the role of the artist in Williams' work, and Donald Pease's more general discussion (in ASSESSMENT) is pertinent.

Joseph Davis discerns in *The Glass Menagerie* themes that recur in later plays—time, the artist, the myth of southern history and southern chivalry. He broadly interprets the play against the background of the actual cultural history of the South. The question is to what extent Williams used the myth of the Old South merely for dramatic purposes. Thomas Scheye emphasizes the role of the gentleman caller in dealing with various aspects of the theme of illusion and reality in *Menagerie*. The author suggests that Jim O'Connor and Laura's ultimate reaction to him prevent the play from being a tragedy.

Philip Kolin finds *The Rose Tattoo* a combination of traditional comic forms and techniques that give the play a substance beneath the superficial overuse of symbolism. Wit, slapstick, character types, and other traditional elements of tragicomedy are well integrated. The author suggests that failure to recognize Williams' handling of these techniques explains the lack of appreciation for this play.

Camino Real also remains intriguing. James Coakley accepts and emphasizes the observations about the play that Williams makes in the foreword and the afterword to the published edition. If either writes an apologia, neither apologizes. Among the more detailed essays that follow is Diane Turner's interpretation of *Camino* as Williams' version of the universal round that Joseph Campbell discusses in *The Hero with a Thousand Faces*. The basic myth and the chance for incorporating numerous allusions may explain Williams' regard for the play.

Philip Wolf's discussion of communication patterns leads far beyond an interpretation of *Camino Real*. The author points out the frequent recurrence of situations and character traits in the Williams canon. Discussion of the play within this very broad framework is intended both to explain why the work was not well received and to suggest why it should be appreciated.

(In a two-part essay appearing in EUROPEAN CONTEXTS Mary Ann Corrigan also studies *Camino*, as an example of Expressionism.)

Charles May studies "Three Players of a Summer Game" in depth as a way of showing the complexity of the later Brick in *Cat on a Hot Tin Roof*. The author talks of Brick's "tragedy" and of Williams' concentration on the ambiguous. The game of croquet in the short story is, the author feels, aesthetically significant; and his close study of "Three Players" makes that short work itself appear significant.

Sy Kahn studies *Baby Doll* as another of Williams' literary productions and not as a mere sensational filmscript, and he discerns much to justify the analysis of a work of art. Leonard Casper's comments on *Kingdom of Earth* (in TECHNIQUES) complement this study.

Alvin Goldfarb finds that *Period of Adjustment*, which Williams called a "serious comedy," emphasizes *serious* rather than *comedy*. The play is, the author claims, no temporary repudiation of the sex and violence of the earlier plays. It is instead composed of variants of the usual Williams character types.

Charles Moorman's brief essay, despite its "long introduction," succinctly deals with both method and themes in *The Night of the Iguana*. The author discerns the triangle of action (see Leonard Casper's essay in TECHNIQUES), the significance of Nonno's poem and the relationship between Shannon and the iguana. He also finds this play distinctly an "affirmation of life" in the Williams canon. Among those who would qualify the conclusion are Jacob Adler (in INTRODUCTORY). And in the immediately following essay Glenn Embrey, by coincidence rather than design, investigates the play in some detail and finds a level of meaning undermining the idea that Williams either affirmed life or changed directions. Sex, the author feels, is the major problem, and he suspects the apparently optimistic resolution of the action. Paradoxically, whatever the libertinism of the playwright, sex, the author suggests, is often the cause of the violence depicted in the plays.

Mary McBride sees *The Milk Train* as belonging to a group of plays dealing with the broad theme outlined in her introduction. She makes interesting observations about the role of Chris, another of the several interlopers Williams introduces into a static environment (see David Matthew on *Orpheus* and *Battle* and Alan Ehrlich on *Streetcar*) and a wry version of Williams' many artists.

Jerrold Phillips has some insights into *Kingdom of Earth* that make what Williams called his "funny melodrama" seem to deserve further study. Undertones of myth enhanced by a meaningful symbolism, especially that of water and the other liquids, suggest fertility and rebirth.

Rexford Stamper's discussion of the several versions of *The Two-Character Play (Out Cry)* suggests Williams may have succeeded in gradually reworking to change an excessively personal statement to a "public" statement resembling that of his earlier plays. These observations should be compared with those of William Free (in ASSESSMENT) and Norman Fedder (in TECHNIQUES).

Since *The Red Devil Battery Sign* of 1975 remains unpublished as the manuscript of this collection goes to press, Sy Kahn relies upon reviews and on his own view of the performance in Vienna to write a brief essay interpreting the last of Williams' plays, except *This Is (An Entertainment)*, and placing it in the context of the Williams canon.

As noted in the preface, though this collection unfortunately has no essay on each of the long plays, each is discussed elsewhere in the text. The index will direct the reader to the appropriate pages.

The Cards Indicate a Voyage
on *A Streetcar Named Desire*

LEONARD QUIRINO

"Art is made out of symbols the way your body is made out
of vital tissue."

Tennessee Williams[1]

" 'They are the souls,' answered his [Aeneas'] father
Anchises,
'Whose destiny it is a second time
To live in the flesh and there by the waters of Lethe
They drink the draught that sets them free from care
And blots out memory.' "

Description of the inhabitants of Elysian Fields
in Book VI of the *Aeneid*.[2]

So MUCH HAS been written about *A Streetcar
Named Desire* in terms of its theatrical presentation as interpreted
by a specific director and set of actors[3] and so much concern has
been lavished on the social attitudes and psychological constitution
of its characters[4] that the author's primary intention as revealed in
his use of mythic symbolism and archetypal imagery to create a
dialectic between soul and body to depict universally significant
problems such as the conflict and mutual attraction between desire
and death has been generally obscured or denigrated as pretentious.[5]
My own intention in this essay is to consider the play neither as
interpreted in any specific production nor as it may embody a
study of satyriasis, nymphomania, or reconstruction in the South,

77

but, rather, as it constitutes what an examination of its symbolism reveals to be Tennessee Williams' intention: a tragic parable dramatizing existence, the fact of incarnation, itself. Far from wishing to dissolve Williams' carefully constructed characters and theatrical effects into illustrations of archetypal figures or myths devoid of the author's particular "signature," I shall try to suggest how Williams' special use of two very ordinary symbols—the cards of destiny and the voyage of experience—aesthetically patterns the mosaic of his literary and theatrical imagery in *Streetcar*, investing the play with an artistry and meaning that transcend the mere theatricality and sensationalism with which it has so often been credited and discredited.

"Catch!" (I, 244) says Stanley Kowalski throwing a bloodstained package of meat to his wife, Stella, at the opening of the first scene of *A Streetcar Named Desire*. Laughing breathlessly, she manages to catch it. "This game is seven-card stud," reads the last line of the play. In between, much of the verbal and theatrical imagery that constitutes the drama is drawn from games, chance and luck. Williams had called the short play from which *Streetcar* evolved *The Poker Night*, and in the final version two of the most crucial scenes are presented within the framework of poker games played onstage. Indeed, the tactics and ceremonial of games in general, and poker in particular, may be seen as constituting the informing structural principle of the play as a whole. Pitting Stanley Kowalski, the powerful master of Elysian Fields against Blanche DuBois, the ineffectual ex-mistress of Belle Reve, Williams makes the former the inevitable winner of the game whose stakes are survival in the kind of world the play posits. For the first four of the eleven scenes of *Streetcar*, Blanche, by reason of her affectation of gentility and respectability, manages to bluff a good hand in her game with Stanley; thus, in the third scene Stanley is continually losing, principally to Mitch the potential ally of Blanche, in the poker game played onstage. However, generally suspicious of Blanche's behavior and her past, and made aware at the end of the fourth scene that she considers him an ape and a brute, Stanley pursues an investigation of the real identity of *her* cards. As, little by little, he finds proof of what he considers her own apishness and brutality, he continually discredits her gambits until, in the penultimate scene, he caps his winnings by raping her. In the last scene of the play, Stanley is not only winning every card game being played onstage, but he has also won the game he played with Blanche. Depending as it does on the skillful manipulation of the hands that chance deals out, the card game is used by Williams throughout *Streetcar* as a symbol of fate and of the skillful player's ability to make its decrees perform in his own favor at the expense of his opponent's misfortune, incompetence, and horror of the game itself.

Equally as important as the symbol of the card game in *Streetcar* is the imagery connected with the mythic archetype of the voyage which Williams portrays both as quest for an imagined ideal and as flight from disillusioning actuality. "They told me," says Blanche in her first speech, "to take a streetcar named Desire, and then to transfer to one called Cemeteries and ride six blocks and get off at—Elysian Fields." Putting together the allegorical names of these streetcars and their destination at Elysian Fields with Williams' portrayal of Blanche as resembling a moth, traditionally a symbol of the soul, we find in her journey a not too deeply submerged metaphor for the soul's disastrous voyage through life. Caged in a body that it attempts to transcend but cannot escape, the moth-soul yearns for the star (Stella) and for rest in the isles of the happy dead; it finds, instead, the flaming "red hot" milieu of the primal blacksmith ("Stanley" or "stone-lea" suggests the Stone Age man and "Kowalski" is Polish for "smith") and a world even more blatantly dedicated to "epic fornications" than its native Belle Reve, a world that shows every sign of prevailing. We are not surprised to learn that the agent of Blanche's journey to Elysian Fields, her school superintendent, is a Mr. Graves, and we can understand the implications of Blanche's statement late in the play, "The opposite [of death] is desire," to be more than merely sexual. Shuttling between yearning and frustration defines the basic rhythm of life itself for Blanche. Opening with her arrival in the land of life in death, the play chronicles the human soul's past and present excursions in the only vehicle that fate provides her, the rattle-trap streetcar of the body; the play closes with the soul's departure for incarceration in another asylum, another kind of living death.

Because the play, so rich in effects, is made to cohere largely by means of Williams' use of the imagery and symbolism of the voyage and the ceremonial and jargon of card games, a detailed exploration of *Streetcar* focusing on these two textural and structural principles might prove rewarding in assessing its artistic achievement. The ultimate aim of such an examination of the symbolism of the play, of course, is to demonstrate that the proper sphere of *Streetcar* is not the socio-clinical one to which it is so often relegated, but the realm of the tragic-universal which is more often than not denied it.

The epigraph to *A Streetcar Named Desire* is taken from Hart Crane's "The Broken Tower":

> And so it was I entered the broken world
> To trace the visionary company of love, its voice
> An instant in the wind (I know not whither hurled)
> But not for long to hold each desperate choice.

Besides focusing attention on Williams' positing of *two* broken worlds, both Belle Reve and Elysian Fields, and on the vision of life as a making of desperate choices, the epigraph introduces Williams' theme of the soul's quest for ideal love in the most unlikely of places —the broken world of actuality. Both the broken worlds which Williams compares and contrasts in the play bear wish-fulfilling names, but neither of these worlds fulfills Blanche's dreams of the ideal and of romantic love.

Blanche's first speech provides the introduction to Williams' treatment of her journey in the universal terms of life (desire) and death (cemeteries). In depicting her destination, Elysian Fields, which proves unwelcome and unwelcoming to Blanche, Williams continues to fuse and juxtapose images of life and death. In the ninth scene, for example, which takes place on the evening of Blanche's birthday (and shortly before the expected birth of the Kowalski child) a Mexican crone hawks "flores para los muertos" through the Elysian Fields offering her funeral "corones" to Blanche. In the previous scene, during the ghastly celebration of her own birthday, Blanche had been presented with a bus ticket back to Laurel (a name which ironically suggests wreaths of immortality) where she is even less welcome than she is in Stanley's domain. The birthday gift is a death sentence, and the soul on its desperate journey through existence finds destinations that are progressively horrifying. "Travelling," Blanche confesses, "wears me out."

Elysium, the paradise of the happy dead for the Greek poets, becomes in *Streetcar* a street which "runs between the L & N tracks and the river." Its flanks themselves suggest voyage although only the train ride, like the journey by streetcar, connotes horror for Blanche: "Out there I suppose is the ghoul-haunted woodland of Weir!" "No, honey," Stella replies, "those are the L & N tracks" (I, 252). But for Blanche whose mental landscape is haunted by her dead husband, the allusion to Poe's "Ulalume" in which the memory of a dead love haunts the narrator of the poem is extremely appropriate. Although she is fearful of further locomotive journeys of desire, Blanche regards the prospect of voyage by water with pleasure. She dreams of cruising the Caribbean on a yacht with Shep Huntleigh (whose first name suggests a pastoral swain and whose last name suggests aristocratic sport) and, in the last scene, even looks forward to death on the sea: "I can smell the sea air. The rest of my time I'm going to spend on the sea. And when I die, I'm going to die on the sea" (p. 410). Throughout the play, Blanche's addiction to water and to the baths which make her feel "Like a brand new human being," her hydrotherapy as she calls it, seems to be connected with the geography and function of the Elysian Fields as represented both in myth and in Williams' play.

In myth, the dead who entered the Elysian Fields were made to drink of the water of the river Lethe to forget all traces of their mortal past. And in Book VI of the *Aeneid*, Vergil depicts Lethe as a kind of watery purgatory where the dead are cleansed of all taint of memory and desire before they can be considered fit for reincarnation. In his adaptation of the concept of Elysian Fields for *Streetcar*, Williams, until the very end when he allows her the refuge of madness, denies the memory-haunted Blanche the full powers of the river Lethe. He depicts Stella, on the other hand, as one of the happy dead: after a night in bed with Stanley, "Her eyes and lips have that almost narcotized tranquility that is in the faces of Eastern idols" (p. 310). While Stella can bridge the two worlds of Belle Reve and Elysian Fields, Blanche is unwelcome in both.

This distinction is important to note because too many critics have made oversimplified, sociologically oriented interpretations of the conflict in *Streetcar* as a representation of Williams' nostalgia for vanished, decadent southern aristocracy and his horror of vital industrial proletarianism. Other critics, noticing that Williams *com-*

pares as well as contrasts Belle Reve with Elysian Fields, claim that his presentation of social conditions is ambivalent and confusing. But Williams, usually little interested in sociology beyond its reflection of the human predicament of survival, does not use Blanche's pretentious cultural standards—which he exposes as pitiful—to measure Belle Reve against Elysian Fields; rather, he emphasizes the uninhabitability of both for his supremely romantic heroine to the extent that she symbolizes the soul. The vitality and "raffish charm" of Elysian Fields is outweighed by its brutality; the fabled graciousness of Belle Reve by its debauchery. The former world with its brawling, bowling cocks-of-the-walk is male-dominated; the latter as its grammatically incorrect name (feminine adjective modifying masculine noun) suggests is a female-oriented, effeminate world whose scions, as symbolized by Blanche's young husband, are apt to be disinclined to propagate. Blanche's remark to Stella about Stanley early in the play, "But maybe he's what we need to mix with our blood now that we've lost Belle Reve . . ." proves, in the light of his (and even Mitch's) rough treatment of her, ironic. There can be no copulation or reconciliation between the world of the "beautiful dream" and the world of death in life actuality that will be mutually and ideally satisfactory. Stella's erotic will to life at any cost, her ability to shut one eye to the claims of the ideal and the other to the horrors of the actual, Williams portrays not as an easy truce between the two worlds but as a "narcotized," quasifatalistic commitment to survival that resolves none of the existential problems it poses.

Elysian Fields, the world that has replaced Belle Reve, will do, Williams seems to be saying, for the insensitive Stanley and the pragmatic Stella just as it provides satisfaction for their upstairs neighbors, the Hubbells, whom he names Eunice (literally "good victory") and Steve (literally "crown"); but it can only further the process of destroying Blanche which Belle Reve had begun. Its amusement-park thrills, its desperately gay and feverish music provide sufficient fulfilment only for the undemanding. The spirit of the whole place is characterized by the name of one of its nightspots, the "Four Deuces"—the poorest of the best hands in poker.

The introduction of Blanche's homosexual husband, Allan Grey, into the design of *Streetcar* has seemed gratuitously sensationalistic to some critics. Mary McCarthy, for example, found Blanche's story of the marriage so "patently untrue" that she took it upon herself to vouch for its incredibility to others: "the audience thinks the character must have invented it" (p. 134). Openly hostile to Williams' symbolism and incapable of interpreting it fairly (she insists on comparing Blanche to a typical sister-in-law—whatever that may be). Miss McCarthy failed to realize that Allan Grey, the deviate poet of Laurel and Belle Reve, is presented as the extreme opposite of the "gaudy seed-bearer" of Elysian Fields, that Blanche's attraction to him is as credible as is her abhorrence for Stanley, and that Blanche's relationship with her young husband proves mutually destructive because Williams' intention was to portray the impossibility of ideally consummating any union in which the body is involved. In Blanche's marriage Williams portrayed the futility of the romantic preoccupation with trying to achieve fulfilment with an epipsychidion or soul mate; in Blanche's intimacies with strangers and with Stanley he portrays the alternative to, and dramatizes the consequences of, that futile quest for fulfilment. "After the death of Allan—," Blanche tells Mitch, "intimacies with strangers was all I seemed able to fill my empty heart with. . . . I think it was panic, just panic, that drove me from one to another, hunting for some protection—here and there, in the most—unlikely places—even, at last, in a seventeen-year-old boy . . ." (p. 386). Throughout the play we are aware of Blanche's being ghoul-haunted by the suicide of her husband and we witness her interlude with the young newsboy whom she envisions as a prince out of the Arabian Nights. Her last attempt to settle for rest with Mitch is thwarted: she has misjudged even that simple soul and is denied even the small demands she makes of this love. All her intimacies have been with strangers to her deepest yearnings. Only when we realize this can we fully appreciate the irony, pathos and horror of her last line in the play: "Whoever you are—I have always depended on the kindness of strangers."

There can be salvation for Blanche neither in the pretentious world of Belle Reve from which she has salvaged only a trunk full of artificial goods and a head full of nightmares nor in the sex-glutted death in life of Elysian Fields because in *Streetcar* Williams has devised a conflict for her which only annihilation can resolve. As a symbol of the soul pitted against and in thrall to the body which fetters it, her natural state, like the moth's, is frustration.[6]

In the fourth scene of *Streetcar*, the following colloquy takes place between Stella and Blanche about the satisfactions of the flesh:

> STELLA: But there are things that happen between a man and a woman in the dark—that sort of make everything else seem—unimportant.
> BLANCHE: What you are talking about is brutal desire—just—Desire!— the name of that rattle-trap streetcar that bangs through the Quarter, up one old narrow street and down another . . .
> STELLA: Haven't you ever ridden on that streetcar?
> BLANCHE: It brought me here.—Where I'm not wanted and where I'm ashamed to be . . . (p. 321).

The banging of the tired old streecar up and down the narrow streets simulates Blanche's view of intercourse just as, in the very first scene, Stella's breathless laughter upon catching the blood-stained package of meat that Stanley throws her simulates *her* reaction to sexuality. In neither case does Williams portray sexuality, which he views as part of a cruel life force, in an attractive light. When Blanche says of Desire "It brought me here" we may take her to mean not only the streetcar that bore her to Elysian Fields, the land of the living dead, but human desire which brought her into existence. Incarnation is what she is ashamed of, and the flesh is what she has abused in her self-punishment for submitting to its importunate demands. "A man like that is someone to go out with," she tells Stella, "—once—twice—three times when the devil is in you. But live with? Have a child by?" (p. 321). Blanche has been conditioned to believe that the anarchy of the flesh must, whenever possible, be transcended in the interests of family and culture; Williams, however, dramatizes the futility of attempts to transcend the limitations of the human animal.

At the end of this fourth scene, imploring Stella to leave Stanley, Blanche delivers a harangue which in its cadence and hysterical rhetoric betrays her desperation and vulnerability. Describing Stanley as the amoral mortal enemy of humanistic aspiration, she says: "He acts like an animal, has an animal's habits! . . . Thousands and thousands of years have passed him right by, and there he is—Stanley

Kowalski—survivor of the Stone Age! Bearing the raw meat home from the kill in the jungle! . . . Night falls and the other apes gather! . . . His poker night!—you call it—this party of apes! . . . Maybe we are a long way from being made in God's image, but Stella—my sister—there has been *some* progress since then! Such things as art—as poetry and music—such kinds of new light have come into the world since then! In some kinds of people some tenderer feelings have had some little beginning! That we have got to make *grow*! and *cling* to, and hold as our flag! In this dark march toward whatever it is we're approaching. . . . *Don't—don't hang back with the brutes!*" (p. 323). Williams frames this speech, just before it begins and immediately after it ends, with the sound of two trains running like the old rattle-trap of Desire: at the same time, he has Stanley enter, unheard because of the noise of the trains, and remain to listen unobserved to Blanche's speech. Her two destroyers, desire and Stanley Kowalski, are thus made to hover like fateful accomplices over Blanche as she implores Stella to join with her in battle against them. That Stanley is placed in the strategically superior position of the unobserved viewer of the scene forecasts his eventual triumph over Blanche. To emphasize the inefficacy of Blanche's appeal and struggle against her fate, Williams ends the scene with Stella's embracing Stanley "fiercely"—joining the "brutes"—as Stanley grins at Blanche in victory. From that point on, Stanley begins to gain the upper hand in the struggle with Blanche.

Though in her long speech Blanche, characteristically rhapsodic, views the main struggle of existence as one between culture and brutality, the context of the play provides the struggle with wider, metaphysical significance. As a soul subjected to existence and hence to a body, her quarrel is not only with apes and brutes but with the apishness and brutality of matter with which she herself is involved and by which her mothlike flightiness is crippled and doomed. She herself has been unable to resist brutal treatment of her husband and she herself has ridden, without discernible satisfaction, on the streetcar of desire whose tracks, unlike the rungs of Plato's ladder of love, pointed to no great destination. Quite the contrary, for Blanche the desire and pursuit of the whole has proved, in practice, to lead to further disintegration.

While Stella and even Stanley would not, by any theological

standards, be considered devoid of a soul, Williams prefers to dramatize the soulfulness of Blanche at their expense because he conceives of the soul not in dogmatically theological but in ideal terms. For Williams, the soul appears to be that impulse in humanity which aspires to transcend the natural corruption and propensity to declivity that he constantly portrays as the informing principle of matter. Whereas he presents Stella and the earthy Stanley as the living dead narcotized by sex, gaming and comic books, characters contentedly buried in what Strindberg in *The Ghost Sonata* called "the dirt of life," Williams portrays Blanche as guiltily drawn to water and baths and as claiming, preciously, that she would die of eating an unwashed grape. The soul, for Williams in this play, seems to be that entity which produces and is sustained by culture but is not synonymous with it. It is that entity which, desiring the Good, is yet powerless to attain it by reason of the inexorable baseness of the matter that incarnates it. When Stanley, overpowering Blanche at the climax of the play says, "We've had this date with each other from the beginning," Williams is portraying what he views as the fated culmination of the soul's struggle against the body. The words "from the beginning"—in the mythic context of the drama—suggest the origins of the human race itself. All of Blanche's mothlike rushing and dashing about, which the stage directions call for her to do, cannot save her from the flame with which she has flirted. Though she was able to frighten Mitch away by shouting "Fire!" she collapses when faced with this more powerful flame to which her treacherous body draws her.

The predominating conflict of flesh and spirit modifies and includes all the other conflicts—sociological, psychological, moral, cultural—which *A Streetcar Named Desire* presents. It would be an oversimplification, as I have stated above, to see Belle Reve and Elysian Fields merely as opposites when Williams has subtly pointed out their similarity and the shortcomings they share in fulfilling the claims of the ideal. And it would be simpleminded to call Williams' presentation of both the attractiveness and failure of these two ways of life as ambivalence and to claim that it mars the play. By pitting the sterility of Belle Reve against the fertility of Elysian Fields, the weakness of Blanche against the insensitive stolidity of Stanley, her cultural pretensions against his penis-status, her sorority-girl vision of courtship and good times against his "colored-lights" orgasms, the simulated pearls of her lies against the swinish truth of his facts, her uncontrollable epic fornications against Stanley's own, less hysterical mastery in this area of experience, Williams attempts to dramatize the inevitable succumbing of the former to the greater power of the latter. If he seems to favor Blanche, it is because she is the weaker and because, at one time, as Stella attests, she showed great potential for tenderness and trust, the qualities of a typical victim. Only her stifled potential and her futile aspirations to transcend or mitigate the harshness of actuality—to cover the naked light bulb with a paper lantern—seem to qualify her, in Williams' eyes, as a symbol of the trapped soul. Not even her moral code, "Deliberate cruelty . . . is the one unforgivable thing . . . the one thing of which I have never, never been guilty," admirable as far as it goes, qualifies her as a symbol of transcendence so much as her pitiful attempts to combat actuality do. And, ironically and tragically enough, it is her very preference for soulful illusion and for magic over actuality which paves the way for her voyage to the madhouse.

Aware of the pity and terror of Blanche's world, Williams is not blind to the same qualities in the world that abides by Stanley's "Napoleonic Code." Stella and Mitch, for example, as creatures less hard than Stanley must nevertheless abide by his rules and even his lies (such as his denial of raping Blanche) if they are to survive in his domain. Though the furies of retribution visit Blanche for her hubris in making too many impossible demands of the "broken world" of mortality, they do not seem powerful enough to affect her antagonist, Stanley. In a way, the plot of Streetcar is modeled on the legend of Tereus, Philomela and Procne—the rape of the visiting sister-in-law by her brother-in-law in the absence of his wife—but Blanche's sister does not cut up her baby and serve it to Stanley for dinner as Procne served her son to Tereus; instead, Stella refuses to believe the story of the rape in order to go on living with Stanley and to provide a home for their child. Nor do the gods enter and transform the triangle into a trio of birds. And, while Mitch appears to believe that Stanley raped Blanche, he is powerless to overthrow his old master sergeant whose code of morality he must continue to endure just as, in the past, he was influenced by it in his treatment of Blanche.

While Williams dramatizes the plight of the incarnated, incarcer-
ated soul primarily in terms of her futile voyage in quest of fulfilment—or, failing that, of peace and rest—he portrays the roles that
fate and luck play in existence primarily in images of gaming. And
the master of games in *Streetcar* is Stanley Kowalski. By reason of
his amoral fitness for survival in a world which, in Williams' Darwinian view, is geared to the physically strongest at the expense of
the meekly vulnerable, Stanley has an "in" with the fates. Though
the intrusion of Blanche into his world rattles Stanley and threatens
to undermine the self-confidence that sustains his power, he systematically allays his own fears at the expense of aggravating Blanche's.
Though he loses at the poker games played in scene three, he wins at
those played in the last scene of the play.

Introducing fate into his play by way of luck at games, Williams
pits Stanley's chances of survival against Blanche's. When Williams
summed up the moral of the play as, "If we don't watch out, the
apes will take over" (quoted in Tischler, p. 137) he expressed the
same view of existence that he delegated to Blanche in her speech
denouncing the poker players as "a party of apes." That the tone
and strategy of the play reveal it not merely as a cautionary drama
but as a tragedy of the futility of attempting to flee the apes, I have
stressed above. What the play really demonstrates is that, willy-nilly,
the apes *must* take over since apishness is presented throughout as
the natural, unavoidable condition not only of survival but of existence itself. A close examination of the Poker Night scene displays
Williams' remarkable use of mythic and symbolic imagery to orchestrate both the "moral" of the play as he is reported to see it and the
wider context in which I have been placing it.

Williams describes the poker players in scene three, Stanley, Steve,
Pablo and Mitch, as "men at the peak of their physical manhood,
as coarse and direct and powerful as the primary colors" of the kitch-
en setting (p. 286). As the scene opens, Stanley is losing and Mitch,
who is shortly to meet Blanche, has been winning and is no longer in
the game. They have apparently been playing games in which specific
cards are "wild," games that depend to a greater extent on luck
(read "fate") than on skill. In the game which we witness, "One-
eyed jacks are wild." The rule of this game seems to describe the wild
players themselves both as knaves and, in the mythic context of the

play, as Cyclopes who, like these players, dwelt apart in caverns, observed no social, moral or legal order and existed by advantage of rude, savage strength unhampered by culture or intellect. By the end of the scene, we will be made witness to their apishness, particularly Stanley's (who as "Kowalski" is linked metaphorically with the Cyclopes who worked as smiths for Vulcan), and we will observe in action the caveman attraction he exerts for Stella whom he carries off to bed with him in their flat which is described as cavelike in the stage directions. Much is made, at the opening of the scene, of Mitch as a mamma's boy. He is playing in a game whose ultimate victors will not be the gentler giants attached to mothers, dead fiancées and flighty moths, but the rougher giants who survive and prevail by means of their brutishness and sheer brag.

The symbolic name of the second game played in this scene, "seven-card stud," is, of course, obvious in the context of these Elysian Fields where values are based on studmanship. While the cards for this game are being dealt out, Steve tells a joke about hens and roosters: the animalistic view of existence is underlined to contrast with Blanche's unsuccessfully transcendental one. As the joke ends, Blanche and Stella, the hens of the household, appear. They are unwelcome intruders in the masculine game. The scene then continues in twin focus on the card game in the kitchen and on Blanche's flirtation with Mitch in the bedroom.

Immediately before Blanche's first conversation with Mitch, Stanley had decided to play "Spit in the Ocean," a game which demands the pushing of one's luck. The name of the game suggests Stanley's attitude to Blanche's dream of ocean voyage and her addiction to the purgative and healing functions of water and, in line with the mythic context of the play, recalls the ancient superstition, popular with the Greeks and Romans, of spitting in the ocean to ward off enchantment and enchanters. The game played by Stanley in the kitchen provides an aptly ironic accompaniment to the game Blanche plays in the bedroom where, in her red satin wrapper, she flirts with Mitch, smokes his "Luckies," has him put up her paper lantern, dances to the music of a Viennese waltz, and tries to create the kind of "enchantment" that is unwelcome in Stanley's world. The romantic bedroom scene is abruptly terminated with Stanley's going as wild as a one-eyed Jack, or Cyclops, breaking the radio, striking Stella, and battling the other apes. Stanley's destructiveness, which Stella fondly rationalizes in the next scene as part of his passionate nature, is also part of the gaudy seed-bearer's physical potency. It is described by Blanche as "lunacy" but Williams ironically emphasizes its normalcy in context of the view of nature he presents in the play, and he has Blanche, instead, carted off as a lunatic at the end.

The poker night scene ends when Stella, unable to resist Stanley's "howling," "baying" and "bellowing" for her, returns to him: "they come together with low, animal moans. . . . [Stanley] lifts her off her feet and bears her into the dark flat." Outside the apartment, terrified, Blanche flits and rushes about like a moth looking "right and left as if for a sanctuary" (p. 307). She is calmed and comforted by Mitch.

Throughout the play, images drawn from gaming, chance and luck compete in number with those suggesting water and voyage. The sixth scene, for example, renders Mitch's marriage proposal to Blanche within the framework of imagery suggesting the game of chance which Blanche is desperately playing with him and with survival. The scene opens with the return home of Blanche and Mitch from their unsatisfactory date. "They have probably," the stage directions tell us, "been out to the amusement park on Lake Pontchartrain, for Mitch is bearing, upside down, a plaster statuette of Mae West, the sort of prize won at shooting galleries and carnival games of chance." At the door to Stanley's flat, Blanche says, "I'm looking for the Pleiades, the Seven Sisters, but these girls are not out tonight. Oh, yes they are, there they are! God bless them! All in a bunch going home from their little bridge party." The presence of the Pleiades in the sky seems to comfort Blanche; her reference to them as bridge ladies not only aligns them with the imagery of existence as a game of chance, but the familiarity with which Blanche treats the seven nymphs who, even as stars, must constantly flee the mighty, devastating hunter, Orion, suggests mythically and cosmically, a parallel to her own danger, pursued as she is by Stanley's vital lust for domination and destruction. The scene ends with Blanche's pathetic belief that Mitch's proposal is a sign that the gods have furnished her with an earthly protector. "Sometimes—," she says, "there's God—so quickly!" The name "Mitch" or "Mitchell," incidentally, is derived from "Michael" and means "someone like

God," but the godlike figure in this play is shown to be less powerful than—indeed in thrall to—the primal savage force represented by Stanley.

Generally, the two major image patterns concerned with voyage (particularly as escape from fate by means of water) and with games (as the framework of human chance and destiny) are only very casually suggested; occasionally they are even joined in a single speech as when Blanche, for example, explains to Mitch why she has come to Elysian Fields: "There was nowhere else I could go. I was *played out*. You know what played out is? My youth was suddenly gone up the *water-spout*, and—I met you . . ." (my italics, p. 387). In the last scene of the play, Williams more forcefully calls attention to his two most important image patterns in a superbly executed finale that boldly juxtaposes them.

Scene eleven opens with these two stage directions:

"It is some weeks later. Stella is packing Blanche's things. Sound of water can be heard running in the bathroom.

The portieres are partly open on the poker players—Stanley, Steve, Mitch and Pablo—who sit around the table in the kitchen. The atmosphere of the kitchen is now the same raw, lurid one of the disastrous poker night" (p. 403). The first words of dialogue in this scene are spoken by Stanley, the ultimate victor in the game between flesh and spirit: "Drew to an inside straight and made it, by God." "*Maldita sea tu suerto!*" says Pablo. Stanley, accustomed to winning by taking unfair advantage of whoever is weaker or of what he cannot understand, says, "Put it in English, greaseball." During the play, Stanley himself has been described in the stage directions as "greasestained" and even by Stella as "greasy"; now, however, as the vanquisher of Blanche, he lords it over the socially inferior, Spanish-speaking Pablo just as, previously, Blanche and Stella, "a pair of queens," had condescended to him. "I am cursing your rutting luck," says Pablo whose choice of epithet aptly describes the reason for Stanley's power in the Elysian Fields, his fabulous rutting. Stanley, "prodigiously elated," then explains his view of luck: "You know what luck is? Luck is believing you're lucky. Take at Salerno. I believed I was lucky. I figured that 4 out of 5 would not come through but I would . . . and I did. I put that down as a rule. To hold front position in this rat-race you've got to believe you are lucky." The combination of physical and sexual potency together with his knowledge of the odds and his capacity for thinking positively assures Stanley, as Williams pictures him, survival in any war or race, human or rat. Mitch, unable to countenance Stanley's self-assurance, blurts out: "You . . . you . . . you. . . . Brag . . . brag . . . bull . . . bull." Even apart from the way Mitch apparently means the terms "brag" and "bull" here, he is appropriately summarizing Stanley's major claims to success. As a noun, *brag* is the name of a card game in which the players *brag* about holding cards better than those that have been dealt them. And *bull*, of course, suggests the awesome fertility that is geared to the successful cowing of other players in any game of seven-card stud.

After introducing the theme of the fatal card game as an analogue of earthly existence, the last scene of *Streetcar* shifts to focus on Eunice and Stella as they prepare Blanche for another journey. Speaking from the bathroom which has been her refuge throughout the play, Blanche asks, "Is the coast clear?" As Eunice and Stella assist her to dress, Blanche treats them like two handmaidens preparing her for a romantic ocean voyage. With "faintly hysterical vivacity" she concerns herself with her clothes and appearance. In having Blanche ask for a bunch of artificial violets to be pinned with a seahorse on the lapel of her jacket, Williams portrays her insignia: the violet which traditionally symbolizes innocence in flower language together with the creature whose natural habitat would be water—not land.

When Blanche meets the doctor who has come for her and sees that he is not Shep Huntleigh, the stage directions read, "There is a moment of silence—no sound but that of Stanley steadily shuffling the cards." As Blanche tries to escape the doctor, "The Matron advances on one side, Stanley on the other. Divested of all the softer properties of womanhood, the Matron is a peculiarly sinister figure in her severe dress. Her voice is bold and toneless as a firebell." When the matron says, "Hello, Blanche," "The greeting is echoed and re-echoed by other mysterious voices behind the walls, as if reverberated through a canyon of rock" (p. 415). The cold, peculiarly sinister figure of the matron whose firebell voice subsumes and awakens echoes of the other voices which have haunted Blanche in the play may be seen as the archetypal embodiment of disaster for her. When Williams states that the matron's greeting must sound like the rever- berations in a canyon, we are reminded of Blanche's speech to Mitch about being "played out" which I quoted above and which intro- duces the image of the world as a rock: "I thanked God for you, because you seemed to be gentle—*a cleft in the rock of the world that I could hide in!*" (my italics, p. 387). However, Blanche's jour- ney has provided her no canyon to hide in and now the hoped-for canyon itself is portrayed as reverberating with inescapable memories of horror. The theatrical image presented by Blanche's "retreating in panic" from the matron on the one hand and Stanley on the other suggests, in the mythic context of the play, the moth-soul trying to evade the grasp both of a cold, earthy, mother-figure (portrayed in imagery that suggests a harsh view of mother nature herself) and that figure's ally described earlier in the play as a type of "gaudy seed-bearer." Blanche's two antagonists here form a theatrical icon of incarnation and existence that graphically summarizes the wider significance of her plight throughout the play.

Only when the old doctor becomes courtly and addresses Blanche gently does her panic abate and does she allow herself to be escorted from Elysian Fields. Blanche's last speech about her continual de- pendence on the kindness of strangers, though terrifying in context of what these strangers have subjected her to, allows her the dignity of repudiating, by implication, what her relations have done to her. At the same time, since the audience knows that Blanche is being conducted to the madhouse and, possibly, to her death there, the dig- nity of her repudiation is gained at the expense of the so-called sanity and brutal vitality of Elysian Fields, the Darwinian state of existence.

As Blanche leaves the scene, Eunice places Stanley's infant son in Stella's arms. Again, the images of destruction and creation are juxtaposed. Stella is sobbing and Stanley comforts her in the only way he knows how: "He kneels beside her and his fingers find the opening of her blouse." Echoing the sinister matron's attempts to subdue Blanche with the words, "Now, Blanche!" Stanley "voluptu- ously, soothingly" consoles Stella with "Now, honey. Now, love. Now, now, love. . . ." The play ends with the "swelling music of the 'blue piano' and the muted trumpet" as Steve says, "This game is seven-card stud."

Throughout *A Streetcar Named Desire*, Williams used every device of theatrical rhetoric to portray and orchestrate existence as a stud game. From the desperate gaiety of the tinny "Blue Piano" which Williams says in his first stage direction "expresses the spirit of the life which goes on here" to the brawling of the Kowalskis and their neighbors, from the cries of the street vendors ("Red hot!" and "Flores para los muertos") to what Elia Kazan called the "ballet" of the passerby in quest of money or sex, Williams created in *Streetcar* a frenetic dramatization of spiritual frustration and physical satiation alike, of life fraught with death (Blanche) and of death burning with life (Elysian Fields). Though not without its quieter moments and lyrical interludes, the play might best be characterized as a syncopated rendition of what Williams views as the basic rhythm of physical existence: tumescence and detumescence, desire and death.

While Williams appears to be primarily concerned with sexuality in *Streetcar*, his symbolic depiction of desire transcends merely sexual passion to include existence itself as its ultimate referent. One need not necessarily accept Freud's theory of the libido as the basic life force to appreciate what Williams means by equating, as Blanche does, desire with life. With more restraint than Williams in *Streetcar*, Paul Valéry in an essay on Flaubert makes much the same equation of desire (and frustration) with life that Williams dramatizes in the play. Variously calling desire "greed," "temptation" and "lack" Valéry writes: "In Nature the root of the tree pushes towards wet ground, the summit towards the sun, and the plant thrives by changing unbalance into unbalance, greed into greed. The amoeba deforms itself in approaching its tiny prey, obeys that which it is going to convert into its own substance, then hauls itself to its adventuring pseudopodium and reassembles itself. This type of mechanism is characteristic of all organic life; the devi, alas! is nature itself, and temptation is the most obvious, the most constant, the most inescapable condition of life. To live means to lack something at every moment—to modify oneself in order to attain it—and hence to aim at returning again to the state of lacking something."[7] It is on this basis that Williams identifies desire with the nature of existence itself and on this basis that he contrasts Blanche's continuous frustration with the narcotized, makeshift fulfilment that prevails in the Elysian Fields of the play.

To point out the symbolic, mythic and tragic implications of the literary and theatrical imagery in *Streetcar* is not to deny that the play is often as jazzy and comic as the vision of existence it depicts (though close inspection reveals that the jazz is usually desperate and the comedy often very cruel). Elements of melodrama, frequently present in tragedy, are also evident in its structure—to such an extent that they have sometimes blinded viewers to its other qualities. Even the usually perspicacious Susan Sontag wrote in her controversial essay of 1964, "Against Interpretation," that *Streetcar* should be enjoyed merely as "a forceful psychological melodrama . . . about a handsome brute named Stanley Kowalski and a faded mangy belle named Blanche DuBois . . ." and that any *other* interpretation of the play would be unwarranted.

What I have tried to do in this essay, however, is to avoid rehashing the most blatantly realistic aspects of the play and to view it, instead, in terms of Williams' persistent concern with creating universal and "timeless" worlds in his plays. In play after play, Williams has consistently (albeit with varying degrees of success) employed symbolism and the mythic mode to universalize the significance of the realistic action he posits, not only, apparently, because he thinks of symbolism and universality as essentials of art, but also because these qualities seem to be characteristic of his personal reactions to life in general. For example, speaking years later of the autobiographical genesis of *Streetcar*, Williams said that whenever he stayed in New Orleans, he lived "near the main street of the [French] Quarter which is named Royal. Down this street, running on the same tracks, are two street-cars, one named DESIRE and the other CEMETERY. Their indiscourageable progress up and down Royal struck me as having some symbolic bearing of a broad nature on the life in the *Vieux Carré*—and everywhere else for that matter."[8]

Read in the light of Williams' personal and aesthetic predilections, all the images, symbols and allusions, even what appear to be only the most casual or realistic of details in *Streetcar*, combine to reveal a tragic parable of the pitiable and terrible fate of the human soul. Incarnated in treacherous, decaying matter, the soul, it appears, has been destined to voyage continually from one broken world to another, the only kinds of environment open to it in a flawed universe. Seeking union with the stars (themselves, whether symbolized as

Stella or the Pleiades, in a precarious situation), or, failing that, at least repose in the extinction of memory and cares in the Elysian Fields, the moth-soul finds, instead, only another broken world, another Darwinian environment in which the brutally fittest rule. As Tennessee Williams dramatizes his vision of existence in *A Streetcar Named Desire*, we see that "from the beginning" the cards of destiny have indicated a seemingly endless voyage for the human soul through progressively disastrous worlds, and the name of the game is tragedy.

Notes to Leonard Quirino, "The Cards Indicate a Voyage on
A Streetcar Named Desire"

1. Introduction to Carson McCullers, *Reflections in a Golden Eye* (New York: New Directions, 1941), p. xiii.
2. Vergil's *Aeneid*, trans. Patrick Dickinson (New York: New American Library, Mentor, 1961), p. 140.
3. The best examples of reviews concerned with the effect of production and acting on the interpretation of *Streetcar* are Harold Clurman's "Review of *A Streetcar Named Desire*," in *Lies Like Truth* (New York: Macmillan, 1958), pp. 72–80 and Eric Bentley's "Better than Europe?" in *In Search of Theatre* (New York: Alfred A. Knopf, 1953), pp. 84–8.
4. See especially Harry Taylor's Marxist view of *Streetcar* in "The Dilemma of Tennessee Williams," in *Masses and Mainstream* 1 (April 1948), 51–8 and Robert Emmet Jones's sociological analysis of Blanche DuBois in "Tennessee Williams' Early Heroines," *Modern Drama* 2 (December 1959), 211–19.
5. For the best example of denigration see, of course, Mary McCarthy's review, "A Streetcar Called Success," in *Sights and Spectacles 1937–1956* (New York: Farrar, Straus and Cudahy, 1956), pp. 131–5.
6. This Neoplatonic dialectic of body and soul or of flesh and spirit is one of the most persistent concerns of Williams. In *Summer and Smoke*, the revision of an earlier play called *A Chart of Anatomy*, Williams developed this dialectic in morality-play fashion; Williams evades resolving the conflict he creates for Alma and John by having each defect, too late, to the camp of the other. While appearing to embrace D. H. Lawrence's gospel of the identity of body and soul, Williams constantly reveals his own fundamental lack of trust in the impertinent body and its power to transcend such physical limitations as age and illness—predicaments which he emphasizes in play after play. Even in his paean to the undying spirit of D. H. Lawrence, *I Rise in Flame, Cried the Phoenix*, Williams depicts Lawrence at a time when, deathly ill, the body he so celebrated was betraying him.
7. Paul Valéry, "The Temptation of (Saint) Flaubert," trans. Lionel Abel, *Partisan Review Anthology*, ed. William Phillips (New York: Holt, Rinehart and Winston, 1962), p. 55.
8. Quoted in Tischler, p. 62. For further elucidation of Williams' preoccupation with universality in life and art, see especially his essay, "The Timeless World of a Play," preface to *The Rose Tattoo*, II, 259 ff.

Complementarity
in *A Streetcar Named Desire*

NORMAND BERLIN

E ACH NEW PRODUCTION of *A Streetcar Named Desire* seems to offer the excitement of witnessing a new interpretation. A great play has within it the potentiality for differing interpretations; indeed, this may be the test of greatness. The different interpretations of *Streetcar* by directors invariably stem from different attitudes toward the two main characters, Blanche DuBois and Stanley Kowalski. Some directors tip the audience toward Blanche, others toward Stanley—and this tipping controls the nature of the tragedy and its effect. The director chooses sides, and the audience, of necessity, must play the director's game.

My aim in this essay is to explore the possibility that Tennessee Williams wishes to keep the sides balanced, that, in fact, complementarity informs the play's art and meaning. My hope is that such a discussion will be fresh enough to be of interest and accurate enough in its scrutiny to add a further dimension to Williams' richest play.

At the outset we must recognize that different interpretations can be caused by fuzziness of writing, blurring of effects, lack of coherence. This, for T. S. Eliot, helps to account for the many and varied interpretations of that artistically inferior play, *Hamlet*. One of our finest critics, Eric Bentley, believes that in *Streetcar* "Williams does not write with complete coherence" (*In Search of Theater*,

97

p. 85). Bentley's view is an echo of and has been echoed by others. But another view is possible: that Tennessee Williams, after O'Neill America's finest playwright, knows exactly what he is doing in *Streetcar*, offering a play with balanced sides built in, dramatizing an attitude toward life based on duality and complementarity. This balancing is achieved in every aspect of the drama—in the treatment of theme and character, in the symbolism, in the movement, in the specific stage actions. Balances are always precarious, in art as in life. Williams maintains his, I wish to demonstrate, and the critics and directors have lost theirs at times.

I begin with Desire, the play's largest idea. Literally, Desire is a streetcar on which Blanche rides until she transfers to a streetcar named Cemeteries in order to arrive in Elysian Fields, where Stella and Stanley live. The symbolic names are characteristic of the dramatic art of Tennessee Williams, for whom symbols are the "natural speech of drama." Their import is obvious. Blanche, in her painful past, has experienced desire and death, and now is entering a "paradise" where she will be considered an intruder and from which she will be expelled. But Desire is a streetcar on which Stanley also rides, for in the specific vocabulary of the play Desire means sexual desires. When Blanche tells Mitch the opposite of death is desire, she goes on to say that she answered the calls of the young soldiers who, when drunk, called her name on her lawn, and she went out to sleep with them. A former soldier, Stanley, also drunk, answering the call within him, rapes her. Sex is the play's great leveler. The genteel Blanche and the raw Stanley ride the same streetcar, but for different reasons. Blanche goes to her sexual affairs to relieve the broken quality of her life, looking for closeness, perhaps kindness, in that physical way. She cannot see herself as a whore because sexual activity was for her a temporary means for needed affection, the only refuge for her lonely soul. Stanley rides the streetcar because that is the necessary physical function of his life, natural, never compensating for emotional agony because his soul is never lost, what Blanche calls "brutal desire—just—Desire!" Desire is the common ground on which Stan and Blanche meet, a streetcar on which both are passengers, the scales on which both are measured. On one side of the scale a fading, fragile woman for whom sexual activity is a temporary release from loneliness; on the other side a crude, physical man for whom sexual activity is a normal function of life. The needs of both are clearly presented by Williams and should be clearly understood by the audience, which must neither wholly condemn Blanche for her whorishness nor Stanley for his brutishness. The scales are balanced so finely that when Stanley condemns Blanche for her sexual looseness and Blanche condemns Stanley for his apishness, each seems *both* right and wrong, right in the light of truth, wrong in the light of understanding.

Desire or sexual impulse, therefore, is common to both Blanche and Stanley and provides one measure of their similarity and difference. They share other measures as well. They compete for the possession of Stella, for the affections of Mitch; they share the bottle of whisky; they dress and undress in the view of others; they both wish to occupy the bathroom. The first and the last deserve brief comment.

Stella shares Blanche's past and Stanley's present. Having a memory of Belle Reve, Stella, according to Blanche, surely cannot live in this place with that beast. Blanche, who allowed sexual affairs to fill her emotional need, cannot understand her sister's need for sexual activity with Stanley. In scene three Blanche physically takes Stella away from Stanley, guiding her upstairs after Stella is beaten by Stanley. But Stella's return down those stairs, when Stanley calls her at the end of the same scene, demonstrates her allegiance to him. Her euphoric state the next morning, after a night of pleasurable lovemaking, seals her bonded fate. Blanche appeals to Stella with tenderness and with arguments about the past and civilization, touching the heart and mind; Stanley touches the body. For Stella, "the things that happen between a man and a woman in the dark" make everything else unimportant.

The bathroom, realistic and unseen, provides an interesting setting for the dialectic of character, with Blanche and Stanley again in opposition, with the bathroom itself a battleground. Blanche needs her bath to calm her nerves, she says. She bathes and bathes, the steaming hot water washing her body but never penetrating to cleanse her soul. The hot water and soap cannot make clean a sordid past, and her perfumes cannot sweeten her tainted mortality. The ritual of the bath is useless; she must ever return to it because, like her sexual activity, it provides only temporary relief. Final relief for

Blanche will come only with her death, and she will die, she claims, "on the sea." The difference between the bath water in Stanley's bathroom and the "ocean as blue as my lover's eyes" is the distance between Blanche's hellish present and her image of a heavenly death. Whereas Blanche needs the bathroom to relieve her nerves, Stanley needs it to relieve his kidneys. The room is one, but the activity is two: for Blanche a bath, for Stanley a toilet. A dialectic between claims in a metaphorical setting.

Light, one of the play's important symbols, provides a wide range of reference, but always reveals Williams' complementary vision. Most fiercely bright is the bulb with a vivid green glass shade which hangs over the poker table. It shines down on men "at the peak of their physical manhood" playing poker. Its glare is the vivid glare of reality. So too is the bulb over Blanche's bed before she puts a paper lantern over it. That she must cover the light and live in the shadow indicates her twilight condition and her attitude toward life: "I don't want realism. I want magic!" Blanche lives between light and dark, avoiding the truthful glare of the former and unable to find the latter. Stanley, on the other hand, can live in light *and* dark. Realism is what he wants, and the world he occupies, *his* world, displays primary colors. But when he wants the dark—for the things that happen between a man and a woman—he can break the bulbs, as he did on his wedding night. Stanley functions in both light and dark; Blanche, delicate as a moth, must avoid strong light. Stanley, himself a garish sun, claims Stella, the star. Blanche neither generates light nor reflects light. She can only sing in her bath about a paper moon in a make-believe world. Paper moon, paper lantern, paper boy collecting money for *The Evening Star*—all manifestations of Blanche's gossamer grip on reality. The light of a bulb, a moon, a star, offering both standard and unique associations, are manipulated by Williams to extend his relentless dialectic.

Complementarity provides the pressure of the play's movement, beginning with the audience's first encounter with Stanley and Blanche. When the curtain rises, the audience witnesses Stanley's sure command of the stage—vigorous, shouting, deftly throwing a package of meat at Stella. Blanche's entrance reveals a delicate creature, frazzled, uncertain, burdened with a suitcase, lost. Within the play's first minute the audience is forced to absorb the dialectic that will give the play its dynamic tension. Within each scene the dialectic continues, becoming more persistent as the play progresses. A brief look at scene three will reveal Williams' method.

Scene three presents the poker night. The men are playing, talking of food, telling vulgar jokes. Stella and Blanche enter. Blanche's "Please don't get up" is answered by Stanley's "Nobody's going to get up, so don't be worried." And the scene's tension begins. Blanche is going to bathe, undresses while standing in the light, and turns on the radio, the central prop of the scene. Stanley, annoyed by the music and the interruptions to the poker game, jumps up and turns off the radio. A soft dialog between Blanche and Mitch follows, in which Mitch reveals his past romance with a sick girl who is now dead. Blanche turns on the radio and begins dancing to the music, with Mitch awkwardly imitating her movements. This brief moment of romance is shattered by Stanley, who fiercely seizes the radio and tosses it out the window. Stella calls Stanley an "animal thing," for which she receives a blow. Stella is guided upstairs by Blanche, who soothingly says: "Stella, Stella, precious! Dear, dear little sister, don't be afraid!" After the men leave, Stanley breaks into sobs, calls for Stella "like a baying hound"— "Stell-lahhhhh!"—who eventually slips down the stairs. Williams' stage direction tells us that they "come together with low, animal moans," that Stanley "falls to his knees on the steps and presses his face to her belly, curving a little with maternity." Stella raises him level with her, and he "lifts her off her feet" to carry her into the flat's darkness. Even so bare a description of the scene indicates clearly the pattern of dialectic, with Stanley and Blanche vying for the attention of the poker players, for the possession of the radio, for the possession of Stella. In each segment of the scene Williams plays with the audience's sympathies, forcing us to side with Stanley when Blanche is teasing and artificially genteel, forcing us to condemn Stanley when he breaks the radio and hits Stella, and forcing us to pity the repentant Stanley who wishes to have his baby back. Balances in our attitude toward character; changes in our emotional responses. And important changes in movement. Stella goes *up* the stairs to escape a raging Stanley, only to come *down* to the baying Stanley. Stanley falls down on his knees to show his repentance, only to rise and lift Stella to show his victory. Stanley's victory is Blanche's defeat. A confused

Blanche ends the scene by talking about the confusion in the world and reasserting her need for kindness. She will give powerful voice to her confusion in the next scene, wondering how her sister could return to the brutal Stanley, calling him "common," "bestial," a "survivor of the Stone Age," and imploring her sister not to "*hang back with the brutes!*" Blanche's "superior attitude," as Stella calls it, will alienate the audience because of the speech's *tone*, but the *content* of her speech offers ideas about civilization and progress that the audience must consider true. And again we have complementarity and balance.

Williams does not even allow the rape, which could be considered the supreme brutalization of Blanche by Stanley, to upset the balance he presents throughout. For Williams betrays a respect for Stanley's "animal joy," for men at the peak of their manhood, for the natural desires of the Stanley Kowalskis, who were born to have women, *and* Williams invests the play with a sense of the inevitability of that violent encounter between executioner and victim, who had that date from the beginning.

What I am suggesting—by my brief discussions of the theme of desire, the characters of Blanche and Stanley, the symbol of light, the movement within the scenes—is that the ambiguity and confusion often felt in specific productions and readings of *Streetcar* are prodded by Williams' delicate art but are not his intent. He aims for complementarity, duality, balance, a difficult challenge for a dramatist, but a necessary one for Williams in this play because it holds the key to the play's meaning and tragic effect. The tensions are present throughout and are basic to the tragedy. We end with pity and terror, themselves balancing emotions, the natural result of all that came before. As Blanche DuBois leaves the stage, we, like Stella, are allowing her to go because we have sided at times with Stanley, we have been annoyed by her falsity and superiority, we have wondered at her cruelty to her now dead homosexual husband, we have considered her a disturbing interruption in her sister's seemingly idyllic life in Elysium. But we feel compassion for this fragile creature who has been living with death, who is trying to hold on to vanishing values, and who needs what we all need, kindness. We feel the terror of her departure to death within the walls of an asylum not only because we pity Blanche, but because we are forced to ask the frightening question: Is the world so possessed by the apes that there is no place for a Blanche DuBois? Both better and worse than those around her—the balance again—Blanche commands our attention as we witness her disintegration. She passes through, and the curtain comes down to block out the light over *that* poker game as we return to *this* one, some of us needing more shade than others, but all, I suspect, affected by Williams' superb dramatization of a basic human dialectic reflecting what our deepest experience tells us is the reality of things, presenting a complementary vision more complex than a one-sided interpretation allows.

Tragedy as Habit:
A *Streetcar Named Desire*

BRITTON J. HARWOOD

A s THE THEATER of Chekhov, Beckett, Pirandello, Ionesco, or Brecht may not, Tennessee Williams' A *Streetcar Named Desire* troubles us with the question of genre. Going no further than the language of the play, we find Williams' stage direction calling for Blanche to assume "a tragic radiance" (I, 406). Yet critical opinion is nearly unanimous that, if Williams intended his play to be judged in the terms of tragedy, it fails.[1] No one, on the other hand, has held that the play is one that makes the question of kind irrelevant. I mean to develop here the answer that *Streetcar* is intended, and ought, to be understood as a sort of *double* of tragedy, the "lurid reflection" of it (to borrow one of Williams' favorite directions in the play) rather than the thing itself—the inevitable continuation of a tragic action already past.[2] As a dramatic action in its own right, *Streetcar* recalls the tragic by redoing it in an ironic register.

The endings of many, if not all, great tragedies are deeply ambiguous. While this is not the place to develop that notion in detail, we can point to Lear, who realizes he is "a very foolish fond old man" only to convince himself at the very end that Cordelia still breathes; or Hamlet, who concludes that "no man knows aught of what he leaves," and yet enjoins Horatio to stay alive for a while to tell the correct version of Hamlet's "story." That is, notwithstanding

104

the protagonist's discovery and the suffering that may attend it, he cannot stop saying or doing the very thing which, one way or another, is the very condition for his guilt.

When Blanche leaves the Elysian Fields, she allows the doctor "to lead her as if she were blind" (p. 418). That might recall the blinded Oedipus, ordered by Creon to go inside where he could not pollute the light of the sun. Yet Blanche enters the play as one who must already "avoid a strong light" (p. 245), her eyes bearing a "blind look" (p. 250). In scene nine, near hysteria, she concedes to Mitch that she has "had many intimacies with strangers." At her first entrance, however, she is already "faintly hysterical," protests too much her blamelessness for the loss of Belle Reve, is terribly fearful, sickens with the memory of her husband's death, and, at the opening of scene two, is in the first of the many hot baths meant to cleanse her from the "filthy tub" (p. 386) of Laurel. Even before Stanley asks her about Shaw (scene five), Blanche frankly admits to Stella that "brutal desire" has "brought me here" (p. 321). I am pointing out not that the action in *Streetcar* is static, but that its ending has certain things in common with its beginning. While not tragic, the action of *Streetcar* is unintelligible except as an analogy to tragedy, and its uniqueness lies in its taking its protagonist, already burdened with perception and guilt,[3] through an experience which has the structure but not the content of tragedy. Like other protagonists at the ends of plays, Blanche at the beginning of this one is unable *not* to recapitulate the stages of her crime. To describe the peculiar distortion which *Streetcar* is intended to work upon the mythos of tragedy, one must risk speaking of tragedy itself.

In tragedy, a hero is aware that he is impinged upon, his existence threatened from without by the blind sweep of an Other. This sense of impingement is signified at the outset—by the lameness which gives Oedipus his name, by Ahab's missing leg, by the "vicious mole" (*Hamlet*). This is to say that the hero experiences the Wholly Other in the boundaries which it sets. In *The Idea of the Holy*, Rudolf Otto writes that "The difference between the 'feeling of dependence' of Schleiermacher and that which finds typical utterance in the words of Abraham . . . might be expressed as that between the consciousness of *createdness* and the consciousness of *creaturehood*. In the one case you have the creature as the work of the divine creative act; in the other, impotence and general nothingness as against overpowering might. . . . [With *creaturehood*] we come upon the ideas, first, of the annihilation of self, and then, as its complement, of the transcendent as the sole and entire reality" (pp. 20 ff.). The source of this annihilation, the nature of this sole and entire reality, is often layered as deep in the poem as it is in the mind of the hero. Nearly eight hundred lines of *Oedipus Rex* have elapsed before Oedipus discloses the "desperate horrors" prophesied for him while he was still in Corinth. Most of *Absalom, Absalom!* is over before we learn that the adolescent Thomas Sutpen came to a sense of himself simultaneously with being turned away from a front door and run off the road. We are three hundred pages into *Tender Is the Night* before we learn of a moment when Dick Diver "realized that he was the last hope of a decaying clan." And it is the fifth act of *Hamlet* before we confront, with Hamlet, the man who has been making graves only since the day Hamlet was born. The hero tries to get out from under what threatens to digest meaning to its own absurdity, in the way that "your worm is your only emperor for diet." To be, which means to be conscious, is what he wants ("conception is a blessing," says Hamlet), and the hero's purpose, as a tragedy begins, is to secure his being by securing his consciousness, by translating flesh into word, by projecting and reifying an idea. So the hero not only moves to a place he imagines to be safe—Thebes, Sutpen's hundred, Dick Diver's Tarmes, "the pales and forts" of Wittenberg, perhaps—but knows that he enjoys it because he acts in consistency with his idea, because he acts on what we may call his ethic. For Agamemnon and Orestes, this means to be just, for Sutpen to be white, for the protagonist of Ibsen's *Master Builder* to make homes, for Dick Diver "to be brave and wise." Hamlet can be a man provided he can be reasonable.

The action of a tragedy is the hero's purposing to be good and then discovering he has always been bad, that his reward for describing an ethic is to find himself guilty in precisely those terms. Agamemnon and Orestes behave compulsively and therefore unjustly, Oedipus finds he does not know himself, Solness burns his own home, Quentin finds himself possessed by the blackness that Sutpen tried to shut out, Dick Diver *inadvertently* cures Nicole by indulging himself with Rosemary. Thus the radical crime, the choice of human existence rather than "impotence and general nothingness," is discovered and understood as the hero's violation of his own ethic. The radical crime becomes understood with a precision that the crime itself—articulating an ethic as a haven for consciousness and therefore as a means for individual existence—has made possible. By trying to circumscribe such a haven, the hero initiates a process which leads to the discovery of criminality within the magic circle of his own consciousness. "I could be bounded in a nutshell and count myself a king of infinite space, were it not that I have bad dreams." (*Hamlet*). Self-knowledge is a crime against the Other; it is the Promethean light, the illusion of individual existence shining like the light and gold of Heorot. Self-knowledge being criminal, it is ironically punished with anagnorisis, self-discovery. At the end, the hero's self-loathing internalizes the Other, which he thought he had fled.[4] The annihilation which is our understanding of the Wholly Other becomes intelligible as guilt. This is the action of a tragedy.

It is part of the specialness of *Streetcar* that the protagonist's confrontation with the nature of the Other,[5] a confrontation which is logically prior to the hero's decision to be, is chronologically first as well. Blanche's insistence that she will near "nice clothes" (p. 257), her bathing to feel "like a brand new human being" (p. 276), to get hold of herself and make "a new life" (p. 313), occur no earlier in the play than her expressed awareness of the Other. Her nervous joke about "the ghoul-haunted woodland of Weir" (p. 252)—only the railroad tracks—anticipates the locomotives that will roar by, making her crouch and cringe, just before she tells Mitch about her cruelty to Allan or just before she is raped. What she must "keep hold" (p. 250) of herself against is annihilation: "Margaret, that dreadful way! So big with it, it couldn't be put in a coffin! But had to be burned like rubbish! . . . the struggle for breath and bleeding" (pp. 261–62). The Wholly Other is the source of "Death—I used to sit here and she used to sit over there and death was as close as you are" (pp. 388–89).

The Other known by our impotence is (as Otto writes) both dreadful and fascinating. "These two qualities, the daunting and the fascinating, now combine in a strange harmony of contrasts. . . . The daemonic-divine object may appear to the mind an object of horror and dread, but at the same time it is no less something that allures with a potent charm, and the creature, who trembles before it, utterly cowed and cast down, has always at the same time the impulse to turn to it, nay even to make it somehow his own" (p. 31). Stanley's "drive" (p. 293) is, of course, exactly this "strange harmony of contrasts." First of all, Blanche feels Stanley as "Violence!" (p. 308). "Somebody growls—some creature snatches at something— the fight is on!" (p. 323). The streetcar leading to Cemeteries leads as well to the "red-stained package from a butcher's" (p. 244),[6] in which the bloodstained pillowcases of Belle Reve (p. 388) represent themselves. Stanley smashes things (p. 312), and at each noise, as he bangs around the flat, "Blanche winces slightly" (p. 328). She recognizes him as an "executioner" (p. 351) and his home as "a trap" (p. 409).

Blanche is nevertheless fascinated by Stanley. When she is alone, she picks up his photo (p. 263) and, in the second scene, flirts with him. If the terrified body, the shaking hand, is something to keep hold of, so is, from the protagonist's point of view, the impulse to make the Other somehow one's own: "A man like that is someone to go out with—once—twice—three times when the devil is in you. But live with?" (p. 321). In fact, since dread is the complement of fascination, not "to bed with him" (p. 319) is not to survive. The "date" which Stanley and Blanche have had from the beginning is a showdown because it is not a tryst.

It is tempting simply to accept Blanche's own account of her promiscuity. Desire being the opposite of death, she reacted to the decay of Belle Reve by going to the arms of young soldiers, much as Mrs. Maartens, in Aldous Huxley's *The Genius and the Goddess*, went to Rivers: "It's the line of a woman who ... suddenly finds herself standing on the brink of the abyss and invaded, body and mind, by the horrible black emptiness confronting her. . . . She had to re-establish her contacts with life—with life at its simplest, life in its most unequivocal manifestations, as physical companionship, as the experience of animal warmth. . . . It was a matter of self-preservation" (p. 119). The soldiers sprawling "like daisies" on the lawn are in their own way "Flores para los muertos" (p. 389). Yet Blanche, who, in common with other tragic protagonists, intends to resist the intuitive or compulsive response, can be only vague to Mitch about her motives: "After the death of Allan—intimacies with strangers was all I seemed able to fill my empty heart with. . . . I think it was panic." The meaning for her of her own sexuality, however, once she has known the blinding Apollonian light (p. 354), derives from, rather than displaces, as we shall see shortly, the meaning of desire in that original Dionysian oneness, voiced in the blue piano and drums, where orgiastic joy and original pain flow endlessly into each other and reverse.[7] The basic character of the sexual for Blanche, then, is a "potent charm" inextricable from repulsive brutality, continuing to threaten her in New Orleans as it had defeated her illusion that Allan was "almost too fine to be human" (p. 364). Blanche's forebears strike at her both with their "epic fornications" and with the horror of their dying.

But Stanley is the Other with a difference. He is vile, not uncanny; sporadic and impromptu, not relentless. He is not only the antagonist, but a member of the chorus, moved in the first place, perhaps, because on the poker night he is getting only a cold supper; he is vain, childishly petulant, ready to lie to cover a mistake, proud to be typical. By arriving at the Elysian Fields in so compulsive a state as to perceive in its "commonness" the annihilation and filth she has known in Laurel both without and within, Blanche raises Stanley to consciousness and to vindictiveness, because she makes him ashamed. Blanche desperately wishes to be away from Stanley, as the tragic protagonist flees the Other. But her flight would have merely the *form* of tragedy, for Stanley is not a tragic phenomenon. Only the tragedy that, for Blanche, is already over could account for her dread in the presence of no more than the leader of the chorus, the captain of the bowling team.

The tragic protagonist, whose life is the Apollonian illusion of individuality,[8] makes consciousness of himself as an individual[9] contingent upon his being conscious of innocence of a certain kind— innocence, more exactly, upon his own terms. If Blanche were to discover something at the crisis of the action, clearly it would not be the knowledge of her own unchastity. Although she works to create for Mitch the illusion that she is a beleaguered virgin, she does not believe her own artifice. That is at least one sense in which she "never lied" in her heart (p. 387). When she tells Mitch she cannot let him do more than kiss her because she has "old-fashioned ideals" "she rolls her eyes, knowing he cannot see her face" (p.

348).[10] Only after the rape and her breakdown does she imagine that a trifle like an unwashed grape might be enough to transport "her soul to heaven" or that her body might bear scrutiny in the full light of "noon—in the blaze of summer" (p. 410). Otherwise, she uses hot water to give herself the physical sensation of innocence and is fully aware of her thirst for the innocence she lacks. When the newsboy tells her he drank a "Cherry" soda, she says: "You make my mouth water. . . . Come here. I want to kiss you, just once, softly and sweetly on your mouth! [She does so.] Now run along, now, quickly! It would be nice to keep you, but I've got to be good—and keep my hands off children." (pp. 338–39). The same thirst—guilt, that is— undoubtedly drew her to the seventeen-year-old boy in Laurel and thus brought her to New Orleans, where she must work so much the harder at her factitious virginity: "little breathless cries and peals of laughter are heard as if a child were frolicking in the tub" (p. 362).

Where the mythos of tragedy leads us to look for the protagonist to articulate the value that is critical for him, we find Blanche affirming a range of values, but with a banality that gives us again, as Williams intends, the structural feature evacuated of the tragic phenomenon. "Sorrow makes for sincerity, I think," she says (p. 298). While she declares she cannot stand "a vulgar action" (p. 300), the triteness of her "favorite sonnet" and of her "attempt to instill . . . reverence for Hawthorne and Whitman and Poe!"— together with her genteelness ("I brought some nice clothes to meet all your lovely friends in," "The Little Boys' Room is busy right now")—has a profound vulgarity of its own.

Although Blanche is genuinely in flight, the security sought against instinct by human self-consciousness—the security imaged for Nietzsche in the high stage, above the orchestra and the dreaming chorus—is represented in *Streetcar* as something already lost. Blanche blesses the "Seven Sisters," the Pleiades, cozily going home "all in a bunch" (p. 342). But the stars, for whom no collections need be taken up, are out of the reach of this "poor relation"; and her own sister, "Stella for star," chooses for her the ironic security of an asylum. The lofty white columns have already been "lost," and Blanche's only crown is rhinestones, "next door to glass"—assimilated, in fact, to the "Corones" for the dead (p. 388). Neither real security nor the possibility of innocence on which it depends is available to her from the beginning of the play; and therefore, despite the genuineness of her flight, the haven she describes clinks like a counterfeit: "my sister—there has been *some* progress . . . ! Such things as art—as poetry and music—such kinds of new light have come into the world since then! In some kinds of people some tenderer feelings have had some little beginning! . . . In this dark march toward whatever it is we're approaching. . . . *Don't—don't hang back with the brutes!*" (p. 323). What Blanche knows is that she must get away: hence the words she believes in are "progress," "march," "don't hang back!" The aim she posits, "such things as art—as poetry and music," is characteristic of the inevitably Apollonian tragic protagonist; but it is an aim she does not believe in. It is expressed in the clichés of the high school English class she draws upon in "improvising feverishly" to Mitch: "Physical beauty is passing. A transitory possession. But beauty of the mind and richness of the spirit and tenderness of the heart—and I have all of those things—aren't taken away, but grow! Increase with the years!" (p. 396). It should have been no surprise when these speeches, spoken by Jessica Tandy, sounded "phony."[11] They serve well enough to isolate Blanche from the choral "commonness" (p. 351) of the French Quarter,[12] although they are doubtless to be associated with her "saccharine popular ballad" (p. 359)—another sample from her "heart-shaped box."

One reason she can be such a propagandist for these values at the same time she drinks heavily and takes "hydro-therapy" is that they are not the ethic she has violated, nor, in a more important way, is chastity. Obviously, she could not relieve her sense of guilt by talking all summer about the terms of it. The ethic which has been peculiarly hers, which she violated, and which, at points when she is in extremity in *Streetcar*, she obliquely reveals comes clearest where, among the eleven scenes of the play, one would expect the crisis— the sixth scene, when Blanche, drinking, on edge since Stanley mentioned Shaw, tells Mitch about her loneliness, and before that how she had fallen in love with Allan, who had come to her for help. "He was in the quicksands and clutching at me—but I wasn't holding him out, I was slipping in with him! I didn't know that. I didn't know anything except I loved him unendurably but without being able to help him or help myself. Then I found out" (p. 354). She recounts Allan's suicide, then "sways and covers her face." "It was

because—," she says, "on the dance floor—unable to stop myself—
I'd suddenly said— 'I saw! I know! You disgust me. . . .' And then
the searchlight which had been turned on the world was turned off
again and never for one moment since has there been any light that's
stronger than this—kitchen—candle . . ." (p. 355). Here her confession of responsibility for Allan's death is collocated exactly with the
dim light in which, throughout the play, she hides herself. The years
that now line her face, which is to say the cycles of guilt and flight
which filled them, followed directly from her saying "I saw! I know!
You disgust me." In self-loathing, she turns the sixteen-year-old girl
that she was into the Tarantula, the female version of the older man
in bed with Allan, repeating the act that disgusts her, then tries to
escape by starting again with virginal boys.[13] Because it was she who
extinguished the "blinding light," she feels every "naked bulb,"
now, as a merciless accusation. She tries to hide, not just her years
and how she spent them, but what caused her to spend them that
way. Not the deaths at Belle Reve extinguish the light, but the criminal knowledge which is death internalized.

Loyalty—standing by someone who needs help—is Blanche's ethic.
She speaks authentically of it in the matter of Belle Reve: "you are
the one that abandoned Belle Reve, not I! I stayed and fought for it,
bled for it, almost died for it!" (p. 260). Although Blanche fears the
consequences if her Laurel reputation gets to New Orleans, the
notion of being unchaste—present, for instance, in her expressed
wish to get her hands on the newsboy or to sleep with Mitch—does
not make her anxious in itself, for it is not the idea on which her
existence depends. By contrast, she is "uneasy" (p. 259) and defensive about the loss of Belle Reve, for that trenches on the question
of loyalty. She defends herself here at length because she can defend herself. Margaret and the others sometimes said "Don't let me
go," and she did not reject them even if she could not stop them.
She not only "Saw! Saw! Saw!" (p. 262) but "stayed." Nevertheless, this loyalty in a situation, however unpretty, where she could
control herself can never remove from her experience her disloyalty
to someone else who was "clutching" (p. 354) at her, whom she
also "saw!"—and to whom she said "You disgust me." [14]

Blanche refers (obliquely again) to loyalty in telling Stanley that
"when a thing is important I tell the truth" (p. 281). She has, in

fact, had to make her way with lies ever since she told the truth to Allan, who did disgust her, after all. But truth, in addition to being a correspondence with the "facts," means fidelity, of course, as in "true blue" (which by no accident, I think, is the color Blanche cares most about). Where her talk of high culture wilts before the animal vitality of the Quarter, the ethic vital for her can be little better than aped: "Mitch is a buddy of mine," Stanley tells Stella. "We were in the same outfit together—Two-forty-first Engineers. We work in the same plant and now on the same bowling team. You think I could face him if—" (p. 365). Stanley calls "conscience" the "deliberate cruelty" with which he avenges an insult. "Deliberate cruelty," a frenzied Blanche will tell him later, "is not forgivable. It is the one unforgivable thing in my opinion and it is the one thing of which I have never, never been guilty" (p. 397). And this is true enough. Where there is deliberation in the rape ("Come to think of it—"), Blanche blurts out the three sentences to Allan ("unable to stop myself"). Allan, essentially a stranger who had depended upon her kindness, she betrayed with an undeliberated cruelty. Only the choice of an ethic is deliberate, however, not the violation of it. Perhaps there is no tragic protagonist whose crime is not compulsive, obscured. It is obscure because, often if not always, it precedes the ethical articulation which will bring it to light. The actual crime (as opposed to the discovery of it) happens before the protagonist posits the terms of it; likewise, conscious intention is clearly not, especially in Blanche's case, a precondition for guilt.

I have been showing, then, that the values explicitly and strenuously defended by Blanche in *Streetcar* ("poetry and music," "richness of the spirit and tenderness of the heart") are meant by Williams to be bogus, the "reflections," however, of the ethic in an antecedent tragic action. They stand to this metonymically, as effect to cause; for the ethic was, as in tragedy it always is, violated. The lies she must tell recapitulate the lie she was not loyal enough to live.

The structural feature of the discovery occurs where we would look for it, but the tragic content is again distorted, for Blanche makes the discovery to Mitch rather than experiences a "recognition" herself. Nor does it result in guilty anguish. To the contrary, Blanche, who is steadily punished from the beginning of the play for urging her imitation illusions, is embraced by Mitch and relaxes "in long, grateful sobs" (p. 356).

The fact of guilt is thus delayed, only to be transformed also. Blanche had reacted to Allan's death self-destructively, internalizing each new death, in effect, by taking another victim into the Tarantula Arms. Each feverish rehearsal of "softness and tenderness" (p. 354) in *Streetcar* glances at the ethic which was to have secured individual existence against dissipation of the "beautiful dream"; it points as well to the betrayal, which was to set death up within the circle of her own consciousness as guilt, expiated in *Streetcar* rather than diminished. That is, following scene six, where ironically the discovery is Mitch's, there is no accession of guilt, because that has been present, of course, since the beginning of the play. After the crisis—again ironically—guilt is displaced into external threats (the bus ticket back to Laurel, Mitch's accusations, Stanley's destruction of her hopes as not "a goddam thing but imagination!" and finally the rape). These punish her for having to "tell what *ought* to be truth" (p. 385), a necessity which results, as we have seen, from her disloyalty. "I hurt him the way that you [therefore!] would like to hurt me . . ." (p. 282). The mobilization of this vengeance is the plot of *Streetcar*. This overdetermines and distorts the reflection of the tragic action: the rape, which consummates the punishment, is also the distorted image of the tragic protagonist's accession of guilt. Raped by a man whom she once described as mad (p. 313), she internalizes, in the final scene, his madness. Thus, in this "doubling" of the tragic, she is more hysterical at the end than at the beginning but not more guilty.

Keats's nightingale ode, it is often suggested, begins where the urn ode ends, when a certain intensity of visual experience is no longer possible. The nightingale ode reproduces the ascent to "heaven's bourne" rather than realizes it, and the reproduction is unsatisfactory: "Adieu! the fancy cannot cheat so well/As she is fam'd to do, deceiving elf." That unsatisfactoriness is, in part, the subject of the poem. This does not make the poem inferior to the urn ode. Only different. A *Streetcar Named Desire* begins where a tragedy has already ended. Its own action transposes the elements of tragedy into ironies, at the expense of the woman whose punishment takes her through a version of the tragic in which no real purpose or perception is possible. That in part is the subject of *Streetcar*, not tragic itself, but referring to tragedy, and generically unintelligible except through that reference.

Notes to Britton J. Harwood, "Tragedy as Habit:
A *Streetcar Named Desire*"

1. See, e.g., Signi Falk, "The Profitable World of Tennessee Williams," *Modern Drama* 1 (1958), 175; R. E. Jones, "Tennessee Williams' Early Heroines," *Modern Drama* 2 (1959), 218–19; Nancy M. Tischler, *Tennessee Williams: Rebellious Puritan* (New York: Citadel Press, 1961), pp. 273–74; J. N. Riddel, "*A Streetcar Named Desire*—Nietzsche Descending," *Modern Drama* 5 (1963), 423; John Gassner, "A *Streetcar Named Desire*: A Study in Ambiguity," in *Modern Drama: Essays in Criticism*, ed. Travis Bogard and W. I. Oliver (New York: Oxford University Press, 1965), pp. 375–77; and J. T. von Szeliski, "Tennessee Williams and the Tragedy of Sensitivity," in *Twentieth Century Interpretations of A Streetcar Named Desire*, ed. J. Y. Miller (Englewood Cliffs, N. J.: Prentice-Hall, 1971), pp. 65, 67.

2. Cf. E. F. Callahan, "Tennessee Williams' Two Worlds," *North Dakota Quarterly* 25 (1967), 62.

3. Cf. Roger Asselineau, "Tennessee Williams ou la nostalgie de la pureté," *Etudes Anglaises* 10 (1957), 440–41.

4. It would be possible to provide either a psychoanalytic description of this, in terms of the instinctual defusion consequent upon the child's introjection of the parent (cf. Freud's *The Ego and the Id*), or a phenomenological one, in terms of the movement from defilement to guilt (cf. Paul Ricoeur's *The Symbolism of Evil*); but there is no need to go into that here. No satisfactory psychoanalytic criticism of *Streetcar* exists, although Philip Weissman has a study of Blanche ("Psychological Characters in Current Drama: A Study of a Trio of Heroines," *American Imago* 17 [1960], 276–84).

5. Cf. Alvin Kernan's remark that Williams is convinced "there is a 'real' world outside and inside each of us which is actively hostile to any belief in the goodness of man . . ." : "Truth and Dramatic Mode in the Modern Theater: Chekhov, Pirandello, and Williams," *Modern Drama* 1 (1958), 111.

6. Cf. Stanley's "licking his lips" (p. 323).

7. See Friedrich Nietzsche, *The Birth of Tragedy*, trans. F. Golffing (Garden City, N. Y.: Doubleday, Anchor, 1956), pp. 38–39.

8. See ibid., p. 56 and passim.

9. Cf. Gassner, p. 376; and Esther Merle Jackson, *The Broken World of Tennessee Williams* (Madison: University of Wisconsin Press, 1966), p. 299 (where she quotes Elia Kazan's comment on Blanche's "compulsion to be *special*").

10. "Blanche has no illusion about her illusions": Benjamin Nelson, *Tennessee Williams: The Man and His Work* (New York: Obolensky, 1961), p. 143.

11. See Harold Clurman, *Lies Like Truth* (New York: Macmillan, 1958), p. 79.

12. Cf. the stage direction at the beginning of scene four: "There is a confusion of street cries like a choral chant."

13. Cf. John J. Mood, "The Structure of *A Streetcar Named Desire*," *Ball State University Forum* 14: 3 (1973), 9; and R. B. Heilman, "Tennessee Williams: Approaches to Tragedy," *Southern Review* (n.s.) 1 (1965), 772.

14. Cf. the way in which Lord Jim's deliberately coming to Doramin to be shot does not substitute, in Marlow's eyes, for his having deserted the *Patna* when his imagination overwhelmed him.

From "Tarantula Arms" to "Della Robbia Blue": The Tennessee Williams Tragicomic Transit Authority

JOHN M. RODERICK

Had William Shakespeare written *A Streetcar Named Desire* it would no doubt head his list of "problem plays." It exhibits a curious resistance to traditional interpretation and utterly defies any insistence upon didactic statement. Reflecting a basic duality or ambiguity which renders comfortable critical statements obsolete, *Streetcar* is often labeled Tennessee Williams' *flawed* masterpiece. An appraisal of the play in the tragicomic terms Williams has set before us, therefore, is long overdue. Williams has not written a flawed tragedy in which our final judgments of hero and heroine are clouded. Rather, through intricate structural control, he has approached brilliant tragicomedy. To commit ourselves solidly to a tragic interpretation would be to do Williams a serious disservice and to deny him that element central to the creative arts —control.

With the tragic implications of so many events in *Streetcar*, one is tempted simply to label the play a tragedy, if an imperfect one. What rises again and again, however, to contradict such a position is a comic spirit that continuously puts the audience off balance. Rather than viewing these comic elements as imperfections in a purely tragic mode, then, or the tragic events as weak melodramatic elements in a comic mode, our appraisal should encompass both modes and allow Williams his tragicomic stance with all of its

116

irreconcilabilities. As Aristotle implies by mimesis, art mirrors life. And if we give credence to Eric Bentley's decree that "contrariety is at the heart of the universe" (*Life of the Drama*, p. 338), we need hardly defend the playwright who illustrates this contrariety in his drama. For the playwright with the tragicomic vision, "the double mask of tragi-comedy reveals the polarity of the human condition." It is the tragicomic sense of life that allows the dramatist to laugh with and through his characters and thereby "cope with the overwhelming burden of reality" (David Krause, *Sean O'Casey*, p. 53).

Williams shows a basic duality at the heart of the tragicomic genre. We begin with the traditional elements of a sacred arena suddenly profaned, but in Blanche DuBois and Stanley Kowalski the complexity of this traditional conflict is compounded. Both are simultaneously attractive and unattractive. Each has elements of both the sacred and the profane. Part of this ambivalence lies in the possibility that the play lends itself to a reading on two levels, one social, the other psychological. Although the levels cannot be isolated in a strict sense, for purposes of discussion one may argue that Blanche, as the last vestige of a dying aristocratic culture, is the heroine on a social level. As heroine she represents all that is sacred within this culture—the love for language, the appreciation of art and music, the "beauty of the mind and richness of the spirit and tenderness of the heart" (I, 396). Stanley, on the other hand, represents the crude destroyer and profaner of this aesthetic sensibility. His violent abuse of Blanche is a destruction of a class as well. In the class struggle neither can brook a coexistence with the other. The negative implication of such a coexistence is seen in Blanche's futile plea to her sister, *"Don't—don't hang back with the brutes!"* (p. 323).

In this same speech Blanche underscores the class struggle and the social tensions which lie behind much of the conflict in the play: "He acts like an animal, has an animal's habits! Eats like one, moves like one, talks like one! . . . Thousands and thousands of years have passed him right by, and there he is—Stanley Kowalski—survivor of the Stone Age! Bearing the raw meat home from the kill in the jungle! . . . Maybe we are a long way from being made in God's image, but Stella—my sister—there has been *some* progress since then! Such things as art—as poetry and music—such kinds of new light have come into the world since then!" (p. 323). It is appropriately ironic that Stanley, in the best "well-made" tradition, is overhearing this entire indictment. As the nature of his adversary's position is revealed, the lines of battle are more sharply defined for Stanley.

On a purely psychological level rather than a social one, however, Stanley emerges as hero. The sexually healthy marriage he shares with Stella stands as the sacred arena defiled by the profane intruder Blanche with her sexual perversity. If Stanley is taken at his word when he confides in Stella, the normalcy of their relationship is convincing: "Stell, it's gonna be all right after she goes and after you've had the baby. . . . God, honey, it's gonna be sweet when we can make noise in the night the way that we used to and get the colored lights going with nobody's sister behind the curtain to hear us. (Their upstairs neighbors are heard in bellowing laughter at something. Stanley chuckles.) Steve an' Eunice . . ." (p. 373). And if we believe that any good subplot is a crucial reflection of the grain of the main plot, then Stanley's allusion to Steve and Eunice also fortifies the position that the Kowalskis share a successful marriage. The relationship of the couple upstairs parallels the marriage of Stanley and Stella in every way—from the violent outbursts to the sensual compensations. Even after the Kowalskis' violent argument, Mitch assures Blanche, "There's nothing to be scared of. They're crazy about each other" (p. 308). Steve and Eunice are likewise able to brook such battles.

In direct contrast to Stanley, on the other hand, Blanche represents the epitome of a psychological malaise. Her sexual perversions with schoolboys are in direct contrast to the normalcy of Stanley's aggressive sexuality in marriage. In the role of psychological profaner, Blanche as much as Stanley is to blame for the rape: "We've had this date with each other from the beginning!" (p. 402), he ominously tells Blanche just before he rapes her. And both he and Blanche recognize the truth in his statement. Earlier Blanche confided to Mitch, "The first time I laid eyes on him I thought to myself, that man is my executioner! That man will destroy me, unless—" (p. 351). Similarly, it is against Blanche as profane intruder into his domain as "a richly feathered male bird among hens," that Stanley violently reacts as his role of supremacy is threatened in his own house. When Stella tells him to help clear the table, "He hurls a plate to the floor," and says, "That's how I'll clear the table! (He seizes her arm) Don't ever talk that way to me! 'Pig—Polack—disgusting—vulgar—greasy!'—them kind of words have been on your tongue and your sister's too much around here! What do you two think you are? A pair of queens? . . . (He hurls a cup and saucer to the floor) My place is cleared! You want me to clear your places?" (p. 371). Psychologically speaking, then, Blanche represents the profanation of Stanley's sacred, if crude, marriage. But we must cope with both the social and the psychological levels simultaneously. Thus the ambiguous duality in our appraisal of Stanley and Blanche is encouraged by Williams, an ambiguity which is not central to the genre of traditional tragedy alone.

If, as Nietzsche claims in *The Birth of Tragedy*, tragedy is begot by the clash between the vital force of Dionysus and the controlling restraint of Apollo, can we make the assumption that somehow the combination of these conflicting forces is to be found in *Streetcar*? It appears that Stanley Kowalski readily lends himself to identification with the vibrant celebration of procreation (as emblematic of the "gaudy seed-bearer") and the frenzied irrational energy of Dionysus. But where do we place Blanche DuBois in this scheme of things? She is hardly the stalwart of control and restraint, order and symmetry we normally associate with Apollo. Hers appears to be a false control, an illusory order whose erupting energy negates her stance. She is a tainted Apollonian or a hypocritical Dionysian who does not allow her welled-up emotions their freedom, except for sordid lapses with young schoolboys and infantrymen.

Stanley, too, on closer analysis, defies stereotyped classification. Where he does represent explosive sexuality and impulsive vitality on the one hand, he nevertheless strives on the other, to retain the status quo of his marriage with himself as cock-of-the-roost. He serves as an Apollonian demagogue in his attempts to discredit Blanche's reputation to preserve his own world. For all of his impulsive behavior, Stanley seeks, above all, to retain the order and symmetry within his created existence. He has his "Napoleonic code" to fall back upon. On this level, Blanche is the Dionysian disrupter of order. What such paradoxical and tautological statements reveal are the shortcomings inherent in attempting to neatly classify complex art. That Williams resists a clearly defined means of measuring tragedy may indicate that we are not wholly in the realm of tragedy in *A Streetcar Named Desire.*

Insufficient attention has been given to Williams' careful juxtaposition of the tragic with the comic—a juxtaposition which underscores not only the ambiguity of the tragicomic genre but, indeed, the ambiguity inherent in an empirical view of reality. Although John Gassner (*The Theatre in Our Times*) acknowledges the paradoxical rhythms in *Streetcar*, like so many critics he appears to be insensitive to the comic spirit which counterpoints the tragic in Williams' play: "But *Streetcar*, for all its dramatic momentum and surge, is a divided work. Ambiguities split the emphasis between realistic and decadent drama, between normal causation and accident, between tragedy and melodrama" (p. 358). Indeed, Gassner goes so far as to parenthetically disapprove of the theatergoing public that does appreciate Williams' humor: "(It was noticed after *Streetcar* had been running for some time on Broadway that audiences, no longer a typically New York playgoing public, reacted to the play as though it were rather comic and prurient.)" (p. 359).

Karl S. Guthke (*Modern Tragicomedy*) is also insensitive to the comic side of *Streetcar* and thereby misinterprets the play as a "so-called naturalistic tragedy, which usually ends on a note of despair unrelieved by the silver lining that appears in the metaphysical reconciliation and religious assurance of traditional tragedy" (p. 98). The greater irony here is that Guthke is dealing precisely with this "bastard genre" tragicomedy and overlooks its most common characteristic, irreconcilability, in a play like *Streetcar*. Traditional reconciliation *is* denied by Williams but in a tragicomic vein, not in an exclusively naturalistic one.

As a significant parallel to the main conflict between Blanche and Stanley, the relationship between Mitch and Blanche serves well to illustrate Williams' contrapuntal technique of juxtaposing the comic with the tragic. Mitch represents the comic contrast to Stanley in almost every way. While Stanley is solidly built, Mitch tends to be on the heavy side, if not somewhat flabby. Stanley is the "gaudy seed-bearer," and Mitch is an anally fixated momma's boy. Similarly, in his first scene with Blanche, Stanley removes his shirt, saying, "Be comfortable is my motto." In contrast Mitch is ashamed of the way he perspires and to his discomfit wears an alpaca jacket in the hottest weather. With these apparent distinctions the audience can more easily laugh at Mitch's ludicrous affectations in his attempts to impress Blanche.

Through Mitch, Williams succeeds in that juxtaposition of the comic with the tragic central to the tragicomic mode. Following immediately upon the tragic implications of a world rapidly closing in upon Blanche and her desperate efforts to seduce Mitch as a potential husband, for example, Mitch brags adolescently that his stomach "is so hard now that a man can punch me in the belly and it don't hurt me. Punch me! Go on! See?" And as Blanche continues to make overtures, Mitch misses the sexual implications altogether and says, "Guess how much I weigh Blanche?" When he hesitates and realizes that his weight is not such an "interesting subject to talk about," for a split second the audience feels that he may turn to more serious issues until he counters with "What's yours?" (pp. 346–7) as if, somehow, Blanche's weight *will* be an interesting subject to talk about. This comic obtuseness is sandwiched between two highly dramatic and potentially tragic confidences which Blanche shares with Mitch—her belief that Stanley will eventually destroy her and her sense of guilt for destroying Allan Grey, as she recounts the incident: " 'Don't go any closer! Come back! You don't want to see!' See? See what? Then I heard voices say—Allan! Allan! The Grey boy! He'd stuck the revolver into his mouth, and fired—so that the back of his head had been—blown away! . . . It was because—on the dance floor—unable to stop myself—I'd suddenly said—'I saw! I know! You disgust me . . .' " (p. 355).

The conflict between Stanley and Blanche is similarly permeated with humorous incidents counterpointing the dramatic action. When Stanley initially feels slighted at Blanche's intrusion and then learns that she has let the Belle Reve estate slip through her fingers, his adherence to the "Napoleonic code" to justify his claim is quite humorous, as is his list of expert acquaintances who will appraise Blanche's furs and jewelry. Similarly, in the midst of a highly dramatic scene when Stanley relates the details of Blanche's past to

Stella and says he has bought her a one-way ticket back to Laurel, Williams inserts the crudely comic, which makes us laugh despite the potentially tragic action.

> BLANCHE: You have such a strange expression on your face!
> STELLA: Oh—(She tries to laugh) I guess I'm a little tired!
> BLANCHE: Why don't you bathe, too, soon as I get out?
> STANLEY (calling from the kitchen): How soon is that going to be?
> BLANCHE: Not so terribly long! Possess your soul in patience!
> STANLEY: It's not my soul, it's my kidneys I'm worried about! (pp. 363–4).

As Wylie Sypher points out, we seek to escape suffering through comedy (*Comedy*, pp. 245–6). And as Susanne Langer indicates, even in the gallows laugh is the temporary elevation above the terror of the moment (*Feeling and Form*, pp. 340–1). One may argue that it is this impulse which motivates Williams' inclusion of the comic with the tragic. But Williams' comic reversals are far too systematic and numerous to be relegated solely to the function of release. The comic elements play their role in aggressive self-preservation just as the tragic possibilities invite the antithetical notion of self-destruction. With the defiant juxtaposition of irreconcilables, ambiguity is at the heart of the tragicomic mode.

Ambivalence seems to be the keynote not only to the judgments made on particular characters but ultimately to thematic statement as well. The two cannot be viewed in isolation, in fact, because one serves as the vehicle for the other. What, in the final analysis, is Tennessee Williams' attitude toward either Blanche DuBois or Stanley Kowalski? For all their obvious flaws, it seems that Williams is also admitting something glamorous in them, some undefinable, appealing trait which ingratiates them to us despite their sordid acts. Williams' sympathies, for example, are certainly with Blanche when her fragile vulnerability carries her to the destructive flame of Stanley's passions. The waste of this aesthete, indeed the destruction of an aesthetic class at the hands of brute power, touched Williams, as it touches his audience.

When Blanche arrives in New Orleans at the beginning of the play, her lines to Eunice serve as a symbolic prophesy of her movement that will echo throughout the play: "They told me to take a street-car named Desire, and then transfer to one called Cemeteries and ride six blocks and get off at—Elysian Fields!" (p. 246). Before she can truly arrive at Elysian Fields—resting place of the blessed dead in Greek mythology—Blanche must travel the sacrificial path from desire to death and be purged for this epiphany. As she tells Stella very early, it is desire that brings her to New Orleans in the first place.

And when Mitch confronts Blanche with the knowledge of the truth about her sordid past, she readily confesses her guilt:

MITCH: Didn't you stay at a hotel called The Flamingo?
BLANCHE: Flamingo? No! Tarantula was the name of it! I stayed at a hotel called The Tarantula Arms!
MITCH: Tarantula?
BLANCHE: Yes, a big spider! That's where I brought my victims. . . . After the death of Allan—intimacies with strangers was all I seemed able to fill my empty heart with. . . . I think it was panic, just panic, that drove me from one to to another, hunting for some protection—here and there, in the most—unlikely places—even, at last, in a seventeen-year-old boy but—somebody wrote the superintendent about it— "This woman is morally unfit for her position!" (p. 386).

It is a guilt, however, for which she is trying to make amends throughout the play. "Now run along, now, quickly!" she tells the Kowalski newsboy. "It would be nice to keep you, but I've got to be good—and keep my hands off children" (p. 339). Indeed, her ritualistic hot baths throughout the play are central to her symbolic purging process. And the suffering or passion necessary for salvation is experienced through her associations with death. The spiritual and physical toll which these deaths have upon her, from the death of Allan Grey for which she feels directly responsible to the deaths of her relatives whose "epic fornications" drained Belle Reve, is readily apparent in her defense to Stella over losing the estate: "I, I, I took the blows in my face and my body! All of those deaths! The long parade to the graveyard! . . . You just came home in time for the funerals, Stella. . . . But funerals are quiet, with pretty flowers. And, oh, what gorgeous boxes they pack them away in! Unless you were there at the bed when they cried out, 'Hold me!' you'd never suspect there was the struggle for breath and bleeding. You didn't dream, but I saw! *Saw! Saw!* . . . Death is expensive, Miss Stella!"

(pp. 261–2). Later, when speaking to Mitch, Blanche draws the explicit polarity between death and desire:

> Death—I used to sit here and she used to sit over there and death was as close as you are. . . . We didn't dare even admit we had ever heard of it!
>
> MEXICAN WOMAN: Flores para los muertos, flores—flores . . .
>
> BLANCHE: The opposite is desire. So do you wonder? How could you possibly wonder! (pp. 388–9).

It is significant that Williams does not wholly condemn Blanche for her indiscretions. Hers, he insists, is too delicate and spiritual a nature to continue to face the harshness of reality. "I don't want realism," she tells Mitch in a frantic plea for sympathy. "I want magic! . . . Yes, yes magic! I try to give that to people. I misrepresent things to them. I don't tell truth, I tell what *ought* to be truth. And if that is sinful, then let me be damned for it!" (p. 385). Where Williams' sympathies lie is quite clear, but he avoids didactic statement, perhaps to a fault to some tastes, when he allows Blanche to be damned, in one sense, precisely for this sin of idealism.

Through her physical and emotional ordeals, however, Blanche has earned a place for herself in the Elysian Fields. She has journeyed from "Tarantula Arms" to visions of "Della Robbia blue" in Williams' mythic statement. Although soiled by reality, Blanche's passion has by the final curtain earned her the right to wear the robes of the Madonna. Williams' functional use of symbolic language strengthens such a reading as cathedral bells are heard in the background and the callous men at the card table stand for the first time for the entrance of Blanche DuBois. Blanche herself speaks in the exaggerated, archetypal language which suggests epiphany:

> I can smell the sea air. The rest of my time I'm going to spend on the sea. And when I die, I'm going to die on the sea. You know what I shall die of? (She plucks a grape) I shall die of eating an unwashed grape one day out on the ocean. I will die—with my hand in the hand of some nice-looking ship's doctor. . . . "Poor lady," they'll say, "the quinine did her no good. That unwashed grape has transported her soul to heaven." (The cathedral chimes are heard) And I'll be buried at sea sewn up in a clean white sack and dropped overboard—at noon— in the blaze of summer—and into an ocean as blue as (chimes again) my first lover's eyes! (p. 410).

Contrary to much critical opinion, however, Williams is not a didactic writer. He is too complex a playwright to offer a saccharine resolution. Blanche's ritualistic epiphany is, to be sure, a tainted one. The audience is too fully conscious that her destination with this gentle doctor is an insane asylum. Likewise, her vision of salvation is mocked by the intrusive violence between Mitch and Stanley. As tainted as this vision is on the temporal plane, though, it is a positive force on the spiritual level. It is a creation of an ideal illusion in the face of a destructive reality. But Williams also avoids the melodramatic condemnation of the portentous force which helps destroy Blanche. In lieu of this condemnation is the ambivalent admiration of a vibrant life force. Unlike the film version of *Streetcar* which deems it necessary to "punish" the recalcitrant Stanley for his crime against nature, Williams honors him with a partial victory of his own. He has preserved his domain. The threat to his dominance has been carried away by a doctor and a nurse. We are left with a "Marriage–New Orleans Style." The idealization of a Belle Reve union cannot survive the light of day in Stanley's world, as Williams readily admits. Thus instead of the manipulated, Hayes-dictated Hollywood ending of Elia Kazan, Williams permits Stanley's final gesture. In fondling the breasts of Stella as she holds his child, Stanley points to a future race not of Shavian Supermen, but of Stanley Kowalskis.

But perhaps even this victory is tainted. The psychic wounds which Stella must surely feel when she asks Eunice whether she did the right thing in sending Blanche away are real:

STELLA: I don't know if I did the right thing.
EUNICE: What else could you do?
STELLA: I couldn't believe her story and go on living with Stanley.
EUNICE: Don't ever believe it. Life has got to go on. No matter what happens, you've got to keep on going (pp. 405–6).

Perhaps it is significant that Stella remains passive to Stanley's overt sexual gesture. Williams' tragicomic vision allows life to go on, but it is a long way from the best of all possible worlds. Tennessee Williams permits reality.

A Streetcar Named Desire Under the Elms:
A Study of Dramatic Space in
A Streetcar Named Desire
and *Desire Under the Elms*

ALAN EHRLICH

A *Streetcar Named Desire* and *Desire Under the Elms* have a much tighter bond than the word "desire." The plays have identical subjects: the threat of the destruction of a family unit by the presence of "desire." The destruction of a family is not a new theme; it has been used in the drama since the Greeks. The house of Atreus, the house of Laius, the house of Lear—the house of Kowalski, the house of Cabot. The disintegration of a family is serious stuff, the stuff of which tragedy is often made. There is no simple answer for a 2500 year popularity of the dramatist's concern for the family unit; but as Gaston Bachelard asserts, the house does assume universal significance. For Bachelard, the house is the center of stability and intimacy—the corner of the world. Everyone yearns for the concentrated, intimate space of a home—the embodiment of his dreams (*Poetics of Space*, I–II). To be without a home can be traumatic. Both Blanche in *A Streetcar Named Desire* and Abbie in *Desire Under the Elms* are homeless; both are unstable, zealous of inhabiting an intimate space.

In this desire to inhabit an intimate space nests the conflict for both plays. Using a traditional literary technique, each playwright sets up an established environment or family unit into which a potentially destructive agent, the catalyst, enters to disrupt the norm. The conflict of the heroine with her environment is the heart of both

126

dramas. O'Neill creates a stronger destructive agent to combat a weaker established environment than Williams does, resulting in Abbie's more successful alteration of her environment.

Both plays adhere to unity of place: they are compact, with the entire action taking place within the confines of one setting. To grasp the potential conflict, an audience must first apprehend the environment established prior to the arrival of the destructive agent. It is crucial that the audience register the set at the initial curtain.

O'Neill's set is distinctive. As the curtain rises we see a New England farmhouse surrounded by stone walls "with a wooden gate at center opening on a country road." In addition to this lateral restriction, the two enormous elms on each side of the house "bend their trailing branches down over the roof" (*Nine Plays*). The vertical restriction complements the lateral restriction. But of course to the audience this limitation might not at first appear threatening. To insure that it does, O'Neill begins scene one with carefully placed dialogue. Eben, Simeon, and Peter all comment on the stone walls built by their father to fence them in. The walls function like a prison to entrap their victims; the restriction becomes a confinement. This prison-house is the established environment for the remaining action of the play. As with any prison, the inmates want out. Near the end of part one, when Simeon and Peter finally gain enough courage and finances to escape, they carry the front gate with them, symbolically opening the door for the possibility of the future escape of their younger brother. Although represented by stone walls, the established environment is initially weakened through Simeon's and Peter's escape.

In *A Streetcar Named Desire*, the confinement inherent in the set is more subtle. With no drooping elms or stones to wall the characters in, the entrapment is less evident. Rather than blatant imprisonment, the play's confinement is the claustrophobia resulting from the loss of privacy, once Blanche arrives. Jo Mielziner, the designer for Elia Kazan's original 1947 New York production, devised a perfect set to depict this loss of privacy: a transparent back wall looking into the courtyard. This transparent wall can function in a manner similar to O'Neill's stone wall and elms. To Cabot, happy on the farm, the wall and the elms remain merely a wall and elms; to his sons, unhappy on the farm, wall and elms are a visual sign of their psychological imprisonment. To Stanley and Stella, happy in their home prior to Blanche's arrival, the transparent wall remains a normal wall; to Stanley, Stella, and Blanche, unhappy in their overcrowded home after Blanche's arrival, the transparent wall becomes a visual sign of their lack of privacy. In *Desire Under the Elms*, the characters are confined to a space that permits escape only after constant effort. In *A Streetcar Named Desire*, the characters are confined to a cramped space that prevents escape altogether.

Both playwrights take great pains to establish their respective environments prior to the arrival of the destructive agent. In addition to their physical settings, both O'Neill and Williams establish a tone for their established environments. A status quo is set up early in both plays as an obstacle against which each destructive agent must combat. In *Desire Under the Elms*, a totally masculine environment has been established. In his stage directions, O'Neill states, "Everything is neat and in order but the atmosphere is of a men's camp kitchen rather than that of a home" (p. 140). Every family unit is governed by its own principles. For the Cabots, with no woman present for years, home is a particular, masculine, established environment. In *A Streetcar Named Desire*, the established environment is simply a happy marriage—the couple lives in "Elysian Fields." Williams establishes this status quo economically in the initial action. Stanley bellows hello to Stella and tosses her a package of meat which she catches, breathlessly laughing—an action that can be interpreted as a symbol of the sex on which their relationship is based. One gives, the other receives; their alliance is established. Stella's whole life is Stanley. She later tells her sister she cannot bear being away from her husband for even one night; in the opening sequence it is only for a few hours, but she must follow him to the bowling alley to watch him bowl.

The order is firmly entrenched; the action impatiently awaits the arrival of the destructive agent. Perhaps, if either Abbie Putnam or Blanche DuBois had entered passively into her respective established environment, there would have been no ensuing tragedy. However, both Abbie and Blanche are powerful individuals accustomed to dominating their surroundings and getting things on their own terms.

The intrusion of any female into a "men's camp kitchen" should be conflict enough, but O'Neill takes no chances. Abbie Putnam, Cabot's new wife, covers all the female archetypes. She is voluptuous and maternal, seductive and matronly, a Helen and a Demeter combined. As soon as she arrives at the farm, she infringes on Eben's territory—the kitchen. When she first sees Eben, "Her eyes take him in penetratingly with a calculating appraisal of his strength as against hers" (p. 159). At first she begins the scene in a playful, seductive manner. "Be you—Eben? I'm Abbie—(she laughs) I mean, I'm yer new Maw" (p. 159). However, the playful seduction turns more and more bitter. After she realizes Eben will be a difficult conquest, she hardens her attack. "This be my farm—this be my hum—this be my kitchen! . . . An' upstairs—that be my bedroom—an' my bed! . . . I hain't bad nor mean—'ceptin' fur an enemy—but I got t' fight fur what's due me out o' life, if I ever 'spect t' git it" (p. 161). Within five minutes Abbie has taken over; she has altered the established order previously weakened by the escape of Simeon and Peter. Eben furiously flings off her arm, calls her a witch, and yells out that he hates her. But the damage is done: Abbie's foot is more than in the door. Part one ends with Abbie washing *her* dishes.

Blanche takes a streetcar named Desire, transfers to one called Cemeteries, and arrives at Elysian Fields—the heart of the New Orleans French Quarter. Like Abbie, she is at first completely out of place. Williams' stage directions read: "Her appearance is incongruous to this setting. She is daintily dressed . . . as if she were arriving at a summer tea or cocktail party . . ." (I, 245). Like Abbie, Blanche immediately tries to alter her surroundings. She covers a naked light bulb with a paper lantern (p. 300); she re-covers a bedroom chair (p. 379). Blanche's arrival mostly affects Stella, who feels compelled to wait on her older sister. In part, Blanche too alters the established environment. She tells Mitch, "I've done so much with this place since I've been here" (p. 382).

Both Abbie and Blanche attempt to revamp the old order and establish a new one. But the situation gets increasingly more difficult for both, as Eben and Stanley wish to maintain the status quo. Both at first resent the women, but strong love/hate attractions and repulsions later occur. The incest incipient in each plot is eventually consummated. Between the action and the setting is a cyclical pattern. The claustrophobic setting limits all alternatives and invites sin, which in turn is a product of the cramped quarters crowding its occupants to the point of desperation. Constraint converges from all sides sealing off all possible modes of escape. The confining environment creates tension for any character who is out of step with it. In *Desire Under the Elms*, Eben feels entrapped. He is the vulnerable character and he gets seduced by the stronger. In *A Streetcar Named Desire*, Blanche feels entrapped. She is the vulnerable character and she gets raped by the stronger. When a character feels entrapped within his environment, extreme desperation and confusion await him.

In *Desire Under the Elms*, Eben feels imprisoned from the beginning. "His defiant, dark eyes remind one of a wild animal's in captivity. Each day is a cage in which he finds himself trapped but inwardly unsubdued. There is a fierce repressed vitality about him" (p. 137). Later, when the brothers talk of their father's strength in comparison to theirs, only Eben is optimistic. "I'm gittin' stronger. I kin feel it growin' in me—growin' an' growin'—till it'll bust out—!" (p. 144). And "bust out" it does, but only after it is indirectly displaced toward Abbie. Abbie too feels the restraint; and as the hot New England sun bakes the suppressed desire, the audience waits impatiently for the explosion. It comes in scene three of part two— the climax of the play as well as of their relationship. Abbie: " 'I'll kiss ye pure, Eben—same 's if I was a Maw t' ye—an' ye kin kiss me back 's if yew was my son—my boy—sayin' good-night t' me! Kiss me, Eben.' (They kiss in restrained fashion. Then suddenly wild passion overcomes her. She kisses him lustfully again and again," p. 178). He backs off here and can overcome the presence of Maw's spirit he feels in the room only after he thinks of her vengeance on his father. He kisses Abbie, "releasing all his pent-up passion" (p. 179) and confesses his suppressed love for her. With this kiss comes a total release of the thing he felt "growin' an' growin' " within him that was seen earlier in the play and felt since his mother's death.

The location of this climactic scene is crucial. Abbie intends to control the entire house, and her final conquest must happen "in the one room hain't [hers] yet." She waits for Eben in the parlor where his mother died and was laid out. This "repressed room like a tomb" with all its "preserved ugliness" (p. 176) has been sealed off to the family for years. The claustrophobic room in which time has been frozen with its stagnant air is about to be given new life. Abbie's attempt at seduction eventually succeeds. With it, Maw's mysterious spiritual presence leaves the farm for good. Abbie: "She went back t' her grave that night we fust done it, remember? I hain't felt her about since" (p. 197). Maw leaves; the old environment is completely altered. Abbie has established a new environment, and her original opponent, Eben, is now a crucial component of the new order.

In *A Streetcar Named Desire,* the weaker character, the one who feels most out of place in the established environment, is Blanche. Like Abbie, she tries to revamp the environment; but unlike Abbie, she is unable to conquer her antagonist. Stella is willing to wait on Blanche, but Stanley is not. Blanche tries to adjust the established environment, but Stanley is not taken in by his sister-in-law's airs. "You come in here and sprinkle the place with powder and spray perfume and cover the light bulb with a paper lantern, and lo and behold the place has turned into Egypt and you are the Queen of the Nile! Sitting on your throne and swilling down my liquor!" (p. 398). Blanche tries to alter the environment but it is too firm. Because her arrival shrinks the two-room apartment in half and prevents privacy, Stanley must defend his home against the enemy. All he wants is to return to the lifestyle he enjoyed before Blanche arrived. "It's gonna be all right again between you [Stella] and me the way that it was. . . . God, honey, it's gonna be sweet when we can make noise in the night the way we used to and get the colored lights going with nobody's sister behind the curtains to hear us! . . . And wasn't we happy together, wasn't it all okay till she showed here?" (pp. 373, 377). Stanley evaluates the problem and pursues the solution. Three into two won't go; Blanche must leave.

After Stanley reveals Blanche's sordid history and gives her the bus ticket back to Laurel, the heroine is clearly awaiting her fate. Scene nine opens with Blanche's tragic theme, the "Varsouviana," playing in the background. "The music is in her mind; she is drinking to escape it and the sense of disaster closing in on her . . ." (p. 379). The air in her small cubicle is hot and stagnant. She artificially attempts refreshening it with her electric fan "turning back and forth across her," but it can only recirculate the stale air, not replenish it. Mitch enters, turns off the fan, turns on the lights, tears the paper lantern off the light bulb, and seals her inevitable doom. In scene ten the fall is continued. This time the agent is Stanley, the "executioner" she had recognized from the beginning. She sits in the claustrophobic room, and confusion, desperation, and destruction await her.

At first the confusion is seen by the workings of her imagination, telling Stanley about Shep Huntleigh's nonexistent phone call. Stanley believes her for a while, but when she is momentarily dazed by his demands for details about the telegram, he finally realizes the truth. "There isn't a goddam thing but imagination!" (p. 398). He follows her into the bedroom. She begins to feel cramped in the congested space. Stanley and the environment close in around her. "Lurid reflections appear on the walls around Blanche. The shadows are of a grotesque and menacing form" (pp. 398–99). Stanley goes into the bathroom and she tries to phone Shep for help. No time. She hangs up and desperately runs to the kitchen for escape, but the house is too small and menacing. "The night is filled with inhuman voices like cries in a jungle. The shadows and lurid reflections move sinuously as flames along the wall spaces" (p. 399). There is no privacy, no escape. The transparent wall now performs its theatrical function and allows the street scenes outside (prostitution, alcohol, looting) to become a part of the calamitous scene inside. All avenues of escape are blocked—her last hope, a desperation telegram to Shep. "In desperate, desperate circumstances! Help me! Caught in a trap" (p. 400). Stanley enters in his "brilliant silk pajamas," deliberately sets the phone back on the hook, as the "blue piano" turns into "the roar of an approaching locomotive," and settles his account once and for all: "We've had this date with each other from the beginning!" (p. 402). And all this while Stella is at the hospital in labor.

Confinement pervades both plays. The claustrophobic environment entraps its victims and eventually leads to their respective tragedies. In Desire Under the Elms, the environment is not as escape-proof. Simeon and Peter escape the farm at the play's beginning. Because the environment is weakened at the outset and because Abbie Putnam is extremely strong, the established order can be altered. Because Eben wants no part of the old order and every part of the new, he is assimilated by it, and a new established order is constructed. In A *Streetcar Named Desire*, the established environment (the happy marriage) is indestructible. Blanche is more delicate than Abbie, Stanley more inflexible than Eben. As a result, unlike Abbie, Blanche cannot alter the environment. Left with no alternative, she must find ways to escape it.

Williams utilizes two devices to demonstrate Blanche's need for escape—her drinking and her baths. Blanche is a heavy drinker and Williams makes her drink to escape her problems. Besides drinking, her only escape is into the bathroom for a "hot tub." As the tension heats, so does the water. Finally, in the tense birthday party scene when Blanche has been stood up, forty-five minutes after her bath, Stanley remarks, "it's hot in here with the steam from the bathroom" (p. 374). But her "hot tubs" are inadequate escape. She remains entrapped and is ultimately crushed by her environment.

In addition to Williams' use of alcohol and baths, both playwrights utilize yet another device of attempted escape for the characters who feel threatened by their environment. These characters are often described as caged animals who long for their freedom. This longing is subdued in every outward direction—the only alternative is upward. In both *Desire Under the Elms* and *A Streetcar Named Desire*, the captive characters constantly cry out to the sky.

Simeon and Peter despise their captivity by their father and his farm and want to escape to California at the play's very opening. They discuss their prospects excitedly. Simeon: " 'Fortunes layin' just atop o' the ground waitin' t' be picked! Solomon's mines, they says!' (For a moment they continue looking up at the sky . . .)" (p. 138). But their longing for freedom (symbolically shown by their gazing to the sky) is ironically juxtaposed with the cruel reality of their situation. Their eyes drop immediately back down to the earth. Peter: "Here—it's stones atop o' the ground—stones atop o' stones— makin' stone walls— . . . to fence us in!" (p. 138). Eben, too, feels his captivity and begins the play with a defiant apostrophe to the sky, "God! Purty!" (p. 137). After being teased by his two older brothers about going to Min's, Eben escapes the unpleasant situation by running out and standing by the gate, "staring up at the sky." A moment later, "Eben stretches his arms up to the sky—

rebelliously" (p. 145). These acts of defiance can only be directed upward. The boundless sky is a perfect device to mock the characters' frustration.

A *Streetcar Named Desire* has no equivalent to the blatant stone walls. The claustrophobia is the result of an overcrowded house. Blanche's arrival shrinks the house in half. She looks to the sky for her salvation. In scene three when she chats with Mitch, "she looks up at the sky" and says, "There's so much—so much confusion in the world . . ." (p. 309). There's "confusion" in the cramped apartment, but there is plenty of room above her head. Later in scene six, Mitch fumbles around for her key. When he finally finds it, Blanche exclaims, "Eureka! Honey, you open the door while I take a last look at the sky" (p. 342). Already the ensuing desperation is sensed. Her "last look" recalls that of a prisoner just prior to his return to the cell.

Rather than for her freedom, Blanche longs for her privacy: "When I think of how divine it is going to be to have such a thing as privacy once more—I could weep with joy!" (p. 396). In fact, freedom is one of the last things Blanche wants; to the contrary, she needs security. Whether it comes in the form of Stanley's best friend, Mitch, or the strange doctor from the state institution who escorts her out, Blanche remains in need of support, always depending "on the kindness of strangers" (p. 418). It is peculiar that Williams chooses such a dependent woman to overcrowd the household. One would suppose such a claustrophobic environment would be ideal for an insecure person. But Williams loves irony, and it is for that he chooses such an heroine. It is the same irony that names the streetcar that carried her to her downfall *Desire*—a "rattle-trap streetcar that bangs through the Quarter, up one old narrow street and down another . . ." until it finally arrives at its destination—"Elysian Fields" (p. 321). The streetcar took her there, and more importantly it can take her away. Just as Williams ironically has the streetcar as a possible vehicle of escape clanging in the background to punctuate the frustration, O'Neill has a big poster of "a ship in full sail and the word 'California' in big letters" right in the middle of the rear wall of the kitchen (p. 140). Both playwrights effectively mock their characters' tragic situations.

If my theory holds true—that the claustrophobic environment is a crucial determinant of the tragedies—then it is reasonable to assume that the more crowded with people, the more confusing the situation. Conveniently, both plays contain group-party scenes.

Stanley has his friends over to the house to play poker. There being no room, the sisters wisely choose to go out for the evening. When they return, the two-room apartment is at its most crowded point in the play, and the result is utter chaos. Stanley is drunk and uncontrollable. When Blanche and Mitch dance to the music of his radio, Stanley vehemently tosses it out the window. The fiasco ends with Stanley's cold shower and warm, tender reconciliation with Stella. This reconciliation occurs, significantly, outside the apartment. It is the one time since Blanche arrived that Stanley and Stella are close to each other. Blanche is inside, still trying to alter the environment, while outside, the happy couple briefly re-establish their old ways.

In *Desire Under the Elms*, Cabot invites the townspeople over to celebrate the birth of his alleged son (part three, scene one). Every-one guesses the true father except Cabot, and a strong element of vicious ridicule prevails. While Cabot dances merrily inside, the young lovers exchange vows outside. Next, Cabot goes outside and informs his son of Abbie's old plan of calculated seduction, which Eben misinterprets. O'Neill's result, like Williams', is also chaotic, with all the simultaneous action going on. Eben "chokes with rage" and threatens to kill his stepmother. Cabot stops him and they grapple for a brief moment. The total misunderstanding directly leads to Abbie's murdering her child—the major problem with the play.

O'Neill's ending is melodramatic. The heroine is forced to kill her son as the only means left her to prove her love for Eben. The man-ner in which Abbie murders her son is revealing. In a play perfused with stone walls, dead rooms, and frustrated desires, Abbie sym-bolically chooses to murder her son in a most appropriate manner—suffocation. However consistent the manner of murder may be, the action itself borders on the incredible. In *Desire Under the Elms*, the outside agent, Abbie Putnam, entered an already established environment and completely altered it to her own standards. The result is a totally new, stronger, established environment comprised primarily of her and Eben. The old environment is initially weak-ened by the escape of Simeon and Peter. Next, Abbie enters to change it even more. Her arrival shakes the household: Cabot is driven from the house to sleep with the animals in the barn; Maw's mysterious spirit finally abandons the farm for good; a new, illegitimate child briefly appears on the scene. Abbie Putnam obviously leaves her mark. O'Neill's final stage direction for the couple reads: "They both stand for a moment looking up raptly in attitudes strangely aloof and devout" (p. 206). Their gazing to the sky has run full circle. Eben utters an identical "Purty" as he did at the play's opening; but because he no longer feels entrapped by his environment, the tone of the line is *devout* rather than *defiant*. Eben and Abbie form a new bond to rise above Cabot and his farm. For Eben to believe his father at the end of the party scene about Abbie's old plan of calculated seduction rather than Abbie seems unlikely, and that Abbie would find it necessary for such a melodramatic murder to convince Eben is highly improbable. Because Abbie takes over, she is the dominating character in the newly established environment that supplanted the old. Actions should conform to the new order, and she should not, therefore, have to resort to such theatrics. The murder is unbelievable because the action is not consistent with the newly established dramatic space that O'Neill created. The inconsistency is a major obstacle for a successful production.

In comparison, A *Streetcar Named Desire* also has a newborn baby appearing at the end. For the finale, Blanche is escorted out by the doctor. Precisely *after* this action is completed, the child appears. The household was too crowded for a sister-in-law, as she is an outsider to the established order, the marriage; but for a son there is plenty of room. Blanche has overstayed her welcome but Baby Kowalski is accepted with open arms. "Eunice descends to Stella and places the child in her arms. . . . Stella accepts the child . . ." (p. 418). The displacement is successful; the family is unified once more. In contrast to O'Neill's final action, Williams has found the perfect gesture to reinforce the dramatic space and environment he created. The established environment, the happy marriage, could not be shaken by a sister-in-law; only a child could be incorporated into it.

Drama of Intimacy and Tragedy of Incomprehension: A *Streetcar Named Desire* Reconsidered

BERT CARDULLO

M∪CH OF THE criticism of Tennessee Williams' *A Streetcar Named Desire* seems to me to miss the point in speaking unqualifiedly of Stanley Kowalski as the destroyer of Blanche DuBois. Harold Clurman, in what otherwise has to be one of the most perceptive commentaries on the play and its original Broadway production, writes misleadingly of a Stanley who, "drunk the night of his wife's labor, . . . *settles his account* [italics mine] with Blanche by raping her," and of a Blanche who "is ordered out of Stella's house" (Hurrell, p. 92). John Gassner, insisting on applying the terms of Aristotelian tragedy to *Streetcar* from without and seeing how well it conforms to them, instead of judging the play on its own terms with their specific implications, concludes that Stanley is a "brutal executioner [who] performs the act of destruction that Blanche *should have* [italics mine] performed for herself, having had within her the seeds of her own destruction" (Tischler, p. 146). The list goes on and on, from Nancy Tischler's "moth beauty" of Blanche destroyed by the "brute ugliness" of Stanley (p. 146) to Jordan Y. Miller's (p. 13) and Signi Falk's (p. 88) bestial Stanley using the "ultimate weapon," rape, to take out his "revenge" on the sensitive Blanche.

Stanley Kowalski may perform the act which seals Blanche Du-Bois' doom once and for all, but, clearly, he has not consciously

137

plotted to destroy her throughout the play. Convinced that Blanche was not a heroine of tragic proportions, critics over the years have looked outside what they have concluded to be a hopelessly demented character to find the agent of her destruction and, quite naturally, come up with an evil, scheming Stanley. But Stella's husband is never so much maliciously intent on destroying his sister-in-law as he is blind to her problems and needs—a "tragedy of incomprehension" (Miller, p. 67) Williams has called this play—however much "truth" he uncovers about her past, however much he reveals her talk to be, in his words, only "imagination . . . and lies and conceit and tricks" (I, 398). Blanche's struggle throughout *Streetcar* is surely more with herself than with Stanley. Her *conflict* with him may be inevitable from the moment she enters his home, given their opposing views of life and each's claim to Stella. The inevitability of her doom, however, springs not from the character of this conflict but from her rejection of Allan Grey on the dance floor of Moon Lake Casino many years before. Stanley's rape of Blanche thus comes to appear the ironic physical incarnation of a defeat[1] whose seeds she herself inadvertently cultivated with "intimacies with strangers" after her young husband's suicide, unable or unwilling to seek consolation, "protection," elsewhere. Such rape must not be defined categorically as his vengeful victory in the struggle to keep her from ruining his marriage and altering or unsettling his way of life.

Indeed, Williams carefully structures act three, scene four, so as to make the rape seem incidental,[2] the result more of Stanley's sudden and uncontrollable drunken lust than of his calculation and deliberate cruelty. Stanley does not rape Blanche because he knows her nervous breakdown and expulsion from his home will result. Rather, he does so because he has been physically attracted to her from the start and has been encouraged by her on at least one occasion, and is able to fuel his desires with knowledge of her checkered past in Laurel. Too, he has probably not been sexually gratified for some time due to his wife's growing pregnancy and the concurrent dearth of privacy created by his sister-in-law's visit to their already cramped quarters. Stanley has no reason to believe his act will have any negative consequences, either for his marriage or for

Blanche's state of mind, since he presumes she will be leaving New Orleans by bus for Laurel on the following Tuesday and since he believes this is what she really wants and is in fact accustomed to getting. When he says, "What are you putting on now?" at the end of the scene (p. 401), he means exactly what he says, thinking Blanche's hysteria is merely an exaggerated reaction to his having trapped her in a lie. (Significantly, Stanley never bothers to ask her *why* she lied, or, for that matter, why she spoke out against him in the first place at the end of act one, scene four. He is interested, has and could only have been interested all along, in maintaining or reveling in his intimacy with Stella, not in questioning Blanche's motives or defending his way of life against hers.) And when he follows with, "Oh! So you want some roughhouse!" (p. 402) he is reacting playfully to what he considers her momentary and obligatory, extravagantly affected resistance to his advances.

Stanley may feel avenged on Blanche as the *result* of the rape, but its *cause* is not his desire to avenge himself on her. Besides, he *has* his "revenge" on Blanche before entering the bathroom in this scene. Having caught her in the lie about the telegram from Shep Huntleigh, Stanley proceeds, in a large expenditure of energy, to condemn her for the "pack of lies" she has told over the past few months. He then signals his victory of *exposure* with a climactic explosion of ha-ha's. That is why the rape appears so incidental, so *anti*climactic. Stanley comes out of the bathroom at a level of relatively low energy and, blind to Blanche's dilemma, grins playfully as he seizes upon *her* demand that he let her get by him. Standing between Blanche and the door to his apartment, he then seizes upon his own laughing dismissal of *her* fear of interference to utter softly, haltingly, "Come to think of it—maybe you wouldn't be bad to—interfere with . . ." (p. 401). His language from this point on is controlled and sometimes implicitly sexual, never angry and overtly revengeful. And it is certainly not unreasonable to assume that, were Stanley bent on revenge, he would characteristically browbeat Blanche into bed in a fierce struggle. Instead, Williams has *Blanche* threaten *Stanley* with the broken end of a beer bottle and him disarm her alertly before carrying her "inert figure" to bed. Her role as the passive victim of an act of incidental, *inadvertent* cruelty, of

sudden lust and immediate "fun" or "diversion," is thus emphasized. Here the active resister of a premeditated, intentionally cruel
act of revenge she is not.

As I have observed, those critics of *Streetcar* who dismiss the play
outright as tragedy point to the character of Blanche as indisputably
that of a clinical case history; they claim that the collapse of her
marriage and the death of her homosexual husband made her a
victim of neurosis. But they fail to take into account, in Leonard
Berkman's words, that "Blanche's most fundamental regret is not
that she happened to marry a homosexual," not the *discovery* of
Allan's homosexuality (*Stella* believes this). It is that, "when made
aware of her husband's homosexuality, she brought on [his] suicide
by her unqualified expression of disgust," her *failure* to be compassionate (p. 253). Confronted in theory with the choice between the
expression of compassion and the expression of disgust at the sudden and stunning revelation of Allan's longstanding affair with an
older man, she at first "pretended that nothing had been discovered"
(p. 355). Then, unable to stop herself, she blurted out abruptly the
words of contempt that drove her first and only love to kill himself.
I say "confronted in theory with the choice" because, as Blanche
herself confesses to Mitch, "[Allan] came to me for help. I didn't
know that. . . . All I knew was I'd failed him in some mysterious way
and wasn't able to give the help he needed but couldn't speak of! . . .
I loved him unendurably but without being able to help him or help
myself" (p. 354). Blanche could hardly be expected to respond with
love and understanding to her discovery, "in the worst of all possible ways," of Allan's homosexuality (though she struggles to—that
is one reason she does not express her disgust immediately), because
she had never had a truly intimate, an open and trusting, relationship
with him. In the same way, Williams leads us to believe she had
never had such a relationship with any of her relatives at Belle Reve
either, nor they with one another, as the DuBois men gradually exchanged the land for their "epic fornications" and the women dared
not admit they had ever heard of death.

The evidence in the present for this conclusion is her relationship
with Stella—hardly what could be called one of confidence and intimacy, despite the genuine feeling the sisters have for each other.

As Blanche dreams airily in act one of Shep Huntleigh's block-long Cadillac convertible and a shop for *both* of them, Stella straightens up her apartment matter of factly and responds to her sister practically, if lightly, even disinterestedly. When Blanche cries out in desperation that she has left only "sixty-five measly cents in coin of the realm," Stella answers this veiled plea for rescue from a life bereft of warmth and affection with little more than an offer of five dollars and a Bromo and the suggestion that she "just let things go, at least for a—while" (p. 319). Stella, out of an overwhelming desire to negate her past and Blanche with it, or out of sheer self-indulgence, will, *can*, concern herself with nothing but the mindless and easy, sensuous pursuit of day-to-day living. When Blanche opens up to her in act two and speaks of "soft people" and "fading," Stella can only reject what she calls morbidity and offer her sister a Coke, even as she offered to pour the drinks in act one, scene one. And when at the end of act three, scene one, Blanche wants to know what has happened, Stella is unable to confront her with what Stanley has reported, even as Blanche herself was unable to confront Allan with what she had discovered until it was too late. In a stunning unmasking of character toward the end of the same scene, Stella reacts to Stanley's purchase of the bus ticket with, "In the first place, Blanche wouldn't go on a bus" (p. 367). She objects to the *means* of transportation instead of expressing immediate incredulity, outrage, and dismay at the *idea* of sending her sister away.

Blanche is closer to tragic heroine than many would like to think, then, "in [her] refusal to shirk a responsibility that the conventional society of her time and place would have eagerly excused . . . ," to quote Leonard Berkman (p. 253). She refuses from the beginning to forgive herself for denying Allan the compassion that would have saved and perhaps changed him, or at any rate made his burden easier to bear. She struggles at the end in his memory to achieve intimacy with Mitch—the only true intimacy within her grasp—which alone can restore her to grace through its inherent linking of sex with compassion. It is thus not arbitrarily or gratuitously, or simply out of her own pure joy, that Williams has Blanche declare, "Sometimes—there's God—so quickly!" at the end of act two, scene two (p. 356). Rather, he has her so reenter a state of grace as a direct result of the embrace and kiss she exchanges with Mitch,[3] of their recognition, finally, of a real need and desire for one another. In this light, the "intimacies with strangers," the sex *without* compassion, she turned to after her husband's suicide come to appear less the free-standing acts of a nymphomaniac than those of a woman trying to find momentary relief or "protection" without having deeply personal demands placed on her. Blanche sought to "fill [her] empty heart" at the same time that she reaffirmed a sexuality lost on Allan's attraction to men and "denied" the death of so many of her relatives. As Stanley himself says, "They [the 'strangers'] got wised up after two or three dates with her and then they quit, and she goes on to another, the same old line, same old act, same old hooey!" (p. 361). This suggests that these "strangers," in "wising up" to Blanche's thinly disguised cries for help and devotion as well as to the artifice and affectation of her ways, were as much to blame for her panic-driven promiscuity as she herself was.

To be sure, the nobility and grandeur of Blanche's character are marred by her intemperance, be it manifested through her passion for drink, her appetite for sex, or her intolerance of Stanley's lifestyle (all of which she strives with varying degrees of willpower, and success, to overcome). But it is not this flaw which brings about her downfall. Neither is it her predisposition to gloss over the harsh realities of life by pretending that they are simply not there, as is popularly believed. (This "flaw" is responsible for her very survival as much as it is for her adversity.) In any case, it is not flaws which precipitate the downfall of great tragic characters. "Truly dramatic flaws," notes Bert O. States in *Irony and Drama*, "are such as . . . to make [tragic heroes] ambiguously fallible," are what "rescues [them] from perfection in the process of being doomed" (pp. 53–54). Blanche DuBois may fall short of traditional greatness as tragic heroine, but doomed she is from the first by the "very different circumstances" under which she grew up and against which she struggled long after Stella had fled to New Orleans. The absence of truth and intimacy from life at Belle Reve is what drove Blanche into an early marriage and on the road to calamity, as is the stagnancy, the decadence, of postbellum plantation life what prompted her sister to opt for the vitality of New Orleans and marriage to a man whose virility could never be questioned. Thus, Blanche's clash with Stanley, specifically, her condemnation of him to Stella at the end of act one, scene four, cannot be construed as the sole, absolute cause of her downfall, without whose occurrence, say, her troubles would eventually have vanished or before which they could scarcely be said to have been pressing. On the contrary, such clash must be viewed as the *result* of her attempt to achieve an intimacy with Stella which had never before existed between them. It is an inevitable *addition* to a long line of unfortunate incidents stemming from the failure of communion over many years to pervade the lives of the DuBois men and women.

Blanche does not criticize Stanley the morning after "The Poker Night" simply for the sake of criticizing him, of extolling the virtues of life at Belle Reve at his expense. Her harangue is designed, above all else, to draw her closer to her sister, to unite them in "light" and "progress" against "barbarianism." Blanche wishes to "get out" and "make a new life" at this point, not so much because she fears Stanley will destroy her as because she deplores his way of life, whose corrupting influence, she feels, prevents her from attaining intimacy with Stella. Departing Stanley's company alone will do her no good, and she knows it. Her sprightly attraction to him in act one, scene two, in spite of his coarseness, tells us she has probably run into his general type in the past, and we are well aware that her flight from Laurel and the assorted "types" of the Hotel Flamingo, among other spots, has done little to alleviate her distress. Escaping Stanley in the company of Stella will lead, she hopes, to the solidification of a bond between them, to their increased compassion for each other's lot, and consequently to a new life some place where the past might at least be brought fully to light, if not somehow atoned for.

Even as Blanche's attack on Stanley at the end of act one has as its foremost objective convincing Stella to leave him and join her, *not* pointing out the shortcomings of "unrefined types," so too does Stanley's failure to come forward and challenge his sister-in-law's remarks have as its objective, finally, less the secret plotting of sweet revenge than the testing of his wife's loyalty toward him. The crux of these moments, then, is the establishment of Stella as an object of contention, not of Stanley and Blanche as mortal enemies. This is why I say "Stanley's failure to come forward" rather than "his decision not to." He does not decide instantly to conceal his presence and figure out how to get back at Blanche upon overhearing bits of her tirade. He *fails* to confront her at once, I believe, because he is as much befuddled by her use of language and her line of reasoning as he is angered by the epithets "common," "animal," "sub-human," and "brute." Blanche brings an element of complexity to his life here that he fails to comprehend. Incapable of coming forward to defend his way of life—the only way he really knows—in words against hers, he hesitates, his attention directed, not unreasonably, to Stella's reaction to her sister's observations. That Stella responds with, "Why, yes, I suppose he is," to Blanche's, "Well—if you'll forgive me—he's *common!*" (p. 322) and, "Go on and say it all, Blanche" (p. 323), to her, "You're hating me saying this, aren't you?" (p. 332) must not be overlooked as a key to the explanation of Stanley's behavior at this juncture. Stanley cannot be absolutely certain whether Stella is defending him or agreeing with Blanche against him (Stella sits in the armchair, her back to him, in the acting edition of the play [p. 50]; also, he has just entered the apartment when the first exchange of dialogue transcribed above takes place). Therefore, rather than step forward and force the issue too soon, he waits apprehensively for that moment which will afford him the best cover and his wife the best opportunity to prove without question her faithfulness to him. With an assist from a passing train, the moment arrives. Seconds after Blanche exhorts Stella, *"Don't— don't hang back with the brutes!"* (p. 323) Stanley calls out his wife's name outside a closed front door. Stella answers by throwing herself "fiercely" at him, and, in the acting edition, he obliges by "swinging her up with his body" (p. 51). In a word, she chooses to hang back with her brute.

Often too much is made in production of Stanley's grin over Stella's head at Blanche here. I would interpret it as one of supreme, perhaps even smug, satisfaction at Stella's choice of action, as his signal of victory to Blanche. To make more of it than this, to make it the knowing or vicious grin of a man hot for revenge, is to suggest that Stanley eavesdropped deliberately and maliciously, intent from the first on one day soon venting his full wrath on this woman so disparaging him. But, as I have attempted to show, Stanley's concern during Blanche's speeches is more with Stella's reaction to their gist and tone than with their every word and notion. The idea of revenge can enter his mind only after he is assured of Stella's continued affection and allegiance, if indeed then. And this "revenge" would take the form of proving Blanche to be as "common" as he is, if not more so, of proving his suspicions about her past to be true. That he would plan rape here, having discovered the clue to its suitability as a mode of revenge in Blanche's "sexy by-play" during act one, scene two, as Signi Falk intimates in *Tennessee Williams* (p. 83), is, in my judgment, nearly inconceivable. It would simply not have served Williams' purposes to portray Stanley completely in the negative light of plotting destroyer here. The point of Stella's union with her husband at the end of act one, scene four, is neither to play up Blanche's role as unjustly doomed, harmless underdog to Stanley's sinister destroyer, nor his as wholesome protector against her deservedly damned, depraved homewrecker. It is to accent the intimacy Stanley and Stella enjoy and for which Blanche yearns, but from which she is excluded. The play *as literature* easily resists the temptation to define the world solely in terms of extremes, of good and bad, right and wrong, strong and weak, even if facile commercial productions of it often do not.

To claim, for all that, as Signi Falk, among others, does, that "part of the confusion in [*Streetcar*] arises from Williams' glowingly wistful admiration for Stan and his friends and for their capacity for unlimited physical pleasure," together with "his sentimental support and sympathy for Blanche, who degenerated pitifully with the same kind of physical indulgence" (p. 83), is not to analyze carefully moments like those at the close of scenes three and four of act one, but to ignore completely the playwright's reasons for their inclusion. These do not exist apart from the rest of the play, the products solely of Williams' incontinent infatuation with the peculiar blend of "childhood innocence" and "vibrant sexuality" to be found in "elemental people." They are not in virulent contradiction to his obvious sympathy for Blanche as a doomed representative of civilization and refinement, or more accurately, of a specific tradition whose effeteness and essential frigidity she seeks to escape, tragically, through impulsive indulgence in carnal pleasures. Perhaps this notion arose in response to the assertion on the part of such noted critics as Brooks Atkinson and Joseph Wood Krutch that the play was about "an unequal contest between the decadence of a self-conscious civilization and the vitality of animal aimlessness" (Donahue, p. 36), between "decaying aristocracy" and "vigorous barbarism" (Tischler, pp. 144, 145). It may appear so on the surface, but it is not. As I stated earlier, Blanche's struggle in *Streetcar* is not so much with Stanley as with herself in her efforts to achieve lasting intimacy.

Critics most often point specifically to the end of act one, scene three, when they charge that there is confusion in the play regarding the placement of its author's sympathies. But their objections to the reunion of Stanley and Stella after the tumult of the poker night as thematically disruptive and filled with a pathos too universally human fail to take into account, tellingly, the part Blanche plays in the situation. The reservations seem based, curiously, on a consideration of the moment virtually out of context. Williams, it is true, does not give us a scene between the two sisters on the balcony of the Hubbell apartment in which Blanche pleads for Stella not to return to Stanley, but he is wise not to. By not including such an exchange of dialogue between the two women (or between Stella and Eunice, for that matter), he conveys the more powerfully by "faint detraction" the idea that there was really never any doubt in Stella's mind that she would return to her husband that night. (Besides, this confrontation need not be depicted here, because it *does* take place in the next scene. Paradoxically, it is the more charged with excitement and suspense for its occurrence *after* the violence and emotion of the previous night, between an even more frenzied Blanche and a Stella completely tranquil after her night of lovemaking with Stanley.) For her, it was only a question of returning at the right moment. It was *Blanche* who suggested she and Stella leave the apartment after Stanley's violent outburst, Blanche who ushered her sister upstairs to Eunice's, not vice versa. And it is Blanche whom Stella leaves upstairs when she comes down to pacify the bellowing Stanley; Blanche who hears, if she does not witness, the emotional reunion of husband and wife; who then "looks into [the] apartment, hesitantly enters, recoils from what she sees, . . . closing [the] door behind her" (acting edition, p. 42). What does she see? Certainly no violent acts. Yet she expresses terror for Stella's safety, despite Mitch's reassurances. So long excluded from real intimacy, she can only recoil at the sight of her sister in bed with her husband. So secretly envious of them, she can only vent her dismay at their acceptance of violence into their lives. Williams' sympathies are not confused at this point, his readers' perceptions are. Or perhaps they have allowed their memories of the overwrought, conceptually unresolved staging of these moments from the Broadway production or the Warner Brothers film of the play to supersede temporarily their critical acumen. The point of Stanley's and Stella's tearful reunion at the end of act one, scene three, is not, then, to make an inconsistent " 'Lawrencian' plea for primitive, spontaneous passion to return to dominance in [the] audiences' lives," as Leonard Berkman phrases it (p. 251). It is rather to stress the intimacy these two people share, and which is absent from Blanche's life.

Had Williams ended the scene on so strong a note as the reconciliation of Stanley and Stella, critics would be in part justified in taking him to task for muddying his sympathies. But he is careful not to. He has Blanche come down the spiral staircase right after Stanley carries Stella into the apartment. Then, in her moment of painful exclusion from the true intimacy she wants and needs desperately to experience for herself, he reintroduces Mitch to the plot, and with him a sudden ray of hope. The possibility now exists that Blanche might yet secure the intimacy so necessary for her survival and happiness.

In this minor peripety, Williams creates a delicate balance of "all that is possible" in the case of Blanche DuBois. He displays in his treatment of Blanche at the end of this scene what Robert Heilman calls "completeness of understanding," "insight into human division" (*Tragedy and Melodrama: Versions of Experience*, p. 26). We see her exposed to her own "full sense of flaw," for instance, when she quickly recoils upon looking into the apartment; when she then proceeds to exhibit intolerance in the face of Stanley's and Stella's loving relationship, going so far as to pretend that her sister is subjecting herself to possible acts of violence by spending the night with her husband. We surmise toward the end of act two, scene two, that she must have recoiled upon suddenly entering a room she thought to be empty and finding Allan and friend in bed. We discover that she pretended nothing had happened. In addition, that she could not suppress her intolerance in the face of a homosexual love relationship to which her husband was party. Finally, that Allan visited lethal violence on himself after Blanche's unqualified expression of disgust and contempt at the revelation of his homosexuality.

We see Blanche exposed to her own "full sense of excellence" in the final moments of the scene. Her look at Mitch after he takes out the inscribed silver cigarette case is surely one of deep compassion, linking them in their mutual sorrow—she over a young boy, he a young girl. We can envision the great compassion she expressed and the great sorrow she felt in her struggle to keep Belle Reve afloat and her relatives alive. Her final lines in this scene are at once a veiled plea for help and an ominous expression of self-awareness, as are several other short speeches of hers in the play (witness, for example, the *resigned* expression of self-awareness in, "So do you wonder? How could you possibly wonder!" p. 389).

"This getting everything into the picture is the ultimate sympathy of the author," says Robert Heilman, "It is his way of 'loving' his characters" (p. 26). And it is by means of irony (referring to the very principle of negation itself),[4] according to Bert O. States, that "[the dramatic poet] seeks out the limits of conceivable proportion and disproportion" in the first place. "He passes through irony, one might say, into dialectic, into arguing *both* sides of the problem fully as opposed to taking one side or another . . . [into] naming nature's limits, finding her out without the complacency or sentimentality of presuming that she can be pinned down and 'dealt with' or, to take the equally sentimental view of the fatalist, that she is bent upon the destruction of our species. . . . What this enables him to achieve in the 'synthesis' of his art is a faint replica of infinitude itself . . ." (*Irony and Drama*, pp. 34, 44–45). "Nature's limits" for Blanche are, in terms of fate, total exclusion from intimacy, on the one hand, and complete achievement of it, on the other. In terms of character, they are her inability to suppress her intolerance in crises or situations of great stress, on the debit side, and her overwhelming desire to achieve true and lasting intimacy, making her kind, compassionate, and devoted, on the credit. The makings of both extremes of fate are contained in the final pages of act one, scene three, but irony has already begun to make its presence felt, and will have arrived once and for all in the next scene.

Stanley Kowalski, convinced, based on the stories he has heard and checked on, that Blanche DuBois is nothing but a scheming floozy who would be little perturbed by her failure to deceive Mitch, attempts to maintain intimacy with his friend by exposing her past to him between acts two and three. Then, after purchasing the bus ticket, he reveals to Stella everything he has learned about Blanche's "recent history" in the belief that she will side with him against her sister. He is unsuccessful in gaining Mitch's friendship, and he is wrong about Stella. Blanche DuBois, unable to conceive of her brother-in-law as a loving and faithful, needing and giving, husband, seeks to achieve intimacy with Stella by selling her on Stanley's commonness and bestiality. She fails. And this the morning after her expression of willingness to enter into an alliance with him, however uneasy, to buy the time necessary to secure an intimate relationship. (She says, "Maybe he's what we need to mix with our blood now that we've lost Belle Reve. We thrashed it [the Belle Reve matter] out. . . . I laughed and flirted and treated it all as a joke" [p. 285].) Needless to say, the alliance did not come off.

Indeed, for all her sensitivity and education, as Leonard Berkman has pointed out, Blanche shows little more understanding of Stanley than he does of her (p. 251). The question in this play becomes, then, one not of opposing, mutually exclusive ways of life locked in mortal combat, but of different ways of life both come to ruin over the basic issue of truth and intimacy in living. Before Blanche's arrival, Stanley and Stella enjoyed, through compromise, an intimate, happy marriage, and in this could be said to have achieved a degree of civilization, of humanity, unequaled by the DuBoises of Belle Reve. Too, if Stanley is so repulsively barbaric, so completely the representative of the Savage State—and, like it or not, this is the sole image of him that most of us carry around in our minds, Marlon Brando's performance notwithstanding—then what is he doing surrounded by the likes of Stella and Mitch, his wife and his best friend, both of whom are in some ways at least as sensitive as Blanche, if not in as desperate need of kindness? (Not accidentally, Stella and Mitch are the only ones who weep at Blanche's departure.) And why would Williams be so careful as to have it pointed up three times that Stanley served in the "Two-forty-first Engineers," and to have Stanley himself brag about his lucky survival at Salerno against the forces of that arch barbarian, Hitler (as he does often, to judge by Mitch's reaction to his speech)? Surely to convey to us his sense of self-esteem, but for another, less apparent reason, too, I suspect: to inform us of his role as a member of "a society which has lost its shape," to borrow a phrase from Joseph Wood Krutch (*"Modernism" in Modern Drama*, p. 128), of a "rat-race." Stanley's is an overpopulated, war-torn world where tradition and civilization have come necessarily to mean, to many, less continuity and refinement than freedom and survival. He and the Allies did not "win" at Salerno, they had "come through," they survived.

Likewise, Stanley does not come out the victor in any contest with Blanche, he survives. And if Blanche is a loser in her struggle to achieve true and enduring intimacy with another human being, Stanley is also a loser in his struggle to remain intimate with Stella at the same time he deprives her sister of her chances for happiness with Mitch. Life for him and his wife will never be the same again— Williams provides plenty of evidence for this conclusion in the last scene of the play.[5] He has gone behind Stella's back to expose Blanche's lurid recent past in an attempt to keep the former's confidence and loyalty, ironically, and then compounds his guilt by denying, in a lie greater than any Blanche ever told, the rape. Stanley is, therefore, as much a victim, in his own way, of a society which has lost its shape as Blanche. Blind to her problems and needs and disaffected by the complexity of a way of life alien to his own, he conceives of her as the enemy almost from the start, a threat to the stability, if not the very existence, of his household. And in his eagerness to protect that household and its associations, as in Blanche's to *secure* one, it was inevitable that he would eschew the uncertainty of compromise and confrontation for the safety and reserve of self-reliance. In his attempts to expose Blanche's past so as to preserve his intimate "present" intact, Stanley conceals his actions in the present, even as Blanche, in her attempts to construct a past that will help her achieve an intimate "present," conceals the actions of her past.

Both are doomed in their essential, existential isolation. No longer at one with Nature and in rebellion against Fate, as were the protagonists of Greek tragedy, they are the inhabitants of a world in which, to recall the title of a recent film by the German director Herzog, it is "Everyman for himself and God against all." Unlike Greek tragedy, which I would call the tragedy of self, of man, Christian tragedy, as epitomized in *Streetcar*, is the tragedy of life, of men. At once burdened with the notion of original sin and tempted with the idea of salvation in the hereafter, Christian man retreats into his mind, becomes uncertain of his position in the universe, and, feeling himself at the mercy of chance, the helpless victim of chance's whims, resolves to insulate himself as much as possible against the arbitrariness, the "cruelty," of life: essentially, the deeds of other men. In this way ever at odds with his fellow men and never at one with himself, he brings about his own downfall at the same time that the specific and final means of destruction comes from without.

Blanche DuBois, the victim of a life without intimacy at Belle Reve, lies about a past she is correct in believing no one will forgive; Stanley Kowalski, the survivor of a world war of murder and destruction, lies about an act which he is correct in assuming no one will forgive. Neither will tolerate the other, since each believes the other a threat to the achievement or maintaining of intimacy in life. Ironically, it is this very lack of tolerance, of real understanding, that causes each to have his chances for or hold on a truly intimate relationship destroyed by the other, ultimately: Blanche's with Mitch by Stanley, Stanley's with Stella by Blanche, inadvertently. And, appropriately, in a final act—rape—from which all true intimacy has been removed. The feeling aroused in the spectator at this is not, to paraphrase W. H. Auden, that aroused in the spectator of Greek tragedy, the tragedy of necessity or fate, of one man, "What a pity it had to be this way." It is that of the spectator of Christian tragedy, the tragedy of possibility or chance, of two or more men, "What a pity it was this way when it might have been otherwise" (see bibliography).

It might have been otherwise, but it was not. The form of this sentence defines *Streetcar's* form, at once suffused with incidentality and inevitability, at once a cross between classic and modern tempers. Ironically, Blanche's doom appears inevitable, yet is essentially pathetic: she will never achieve true and lasting intimacy with another human being; at the same time, her tragedy is made to occur incidentally: Stanley rapes her and she leaves for an asylum with some measure of dignity, never having ceased to accuse him. Blanche herself, representative of "the decadence of a self-conscious civilization," is now lucid, now unstable. Defined by "the vitality of animal aimlessness" of the relationships between Stanley and Stella and the slightly older Steve and Eunice, the play's rhythms are likewise now violent and passionate, now calm and reconciled. (Brooks Atkinson's categories apply in part here, if his entering them in an "unequal contest" does not.)

In this unresolved tension of its form and life, more accurately, in the embodiment of this tension, this dialectic, in the character of Blanche DuBois, *Streetcar* stands as a unique contribution to the body of world dramatic literature. If classical tragedy's completeness, infiniteness, was its insistence on marking for certain destruction the man in the middle, the man who was neither flawless nor hopelessly flawed,[6] *Streetcar's* is its depiction of life's workings as inexplicable, ultimately, in terms of fate or chance exclusively, indeed, as seemingly simultaneously inevitable and incidental. No small part of this "completeness" is the play's marking for spiritual death Stella and Mitch, the former in a life tortured by self-recriminations and lived vicariously through her children, the latter in one haunted unceasingly by the thought of love rejected and happiness lost. Through all this Williams manages, nevertheless, to leave to the Absurdists to come the task of sacrificing the essential humanity, the excellence and flaw, of his characters to the vagaries of a world devoid of all order, meaning, and purpose.

Notes to Bert Cardullo, "Drama of Intimacy and Tragedy of Incomprehension: *A Streetcar Named Desire* Reconsidered"

1. Leonard Berkman, "The Tragic Downfall of Blanche DuBois," *Modern Drama*, 10: 3 (December 1967), 255.
2. Cf. the analysis of the structure of act three, scene two, in Bernard Beckerman, *Dynamics of Drama* (New York: Alfred A. Knopf, 1970), pp. 98–100, 112–113, and passim.
3. Berkman, p. 254.
4. "Irony is the dramatist's version of the negative proposition: it helps him to avoid error, and by this I mean that it widens his vision, allows him to see more circumspectly the possibilities in his 'argument'; and in so doing it ensures his not falling into the incomplete attitudes of naiveté, sentimentality, self-righteousness, or unearned faith." Quoted from Bert O. States, *Irony and Drama* (Ithaca, New York: Cornell University Press, 1971), p. xviii.

5. Stella's absence from scenes three and four of act three, coupled with her reappearance on stage in scene five after giving birth, serves to distance her in our minds from Stanley and to prefigure her relationship with him beyond the perimeters of the play. That Stella does not once speak to her husband in the last scene of *Streetcar* (even when addressed by him one time) is indicative of the essential silence which will permeate the rest of their lives together. That she comments on the ache she feels when she is not in the same room with her child (while Stanley, significantly, never refers to the son he so celebrated before Blanche in act three, scene four) and says nothing of having missed Stanley while she was away in the hospital (in act one, scene one, she tells Blanche, "I can hardly stand it when he is away for a night" [p. 259]) is significative of the role her son will now play in providing her with the opportunity (however limited) for self-fulfillment implicitly denied her from the start by her husband.

It was the imminent birth of the child which decided, *incidentally*, that Stanley's and Stella's strained bond would be momentarily strengthened, reinforced, that Stanley would prevail over Stella in his efforts to expel Blanche from his home (act three, scene two). And ironically, it is the child's final presence which signifies the inevitable dissolution of their bond. It is not by accident that, as Stanley goes to placate his wife on the stairs at the end of the play, the child, whom Eunice has placed in Stella's arms, stands between them. Even as he kneels here, so too did Stanley kneel on these stairs in intimacy with Stella, his face pressed to her belly, at the end of act one, scene three.

The child itself, by remaining unnamed and unspoken of as someone with a psychological life of his own, and by being kept offstage until after Blanche's exit, comes to function as an almost pure symbol not only of all the children Stella will bear in her steady retreat from Stanley, but of the result of things, the ironic and abrupt end of his benign domination of her. It is Stanley's lust after Stella—the epitome of this domination and crux of their relationship—which frees her, finally and ironically, to direct her attentions away from him and toward the son born of his lust. The delayed introduction of the child, whose absence from the plot up to this point lends its now unique presence the urgency of allegorical simplicity, thus sets the final moments of the play off as the anticipated, yet anticlimactic, culmination of Stanley's and Stella's relationship.

6. States, p. 54.

A *Streetcar Named Desire:*
Its Development through the Manuscripts

VIVIENNE DICKSON

IN THE Tennessee Williams Collection of the Humanities Research Center at the University of Texas at Austin are some 140 pages of early drafts of A *Streetcar Named Desire*, five complete play and screen scripts of the later drafts, and a particularly full record of the first production of the play.[1] Although the collection is weakest in the early material, it is with these fragmentary first drafts that this paper will be chiefly concerned, for it is through them that the evolution of the play from a romance to a tragedy can be traced. The many revisions in the later drafts have a considerable cumulative effect, but they serve only to confirm and clarify Williams' conception of the play. It was in the earlier stages that the conception itself was shaped. This paper, then, is an attempt to describe, largely from the early manuscript record, the evolution of A *Streetcar Named Desire*.

The play that was to become *Streetcar* was not written from a solid outline that needed only to be fleshed out and revised to take its final form. The earliest drafts show that Williams started with little more than the basic situation in mind: an unmarried teacher visiting her younger sister and brother-in-law meets a prospective husband. The teacher is more refined and delicate than her sister, but her looks are fading, and she and her family are conscious that she has one last chance of avoiding a lonely future as a single woman.

154

From this initial situation, Williams explored the possible complications, making false starts and rejecting many resolutions, but always returning to the original idea with something salvaged from the discarded material—an image, a few lines of dialogue, or a refinement of character or plot.

The lack of comparable scenes in the fragmentary early manuscripts makes a firm chronology impossible, but changes in the title, in the location of the play, and in the characters' names and nationalities, provide sufficient clues for a tentative ordering to be made. In the following table, pages which are either too reticent or too brief to be placed with certainty *are marked with asterisks*. A 57-page typescript which was catalogued as a composite manuscript has been divided between [The Primary Colors] and The Poker Night. Other untitled fragments which are separately catalogued in the H.R.C. collection have been grouped in my table under "miscellaneous."

Using these materials, I shall discuss the titles and epigraphs; the stage setting; the locations of the play and the nationalities of the characters; and the names of the characters. The second section of the paper concerns Williams' characteristic handling of images and dialogue salvaged from discarded drafts. The final section, which is largely drawn from the late manuscripts, uses Williams' revisions of the ending of the play to illustrate his constant reworking of portions of the material long after the body of the play had been given its final form.

In a letter to Audrey Wood, dated March 23, 1945, Tennessee Williams said he was considering four different titles for the play: *The Moth; The Poker Night; The Primary Colors; Blanche's Chair in the Moon*. Like their predecessors, which Williams does not list, these titles reflect the evolving conception of the characters and their fates. Typically, when a title was rejected, some trace of the idea which inspired it remained in the body of the play itself.

The manuscript of *The Primary Colors* is prefaced with a quotation which Williams attributes to Saint John Perse (sic): "And life! Life beautiful as a ram's skin painted red and nailed to the wall above a bolted doorway!"[2] In this early version, Blanche and Mitch/ Howdy do discover the beauty of life when they joyously overcome their inhibitions. Although Ralph's lust is ultimately frustrated, the tension between him and Blanche is dramatically underlined in a

Title	Location	Names of Chief Characters	Nationality of:			Town where Blanche teaches
			Stanley	Blanche & Stella	Mitch	
(untitled) (3 pp.)	Southside Chicago	Lucio Bianca Rosa —	Italian	Italian	—	Baton Rouge, La.
The Primary Colors (32 pp.)	Atlanta	Ralph Stanley Blanche Collins Stella Mitch/Howdy	Irish	Southern U.S.	—	Macon, Ga.
[*The Primary Colors*] (*42 pp. of a composite 57 pp. ms., plus * 8 pp. misc.)	Atlanta	Ralph Kowalski Blanche, Stella Mitch (Harold Mitchell)	Polish	Southern U.S.	—	Columbus, Ga. Laurel, Miss.
Electric Avenue (4 pp.)	—	Stanley Landowski Blanche Stella Eddie Zawadski (Mitch)	Polish	—	Polish	—
*(untitled) (6 pp.)	N.O.	Jack, Blanche Stella, George	—	—	—	Blue Mountain
The Poker Night (title page, complete typescripts, *15 pp. of a composite 57 pp. ms., *19 miscellaneous pp.)	N.O.	Ralph/Stanley Kowalski Blanche Boisseau/ DuBois Stella Mitch (Harold Mitchell)	Polish	Southern U.S.	—	Laurel, Miss.

scene where Ralph wears a brilliant green bowling shirt and Blanche a scarlet kimono. A discussion of stop/go signals is excised in later drafts, but the color symbolism is retained, and a direct reference is made to the earlier title in the stage directions for scene three of *Streetcar* where the men are described as being "at the peak of their physical manhood, as coarse and direct and powerful as the primary colors" (I, 286).

In the same stage directions, "an electric bulb with a vivid green glass shade" lights the kitchen with a "lurid nocturnal brilliance, the

raw colors of childhood's spectrum." Here are echoes of two titles—
The Primary Colors and its successor *Electric Avenue*—and, of
course, a very clear reference in the whole passage to the penultimate
title, *The Poker Night*. *Electric Avenue*, of which a title page and
three pages of the final scene survive, is closely related to *The Primary
Colors* in that both have happy endings to the romance. Eddie offers
to marry Blanche, although she is no longer a sexual innocent. An
epigraph to *Electric Avenue* suggests the tone of the final scene:

Prometheus: I caused mortals to cease forseeing [sic] doom . . .
gave them blind hope . . . besides this I gave them
fire! [possibly an inaccurate version of David Grene's translation]

The marked similarities between the intent of the epigraphs to
The Passion of a Moth and *Go, Said the Bird!* suggest that Williams
considered these titles after he had rejected a happy solution to
Blanche's problems. Only the title pages remain, but they illustrate
how closely Williams had come to his final conception of Blanche.

The epigraph to *The Passion of a Moth* is a version of the last
stanza of "Lament for the Moths" (*In the Winter of Cities*, p. 31):

Give them, O Mother of Moths and Mother of Men,
Strength to enter the heavy world again.
For delicate were the moths and badly wanted
Here in a world by mammoth figures haunted!

Light—both physical and symbolical—is now too harsh for Blanche's
world, and her contact with its flame proves fatal to her. She could
live only in a world of shaded lights after the searchlight was turned
off at her young husband's death. When Blanche first appears in
Elysian Fields, Williams comments: "There is something about her
uncertain manner, as well as her white clothes, that suggests a moth"
(I, 245). And in the rape scene she wears "a somewhat soiled and
crumpled white satin evening gown and a pair of scuffed silver
slippers with brilliants set in their heels" (p. 391)—a tattered moth.

In an untitled draft of the play, Williams experimented with
giving a visible shape to the mammoth figures alluded to in the
epigraph. "A ghastly phantom head . . . half-human half-ape the
very person of lunacy"[3] glows dully at the open window, stirring
Blanche from her catatonic trance. It reappears when she springs

free from the Matron. In *Streetcar*, the "mammoth figures" take the shape of "lurid reflections" (398, 417), shadows "of a grotesque and menacing form" and "inhuman voices like cries in a jungle" (398–9). They fade when the doctor speaks to her gently.

The lines from T. S. Eliot which form the epigraph to *Go, Said the Bird!* were used again as the epigraph to *The Poker Night*. Williams, slightly altering Eliot's punctuation, wrote: "Go, said the bird, go, go, go, said the bird! Human kind cannot bear very much reality" ("Burnt Norton"). The bird imagery was developed in a long passage in the composite manuscript of [*The Primary Colors*] where Blanche talks of the many birds that came to the family home in the last few summers. She sees the birds as "signs of—God's approval," curing her insomnia with their singing.

The last title Williams mentioned in his letter to Audrey Wood (*Blanche's Chair in the Moon*) seems to have had a deservedly brief life. A number of references to the moon were later deleted, but the only direct reference I have found which seems relevant is a pencil note on the back of the letter:

> Legends!
> *first* =
> Have you ever been afraid to go somewhere you are going?
> *Last* =
> But I suppose I will find some chair in the moon . . .

Presumably Williams was considering opening and closing the play with these lines or using them as an epigraph. They would have been appropriate for one of the plot resolutions Williams sketched out: Blanche and Stanley, on the morning after their momentous lovemaking, agree to part for the absent Stella's sake. Blanche, who is possibly pregnant, plans to keep searching, and drifting.

Although the title of the play changed frequently as the characters increased in complexity and different plot resolutions were worked out, the stage setting did not. It consistently suggested a milieu where the expression of violent passions would not be submerged by the tinkle of teacups. The action always took place in a two-roomed apartment whose rear window (or windows) looked out on a bleak urban landscape against a clear, light sky. In the downtown business district of Atlanta the view is of "a vacant lot with bill-boards to the skyline" (*The Primary Colors*). The implied contrast between the sterility of the outside world and the rich sense of life within the small confines of the apartment walls was to become a powerful motif in the play, gaining additional point when, in New Orleans, the view changes to the desolate railroad tracks and signal towers. A symbolic link is forged between Stanley and the powerful modern engines of the railroad, and Williams once considered ending the play with Blanche throwing herself in front of a train in the freight-yards (see letter to Audrey Wood).

The two-roomed apartment where the characters fought and loved was moved to various geographical locations, the moves accompanied by changes in the nationalities of the characters. But whether Stanley and the sisters are Italians living in Chicago, Irish and Southerners in Atlanta, or Poles and Southerners in New Orleans, they belong to racial groups not traditionally reticent about their feelings. Poles, Blanche suggests in the published play, are "something like Irish" and Mitch, who is usually depicted as that ill-defined hybrid, an Anglo-American, acquires a Polish nationality in *Electric Avenue* when he is stiffened into a self-confident suitor.

When Williams made Stanley a son of peasant immigrants and the sisters relics of a decayed southern aristocracy, he retained their national temperamental resemblances while creating a new dimension to the conflict with the addition of cultural differences. He may have been unconsciously moving towards exploring the potential of such a clash of cultures even in the earliest draft of the play; for while the play itself is set in Chicago, the Italian Blanche is employed as a teacher in Baton Rouge, a town some ninety miles from New Orleans. In this early draft nothing is made of the Blanche/Bianca connection with the South—she simply happens to be living there and could as well have been living in any other small town in the United States. However, when the play is moved to Atlanta, the thematic possibilities of the clash of cultures begin to enrich the original clash of personalities. The point was made explicitly in a speech by Ralph which Williams later omitted: "You folks are pretty refined compared to my folks, I guess. We're just old shanty Irish. You know—pigs in the parlor and all that sort of thing. Never had a lace-curtain in the home!" ([*The Primary Colors*], composite ms.). The change of location to New Orleans ironically underlines

Blanche's situation. An outcast from a town which has replaced the plantation culture with that of twentieth-century America, she is now living in Elysian Fields, an immigrant area on the fringe of the once-aristocratic French Quarter. Blanche is a beautiful but pathetic anachronism, clinging in spirit to "La Belle Reve," from which she has been physically severed. The image was pointed in a late draft of the play when the original name of her ancestral home, "The Columns," was changed to the more evocative "La Belle Reve." The original name lingers in the several references in the play to the columns of the old house.

The changes in the nationalities of the characters reflect the growing complexity of Williams' conception of the characters and the concomitant dramatic conflict. Similarly, the evolution of the characters can be partly traced through the changes in their names, not all of which were necessitated by the changes in nationality. The names of the minor characters underwent several changes, perhaps the most significant of which was that of the gentleman Blanche believed, or pretended to believe, had asked her to accompany him on a cruise. He originally bore the first name of the hero of Margaret Mitchell's *Gone With the Wind*: Rhett. The change to Shep (Huntleigh) perhaps made his existence more probable, but it also closed a fascinating glimpse into Blanche's dream-world. The young newsboy was named Isaacs Shapiro, then Lucio Francesco Romano, and finally became anonymous. Steve and Eunice Hubb became Hubbs and, finally, Hubbell, and the fourth poker player was Jack O'Shaughnessy and, later, Pablo Gonzales.

Of the four main characters, Stella changes least from Williams' original conception of her to his final portrait. Her character is deepened with subsequent drafts, but her somewhat blowsy maternity, her frank sensuality and her uncomplicated nature are established from the beginning. As Rosa, in the draft set in Chicago, her "vivid good looks" are described as having "suffered from maternity and spaghetti," but "she is unaltered in Lucio's uxorious eyes." Her popular Italian country girl's name is not translated into its English equivalent when she loses her Italian nationality, perhaps because to the English ear "Rose" too strongly suggests the qualities of the flower which has become the standard symbol of beauty. When the play is moved to Atlanta, Rosa becomes and remains, Stella, "Stella for Star!" as Blanche exclaims in *Streetcar*. In the composite manuscript of [*The Primary Colors*] Stella becomes sharper with Blanche, and her early resentments of her spoiled elder sister are clearly suggested; but when Stanley's antagonism to Blanche increases, Stella reverts to a more sympathetic character.

In the early drafts, Stella has already borne her husband a son. In the later drafts when the tension between her sister and her husband develops to the point where they make love, the enormity of their action is underlined by having Stella give birth to her first child on the night when they consummate their affair. The adultery is shocking in a conventionally moral sense, as they themselves admit when they agree to part on the following morning. They are both guilty of an unfortunate passion. However, when adultery becomes, in the later drafts, Stanley's destructive, life-denying rape of Blanche, the contrast with Stella's life-giving actions suggests a far more powerful moral point. It may have been with this point in mind that Williams once considered ending the play with Stella rejecting Stanley's advances. The destructive ripples of Stanley's act would then have widened to engulf his marriage. Williams also considered having Blanche hold the baby briefly before leaving for the asylum. However, he eventually rejected both endings in favor of one which underlined Blanche's isolation and stressed Stella's acceptance of passion, of life. In choosing to believe Stanley rather than Blanche, to accept his way of life rather than her way of death, Stella is affirming the choice she made when she left Belle Reve for New Orleans.

The frequent changes in the name of Blanche's suitor—Mitch, Howdy, Eddie Zawadski, George and, again, Mitch (Harold Mitchell)—suggest that he was the least defined of the characters when Williams began writing. In the first draft the suitor is not named, although the play seemed, at that stage, to be focused on his courtship of Bianca. In the later drafts where the emphasis shifts to the Blanche/Stanley relationship, it becomes apparent that the suitor's character is not developed independently, but is, rather, a kind of by-product of the central relationship. In those versions wherein the suitor wins Blanche, he is made stronger than the brother-in-law. Halfway through the first draft of *The Primary Colors* the suitor's name is changed from Mitch to Howdy, a change which reflects his transformation into "a more attractive caller than might be expected ... a more positive young man than Ralph, bigger and firmer looking" (*The Primary Colors*). This version ends with Howdy and Blanche giggling in bed together, and the initially disapproving Stella and Ralph joining in the laughter. Eddie Zawadski, in *Electric Avenue*, shoulders aside a weakly protesting Stanley Landowski to claim his bride.

In a six-page fragment of scene nine of an untitled draft, the suitor is called George, the brother-in-law Jack. George leaves Blanche, as in the final version of the play, but is here a much more determined, even brutal, character than the later Mitch. Simply, his woman has been cheating on him and his masculine ego has been bruised. After a bitter quarrel, with Blanche maintaining a poise of brittle sophistication, and George sarcastically goading her, he goes—leaving no doubt in the reader's mind that his heart will mend rapidly.

With the return to one of the first names Williams considered for Blanche's suitor, Mitch becomes a milder, less worldly character. Stanley is now firmly established as the dominant male, while Blanche is not yet the desperately vulnerable woman she eventually becomes. She is still capable of selflessly sending Mitch away, telling him to "find somebody who dates in the afternoon" ([*The Primary Colors*], composite ms.). In the final version, Mitch's rejection of Blanche was made more credible by two elements which were added: his drinking before he visits her and his fondness for his mother. His rejecting her, rather than her rejecting him, exposes her weakness and prepares for her end. This Blanche is fighting for her life, not making the gestures of a romantic heroine.

The frequent changes in the name of the suitor reflected Williams' handling of him as a "reactor," a character created largely in response to the personalities of the "actors," Blanche and Stanley. And of the two "actors," Blanche seems to have been most clearly conceived from the beginning. Significantly, her first name is changed only once. In the first, Chicago, draft she is Bianca, a name which suggests innocence and purity as well as recalling the submissive gentleness of Shakespeare's heroine. The Bianca of the first draft is such a person, speaking "sweetly in a small, hesitant voice," quivering nervously as she prepares for her date, convinced that either her gentleman caller will not call or that he will not propose if he does. When she becomes Blanche in the next draft, the Shakespearean allusions are lost and with them the submissiveness, but her essential innocence is retained, even accentuated, through all the later developments in her character and the vicissitudes of her fate. The Blanche of New Orleans is a tarnished, battered, but still recognizable older sister of the Bianca of Chicago.

When the play moved to Atlanta and the characters lost their Italian nationalities, Blanche was given the plain English last name of Collins. This Blanche is more forthright and better equipped to survive her battles: her clashes with Stanley dent her armor of sophistication but do not sever an artery. Of the Blanche Shannon phase (which may have come next), only the title page with the part inscribed to Tallulah Bankhead survives in the Humanities Research Center Collection. Blanche Boisseau, as she becomes when the action is set in New Orleans, retains some of Blanche Collins's mannerisms, though her armor has worn thin and can no longer protect her. The fading beauty gaily explains to Mitch that her last name means "woods and Blanche means white, so the two together mean white woods. Like an orchard in spring!" A moment later she asks Mitch to put a lantern over the light bulb, conscious that she is not in the spring of her days. Her youth is illusory, her innocence smudged, her descent from French Huguenots irrelevant in an America that sees no continuity between past and present; yet Blanche DuBois, through all her self-deceptions, has not lost her affinity with the "white woods."

Whereas Blanche was recognizably the same basic character through all the drafts, her brother-in-law underwent a complete metamorphosis as his role in the play developed. The changes in his names, both first and last, signal his progression from a relatively minor character to center stage, from a "reactor" to an "actor." The focus in the first draft of the play is on the courtship of the school teacher by the man she has met in Chicago. Thus her sister and her brother-in-law are in the background, sounding boards for Bianca's doubts. Lucio, the brother-in-law, is described as a "weakly good-looking young man. He has a playful tenderness and vivacity which would amount to effeminacy if he were not Italian." His passionate involvement with his wife embarrasses rather than threatens the innocent Bianca.

The amiable Lucio becomes the more aggressive, though still not dominant, Ralph Stanley as the sexual tension between him and Blanche develops. Ralph is described in the first draft of *The Primary Colors* as a "healthy Irish peasant type with urban modifications and a keen sense of the fact that he is one man in a house with two women." Blanche is "charged with plenty of that blue juice which is the doves of Aphrodite's or anyone's car." The pipe-smoking Ralph and the brittle, superior Blanche spar viciously, with Blanche finally accusing him of compensating for his lack of height, and remarking, "I think you have a very wide streak of the feminine in your nature. You think you'll obscure it by acting with the greatest possible vulgarity. But what you sometimes really remind me of is a vicious little fourteen year old girl that I've had in my class for two years." Such an explicit "explanation" of Stanley's aggressive masculinity is omitted in *Streetcar*, but his behavior does indeed suggest he is a man who fears the feminine in his nature.

The sexual tension between Ralph and Blanche in *The Primary Colors* becomes apparent even to Stella, who concludes that "you pick at each other so much [because] underneath I think you like each other." In this draft, however, Blanche is in control, and Ralph can do little more than reject Stella's sexual advances and smash his pipe in frustration. Here, Mitch/Howdy wins Blanche, just as the more powerful Eddie Zawadski (Mitch) pushes Stanley Landowski aside in *Electric Avenue*.

Included in the first manuscript of *The Primary Colors* is a short scene which expands an incident in the main draft. A brief encounter between Ralph and Blanche (watched by Stella) is rewritten as a more direct confrontation. Stella is removed (sent to watch a film at Loew's State), and Ralph, in a green bowling shirt, asks Blanche whether her red kimono signals stop or go. He "comes up very close to her, extending the cigarette." Untitled drafts of the play which followed developed this scene, with Blanche, after a short struggle between her desires and her conscience, taking up the challenge of Ralph (now Ralph Kowalski). Succeeding scenes show them, exhausted and stunned by their passionate encounter, nobly agreeing that they must part. This scene is, of course, the genesis of the rape scene in *Streetcar*. The growing dominance of the male is accompanied by changes in his nationality and name from the relatively soft-sounding Irish Ralph Stanley to the stronger Polish Stanley Kowalski (which is still more feminine than the Polish *Stanislaus*). The connotations of *Ralph* are not those of a victor, of a triumphant aggressor; and in the drafts of the play where he retains this name he is matched by Blanche, sometimes overmatched by Mitch, but never becomes the supremely destructive male, Stanley Kowalski of *Streetcar*.

These frequent changes in title and setting, in the characters' nationalities, names and ultimate destinies, might suggest only general resemblances between the first and last drafts of *Streetcar*. In fact, however, there are many detailed resemblances, for Williams seldom discarded material which would help define the characters or increase their complexity. Images (particularly visual ones) and dialogue (its matter, not the exact words) which appeared in very early drafts were often retained, though in a changed form, in the final drafts. They either decreased or increased in importance, but seldom disappeared completely.

It is characteristic of Williams' method of composition of *Streetcar* that he develops an idea to make an explicit statement, and then reduces it to no more than a suggestive role. Examples of this method have already been given in the discussion of Stanley's latent femininity and Stella's perception of Blanche's and Stanley's quarrelling as a concealment of their mutual attraction. Similarly, Stella's admission in one draft that it was largely sex that attracted her to Stanley, and Stanley's statement to Blanche that he was not acting to protect Mitch but to have her for himself, do not appear in the final version where their motives, unchanged, are made implicit in their behavior. The final draft has no discussion of the events that caused Blanche's final breakdown. In earlier drafts, however, Stella expresses her fears that Blanche's story about the rape was in fact true, and it is partly because Stella does not dare accept Blanche's story that she agrees to her sister's going to an asylum.

The association of Stanley with hunting and with death was more obviously emphasized in the early drafts. His job was once that of a salesman of mortuary goods, and the package of meat he throws to Stella in the first scene of *Streetcar* once led Blanche to ask what was in the package. "I had a horrible notion it was part of some—dismembered body." Stella replies, "He brought home squirrels" ([*The Primary Colors*], composite ms.).

A rainbow-colored silk scarf which Stella lends Blanche was used emphatically in several drafts to suggest happiness, hope and joy. Blanche wears it when she leaves with Eddie (in *Electric Avenue*) and again in a later draft with Mitch, where it has become "a shawl in tender moth-like colors" (*The Poker Night*, misc. pp.). In the final version it plays a minor role, becoming simply the "gossamer scarf" she wears on the night Mitch proposes. Williams once considered expressing Blanche's frustration and fears by having her react violently to the howl of an alley cat outside. In *The Primary Colors*, for example, she leans forward, then "twists her mouth down and imitates the cat's cry, long and hideously!" The incident was rewritten a number of times, but in the end Blanche's reactions to the howls of the cat were more subdued, expressing only her jumpiness. Her haunting memory of her husband's death, suggested by the polka tune (Var Sous Vienna—later Varsouviana) and the revolver shot, originally included her memory of the words she shouted at him on the dance floor: "I saw, I know, you disgust me!" ([*The Primary Colors*], composite ms.). The tragedy of her husband's death was a late addition, the first record of which is in the composite manuscript of [*The Primary Colors*].

Another method of composition Williams used in writing *Streetcar* was retaining ideas and either using them for different purposes or expressing them through different characters. When Mitch acquired a mother to whom he was devoted, it was she who suggested, in *Electric Avenue*, that he bring Blanche to her, for "the woman has suffered." Later, his mother becomes a reason for rejecting Blanche. Blanche is disgusted when Ralph watches her undress through the portieres, but she later undresses to tempt Mitch. It was originally Ralph/Stanley to whom Blanche explained why she left her school, adding that she had seen Mitch "as a possible refuge, a cleft in the rock of the world that I could hide in."[4] In *Streetcar*, roughly the same words are spoken directly to Mitch. Originally it was Stella, not Stanley, who sharply questioned Blanche about the loss of her old home. The speech about dying of eating an unwashed grape (which appears in the last scene of *Streetcar*) was first made by

Blanche when she and Stanley decided to part after their lovemaking. In the same draft Blanche noted that the only reminder of her visit would be the spilt talcum and empty perfume bottles—a comment Stanley was to savagely rephrase in his last words to Blanche in *Streetcar*.

Not all of the images and dialogue were either reduced in significance or used in different contexts. Visual images associated with a character in the early drafts were frequently developed into strong symbols in subsequent drafts. The process can be illustrated by an examination of the changing significance of Blanche's clothing. Blanche/Bianca's essential innocence was suggested visually in the first draft by her wearing a white suit with slightly tired violets pinned to her fluffy blouse. The image here simply supports Williams' portrait of Bianca, who is obviously pure and innocent, though ageing like the violets. In the final version of the play, however, the white clothes Blanche wears suggest a core of innocence, despite her more obvious immoral sexual behavior. Blanche arrives at Elysian Fields in a white suit which, although incongruous in this setting, expresses her need to start afresh, to be seen by others as an innocent. The coke spilt on it later does not stain; but she wears a "somewhat soiled and crumpled" white satin evening gown on the night she is raped (p. 391). When Blanche dresses to leave in the final scene she plans to wear a bunch of violets on her dress. The violets are now artificial, relics of her youth, and the dress she proposes to wear is yellow, which, in this context, can be seen as a stained white, the color of a Roman prostitute's clothes. In the end, however, she chooses a dress which is explicitly described as being "the blue of the robe in the old Madonna pictures" (p. 409).

In the first draft, Bianca wears a "vivid silk robe" before putting on the white suit in preparation for Mitch's visit. The robe later becomes a kimono with poppies printed on it, and then the kimono itself becomes scarlet, quite clearly representing the passionate side of Blanche's nature. She is wearing it in the draft where she and Stanley make violent love, unable to control their mutual desires; and in the final version it is a constant reminder that Blanche is a passionate woman, wearing scarlet in private, white in public. Blanche wears the kimono before and after she bathes; she is wearing it when she attracts Mitch by letting him see her undress; she is wearing it when Mitch, unable to accept her past, leaves her; and she wears it before she changes into the blue dress for her departure.

Just as visual images were given larger significance, so a passage of dialogue—perhaps only a phrase—which in its original context had little significance would be worked up in later drafts into an important indication of character. In *The Primary Colors*, Blanche, panicking like any woman whose suitor is unexpectedly calling, cries, "Oh, but honey, I haven't had my bath yet! That's the trouble, I've got to *bathe—bathe!*" Later in the scene her love of looking fresh, "as cool as a cucumber," is mentioned, though it is little more than nervous chatter in this context. The Freudian implications of Blanche's obsession with bathing and appearing virginally fresh are developed only in a later draft. Similarly, her giggly offer to Howdy/ Mitch of a drink of Southern Comfort is nothing more, here, than a nervous social gesture, and does not lead, as in the final version, to an accusation that she has been "lapping it up all summer like a wild-cat!" (p. 383). Her age became another neurotic obsession only in later drafts. Blanche, to begin with, was simply a high-strung woman. When Williams exaggerated the signs of her nervousness— her desire to bathe before her suitor arrives, her offering Mitch a drink, her consciousness of her age—she becomes a psychotic. Her behavior, no longer "normal," made her end not merely credible: it made it inevitable.

The actual details of Blanche's end gave Williams considerable trouble. The manuscripts show that even after the body of the play was complete but for minor revisions, Williams was still dissatisfied with the ending. Fortunately, exceptionally full records of the last scene survive in the manuscript collection. Because of the uncertain chronology of the fragments, a neat diagram of the development of the scene is impossible. Nonetheless, they provide the clearest illustration in these materials of Williams' creative methods and of the tenacity with which he sought a satisfactory resolution to the play.

As late as March 1945 Williams had not decided among three possible endings: "One, Blanche simply leaves—with no destination. Two, goes mad. Three, throws herself in front of a train in the freight-yards, the roar of which has been an ominous under-tone throughout the play" (letter to Audrey Wood). The first possibility is developed in two of the eight miscellaneous pages I have tentatively ascribed to [*The Primary Colors*]. Of the third possibility, Blanche's suicide, no draft survives. Once Williams had settled on the second ending (Blanche goes mad), he still had to work out the details of the final scene.

Three versions of parts of the last scene are recorded on a single page of the eight miscellaneous pages I have ascribed to [*The Primary Colors*]. In one, a typescript with holograph revisions, Stella lets Blanche hold her child, despite a poker player's protest that Blanche is a lunatic. Blanche quietly returns the child and goes out through the front room, saying, "Don't get up. I'm only passing through." She asks Stella to walk with her to the corner, for "It's a beautiful night." The second version (in holograph) establishes Blanche's madness more firmly by having her calm discussion of her need for treatment end in an insane scream. The doctor and the nurse waiting on the street corner drag her away. A holograph outline, which may not be contemporaneous with the two other versions on this sheet of paper, introduces the idea that Blanche believes she is leaving for a trip with a Dallas millionaire. The "grape" speech, salvaged from a miscellaneous manuscript of [*The Primary Colors*], where Blanche simply leaves at the end, is marked for insertion here. The doctor and the matron wait at the corner, from where Blanche waves goodbye to Stella, standing on the steps with the baby. Eunice, whose original dramatic purpose seems to have been to give Stella someone to talk to, returns to the poker players.

A four-page typescript which forms part of the nineteen miscellaneous pages I have grouped under *The Poker Night* may represent the next stage in the development of the last scene. Blanche, having returned from a two weeks' stay in the hospital, is preparing to leave voluntarily for the asylum. At the last moment, she panics, but now the doctor and the matron use a hypodermic and strait jacket to subdue her before carrying her around the corner. Stella, half convinced by Blanche's story of Stanley attacking her, shrinks from Stanley's embrace.

In two slightly different drafts (of nine and six pages) which I have ascribed to *The Poker Night*, Blanche is catatonic. Stella and Eunice discuss Blanche's illness and her allegations about Stanley. When the doctor and the matron try to lead the silent woman away, she breaks out of her trance and screams. She is subdued as before, and Steve (in one version) or Stanley (in the other) helps to carry her out. Stella sobs on Stanley's shoulder while Eunice returns to the poker players, who continue their game unruffled.

In the first complete script we have of *The Poker Night* (a 132-page typescript with holograph revisions), Blanche is an Ophelia-like figure, singing a song which leads into the "grape" speech. After she has been immobilized, Stanley steps forward to assist the doctor, but is stopped by Stella shrieking, "She'll die if you touch her!" and accusing him of having caused her sister's breakdown. So it is Steve who helps the doctor. Stanley and Eunice rejoin the players, and Stella sits on the steps outside with the baby. The play ends as she stands and "elevates the child in her arms as if she were offering it to the tenderness of the sky. Then she draws it close to her and bows her head until her face is hidden by the child's blanket."

The first typescript to be given the *Streetcar* title was a 131-page revision of the 132 page script referred to in the previous paragraph. Unfortunately, the last scene is missing in this revised script, but a later 136-page typescript (originally intended for the printer's copy) includes the last scene—the only scene in the manuscript substantially different from the New Directions edition of *Streetcar*. It includes a lengthy discussion between Eunice and Stella of the events of the night of the rape. Stella, half believing Blanche's story, shows Eunice Stanley's torn pyjama jacket, and Eunice describes Blanche's state when she fled upstairs to Eunice's apartment that night. Stella's agreeing to commit Blanche is shown to be a deliberate decision to preserve her marriage. Stanley stands in the room after Blanche has gone "holding the paper lantern. He revolves it slowly in his hands as if he were perplexed by its meaning. He crumples it up, finally, and tosses it into a corner of the room. After dumping some empty perfume bottles and a box of powder on top of the crushed lantern, he walks back into the kitchen." As in the final script, Stella sobs luxuriously in his arms as the play ends.

Although all the differences between this late 136-page manuscript and the earlier complete scripts are striking, none is more important to the tone of the whole play than the difference in the handling of Blanche's confrontation with the doctor. For the first time in a complete typescript, the hypodermic and strait jacket are not used in this scene. Williams' desire for Blanche to leave with dignity was implied in the earliest drafts, but his need to establish her madness unambiguously and to hint at her ultimate fate, led to the introduction of the violent struggle with the doctor and the matron. It was not until this very late stage in the development of the play that Williams resolved his dilemma by changing Blanche's reaction to the doctor. Her insanity is affirmed without reducing her to a raving maniac, and Blanche can leave with dignity, her tragedy poignantly expressed in the fine lines, "Whoever you are—I have always depended on the kindness of strangers" (p. 418).

Notes to Vivienne Dickson, "A *Streetcar Named Desire*: Its Development through the Manuscripts"

1. I am grateful to both Mr. Tennessee Williams and the Manuscript Committee of the Humanities Research Center of the University of Texas at Austin for giving me permission to work with and quote from these manuscripts. Dr. David Farmer, Ms. Sally Leach and Mr. John Ramington, all of the H. R. C., gave me invaluable assistance.

2. The lines from St.-John Perse which seem to be the source are: "et ce monde est plus beau/qu'une peau de belier peinte en rouge!" *Anabasis*, trans. T. S. Eliot (New York: Harcourt, Brace, 1938), p. 27.

3. *The Poker Night*, 15 pp. of a composite 57 pp. ms.

4. Uncatalogued page filed with single title page of *The Poker Night*.

"Towards Bethlehem":
Battle of Angels and Orpheus Descending

DAVID C. C. MATTHEW

BATTLE OF ANGELS was the first play by Tennessee Williams to be given a professional production (30 December 1940), and, despite its unfavorable reception, Williams stubbornly continued to revise for seventeen years, until the play emerged as *Orpheus Descending*. He said then, "I have never quit working on this one, not even now" (III, 224). Indeed, it was to return still later as a film, *The Fugitive Kind*.

Battle of Angels is much more than "a lyrical play about memories and the loneliness of them" (III, 223). Williams has erected an elaborate structure of symbols and characterizations upon which to reenact a modern version of the self-immolation of a divine artist, who propels himself toward his fate in a search for some instinctively sensed catalytic perception or experience. This search has no practical reality at all; the hero's self-realization is his only goal. And in exactly the Arthurian mode, the quest of the knight for self-definition is pursued by making himself open or available to any and all adventure (Auerbach, *Mimesis*, pp. 116, 117). Williams has recognized the power of the myths accompanying and underlying the search of the knight errant and has interwoven the ancient myth of sacrifice with the very modern idea of the drama of what Robert Brustein terms "existential revolt," wherein "existence itself be-

172

comes the source of the playwright's rebellion" (*Theatre of Revolt*, p. 26). Williams' hero finds that his knightly quest results in the discovery that he, like all other men, is "alone in a terrifying emptiness . . . doomed, as it were, to a life of solitary confinement" (Brustein, p. 27). The divine artist's enlightenment as the culmination of his quest leads inexorably to his self-sacrifice.

Williams uses the same setting in each play—a small southern town located in Two River County somewhere in the Deep South, a place where sex, death, and disaster are the staples of conversation. When the play opens, it is winter, and death is ominously announced in the person of Jabe Torrance, who has just returned home to die of cancer after an unsuccessful operation in Memphis. His wife (Myra in *Battle* and Lady in *Orpheus*) is Italian, passionate, and sexually frustrated, like Serafina delle Rose of *The Rose Tattoo*.

Into this setting Williams introduces his hero, Valentine Xavier, also known as Snakeskin because of the garment he wears. His car axle has broken in the midst of a storm, and this southern Bethlehem is to be the ultimate stop in his lifelong quest. In the first version, he is a somewhat naive young writer of twenty-five; in the second, he has aged to thirty years and has become a knowledgeable, worldly-wise guitarist. He is a wanderer, an artist—and a daydreamer.

In *The Creative Unconscious*, Hanns Sachs says, "The traditional figure of the future poet—and, generally speaking the tradition is here true to life—is that of a boy who has not much interest in the realities of life as they offer themselves to him, but walks the earth in a world of his own, surrounded by the shadow-play of his daydreams and fantasies. It is also common knowledge that this day-dreaming habit forms the initial stage for all future creation, no matter how straight or how tortuous the line of the poet's life may become" (p. 12). Use of the tradition automatically allows Williams to suggest a character more imaginative, sensitive, and creative than his actions might indicate.

Yet, Val Xavier has more than the characteristic of daydreaming to portray him as an artist. In *Battle of Angels* he is writing a book, the manuscript of which is in a shoebox. He even daydreams a few lines into the action. In *Orpheus*, Val's artistic temperament is symbolized by his guitar and attested to both by Carol Cutrere's prior knowledge of his New Orleans fame and by the many signatures of still more famous musicians inscribed on his instrument. Val occasionally plays on his guitar and even sings "Heavenly Grass," one of Williams' "Blue Mountain Ballads" (*Winter of Cities*, p. 101).

In *Orpheus*, Val is very careful with his guitar. (Perhaps it is the one purchased from the black musician Loon in Val's previous dramatic incarnation.) The guitar is also a phallic symbol, of course, reminding us of Val's artistry in the bedroom as well as his association with Dionysus. When violence threatens Val personally, he is calm; but when Dog Hamma and Pee Wee Ginnings threaten to harm his guitar, he goes into a frenzy and is oblivious to their drawn knives and superior numbers. Sheriff Talbott remarks with what must be deliberate sexual irony, "Awright, boy. Git down off th' counter, I ain't gonna touch y'r guitar" (III, 320). Val's physical identification with the art object is a most emphatic way of showing the man as a personification of the image of the artist.

But Val is also an unfulfilled artist. In one case, he has not finished his book. In the other, he has abandoned his career as a musician because of a longing for something more. He asks, or seeks to formulate, Big Questions, sometimes in spite of his deficient articulation, sometimes inspired with Williams' romantic rhetoric. He is a wanderer who feels lost in a land which may at first offer fulfilment but then snatches it away as illusory. He is, therefore, not only an artist in the literary or musical sense, but, more important to Williams, an artist-philosopher seeking an ultimate answer. That he may be so limited in intelligence as to be inarticulate is immaterial. For Williams, the concept of being the artist defines one as a philosophical questioner of the static and the status quo. The existential awakening of this artist-searcher to the solitary nature of man's fate catapults the artist and god to his fate.

The biographical anecdote narrated in each play in virtually the same language shows the origin of Val's quest. When still a young boy, he was orphaned and lived at one with nature in a swamp. There, however, he was not satisfied; he was waiting for something, though he did not know what. Finally one day he discovered a young girl in the swamp, and he thought she was what he wanted. Although he taught her "love," he found after a time that this relationship was not the fulfilment for which he had been waiting. So he began his search in the world of men, not for the make-believe answer of "love," but for something more profound and permanent.

This notion of the symbolically divine artistic wanderer is essential to the entire oeuvre of Williams. Tom in *The Glass Menagerie*, Kilroy in *Camino Real*, Chance Wayne in *Sweet Bird of Youth*, and Sebastian Venable in *Suddenly Last Summer* are only a few examples of this omnipresent type. In "The Malediction," Williams even imputes this search to the deity: "God was, like Lucio, a lonely and bewildered man Who felt that something was wrong but could not correct it, a man Who sensed the blundering sleep-walk of time and hostilities of chance and wanted to hide Himself from them in places of brilliance and warmth" (*One Arm*, p. 48). This notion of a reluctant God who wishes to hide himself in warmth seems simultaneously to suggest that he is seeking surcease from his quest in the warmth of either sex or suicide. Val seeks solace in sex, while Lucio seeks it in suicide, a suicide deliberately suggesting a parallel with Christ. Williams' works often find sex and suicide essentially linked in what a Freudian might term a symbolic association reflecting masochistic homosexual predilections. The spent seed which offers no prospect of procreation is truly the spender dead, a part of the self killed. The similarity between death and the sexual act is also generally recognized as a familiar literary metaphor.

That Val Xavier is a wanderer suggests another facet of his personality—the role of scapegoat. The responsibilities for sins are heaped upon him. Jabe Torrance in each case blames him for the murder of Mrs. Torrance; in *Battle*, the sheriff holds him responsible for the unconsciously amorous actions of Vee Talbott. And in both plays, the sacrifice required is either exile or death, death finally being the hero's fate.

Williams uses several obvious allusions to the divinity of the hero. Val's last name is a pun on "savior." Jabe Torrance is the Old Testament Jehovah, demanding a sacrifice for the corruption rampant in the town and getting his wish on Good Friday, the day on which the last act takes place. Williams has used the Christian myth so obviously throughout the play that a cataloging of references would serve little purpose. One descriptive passage will show the tenor of the Christian allegory. In *Orpheus*, Val has some rather grotesque characteristics that can be explained only as presenting a down-home version of the deity. He says, "I can sleep or not sleep as long or short as I want to. . . . I can sleep on a concrete floor or go without sleeping, without even feeling sleepy, for forty-eight hours. And I can hold my breath three minutes without blacking out; I made ten dollars betting I could do it and I did it! And I can go a whole day without passing water. . . . Well, they say that a woman can burn a man down. But I can burn down a woman" (III, 264).

Unlike the conspicuous Christian allusions and those to the Orphic myth suggested primarily by the title of the second version, these plays have as a center the myths of Attis and Dionysus, both of which are keystones of Williams' dramaturgy and not merely conscious superficial referents.

Henry Popkin has suggested that Val fits an archetypal pattern for a Williams hero: "These magnificent, untamed creatures are threatened by corruption. Before our eyes several of them give way to it. . . . All are threatened because their superb qualities attract the lightning, bringing love, envy, and the danger of corruption. . . . We may say that Williams starts with his Adonis for the same reason that Sophocles begins with his king of Thebes. Each is great enough to attract the lightning" ("The Plays," p. 46). Val's ability to charm women, which seems to border on hypnotism in the case of Vee Talbot, suggests Dionysus rather than Adonis. In a scene added in *Orpheus*, Val is calming Vee by explaining that her religious art and its fascination with Christ derives from the chaos by which she is surrounded. That chaotic ethos is uncannily reminiscent of the violent celebrations of the rites of Dionysus:

> VAL: Before you started to paint, it [existence] didn't make sense. . . .
>   You lived in Two River County, the wife of the county sheriff. You
>   saw awful things take place.
> VEE: Awful! Things!
> VAL: Beatings!
> VEE: Yes!
> VAL: Lynchings!
> VEE: Yes!
> VAL: Runaway convicts torn to pieces by hounds!
>
>   .   .   .   .

VEE: *Chain-gang dogs!*
VAL: Yeah?
VEE: Tear fugitives!
VAL: Yeah?
VEE: —to *pieces.* . . .

. . . .

VAL: Without no plan, no training, you started to paint as if God touched your fingers. . . . You made some beauty out of this dark country with these two, soft, woman hands . . . (III, 290–92).

The symbolic rending of the god Dionysus by the Maenads is evoked by this imagery of violent dismemberment, from which emerges the messianic paintings which are Mrs. Talbot's art.

Only a few minutes later, Val will explain to Lady that he feels he is the "brother" of the convict pursued by the dogs outside (III, 294). Val is Dionysus not only in being the game in this fatal pursuit but also in his assumption of animal forms and his constant association with the beasts of the wild. In *Battle*, he tells Myra he used to "live like a fox," and also compares himself to a "fox pursued by hounds" (I, 49, 51). This symbolic linkage with the animal kingdom is extended by the relationship between Val and the animalic "Choctaw cry," given by Uncle Pleasant, the aged mysterious Negro in *Orpheus*. Carol asks Uncle Pleasant to give the cry, described as "a series of sharp barking sounds that rise to a sustained cry of great intensity and wildness. . . . Val sweeps back the alcove curtain and appears as if the cry were his cue." At this strangely heralded entrance, Carol says, "Something is still wild in the country!" (III, 326–27).

This Dionysiac savior is introduced into Two River County (a possible echo of the legendary location of Eden amidst the Tigris and the Euphrates) by Vee Talbot, a member of the Church of the Resurrection, who uses Val's features for her portrayal of Christ in her "Last Supper." In *Battle*, Williams repeats a crude bit of business wherein Val's plausibly naturalistic expletive "God, I—! Lady, you—!" is reinforced by Lady's response, "God you an' lady me, huh" (I, 33). This is a god who communes directly with Lady and, in the penultimate scene, brings life where all had been dead, by making her conceive to bear fruit. The spring succeeds the barrenness of winter, just as Lady's fruitfulness succeeds her winter of sterile marriage with Jabe.

The subject matter of the song Val sings in *Orpheus* reinforces the suggestion that Val is an extraordinary wanderer who has come from the heavens to linger but awhile on earth:

> My feet took a walk in heavenly grass.
>
> . . . .
>
> Then my feet come down to walk on earth,
> And my mother cried when she give me birth.
> Now my feet walk far and my feet walk fast,
> But they still got an itch for heavenly grass
> But they still got an itch for heavenly grass.
> (Winter of Cities, p. 101)

One of Val's lines in his final scenes with Lady is an echo of Christ's valediction, "It is finished." In *Battle*, Val actually uses the phrase, "It's finished!" (I, 115), and in *Orpheus* he says, "My time is up here" (III, 330). When the blowtorch is lit in the last moments of *Orpheus*, the expletive "Christ!" is repeated twice.

If then Val Xavier is a wanderer, an artist, a visionary, and a composite of various divinities, how do all these symbolic elements form a coherent entity? This was one of the problems with which Williams was forced to wrestle in his seventeen years of rewriting; it is most important to notice and examine the elements of character, plot structure, and symbolism retained in each version. Clearly Williams is using the device of the romantic quest and imbuing his knight errant with the attributes of both an ancient god and a twentieth-century self-exploratory artist.

Undoubtedly Val's character is the motivating force behind his tragedy. He goes to his death because of his own commitment. Williams' revisions stress this classical concept that character determines fate. Elimination of the woman from Waco was the result of Williams' wish to simplify his concept of fate as the idea that all men gradually kill themselves from day to day. In "Moony's Kid Don't Cry," published in the same year as *Battle*, Williams describes a lumberjack whose life had been defined by the ecstasy of freedom, of "swingin' my axe in the north woods" (*American Blues*, p. 7). But he yielded that freedom to his sexual needs and took a wife. She

wished to move to the city, and a child has also been produced from
Moony's passion. Moony finds himself in a living death, the purgatory of a monotonous job with no future and a present built only of
endless minor frustrations. It is, however, his family, the physical
embodiment of his own desires, that has enslaved him. This quality
of being the victim of an inevitably self-inflicted fate gives Val and
other Williams characters tragic stature. They struggle and fail because they have sought to escape the morass of the self-satisfied
middle class.

In each play Val tells Myra the same story of his early life. Left
behind in the swamp by his parents, he "lived like a fox," but a fox
who has an inchoate notion of a Romantic quest: "I know I had
some peculiar notions . . . I used to lay out naked in a flatboat with
the sun on me. . . . I had a feeling that something *important* was going
to come *in* to me. It would come *in* to me. Through my eyes—see?
. . . Like a net—see? If you don't spread it out, you won't catch nothing in it. But if you do, you *might*. Mine I used to spread it out, wide-
open, those afternoons on the bayous—ears pricked, eyes peeled—
watchin', waitin', listenin' for it to come!" (I, 51–2). Although
presented as physically passive, the young knight errant is here ready-
ing himself for his quest although its physical bounds are not to be as
far flung as its psychological ones.

Val's first challenge episode comes appropriately with the sudden,
almost magical appearance of a young girl in the swamp. He is at
first simply an observer, but the element which activates him, which
in fact introduces him consciously to the existence and meaning of
the sexual impulses, is a bird. "Oh, God, I remember a bird flown
out of the moss and its wings made a shadow on her! . . . An' then
it sang a single high clear note. An' as though she was waitin' for
that as a kind of signal—to *trap* me—she turned and smiled an'
walked on back in the cabin!" (I, 53). This is the first of many times
Williams will use bird imagery to suggest something about the sexual
encounter of man and woman. Here the bird seems to be the signal
to Val, the observer, of a separateness in the sexes and in the persons,
a separateness that appears to offer the possibility of a true union,
a fulfilment. This possibility or hope is denied, of course, not only
in the attempt at realization of the union sexually, but even in the
initial metaphor, with Williams' emphasis on *trap*. The eternal

elusiveness provided by the bird's facility of flight is an important symbolic connection for Williams. The bird offers an attractive colorful appearance of vibrant life, yet the very alienation from the earth given it by its wings denies the possibility of any realization or consummation of a terrestrial relationship.

This concept is explained in the most important bird image in *Orpheus*, that of the tiny blue bird with no legs. Val is impressed profoundly because these birds never come to earth throughout their lives. He and Lady both see the bird as an embodiment of perfect freedom. Lady even doubts that anything can be so free as that blue bird, and she says she would give the entire store and all its stock if she could be that bird for only one night (III, 266). Williams is very careful to emphasize the color of these birds; Val says not only that the bird was "light-blue colored" but also explains that its wings were "the color of the sky" and that, "You can't tell those birds from the sky and that's why the hawks don't catch them, don't see them up there in the high blue sky near the sun!" (III, 265).

The sky color is repeatedly linked to Val in counterpoint to this blue bird of happiness and freedom. When Val arrives, he is wearing blue serge. Lady gives him a blue suit to work in. Carol calls his blue business suit "the nice blue uniform of a convict" (III, 283). When Lady is celebrating the opening of her store, she wears a dress which she says is "ecstasy blue." Clearly Williams associates the color with Val's special embodiment of freedom and joy desired but not possessed by any of the other characters, except Lady in her final moments when she wears her ecstasy-blue dress. Val's various jobs do not make him a prisoner, for he had this special air of detachment, the special freedom of the one who does not belong, when he was the musician Snakeskin playing in New Orleans night clubs, as obviously as he has it as a clerk in the Torrance General Store. But Val himself has seen one of these fantastic birds only once— when it was dead. So the blue bird of freedom (Maeterlinck?) eludes even its most ardent hunter, a hunter so ardent that the reflection of his quest is almost visible on his countenance.

Just as the knight errant's character is defined by his adventures, Val's self is a reflection of all that he has been and done. When he lived in Texas (*Battle*), he was known as Jonathan West, a name which combines the name meaning "the Lord has given" with the direction associated colloquially with death ("gone West"). While in Texas, he became involved with the woman from Waco, who pursues him thereafter like some Fury. But Val had allowed himself to become involved with the woman, and it was his decision to abandon her. Thus he has brought about his outlaw status. His passion is his fatal flaw. When he arrives in Two River County and refuses a room at the jail because of a personal phobia (*Battle*), he puts himself in a position that leads to his sleeping in the Torrance store, a situation clearly provocative of the subsequent action. In *Orpheus*, Val's actions are slightly less obvious; he first moves into a motel near town, and Lady eventually persuades him to stay in the store; but his action and its ramifications are even more obviously his own responsibility.

One of his phobias, clearly stated in *Battle* and implied in *Orpheus*, is fear of fire. He tells Myra that a fire caused him to move on from his previous job:

> VAL: The place next door burnt down.
> MYRA: What's that got to do with it?
> VAL: I don't like fire. I dreamed about it three nights straight so I quit. I was burnt as a kid and ever since then it's been something I don't forget (I, 30).

The fire he fears is more than the element of flame; it is the fire of his own passion. He is constantly battling with this internal fire, in an attempt to keep it inside. As he explains to Myra, "You said this morning I touched the women too much when I tried shoes on them. Maybe I do. My hands—I'm afraid of my hands. I hold them in so hard the muscles ache. . . . You know what it's like? A herd of elephants, straining at a rope. How do I know the rope won't break sometime? With you or with somebody else?" (I, 74). This fire from inside breaks into the open in this same scene with Myra, when Val deliberately breaks into the back room of the store, after Myra has explained it is locked. This is a frank, physical action taken by Val to enter into a sexual and emotional relationship with Myra. It is not a casual passion of the instant, for he has rejected such a liaison with Cassandra Whiteside. Val acts deliberately, even though he has explained to Myra that this physical action must inevitably fail to draw two persons closer together (I, 50). Val has shown himself capable of other types of love; his "laying on of hands" with Vee Talbot illustrates a spirit of charity and sympathetic pity. Thus Val is not acting on the spur of the moment without an awareness of an alternative expression of emotion or of the probable outcome.

In fact, the outcome is worse than the outcome of the affair with the woman from Waco. Myra points out that he cannot escape, that the results of their fiery passion are growing in her womb, and that he will never achieve his idyll. Val has explained that it is his utmost wish to be alone on the desert so that he might stretch out his brain, "so far, it's pushing right up against the edges of the stars!" This condition can be reached only in a state of absolute loneliness: "when you're out there alone by yourself (not with nobody else!) ..." (I, 108). Instead of reaching the desert alone, Val is faced with the prospect of living in Two River County with a woman and child, and death knocking upstairs in the person of Myra's husband, Jabe. Yet it is nothing external, not Sheriff Talbott, not Jabe Torrance, not the woman from Waco who has put Val in this position. When the woman from Waco has just appeared in the store with the sheriff, Val's description of his feelings uses imagery to suggest that he knows his enemy is not an external one, rather one from inside him. He says, "I'm not so scared. I'm sick. . . . Like something was crawling on me. Something that crawled up out of the basement of my brain" (I, 104).

Even at this last minute, Val has options. He could compromise his principles, play along with Myra, and possibly fool Jabe (Battle). But he deliberately maintains consistency of character, and insists on leaving, on driving west into the storm, without Myra. He has been warned of the consequences of his actions, as has Myra. Cassandra prophesied, "Whoever has too much passion, we're going to be burned like witches because we know too much. . . . my lips have been touched by prophetic fire. . . . I have it on the very best of authority that time is all used up. There's no more time" (I, 99–100).

Although in Orpheus the warning comes from Sheriff Talbott, and is more direct and less poetic, in that play the deliberate nature of Val's decision to stay is also accented. He twice changes his mind about leaving, once at the end of act two, when Lady pleads that she needs him to live, and again in the final scene when she tells him of her pregnancy. This decision to stay is tantamount to an acceptance of his violent end. Jabe's melodramatic entrance and murder of Lady in both plays should not conceal Val's contribution to his own destruction.

Val's motivation, as noted above, is the "romantic quest." In such romances as Malory's *Morte d'Arthur*, the episodes fall into a general pattern of a knight leaving his home in quest of adventure, serving a lady, and meeting challenges on her behalf. The knight may assume as his public identity a cognomen drawn from his apparel or his past adventures. Val was known only as Snakeskin in his prior career, and in *Orpheus* Williams renames his female lead Lady, to accentuate the atmosphere of romance. But Val came not from a court, nor even, indeed, out of a family, since he says he allowed his parents to desert him in a swamp. Thus he comes from an existential loneliness. His adventures are hardly in the tradition of courtly love, but then Val is a modern knight. In his state of loneliness, he is eagerly awaiting something to come *into* him. Instead, he physically moves into an adventure, with the girl in the swamp. Several other adventures are alluded to, none of them removing Val's sense of dissatisfaction.

His first word, "Why?" is also the big question which epitomizes his quest for the meaning of his own existence. It is a search in which Val is unsure of the mode in which the adventure bearing the answer to his question will come, but he persists in his quest despite continual disappointments. At one point he says, "What does anyone wait for? For something to happen, for anything to happen, to make things make more sense. . . . It's hard to remember what that feeling was like because I've lost it now, but I was waiting for something like if you ask a question you wait for someone to answer, but you ask the wrong question or you ask the wrong person and the answer don't come" (III, 271). And at another point in the conversation, he explains a different approach to answering his question: "How do you get to know people? I used to think you did it by touching them with your hands. But later I found out that only made you more of a stranger than ever. Now I know that *nobody* ever gets to *know* anybody. . . . We're all of us locked up tight inside our own bodies. Sentenced—you might say—to solitary confinement inside our own skins" (I, 50). Certainly if the knight is trapped inside himself, he cannot succeed in his quest to break out, to touch others, to have them tell him "Why." His quest has taken him to a town suffused with death, almost a Hades above the ground (see Quirino, "Darkest Celebrations of Williams," pp. 24, 30, 34). He is fated to conclude his quest in a violent death, the ultimate loneliness.

If the structure of the play is focused on Val as the unsuccessful seeker after happiness, Williams has reinforced that theme with the two women, Myra (Lady) Torrance and Cassandra Whiteside (Carol Cutrere). In *Orpheus*, Williams adds Lady's full history, telling of her early life with her father at his Moon Lake Casino, when the young Myra Romano sought and found youth and romance. This idyllic period ceased abruptly with the violent destruction of her father and his resort, a tragedy which drove Myra to embrace death in the person of the cancer-wracked murderer of her father, Jabe Torrance. She endures this winter of desolation by looking for and dreaming of a savior who might rejuvenate her and make her bloom with life. Val's engendering life in Lady's womb marks a fulfilment of her search. In *Orpheus*, Val's attitude toward Lady's annunciation is much more sympathetic, indicating his increased willingness to acknowledge this fulfilment as the convergence in life of both his search and hers.

Carol Cutrere (Cassandra Whiteside) is like Myra and Val in being a night person, and she reinforces Val's role: "You—savage. And me—aristocrat. Both of us things whose license has been revoked in the civilized world. Both of us equally damned and for the same good reason. Because we both want freedom. Of course, I knew you were really better than me. A whole lot better" (I, 45). Val is an outcast because he is an artist, a daydreamer, and a messiah of sorts. Myra is an outcast from the land of the living because of her voluntary marriage with death. Carol is an outcast because of her convictions. She too is more fully developed in *Orpheus*, able to communicate less oracularly with a more reticent, less flamboyant Val. In one conversation she draws him out, saying "*I'm an exhibitionist!* I want to be noticed, seen, heard, felt! I want them to know I'm alive! Don't you want them to know you're alive? VAL: I want to live and I don't care if they know I'm alive or not. CAROL: Then why do you play a guitar? VAL: Why do you make a goddam show of yourself? CAROL: That's right, for the same reason" (III,

251). Notwithstanding his seeming reticence, Carol knows that Val and she are traveling the same road for the same reasons.

She has tried to be a messiah, a savior for causes, civil rights, free clinics, equal justice for all. But now she has devoted her energy to following the advice of the dead, who she says speak to her and tell her to "Live, live, live, live, live!" (III, 252). She interprets this message to mean that free vent should be given to passion, the fires of which will eventually destroy her, just as they will destroy Val and Lady.

Cassandra's passion is always close to death. She says her "jook-ing" usually ends in Cypress Hill Cemetery, her favorite spot for copulation. She is very fond of the cemetery and often goes there alone to commune with the dead. She speaks casually of suicide and, in fact, has attempted it several times, succeeding only in cracking up her car seven times and killing a mule. The epilogue to *Battle of Angels* indicates that she finally succeeds in killing herself after Val's death, drawing the three parallel lines together into a single point of lonely loss (her body never recovered from the river). *Orpheus Descending* ends with Carol's speech upon the reception of the snakeskin jacket, and in that speech she says the fugitive kind always follow their kind. She exits, ignoring the sheriff, supposedly to fol-low the road of the fugitive kind, Val's road. She is more free than Val, because he refuses her solicitations, and therefore she has no lover except for an occasional pickup or her black chauffeur. Thus she is closer than Val to the blue bird of freedom which epitomizes Val's desires. In fact, Val himself draws attention to the resemblance between Carol and the blue bird. Her brother is on his way to pick her up in his "sky-blue Cadillac," and Carol is attempting once again to seduce Val, when he replies, "Little girl, you're transparent, I can see the veins in you. A man's weight on you would break you like a bundle of sticks. . . ." When Carol agrees that she is too frail for childbearing and that even lovemaking is painful, Val says, "Well, then, fly away, little bird, fly away before you—get broke" (III, 282). If Carol is the blue bird of freedom, the linking of death and sex here is very significant. When Carol relieves her loneliness in the act of lovemaking, she risks her life, courts death. Thus, free-dom is purchased only at the price of a loneliness which is finally unbearable. Even death will be courted as a companion if it suggests, even momentarily, the communality of humanity. Williams thus shows symbolically in Carol the fate of the perfect ideal of freedom for which Val and Lady strive. Their quest can end only in the embrace of death.

Carol Cutrere is, of course, also the heir to the snakeskin jacket which Val leaves behind, and she draws attention to its totemistic importance in her final speech: "Wild things leave skins behind them, they leave clean skins and teeth and white bones behind them, and these are tokens passed from one to another, so that the fugitive kind can always follow their kind . . ." (III, 341). The snakeskin jacket is one of several symbols of mythic origin which Williams uses in the play to reinforce his dramatic structure.

Frazer points out that Dionysus would occasionally appear clad in the skin of various animals associated with him, among them the serpent and the goat (p. 453). The totemistic treatment of the snakeskin jacket also suggests the myth of Attis. Frazer explains that the legend of Marsyas reflects the treatment of some of the human representatives of Attis: "Marsyas . . . was said to be a Phrygian . . . herdsman, who played sweetly on the flute. A friend of Cybele, he roamed the country with the disconsolate goddess to soothe her grief for the death of Attis. The composition of the Mother's Air, a tune played on the flute in honour of the Great Mother Goddess, was attributed to him by the people of Celaenae in Phrygia. Vain of his skill, he challenged Apollo to a musical contest, he to play on the flute and Apollo on the lyre. Being vanquished Marsyas was tied up to a pinetree and flayed or cut limb from limb either by the victorious Apollo or by a Scythian slave. His skin was shown at Celaenae in historical times" (*Golden Bough*, Macmillan Paperbacks, 1963, p. 411). The preservation of the skin and the hacking to death of the wandering musician clearly seem to be reflected in the fate of Val Xavier.

If Carol implies in her final speech that the snakeskin jacket has a life of its own, she is associating it with a well established tradition in folk tales, that of the external soul. According to this tradition the soul can be separated from the body and treated as a physical object, even hidden from prying eyes (Frazer, p. 774). In *Battle*, the epilogue notes that the jacket never seems to get dusty, even though it hangs in the store museum where everything else is coated with the dust of disuse. A connection between the totem and its owner clearly still exists. Williams made the link even closer in *Orpheus Descending*, where he added the details of Val's stage career in the past when he was known as Snakeskin. Carol Cutrere calls him by that name throughout the play. Val's leaving the snakeskin behind him emphasizes his connection with both Dionysus and Christ. The followers of Dionysus would wind themselves in symbols of the god after tearing him to pieces in their frenzied worship. The Christian notion of resurrection and rebirth is suggested by the snake's shedding of an old skin, which happens in nature when the animal has reached the limit of growth in one stage of development.

Another interesting symbol in this play as well as in many other of Williams' works is that of water. Jung (*Basic Writings*, p. 302) has said that water is the most common symbol for man's unconscious mind, and this symbol appears in the literature of romance even as far back as Chrétien's *Lancelot*. Gawain, held back by unique moral scruples, is trapped by the underwater bridge passage to Baudemagus, while Lancelot proceeds over a sword bridge to rescue and bed Guinevere. Williams has identified his southern town only by saying it is located in Two River County. Spring comes in the course of the play, bringing rain and floods to the rivers, rivers which consume and carry away Cassandra Whiteside.

Of course, water does not always mean danger in Williams. In both these plays, as well as in *Sweet Bird of Youth, Streetcar Named Desire*, and *Summer and Smoke*, Moon Lake is a place of freedom and pleasure removed from the present. The pleasures associated with the Moon Lake Casino are sensual ones; it is the place of assignations for the population, including the young Myra Romano, who has had her first love affair there. It is, however, an image which exists only in the past for Myra. The most she is able to do is to redecorate her confectionery to resemble the orchard on Moon Lake where her father ran the garden of pleasure. In this redecorated confectionery Myra keeps her dreams. Since water is a familiar element of the Christian baptismal ritual, dreams of regeneration, rebirth and salvation are suggested. But these dreams too will remain unfulfilled, because there is no water in the confectionery: only "Death's in the orchard" (I, 113)—probably a reference to the Garden of Eden and the idea that death came to man after the Fall, in association with the traditional interpretation of the Fall as being the result of carnal (sexual) awareness. Myra's past is buried at Moon Lake with her father and her aborted child; her present and future, herself and her second child, die in the confectionery's reconstruction of Moon Lake. As if she had never lived except in her unconscious, in a dream, she says, dying, "The show is over" (III, 339). In keeping with the Jewish myth, expulsion from the Garden of Eden (Moon Lake) is mandatory, and this Adam and Eve cannot have their child (Seth) there.

Using these complex and multilayered references to myth, Williams apparently intends the characters to live on in the ritual recapitulation of their story, an intent openly stated by the structure of *Battle* and more subtly implied by the stage directions of *Orpheus*. *Battle* includes a prologue and an epilogue in which the Temple sisters guide tourists through the shrine of the store-museum. The totemistic snakeskin jacket hangs prominently in the dusky store, and the celebration of the departed Xavier is presided over by the two Temple sisters, Eva and Blanche, whose names suggest their roles as vestal virgins and custodians of the temple. It is Williams' ironic comment on the institution of the church that they charge a twenty-five cent admission to their sacred realm, while he also suggests the required payment to Charon for transportation to Hades.

Orpheus omits the epilogue and moves the prologue into the time of action of the remainder of the play, thus tightening the dramatic coherence and forcing Williams to indicate the ritual nature of the action in his directions to the players and producers. He stresses that the setting should be "nonrealistic," that the merchandise should not be realistic, the confectionery should be "shadowy and poetic," and the two women are to be dressed "in a somewhat bizarre fashion" (III, 227). Beulah's initial monologue "should set the nonrealistic key for the whole production" (p. 230). Near the climax of the play, Williams reminds the director that the finale of act three, scene two where Val confronts Sheriff Talbott and is ordered out of town "should be underplayed, played almost casually, like the performance of some familiar ritual" (p. 317). The final scene of this last act of the play is to have lighting even "less realistic than in the previous scenes of the play. . . . A singing wind sweeps clouds before the moon so that the witchlike country brightens and dims and brightens again" (p. 322). Williams uses music throughout the play to reinforce action and mood and employs only lighting changes to indicate changes in time. He thus suggests the timelessness of an oft repeated ritual. The stage is a kind of sacred ground on which the play is played out, always with the same players and the same ending.

This play in both its versions has presented a view of a hero who seems certainly to partake of the characteristics of the messianic hero, in the sense that he has come into the life of the world of the store and replaced in one sense the old god, Jabe, a god of death, and brought a change to the lives of those around him, Lady, Vee, and Carol. "Like most saviours, he suffers the fate of the scapegoat at the hands of the multitude; and the betrayal of the messianic hero provides the dramatic climax of the messianic play" (Brustein, *Theatre of Revolt*, p. 19).

For a play to be a drama of messianic revolt, the messiah's doctrine need not be any more profound or original than Val's ideas about solitude, perfect legless blue birds, and deserts of loneliness. Brustein comments, "As for its doctrine, this is not usually very impressive when separated from the play proper. For the various messianic creeds . . . are neither very comprehensive nor even very original (most of this material is borrowed from other rebel thinkers like Kierkegaard, Schopenhauer, Nietzsche, Dostoyevsky, or D. H. Lawrence)" (p. 19).

However, Williams is dramatizing more than messianic revolt. He continually suggests the animal nature of Val, through stage directions such as, "He is standing . . . in the tense, frozen attitude of a wild animal listening to something that warns it of danger . . ." (III, 314) or more openly as when Val compares his temperature to that of a dog (p. 259). Val's sexual prowess and earlier profligacy are immediate products of a kind of animalistic nature, not an idealized messianic one. This idea of the artist as a product not of a divine muse, but of earthier origin was pointed out by Northrop Frye when he spoke of Byron and Byronizers, including D. H. Lawrence: "From Rousseau's time on, a profound change in the cultural framework of the arts takes place. Man is now thought of as a product of the energy of physical nature, and as this nature is subhuman in morality and intelligence and capacity for pleasure, the origin of art is morally

ambivalent and may even be demonic" (*Fables of Identity*, p. 186).
This observation helps to explain the reflections of Dionysus and
Attis in Val's nature.

Both romantic tradition and the basic myth require the artist to
die. However, Williams is not writing a romantic paean to a dead
hero; a darker vision is operating in his characters, a vision which Brustein says is reflected in what he calls existential drama, "in tone and
atmosphere, the most tragic of the modern genres. . . . The existential
dramatist projects himself into his characters' melancholy and complaint, and often manages to transcend his disgust with genuine
feelings of compassion. 'Humankind is pitiable,' Strindberg's Daughter of Indra intones repeatedly, while the author, recoiling from the
abyss of absurdity, forces himself to accept the painful riddles and
contradictions of life. Strindberg's stoicism is rather typical of existential drama, which frequently subsides into a kind of resignation—
an acceptance of waiting, patience, ordeals. O'Neill's derelicts wait
for death, Beckett's tramps wait for Godot, Gelber's junkies wait for
their connection . . ." (pp. 29–30). Val, accepting his fate, awaits
the final resolution—his death.

In attempting to delineate the distinctions between messianic and
existential drama, Brustein incidentally describes Val Xavier: "the
central figure of existential drama" engaged in the "revolt of the
fatigued and the hopeless, reflecting—after the disintegration of
idealist energies—exhaustion and disillusionment. This explains its
close relationship to messianic revolt, for it is actually an inverted
development of the messianic impulse. As a matter of fact, a number of modern dramatists, messianic in their youth conclude their
careers as existential rebels, their urge towards Godhead dissipating
in anguish and frustration" (pp. 27, 29). In *Battle of Angels/
Orpheus Descending*, Williams anticipated and combined impulses
of the messianic play with those of the existential drama, to provide
a work more insightful than the messianic and more allied to deeply
moving mythic roots than the existential. In 1957 producer Robert
Whitehead called *Orpheus Descending*, "Williams' biggest play to
date so far as philosophy, clarity, strength and social reference are
concerned. . . . Its theme is that the poet's life blood is protest, even
though when he does protest, he is destroyed . . ." (quoted in
Donahue, p. 88).

Although critics have not cited this work of Williams for its clarity, it is certainly a powerful play. Its power comes not from the too numerous classical allusions such as its second titling, but from the basic conception of the play, a dramatization or ritual celebration of the immolation of the artist-god on the altar of his own awareness of the nature of being. Tapping this ancient myth, Williams has created an important work that transcends labeling, because it is at once young and old, worshipful and cynical, myth and ritual. In 1957 Williams termed it a sort of bridge between his early years of playwriting and his "present state of existence as a playwright" (III, 224). This is an accurate statement, since this play, in its first and its second versions, embodies the central unified approach that may be found in the remainder of the Williams canon, an approach which survives even in the latest works.

Landscapes of the Dislocated Mind in Williams' *The Glass Menagerie*

JOSEPH K. DAVIS

The DRAMATIC PATTERN Tennessee Williams worked out in *The Glass Menagerie*—and one which assured it not only initial but continuing theatrical success—manifests two significant features: (1) the dramatization of men and women by a display of their fragmented, tortured psychologies; and (2) the depiction of these characters against a haunting environment which is itself a condition of their alienation and unhappiness. This dramatic realization of what are essentially *landscapes of the dislocated mind* constitutes typical Williams theater. The pattern developed is one Williams consistently uses, though with refinements, in later plays.

In achieving what in the "Production Notes" he terms "a new, plastic theatre" (I, 131), Williams adapts to the stage a technique already familiar to modern art media, especially to fiction and film. The entire play is staged literally with an actor, Tom Wingfield, who is not only the principal character but who also supplies the point of view for both events and theme of the drama. The effect recalls a cinemagraphic montage, with simultaneous use of interrelated memories, scenes, symbols, and musical motifs. Tom's presentation is characterized, as he himself says, by "truth in the pleasant disguise of illusion" (p. 144). The story he stages is not simply an account of how an individual gifted with a poetic temperament is denied a useful, creative life because of a hostile environment and

192

cruel family circumstances. And if Tom himself recalls similar modern individuals who search for self-expression, he is also concerned with reminiscences that quickly suggest much more than his own quest. Both as a major character and as a narrator he is unable to construct out of the materials he offers either a coherent or a personally satisfying explanation of reality. Nor is he able to establish with any confidence a genuine relationship with his family, his environment, or indeed with himself. The world of Tom Wingfield is clearly that of twilight, memory, and fantasy, from which images and shadows of the past loom threateningly over the present.

Tom's mode of dramatic presentation is clarified by a definition of two very different types of thinking. *Directed thinking* is logical in its verbal formulations and intentions, for it is causally linked with the external world by a more or less direct relationship with what it seeks to communicate. *Nondirected thinking* is spontaneously produced and unconsciously motivated. The former is occasionally referred to as progressive because it is oriented to reality and the demands of reality; the latter, as regressive because it is associated with formulations which have no apparently useful, sensible meanings (e.g., as in the materials of most day- and night-dreaming). Directed thinking seeks as its object adaption to reality and productions which reality esteems, while nondirected thinking turns away from reality and is concerned with a subjective content often bizarre and unacceptable to the normal modes of human consciousness. Tom's narrative throughout consists of nondirected thinking, a concept that may explain the entire play.

The function of Tom extends beyond any thematic intention to render inner experience or some quality of expressionistic reality. In its dramatic mode and theme, in fact, *The Glass Menagerie* portrays individuals not only fleeing from reality but also wishing to escape time and history. Each of the major characters is unable to accept and live with daily events; and each compensates for this failure by rejecting the present through wish-projections and fantasizing. Unable to live in the present, each character retreats into a time appropriate to his or her individual fantasy. Tom Wingfield cannot endure his home life or his job in the shoe factory and uses the motion pictures as a temporary means of escape. Seeing himself as a poet he eventually leaves home and hopes to find a life as an artist. His sister Laura tries to live in the present, but her crippled body and grim prospects in the secretarial school overcome her fragile sensibilities. She withdraws into the world of her glass animals, and so flees into a no-time of approaching mental collapse. The mother Amanda Wingfield cannot accept life in the St. Louis tenement and returns in fantasies to the past—an earlier period of gracious living on the plantation in Mississippi where, as she chooses to remember, she was surrounded by chivalric men of wealth and fashion who wanted to marry her. Each character is capable only of the briefest moments of realistic thinking; none can sustain anything like a vital relationship with another or with the facts of daily existence.

Not surprisingly, then, the dramatic structure of *The Glass Menagerie* cannot be worked out on the level of direct action. The present is avoided and actually repressed as too painful and monstrous to be faced and accepted. The landscape in which each of the three characters seeks refuge is one within his or her mind. Thus the entire play consists of an interplay of shadow and act—a structural movement which supports Williams' theme of flight from the present time and indeed from history.

Laura Wingfield is both the lyrical and the symbolical center of the play. Her shattered sensibility and delicate mental balance compel the only instance of genuine affection and compassion either Tom or Amanda shows in the drama. Unable to cope with her crippled body or the mechanical routine of the business school she briefly attends, she fabricates a nether-nether world out of the glass animals she collects. Quite literally they offer her the only security, intimacy, and permanence she can find in the brutal environment of her St. Louis tenement. Fragile and artistic, these glass figures, like Laura herself, suggest a world other than the one Williams depicts in the play. They symbolize all the artistry and beauty which to her, and perhaps to Williams, are missing in the secular-urban order of the modern era. In high school Laura attempted unsuccessfully to relate to a fellow student. Her secret beau turns out to be Jim O'Connor, the "gentleman caller" whom Tom brings to dinner. Once more Laura is betrayed, for Jim is already engaged to another girl. The idea of Jim as "savior," suggested by Stein (pp. 141–153), provides a final cruel moment in the play. Laura withdraws completely from the present, defeated by the world around her; she moves into the no-time of her glass animals and thus suffers a devastating mental collapse. Williams offers no "saviors," it seems. Art and beauty are given no way to exist in the world of *The Glass Menagerie.*

In addition to his role as stage narrator, Tom Wingfield emerges as Williams' prototypical "fugitive"—a sensitive, modern individual who is artistic in impulse and temperament. Tom rejects both his present menial job at the warehouse and his mother and her professed recollections of a chivalric, heroic past in Mississippi. He can only project his life into the future by means of fantasies as a poet. Tom exemplifies, in fact, two related patterns Williams consistently employs in his plays: (1) a rejection of past and present—both the romanticized past of his southern men and women and the bourgeois everydayness of contemporary secular-urban life; and (2) the Orphean compulsion toward the deeply instinctive regions of sexuality and violence. These areas cluster around what William Barrett in *Irrational Man* terms the Oresteian "Furies," or feminine earth-spirits, who demand a place in a society that is increasingly rationalistic and organized to serve the machine. The older Promethean/Faustian lifestyle of post-Renaissance times, represented in *The Glass Menagerie* by the gallantry and heroic order of the South, no longer are viable. Indeed, Tom cannot accept either as real or as desirable the way of life Amanda challenges him to emulate. The brutal fact of the commercial-industrial state cancels any possible return to such behavior. Caught between past and present, therefore, Tom retreats into fantasies and at last flees the stifling apartment.

Only in instances of wish-projections of himself into the future as poet-artist can Tom relieve the terrible depression and anxieties of his deadly lifestyle in St. Louis. Using various literary allusions—Jim O'Connor, for example, calls Tom "Shakespeare"—Williams reinforces Tom's hope that by means of art he might in time escape the world he now lives in. As a further act of rebellion, he identifies with the father who deserted them some years earlier and so, thief-like in the night, at last flees. Yet this act occasions the Angst and guilt Tom clearly admits during his troubled narrative. Survival in today's world, Williams implies, is bought at the cost of these debilitating inner conflicts.

The second Williams theme Tom exemplifies is the Orphean

plunge into the life of the body. At one point, Tom exclaims to his mother: "Man is by instinct a lover, a hunter, a fighter, and none of these instincts are given much play at the warehouse!" (I, 174). These activities are markedly predatory, but to Tom they belong to a side of human life repressed by the sterile organization of contemporary society. Yet they too must have a place in the full life of individuals; for if they are denied, they will rise in behavior that is ugly and violent. In *The Glass Menagerie* this theme is not treated in great detail; but in later plays it emerges with tremendous force and often with terrible consequences for Williams' men and women. So significant is it, in fact, that some clarification of it here is useful.

The Orphic theme, only foreshadowed in Tom's affirmation of man's beastlike aspects, points to several related emphases in Williams' plays. At one level it suggests the supernal power and role of art and artist. The legendary Orpheus, son of a divine Muse and a Thracian prince, was a master musician who rivaled the Olympians themselves. His lyre enchanted human beings and animals who heard it; it even saved Jason's mariners from despair and the bewitching songs of the Sirens. Orpheus, then, recalls the artist whose music calms and heals; for his incomparable songs purge the weariness and pain of life, uniting all who hear their ethereal melodies. At another level Orpheus alone dares the dark powers of the Underworld in search of his beloved Eurydice, taken from him by the sting of the poisonous viper. So beautiful is his music that the rulers of Hades agree to return her to him if he departs immediately and never looks back. Unfortunately he looks back too soon upon regaining the world above, and Eurydice, still within the gloomy shadows, is lost forever. But in seeking her he has challenged the fearful depths and so is one who quests for the reunification of body (the animal, sexual body) and spirit (the cognitive, enlightened heights of thought). Orpheus attempts to bring nature and man into harmonic unification. Williams clearly introduces both of these characteristics into his dramas.

This Orphean quest for unification of man's animal and intellectual dimensions through artistic means is a persistent dilemma in Williams' plays. Williams is never able to reconcile the split between man the artist and man the thinker. The body in its full, free life always becomes either a brutal punishment or an agent of tragedy. The Orphic dilemma, expressed by the ancient warning, soma sema (*the body, a tomb*), is one of the consistent mythopoeic themes in Williams' work. As the half-crazed Maeneds tear Orpheus to pieces, tossing his parts into the river Hebrus, so the heroes and often the heroines in Williams' plays must suffer dismemberment in their attempts to live the full life of the body.

If *The Glass Menagerie* only introduces Williams' Orphic dilemma, later works deal more or less consistently with it. *A Streetcar Named Desire* (1947), for example, rejects as dangerous and damaging the idea that individuals can live exclusively for unlimited self-indulgence, especially sexual gratifications. At the same time Williams recognizes that in attempting to seize their lives men and women experience definite limits. Each of us, after all, is not simply situated in this universe; and Williams undertakes specific explorations in his dramas of the 1950s of what moral order, if any, exists. In these plays he examines the terms whereby individuals may purposively act and thus the standards which can effectively measure their actions as creative or destructive. These plays reveal that Williams' investigations are undergirded by the conviction, never entirely absent from his work, that limits exist beyond which persons may not venture except at supreme risk and perhaps inevitable retribution.

That Williams came to such a view of human existence is seen in a growing preoccupation in the works of the 1950s and later with the problem of moral guilt and the violence which all too frequently this guilt generates. In *Camino Real*, a radical reworking of a 1947 play, *Ten Blocks on the Camino Real*, and in *Orpheus Descending*, also a completely reworked version of a 1940 play *Battle of Angels*, he gives us characters who express what Williams himself terms, with reference to the earlier play, "the romantic nonconformist in modern society" (as quoted in Donahue, p. 58). Both Kilroy in *Camino Real* and Val Xavier in *Orpheus Descending* attempt to live in this world by their own individualistic codes of behavior. Each would realize his life in ways personally satisfying, but at the same time each would act outside the social and moral order of his particular environment. In the end each is frustrated: Kilroy becomes a personification of sterility and thus is thrown into a kind of hell; Val is rendered literally impotent by a murderous act of physical castration.

The dilemma of Williams' Orphean hero is further explored in the controversial treatment given to the martyred homosexual Sebastian Venable in *Suddenly Last Summer* (1958) and in the portrait of the defrocked clergyman Shannon in *The Night of the Iguana* (1961). Despite Williams' clear dramatic presentation of ways in which both these heroes suffer and are punished, we are never quite sure that they themselves are entirely to blame or in fact deserve what happens to them. The framework of the problem of moral guilt is ambivalent; and Williams' handling offers us no easy access to his own views. The theatrically successful plays, *Cat on a Hot Tin Roof* (1954) and *Sweet Bird of Youth* (1959), for example, may be regarded as instances in which moral guilt brings pain and suffering, perhaps justifiably in the cases of Brick Pollitt and Chance Wayne. We may be entirely correct to say that for Williams man is finally a sinner and that through suffering he must expiate his sin and lose his guilt, but it is far too easy to pass over these complex dramatic presentations with such remarks.

It is more likely that Williams' dramatizations of the problem of guilt and moral ambiguity contain no successful way out. Indeed, his Orphean hero has necessarily become something of an Oresteian hero—a representative modern individual driven by self-admitted guilt and obsessive fears but who has a deep-felt longing to experience a redemptive vision and win back his peace of mind. Unlike Aeschylus' hero, Williams' hero is yet pursued by the Furies; thus far no divine intervention has occurred to save him and cleanse his tortured soul.

These ambiguities clearly emerge in Williams' delineation of Tom Wingfield and the dramatic pattern of *The Glass Menagerie*. But if Tom is the narrator and central character of the play, the pivotal figure is the mother Amanda; for she is instrumental in bringing her two children to such a desperate situation. She has consistently indulged in illusions and failed completely to meet life directly; and her bitter disappointments have left her impotent, as both adult and mother. Amanda's response to life generates devastating consequences for her children, crippling them psychologically and seriously inhibiting their own quests for maturity and self-realization.

From the opening scene of the play she constantly reminds everyone that she belongs to an earlier time on her family's plantation in Mississippi. As she exclaims to Tom and Laura: "One Sunday afternoon in Blue Mountain—your mother received—*seventeen!*—gentlemen callers! Why, sometimes there weren't chairs enough to accommodate them all. We had to send the nigger over to bring in folding chairs from the parish house." These gentlemen callers were, as she never tires of saying, "some of the most prominent young planters of the Mississippi Delta—planters and sons of planters." A woman was secure in this past time, Amanda thinks, for it was an age of chivalry and elegance. It was a time characterized by what she calls "the art of conversation" and by young ladies "possessed of a pretty face and a graceful figure" and also "a nimble wit and a tongue to meet all occasions" (I, 148). All too sadly, however, it is a time now irrevocably lost. Later in the play she tells Jim O'Connor, the gentleman caller of the present: "Well, in the South we had so many servants. Gone, gone, gone. All vestige of gracious living! Gone completely! I wasn't prepared for what the future brought me" (I, 204). Her admission that she "wasn't prepared for what the future brought me" is, of course, an explanation of her present need to live in the past by means of fantasizing: she deeply believes that she belongs to this earlier age of aristocratic life, not to the grinding daily routine of her St. Louis tenement.

Amanda Wingfield's past not only animates but also sustains her in the present, becoming in effect her point of reference for everything connected with goodness, truth, and reality. She is simply unable to break out of the framework of her dreamy recollections and to achieve any degree of perspective on them as real or imagined elements. She makes invidious comparisons between her former life and her current situation, and she emphatically rejects the present in favor of the past. Her instability is frighteningly apparent in her inability to sustain a relationship between her almost lucid moments of realism and her constant fantasizing. She vacillates from urging Laura and Tom, on the one hand, to prepare for the gentleman callers she believes are about to arrive to warning Laura, on the other, that she must get training for a business or a professional career. Amanda warns that she has seen "such pitiful cases in the South—barely tolerated spinsters living upon the grudging patronage of sister's husband or brother's wife!—stuck away in some little mousetrap of a room—encouraged by one in-law to visit another —little birdlike women without any nest—eating the crust of humility all their life!" (I, 156). These instances of grim realism are unfortunately rare with Amanda; she usually persists in fantasizing about the past and projecting its remembered images upon her present circumstances.

On the all-important evening when a gentleman caller finally appears, Amanda indulges in the consummate fantasy. Entering the room wearing "a girlish frock of yellowed voile with a blue silk sash," she proudly announces: "This is the dress in which I led the cotillion. Won the cakewalk twice at Sunset Hill, wore one Spring to the Governor's Ball in Jackson!" (I, 193). The triumph of the past is seemingly now complete, for Amanda has regressed in her fantasizing to the years of her youthful innocence as a "southern belle."

The past replaces the present; illusion overcomes reality, yet cannot reverse events. In the following scenes Jim O'Connor, the gentleman caller, is only, as Williams himself warns, "a nice, ordinary, young man" who works with Tom at the warehouse. As Laura's former high school idol, moreover, he occasions her final withdrawal from reality. When he confesses he is soon to marry a young girl he has courted for some time, all illusions are shattered. The play ends with Tom determined to leave home and go to sea, with Laura completely crushed and "huddled on the sofa," and with Amanda trying to comfort her. Williams seems to suggest in his closing stage directions that Amanda gains a degree of "dignity and tragic beauty" by her act of comforting Laura; but audiences may find it difficult to accept this assessment. It is perfectly in character for Amanda to assume a role that is only another of the bad games she constantly plays. Regardless of the individual interpretation of the ending, the play clearly shows the destructive, tragic consequences of Amanda's fantasizing, the results of which are only too apparent in the lives of Tom and Laura.

The outcome of events in *The Glass Menagerie* dramatizes the tragedy of indulging in the kinds of behavior and thinking that negate the possibilities of living fully and honestly in the present.

Laura is no doubt the individual who shows the deepest personal ravages of these cruel scenes, but Amanda is still the best illustration of how such a mental condition works its corrosive destruction. Not only does she deeply and permanently injure her children but she herself is a victim of an illusory way of life—that generated by her beloved plantation South. The very nature of this civilization and her relationship to it have created in her habits and attitudes which encourage fantasies and illusions. To understand Amanda and the South, we must explore precisely what her southern background means and how its environs have fostered in her such romantic notions and wistful ideas.

The South that we encounter in *The Glass Menagerie* through Amanda's recollections is actually a pseudo-history of the region and thus a kind of myth. It is, however, a particular myth that is highly significant for Williams and for his men and women, since it functions as a mediating image by means of which his dramatic characters understand and measure their lives and current situations. Certain major characters in all of Williams' works are trapped within a mode of thinking oriented to the past, to a psychological impulse to withdraw into a fabricated "lost" time. The present exists for these men and women only to the degree that it can be verified by constant references to the past. And the most important of his representations of the past is that of the American South, with its special commitment to a ruined former time and to a haunting awareness of a paradise now lost. In those works which develop themes and characters out of the South, beginning with *The Glass Menagerie*, Williams employs the South of history and myth as an image that mediates between what is and what might be, and thus between life caught as human expectation, desire, anxiety, and life actually realized as human creativity and individual fulfilment. Whether in memory or in fantasy, it animates and informs the consciousness of his dramatic characters, drawing them back ceaselessly into themselves and finally into some sense they have of their relationship to the past.

Elsewhere (see bibliography) I have argued that in the popular imagination both the ante- and the post-bellum South are aspects of the American dream of the creation of a new world and the emergence of a new man who will in time bring forth a new Golden

Age. The relationship between the American dream and the South, if crucial, is not actually difficult to establish and trace. According to the widely accepted view of southern history, the Old South is believed to have become, soon after settlement in the sixteenth century, a cultural region dominated by manorial plantations graced with beautiful ladies and guided by elegant gentlemen of noble birth and heraldic virtues. Despite the fact that the educated and better informed have always understood the fundamental inaccuracy and romantic idealization of this view, the illusion that the area was a land of nobility and courtly manners persists, largely untarnished by events and time. It is yet argued, in fact, that the South which fought the Civil War was, as W. J. Cash said thirty-odd years ago in *The Mind of the South*, "home of a genuine and fully realized aristocracy, coextensive and identical with the ruling class, the planters" (p. 4). The second view, and a corollary of the first, is that the Civil War and the thirty years following saw the destruction of civilization in the Old South, with the result that except for scattered and isolated remnants the entire structure, with its splendid men and women and its cultivated way of life, disappeared, only to be replaced by a new order of life derived from the powerful commercial and industrial interests then working to transform all of America into a modern technological nation. The Old South remains only in memory; and there it endures today, to serve in its principal features as the idealized model for worthwhile imitation and future approximation.

This account of southern history is hardly credible; it is nevertheless a very important account of the region, embodying a view of the past commonly regarded as essentially correct and true. Actually the Old South of the popular mind is best regarded as myth—but a myth vital and important in grasping the spirit of this geographical region and in seeing its relationship to its own history and to the rest of the United States. As myth this account of the South has exactly the function which Mircea Eliade in *Myth and Reality* (p. 5) explains as "sacred history"; namely, the transformation of the origins and development of the region—from its settlement and colonization to its deep frustrations over Negro slavery and complete defeat in war—into a rendition of its history that is mythic in form and intention. In barest outline, the Old South emerges as an almost idyllic agricultural society of genteel people and an aristocratic way of life, exemplary in its pattern and content. A visionary moment of the American dream occurred and passed; now its history is transformed into the story of a fallen order, a ruined time of nobility and heroic achievements that was vanquished and irrevocably lost. In this way the actual facts of the Old South have been translated by myth into a schemata of the birth, the flowering, and the passing of what others in an earlier era might well have called a "Golden Age."

The significance of the Old South understood as myth is considerable and far reaching in implications. It is above all a kind of pseudo-history accepted as genuine history, and thus as a view of the past by which many people—foreigners as well as Americans—orient themselves in their attempts to comprehend and relate to the American experience. Reliable, accurate history is one thing and myth quite another. History provides the living context to which man turns, to discover not only himself but also his world. There always exists a vital way in which man himself and his emerging life are created by the fact of his being in and of history. At this junction of man and history in their mutually creative union the dynamics of historical consciousness become important. Indeed, for the individual's own continuity, and for his own deep need to experience himself defined within some grasp of origins and the spirit of his own time, he must possess a reliable historical consciousness. It becomes not merely a necessary condition of his full existence in time but also something which takes on the power of a faculty by which he is able to come into possession of his own life and thus to seize, if he can, his possibilities in relationship to himself and his environment.

To find oneself with a largely inaccurate and faulty historical consciousness is to be condemned to a marginal, inauthentic existence. Such an individual is all too likely to be delivered over to those basic impulses we associate with man's bestial life. He is also subjected without aid or relief to those doubts and fears which rise from shadowy suppositions and ancient superstitions. The late German philosopher Karl Jaspers in *The Origin and Goal of History* speaks to this point with great persuasion: "If no ground is firm enough to stand on—if there is no echo for authentic selfhood—if there is no more respect because masks and wrappings do not command respect, but only make possible fetishistic deification—if men do not bring me to an upsurge through the hidden demand of their selfhood speaking out of their existence—then the troubled mind grows into the despair that was prophetically lived through by Kierkegaard and Nietzsche and that attained its most lurid expression in their interpretations of the epoch" (p. 99). A properly functioning historical consciousness grounds one in the present, in real-life activities and situations, and thus in a definite time and place. It "authenticates" man's existence, as if by means of what Jaspers calls an echo (*Widerhall*), by generating an awareness in him of who he is and what and where he is. Without a reasonably accurate historical consciousness, one is confused and bewildered; a faulty, distorted view of history frequently leads one into tragic illusions and even into utter personal darkness (see Jaspers, pp. 231–33).

The relationship between actual history and the way an individual looks at history are important in the successful rise of the myth of the Old South. By the middle of the nineteenth century the southern dream of empire had come painfully to grief. And by the ending decades of the nineteenth century the Southerner began to withdraw into an insular view of his region and its heritage. The still unrealized demands of the Negroes for justice and some measure of human equality, as well as the mounting tensions caused by the rapid industrialization and urbanization of the Old Confederacy, contributed significantly to the impulse to retreat into the legacy of the southern past. Now, however, the order and achievements of that earlier time are fully translated into the myth of the Old South. This tendency is only another instance of projecting on the recent past what are actually wish-fantasies of the present—here, a yearning for recovery of a lost time now transformed by means of a pseudo-myth into a marvelous and heroic era associated with the idea of a Golden Age. As a kind of history the myth will serve as deeply revered consolation and refuge for the white Southerner as he struggles with the actual heavy burdens of his daily situation and as he lives with the sharp consciousness of his defeated, ruined dreams.

The image of the South contained in *The Glass Menagerie*, as indeed in all of Williams' southern plays, is neither accurate history nor proper myth. What we are given in both cases is a falsification of history and a distortion of myth. That is, the South portrayed in Williams' works is an instance of how the popular imagination rewrites history and counterfeits myth, doing so largely out of a mentality that is incapable of handling the actual situations of life and thus of working through difficulties to establish a creative relationship between the past and the present. According to Nancy Tischler (pp. 1–3), Williams himself apparently accepts this mythopoeic reading of southern history. Certainly the image of the South he employs brilliantly serves his dramatic purposes. Unable to confront and accept their present lives, his characters are in desperate flight from time and actual history—literally, from a defeated present and thus from their fears of what they have become. None takes responsibility for his or her acts, and none is able to achieve an authentic, creative life. Trapped in time past or time future, each falls victim to illusions, illnesses, fantasies, violence—or, worse—to definite kinds of insanity. Such then are the results of repression and attempts to avoid contemporary situations.

The best dramatization of what a false historical consciousness means to an individual is Williams' portrayal of Amanda Wingfield in *The Glass Menagerie*. The view she holds of her own origins and early life in the South—or, specifically, that wistful remnant of the Old South surviving in recollections of her home at Blue Mountain, Mississippi—is so distorted by illusions and fantasizing that her integrity and character have been thoroughly undermined. The prototype of all of Williams' southern women, Amanda is directly responsible for the terrible and permanent alienation of Laura and Tom. Because she herself has withdrawn from reality, preferring rather dreams of a lost time in the South, Amanda has handed her children over to a similar, if not a worse, psychology and grim fate. *The Glass Menagerie*, in effect, gives us Williams' poignant dramatization of the dreadful human waste of illusions. The major characters in this play are so warped and their lives so distorted and perverted by fantasies that each is left with only broken fragments of what might have been.

Seen in its larger implications, the image of the South, whether approached as history or as myth, constitutes the ultimate landscape of the dislocated mind for Williams' characters. It is not merely the vital context in which his men and women exist; it is for them a final possible "environment"—the extreme of their psychological fantasies—for it must somehow provide them with the means to establish values and to measure the possibilities of life. We are hardly surprised when bitter frustrations and violence result from their efforts.

The Glass Menagerie:
"It's no tragedy, Freckles."

THOMAS E. SCHEYE

A T THE OPENING of *The Glass Menagerie,* Tom comes out of the shadows of the Wingfield apartment, the stage magician promising to explain the tricks in his pocket. But Tom is a creature of the shadows who never really admits what he has up his sleeve. He says "the play is memory"; it is also forgetting. In another version of *The Glass Menagerie,* the story called "Portrait of a Girl in Glass," the narrator is more honest about what he re- members: "In five years' time I had nearly forgotten home. I had to forget, I couldn't carry it with me" (*One Arm,* p. 112). That is what Tom would say too, except that he has been unable to shake his memories of home because his sister will not be forgotten: "Oh Laura, Laura, I tried to leave you behind me, but I am more faithful than I intended to be!" (I, 237).

In this "memory play" Tom remembers in order to forget. The contradiction in terms can be explained by the double game Tom is playing in the theater as "the narrator of the play, and also a char- acter in it." He is inside the illusion that he calls "truth in the pleasant disguise of illusion," and he is on the outside, "an emissary from the world of reality" (pp. 144–45). In his first appearance, already dressed as a merchant sailor, Tom seems safely outside. But he is still haunted by the memory of his sister, still searching for anything that can relieve his feelings of guilt, "anything that can blow your candles out!" (p. 237). The intention of *The Glass Menagerie* is to leave Laura in the past, in the shadows on the other side of the scrim, to plunge her "into everlasting darkness." The shadows fall across the stage after Tom uses the money for the light bill to pay his dues to the merchant marine; and at the end when he directs Laura to blow out the candles, the darkness is complete. Tom has to re-enter the past a final time, to make a play out of his memory, in order to leave memory behind. Once Laura, as a character in the play, can be brought to forgive and forget Tom's running away, he can make good his escape.

From the first moment he enters the play, Tom is trying to escape. He no sooner comes to the table than he pushes away because Amanda is carping at his table manners, and he plays most of the scene while standing at the portieres. Like the transparent scrim, the portieres curtain off an inner stage; they are another dividing line between illusion and reality or one kind of truth and another. According to Williams' stage directions, Amanda addresses Tom as if he were still at the table, and Tom answers her. Otherwise, "he plays this scene as though reading from a script" (p. 148), motioning once for music and then for a spotlight on Amanda. Tom is divided between two roles: the actor inside the illusion and the narrator or playwright on the outside. From the start he is trying to keep his distance. And his direction is clear: he is on the way out.

Scene three, which opens with Tom's soliloquy on the fire escape, closes with his making his move to escape. This time it is not Tom's table manners that provoke the quarrel with his mother, but his writing, Amanda's "interruption of Tom's creative labor" (p. 162). There is a contradiction between what Tom is doing and what he dreams of doing, between the day job which ties him to the apartment and the nightly creative labor which demands his freedom. "I'm leading a double-life," he tells his mother, "a simple, honest warehouse worker by day, by night a dynamic *czar* of the *underworld*" (p. 164). The foolishness here hardly disguises the terms of the conflict; it is the same conflict as between his two roles in the play. Either Tom stays inside, working for the Continental Shoemakers to pay the rent on the apartment, or he runs away to the merchant marines, gets free to write his play. And that course is threatening to the Wingfields.

After threatening to explode all their illusions Tom charges for the door. When he is caught up in his coat and throws it off, striking the shelf where the glass collection is, "there is a tinkle of shattering glass. Laura cries out as if wounded" (p. 164). Tom is drawn back into the room, into the world of the glass menagerie, in an attempt to comfort her. The symbolism, which is obvious without being a nuisance, states the predicament: Tom cannot escape until he finds the way to leave without shattering Laura's fragile self.

That is a trick he learns from the stage. At the movies' stage show the headliner was Malvolio the Magician—Tom came out of the audience to help him—and the magician proves to be his savior. Malvolio can turn water into wine, and triples the miracle of the wedding feast by turning the wine into beer and the beer to whiskey. "But the wonderfullest trick of all was the coffin trick. We nailed him into a coffin and he got out of the coffin without removing one nail. . . . There is a trick that would come in handy for me —get me out of this two-by-four situation!" (p. 167). In *The Glass Menagerie* the sorcerer's apprentice becomes the stage magician. He brings home a conjuring scarf which he gives Laura as a "souvenir," something to remember him by. And it is a conjuring trick— turning Jim O'Connor into a gentleman caller—that will solve Tom's predicament.

Tom conjures up Jim O'Connor as his surrogate after Amanda agrees that once "there's somebody to take your place" (p. 175), he is free to go. Turning Jim O'Connor into the gentleman caller turns the trick because he can do what Tom could never do by himself: get out of the two-by-four situation without removing one nail. Jim deserts Laura and she is not shattered by it; in fact she is able to say, "It's no tragedy" (p. 226).

Tom offers no reason why the incident with the gentleman caller should be his cue to leave, but Jim's identification with Tom provides a clue. Like Tom, Jim leads a double life, by day and night. Or, as he puts it more prosaically, "I have a couple of time-clocks to punch. . . . One at morning, another one at night" (p. 233). In the world of the play, he is as much a contradiction as Tom, both inside and outside the illusion. Tom captures the contradiction when he describes the gentleman caller in the opening monologue as "the most realistic character in the play" and also as a symbol. He is Tom's friend at the warehouse and the playwright's personal symbol. Tom calls him "an emissary from a world of reality that we were somehow set apart from" (p. 145). But it is precisely from that world that Tom returns in scene six, to usher on the gentleman caller. The acting edition of *The Glass Menagerie* specifies that Tom is dressed as a merchant sailor for the monologue in scene six as he is at the opening and close of the play.

The gentleman caller is "the long delayed but always expected something that we live for" (p. 145). All the Wingfields are living for the day he comes to call. "Haven't you ever liked some boy?" (p. 156) Amanda asks; Laura has never stopped loving Jim. Williams describes Laura's scene with the gentleman caller as "the climax of her secret life" (p. 210). He is what Amanda has wished for on the "little silver slipper of a moon" (p. 180) rising over Garfinkel's delicatessen and what Tom has wished for too.

Jim O'Connor is "A nice, ordinary young man" (p. 129) who is transformed, as if by magic, into the romantic figure of a gentleman caller. Tom refers to this image as an "archetype of the universal unconscious," "this spectre, this hope"; he is drawn not from life but from the "serialized sublimations of ladies of letters" (p. 159) in the magazines Amanda sells over the phone. The sort of gentleman caller Amanda herself had known once has died out or disappeared; in the violence and confusion of the thirties, the world "lit by lightning" instead of candles, he no longer exists except in books—or plays.

Jim O'Connor seems the unlikeliest choice to fill the role. He is a great believer in the importance of the "right connections," the power of positive thinking, and the virtues of a night school course in public speaking. He is confident that "social poise" allows anyone to hold his own on any social level; he even tries to sell Laura on his own naive faith in "the cycle democracy is built on" (p. 222). All men are created equal, everyone is just like everyone else, only better: "Why, man alive, Laura! Just look about you a little. What do you see? A world full of common people! All of 'em born and all of 'em going to die! Which of them has one-tenth of your good points! Or mine! Or anyone else's as far as that goes—gosh!" (p. 221). But as he becomes aware Laura is truly different, he turns into something surprisingly different too. Under the spell of Amanda and her jonquils and romantic candlelight and the strains of "La Golondrina" he emerges as an emissary not from the world of reality but from Blue Mountain. When he observes that Laura's principal trouble is "a lack of confidence in yourself as a person" and tries to convince her to "think of yourself as *superior* in some way" (p. 221), he is using the words he has learned will make friends and influence people. When he asks Laura to dance, he is fumbling for the accents of the spectral gentleman caller: "Or is your program filled up? Let me have a look at it. . . . Why, every dance is taken! I'll just have to scratch some out. . . . Ahhh, a waltz!" (p. 224). And to the music from the Paradise Dance Hall he waltzes her uneasily around the room.

It is during their dance that the unicorn is knocked to the floor, the second time in the play that something from the glass menagerie is broken. The first time, Laura cried out as if she herself were wounded; now she can say, "It doesn't matter" (p. 226). All the figurines are part of Laura's own little world, but the unicorn is different, as Laura is different. It is, she says, her favorite of the glass menagerie; given the playwright's "weakness for symbols," the unicorn can be identified with Laura. And yet she can say, "It's no tragedy, Freckles" (p. 226), calling Jim by a special name.

In "Portrait of a Girl in Glass," Freckles is a character in a book that Laura reads over and over, "actually lived with." When Jim comes to dinner Laura mentions his freckles, and Jim says Freckles is his nickname. "She looked toward me," the narrator says, "as if for the confirmation of some too wonderful hope. . . . Yes, he had undoubtedly assumed the identity—for all practical purposes—of the one-armed orphan youth who lived in the Limberlost, that tall and misty region to which she retreated whenever the walls of Apartment F became too close to endure" (p. 109). But Jim's identification with the gentleman caller, and Laura's with the unicorn, are broken after the horn is broken.

Losing the horn, Laura thinks, is a "blessing in disguise" because it makes the unicorn less freakish, more like the other horses. "I'll just imagine he had an operation" (p. 226), she says. The line takes on nightmare proportions if the breaking of the horn is taken to symbolize Williams' own sister Rose's prefrontal lobotomy. But Rose's fate is not Laura's. By his stumblejohn gallantry Jim teaches Laura to have some confidence in herself, shows her that she is different from other people and should stay that way—even if it means never moving from the shelf, being left alone. It is the *gentleman* caller who speaks: "The different people are not like other people, but being different is nothing to be ashamed of. Because other people are not such wonderful people. They're one hundred times one thousand. You're one times one! They walk all over the earth. You just stay here. They're common as—weeds, but—you—well, you're— *Blue Roses!*" (p. 227).

Jim makes the final romantic gesture when he sweeps her up in his arms to kiss her. And having kissed her he takes leave— but not before she presses the broken unicorn on him as "A—souvenir" (p. 231). Since it is "just like all the other horses" now, it belongs in the world of reality where Jim lives; Laura does not. The unicorn is a painful reminder of what might have been but had better not, something for him to remember and for her to forget: the dream of ever liking some boy or ever having a gentleman caller.

Jim O'Connor has played the role in which he was cast, and played it well by playing it badly. His impersonation of a gentleman caller is so clumsy that Laura can see the apparition for what it is. And perhaps she sees that if her dream did come true, come to life, he might look like Jim O'Connor, he would not be made of glass and he could crush her fragile existence as he had broken the unicorn. And so she can say, "It's no tragedy, Freckles."

Tom's leaving her is no tragedy either; at least Tom can convince himself of that now. In his last speech, he describes his life from the day the gentleman called to this moment as a failed attempt to put some distance between past and present, Laura and himself. He has always been pursued by guilt, the memory of his sister; it is what he tries to forget: "I reach for a cigarette, I cross the street, I run into the movies or a bar, I buy a drink, I speak to the nearest stranger —anything that can blow your candles out!" (p. 237). During the monologue, with the scrim being lowered, the play comes back on itself; Tom is left safely outside. On stage he has cast his memory in the form of a play, and the play succeeds where everything else has failed. In the final scene, Laura stops her pursuit and takes her place in the past. A conjuring trick, the gentleman caller, has shown Laura what Tom could never tell her: that her life is on the other side of the scrim which divides illusion and reality, in the dark.

Though Tom has tried every other trick to blow the candles out, it is only Laura who can do that for him and only as a character in the play that she will. The final line of *The Glass Menagerie* is a stage direction.

"Sentiment and humor in equal measure": Comic Forms in *The Rose Tattoo*

PHILIP C. KOLIN

WHEN *The Rose Tattoo* made its Broadway appearance on 3 February 1951, Tennessee Williams did not have a reputation as a comic writer. Quite to the contrary, his two hits, *The Glass Menagerie* and *A Streetcar Named Desire*, had, according to *Life*, established him as a dramatist who "could write only about doom-ridden damsels." For his comic efforts in *The Rose Tattoo*, Williams was promptly whipped. As the reviewer in *Newsweek* put it, "there is an uneasy feeling that his new play is sometimes funny without quite intending to be." Williams' humor was labeled in the basest terms. The more serious events in act one "descend into cheap farce which must be seen to be believed," wrote Margaret Marshall in *The Nation*. The reviewer for *Time*, contemptuous of the rapid changes of mood, renamed the play Banana Truck Named Desire. F. W. Dupee ("Literature on Broadway," *The Partisan Review*, May 1951, p. 334) quickly summarized the critical opinion of Serafina and much else in the play when he said it was "farced-up."

In the 1966 revival of *The Rose Tattoo*, Williams' comedy had evidently changed for reviewers—it had become appropriately grotesque. If they could not assent to it as it was, they could at least praise the absurdist elements, in vogue in avant-garde theater both here and abroad. Williams' play had been acceptably reclassified through making virtues of its earlier vices. Absurdity by any other

214

name is just as meet for neurotically-conditioned audiences. Henry Hewes offered an explanation for the approval: "Now it very probably was not Mr. Williams's intention to write *The Rose Tattoo* as a grotesque comedy, but that is what this new presentation seems, and that is why it appears not in the least bit dated" (*Saturday Review*, November 1966). Jan Kott, who has found Shakespeare so relevant to our "absurd" world, would readily have approved of the change. Yet, regardless of the revival, and perhaps because of it, critics, with a few exceptions, have dismissed *The Rose Tattoo* as one of Williams' lesser accomplishments, better left on the rose heap. Ruby Cohn has given the play its death-knell: "He probably intended *The Rose Tattoo* to be something of a saturnalia, a joyous celebration of sex, but (when we are not simply bored) we tend to laugh *at* rather than *with* the celebrants" (p. 110). To his credit, though, the play was and is still good box office.

Why in 1950–51 did Williams write a work which seemed in so many ways to differ from his previous, and successful, plays? Biography provides a few clues. Williams had just returned from a sojourn in Italy, the land of warm sunshine and fiery passions, and said, "I have never felt more hopeful about human nature as a result of being exposed to the Italians" (quoted in *Saturday Review*, March 1951). While in Sicily Williams must have soaked up enough local culture to write knowledgeably about the folklore, language, and characters of the region and create the Dionysian elements he claims to have captured in the play (*Vogue*, March 1951). Birds, children, goats, sky, fruit, earth, sun, and air—all are found in *The Rose Tattoo*.

Biography aside, Williams' neglected yet strong flair for the comic is found not only in *The Rose Tattoo* but elsewhere in his work. In a provocative article ("The Comic Tennessee Williams"), Charles Brooks calls Williams "an essentially comic playwright" whose "greatest power and appeal derive from a comic vision which he seems unwilling to trust fully" (p. 275). In his review Hewes had said that comedy—even the more grotesque variety—could "open up a green territory in which Tennessee Williams might profitably exercise his talent." Classifying Williams' plays by genres—tragedies or comedies—is gross oversimplification. Comedy is as difficult to define as tragedy. Socrates long ago said (in *The Symposium*) they were similar, often reaching the same ends; and Aristotle unfortunately never discussed that tragedy which, like a comedy, has a happy ending. *The Rose Tattoo* is easier to type than other Williams' plays because of both its virtues and its faults. It successfully dramatizes the fulfilment of hope and love. The play is an experiment in comedy, a potpourri of comedic forms, sometimes blended and sometimes juxtaposed. Comic forms range from slapstick humor, including farce, music hall antics, and vaudeville to folk, satiric, and romantic comedy, and, occasionally, tragicomedy. Even sadness is assimilated into the comic vision.

The Rose Tattoo has characteristics of low comedy or farce. But within this broad category are elements of vaudeville, Chaplinesque humor, and vestiges of the commedia dell'arte. Though dissatisfied reviewers and critics have lampooned Williams for his cheap and unsophisticated displays, jests and clowning are part of his stagecraft from his early works to his middle ones (*Camino Real*) to his late ones (*Gnädiges Fräulein*). Williams is a shrewd man of the theater, keenly aware that laughs as well as tears sell tickets. He incorporates many comic gags, verbal and physical, to entertain and cajole his audience, and, at times, make them feel superior to his characters.

One of Williams' greatest achievements as a comic dramatist is his use of dialogue, though Ruby Cohn observes: "Larded with Italian phrases and locutions, the English is surprisingly grammatical, the vocabulary extensive, and the emotions self-consciously expressed" (p. 111). Regardless of Serafina's regular syntax, the play is fastmoving, speeded along by a series of one-liners that are the classic tool of the comedian's art. These are hurled at and by Serafina, some of them as cutting as the knife she will use on Estelle, others as sharp as a courtier's rapier.

These one-liners are well-suited to the Italian temperament. Angered by Serafina's delay in sewing their daughters' graduation dresses, local mothers pounce on her. One of them exclaims: "Listen, I pay in advance five dollars and get no dress. Now what she wear, my daughter, to graduate in? A couple of towels and a rose in her hair?" (II, 295). She thus makes sport of both the Delle Rose name (and emblem) and Serafina's impoverishing profession. When Rosa stands naked in the window, her clothes hidden by her suspicious mother, Williams demonstrates his agility with an Italian pun when a neighbor says: "In nominis padri et figlio et spiritus sancti. Aaahh!"

(p. 294). *Figlio*, the child of naked vulnerability, such as Rosa is judged to be, replaces the *filio* of the invocation. Later, Rosa catches her mother in an embarrassing lie when Serafina explains Alvaro's presence by saying he was chased by the police. Rosa shrewdly inquires: "They chased him into your bedroom?" (p. 410). And the disarray in which Serafina finds herself after her boisterous fight with Father De Leo gives rise to even more humor because of the sham politeness with which the salesman addresses her: "I sell directly to merchants but when I stopped over there to have my car serviced, I seen you taking the air on the steps and I thought I would just drop over . . ." (p. 348).

Serafina's verbal assaults match her muscular defenses. At the start of the play, Serafina can counter the potion-selling Assunta's attempts to bring aphrodisiacs when they are not wanted by observing that it is not the sound of Venus that the old woman hears: "Naw, them ain't the star-noises. They're termites, eating the house up" (p. 275). To those who say she is improperly, scantily dressed, Serafina proclaims: "I'm dressed okay; I'm not naked!" (p. 301). Her invectives are charged by her shrewish wit. High school for her is as "high as that horse's dirt out there in the street!" (pp. 300–301). Equally facile retorts face Jack Hunter, as Serafina, punning on his name, asks: "What are you hunting?—Jack?" (p. 326). But Serafina reveals her own narrow limits and calls down laughter on her head when she utters the understatement of the play: "But we are Sicilians, and we are not coldblooded" (p. 329). Serafina's claim to recognize religious denominations in body types is of course ridiculous. Yet she bounces back into control when she plays a game with Alvaro. When he tells her of his previous amorous mishap because he gave the girl a fake diamond (a zircon), Serafina responds that she too would have slammed the door in his face. Williams sees the folly of his characters' lives and captures it in their dialogue as well.

With Alvaro, Williams invents another comic portrait in prose. Alvaro's description of his family and their petty vices sounds almost as if it came from Eudora Welty's pen: "One old maid sister, one feeble-minded grandmother, one lush of a pop that's not worth the powder it takes to blow him to hell.—They got the parchesi habit. They play the game of parchesi, morning, night, noon. Passing a bucket of beer around the table . . ." (p. 364). Alvaro's wry detachment from his inherited handicaps fills out the picture of his family. He asks Serafina what in his heritage as the grandson of a village idiot he has to be thankful about: "What have I got to respect? The rock my grandmother slips on?" (p. 366). Williams is at his best in these comic vignettes, as the comments exchanged between Bessie and Flora well illustrate. The two prigs, eager for some sexual titillation, discuss one such prank that may promise pleasure: "I heard, I heard that the Legionnaires caught a girl on Canal Street! They tore the clothes off her and sent her home in a taxi!" (p. 370). Of course they disavow any interest in this nonsense, but they obviously enjoy it.

The Rose Tattoo also shows a mastery of other standard comic conventions, including physical deformities. Serafina's exaggerated ego and passion match the rotundity of her shape. Hers is a big, often stricken body, described as a "heavy, sagging bulk" (p. 297). Her hips have exceeded their girlish limits, suggesting a comparison to a "parading matador" (p. 301). Moving to the other side of the ring, Williams labels her a bull (p. 338). She is like a "strange beast in a cage" (p. 337). All these remarks suggest that Serafina is like an animal in heat, her plump body always charging her enemies or her lover. Her struggles with her girdle call attention to the incompatibility of her form and the restraint she seeks to impose on it. In these pantomimes, Serafina is both laughable buffoon and frustrated lover. The girdle represents an impediment to her passions; and the more she struggles, the funnier are her attempts. Nor has Williams spared other parts of her anatomy. Her hair is wild, greasy, always out of control like Serafina herself. No make-up, it seems, will help. Rosa's "cosmetic enterprise" (p. 321) does not improve her mother; it leaves her only with a "dazed look." Serafina's deprecatory gestures, signs of her ethnic background and feverish anger, also make her look ridiculous.

Her new lover, Alvaro, and his body are also exploited for comedy. This clown seems like an appropriate visitor to the carnival booth (p. 269) that is Serafina's house. He is as awkward as Serafina is accusatory. His ears stick out, he is short, and he hitches his shoulders —traits that certainly call attention to his comic torso. Williams refers to him as one of the "glossy young bulls" (p. 348) as if to emphasize his sexual powers. Alvaro is doubtless the bull in the dress shop. He is so clumsy that he drops everything from ice cubes to condoms. His trance after his first night with Serafina has "the pantomimic lightness, almost fantasy, of an early Chaplin comedy" (p. 405). Like the silent movie star, Alvaro finds mischief where he least expects it. He collides with Serafina's furniture and, finally, her daughter. Thinking he is raping her daughter, Serafina lunges at him, beating him all the way out of the house. Alvaro scurries around the house with "his shirttails out" (p. 408) much as Chaplin tries to evade the comic Furies hounding him.

The fight and the ensuing chase—the two most common and oldest comic tricks—fill up much of the action in *The Rose Tattoo*. Serafina tells Alvaro that "I had two fights on the street" (p. 353), but she underestimates the number of her quarrels. She battles with her daughter, jerking her away from the window; she does much the same with her clownish customers, except she chases them out of the house with a broom (p. 314). She is forever fighting with the Strega whom she orders "Getta hell out of my yard!" (p. 341). Not even the clergy is exempt; with Father De Leo Serafina is "on the point of attacking him bodily" (p. 346) when he is rescued by her neighbors. On stage these incidents elicit laughter. Yet they also point to the turmoil inside Serafina. She is out of control, as her anger and the shrewishness arousing it demonstrate. One beating, though, which does not fit with the rest is that given Estelle early in the play by Serafina's neighbors. As she comes to see Rosario's body, "The bouquet of roses is snatched from her black-gloved hands and she is flailed with them about the head and shoulders" (p. 291). Though not comic, this incident precipitates and parallels other quarrels. Serafina's revenge lasts so long and is so violent that we automatically seek a cause: The community punishment of Estelle anticipates Serafina's punishment of the community. The difference between the two beatings shows how funny Serafina's struggles have become.

These quarrels often result in chases among objects with people falling down or being torn apart. The slapstick humor is transparent; the angrier characters become, the less successful are their attacks. But when Serafina gets into the act, all discord follows. At first she locks Rosa in the house; then a little later Rosa is locked out of it, having to run around outside. The neighborhood children often flee in panic when Serafina threatens them. In her fury, she pursues her customers, Bessie and Flora, turning over a table. The most obvious flight, however, is the goat chase, a sign of Serafina's passionate dilemma. Next comes Father De Leo, who is hounded by the widow. Then another goat chase. The pattern—chase after chase—characterizes the comic deception befalling Serafina and pinpoints Williams' hilarious if conventional source of comedy. The opportunities for improvisational comedy are unlimited here.

Alvaro's arrival brings more chases and even greater damage. His precursor, the salesman, signals further debasement for Serafina. The new product he offers "explodes in Serafina's face" (p. 349). The scene recalls Punch and Judy antics, but it prefigures the eruptions with Alvaro. While talking to him about vicious rumors, Serafina hurls a glass to the floor. Twice, in a few minutes, she explodes at Alvaro, both times chasing him for his life and crushing anything in her way. First, "she springs up and runs into the parlor. He pursues. The chase is grotesquely violent and comic. A floor lamp is overturned. She seizes the chocolate box and threatens to slam it into his face if he continues toward her" (p. 386). After a few calm moments, Serafina disrupts the peace when she hurls the phone to the floor (p. 392). She even addresses the Blessed Virgin with "explosive gestures" (p. 395). The second time, the termagant flies at Alvaro "like a great bird, tearing and clawing at his stupefied figure" (p. 407) in retaliation for his bumping into Rosa. Alvaro is the butt; even when he walks he "topples over" (p. 406).

But this rampage provides no release for Serafina; nor was it meant to. These chases only increase her frustration and rekindle the fires of her anger. For it is herself Serafina chases most often. She lunges, plunges and trounces all over; but, as Williams deftly points out, "she swiftly and violently whirls about in distraction." In desperation for clothes, she grabs at her dummies, one of which collapses. She tears things apart and threatens death to those who cross her. But she can have no honest release until she breaks the urn holding Rosario's ashes. All the other acts may be gratuitous, there for the laughs pure and simple, but when she "seizes the marble urn and hurls it violently into the furthest corner of the room" (p. 394), she finally can escape from the whirligig of the time past and confront the love Alvaro has to offer. She can break away from the comic captivity of her previous actions; she can stop being "dressed in the rags of a convict" (p. 341). Inserted among the other humorous acts, destruction of the urn may at first seem to be the result of Serafina's rage. But Williams has juxtaposed this act with other slapstick gestures to suggest how it differs from them and how, in effect, it points to the climax of the play. Within Williams' slapstick comedy is more serious business, but an appreciation of the relationship between events, however foolish, reveals the unity.

Among the most obvious but, surprisingly enough, least valued elements in *The Rose Tattoo* is the folk comedy. The passions of Rosa Gonzales, her revengeful father, and the symbolic cock fight of *Summer and Smoke* are examples of Williams' use of folk habits. Natives appear in both *Camino Real* and *The Night of the Iguana*. And insofar as his plantation caste in *Cat on a Hot Tin Roof* or *Sweet Bird of Youth* comprise separate, regional and rural subcultures, Williams reveals some knowledge of folk drama, twentieth-century style. Because of their obvious "foreignness" and importance, the Italians and Sicilians of *The Rose Tattoo* stand out most distinctly in Williams' use of folk materials. Their language, religion, and superstitions give the play its zest and shape its humor. Their music permeates the play, since a folk player appears at all the major breaks. Although living in the American South, Serafina and her neighbors lost not a whit of their native hopes and fears in steerage. They are close to the earth and to the animals and the children bred on it.

The lingo of these southern Europeans—the patois of the peasant —is liberally sprinkled throughout *The Rose Tattoo*, often adding to both the romantic and the humorous depiction of Serafina and her neighbors. Born of "contadini," Serafina becomes a "baronessa" even if her estate is no more than the sewing shop which is also her house. The Sicilian vocabulary makes Serafina's ire even more passionate and her love more earthy. Alvaro is a "cretino," a "buffone," or, even worse, a "maleducato" when he alarms her, but he is her "amore" at the end of the play; and her once intractable daughter is her "carissimo." The small house on Front Street, with the highway before it, is closer to Palermo than to New Orleans.

This language also reflects the many superstitions and taboos that prey so humorously on Serafina's psyche. Her goattending neighbor is always addressed as the Strega, the witch. So foolish is Serafina that she believes this spindly, hairy-legged creature possesses evil powers. She has "malocchio," an evil eye according to Serafina, though to the less impressionable Rosa it is only a cataract. When the Strega touches Rosa, Serafina at once supplies a folk cure—the girl must "wash [her] face with salt water and then throw the salt water away!" (p. 286). The Strega takes her place alongside Williams' other hags, comic and serious. She is part of the tradition which produced the blind woman selling flowers for the dead in A *Streetcar Named Desire* and Leona in *Confessional*; they serve as reminders of impending doom. The Strega, moreover, infrequently serves as the play's narrator, pointing out comically Serafina's excesses—"The Wops are at it again" (p. 296)—while she and her rampaging goat are also grotesque. The "little procession" of her and the goat home really begins in her having let him loose in the first place. The superstitions associated with her must be judged against those of Assunta, the "fattuchiere" with her miraculous aphrodisiacs, and the more prosaic powers of the "imported Sicilian spumanti." The artifacts of this culture—goat, potions, wine—are among the leading stage symbols, however much they are abused through repetition and obviousness. From them Williams tries to create a comic (and folk) atmosphere; they are the legerdemain of his dramatic artifice.

Even the plot of *The Rose Tattoo* reads like a series of folk motifs, many of them documented in the Stith Thompson index. A duped widow who strikes out at all around her because of their mockery of her love finds a solution to her problems with another man who, in many ways, is the muscular though comic reincarnation of her deceased husband. At first, Serafina is attracted to Alvaro because, as she claims, he has "My *husband's body*, with the head of a *clown!*" (p. 354). Alvaro is the lover disguised as a fool, an old motif that Williams adopts for his own purposes by fusing suitor and fool into one role. Alvaro's disguise is laughable to Serafina who at first fails to see the love he brings.

This mysterious attraction is demonstrated through the rose symbolism. The rose appears in folk beliefs as a magical love-producing object. In fact, it is the talisman which often draws a lover to a woman, though Williams uses it to draw the woman to the man.

The sexual bonds between Rosario and Serafina need little comment. But an even more interesting folk motif about roses is associated with Alvaro. Even though Serafina is already aroused by Alvaro, when he has the patronymic emblem of her first husband emblazoned on his chest, she finds Rosario Delle Rose again, or a more faithful though less attractive version of him. In essence, her "rose" has been transformed into a human being, a folk motif which is at the center of Serafina's discovery of self and the audience's demand for comedic harmony. Folklore also associates sexual powers with roses. By eating a rose, according to one superstition, a woman could conceive. Serafina's pregnancy by Rosario and her conception after sleeping with his humorous incarnation, the tattooed Alvaro, recall the motif. As long as Serafina has a rose in her life, she does not need the sexual stimulation promised by Assunta's potion.

Much in *The Rose Tattoo* derives from the conventions of romantic comedy. Williams, who elsewhere is the frustrated romanticist or the rebellious puritan, here successfully gives the upper hand to the forces of love and nature. The fecundity of nature and man, and the desire, voiced by all romantic comedies, to unite every eligible female with every suitable man, frequently appears. Williams' pastoral setting—on the Gulf Coast between the magic city of New Orleans and the port of Mobile—displays a territory of passion and a land of sexual fulfilment. References to vegetation are numerous, and fruitful. The "Author's Production Notes" call for "palm trees," "tall canes with feathery fronds and a fairly thick growth of pampas grass" (p. 269). Rosario hauled bananas for the Romano Brothers; and Alvaro arrives with "a great golden bunch of bananas" (p. 373). The shape of this fruit leads Henry Popkin ("The Plays of Tennessee Williams," p. 59) to see it as a phallic symbol, which seems appropriate for the context. Estelle Hohengarten's last name, which literally means a high garden, likewise suggests the fruitfulness of sex. The young Jack Hunter gives Rosa a bunch of roses for her graduation. And Serafina more than once breaks open a bottle of spumanti, highly suitable for the Bacchic entertainment serving as a preamble to love. Above the fertility of the earth shines Venus, "the female star with an almost emerald luster" (p. 273), and this star appears above Serafina's porch near the end of the play "still undimmed" (p. 405).

The surge toward fertility—and reproduction—is even stronger among the characters for whom this vegetation serves as a background. The play begins and ends with Serafina pregnant, once by her unfaithful husband and once by her foolish paramour, Alvaro. Serafina's rejection of the creative rhythms of life brings only reminders of how fruitful she should be. Father De Leo cautions her: "You are still a young woman. Eligible for—loving and—bearing again!" (p. 341). Later in the play, Alvaro tells her, in his awkward proposal, that his old maid sister wants nephews and nieces (p. 387). Serafina can be happy only when she is loved and loving— whether it is every night with Rosario or not quite so often with Alvaro. Serafina's comic problem rests in acknowledging and triumphing over obstacles to love. She must ignore Estelle's illicit affairs and forgive Alvaro's fumbling attempts to use contraceptives.

If the specific pastoral location lends itself to romantic comedy, so too does the particular time of the action. It is June, near midsummer, the time of love, passion, fulfilment, weddings. It is a highly festive day on the calendar. Even the clowns Bessie and Flora are eager to see the Veterans Parade in New Orleans. But it is also a highly symbolic day—Rosa's graduation day and Serafina's as well. This occasion suggests Rosa's development, her commencement of sexual maturity. As Rosa tells Jack, "Just think. A week ago Friday— I didn't know boys existed!" (p. 318). It is her initiation, so to speak, receiving the *Digest of Knowledge* and Jack Hunter's pristine love on the same day. Their trip to Diamond Key (the place name suggesting some kind of engagement) in a sense charts their rite of passage into sexual maturity, soon to be concluded in a New Orleans hotel room. But on this very special day, Williams reminds his audience, they are the quintessence of young love. As Brooks Atkinson said in a *New York Times* review of the original production, their affair "has all the lyric rapture and sincerity of young poetry. As sheer writing, it is one of the finest things Mr. Williams has done."

But as in so many other romantic comedies, the young lovers are frustrated in meeting and marrying. Usually, a blocking figure, some pitiful and laughable parent, stands in their way. This is one dimension of Serafina's role. She is the obstacle to their love as well as a blatant contrast to it. It is hard to agree with Charles Brooks who

sees Serafina as "the healthy one in the play" and Rosa as the "sentimental" embodiment of her mother's faults who "weakens an otherwise fine comedy" (p. 277). If nothing else demonstrated how wrong
this view of Rosa is, Serafina's reactions to graduation day would
certainly be enough. To the embittered widow, the festive day brings
only anxiety and fear. She tries to spoil the holiday at first by locking
her daughter up; the celebration, she thinks, is the public declaration
of all the wrong things the high school did to Rosa. Even when Rosa
is released through the intervention of Miss York, Serafina still cannot participate in the ceremonies. She tries to attend, but she never
does, for she is detained by her customers. And the music she hears
does more to annoy than uplift her. When Rosa returns, elated by
her honors, Serafina tries to fight off the future she brings with her
diploma by saying: "Va bene.—Put it in the drawer with your
father's clothes" (p. 324). Serafina hopes to keep Rosa in the stagnant past with the memory of Rosario. Rosa's youthful innocence
and Rosario's faithfulness are tied together. Serafina does not want
change. As she tells Jack Hunter: "Two weeks ago I was slapping her
hands for scratching mosquito bites. She rode a bicycle to school.
Now all at once—I've got a wild thing in the house" (p. 330). Graduation day has caused all of Rosa's problems and most of Serafina's
trouble.

But Serafina, like so many other foolish parents in comedy, has
problems both more serious and more comic than those she anticipates. She tries to protect Rosa from sexual abuse and dishonesty.
Yet she herself is the victim of one of the oldest and funniest deceptions of romantic comedy. She has been cuckolded by Rosario
and refuses, until shown otherwise, to believe it. In setting up a
shrine to her late and beloved husband, she makes a mockery of her
injunctions to Rosa not to trust a boy. Her religious fanaticism is,
therefore, not without humor. Even her name suggests some comic
duplicity. Not only does it imply her own nocturnally amorous
ability ("sera fina"—"fine nights"), as Ruby Cohn has pointed out
(p. 111), but Williams may have had an actual Saint Seraphina in
mind when he decided to name his heroine. *The Catholic Encyclopedia* states that Saint Seraphina was a virgin who "led a religious
life in her parental home and was an example of piety, charity, mortification, and patience during a long serious illness . . ." (p. 105).

The Saints: A Concise Biographical Dictionary (ed. John Coulson, New York, 1958) says she was associated with white violets, which "were found to be growing on the board on which she had lain" (p. 183). The widow Delle Rose is hardly a young, suffering virgin, and the contrast between her activities and those suggested by her holy namesake emphasize the folly of her devotion. Her wifely piety and the shrine she erects come in for constant comic attacks. Her house is noted more for brawls than prayers. In fact, at one point it even turns into a kind of "casa privata" (p. 385).

But it is her opposition to Rosa and Jack that makes Serafina a foe to love. Only when she relents and sends her daughter off with a blessing does she overcome her own ignorance and accept love herself. Breaking Rosario's urn and honoring Rosa's desire to love Jack indicate the change. She moves from hostile enemy to confidant, from a blocking figure to a woman who can see the world romantically. Serafina graduates by throwing off the bonds of the past, which enshackled her in buffoonery, and accepts the love and promise of the future.

The use of festivity in *The Rose Tattoo* derives from some of the major elements of romantic comedy. These include the so-called "green world" which the lovers inhabit, the opposition of the parent to their love, the easy and comic deception of the parent, the hypocrisy of the parent's advice, and the holiday occasion giving rise to these opposing views. Unlike other comic butts, though, Serafina finally joins the lovers' cause. Williams' tone of satire is replaced by a strong and unmitigated sense that harmony will finally reign.

Much in *The Rose Tattoo* does not quite fit into the categories of vaudeville, farce, or romantic comedy. The serious moments of grief early in the play, the agony Serafina encounters in act two, and the union of Serafina and Alvaro at the end of the play amidst tears and laughter, defy comic label. Shifting tones and modes, many of them branded as Williams' faults, suggest that *The Rose Tattoo* is a tragicomedy, a genre that allows comedy full and varied play, even giving it the last word, while acknowledging the undercurrent of tragic love and pain.

The playwright's inability to write pure comedy throughout the play may explain why *The Rose Tattoo* is a tragicomedy. Williams may have explained his play as a Dionysian celebration, a dream of life's juices flowing through herbs, children, and lovers, but his preface on "The Timeless World of the Play" turns the reader's eye in another direction. There Williams speculates about "plays in the tragic tradition" and discusses his own version of catharsis by which "our hearts are wrung by recognition and pity" (p. 262), a strange introduction for a saturnalian comedy. But perhaps these autobiographical assessments to some extent explain the work. Williams wants us to laugh and suffer with Serafina; she is both the dummy bride and the dummy widow. He wants "sentiment and humor in equal measure" (p. 270), an almost impossible feat in an age grotesquely divorcing the two and a difficult task for a playwright whose comedy usually reflects irredeemable futility. Still, as Henry Hewes recognized when seeing the 1966 revival, "we laugh at the ridiculousness of the events at the same time that we recognize the characters' agonizedly sincere involvement in them." Laughter may provide a better catharsis than either pity or fear.

Coarse, vulgar, foolish love exists alongside more noble kinds. The Strega, Estelle, and the taunting children get billing with Alvaro's shrewd recognition that Serafina laid her "heart in the marble urn with the ashes" (p. 372) and Rosa's advice that "Everybody is nothing until you love them" (p. 319), perhaps the topic sentence of the play. Serafina is likewise the nothing turned to everything, comic scapegoat and sympathetic heroine. Williams debases and enthrones her, often at the same time. She sinks into "comic desolation" (p. 300), and her appearance is at once "comic and shocking" (p. 321). Her former beauty is often mentioned, nowhere more poetically expressed than in Father De Leo's description of her as being "like a lady wearing a—piece of the —weather!" (p. 341).

But his view is challenged by her present appearance; she has become a hobgoblin scaring the children away. Williams seems to transfer some of his former heroines' problems to Serafina. Starnes ("The Grotesque Children of The Rose Tattoo") has concluded that, "In terms of Williams's typical character deployment, Serafina is actually a direct descendant of Laura Wingfield in The Glass Menagerie and of Alma Winemiller in Summer and Smoke" (p. 368). Although Serafina lives in her own world, a victim of her own dreams, the affinity with Williams' earlier female characters is tenuous. Serafina is much more adaptable than, say, Blanche Du-

Bois. Serafina throws off the deception in time to marry Alvaro. But it is too late for Blanche and her Alvaro (Mitch), whom she loses too soon and wants too late. In short, Serafina is a complex, often contradictory figure whose failures and successes in love combine farcical comedy with tragic implications. The rapid changes, especially after Alvaro reveals his rose tattoo in act three, are characteristic of and suitable for a tragicomedy.

Another major feature of tragicomedy is surprise, the unexpected resolution of the tragic dilemma that leads to a happy ending. Poorly used, this deus ex machina, the manipulation of events, can descend to cheap melodrama. But Williams has made some attempts to prepare his audiences, and characters, for the unexpected comedic resolution of events. The numerous references to the Blessed Mother, whom Serafina at first worships, then rebukes, then adores, suggest that these Sicilians feel providence can work out their problems. And Williams cautioned his crew and cast not to scoff at the "religious yearnings" (p. 270) these people feel. Everywhere, Serafina looks for signs. In sympathy with her, the audience should too. It is significant that the play begins and ends with Assunta saying that "It is impossible to tell me anything that I don't believe" (p. 414). The appearance of Alvaro is just that strange event which, on the face of it, seems incredible, for as he tells Serafina: "If strange things didn't happen, I wouldn't be here. You wouldn't be here. We wouldn't be talking together" (p. 361). Some have dismissed *The Rose Tattoo* as a contrived work, with Williams pulling all the strings in open view of the audience. And while there is some truth to the stricture that Alvaro is clumsy, and even stupid, his gift of love to Serafina does bring her out of despair and back into the world of love. Just as Serafina is filled with joy waiting for her first husband when the play begins, she is flowing over with excitement and love when running to meet her second husband as the play closes. That they rush to meet each other on the embankment signals their ascendancy over the neighborhood and the individuals who ridiculed and railed at them. Alvaro's strange and comic visit to Serafina's house results in the triumph of love.

The theme of time adds to both the tragic and the comic dimensions of the play. In his preface to *The Rose Tattoo*, Williams says that if time is arrested the events on stage acquire more tragic worth and contribute to the dignity of the characters. Were *The Rose Tattoo* pure tragedy, such observations might clearly apply. But the cessation of time for Serafina is both cause and effect of her comic debasement and our sympathy for her. When she is bound by time, or restlessly fights its pull, she is most pathetic and least likely to accept a new and fruitful life.

The time of the play may be the present, but for Serafina it is, until Alvaro's successful wooing, always the past. Before she learns of Rosario's death, she rapturously recalls her previous nights of love. All time is measured by and included in her husband's embrace. "Each time is the first time with him. Time doesn't pass . . ." (p. 280), she tells Assunta. But when Assunta reminds her of time's witness, the clock, Serafina has only contempt for it: "No, the clock is a fool. I don't listen to it. My clock is my heart and my heart don't say tick-tick; it says love-love!" (p. 280). The action reveals both how foolish and how sad Serafina's sense of time is when Estelle imposes another interpretation on the same hours: "Tomorrow's the anniversary of the day we met . . ." (p. 282), she tells Serafina, who is of course unaware of Rosario's infidelity.

Serafina is not concerned with the future, despite reminders of time's passing. She tells Assunta that Rosario will no longer conceal drugs under his load of bananas. "Tonight is the last time he does it! Tomorrow he quits hauling stuff for the Brothers Romano" (p. 279). Tomorrow never comes, even though Williams manipulates stage time so as to make years pass between scenes three and four of act one. All of a sudden, it is "A June day, three years later" (p. 293). (One recalls the passing of sixteen years between acts in Shakespeare's tragicomedy *The Winter's Tale*.) Williams admits that "The diminishing influence of life's destroyer, time, must be somehow worked into the context of . . . [the] play" (p. 263), but Serafina's struggle against it or imperception of it causes her grief. Williams' critical views are at odds with his dramaturgy, not an unusual conflict considering that sometimes his dramatic criticism fails to provide the most trusty guide to the work it discusses. When Serafina understands and appreciates time's changes, she is saved. Until then, she has only memories, views of the past which remove her from time's obligations and successes. As she tells Alvaro, "The memory of a love don't make you unhappy unless you believe a lie that makes it dirty" (p. 363). She clings to the lie because it protectively confines her in a beautiful past. She dwells on the social honors of the past. Rosario's uncle was a baron; she is a baronessa. But this claim brings only ridicule. She forestalls giving the mothers their daughters' dresses, promising them "Domani-domani-domani" (p. 293), even though, ironically enough, the dresses are done. In front of Bessie and Flora, she speaks of her previous work for them but spurns future jobs. When Serafina snarls at Flora that she is "late for the graduation of my daughter," the angular prig cruelly retorts: "You got plenty of time" (p. 305). Serafina has plenty of time except that all of it is recounted in her past sexual feats.

It is with Rosa that Serafina's distorted sense of time is most carefully treated. So harassed is Serafina that she never attends the graduation exercises; instead, she sits in the gloomy shadows of her house, surrounded by the manikins of both bride and widow, images of time past and time present. Ironically, the time-fettered Serafina buys Rosa a Bulova watch for her graduation present. But as Rosa leaves, the "gift still ungiven" (p. 411), the action means Serafina's sense of time cannot be transferred to her sexually unhindered daughter. That the watch does not work properly to begin with is further proof that this present represents Serafina's own limits; she has been frozen in time and must be unlocked from the past. Starnes has argued that when the watch does work, "time's passing and the transcience of all meaning are now all she can see"; and that when the watch ceases ticking "Time has been arrested for her again, and is significant of Serafina's spiritual rebirth" (p. 369). This view runs counter to the unfolding of events, for it is only when Serafina gives up on the defective watch that she can run to Alvaro who offers her a new love which releases her from her past folly.

In this role as time's new man, the new watchman of Serafina's heart, some of Alvaro's silliness vanishes, and much of his thematic significance is stressed. Though an awkward lothario, Alvaro plans for the future. Although his dreams are not as grand as Jim O'Connor's, Alvaro seeks security in the household of an older, financially stable and physically developed woman. But his youth and sexual prowess make him attractive to Serafina; he can offer her new hours of pleasure in bed while granting her wish not to be saddled with "some middle-aged man, not young, not full of young passion, but getting a pot belly on him and losing his hair and smelling of sweat and liquor" (p. 312). With Alvaro, Serafina's heart will again be in step with the fluidity and fruitfulness of time. Licking the chocolate from her fingers, Alvaro reminds Rosario's widow that "You're as old as your arteries, Baronessa. Now set back down. The fingers are now white as snow!" (p. 383). This ridiculous gesture is symbolically an act of purification, or a preview of sexual delights awaiting Serafina. When she protests his advances, Alvaro says, "Is it my fault you have been a widow too long?" (p. 388); and he even agrees to "go out and come in the door again" (p. 389) if the day is wrong. Timing is important for Alvaro, for he is conscious of his past failures in love. Once Serafina exorcises the lie from her memory, comes back into time, and accepts Alvaro's youthful love, she can escape the sadness of the past and the folly of the present. Giving assent to the passing of time shifts characters and audience away from tragedy and into the joy of comedy.

The Rose Tattoo is not one of Williams' best plays, but it does show his ability to write fulfilling comedy, comedy which is indebted to a number of different dramatic traditions. From farce and slapstick humor, Williams takes the lively action of his play—fights, chases, one-liners, grotesque characterization. But he dignifies, or at least tones down, some of these antics by incorporating elements of romantic comedy. Rosa's attempts to run away with Jack Hunter are successful only when Serafina finds love herself. That recognition is placed within a tragicomic frame, allowing Williams to introduce more serious moments into the play. All this action is set within a folk community from which Williams derives further comedy. If the play never won critical approval, possibly Williams was too ambitious, too eager to make sure his play left no comic form untouched.

Time and Tide
on the *Camino Real*

JAMES COAKLEY

A MONG THE PLAYS of Tennessee Williams *Camino Real* remains an enigma. A failure on Broadway, subjected to drastic revision as if its author refused to let it ever congeal into some finished form, and regarded by its critics as no more than the reworking of a jeu d'esprit, it received, Williams tells us, "more conscious attention to form and construction than . . . any work before" (II, 420). Well and good, we might say, but after decades of exposure to European experimentalists, audiences are still baffled by, indeed scornful of, this fascinating and demanding play.

One need not invoke esthetics, literary theory, or that tiresomely incantatory phrase "avant-grade" to see that *Camino Real* is a different kind of play. Its persistent dramatic method is via the sharpest possible contrast and juxtaposition of style. Indeed, stylistic disparity promotes the play's bold efforts to break loose from the stage and spill into the house, enhancing the dramatic action's reliance upon theatricalist conventions (mime, dance, and lavish technical effects) as the source of the drama's attempts to plunge the audience directly into its reality. Yet, this eclecticism of method does not mean that the piece's structure is loose, flimsy, or haphazard. On the contrary, in no play of Williams before or since does his sense of form, of where he is going and how he is going there, serve him more faithfully.

Camino Real is nonlinear in structure, and the use of such a pattern immediately prescribes hard and fast rules: (1) to relinquish forward movement of narrative and action is to lose the easy tension in the rigidly selective organization common to linear drama where one event plunges irreversibly onto the next; (2) to deny the melodramatic core of such an action is to reject what Ionesco (see *Victims of Duty*) calls, for example, the "detective story" nature of drama ; (3) and, finally, to deal in episodic units (Williams calls them "blocks," or, more familiarly, French scenes) is to present experience as fragmented, often seemingly aimless or ambiguous. This fragmentation of experience (common to films, but risky business in the theater) suggests the momentary focus on the instant, the episode caught in time and frozen in space, in which we are permitted to discover in vertical movement layers of personality often impossible to consider in the linear form's horizontal progression. In theory, at least, the nonlinear mode chooses to linger in the hidden corners of human motivation, where behavior has the clarity of true complexity. Finally, the most serious challenge of this play is its refusal to accept time either as sequential or as the fundamental common denominator of human affairs. To achieve this immediacy it presents time as discursive, arbitrary, and above all subjective. This particularly modern notion of time is the organizing principle of *Camino Real*, a method perfectly suited to the presentational production style which should, as Williams insists, aim for the freedom of improvisation in performance. It should give that sense of the "perpetual present" where the play is poised, in the words of Thornton Wilder, on a "razor-edge, between past and future, which is the essential character of the conscious being."

So restless a method as fluidity, however, requires control over the diffuse vignettes sprawling across the stage. To absorb an audience in a free association of disconnected images invites chaos or, worse, the private vision of a dilettante. Williams is too shrewdly in control of his materials, however, too aware of the dangers of excessive fragmentation, to allow his play to wander off in meaningless montages. To be sure, time interiorized and discontinuous provides unity, but *Camino* resides paradoxically in the best of two possible worlds: bracketed by Don Quixote's dream, its interior plunges ceaselessly across the country of the mind revealing a completely subjective spectrum of colors, shapes, and images, while retaining a semblance of direction in the adventures of its three quasiheroes, the Don, Kilroy, and Lord Byron. Melodramatic considerations suggesting progressions and resolutions bristle within the play's busy frame, but the truth is that while, much in the fashion of Chekhov, the arrivals and departures of characters imply movement to a destination, they really lead to perpetual wandering (the Don and Kilroy), or to death (Lord Byron). This trio is as rootless and spiritually displaced as any who are trapped forever on the Camino.

The effect of this calculated disorder upon characterization, however, allows for the play's most remarkable achievement. Normally, theatricalism robs character of dimension and consistency; tends, in fact, to dehumanize. In *Camino*, it seems to me, Williams withstands any impulses to present his people as mere style with no matter. Avoiding traditional treatment of his gallery of familiar literary types, he does rely on overtones, the suggestions of myth surrounding them, but in no way are they simply dusted off, refurbished, and reused. They are deployed and developed solely in terms of their perception of time. The persistent contrast is what they once were with what they are now: Quixote is an old desert rat, Casanova an impoverished, seedy roué, and Marguerite Gautier a frightened and lonely woman, addicted to drugs. Here, indeed, is the nub of the drama: the stasis of the present vs. the motion promised by the future, both of which are frustrated by the past's refusal to disappear. For time halted does not erase memory; it encourages the reflection proper to dimensioned characterization. The characters can be understood only by what we might call reflexive reference, their passions and problems darting back and forth; and, like the heroes of Pirandello, condemned to the limbo of the present, they are able to summon nonsequential, past experiences on the instant.

Three groups inhabit the Camino: the outcasts—the bums and drunks of a flophouse; the decadents—Marguerite Gautier, Jacques Casanova, and the Baron de Charlus; and the idealists—Don Quixote, Kilroy, and Lord Byron. Each is tainted (humanized) by the problem of time's meaning; each is dramatized (rather than merely represented) downward to the essence of human existence, forced to examine his problems in the arrested depths of the moment. External reality, the movement of life from point to point, is rejected, for the truth is to be discovered only in context, only in the fusion of past, present, and future: an amalgam of hurts, questions, and no answers. The outcasts (technically they also provide background) elect to ignore time, escaping into drugs and alcohol; for them life is a scavenger hunt "in a bazaar where the human heart is part of the bargain" (II, 452). There is no struggle—nothing in fact, but the cynical acceptance of things as they are. The sentimental comfort of memories is useless; the satisfaction of appetites is all that remains; and the moral principle is all too clear; indifference to time, to the world, in effect, breeds disaster, self-destruction. To shirk the issue is to end up, as Casanova does, on Skid Row, life hastily collected in a battered portmanteau.

But the decadents, the transients of an expensive tourist hotel, are, like all practicing romantics, terrified of time. Anguished over past glories and present stalemate, their attainment of spiritual freedom (the original reason for their rebellion against the world's order) is movement, flight, escape from the immobility of the Camino. They are morally, however, no better than their counterparts across the plaza. Practicing the same vices, they have more money, but the same fears. And for them to contemplate temporality in human affairs is only to see existence as no more than a series of waystations towards death. With these characters, as we might expect, are posed the play's most serious questions in set speeches of important thematic weight; the chance, as Williams sees it, to play upon his central perception: life is no more than "dim, communal comfort" (II, 527) eroded by change; values are illusory, perpetually in transit. How, in short, is one to live? It is a despair worthy of Beckett, priding itself upon no more than the black honesty of its vision. Neither psychological in origin (as in *Streetcar*) nor diluted with the panacea of the social worker preaching adjustment to the human condition, this despair is metaphysical and profoundly moral. Suspended and viewed in the pity and terror common to all, it is not sentimental; it is artistic, it seems to me, its logic and worth predicated upon the givens of the structure in which it operates. Indeed, in Block Ten, a brief scene between Marguerite and Jacques, Williams drops the theatricalist mask and allows his heroine to proclaim the dilemma correctly:

What are we sure of? Not even of our existence, dear comforting friend! And whom can we ask the questions that torment us? "What is this place?" "Where are we?" (p. 526).

In the microcosm of the moment all is visible; character, in effect, becomes symbol, the inner life of these people bursts forth, projecting the scope of the play outward to an indictment not only of the world of the play but of a universe equally perverse and corrupt.

The idealists do retain symbols of past achievements (Byron's pen, Kilroy's Golden Gloves, Quixote's blue ribbon), but each chooses, despite the consequences, merely to depart into life against time's ravages. Each makes that deliberate and existential choice by which the self is defined in this world. Yet the promise of self-fulfilment is slight. The Don does forbid Kilroy the pleasures of self-pity, and his only answer to the dilemma is that we must smile, making the best of what we have. To do less is immoral.

Thematically and structurally, then, *Camino* is a most ambitious play; or rather, a scenario, as Williams says, fit only for the "vulgarity of performance" (p. 423). One need not become its apologist to see that its intention and execution are evenly matched. To deprecate it as the triumph of the theatrical over the literary imagination is to miss the most important of matters: its form is its meaning, its central perceptions are stated directly, sincerely, and insistently: a dark message in the garish colors of a circus sideshow.

The Mythic Vision
in Tennessee Williams' *Camino Real*

DIANE E. TURNER

> Through me is the way into the woeful city.
> Through me is the way into eternal woe.
> Through me is the way among the Lost People.
>
> Dante[1]

AT THE HEART of Tennessee Williams' *Camino Real*, as in his other plays, lie the remnants of a great comic myth, the myth of rebirth, renewal, and rededication. What the mythic structure is, how it operates through both profane and sacred time, and how this brazen dream travesty ultimately becomes "a pageant, a masque in which old meanings will be remembered and possibly new ones discovered" (II, 437) is the subject of this article.

Camino Real begins where the *Camino Real* ends, in disillusionment and frustration. Although the play functions in a traditional mythic mode of rebirth through initiation, the rituals do not recreate sacred time but have on the contrary been distorted by the profane time of the modern, secular world. Ubiquitous cultic themes such as the quest, the fertility ritual and divine sacrifice, death and resurrection, divorced from their original context, have degenerated into a grotesque parody of their classic versions.

The "heroes" of the quest—Kilroy, Casanova, and the rest are tattered and fallen heroes—their ideals half lost and half forgotten, their sacral functions little more than a dream memory. But the dream and the ideal are those the myth has always celebrated—Byron's freedom, Casanova's honor, and Kilroy's One True Woman. These ideals are not finally or irrevocably lost, only grown older in the profane time and hence a little harder to recognize. Still, as

237

theater (which is but the sophisticated daughter of ritual-myth), *Camino Real* retains an especially strong link with its ancient heritage. Its characters share a vast mythic and heroic past, however shadowy, and they hope for a future, however uncertain, a future apart from the absurd and confused present in which the play finds them. Somehow our heroes have survived, and the fact of that survival into our time makes it certain they have kept something of the eternal time and eternal spirit. This spirit reveals them at last as being as truly noble in the bitter experience of mankind as they were in its callow and hubristic youth.

The structure of *Camino Real* is that of the dream-vision, a very old device which Northrop Frye has linked with the development of ritual drama; both are composed largely of a series of archetypal dream images.[2] In *Camino Real* the concept of dreaming is employed again and again—indeed the entire drama is a dream fantasy of Don Quixote, that master dreamer of ideals. One character is called simply The Dreamer, an ambivalent figure treated in more detail below.

In Frye's view, dream is the basic content of all romance, and certainly *Camino Real* bears close resemblance to the typical examples of the genre in three important ways: its major theme is the search or quest, a structural motif that connects various episodes in the plot action and unites the characters in a common purpose— escape. Both the spatial and the chronological patterns of the play emphasize this quest motif; the hero (Kilroy) acts not as a representative of a country or group but purely as an individual: "I'm a free man with equal rights in this world!" (p. 481). The Camino itself is a vague and exotic setting. The similarity to a standard romance is most valid from this purely structural viewpoint, however, for on a more profound level this particular quest is one for meaning and salvation, and both the horrors and the glories of the Camino have a more real counterpart in existential philosophy than in a remote never-never land or even some South American dictatorship.

But after all *Camino Real* is not a conventional romance. Side by side with the romantic dream motif is that of its companion, ritual. And while the dream concept adds color and symbolism to the play, the ritual aspect provides impetus and direction. The key themes of initiation and rebirth are *acted out*, made *visible and real*.

Deriving from both the dream and the ritual are the characters, who seem, especially at the beginning, to be highly stylized images, almost caricatures. This device is of course intentional and in keeping with the mode. For as W. H. Auden writes, "The Quest tale is ill-adapted to subtle portrayals of character; its personages are almost bound to be Archetypes rather than idiosyncratic individuals."[3]

In *Camino Real* both the "archetypes" (the Gypsy, Esmeralda, La Madrecita) and the historically real "idiosyncratic individuals" are found in abundance. The most successful creations, however, are those characters whose significance derives from a skilled blending of these aspects: Kilroy, Camille, and Casanova. The names do more than denote specific "historical" personages—they have become symbols. Kilroy, for example, is transformed from a very specific young American boxer into the chosen hero of the Camino Real and finally into the universal dying and resurrected god.

The major symbolic device in the play is the Camino Real itself, which, like the other mythic symbols, operates in two ways—as a literary model of the original, factual Camino Real (a road stretching from Santa Fé, California to Chihuahua, Mexico) and, in an extended reference, as a mythic road, a vital image of the quest theme which so dominates the action of the play. The road motif itself is an archetypal one, figuring predominantly in folk tales— from the golden road in the Grimm brothers story to the yellow brick one in *The Wizard of Oz*.

Yet the Camino is not merely a road, mythic or otherwise. It is also a destination, again both symbolically and actually. People stagnate in the Camino (Prudence, Olympe), flee from it (Sancho Panza), overcome it (Kilroy), or by submitting to their destiny there, transform it (Camille and Casanova). The ultimate journey is to salvation, and in this sense the Camino unveils a third aspect, neither journey nor goal, but obstacle and proving ground.

Gutman, the Camino's host, puts it this way: the Camino "is a port of entry and departure. There are no permanent guests" (p. 503). It thus becomes a fitting environment for all the rites of passage, the fertility celebration, and the sacrificial death. It is at last neither heaven nor hell but a purgatory in which the candidate must suffer the torments of the damned to reach the gates leading to salvation.

The design of the play makes Kilroy's material quest theme (to find the Way Out) symbolic of the initiation rite. By so doing, it brings together a complex of motifs, which revolve around a concept of threefold time: the rectilinear, the cyclical, and finally a transcendent, eternally sacred, mythic time. Although Kilroy begins his journey in linear time, our time (whose inexorable passage weakened and distorted our image of traditional heroes), he is soon plunged into the cyclic and ultimately meaningless time of the Camino. The Gypsy jeers, "Have you arrived at a point on the Camino Real where the walls converge not in the distance but right in front of your nose? Does further progress appear impossible to you? . . . Do you wish that things could be straight and simple again as they were in your childhood?" (p. 458). At last Kilroy is transferred, through his initiation beyond the Camino and into the realm of sacred time. His metamorphosis into the chosen hero proceeds by phases, in a pattern corresponding to Van Gennep's classic analysis of the typical stages involved in a rite of passage.[4] The Prologue through Block Six enacts the rite of separation; Blocks Seven through Eleven that of transition; and Blocks Twelve through Sixteen that of incorporation. Intermissions divide the stages. Each of the three great changes Kilroy undergoes occurs at the end of one of these phases. He takes on the role of scapegoat at the end of the separation phase, ritual lover at the end of the transitional phase, and finally the dying and reborn god hero at the end of the incorporation phase. It is through this series of rebirths that the entire mythic vision of the play is developed.

PART ONE: SEPARATION PHASE

The first words of *Camino Real*, Don Quixote's cry, "Blue is the color of distance," reflect both the separation from the old life and the void ahead of him. "It serves to remind an old knight of distance that he has gone and distance he has yet to go" (pp. 432, 433). For Quixote, the journey is largely a physical and emotional one, measured in miles and years. His own personal Golden Age, the land of innocence and mythic time, is fondly recalled. "It also reminds an old knight of that green country he lived in which was the youth of his heart" (p. 433). In fact, all the characters in the Prologue reminisce about that Golden Dream Time and contrast it with their present unhappy reality. The sense of separateness is universal, and Quixote takes pity on the Camino. "When so many are lonely . . . it would be inexcusably selfish to be lonely alone" (p. 436).

The proscenium arching the Camino marks the point where Quixote must separate altogether from his former life, a life represented by his uninitiate comrade, Sancho Panza.

> SANCHO: Let's go back to La Mancha.
> QUIXOTE: Forward!
> SANCHO: The time has come for retreat.
> QUIXOTE: The time for retreat never comes! (p. 435).

Thus Quixote strikes again the keynote of the play: time and trial. The heroic struggle against vast odds can never be won until time itself is transformed.

The setting which the proscenium arch reveals is a true underworld, a land of death and sleep, located in some unspecified but vaguely familiar tropical port. It is a Hades divided into its Erebus and Tartarus (represented by the Sieta Mares on one side and the Ritz Men Only on the other.) Like the Hades in another quest romance, the *Odyssey*, it is separated from the upper world by water. Pluto's palace is admirably suggested by the Siete Mares hotel, and the entire area is both surrounded by illimitable wasteland and guarded by two slightly unconventional "porters"—armed and uniformed guards.

In the midst of all this lonely desolation, however, is the perennial emblem of resurrection, the phoenix, painted on a silk cloth and spotlighted. Birds furnish some of the most persistent imagery of the play, beginning with the stage direction of the prologue, which suggests that daybreak was "a white bird caught in a net and struggling to rise" (p. 431). Aurora, the Gutman's imprisoned cockatoo, is the white dawn bird. And Don Quixote reads solemnly from a parchment that "there are no birds in the country except wild birds that are tamed and kept in—" (p. 435) cages of course. Casanova, the old hawk, and Camille, are like the birds, also prisoners, "a pair of captive hawks caught in the same cage" (p. 526). The only bird ever freed is the soul of Kilroy at his "death." The Pink Flamingo, the Yellow Pelican, the Blue Heron, and the Prothonotary Warbler, the Camino's "hot spots," are pits of depression and despair.

The first two blocks introduce many of the major characters: Gutman, Casanova, Camille, the Gypsy, Esmeralda, La Madrecita, and her son, the Dreamer. The strange figure called La Madrecita is the most easily recognized as well as the most complex of the mythic characters. She is first seen in the attitude of the Pietà, cradling in her arms the ironically named Survivor. She is the incarnation of many ancient goddesses—Demeter (although the vegetative motif associated with her is subdued because of the "urban" environment of the Camino), the Anima, the Magna Mater, the blind seeress, and the Virgin Mary, the last allusion made explicit by Kilroy's agonized cry, "*Mary, help a Christian! Help a Christian, Mary!*" (p. 482).

At the death of the Survivor and the entrance of Kilroy (a simultaneous occurrence), the Madrecita becomes Kilroy's protectress, thus acting the part of the old woman or crone (often replaced by the Virgin Mary in Christian myth) who helps the hero along in his quest (Campbell, p. 71). She not only provides material aid by giving bread (Block Six) but also effects the spiritual resurrection of Kilroy at the end of the drama.

The Dreamer, her son, is a more ambiguous character. A guitar-playing Orpheuslike figure, he makes his entrance leading La Madrecita, an action typical of Dumuzi-Tammuz, who on ancient urns is generally depicted as leading his mother and consort, Inanna-Ishtar. His reiterated cry of *hermano*, the taboo word, nearly incites the inhabitants to riot. Taboo is ritually connected with a festival, and in this case the utterance of the forbidden word signals the beginning of the festivities. It is a magico-celebrative fertility rite that restores the virginity of Esmeralda, the Gypsy's daughter and local whore, whose name means *green*, and by connotation both *virginal* and *fruitful*. Her restoration to a pristine state is a rite of sympathetic magic, performed in hopes that the Camino itself can be likewise reborn.

At the close of Block Two, Kilroy makes his entrance from the orchestra aisle, as Don Quixote did before him. His essential likeness to the old knight is at once apparent. Like Quixote, he bears all the paraphernalia which properly belong to the chosen hero: the magic weapon (his golden boxing gloves) and the outer sign of election—his bejeweled belt marked CHAMP. The fact that Kilroy is an athlete has significance. Very early Greek religion, for example, "consisted in the sacrificial worship of heroes. . . . There is a great deal to suggest that the winners at the games became kings."[5]

Kilroy also is marked by the inner sign which isolates him from others, a sign he declares in his first long speech. "I've got a heart in my chest as big as the head of a baby" (p. 455). This heart turns out to be solid gold. Gold is not only the most precious metal but is also a traditional efficacy against evil. But these physical accoutrements are of little avail to Kilroy; his greatness does not depend on them. Belt, gloves and heart—by the end of the play he loses them all, one during each phase of initiation; they are the price of redemption, and they evidence Kilroy's removal from the ordinary spheres of life.

In Block Three, Kilroy, like Quixote, relives his separation from the "green country" he lived in, which was the youth of his heart, and he enumerates what he has sacrificed—so as to purify himself—all on account of his heart, his magical sign. "They said to give up liquor and smoking and sex!—To give up sex!—I used to believe a man couldn't live without sex—but he can—if he wants to" (p. 456). This purification ordeal further involves a rupture with his family, another form of leavetaking from his old life. He adds, "So one night while . . . [his wife] was sleeping I wrote her good-bye." This separation from the past is only the first step, though, and it leaves the hero vulnerable. As he states, "One: I'm hungry. Two: I'm lonely. Three: I'm in a place where I don't know what it is or how I got there!" (p. 461). This is simply another aspect of Kilroy's candidacy. "So too in the case of initiation: by means of fasting and abstinence, the candidate evacuates his former selfhood preparatory to merging in the corporate personality of the group."[6] The loneliness of which he complains is a deep sense of alienation—Nietzschean in its feeling of rootlessness and isolation, but which is also the mark of the chosen. Kilroy must still wander for a dark time among the wretched of the Camino before he can transcend them through his final sacrifice and resurrection.

In Block Five, Kilroy begins his spiritual preparation for divine kingship and eventual sacrifice by undergoing the traditional rites of instruction of the novitiate in order to learn the secret and forbidden facts about "the tribe" from the initiatory priest, Casanova, who indicates to Kilroy the Way Out, an arch opening onto the limitless desert beyond. But Kilroy is not ready to accept the challenge. "It's too unknown for my blood" (p. 474).

Block Six is the last and crucial stage of the separation phase. It begins with the bread which the Madrecita offers Kilroy. This action, signifying the sacred meal (which is the original meaning of the word *festival*) immediately sets into motion the inauguration of Kilroy as scapegoat. He is dressed in a clown suit, "the uniform of a patsy," ceremonially pursued through the orchestra, beaten to his knees (originally a presage to the fertility rite), and humiliated. This sequence is mirrored in the pursuit and capture of Esmeralda by the androgynous Nursie, thus linking the fates of the two. At this point, the end of Block Six, Kilroy has made a complete break from his old status. From the champion to the patsy-scapegoat, he has become what Ihab H. Hassan has called the "rebel victim, a grotesque effigy to the rule of chaos. . . . in this he does not differ greatly from the ancient heroes and scapegoats of myth."[7]

PART TWO: TRANSITION

The greatest transition of all is one from life to death and vice versa. The former process, that of dying, is enacted in Block Seven. The hour, sunset, emphasizes the mood of death and change, which Northrop Frye associates with the isolation of the hero and the related theme of the dying god (pp. 158 ff.). "The fire's gone out of the day but the light of it lingers . . ." says Gutman. Even he feels the need for a renewal of purpose. "And these are the moments when we look into ourselves and ask with a wonder which is never lost altogether: 'Can this be all? Is there nothing more? Is this what the glittering wheels of heaven turn for?'" (p. 485).

This section of the Camino, the transitional phase, belongs primarily to Casanova and Camille, the lost people. They are the tragic dying characters in a comedy of rebirth. For Kilroy, it is the waiting period, and like other traditional waiting periods (pregnancy or betrothal) it is a suspended state for him. He takes no further part in the play until the very end of Block Eleven and spends the mean-time in the pawnbroker's shop, the Camino's warped version of an initiation hut. "During the second phase initiates usually endure periods of seclusion in a dark and threatening place. As Eliade states, 'a considerable number of initiation rites reactualize the motif of death.'"[8]

Block Seven does in fact concentrate on the dead and the dying, the necessary pruning that will clear the way for new life. Williams uses Lord Mulligan for this purpose, holding up his enervation and weakness as a vivid (and hilarious) contrast to Kilroy's youth and energy. The Streetcleaners soon arrive to take him away.

Between the life past, represented by the Mulligans, and the life to come, represented by Kilroy, are Casanova and Camille, who are in the transitional phase of dying. Their conversations consist of reminiscences and references to death. Camille's first speech will supply an example, when she chooses the flower she will wear. "It's always a white one now . . . but there used to be five evenings out of the month when a pink camellia, instead of the usual white one, let my admirers know that the moon those nights was unfavorable to pleasure" (p. 489). These words carry a rich inheritance from mul-tiple sources—literary, mythical, and anthropological. Red flowers suggest most obviously in this context the menstrual cycle and its consequent taboo, while white connotes purity, but both have a deeper significance. The red flower is the timeless symbol of renewal and resurrection through blood sacrifice (a point made explicit later in the play) while white has all the negative qualities of sterility and death. The Streetcleaners, as Lady Mulligan notes, are "two idiots pushing a white barrel!" (p. 487). Death is, after all, the final purification.

The association of death with whiteness recurs later in the block, and this time it is Camille who draws upon it. "And when the last bleeding comes . . . you're wheeled discreetly into a little tent of white gauze, and the last thing you know of this world, of which you've known so little and yet so much, is the smell of an empty icebox" (p. 498). The block closes on a note of despair, Camille and Casanova imprisoned and dying on the Camino.

The controlling image on Block Eight is the figure of Byron, the first to make the transition "From my present self to myself as I used to be!" (p. 503), deliberately going backward in time in a desperate attempt to find himself. The words "used to be" on the Camino always evoke in the speaker's mind his own Golden Age, from Camille's regretful "but there used to be five evenings out of the month" to Kilroy's more pragmatic, "Oh, well. Sometimes a man has got to hock his sweet used-to-be in order to finance his present situation . . ." (p. 462). The whole tone of Byron's speeches in this block recall the past—the war in which he died a hero, Athens, freedom, the Acropolis. He exits—into his past, so largely mythic, and carries with him the birds of his soul—still caged. He is the modern absurdist caught in the net of his past, left alone to face an alien universe. "There is a time for departure even when there's no certain place to go!" (p. 508). But he goes anyway, even though his Golden Fleece is nothing but a memory.

Blocks Nine and Ten, which contain the Fugitivo scene and its aftermath, present the Camino at its cruelest and most desperate, and the question is whether those aboard the plane represent the saved or the damned. Block Ten also marks the last appearance of the Orpheuslike Dreamer, whose music has supplied both harmonious and contrapuntal comment on these proceedings.

In Block Eleven the Festival proper begins. "The first event is the coronation of the King of Cuckolds" (p. 530). The celebrants form a circle around Casanova, chanting, while the Hunchback places a crown of gilded antlers on his head. The mythic meaning of this crown is very old and has significance far other than indicating the dupe or cuckold. In the Punjab and other places in the East is a cultus of male horned figures which corresponds to the worship of the Great Mother and has the same function—to represent fertility. The main difference is that the latter emphasizes the floral and the former the faunal aspect. The more familiar connotation is immediately clear, of course, but Jacques takes pains to assert the more ancient meaning of the sacral horns as well. He shouts, "Yes, I said GREAT LOVER! The greatest lover wears the longest horns on the Camino! GREAT! LOVER!" (p. 531).

At this point two things happen almost simultaneously. Esmeralda reappears, and Kilroy discards his clown suit. Esmeralda's transformation is a good deal less obvious than Kilroy's—the Gypsy must proclaim it. "The moon in its plentitude has made her a virgin!" (p.

532). The moon, of course, is the age-old emblem of cyclic time; the purity it bestows can never be permanent. Thus, the two primary facets of the mother cult, fertility and renewal, unite in the figure of Esmeralda. She must now perform her most important task; she must "choose the hero," so the cycle can start again.

By now Kilroy has emerged from the Loan Shark's place, whose darkness bears resemblence not only to the initiation hut but also to its prototype, the womb. Kilroy's emergence from it indicates a new birth. He has attempted a disguise, but "He has no sooner entered the plaza than the riotous women strip off everything but the dungarees and skivvy which he first appeared in" (p. 534). The celebrants have become Maenads who strip the Pentheuslike king-scapegoat of his disguise; he is ready now to join the cult of Dionysus, a religion very closely allied with the cult of the Great Mother in the Eleusinian mysteries.

The transfiguration is complete. Kilroy, lifted hight into the air by the revellers, becomes the Chosen Hero; and to herald the renewal and rebirth, Esmeralda tosses to him the red flowers—symbols of fertility and eternally resurrected life. Their first function is enacted almost at once.

PART THREE: INCORPORATION

Blocks Twelve through Sixteen trace Kilroy's incorporation into a renewed order wherein he takes on the characteristics of the divine hero. His name itself provides a useful clue about his destined part in the drama—"kil-roi," the king who must be killed. Frazer describes him as young and beautiful, beloved of a goddess, and the victim of a tragic and untimely death.[9] At the same time he is the counterpart of the folk tale's youngest son (of whom Chrétien de Troyes's Percival may serve as the classic example)—the last person in the world one would expect to achieve anything. *Inadequate* seems the kindest word. The Gypsy sums up this sentiment in disgust. "Chooses a Fugitive Patsy for the Chosen Hero!" (p. 538).

The Gypsy is one of Williams' most marvelous creations. She is the Madrecita in a comic vein—Mamacita, as Kilroy once calls her. She is the madam of her establishment and the outrageous mother of Esmeralda, who becomes in this block the divine Virgin-Prostitute. Campbell would recognize in the Gypsy the archetype of the hag, who takes charge of Kilroy's initiation into yet another role. "Well, how does it feel to be the Chosen Hero?" (p. 540). She makes dutiful inquiry as to the identity of his parents. "Both unknown" (p. 541) is the reply. Like many of his mythic forebears, Kilroy's true origins remain shrouded in mystery. The Gypsy also dabbles in all the accoutrements of magic—astrology, crystal gazing, cards, and tea leaves. Magic is the pragmatic, profane cousin of ritual and myth, and its use here instead of myth illustrates the Gypsy's essentially practical approach to the rite to come.

The verbal testing of Kilroy (a brief, but gruesome enough experience) ends abruptly as Esmeralda is carried in and the parody of a fertility rite begins. Esmeralda is adorned with "a pair of glittering emerald snakes coiled over her breasts" (p. 547). The mythological references are legion, foremost among them perhaps an allusion to the snake goddess of Knossos, who was similarly attired. Snakes are a suitable choice at any rate, their subconscious sexual connotations now being familiar to everyone.

The scene gets underway with the utterance of the magical and formulaic charm, "Pretty please" (p. 556), which allows Kilroy to lift the veil. The veil symbolizes not only the hymen (which is in this case symbolic to begin with) but also very possibly a blasphemous version of the veil surrounding the Ark in the Holy of Holies.

Also a dark hint of the human sacrifice is implicit in the fertility rite. "But just the same, the night before a man dies, he says 'Pretty please—will you let me lift your veil?—' while the Streetcleaners wait for him right outside the door!" (p. 558). Then the ritual words, "I am sincere" (p. 562) are repeated four times each by the lovers, the veil is lifted, and the rite accomplished. But immediately following, Kilroy realizes, "It wasn't much to give my golden gloves for" (p. 563). Esmeralda has not been the fulfilment of the hero's quest, but a temptation drawing him away from it. "The seeker of the life beyond life must press beyond her, surpass the temptations of her call, and soar to the immaculate ether beyond" (Campbell, p. 122).

But first, before he tastes the ether, Kilroy, now type of the suffering god, must taste death, the final degradation, and end of both scapegoat and chosen hero. He is aware of the end drawing near. "Washed up!—Finished!" (p. 576) he despairs, and, in accordance with established custom, submits to the sacrifice. The killing of the hero-king at his first sign of weakness is well documented by Frazer, and Kilroy is no exception. The Streetcleaners surround him, as the Titans around Prometheus, and ritually beat him to death. La Madrecita, Madonnalike, is present at the execution.

Block Fifteen opens with La Madrecita cradling Kilroy's body as she had that of the Survivor—in the attitude of the Pietà. She mourns him as Isis and Inanna mourned for their beloved. "Think of him, now, as he was before his luck failed him. Remember his time of greatness, when he was not faded, not frightened" (p. 578). She evokes his mythic and heroic past. "You should have seen the lovely monogrammed robe in which he strode the aisles of the colosseums!" (p. 579).

Attention shifts as the anatomy instructor, who plays the part of the shaman, proves Kilroy's divine kingship. "There is no external evidence of disease" (p. 578). This remark is important, for as Frazer makes clear in *The Golden Bough*, freedom from deformity is a "must" for the sacral king. It was an equally stern custom that the public pretend complete ignorance of the ritual murder. Note the anatomy instructor: "His death was apparently due to natural causes" (p. 579).

The dismemberment (sparagmos) of Kilroy, a necessary part of all fertility sacrifices, follows in the form of the time-honored Aztec method—the cutting out of the heart. The dummy upon which this operation is actually performed, Kilroy's substitute, also appears to have very ancient origins. It is the surrogate sacrifice (a custom which grew up after a time in more sophisticated cultures as it became harder and harder to find anyone willing to become a king, with a knife almost literally hanging over one's head). While the heart is being removed, the moment of revelation (epopoteia) breaks upon the Camino. "This heart's solid gold!" (p. 581). As the golden heart is removed, La Madrecita can now restore and free the soul of Kilroy. "Rise, ghost! Go! Go, bird!" (p. 580).

Block Sixteen is the final block on the Camino. The course of the traditional Orphic hero is likewise a journey of sixteen stages— the last of which, depicted on the sacramental Orphic bowl, shows the rebirth of the hero into a realm of light. Block Sixteen begins with the experience of being born again; consequently, the dream motif is heavily accentuated, as it was in Block One. The processes of birth and dreaming are psychologically similar, and bound up with both is the sensation of lostness in a new environment. Kilroy cries at the beginning of the last block, *"Gee, I'm lost! I don't know where I am! I'm all turned around, I'm confused. . . . it's like a— dream, it's—just like a—dream. . . . Mary, help a Christian!! . . . Mary!—It's like a dream. . . . Yes, it's—like a—dream . . ."* (pp. 582– 3). The confusion grows more wild, until Kilroy is "Stewed, screwed, and tattooed on the Camino Real! Baptized, finally, with the contents of a slop-jar!" (p. 587).

And here the dream myth ends, with the awakening of Don Quixote and the flowing of the fountain that has until now been dry. The rebirth of the hero has resulted in the salvation and renaissance of society. As for Kilroy, in a very typical folk motif, the final act of degradation—giving up to the Loan Shark the last and best of what remains to his old life, his golden heart—has meant a transfiguration into a new world. "The young god dies annually in the rotation of the seasons and has to be rescued and restored from the land of the dead by his mother-lover. It was she who resuscitated him, and by so doing brought about the revival of life in nature and in mankind."[10]

Kilroy, with his new mentor, Don Quixote, undergoes the last rite of passage, as he proceeds through the Arch into the Terra Incognita, in fulfilment of his destiny, a destiny which identifies the seeking after truth with truth itself. The spiritual sun comes out, and Kilroy, hero, fool, scapegoat, and resurrected god, comes under its influence.

Now the journey, however perilous, must be attempted. "As 'the faithful son of the waters . . .' [Kilroy arrived by water, of course, but the reference can equally be applied to the renewed flowing of the fountain] he was the youthful suffering god who died . . . and passed into the nether regions from which normally there was no return" (James, p. 78). They exit, and Don Quixote shouts, *"The violets in the mountains have broken the rocks!"* (p. 591). He refers not only to the fragile tenderness of Casanova and Camille but also to an ancient mythic symbol, for violets are said to have sprung from the grave of Attis. They promise rebirth.

Having fulfilled the regenerative cycle, the new Kilroy can now move forward. The quest for truth is renewed and purified, the last rite of passage endured. Profane time itself, both cyclic and linear, has been reborn into sacred time. The Camino has no power left to assert, for its cycle is broken forever. "The Curtain Line has been spoken!" says Gutman. "Bring it down!"

Notes to Diane Turner, "The Mythic Vision
in Tennessee Williams' *Camino Real*"

1. Quoted in Joseph Campbell, *The Hero With a Thousand Faces* (New Brunswick: Princeton University Press, 1966), p. 21.

2. Northrop Frye, *Anatomy of Criticism: Four Essays* (New York: Atheneum, 1967), pp. 104–08.

3. W. H. Auden, "The Quest Hero," *Texas Quarterly*, 4 (Winter 1961), p. 86.

4. Arnold Van Gennep, *The Rites of Passage* (Chicago: University of Chicago Press, 1960).

5. Lord Raglan, *The Hero* (New York: Vintage Books, 1956), p. 60.

6. Theodore H. Gaster, *Thespis: Ritual, Myth, and Drama in the Ancient Near East* (New York: Harper and Row, Torchbooks, 1950), p. 38.

7. Ihab H. Hassan, "The Character of Postwar Fiction," in *On Contemporary Literature*, ed. Richard Kostelanetz (New York: Avon Books, 1964), pp. 40–1.

8. Charles W. Eckert, "Initiatory Motifs in the Story of Telemachus," in *Myth and Literature*, ed. John Vickery (Lincoln: University of Nebraska Press, 1966), p. 164.

9. J. G. Frazer, *The Golden Bough*, 3rd ed. (rpt. New York: St. Martin's Press, 1955), part 3.

10. E. O. James, *The Ancient Gods* (New York: Putnam's Sons, 1960), p. 48.

Casanova's Portmanteau: *Camino Real* and Recurring Communication Patterns of Tennessee Williams

MORRIS PHILIP WOLF

T HE YEARS 1945–55 were notably productive and controversial for Tennessee Williams. Excluding *You Touched Me!* which he wrote in collaboration with Donald Windham, Williams published during that single decade the twenty-five plays and twenty-one stories upon which this essay rests. Among those works were *The Glass Menagerie* and *A Streetcar Named Desire,* both of which earned tumultuous acclaim. On 31 March 1945, at the premiere of *Menagerie,* his first Broadway play, the audience cheered persistently, compelling Williams to appear on stage. He was the only Broadway playwright to receive an "Author!" ovation during that season. Then, on 3 December 1947, *Streetcar* opened in New York. It received the Critics' Circle Award as well as the Pulitzer Prize. No American play before it, other than William Saroyan's *The Time of Your Life,* had been so honored. Tennessee Williams had won general endorsement from professional critics and from the public.

But on 19 March 1953, *Camino Real* made its Broadway debut, and heated controversy ensued. Williams provided an apologia in his foreword and in his afterword to the text; yet *Camino Real,* which he said represented his highest hope as a communicative work, bypassed many of its spectators . . . and vice versa. In his foreword, Williams acknowledges that *Camino* exasperates and confuses members of its audience; however, the same foreword asserts Williams' desire to share with many theatergoers the sensation of release that he experienced through writing *Camino Real*. What accounts for this communication gap?

Perhaps more things are wrought by patterns—patterns of characterization, of settings, of lights, and of colors—than even their authors dream of.

Throughout the plays and stories of Tennessee Williams, the violent, incessant, screaming rush of moments and years robs human life and threatens the loss of human dignity. Confronted by present urgencies, many of Williams' characters plunder the past, striving to secure defense against the present. Those patterns of characterization appear certainly in *Camino Real*; but in *Camino* they have names of extraordinary fame, names that are well known in history and tradition, names with which knowledgeable audiences previously have established symbolic associations derived from earlier sources. Although the people of *Camino Real* are called Don Quixote, Lord Byron, Casanova, Camille, and the like, they are uniquely the creatures of Tennessee Williams; and it is this fact which their author and their audiences must realize if effective communication is to occur. Apparently, however, playwright and audiences have not shared a basic view of *Camino Real*: In *Camino* Williams uses prototypical and symbolic names to represent the characters and themes of *his own* recurrent communication patterns.

Few reasonable persons would deny an artist the privilege of applying his own interpretations to conventions, including the conventions of literary symbolism, even of names. But if that artist declares, as Williams does, an intention to share his work with many audiences, he must convey his special uses of referents which are already familiar in contexts other than his own. Only then can he establish and maintain rapport between his play and its spectators or readers. In the *Camino* foreword, Williams declares that he is impelled not merely to express but to share with many persons his interpretation of contemporary life. Is such sharing possible when an author assigns to characters of his own creation an array of symbolic patterns which evoke traditional association with one kind of response while representing quite another kind of response in the mind of that author? Despite his sincerity of purpose, does Tennessee Williams risk plunging *Camino* from fantasy into farce by portraying diverse characters, apparently legendary, within the carnival atmosphere of a timeless, placeless arrest-point; by presenting seemingly incongruous stage effects; and by using celebrated names that evoke inappropriate audience response to what are essentially his own characters and his own themes? These questions invite detailed examination—and appreciation—of *Camino Real* in terms of its relationship to Williams' recurrent patterns of communication.

As parts of those characterization patterns which permeate Williams' works, his *Camino* Quixote and Byron use memories to escape snares whereas his Casanova and Camille remain entrapped because, in large part, of dependence upon nostalgia. A bit of blue ribbon reminds Quixote of his youth, of distances that he has traveled but also of his need to go onward; the discussion of a poet's vocation reminds Byron of his lavish escapades and, more urgently, of his imminent journey beyond the Camino Real plaza. Conversely, Casanova's memories of past glory only aggravate his anxiety, displayed especially by his sobbing in the Fiesta episode of Block Eleven. (Significantly, perhaps, Williams labels "scenes" in *Camino Real* as "blocks." In a city or town, people may progress from block to block, and in a pilgrimage they may go by "way stations." But "blocks," also, are obstacles to progress, barriers to escape.) Camille's reveries of past joys merely intensify her despair when, having been abandoned by the Fugitivo (an instrument of potential escape in the form of an airplane), she remains trapped in the plaza. Here, then, emerge two variations on the characterization of what may be called, or miscalled, romantic dreamers: The first, which, for convenience, may be termed Pattern A, is stimulated by memories to escape from a trap in present time; the second, Pattern B, depends so desperately upon memories that satisfactory escape is impossible. Although distinct, these categories are not so exclusive as to prevent a character from displaying primary traits of one pattern and secondary traits of another.

Pattern A

Joe Bassett of Williams' one-act play "The Long Goodbye" may be seen as representing what has been identified in *Camino Real* as Pattern A with modifications of Pattern B. His loved ones, through death or other modes of escape, have left the trap of their apartment-home; and, at the moment of crisis in this short play, Joe, too, must move out.

Joe brings himself to quit his tenement of conventionality, to leave a breeding-place of memories which, although frequently painful, are reassuring in their familiarity. Breaking from what he has known, he is reluctant to abandon voluntarily the safety of a place that symbolizes his former life. To Joe, a romanticist contending with "practical" people, reminiscence is both goad and inhibition. The yearning for what has drifted through time and space floods his mind now with dreams, with images of his dead mother, with memories of his impetuous sister. Joe, himself, seems adrift in time and space, floating between what has been and what is, knowing no security as he drives himself and is driven by others. When the Movers and his friend, Silva, cavil and blare at him, Joe returns—only momentarily—to the present; and he *physically* abandons a trap to which *he* had been abandoned by the defections of his father and his sister as well as by his mother's death. Thus Joe may be classified within Pattern A because he does progress to new adventures; but he reflects the traits of Pattern B insofar as he carries with him the fetters of chronic retrospection that insure his own despair.

The Pattern A characterization of Tom Wingfield in *The Glass Menagerie* is closely related to that of Joe Bassett. Joe writes fiction or drama; Tom writes poetry. Striving to snap the web of circumstance which threatens his own individuality, Tom must break away, at least ostensibly, from the place that represents family responsibility. Tom sympathizes with his sister, Laura, as does Joe Bassett with Joe's sister, Myra. Each brother lovingly advises the girl concerned. Joe admonishes Myra harshly; Tom counsels Laura gently. Tom, like Joe, leaves the family environment behind him physically but carries it with him in the bonds of memory. Tom, like Joe, rebels against the forces of entrapment; and this defensive rebelliousness sends Tom physically into the present world while it keeps him, like Joe, psychologically at home in the past. Moreover, the narrator of "Portrait of a Girl in Glass"—the short-story nucleus of *Menagerie*—is identical to Tom Wingfield and, therefore, another specimen of Pattern A characterization with Pattern B modifications.

Several of Tennessee Williams' female characters also follow the Pattern A development. Alma Winemiller of *Summer and Smoke*, rejected by the man she loves and improperly appreciated by her parents, repeats Joe Bassett's farewell gesture to familiar convention. Joe puts his hand to his forehead in a mocking salute; Alma's salute is valedictory. These salutes are not implied; they are specified by Williams in the final stage directions for "Goodbye" and for *Summer*.

Within the context of Pattern A, Alma attempts to escape from her trap by courting the attentions of a stranger. Karen Stone makes a similar attempt at the conclusion of Williams' long story *The Roman Spring of Mrs. Stone* by signaling an invitation to a secret admirer or pursuer. Blanche DuBois's trial with this technique is disastrous, as the exposition of *A Streetcar Named Desire* pointedly reveals. But Serafina Delle Rose of *The Rose Tattoo* escapes successfully from the trap of enervating memory by finally accepting a new lover in place of her dead husband. Mrs. Holly of the whimsical story "The Coming of Something to the Widow Holly" follows Pattern A by emerging from the snare of routine existence and admitting a handsome young man to her house and her bed. Dorothy Simple of the short play "The Case of the Crushed Petunias" escapes the restraint of her Primanproper Shop by setting off, hellbent for heaven, in search of a dynamic male and new adventure. Also, in "Ten Blocks," the earlier version of *Camino Real* which does not contain Byron, Don Quixote offers to lead Kilroy and Sancho out of the plaza-trap and away from the self-pity of loss.

These specimens from works published earlier than *Camino Real* attest Tennessee Williams' characteristic concern with the theme of escape by means of rebelliousness. Margaret Pollitt's action in *Cat on a Hot Tin Roof*, the long play immediately following the appearance of *Camino Real*, corroborates this evidence; by refusing to submit to the tyranny of memory, Margaret (Maggie the Cat) snaps restraint, endeavoring to save both herself and her husband through the sex act. Thus, related to Williams' other works under discussion, the major characters of *Camino Real* may deserve their author's classification of them as archetypes of basic attitudes and qualities. Indeed, Williams describes them so in his foreword to *Camino Real*. The thesis being advanced here, however, is that they appear to be archetypes not of history or legend that their names— *Quixote, Byron, Casanova*—imply. Rather, they serve as members of a characterization pattern that Tennessee Williams develops within the canon of his own works: They are archetypes of the restless human spirit which perseveres, sometimes successfully, in meeting the demands of present time and place despite the debilitating force of nostalgia.

Pattern B

As identified in *Camino Real*, Pattern B represents the person who, struggling to retain a sense of present security by clinging through memory and delusion to the remnants of alleged success or happiness, does not escape the trap of the present.

Throughout his works Williams depicts this archetype at a climax pivoting upon the defensive use of imagination, a dependence frequently preventing socially approved adjustment to ordinary problems of current life. The representatives of Pattern B, intent upon preserving a sense of personal worth and of personal grandeur, are confronted by pragmatic antagonists. Williams' specimens of Pattern B are sensitive, vain, withdrawing idealists whose standards seem appropriate to themselves but immoral to others and whose attempted compensation for loss is futile rebelliousness. The personalities of Pattern B cling to yesterday despite and because of today. Unlike the personalities of Pattern A, they do not escape entrapment.

For example, Mrs. Hardwicke-Moore in Williams' short play "The Lady of Larkspur Lotion" represents herself to others—and believes herself to be—not merely a woman but a Lady. She displays a sense of grandeur, a fortification of dreams, that enables her to exist in a vermin-infested rooming house without surrendering her preciously elegant gestures and speech. Her happiness, indeed her identity as Mrs. Hardwicke-Moore, requires the active preservation of a delusion: the notion that she derives her income from ownership of a fabulous Brazilian rubber plantation. Mrs. Hardwicke-Moore's deterioration is climaxed by the threats and chastisements of her landlady, Mrs. Wire, who, demanding the rent, assaults the fragile bastion of Mrs. Hardwicke-Moore's dream. Thus the image of past splendor, of a lineage that boasts a coat of arms and a magnificent estate, of things remembered as indescribably beautiful—this systematized lie that becomes truth to the person who has created it—is attacked by the crass urgency of present events. Mrs. Hardwicke-

Moore cannot bear, and consequently rejects, criticism of her life-style. She suffers despair, even panic, when confronted by refutation. Reinforced by the delusion of her wealth, she struggles to retain her social ideal as a Lady. The tone of her voice is shrill, her elocution affected, her attitude condescending. Absolute and unchanging is her conviction that the rubber plantation is real; to recognize this conviction as a figment of imagination would be to dissolve the chief of her reasons for being. She is noticeably vain, especially when, at the play's end, she smiles a coquettish invitation to the Writer. Confronted by direct threat, Mrs. Hardwicke-Moore defends herself; but her defense is psychological withdrawal from circumstances of stress.

Lucretia Collins in Williams' short play "Portrait of a Madonna," like Mrs. Hardwicke-Moore, clings to imagination for security. Miss Collins' pattern of decline is associated with proffered but rejected love; even in middle age, she offers herself to the lover of her youth. (cf. the actions of Camille in *Camino Real*, Marguerite in "Ten Blocks," Serafina Delle Rose in *Tattoo*, Alma Winemiller in *Summer*, and Blanche DuBois in *Streetcar*.) Denying the trauma of rejection by that lover, Miss Collins refuses to admit her spinsterhood. The drift of her decline is signalized, as is that of Blanche DuBois in *Streetcar*, by her removal to a mental hospital. Throughout the events leading to this climax—and at the moment of the climax itself—Lucretia Collins (like Mrs. Hardwicke-Moore and Blanche DuBois) insists upon remaining a Lady. Her fervent desire to retain the memory of an imaginary young lover requires her to preserve tangible as well as intangible mementoes of the time when she too was chronologically young. Her hair is arranged in curls that would be attractive for a young girl; her costume is frilly, perhaps a negligee from a hope chest. Lucretia Collins is even less capable than Mrs. Hardwicke-Moore in meeting the demands of the Now. Miss Collins insists that she is being ravished by her imaginary lover, that she is being persecuted by strangers, that the world is remorselessly maligning her. She is calmed, confused, and terrorized by a religious fixation. She retires from Now and plunges into the refuge of What-hasbeen. Like Mrs. Hardwicke-Moore, she rejects criticism, ignores slurs and snide remarks, primps often, compulsively touches her curls to reassure herself. The unflattering glare of direct light horrifies her

—as it does Mrs. Stone of *Roman Spring* and Blanche DuBois of *Streetcar*—even in remembrance. Psychological withdrawal into her isolated, private reality is Lucretia Collins' defense and her disaster.

Like Mrs. Hardwicke-Moore and Miss Collins, *Menagerie's* Amanda Wingfield, *Streetcar's* Blanche DuBois, and *Summer's* Alma Winemiller proclaim themselves to be *Ladies*. They, too, affect an air of grandeur, maintaining preciously elegant gestures and speech in situations that render those traits incongruous. Amanda persists in clutching the fragments of dreams, the tatters of memory, for psychological sustenance. Vociferously recollecting the battalions of gentlemen who formerly called on her at Blue Mountain, she complicates for her family the trials of ordinary life in the present. However, Williams enables Amanda to calculate shrewdly when necessary. In this respect, as in their bonds to the past and in their affected mannerisms, Amanda Wingfield, Mrs. Hardwicke-Moore, Blanche DuBois, Camille, and the other specimens of Pattern B are closely related. For example, Mrs. Hardwicke-Moore possesses marked self-control as she humorously but decisively complains to her landlady of cockroaches. The Lady of Larkspur Lotion is disturbed particularly, it seems, because those roaches *fly*. She experiences, moreover, not merely disgust but what she describes as horror of even "pedestrian" roaches. This incident reveals Mrs. Hardwicke-Moore's ability to confront the Now unless present circumstances threaten her inner security, compelling her retreat into imagination. Similarly, Blanche DuBois of *Streetcar*—despite and because of herself—attempts to resubjugate her younger sister. Likewise, Tom's mother in both *Menagerie* and "Girl in Glass" displays acumen in her subscription-selling and in her businesslike preparations for Laura's gentleman caller. Also Camille of *Camino Real* and "Ten Blocks" is businesslike in purchasing the society of young men.

Other specimens of Pattern B characterization abound in Williams' works: Laura, the wistful creature of *Menagerie* and of "Girl in Glass," resembles Blanche and Alma in being a hypersensitive dreamer. Her retirement from reality is symbolized and effected by her fetishlike addiction to a glass collection that protects, isolates, and imperils her. When she discovers that her gentleman caller is Jim O'Connor, whom she has adored privately and faithfully since her high school days, she cannot cope with present events. Jim is attracted to her but is deterred by her formidable Ladyness. This ambivalence provides another parallel in the characterization patterns of the Williams canon, for such is the reaction, initially, of Mitch to Blanche in *Streetcar* and, eventually, of John to Alma in *Summer*. The entire gentleman-caller episode fails for the Wingfields when Jim discloses his engagement to a girl other than Laura; similar fiascoes wreck Blanche's opportunities with Mitch and Alma's with John. Alma is capable, at least temporarily, of escape; Blanche remains the prisoner of her antagonists, including herself.

In their physical as well as their psychological composition, the characters of Pattern B resemble one another. Camille's hypertension disposes her to drugs, fainting, and hectic emotionality. Amanda Wingfield and Lucretia Collins declare their susceptibility to malaria. Miss Collins, Laura, Alma, and Blanche all have the habit of dabbing their faces with handkerchiefs when distraught. Camille performs this gesture in *Camino Real*, but her sorrow is so passionate that the handkerchief is bloodied. Preoccupation with physical attributes and appearances is typical of these personalities. Amanda's hair, like Miss Collins', is set in girlish ringlets. Blanche DuBois avoids direct light and repeatedly asks: "How do I look?" The prospect of losing the physical attributes of youth and beauty terrifies Blanche. Lucretia Collins, on the other hand, chooses not to admit such loss; Amanda Wingfield seizes vestiges of glory and glamorizes them with memory; but Blanche, like Camille of *Camino Real* and Marguerite of "Ten Blocks," senses the disintegration of her physical charm and the fading of her life.

At least eight of Williams' short plays provide examples of the Pattern B characterization. "The Last of My Solid Gold Watches" depicts the living death of Charlie Colton, a salesman whose pride, reinforced by mementoes of former success, is assaulted by new products, new values, and the insinuation of death. He is a Gentleman, "Mr. Charlie Colton," imperious, vain, and bypassed. "Lord Byron's Love Letter" presents two women who depend upon the past for their very livelihood. Supposedly, the Old Woman had a tryst with Byron, and the Spinster is the illegitimate issue of that affair. These stage-persons, hardly characters, attempt to earn money by exhibiting a letter, the token of romantic seduction, for a fee.

They are locked away from the present in the cell of their musty room, a niche in time and space isolated even from the carpe diem insistence of the New Orleans Mardi Gras that surrounds them. The physically ill Bertha in "Hello from Bertha" apparently suffers from delusions of persecution. She accuses former coworkers of robbing her and of conspiring to have her hospitalized. She insists that she is a person of influence, and delusionary hope of rescue is associated with memories of a former lover. Her former lover is a salesman named Charlie; Williams includes salesmen as characters in *Summer and Smoke*, *The Rose Tattoo*, and "The Last of My Solid Gold Watches"; *The Glass Menagerie* and "Portrait of a Girl in Glass" contain dramatic references to the personality of a salesman-father. Other dramatis personae trapped in present time and place by bonds to the past include the mutually dependent Man and Woman of "Talk to Me Like the Rain," the aggressive Cornelia Scott and submissive Grace Lancaster of "Something Unspoken," the balky Moony and romantically retrospective Jane of "Moony's Kid Don't Cry."

In Williams' stories too the Pattern B characterization is discernible. Oliver Winemiller of "One Arm"—like Kilroy of *Camino* and "Ten Blocks," as well as Brick Pollitt of both *Cat* and "Three Players of a Summer Game"—is a former athlete whose lost prestige, the result of lost physical prowess, incapacitates him. For the mutilated Oliver, for the alcoholic Brick, and for the muddleminded Kilroy, time past reinforces the trap of time present. Brick and Kilroy endure, dependent upon other people; Margaret becomes Brick's prop (and conqueror?), whereas Quixote rescues Kilroy.

Perceived as archetypes of history or of legend which their names imply, the *Camino Real* characters can confuse the audience and can elicit spectator responses that are inappropriate to the communicative purposes stated by Williams in his foreword and afterword to *Camino Real*. Recognized, however, as archetypes of characterization patterns that permeate and tend to unify the many plays and stories of Tennessee Williams, those *Camino Real* stage-persons assume meaningful identity. Quixote and Byron are romantic dreamers stimulated by memories to escape a trap in present time (Pattern A). Casanova and Camille emerge as romantic dreamers incapable of coping with the present because they will not relinquish the past (Pattern B).

But what of other characterization patterns recurring throughout and tending to integrate the plays and stories of Tennessee Williams?

Pattern C

Gutman, proprietor of the Siete Mares Hotel in *Camino Real*, is another of Williams' archetypes: a character who threatens, with weapons of present urgency, the delusions and memories of his fellows. Functioning as actor-announcer-commentator, Gutman is comparable in relatively recent theatrical literature to the druggist-stage manager of Thornton Wilder's *Our Town* and perhaps ultimately to the chorus of classical drama. It is Gutman who notifies the audience and dramatis personae of the scene divisions, or blocks, as Williams terms them. It is Gutman, also, who stimulates much action: He orders the barrier guards to admit Quixote; describes for the audience the idiosyncrasies of his Siete Mares hotel guests; frustrates the desires of the Survivor, of Casanova, of Kilroy, and of other dreamers; sounds the klaxon of ordinary reality in extraordinary situations (for example, in the Fugitivo and in the Fiesta episodes). It is the realistic Gutman who rips the fabric of illusion even as he impels the fantastic action of *Camino Real*.

In *The Glass Menagerie* Tom Wingfield performs a function similar to Gutman's; but whereas Tom is himself a prisoner striving to escape his penitentiary—and that last word seems particularly appropriate here—Gutman remains a warden. (Perhaps that job is Gutman's "punishment"?) Whereas Tom carries with him the necessity of his own penance, Gutman sees that penance is done by others. Tom is recognizable as a variation of Pattern A with modifications of Patterns B and C; Gutman sustains Pattern C characterization throughout *Camino Real*.

Also, Mrs. Wire of "Larkspur Lotion" emerges fundamentally as a Pattern C character, a pragmatic and brash landlady counterposed to the dreamer-protagonist. Under Mrs. Wire's assault, the Lady of Larkspur Lotion retreats into the private reality of dreams. Similarly, in "Portrait of a Madonna," the Elevator Boy personifies Pattern C; he snickers, insinuates, ridicules Lucretia Collins with deliberate rudeness. As Gutman represents the insistent threat of present circumstances to the people of *Camino Real* (and to those of "Ten Blocks,"), as Mrs. Wire castigates Mrs. Hardwicke-Moore, and as the Elevator Boy baits Miss Collins, so the Movers and Silva confront Joe Bassett of "The Long Goodbye" with present urgency. The Movers' salacious comments and Silva's beer-drinking prescriptions serve to counterpoint Joe's reverie. Bob Harper likewise intrudes upon the musings of Charlie Colton in "The Last of My Solid Gold Watches." The Husband abruptly returns the other characters of "Lord Byron's Love Letters" to present time and place. Goldie attempts, unsuccessfully, to do the same thing for Bertha in "Hello from Bertha." Even young Tom, the boy in "This Property Is Condemned," counters little Willie's extravagant pretensions. In "The Long Stay Cut Short, or, The Unsatisfactory Supper," Archie Lee personifies Pattern C; he refers pointedly to Aunt Rose's delusions of grandeur before he and Baby Doll abandon the old woman, accompanied by only memories, to a storm. Stanley Kowalski of *Streetcar* seizes every opportunity to penetrate Blanche DuBois's defense of memory and of dream. To Stanley, Belle Reve ("Beautiful Dream") is a wasted financial investment instead of the estate which, for Blanche, symbolizes justification of her claims to social prestige and personal distinction. Stanley mocks Blanche's mannerisms, destroys her romance with Mitch, attacks the delusion of her Ladyness with the facts of her sexual promiscuity. Blanche's refuge is in the past and in her imagination; Stanley, personifying Pattern C characterization, works to annihilate not only the refuge but the refugee.

As with his other archetypes, Pattern C characters appear frequently not only in Tennessee Williams' plays but also in his stories. For example, the cousins of "Hard Candy" claw at the private reality of Mr. Krupper. The passerby and Jane Austin shatter Donald's defense against the world in "The Vine," driving him back to the warm shelter of Rachel's reciprocal dependence upon him. Also functioning as Pattern C personalities are Paolo, Meg Bishop, and the Contessa, who snap the threads of Mrs. Stone's romantic imagination in *The Roman Spring of Mrs. Stone*.

Within the context of this discussion, Gutman of *Camino Real* emerges with special (and perhaps previously unperceived) importance to the audience. For what Tennessee Williams hoped would be his most communicative play, Gutman serves as the archetype of Pattern C.

Pattern D

Kilroy of *Camino Real* and "Ten Blocks" apparently represents a fourth characterization pattern: that of an athletic, unsophisticated dreamer who, suffering mutilation or loss, elicits audience sympathy.

For all his buffoonery and clownishness, this former boxer is a stage-person who radiates the appeal of spectacular failure. He is easygoing, open-hearted, gregarious, and weak. Kilroy's weakness is his utter dependence upon the aggressiveness of other characters so far as the highlighting of his own personality is concerned. He stands out boldly, but that boldness is one of sculptured relief against the dynamic background provided by Quixote, Gutman, the Gypsy, and the other dramatis personae. Kilroy, usually muddled, is pathetically ineffectual; but his very naiveté and his lack of affectation arouse sympathy. His souvenirs—the jeweled championship belt and the golden gloves—betoken his dependence upon Whathasbeen. His preoccupation with heart disease and implied abhorrence of time's tyranny are punctuated by the squawk of the Gypsy's loudspeaker and by the laboratory-pursuit sequences. Kilroy's present distress, piqued by his drive to escape from the plaza, is resolved not through his own volition but by the action of other characters. Even his lurid scenes with Esmeralda are motivated by the Gypsy and by Esmeralda herself. Unable to match Byron's courage in quitting the Camino Real plaza, Kilroy loses his nerve. Ultimately, this baby-hero is rescued only through the zeal of Quixote. Even at the last, Kilroy speaks with wistful uncertainty as he follows the aged knight into an unknown land.

Moony of "Moony's Kid Don't Cry" is another personification of Pattern D. This young, strong workman shares many physical qualities with Stanley Kowalski of *Streetcar*: pride in bodily prowess; a conqueror's attitude toward women; energetic awareness of his would-be independence. Moony's zest for personal freedom tempts him to abandon his home (cf. the motivation of Tom in *Menagerie* and "Girl in Glass" as well as that of Joe in "Goodbye"); but the pride of fatherhood, nourishing his vanity, blocks the temptation.

Jim O'Connor (*Menagerie*, "Girl in Glass"), Mitch (*Streetcar*), and John Buchanan (*Summer*) exhibit Pattern D traits in their associations, respectively, with Laura Wingfield, Blanche DuBois, and Alma Winemiller.

Oliver Winemiller of "One Arm"—like Kilroy of *Camino Real* and "Ten Blocks"—is represented by Williams as charming and defeated, a characteristic representation also for Brick Pollitt in both "Three Players of a Summer Game" and *Cat on a Hot Tin Roof*. Except for the loss of his arm, Oliver's physical appearance corresponds even to details of costume with Kilroy's in *Camino Real*; both of the young ex-boxers wear skivvy shirts and dungarees. Oliver shares with Kilroy a penchant for comic-book buffoonery. Oliver's torso—like Alvaro Mangiacavallo's in *The Rose Tattoo* and the younger writer's in "Night of the Iguana"—is represented by sculptural epithets. And his appearance—like Stanley Kowalski's (*Streetcar*) and Moony's ("Moony's Kid")—is compared with that of an animal.

Other specimens of Pattern D characterization, whose *Camino Real* archetype is Kilroy, include the following: the Boxer in "The Strangest Kind of Romance," Christopher Cosmos in "The Coming of Something to the Widow Holly," and Richard of "The Resemblance between a Violin Case and a Coffin."

Unexplicated, *Camino Real's* Kilroy may appear to audiences as merely a somewhat pitiable fool of a former athlete. But *related to* Williams' other plays and stories, Kilroy becomes recognizable as the embodiment of a characterization theme (here called Pattern D); he emerges as the personification of an athletically inclined, unsophisticated dreamer who, associated with loss, invites audience interest.

Other Categories

The aforementioned classification system is offered as one approach to the study of characterization patterns in Williams' plays and stories. Those interested in other categories may find the following guides useful.

A. Forty-three characters whose defensive, private reality is assaulted by ordinary existence:
　　1. Amanda ("Rubio y Morena")

2. Joe Bassett ("The Long Goodbye")
3. Bertha ("Hello from Bertha")
4. Anthony Burns ("Desire and the Black Masseur")
5. Camille (*Camino Real* and "Ten Blocks on the Camino Real")
6. Casanova (*Camino Real* and "Ten Blocks on the Camino Real")
7. Donald ("The Vine")
8. Blanche DuBois (*A Streetcar Named Desire*)
9. Lucretia Collins ("Portrait of a Madonna")
10. Charlie Colton ("The Last of My Solid Gold Watches")
11. Eloi Duvenet ("Auto-Da-Fé")
12. Flora ("The Important Thing")
13. Pablo Gonzales ("The Mysteries of the Joy Rio")
14. Mrs. Hardwicke-Moore ("The Lady of Larkspur Lotion")
15. Mrs. Holly ("The Coming of Something to the Widow Holly")
16. Jane ("Moony's Kid Don't Cry")
17. Edith Jelkes ("The Night of the Iguana")
18. John ("The Important Thing")
19. Kamrowski ("Rubio y Morena")
20. Mr. Krupper ("Hard Candy")
21. Lawrence (*I Rise in Flame, Cried the Phoenix*)
22. Lucio ("The Malediction")
23. The Little Man ("The Strangest Kind of Romance")
24. The Man ("Talk to Me like the Rain . . .")
25. Narrator ("The Angel in the Alcove")
26. Narrator ("Chronicle of a Demise")
27. Narrator ("The Resemblance between a Violin Case and a Coffin")
28. Narrator's Sister ("The Resemblance between a Violin Case and a Coffin")
29. Poet ("The Poet")
30. Brick Pollitt (*Cat on a Hot Tin Roof* and "Three Players of a Summer Game")
31. Rachel ("The Vine")
32. Aunt Rose ("The Long Stay Cut Short, or, The Unsatisfactory Supper")
33. The Saint ("Chronicle of a Demise")
34. Dorothy Simple ("The Case of the Crushed Petunias")
35. The Son ("The Purification")
36. Homer Stallcup ("The Field of Blue Children")
37. Karen Stone (*The Roman Spring of Mrs. Stone*)
38. Willie ("This Property Is Condemned")

39. Alma Winemiller (*Summer and Smoke*)
40. Oliver Winemiller ("One Arm")
41. Laura Wingfield (*The Glass Menagerie*) and
    Tom's Sister ("Portrait of a Girl in Glass")
42. The Woman ("Talk to Me Like the Rain . . .")
43. The Writer ("The Lady of Larkspur Lotion")

B. Thirty-seven characters whose instrument of survival is aggressive self-assertion:

1. Jane Austin ("The Vine")
2. Archie Lee Bowman ("The Long Stay Cut Short, or,
   The Unsatisfactory Supper")
3. Baby Doll Bowman ("The Long Stay Cut Short, or,
   The Unsatisfactory Supper")
4. Meg Bishop (*The Roman Spring of Mrs. Stone*)
5. The Elevator Boy ("Portrait of a Madonna")
6. John Buchanan (*Summer and Smoke*)
7. The Contessa (*The Roman Spring of Mrs. Stone*)
8. Christopher Cosmos ("The Coming of Something to
   the Widow Holly")
9. The Cousins ("Hard Candy")
10. The Saint's Cousin ("Chronicle of a Demise")
11. Goldie ("Hello from Bertha")
12. Rosa Gonzales (*Summer and Smoke*)
13. Gutman (*Camino Real* and "Ten Blocks on the Camino Real")
14. The Gypsy (*Camino Real* and "Ten Blocks on the
    Camino Real")
15. Bob Harper ("The Last of My Solid Gold Watches")
16. Olga Kedrova ("The Mattress by the Tomato Patch")
17. Stanley Kowalski (*A Streetcar Named Desire*)
18. The Landlady ("The Angel in the Alcove")
19. The Landlady ("The Strangest Kind of Romance")
20. The Landlady ("The Malediction")
21. Luisa ("The Purification")
22. The Young Man ("The Case of the Crushed Petunias")
23. The Masseur ("Desire and the Black Masseur")
24. Jake Meighan ("27 Wagons Full of Cotton")
25. Moony ("Moony's Kid Don't Cry")
26. The Movers ("The Long Goodbye")
27. Myra ("The Field of Blue Children")
28. Myra ("The Long Goodbye")

29. Paolo (*The Roman Spring of Mrs. Stone*)
30. Margaret Pollitt (*Cat on a Hot Tin Roof* and "Three Players of a Summer Game")
31. Richard ("The Resemblance between a Violin Case and a Coffin")
32. Silva ("The Long Goodbye")
33. The Usher ("The Mysteries of the Joy Rio")
34. Silva Vicarro ("27 Wagons Full of Cotton")
35. Alma Winemiller ("The Yellow Bird")
36. Amanda Wingfield (*The Glass Menagerie*) and Tom's Mother ("Portrait of a Girl in Glass")
37. Mrs. Wire ("The Lady of Larkspur Lotion")

Still other classification systems can be devised, reflecting, for example, the recurrence of characterization patterns involving spinsters, prostitutes, seekers of romance, and sexual adventurers. Perhaps, however, the foregoing illustrations suffice to support this opinion: Recognizable archetypes of characterization, classifiable under more than one system, permeate and tend to unify the whole of Tennessee Williams' drama and fiction. A corollary belief is that the stage-persons of *Camino Real* must be perceived *as creatures of Tennessee Williams' talent* rather than misidentified as the personalities of legend or of literary history whose names they wear. Indeed, the unclarified assignment of "Quixote," "Camille," "Casanova," and other stock names *to Williams' own characters*, who are presented in a kaleidoscope of carnivalian fantasy, may block rather than promote communication between the author and the audiences of *Camino Real*.

Physical Settings

The *Camino Real* setting contains three main areas: the Siete Mares Hotel with its terrace and balcony; Skid Row, comprising the Ritz Men Only and the Gypsy's Establishment; the plaza with its fountain and stone stairs leading to the Way Out. This triune organization corresponds to *Summer and Smoke*'s arrangement of two houses and the public square.

The *Camino* plaza has its counterpart of a central playing area in the public square of *Summer*. The plaza fountain serves, visually, to unify the action of *Camino*: At *Camino*'s opening, the Survivor dies and Don Quixote slumbers near the fountain base; the Fiesta and the Fugitivo scenes occur in the fountain area instead of on Skid Row or at the Siete Mares; and, at the end of the play, Don Quixote bathes in the fountain's waters. Similarly, the *Summer* fountain with its stone angel of Eternity provides a visual focus: Alma's first action is to drink at the fountain; the stone statue is literally high-lighted during and between the scenes of *Summer*; and, finally, Alma addresses her valedictory salute to the fountain angel.

The flight of stairs leading to the Way Out, another visual focus in *Camino Real*, has a counterpart in the piazza stairway for *The Roman Spring of Mrs. Stone*. The luxurious trappings of the Siete Mares Hotel in *Camino* correspond in quality to those of Mrs. Stone's rented palazzo and to Miss Scott's household in "Something Unspoken." The Ritz Men Only is one of many cheap hotels and rooming houses that serve as settings for Williams' plays and stories, including *A Streetcar Named Desire*, "Hello from Bertha," "Moony's Kid Don't Cry," "Portrait of a Girl in Glass," "Rubio y Morena," "Talk to Me Like the Rain . . . ," "The Angel in the Alcove," "The Dark Room," *The Glass Menagerie*, "The Lady of Larkspur Lotion," "The Last of My Solid Gold Watches," "The Long Goodbye," "The Malediction," "The Strangest Kind of Ro-mance," "The Yellow Bird," "Portrait of a Madonna," and "This Property Is Condemned."

Lights, Colors, and Music

Besides its patterns of characterization and of setting, *Camino Real* is related to Williams' other works by recurring patterns of lights, colors, and music. Gauze transparencies, string curtains, and similar scrims modify the lighting not only of *Camino* but also of "Goodbye," *Menagerie*, *Streetcar*, and *Tattoo*. Transitions for the "Goodbye" flashback scenes involving Myra and Mrs. Bassett occur through special dimming and brightening effects complemented by symbolic colors and music to convey the impact of memories. The *Menagerie* screen device, specified in the published version but omitted from the original Broadway production of the play, is a sur-face upon which images and titles are projected for visual emphasis. As in Williams' other works, his detailed manipulation of lights and transparencies in *Menagerie* apparently reflects an effort to achieve fluidity of time, space, and action. Similar lighting effects are found in *Streetcar*, whose spectators (like those of *Menagerie*) are enabled by stage transparencies and adjustments of illumination to peer through a "fourth wall." The major divisions of *Summer*, also, are expressly signified not by the rise or fall of proscenium curtains but by adjustments of lighting. But continuing his efforts to achieve flexibility of physical form, Williams dispenses altogether with transparencies in *Summer*; even wall-sections appear only when set-pieces are functionally necessary to that play. With *Tattoo*, however, Williams returns to his earlier *Menagerie* scrim.

Williams' patterns of lighting reinforce the suggestion of a time-space drift for his characters. And besides establishing the memory-context of flashback scenes, his purposeful adjustments of illumination also suggest a transition to after-action transcending the play proper at the moment that they conclude action immediately at hand. Drifting among losses, suspended between time present and time past, Williams' dramatis personae who look so frequently upon the world as if it were a dream are themselves occasionally rendered almost dreamlike by lighting effects. They live and die behind screens of gauze, webby transparencies, pseudodefensive devices that reveal but do not always safeguard.

Many of Williams' characters exhibit almost panicky and usually ineffectual aversion to direct light. During the *Camino Real* chase scene (Block Six), Kilroy, his pursuers, Esmeralda, her nurse, and other play-persons are plunged into confusion that spews through the playhouse auditorium and spills back upon the stage. The climax of this spectacular episode occurs when the police close upon the distraught Kilroy and a dazzling spotlight illuminates him. Lighting becomes a medium of proclaiming Kilroy's dismay and degradation. Compelled to assume a patsy's costume, Kilroy lights his nose, which then blinks with firefly rhythm until the stage is dimmed to darkness. Direct light also accentuates Camille's despair when she is abandoned by the Fugitivo which, to her, is the symbol as well as the means of flight. In Block Nine Camille is caught by a dazzling follow-spotlight that blinds her; and in Block Eleven blinding shafts of light intensify Casanova's anguish as well.

These visual effects may alienate theatergoers who, jolted by the sudden intrusion of a technical device, do not recognize direct, intense lighting as an accent-mark of Williams' work patterns. Perceived solely as a heavy stroke of theatrical mechanics, Williams' light-play may distract and offend; interpreted, in part, as a feature of plot and characterization, it merits revaluation. Williams' men and women, psychologically, are creatures of darkness; what, therefore, could be more damning to them than the assault of ordinary reality through the medium of sudden and concentrated light?

This pattern is consistent: *Streetcar's* Blanche DuBois, who cannot endure strong light, is exposed to the glare of a locomotive headlamp and to the stark rays of a naked light bulb. Unshaded light punctuates also the woes of Mrs. Hardwicke-Moore in "Larkspur," Lucretia Collins in "Madonna," the Little Man in "Romance" (called Lucio in "Malediction"), the Narrator of "Angel," Edith Jelkes of "Iguana," and Karen Stone of *Roman Spring*. Lucretia Collins' and Mrs. Stone's nemesis is bright sunlight; bare light bulbs distress the other characters.

Williams' symbolism accommodates less intense forms of lighting, also. Associated especially with hopeful situations, for example, are shaded lamps and glowing candles. Again Williams' pattern is consistent: Candles are traditional emblems of romance, of imagination, of persons who seek solace in shadows. At the same time, candles are weapons whereby one can ward off evil (utter darkness); candles are sources of flattering (unglaring) light; and candles are symbols that appear often in the works of Tennessee Williams.

For instance, hoping to create a romantic atmosphere of courtship, Blanche DuBois declares to Mitch in scene six of *Streetcar*: "I want to create—*joie de vivre!* I'm lighting a candle ... (She lights a candle stub and puts it in a bottle.) Je suis la Dame aux Camellias!" In scene eight, Blanche counterposes birthday candles (the symbols of joy and hope) with her fear of glaring light (the antithesis of romance and illusion); she voices her hope that the eyes of her sister Stella's yet unborn child will resemble two big candles, lighted and festive; Blanche observes that when light bulbs replace candles, one sees too plainly.

The pattern remains consistent: In *Menagerie* candles symbolize romantic imagination; they help to create the diffused atmosphere of the dinner episode (scene seven), and there is pathos in Laura's extinguishing the candles of her hopeful dreams at the final moment of that play. Williams' candles of hope appear again as vigil lamps for Serafina in *Tattoo* and for Amada in "Rubio." The *Camino Real* action involving a candle, although incidental and easily obscured by simultaneous plot development, is relevant here: During the Byron episode (Block Nine), the theme of which is hope and honest valor, Camille and Casanova are seated at a screened, candlelit Siete Mares table. Following Byron's exit, a minor character runs across the plaza; he carries a billowing flambeau. At this moment the Fugitivo's engines are heard. Recognizing the Fugitivo as her only vehicle of escape, Camille performs a paradoxical gesture; to perceive the symbol of flight, she extinguishes the symbol of hope: Trying to see the Fugitivo airplane, she blows out the flame of her candle. And, subsequently, flight is denied her.

Perhaps more spectacular in Williams' pattern of lighting is his fire symbolism. Recounting Shelley's death, Byron of *Camino Real* associates the flames of cremation with the idea of purification. And in "Black Masseur" fire serves as the portent of ultimate atonement (purification of sin) as well as death for Anthony Burns, whose name itself may be a symbolic pun. Elsewhere in the Williams canon, the landlady of "Angel" contends that she accomplishes purification, not merely destruction, when she causes the mattress of a tubercular and homosexual artist to be burned. And "Auto-Da-Fé" (a play whose very title, alluding to the burning of a heretic, connotes a fire image) is climaxed by the suicidal arson of Eloi Duvenet. Eloi's mother synthesizes the effects of light, color, sound, characterization, and action with one word that she, like Blanche of *Streetcar*, shrieks in hysterical refrain: *"Fire!"*

In his afterword to *Camino Real*, Williams asserts his awareness of form, color, line, light, and motion; and stage directions throughout his works reflect that awareness. In *Menagerie*, for example, directions stipulate that Laura's light should resemble the lighting of early religious portraits and of paintings by El Greco. Williams' directions for the fragmentary setting of *Summer* also refer to visual art, specifically to Chirico's painting "Conversation among the Ruins." And Williams' stage portrait of the young Rosa in *Tattoo* corresponds to a blending of Botticelli's "Birth of Venus" with Giorgione's "Sleeping Venus." In faint light Rosa sleeps upon a concave surface of white cloth that resembles the lustrous hollow of a shell; in the sky above her, Venus shines as a planet. *Streetcar,* also, sustains Williams' pictorial pattern: Blanche tells Stanley that she likes an artist who paints in strong and bold colors (scene two). The detailed directions for scene three require a Van Gogh picture of a billiard parlor at night. And Williams describes the pokerplayers—Stanley, Steve, Mitch, Pablo—as men at their physical prime, coarse, direct, and powerful as primary colors.

Two of the primary colors—blue and red particularly—course through the mosaic design of *Camino Real.* As the curtain rises for the *Camino* Prologue, a shaft of blue light discloses Don Quixote, who explains that blue is the color of distance, nobility, and remembrance. Blue serves as a color symbol of remoteness in place as well as time; Williams surrounds those *Camino* characters who have legendary names with flickering, blue radiance. Blue also signifies purification; Byron refers to the purifying flame, the blue flame, of Shelley's cremation. Thus, in Williams' work patterns, blue functions as a color symbol of what is noble, pure, and remote by association with memory. Conversely, red is linked in *Camino* to qualities of emphasis, vigor, passion, and peril. The Guards who challenge Quixote carry red lanterns. Prudence's hair is henna-streaked. A red stain signals the Survivor's death. Kilroy's championship belt, the souvenir of his success as a boxer, contains rubies. The white jackets of the macabre Streetcleaners are punctuated with flecks of red. Block Ten, a scene of intense despair and increasing danger, opens with a flickering of red lights. A cryptic, rice-paper banner is, in part, scarlet. Kilroy's frustration is made visual by the blinking red nose and the red fright wig of his patsy costume. The sign of Esmeralda's invitation to Kilroy in Block Eleven is her tossing roses to him, one of which he places between his teeth. Camille mentions wearing a pink flower as the token of menstrual limitations to pleasure. Manifestations of red, moreover, are aural as well as visual; the name of the plaza prostitute, for example, is Rosita.

Williams' pictorial conception of literary art emerges through his efforts to create portraits and tableaux apparently intended to transcend a proscenium, an arena, or a page, much as pieces of sculpture are at once static and dynamic or as paintings are contained by, yet transcend, the time-space limits of their frames.

For example, the color-lights of *Tattoo* mirror Serafina's conflict: the struggle between entrapment by memory, exemplary of Characterization Pattern B, and escape from the prison of nostalgia, indicative of Characterization Pattern A. Half of *Tattoo* is set in blue light, the light of evening or of predawn hours, the light of romantic entrapment or refuge. The other scenes are staged contrastingly in the glaring brilliance of daylight, the light of vigorous realism. Thus the principal cause of a memory trap (Serafina's apotheosis of her dead husband Rosario) and the instruments of rebirth-escape (Alvaro's wooing of Serafina, Jack Hunter and Rosa's love) are visually reinforced by key color-lights as well as by characterization and action.

Verbal and physical nuances of red abound in *The Rose Tattoo*, as the very title of that play suggests. The stage setting contains rose-patterned wallpaper, a rose-colored carpet, and ruby articles such as a vigil light in its glass cup. Roses and rosy tints pervade Williams' choices of words, stage-props, costumes, and music, as evidenced by the name of the delle Rose family, two of whose members are called Rosario and Rosa; by the rose tattoos of Rosario, Serafina, Estelle, and Alvaro; by the rose-silk shirt designed for Rosario but received by Alvaro; by Serafina's mourning dress, which is a soiled pink slip; by the roses in Serafina's hair and on her fan; by Estelle's funeral bouquet of roses; by Jack's friendship bouquet of roses; by bottles of wine; and by bowls literally filled with roses passim. Also, the *Tattoo* dialogue sustains Williams' rose pattern and occasionally evokes humor. For instance, in act one, scene four, a neighborhood woman, incensed by Serafina's delay in finishing a dress, exclaims: "Now what she wear, my daughter, to graduate in? A couple of towels and a rose in the hair?" Williams' rose also symbolizes the attempted defense of beauty and love by imagination. For example, in act three, scene two, Jack echoes Serafina's description of Rosa as a rose and says that his beloved sees him through rose-colored glasses. Indeed, the color-pattern of *Tattoo* begins and ends with red. Initially, the spectators see a small boy with a red kite (who, incidentally, prompts comparison with Tom in "This Property Is Condemned"). Finally,

Rosario's rose-silk shirt finds its way to Serafina's new lover; and the romantic vigor of new passion (red) replaces the idealized restraint of retrospection (blue).

Again Williams is consistent: His red-blue pattern appears in the setting, props, words, and actions of *Summer* also. The sky, with varying shades and tints of blue, is the prevailing backdrop of that play; Gonzales' daughter is named Rosa; Alma's family name is Winemiller (so is Oliver's in "One Arm"); and Alma, entertaining *Summer* memories of passion, accepts a gift of sachet rose. In *Streetcar*, when the trap of memory shuts completely upon her (scene eleven), Blanche DuBois wears a jacket of Della Robbia blue. Even the grapes that she eats in this scene maintain the red-blue motif as does, too, her fancy that she will be buried in an ocean as blue as the eyes of her first lover. Not only *Streetcar*'s words, costumes, and props but also its music convey the blues; Williams' "blue piano" is heard throughout the play. Subdued, however, for Laura Wingfield's story, the nostalgic quality of blues music imbues *Menagerie* with what Williams describes as light, delicate, sad, nostalgic sound which links the episodes of that play. Furthermore, the setting of *Cat on a Hot Tin Roof* continues Williams' red-blue pattern. The *Cat* cyclorama suggests a summer sky that fades into the blues of dusk and night. Against this blue background appear Brick Pollitt's red hair, major action colored by rose-silk drapes, and, in the original script, a rose-silk shaded lamp beside the bed that promises replacements for souvenirs of past sorrows.

Two prominent illustrations of Williams' color-values occur in *Streetcar* and in *Menagerie*. In scene ten of *Streetcar*, Blanche DuBois causes a visual explosion by slamming her mirror so violently that it cracks. Moments later the violence of Stanley's attack upon Blanche is reflected in colors, lights, and sounds. On the walls surrounding Blanche, lurid reflections appear like flames; and the bestial cries of a jungle are heard. Williams' patterns of color, light, sound, music, word, characterization, and action are synthesized when, at the climax of Mitch's rejection of her, Blanche hysterically screams "Fire!" At that instant Williams' patterns indeed merge, with the red fury of fire affording stark relief for Blanche, whose name is *white*, clad in her scarlet robe against a frame of blue light. Perhaps not quite so sensational but nonetheless notable is Williams' merger of his favorite symbols in *Menagerie*; his sobriquet for Laura Wingfield when she reaches the crux of conflict between romantic isolation and vigorous realism is "Blue Roses."

Camino Real as Tennessee Williams' Portmanteau

To other essayists remain, for the present, evaluation of moral aspects and literary merits in Tennessee Williams' works. To them also remains the tracing of influences exerted upon his plays and stories by these factors: his childhood; residence at his grandfather's rectories in Tennessee and Mississippi; family hardships in Missouri; friendships and enmities in Iowa, Louisiana, California, Florida, and countries abroad; his love of his sister Rose; Kip's memory; Ozzie's relationship; and the biographical allusions of his poems.

This study has explored the 1945–1955 plays and stories of Tennessee Williams in an attempt to disclose patterns of expression, patterns of words and other symbols, symbols subjected from the moment of their making to dire misconception or to appropriate interpretation or most probably to some territory in between. *Camino Real* has provided a focal point and now offers a conclusion for this essay: Williams' foreword to *Camino* cites Casanova's eviction from the Siete Mares. Casanova's portmanteau is flung from the balcony of that luxurious hotel. While the portmanteau is in the air, Casanova shouts a caution. The suitcase crashes upon the street; it had contained fragile mementoes of unique value. *Camino Real* may well be Tennessee Williams' portmanteau.

Brick Pollitt as Homo Ludens: "Three Players of a Summer Game" and *Cat on a Hot Tin Roof*

CHARLES E. MAY

IF MAGGIE THE CAT is one of Tennessee Williams' most dramatically engaging characters, her husband, Brick Pollitt, is one of his most metaphysically mysterious. Brick's enigmatic detachment in *Cat on a Hot Tin Roof* has been the subject of more problematical commentary than either Maggie's feline restlessness or the spirit of mendacity that dominates the thematic action of the play itself. With his cool ironic smile and relative immobility (suggested both by his literal crutch and by the crutchlike liquor cabinet from which he never strays very far), Brick is, by contrast, the ambiguous center for all the characters in *Cat* who dance about on the hot tin roof of their "common crisis." Because Brick's detachment is thus so crucial, and also because Williams makes him so teasingly mysterious, the central question of the play that has always puzzled critics, a question still unanswered, is: What, apart from its function as catalyst for the dramatic action, does Brick's detachment mean?

In his "Note of Explanation" in the published version of *Cat*, Williams makes it quite explicit that for him Brick's "moral paralysis" is central to the play, a "root thing" in Brick's "tragedy." In fact, Williams felt Brick's problem was so basic to his own conception of *Cat* that of the three changes Elia Kazan urged him to make in the Broadway version of the play, the alteration in Brick's character in the third act is the change to which he devotes most of his ex-

277

planation. Williams complains that such a dramatic progression tends to obscure the meaning of Brick's tragedy, for no matter how revelatory the conversion, it never effects such an immediate change in the "heart or even conduct of a person in Brick's state of spiritual disrepair" (p. 168). Indeed, Nancy Tischler says that as a result of the change in Brick in the third act of the Broadway version, audiences may leave the theater suspecting that the "whole truth" about him has not been told (p. 210).

However, even those critics who consult Williams' original third act, included in the published version of the play, complain that the meaning of Brick's tragedy remains obscure. Williams' own commentary offers no clarification. He is well aware of the mystery of Brick's personality, and he wishes to leave it that way. "Some mystery should be left in the revelation of character in a play, just as a great deal of mystery is always left in the revelation of character in life, even in one's own character to himself" (pp. 114–15). Although everyone familiar with the play is aware that Brick's disgust with life and resultant detachment has something to do with his homosexual relationship, latent or otherwise, with his friend Skipper, most readers sense that this is not the whole truth. Again, Williams encourages rather than clarifies the ambiguity. As Brick and Big Daddy "timidly and painfully" try to discuss the "inadmissible thing that Skipper died to disavow," Williams comments that the "fact that if it existed it had to be disavowed to 'keep face' in the world they lived in, may be at the heart of the 'mendacity' that Brick drinks to kill his disgust with. It may be the root of his collapse. Or maybe it is only a single manifestation of it, not even the most important" (p. 114).

Throughout the published version of *Cat*, Williams' comments suggest that Brick's problem is spiritual or metaphysical in nature, not simply psychological, and therefore not so liable to "pat" conclusions or "facile definitions which make a play just a play, not a snare for the truth of human experience" (p. 115). What Williams says he wishes to capture in the play is not the solution of one man's psychological problem, but rather the "true quality of experience," the "interplay of live human beings in the thundercloud of a common crisis" (p. 114). However, since much of this "common crisis" is the result of Brick's disgust and detachment, many critics have argued that Brick himself should be more adequately explained. As Benjamin Nelson says, "A true quality of experience cannot be grasped when the situation and characters involved are left unexplained" (p. 211). Signi Lenea Falk even goes so far as to suggest that "Williams writes as if he himself did not know the physical and moral condition of his hero and the reason for his collapse" (p. 107).

Nelson, Falk, and other critics who have accused Williams of obscurantism in regard to Brick have done so precisely because they do not see that Brick's problem is not simply psychological and therefore not solvable by "facile definitions." What is wrong with Brick is rather metaphysical in nature and thus not "knowable" or "explainable," at least not in the way that Nelson and Falk expect when they use those terms. Brick's mysterious disgust can perhaps best be approached by comparing it to the problem of a similar disgust in *Hamlet* as it is analyzed by T. S. Eliot. As Eliot says, although Hamlet's disgust may be occasioned by his mother, she is not an adequate "objective correlative" for it. Similarly, Brick's disgust exceeds the so-called homosexual problem with Skipper. As a result, he, like Hamlet, is unable to understand the cause of his dilemma. In one of the stage directions in act two, when Brick tries to explain himself to a skeptical Big Daddy, Williams describes Brick as a "broken, 'tragically elegant' figure telling simply as much as he knows of 'the Truth' " (p. 122).

The "true quality of experience . . . , that cloudy, flickering, evanescent—fiercely charged!—interplay" (p. 114) that Williams wants to catch in *Cat on a Hot Tin Roof*, does not stem from a psychosexual problem, but rather from the metaphysical implications of some "inadmissible thing" that Williams attempts to objectify by means of Brick's "homosexuality." If the objectification is inadequate, it is not because Williams does not know what the problem is but because it is simply not knowable or explainable in psychological or sexual terms. However, since the psychosexual answer is such an easy if not completely satisfactory one, it has been used to account for Brick's malaise just as Hamlet's disgust has been explained as a reaction to his incestuous desires for his mother. Similar explanations have been given for Claggart's mysterious hatred for Billy Budd in Melville's novella and Gustave Aschenbach's degeneration in Mann's *Death in Venice*. In fact, much of the metaphysical mystery of the so-called southern Gothic school of literature, a group in which Williams is often placed, has similarly been attributed to suppressed homosexuality, incest, pederasty, and other sexual "perversions."

That such explanations miss the point quite a bit more than they hit it is suggested by Williams in his introduction to the New Directions edition of Carson McCullers' *Reflections in a Golden Eye*. In this mock dialogue with a puzzled representative of the "everyday humdrum world" in which Williams compares the southern Gothic writers to the French existentialists, he also gives us a clue to the metaphysical mystery of Brick Pollitt. The true sense of dread in life, says Williams, is "not reaction to anything sensible or visible or even, strictly, materially, *knowable*. But rather it's a kind of spiritual intuition of something almost too incredible and shocking to talk about, which underlies the whole so-called thing. It is the incommunicable something that we shall have to call mystery." Brick's detachment is an existential leveling of values that makes no one thing more important than another. It is the result of an awareness of absurdity that, as Albert Camus says, can come at any time with no discernible cause and that resists any attempts at psychological explanation. Like Hamlet who senses that the rottenness in Denmark reflects a rottenness at the heart of existence, Brick is existentially aware of the universality of the mendacity on Big Daddy's plantation kingdom, and in face of it he too would wish that his too solid flesh would melt.

However, whereas Hamlet cannot find anything to do that is adequate to resolve the disgust he feels, Brick no longer tries to do anything. This withdrawn impassivity, Brick's refusal to act, even to think, makes his basic situation difficult for the reader to understand. When a fictional character faces a problem that he cannot articulate, a problem that evades attempts to conceptualize it, perhaps the only way the artist can communicate the nature of the problem is to show how the character attempts to deal with it. Thus, the "inadmissible thing" that lies at the heart of *Oedipus* cannot be presented directly. Rather, the play unfolds as a series of attempts by Oedipus to resolve a problem which, while symbolically objectified by the plague, truly hides within metaphysical mysteries that evade all "pat conclusions" and "facile definitions."

Ernest Hemingway, who was always concerned with the artistic problem of finding objective correlatives for the sense of metaphysical dread that Williams calls an "incommunicable something that we shall have to call mystery," also found that he could best present it by objectifying the attempts of his characters to deal with it. For example, in "A Clean, Well-Lighted Place," there is no objective correlative adequate to the old waiter's sense of nada which has seized him. However, the clean, well-lighted place itself is a communicable symbol of a way to live with that sense of nada. Similarly, the mysterious fear and dread that have taken hold of Nick Adams in "Big Two-Hearted River" is not adequately objectified by the "tragic" nature of the swamp, but the way to deal with the dread is adequately communicated by the detailing of Nick's fishing activities that make up the story.

However, in *Cat on a Hot Tin Roof*, because Brick makes no effort to deal with his problem, we are given no clues as to the nature of Brick's problem via an objectification of a possible solution or even, as in Hemingway's stories, a possible palliative. The click in his head that Brick drinks to achieve seems merely an intensification of his already withdrawn state. It gives no hint of why he wishes to withdraw. And, as noted, Brick's disgust seems to exceed its ostensible cause as objectified by the relationship with Skipper. The result is that while a great deal of action goes on around Brick in the play, action which reveals the motives of the other characters, Brick remains inactive and thus unrevealed.

I suggest that Williams does not have Brick make any effort to resolve his problem in *Cat on a Hot Tin Roof* because in an earlier fictional account of the dilemma Brick does make such an effort, the only kind of effort that can be made, and it is inevitably doomed to fail. Tom S. Reck, in an essay on the relationship between Williams' stories and plays, suggests that "Three Players of a Summer Game," published in *The New Yorker* only two years before Williams wrote *Cat*, may come closer to the "whole truth" (p. 147) about Brick than the play does. However, Reck makes no more effort than any of the other critics to determine what that whole truth is.

The truth is certainly not to be found in the ostensible cause for Brick's disgust given in the story, for that is left even more mysterious than in the play. Williams' story-telling narrator says only that his "self-disgust came upon him with the abruptness and violence of a crash on a highway. But what had Brick crashed into? Nothing that anybody was able to surmise, for he seemed to have everything that young men like Brick might hope or desire to have" (*Hard Candy*, pp. 13–14). The only strictly "knowable" thing suggested in the story that might be the cause of Brick's "dropping his life and taking hold of a glass which he never let go of for more than one waking hour" (p. 14) is, as it is in *Cat*, a sexual problem—in this case, his emasculation by his wife Margaret and a consequent sexual impotence. This is hinted at in Brick's drunken monologue to the house painters in which, "explaining things to the world," he is, as he also is in *Cat*, "like an old-time actor in a tragic role," telling as much as he knows of the Truth: "the meanest thing one human being can do to another human being is to take his respect for himself away from him. . . . I had it took away from me! I won't tell you how, but maybe, being men about my age, you're able to guess it. That was how. Some of them don't want it. They cut it off. They cut it right off a man, and half the time he don't even know when they cut it off him. Well, I knew it all right. I could feel it being cut off me." A bit later Brick continues the castration allusion by explaining how he is going to solve his drinking problem. "I'm not going to take no cure and I'm not going to take no pledge, I'm just going to prove I'm a man with his balls back on him!" (pp. 21–6 passim).

The irony and seeming contradiction of trying to prove one's masculinity by learning to play what Brick himself calls the "sissy" game of croquet should be hint enough that Brick's problem is not emasculation and impotence in the psychosexual sense in which we usually understand such terms. Rather as in *Cat*, Brick's problem is a more basic and pervasive one for which his sexual dilemma is merely a symbolic objectification. The complexity of the problem can best be seen by examining the way Brick seeks to deal with it, that is, by examining the summer game itself—both the purely aesthetic game of croquet and the psychological game Brick plays with the other two players, the young widow Isabel and her daughter Mary Louise. Brick's impotence is not a reaction against the emasculating Margaret, but rather a revolt against the flesh itself. His flight into the chaste, because death-purified, arms of Isabel is the search for Truth in its Keatsean equation with Beauty. It is an attempt to escape from flesh into art, to escape from the intolerable, because contingent, real into the bearable, because detached and fleshless, ideal of artistic form.

However, this attempt to escape the contingency of existence by means of aesthetic patterning and idealizing is doomed from the start, for Brick's hoped-for ideal relationship with Isabel as well as his effort to play the superior game of art and form with human beings as counters comes crashing against the "real" fleshly and psychological needs of the other two players. The problem is similar to the one facing Aschenbach in *Death in Venice*. He, too, wishing for the form and detachment of Beauty, finds that unless it is embodied in the flesh it is inhuman; but if it is human, it must therefore be fleshly and consequently be that very thing from which he wishes to escape. It is this intolerable aesthetic and metaphysical dilemma that destroys him.

Tennessee Williams offers several suggestions throughout "Three Players of a Summer Game" that this indeed is the inadmissible, because unnamable, thing that so plagues Brick. At the end of the major events of the story, after Brick has realized the impossibility of his summer game and no longer comes to the widow's house, the narrator says, "The summer had spelled out a word that had no meaning, and the word was now spelled out and, with or without any meaning, there it was, inscribed with as heavy a touch as the signature of a miser on a check or a boy with chalk on a fence" (p. 41). Any attempt to "spell out" the problem, even the attempt the story itself makes, is inadequate to get at the Truth. However, even as the attempt to escape from life through art is the subject of the story, art is the only means to present such a subject; for it is a subject that must be presented obliquely and metaphorically through symbolic objectifications.

At the very beginning of the story the narrator establishes the metaphor that identifies the summer game with the nature of the art work, and he does so in language that Williams later uses in *Cat on a Hot Tin Roof* to refer to that "fiercely charged!—interplay of live human beings" that he wishes to capture in the play—"flickering, evanescent" (III, 114). The game of croquet itself, says the narrator, "seems, in a curious way, to be composed of images the way that a painter's abstraction of summer or one of its games would be built of them. The delicate wire wickets set in a lawn of smooth emerald that flickers fierily at some points and rests under violet shadows in others, the wooden poles gaudily painted as moments that stand out in a season that was a struggle for something of unspeakable importance to someone passing through it, the clean and hard wooden spheres of different colors and the strong rigid shape of the mallets that drive the balls through the wickets, the formal design of those wickets and poles upon the croquet lawn—all of these are like a painter's abstraction of a summer and a game played in it" (p. 9).

Likewise the characters in the story become images and abstractions, not so much real people as stylized gestures which are pictorially woven within the lyrical narrative that make up the "legend" of Brick Pollitt. The narrator is well aware that he is playing the game of detachment of form, the rule-bound ritualized game of arranging images in a formal design that both reveals and conceals, the game of art. "These bits and pieces, these assorted images, they are like the paraphernalia for a game of croquet, gathered up from the lawn when the game is over and packed carefully into an oblong wooden box which they just exactly fit and fill. There they all are, the bits and pieces, the images, the apparently incongruous paraphernalia of a summer that was the last one of my childhood, and now I take them out of the oblong box and arrange them once more in the formal design on the lawn. It would be absurd to pretend that this is altogether the way it was, and yet it may be closer than a literal history could be to the hidden truth of it" (pp. 11–12).

This engagement in the formally-controlled, ritualized patterning of the art work that one plays to deal with the incongruity and contingency of life is of course the same game Brick wishes to play. The croquet game means the same kind of control to Brick that the fishing trip does to Nick Adams in "Big Two-Hearted River." As Brick explains to the painters and thus to the world, croquet is a wonderful game for a drinker. "You hit the ball through one wicket and then you drive it through the next one. . . . You go from wicket to wicket, and it's a game of precision—it's a game that takes concentration and precision, and that's what makes it a wonderful game for a drinker" (p. 26). The game for both Brick and the narrator of "Three Players of a Summer Game" is thus an Apollonian means to deal with the Dionysian drunkenness and incongruity of raw existential reality.

Although the relationship between the process of art and the process of game has often been noted, it has perhaps been given its most profound treatment in Johan Huizinga's *Homo Ludens: A Study of the Play Element in Culture*. Huizinga says that engagement in both play and art involves the assertion of freedom, the abolition of the ordinary world, and the participation in an action that is limited in time and space. In both the game and the art work, something invisible and inchoate takes form and transcends the bounds of logical and deliberative judgment. As Huizinga says, "All poetry is born of play. . . . What poetic language does with images is to play with them. It disposes them in style, it instills mystery into them so that every image contains the answer to an enigma" (pp. 129, 134). However, as Huizinga suggests, it is not the psychological meaning of the action that reveals the answer to the enigma, but rather the ritualized pattern that is formed from the bits and pieces, the actions and images, that make up the art work. It is this spatializing of the temporal, the transforming of the historical into myth, that the narrator of Williams' story says may come closer to the hidden truth of Brick Pollitt's summer game than a literal history.

That the summer game Brick plays with Isabel and her daughter is bound up with his own aesthetic search for detachment and form, his search for an escape from the temporal into the spatial, can be seen in what he desires of the relationship with Isabel. Williams must have had Keats stirring about in his mind when he wrote "Three Players of a Summer Game," for Keatsean aesthetic motifs echo throughout. Even the name Isabel and the fact that Isabel's husband's illness begins in a shocking way in which "An awful flower grew in his brain like a fierce geranium that shattered its pot" (p. 16) suggests Keats's Isabella and her beloved but gruesome pot of basil. Just as in Keats's poem, in Williams' story, hoped-for love and beauty germinate in death itself and remain inextricably tied to the horrors of the flesh.

Brick is initially drawn to Isabel because her actual encounter with the contingency and horror of flesh reflects his own metaphysical encounter. As together they watch the young doctor die, "God was the only word she was able to say; but Brick Pollitt somehow understood what she meant by that word, as if it were in a language that she and he, alone of all people, could speak and understand" (p. 16). After Brick pumps the death-delivering contents of the hypodermic needle into the doctor's arm, he and Isabel consummate their communion of metaphysical despair by lying together chastely in bed, "and the only movement between them was the intermittent, spasmodic digging of their fingernails into each other's clenched palm while their bodies lay stiffly separate, deliberately not touching at any other points as if they abhorred any other contact with each other, while this intolerable thing was ringing like an iron bell through them" (p. 17). The summer game thus becomes, says the narrator, a "running together out of something unbearably hot and bright into something obscure and cool" (p. 17); it is the running out of the hot, unbearable world of existential reality into the cool, obscure world of the art work.

However, when Brick realizes, as does Gustave Aschenbach, that form must inevitably become involved and entangled with the reality of flesh, he finds himself caught on the horns of an unresolvable metaphysical dilemma. Thus, in "Three Players of a Summer Game," the ideal game of art as Huizinga describes it becomes enmeshed with the real game of existential reality as it has recently been analyzed by Eric Berne in *Games People Play*. Because two other players are involved in Brick's game, players who have real fleshly, emotional, and psychological needs, the game is contaminated when it must be played at the expense of Isabel and Mary Louise. Brick's motive for his game, concealed by its metaphysical and inchoate nature, results in the "real world" of the story in what Berne calls an "ulterior transaction" in which others are exploited by the player. Thus, the artistic game, at the same time that it is the most noble and ideal of all games, becomes a "substitute for the real living of real intimacy" as Berne says most of our social games are (p. 18).

The exploitation is made quite clear in its effect on Mary Louise, lonely already because of the "cushions of flesh" which her mother promises will "dissolve in two or three more years" (p. 31), who is made even more lonely during the summer by being shut out of the house when Brick is there. However, as the summer passes, it also becomes apparent that Brick's need to play the artistic game of inhuman form is not satisfying to Isabel either. Although the conflict between Brick's ideal and Isabel's flesh is suggested in various ways in the story, the scene that makes it most obvious occurs one evening when, after setting up the croquet set, Mary Louise stands beneath her mother's bedroom window and wails for her and Brick to come out and play: "Almost immediately after the wailing voice was lifted, begging for the commencement of the game, Mary Louise's thin pretty mother showed herself at the window. She came to the window like a white bird flying into some unnoticed obstruction. That was the time when I saw, between the dividing gauze of the bedroom curtains, her naked breasts, small and beautiful, shaken like two angry fists by her violent motion. She leaned between the curtains to answer Mary Louise not in her usual tone of gentle remonstrance but in a shocking cry of rage: 'Oh, be still, for God's sake, you fat little monster!'" (p. 30). The imagery of flight into an unexpected obstruction and the breasts like fists suggest the frustratingly unyielding obstruction her own flesh has met in Brick's gauze-like ideal.

The contrast between that ideal of the frozen art work that Brick desires and the real physical life that he must live with is perhaps indirectly suggested by an incident the narrator relates about a visit he and Mary Louise pay to an art museum. The scene may have more than accidental significance since it did not appear in the original version of the story in *The New Yorker*, but rather in the revised version that was published the following year in *Hard Candy*. When the two children enter a room with a reclining male nude entitled the "Dying Gaul," Mary Louise lifts the metal fig leaf from the bronze figure and turns to the narrator to ask, "Is yours like that?" (p. 19). Since the added incident has nothing directly to do with the problem of Brick, it may be another of the bits and pieces that reflect Brick's basic dilemma—being caught between the ideal Greek beauty of idealized body and the real and therefore ugly flesh of physical body .

Williams adds another passage to the *Hard Candy* version of the story. In the concluding description of Brick's being driven through the streets of town by Margaret, much the way a captured prince might be led through the streets of a capital city by his conqueror, Williams has the narrator describe him as the handsomest man you were likely to remember, adding significantly, "physical beauty being of all human attributes the most incontinently used and wasted, as if whoever made it despised it, since it is made so often only to be disgraced by painful degrees and drawn through the streets in chains" (p. 44). Thus, what Brick and the narrator learn in the story, although they learn it only in an inchoate and oblique way, is that when one uses human beings in an effort to play the game of art and reach the beauty and detachment of form, the result is the inevitable disgrace of the flesh. The beauty of the art work alone can remain pure, but only because of its inhumanness, its noninvolvement. Ike McCaslin's attempts to realize the Keatsean equation of Beauty and Truth in Faulkner's *Bear* by relinquishing all claims to the world and the flesh meet with the same ambiguous and inescapable paradox.

When Brick realizes the hopelessness of his aspiration, he is transformed from tragic actor to clown. The croquet lawn becomes a circus ring. Brick's tragicomic efforts come to a climax one night when he turns on the water sprinkler, takes off his clothes, and rolls about under the cascading arches. No longer the Greek statue, Brick is now "like some grotesque fountain figure, in underwear and necktie and the one remaining pale-green sock, while the revolving arch of water moved with cool whispers about him" (p. 33). The degeneration of the tragedy can also be seen in what the narrator calls a conclusion "declining into unintentional farce" as Isabel and Mary Louise carry on trivial conversations in the face of Brick's absence from the house. The conversation about the ice that Mary Louise uses to ease her mosquito bites is the culmination of a pervasive motif of frozen coolness interwoven throughout the story. A game that began with a running out of something hot into something obscure and cool, a game that took place among frozen stylized figures on the cool, dark lawn of a house that has the appearance of a block of ice, has now become a banal banter between "two ladies in white dresses waiting on a white gallery" (p. 35) in which the ice is reduced from its symbolic significance to the practical utility of cooling Brick's drinks, easing Mary Louise's mosquito bites, and putting in the ice bag for Isabel's headaches.

This analysis of how Brick attempts to deal with his problem in "Three Players of a Summer Game" should make clearer the metaphysical mystery of Brick's detachment in *Cat on a Hot Tin Roof*. The basic tension between the ideal and frozen art work and the unbearable hot tin roof of reality is the tension of both the story and the play. Even the "Person-to-Person" preface which Williams writes for *Cat* contains a clear reference to the problem of the Keatsean equation of Truth and Beauty that he is concerned with in the play. However, because Williams sees that such an equation is possible only in death or in the deathlike art work, the poem he chooses to reflect the dilemma is not from Keats, but from Emily Dickinson. In "I Died for Beauty," it is only in the grave that Beauty and Truth recognize that they are "brethren."

Perhaps one of the reasons for Williams' often expressed admiration for Maggie the Cat is that she alone in the play seems to realize what Brick's desire is. However, she also realizes that it means death and rejects it in her famous cry, "Maggie the cat is—*alive! I am alive, alive! I'm . . .—alive!*" (p. 60). Against Brick's protestations she tries to explain that she made love to Skipper only because of Brick's detachment, only because he refused to return the love of those who cared for him. "Skipper and I made love, if love you could call it, because it made both of us feel a little bit closer to you. You see, you son of a bitch, you asked too much of people, of me, of him, of all the unlucky poor damned sons of bitches that happen to love you . . . you—superior creature!—you godlike being!—And so we made love to each other to dream it was you, both of us! Yes, yes, yes! Truth, truth!" (pp. 55–6). Maggie insists she does understand about Brick and Skipper, knows "It was one of those beautiful, ideal things they tell about in the Greek legends. . . . Brick, I tell you, you got to believe me, Brick, I *do* understand all about it! I—I think it was—*noble!* Can't you tell I'm sincere when I say I respect it? My only point, the only point that I'm making, is life has got to be allowed to continue even after the *dream* of life is—all—over . . ." (p. 57).

It seems obvious that what Brick hoped to achieve in his games with Skipper is the same thing he aspired to in his croquet game with Isabel and Mary Louise, and it is also obvious that his effort fails for the same metaphysical reasons in both the story and the play:

human needs always interfere with purely ideal aspirations. As a result, in *Cat* Brick stops playing altogether, or at least thinks he does; however, the click he waits to hear in his head is a metaphoric echo of the click of the croquet mallets that can be faintly heard offstage in act one. Maggie understands Brick's game-playing posture when she tells him he has always had a detached quality as though he were playing a game without much concern over whether he won or lost. Now that he has quit playing, she says he has the "charm of the defeated.—You look so cool, so cool, so enviably cool" (p. 30).

However, everything is not so cool for Brick, or else he would not continue to drink and wait for the click in his head; he would not stare out the window at the moon in act three and envy it for being a cool son of a bitch. Brick continues to try to play the ideal game in which the goal is not to win or lose, but rather to carry the game through. This time, though, he tries to play it alone. As Huizinga says, the essence of play can be summed up in the phrase, "There is something at stake"; yet this something is not the material result of the play, but rather the "ideal fact that the game is a success or has been successfully concluded" (p. 49). Now, however, Brick's problem is that the human games of others are always breaking in on the ideal game of cool withdrawal he wishes to play. If it is not what Maggie calls the "cardsharp" games of Gooper and Mae as they use their children as counters to win the legacy of Big Daddy, it is Maggie's own game of attempted seduction of Brick. The most pervasive game, however, that surrounds the action of the play and threatens to shatter Brick's detachment, is summarized in an offhand phrase by the insensitive Reverend Tooker as a game of life and death in which "the Stork and the Reaper are running neck and neck!" (p. 72).

In *Cat on a Hot Tin Roof*, Brick's game of detachment is as destructive and exploitative as his more directly involved game in "Three Players." This time Brick preserves his "charming detachment" by that "simple expedient" of not loving anyone enough to disturb it. Consequently, he damages Skipper, Maggie, and Big Daddy, all who need his love and involvement. However, as much as Brick realizes these needs, he can do nothing to satisfy them without entangling himself in the chaos of that real life that so disgusts him. He intuits that love of another human being not only is insufficient to fulfill the ideal demands of the human spirit; by its very nature such a love negates the possibility of such fulfilment. Perhaps it is this realization that made Williams object to the change Kazan wanted effected in Brick in the third act. In the original version of the play, when Maggie makes her announcement that she is pregnant, Brick simply keeps quiet, not as an attempt to save Maggie's face, but rather as a result of his own continued indifference. In the stage version, Brick actively supports Maggie's false claim, as if it truly makes a difference to him. His last words in the Broadway version are: "I admire you, Maggie" (p. 214). The implication is that he has found a solution to his problem and will henceforth be "alive" as Maggie says she is. The conclusion to the original version of the play is more ambiguous. As Maggie turns out the lights in the bedroom and the curtain begins to fall slowly, she says to Brick, "Oh, you weak people, you weak, beautiful people!—who give up.—What you want is someone to—. . . take hold of you.—Gently, gently, with love! And—. . . I *do* love you, Brick, I *do!*" Brick's final words before the curtain falls are uttered with that charming sad smile still on his face: "Wouldn't it be funny if that was true?" (pp. 165–6). This final question of the play is not just in response to Maggie's declaration of love, but rather it is a fittingly enigmatic and ironic response to Maggie's claim that all such people as Brick need to resolve their metaphysical dilemma is for someone to take hold of them with love. Brick's final skeptical query then bears a striking resemblance in its hopeless ambiguity to Jake Barnes' reply to Lady Britt at the conclusion of Hemingway's *The Sun Also Rises*: "Isn't it pretty to think so?"

It is thus with Brick's mysterious metaphysical problem still unresolved that Tennessee Williams wished to end his play, for it is a problem that is not knowable by any ordinary epistemology nor solvable by any ordinary psychology. In "Three Players of a Summer Game," Isabel is obliquely referring to Brick when she responds to Mary Louise's question about why the sun goes south: "Precious, Mother cannot explain the movements of the heavenly bodies, you know that as well as Mother knows it. Those things are controlled by certain mysterious laws that people on earth don't know or understand" (p. 36).

Baby Doll: A Comic Fable

SY KAHN

I F NOT AMONG the most arresting and brilliant of Tennessee Williams' works, *Baby Doll* is unique. It was written as a film script and melds two earlier one-act plays: *27 Wagons Full of Cotton*, and the shorter, less frequently performed *The Long Stay Cut Short, or, The Unsatisfactory Supper*. Although Williams worked on film scripts before, helping to adapt some of his plays to the screen, *Baby Doll* is his only original film scenario. No less characteristic of Williams' fictional world in other literary forms, it is more obviously comic. Williams' rich sense of comedy is often adumbrated by the remembered images and power of tense confrontations and moving revelations of character in his full-length plays.

In constructing the film script, Williams almost evacuated the two short plays, with much of the dialogue intact. Besides the task of bringing the plays into the single focus of the longer work, he necessarily added scenes, most notably the long hide-and-seek sequence in the rooms and precarious attic of Archie Lee and Baby Doll Meighan's house, in and around which most of the action takes place. More important than the literary carpentry involved in connecting the plays into a shooting script is that the scenario reveals an expansion and enrichment of characterization and themes in the plays, and necessarily alters and adds significant details. For example, in *The Long Stay Cut Short* old Aunt Rose Comfort at the end of

292

the play is blown by a powerful wind toward a "sinister-looking" rose bush in the front yard. Although she calls these roses "poems of nature," their ambiguous symbolism also makes them emblems of lurking death. The film script retains the rose only as "poem of nature" (*Baby Doll*, p. 27), and in it she experiences a happier fate, saved by Silva Vacarro from rejection and a lonely death.

However, it is not my intention to explore the literary architecture that made of two smaller structures a single edifice but rather to examine the script as one might any other of Williams' discrete works, and with a greater leisure than the film itself permits. Indeed, the film script may easily be imagined as metamorphosizing into a play again, though still different from the two works that generated it. Certainly there is less characteristic scene and mood description in the film script than in a Williams' play, and, of course, rapid shifts of locale impossible for the stage, but perhaps not impossible to reorder and recompose, were that the medium. Williams knew enough about filmmaking, and particularly about Elia Kazan, the director of *Baby Doll*, to leave considerable latitude of interpretation to a man who had been so influential as a director of his previous plays and their film interpretations.

In fact it was Kazan who urged Williams to the project of writing the film script. While Williams was on one of his frequent trips to Europe during the summer of 1955, and following the successful opening of *Cat on a Hot Tin Roof*, he began refashioning the two ten-year-old plays into *Baby Doll*—at various times entitled *The Whip Hand* and *Mississippi Woman* and *A Mississippi Delta Comedy*. Events moved quickly once Williams mailed the script to Kazan, and in a ten-week period during the winter of 1955–56, in Benoit, Mississippi, most of the film was shot. The principal roles of Baby Doll, Silva Vacarro, Archie Lee and Aunt Rose were played, respectively, by Carroll Baker, Eli Wallach, Karl Malden and Mildred Dunnock, with many supporting roles recruited from the locals of rural Mississippi. For part of the time Williams was also on location and was urged by Kazan to continue working on the script. Just as Williams trusted to Kazan's inventiveness and emphasis of script values with the camera, Kazan in turn gave considerable rein to improvisation by his main actors. Both Wallach and Malden cite examples of how they were able to invent action or intensify moments during the filming, but both insist they did not alter dialogue. (See Mike Steen's *A Look at Tennessee Williams*, 1969.) This process, of course, is no different in play production when director and actor collaborate to best realize the script without violating its language and meaning.

Set in rural Mississippi, as were the two short plays, *Baby Doll* is a comic fable of frustration and fury. On its most apparent level of meaning, it depicts the impact of the new industrialism on the Old South, already outmoded and fated to be undone by the engines and energy of syndicated technology. The impact reverberates through and shakes the whole society, bringing down its already decayed mansions and threatening the livelihood of its lackadaisical rural clans. As in fable, the characters are broadly rendered through distinct types, the Southerners particularly reminiscent of Erskine Caldwell's novels or the comic passages of William Faulkner's stories and novels, as well as of Williams' own gallery of southern portraits.

In the film script, Archie Lee, of indeterminate middle-age and owner of a rickety cotton gin, is married to nineteen-year-old Baby Doll. This marriage of May and September is complicated by the agreement Archie made with Baby Doll's father on his death-bed that the marriage would not be consummated until Baby Doll reached twenty. Loud, crude and mean-tempered to begin with, Archie Lee, suffering the terms of this agreement, is now sweatingly frustrated, apoplectic and explosive. The scenario opens two days before Baby Doll's birthday, and we discover her, in all her "mindless, virgin softness," asleep and thumb-sucking in a cradle with the slats let down. Her bedroom, apart from her husband's, is in the nursery of their dilapidated house which once knew affluence. Though "voluptuous," and aware of her attractiveness and sexual power, Baby Doll is still as essentially innocent and girlish as she is virginal. Her threat not to keep the marriage agreement unless Archie Lee can pay for five rooms of furniture, bought on credit from the Ideal Pay As You Go Plan Furniture Company, gives him, along with his long sexual abstinence and frustration, additional reason to sweat. The company is presently hounding him for delinquent payments. The third member of this faded house is Baby Doll's Aunt Rose Comfort, a withered, superannuated lady, whose fumbling semisenility adds to Archie Lee's exasperation. An inept but good-hearted cook and housekeeper, she also suffers Archie Lee's bullying and redirected frustrations. Her remaining passion in life is to consume the gift candy, particularly chocolate-covered cherries, of her friends who are committed to the hospital. Her appetite is a comic parallel to Archie Lee's unslacked lust for his virgin wife. Indeed, one scene makes much of his desire to "consume" her. "What would I do," he asks, "if you was angel food cake? Big white piece with lots of nice thick icin'?" (p. 38).

During the opening moments of the script, a mouselike scratching sound awakens Baby Doll; Archie Lee is attempting to play Peeping Tom by gouging a hole in the wall between their bedrooms. Unshaven and in sweaty pajamas, he is discovered among such character-revealing props as a half-empty liquor bottle, an old, ticking alarm clock, a copy of *Spicy Fiction* and a tube of ointment. Baby Doll ridicules his spying and then rebuffs him when he attempts to enter her shower. When he emerges dripping and crestfallen, one gathers this is simply the last of many such clumsy defeats and that he is a figure fated for repeated humiliation.

During the swift and early opening sequences, Williams orchestrates and amplifies a series of sounds. From wall scratching and ticking clock, he makes a transition to the louder sound of the recently constructed Syndicate cotton gin, "like a gigantic distant throbbing heart," a modern machine that threatens Archie Lee with the loss of work, house, furniture and Baby Doll. His ineffectual response is to close the window and dolefully consider his appearance in a mirror. "Yeah," comments Baby Doll, "just look at yourself! You're not exactly a young girl's dream come true" (p. 10). With the later revelations that the new gin is operated by the young and vital Silva Vacarro, and in its strong beat expressive of his energy and sexuality, one can see in retrospect how carefully Williams has orchestrated sound, symbol and dialogue. The rhythm of the gin gives way to a ringing phone and the characteristic cacophony of shrill screams it always occasions from skittish Aunt Rose. It is the furniture company dunning Archie Lee. Thus this quick series of scenes illustrates the economic and personal consequences of the Syndicate gin on Archie Lee. In short, *Baby Doll*, for all its broad effects, under scrutiny proves to be no rough job of literary carpentry but rather a carefully constructed shooting script by a practical and poetic playwright. As Mildred Dunnock, who played Aunt Rose, said, "I think *Baby Doll* is a sophisticated picture. If people do take it on its face value, then it is disaster" (Steen, p. 3).

Besides illustrating economic collision in the South, *Baby Doll* also depicts the powerful force of sexual vitality. These are among Williams' most familiar themes, as serious here as in his other work, despite the comic surface of this work. This last theme brings us to the fourth and last major character, Silva Vacarro, an energetic Sicilian, booted, whip carrying, dark, wiry—a phallic figure of a man. We have met him before in various guises, in D. H. Lawrence's work, to be sure, and in earlier plays by Williams—nor are we to see the last of him. He is always the seed-bearer, the outsider, the new quick and quickening energy and the threat to an old, established social order that stifles, frustrates, even perverts passion. From *Battle of Angels* (1940), Williams' first major play, to his latest Vienna premiere of *The Red Devil Battery Sign* (1976), a Vacarro variant makes his appearance. Vacarro's new, pulsating cotton gin is a symbol of his personal vitality and contrasts with Archie Lee's deteriorating and eventually disabled "pile of junk" (p. 20), as Baby Doll characterizes it, and by implication Archie Lee himself. When Archie Lee's equipment breaks down as he attempts to gin Vacarro's twenty-seven wagons of cotton, Vacarro says "this equipment was rotten" (p. 87). The observation precisely judges the old gin, the Old South, and that "good old boy" Archie Lee.

More desperate than his Mississippi cohorts, because of his anxiety about Baby Doll, Archie Lee turns arsonist and burns down Vacarro's gin. He then intimidates Baby Doll into supporting an alibi that will account for his time away from the house while he set the fire. In a scene in which he, by turns, both physically hurts and flatters her, he manages, in the hot and fire-inflamed air, virtually to mesmerize her, coming as close to successful seduction as he is to come. However, rehearsing the alibi is more pressing to Archie Lee than his momentary advantage. The scene is decadent, cruel, cunning and sensual; there is the shine of decay, the glistening sweat of evil. In Baby Doll some latent sexual feeling has been perversely touched, but Archie Lee, more concerned with safety than sex, permits her to escape the hypnotic moment. "Nice quiet night. Real nice and quiet" (p. 40), he soliloquizes after her release. Vacarro's gin can no longer be heard. This still moment and temporary triumph is the only brief interlude of satisfaction Archie Lee is to enjoy.

The fire set by Archie Lee which destroys Vacarro's gin illuminates several meanings in the script. The first of these is suggested by the failure of the firemen to extinguish the flames, partly because of their own laxity—the Syndicate cotton gin has put too many friends and neighbors out of business—and also because the hose falls short and there is insufficient water. This large, even expressionistic, phallic symbolism comments on Archie Lee's sexual frustration and failures with Baby Doll as well as on the viciousness and ineptitude of the small town clan. In contrast, Vacarro lashes at the man holding the hose, seizes the nozzle and walks directly into the flame after having driven the men back with a stream of water. After he disappears into the fire, the hose "suddenly leaps about as if it had been freed" (p. 33). Soon returning, singed, smoking, injured, at the point of collapse, he has recovered the incriminating gasoline can used to set the fire. Recovering himself, he looks up into a circle of hostile faces lit by the shaking radiance of the fire. Phoenixlike, he rises, smudged and ash-covered and smoldering, and sets upon the trail of the arsonist, since he notices that Archie Lee is not among the townspeople. This fire-inspired quest is to bring Archie Lee to further humiliation, as well as to awaken and to attract Baby Doll's unfocused sexuality. However, the meaning of the fire extends beyond its dramatization of Archie's, and the town's, desperations in dealing with new and efficient competition, impelled by Vacarro's tense energy.

In a later conversation between Vacarro and Baby Doll, Williams expands the meaning of the fire as well as stretches Vacarro's heroic proportions. Having revealed that she believes the house she lives in is haunted, Baby Doll is about to retreat indoors to escape Vacarro's questions and suspicions about the fire, but is restrained by the following dialogue.

> SILVA: Do you believe in ghosts, Mrs. Meighan? I do. I believe in the presence of evil spirits.
> BABY DOLL: What evil spirits you talking about now?
> SILVA: Spirits of violence—and cunning—malevolence—cruelty—treachery—destruction. . . .

BABY DOLL: Oh, them's just human characteristics.

SILVA: They're evil spirits that haunt the human heart and take pos-session of it, and spread from one human heart to another human heart the way that a fire goes springing from leaf to leaf. . . .

BABY DOLL: You have got fire on the brain.

SILVA: I see it as more than it seems to be on the surface. I saw it last night as an explosion of those evil spirits that haunt the human heart—I fought it! I ran into it, beating it, stamping it, shouting the curse of God at it! They dragged me out, suffocating. I was defeated! (pp. 78–9).

Silva goes on to explain that the fire was an expression of the human will to destroy, that the human heart is not only haunted by the demons of hate and destruction, but places may be as well—as the old, ruined mansion—and the implication is left for us to draw, as is the whole locale.

As well as expressing human malevolency, the "natural depravity of the human heart," as Nathaniel Hawthorne would have rendered it, and more particularly Archie Lee's personal frustrations, the fire also satisfies "some profound and basic hunger" (p. 40) as Williams says in a scene direction. It unleashes a holiday mood in the com-munity, especially in the Brite Spot Cafe where the local clan gathers to drink and to celebrate the destruction. The scene invites the image of a demon dance around a bonfire lit for human sacrifice.

Archie Lee's bedeviled house, his debris-scattered yard, his be-leaguered livelihood, and his sweaty disarray suggest the dissolution and moral bankruptcy of the region. An old and rusting Pierce-Arrow limousine, immobile and decaying, in his yard recalls a previous grandeur and ease Archie has never known, as do the old chandelier and grand staircase in the deteriorating mansion. The house is sup-posedly haunted by its previous mistress; it also is haunted by the relics of a more gracious past. Archie Lee's inability to consummate his marriage, his frequent humiliations, as the dupe of boys, blacks, and circumstances in general, make him and his decaying possessions the symbols of impotency, ripe only for dissolution.

With inconclusive evidence, but with correct assumptions about Archie Lee as the perpetrator of the fire, Silva Vacarro pays a visit to the Meighan house to make arrangements to have Archie Lee gin his cotton. Elated beyond tact, Archie grasps the job—it will save his threatened furniture and insure the sexual compliance of his wife. However, the rotten machinery soon breaks down; and under threat of losing the job, he rushes off in his battered Chevy to search for a replacement for the faulty part. In the meantime, Vacarro has the gin repaired with a spare part he has—all of this permitting him time alone with Baby Doll.

Before going off to gin Vacarro's cotton, Archie Lee confides to Vacarro that since he believes in "the good neighbor policy," and since Vacarro is his closest neighbor, they can do each other good turns. "Tit for tat," he says. "Tat for tit is the policy we live on." A moment later he refers Vacarro to the blushing Baby Doll, saying, "This is my baby. This is my little girl, every precious ounce of her is mine, all mine" (p. 51). The bawdy implication of this scene can hardly be missed, with the unconscious suggestions that the full-breasted Baby Doll may serve for the "tit" in exchange for the "tat" of cotton. This notion is reinforced when Silva says later, privately, to Baby Doll that indeed she makes him think of cotton. Further, if we refer to 27 Wagon Loads of Cotton, the exchange of work for sex is more explicit and precisely how the play concludes.

One of the two prototypes for Baby Doll, Flora in 27 Wagon Loads of Cotton, is a much grosser woman, less young and more slow-witted than Baby Doll in the film script. We have in the play a similar Archie Lee (then Jake) and Vacarro, but Jake, though cuckolded by Vacarro, is less a buffoon figure, though as desperate. Vacarro is the same compact and cocky Latin. In the play, the sound symbols are also revealing: Flora is echoed by mooing cows, suggesting her bovine and slow-witted nature, and Vacarro predictably by the rooster. The drama, unlike the film script, is an unrelieved picture of decadence, of desperate acts and the coarsening of human relationships. Flora is clearly in the "tit for tat" situation, and Jake's cuckolding seems poetic justice for the fire he set to burn down the rival Syndicate gin. Oblivious to what has transpired between Vacarro and Flora, Jake is content that she will entertain him with gin and lemonade when Vacarro continues to have his cotton processed. Also, he is equally unrecognizing of the transformation that Vacarro's ravishment of Flora has worked on his mesmerized wife at the end of the play—who, though probably beyond childbearing age, seems transported into a second motherhood. When Jake asks from

inside the house, "What did you say, Baby?" she responds, "I'm
not—Baby. Mama! Ma! That's—me. . . ." A few brief passages later,
she is laughing in the moonlight, sensual and maternal instincts fog-
ging her mind, and while clutching a white kid purse (her "baby"),
croons the "Rock-a-bye" nursery song (27 *Wagons*, p. 28).

The other prototype for Baby Doll is the indolent and ample
Baby Doll of *The Long Stay Cut Short.* This brief one-act turns on
the situation of Archie Lee's attempt to disburden himself of old
Aunt Rose. At the end of the play, the wind that drives the withered
Aunt Rose toward the sinister rose bush seems a wind generated by
Archie Lee's mean temper and ungenerous nature. Yet wind and
bush are ambiguous symbols, suggesting death as blessing and relief.
Baby Doll here is simply benign, and incompetent in dealing with
her husband or as his effective agent in urging Aunt Rose to cut
short her stay.

From the six characters of the two plays, Williams reconstructed
four, but of these Baby Doll is at once the most blended and renewed.
However, certain scenes make her heritage clear. She has the dormant
sensuality of Flora and is subject to the same sexual mesmerization;
she has the physical amplitude and lushness of the earlier Baby Doll
and at times something of her helplessness. Unlike her two dramatic
predecessors, she is young, physically attractive, less dull-witted,
shrewder and more spirited.

To understand the generating line and full significance of Baby
Doll, we must go back not only ten but twenty years and refer to
a different literary form. In the summer of 1936, Williams and a
friend, Clark Mills McBurney, shared a cellar workshop they called
"the literary factory." At that time Williams wrote a short story
about an elephantine woman, mistress of a plantation, who is im-
portuned by a Vacarro-like employee to go to bed. Like his later
version, he also carries an impatient whip. When she consents, her
mountainous flesh looming over him, she coquettishly admonishes
him to promise "not to hurt me!" The story was extremely humorous
to both young men, and was, in its turn, a literary expression of Williams' youthful interest in plump girls, according to McBurney. He
also recalls an evening at a party where the characteristically shy
Williams was attracted to an extremely fat girl ignored by everyone
else, and that, at least for the evening, Williams was enraptured by

her (Falk, p. 35). The situation recalls the hoary joke of the circus midget who falls in love with the fat lady and when introducing her says with great satisfaction, "Acres and acres of her, and she's all mine." Whether Williams knew this joke or not, the line is echoed in *Baby Doll* when Archie Lee introduces his wife to Vacarro and says, "This is my little girl, every precious ounce of her is mine, all mine" (p. 51). Though Baby Doll is not an acre of a woman, the line responds to the male feeling of domain over a vast and voluptuous treasure—one that Archie Lee will never spend but that the small Vacarro will. From Vacarro's point of view, as well as Baby Doll's, she remains big, as revealed by their references to her size, but in context the innuendo of "size" is sexual (p. 72).

Whether the situation of mountainous woman seduced by small man responded to Williams' fantasy as much as it appealed to his sense of humor remains speculation. However, the joke, the short story, the one-act and film script may be taken as testimony to the prevailing image of woman as inevitably vulnerable to sexual prowess. He frequently dramatizes sex as having the hypnotic power to subordinate the consciousness of women and to transform them. Furthermore, under the narcosis of sex the subconscious mind can release the potential poetic statement or gesture. Whether the flesh be abundant or voluptuous, in every pound of female flesh the sleeping cell can be quickened to dream. It is at once woman's vulnerability and power.

The verbal, physical and emotional sparring between Baby Doll and Vacarro, and the eventual hide-and-seek game they play in the old house, presage her transformation. Although no physical seduction takes place, it is clear in the end that Vacarro has won Baby Doll and that there will probably be a sexual conclusion later—perhaps as soon as her twentieth birthday. Vacarro perfects his triumph over and humiliation of Archie Lee by offering Aunt Rose sanctuary as well by inviting her to become his cook and housekeeper. For Baby Doll, first encountered as petulant, willful and contentious, there is an unlayering of the girlish personality and a woman revealed.

In provoking Baby Doll's transformation, Vacarro not only sexually awakens but also instructs her. Having suffered Archie Lee's crudity, she is prepared to understand and to accept Vacarro's reading of the world. For example, when Archie Lee earlier complains of his public humiliation by "people who know the situation between us," she responds with uncharacteristic pithiness, "Private humiliation is just as painful" (p. 18). Later, when she expresses her vulnerability by clutching her purse, Vacarro takes the prop as cue to explain "what a lot of uncertain things there are," and the need people have for "something to hold on to" (p. 67). However, few "things" offer personal protection, or "instruction," as he has noted earlier—whether against fires, inept fire departments, ghosts in haunted houses—and the least protection of all is a husband who is "across the road and busy" (p. 67). At that moment her defenselessness against all the demons of the world, even the menace of Vacarro's vengeance, becomes parabolic of the general human situation. The assumption that people live in a threatening world, that they are "spooked," as Shannon in *Night of the Iguana* says, is basic to Williams' work, as is the idea that one is pitifully defenseless against the malevolency of both man and nature.

Throughout the conversation between Baby Doll and Vacarro is the flicker of sexual innuendo. Vacarro's goal, however, is not vengeful seduction but rather to disarm and to confuse her in order to break down the alibi protecting Archie Lee. Brushing physical contact with Vacarro, and the light switch of his riding crop on her legs—to drive away flies—increases the pitch of her giggle and hysteria. At one point all she can manage is a comically weak cry for help, not really desired in her nervous titillation. When she retreats to the house to make lemonade, locking the door, Vacarro neatly rips the screen with his pocket knife and easily enters. The action parallels but contrasts with the opening scene when Archie Lee ineffectively works a hole through the plaster. Where Archie fails even as a Peeping Tom, Vacarro insinuates his whole body. Meanwhile, Baby Doll in her nervousness cuts her finger and draws blood. The symbolic action foreshadows her loss of virginity and predicts their sexual intercourse.

After Vacarro raids the ice-box, "gnawing" the meat off a chicken and swilling gin and lemonade (pp. 95 ff.), he follows the trail of blood from Baby Doll's cut finger to the upstairs nursery, always swishing the riding crop. There he mounts a wooden hobby horse, rocks and lashes it with the crop—a scene reminiscent of D. H. Lawrence's "The Rocking Horse Winner." Soon Baby Doll's real, but delicious, fright, and Vacarro's serious search give way to a new, ambiguous mood which dominates the script until the end. The hide-and-seek game which follows becomes a sexual romp of hunt and be hunted, and at the same time becomes the innocent exuberance of children—Adam and Eve playing tag in Paradise. Retreating to the altogether rickety attic of the house, locking the door behind her, Baby Doll proclaims she is most frightened of Vacarro's whip. As plaster disintegrates beneath her, leaving her perched on bare beams, Vacarro is able to get her signed confession of Archie Lee's guilt. When he starts to leave, Baby Doll is crestfallen. "Was *that* all you wanted . . . ?" (p. 105). Never having lost his primary goal in the game, he responds, "You're a child, Mrs. Meighan. That's why we played hide-and-seek, a game for children. . . ." When he is about to return home for a "siesta," Baby Doll invites him to sleep in her crib in the nursery, and the effect, as Williams says in the scene direction, is "of two shy children trying to strike up a friendship" (p. 106). The sequence ends with Vacarro asleep in the crib, his thumb in his mouth, and Baby Doll, now gentle mother, rocking him in her arms. The conclusion recalls 27 *Wagons Full of Cotton*, parallel in their effect of symbolically moving both women, though of considerably different ages, to images of motherhood. In both instances there is a shift to a type of peaceful, even blessed, innocence—whether or not the agent has been actual or symbolic sex.

At about this time, Archie Lee returns after a long and finally successful trip in locating a new saw-cylinder for his faulty gin, only to be refused it in the end for lack of cash. He returns not only to find his gin functioning but Vacarro absent. Sweaty and irritated, he retreats to his house to a repeated chorus of Negro laughter, feeling ridiculed, somehow a patsy—laughter that is later repeated in the script. Karl Malden has remarked on these scenes that both Williams and Kazan "were making a subtle comment about the Negro situation." Malden recalls that in the film script "Negroes were always in the background, looking at the Caucasians, at the whites, and kind of laughing." Malden interprets this as a black comment on the sound track, the rock-and-roll music that was derivative from black music—and in general a mocking of all white derivations from black originality (Steen). Whether or not that was the specific comment intended, it is clear from the script that the derisive laughter is also derivative of Sherwood Anderson's novel *Black Laughter*, in which the easy, natural laughter of blacks is in counterpoint to white rigidity and neurosis. More particularly, the laughter in *Baby Doll* further ridicules and infuriates Archie Lee. He returns to his further deteriorating house with its collapsed attic floor and discovers a semiclothed Baby Doll. His bellows cause further destruction in the kitchen when Aunt Rose is startled and breaks china. Clearly, Archie Lee's precarious world enters the stage of final disintegration. When he says that there is a "U. W. Bureau" in Washington, standing for "useless women," with secret plans to round up and shoot them, Baby Doll retorts that they may have similar plans for destructive men. "Men that blow things up and burn things down because they're too evil and stupid to git along otherwise. Because fair competition is too much for 'em. So they turn criminal. Do things like Arson" (pp. 113–14).

Baby Doll's rejection of Archie Lee, as unattractive lover and boggling provider, now has the force of moral outrage and judgment. She soon declares that she feels herself no longer bound to her marriage agreement. A few pages later her new mood and decision are marked by Vacarro, having descended from his cradled nap, when he says to Baby Doll, "I find you different this evening in someway. . . . Suddenly grown up!" (p. 122). Vacarro's abrupt presence in Baby Doll's life urges her rapid transition from "baby" and "doll" towards womanhood.

When Vacarro first enters the grounds, Williams quickly establishes water as one of Vacarro's major symbols. Offered coffee, he requests water, and Baby Doll refers him to an old cistern at the side of the house, if he has "the energy to handle an old-fashioned pump." He retorts that he has "energy to burn." While he seeks the water, Aunt Rose is heard singing "Rock of Ages" (pp. 53–4), a significant detail, as we shall see, in that she repeats the hymn at the end of the script. Vacarro is accompanied by his foreman, "Rock," thus establishing the symbolic connection among young men, water and the hymn. A scene direction informs us that Baby Doll is "unconsciously drawn by the magnetism of the two young males," and by implication to their protective and lifegiving abilities, symbolized by rock and water. Much is made of Vacarro's drawing the cool well water. Aunt Rose warns that sometimes it comes, sometimes not, and that she herself lacks strength to draw it. Vacarro, "touched by her aged grace," offers her water, at which point Baby Doll appears exclaiming that "They's such a difference in water!" (pp. 54–5). Bringing up more water, Vacarro strips off his shirt and empties a dipperful over his head. He then sends Rock away to the cotton, and for the first time Vacarro and Baby Doll are alone.

He is one "gentleman caller for whom we all wait," as Williams has it in *The Glass Menagerie*, who, unlike the disappointing Jim of that play, will bring protection and relief to both women of the house. Vacarro's pure energy can draw lifegiving water from the parched earth for both a desiccated old lady and a flourishing girl. He is also the "rock" upon which something can be built.

Much later in the scenario, the pump/water symbolism occurs immediately after Baby Doll informs Archie Lee that she considers herself free from their bargain. Hearing Vacarro at the pump, she and Archie cross to him and see him dousing himself again "with the zest and vigor of a man satisfied." The "satisfaction" as we know has been his innocent nap in the cradle and Baby Doll's cradling arms, but now Archie Lee's suspicions are fired and continue to build to the end of the script. With rare hilarity, Baby Doll exclaims when seeing Vacarro's ablutions, "HEIGH-HO SILVER." Almost every American, at least of a certain age, will identify the old cry of the "masked stranger" who was the Western hero of our youth, righting wrongs and saving countless distressed ladies. "Silva" and "Silver," the Lone Ranger's heroic horse, are blended by the pun, and her identification of Silva Vacarro as her savior completed. This image is reinforced reflexively by the earlier scene of Silva on the hobby horse in Baby Doll's bedroom. The motifs of her rescue and transformation are perfected when she asks Vacarro for another drink "of that sweet well water," and observes, "You're the first person could draw it." Williams' scene direction at this point reveals that "There is a grace and sweetness and softness of speech about her, unknown before . . ." (pp. 116–17).

In the remaining scenes Archie Lee resorts to drinking too, breathing "loud as a cotton gin" and his face "fiery" as he fuels his anger with liquor, in contrast to Baby Doll's and Vacarro's almost ritualistic drinking together of cool water. All his actions amplify his buffoonery. Convinced he is a cuckold, he resorts to ineffectual and ludicrous ranting about his "respected position" in the community and darkly suggests that his "associates" will eliminate this intruding "dago." Verbal lava hotly flows from this exploding volcano; and although his raving is comical, his frustration richly deserved, Williams would have his violence at one climactic moment "give him almost a Dostoevskian stature" as he reaches a state of "virtual lunacy" (pp. 131–32).

As Baby Doll goes to help Aunt Rose pack, and Vacarro retreats through the debris-littered yard and climbs into a tree, Archie Lee goes for his shotgun, liquor bottle in hand. In terror, Baby Doll calls the police, then runs into the yard where Vacarro hoists her into the tree with him.

There follows an ineffectual fusillade at pointless targets as Archie Lee vents his sexual and general frustration. Above the barrage and maniacal rant, Vacarro and Baby Doll safely share pecans from the tree, while Aunt Rose comes to the porch with her battered suitcase. Baby Doll says, "I feel sorry for poor old Aunt Rose Comfort. She doesn't know where to go or what to do. . . ." Vacarro answers, "Does anyone know where to go, or what to do?" Meanwhile the police arrive and drag off Archie Lee's limp figure—and the script concludes with Aunt Rose singing in the dark, "Rock of Ages, cleft for me/Let me hide myself in Thee!" (pp. 139–40). The final image is of Vacarro, arms uplifted, to help Baby Doll, "the ex-Mrs. Meighan" (p. 137) as she said to the police on the phone, down from the tree.

Clearly, the concluding hymn sings the value of Vacarro for Aunt Rose who has found a "cleft" in the rock in him—and unlike, as one may recall, the beleaguered Blanche DuBois in A *Streetcar Named Desire* who used the same metaphor for Mitch, another gentleman caller who fails to provide that saving niche. (Coincidentally, it was the same Karl Malden who played Mitch as well as Archie Lee.) The cleft image also works to extend the picture of Vacarro and Baby Doll in a tree crotch and strongly suggests, beyond the equivocal final exchange of dialogue, that Baby Doll as well has found a cleft in a rock.

The film scenario explores the major themes of Williams' plays. Once again the South is a microcosm, expanded by means of symbol and generalized dialogue to permit observations on the human condition. The ruined house in Mississippi and the clannish town argue for a constricted, indrawn South, strewn with the relics of past affluence and gracious living. The house is not only, however, a symbol of a particular perception of the South but also brings into focus Williams' larger view of the world, which for him is also "spooked." In particular, just as evil and viciousness haunt the human heart, the world in general is bedeviled by the malevolency of man and nature, and is especially quick to prey on persons in vulnerable social or psychic conditions.

Though Baby Doll is potentially vulnerable as the wife of Archie Lee, she is not Williams' typically cracked southern belle. She is too young, willful and vigorous to be yet undone by the world, and luckier in finding a gentleman caller who proves to be a secular savior. These differences, along with broad characterization, insure Baby Doll's comic mode. In this mode sexual frustration, which in Williams' other plays generally serves to distort and crack the psyche, as with Blanche (in Streetcar) or Shannon (in Iguana), here serves to torment an all too deserving comic monster in Archie Lee, while sexual energy impells Baby Doll and Vacarro toward human intercourse. Here, too, the outsider, the foreigner, triumphs over southern and general circumstances of danger, mendacity and viciousness to outwit the Archie Lees of the world, win the girl and the woman latent in her, and save an old lady as well. And if a ruined and debased South can still in the agony of its dissolution destroy by fire, the victory is brief, and in the end as ineffectual as Archie Lee's drink and rage-blinded barrage. Though all is never right with the world in Williams' view, in Baby Doll it comes as close to being so as it ever does.

Despite the comedy and optimism of Baby Doll, the film came under heavy public attack. The outrage occasioned by the film's sexual suggestiveness seems almost quaint twenty years later, with much more explicit sexual scenes available at every neighborhood movie. Initially, no doubt the sensational publicity attending the film's New York premiere offended some. The lifted eye was assailed by a block-long billboard of Carroll Baker as Baby Doll, in scant pajamas that were to be trademarked by her name, thumb-sucking and sloe-eyed, reclining above Times Square in the blatant vulgarity of seventy-five-foot-long nude legs and eight-foot eyebrows. Though the film passed under the old Hayes Code (the motion picture industry's board of censors) as well as the New York board of censors, it was denounced by Mayor Wagner, whose name had erroneously appeared as a sponsor for its Actor's Benefit premiere at fifty dollars a seat. The Roman Catholic Legion of Decency totally condemned *Baby Doll*, and Cardinal Spellman excoriated it from the pulpit as revolting in theme, a defiance of natural law, morally corrupt and a clear violation of the motion picture code. Critics writing for popular magazines also recoiled. *Time* reported it was "the dirtiest American-made motion picture that has ever been legally exhibited," and the *Saturday Review* found it "one of the most unhealthy and amoral pictures ever made in this country."

If memory serves, Kazan's filmic interpretation of the script did intensify the general sense of decay and heightened the effect of moral decadence by emphasizing the lascivious elements of the film's sexual theme. Even Williams admitted that parts of the film made him "cringe." Carroll Baker did "a little too much licking of ice-cream and thumb-sucking." No doubt, for many, Baby Doll was too brazen, her contract with Archie Lee too sadistic and unnatural, and the miasma of a rotting, rural South too offensive. Williams was not responsible for the directorial emphasis and interpretation which doubtless intensified critical ire. From Williams' point of view, *Baby Doll* was a comedy.

It was scarcely the first time Williams experienced critical and public outrage. As early as 1940, with the Boston opening of *Battle of Angels*, his work came under bombardment. On opening night the audience was so restive that Miriam Hopkins ended by literally yelling her lines from the stage over the angry clamor. Furthermore, despite increasing critical appreciation of Williams during 1945 to 1955, and the granting of important awards to his plays, Williams came under continued critical attack by those who found his work obscene, decadent and immoral. His posture in 1956, as in 1940 with *Battle of Angels*, was similar; he played the role, whether as much ironically as by conviction, of hurt innocent whose work was essentially "pure as the driven snow" as he said about the earlier play, and said he himself felt "clean." As for the clerical attack on *Baby Doll*, and despite only partial responsibility for its filmic treatment, he said, "I can't believe that an ancient and august branch of the Christian faith is not larger in heart and mind than those who set themselves up as censors of a medium of expression that reaches all sections and parts of our country and extends the world over" (Donahue, pp. 173–5). It is difficult to believe that Williams, by this point in his career, if ever, could be innocent of the impact his characters and situations would have on general sensibility and defenders of public morality. His devotion to the work of D. H. Lawrence and Hart Crane, and his knowledge of the outrage that either their work or lives provoked, as well as his own previous experience of hostile criticism, argue against this.

What is disappointing in these outraged critical responses is the failure to discover in Williams' work the moral values that undergird it and his consistent defense of them. Williams' implicit plea for honesty, justice, and especially compassion are everywhere discoverable. However, the sensational surfaces of his work, his impulse toward broad symbolism, expressionistic characterization, even melodrama can outrage propriety and becloud judgment. Consequently, both the comedy and the seriousness of *Baby Doll* escaped a less impassioned and more considered critical assessment.

As noted, *Baby Doll* is linked to some of the major themes in Williams' work. However, its classic situation of the cuckolded older husband, foolish and desperate in a mismatched marriage, its broad characterization and extravagant humor, its moral injunctions for honesty, justice and typical sexuality, give the work the characteristics of comedic fable. As such, it indicts perversity and celebrates human vigor and compassion.

Period of Adjustment and the New Tennessee Williams

ALVIN GOLDFARB

O N NOVEMBER 30, 1960 a Broadway audience saw Tennessee Williams' first play of the sixties. While it was to be a decade of frustration for both the nation and its most prominent living playwright, this new work, *Period of Adjustment* or *High Point Over a Cavern*, was written for laughs. It was a "serious comedy."

The comedy was not a new work, having been revived from Williams' famous play trunk (? Casanova's Portmanteau). Also, it was not really a sixties drama, for this domestic comedy had premiered at Miami's Coconut Grove Playhouse on December 29, 1958 (Donahue, p. 123). Despite the favorable reactions, Williams let the play get cold: "I have put it away for the time being. I like to let things get cold for awhile" (Donahue, p. 124). Two years later, after his usual revision period, the work premiered in New York, receiving mixed notices. Yet even those critics who reacted positively were condescending. The critical majority found the comedy too slick, too reminiscent of a sexually liberated television situation comedy. However, those who had reacted positively talked of a new, more compassionate Tennessee Williams, a Williams who had finally disinherited cannibalism, mutilation, and castration. In a pre-premiere *New York Times* article the playwright stated that he had liberated himself from "false intensities" and learned to "stop taking a problem as if it affected the future of the world" (Gassner, "Broadway," p. 53). Yet, neither the positive nor the negative critiques did justice to the "serious comedy." Instead, *Period of Adjustment* must be analyzed in its relationship to the rest of Williams' dramaturgy. Through such an analysis the play's strengths and weaknesses become apparent.

Dealing with two couples suffering from marital unrest and attempting to weather their periods of adjustment, the serious comedy *is* quite reminiscent of a television situation comedy. Ralph Bates's once homely, now redone spouse, Dorothea has on the day before Christmas walked out simply because Ralph has quit his job, liberating himself from his boss, Dorothea's tyrannical, penny-pinching, millionaire father. Enter George Haverstick, Bates's ex-army buddy, with his wife of one day, Isabel. Apparently, they too are going through a period of adjustment for their marriage is still unconsummated, partially because of George's physical tremors and partially because of Isabel's professional virginity. By evening, however, army buddies and both couples are reunited, with the four neurotics having adjusted.

Period of Adjustment's characters all bear striking resemblances to earlier Williams heroes and heroines. All four are variations of previous types that roam the pages of Williams' dramaturgy.

Ralph Bates is a thirty-five-year-old Jim O'Connor, the gentleman caller, in *The Glass Menagerie*, and basically another variation of the playwright's degenerating dreamer. While the youthful O'Connor has plans for success, dreaming of an electronics career, in reality he has not gone on from his high school triumphs to be the one most likely to succeed. Instead, he merely works in a shoe factory. A returned war hero, as opposed to a high school football hero, Bates too was going to make the American Dream a reality. Yet, even after his marriage to the boss's daughter, the monotonous job remained the same, and the idea that his life had become an "affliction" became an obsession.

Ralph Bates dreams; he dreams of going, not to the moon, but to Mars, to Venus, to the stars: "Hell, I'd like to be transported and transplanted to colonize and fertilize, to be the Adam on a—star in a different *galaxy*, yeah, that far away even!—it's wonderful knowing that such a thing is no longer inconceivable, huh!" (IV, 199).

Just as Tom Wingfield, in *The Glass Menagerie*, escapes into films, Bates escapes into television, half-watching his set throughout his period of adjustment. Ralph also lives in his past, as does Brick, another dreamer, in *Cat on a Hot Tin Roof*. Obviously then Bates is becoming a middle-aged, middle-class American, unable to break the stranglehold of bourgeois existence. His weakness in character, a weakness inherent in the majority of Tennessee Williams' male protagonists, forces him to escape into another dream world rather than attempt a real escape.

George Haverstick is a combination of Stanley Kowalski in *A Streetcar Named Desire* and Brick. Haverstick views females as sex objects desiring to be sexually ravished. He is the violent, rambunctious male for whom sex symbolizes conquest; or so he pretends. In reality George is a frustrated Stanley. All his "sex talk" is simply talk. In Japan he taught the geishas English while later bragging of sexual gymnastics. On his wedding night he has had to be brutal with Isabel to mask his fear of impotence, to hide his terror of "shaking" while they are making love. Afraid of being unable to consummate his marriage, he, like Brick, turns to alcohol, drinking throughout his honeymoon. In many respects, Haverstick's tremors parallel Brick's broken leg. Both are excuses for avoiding sex; both are symptoms of a far deeper affliction. George, as do Ralph and Brick, rests on his laurels, continuously citing the fame of the Haversticks who died at the Alamo or his own war exploits. The relationship between George and Ralph is similar to the relationship between Big Daddy's son and Skipper. Both duos suffer from an affliction common to Williams' various protagonists: "Williams is a dramatist who delineates the problem of growing up, the difficulties of becoming an adult; and in an age that has no real concept of what an adult is, this problem is a real one. . . . Williams' plays deal with middle-aged adolescents" (Sharp, p. 168).

Dorothea Bates is a personage who is changing. At the time of her marriage, Mr. and Mrs. McGillicuddy's daughter was a combination of Laura in *The Glass Menagerie* and Alma in *Summer and Smoke*. Because Miss McGillicuddy was a plain, introverted young woman, her father was forced into collaring Ralph and coercing him into marriage. Mr. McGillicuddy's entrapment of Ralph is reminiscent of Amanda's desperate search for Laura's gentleman caller.

Also, bucktoothed Dorothea was suffering from psychological frigidity. Her sexual inhibitions parallel Alma's. Yet Ralph cured Dorothea. Mrs. Bates, therefore, has become reminiscent of Carol Cutrere in *Orpheus Descending*, Maggie in *Cat on a Hot Tin Roof*, and the sexually insatiable Princess Kosmonopolis in *Sweet Bird of Youth*. According to Ralph, "I wasn't excited enough by Dotty to satisfy her, sometimes. . . . Poor ole Dotty. She's got so she always wants it and when I can't give it to her I feel guilty, guilty" (p. 202). Dorothea has obviously metamorphosed into a variation of Williams' battling southern female. By the close, she has gained the forcefulness of a Maggie. She too learns to fight for survival. Dorothea sends her parents away, ignoring their protestations; allows Ralph to denigrate her and, ultimately, sexually revives her husband.

Isabel also resembles various Williams' female prototypes. As a weak, vulnerable woman, who has discovered herself in the grips of a bestial male, she is in a situation similar to that of Blanche in *A Streetcar Named Desire*. Possessing Blanche's strong sexual desires, hinted at by her perfume and alluring nighties, Isabel has, as did Alma in *Summer and Smoke*, kept these desires unhealthily under control. Mrs. Haverstick seems to be suffering from an Electra complex: "I just hope I stop crying! I don't want Daddy to hear me. . . . Poor ole thing. So sweet and faithful to Mamma, bedridden with arthritis for seven years, now. . . . I'm going to tell him that I am blissfully happy, married to the kindest man in the world, the second kindest, the kindest man next to my daddy!" (p. 188). It is a complex that Boss Finley's daughter, Heavenly, suffers from in *Sweet Bird of Youth*. Interestingly, Isabel's Electra complex is antithetical to Dorothea's relationship to her father. According to Ralph, his wife's psychological frigidity stemmed from paternal hatred.

The comedy's minor personages are interjected for slapstick. Mr. and Mrs. McGillicuddy are caricatures, quick, undeveloped sketches. They are elderly versions of Mae and Gooper. Dorothea's parents' materialism has replaced emotions. Their daughter is no more than the sum total of her belongings in the Bateses' home. Money is the McGillicuddys' god, Mr. McGillicuddy's avarice being symbolized by the single penny he has deposited in Ralph's good-luck statuette. The relationship between Bates's in-laws and the relationship between Mae and Gooper are identical; the loud-mouthed upper middle class wife making the decisions, the husband coerced into enforcing them.

Period of Adjustment is also saturated with symbolism common to much of Williams' dramaturgy. The action (as in *The Mutilated*) occurs at Christmas. Ralph's wife has left him just before Christmas, while Isabel and George are apparently separating on Christmas eve. However, the holiday hints at the eventual positive conclusion. The eventual reconciliation, the eventual birth and rebirth of relationships, is obviously foreshadowed by the Christmas setting. (References to "White Christmas" also set the scene for the positive denouement.)

Furthermore, the drama's mise en scène is also a major symbol. Ralph Bates's home is Ralph Bates. The living room, quite reminiscent of the setting for *Cat on a Hot Tin Roof*, with the constantly operating television set and the Christmas tree, and the cozy bedroom with the "His and Her" beds with the long gap in between, represent the Bateses' plastic, middle class existence. The house is swallowing up Ralph. It is from this environment, not from Dorothea, that Ralph really wants to escape.

The Bateses' home is also literally being swallowed up by a cavern. Each new shift puts a new crack in the wall and foreshadows the building's eventual destruction. The absurdity of Ralph's middle class existence is mirrored in the fate of his home. With each new middle class trauma Bates suffers, his universe sustains a new crack and sinks. Like his home, he too will eventually sink into the bottomless cavern of bourgeois existence.

One symbol, however, holds hope for Ralph, "the dignified Texas Long Horn." George suggests that if he and Ralph breed these cattle, they can escape the middle class rat race. By adopting an agrarian lifestyle they will break the chains of their undignified existences. In a speech strikingly reminiscent of Biff's final monologue in Arthur Miller's *Death of a Salesman*, George presents the proposition to Ralph: "There *is* dignity in that sky! There's dignity in the agrarian, the pastoral—way of—existence! A dignity too long lost out of the—American dream . . . as it used to be in the West Texas-Haverstick days" (p. 197). *Period of Adjustment* is one of the few instances in which Williams employs the "earth" as a symbol of purity. Otherwise, throughout the playwright's oeuvre the earth destroys man. Both Blanche and Stella are products of an agrarian system. In *Orpheus Descending* Val Xavier discovers destruction in an agrarian southern hamlet. Unfortunately, for Ralph and George this agrarian lifestyle is just another of their many dreams.

Williams labels *Period of Adjustment* a "serious comedy." More accurately, the work is a stinging social satire, and an analysis of the play's subtitles reveals the targets of Williams' ridicule. Apparently, *Period of Adjustment* has two different subtitles. The one given in *The Theatre of Tennessee Williams* is *High Point over a Cavern*; that given in the acting edition is *High Point is Built on a Cavern*. The shorter title is a sexual double entendre indicating the sexual frustrations and lack of sexual satisfaction in both the Bateses' and the Haversticks' marriages. The longer subtitle stresses High Point as a symbol of existences built on shaky grounds, of individuals sinking into quagmires along with their homes.

Primarily, the "serious comedy" satirizes middle class American life. Ralph Bates's High Point is representative of all American suburbs, for as he tells Isabel, "I guess all fair-sized American cities have got a suburb called High Point" (p. 140). From the opening moment of the play, when the television blares a stereotypical detergent commercial, it is apparent that *Period of Adjustment* is attacking a lifestyle epitomized by television commercials and Spanish-type stucco houses with "sweet" little Christmas trees, "sweet" little kitchens and "sweet" little bedrooms. The focus of *High Point over a Cavern* is the purposeless, unfulfilled, middle class lives the Bateses and Haversticks lead. None of these characters can honestly answer Isabel's questions: "Where do we *come* from? *Why? And where, oh where, are we going!*" (p. 148).

That Williams mocks the difficulties inherent in marriage, particularly sexual difficulties, is also quite obvious and is in keeping with his bleak portrayal of suburban life. While Ralph insists that all couples suffer short periods of adjustment, what the playwright presents instead are two marriages that are continual periods of adjustment. Neither marriage developed out of mutual understanding, Ralph having married Dorothea for financial rewards and Isabel having married George out of sympathy. Tenderness is also lacking. The final stanza of Williams' poem "Shadow Wood" which, in a slightly altered version, prefaces the play's acting text accurately describes all of High Point's personages: "For tenderness I would lay down/the weapon that holds death away,/but little words of tenderness/are hard for shadow man to say" (*In the Winter of Cities*, p. 125). Neither the newlyweds nor their already married friends have adjusted to one another. That their relationships are superficial is seen in the Bateses' reconciliation which is brought about by a beaver coat costing $745. Materialism, rather than mature adjustment, reunites the couple. Tennessee Williams' scornful view of such marriages is most clearly symbolized by the Haversticks' honeymoon vehicle, a rundown 1952 funeral limousine.

It should, therefore, be apparent that as in Williams' earlier tragedies, the comedy here is deadly serious. The characters in *Period of Adjustment* are desperate over their tragicomic predicaments. The basic difference between *High Point* and the playwright's earlier dramaturgy is that "what previously had been cause for catastrophe is now cause for comedy" (Nelson, p. 286). If not for the positive resolution, generically the "serious comedy" would be almost identical to Williams' previous works.

Finally, then, is the play atypical Tennessee Williams? As indicated, *Period of Adjustment* contains the basic Williams elements. Apparently, the 1960 critics disagreed basically about the drama's positive conclusion. What many failed to notice was that while the reconciliation does have the makings of a situation comedy, Williams' sardonic humor is at play. Dorothea closes the drama by warning Ralph, who is attempting to remove her nightgown, "Careful, let me do it!—It isn't mine!" (p. 246). Again, the middle class plasticity, the bourgeois materialism interjects itself into the "happily-ever-after" ending, with the nightgown being more important than their spontaneous lovemaking. If the final line indicates that Dorothea can never truly change, it also makes Ralph's, George's, and Isabel's transformations dubious. Also, throughout the dramatic action each character expresses a desire to leave; to leave the home, to leave a spouse, to leave an existence. Almost tragically every character remains.

When we begin to question Williams' newfound compassion in *Period of Adjustment* we discover that he is humorously dissecting the middle class angst of all the Ralph Bateses, Dorothea Bateses, George Haversticks, and Isabel Haversticks in his audiences. In many ways *Period of Adjustment* is the same old Tennessee Williams.

The Night of the Iguana:
A Long Introduction, a General Essay, and no Explication at All

CHARLES MOORMAN

T. S. ELIOT WAS, of course, right about *Hamlet*; it is an artistic failure. For Eliot believed that "the only way of expressing emotion in the form of art is by finding an 'objective correlative'; in other words, a set of objects, a situation, a chain of events which shall be the formula for that *particular* emotion; such that when the external facts, which must terminate in sensory experience, are given, the emotion is immediately evoked." And "Hamlet is up against the difficulty that his disgust is occasioned by his mother, but that his mother is not an adequate equivalent for it; his disgust envelops and exceeds her."[1]

One can think immediately of other such failures to find "a set of objects, a situation, a chain of events" sufficiently correlative to the author's conception of life to transmit it adequately: Melville's *Pierre*, Crane's *Maggie*, "The Idiot Boy," all of them vehicles too weak to carry the massive philosophical baggage assigned to them.

One senses, however, that Eliot's dictum, however useful it may be in defining in a very specific way the failure of the artist to conceptualize successfully, is of limited critical use; it cannot, for example, aid the critic in exploring the artist's successful use of symbols. Once one has said that in *Moby Dick* the whale does indeed symbolize the incomprehensibility of the universe, that in *1 Henry IV* the triangular opposition of the King, Falstaff, and Hot-

318

spur adequately dramatizes Hal's choices, that Yeats's Byzantium precisely stands for the perfection of art, then how can the doctrine of the objective correlative lead him further into the work? Patently, it cannot.

Our inability to progress under the doctrine stems, I think, from the fact that Eliot has placed the cart before the horse, the artist's intention, his "*particular* emotion," before the nature of the objective correlative itself. In reading the prefaces of Henry James, for example, one recognizes that James, unlike Eliot, does not venture forth into nature, preconceived theme in hand, in order to find there a plot to fit it; he discovers instead his theme among and within the objects of the world as he perceives them. As R. P. Blackmur says, "often a single fact reported at the dinner-table was enough for James to seize on and plant in the warm bed of his imagination";[2] and James himself remarks of the genesis of *The Ambassadors*—a friend's report of a conversation overheard at a Paris garden party— that "never can a composition of this sort have sprung straighter from a dropped grain of suggestion, and never can that grain, developed, overgrown and smothered, have yet lurked more in the mass as an independent particle" (*Art of the Novel*, p. 307). Granted, of course, that I have perhaps falsely identified Eliot's author's "*particular* emotion" as a "preconceived theme" and granted also that James was interested only in certain kinds of situations—he would have found as few "germs" at a prize fight as Hemingway would have at that Paris garden party—nevertheless for James—as for Wordsworth perceiving a field of flowers or Yeats a chestnut tree or Dante a Florentine girl—the nature and character of the image preceded and contained within itself the poet's conception and use of it.

In spite of its limitations, however, Eliot's notion that intent precedes and determines symbolization is of great use in leading the reader to perceive the tricks and distortions of the manipulated, the "thesis," work where unnaturally contrived symbols join to form patterns of coalition and confrontation, where one is forced by the author to see that, ah yes, the processes of a Salem witch trial are indeed like those of a congressional committee and that, agreed, modern man is very like a cockroach or a hippopotamus. At times, the student of literature comes to realize that the most ideologically

tractable play is the least convincing piece of stagecraft; the pre-
ciseness of symbolically and thematically oriented structure that
makes *The Wild Duck* and *The Plough and the Stars* eminently
suitable for academic analysis accounts for their being less dramatically convincing than the less cleanly structured *Hedda Gabler* and
Juno and the Paycock. What one always hopes to find in experiencing a work of literature is that having accepted the objective correlatives all along for what they in themselves are, he comes eventually,
either slowly and imperceptibly or with a violent shock of recognition, to witness an epiphany, to feel that "knowledge carried alive
into the heart by passion," to see those objects at last as the artist
sees them, with, as Sir Joshua Reynolds put it, "common observation and a plain understanding."

What I am saying—that symbolic objects must be objects first
and symbols second—is certainly commonplace; indeed one of my
reviewers once remarked that my "common sense" could reduce
great literature "to a shambles." But commonplace is not necessarily
false and may even be rewarding. And this particular handle (which
is all critical theories are) seems to me to be especially rewarding
in the appreciative understanding (which is the highest aim that
criticism can aspire to) of drama in general where the objective
correlative must be *at once* visually and audially convincing and of
Tennessee Williams in particular, whose name, I will warrant, the
reader thought I had forgotten how to spell.

For those first plays upon which Williams' reputation still largely
depends—*The Glass Menagerie* and *A Streetcar Named Desire*—
whatever their particular successes in dialogue and stagecraft and
dramatic force, strike one, especially in the raw light of the study
rather than the filtered one of the stage, as being manipulated. One
somehow imagines Williams saying: "Let us take one strongly
stereotyped, deep-South, poverty-stricken, genteel, foolish, garrulous,
dislocated southern widow, add her two children, an introspective
crippled (good touch, that!) girl, and a poetical, philosophical
(though realistic!) son (enter chorus!) and, to set the puppets in
motion, introduce a shy gentleman caller. Mother will, of course,
talk; daughter will, of course, not; and son can comment away on
isolation and alienation on the fire escape. And, oh yes, let us have

us a really symbolic symbol, a set of glass animals, which we can break in the end."

OR: "How about conjuring up two one-dimensional, deep-South sisters, one the wife of a brutish Polack factory worker and the other a supposedly genteel widow who is really the aging village nympho, then letting the Polack rape the widow, while a symbolic streetcar roams around the French Quarter."

I do not intend to demean these two plays (they are, after all, the pride and joy of the American theater) only to satirize their manifestly contrived use of character and incident and symbol. That Williams manages to conceal his shopworn characters and conflicts behind a façade of brilliant theatrical magic is a tribute to his genius. But it may well be that in *The Night of the Iguana* (and perhaps in a few other late plays as well, notably I think *Suddenly Last Summer*) one can detect a growing awareness that theatrical characters need not be entirely stereotyped nor immediately classifiable to be convincing, that plots need not be either contrived or labored to be effective.

The germ of *The Night of the Iguana* is contained in a short story of the same name which appeared in 1948 in *One Arm*.[3] *The Night of the Iguana*, however, produced some thirteen years later, is so different from its fictional first version that one can hardly believe them to be by the same writer. Indeed the short story—sketch really —is embarrassing, the sort of thing college teachers of English send to *The New Yorker*. Four characters are involved, "a Miss Edith Jelkes who had been an instructor in art at an Episcopalian girls' school in Mississippi until she had suffered a sort of nervous breakdown and had given up her teaching position for a life of refined vagrancy" (pp. 169–70); two "young writers" (though one is somehow "the older") much given to secret conversations, arguments, and seminude bathing; and the rough and ready patrona of the Costa Verde hotel near Acapulco. All four are predictable reliques of Early Williams; one could exchange them unnoticed for the Blanches and Toms and Serafinas of *Streetcar* and *Menagerie* and *Tattoo*.

The story is simple enough: Miss Jelkes, a virginal artiste "trying to evade her neurasthenia through the distraction of making new friends" (p. 170)⁴ attempts to invade the privacy of the writers and is rebuked by both. She finally provokes an unsuccessful assault by the "older" of the two and withdraws muttering "*Ah, Life*" as she touches the writer's ejaculation "still adhering to the flesh of her belly as a light but persistent kiss" (p. 196). The meaning of all this is symbolized by Williams in an Iguana, caught and tortured by the patrona's son and liberated by God-knows-whom in order to show Miss Jelkes that "in some equally mysterious way the strangling rope of her loneliness had also been severed by what had happened tonight on this barren rock above the moaning waters" (p. 196).

If I am inordinately critical of the short story version of *The Night of the Iguana* it is because I see it in terms of what it is to become, the brilliant play of thirteen years later. The neat pat symbols of the story (and of the early plays) disappear. Miss Edith Jelkes becomes Hannah Jelkes of Nantucket, a gentlewoman still, a virgin still, but also an open-eyed realist, a confidence artist, forced by circumstances to an itinerant existence to support her father, at ninety-seven "the world's oldest living practicing poet." Hannah is "a Gothic cathedral image of a medieval saint, but animated" (IV, 266); unembittered, though exhausted, warm and sympathetic, though desperate, she has arrived penniless with her dying father at the Costa Verde, no longer a smart resort in its off-season, but the seedy establishment of Maxine Faulk, lately widowed and randy. The Costa Verde is also the refuge of the unfrocked Reverend T. Lawrence Shannon, who has drunkenly conducted a female party of Texas schoolteachers to his old friend Maxine's hotel. Discredited, drunken, discharged from what is obviously to be his last hope of respectable employment, Shannon, like Hannah, has come to the end of his rope. The hotel is also inhabited by an exuberant party of honeymooning Germans, all "pink and gold like baroque cupids"; they are the New Order, "splendidly physical," perpetually romping and cheering Hitler's speeches on the radio. Conflicts quickly develop. Maxine offers Shannon security, protection; he can become both proprietor and house stud. Shannon, however, resists Maxine's easy degeneracy and sees in the sensitive, though sexless, Hannah some hope of retrieving his former, better self. Hannah, rejecting Shannon, wants only peace. And, miraculously, all find themselves in Williams' cosmic jungle Lost and Found.

Around this simple triangle, Williams has created a world of symbols and minor characters, all of which in their integrity and unforced faithfulness to their own natures become in fact objective correlatives of the emotions and states of mind of the principal characters and hence of the author's *"particular* emotion": the violent storm at the end of act two, a natural enough occurrence in Mexico, which marks the beginning of the cleansing of Shannon; the beach boys who typify and satisfy Maxine's libido, the Texas schoolteachers who represent the aberrations, nymphets, and lesbians of the world from which Shannon is escaping; the Nazi family from whose insensitive paganism they all must escape; the final poem of Hannah's father, with its willing renunciation of golden innocence and its courageous acceptance of earth's corrupting love; and, of course, the iguana, the word no longer capitalized, which Shannon frees at almost the very moment of Hannah's father's death, so that, like all of them, it can "scramble home safe and free."

And scramble home they manage to do, though all must accept alternate solutions with, as Nonno's poem says, "frightened hearts": Shannon to the security of Maxine, if not to the purity of Hannah; Maxine to an end of loneliness and frustration, if not to a renewal of the "patient, tolerant" love of the bigger-than-life size Fred; Hannah, freed from the burden of her father, to some hope of peace, even if not to a world where unkindness and violence do not exist. In the midst of a world rapidly yielding either to the puritan values of the faculty of the Baptist Female College of Blowing Rock, Texas, or to the exuberantly efficient, though sinister, sensualism of the German family Fahrenkopf, all of them find in this Mexican Shangri-La a renewal of life, a "second history," as Nonno's poem has it, after the "zenith of life" has past, a "chronicle" which "if no longer gold" is at least endurable. Like the kinsmen in the Emily Dickinson poem which stands as headnote to the play, all have talked "between the rooms," but Nonno's poem of courage replaces Miss Dickinson's poem of despair, and in the end the iguana goes free.

The line-by-line demonstration or refutation of these matters I cheerfully leave to others. As my title suggests, this is an essay, a trial-run, a fungo. But *The Night of the Iguana* is so palpably strong a play, so patently an objective correlative of Williams' late, if not his final, set of themes, so organically unified a work of art, that explication de texte seems an unnecessary intrusion upon its affirmation of life.

Notes to Charles Moorman,
"*The Night of the Iguana*"

1. *Selected Essays* (New York: Harcourt, Brace, 1932), p. 124.

2. "Introduction" to *The Art of the Novel: Critical Prefaces by Henry James* (New York: Scribner's, 1947), p. xv.

3. A similar relationship exists between, for example, "Portrait of a Girl in Glass" and *The Glass Menagerie*. Unlike the two "Night" pieces, *The Glass Menagerie* is hardly better than "Portrait."

4. Williams explains that she is a member of "an historical Southern family of great but now moribund vitality whose latter generations had tended to split into two antithetical types, one in which the libido was pathologically distended and another in which it would seem to be all but dried up" (p. 170).

The Subterranean World
of *The Night of the Iguana*

GLENN EMBREY

M OST OF TENNESSEE WILLIAMS' characters eventually discover there is no fate worse than sex; desire maims and kills, often in the most violent fashion. Val Xavier is burnt to death, Blanche DuBois is raped and driven insane, Chance Wayne waits to be castrated, and Sebastian Venable is torn apart and devoured by children—all because of sexual drives. Many other characters in Williams' plays are destroyed by their passions, only in less physical and sensationalistic ways.

The idea that sex is fatal is not always easy to catch in the plays, for it is usually not developed explicitly. Instead, it lurks in the background, like a vague but persistent nightmare that affects the shape of whatever else the plays have to say. Also, it contradicts some of the popular notions about Williams. After all, his heroes and heroines often openly revel in their sexual exploits. He is considered the champion of the promiscuous, the passionate, the deviant. When these characters are destroyed, they appear to be the victims of an insensitive or sadistic world that will not tolerate their differences, especially their sexual differences; they seem to be brutalized not by their own desires, but by cruel, external forces. Blanche DuBois, for example, is assailed by a crude society that has no room for her sensitivity, her ideals, or her need to find comfort in sexual encounters. But this view of Blanche is only half true. There is in *Streetcar* what

325

Shannon would call a "subterranean" or "fantastic" level. On this level, the play is really a dramatization of how Blanche and her delicate nature are devastated by the promiscuous behavior her sexual nature drives her to, a fate paralleling the way her family's plantation was lost through the "epic fornication" of their ancestors. When Stanley ravages her mind and body at the end of the play, he is not so much an agent of the real world as he is a symbol of the sexual drives that have ravaged her throughout her life.

The main character of *The Night of the Iguana* seems to escape the violent fate usually in store for Williams' heroes. True, desire has been ruining Shannon's life for the past ten years, but at the climax of the play he manages to form what promises to be a lasting sexual relationship with a mature woman. This optimistic ending appears to make *Iguana* very different from the serious plays that precede it; for the first time hope breaks across Williams' bleak world. But appearances are deceptive, for there is a "subterranean" world within *Iguana*, as there is in *Streetcar*, and this world makes *Iguana's* optimism naive and unjustified, and makes the play just another variation on the theme that haunts all of Williams' works—that sex kills, that it is disgusting and dangerous. The conflict that exists between the different levels of *Iguana* is also typical of the playwright's works, and the play provides a clear example of how they collapse into confusion because unacknowledged fears of sexuality undermine their more overt and positive levels.

Shannon arrives onstage in the condition of the typical Williams hero—on the verge of going to pieces. Emotionally, physically, psychologically, financially, in almost every possible way, he is at the end of his rope, just like the frantic iguana. The play provides a surfeit of explanations for his imminent breakdown. One is simply his bizarre lifestyle: he roams about the world, towing his unsuspecting tour groups after him, in search of the most horrifying and disgusting scenes he can find. The understandable complaints posted by his parties, along with his seductions of the youngest ladies of the groups, get him fired from one travel agency after another. He is currently employed by the sleaziest of the agencies, and none is left to hire him if he is fired again.

Another reason for his collapse is that he is so preoccupied with himself he is cut off from everyone else. Despite his busloads of companions, some more intimate than others, he is abjectly lonely. In his conversation with Hannah during the second act he explains what has led to his miserable way of life. Ten years before, his brief career as a minister ended after he committed both fornication and heresy in the same week. A young Sunday school teacher had come to the rectory and wildly declared she loved him. When he knelt with her to pray for guidance, they suddenly found themselves making love. Afterwards, he slapped her and called her a tramp; when she went home she tried to commit suicide. On the following Sunday, facing a congregation expecting an explanation and apologies, he suddenly threw away his prepared remarks and shouted an impromptu sermon that drove the people from the church. The gist of his outburst was that he refused to conduct services for the kind of God he felt they believed in: a *"senile delinquent,"* "a bad-tempered childish old, old, sick, peevish man" (IV, 303–4).

He was locked out of his church and committed to an asylum to recover from his apparent nervous breakdown. When released he became a tour guide, and his itineraries show he never fully recovered from whatever had possessed him. On each of his tours he clearly reenacts the dual sin of fornication and heresy. He seduces one or more of the youngest members of the party, afterwards treating them as abusively as he did the Sunday school teacher. The tours themselves are a continuation of his heretical sermon, for on them, he tells Hannah, he is trying to "collect evidence" of his own "personal idea of God" (p. 304), evidence that attacks his congregation's notion of God. And the results are just the same: he is fired by his tour groups as he was fired by his congregation.

Shannon's concept of God needs some explaining for it seems at odds with the kind of evidence he gathers. He is primarily interested in examples of the disgusting misery of human life. The story that Hannah finds nauseating about the aged filthy natives crawling about a mound of excrement looking for bits of undigested food to eat epitomizes what Shannon collects. So does the iguana. Jerking about desperately and uselessly against its noose, destined to become Maxine's dinner, the iguana is a metaphor not only for the major characters of the play but also for all human beings, creatures made grotesque by suffering and terror, frequently forced to live in the most degrading of conditions.

Shannon's God provides quite a contrast to these images. He is personified as a "terrific electric storm"; he is the "God of Lightning and Thunder" and of blazing, apocalyptic sunsets. Shannon's descriptions recall the Old Testament God of overwhelming majesty and righteous wrath. And although this is the kind of God he really believes in, he overtly rejects the idea by arguing that his God is in no way interested in punishment or suffering.

The key term in Shannon's theology is "oblivious"; when he points out the nearing thunderstorm to Hannah, he says, "That's him! There he is now! . . . His oblivious majesty" (p. 305). According to Shannon traditional theologies see suffering as purposely sanctioned by God as an opportunity for men to atone for their sins and rise to him, but Shannon feels that suffering is simply the result of the world's "faults in construction." They are architectural imperfections, God's accidents, and men do suffer because of them; but no divine plan lies behind the misery. To claim design, as Western theologies do, says Shannon, makes God either a cruel child or a sadist; Shannon refuses to conduct services for such a God. The logic connecting human degradation and divine majesty is somewhat tenuous. Apparently Shannon's twisted thinking runs along these lines: God is awesome, powerful, majestic (this idea is a product of his childhood, and he never seems to question it; it is a given). But a God who is all these things could not possibly be aware of man's extreme misery and let it continue to exist; therefore God must be unaware of it. Thus, the more examples of suffering Shannon can collect, the more he is demonstrating that God is oblivious, and consequently the more he is proving God's majesty.

Williams takes the explanations of Shannon's crack-up a step further in the third act, when Maxine uncovers the psychically damaging events that eventually led to the eruption of Shannon's double offense. She recounts to Shannon, surely for the audience's sake rather than his, what she once heard him telling her deceased husband. His problems supposedly began when his mother caught him masturbating; after spanking him she said his behavior made God even angrier than it made her and that if she did not punish him, God would, and much more severely. Maxine continues, "You said you loved God and Mama and so you quit it to please them, but it was your secret pleasure and you harbored a secret resentment against Mama and God for making you give it up. And so you got back at God by preaching atheistical sermons and you got back at Mama by starting to lay young girls" (p. 329). A simplistic psychological explanation, to be sure, but one that Williams apparently intends us to take seriously, for none of the characters or Shannon's actions contradict it. On the contrary, his theology and behavior are perfectly in tune with it. It reveals, for example, the origin of his belief that God is awesome, threatening, and by extension, majestic; this is his adult version of his mother's warning that God was angry and ready to punish him severely. It also explains why fornication is always linked with heresy. He was told that he would have to suffer for his sexual pleasure; thus, to ward off the punishment he has earned whenever he indulges his sexual desire, he must immediately assert that God is actually oblivious to mankind. Sex becomes safe if he can deny his mother's idea of God, so he tries to collect evidence for this denial.

Maxine's comments also explain the sudden, powerful emergence of his sexuality that occurred that day on the rectory floor. Fear of punishment caused the young Shannon to repress his sexual nature; the consequences of his repression are the same as those suffered by other Williams characters. Driven underground for whatever reason, sexual urges grow more powerful and more threatening. The vicious circle in which repression causes a strengthening of the desire repressed, which in turn causes renewed effort to repress, can end only disastrously when desire breaks through its restraints. By this time it has grown so powerful that it is virtually uncontrollable and blasts away the character's former life. This pattern appears in the lives of Blanche in *Streetcar* and Alma in *Summer and Smoke*. The dangerous energy that repressed desire takes on is manifest in Stanley Kowalski and John Buchanan, menacing sexual supermen who are really the women's sexual alter egos. Since that first incident, Shannon has learned what Blanche and Alma learned. Initially he was able to smother his sexual nature so thoroughly that he became not only a minister of the God who opposed his sensual pleasure; he also became what he calls "the goddamnedest prig" imaginable.

Desire burst free while he was kneeling with the Sunday school teacher and has remained irrepressible ever since. His continual seductions are not so much a way of getting back at his mother, as Maxine suggests; they are something he is driven to, in spite of his conscious reluctance, by his voracious sexual appetite.

And he obviously has a great deal of reluctance. I have said that his initial trauma explains Shannon's wanting to make God oblivious and unvengeful, but it should be clear by now that all his efforts in this direction are a case of his protesting too much. Shannon is afraid that God is full of righteous wrath, and naturally he is terrified about what his uncontrollable passion will bring down upon him. His panic and anxiety are very understandable in this light. No doubt even his feeble efforts to avoid God's wrath by preaching about a different kind of God aggravate his guilt and fear—he is aware rebellion will not escape notice or punishment.

There is plenty of evidence that Shannon still believes in the God he pretends to dismiss. We have his latest lover's word that he continues to feel as guilty about sex as he did after his first transgression: "I remember that after making love to me," Charlotte tells him, "you hit me, . . . you struck me in the face, and you twisted my arm to make me kneel on the floor and pray with you for forgiveness" (p. 298). An oblivious God would hardly be interested in forgiveness. Shannon's continuing fantasy that he will write to his former bishop and be reinstated as a minister suggests how ineffectual his efforts have been to break away from the God his mother warned him about. He dreams of giving up his heretical and sexual offenses and being forgiven by one of God's agents. In effect, he wants to become a good boy again.

Shannon's parody of Christ's crucifixion is the most blatant evidence of his failure to get free from this God. He is so far from truly believing that God is oblivious to suffering and atonement that he plays at being God's son. In the third act when he has finally cracked up, Maxine has him tied in a hammock to keep him from drowning himself. He struggles melodramatically against the rope, and Hannah, a quick-sketch artist who specializes in accurate psychological portraits, accuses him of being a perverse Christ figure engaged in a self-indulgent passion play: "There's something almost voluptuous in the way that you twist and groan in that hammock—no nails, no blood, no death. Isn't that a comparatively comfortable, almost voluptuous kind of crucifixion to suffer for the guilt of the world, Mr. Shannon?" (p. 344). How useless all his evidence has been. Afraid of being punished for his sins, he tries to stave off God's wrath by "suffering" like Christ, to atone for his offenses. Ironically, he is never totally free from either his dread of God or his sensual nature; each aspect of his personality corrodes the other. His guilt and fear keep him from ever enjoying sex fully, and his sexual instincts manage to corrupt his attempts to suffer for his sins since he derives sensual pleasure even from his suffering.

Caught between his sexual drives and his religious fears, between his need to deny God and his yearning for forgiveness, Shannon can find momentary relief from this tension, from his "spook," only in periodic crack-ups. During such times he loses control of himself and can no longer be held accountable for his sins.

Williams captures Shannon's predicament brilliantly in a brief and wordless scene in act three, after Shannon has lost the last vestiges of control over his touring party. He stands onstage wearing a few pieces of his ministerial garb; suddenly, he "with an animal outcry begins to pull at the chain suspending the gold cross about his neck" (p. 340). He jerks savagely back and forth on it, slashing himself. His actions illustrate how he is tied to his warped theology, just as the iguana is tied to the stake. He shows how his religious beliefs make him suffer, how his efforts to free himself from them are useless and only make him suffer the more. And he shows how willingly he punishes himself.

This masochistic pantomime ends in a very significant way, and this is where *Iguana* begins to differ from Williams' prior works. Hannah rushes over to help him and soon frees him from his chain and his self-laceration. During the rest of the play, she will accomplish in actuality what she does here symbolically— she frees him from his obsessive, self-destructive notions so that he can move completely out of the previous pattern of his life, find a measure of peace, and establish a healthy sexual relationship. To underline Hannah's triumph, at the end of the play Williams has Shannon give his cross and chain to her.

Hannah begins her therapy by pointing out to him how self-indulgent and voluptuous his struggles actually are. Then she focuses on the problem of his miserable loneliness. He has been so obsessed with himself and his fears, she tells him, that he hasn't been able to see that people might help him. Even his sexual escapades have been cold and lonely, she says, and isolate rather than connect him with others. Her initial advice echoes Big Mama's plea in *Cat*: "we just got to love each other an' stay together" (III, 157). Hannah tells Shannon he needs to find relief in "Broken gates between people so they can reach each other, even if it's just for one night only . . . communication . . . A little understanding exchanged between them, a wanting to help each other through nights like this" (IV, p. 352). People must struggle to break through the walls that keep them apart and come together, even if only momentarily, with understanding, kindness, and sympathy. Hannah reinforces her advice by becoming an example of what she is talking about. She reaches out to him with compassion and respect. And her advice and example are very effective; he is finally able to put aside his obsessions and establish a healthy connection with another human being, Maxine.

Hannah also makes two other important suggestions. She tells him he must learn simply to endure the tension and terror that are part of his life. Later she advises him to go beyond endurance to acceptance; after recounting the two bizarre incidents that comprise her "lovelife," she tells him "the moral is Oriental. Accept whatever situation you cannot improve" (p. 363). It's no accident that "the moral is Oriental" for the play creates a definite contrast between East and West, in which the Eastern attitudes of stoicism and fatalism are offered as a positive alternative to the Western preoccupations with guilt and suffering.

Iguana conveys the superiority of East over West in a number of ways. For example, near the end of the play Hannah tells Shannon how moved she was by the peaceful deaths of the poor in Shanghai: their "eyes looked up with their last dim life left in them as clear as the stars in the Southern Cross. . . . Nothing I've ever seen has seemed as beautiful to me" (p. 356). In this respect, Nonno's calm resignation before death is "Oriental," as Hannah makes clear, and is in stark contrast to the terror and hysteria the approach of death usually evokes in Williams' characters. The East-West theme is also established visually. Close to the beginning of the third act Hannah puts on a Japanese Kabuki robe, so that when she later manages to free Shannon from his cross and chain her exotic Eastern attire makes her look a world apart from the neurotic minister. She wears the robe throughout the act, reminding us of the source of her compassionate advice.

The Fahrenkopfs provide an even more vivid contrast to the Oriental Hannah. In their Rubensesque proportions and Wagnerian exuberance they represent the culmination of Western civilization. Their boisterousness and frenetic activity counterpoint Hannah's demeanor, and as Nazis they epitomize the cruelty and violence of the Western world.

Williams even manages to have Maxine reinforce the theme—in her characteristically crude way. Early in the third act, in an effort to soothe Shannon's nerves, she tells him her cook's philosophy of life, one she appears to share: "The Chinaman in the kitchen says, 'No sweat.' . . . 'No sweat.' . . . All the Chinese philosophy in three words, 'Mei yoo guanchi'—which is Chinese for 'No sweat'" (p. 330). And at the very end of the play, in a surprising transformation, Maxine *becomes* Oriental; in a stage direction Williams writes: "It is apparent that the night's progress has mellowed her spirit: her face wears a faint smile which is suggestive of those cool, impersonal all-comprehending smiles on the carved heads of Egyptian or Oriental deities" (p. 373). No doubt this metamorphosis is a major reason Shannon can accept her at the climax of the play.

This climax sets *Iguana* apart from Williams' other serious works. Shannon survives. He attains some measure of peace. He is neither returning to the ministry nor continuing his rebellion against it and his mother. Instead, he has been led beside the "still waters" of the Costa Verde Hotel. Much more than this, he enters what is apparently a healthy sexual relationship. Other Williams characters have found momentary stays against despair in brief, casual encounters with strangers, but Shannon seems to be entering into something more lasting with Maxine. His decision to stay with her fulfills both parts of Hannah's advice: he is finally reaching outside of himself, and he has decided to accept Maxine and his present situation. He leaves the play chuckling happily, with Maxine "half leading half supporting him" (p. 374). Anyone familiar with the bulk of Williams' work can appreciate how unusual, how positive this description of their relationship is.

Shannon's loosing the iguana at the end of the play is obviously a symbol of the optimistic resolutions that are simultaneously occurring. The lizard is set free at the same time Nonno is set free from his poem and his life, at the same time Hannah is unburdened of her dying grandfather, and at the same time Shannon escapes from his God, his mother, and his loneliness.

Unfortunately, the ending isn't as believable as it is formally pleasing and optimistic. Even according to the overt level of the drama, the ending sounds suspiciously like the product of wishful thinking. For one thing, it comes rather suddenly and unexpectedly; an hour's exposure to human compassion, a cup of poppy tea, and a bit of Oriental wisdom hardly seem sufficient to eradicate habits and attitudes hardened over the past ten years. For another, the advice Hannah gives him doesn't really speak to the main sources of his problems: terrible guilt, fear of God, and an overpowering sex drive. The two characters never mention these things, much less work through them during their conversation. Hannah could conceivably convince him that human contact is worthwhile, but she never points out or tells him how to combat those feelings that have made human contact so difficult for him. The optimistic conclusion simply ignores the psychological portrait Williams works out so carefully during the course of the play.

And if the ending isn't entirely convincing on the overt level, it is completely incompatible with some less explicit, subterranean elements which work like an undertow to suck the mood of the play back into bleakness and despair. The difference between acceptance and endurance is a key to the nature of the shadow side of the play. Acceptance is a more positive notion. A person is able to accept an undesirable situation by putting aside his own needs or expectations and seeing beyond the negative aspects to find something positive he can embrace. Endurance is more pessimistic. It implies that the unsatisfactory situation remains exactly as it seems—painful, destructive, threatening, or whatever. Nothing redeeming is to be found in it. Maggie in *Cat* provides an example of this notion. Tense and frustrated by her husband's physical and emotional rejection of her, she wonders what victory a person who feels like "a cat on a hot tin roof" can achieve; she decides, "Just staying on it, I guess, as long as she can . . ." (III, p. 31). Endurance implies that the roof never cools down; the cat merely grins fiercely and bears it. This is the implication of Hannah's remarks when she tells Shannon she showed her own spook "that I could endure him and I made him respect my endurance." Shannon asks how and she replies, "Just by, just by . . . enduring" (p. 353). Though she will later speak of *acceptance*, much in the play makes this concept out of the question for Shannon and indicates he is in a situation he can barely endure.

In a way, we have Williams' own word for this point. In an interview during the rehearsals for *Iguana* he said the theme of the play is "how to live beyond despair and still live" (Funke and Booth, p. 72). The context makes clear that *beyond* means not *without* but *in a state worse than* (despair). Many elements of the play itself reinforce this feeling of utter bleakness. Nonno's poem, his best, coming as it does at the climax, is a poetic commentary on what the play is about. Implicit pessimism in the first stanza is emphasized because the penultimate stanza is almost identical:

> How calmly does the orange branch
> Observe the sky begin to blanch
> Without a cry, without a prayer,
> With no betrayal of despair (p. 371).

The implication is clearly that there is a great deal of despair—however, the tree heroically refuses to give any sign of it, much as Hannah tries to keep hers under control with her deep breathing.

But what is it that can only be endured, that is the cause of this vast despair? The poem suggests initially that it is death, or the ageing or ripening accompanying it. But the fourth stanza carries a much more important idea. According to the poem, when the fruit grows ripe it falls to the earth where it must suffer

> An intercourse not well designed
> For beings of a golden kind
> Whose native green must arch above
> The earth's obscene, corrupting love.

This is an accurate description of the basic dilemma of most of Williams' major characters: they are sensitive idealists forced to indulge in sexual activity, which they find corrosive and obscene. The assumption that sex is disgusting and threatening is the real motive for Shannon's behavior; in fact, the play itself seems to foster the same feelings about sex. It is this underlying fear that makes Shannon's final situation at best only endurable.

What makes this attitude hard for the audience or reader to catch is that it is never explicitly discussed by any of the characters, much less identified as the basis of Shannon's problems. As we've seen, all three main characters offer a variety of other plausible explanations, and these keep us from seeing this one clearly. It is a very real part of the play, nonetheless, and makes itself felt in a number of ways. We sense, for example, that much more than either guilt or rebellion accounts for Shannon's sexual behavior. At the end of the play he speaks of "Always seducing a lady or two, or three or four or five ladies in the party, but really ravaging her first by pointing out to her the—what?—horrors? Yes, horrors!—of the tropical country being conducted a tour through" (p. 369). It is as if for a select few the last stop on his repulsive itinerary is his own bedroom. Sex for him is on a par with the other ravaging horrors he subjects himself and his tours to.

His penchant for the very youngest ladies suggests that he is afraid of more mature women. His attitude toward Maxine reinforces this idea and reveals his feelings of disgust as well. Whenever she makes sexual advances, he draws away vehemently, uncomfortably, or cruelly. At the beginning of the play, he disgustedly tells her she looks as if she's "been having it" and then pleads with her to button up her blouse so she will look decent. Later he suggests she has turned into a pig. At another point he says she is "bigger than life and twice as unnatural" (p. 270). His fear of her is apparent in his calling her a "bright widow spider" (p. 317), referring to an insect that proverbially devours her mate after intercourse. The audience itself tends to see her in much the same way. Nothing whatever in the play suggests that Shannon is incorrect about her, that his feelings are a product of his demented imagination. On the contrary, the playwright seems at pains to validate this vision of Maxine. In a stage direction at the beginning she is described as "rapaciously lusty" (p. 255). We are quickly made aware to what excess her sexual appetite runs—she has hired not one but two young Mexicans to serve her desires. Williams' description of her constantly recurring laugh emphasizes her animallike nature: "*Maxine always laughs with a single harsh, loud bark, opening her mouth like a seal expecting* a fish to be thrown to it" (p. 255). Throughout the play she is coarse and suggestive, and at one point she tells Shannon that her interest in him is primarily sexual: "I know the difference between loving someone and just sleeping with someone—even I know about that. We've both reached a point where we've got to settle for something that works for us in our lives—even if it isn't on the highest kind of level" (p. 329). Even her name, Maxine Faulk, is unattractive: her first name suggests that she is manlike, aggressive, and her last name is a crude pun. Given all this, the audience has little chance of regarding her in a way fundamentally different from Shannon's.

The central symbol of the play also points up the frightening nature of Maxine's desires. The iguana scrambling frantically at the end of its rope represents all the main characters, but it has a special affinity with Shannon. Not by coincidence is it supposed to become Maxine's dinner—its intended fate reinforces Shannon's fears that she will devour him, too. He may free the lizard at the end of the play, but he himself is tied more closely than ever to the "bright widow spider." The director of the original Broadway production must have sensed how inappropriate optimism is in the conclusion, for when Shannon returned to the stage after cutting the iguana loose, he was wearing the rope around his own neck (see Adler, "Night," p. 63).

No wonder, then, that Shannon feels threatened by Maxine, this female version of Big Daddy Pollitt. The wonder is that at the end of the play she can abruptly change, somehow, somewhere offstage, into a mellow Oriental goddess. To be believable such a radical transformation requires much more than the stage-direction and the few lines of dialogue Williams supplies. As it stands, the ending comes as quite a jolt. A character we have been forced to see as vulgar, aggressive, and menacing suddenly acquires alluringly soft edges. More than this, throughout the play Shannon has drawn away from the rapacious widow in apprehension, an apprehension the play helps the audience to share; now in a bizarre about-face he willingly agrees to live with her. Blanche DuBois might as easily become more receptive to the sexual overtures of a Stanley who has become suddenly more gentle and solicitous. (The arrangement Shannon and Maxine come to at the very end makes the conclusion even more outrageous. He agrees not only to live with Maxine but also to cater to the sexual needs of the female guests of the hotel. Incredibly, he "chuckles happily" at the thought—this from a man who previously has been obsessively guilty about, disgusted by, and terrified of sex. Their interchange—at least his response—violates the seriousness of the play and of Shannon's problems. This interchange ought to be dismissed simply as a momentary lapse, or as one of the occasions on which the playwright falls victim to his popular reputation of being obscene and shocking.)

Even Hannah, the most positive and sympathetic of the main characters, contributes to the underlying feeling that sex is dangerous or dirty. In stage directions, Williams describes her as appearing "androgynous" (p. 266) and as having "a fastidiousness, a reluctance, toward intimate physical contact" (p. 348), a description made concrete when she hesitates to touch Shannon to find his cigarettes. She admits to Shannon that sex is definitely not a part of the "broken gates" between people that she sees as an antidote to loneliness. She has clearly never accepted or enjoyed her own sexuality. Her lovelife consists of two pathetic incidents in which she was hardly a willing participant and which, in spite of her protest to the contrary, add to the suspicion that sex is degrading. The only lasting relationship she has formed is the very safe, asexual one with her grandfather. She quickly and surely squelches Shannon's suggestion that the two of them travel together, even after they have grown close through their compassionate nighttime exchange. There is obviously a very definite boundary to her willingness to communicate and share: it comes to a complete halt this side of the physical. In effect, Hannah creates in the audience the impression that withdrawing from sex is positive or healthy, since we tend to see all the behavior of an admirable character as admirable, unless something indicates we should feel otherwise. And nothing in this play indicates that her sexual reluctance is a problem.

Hannah's attitude, however, adds to the improbability of Shannon's final decision. Why would his feelings toward the sexually voracious Maxine turn around after a conversation with this sexless spinster? In fact, it seems likely that a major reason he is able to communicate with Hannah to any degree is that she *is* sexless; since she does not arouse his desires, he does not have to be afraid of her. In this regard *Iguana* reflects a pattern typical of Williams' works:

a character can offer or find either love or sex, but not both. The underlying attitude toward sex explains why this dichotomy occurs: love is an ideal, something only "beings of a golden kind" can attain; sex is obscene and corrupting and so must be kept separate from the ideal. Thus Hannah can give Shannon a momentary glimpse of what it means to love only by being asexual; and Maxine's sexual drives keep her from being able to offer him real love.

A glance at the play as a whole shows how everyone in it contributes to the feeling that human desire is obscene and fearful. Not a single sexually healthy character appears; no figure can define for the others (or for the audience) what sexual normalcy is, or give any hope that such a state can even be attained. (Where in any of Williams' work is such a figure?) Miss Fellowes is more than a strident castrating woman who reduces Shannon to feebly demonstrating his manhood by urinating on the luggage; she is a butch lesbian. Her protegé, Charlotte Goodall, flings herself hysterically, masochistically at Shannon "like a teen-age Medea" (p. 294). Both women make celibacy attractive. The Fahrenkopfs may be the most telling of all. No one could be more exuberantly physical and sexual than these caricatures who charge in and out of the drama bulging out of their scant swimming suits, clutching at one another, swilling beer, and booming out marching songs. It is no accident that these gross honeymooners are also part of the most monstrous political machine in Western civilization. The most overtly sexual characters, they are also the most grotesque, dangerous, and genuinely obscene.

Clearly, then, some less explicit elements in *Iguana* make its optimistic conclusion untenable. Considering the subterranean aspects of the play, Shannon's staying with Maxine means he is putting himself in the maw of a devouring monster. Obviously he cannot do so optimistically or happily. In effect, the different levels of the play pull the audience in opposite directions, an uncomfortable feeling created even in Williams' best works. *Cat* is another example. Overtly, the play demonstrates that Brick's extreme idealism, his refusal to grow up or old, is unhealthy and damaging, presaging death rather than life. But the abundant animal imagery and the behavior of the other characters graphically support his attitude toward reality and sex: human beings are mean, greedy, pathetic, cruel, and beastlike, and when they make love they are no different from, or better than, "two cats on a—fence humping" (III, 123). As in *Iguana* we are made to think one way and feel another.

What is usually at the heart of the internal conflict in Williams' works is a disgust with and terrible fear of the sexual act. As I mentioned at the outset, these ideas are not always easy to discern. They are contrary to his general reputation as a sexual libertine, in his life and works; and though his plays are obviously about sex and violence, critics and reviewers usually do not recognize that sex itself, not the brutal world, causes the violence. The fundamental rejection of sexuality is hard to see also because sex usually is made to bear a heavy and confusing burden. A character may behave at various times as if sex is an immensely pleasurable activity, an assertion of life in the face of death, a means of staying young, a degrading or bestial act, a source of guilt, and a means of expiating this guilt. Add to them the feeling that sex is dangerous and obscene, a feeling that is the more insidious because it is not explicit, and the works add up to a welter of confusion about how to regard human sexuality. It is not as if sex is presented as a complex phenomenon; rather, the characters act, at successive moments, as if one particular attitude is true and all the others are nonexistent. The plays themselves reinforce this problem by providing nothing or no one to point out that at these moments the characters are confused, incorrect, or self-contradictory.

Iguana may look like a new kind of play for Williams, but it is not. What makes it more of the same, despite its surface optimism, are the feelings about sex that emerge from the subterranean world of the play. Early in his career Williams captured vividly the nature of these feelings in the short story "Desire and the Black Masseur." It is a grotesque and violent tale of a helpless little man who puts himself in the hands of a huge black man. The masseur beats him repeatedly and cruelly and at the climax of the story, after beating him to death, eats him. Desire, the story suggests, *is* the black masseur, is a gigantic dark force that batters human beings and finally devours them. *The Night of the Iguana* shows that thirteen years after the publication of the story, this fear of sex is still a part of Williams' work and undermines whatever positive values the playwright consciously wishes to attribute to human relations.

Prisoners of Illusion:
Surrealistic Escape in *The Milk Train Doesn't Stop Here Anymore*

MARY McBRIDE

A COMMON SITUATION among the characters of Tennessee Williams is self-induced imprisonment—ironically the result of an effort to escape. The problem of Mrs. Goforth in *The Milk Train Doesn't Stop Here Anymore* is correlative with the problem of Amanda in *The Glass Menagerie* and various other Williams characters; thus its manifestation may be identified as a thematic process in Williams' predominantly surrealistic characterizations. (*Surrealism* refers herein to a state of illusion.) Each character, unable to accept reality, seeks escape—he may dream (like Amanda); he may drink (like Brick in *Cat on a Hot Tin Roof*); he may lie (like Margaret in the same play); he may become mad (like the dadaistic Blanche in *Streetcar Named Desire*); or he may withdraw to a mountain above the sea and thrust himself into the past (like Mrs. Goforth in *The Milk Train Doesn't Stop Here Anymore*).

Ironically, the escape of these characters becomes a prison, confining and degrading the prisoner and sometimes others with him. It is this basic inability to cope with reality, this deliberate and destructive evasion of the truth, that Williams seems to emphasize as a dominant trait of his problem characters. Much of the substance of his plays follows the thematic process of uncovering such evaded and veiled reality—a revelation which inevitably resolves into crumbled illusions.

341

Amanda (*The Glass Menagerie*) fancies herself a former Delta belle, an illusion into which she attempts to escape from the confinement of a tenement house in St. Louis. In part because of her mother's frequent references to a romanticized past, the daughter Laura imprisons herself in the world of her glass figurines. After a brief period with her one gentleman caller from her own past, she returns, devastated, to the world of illusion. Her brother Tom, in spite of strong literary ambition, is forced, by the responsibility of caring for his mother and his sister, to work at a stultifying job. Tom first escapes into a world of literary diversion. His literal escape comes at the end of the play when he deserts the family.

In *Cat on a Hot Tin Roof*, Brick finds escape in alcohol and Margaret in lies. The reality from which Brick escapes is made grim by two intense provocations: his latent homosexuality and his father's impending death from cancer. Margaret, Brick's wife, intensely concerned about the inheritance, is driven to tell her famous lie about her pregnancy.

Blanche in *A Streetcar Named Desire* is, like Amanda, an aristocrat who has lost her social status and is unable to break from her past. Unlike Amanda, she attempts to escape *from*, not *into*, the past, with its sordid reality. Stanley's revelations about her many deceptions both prevent her escape and show her more complex entanglement. She retreats into the prison of madness, where finally she takes refuge from both past and present.

In *Milk Train*, Mrs. Goforth is forced to confront the grimness of reality. Her attempt to escape into surrealistic illusion imprisons her, then fails, leaving her more weakened, again in the grim presence of reality.

Mrs. Goforth's attempted escape is chiefly *from* three elements of reality—society, illness, and death—and *into* two areas of surrealistic illusion—the past and pretense. Using riches left her by deceased husbands, she achieves physical withdrawal from society by moving to a mountain inhabited by only herself and her servants, and very nearly inaccessible to the outside world. This physical withdrawal is, moreover, a means to the end of metaphysical withdrawal into the past and pretense, from the society and illness of life, and subsequently from death. Thus she struggles to elude the present and the future by isolation on the mountain and by the immersion of her being into the urgent task of writing her memoirs, an escape into the past. Her own iteration of this evasion of reality is given in her statements concerning the meaning of life: "I've often wondered, but I've wondered *more* lately . . . meaning of *life*. . . . Sometimes I think, I suspect, that everything that we do is a way of—*not* thinking about it. Meaning of life, and meaning of death, too. . . . *What . . . are we doing?* . . . Just going from one . . . frantic distraction to another, till finally one too many . . . frantic distractions leads to disaster, and blackout? Eclipse of, total of sun?" (V, 62).

Concerning her physical and nonphysical escape from society, she says she was still meeting people until they all seemed like the same person and she grew tired of the person. She repeatedly expresses and demonstrates her distrust of people. Asked by her mysterious visitor Christopher (the "Angel of Death") if she trusts anybody, she replies, "Nobody human, just dogs" (p. 99). In an earlier statement, she makes a similar reference to cats. Refusing to accept her visitor's mission as "Angel of Death," she states that she is not superstitious: "I couldn't be less superstitious, deliberately walk under ladders, think a black cat's as lucky as a white cat, am only against the human cats of this world, of which there's no small number" (p. 72). And again near the end of the play when she is very ill, she puts her valuable rings on her fingers and provokes a cogent comment from Blackie, her perceptive secretary: "she's put on all her rings so they won't be stolen. She's more afraid of being robbed of her jewelry than her life" (p. 104). Mrs. Goforth's heart, in her own words, is encased in a "hard shell" (pp. 14, 117) and she says the sun is "just a big fire-ball that toughens the skin, including the skin of the heart" (p. 87). She constructs her own literal and figurative Alcatraz, by withdrawal into pretense and the past on her own mountain above the sea, ostensibly isolated from society.

A second element of reality from which she attempts to escape is her serious physical illness. Though she is afflicted with a severely abscessed lesion of the chest, she shouts at Blackie, "*I don't have a chest abscess!*" (p. 34). "Are you in pain? Do you have a pain in your chest?" asks the visiting Witch, when Mrs. Goforth keeps touching her chest. And Mrs. Goforth's evasive reply is "Emotion. I've been very emotional all day" (p. 47). Earlier the sick woman has pushed her doctor's X-ray machine over the cliff. Throughout the play, even—especially—in the midst of violent attacks of physical infirmity, she refuses to accept the reality of her illness, pretentiously boasting of a healthy, attractive body.

A third and closely related element of reality—her impending death—evokes an even more vehement effort to escape, and this effort constitutes a main thrust of the play. Her conflict with death involves four overlapping manifestations: (1) she fears it; (2) she is forced to face it; (3) she tries to escape it; (4) she is overcome by it.

In a brief soliloquy near the beginning of the play, she bares her fear of death as she speaks to the absent Blackie: "Oh, God, Blackie, I'm *scared*! You know what I'm scared of? Possibly, maybe, the Boss [a reference to herself] is—dying this summer!" (p. 13). Very soon after she makes this statement Chris, her mysterious guest, arrives uninvited.

Despite his difficulty of passage to her villa on the mountain and despite the violent resistance of her watchman and watchdogs, Chris reaches his destination and thus forces Mrs. Goforth to face the reality of death. Before he gains audience with Mrs. Goforth, he discusses her condition, and his mission, with Blackie:

> CHRIS: She doesn't know she's—
> BLACKIE: Dying? Oh, no! Won't face it! Apparently never thought that her—legendary—existence—could go on less than forever! . . .
> CHRIS: I've had a good bit of experience with old dying ladies, scared to death of dying, ladies with lives like Mrs. Goforth's behind them, which they won't think are over (p. 30).

Later Chris talks with Mrs. Goforth, who asserts that she never thinks of death, then admits that she wonders every night if she will die before morning:

> CHRIS: Mrs. Goforth, are you still afraid of—(He hesitates.)
> MRS. GOFORTH: Death—never even think of it. . . .
> CHRIS: Death is one moment, and life is so many of them. . . . Yes, life is something, death's nothing. . . .
> MRS. GOFORTH: Nothing, nothing, but nothing. . . . Oh, I don't think I'm immortal—I still go to sleep every night wondering if I'll—wake up the next day . . . (p. 86).

Yet, on her mountain, the bugle never plays taps—always reveille. Irony and mitigated pathos characterize her early statement about the prospect of young Chris's presence on the premises during the summer. "Hmmm," she exults, "the summer is coming to life! I'm coming back to life with it!" (p. 39). Ironically, Chris has come to bring death, not life. She continues to deny acceptance of the reality of his mission when she remarks that she will not subscribe to superstitious belief in an "Angel of Death" and again when she expresses determination to overcome her cough. "I'm going to beat it," she exclaims, "it isn't going to beat *me*, or it'll be the first thing that ever *did* beat me!" (p. 80). Chris emphasizes this dogged resistance to the reality of death in his explanation of the griffin depicted on the flag flown over Mrs. Goforth's mountain. "What's a griffin?" Mrs. Goforth asks; and Chris replies, "A force in life that's almost stronger than death" (p. 68). Later when she is dying, a stage assistant observes, "The griffin is staring at death, and trying to outstare it" (p. 105). Strong resistance notwithstanding, death prevails; and the griffin is lowered in final subjection to reality.

Unable or unwilling in later life to accept society and illness in the present and death in the future, Mrs. Goforth turns to the illusion of pretense and the past for surrealistic escape. Life is "really all memory," she says, ". . . except for each passing moment" (p. 46). Her most congenial associate is the beastlike watchman who by force guards her "prison of the past" to prevent intrusion by the reality of the present or the future. Her least congenial associate is her secretary Blackie, who fearlessly speaks the truth, crumbling Mrs. Goforth's walls of illusion by forcing her at intervals to face reality and by exposing her pretenses. But though Mrs. Goforth herself resorts to lying and various other manifestations of pretense, she detests falsehood in things and in other people. For her false visitors, she has prepared a special little grass hut called "Oubliette," where she puts them away to be forgotten. "I can't stand anything false," she declares ironically. "Even my kidney stones, if I had kidney stones, would be genuine diamonds fit for a Queen's crown" (p. 41). Later she proclaims "No more pretenses" (p. 72)—and goes on pretending.

Consequently, she dwells on her youth. Frantically writing her memoirs, she rejects her real self—old and ill—and imagines she is still a beautiful dancer. The truth-bearer Blackie tells Chris that the sick woman stumbles about at night, "raving . . . her demented memoirs, her memories of her career as a great international beauty which she thinks she still is" (p. 30). On one occasion Mrs. Goforth tries to dance as in earlier years, becomes dizzy and staggers, then tries to laugh it off.

Her attempted reversion to youth is activated in part by the arrival of the young Chris, whom she identifies, from first sight, with Alex, her deceased lover and the latest of her husbands. Throughout the play, even during the last scenes of her death, she boasts to Chris of her physical endowments, flaunting her body before him and making suggestive advances, to which his responses are void. "Know how I've kept in shape, my body, the way it still is? [By exercise] In bed!" (pp. 82–3) she says to him in one scene; then in the same scene she asks him, and he refuses, to kiss her for a cigarette. Unwilling to accept the real Chris, she makes him a part of her past. Once he gains admission into her prison of illusion, he is able to complete his mission as "Angel of Death." He confronts her squarely with a reality no longer resistible. Her illusion is destroyed, and she is forced out of her prison into the world of reality from which she has fervidly sought to escape.

Mrs. Goforth also recognizes, perhaps grudgingly, that even she must submit to forces beyond her control. Writing memoirs of a former husband, she dictates, "I confessed . . . that over this young poet with Romanav blood in his veins, I had no more control than my hands had over the sea-wind or the storms of the sea" (p. 9). Likewise, she must succumb to death, represented to her by the "Angel of Death," Christopher Flanders, bearing the name of the famous burial place immortalized by poets like John McCrae in descriptions of poppies and crosses in Flanders field. Mrs. Goforth can no longer resist going forth.

Nature, throughout the play, supersedes and interacts with man's experience, in effecting the ultimate predominance of reality and the irresistible force of fate. Mrs. Goforth, smug in her "prison" of surrealistic escape, is jolted by the metal work of art brought her by Chris. It is a mobile that he has named "The Earth Is a Wheel in a Great Big Gambling Casino." It is constructed so that if hung in the wind the wheel of fortune, like an Aeolian harp, is turned by nature, a force beyond the control of man.

Another gift brought by Chris is his book of verse titled *Meanings*

Known and Unknown, significantly representative of two areas of life: comprehended reality and the mystery of the unknown. In the death scene, Chris relates to Mrs. Goforth the meaningful example of the Swami of whose works Chris's book is a verse adaptation. The Swami's message, conveyed in silence, was acceptance, Chris tells Mrs. Goforth—acceptance of "many things, everything, nearly. Such as how to live and to die in a way that's more dignified than most of us know how to do it. And of how not to be frightened of not knowing what isn't meant to be known, acceptance of not knowing *anything* but the moment of still existing, until we stop existing—and acceptance of that moment, too" (pp. 115–16). Thus Chris gently cushions Mrs. Goforth's ejection from smug escape into the inexorable force of fate by which she is being hurled into the reality of the unknown realm called death.

Chris's next mobile, conceived during the course of Mrs. Goforth's ejection into the reality of death, will be called "Boom." "The sea is saying the name of your next mobile" (p. 120), Blackie comments as she and Chris look out over the sea beneath the mountain after Mrs. Goforth's death. *"Boom!"* answers Chris, echoing his own repeated utterance of *Boom* throughout the play. Early and frequently he uses the word as an exclamation accompanying the crashing of waves in the sea beneath Mrs. Goforth's mountain. *Boom* becomes synonymous with the agitated force of crashing waves, a force beyond the control of man—the reality of inexorable fate from which man is unable to escape.

Crashing waves indeed mark points of awesome emphasis and revelation in the play. The waves crash and Chris exclaims "Boom" when he arrives on the mountain hungry and exhausted and finds that both he and his lederhosen have been mutilated by Mrs. Goforth's watch dogs. Again soon a crashing wave punctuates his imperious and temporarily unanswered call to Mrs. Goforth in an urgent effort to see her, now that he has arrived on her mountain despite the perils of his journey. Later in the play a wave crashes loudly below when Mrs. Goforth, raving in illness at night, stands swaying at the edge of the cliff and is barely saved by Blackie. The wave punctuates with emphasis the real and uncontrollable force of fate in Mrs. Goforth's world of attempted escape. Such force may be further implied when Chris explains to Mrs. Goforth that her signal, the griffin, is a life force almost stronger than death, then "springs up and turns to the booming sea" (p. 68), symbolizing the ultimate force. Later he "turns to the booming sea and says 'Boom' " (p. 71) to emphasize an agitated experience of ostracism that he is relating to Mrs. Goforth. He has been ostracized by the people in Naples, he says, because his own sense of reality disturbed theirs. His "Boom" at this point bespeaks his awesome recognition of his own forced submission to fate, to forces outside himself and beyond his control. He exudes the word again when the dying Mrs. Goforth, helpless in the clutches of fate, coughs blood (p. 100). Chris tells Blackie, as a wave crashes under the mountain, "Boom! I'd like to make a mobile. I'd call it 'Boom' " (p. 106). *Boom*, then, is a word symbol of the infinite, a signal of the irresistible force that controls the destiny of man. It is this irresistible force that crumbles the walls of Mrs. Goforth's prison of illusion, exposing and compelling her out of surrealistic escape into the realm of stark, tempestuous reality, the common human realm of despotic fate.

In his frequent use of this technique of displaying illusions destroyed, as characters attempt to avoid reality, Williams recalls a central doctrine of Greek tragedy. Whatever the character does in the attempt to avoid his fate merely, as if by design, contributes to the inevitability of fate.

Kingdom of Earth: Some Approaches

JERROLD A. PHILLIPS

I N *Memoirs*, Williams flippantly refers to *Kingdom of Earth* as his "funny melodrama" (p. 40), and it has struck some critics as self-parody. On its surface it is a tale of a one-lunged transvestite dying of tuberculosis, who, to keep his half-brother from inheriting the farm, marries a prostitute he met on a television program and takes her back to the farm at a time when the Mississippi River is about to flood the entire county. Certainly the stuff potboilers are made of, the play, taken at its surface level alone, is indeed a funny melodrama, both strange and difficult.

Only when the material lying beneath the surface is examined does the work come into focus. What follows is a view of the play that regards it as a work of great imaginative power and compelling intensity.

First produced in 1968, the play derives from "The Kingdom of Earth," a short story published in 1954 and included in *The Knightly Quest and Other Stories* (1966). The story is told in the first person, with Chicken as narrator. The characters of the story are the same as in the play, only considerably less exotic. The final union of Chicken with Myrtle takes place without an external crisis (the flood) but as a result of the physical attraction the two have for each other. According to Chicken, Myrtle confesses, "The minute

I laid eyes on you, the first glance I look at that big powerful body, I said to myself, Oh, oh, your goose is cooked, Myrtle! . . . Well, I said, when somebody's goose is cooked the best way to have it is cooked with plenty of gravy" (*Knightly Quest*, p. 161). The simple outline of events that comprise the story becomes but a starting point for a profound, hallucinatory examination of human existence in the play.

In the final scene of the play, Chicken defines the Kingdom of Earth: "nothing in the world . . . can compare with one thing, and that one thing is what's able to happen between a man and a woman, just that thing, nothing more, is perfect. The rest is crap . . . , and if you never had nothing else but that, no property, no success in the world, but still had *that*, why, then I say this life would be worth something. . . . Yes, you could come home to a house like a shack, in blazing heat, and look for water and find not a drop to drink, and look for food and find not a single crumb of it. But if on the bed you seen you a woman waiting, maybe not very young or good-looking even, and she looked up at you and said to you, 'Daddy, I want it,' why, then I say you got a square deal out of life, and whoever don't think so has just not had the right woman" (V, 211). Sex transforms existence from something barren and empty into something rich and glorious.

In opposition to the Kingdom of Earth, which Chicken apostrophizes, is the Kingdom of Heaven. Chicken talks of his religious experience with an evangelist who temporarily persuaded him to restrain his "lustful body" and seek the Kingdom of Heaven. Lot emphasizes the contrast in telling Myrtle, "You've married someone to whom no kind of sex relation was ever as important as fighting sickness and trying with his mother to make, to create, a little elegance in a corner of the earth we lived in that wasn't favorable to it." To this ironic asceticism, Myrtle, the sentimental whore, replies, "I . . . Understand. And I'm going to devote myself to you like a religion" (p. 160).

The sexless Kingdom of Heaven Lot describes is a world represented by the furnishings of the parlor. Velvet draperies, gold chairs, a crystal chandelier, elegance and taste, grace and style, present an ironic version of the streets of gold and the pearly gates. Refined sensibility is contrasted with sensuality; spirit is opposed to body, as in *Summer and Smoke.*

Yet, closer examination reveals that neither Lot nor Chicken is really pursuing his objective; each is false to his kingdom as he defines it. Lot is false as was his mother, an avid sensualist, who "begun to cheat on" her husband soon after her marriage, "with a good-looking young Greek fellow that had a fruit store in town" (p. 187). The elegant parlor was only a façade to mask the pursuit of the Kingdom of Earth. Lot's revelation about his bleached blond hair symbolizes the falsity of his spiritual quest. Marrying Myrtle is but a calculated attempt to deprive his half-brother of the farm. His grace and elegance conceal his meanness and his desire for vengeance against the stronger Chicken (an inversion of the situation in *A Streetcar Named Desire*).

As the parlor indicates, Lot's Kingdom of Heaven was no more than his relationship with his mother whom he attempts to "resurrect" through his transvestistic donning of her clothing. This false and sterile Kingdom of Heaven, however, is also the kingdom of death, fully manifested in Lot's demise near the end of the play.

Chicken's pursuit of the Kingdom of Earth is hardly more rewarding. Although he speaks reverently of sex, what he pursues is ownership of the farm. He even sleeps with the will he forced from Lot. For one who would give up food and water to bed in a shack with an ugly middle-aged woman, he is remarkably materialistic. And while his name seems to derive from his brutal practice of catching chickens, biting their heads off, and drinking their blood during those occasions when he was waiting out the Mississippi's floods while perched on the roof of the farmhouse, the name also suggests cowardice in his fear of finding a woman to live with him. Instead he hangs a picture of a nude woman in the kitchen and fondles his genitals when he looks at the picture. When Lot arrives with Myrtle, he crouches behind the door and remains in the kitchen until he has fortified himself with whisky. His sexual act with Myrtle is apparently fellatio only, and he at once says he does not like to be near a woman for a while after the sexual act.

At another level, the play is a confrontation between aspects of the human psyche. The rational (conniving) Lot spends much of his energy in the attempt to deprive Chicken of the farm. Williams, in an attempt at subtlety, may even intend Lot's chills to suggest the coldness of rationalism or at least of calculation. The delicately ordered parlor is the proper setting for such a character.

In contrast, Chicken's primeval animality is obvious. He brutally and singlemindedly *survives*—survives the floods—and brutally mishandles Myrtle. He lives in the disordered kitchen, where the food and heat (passion) are, amusing himself by carving obscenities on the kitchen table. Fear of the flood is inconceivable for him, since he is as elemental a natural force—"Life, rock. Man, rock. Both rock" (p. 199), he says.

The water symbolism emphasizes Chicken's association with elemental nature. Beneath the parlor, beneath the upstairs bedroom where Myrtle virtuously promises Lot to devote herself to him, is the cellar swirling with water. Symbolically, its depths are unknown, and symbolically Chicken throws in the cat which also instinctively survives.

The flood itself recalls the deluge of the Old Testament and numerous older documents. Everything will be cleared away, including the weak and corrupt. Myrtle's technological contraptions will be ruined, along with all the fragile contents of the parlor.

Myrtle's difficulty with heating the water for Lot's comfort suggests her attempt to repress her own elemental nature—her sexuality—as she tries to reform her promiscuity to wifely virtue and motherly kindness. Chicken's furnishing her with fresh rain water from the outside barrel may hint of her real conversion and her baptism.

Instead of merely inventing another grotesque incident, Williams possibly attempts a meaningful subtlety in confining the sexual act to fellatio. Myrtle's rebirth derives in part from drinking the fluid of life—Chicken's semen. She eats *and* drinks with Chicken. Immediately after their sexual act, Chicken says, "Let there be light," then inquires whether Myrtle has ever been saved. He tells of his own temporary conversion and, in one version of the play, points out that the house is built of wood and not of rock—on which St. Peter (the rock) was to help build the church. Chicken builds his church, safely on the roof top, one assumes, at the spire, with at least one disciple.

But the play was originally *The Seven Descents of Myrtle*, and possibly, with all the changes, it is Myrtle's play—to pun, a play for Myrtle, the "warm-natured woman. You might say passionate, even" (p. 201)—whose little white pills from the Memphis doctor fail to restrain her natural inclination to give herself in service to all comers. The instinctual Chicken at once realizes she is a mother to all men. And each descent from the upstairs room takes her closer to Chicken. (Lot, incidentally, descends to die.)

And in this complex symbolism, is Myrtle Kain somehow also Cain? Each brother, neither of them a brother to the other, attempts to use her against the other. And considering his interest in Classical mythology, did Williams think of Myrtilus, the legendary Greek involved in the intrigue that led to the curse on the house of Pelops and on to the conflict between Atreus and Thyestes? And Aphrodite was associated with the myrtle: Myrtle's seven descents also reveal a changing definition of love that occurs during the course of the play. She moves from her sacrificial motherliness to a resumption of her real self. The house made not of rock but of wood may be eventually made of Aphrodite's myrtle wood.

The play may even be Myrtle's nightmare of repressed sexuality; the inexorable flood symbolizing the orgasm she is struggling to avoid. Myrtle dreams of giving up her anomalous position as whore to all men to become dedicated wife to one, only to discover that her husband is an impotent child, her house no home, no sanctuary, and her husband's half-brother a muddled hybrid like Stanley Kowalski, determined to survive—eating his raw meat, which she also must eat in various ways. She finds she must face the depths of being in a way never faced before, for all her experience has failed to diminish her innocence. She is, finally, Lot's wife. She disobeyed the commandment. She looked back at Sodom and Gomorrah. She lost the Kingdom of Heaven which Lot represents. But in an inversion characteristic of Williams, she becomes not a pillar of salt but possibly —just possibly—a live inhabitant of the Kingdom of Earth. After the flood, she will bear Chicken's child, conceived by the only natural means, and, despite the dirt of their lives, begin to populate a Kingdom of Earth.

The Two-Character Play:
Psychic Individuation

REXFORD STAMPER

T HE *Two-Character Play* is an important play. It is not a good play; it is too long, too opaque, and too obviously therapeutic to be good, but it is important because it establishes a new subject and a new theme for an artist who has already contributed significantly to American drama. Tennessee Williams has staged at least four versions of *The Two-Character Play*, a remarkable effort even for a dramatist known for revision. The first production was in London in 1967; four years later the revised play came to the stage in Chicago under the title *Out Cry*; following another revision, *Out Cry* opened in New York in 1973. Williams subsequently reworked the material, returned to the original title and presented *The Two-Character Play* in New York in 1975. The latter version apparently satisfied Williams that the work was in its final form; it is the version included in the recently issued volume five of his collected drama (1976).

Beyond the effort Williams has exerted on this play, the number of references he makes to it in *Memoirs* emphasizes his estimate of its importance. He refers to the play as "the big one" (p. 129), a play "close to the marrow of my being" (p. 228), a work in which he was "very deeply emotionally involved" (p. 229). He states that his only reason for accepting the role of Doc in *Small Craft Warn-*

354

ings was to generate sufficient interest in himself and his work to insure that *Out Cry* would be a success (p. 127).

Everyone concerned with modern American drama recognizes, however, that Williams' recent plays have been failures; and although many reasons have been offered, perhaps not enough attention has been paid to the most apparent reason for this failure: he is no longer writing the type of drama which won him his reputation. Williams himself confesses that his theater productions during the 1960s were disastrous, and the reasons he gives for this disaster are germane to understanding his recent works, as well as the importance he places on *The Two-Character Play*.

Williams says the failures are "due to my inability to cope with the preparations for them and with a turn, in my work, towards a new style and new creative world with which the reviewers and the audiences found it very hard to empathize so abruptly" (p. 207). It is this shift to a new creative world that makes *The Two-Character Play* an important work in Williams' canon. The play is blatantly confessional and therapeutic, but it is also an objective presentation both of the discriminatory separation of the psyche and of the integration that is necessary if the artist, or everyman, as Williams uses the concept of artist, is to achieve psychic individuation. In *The Two-Character Play*, Williams tentatively establishes himself in the new creative world he first explored in the 1960s; he turns away from the symbolic South as his creative source, away from the naturalistic theme of the individual crushed by biological and social forces, and concentrates instead upon the subjective self in order to demonstrate that the artist's greatest struggle is not with his society but within himself.

Williams' obviously Jungian view of the subconscious is reflected in his three conclusions for this play, in the dominant symbolism of the play, and in the androgynous nature of the two characters, Felice and Clare. As *The Two-Character Play* opens, Felice is alone on the stage writing the script for a play he and his sister Clare will later perform. On the stage are two interior sets containing the properties for the ensuing performance. The two flats of the interior set reveal a bizarre, astrologically furnished interior of a living room as it would appear during the afternoon of a southern summer. One of these sets contains a door, the other a large window through which the audience can see a yard dominated by a thick growth of tall sunflowers. The rest of the stage is cluttered with the unremoved properties from previous performances. Just as sunflowers dominate the interior set, a sinister statue of a giant towers over the off set. Juxtaposed, these two symbols suggest the emotional and the thematic contexts of the play.

Clare joins Felice on the stage, and he tells her they will have to perform alone because the other members of the troupe deserted them earlier in the day, leaving a note saying "your sister and you are—insane!" (p. 321). They are alone, in the state theater of an unnamed arctic country, and the only play in their repertory which requires only two actors is a work by Felice entitled *The Two-Character Play.* They perform the play, which deals with a brother and sister named Felice and Clare who are afraid to leave their home. They fear social recriminations because their father, an astrologer, killed their mother and himself. In Felice's *The Two-Character Play* the brother and sister argue, plan to leave the house to get provisions, reveal that one or both have been committed to the state mental hospital, suggest that they may be involved in an incestuous love affair, and discuss their father's murder of their mother and his suicide. After several attempts to muster courage to leave the house for provisions and failing each time, they begin a search for their father's gun. As they approach a point in the dialogue where the location of the gun will be revealed, the inner play breaks off without a conclusion.

Felice and Clare, obviously drained by the performance, prepare to leave the theater; however, they find they are trapped. The audience, in either disgust or boredom, has long ago departed, leaving locked the only door in the windowless theater. Even the phone is dead, and they soon realize that their situation is desperate as the houselights dim and the cold of the arctic climate begins to creep into the theater. They decide their only hope for survival is to reenter the play and lose themselves imaginatively in the sunlit world of New Bethesda. Once they reenter the play, Felice and Clare begin searching for a conclusion to *The Two-Character Play.* They skip rapidly through the work until they reach the dialogue concerning their father's murder-suicide and the location of his revolver. Both intuitively grasp that the logical conclusion of the imaginary work is that Clare should kill Felice and then herself. At this point the play ends for the final time.

Williams' three conclusions to the play reflect his changing view that the artist's struggle is not external but internal. The conclusion to *The Two-Character Play* of 1969 is almost Freudian in its suggestion that the artist must destroy a part of his psyche if he is to survive. The play ends ambiguously, but the stage directions indicate that the only escape from the psyche is to destroy it: "She raises a hand, not quite to her eyes but toward her eyes as if to shield them from a blinding light. Then, as she turns to the sofa to lift the pillow, she draws an audible breath. The stage is dimmed out" (p. 96).

In *Out Cry*, however, Williams has changed the stage directions and drastically altered the thematic core of the work. *Out Cry* ends with Felice and Clare in an embrace, failures in both the real world of *Out Cry* and the world of Felice's *Two-Character Play*, but, as the final stage direction indicates, still able to function and to triumph over their failures. As the play ends, "The lights fade, and they accept its fading, as a death, somehow transcended" (*Out Cry*, p. 72). This conclusion marks a retreat from the new creative world Williams had attempted to enter earlier. With this conclusion he has returned to the themes of his first works by extolling the superiority of the "beautiful little people" who are crushed by their surroundings but who find completion even if they must pay for it with their own destruction.

Williams, obviously realizing that a return to past success is not exploration, provided another, more satisfactory, conclusion for the 1976 version of the play:

> (She quickly retrieves the revolver from beneath the sofa cushion, and resolutely aims it at FELICE, holding the revolver at arm's length. There is a pause.)
>   FELICE (harshly): *Do it while you still can!*
>   CLARE (crying out): *I can't!*
> (She turns convulsively away from him, dropping the revolver as if it had scorched her hand. As it crashes to the floor, FELICE turns from the window, his motion as convulsive as hers. Their figures are now almost entirely lost in dark but light touches their faces.)
>   Can you?

(He moves a few steps toward the revolver, then picks it up and slowly, with effort points it at CLARE. FELICE tries very hard to pull the trigger: he cannot. Slowly he lowers his arm, and drops the revolver to the floor. There is a pause. FELICE raises his eyes to watch the light fade from the face of his sister as it is fading from his: in both their faces is a tender admission of defeat. They reach out their hands to one another, and the light lingers a moment on their hands lifting toward each other. As they slowly embrace, there is total dark . . .) (V, 369–70).

This conclusion is cauterized of the cancerous romanticism that mars *Out Cry*. In both conclusions the individual faces defeat, but in the conclusion to the last play, his defeat is not proof of his moral superiority: it is, rather, acceptance of his mortal lot. Williams' three conclusions form a pattern that reveals his conception of the psyche changing from a quality that must be destroyed to one that assures the artist's moral superiority, to one that must be recognized and accepted as a part of the creative life.

The Two-Character Play is important; Williams is dealing with the unconscious on a formal basis for the first time in his dramatic career. *The Two-Character Play* dramatizes a confrontation with the unconscious. The panic on the stage is not caused by boys who throw stones, nor by neighbors who point accusing fingers, but by a fundamental problem of psychic individuation. Felice and Clare clearly symbolize two parts of the creative personality. This personality, in coming to terms with the problems of isolation, communication, and death, is beginning to realize the absolute necessity for integration and love if it is to overcome the sociological and biological trap in which it finds itself. The conflict in the play centers on psychic entrapment, and whether the location of the trap is the theater or the imaginary sunlit world of New Bethesda, the problem is one which must be solved if the artist is to fulfill his creative function.

The dramatic characterizations and dual sets for *The Two-Character Play* are giant symbols for the psychic state of the artist. The introductory comment, "a garden enclosed is my sister," suggests the antithesis to the prime symbol of the present era, "the wasteland," represented by the outer set propertied with unassembled pieces of scenery from other plays. Williams uses this garden enclosed in a traditional sense as a symbol of fulfilment. Yet, as he explores the relationship within the psyche, he demonstrates that the inner world, usually a source of strength and renewal, is near exhaustion as the result of the jarring incompatibility between its feminine and masculine elements.

The two chief symbols of exhaustion and regeneration within the inner play are the faded rose on the carpet and the sunflowers surrounding the house. The rose, a relic from their father's astrological past, is traditionally a symbol of beauty and perfection. Although its presence in the play suggests a mythological, arcane tradition, its modern meaning is fairly standardized. The rose is the one flower which almost always suggests a positive value. "It blossoms," according to Barbara Seward, "in abundance where despair has been routed or defied" (*The Symbolic Rose*, p. 122). Yet, this rose is faded, and its dilapidated state suggests that a "desperate situation" exists between the structural components of the psyche. The cause of this struggle is archetypal, representing inherited tendencies of the psyche contained in the collective unconscious.

The struggle between masculine and feminine elements within the psyche, and its resolution, is symbolized by the giant sunflowers that dominate the inner set. The sunflower, with its earthbound following of the sun, represents most basically the aspiration of man and the longing for transcendence. However, in this play the sunflower also suggests the ancient integration of the two elements sun and flower which represents the sexual union of male and female creative forces and the ultimate harmony to be found in spiritual attainment. Not only the struggle, but also its resolution, is symbolized by the sunflowers. The sunflower symbolizes masculine dominance over the feminine, or the mythological metamorphosis known as solarization, the victory of the male sun god over the female moon goddess. However, it is not dominance but acceptance that will calm the psyche, and Williams uses a large two-headed sunflower to represent the possibility of an androgynous personality with a predominance on neither the masculine nor the feminine side.

This flower, which Felice refers to as "a wonder of nature," becomes the symbol of reconciliation within the play. The theme of the play is that the contrary elements of the psyche must cease their struggle for supremacy and live in androgynous harmony, not only in the actual world of time and place but in the subjective world of imagination and fantasy. The struggle on the stage before the performance and during the actual performance itself indicates that for Williams the war within the psyche is a very real one and that only when the struggle is resolved through the integration of supposedly incompatible elements can personal and artistic individuation occur. The symbol Williams uses to represent the possibility for individuation, the integration of opposites within the personality, is the giant two-headed sunflower. This sunflower, although a freak of nature, represents the possibility of androgynous integration, and it dominates the inner set much as the giant statue of despair dominates the outer set.

The Two-Character Play is not a good play, but it is an important one. In this play, as in *The Gnädiges Fräulein, The Milk Train Doesn't Stop Here Anymore, In the Bar of a Tokyo Hotel,* and *Small Craft Warnings,* all recent works, Williams has used the theater to work out his personal and artistic problems. These plays are not intended to tell a story or to present a slice of life but to communicate—through a series of images, symbols, and clever language—his uniquely changing conception of reality. The effort, while admirable, has failed to produce good theater because the scope of his art, as the various versions of *The Two-Character Play* demonstrate, has become so narrow and so uniquely subjective that Williams is unable to communicate to his audience the significance of his vision.

In his earlier, successful plays, Williams presented a view of reality that was predicated on a dichotomy, usually symbolized by the schizophrenic character who represented the inseparable schism between the world of reality and the world of imagination. In his recent drama, Williams has, unfortunately, narrowed the referent for this symbol to such a limited range of experience that the audience can no longer accept its validity. Williams' earlier works take as a thematic basis the cultural schizophrenia of the South; his most recent works deal with personal adjustment. By changing the referent of his symbol from public myth to personal neurosis Williams has committed the subjective fallacy that undermines many artists: he fails to see that his work has become a personal statement which, by its very nature, is unintelligible to anyone except himself.

Until recently this shift in emphasis has adversely affected Williams' drama. By focusing on himself instead of his culture and by utilizing his drama as personal therapy, he has lost the mythic, public spectacle necessary for all great drama. Williams' recent plays, as illustrated by much of the opaqueness in *The Two-Character Play*, have become exercises in which he uses the actors as projections of his own mental anguish, with his personal psychosis serving as his thematic basis. Such a conception of drama, as in the case of Strindberg or Maeterlinck, can lead to powerful theater because the play provides a model by which the audience can come to recognize, through an examination of the dramatist's psychic state, its own or its culture's psychosis. Theater of this type returns drama to its origins and becomes a public ritual that is therapeutic for both the author and his audience. To succeed, as this form of drama does for the plays of O'Neill and for the earlier works of Williams, the psychosis must be so widespread with roots so deep in the psychocultural history of the audience that the malady is immediately recognized. Failing that, the work is nothing more than an exercise in ego.

Williams' last plays have failed because in these works he relied on a too narrowly conceived psychological awareness and idiosyncratic symbology to interest a general, informed audience. The final version of *The Two-Character Play*, in which he has utilized a structured psychological profile and a traditional use of symbols, hints that Williams may have finally established a small, but important, beachhead in this territory of ritualistic drama. This play reveals that he is once again, as he did in his earlier works, drawing upon his own psychic awareness as a source for public drama. One can only hope that he has the energy and the will to pursue this exploration and that his future work will fulfill the need for mythic, public theater— Felice's total theater—that is obviously missing in current American drama.

The Red Devil Battery Sign: Williams' Götterdämmerung in Vienna

SY KAHN

THE SECOND PRODUCTION of Tennessee Williams' *The Red Devil Battery Sign* had its "world premiere" on January 18, 1976 in Austria at Vienna's English Theatre. Although the play had a previous run in Boston, it was announced in Vienna as a "premiere" in that Williams had revised the play—and it would be presented with an entirely different cast. Prior to the play's official opening, there were several weeks of well-attended preview performances which were reviewed by various Austrian and German newspapers. I was in Vienna during the preview period and saw the play only a few days before its official opening. (I am indebted to Professor Martha Raetz of The University of Vienna for her painstaking translations of numerous German and Austrian reviews.)

Although Williams was not in Vienna at that moment, having returned to San Francisco for the run of *This Is (An Entertainment)*, he had been in Vienna during the early weeks in January to confer with the director, Franz Schafranek, and others about the production. Interviewed by Ludwig Heinrich for the *Abendpost-Nachtausgabe* (Frankfurt/Main, December 27, 1975), Williams revealed that in the earlier production of *Red Devil*, directed by David Merrick, he had been beset by requests for revisions and changes to the point where he withdrew the play. He also observed that a new production in New York involves high costs, about

362

$400,000, and that producers are reluctant to take expensive risks with plays that are not all entertainment. After withdrawing the play in Boston, Williams made the acquaintance of Schafranek, and the director's ideas about the play, as well as the modest proportions of his stage and house (275 seats) convinced Williams that in Vienna his play would not be "ruined by the technicians." Asked to comment on the play, Williams said it was about the fate and destiny of two people and at the same time a parable of a world corrupted and eroded by civilization. Interviewed in Vienna by Lothar Schmidt-Mulisch of *Die Welt* in West Berlin (published December 29, 1975), Williams gave further reasons for having *Red Devil* produced in Vienna. He explained that he wanted to "try out a few things" and not be "torn apart" by American critics. Also, Williams added, people in Europe love artists better and forgive them for being sometimes less than good. As for *Red Devil*, Williams ranked it in its new version as equal to his greatest works: *A Streetcar Named Desire*, *The Glass Menagerie*, *Camino Real* and *Cat on a Hot Tin Roof*, which he considers his best.

Williams' recently published *Memoirs*, and the parallel runs of two plays opening in San Francisco and Vienna led a number of European newspaper reviews and interviews to dwell on the theme of Williams' "comeback." Though his work had never been off the boards, in either the United States or Europe, since the 1940s, surely Williams did not often equal the power of his earlier successes in the 1940s and 1950s with his later work. If one were to judge from reviews that appeared during the preview run and after the official opening, the comeback trail is going to be difficult. The play itself received mixed reviews at best. However, the "event" of the Vienna run and the presence of Williams in Europe at the time were more gently treated in the articles appearing during the preview run.

When the play came into focus in these reviews, they remarked almost uniformly on the failure of the play to develop organically its realistic and parabolic elements. The apocalyptic conclusion of the play seemed, for many, too unlikely a consequence of its realistic plot and playing style. Otto F. Beer in *Süddeutsch Zeitung* (Munich, January 7, 1976) in the course of accurately observing the similarity of *Red Devil* to Strindberg's *Dream Play*, as well as to Williams' earlier *Camino Real*, comments on the "two-track design" of Williams' latest play. For Beer, the private lives of the two main characters, their passionate bedroom scenes, and the play's tough and brutal plot so dominate the work that he finds difficulty in accepting its "visionary effects," especially as these find culmination in the final scene. This dichotomy in the play between its realistic and its visionary, expressionistic elements frequently troubled the reviewers, and indeed the Götterdämmerung conclusion of the play may seem to many too intellectual an imposition, or too fond a dream, for its structure, style and premises.

At the end of *Red Devil*, the main female character called the "Woman Downtown" stands in a bleak landscape, uniting the warring and tattered street gangs into a revolutionary force that will destroy a civilization corrupt beyond redemption. The scene is rendered as vision or dream. The Woman appears as a secularized type of Joan of Arc, mesmerized, refined to pure, silent symbol of leader and avenger, dominating and giving focus to the street tribes whose program is to destroy society by fire. The stylized, slow physical movements of the scene, amid cataclysmic sound effects, suggest the final moments be understood as an expressionistic and emblematic representation of a desperate alternative to a power-crazed and dehumanized world. The most dominant of the gang leaders, named Wolf, moves magnetically toward the Woman who appears transfixed by the concentration, and consecration, of her vision. Since the role of Wolf was played by a former drama student of mine, we had occasion to discuss this moment in the play, especially since he felt some difficulty with his motivation in the final scene. He was directed to see in the Woman's eyes all of humanity—to see, one would gather, beyond the moment and into the future.

The play is set in Dallas, significantly as we shall see, and its long, multiscened first act takes place in a luxurious, modern hotel owned by the former husband of the Woman. He is also the business tycoon who heads the Red Devil Battery Sign Company, an organization with worldwide business and political connections. The implication is that this powerful and ruthless company has secret plans to dominate the United States as well as other countries. Projection panels alongside the stage reveal pictures, at various moments, of Americans assassinated during the 1960s, most notably John F. Kennedy in

Dallas, as well as shots of the war in Viet Nam. By this device we are meant to understand that the company which bedevils the Woman in Dallas has the power to kill, to cause war, to hold the world in its grip. The Woman's distress is in small the agony of nations. The ominousness of Red Devil power is dramatized in various ways: by the metaphors embedded in the title of the company and the name of the play itself, by the fact that the man controlling the company is never seen in the play, but his power felt everywhere, by the virtual incarceration and constant surveillance of the Woman by Red Devil agents, who in their neat business suits and crewcuts resemble stereotypes of FBI and CIA agents, by the turns of plot that eventually involve rape and murder, and by the pulsing red lights that punctuate certain moments of the play. Williams, we know, is not reluctant to dot his "i's" with pumpkins, but whether or not the Brechtian devices of side panels and pulsing lights are part of Williams' script or directorial interpretation and latitude must await the availability of the script itself. Williams intends to revise the play further for a possible Broadway production, and therefore the script is not available at this time. Consequently, my discussion of the play in its Vienna production is of a work that is, in a sense, still in progress.

The evil power of the battery sign corporation is made blatantly clear by its "devil" symbol. The word *battery* suggests that the organization, an example of the interdependence of the big-business-military-political complex so much remarked upon during the 1960s, is the power source for international conspiracies which generate assassinations and wars. The pulsating red sign is a bloody and vicious hex upon mankind. All the power of the organization is brought to bear on the Woman Downtown who particularly dramatizes how the corporation, directed by a tycoon, can victimize individuals who run counter to organizational power. She has stolen some incriminating company documents and given them to her warden, a judge, whose age and illness comment on the state of American justice. Having been discovered, the Woman was first put away in an asylum, then released by her husband, and we find her at the beginning of the play restricted to the hotel and carefully guarded by the hotel keeper as well as the company agents. Meanwhile the judge has had the documents decoded and attempts to rescue his ward, to fly with her to Washington, where he intends to reveal the conspiracy to a special Congressional committee. Eventually the judge is murdered and this attempt at revelation foiled.

Early in the play we discover the Woman as a distressed, harried victim, a type reminiscent of earlier Williams heroines pressed to the border of insanity, a kind of Blanche DuBois. In her portrayal it seems Williams has returned to that kind of female character he depicts so effectively—women under great emotional stress given to moving self-revelations. In the hotel she encounters King del Rey, once the leader of a successful band, restlessly married, worried about his daughter, La Niña, who once sang with him, but is now pursuing a seedy, troubled career in Chicago. In time we learn that he is afflicted by a brain tumor which soon will kill him. As his name suggests, King is a strongly masculine character who proves quickly responsive and sympathetic to the Woman; she, in turn, is desperately in need of a defender and confidant. The Woman, once the wife of a Texas tycoon, and the doomed King soon are in love, but we come to see them both as deposed royal lovers, victims of inexorable forces that permit neither love nor justice to persist. Though not so specifically symbolized in this play, King's brain tumor is like Big Daddy's cancer in *Cat on a Hot Tin Roof*, in which the cancer is a symbol of "mendacity"—of corrupted and vicious human relationships. King's malignant tumor is another way Williams expresses the malevolency of the *Red Devil Battery Sign* world. The Woman, as so many of Williams' earlier heroines, has experienced a repressed and abused sexual life—but in this play it is not sexual frustration that primarily accounts for psychic distortion and disharmony; rather it is the evil of super-organizational power. This is not to say that the earlier Blanche or Maggie the Cat was entirely motivated by sexual frustration. Blanche was also fleeing from the crumbling family plantation, Belle Reve, and economic ruin, while Maggie clearly was vying for a piece, if not all, of Big Daddy's vast estate—so both characters were driven by economic concerns too. But in *Red Devil* the emphasis is changed: manipulative economic and political power rather than sexual frustration and repression are the victimizing forces.

During a long night of sex and love, the Woman and King seal their relationship, reveal to each other their individual histories and woes under duress of their separate, now joined, dilemmas. In a series of bedroom scenes, explicitly sexual (including King in the nude), the Woman tells King of her childhood, her sexual ignorance and suffering, her abusive marriage, and her victimization by the "Red Devil" conspiracy. It becomes clear that the hotel bedroom is a kind of last refuge for doomed lovers, ambiguously as much a cell of incarceration as retreat. Soon after these scenes, and King has left, the Woman is raped by a Red Devil agent; then she escapes to seek King at his home located in the outskirts of the city amid rubble heaps and marauding street gangs.

The second act of the play, removed from the hard glitter and luxury of the hotel, reveals a pattern of dire events in a darkening landscape. In an act punctuated by explosions caused by the surrounding gangs, King is increasingly paralyzed by the tumor and finally hemorrhages out his life on stage. The laments of his wife, Perla, enhance the dirgelike quality of these scenes during which various confrontations take place. King does manage to kill the Woman's rapist; his daughter, another victim, returns with McCabe, revealing her unhappy fortunes in Chicago. However, McCabe wants to marry her and must win the approval of the predictably hostile King, and finally succeeds. Thus in various ways King is deposed: as husband, as protective father, and as lover, leaving Perla to weep and the Woman Downtown to become the matriarchal leader of the lurking and violent gangs. Increasingly during this act, and ultimately in the final scene, the play moves from realistic situation and dialogue toward phantasmagoria, toward dream and vision. The final tableau attempts to fashion an answerable myth to the world of inexorable power. Some reviewers, such as Harold Sterk (*Arbeiter-Zeitung*, Vienna, January 4, 1976) see in the Woman a kind of "Mother Meinhof," that is a type of terrorist who several years ago led a violently revolutionary group in Germany, was captured, and recently committed suicide in her cell. Sterk also notes that Williams' play recalls a recent play by the Austrian playwright Zuckmayer, whose *Rattenfänger* (*The Pied Piper*) depicts in its finale youth being summoned by a maternal "führer" to acts of terrorism meant to cleanse and renew the world. Sterk decries these plays as old men's desperate and despairing answers to a violent world.

Whether the Woman is savior, terrorist leader and avenger, or violated idealist and renewed realist—or all these—is, I believe, purposely ambiguous. Clearly, though, she is meant as an alternative to the world of big business conspiracy and power, as a focal point for the diverse, warring gangs to join in the common purpose of militant opposition to the "Red Devil" complex.

In some ways the Woman is a parallel to the Daughter of Indra (Agnes) in Strindberg's *Dream Play*, who, one may recall, descends to Earth in human form in order to experience human life and comes to the conclusion that "Humanity is to be pitied." However, in that play Agnes is a figment in the head of the dreamer, the whole play being a dramatization of the dreamer's dream. Though every play is, in a sense, a playwright's dream made manifest on stage, most plays attempt to create an illusion of reality, and this is no less true of *Red Devil* for the most part. However, the play does move toward dream and vision, toward a patently symbolic statement of its meaning—a projected consequence of Williams' reading of contemporary society. The Woman, though no innocent goddess, was the innocent who became the wife of a powerful Texas tycoon. Because of harsh treatment, she defects to become the Woman Downtown, trapped in a hotel, descended, like the Daughter of Indra, into the brutal center of urban society. In the *Dream Play*, the Daughter reascends, a goddess now informed of human paradox, irony and suffering; the Woman Downtown is apotheosized into a kind of secular goddess-mother who will lead, not merely learn from, a bedeviled, fallen humanity. In Williams' play, unlike Strindberg's, no magical flower bursts into bloom at the top of a castle, no ultimate vision promises humanity salvation. Instead, we are left with the promise of severe confrontations between inspired street people and the organizers of established wealth and power.

This shift in the final moments of the play from realistic plotting ＇ dialogue—with its extension of expressionistic devices—to its ＇ purely metaphorical theatricality most provokes the early critics ＇ play. The transformation of the Woman, through a satiating ＇ brief love affair, from harried, frustrated and frightened victmost a deified vision, seems to some reviewers too long and ＇ evolutionary leap. It may be that Williams' vision of ＇umanity, doomed in a twilight world, requiring miracles ＇nal transformation for its salvation, is at once too dark a reading and too extravagant a hope for even theatrical credibility.

Williams offers us in *Red Devil* a grim parable of the contemporary world divided into two sets of menacing images: the slick power conspiracies, with the red devil sign as cosmic symbol of hex and hell, and the alternate savagery of fugitive street gangs shaped into a menacing counterforce. Between these alternatives there is no crevice of escape for the individual. In earlier Williams plays, and even as late as *Kingdom of Earth*, psychologically uncomplicated sex offered some defense against, or recompense for, the natural terrors of the world, as well as a basis for love; in *Red Devil* sex is debased and love doomed. King del Rey, wrecked, debilitated image of virile man, staggers about the stage in the end, bleeding from the mouth, threatening suicide before he painfully dies. The King is dead; long live the Queen—since there is no King to inherit his particular mantle. Always given to a rather paranoic and pessimistic view of the world, Williams in this play gives full expression to his feelings of oppression, alienation and inevitable defeat, particularly for the injured underdogs of the world. Without King and the human qualities of love, protection and succor he represents, the Woman Downtown becomes the Woman Underground—a mysterious leader of the dispossessed in a twilight, barren landscape. In the world of *The Red Devil Battery Sign* the southern evil of his earlier plays has become cosmic evil requiring a dark goddess in strange alliances to combat its menace.

Though the play may have structural faults, the production itself suffered problems not necessarily inherent in the script nor in the limitations of a modest stage. During its preview run the play was reported as running as long as four hours, and did run for three and one-half hours on the evening I saw it. As it neared its official opening, it tightened even more. Though the play is lengthy, with many scenes, some necessitating shifts, clearly it was prolonged by slow-pacing and noisy, laggard shifts, but these are problems of direction and playing tempo more than of the script. Another feature of the play contributing to its slow pace was the periodic appearance during scene breaks of three authentic mariachi players whose smiling renditions were as much a novelty in old Vienna as were the great variety of accents, both intended and unintended, in the production. The principal roles, played by Ruth Brinkman (American) and Keith

Baxter (English)—played in the Boston run by Anthony Quinn and Claire Bloom—were rendered in authentic accents, Baxter affecting Quinn's hoarse, gruff, masculine voice. The supporting cast, however, drawn from English, American and Austrian acting ranks, rendered some roles in accents redolent of their native speech. Of course this probably was less identifiable to most Austrian ears not so finely tuned to variations in American speech. However, when one actor rendered English with a clearly Austrian accent, it created some humor in the audience.

The play was well received the evening I saw it, though a few in the audience were too restless or befuddled to bear the three and a half hours playing time. We may judge from the reviews of Liselotte Espenhahn, writing for the *Kurier* in Vienna before and after the premiere (January 3 and January 20, 1976) that certain production faults were corrected. In her review of the premiere she remarks, "the performance has been speeded up, has become more compact, its quality and inventiveness have been improved, the acting of the major parts . . . has become more passionate, more solid, so that the various styles (realism and symbolism) now blend more harmoniously." An anonymous review in Vienna's *Die Presse* (January 20, 1976) remarks that the premiere ran twenty minutes shorter than a preview performance reviewed by the writer, and the tempo in general increased. The premiere, the reviewer remarks, was attended by a distinguished Austrian and international audience, headed by Austria's head of state, President Kirchschläger. The audience applauded the play for "four minutes and seven seconds," notes the reviewer, and discussion continued long after the premiere ended, in the Palais Pallavicini where the dignitaries and the famous in the audience gathered. "The theatre crowd," according to the reviewer, "deplored Williams' stubborn refusal to part with the crude end of the play where the Woman Downtown, tormented by her persecutors, descends from her penthouse into the armed underground."

My own impression of the play, based on the preview I saw, is that *Red Devil*, despite its production flaws at that moment, and its mélange of unintended accents, generated considerable power, especially in the first-act scenes that rendered the Woman Downtown as a distraught, apprehensive fugitive, and in the interchanges between King and the Woman. In these scenes Williams' former power in dialogue, situation and characterization again makes itself felt. There were, however, too many short, interrupted bedroom scenes. The brief male nude scene seemed more gratuitous than dramatically effective, and King's debilitation and death on stage appeared protracted. I have less quarrel with Williams' shift in style to his visionary and ambiguous conclusion than do most of the European reviewers of the play—nor is the blend of realism and expressionism unprepared for in Williams' work for those who know *Camino Real*. However, one can certainly quarrel with Williams' reading of society as oversimplification, and with his image of revolutionaries led by a too swiftly metamorphosed matriarch as a vision too unlikely to square with reality.

It was clear, too, that some members of the audience were disturbed by the play, but none more so than one middle-aged Austrian lady who, following the performance, told the world in general, and no one in particular, that she was outraged by the play, that it was "sick," and that she had been robbed in paying three hundred schillings (about fifteen dollars) to see it. Finally she was informed by one of the theatre personnel that "when one attends a play by Tennessee Williams, one does not expect to see *Die Fledermaus*." When I reported the incident to my former student in the cast, he gave me an actor's and a playwright's answer: "Well, at least we got to her." The lady continued her soliloquy down the street. I suspect the play sent more than one person howling from the theater into the night.

European
Contexts

One often hears that Tennessee Williams is more appreciated abroad than he has been in America. He must, in any case, be perceived within the context of Western literature and not merely of southern or American literature. Esther Jackson suggests an approach in her essay (in INTRODUCTORY), and the essays in this section deal with other European movements of the last century and more.

Part one of Mary Ann Corrigan's essay is far more than an oversized introduction to part two, which analyzes the Expressionistic aspects of *Camino Real*. The first part was requested of the author specifically to show all the possible European latitude in Williams' background. Part one has frequent references to other Williams plays and to his techniques, in addition to references to both American and European Expressionists.

June Larsen's study might have appeared in any of several other divisions of this collection. But her essay also expands the context for the study of Williams' work. By locating him among the Symbolists, ironically influenced by Poe, the author explains theme and technique in some plays. While she makes observations about *Out Cry* and the neglected *Slapstick Tragedy*, she concentrates on a perceptive analysis of *Camino Real*.

Beate Hein Bennett has at the editor's request expanded a short essay into an investigation that attempts to locate Williams in the broad context of the most recent experimental drama of Europe. The point was not mere name dropping but the hope to suggest lines of study beyond the regional. The first part of the essay deals with "infernalists" and the second with those attempting to revivify myth. The essay as a whole deals with the important and absorbing theme of the artist's relationship to society. The author has the ad-

373

vantage of being able to see Williams from the viewpoint of a German background but has unfortunately the difficulty of trying to condense a book into a relatively short essay. The reader may find it helpful to know that a possible subtitle for the essay is "The Tattered Masks of Existential Revolt."

Beyond Verisimilitude:
Echoes of Expressionism
in Williams' Plays

MARY ANN CORRIGAN

I

E XPRESSIONISM DOMINATED the visual and literary arts earlier in this century and made a lasting impression on the drama. Tennessee Williams reveals his critical awareness of dramatic Expressionism in his production notes to *The Glass Menagerie* and goes so far as to revive a defunct variation of Expressionist drama in *Camino Real*. To illuminate the nature and function of Expressionism in Williams' plays and to analyze the Expressionism of *Camino Real* is the purpose of this essay.

Expressionism in drama occurs when a playwright objectifies the subjective, when he deems an accurate reflection of the world of sense impressions less important than a direct expression of the thoughts and emotions of a character or of himself. Since the only method of representing the unseen and impalpable of subjective experience is through the seen and palpable of concrete reality, distortion of literal reality, now become symbolic, is often, though not always, necessary in Expressionist art. Peter Bauland says, "Expressionism is not nearly so impossible a concept to deal with concretely if we do not expect rigid rules and limitations within the genre and if we avoid the fallacy that it is an isolated manifestation of Germany in the years between 1910 and 1925" (pp. 64–5). The soliloquy and the aside, for instance, are among the more familiar Expressionistic theatrical conventions. Although Expressionism made an occasional appearance in the drama of other ages, it gained the force of a movement early in this century because it was consciously pursued as an alternative to and reaction against the dominant theatrical method of verisimilitude. Expressionism of this century sprang from a desire to depict on stage what the "peephole" drama, in limiting itself to what is seen and heard in a middle-class drawing room, effectively excludes: the thoughts, emotions and dreams that a person is unlikely to reveal to others.

August Strindberg's experimental plays provided a model for later Expressionist drama. Composed of thematically related discrete incidents, these plays are highly autobiographical, symbolizing events in Strindberg's life (*To Damascus, The Great Highway*), as well as metaphysical, probing the nature of man and human experience (*A Dream Play, The Ghost Sonata*). Both Strindberg's reduction of characters to types or to projections of the protagonist's mind and his metaphoric use of setting and props were imitated by the German Expressionist playwrights, who aimed, like Expressionist painters, at the depiction of intensest emotion. On the German stage, revolt, personal or social, was the keynote; the rallying cry was Georg Kaiser's *Erneuerung des Menschen*, the regeneration of mankind. The exporting of plays like Ernst Toller's *Man and the Masses* and Walter Hasenclever's *Beyond* resulted in the facile association of German Expressionism with left-wing political movements and/or deliberate obscurity, a conclusion based on allowing the lunatic fringe to speak for the whole movement. The German Expressionist dramatists were responsible for bringing attention to the aims and methods of Expressionism, but their imitators abroad conscientiously avoided the solipsism and stridency that had marred much of the Germans' work. Expressionism began to have an effect on American drama at about the time it sank into disrepute in Germany—in the twenties. Ludwig Lewisohn says that after World War I "expressionism was in the air. None could escape it, however ignorant of the German originals" (p. 398). The production of the German "originals," as well as Expressionistically staged classics, like Robert Edmond Jones's *Macbeth*, resulted in a veritable Expressionist fever in the American theater. American practitioners of Expressionism—Eugene O'Neill, John Howard Lawson, Elmer Rice, Francis Faragoh, Sophie Treadwell, Paul Green, George S. Kaufman and Marc Connelly—used Expressionistic devices selectively, often abandoning telegraphic dialogue and character reduction, the stylistic features of Expressionism least congenial to audiences.

Tennessee Williams' academic study of drama at Washington University and the University of Iowa in the 1930s would have familiarized him with a movement so widespread in the previous decade. Although Expressionism in the American theater had died down before the mid-1930s, its experimental techniques were available to later dramatists and cropped up even in essentially non-Expressionist plays, like the Living Newspaper productions of the Federal Theater Project. An active participant in college and little theater groups, Williams knew contemporary plays and came into contact with "epic theater" director, Erwin Piscator, at the New School. The movie houses which Williams frequented in the 1920s and 1930s provided him with his most concentrated dose of Expressionist style. The techniques of the film, which came of age during the same period as the development of Expressionism, always had much in common with those of Expressionism, with its emphasis on the visual and episodic. Through montage the film accomplished naturally and with finesse what Strindberg had had to revolutionize the drama to achieve—a breakdown in the continuity of time and space. Walter Sokel notes the attraction that the silent films with their "mixture of sentimental pathos, social protest, and grotesqueness" held for the German Expressionists (*Anthology*, p. xx), whose plays depended far less on the verbal element than those of American Expressionists. O'Neill, who acknowledged his debt to Strindberg, though not to the German Expressionists, admitted that the German Expressionist film, *The Cabinet of Dr. Caligari* (American release, 1921), which used angled sets and chiaroscuro lighting in exploring the mind of a madman, suggested to him dramatic possibilities that he had not before considered (Valgemae, p. 34). Although few films as wholly Expressionistic in method and aim as *The Cabinet of Dr. Caligari* appeared, Expressionistic distortion became part of the repertoire of cinematic techniques. American films, with characteristic light touch, adopted the comic-satiric form of Expressionism, illustrated by Kaufman and Connelly's *Beggar on Horseback*. The line of development is from this comic dream play of the 1920s to the grotesque antics of the Marx Brothers (Bauland, p. 94) and the musical extravaganzas of the 1930s—the locus of action in all firmly outside the realm of daily reality.

That Williams was familiar very early in his career with not only the theory of Expressionism but also its earlier dramatic manifestations seems evident from his unpublished play, *Stairs to the Roof*, a fantasy reminiscent of Kaiser's *From Morn to Midnight*, Rice's *The Adding Machine* and Lawson's *Roger Bloomer*. According to Benjamin Nelson, this episodic play depicts the dissatisfaction of a "little wage-earner," Benjamin Murphy, with his work in a shirt factory and with his domestic life. Like Roger Bloomer and Mr. Zero, Benjamin finds a kindred soul in his coworker, known only as "The Girl." After the two of them symbolically release animals from their cages at the zoo, they watch a troupe of mummers perform a fairy tale containing an obvious lesson for them. They resolve to leave their old lives behind and climb the "stairway to the roof" at the factory, despite the best efforts of the stockholders to prevent them. A mysterious Mr. E. with flowing white beard meets them on the roof and whisks them away "to another world to begin the story of man anew" (Nelson, 68–73). Here is Kaiser's *Erneuerung des Menschen* tempered by the whimsy of *Beggar on Horseback*. The enemies in this play are the same enemies who appeared in earlier Expressionist plays—assembly lines, ticking clocks, managers, stockholders, zoo-keepers, and other representatives of a repressive materialistic culture. A description of a 1947 production in Pasadena of *Stairs to the Roof* demonstrates that the play is Expressionistic in effect: "A symbolic representation of the struggle of the 'little man' against the stultifying economic and spiritual forces, the play is set in a shirt factory and such haunts of its workers as bars and carnivals. The production has a cast of forty and twenty scenes, with sets designed especially for constantly changing 'mood' lighting, and periodic mood music" (*New York Times Theater Reviews*, February 25, 1947, p. 35). If this unpublished play and *Camino Real* are inadequate testimony to the effects of Expressionist dramaturgy on Williams, one need only glance at the more "realistic" plays to find a variety of formal characteristics of Expressionist drama in undiluted form or with small modifications.

A salient feature of dramatic Expressionism is its abandonment of tight causal, chronological plotting in favor of a looser organization by theme or motif and, often, an episodic structure. Thus the episodes of Strindberg's A Dream Play, in which characters switch roles, and architecture and props acquire different functions as the backdrop changes (a tree is treated as a hat rack, a bed as a tent), are held together by common themes of the necessity and irreconcilability of opposites and of man as prisoner of his flesh. A more limited treatment of a similar theme (with static characters and confined locale) occurs in Summer and Smoke, in which Body and Spirit do not so much vie with each other as pass each other by in twelve episodes. The three fairly discrete acts of Cat on a Hot Tin Roof, among Williams' more conventional plays, are connected to one another by the mendacity motif. Often the episodic structure (in, for instance, Strindberg's To Damascus, Reinhard Sorge's The Beggar and O'Neill's Emperor Jones) reflects the pattern of the dreaming or reminiscing mind. Such is the function of the seven scenes in The Glass Menagerie, vignettes etched on Tom Wingfield's memory, and the sixteen "blocks" of Williams' rather literal dream of life on the Camino Real. In some earlier Expressionist plays, Stationen dramas like Toller's Transfiguration and O'Neill's Hairy Ape, the episodes depict the progress of the main character toward a new understanding of his position in the universe. The end of the pilgrimage is ironically inverted in Williams' Stationen drama, A Streetcar Named Desire, as Blanche moves in each of eleven scenes inexorably closer to the disintegration of her mind and the total rejection of reality. The episodes of The Glass Menagerie reveal Tom's gradually moving toward a break with his family that only years later he recognizes as a futile gesture. Although Williams' later plays, perhaps as a concession to the commercial theater, use the traditional three-act structure, the scene—a short encounter possessing a single emotional theme—is his forte, as the control and concentration achieved in the one-acters and the early episodic full-length plays indicate. Whether Williams consciously imitated the loose structure of Expressionist plays is moot. Once Expressionism had made an impact on the theater, the choice of an episodic structure to reflect progressive internal action was not unusual.

Perhaps the most significant change effected by the Expressionists was an increased emphasis on the visual elements of theater.

Whereas in the theater of verisimilitude the setting, props, and lighting provide an environment for the action or further the plot, they serve a more metaphoric purpose in Expressionist drama. Expressionist staging attempts to "make the decor act" (Roberts, p. 188). Thus the home of Elmer Rice's Mr. Zero, a slave in life and in death to his monotonous work at the adding machine, is papered with "foolscap covered with columns of figures." Williams designs sets for both functional and metaphoric purposes. The dichotomies of the Manichean *Battle of Angels* (light vs. darkness, nature/ imagination vs. commerce, life vs. death) are reinforced by a divided set, downstage a shuttered utilitarian dry goods store, upstage a confectionery decorated to resemble an orchard in full bloom, lit by the "soft rosy-glow" of Japanese lanterns. The divided stage in *You Touched Me!*, an adaptation of a D. H. Lawrence short story, visually establishes the conflict between female gentility and male vigor and, in *Summer and Smoke*, between the doctor's physical world and the parson's daughter's spiritual one. In the latter play Williams also calls for frequent spotlighting on a stone statue of the angel Eternity and on an anatomy chart. With a little more subtlety, Williams tries to make "landscapes reflect the emotional situation of the characters" (Sokel, *Extremis*, p. 38), a feature of German Expressionism, in later plays. In *Suddenly Last Summer* the jungle garden with its "massive tree-flowers that suggest organs of a body, torn out, still glistening with undried blood" (III, 349) sets the emotional tone for the story. The backdrop for the original production of *A Streetcar Named Desire* was designed by Jo Mielziner, who incidentally was influenced by German Expressionist stagecraft while in Berlin; its angled telephone poles, lurid neon lights and ornately decorated façades on crumbling structures express the quality of life in the Vieux Carré as seen by Blanche. Costuming, props and lighting convey the emotional strength of the characters in *A Streetcar Named Desire* and reinforce the dichotomy between Blanche and Stanley. The overwrought, emotionally drained Blanche always wears pastels in half-lights; Stanley, "the richly feathered male bird," appears in vivid primary colors under strong, garish light. Stanley's initial appearance, as, dressed in work clothes, he hurls a blood-stained package of raw meat at his wife, contrasts with Blanche's: "Her appearance is incongruous to this setting. She is daintily dressed in a white suit with a fluffy bodice, necklace, and earrings of pearl, white gloves and hat, looking as if she were arriving at a summer tea or cocktail party in the garden district. . . . There is something about her uncertain manner, as well as her clothes, that suggests a moth" (I, 245). A moth indeed, cowering beneath the glare of a naked light bulb, ill-disguised behind a tawdry artificial lantern, as the reality of her life is poorly cloaked by the illusions she holds. Val's snakeskin jacket, Hadrian's penny flute, Brick's crutch, Alma's plumed hat, Kilroy's golden heart are all attempts to express an internal state in objective terms. The glass unicorn, possibly Williams' most famous symbol, is an analogue for Laura's subjective state and enables the audience to understand the emotional stages through which she passes in her encounter with Jim. The "freakish horse" with a single horn, her favorite piece in the menagerie, reflects her self-image, which undergoes a transformation as Jim treats her as an attractive, normal young woman. When he knocks over the fragile figure, breaking its horn off, Laura responds with delight to the newly conferred normality of the unicorn. Her gesture in giving him the no longer freakish figure conveys to the audience how fleeting is her adaptation to the world, an event to be commemorated by a souvenir.

Exploiting the symbolism of setting and props is a tendency even in wholly verisimilitudinous dramas: the Cherry Orchard is more than a background in Chekhov's play, and Hedda Gabler's guns are as important in revealing her psychological nature as they are in furthering the plot. John Gassner says, "When anti-realists belabor illusionism, they are actually flogging a dead horse—and one that never had much life in it anyway, so far as Ibsen, Strindberg, Chekhov and Shaw were concerned. No one despised mere verisimilitude as much as they" (*Directions*, p. 87). With respect to the use of stage properties, the difference between the Expressionists and the best writers of the "realist" tradition is one of degree rather than kind. Seldom in plays by Ibsen and Chekhov does the symbol interfere with the illusion of fidelity to tangible reality, as it does with impunity in Expressionist plays. When a dramatist working within the conventions of verisimilitude is too insistent upon the symbolism of properties, the result can be ludicrous: thus, Chekhov's "embarrassing seagull" and "Miss Julie's over-strident birdcage"

(Styan, *Drama, Stage and Audience,* p. 42). But the Expressionists' attempts to reveal a character's emotional response to a situation can easily result in distortion that enhances the experience of the play. Thus the college examiner in Lawson's *Roger Bloomer* "sits on a throne-like chair" high above the test-takers, and the "little formless fears" of O'Neill's Emperor Jones are objectified in small "black, shapeless" beings with glittering eyes. Williams, with no regard for realist propriety, asks that a screen for slides and legends be placed in the Wingfield apartment and that the back wall of the Kowalski flat become transparent so that Blanche's fears may be objectified.

Williams' often rather explicit directions for lighting reveal an attempt to make an expressive device of theatrical necessity. In *The Glass Menagerie* the ethereality of events occurring in memory is conveyed by the comparative dimness of the lighting throughout the play. Sofa lighting creates an aura of romance or sentimentality. More dramatic lighting effects set an emotional tone for a single scene or bring a particular character's internal life into focus. When Tom and Amanda are arguing upstage, this area "is lit with a turgid smoky red glow" (I, 162). Frequent spotlighting of Laura polishing her glass animals produces the stage version of a movie close-up. Williams describes the effect he wishes to achieve: "The light upon Laura should be distinct from the others, having a peculiar pristine clarity such as light used in early religious portraits of female saints or madonnas" (pp. 133–34). Later, when describing Amanda in her peevishness over the argument with Tom, Williams writes that the "light on her face with its aged but childish features is cruelly sharp, satirical as a Daumier print" (p. 169). Such lighting is intended to reflect Tom's emotional response to the other characters: his memory canonizes Laura and criticizes Amanda. His light cues indicate that Williams is the beneficiary of earlier attempts to practice Adolphe Appia's ideas on the free use of diffused, focused and colored lighting to convey the emotional implications of the stage action. In using spotlights to draw attention to discrete incidents related only by thin threads of association to the main action, Sorge's *The Beggar* demonstrates the power of light to heighten the experience of the subjective in an Expressionist play. Similarly, in Williams' early one-act play, *The Long Goodbye,* the stage lights are dimmed for flashback sequences. Williams is not above using lighting to reinforce symbolic meaning. The murder scene in *Battle of Angels* is played entirely in darkness, until at the moment of Myra's release from death-in-life the lights in the confectionery go on, signifying her life-in-death. In *Iguana* Shannon's search for meaning is underscored, as a "clear shaft of light" mysteriously pierces the darkness of a stormy night to focus on his "reaching-out hands" (IV, 326).

Attempts to "make the decor act" reflected the Expressionists' desire to revive Wagner's ideas on the Gesamtkunstwerk of theater, a work which unites all other arts. German Expressionists did not feel themselves confined to creation in only one art form. Indeed, some early Expressionist playwrights are better known for their work in the visual arts: Oskar Kokoshka, Ernst Barlach and Vasily Kandinsky. Williams' production notes reveal his consciousness of the special relation that exists between drama and the visual arts, for he frequently refers to specific works, artists or movements to explain the mood that he wishes to create. Possibly the most famous example of his use of a painting as a model for an effect is in *A Streetcar Named Desire*'s poker night scene, designed with Van Gogh's *Night Café* in mind. Williams refers to Giorgio De Chirico's *Conversation among the Ruins* to explain the use of fragmentary walls and interiors for the set of *Summer and Smoke*; a Japanese line drawing sets the mood for *The Mutilated*. In *Ten Blocks on the Camino Real* the appearance of the streetcleaners is suggested by old German prints of the Dance of Death, and the decor at the gypsy's stall is of "Moorish opulence . . . as it might be drawn by Rube Goldberg" (*American Blues*, pp. 58–9). Far from depicting reality with photographic accuracy, Williams' stage settings are artistic distortions.

Music and sound effects are likewise elements of composition in Williams' plays. Walter Sokel discusses the tendency for Expressionist literature to strive for the effect of music, the art in which emotion is most directly embodied (*Extremis*, pp. 24–54). Strindberg's *To Damascus*, with its funeral march, organ music and church bells, provides an early example of music to establish mood in an Expressionist play. Jazz sequences, often accompanied by choreography, appeared in American Expressionistic plays of the 1920s (John Dos Passos' *The Moon Is a Gong*, Faragoh's *Pinwheel*, Lawson's *Processional*). The silent movies probably influenced Williams' use of music in *The Glass Menagerie*. The play's scenes are framed by music, which mediates between the present and the past. Each major character has a personal musical theme, symbolizing his illusions: Laura's theme, "The Glass Menagerie," is light, delicate, poignant; nostalgic fiddling accompanies Amanda's reveries; "theme three" adventure music calls Tom to his wandering future. In *Summer and Smoke* intermittent mood music seems to express the vague, unfulfilled longings of John and Alma for each other. A *Streetcar Named Desire* uses music more extensively and functionally. Whenever Blanche feels threatened, she and the audience hear the polka tune that was being played as her husband shot himself. Other music in the play—blues, jazz, honky-tonk—is justified by the presence of a nearby night spot. The blues, expressing loneliness, plays as Blanche arrives in the Vieux Carré and is particularly dominant when she recounts the deaths at Belle Reve and when she kisses the newsboy. As Blanche is being led away to the asylum and Stella cries uncontrollably, the music of the blue piano swells. At one point this music catches Stanley's mood too: when Stella leaves him, and he sobs, "I want my baby," the "'Blue Piano' plays for a brief interval" (I, 306). But normally the uncomplicated, obtrusive rhythms of the honky-tonk express Stanley's personality. This music dominates the rape scene. Williams' most extensive use of music and choreography, as well as a variety of other symbolic effects popularized by the Expressionists, is in *The Purification*, a short play which, as a result of its Spanish-American setting and emphasis on ritual, seems to resemble the work of Garcia Lorca more than that of the Expressionists. The subjective visions that two men have of the same dead girl come to life on stage; a smiling Elena enters with flowers as the "guitar weaves a pattern of rapture" (*27 Wagons*, p. 36) and the sky lightens; the loveless Elena, bearing a cactus, enters to the tune of dissident notes and the blowing of a dry wind.

A sound score is often a necessary concomitant to the text of an Expressionist play. Treadwell says in the stage directions for her Expressionist *Machinal* that the play uses sounds (steel riveting, a priest chanting, a Negro singing, a jazz band) for their emotional impact as well as their ability to create a background for the action. Williams employs sound effects for the same purpose in his earliest play, *Battle of Angels*. Myra's and Val's conversations are often punctuated by sounds suggesting nature and wildness, like the baying of hounds and the shouts of a peddlar selling vegetables—"Ahhhh ahhhh. Turnip greens, new potatoes, rutabagas. Ahhh-ahhh" (I, 49). As the passion between Val and Myra increases, a cotton gin, which "makes a sound like your heart was pounding a lot too fast" (p. 74) gets louder and louder. Thunder heralds the beginning of the battle of angels, and a gong tolls its end. Incidental sound effects are less obtrusive, but no less symbolic, in A *Streetcar Named Desire.* As Blanche is confronted by Stanley clad in "brilliant silk pajamas," the barely audible blue piano music "turns into the roar of an approaching locomotive" (p. 400). Jungle sounds are heard in the background during the rape scene, as they are during the whole of *Suddenly Last Summer.*

The focus on internal reality rather than external appearance results in early Expressionist plays in a reduction of character to type, abstraction or caricature and of dialogue to emotional utterance with minimal denotative significance. At the extreme are plays like Strindberg's *To Damascus,* in which minor characters serve only to symbolize the personality traits of the main character, and Hasenclever's *Humanity,* with its oblique, staccato dialogue. Expressionists frequently used nameless figures (Old Man, Mother, Aristocrat), believing that individualizing characteristics, so important to slice-of-life dramatists, only obscure the inner nature of human beings. German Expressionist playwright and critic, Paul Kornfeld, contrasts "psychological man," who is "seen from the outside, as an object of portrayal and scientific analysis" with "souled man" who is "felt from the inside" (Sokel, *Extremis,* p. 52). Whatever the strength of the theory, the practice of typification and telegraphic dialogue was never popular with writers outside Germany, who recognized that "externalizing a state of mind does not have to result in a complete annihilation of individuality" (Broussard, p. 49). O'Neill says that Expressionism without character is unworkable: "I personally do not believe that an idea can be readily put over to an audience except through characters. When it sees 'A Man' and 'A Woman'— just abstractions, it loses the human contact by which it identifies itself with the protagonist of the play" (Cargill, p. 111). O'Neill's *Hairy Ape* and Lawson's *Processional* demonstrate the compatibility of Expressionism with not merely familiar dialogue, but even regional dialect. Broussard summarizes the "sea change" that Expressionism underwent in coming to the United States: "There can be no better illustration than *The Adding Machine* of the essential difference between Continental expressionistic drama and its American counterpart. To his principal characters—to Zero, Mrs. Zero, Daisy— the author gives the breath of life in a dialogue that is homely, sharp, at once American, and with an emotional dimension from which they emerge as human beings and not as abstractions" (p. 49). Apart from a few isolated appearances, such as in the office scene in *Machinal*, telegraphic dialogue was an insignificant feature of American Expressionism.

Despite Williams' occasional use in the early plays of nameless figures (*The Strangest Kind of Romance, The Purification, Talk to Me Like the Rain . . .*) and abstract characters (Jabe is Death, Cassandra is Sex in *Battle of Angels*), he clearly reveals the American tendency to individualize characters and, indeed, adds his own fillip to the exploration of inner states by delving into highly idiosyncratic minds. It is the *atypicality* of Williams' characters that is obtrusive. Miss Collins, Willie and Eloi of the early one-act plays, Alma, Blanche and Sebastian are all individuals set apart by psychological quirk from the mass of mankind, perhaps, after all, the best subjects for internal exploration, their emotional excesses suiting them for Expressionistic treatment. John Gassner discusses the importance of combining realism and theatricality in stage characters and cites as paragons Shakespeare's "actor characters." Beatrice, Falstaff, Hotspur, Hamlet are "characters who are highly articulate, histrionic, self-dramatizing" (*Directions*, p. 223)—existing on two planes simultaneously: "real" in their depth and complexity, "theatrical" in their capacity for self-expression. Williams' best characters are maddening and delightful self-dramatizers—Amanda, Blanche, Maggie—who likewise combine realism and theatricality. For dialogue, Williams prefers familiar, if somewhat heightened, regional speech; only in the short *Auto-Da-Fé* does he approach anything resembling the telegraphic utterances of German Expressionism.

Williams' spiritual kinship with earlier Expressionists accounts in part for his adoption or adaptation of their techniques. Walter Sokel notes the Expressionist tendency to use art as an escape from the agony of life (*Extremis*, p. 128). Elmer Rice defines the process of creation as the artist's impulse to "get his trouble off his mind or his chest . . . by symbolically externalizing it" (p. 1). Williams shares with Strindberg a tendency to escape into his own writing and to reshape his personal experience through it. Williams says, "I'm a compulsive writer because what I am doing is creating imaginary worlds into which I can retreat from the real world because . . . I've never made any kind of adjustment to the real world" (Funke and Booth, p. 73). Time and again he creates characters in his own image; his plays are full of people who cannot adjust, who escape into reverie, fantasy, dream, alcohol, drugs, insanity. Williams' own life forms the obvious basis for the plot of his first successful play. Like Tom Wingfield, Tom Williams was an aspiring writer who worked in a shoe factory during the Depression, an experience that Williams characterizes as "indescribable torment." Williams' father, a traveling salesman, and his southern-bred mother bear some resemblance to the father "who fell in love with long distances" (I, 145) and to the ageing belle, Amanda. Williams' sister's emotional instability, which eventually caused her to be institutionalized, becomes in the play Laura's physical handicap. Robert Rice reports that Williams' sister even had a menagerie of glass animals (p. M2). In later plays Williams externalizes his own feelings through female characters: "Alma went through the same thing that I went through —from puritanical shackles to, well, complete profligacy" (Gaines, p. 27). In his *Memoirs* Williams writes of accepting with equanimity the nickname of Blanche. Most recently, the sensitive artist homosexual of *Small Craft Warnings* speaks for Williams.

Although Expressionistic techniques often appear in dramas without Expressionistic tenets, Williams' writing reveals a commitment to Expressionist subject matter and themes as well as methods. Criticism of the factory and city, of the plight of the working class and the dehumanizing conditions of modern life, so central to Kaiser's *Gas*, Rice's *The Adding Machine* and *Subway* and Lawson's *Roger Bloomer*, appears in Williams' earliest plays, which reflect the influence of the social action plays of the 1930s (*Moony's Kid Don't Cry, The Case of the Crushed Petunias*, and *Candles to the Sun*). The leap into a new, more nearly perfect society effected by the lovers in *Stairs to the Roof* recalls the ending of Edmund Wilson's Expressionistic *Crime in the Whistler Room* (produced by the Provincetown Players in 1924) and countless heralds in German Expressionist plays of the coming of the New Man. But already by the time of *The Glass Menagerie*, the social theme seems tacked on, insisted upon in Tom Wingfield's direct addresses to the audience, but less central to the fate of the characters than their own natures are. For Williams, as for Strindberg, the problems lie less in transient social conditions than in the immutable nature of human beings, whose aspirations make them strive for a perfection that their physical limitations prevent them from achieving. A Manichean conflict between Soul and Body, waged externally in *Battle of Angels*, possesses Alma, Blanche and Shannon, who, like the dissolving characters of *A Dream Play*, strive in vain for wholeness.

At its heart Expressionist drama is Platonic, whether the perspective is metaphysical (presenting a character's longings for the Ideal), political (depicting the struggle for Utopia), or social (revealing the meaninglessness of earthbound existence). The myth that explains the suffering in Strindberg's *A Dream Play* lies behind the quest of the Expressionist hero for a never-to-be-realized perfection: the mating of Brahma, divine force, with Maya, Mother Earth, "constituted the fall of heaven into sin. Thus the universe, mankind, existence are merely a phantom" (p. 401). Quotidian experience, as impermanent as the sixteen blocks on the Camino Real or the swift "stations" that Kaiser's Cashier stops at on his way to enlightenment-destruction, is a hindrance to vision. At the highest level of generality, Expressionist art asserts the primacy of the "inner" life over the "seeming" of external existence. The moral superiority of those who rebel against what is in the name of what ought to be is attested by a spiritual victory that affirms the worth of the struggle (the conversion of the two women through the execution of the heroine in Toller's *Man and the Masses*; the "Ecce Homo" of the dying Cashier in *From Morn to Midnight*; the nobility of Blanche as she leans on the arm of the doctor; Chance Wayne's "I do not ask for your sympathy . . ."). The ruling principle for many Williams characters is expressed by the student in Strindberg's *Ghost Sonata*: "What do we find that truly lives up to what it promises? Only things in our dreams, our imagination!" (p. 492). So, in *The Lady of Larkspur Lotion*, The Writer defends Mrs. Hardwicke-Moore: "Is she to be blamed because it is necessary for her to compensate for the cruel deficiencies of reality by the exercise of a little—what shall I say?—God-given—imagination?" (27 Wagons, p. 70). Illusions, whatever their shortcomings, are necessary. Amanda's embellished memories and Tom's pipedreams are ridiculous, but ennobling, raising the Wingfields above the obtuse who accommodate themselves to reality. The need for ideal constructs of mind and imagination to redeem the shortcomings of mortal existence is reiterated in Camino Real, the living hell from which only a knight-errant, a romatic poet and a pie-eyed American optimist escape. To possess "illusions" is to have a higher truth, albeit a self-destructive one. Characters like Val Xavier, Blanche, Chance Wayne, Sebastian Venable, having perceived a vision, however inadequate, that redeems their lives, return to the darkness of the cave to be destroyed by the prisoners inside, who are satisfied by the shadows on the wall.

Although Williams may come down ultimately on the side of Idea over Experience, his characters, unlike those of the German Expressionists, mercifully lack a sense of mission. They are unwilling idealists, ambiguous saviors, embracing a more nearly perfect vision, not because they want to but because they must, having been endowed with the curse of sensitivity. A verdict of mental health is not likely to be accorded to those who cling, in the face of recalcitrant matter, to their own illusions. Society makes one judgment; the playwright makes another. Walter Sokel says madness, or "an escape into retrogression from an inner complexity too difficult to bear, was for most Expressionists . . . a consummation devoutly to be wished" (Extremis, p. 96), and one repeatedly evoked in their dramatic compositions. The characters who have an emotional breakdown because of their inability to adjust to the imperfection of the world are the heroes: Kaiser's Cashier driven to suicide, O'Neill's Hairy Ape caging himself with his spiritual brother, Rice's Sophie, a victim of man's prurience, who throws herself in front of a subway, and Treadwell's Young Woman who murders as an act of freedom. So too Williams depicts social misfits as heroic. The harmless dream of Mrs. Hardwicke-Moore is preferable to the roach-infested reality of the Landlady; the frenzy of Eloi to the practicality of his mother; the incestuous love craze of The Son to the reason of The Rancher

(*The Purification*); the madness of Blanche to the sanity of Stanley. With its various techniques for concretizing subjective experience, Expressionism lends itself to the depiction of mental disintegration and withdrawal into a private reality.

A principal theme of the German Expressionists (e.g., Sorge, Kornfeld, Hasenclever), which Williams explores in even his most "realistic" plays, is the father-son conflict, the adolescent revolt against authority and convention, symbolized by members of an older generation. Sorge's autobiographical *The Beggar* (considered the archetypal German Expressionist play by Samuel and Thomas, *Expressionism in German Life, Literature, and the Theatre*) adds another dimension to this theme by making the son a poet and his father an engineer. *Beggar on Horseback*'s dream sequence comically depicts the stifling of artistic impulse in the young by the demands for standardization of an older generation. In defiance of factory regimentation, Tom Wingfield writes poems on shoe boxes. Chance Wayne, youth incarnate, takes on and loses to Boss Finley. Brick delights in defying Big Daddy. Val Xavier, on the surface little more than a coy sexual adventurer, is accorded dignity by his defense of a black guitar player persecuted by the white elders in a southern town. The "little man," free of emotional attachments, social position and political power, is the revolutionary hero in Expressionist plays. Bernard Myers says that the Expressionist artists' antiauthoritarian stance is often traceable to "unsatisfactory emotional relationships" with a father (p. 11), an experience shared by Williams. The male authority figures in Williams' plays are like his father, robust, domineering, righteous materialists, who attempt to impose their value system on others. Often left in the care of his mother while his father traveled, Williams is no stranger to the more subtle repression that a woman in authority can practice. The sins of maternal protectiveness of which Amanda is guilty appear less sympathetic when perpetrated by Violet Venable in *Suddenly Last Summer* and Aunt Emmie in *You Touched Me!*

Although the staging techniques and the themes associated with Expressionism are apparent in many of Williams' plays, his early plays, those up to and including *Camino Real*, seem the most affected by Expressionism. His first professionally produced play, *Battle of Angels*, employs a ragbag of symbolic techniques to confer metaphysical implications on a sordid melodrama. The stage lights flicker on or off at significant moments, Christ-figures abound, church bells toll and thunder rumbles to underscore the Manichean power struggle, which the love affair between Val and Myra precipitates. Here are Expressionist trappings without Expressionist essence. Although the play's action appears in flashback, the events are not rendered from the perspective of those ostensibly telling the tale; the inward vision that justifies Expressionistic distortion is lacking. The characters, mostly one-dimensional and static in their roles as good or bad angels, are yet unlike the type characters of Expressionist plays, who are either projections of the mind of the protagonist or representations of a recognizable class of human beings. The dichotomies in *Battle of Angels* resemble those of Strindberg's *A Dream Play*. Strindberg's vision, however, more nearly approximates human experience: his internal perspective enables him to reveal a struggle between good and evil *within* each person, whereas Williams' external focus depicts the conflict *between* unambiguously good and bad people. *Battle of Angels* is the first crude step in Williams' decade-long search for a workable combination of realism and theatricalism.

As a collaboration and adaptation, Williams' next work, *You Touched Me!*, does not merit as much consideration as his other early plays. Symbolic staging, including the attack of a fox on the hen yard, and props (a flute for the Pan-like Lawrentian hero) lend a veneer of symbolism to a fairy tale love story. Characters, like those in *Battle of Angels*, are categorized by their positions in the sterility-fertility tug of war. A functional divided stage, used for comic juxtaposition in this play, is a device Williams exploits for Expressionist purposes in later plays.

Possibly as a result of the concentrated character exploration Williams practiced in the one-act plays, his next work, *The Glass Menagerie*, avoids the fatal flaw of wooden characterization exhibited by *Battle of Angels* and *You Touched Me!*, although Expressionistic devices are not yet wholly integrated into the play. A memory play, *The Glass Menagerie* is Expressionistic in actualizing the subjective vision of a single person. It is important to emphasize that Tom Wingfield manipulates the action, for *The Glass Menagerie* has often been used merely as a vehicle for superannuated actresses, although it makes sense only as the private musings of the Williams surrogate, Tom. The characterization of Amanda and the gentleman caller, both so close to caricature, and the sentimentalized portrait of Laura are rendered from Tom's unique perspective. Williams reminds the audience of the inward vision in the narrative frames, full of purple passages typical of one who fancies himself a writer ("In Spain there was Guernica! But here there was only hot swing music and liquor, dance halls, bars, movies, and sex that hung in the gloom like a chandelier and flooded the world with brief, deceptive rainbows," p. 145). The play's nonrealistic lighting, its musical themes and the symbolic glass figures are useful devices to fix the audience's attention on the emotions of the characters; less useful is the screen for slides and captions that the published version of the play describes in detail. Williams may have originally intended the screen as a means to give objective shape to the subjective (Amanda's reveries are underscored by the picture of her greeting callers, Tom's plans by the image of the sailing vessel, Laura's dreams by the portrait of Jim O'Connor as high school hero), but in practice the device generally either repeats the objective or provides an ironic commentary on action and character. Although projecting captions on the screen may be psychologically valid as a reflection of the memories of a character literally bred on silent movies, the device is offensive to the audience in its redundancy and obtrusiveness. Laura's trauma is trivialized by captions like "Terror!" and "Not Jim," just as Amanda's and Tom's illusions appear ridiculous when concretized in images. With the screen device the boundary between Expressionism, which appeals to the emotions and seeks an alliance between stage and audience, and "epic theater," which appeals to judgment at the expense of empathy, has been crossed. The images and captions alienate the audience from the action by ridiculing the idealizations of reality that the rest of the play posits as necessary to the survival of the sensitive. Most directors of *The Glass Menagerie*, in wisely dispensing with the screen, produce a rare dramatic experience, a fairly subtle Expressionist play.

The resemblance in theme and character between *Summer and Smoke* and *A Streetcar Named Desire* may be the result of Williams' writing the plays almost simultaneously. *Summer and Smoke* was

MARY ANN CORRIGAN 393

completed first, having been produced in Dallas in the summer before A *Streetcar Named Desire*'s premiere on Broadway. Although Alma is the focal point in the earlier play, being its only fully developed character, her central role differs from that of the main character who typically dominates the stage in Expressionist drama. It is not the inner reality, but the outward "show" of Alma that Williams depicts. The play's action, showing the movement of a soul from excessive spirituality to excessive sensuality, is internal action and therefore suited to Expressionist treatment, which it does not receive. Alma is developed "from the outside looking in." The audience never knows what is going on inside her mind; its only access to her is through the reactions of the other characters to her. This technique is different from an Expressionistic attempt to objectify the main character's personality traits by embodying them in minor characters, for the secondary characters of *Summer and Smoke* are not aspects of Alma's mind. The stage symbolism, dual set, angel and anatomy chart, aid Williams in demonstrating the proposition that Body and Soul are irreconcilable, but Alma's internal strife, which issues in her transformation from Puritan to profligate, occurs between the acts.

By contrast, the symbolism of A *Streetcar Named Desire* indicates the stages in Blanche's progression toward insanity. As much as possible, Williams remains within the conventions of verisimilitude in using theatrical devices to objectify Blanche's distorted vision of reality. The audience is, however, aware that baths (purification) and light bulbs (factual reality) have a meaning for Blanche apart from their functional existence. The further Blanche retreats from reality, the more Williams distorts the surface realism of the play. The occasional playing of a musical theme imagined by Blanche in moments of stress gives way to more concentrated expressions of subjective experience. Thus, the back wall of the Kowalski flat becomes transparent in the rape scene to allow for concrete depictions of Blanche's terrors in the violent, immoral, bestial behavior of the New Orleans street figures. She and we hear the sounds of jungle life as Stanley is about to pounce. Largely through visual and aural devices the disintegration of Blanche's mind is made apparent to the audience. Exercising more control over theatrical devices than he did in *The Glass Menagerie*, Williams writes in *A Streetcar Named Desire* a play that integrates psychologically valid character study and Expressionist distortion.

The Expressionism of *Camino Real*, examined in detail in part two of this essay, is blatant and without the basis in objective experience that grounds the subjective visions of the best of Williams' early plays. Between the writing of *Ten Blocks on the Camino Real* in the late forties and the production of the expanded version, Williams wrote *The Rose Tattoo*, a thin romantic tale embellished by suggestive symbols and music. The 1953 production of *Camino Real* seems to have exorcised a devil for Williams. His next play, *Cat on a Hot Tin Roof*, which lacks the episodic structure of short emotional scenes that Williams had favored for a decade, is stylistically at the opposite extreme from Expressionist spectacle. It is the play that relies least on symbols to express the inner life. Instead, characters vent their feelings and thoughts in confessional monologues. The medium of *Cat on a Hot Tin Roof*, like that of most of Williams' later plays, is not visual, but verbal, using monologue and verbal imagery to reveal the unseen. This method allows Williams to remain within the bounds of strict verisimilitude, but precludes the depiction of unconscious or deliberately concealed subjective responses. For the most part, Williams remains resolutely within the confines of "slice-of-life" theater in his later plays. The most experimental of his later plays, *Out Cry*, though abjuring readily recognizable situations, relies primarily on dialogue to extend the boundaries of drama beyond verisimilitude. Even in *Suddenly Last Summer*, which exists to concretize the metaphor of the strong devouring the weak, the action is contained in the monologue of one character who speaks under the influence of a "truth serum." The closest Williams comes to Expressionism in his later full-length plays is in *Night of the Iguana*, in which various female characters might be considered as objectifying aspects of the hero's personality, although their function as individuals in the objective realm is far more important in the play. The epitome of Williams' dependence on the verbal elements of drama is reached in *Small Craft Warnings*, a play composed of a series of engrossing monologues—an inherently undramatic play. Although all of Williams' plays reveal the influence of the techniques of symbolic staging popularized by the Expressionists, Williams' dedication to the Expressionist purpose of directly depicting subjective experience, regardless of the distortion of verisimilitude, abates after the 1940s. *Cat on a Hot Tin Roof* and *Night of the Iguana*, the best plays of Williams' later career, are generally deemed inferior to the Expressionistic plays, *The Glass Menagerie* and *A Streetcar Named Desire*. Even *Camino Real*, despite the criticism leveled against it, continues to fascinate, as frequent revivals here and abroad testify; it is one of Williams' more successful failures.

How can we account for this change in emphasis in Williams' plays? Williams has often displayed his sensitivity to critical and box office success. *Camino Real's* run of a mere sixty performances was shorter than that of any of his plays since *Battle of Angels*, including *You Touched Me!* Williams may have concluded that Expressionism, rather than his own use of it in that one play, was unacceptable to audiences. He may have recognized the instant appeal to Broadway audiences of sex and violence, unadulterated by experimental stagecraft and philosophical estimates of society. Otto Mann, in characterizing Expressionism as a youthful movement in its espousal of extreme positions and use of exaggerated techniques, offers another explanation for such a change; most Expressionist writers abandoned Expressionism as they grew older (p. 24).

It is unfortunate that Williams turned away from the kind of drama he attempted to write in the first decade of his career, for he had the best of two worlds in the earlier successful plays. In the words of Joseph Golden, Williams had learned "from expressionism, a bolder use of symbol and metaphor and a freer handling of time and space; from naturalism, a continuing appreciation for the special characteristics and resonances within the individual characters" (p. 113). Because of Williams' "dual allegiance" in the early plays, he was able to bring to life on stage characters who lose themselves in illusions, dreams and ideals, and for whom the borderline between reality and fantasy is blurred.

John Gassner says, "The solution of the esthetic crisis in the theater depends on our knowing when and how to combine the resources of realistic and theatricalist artistry" (*Directions*, p. 138). A workable combination of realism and theatricalism occurs in Williams' earliest plays in which Expressionistic techniques deepen and refine the characterizations of unique, wholly believable human beings. The second part of this essay, analyzing Williams' most obviously Expressionistic work, illustrates that the most viable form of Expressionism for Williams, and indeed for other playwrights as well, does not sacrifice dramatic structure or complexity and realism of character in its attempt to depict the unseen.

II
Camino Real: Two Roads Diverge in a Dark Wood

Nothing quite like *Camino Real* had appeared on the stage for over thirty years, says Louis Broussard in *American Drama* (p. 7). Its technique and subject matter recall the Expressionistic extravaganzas popular in the American theater during the 1920s. It is written in the tradition of Strindberg's dream plays, *Stationen* dramas, like Kaiser's *From Morn to Midnight* and Rice's *The Adding Machine*, O'Neill's dramatizations of subjectivity, and free-wheeling fantasies with a social message, like *Beggar on Horseback* and the films of Chaplin. Since all such drama has an inbred freedom from strictures of verisimilitude in plot, characters, and setting, fair evaluation of *Camino Real* must consider the unique rules for such compositions.

Williams prefaces his serious fantasy with an epigraph from Dante's *Inferno*: "In the middle of the journey of our life I came to myself in a dark wood where the straight way was lost" (II, 417). Williams' dark wood is the Camino Real. His demand for an anglicized pronunciation (*Camino Real*) suggests the play on words that the drama makes explicit: here is a real road where once was a royal road. The setting is the plaza of a "tropical seaport." On stage left is the terrace of the luxurious Siete Mares Hotel, and on the right is Skid Row, with its loan shark's establishment, gypsy's stall, and flophouse. Like the Fairhaven and Foulstrand of Strindberg's *A Dream Play*, the two sides of the plaza are materially different but spiritually the same. The side of the plaza one inhabits matters little, for on the Camino Real everyone knows suffering and degradation. The fountain in the middle of the plaza has gone dry. The only escape from this arid world is through the upstage archway leading to "Terra Incognita," a wasteland between the plaza and the snow-capped peaks in the distance.

The play is divided into sixteen short "blocks," resembling Expressionistic "stations." Williams' final revision contains a prologue and a few characters not in the 1953 production. In the prologue Don Quixote arrives at the plaza where Sancho Panza deserts him because Camino Real is a place where "the spring of humanity has gone dry." The tired Quixote decides to sleep: "And my dream will be a pageant, a masque in which old meanings will be remembered and possibly new ones discovered, and when I wake from this sleep and this disturbing pageant of a dream, I'll choose one among its shadows to take along with me in the place of Sancho" (p. 437).

What follows is as illogical and disjointed as dreams usually are. A procession of characters from different epochs with their various torments appear on the plaza. Among them are the survivor of an exploring expedition who is brutally shot down as he seeks water at the Siete Mares; the aging Casanova forced to don cuckold's horns; Marguerite Gautier, the formerly beautiful courtesan, whose clients now rob her of both her dignity and her material possessions; the all-American Kilroy, who for reasons of health has given up a successful career as a prizefighter and finds himself cast in the role of professional buffoon, able to communicate only by lighting up his nose. In the background of the action on the Camino Real are the piping street cleaners who have the pleasant job of removing the corpses of those who perish on the plaza. Baron de Charlus, the effete aristocrat from Proust, and Lord Mulligan, a business tycoon, are among their victims. Lord Byron alone escapes the street cleaners by venturing out on the Terra Incognita, whatever the consequences. All other attempts to leave the Camino Real are futile: the unscheduled Fugitivo, the airplane which Marguerite tries unsuccessfully to board, crashes. A thread unifying the various scenes of the play is the growing tenderness between Casanova and Marguerite.

The slight narrative in this pageant of human suffering is Kilroy's. This American dreamer comes to the Camino Real with his ideals and his mementos of a happier past. He learns that Camino Real is not "a free country," when he is made to play the role of clown. Eventually helped out of his costume by Casanova, whose horns

Kilroy has kindly removed, Kilroy does what previously was inconceivable for him—sells his golden gloves for money to escape. Meanwhile the fiesta starts, and Kilroy is waylaid by the gypsy's daughter, who becomes a virgin again with each new moon. He gives up his money for the dubious pleasure of "having" the gypsy's daughter because he hears the piping of the street cleaners and realizes that "to be warm for a little longer is life"—a line which echoes Blanche's assertion that desire is the opposite of death. Kilroy faces the inevitable with courage, fighting the street cleaners off as long as he can. When he finally dies, an old woman embraces him in the manner of the Pietà. As she touches him with flowers and says, "Humankind cannot bear very much reality," he is resurrected. His embodied spirit rescues his heart—made of solid gold—from a medical research team. He pawns the heart for riches with which to tempt the gypsy's daughter and is once more degraded. In the finale Don Quixote awakens and, after admonishing the hero against self-pity, takes Kilroy with him on his journey through the Terra Incognita. In a simultaneous pantomime Casanova and Marguerite are reconciled. The waters of the dried up fountain on the Camino Real flow once more.

The prologue, which establishes the play as the dream of Don Quixote, was added to the play in a revision, perhaps to justify to puzzled audiences the play's unconventional technique. The dream is actually Williams': "my conception of the time and world that I live in" (p. 419). Williams' intention to dramatize "the continually dissolving and transforming images of a dream" (p. 420) recalls Strindberg's similar pronouncement in the preface to A Dream Play. Both dream plays are episodic; the events in the various scenes are thematically, rather than causally, related to one another. But unlike Strindberg's characters, who split, multiply, and take on different roles in each scene, Williams' characters remain "archetypes of certain basic attitudes and qualities" (p. 419).

Williams' archetypal characters come from history, legend, and literature, as well as from his own head. Don Quixote is not the only one among them who mourns "the youth of his heart" (p. 433). For all of them the royal road of beauty, health, wealth, and happiness has become the real road of age, sickness, poverty, and misery, a prelude to an undignified death as inane as the street cleaners who herald it. On the Camino Real the archetypal figures continue to act in their characteristic ways, but without the success that crowned their youthful efforts. The legendary lover, Casanova, fails in his attempt to woo a woman whom he surely would have scorned in the past. Marguerite, Dumas' Lady of the Camellias, a highclass whore, now must pay for the attention of lovers. Byron, experiencing the corruption of success, writes only bad poetry. Lord Mulligan, Williams' archetype of the wealthy businessman, learns that the death-bringing street cleaners are the only officials on the Camino Real who cannot be bribed. The Baron de Charlus, despite the nobility of his birth, cruises the poor side of the plaza, hoping to find partners for his sexual appetites. Kilroy, once in the limelight for his boxing skill, now commands attention only as a clown. As Marguerite says, "Time betrays us and we betray each other" (p. 529). So obsessed are the characters with their own problems that they offer little comfort or assistance to their colleagues. As indicated by the stage directions, the legendary characters wear "modern" clothes with only vestigial touches of the period costume. Each character then represents a legend or myth still operative in the present. The drama indicates which Williams considers the "saving myths."

Camino Real is a paean to dreamers and idealists, artists and knights errant. The only way out of the horror of the plaza is through the Terra Incognita, and the only characters to take that route are Byron, Don Quixote, and Kilroy. Byron appears only once in the play, to make a long speech in Block Eight. He proposes to go through the Terra Incognita in hopes of regaining the pure vision of his youth: *"There is a passion for declivity in this world!* And lately I've found myself listening to hired musicians behind a row of artificial palm trees—instead of the single—pure-stringed instrument of my heart . . . Well, then its time to leave here!—There is a time for departure even when there's no certain place to go" (p. 508). Like the historical Byron, Williams' character turns to classical art for inspiration and makes Greece the goal of his journey. Byron is no more likely to be effectual than Williams' other characters who seek a lost past—Amanda, Alma, Blanche. But Williams admires the mere attempt to escape human entanglements and the suffering that attends mortality. The gesture matters, not the result. Those who watch Byron disappear into the Terra Incognita—Casanova,

Marguerite, Lord Mulligan—cannot follow him, for they lack the poet's vision. For Don Quixote also the dream of what life should be is more potent than the knowledge of what life is. Having lost his companion, Sancho, and witnessed the horrifying pageant of life on the Camino Real, he yet can smile, for he believes, "the time for retreat never comes" (p. 435). In him, Williams has a ready made symbol for persistent romantic idealism. Kilroy is the knight's perfect companion, because experience teaches him nothing. His incorruptibility is a source of pride to him: the fixers never bought him, nor has he ever been unfaithful to his wife, his "real true woman." Kilroy perishes in a world where the honest and pure of heart are patsies, the official butts of fate's cruel jokes, but he struggles against that world until the very end. Although he has seen how futile it is to fight the street cleaners, he calls to them with clenched fists: "COME ON, YOU SONS OF BITCHES! KILROY IS HERE! HE'S READY" (p. 577). Even after he is dead, when he should have his mind on "higher things," he makes the same mistakes again, for he returns to the gypsy's daughter.

Byron and Don Quixote, who appear only momentarily, are undeveloped characters. Williams exploits one dimension of the personality of each for his symbolic purposes. Unfortunately, the play's major figure, Kilroy, also lacks the depth of a good dramatic character. As Walter Kerr says, "Kilroy was not here. . . . Blanche DuBois was, but not Kilroy. Kilroy was not here because Tennessee Williams forgot to invent him. He just named him, and put the name on the stage" (God on the . . . Floor, p. 172). Williams' choice of a name makes a claim for the universality of the character, who should have uniquely American personality traits. Kilroy has possibilities as a character. A sentimental prizefighter, he embodies the curious American blend of violence and innocence, but these contradictory aspects of his personality are unexplored. Williams so emphasizes Kilroy's naiveté that all other character traits recede. It is a brilliant stroke to make Kilroy wear the uniform of a patsy, but again Williams fails to realize the potential of this device. The buffoon, a figure who appears in the literature of many different ages, reflects the absurdity of the world and, in his foolishness, proves himself superior to those who treat life seriously. The buffoon is "physically undignified but eternally resilient, incapable of foresight or prudence, single-minded and simple-minded, who in his naive and unselfconscious way 'breaks down the distinction . . . between folly and wisdom'" (Pearce, p. 102). This is just the figure Williams would like Kilroy to be, but costuming alone does not make him that. Apart from blinking out the word "brother" in Morse Code with his nose, Kilroy never *acts* in his capacity as clown. Forbidden to speak in Block Six, he remains an onlooker until he sheds his costume in Block Eleven. But the inability to speak never stopped a real clown from playing his part. Kilroy is not a real clown any more than he is a real prize fighter or a real altruist. His clown outfit, golden gloves, and heart of gold are the material symbols of qualities that the character does not seem to possess.

When he first arrives on the Camino Real, Kilroy provides his whole medical history to anyone willing to listen and gives a detailed account of his experiences on "the lousiest frigging tub I ever shipped on" (p. 455) with no sick bay, no doctor, no medicine. At the end of the play he is still complaining: "Stewed, screwed and tattooed on the Camino Real! Baptized, finally, with the contents of a slop-jar! —Did anybody say the deal was rugged?!" (p. 587). No profession of faith accompanies the baptism. Though Kilroy goes with Don Quixote in search of a new life beyond Terra Incognita, he calls him a "crazy old bastard." If for no other reason than dramatic effect, Kilroy should learn something from his experiences, purge himself of baser instincts, and thereby earn his escape from the Camino Real. But by making Kilroy such a consummate example of the naive, sentimental, platitudinous American optimist, Williams precludes the character's developing. Kilroy is too obtuse to achieve enlightenment from his suffering and too inarticulate to convey a new depth of understanding. Whatever nobility the character has lies in his willingness to struggle, as strong at the beginning of the play as at the end, and not in his progress to knowledge or virtue. Kilroy, like the other archetypal figures in this play, has an unchanging, simple attitude. Possibly a good symbol for the none too bright American dreamer, Kilroy is nonetheless boring on stage. Those who have seen *Camino Real* might be tempted to repeat the words of the adjutant general's spokesman who announced on September 27, 1946: "As far as we're concerned, this Kilroy simply doesn't exist."

The other denizens of the Camino Real could use some of the consistency that the archetypal figures have in too great a measure. Gutman, the proprietor of the Siete Mares, changes personality according to the mood of the moment. He is obviously one of the persecutors on the Camino Real. He is in league with the fascist police, sneers at his guests, orders Kilroy dressed as a patsy and Casanova evicted from the hotel. Sometimes, however, he acts as a neutral master of ceremonies, introducing the characters directly to the audience. Occasionally his words belie his apparently cruel nature, as when he remarks on the pitiful effects of aging on the most cavalier adventurers. "When I observe this change," he says, "I say to myself: 'Could it happen to ME?'—The answer is 'YES!' And that's what curdles my blood like milk on the doorstep of someone gone for the summer" (p. 488). Although he knows that he too will become a victim on the Camino Real, Gutman persists in degrading the others.

Esmeralda also lacks a consistent personality. At times she is obviously her selfish money-grubbing mother's daughter, relishing the festival that restores her virginity and fills the gypsy's coffers, coy about delivering "goods" that have been paid for, insisting that Kilroy finance her trip to Acapulco. Still, she seems genuinely attached to Kilroy. She shares his pain when he is caught by the police: "Each time he is struck, Esmeralda screams as if she received the blow herself" (p. 483). The play fails to explain why she is thus set apart from the others on the Camino Real. She both contributes to and suffers from the way of life on the plaza. Finally she, like Gutman, becomes Williams' mouthpiece, asking a blessing on each of the archetypes and praying, "sometime and somewhere let there be something to mean the word *honor* again" (p. 586). At such a time Williams' dream becomes far too literal.

Apart from some conversations between Casanova and Marguerite (pp. 593–99, 513–14, 525–26), the dialogue of the play is neither believable nor consistent, suffering alternately from exaggerated colloquialism and pretensions to profundity. It is a relief to the audience when Kilroy can communicate only by lighting up his nose, for his speech is a bundle of clichés, outdated slang, and unspeakable lines ("Sometimes a man has got to hock his sweet used-to-be in order to finance his present situation," p. 462). Williams uses the exaggerated homey idiom to persuade the audience that Kilroy is the boy next door, typical product of a society that distrusts intellectual and verbal talent as much as it admires physical prowess. Because it is unnecessary to convince the audience of the reality of his developed characters, like Amanda and Blanche, Williams permits them to speak "poetically." *Camino Real* allows no respite from pedestrian dialogue. Various characters engage in "significant" word-play: "Used to be is the past tense, meaning useless" (p. 467); "I been in countries where money was not legal tender. I mean it was legal, but it wasn't tender" (p. 476); "Continue until you come to the square of a walled town which is the end of the *Camino Real* and the beginning of the *Camino Real*" (p. 435). Even more synthetic are the gypsy's flippant and trite aphorisms that summarize the play's events: "We're all of us guinea pigs in the laboratory of God. Humanity is just a work in progress" (p. 543); "The Camino Real is a funny paper read backward!"(p. 544).

Williams relies on symbolic settings and props, as well as verbal images, to objectify his nightmarish vision of modern life. The plaza, with its rich and poor sides, is a microcosm of the world of daily existence. The stairway at the rear leads to the realm of imagination, its snowcapped peaks reminiscent of Kilimanjaro (Broussard, p. 112). Most of the play's visual and verbal images are archetypal, communicating their meanings instantaneously. The plaza's dried up fountain, which flows again for Don Quixote, scarcely requires Sancho's interpretation: "the spring of humanity has gone dry in this place" (p. 435). Williams calls for a phoenix wall hanging to "be softly lighted now and then in the play, since resurrections are so much a part of its meaning" (p. 431).

The other birds mentioned in the play are not so fortunate as the phoenix, for they are caged and, for the most part, doomed to remain so. Don Quixote reads from the chart that guides him to Camino Real: "there are no birds in the country except wild birds that are tamed and kept in—*Cages*" (p. 435). Marguerite often compares herself and Casanova to caged birds: "we're a pair of captive hawks caught in the same cage, and so we've grown used to each other" (p. 526); "Caged birds accept each other but flight is what they long for" (p. 501). Byron's luggage consists "mainly" of caged birds that presumably will be freed on the Terra Incognita. When Madrecita, the old woman who symbolizes mercy, awakens Kilroy's spirit after his death, she says, "Rise, ghost! Go! Go bird" (p. 580).

Kilroy and Byron are united in their obsession with heart. Byron tells of seeing Trelawney snatch Shelley's heart from the funeral pyre and asks: "What can one man do with another man's heart?" Casanova's reply illustrates his experiences on the Camino Real: "*He can twist it . . . He can tear it . . . He can crush it under his foot!*" (p. 506). Byron replies, "That's very true, Señor. But a poet's vocation . . . is to influence the heart in a gentler fashion." A heart is "a sort of—*instrument!*—that translates *noise* into *music, chaos* into—*order*" (p. 507). Kilroy, too, "has heart," big as a baby's head and made of solid gold. In this play Williams employs all of the usual associations of heart: in Casanova heart is the seat of love; in Byron it is the source of inspiration; in Kilroy, an indication of generosity. The function of the heart symbol in the last scenes is less clear. Kilroy's snatching his heart from the medical research team is parallel to Trelawney's act. But apart from associating Kilroy with other romantics, this incident has little point. In fact, Kilroy proves that one man is unable to do very much with his own heart, even when it is made of gold. Is it misplaced romanticism, persistent obtuseness, or a refusal to admit his own death that prompts Kilroy to pawn his heart?

Despite Williams' assertion that he hates a "parade of images for the sake of images" (p. 421), Camino Real comes dangerously close to being just that. The play's imagery does not attain its significance in and through the action. Phoenixes, fountains, caged birds, and hearts are symbols independent of Williams' play. Instead of deepening or altering the usual meanings associated with these symbols, Williams uses the symbols to bestow significance on characters and actions in themselves superficial. Here are no "images for the sake of images," but images to rescue the play from triviality.

The street cleaners rightly belong in a discussion of the play's symbolism, not its characters; though they talk, laugh, and pipe tunes, they are simply death personified, if not in an archetypal, certainly in an oft-used image. Possibly Williams knew Dos Passos' Expressionist play of the 1920s, *The Moon Is a Gong*, in which death appears as a garbage man. In a German play of approximately the same period as the conception of *Camino Real,* Wolfgang Borchert's *Draußen vor der Tür,* produced in America in 1949, death is personified as a street sweeper (Bauland, pp. 167–68). The weird tune piped by Williams' street cleaners is a constant reminder of the nearness of death on the Camino Real.

Most of the remaining theatrical effects in *Camino Real* are intended to heighten spectacle. Casanova's striking the stage with his cane sets the rhythm for percussive instruments, which become louder as carnival mummers take over the plaza. Williams leaves the particulars of staging the fiesta to the director and choreographer, but describes in detail the two chase scenes that extend into the theater aisles, accompanied by searchlights and appropriate sounds: sirens, screeching brakes, pistol shots, thundering footsteps. The Keystone cops are apparently just around the corner.

That *Camino Real* has a serious theme is obvious, despite Williams' occasional lapses into slapstick. In the theme, as in the method, echoes of an earlier Expressionism are apparent. "For the expressionist," John Gassner says, "the stage was to be a means of projecting the disintegration of modern man and twentieth century society" (*Directions,* p. 109). The characters of *Camino Real* are wanderers in search of stable values in a world gone awry. Gutman says, "this is a port of entry and departure. There are no permanent guests" (p. 503). The Camino Real is a way station, albeit a most depressing one, on the journey from birth to death. The play's epigraph from the *Inferno* reinforces the pilgrimage theme. A quest for the "straight way," for meaning and happiness, figures in such Expressionist plays as *To Damascus* and *From Morn to Midnight.* Ruby Cohn says, "A quest play like *A Dream Play, Camino Real* mirrors Kilroy's quest by the separate quests of Jacques Casanova, Proust's Baron de Charlus, Lord Byron, and the arch-dreamer Don Quixote" (p. 122). Kilroy is not, however, sufficiently complex to mirror the experiences of the other characters. The poet, lover, rich man, effete noble, and naive American seem rather to be fragments of Williams' personality. The suffering that the archetypal figures undergo may reflect Williams' own experience generally, though not strictly autobiographically. Williams shares with earlier Expressionist dramatists, including Strindberg and O'Neill, a tendency to rework his personal life in his plays.

In the course of the scenes depicting the suffering of those on the quest, Williams satirizes some institutions of modern civilization. Thus he has "Grotesque mummers act as demon customs inspectors and immigration authorities" (p. 515). The gypsy engages with Kilroy in a spoof of the official interview when she asks him about his childhood diseases, makes him sign a meaningless form, and tells him to roll up his sleeve for "a shot of some kind." In another scene she expresses the malaise of modern life in the form of an advertisement for tonic (p. 458). Although Williams says that the fiesta is a "serio-comic, grotesque-lyric 'Rites of Fertility' with roots in various pagan cultures" (p. 533), its relation to all kinds of religious rituals is apparent. Williams also satirizes some less institutionalized rituals. Kilroy and Esmeralda engage in a ridiculous parody of lovemaking in which climax is reached by raising Esmeralda's spangled veil. In the satirical scenes, which are the play's best, Williams writes in the tradition of Expressionism popularized by Kaufman and Connelly in the 1920s in *Beggar on Horseback*. Expressionism's verbal and visual exaggerations are effective tools for revealing the absurdity of mechanistic procedures and conventional behavior.

But indicting society is not Williams' primary purpose in *Camino Real*. Like Strindberg, and unlike most German Expressionists, Williams locates the ultimate source of man's problems not in social institutions but in the conditions of mortal existence. Hope necessarily gives way to despair as youthful idealism ceases to transform cold facts. The characters on the Camino Real suffer because time, not society, has betrayed them. All of them would like to make the journey that Byron alone undertakes, "From my present self to myself as I used to be!" (p. 503). Like many of Williams' characters, they are obsessed, even immobilized by thoughts of a happier past. Casanova saves fragile mementos in his portmanteau, Marguerite balks at substituting black gloves for white ones, Kilroy clings to his golden gloves. The happier past, which in some of Williams' plays is a mere product of the imagination of congenital have-nots, is a reality for those on the Camino Real. Success, far from insulating one from the ravages of time, makes one more vulnerable. To these victims of time, Williams offers the cold comfort of Terra Incognita.

Although the play ironically undermines romantic notions about love, fame, and death, it is designed to perpetuate romantic idealism. *Camino Real* affirms the ability to rise above the world, time, and necessity. When the conditions and events of daily human existence become intolerable, they can be left behind. A leap of faith takes one over the wall. The escape from Camino Real is reminiscent of the ending of Williams' early unpublished fantasy, *Stairs to the Roof*, in which the persecuted protagonists are simply whisked away to a better world. Terra Incognita, whether or not it leads to a better world, is preferable to the plaza. The movement of Byron, Kilroy, and Don Quixote away from the Camino Real reflects Williams' own response to life, for he admits his writing provides an escape from unbearable reality. Each of the three romantics in *Camino Real* has his own reasons for retreating from the plaza. Byron seems inspired more by nostalgia than by artistic considerations. A touch of madness prompts Don Quixote to go on. After some false starts, Kilroy finally enters Terra Incognita on impulse. While the play mocks naive optimism, expressed in Kilroy's belief that the American Consulate and the Y.M.C.A. can right all wrongs, it ends by endorsing an even more profound belief in pie in the sky. Whatever the source and motivation, the renunciation of reality for the pursuit of a dream is superior to adapting to life on the Camino Real.

But since few are equipped for an escape into the imagination, and many might deem it futile, Williams uses the Casanova-Marguerite subplot to present another "cure" for the pain of living. Casanova's role is to pursue Marguerite, offering her quiet companionship if she will not accept love. In Block Ten Marguerite expresses her discouraging view of the possibility for meaningful relationships on the Camino Real: "we huddle together for some dim-communal comfort—and that's what passes for love on this terminal stretch of the road that used to be royal. . . . But tenderness, the violets in the mountains—can't break the rocks!" (p. 527). Yet in Block Sixteen, under the influence of the romantic Don Quixote, she gives her hand in love to Casanova, as Quixote announces: *"The violets in the mountains have broken the rocks!"* (p. 591). Marguerite's change of heart is inexplicable. True, she has had another unhappy encounter with a younger man, but previous similar experiences did not reconcile her to the old Casanova. Nor does the plot support the supposition that love on the Camino Real is lasting. Williams' point is clear: idealism conquers the limitations of mortality, love temporarily makes them bearable.

Like Strindberg's *A Dream Play*, in which a bud on top of a castle mired in dung suddenly bursts into flower just before the play ends, *Camino Real* extends its ray of hope only in the last minute. Both plays are monuments to the overwhelming strength of evil in the world. The happy end to the quest seems almost tacked on. The Terra Incognita appropriately remains hidden behind a high wall, unknown, insubstantial, without artistic realization. In his failure to give form to his "solution," Williams is no different from his German Expressionist forebears, who were rather less specific about the nature of the new society they heralded than about the forces preventing its emergence.

In this play Williams conveys the same theme that *The Glass Menagerie* and *A Streetcar Named Desire* embodied: survival with dignity is possible only when the inner life and the imagination maintain primacy over the outer life and the mere facts of existence. In the earlier plays the theme arises organically from Williams' depiction of the problems which Laura and Blanche face in a world in which sensitivity is not valued. The audience readily agrees that Laura's voluntary and Blanche's involuntary exile from the world are necessary and preferable to adjustment. Assent to *Camino Real's* similar proposition is not so readily given. In failing to come to terms with the problems inherent in the play's highly subjective form, Williams obscures the relevance and seriousness of his theme.

In a dream play a dramatist must work with a structure, theatrical conventions, and methods of characterization vastly different from those of a play which seeks to imitate objective reality. Because a chronological and causal sequence of events is not suitable for dramatizing internal action, Expressionistic drama is often episodic, but not necessarily lacking in dramatic structure. O'Neill's *The Emperor Jones* uses reverse chronology to dramatize the reversion to primitive fears of a black potentate as he relives the history of his race. The structure of Strindberg's *A Dream Play* is more subtle; Evert Sprinchorn diagrams the scenes to show that the drama reflects the action of the subconscious in sinking into a dream and awakening from it

(p. 354). Notwithstanding Williams' remarks in the foreword about the "painstaking design" of *Camino Real*, his play suffers from a lack of structure. The scenes occur in no necessary order; reshuffling them would not alter the play. Byron enters and leaves in Block Eight, but he could just as well say his speech in Block Three or Block Sixteen. Apart from the notion that it is nice to have a spectacle near the end of the play, no dramatic necessity requires the fiesta and the encounter between Kilroy and the gypsy's daughter to occur when they do. No sense of development ties the discrete scenes of *Camino Real* to one another. Thus the whole point of the *Stationen* drama, depicting progressive stages of internal action, is lost in this play. *A Streetcar Named Desire*, with scenes that reveal the increasing desperation of Blanche, is far closer to the spirit of *Stationen* drama.

The writer of a dream play has more freedom in his use of the elements of theatrical art; for setting, props, lighting, movement, music, sounds, even language need not reflect only what may occur in actuality. He can, as Williams does, conjure up a place that could not exist and make a metaphor visible, like Kilroy's golden heart. But distortions of objective reality must be handled with care in a play with a serious theme, because unnatural and exaggerated things tend to be funny. Williams employs Expressionistic techniques derived from comedians of the silent film and from the Marx Brothers, when he has his characters abandon the stage to pursue one another into the theater aisles and the balcony. But Williams' assignment of a ponderously serious meaning to these amusing interludes results in a tonal inconsistency. The audience is asked to accept as real and significant the persecutions of Kilroy which are punctuated by scenes of horseplay and burlesque. The Keystone cops hardly belong in a play with an epigraph from Dante's *Inferno*. The bum in the window, with his drunken rendering of "appropriate and contrapuntal song titles," is another gratuitous and heavyhanded device. Williams' combination of the humorous and the serious functions best when his touch is light, when he intertwines in a single gesture comedy and pathos (Amanda's selling magazine subscriptions) or comedy and menace (Stanley's speech on the Napoleonic code). Broad comedy and no less subtle "intellectualism" vie with one another in *Camino Real*. The audience must adjust its responses to the constantly shifting tone of the play, which partakes alternately of slapstick, nightmare, and sermon.

The most serious flaw of *Camino Real* is the failure in characterization. According to Eric Bentley (*Life of the Drama*), a playwright should avoid "static portraits on the analogy of painting" and present instead "the dynamics of relationship" (p. 63). Bentley is right, whether the playwright employs the type characters that have been drama's staple for centuries or the psychologically developed characters of the verisimilitudinous drama. The characters of *Camino Real* are static portraits—portraits not drawn by Williams, but lifted from his wide but superficial reading. They are static because they scarcely interact with one another or alter in the slightest in the course of the play. Plays like *To Damascus, From Morn to Midnight*, and *The Adding Machine* also reduce characters to one or two salient traits, but for the purpose of exploring the mind and emotions of the central character, who is defined by the fragmentary figures around him and who changes through his contact with them. Neither Don Quixote, whose dream *Camino Real* is supposed to be, nor Kilroy, who is the play's ostensible hero, is defined by the other figures; neither is more than one-dimensional. Williams takes the easy way out in fashioning the characters of *Camino Real*. "Rather than building a character to reflect a universal attitude," Nelson says, "Williams simply uses a known character and relies on allusions to do the work for him" (p. 192). The choice of figures familiar to the audience simplifies exposition, but does not obviate the need to develop the characters. Believable, rounded characters help establish the "realism in the objective or literal sense which seems to be necessary to hold the spectator and his interest in Expressionism" (Milton, p. 114). Although characters in dream plays need not possess detailed psychological histories, nothing is lost by giving them individualizing traits—and much can be gained. One method of injecting believable characters into a dream play is to use, as Kaufman and Connelly do in *Beggar on Horseback*, an extended realistic frame to establish the literal reality of the figures who then behave in fantastic ways in the dream sequence. Strindberg even manages to convince the audience of the reality of characters who "split" and "multiply" in *A Dream Play*, by having them adopt familiar roles—wife, husband, lover, mother. In *Camino Real* the only character who seems to reveal genuine human emotions is Marguerite as she suffers the pangs of aging. She alone changes in the course of the play, but Williams frustratingly provides no explanation for her actions. On stage are attitudes and qualities, not people.

Williams fails to do in this play what he does so well in *The Glass Menagerie* and *A Streetcar Named Desire*—elicit sympathy for the desperate and powerless. Comedy makes Kilroy's sufferings seem slight. The other characters, limited to basic personality traits, can suffer only as befits their narrow natures. Thus, Casanova is cuckolded. Marguerite, who accepted jewelry as payment for the love she gave, now pays in kind. What Williams insists the audience view as torment seems little more than poetic justice. The degenerate Baron and the haughty Mulligans complete the cast of the "downtrodden" who "cannot bear very much reality." Without constant reminders that these are faded, frightened, broken souls, one might think that Williams was mocking them.

Just as *Camino Real* should not be condemned for failing to possess traits proper only to the drama of verisimilitude, it ought not be excused for faults that dream plays can avoid. John Styan writes of dream plays that "the one consciousness must not be the author's alone: it must be no less than the spectator's in the theatre" (*The Dark Comedy*, p. 119). The consciousness of the author and that of the spectator do not merge in a production of *Camino Real*. The summary of the action in the prayer of the gypsy's daughter and the moral delivered by Don Quixote are Williams' admissions of the failure of the play's action to communicate the meaning he assigns to it. *A Streetcar Named Desire* presents no moral, for the action speaks for itself. Harold Clurman (*Divine Pastime*) rightly points out that *Camino Real*, "Instead of being the surrealist phantasmagoria it intends to be, is far too literal" (p. 22). Because of Williams' fear that the audience may miss the serious point of the spectacle on stage, *Camino Real* explains itself ad nauseam.

Although nothing quite like *Camino Real* had appeared on the American stage for thirty years, the play is not an aberration in Williams' dramatic development. Throughout the 1940s Williams had attempted to use theatrical devices for depiction of subjective experience, regardless of any violation of verisimilitude. The screen device of *The Glass Menagerie,* the transparent wall of *A Streetcar Named Desire,* and the haunting music of the early plays are embryonic forms of the Expressionism that dominates *Camino Real.* In *The Glass Menagerie* and *A Streetcar Named Desire,* however, Williams first created believable characters and then set about delving into their minds through stage devices, and thus he avoided the fatal pitfall of Expressionism, described by Galsworthy as picturing "the inside of things without showing their outside" (quoted in Gassner, *Theatre,* p. 203). True, the inside of things lies bare in *Camino Real,* but we don't believe in it, because the outside fails to carry conviction. *Camino Real's* epigraph is an apt comment on the play's creation as well as its action, for Williams, no less than his characters, has lost the straight way. Two roads diverge in a dark wood: Williams' royal road and the real road to drama.

Tennessee Williams:
Optimistic Symbolist

JUNE BENNETT LARSEN

TENNESSEE WILLIAMS is a direct descendant of the Symbolists, whose concern with man's struggle against the void led them to seek refuge in dreams. Their wish for surroundings congenial to the fragile poetic spirit meant a rejection of realism in drama. To communicate through a medium transcending ordinary language, they created an evocative new language of symbols. They were fascinated with the past, especially with the Medieval period. Their work often resulted in mixed dramatic forms that included music. The new drama abounded with dualisms, especially dream-reality and life-death. Rejecting the old concept that art imitates nature, the Symbolists demanded that nature imitate art. To the Symbolists, artificiality was a way of being true to nature. Unlike Williams, theirs was not an actors' theater, for, ideally, actors in Symbolist plays were little more than marionettes.

At the core of the Symbolists' retreat from reality was the decadent spirit. One aspect of decadence revealed a taste for the morbid and the perverse. Androgynous figures were popular subjects in many Symbolist paintings. The darker Symbolist artists, such as Fernand Khnopff, often painted fierce deathlike chimeras, whereas the lighter Symbolists featured more benign androgynous figures as subjects in their paintings. In literature, the central figure in Karl Huysmans'

413

novel, *A Rebours*, is a hyperaesthetic effete who seeks new sensations in attempting to relieve the ennui of daily existence. In the theater one of the first Symbolist plays was the lengthy *Axël* by Villiers de l'Isle-Adam, in which the central characters, Axël and Sara, seem to be two parts of an androgyny. In a recent interview in *Playboy* (Jennings, p. 72), Williams discusses his fascination with androgyny, especially androgynous males.

Yet another and more significant aspect of the decadent spirit was the Symbolists' concern with the mystery of life. They recognized the immediacy of death and were always haunted by isolation and mortality. Edgar Allan Poe, especially as presented by Baudelaire, was the inspiration for many of these writers. Poe influences Williams both directly and by way of the French and German Symbolists. Poe and Williams, both Southerners, share a mystique about death that has always been a preoccupation in the South. Edward H. Davidson says, "It is not enough to say that Poe . . . capitalized on a popular commodity of his day . . . in the dramaturgy of death and the dead. . . . from the Gothic romances to the very popular gift annals and periodicals of the day, the corpse, the tomb, the mourning survivor were so frequent as to be almost overwhelming. The first half of the nineteenth century, at the popular level at least, shuddered to its heart's content; and the delight in fictive death did not abate until death became a real matter of common life in the Civil War" (*Poe: A Critical Study*, pp. 105–6). So indigenous was the South's preoccupation with death, and with death made fashionable, that Mark Twain brilliantly satirized the subject in *The Adventures of Huckleberry Finn*: Emmeline Grangerford pastes newspaper obituaries, accounts of gory accidents and tales of human suffering into scrapbooks and writes odes to the dead. Despite the shock of death as a daily living reality, the South renewed and even intensified its preoccupation after the war was over; and, indeed, the fascination persists today.

Paradoxically, death has been a life-force for the greatest portion of Tennessee Williams' work. He has almost consistently written during periods when he believed himself to be dying. The belief that he is dying appears crucial to his creativity and also provides much of the content of his work. Despite Williams' acknowledged preoccupation with death, he also believes it can be put off: "I've almost

died so many times, but I didn't die because I didn't really want to.
. . . I think I can delay death. . . . I think a lot of my work has dealt
with death. I have a preoccupation with death and a preoccupation
with sensuality—" (*Playboy*, p. 76). Consequently, much of his work,
while concerned with the grotesqueries of life, is often very optimistic. Williams here parts company with the early Symbolists; for
while he is acutely aware of man's inevitable fate, he does not believe that life is futile. Most of his characters never really abandon
life for they are always reaching out for something and usually someone. A word appearing with uncommon frequency in his work is
outcry. It is even the title and the major symbol of a recent Williams
play that Clive Barnes said "will one day be regarded as one of the
most remarkable symbolist plays of the 20th-century" ("Tennessee:
A National Treasure," Washington, D.C.: *Stagebill*, February 1975,
p. 27). Although the cries of his characters are seldom heard, they
do cry out. When asked in the *Playboy* interview why he had changed
the title of *The Two-Character Play* to *Out Cry*, Williams replied,
"It fits so perfectly. I had to *cry out*, and I did. It's the only possible
title. At one point, the actress cries out, 'Out, out, human out cry.'
It's about two people who are afraid to go out. 'To play with fear is
to play with fire,' one of them says, and the other replies, 'No, fear
is worse'" (p. 80). (The lines as Williams quotes them to the interviewer do not appear in *Out Cry*, 1973, a revision of *The Two-
Character Play*. But see the variants on pp. 66, 67. The most recent
published version, reentitled *The Two-Character Play*, has most of
the lines. See V, 309, 334, 363.)

Williams was referring not only to his play but also to what he
personally endured during the sixties with alcoholism, drug addiction, severe depression, nervous breakdowns and heart attacks,
largely caused by the criticism and consequent failure of his plays.
He, like Poe, was for a time confined to an asylum. Williams differs
from Poe, however, in being a *survivor*. Through sheer force of will,
he extricated himself from the chasm. "Well, that was the end of
my long death wish," as he said in the *Playboy* interview (p. 78).

Williams denounced critics for their treatment of *Slapstick
Tragedy*, *Kingdom of Earth*, *In the Bar of a Tokyo Hotel*, and of
course *Out Cry*. A much earlier work, *Camino Real*, was also rejected. This group of plays shares with others the influence of the

Symbolist aesthetic. Williams says the critics "want to try to judge you on traditional form when you're trying to move to something freer, like presentational theater, when you depart from realism—... The critics still want me to be a poetic realist, and I never was. All my *great* characters are larger than life, not realistic" (*Playboy*, p. 80).

"Plastic" is Williams' term for the antirealistic theater that he described as long ago as 1945 in his production notes for *The Glass Menagerie*. The passage reads like a Symbolist manifesto: "Expressionism and all other unconventional techniques in drama have only one valid aim, and that is a closer approach to truth. When a play employs unconventional techniques, it is not, or certainly shouldn't be, trying to escape its responsibility of dealing with reality, or interpreting experience, but is actually or should be attempting to find a closer approach, a more penetrating and vivid expression of things as they are. . . . These remarks are not meant as a preface only to this particular play. They have to do with a conception of a new, plastic theatre which must take the place of the exhausted theatre of realistic conventions if the theatre is to resume vitality as a part of our culture" (I, 131).

The idea of a plastic theater derives from Wagner's concept of synthesis and the ideas of his Symbolist followers whose goal was to create a new syntax of poetic conventions that transcended ordinary language. Wagner sought a fusion of music, poetry, and all areas of design. Similarly, Williams strives for a synthesis of poetry, music, dance, mime, and all theatrical elements of design, including such modern devices as the film screen. Wagner insisted on complete control over production, and all evidence seems to point toward his subordination of other theatrical components to the authority of music. Williams' concept seems more theatrically successful, for he has achieved a more nearly perfect fusion of all components. No single element towers over another—not even language, for Williams' drama is not primarily didactic. His theatrical goal is transformation through sensual evocation by synthesizing all artistic components (cf. Jackson, pp. 88–108).

Many of Tennessee Williams' plays employ symbolic titles (*The Glass Menagerie, A Streetcar Named Desire*). Yet, ironically, those plays that most clearly reflect the Symbolist aesthetic are devoid of symbolic titles. Among the best examples are *Suddenly Last Summer, Out Cry, Camino Real,* and the two plays comprising *Slapstick Tragedy: The Mutilated* and *The Gnädiges Fräulein.*

On the surface, *Suddenly Last Summer* (1958) least resembles a Symbolist play because the set would not seem to be stylized although its appearance should be exotic. However, Williams notes in his stage directions that "The set may be as unrealistic as the decor of a dramatic ballet" (III, 349). The mise en scène is a tropical garden, part of a Victorian Gothic mansion in an area of New Orleans known as the Garden District. Williams further notes that, along with giant ferns and other tropical foliage, "There are massive tree-flowers that suggest organs of a body, torn out, still glistening with undried blood; there are harsh cries and sibilant hissings and thrashing sounds in the garden as if it were inhabited by beasts, serpents and birds, all of savage nature" (p. 349).

Mrs. Violet Venable is a wealthy, elderly woman who has secluded herself in her palatial home since the demise of her only child, Sebastian, whose death dominates the play. Mrs. Venable has summoned a very young, very handsome doctor to her home to bribe him to perform a frontal lobotomy on her niece who has been confined in an institution for the emotionally disturbed. The niece Catharine arrives, accompanied by her avaricious mother and brother, and a nun, ironically named Sister Felicity, who guards Catharine's every move. The dualism of life and death pervades the play. On one of their annual summer retreats to remote areas of the world, Mrs. Venable and Sebastian visited the Galapagos Islands where they witnessed the hatching of giant sea turtles: "It's a long and dreadful thing, the depositing of the eggs in the sand pits, and when it's finished the exhausted female turtle crawls back to the sea half dead. She never sees her offspring, but we did. Sebastian knew exactly when the sea turtle eggs would be hatched out and we returned for it . . ." (III, 355). Mrs. Venable goes on to describe the volcanoes known as the Encantadas, the beach that was "the color of caviar," and the sky full of flesh-eating birds waiting for the hatched turtles to make their race to the sea. As Violet Venable completes the description the "wild, ravenous, harsh cries" of birds are heard in the background: "And the sand all alive, all alive, as the hatched sea turtles made their dash for the sea, while the birds hovered and—swooped to attack! They were diving down on the hatched sea turtles, turning them over to expose their soft undersides, tearing the undersides open and rending and eating their flesh" (p. 356).

In that far off Galapagos Island, Sebastian Venable was looking for God. He was a self-styled poet who wrote one poem a year; and, reminiscent of a Symbolist recluse, he printed it himself on an eighteenth century handpress at his atelier in the French Quarter so no one could see it. Williams describes Mrs. Venable showing the doctor the book of poetry: "She lifts a thin gilt-edged volume from the patio table as if elevating the Host before the altar. Its gold leaf and lettering catch the afternoon sun. . . . At the same instant a bird sings clearly and purely in the garden" (p. 353).

As the play unfolds in the blaze of an afternoon sun, Catharine reveals the truth about Sebastian Venable—the truth that his mother wants cut from her brain. Sebastian was an effete homosexual who sought the beautiful, the talented, and the young, who used his mother to procure for him until she was disfigured by a stroke. In the last summer of his life, Sebastian asked Catharine to accompany him to a Mediterranean island called Cabeza de Lobo where he changed his fastidious ways. Using Catharine as a procuress, he went to a public beach where his activities eventually antagonized a band of starving boys who devoured parts of his body. The analogy in the deaths of the sea turtles and Sebastian Venable is unmistakable. His death sets in motion the action of the play. In the reclusive life that he led, in his retreats to remote areas of the globe in search of God, Sebastian bears remarkable resemblance to his turn-of-the-century counterparts. Ironically, however, he is never seen. Yet it is principally through this character that Williams evidences the influence of the Symbolist aesthetic, for it is through Sebastian that he threads the themes of perversity and death. The ending of the play, however, is positive, for the doctor considers the possibility that Catharine's story might be true.

Unlike the two plays that comprise *Garden District* (*Suddenly Last Summer* and *Something Unspoken*), the two plays of *Slapstick Tragedy* (1966) are companion pieces. Both *The Mutilated* and *The Gnädiges Fräulein* deal with outcasts from society, the dualities of life-death and flesh-spirit, and dwell on the grotesque. Williams treats the grotesque humorously, which explains the slapstick of tragedy. In this approach he differs from the early Symbolists, who found little or no humor in life.

In his production note for *The Mutilated*, Williams describes the two sets to be "as delicate as Japanese line drawings; they should be so abstract, so spidery, with the exception of Trinket Dugan's bedroom, that the audience will accept the nonrealistic style of the play" (*Dragon Country*, p. 79). The mise en scène is a slum hotel in New Orleans. It is Christmas and carollers sing verses in a sort of prologue, after various scenes, and at the end of the play in a sort of epilogue. They are led by the character of Jack In Black, symbol of death.

The two main characters embody the duality of flesh and spirit. Celeste is a frumpish, alcoholic whore whose chief attraction is a more than ample bosom. Trinket poses as a ladylike ex-stripper turned wino recluse because of a mastectomy—her mutilation. Despite a conflict between the two women, they need each other, for they are outcasts—"freaks"—Celeste by birth and Trinket by choice. They are inhabitants of a small and isolated world of outcasts who have been abandoned by, or who have abandoned, society. Their companions in the play include whores, pimps, hotel clerks, sailors, bartenders, and "drag queens" who populate the Silver Dollar Hotel and Cafe Boheme. Another "freak" in their midst is the "Bird-Girl." Offered as a street attraction, she is the embodiment of human degradation. When she loses some of her glued-on feathers, Celeste speaks a bitter truth about the human condition: "If she was a bird, the humane society would be interested in her situation but since she's a human being, they couldn't care less" (p. 87). Williams' implication is clear. Throughout the play, bitterness and humor are woven into a single strand of dramatic irony.

With the nearness of death, the earthy Celeste convinces the deeply religious Trinket that the spirit of the Virgin Mary has entered Trinket's heart. The pain leaves Trinket's breast, and yet another miracle occurs on Christmas Eve. Death is forestalled as the spirit triumphs over the flesh. In the epilogue Jack In Black sings solo:

I'm Jack In Black who stacks the deck,
Who loads the dice and tricks the wheel.
The bell has stopped because I smile.
It means forget me for a while.

He then "moves his lifted hat from left to right in the style of a matador dedicating his fight to the audience" (pp. 129–130) as the curtain falls.

The characters in *The Gnädiges Fräulein* are equally grotesque and comic. Molly and Polly are, respectively, a proprietor of a shabby boarding house and an undistinguished member of the fourth estate. The star boarder at Molly's establishment is the Gnädiges Fräulein, an ex-soubrette fallen on hard times, given to singing and reading her press clippings when not engaged in competition with the coca-loony birds for fish to pay her rent. The object of the women's admiration is a character named Indian Joe, who has little dialogue and who "doesn't have to be anything but an erotic fantasy in appearance, but with a dancer's sense of presence and motion onstage" (*Dragon Country*, p. 218). They reside on a southernmost Florida key that Williams calls "Cocaloony" after the overgrown sea birds that inhabit the reef and the play. The sense of distance and proximity of water is consistent with the sense of isolation so apparent in early Symbolist plays.

The stage set is the porch of Molly's frame cottage which requires a stylized arrangement of wicker rockers and other assorted porch props, steps, yard, and picket fence. It is to be in "the subtle variety of grays and grayish whites that you see in pelican feathers and clouds. Even the sun is a grayish-white disk over the lustreless gray zinc roof that sits at the angle of Charlie Chaplin's derby" (p. 217). In contrast to this exterior is the interior of Molly's boarding house to which the audience is afforded only brief glimpses: "once or twice in the play a bloom of light behind the window reveals a poetically incongruous Victorian parlor, like the parlor of a genteel bordello in the eighties or nineties, and this alone violates the chromatic scale of the pelican: it is a riotous garden of colors, provided by crimson damask, gilt frames and gilded tassels, a gaudy blackamoor pedestal for a light fixture" (p. 217). This contrast is symbolically reflected in costumes as well as set. Molly and Polly are in pelican shades while the Fräulein wears the remnants of a theatrical costume which "would not be out of place at the Moulin Rouge in the time of Toulouse-Lautrec" (p. 230). A conspicuous article of her costume is a blood-stained eyepatch.

Like *The Mutilated*, *The Gnädiges Fräulein* uses music and dance. Williams indicates that the role of the Fräulein should be played by a singer since she is an ex-soubrette who, to paraphrase one of Molly's speeches, is long past the zenith of her career in show business and as a bar girl at local juke joints and has transferred her battleground for survival to the fish docks. Like Trinket Dugan, she is mutilated: she loses both eyes to the cocaloonies in a fight over fish. Swooshing sounds of cocaloonies are heard throughout the play, and one appears briefly and has a stylized dance with Indian Joe. (The Bird-Girl of *The Mutilated* doubles as the cocaloony in this second play.) The Fräulein gradually takes on the characteristics of the cocaloony as she increasingly begins to waddle and flap about the stage.

In the union of cocaloonies, the Fräulein is looked upon as a "wildcat operator." Molly says, "Nothing is more intolerant . . . than one parasite of another" (p. 238). In the daily battle for survival when the fish boats whistle, the cocaloonies and the Fräulein swoop to the docks to claim their haul for the day. When the soubrette triumphantly returns with a mackerel she is challenged by a cocaloony. The duel occurs offstage and a human outcry is heard. The Fräulein re-enters in defeat, singing with her hands clasped spiritually together, and a large bloody bandage is tied around her orange-pink curls in a butterfly bow. Williams is very specific about her appearance: "Her costume is the same except that her tulle skirt, or tou-tou, is spangled with fresh drops of blood that glitter like rubies and her legs, bare from mid-thigh to ankle, are likewise streaked with blood. However, her voice is clear and sweet as a bird's: I mean songbird's. Her motions are slow, very slow. Now and then she extends a thin arm, to feel her way forward as she is still moving forward. She is transfigured as a saint under torture" (p. 245). Maimed and mutilated, she is nevertheless undaunted, for at the end of the play when the fishboats are heard again, the Fräulein grabs her bucket and runs with the cocaloonies to compete for the catch.

In its theme of survival, *The Gnädiges Fräulein* veers in the direction of realism rather than Symbolism. The significant element, however, is Williams' *treatment* of his material. The antirealistic style is organically related to that of the Symbolist aesthetic.

Out Cry is not only a two-character play but also a play-within-a-play. With its sense of isolation, the dualisms of dream-reality and life-death, its enigmatic quality, and foreboding ending, *Out Cry* is perhaps the purest example of the Symbolist aesthetic.

The external play that frames the interior action involves a brother and sister who have been deserted by other members of an itinerant theatrical troupe of which they were the heads. The pair find themselves in a "state theater of a state unknown" (p. 9) with no clear memory of how they got there. The departed company sent a telegram saying they left because "Your sister and you are—*insane!*" (p. 17). Clare explains to her brother, who had once been confined in an asylum, that they were abandoned because of his wild and erratic behavior. Felice, as his name suggests, is an androgynous male whom his sister calls "hermaphroditic." He insists that they fulfill their engagement by performing *The Two-Character Play*, to which Clare objects because she knows the play has no ending. Felice warns that *The Two-Character Play* must continue. The performance of the "play" comprises the interior action.

Williams specifies that the stage should be naked and almost bare except for a fragmented set dominated by a huge, dark, monolithic statue, symbolic of "things anguished and perverse" (p. 7), which Felice demoniacally and unsuccessfully tries to remove. A stairway spirals upward and stops in space. Images are projected on a backdrop. Felice announces the presentation of *The Two-Character Play* to an audience that is, in reality, not there. The *imagined* setting of the "play" is a house shielded by giant golden sunflowers in a small southern town called New Bethesda.

The "reality" of the play becomes confused with the supposed fantasy of the play-within-the-play since Felice and Clare are *themselves* the characters in the "play." This second interior plot reveals the brother and sister together in the house bereft of provisions or money. They are too frightened to leave even to seek urgently needed help. It soon becomes apparent that they are imprisoned by fear and guilt, symbolized by the giant golden sunflowers surrounding the house. It also becomes apparent that the two are acting out their past. Their fear of the truth, as well as the truth of their fear, finally surfaces when we discover that their father had killed their mother and then turned the gun on himself. The tragedy resulted in the insurance company withholding payment of the death claim, with ostracism and ridicule by neighbors, and creditors causing seclusion to the point of starvation. To no avail, each prompts the other to seek help in the outside world. The tension builds on two levels: that caused by their confinement in the "house" as they deliberate what action to take and that caused by their confinement in the otherwise empty theater. It reaches a climax when the past and the present converge and the dark secret of incest is obliquely revealed. Clare frantically attempts to stop the "play" by calling out "Line!" for a line of dialogue. She eventually succeeds, and the "performance" is momentarily suspended. The two prepare to leave the theater only to discover that they are locked inside a building that "is windowless as a casket" (p. 66). Confinement in the cold, dimly lighted theater, like confinement in the "house," is a projection of their emotional states. As Clare realizes that her brother is truly mad her fear increases to panic. Screaming "Out! Out! Out!" she grabs a prop phone only to realize that it, like the spiral stairway, will get her nowhere. Her human outcry cannot be heard. Imprisoned in a fusion of reality and fantasy, she defeatedly goes back into *The Two-Character Play*.

Actually, *Camino Real* (1953) was Tennessee Williams' first major work reflecting the Symbolist aesthetic. In his foreword Williams wrote that it was his "desire to give these audiences my own sense of something wild and unrestricted that ran like water in the mountains, or clouds changing shape in a gale, or the continually dissolving and transforming images of a dream. This sort of freedom is not chaos nor anarchy. On the contrary, it is the result of painstaking design, and in this work I have given more conscious attention to form and construction than I have in any work before. Freedom is not achieved simply by working freely" (II, 420).

Camino Real is the quintessential example of Williams' concept of plastic theater. It presents a synthesis of poetry, music, mime, dance, lighting and spectacle. The action is not confined to the stage. The entire theater auditorium was utilized by Williams and the director Elia Kazan.

Consistent with the Symbolists' sense of isolation from the real world, the setting is a walled seaport town of no specific locality called the Camino Real. The action exists outside of time. Structurally the play is divided into a prologue and sixteen blocks (scenes) on the Camino Real. Again like his Symbolist antecedents, Williams looked to the past: his characters are an archetypal mixture from legend and fiction as well as history. Along with the familiar dualities of life-death and dream-reality is the added duality of past-present. The theme is evident in the character of Kilroy, the name of the fictitious and ubiquitous American soldier who left the inscription "Kilroy was here" on walls and property all over the world during and after World War II. As a symbol of one who travels a great deal, Kilroy brings together the present with the past. The journey of yet another traveler, Don Quixote, frames the action. In the prologue he enters by an aisle of the theater accompanied by Sancho Panza. They have lost their way, and Sancho reads from a chart: "Continue until you come to the square of a walled town which is the end of the Camino Real and the beginning of the Camino Real. Halt there . . . and turn back, Traveler, for the spring of humanity has gone dry in this place . . ." (p. 435).

Sancho refuses to accompany his master into the town and returns to La Mancha. Quixote falls asleep to dream and does not awake until near the end of the play. As "The Nightingale of France" is played on a mandolin, Quixote says before falling asleep: "And my dream will be a pageant, a masque in which old meanings will be remembered and possibly new ones discovered, and when I wake from this sleep and this disturbing pageant of a dream, I'll choose one among its shadows to take along with me in the place of Sancho" (p. 437).

The characters are allegorically divided into dreamers and realists, good and evil. All are trapped in the squalor of the wasteland known as the Camino Real. The phantasmagoria unfolds, and a hunchback shakes a hoop of bells announcing the appearance of each of the legendary characters, all of whom are dreamers and therefore "good." In addition to Quixote are Marguerite Gautier, Casanova, Esmeralda (from Victor Hugo's The Hunchback of Notre Dame), and even the once real poet, Lord Byron (played by the same actor who plays Quixote). Also among the dreamers are La Madrecita and her son; The Survivor; and The Dreamer, who never speaks but plays melancholy music on the mandolin. Those who personify evil (realists) include Gutman, the archetypal stormtrooper who governs the Camino Real and, as narrator, announces the block numbers in the procession of scenes; The Gypsy, mother and prostitutor of Esmeralda; Nursie, an effeminate man "in drag" as a duenna; and an assortment of officers and street people, including the aging and avaricious whores Prudence and Olympe (antitheses of Marguerite Gautier in *La Dame aux Camélias*), and the Streetcleaners in swallowtail coats who are symbols of death.

Into this mélange enters the beaten hero, Kilroy, the naive young southern American whose heart, though weak, is as big as a baby's head and made of solid gold. He is a former boxer who wears a pair of golden gloves slung around his neck and a ruby and emerald studded belt proclaiming *Champ* in bold letters. In Kilroy's fight for life and dreams, the evil realist Gutman pronounces him "The Eternal Punchinella" and makes him wear the "patsy" outfit of a clown. Kilroy desperately tries to escape from the Camino Real and, failing, enters into various encounters with the inhabitants. His heart is weak, however, and finally the Streetcleaners come for him. He goes down fighting, but he does not die. Even after undergoing an autopsy, he does not die. A medical student holds high a golden sphere—the heart of Kilroy. He retrieves his heart only to hock it for riches for Esmeralda, who rejects him, for she wants only to *dream* of her chosen hero. Nevertheless, Esmeralda offers a prayer for some of the inhabitants of the Camino Real: "God bless all con men and hustlers and pitchmen who hawk their hearts on the street, all two-time losers who're likely to lose once more, the courtesan who made the mistake of love, the greatest of lovers crowned with the longest horns, the poet who wandered far from his heart's green country and possibly will and possibly won't be able to find his way back, look down with a smile tonight on the last cavaliers, the ones with the rusty armor and soiled white plumes, and visit with understanding and something that's almost tender those fading legends that come and go in this plaza like songs not clearly remembered, oh, sometime and somewhere, let there be something to mean the word *honor* again!" (pp. 585–86). Quixote awakens, hears the prayer and calls out a loud "Amen!" which Kilroy echoes. Quixote steps to the fountain, and for the first time water begins to flow. He chooses Kilroy as a replacement for his former companion and the two dreamers plan to go on from *there*. When Kilroy asks, "Donde?" Quixote replies, "Quien sabe!" Together they face the brilliant light of morning as they go through the arch that leads into "Terra Incognita." Quixote cries out triumphantly, *"The violets in the mountains have broken the rocks!"* Gutman turns to the audience and says, "The Curtain Line has been spoken!" And to the wings he calls out, "Bring it down!" (p. 591).

In reaching back into the past, in its sense of isolation, in its use of nature, in its use of color (especially gold and red) to evoke emotion, in its sense of hopelessness, and in its defiance of realism, *Camino Real* bears the imprint of the Symbolists. Yet it was Williams' tribute to the triumph of the human heart over adversity, anguish and despair. Esmeralda's prayer is clearly Tennessee Williams' plea to humanity. Further, in depicting Kilroy as a fighter with a golden heart who outwits evil (Gutman) and death, Williams' statement is clearly symbolic as well as symbolically clear. The play's positive denouement, therefore, sharply separates *Camino Real* from the pure Symbolist dramas.

Tennessee Williams uses a syntax of Symbolist poetics. It is most evident in the plays mentioned herein, yet the Symbolist influence, whether conscious or unconscious, is discernible in a great portion of his work. Williams' characters occupy worlds in which nature is ever present: exotic birds and animals play both real and symbolic roles, serving as character-metaphors or as characters themselves; insectivorous Venus Flytraps are nourished on Florida fruit flies, roses are usually crushed, yet violets are capable of breaking rocks. The vast expanse of sky spreads over it all like a colossal canopy, the purifying Gulf breezes sweep in and out, and looking down from its lofty position is the unreachable moon—that "cool son-of-a-bitch" as Brick often refers to it in the original Broadway version of *Cat on a Hot Tin Roof*—that consummate emblem of nonlife that dominated early Symbolist plays. Discernible dualities are woven into bright and dark patterns. The duality of flesh and spirit is often personified in the characters of doctors and ministers ubiquitous in Williams' plays. In his characters' quests for identity, reality, fantasy, or God, doctors and ministers are of little assistance, but they appear nevertheless. (As Flannery O'Connor says in "The Grotesque in Southern Fiction," *Mystery and Manners*, p. 44, "I think it is safe to say that while the South is hardly Christ-centered, it is most certainly Christ-haunted.") "The eccentricities of a nightingale" (the phrase a title of one version of *Summer and Smoke*) are in conflict not only with the duality within herself, but also with the duality of time and timelessness as Alma Winemiller's lost and unfulfilled youth moves closer to middle age in the shadow of the stone angel symbolizing eternity. And often, very often, visible and invisible presences act as forces on the action: the father's picture in *The Glass Menagerie*; Belle Reve and a lost way of life in *A Streetcar Named Desire*; the statue of the angel in *Summer and Smoke*; the urn of ashes and the rose tattoo in the play about the earthy and superstitious Serafina delle Rose; Jack Straw and Peter Ochello, and especially Skipper, whose unseen presences haunt the bedroom of Maggie and Brick in *Cat on a Hot Tin Roof*; the dead Sebastian in *Suddenly Last Summer*; the monolithic statue suggesting anguish and perversity in *Out Cry*; and the banner on which is painted a large phoenix in *Camino Real*, a play in which "resurrections are so much a part of its meaning" (II, 431).

Tennessee Williams is clearly an eclectic writer. He is also a very American writer who draws on his southern background for the environmental circumstances of his plays as well as the southern mystique in which his characters are often enveloped. Yet, through universality of idea, expert craftsmanship, and sheer theatricality, he transcends region. Williams is not a literary writer. His larger-than-life characters are forced into *conflict* which is the lifeblood of drama. His plays are unified by action as well as theme. His concept of plastic theater is a means of capturing truth, rather than the appearance of reality. Certainly it is his treatment not his philosophy of life that binds him to the Symbolists. Yet his roots and his purpose are clearly traceable to Poe and Wagner. Although his work is death-haunted, Williams deviates from the Symbolists in his belief in resurrections, thereby presenting a more optimistic outlook. It is because of this optimism that his characters often elude death. It is also because of this optimism that even the most pathetic of his characters, Blanche for instance, is possessed of a sense of humor.

Laughter is essential to Williams. The Symbolists' view of life was devoid of humor. Williams' optimism may be cockeyed, but it is there nonetheless.

Tennessee Williams is tortured by the commercial failures of his later plays. In attempting once again to find an audience he has turned to off-Broadway production where the unusual and "experimental" are welcomed. Off-Broadway, while serving a dedicated purpose, is less prestigious than Broadway. It is still more or less considered a showcase for the less experienced. The bitterness of being reduced to lesser theaters is illustrated in a small segment of Williams' recently published novel, *Moise and the World of Reason*. The young and unsuccessful writer-narrator of the book meets an aging, once distinguished playwright who is trying to stage a comeback at a less than grand off-Broadway, off-Bowery theater. There is a duality of illusion and reality, for both characters represent Tennessee Williams: one early in his career and the other past his zenith. The latter is Williams in the 1960s and 1970s, a time of great despair for him as one new play after another folded, often in less than a fortnight. Most of these plays reflect the Symbolist aesthetic.

In perhaps no other play is the personal anguish of the playwright Tennessee Williams so Symbolistically projected as in *The Gnädiges Fräulein*. With the nearness of death, with the commercial failures of the new plays, Williams was like the soubrette who answered the call to compete with the cocaloonies for survival, always at the mercy of newspaper critics (it can be no accident that the character of Polly has journalistic connections). Even as the Gnädiges Fräulein returned to her book of press clippings after each defeat, Williams fled to Tokyo and his homes in New Orleans and the Florida Keys, and was even temporarily institutionalized, until *he* answered his own outcry. In his battle for personal and artistic survival, Williams, like the Gnädiges Fräulein, was never completely defeated. His position as one of the greatest playwrights in the history of the American theater has become like her tattered theatrical costume, made all the more brilliant as he wears his commercial failures like spangles of blood that glitter like rubies.

Williams and European Drama: Infernalists and Forgers of Modern Myths

The *Impromptu of Alma* (1955), one of the less known works by Eugene Ionesco, bears a title curiously suggestive of Tennessee Williams. At one point in the play a character named Ionesco says the theater is for him "a stage projection of his inner world." The statement is no enigmatic novelty, since the "inner world" has been the source of creativity for most artists in the Romantic tradition. Tennessee Williams' preoccupation with his inner world, as it absorbs, rejects, and rebukes the outer world, belongs to the same tradition. The alma assumes many public guises reflected not only in the rich variety of Williams' characters, who are in many ways the sludgy silt of Western culture, but also in the variety of dramaturgic forms which serve the plays as autonomous frames and structures. Indeed this sort of experimentation with forms, the eclecticism with which he examines and utilizes both dramatic techniques and techniques gleaned from other arts aligns him with the experimentation apparent in European dramaturgy ever since August Strindberg. The projection of the "inner world" and the fascination with forms and forces reflect the peculiar dilemma of the modern artist as a public and a private figure.

Throughout this century, culminating with the inferno of World War II, European playwrights, along with other artists, were faced with pressing demands from the public, who looked to the artist for

429

help in defining the immediate past and in formulating a future. He
was to help exorcise once and for all those haunting visions of recently displayed human evil and atavism, to mend the broken spirit
of people, and to aid in the erection of a new and positive image of
the middle classes who had disintegrated during the century into fearfully acquiescent, or ineffectually rebellious masses, denouncing and
renouncing, heroic and cheap, but mainly spent and wary. Those
demands had occurred after World War I, but the later search for
some expression of hope was even more desperate. In general, artists
did not meet that demand in the desired simplistic terms and above
all shunned any kind of nationalistic positivism. Nevertheless, the
experiences of the century and the human condition found an artistic
reckoning based for the most part on an *existential metaphysics of
time*, and a manner of perception which I call *imagistic analysis*,
both explained below. Instead of order, a variegated dramaturgy
emerged—one of almost "primitivistic" strength, to cite Ionesco,
"where the corners are not rounded" ("Experience of the Theatre").
Keeping in mind that modern artists change their paths of expression, that in the Romantic tradition of experimentation they tend
to discard a style deliberately as soon as they have penetrated its
possibilities, one may yet discern basic rubrics: *one is infernalism and
the other is mythmaking*.

Tennessee Williams may be properly placed within the context
of these European dramaturgical forms. His manner of filtering experience, of self-reflection, his eclectic sense of social engagement
based on a bifurcated perception of being an artist in an indifferent
universe, his continuous effort to transcend the paralyzing negative
state of existential absurdity by dint of work and thus come to an
affirmative arrangement with life—all parallels fundamentally the
efforts of the Europeans to deal with art and existence. At the heart
of most of these works is the Absurd point of view, as expressed by
Albert Camus in *The Myth of Sisyphus*. Jean-Paul Sartre (in his
essay on *The Outsider*) and Martin Esslin have both referred to
this work as a seminal explanation of the bifurcated nature of the
Absurd, as an idea and a sense, as affirmative and negative, as the
link between existential metaphysics and the metaphor of the human
condition, to echo Esslin (*Theater of the Absurd*, p. 373).

The Myth of Sisyphus fundamentally reinstates what Thomas

Carlyle had expressed in *Sartor Resartus*, that the artist must necessarily transcend the "Everlasting Nay," the negative awareness of the absurd human condition, and choose to affirm by work itself the fluidity of the "Everlasting Yea." Carlyle saw both states, the negative and the positive, as necessary stages in the artist's perception of the human condition, but he also saw the danger of halting in the negative stage because of an increasingly secularized and nonredemptive vision. Camus expresses the same apprehension metaphorically. His Sisyphus comes to an actively lucid, nonvalidative cognizance of his condition during his descent. He knows he will face the rock again and again, but he also knows his rock to be the limit of his fate, and thus he experiences in his descent a temporary suspension of limits; and he is able to rejoice in the moment. He experiences the freedom of the man condemned to death, devoid of hope and thus devoid of expectation. He knows himself, and he feels himself a part of the perennial flux of creation and destruction without any ulterior motive. Camus stresses the sense of celebration, of exuberance, in the face of ineluctable fate, much as Friedrich Nietzsche had stressed the Dionysian exuberance in the face of Dionysian cyclical destruction and rebirth. The sensory aspect of this metaphysical explanation is important to the artist, for he, after all, does not wish to explain but to describe and thus provide alternatives for explanation. The Absurd artist thus deals with external phenomena, which may include externalizations of his own personalities like someone who has placed himself consciously outside the limits. He may thus socially be condemned, but he is able to look at the human condition and convey its disturbing ambiguity. However, he too suffers, for the air of freedom in exile is thin and, despite exhilaration, makes him giddy. The lucidity may be too strong, for despite the empathetic suffering and joy, the artist has lost social intimacy and often bemoans the loss.

The ambiguity of the Absurd artist's relationship to his environment and also to himself as a social man is evident in Tennessee Williams. It is particularly evident in his later works, notably in the novel *Moise and the World of Reason* (1975), but also in such plays as *Out Cry* (1969, 1973), *In the Bar of a Tokyo Hotel* (1969), and *The Two-Character Play* (1975). The serene sense of exile in these works recalls Beckett, even as things become comically ominous by their exclusion. But the sense of suffering from the dichotomous demands upon his own self both as artist and as man emerged as early as *The Glass Menagerie* (1944) and may thus be considered essential in his artistic development. The deepseated dilemma of existential commitment to be a probing, analytical artist in a society which demands above all social commitment in the form of synthetic approval of its criteria is what relates him to the European artist. He has looked with great admiration upon certain European writers who managed to bring this dilemma under some profitable control by an apparent reconciliation between the artist and the social man. Bertolt Brecht, Sartre, and Anton Chekhov impressed him in this way as well as by their artistic abilities. By contrast he was drawn in a sort of empathic sympathy to D. H. Lawrence and Arthur Rimbaud, and to painters like Jackson Pollock or Vincent Van Gogh.

Because of the problematic relationship between artist and social man, stimulating phenomena necessarily undergo some sort of metamorphosis in the creative process. Though Williams' primary response to the phenomena of life is not precisely intellectual, it is, nevertheless, analytical. His senses are quick in discerning the minutiae of an image, a gesture, or an expression. Beyond that he has cultivated a visual memory to store these impressions. Of course he needs people, events, other arts to feed his writing. In fact, he always seems to have relished some exposure to extreme situations and eccentric people which he then incorporates as concentrated images in his work. The ability to perceive the components of phenomena which can be exaggerated and reorganized to create dramatic images larger than life is a major characteristic of the creative, analytical activity by which the Absurd artist is able to link metaphor with metaphysics and provide an allegorical underpinning to his symbols. Phenomena are comprehended by imagistic analysis which demonstrates a peculiar simultaneity of sensory input, categorization, and artistic transformation. This particular manner of comprehension has also kept Williams from psychological pedantry and social verismo and is the magic ingredient which may explain his having outlasted Miller. Intricately related to the imagistic analysis of phenomena is Tennessee Williams' conception of dramatic time, which too is based on a metaphysical comprehension. As early as 1951 in his preface to *The Rose Tattoo*, he points to "the timeless world of a play" as the basis for its significance. He sees dramatic action, the structural skeleton of any play, as an "arrest of time." He means that any given image or action may be lifted from its temporal confinement of reality and manipulated into a different dynamic tension. The playwright may take that image or action and freeze it, distort it, even split it up into stroboscopic elements, or he may graft the original image or action onto a different environment. Thus the writer is able to take a trivial occurrence and remold it into a significant event, or he may imbue the original triviality with a higher metaphysic. The latter course has certainly been taken frequently by the Absurd dramatist, and both methods can be observed in Williams' work. His dual conception of time vaguely echoes Henri Bergson who conceived of time as being both duration, which is related to subjective perception, such as the moment perceived as eternity, and a series of more or less objective but mechanical historical occurrences. Bergson had indeed a great influence on twentieth century art, particularly on the experiments of simultaneity by the Surrealists, and of course on the subjectivism of existentialists, for instance Sartre, whose plays also deal with the "arrest of time." About thirty years after Bergson, Beckett constructed a similar dualistic metaphysic of time in his seminal work *Proust* (1931), which may well be considered a theoretical foundation for much of Beckett's and the Absurdists' dramaturgical experimentation with time.

Like an alchemist, the modern playwright distills time elements and recombines them on stage. Past, present, future may be fused into surreal dreamlike images which congeal into immediate dramatic reality at the moment of their appearance on stage. The directness of dramatic duration allows the playwright to manipulate the precise degree of significance for each element in an action or an image. This type of dynamic control is not new in the visual arts or music, or even poetry. In those arts the perceptual impact has always been heightened by dynamic, spatial or temporal, manipulation. It had also existed in drama; for instance both Sturm und Drang and Symbolist drama experimented with adjusting dramaturgical time forms to psychoesthetic innovative speculations, but most of those plays, if performed at all during their own times, were unsuccessful. In any case, naturalistic and "message" drama largely undermined these efforts and abetted the tenacity with which theater audiences and practitioners resist this necessarily estranging manipulation.

Closely related to concepts of time is the idea of universality. The timeless and the timely are the dual considerations of the playwright who aspires in his work toward universal significance at least within his culture. On the surface these two aspects are difficult to unite, yet certain fundamental elements in culture transcend fixed historical units of time. The desire to connect our century's experience to previous experience is not merely apologetic; rather it is the profound attempt to overcome the increasing sense of disjunction and fear of solipsism. The findings of C. G. Jung were appealing because they opened a new lode of metapsychological explanations. His thoughts, though anticipated in many ways by Strindberg, brought renewed vitality into a dramaturgy somewhat jaded by pointless and diffuse naturalism and simpleminded realism as well as obscure symbolism. Jung's theories underlay most of the early Expressionist dramaturgy, for instance that of Ernst Barlach, Oskar Kokoschka, and the very early Brecht. The Absurdist writers too, despite their variegated expression of metaphysical dismay about the triviality in human experience, strained toward achieving universality in significance and meaning, and thus they sought out and imbued with fresh images certain archetypal configurations and emotions. This is not to say that Jung became a textbook for artists but that his ideas seemed to encourage and corroborate certain configurative, creative stirrings, and provided a new-old fund for allegorical structure. Actually, some of the Absurd dramatic techniques recall in a peculiar fashion Baroque allegorizations which were also an attempt to make universally understood those experiences, motivations and fears which, though deeply lodged within the individual, bound him nevertheless inextricably to the rest of society, to his ancestors, and to his descendants. At the base of this similarity may be a cyclical vision of history and experience which seems to underlie Jungian and Baroquian thinking, with the main difference of course that Baroquian cycles formed an ascending hierarchy with God and Superior Spirit at the top. In this sense the Baroquian universal vision may be considered a transition from the medieval Dantean conical-spiral vision to the modern atomic-cyclical vision.

Thus the cyclical cosmology in any case lets nothing disappear but locks everything into the confinement of universal history. Therefore what may appear to us as our most private incubus of our individual solitude actually binds us to the universal demon, the fear of insignificance in the midst of the eternal recycling. With the pressure of individualization in a culture which also rewards social adaptability, the individual can escape a paralyzing negativism only after passing through an inferno of experience by a Nietzschean espousal of dynamic affirmation itself. But the inferno comes first.

Williams' fascination with the inferno vision has apparently not subsided with increasing age. In fact, his latest play, *The Red Devil Battery Sign*, is another manifestation in the style of *Camino Real*. An illuminating review (Beer) of the play's premiere at Vienna's English Theatre in Austria (January 1976) provides insight into the dramaturgy. According to the reviewer the play bursts all previous dimensions of Williams' dramaturgy and may well represent an abstract of his opus. A kind of *Faust*! This view fairly corroborates Williams' own assessment of the play toward the end of his *Memoirs*. Like *Camino Real*, it apparently follows basically a Strindbergian *Dream Play* dramaturgy, marked by a tectonic structure of realism and phantasmagoria. (The reviewer could not withhold a stab against New York producers by claiming they could not gumption the phantasmagoric part and tried to have Williams retract it. Williams retracted the whole play instead and adjusted it for its opening in the intimate English Theatre of Vienna. The reviewer is quick to add that a similar resistance had prevailed against *Camino Real* when it was first produced in the United States, while European audiences had responded with favorable puzzlement. In short, he presumes that Williams may have responded to the traditionally warmer climes toward his theater in Europe. However, I must add that Williams in Germany despite his great popularity, according to the frequency with which his name appears on playbills, has been mostly praised for his adept portrayal of psychopaths. And that is a thoroughly middle class assessment.)

The story of *Red Devil Battery Sign* is of the ex-wife of a magnate of a powerful battery corporation in Dallas, with the trademark of a red devil. The woman holds damaging evidence about her former husband's corrupt political dealings and is therefore kept under constant surveillance by the rough Red Devil Gang of strongmen, though she ostensibly lives a leisurely life in a luxury hotel. She has the familiar traits of other Williams heroines: she is haunted and persecuted by a brutal society, she has experienced alcohol and madness, and she is aging. However, she transcends these other women ultimately, as indicated by her namelessness and later transfiguration. She has a lover, also a burnt-out figure, the musician King del Rey whose career has been destroyed by a brain tumor and who, until his encounter with the mysterious lady, had been living off a somewhat picayunish older wife. When the two, the nameless lady and her musician, attempt to break out of their shackles and rise against corruption, the musician invites his own death while she, after being raped by one of the Red Devil gangsters, escapes death because a horde of young revolutionaries storming the building provide cover for her getaway. And here the phantasmagoria, which had been interwoven into the gangster and love plot all along, reaches its climax. The nameless lady reconciles and unites the young people who take her as their Madonna while they cry out for a holocaust.

Ever since Dante described the Inferno as an immense prison where individual souls were subjected to systematized, extreme physical and spiritual torment, poets have rendered their infernal visions as condensations of personal hell. Dante's influence on the poetic and dramatic vision of the twentieth century is documented by such diverse writers as T. S. Eliot, Luigi Pirandello, and Beckett, and of course Williams himself, who have made numerous references to Dante. The implicit influence can hardly be measured, but it is evident in the works of the French Jean Genêt, Sartre, Camus, and Jean Cocteau, to name but a few, and also such remarkable Polish dramatists of this century as Stanislaw Witkiewicz and Witold Gombrowicz, and at the turn of the century there is of course Strindberg. (An interesting sideline of this contemporary fascination with Dante are Robert Rauschenberg's exquisite illustrations of the *Inferno*.) In Dante as well as the modern artists one important sense pervades the variations of a personal inferno: it is the sense of confinement and of the ineluctable repetitiousness of torture. This sense grows out of a metaphysical speculation about death, be it spiritual, emotional, or physical, namely a fear of absolute stasis. When Dante finally penetrates to the center of evil, he finds Lucifer stuck upside down in the frozen lake of Cocytus. Satan is thus absolutely static, his vision inverted, and he is literally stuck in his own hell, an ironic inversion of the holy trinity with his three heads forever devouring. Everything in his immediate vicinity is in a perpetual frozen position. Up to that point Dante had evoked numerous grotesque visages of corruption and pain belonging to friends and foes he had known in life on earth. With Lucifer's static image the compounded realization emerges that these masks are no longer changeable, that they have become fixed in time and space, and that the soul, encapsuled in that mask, will be forever tormented by tortures pitched against the mask as well as by the lucid knowledge about the origin of the mask. Dante thus saw hell as an irreversible rigidification of evil and suffering which on earth at least seemed subject to changes. In hell, man is knowingly fixed to the most prominent role he chose in life. The fear of being confined to one mask is powerful indeed, and the fear of being railroaded into such confinement is as pervasive in contemporary thought as is the opposite fear of disintegration into fragmented and unrelated bits and pieces of personality. Williams' play *Summer and Smoke* for instance traces such a gradual rigidification of a mask and the subsequent horror when Alma realizes how she had cloistered herself. Even though modern man no longer possesses the assurance of an ultimately harmonizing god, such as Dante had, various modern conclusions may still be drawn from Dante's metaphor of evil. Though Dante is able to climb out of the Inferno while we are left with dichotomous fears from which we take brief respites in temporary states of oblivion or some provisory phantasmagoria of apotheosis, Dante's basic conception of the Inferno can still be appreciated in our times. While Dante is granted the grace of Beatrice and Vergil as spiritual leaders out of the morass, the modern poet has the option of either a graceful temporary suspension in phantasy or of a conscious reckoning of the past. The end of *Red Devil Battery Sign* thus is apparently an attempt to transcend paltry reality with a consciously chosen phantasmagoria. However, while Dante eventually finds redemption, Williams' phantasmagoria is by no means redemptive, although he has been suspected of such simplistic sentimentality. The conclusion of *Camino Real*, too, has often been construed as a redemptive solution, although the constellation of characters and situation ironically undermines such a hope. The difficulty with modern works lies precisely in that ironic attitude toward any conclusive solution which would not befit a truly secular metaphysic, or a metaphysic allegorized by Sisyphus. Thus to end a play like *The Red Devil Battery Sign* with an obviously glorified revolution may say something about the poet's ability to transcend and metamorphose his experience; it may express a certain trust in the dynamic flow of human existence, but it does not mean a simple trust in the ameliorative effect of human progress.

Genêt's *The Balcony* (1956, 1961) is also structured as an infernal vision of a social microcosm in which individual guilt and innocence become masks of torture and suffering, of power and submission. The setting of this play, like that of *The Red Devil Battery Sign*, is confined in this case to Madame Irma's brothel or "hall of mirrors," with the exception of one other interior scene. Though each of the nine scenes shifts to a different room in the brothel, the interconnection of the rooms with the control room (Madame Irma's boudoir), via closed circuit television, emphasizes the sense of inescapable constriction. The visual is underscored by sound: each scene is concluded by intruding machine gun sounds from the revolution raging outside. Though the characters leave at the end of the play and Madame Irma dismisses the audience from the immediate prison of the Balcony, the effect is merely the release from a microcosmic prison to the prison-at-large, where mirrors surround us giving us the illusion of alternatives and freedom of action.

The mirrors function in two ways: we can see our own masks in them, and we can be observed; stimuli can be served to us clandestinely, and what we consider our original and aggressive action may actually be the motions of a response mechanism. The tragic moment occurs when the character becomes conscious of his actions as nothing more than delaying defense motions against the ineluctable. Genêt shows this shift of consciousness when the characters are forced to play their roles for real, when the ideal, which they had thought sheltered, is transformed by force into public pretense. If Genêt's characters speak of freedom in the end, as Solange does in *The Maids*, they express their realization and acceptance of their ultimately choiceless existence. The freedom of playing at freedom grows out of the distinction between the illusion of freedom and the mastery of consciously playing roles. The inferno is the extended dramatic metaphor by which these distinctions are brought to light. The early version of *Camino Real*, the 1948 *Ten Blocks on the Camino Real*, stops at this point of expression, as do the earlier plays by Genêt, *The Maids* and *Deathwatch*. The later version of *Camino Real* and *The Balcony* go further to show the possibility and subsequent tortures of the continued act. The expected resolution is now seen as a temporary stop, as "the curtain line" which is spoken but which does not really terminate the life of the act. Pirandello's *Henry IV* (1922) is another example of the implied continued act in the end. Sartre's *No Exit* (1949) which Williams greatly admires also ends on a note of infinite continuation when the characters consciously choose the confines of their masks and Garcin proclaims "Let's get on with it." The inferno is thus felt keenly as a spatial limitation also in the sense that the character himself can no longer change or expand. A compulsive struggle ensues which is a kind of "dead reckoning" with human history as Skipper in John Hawkes's *Second Skin* explains the effort after the attempts at escaping.

The dramaturgy of the infernal vision is thus formed by two fundamental compositional elements, the evolving configuration and almost simultaneous exorcism of the particular incubi and succubi, and the final embrace with the demons. The pictorialization of the inferno is derived from reality: there may be elements of junkyards, or, in Fernando Arrabal's case, the automobile graveyard, there may be the horror of hotel lobbies, as in Williams' *The Mutilated*, or *Gnädiges Fräulein*, or *In the Bar of a Tokyo Hotel*, or Alfonso Sastre's *Anna Kleiber*; of waiting rooms, as in a strange play by Witkiewicz, *Gyubal Wahazar*, where one character comments that "Hell is one big waiting room." Even the dead end of a highway where human refuse and compulsive idealists collect, as in *Camino Real*, or Strindberg's *The Great Highway*, becomes an inferno. Usually there is one exit gate, but the traveler does not reach it until he realizes that the expanse beyond is not absolute freedom but merely another potential prison, dark, unknown and visibly arid. The aridity or icy quality of the space glimpsed beyond the exit intensifies the sense of metaphysical confinement. At the same time, however, the individual soul is voided of the illusion of the unattainable, or rather the hope that the unattainable may be attainable by some act of virtuous blackmail. Thus the landscape of the inferno becomes transmuted into the inscape of the inverted universe which must be traversed before existence can be grasped in its totality. It is that part of negation, of destruction, which also contains the seed for creation, for reassemblage.

The masks populating these infernos may be as brittle and as disconnected as the onion peels with which Peer Gynt identifies the phases of his existence. The preponderance of fugitives and feigned madmen caught in the corners of these hells reflects the strong human desire to escape the sense of the ineluctable. Since the escape cannot happen in actuality, it is often performed in a form of phantasmagoria, thus leading to the realization that any form of escape can be effected only by the power of imaginative will. The fragility and therefore temporaneity of this will is captured by Rimbaud in a beautiful image in his "Bateau ivre," which has also haunted Tennessee Williams for a long time; for he refers to it in his *Memoirs* and paraphrases it in *Moise*: It is the image of a child crouched over some frozen ditch releasing a paper boat as "frail as a butterfly." Mad innocence in face of frozen reality! The ice in midst of hell! Yet the act also conveys a lucidly defiant acceptance of existential givens. This is the madly cognizant transcendence over the impossible where the act itself triumphs, the act of imagination. The child after all does not even attempt to break the ice; it rather disregards the hostility.

Just as the spatial definition of the inferno is derived from elements of reality or from elements of literary or mythopoeic tradition, some of the masks which people these infernos are frequently made of reassembled components from literary or historical figures who have become part of the archetypal fund. Thus the personal inferno is firmly anchored within a larger cultural framework and the acts of personal psychic exorcism may be also regarded as the exorcism of cultural psychic myths as well. The masks are often reduced to fossilized versions of human dreams, such as the dream of inexhaustible discovery, or the dream of the consummate lover, or the dream of the conqueror par excellence, of the savior of mankind, and finally of the all-transcending artist, the god-challenger. In *Camino Real* appear a number of these masks: Jacques Casanova and Marguerite Gautier are the proverbial lovers by profession but they are uncomfortably locked into their roles. Lord Byron and Don Quixote are compelled to be adventurers forever. The Proustian figure Baron de Charlus is but a reduction of Proust's reduction of Robert de Montesquiou, a dandy in rigor mortis. Max Frisch juxtaposes in his play *The Chinese Wall* (1955) similarly historical and legendary figures with imaginary timeless figures. But in this play such perennials as Romeo and Juliet, Napoleon Bonaparte, Don Juan, Cleopatra and many other half-legendary, half-historical and thus quite mythical figures are forever caught in their moments of crisis. Like Dante's Francesca da Rimini they keep whirling by in a sort of Walpurgisnacht turned marionette roundel, passing just long enough to repeat their tales of trauma. The structural metaphor of figures caught in a sort of neverending dance which compels them to move in a set way corresponds to the constriction of the masks. It exemplifies the paradox of motion within immobility, of the longing for fertile growth within dearth and aridity. As the fire of Dante's City of Dis is cancelled by the ice of Cocytus, so is the external expression of passion cancelled by the ice within. The tension of what the self or soul had aspired to be and the realization of the masks that have frozen into one conglomerate grimace marks the characters of many plays in what Camus in *The Rebel* calls "the literature of damnation." The conqueror Pizarro in Peter Shaffer's *The Royal Hunt of the Sun* (1964) faces in the end also the slavishness with which he had pursued the chimerae of absolute conquest and joins the conquered Inca king in snowbound earth with the sun roaming "uncaught over his empty pasture." The damnation lies in the ultimately irresolvable tension of a longing for redemption and the realization of the futility of that hope. The paradox is often embodied in the characters themselves, like Pizarro, in their appearance and their behavior. They may be locked into a role which symbolizes basic human aspirations, such as love, wisdom, adventure, success, and variables thereof. If these figures are literary or legendary versions of these aspirations the paradox lies in revealing that these idealized, symbolic figures were actually involved in quite realistic situations that history has gradually transformed and concealed for the purpose of sustaining a traditional social order.

Michel de Ghelderode's *Christopher Columbus* (1928) shows a Columbus who discovers not a New World but a dying civilization from which he learns to deal with death as the ultimate affirmation of life. He joins the "everlasting dance on the tombs," a brightly colored "carnival of blood and plumes," an "everlasting departure." As a result, he is imprisoned by the King of Spain on crutches, who first wishes to silence such iconoclasm but later shares the glory with Columbus by freeing Columbus through a pretense at justice. While in prison Columbus embarks on the loveliest of his journeys where imagination joins death. However, this ends in ambiguity too, for the statue of Columbus raised by The American and Buffalo Bill comes to life after a cacophonous mocking procession in his honor and complains about having become the mock-heroic object of a nation's institutionalized ideal which is callous replacement in the name of progress. Ghelderode had explained in *The Ostend Interviews* that his dramatic visualizations had been greatly influenced by those phantasts who struggled to materialize their existential visions. He mentions E. T. A. Hoffmann, E. A. Poe, Villiers de L'Isle-Adam, Comte de Lautréamont (Isidore Ducasse) and painters of his country, the Flemish masters Hieronymus Bosch and Pieter Breughel, and the modern James Ensor, whose infernos combine personal trauma with cultural allegories of anxiety.

Psychological forces may also be reduced to masks which reveal the delusive game for existential redemption. Psychological myths have been created as much as religious or metaphysical myths and for a similar purpose of maintaining a precarious functional balance within social institutions. Thus we have created the idea of a Hero, a Mother, a Son or Child, or a Martyr, and we have created the necessity of an ideal Scapegoat with which to extirpate periodically the miscarriages of those ideals. We have also mythologized psychological interrelationships, such as the master/slave, the husband/wife, and the hunter/prey, and we have created a whole mimetic system of expressive conventions within such interrelationships. The modern playwright frequently uses these fossilized conventional expressions like masks which are in conflict with a submerged counterforce. The masks may split into various allegorical configurations as in Strindberg's dreamplays *To Damascus, Dream Play*, and *The Great Highway*. Williams' *Gnädiges Fräulein* and more covertly his *Streetcar Named Desire* break up into various masks of conventional expressions. Another interesting example is contemporary Greek playwright Notis Periyalis' little carnevalesque *Masks of Angels* (first produced in 1959) wherein characters, an allegorical lame man and a prostitute, go through the painful experience of tearing their masks off only lyrically to replace them with angel's masks in the end. The internal friction and tension between the mask in which these characters are confined, for instance Blanche's obsessive yet fastidiously studied fragility in the face of the equally studied brutishness of Stanley, and the underlying discomfort with these masks of behavior, emerge as the ineradicable source of personal hell. Gombrowicz speaks at one point about the deforming process which the individual undergoes through interrelationships. His plays, *The Marriage* (1953, 1957), *Princess Ivona* (1939) and the highly amusing *Operetta* (1969, 1970), show characters as they become distended and swollen only to collapse and contract again, as their role behavior becomes distorted in a given situation. The distortion gives an illusion of change; first the compulsion to form a mask (in *Operetta* even the mask of nudity in the name of haute couture) gives way to painful awareness of the rigidly grotesque mask until finally acceptance of the mask through playful manipulation leads to serenity. However, the process is one of gradual fossilization and confinement, not change, until the sense of freedom occurs when all hope of and attempt at freedom are exhausted. As Williams quotes so aptly in his preface to *Cat on a Hot Tin Roof*, "you can't get out of your own skin" (actually a very popular German saying!).

Even a highly religious writer, Paul Claudel, created in his major opus *Tidings Brought to Mary* (1910, 1948) a collection of allegorical masks whose very names symbolize the inherent constriction. The dynamics of inner conflict are brought to surface as each character gropes to find a channel for transcendence. Violaine, her father Anne Verscors, and the leprous master builder Pierre de Craon, choose to confront, explore, and come to terms with their fate. In the midst of seeming happiness and order, they seek out their human mission. Through intimate knowledge of disease and chaos they wish to sound the limits of human existence, faith, and fate. Claudel imbues his characters with an intense zest, reminiscent of Nietzsche's and Bergson's demands to test the life force to its extremes. He sees the act of seeking and withstanding the infernal part of life as a conscious exploration and cognition of death which, in Claudel's case, leads to an affirmative vision of God because only conscious suffering and death make creation meaningful. His vision too somewhat resembles Dante's vision since Dante, before he can reach the Mount of Joy, must first recognize suffering by his descent into hell. Violaine deliberately infects herself with leprosy by sealing a secret bond with Pierre de Craon. By this act of will she recognizes the depth of suffering as well as the source of life and is thus able to give life while tainted with death. Her sister Mara who, like her mother, chooses the simple path of happiness and refuses to acknowledge the power of death and the necessity of suffering, cannot come to terms with existential limitation. Claudel's vision despite its Dantean form is tempered by Nietzsche in the sense that while Dante saw the descent into the inferno as a means to an end, the Nietzschean vision sees in the willful descent itself a transcendence and conquest of the abyss. And this vision again relates to Camus' Sisyphus who consciously descends to his rock. Modern dramaturgy is replete with such deliberate encounters with hell and the various configurations of our incubi and succubi as they beset both the individual and human culture as a whole. Since modern playwrights like modern poets and other artists have inherited the Romantic task of being the high priests and prophets of the evolution of humanity, they are compelled to share their visions and proclaim their testimony though in our age without the benefit of a religious or philosophical superstructure.

Jan Kott comments in his *Theatre Notebook: 1947–1967* that modern writers, playwrights included, are primarily concerned with demythologizing culture and demystifying human nature, whereas the poets of old were creators of myths (p. 262). In view of a drama which translates inner emptiness into silence and virtual paralysis the observation is correct, and it is appropriate for a formulaic realism. However, a part of modern drama continues the mythopoeic tradition, albeit in a nonillusionistic manner. The myths, which may be contemporaneous reifications of sociopsychological currents, are dramatically created as myths in order to be exposed as myths. Thus what may exist as an illusion in reality is also exposed dramatically as an illusion in order to be exorcised. New masks and new roles appear, or classical myths, classical masks and roles may acquire new robes. In any case they are shown as symptoms of important underlying forces which also must come under some "dead reckoning." Those underlying forces come to the surface when challenged by an appropriate situation. The friction between the delimiting external forces and the expansive internal forces necessitates the mask and the role playing. Modern dramaturgy uses the mythopoeic mode as another demasking method, and in this sense the mode is related to the infernal vision.

Before World War II the common conception of man's responsibility for the quality of existence rested on the belief in a fundamentally ameliorative evolutionary process. Man was presumed to make his choices subconsciously or instinctively for the ultimate benefit of human evolution. Thus even individual destruction could be explained as a weeding of decadent elements. Artists had warned against such simplistic trust as one can see in such poems as Yeats's "Second Coming," or in the brilliant guignolade, Alfred Jarry's *Ubu* plays, or the prophetic works of Strindberg and Ibsen. And then there are those haunting paintings by Edvard Munch, Ensor, and Ernst Barlach to name but a few. World War II destroyed the trust finally on a wide scale. Questions arose about the predominant factor in the control of human existence. "Human nature" had clearly failed the test on a large scale; the overwhelming situation had paralyzed and disoriented it in such a way that Europe seemed to go the way of lemmings. The negative heroism of plain survival became an art, and human dignity rested in the resilience the individual could muster. Masks and roles were created for makeshift substance until, it was hoped, the soul could restore itself. However, much of this makeshift became permanent and provoked playwrights to a new kind of mythopoeic activity, namely the simultaneous building and dismantling of the newly created or revamped myths. Sartre's essay "The Forgers of Myths" (1945–46) explained French dramatic interest in myth as a renewed attempt to distill profound passions and tensions as they are aroused by extreme situations and to crystallize them into metaphors commensurate with their primitive and pure power.

Though the cataclysm of the Civil War in the southern United States could obviously not have been personally experienced by Tennessee Williams, he, like so many of the other modern southern writers, was nonetheless drawn to its after effects, feeling the need to reflect the particular ordeal of a society's reordering. In this sense and despite different premises the metaphysical needs of the South have resembled those of post-World War II Europe as Sartre explained them in his essay, namely as a need to reconstruct while seeking new principles. Individuals are thus often placed in extremely strained situations with contradictory demands. The situations though extreme are also basic, usually about conflicts of right, of survival, of power, with disturbing interlacings of love. The characters are forced to respond to the demands of the situation, which brings out sharply certain fundamental inconsistencies within the characters themselves. To overcome the situation, the characters may choose to comply with some sort of modus operandi displaying a behavioral pattern which attempts to cover inner uncertainty but which in the course of crisis proves to be the insufficient moultings of an outdated myth. Yet, some characters dare to take upon themselves the creation of profound new and contemporaneous myths. Thus Williams creates in *Orpheus Descending* (1955) a curious mixture of archetypes found in the classical myth of Orpheus with a southern topology and at the same time a uniquely modern application. The southern twist lies in the rendering of the cannibalistic death as that peculiar vigilante lynch mob action which has been a frequent southern judicial execution. Val Xavier's fate combines the classical hero's cannibalistic death with contemporary motifs. Val is torn to pieces by chaingang dogs; Orpheus was torn asunder by Bacchantes.

The play belongs to a whole symbolic tradition in the quest myth which Northrop Frye (*Anatomy*) calls the dying-god myth where heroic action is dissipated into confusion. However, as in all Dionysiac myths, to which the Orpheus myth belongs, in the very destruction lies the seed for rebirth though death is again in store. And so the Conjurer brings Val's snakeskin jacket to Carol Cutrere, and she consciously takes it up as a legacy to follow the fugitive kind. The rebirth motif is thus not associated with the expected child engendered by Val and Lady, since Lady is killed, but rather with the continuation of a certain type of human being who will perpetuate the myth. The universal modernity lies in the motif of the rootless fugitive. The Orpheus myth has been the motif for a considerable

number of twentieth century plays ranging in variety from the surreal collage of Cocteau's *Orphée* (1925) and his *Blood of a Poet*
(1932) to the lyrical Jean Anouilh play *Legend of Lovers* (1941)
which uses another facet of the Orpheus myth, the retrieval and
later joining of Eurydice in the realm of the dead. The conciliatory
lyricism of Anouilh's play strikes one now as somewhat sentimental
and oldfashioned in comparison with Williams' sharp cutting of the
myth.

The two archetypes in Williams' play are the fugitive exile and
death by some form of cannibalism, both prevalent in his work and
both found in much European drama since the early part of the last
century. The disillusionment with the French Revolution began a
gradual estrangement from Enlightenment thinking that culminated in the experience of World War II. The mythological models
which could analogically allow for this experience were devouring
and resurrection myths along with plague and expulsion myths, and,
for a more solipsistic vision, the epiphanal myth. Plays dealing with
Prometheus, Ahasuerus, Tristan and Isolde abound. Von Kleist's
Penthesilea (1804–5) as an early example and Edward Bond's *Early
Mourning* (1969) as a modern example represent the extreme fascination with the implications of the devouring of gods, whereby the
eating connotes a simultaneous eradication of the other's separate
entity as well as complete absorption of the other. American authors
who have taken up those mythoi include Poe, Ezra Pound, John
Hawkes, to some extent Eugene O'Neill, and the southern writers
Flannery O'Connor and Williams. Belonging to this tradition were
also the theater experiments of the 1960s; notably The Living
Theatre and Schechner's Performance Group relied heavily on
mythical material of that sort. What makes these visions so un-
palatable to the mainstream of post-Enlightenment thinking (most
middle class thinking) is the affirmative confrontation with an inherent chaos and destructive urge in the human condition. This
tendency has provoked much speculation about a nonconciliatory
vision or, as some have said, decadent olfactory and scatological obsession. Many dismiss it as an aberration. The result is often a misunderstanding of the dramatist's ironic thrust; or, if his work is
malleable and ambiguous, he may be sentimentalized. The latter
has often been Williams' fate, at least in America. The American

critic, being part of a society which is extremely conciliatory and pragmatic, thus allowing for little "pathological deviation," has been as responsible in sentimentalizing Williams or dismissing some of his work as interestingly psychotic as those American directors who have directed the plays in a strictly American Stanislavskian tradition which allows for no unmodified and unmotivated character cracks. Some naive and persistent redemptionism in the American consciousness denies any affirmative value to a Nietzschean or fundamentally Absurd vision. The democratic American myth is rooted in the idea of progress through good will. It is fundamentally unlyrical as it is directly derived from Enlightenment thought. It cannot abide chaos for it rests on order. Tennessee Williams prefaces the acting edition of *Orpheus Descending* with a note by Strindberg to Paul Gauguin, in which he speaks of "an immense need to become a savage and create a new world."

After *Orpheus Descending, Suddenly Last Summer* (1959) uses the motif of cannibalism though more in a symbolic than mythical manner, since the character who was actually destroyed by a cannibalistic murder functions by his absence more as a catalyst than as a tragic nexus. However, the theme of cannibalism dominates the scenery, the past as it is revealed, and, most of all, the psychic interrelationships among all characters, not just between Mrs. Venable and Catharine. Destructiveness is complete and without reprieve since no seed is left to flourish; the infection has spread to endemic proportion in the prolonged devouring process. Nevertheless, the play has a mythic quality in that it displays human relationship in archetypal magnitude. In this play man's behavior is as doomed and meaningless within the course of nature as that of the poor turtles scrambling for life between hostile land and hostile sea. Human relationship is distorted from the very beginning by the pain felt at birth, by the vulnerability of youthful senses, by the callousness of the survivers, and by the equivocation of all at death. These tensions are displayed lyrically in *Suddenly Last Summer*; and though they form an archetypal substructure, the characters who experience them are not mythical. To be sure they are no mere psychological studies; they are symbolic, perhaps even allegorical, but they do not contain the implication of any cyclical continuation, of rebirth.

In Williams' work familial relationships are frequently archetypal, particularly that of brother and sister. Often these are subjected to the breaking of a taboo which equals a regression into presocial, anarchic communion. To confine a brother-sister relationship or any familial relationship to a Platonic relationship was an early act of social structuring. However, the privileged class was often exempted from this ruling and thus separated from the rest of society. Aristocratic or near-divine orders in human culture seemed to have an official sanction to propagate by incest. The fact that the law has been broken by isolated peasantry and tribes (as Jung had noted) seems to indicate a relative sophistication with regard to social hygiene exhibited by evolving major civilizations. But it is the decay and breaking of these civilizations which concern a good many modern writers, Williams included. The topoi are not new. Ancient myths testify to the trepidations with which societies have always observed internal corrosion. The stronger a sense of tradition is associated with a sense of social accomplishment, the more the society fears changes because these necessarily erode a status quo. Within the United States the South is the most stringently tradition bound; in fact "Southern Tradition" has become such an abstract notion it is nearly mythically removed and a nightmare or dream fixation for the inheritors. Since this society is derived from an agrarian culture where family is the core of any social structure, the innermost fears about its crumbling state will first substantiate there. In *Suddenly Last Summer*, the mother-son and son-cousin relationships apparently broke taboos at least in spirit, though the son's implied impotence apparently prevented the actual physical act. The implication, however, of the son's desire to vicariously devour, as his fanatic collection of flesh-eating plants indicates, is a sublimation of the sexual act with the consummate rigor of a praying mantis. The metaphor seems to express the symptomatic desire of the son to destroy in its very heart a sterile and dying culture of which he was a part and by consuming it attempt to convert dead matter to a possible new energy. However, as noted above, no new energy is indicated at the end of the play because the son had been utterly destroyed, leaving behind only horror.

Incest may show a similar desperate and self-destructive urge, a breaking through bonds by devouring them and thus clearing the surface for new creation and new energy. Williams in any case had some interest in the question, as his early, little known one-act play *The Purification* (1940) deals with the subject. The incest between brother and sister in this play gives the sense of an act of solipsistic and desperate self-love by a dying culture in the face of an encroaching yet prematurely exhausted new culture. The visionary Elena of the Springs and Elena of the Desert are united in one girl who embodies death and life simultaneously as she loves her brother, an act beyond bounds, but remains cold to her husband, "the burnt out shell of a longing" (p. 30), because he cannot serve her desire "to dive skyward" (p. 59) toward nothingness, which is her only alternative to dead matter. Music accompanies the verse throughout, as commentator and conveyor of the passions when words no longer suffice; but sometimes too as an ironic counterpoint. In any case music is the reminder of the spiritual content of this passion play.

The brother-sister theme reappears in one of Williams' latest plays, *Out Cry*. While the lyricism of *The Purification* recalls the mystique of Garcia Lorca's plays, the broken severity of *Out Cry* recalls the poetic abstraction of Beckett's strange monologue *Imagination Dead Imagine* (1970). The taboo passion is recapitulated in both of Williams' plays; it is verbally reckoned with and put into form. The myth is created on stage, if we understand the representation of a myth to be a verbal and gestural configuration and delimitation of an internal polarizing tension between the self's longing both to become absorbed in the universe and to establish its separate autonomy. In the early play the abstraction is musical and poetic; in the later play the abstraction is spatial, metaphysical. In either case it is the enactment of the individual's dead-end encounter with the Ineluctable which may be culturally perceived (in *The Purification*) or entirely individually as in *Out Cry*. The "unalterable circumstance," as Felice calls it in *Out Cry*, turns out to be the necessity to enact *The Two-Character Play*, though with no external reason to do so. As characters, Felice and Clare are by themselves, but as actors they are not. The implication is that we are driven to aggressively impose a form onto our passions and fears even if the act itself means sealing shut the very source of our creative energy. Clare fears precisely this, but at the same time she is drawn into arranging the props and formulating her role because she is part of this "unalterable circumstance." Their roles, their play is their prison which not only shuts them away from others but which also locks them into their barren union until they realize that through imagination they can transcend this real prison, at least temporarily. With the brother and sister players Williams has returned to an old motif which also plays an important part in the Electra and Orestes topology. Jean Giraudoux and Hugo von Hofmannsthal connect Electra and Orestes as lovers in their fateful commitment to an internal necessity or "unalterable circumstance," as one might call the urge to bring about the final conflagration which will free the stage for new life. They have to fulfill their roles. In Sartre's *The Flies* (1943) Electra and Orestes are also lovers bound to fulfill their roles as the autonomous executors to clear the earth of the "bad blood," the "sangre mala" as Williams expressed it in *The Purification*. The willingness and passion with which the characters fulfill their parts aligns them with the modern existentialist concept of human responsibility. It is a conscious participation in the universal principle of matter striving to dissolve into spirit, into meaningful nothingness, which is enacted in these danses macabres. The juxtaposition of specific classical myths with modern times is a metaphoric expression of the critical point in a culture's development when old values must be shed to give as yet unformed forces free flow and recognition.

But each age creates also its own specific mythology. The same process exists: the poet or mythmaker is visionary and alchemist distilling and combining from the real phenomena the undercurrents of energy for which he has no name but for which he can create analogous metaphors. Rimbaud, Strindberg, the Expressionists were contemporaneous mythmakers in this alchemical way. Today playwrights such as Ionesco, Friedrich Dürrenmatt and Bond have contributed to a body of contemporary mythoi. Bond, for instance has been concerned with creating a body of works which reflects the pervasive and manifold phenomenon of money power, the pounds of flesh we demand so coldly of one another. Dürrenmatt is interested in creating an iridescent phenomenology on stage where things are representative of the contemporary mania for diversity, as in that ironical *An Angel Comes to Babylon* (1952). And Ionesco creates haunting dramatic spaces where figures are stealthily deprived of their faces, as in *Rhinoceros* (1958). Williams has also found certain contemporary phenomena which he represents on stage in mythic size. These are not necessarily rooted in an archetypal tradition as his devouring and fugitive myths are, though those contain contemporary references, as pointed out, but rather they are calcifications of one contemporary American problem, the systemic paranoia which silences lyrical vision by denigration or indifference. Williams mythologizes this problem into particular situations where figures appear in various stages of disintegration depending on the intensity of their prophetic vision and the resistance they encounter. These figures are odd in that they contain in excess qualities which have been embraced as positive ideals by the American character, such as ingenuousness, trust in humanity's goodness, generosity, individuality, respect and love for parental heritage, absolute loyalty to a creed and/or ideology. By distilling these behavioral virtues from a common canon of a culture's ethical direction, and condensing them into single figures, Williams exposes a number of incoherences which plague American culture, the main one being the cultivation of individuality in a culture which translates the ideal of equality into homogenous mediocrity. There are those female figures, like Blanche, Laura, Alma, Trinket, and Hannah who seem to be so encapsuled in their private ingenuous perceptions of themselves and the reality around them that they elicit nothing but envious contempt from others; and, when contempt is not enough to unsettle their blithe generosity, the others are driven to vicious destructiveness. Their outward eccentricity, which exposes them to the uneasy ridicule from others, is brought about by an abnormally consistent externalization of their self-images and the near fanatic attempt to preserve the profound innocence of their vision in face of shallow brutality. The conscientious, though illusory, attempt to cultivate a face instead of a mask causes discomfort in a society where masks are essential for functional efficiency because the prevailing social habit of dispensable masks is sensed as the cause of the loss of human dignity. Thus these figures are made the scapegoats for the sins committed by society against society's proclaimed ideals. These figures then become the literal pounds of flesh with which society balances its shortchanged account of ideals.

Arthur Kopit's *Indians* (1969) is another example of an American myth being demasked by a scapegoat sacrifice, though the topic and the format of the play are far removed from any of my Williams references. Nevertheless, I find that the figures and their subjection to ineluctable dynamics have the same mythic undertone. Another American, Edward Albee, has attempted in *Tiny Alice* (1965) a mythologization of the contemporary dilemma to accept by act of faith the validity of an ideal, to overcome by act of faith a materialistic hypostatization of God. In short, Albee has created with this play not a vaguely universal symbol, but rather distilled an essentially American metaphysical problem, namely the difficult reconciliation of a secularly pragmatic materialism with a proclaimed foundation in a God who is represented by a multitude of organizations, largely social not spiritual in function. Little room is left for the spirit to expand, and it has little peace to rest unless the choice of self-exile is made. Thoreau had recognized that. Thus Williams, Kopit, and Albee have perceived that fundamental irony in American existence, that the original desire to find a space for the soul to expand and the individual to unfold disappeared under the rubble left by rapacious invaders and was soon superceded by a flaccid notion of the "pursuit of happiness." Even Jean-Claude van Itallie's *America Hurrah* which is dramaturgically somewhere between Clifford Odets Expressionism and Second City cabaret, can be considered in this light, as a mythologization of sterile forms, be they interviews, television programs, or motel rooms, and their palpably disjunctive influence on the individual.

At this point the difference between the mythological and the symbolic approach needs to be clarified since these playwrights have often been categorized into presumably mutually exclusive slots, either realistic, Absurdist, or symbolic, rarely mythic. Northrop Frye's distinction in *Anatomy* between symbol and myth, adapted to the form of drama, shows mythos to be the direct mimetic rendering of meaning in movement, or the enactment of a real phenomenon in terms of its historic emergence. In other words a dramatic mythos is history in dynamic flux, in its process of reification. Drama which employs symbolism deals with real phenomena in terms of their already fossilized appearance and is thus what Frye would call "*dianoia* in stasis," or stabilized meaning. Though symbolism or archetypes often perform important functions in mythic drama, the mythos usually develops independently. Thus *Cat on a Hot Tin Roof* displays the mythos of a life force as it furiously attacks and tries to drive out life-negating sterility. On the surface the play appears quite realistic, though a symbolic interpretation is encouraged by Williams' scenic instructions and may be accomplished by emphasizing certain "things," such as the predominant bed, the crutches, and alcohol. However, an imbalanced emphasis on either the realistic or the symbolic elements would seriously flaw the dynamic flux of the play which is dependent on a subtly ironic counterpoint of meaning and appearance, in the competition between priorities. The mythos is enacted like a game in which ruses are used to cover up the essential truth. Even Maggie's naively touching final attempt to literally press life into Brick has something of an animal desperation as when a mother animal covers and nurses its dead young, waiting for it to revive. The play thus deals with one facet of the life force which has been mythologized universally but which has had an enormous impact on American existence: motherhood and its instinctual, naive refusal to acknowledge death and its fierce opposition to anything that might undermine fecundity. I think Williams indicted in this play the sort of illusionism which accompanies the idolization of motherhood because it disregards other life-giving impulses and distorts the meaning of death. (Unfortunately, Kazan failed to recognize as much when he directed the play for Broadway, for the ending which Williams had to change is falsely sentimental and actually quite "unrealistic" and illogical, as Williams himself has acknowledged.) Here too, a myth is enacted on stage; it is created only to be eventually demasked.

In *Summer and Smoke* (1947) Williams created a mythos of the soul and how it is made the target of believers and nonbelievers alike. The believers attribute to it an illusionistic, lyrical quality like a veil behind which they seek protection from the sharp edges of life. Thus being a lady is to Alma almost synonymous with having a soul, until an internal fire destroys this illusion. The nonbeliever John Buchanan applies the typical "scientific" doubt when he cannot locate the soul in his anatomical chart. His doubt is no less naive than Alma's illusion; both are ultimately static. Once they learn that soul is more akin to the soothing water which is graciously offered by the stone angel as temporary relief and that it wells up from deep within, they can understand its actual value as a succour in human relationships, and they learn that its flow must be controlled to prevent a drying up. The connection between the larger mythos, the search for a soul, and the specific American version of this mythos is in the cultural incoherence which the two main families illustrate, the strict separation in the social fabric of spiritual and physical needs and the slightly denigrating attitude of one set of administrators towards the other. The result is a codified and regimented spiritual and physical culture, and never the twain shall meet.

Inasmuch as the poet is mythmaker he also partakes in the mythopoeic process, as Pirandello demonstrated in *Six Characters in Search of an Author*. He creates myths to exorcise certain painful concerns. The figure of the artist becomes therefore frequently the most relevant modern vehicle to exorcise the peculiar concerns of the poet himself in his own time. The poet's role has in our age become the role of the visionary prophet, but he is a sort of Cassandra whose profoundest visions were derided as the spoutings of a mad woman. Thus the alienation of the poet from society is not only painful but also dangerous if it turns into solipsism. At the same time self-alienation of the poet is necessary to his art. In a time when the creative process itself is considered the source for existential affirmation, the artist has to guard quite defensively the environment which allows the process to unfold. Since the emphasis has shifted from result to process, both sensitivity toward creative work itself and a self-consciousness about social usefulness have increased. The fear of "drying up" has become almost endemic among modern artists. This fear becomes subject to mythologization. In Tennessee Williams' work artists have occupied special positions for some time: the autobiographical Tom in *Glass Menagerie*, Nonno the poet and his granddaughter, the painter Hannah, in *The Night of the Iguana*, the writer in *The Lady of Larkspur Lotion*, the actors in *Out Cry*, the painter and the writers in *Moise*, and that most devastating figure of a painter, Mark of *In the Bar of a Tokyo Hotel*. Since the lastmentioned play best exemplifies the depth of the problem and its perfect mythologization I shall concentrate my analysis on it. First of all, the play dissects the various demands which society, in this case the consuming higher society, places upon the contemporary artist. Most of these demands are inhibitive if not destructive to his creativity. Secondly, the self-conception of the modern artist rests frequently on his obsession to reveal, with every work, essential tensions and nerve fibres. Thus he is involved in a continuous effort to reduce, to peel away, with the inherent danger that he will reach an impasse when there is no more to say. Thirdly, the modern artist is frequently unable to separate himself from his art because the process consumes him; thus his capacity for a private life, for companionship decreases though elemental needs persist. And with the increasing isolation the fear of creative and personal sterility heightens from which he can save himself only by plunging back into the world of phenomena, by splitting himself and his existence into phases. The Romantics were keenly aware of the artist's existential problem, and some of them never could come to an arrangement: Shelley, Christian Grabbe, Rimbaud—the list of casualties goes on. Perfect examples of the solution were painters like Picasso and Matisse, but Mark is the opposite. He has burnt himself out in the struggle to become one with his art, which he considers the only moral existence for an artist. However, he has made the mistake of identifying his art with his entire person, and thus has cut himself from the source of his creative process because he has alienated himself from essential perceptive channels. His cruel wife Miriam perceives this failure and uses it to destroy him. She is in a way like Maggie the cat, in that she absolutely refuses to accept and tolerate such solipsism. Leonard, the art dealer and financial backer of Mark, understands and tolerates Mark from an intellectual or rather mercantile point of view, but his ability to help stops where Mark's marketability stops. The Barman completes the microcosm of a modern sophisticated high society which seems to be the only part of society concerned with the artist. It supports him financially and gives lip service to his extravagances which often are nothing but desperate cries for serious attention in his isolation. He has been relegated more and more to the position of a talented child who is encouraged but who is ultimately not taken seriously. The supporters are financial wizards who can afford to be generous with their tax-deductible gifts because it enhances their position in culture. They pay for creative inspiration, for amusement, take the product and bother themselves little about replenishing the source. Leonard is therefore worried about Mark's physical decline because Mark is an investment not yet amortized. The ivory tower is created materially, thus putting to a special test the source of creation which is conflict.

Camus would say (in *The Rebel*) "the organic intolerance" is put to a test of authenticity. The connoisseur pays for vicarious suffering so that his conscience may be purged of the sin of callousness; therefore the artist must provide the image of suffering. To do so authentically, he must expose himself to conflict, that is, if he sees art and life united within himself.

The Surrealists had made playful use of this desire to wipe out the distinction between life and art, by making deliberate constructs of their lives. For instance, the phenomenon of their soirées, later action painting in public and happenings, carried the act of art into public life, though of course much of it was spoofish and no more than a fad. Mark attempts the opposite way: he wants to make his art a work of life, realizing too late the cul-de-sac of such an attempt. An early play by the German poet Gottfried Benn, *Der Vermessungs-dirigent* (1916, *The Surveyor*) reveals the dilemma in the two main characters Pameelen and Picasso. Picasso solves it for himself in some benevolent form of schizophrenia, asserting in the face of Pameelen's disintegration and death that "we are not born" but rather that "we are admitted to existence" and that "we create ourselves." Cocteau devises a comic mask for the painter in *The Wedding on the Eiffel Tower* (1921) where he creates the actual wedding and "sells" it to his dealer. The Surrealists, even Artaud in the 1920s, were able to transcend the cleft existence of artist and man by assuming, as Santayana would have it, with "panache" the comic mask and create "prodigious allegories for the mere sport and glory of it" ("The Comic Mask"). In *Moise and the World of Reason* Williams creates an allegory of that sort though with a bit more harsh irony than Santayana would allow for, but then Williams has always opted for irony to pull himself out of the rather dismal notion that "Personal lyricism is the outcry of prisoner to prisoner from the cell in solitary where each is confined for the duration of his life" (III, 3).

Ionesco too is a bit grimmer than the Surrealists when he deals with the topic of the exploited artist, as in *The Painting* (1954), in which the artist ends up paying an outrageous sum for the privilege of being "created" by the Businessman. The preoccupation with showing the artist's predicament is apparent in the number of plays which show him either exploited as a madman (for instance in that wonderful Witkiewicz play *The Madman and the Nun*) or as the

butt of ridicule (as Chekhov had done in *The Sea Gull*). The problem of the artist's integration in society while maintaining a necessary distance had already occupied Goethe, for it formed the theme
of *Torquato Tasso* (1795). But the indictment in our century is
sharper because the alternatives have narrowed between the buffoon,
the madman, and a living, working artist. Withdrawal is no longer
possible because there is no more a separate Sublime Being which
could be celebrated as a cosmic foundation. Mark keeps referring
with envy to Michelangelo's escape up the "stepladder" to create
"the creation of the creation of the creation." Instead of spiritual
sustenance, the modern artist Mark is offered liquor and tranquil-
izers, and trips to Japan. The modern artist must also be internation-
ally visible; it increases his marketability. Thus *In the Bar of a Tokyo
Hotel* deals with the pressure of being a successful artist, i.e. an
investment article whose idiosyncrasies are fostered as long as they
are profitable, the pressure of being metaphysically isolated from any
possible close relationship, and the psychophysical disintegration
from frequently self-inflicted abuse which brings about the final
despair and inability to work. By compressing into a single situation
the whole spectrum of the problem and focusing upon the fear, Williams has mythologized his material as Strindberg had mythologized
a particular kind of marriage in *Dance of Death*. Both plays let the
ineluctable night draw near, and the characters perform their ritual
in the circle of that dimming light.

Williams' recently published *Memoirs* (1975) bear out implicitly
and at times even explicitly the ambiguous sense of alienation. Repeatedly he presents himself as a fugitive in flight from his inadequate
social self, one who feels safe only in the isolation which his work
provides him. Yet his memoirs are above all a list of the abundant
social contacts and events throughout his life; the profoundly sensitive relation to his work is revealed very reluctantly through some
scattered bits and pieces of insight. Thus in Tennessee Williams
the problem of coexistence of social man and writer appears to be
the source of much of his malaise, apparently more than the often
cited problem of being a homosexual in a heterosexually oriented
society. Again one must emphasize that this awareness really crystallized and emerged so clearly only in later years, though metaphors
of the tension exist throughout his work. He tells with a deep un-

derstanding in his *Memoirs* of one remarkable meeting with the Japanese novelist Yukio Mishima shortly before the latter's suicide. He explains, in retrospect, this suicide as the act of an artist who had reached an insurmountable impasse in his art, the completion of his trilogy. Apparently he perceived Mishima's act as an entirely logical and harmonious fusion of artist and man. Since he has apparently never considered any of his works as a final statement, his work has kept him from self-destruction. Thus he fulfills Carlyle's dictum: Know what thou canst work at, setting his stage anew with each outcry.

Themes

George Niesen uses *Suddenly Last Summer,* in which the artist (also the main character) does not appear, and the most recent version of *The Two-Character Play* as a frame for his discussion of the artist's role in Williams' work. But in tracing his theme he discusses numerous other plays and adds insightful observations about their significance. The essay deals with one of the most prevalent themes in Williams.

Nancy Tischler uses Jungian theories (and specifically Neumann's *Great Mother*) to restudy the women in Williams' work. While others may argue cogently about one theory or another, the author as firmly argues that the women are distinctly females even if categorizations of women are made from a masculine point of view. Jeanne McGlinn states her purpose in the second paragraph of her essay, and she moves on to show that the female characters are too complex for stereotyping. The discussion involves studies in characterization that lead on by implication to observations about Williams' technique in contrasting his female characters.

No honest discussion of Williams can omit references to sex, when Williams himself so obviously and adamantly insists on using autobiography in his art. Edward Sklepowich manages a discussion of what some may still consider the most bizarre and grotesque of the playwright's themes. The author traces the changing views that develop during Williams' career, and he places his study within a broad context of American culture. Robert Jones, as his title suggests, also has no interest in the sensational but in an aspect of the playwright's dramaturgy and in themes associated with the unisexual character. His classification of male and female roles gradually leads to an interesting view of the roles in *A Streetcar Named Desire.*

Williams' autobiographical preoccupation with death is discussed with reference to the plays named in the title of Philip Armato's essay. The index will indicate that numerous other essays unavoidably discuss the subject, and June Larsen (in EUROPEAN CONTEXTS)

461

suggests a peculiarly southern preoccupation expressed at least as early as Poe. But the juxtaposed theme of survival is therefore the more important. This essay, in discussing death, also interprets the plays mentioned: the plots of *Suddenly Last Summer, The Night of the Iguana,* and *The Milk Train Doesn't Stop Here Anymore* present contrasting views by juxtaposed characters. Distinguishing the point of *Suddenly* from those of the other plays, the author claims Williams is a "Christian playwright." (His conclusion may be compared with those of Delma Eugene Presley and John MacNicholas at the end of this section.) The concept of the inferno is much elaborated in the essay by Beate Bennett (in EUROPEAN CONTEXTS).

Delma Eugene Presley looks at Williams from a Christian theological point of view and comes up with some unusual comments about the usual themes. The author suggests that Williams unsuccessfully deals with theology and that his attempt may in part account for the weakness of his less successful plays. Comments on *The Night of the Iguana* may be compared with those of Charles Moorman and Glenn Embrey (in PLAYS) and the comments about *Camino Real* with those by Morris Wolf and Diane Turner (in PLAYS) and Mary Ann Corrigan (in EUROPEAN CONTEXTS).

John MacNicholas explains his title and his point in the second paragraph of his essay. The title has an ironic theological connotation related to a discussion of damnation and redemption in Williams' work. In a universe with a deus absconditus (hidden god), redemption depends upon humanity, according to the author's interpretation of Williams. The discussion of the artist-priest leads to interpretations that offer insights into many of Williams' plays. The section closes with a discussion complementing that of George Niesen at the beginning of the section while it also makes original comments on numerous other important themes.

The Artist against the Reality in the Plays of Tennessee Williams

GEORGE NIESEN

What can be Created Can be Destroyed.
(William Blake, "The Laocoön")

From VAL IN *Battle of Angels* (1940) or the Writer in *The Long Goodbye* (1940) to the two players in search of an author, a cast, and an audience in *The Two-Character Play* (1976), Tennessee Williams has indulged his penchant for creating in his plays characters who are artists of one sort or another. Not all his plays feature such characters, but most of the plays include someone in the cast with the qualities if not the title of an artist. In each case the figure is sensitive, creative, and, paradoxically, destructive. He is sensitive to time, to his own feelings, and to others and their feelings. He is generally so sensitive, in fact, that he cannot function well in the real world. He creates, of course. The artist attempts to give some kind of meaning to life and death. He reaches for the unobtainable and often fashions an idealistic fiction to replace a frustrating reality. Finally and surprisingly, the artist is invariably associated with destruction, either his own or that of someone close to him. *In the early plays his sensitivity usually leads to his death. In the later plays he is an "angel of death."*

However, the artist never withdraws from his world in the face of his problems—which may help to explain Williams' popularity. The artist never appears in the ivory tower, but is instead tested in the crucible of the reality of the play—a reality which, with its brutality and cruelty, and despite its strangeness and grotesqueness, is created

463

carefully enough that it is acceptable and believable to the audience. The result is standard dramatic conflict with strong social content. As Nathan A. Scott (*The Broken Center*) puts it, "the self achieves definition only as it pits itself against the hard, recalcitrant stuff of social and political reality" (p. 225). Clearly Williams is telling his audience something about their world and the problems that a sensitive individual faces in dealing with it (cf. both Weales and Skloot).

Williams' ideas are most strikingly stated in *Suddenly Last Summer* (1958) which dramatizes the entire world view of the dead poet. Sebastian's reactions to social and human pressures reveal the playwright's most significant delineation of the artist figure, even though the artist himself never appears. Furthermore the play is a restatement of nearly all Williams has said about art and the artist in his earlier plays. In none of Williams' plays is the designing influence of an artist so strong, so oppressive, in fact, as is Sebastian's in *Suddenly*. The poet or creator who refuses to "correct a human situation" or to "interfere in any way," nevertheless exerts, even when dead, a profound control over the lives of the members of his family.

The artistic influence for Williams, then, in *Suddenly* and in the earlier plays, is destructive rather than creative. Sebastian sees horror beside beauty wherever he turns. The God he sees in the caviar-colored beach and the equally black sky, for example, is the destroyer as well as the creator of the world. The lush hothouse plants suggest "organs of a body, torn out, still glistening with undried blood" (III, 349). His mother and procurer, Violet, loses her beauty to a disfiguring stroke. Sebastian's horrible death may mean life to the starving urchins who devour him. In any case the artist (who is frequently a Christ or other sacrificial figure) cannot relate the horror to the beauty and can do little more than imbue an inevitable death with some semblance of meaning. He does not create life. Rather, he makes death stand for something.

Suddenly also marks a major turning point for Williams, for in the plays following *Suddenly* he assumes a different view of existence, one in which his characters generally opt for survival. Although they are often in some way impotent (as with the destructive nature of creators, impotence is also a paradoxical trait for the supposedly productive character), they manage somehow to come to grips with their world and function well enough in it to remain alive at least. Of course a great, dramatic death, and usually even a pathetic one, is inherently more interesting dramatically than survival, no matter how great the struggle, and Williams' earlier plays have been more successful on stage than the later ones. Furthermore, as Williams turned his thoughts after *Suddenly* to a new appreciation of life, he had to learn a new dramatic mode and has not again reached his former dramatic heights. With *The Two-Character Play*, however, Williams has finally achieved a new intellectual statement which ranks with that of *Suddenly*. *The Two-Character Play* is a cri de coeur, a plea for survival and for a place to be somebody, a play which, despite its dramatic failings, clearly delineates the problems the artist faces in trying to survive in a hostile environment.

Tennessee Williams is telling us all how to survive. He insists that both horror and beauty surround us and that we must learn how to relate to them. He also sees that it is impossible to reconcile them and that the artist, who must create beauty and still face the horror, is forever in an untenable bind. That bind is my subject; and to determine the qualities that define the Williams artist and discover the nature of the reality with which the artist must deal, I will examine the plays of the Williams canon. In addition I will analyze the two phases of Williams' career which *Suddenly Last Summer* and *The Two-Character Play* represent especially well. Both plays focus sharply on the sensitive artist, yet they offer two distinct answers to the question of the artist's relationship to an insensitive society. In the early plays the artist cannot deal with his reality, except by escaping it, usually through death. In the later plays the artist endures the impossible bind. He is never reconciled, certainly, but he survives. In neither case can the artist create in the traditional manner, and in either case he is more or less destructive. Williams' world view is indeed bleak.

Williams' early plays show a wide range of destructive tendencies, from a simple denial of the real and the substitution of fiction—to holocaust. *The Glass Menagerie* (1945) and both Broadway and Hollywood versions (see Sacksteder) of *Cat on a Hot Tin Roof* (1955) represent Williams' successful resolution of his soft line, wherein the protagonist survives and presumably goes on to create something from the ruins of his past. *Battle of Angels* outlines Williams' hard line—wherein the protagonist cannot survive—which has bedeviled Williams ever since. In any case, however, little in the plays is creative or constructive.

The Long Goodbye is an early one act version of *The Glass Menagerie*, in which Joe, a young writer, talks to Silva and watches the moving men empty his flat of its furniture. In flashbacks Joe's sister enters three times and his mother once. Toward the end Joe says, "You're saying goodbye all the time, every minute you live. Because that's what life is, just a long, long goodbye! To one thing after another! Till you get to the last one, Silva, and that's—goodbye to yourself!" (*27 Wagons*, p. 178).

Very near the beginning Joe tells Silva that he is leaving. "All of this here is dead for me. The goldfish is dead. I forgot to feed it. . . . I shouldn't have left the bowl setting right here in the sun. It probably cooked the poor bastard" (p. 163). A short time later Joe and Silva watch the movers carry out the bed: "JOE: Mother died on it. SILVA: Yeah? She went pretty quick for cancer. Most of 'em hang on longer an' suffer a hell of a lot. JOE: She killed herself. I found the empty bottle that morning in a waste-basket. It wasn't the pain, it was the doctor an' hospital bills that she was scared of. She wanted us to have the insurance" (p. 165). Joe calls his sister Myra a whore on her third appearance and she leaves, saying "they'll move every stick a furniture out a this place before they do you!" (p. 177). The father disappeared years before, "tired of living a regular middle-class life" (p. 177). Finally the movers remove the last stick of furniture and a child in the background cries "olly—olly—oxen-free!" (p. 179), which suggests Joe's new freedom now that he has shed his family and his past.

The Glass Menagerie is a memory play, soft in tone, which nevertheless uses both the family and the destructive overtones of *The Long Goodbye*. The individual members of the family are totally different in the long play—more sympathetic certainly—but retain the basic interpersonal relationships and individual drives of their counterparts in the early sketch.

Laura, the fragile figurine of *The Glass Menagerie*, is a much revised Myra, delicate and pitiable. The gentleman caller who provides "the climax of her secret life" (I, 210) also, by announcing his engagement, snuffs out "The holy candles in the altar of Laura's face" (p. 230). Amanda, the mother, is no longer the passive victim of *The Long Goodbye* but a dictatorial force who plans either marriage or a business career for Laura (p. 157) and who insists that Tom not "jeopardize" a secure job he detests (p. 163). The father, much as in the shorter play, "was a telephone man who fell in love with long distances . . . and skipped the light fantastic out of town" (p. 145).

Tom, however, a poet who eventually is fired for writing a poem on the lid of a shoe box, is the artist character who must escape the reality of his existence (cf. King). He finds some solace in the fantasy world of movies but he is still ensnared by the responsibilities which his father abandoned—a dominant, security conscious mother and a weak, dependent sister. Tom has "no single thing" (p. 161) he can call his own. He is not "in love with the Continental Shoemakers" (p. 163). He is afraid of getting himself nailed into a coffin (p. 167), of finding himself trapped by a dismal life.

When the gentleman caller arrives, though, we learn that Tom is "waking up. . . . The signs are interior" (p. 200). He has paid his Union of Merchant Seamen dues with the light bill money. Shortly afterward, of course, the lights go out—in the house, in Laura's face, in Amanda's life. Amanda berates Tom for not knowing of the gentleman caller's engagement. When Tom protests that "The warehouse is where I work, not where I know things about people," Amanda replies, "You don't know things anywhere! You live in a dream; you manufacture illusions!" (p. 235). Tom then "smashes his glass," which causes Laura to scream out, and he goes off to the illusory world of the movies, a world which is his only antidote to the reality of the play. Eventually Tom goes even further than the movies and, like his father before him, abandons his family in his search for self. Amanda is easy enough to leave, but Laura continues to haunt him. Since Tom is not about to return to the stifling world of St. Louis tenements, however, his only escape from Laura is through mindless activity, drink, the movies or strangers, through whatever can blow out her candles (p. 237) and destroy his image of her.

A look back at *The Long Goodbye* clarifies Tom's situation and the destructive nature of his actions. Joe, like Tom, is trapped, though less by responsibility than by an inability to leave. Joe's release comes only with the dissolution of the family and all mementos of it (from the bed the mother died on to the last stick of furniture), only after everything in the home is dead, including the goldfish which he inadvertently destroys. The mother kills herself for the sake of Joe and his dreams. He drives his sister away. Joe is in no way directly responsible for his family's fate, yet his freedom is contingent on its death.

Tom, like Joe, represents a destructive force, though more subtly. Tom's final lines, for example, indicate that he is trying to erase Laura and her candles from his memory. Laura is identified with light—her school yearbook is *The Torch*, "she is like a piece of translucent glass touched by light" (p. 191)—yet an important metaphor in the play is that of snuffing out her candles. If the gentleman caller arrives at the climax of her life, her future looks dark. Tom's departure at the end of the play, when he smashes his glass and causes Laura to scream, recalls his earlier attempted departure when, after calling Amanda an "ugly . . . old—*witch*," he rips off his coat and throws it across the room, shattering some of Laura's glass menagerie. She "cries out as if wounded" (p. 164). Since Laura is closely identified with her menagerie, and since she cries out when glass is broken (her unicorn is only altered, not destroyed, and Jim's clumsiness elicits no scream), I see in Tom's thoughts and actions an attempt (perhaps conscious, perhaps not) to destroy her. On Tom's command, Laura blows out her gentle candles to end the play.

Tom cannot abandon Laura without destroying her, however, for they are kindred spirits. They both "live in a dream" which is for them an omnipresent world. Tom has no such attachment to Amanda and can leave her freely. He destroys some of her hopes and dreams, he shatters her dictates, but she remains, finally, with her "dignity and tragic beauty" (p. 236).

Joe and Tom, in their attempts to become artists and to fulfill themselves, must break away from their environments and families. Like the phoenix, they must create from the ashes of the past they have destroyed.

Presumably Joe and Tom, who escape with psychic wounds and intact bodies, will become artists. Valentine Xavier of *Battle of*

Angels (Williams' early hard line play) and *Orpheus Descending* (1957) fares far less well.

In both plays Val, a young, virile artist, enters the Hell of the small southern town on the note of a Choctaw cry. He becomes involved with two women who are in many respects similar to the mother and the sister in each of the plays discussed above. He ends up in a situation analogous to Tom's and Joe's but far grimmer.

Val is searching for something. He thinks it is love and he teaches "love" to the Cajun girl but, as he says, "afterwards I wasn't sure that was it, but from that time the question wasn't much plainer than the answer. . . . I went to New Orleans in this snakeskin jacket. . . . I learned that I had something to sell besides snakeskins and other wild things' skins I caught on the bayou. I was corrupted! That's the answer" (III, 273).

Lady (Myra in *Battle*) knows that "corruption ain't the answer" (p. 273). In act one she says to Val, "I'm not interested in your perfect functions, in fact you don't interest me no more than the air that you stand in" (p. 266)—air which she must breathe to remain alive. Yet a short time later Lady tries to buy life from Val. "NO, NO, DON'T GO . . . I NEED YOU! ! ! TO LIVE. . . . TO GO ON LIVING! ! !" (p. 305). She offers him a room that will cost him nothing. She threatens to withhold money. "If you try to walk out on me, now, tonight, without notice!— You're going to get just nothing! A great big zero" (p. 331). She offers him money. "Everything in this rotten store is yours, not just your pay, but everything Death's scraped together down here!—but Death has got to die before we can go" (p. 333). Val takes the first bribe and stays at the store, collecting his "commissions" (p. 310) and bringing life and subsequent death to Lady.

After the sheriff tells him to leave town, Val can very nearly resist Lady's offers. When he learns she is pregnant, however, he looks back once, and Jabe, her dying husband (who killed her father), kills her. Orpheus himself must die, of course, and he does at the hands of a lynch mob after Jabe accuses him of murdering Lady.

The Carol of *Orpheus* is quite different from the Cassandra of *Battle*. Cassandra clutches passionately for Val, almost as strongly as Myra. Val is torn between the two women. But Carol is less developed as a character and less central to much of the action. After

Val is killed, Cassandra drives into the river, while Carol only suggests suicide, "so the fugitive kind can always follow their kind" (p. 341). Some of their traits are identical, however, They both have a translucent "fugitive beauty" (p. 236). They are both "lewd vagrants" (p. 252) who want to live but die instead. They remind one of Laura with their "transparence," their fragility and lonesomeness —"The act of lovemaking is almost unbearably painful, and yet, of course, I do bear it, because to be not alone, even for a few moments, is worth the pain and the danger" (p. 282)—and their pathetic sterility: "I'm not built for childbearing" (p. 282).

And Lady is like Amanda in some respects. Both are burdened with metaphorically dead husbands. Both grasp for a type of security embodied in a young male figure. Each reaches for the memory of a romantic past, Amanda in receiving the new gentleman caller and Lady by redecorating the confectionery in the style of her father's wine garden.

Val, like Tom, is an artist who finds himself a slave to his environment and its women. In Williams' more violent plays, though, the definition of the environment is much more profound than in *The Glass Menagerie*. Val cannot simply escape the environment of the play, as Tom does, for he has found in his wanderings that corruption *is* the answer, everywhere. Lady has "sold" herself (p. 285) and she tries to buy Val. Carol has become a "lewd vagrant." Each character is a synthesis of life and death—Lady conceives and then dies because of it, Carol goes to the Cypress Hill cemetery to hear her ancestors say "live," and Val himself becomes the true "angel of death" who brings life and hope to Lady and Carol just before he brings them destruction. Even basic life and death is a corruption, however, and the artist's answer, for which Val has looked so long, is a phoenixlike self-destructive purification by fire. To achieve his escape he too must first be instrumental in the destruction of those to whom he is tied.

Williams' notions of fire, destruction and purification are obvious in the early one act *Auto-Da-Fé* and appear again in *I Rise in Flame, Cried the Phoenix* (1951), where the symbolism of light, heat, gold, fire, the phoenix, and the sun is almost overbearing. D. H. Lawrence is the artist hero who insists "there will always be light— And I am the prophet of it!" (*Dragon Country*, p. 74) and that if he ever finds his god he will "tear the heart out of my body and burn it before him" (p. 62). Here too is a version of the image of the sun killing goldfish. Frieda accuses Lawrence of "sucking the fierce red sun in your body all day and turning it into venom to spew in my face!" (p. 61). Lawrence's "body's a house that's made out of tissue paper and caught on fire" (p. 67). The sun, heat, and fire are clearly destructive and can bring about a renewal only after death, consummation, and the resulting purification. The sun itself, according to Lawrence, dies nightly in copulation with the "harlot of darkness" (p. 74), and the masculine sun becomes as tied to cycles as any feminine symbol.

The Dylan Thomas poem, "Do Not Go Gentle into That Good Night," is a far more appropriate epigraph to *I Rise in Flame* than to *Cat on a Hot Tin Roof*, where it appears. Lawrence does not want to die and rages against his death, yet in taking the phoenix for his symbol he has already accepted death (and presumably resurrection).

The point is that in the Williams play Lawrence is preoccupied with destruction and his own death. His art leads to book bannings and near burnings of canvases. His raging hastens his own death. All his creative impulses, in the world of the play at least, lead to destruction, and once again Williams confirms the artist's untenable position in the world (at least during the artist's own lifetime).

The phoenix is the appropriate symbol for Williams' destructive plays. Tom deprives his family of light and is, in a way, the "harlot of darkness." Val burns, and Lawrence is consumed with fever. Sebastian dies under the blazing white sun. Some sort of resurrection may later occur but in each play Williams is concerned only with the end of past and present.

The heart is the symbol of Williams' plays of denial; and it offers a suitable contrast to the phoenix, even though frequently rent from the body and burned (as Lawrence threatens). The heart represents or creates reality as it ought to be. The heart's function is to turn "chaos into—*order*," as Byron puts it in *Camino Real* (II, 507), and to create a fiction which is more bearable and more sympathetic than the real world which, according to the Writer in *The Lady of Larkspur Lotion* (as for Big Daddy years later in *Cat*), "is a hideous fabrication of lies! Lies! Lies!" (27 *Wagons*, p. 71).

The Lady of Larkspur Lotion (1941) is another early short play which features a writer as character and which prefigures a number of later plays. It is the first in the line of those plays which in one way or another deny reality, and its bleak but less than totally destructive viewpoint points to Williams' later period. "What if there *is* no rubber king in her life!" the Writer says. "There *ought* to be rubber kings in her life! . . . Suppose that I live in this world of pitiful fiction! What satisfaction can it give you . . . to tear it to pieces, to crush it—call it a *lie?*" (*27 Wagons*, pp. 70–1). And thus the Brazilian rubber plantation is on the Mediterranean and in full view of the cliffs of Dover. "Compassion and understanding" take over to destroy the reality of cockroaches, prostitution, "body vermin," and a hard nosed, tightly drawn landlady (Mrs. Wire). The fiction makes life in such surroundings passable for the Lady and the Writer for at least one more night. Yet, the denial of reality is not far removed from destruction. Neither has much hope; for both the Lady and the Writer must deny the real world of rent payments— at who knows what cost—to create an alternate fiction.

Aspects of denial leading to destruction appear in Williams' two most experimental plays, *Camino Real* (1953), with its Lord Byron as artist character, and the early verse play, *The Purification* (1944), which does not include an artist in the cast but which is, in many ways, *Camino Real*'s forerunner. The Son and Daughter (Elena) of Casa Blanca in *The Purification*, for example, share the usual qualities of Williams' artists. They are sensitive, passionate, and unable, because of their passion and incestuous relationship, to exist in the usual real world. They attempt to transcend that world through their passion. "Resistless it was,/this coming of birds together/in heaven's center . . ./Plumage—song—the dizzy spirals of flight/all suddenly forced together/in one brief, burning conjunction!" But "Afterwards, shattered,/we found our bodies in grass" (*27 Wagons*, p. 45). The only reality for an unacceptable love affair is purification through death and a psychic or spiritual resurrection. The end of the play, in fact, suggests that it has been an analogue to the celebration of the Mass. "The play is done!" the Judge announces (p. 62). And the incest, the passion, and the religiosity of the play link it to *Camino Real* generally and to Byron in particular.

Byron appears in *Camino Real* only in Block Eight. He tells the story of Shelley's cremation and the snatching of the heart from the "blistering corpse" and "the purifying–blue flame" (II, 506). Byron speaks of the poet's vocation, which "is to influence the heart," which is in turn "A sort of—*instrument!*—that translates *noise* into *music*, chaos into—*order* . . . —*a mysterious order!*" (p. 507). He crosses the Terra Incognita on his way to Athens where "the old pure music" will come to him again. He will "Make a departure!" he says, "From my present self to myself as I used to be!" (p. 503). "*Make voyages!—Attempt them!*—there's nothing else. . . . THIS WAY!" (pp. 508–9).

There are other, mechanical links between the plays. In *The Purification* the brother tells the story of Peeto the pony (pp. 60–61). The survivor in Block Two of *Camino Real* repeats it. The words of the chorus of women in *The Purification*, "rojo de sangre es el sol!" (p. 58), are spoken by La Madrecita in *Camino*. "Rojo está el sol! Rojo está el sol de sangre! . . . Blanca está la luna de miedo!" (p. 451). Red is the sun of blood. White is the moon of fear. Furthermore the tone of Williams' verse play is often reflective of T. S. Eliot's *Murder in the Cathedral*, in which the Archbishop attempts to justify to himself his death while society attempts to justify to itself his murder. In fact, a line from the play appears in *Camino Real*. "Humankind cannot bear very much reality" (p. 580).

Undoubtedly the three plays are linked. The meaning of *The Purification* and *Murder in the Cathedral* is clear enough. The Son joins his sister in death, for "nothing contains" her where she is, in "the wildest and openest places" (p. 59). The Archbishop makes his decision "out of time" to give his life "to the Law of God above the Law of Man." Each character reaches for something beyond the rational and the physical, much as Val in *Battle* wants space around him and wants to stretch his brain out, "right up against the edges of the stars!" (I, 108). Each character wants to substitute an unrealistic fiction for an unbearable reality. Each, facing an inevitable death, wants, at the very least, that final act to be symbolic in some way. Each wants to make his splash against the sky.

The destructive message in *Camino Real* becomes clear. Byron's brief appearance represents a dialogue between body and soul, with the body at once both fascinating and repulsive. Byron ends his lurid story with the statement that "I thought it was a disgusting thing to do, to snatch a man's heart from his body!" (p. 506). Nevertheless what he searches for is not in the clearly corrupt physical realm, a realm which he must transcend. He attempts to return to himself as he used to be—the poet (instead of the versifier) with an uncorrupted vocation, "before it was obscured by vulgar plaudits!" (p. 507). Living and dying is the only true poetic act. He voyages across the great unknown, to the war in Athens where he is killed. His search is not for innocence but for "the old pure music"—the purity which is indeed characteristic of art, which transcends the physical, and which may very well be expressible only in the irreversible act of death. For as Val knows, corruption is really the fact of physical existence.

Basically, purification is the destruction of the physical and an assault on the unknown. Purification is most effectively initiated through ritual death. Of course Kilroy, the great American pragmatist, is incapable of even imagining the suprarational or supraphysical and dies like the survivor, senselessly, without meaning and with the rattle of a dry gourd. His Blakean soul appears, however, enfolded in the humanity of La Madrecita, and after his heart is cut from his body he seizes it and pawns it in a futile and regressive attempt to buy paradise in the person of Esmeralda. As Byron discovered, however, at Shelley's vivisection, the physical heart is corrupt, and it is only after the Gypsy forces him to face the real camino that Kilroy sees the physical world for what it is—"a pile of excrement" (Weales, p. 23, discussing Shannon's view). Idealism, in the person of Quixote, then awakes, Kilroy sees it, and water begins to flow (much as the rains come in *The Purification*) only after the reduction of the world to absolutely basic terms and only after the destruction of all illusions. The play opens with the same basic term when "Sancho mutters the Spanish word for excrement as several pieces of rusty armor fall into the aisle" (p. 433). Only through the course of the play, however, can the characters (and presumably the audience) realize the nature of physical reality.

Thus a baptized, purified Kilroy, embraced by idealism, escapes at last from the camino real to attempt the exploration of the unknown, the Terra Incognita—much as Byron has escaped, much as Jacques and Marguerite escape into the unknown land of love, much as the fugitive kind have flown. Art represents less the destruction than the denial and transcendence of the physical, although the artist must frequently destroy the real world to go beyond it. For Byron, the physical heart may be burned or not; it may be twisted and torn like a loaf of french bread, for it does not matter. What is important to him is the artist's heart, which is a spiritual instrument of order and not a physical organ. What matters is that, as in *Larkspur*, the artist create an acceptable world and reject the real world. Imagination and the ideal are what should exist.

In two important plays preceding *Camino*, *Streetcar Named Desire* (1947) and *Summer and Smoke* (1948), Williams examines the age-old question of the relationship of the physical and real to the ideal and spiritual, and he examines it again much later in *Kingdom of Earth* (1968, 1975). *Kingdom* is very nearly a rerun of *Streetcar*, with Lot analogous to Blanche, Chicken to Stanley, and Myrtle to Stella. Both Myrtle and Stella "choose life." Williams' emphasis on the dichotomy of flesh and spirit in the plays and his refusal to take sides underscore the estrangement of the sensitive person from society. (William Blake is used ironically in *Summer and Smoke*, for no poet was more opposed to the dichotomy of body and soul.) And even though no specific character in either of the earlier plays is an artist, the plays are important since the theme of estrangement recurs often in Williams' work and adds a significant dimension to the role of the artist.

Williams carefully polarizes John and Alma in *Summer and Smoke*, with the only possibility of synthesis embodied in the earthbound angel, eternal and lifeless. John moves away from total sensuality in the course of the play while Alma moves away from complete spirituality. Somewhere near the end of the play the two cross each other's paths with no hope of meeting, and Alma is apparently on the way to becoming another Blanche (see Popkin, p. 47). In *Eccentricities of a Nightingale* (1964), a later and very different version of *Summer and Smoke*, Alma is more clearly a singer and more clearly eccentric (hence the title). She is more nearly an artist figure —sensitive, unable to cope adequately with her environment, passionate, and mildly destructive, at least as far as her own reputation goes. She hazards all for one night of love. She is gentle and pathetic, however, and more akin to Laura Wingfield than to Val or even Tom. She is, after all, a post-*Suddenly* character who does survive.

Blanche, in *Streetcar*, contrasts herself to Stanley. "He acts like an animal! . . . Maybe we are a long way from being made in God's image, but Stella—my sister—there has been *some* progress since then! Such things as art—as poetry and music. . . . In some kinds of people some tenderer feelings have had some little beginning! That we have got to make *grow*! And *cling* to, and hold as our flag! In this dark march toward whatever it is we're approaching. . . . *Don't— don't hang back with the brutes!*" (I, 323). Blanche's remarks reveal her nature. She can't abide the brutality which surrounds her. Even though Stella, the star married to the brute, offers Blanche an example of synthesis, and even though Blanche herself is considerably more free to act than Alma, Blanche is like Alma in succumbing to the sensual at the expense of her ideals and her own wellbeing. In the light of the thrusts of the previous plays, such a resolution suggests two lines of thought.

As Byron and Val state, the submission to the physical (and therefore corrupt) world demands the destruction of the artistic temperament. Thus for Alma and Blanche (who are spiritual characters) a movement toward sensuality represents psychic if not physical destruction. Indeed their attempts to come to terms with the corruption of the physical world end only in corruption. Yet the continued existence of the spiritual person in the physical world is equally impossible. As noted the only solution to the artist's bind is some form of escape from it, often in the form of death. A spiritual beauty and a real horror cannot exist together.

Brick in the original version of *Cat on a Hot Tin Roof* is another early character who will, with a dream, destroy himself and his world rather than submit to its corruption. Brick is an artist, as Gerald Weales notes (p. 19). He is an extremely sensitive person: "One man has one great good true thing in his life. . . . I had friendship with Skipper" (III, 58). Furthermore he wants to transcend the physical, yet is aware of the ravages of time. He wants to "keep on tossing—those long, long!—high, high!—passes that—couldn't be intercepted except by time" (p. 122). Brick is also a destructive power. He tortures Maggie. "*Oh, Brick!* How long does it have t' go on? This punishment? Haven't I done time enough, haven't I served my term, can't I apply for a—pardon?" (p. 39). And "you asked too goddam much of people that loved you, you—superior creature!— you godlike being!—And so we made love to each other to dream it was you, both of us!" (p. 56). Brick drives Skipper to his death. "Yes—I left out a long distance call which I had from Skipper, in which he made a drunken confession to me and on which I hung up! —last time we spoke to each other in our lives" (p. 124). He pronounces Big Daddy's death sentence. "*How about these birthday congratulations, these many, many happy returns of the day, when ev'rybody but you knows there won't be any!*" (p. 125). When Brick tells Big Daddy to "Leave th' place to Gooper and Mae" (p. 126) he attempts to dispose of his past, his family, and his environment. He in effect sells his birthright.

Brick might insist that he is less interested in destroying his environment and escaping it than in simply transcending it. He drinks to activate a "Switch clicking off in my head, turning the hot light off and the cool night on and . . . all of a sudden there's—peace!" (p. 98). Still, his attempts to transcend the physical have strong self-destructive overtones. "Mendacity is a system that we live in. Liquor is one way out an' death's the other. . . . I'm sorry, Big Daddy. My head don't work any more and it's hard for me to understand how anybody could care if he lived or died or was dying or cared about anything but whether or not there was liquor left in the bottle. . . . Maybe it's being alive that makes them lie, and being almost *not* alive makes me sort of accidentally truthful" (pp. 127–28).

Thus Maggie must lock up Brick's liquor and force him to submit to her. She wins the battle of the physical and indeed wins the physical itself, the plantation which is necessary to support Brick's drinking, but she loses the war. Brick is not concerned with the physical; and at the end (particularly in the original third act) Brick remains as detached as ever. "I don't say anything. I guess there's nothing to say. MARGARET: Oh, you weak people, you weak, beautiful people!—who give up.—What you want is someone to—take hold of you.—Gently, gently, with love! And—I *do* love you Brick, I *do*! BRICK (smiling with charming sadness): Wouldn't it be funny if that was true?" (pp. 165–66). Wouldn't it be funny if anything were true? The frequent repetition of the phrase suggests that very little is true in life aside from death and maybe birth. Perhaps man's only meaningful statement within the mendacious system is in death— a death imbued with some sensibility and meaning.

Sebastian's death as related in *Suddenly Last Summer* is not only extremely symbolic but, in perverse and destructive terms, an artistic triumph. Sebastian's mother, Mrs. Violet Venable, tells Dr. Cukrowicz that "Without me he died last summer, that was his last summer's poem" (III, 354). Too, she says, "nothing was accidental, everything was planned and designed in Sebastian's life and his—(She dabs her forehead with her handkerchief which she had taken from her reticule.)—work!" (p. 351). Her hesitancy to say *work* suggests that had she not paused to think, she might have concluded her statement with the verbal opposite of life—*death*. A few lines later she says "strictly speaking, his *life* was his occupation." Clearly (for Catharine neither disputes nor denies any of her aunt's statements) Sebastian meant his very existence to be meaningful. His death, which is his poem and his last artistic statement, tells a great deal about art and death and the artist's untenable relationship with reality.

Mrs. Venable says that Sebastian "always had a little entourage of the beautiful and the talented and the young!" and that "Both of us were young, and stayed young, Doctor" (p. 359). She would have us believe that Sebastian was chaste, that he was "*Forty*, maybe. We really didn't count birthdays" (p. 361). She is obsessed with youth and grandeur and the necessity of being a cynosure. "Most people's lives—what are they but trails of debris . . . with nothing to clean it all up but, finally, death. . . . My son, Sebastian, and I, . . . we would—carve out each day of our lives like a piece of sculpture. —Yes, we left behind us a trail of days like a gallery of sculpture! But, last summer—I can't forgive him for it, not even now that he's paid for it with his life!—he let in this—*vandal!*" (p. 363). In describing the "vandal" Catharine, Violet in effect describes herself; "they want your blood on the altar steps of their *outraged, outrageous* egos!" (p. 364). Finally, a few sentences later, she admits to having turned into an elderly lady. "We had an agreement between us, a sort of contract or covenant between us which he broke last summer when he broke away from me and took her with him, not me!" (p. 408). Catharine says, "She had a slight stroke in April. It just affected one side, the left side, of her face . . . but it was disfiguring, and after that, Sebastian couldn't use her" (p. 396). Catharine says too, "a—sort of—*umbilical* cord" had broken. "All I know is that suddenly, last summer, he wasn't young any more" (p. 409).

It is nearly impossible to separate Violet and her story from Sebastian's, for, as Catharine says, "I think it started the day he was born in this house" (p. 405). Violet presents herself quite clearly as a woman afraid of mortality, mutability, and death. Her refusal to accept her mortality, however, brands her as the antiartist, in opposition to Sebastian who has seen God only in a cruel, carnivorous universe where violent mutability is the rule. He has seen the need to transcend the corrupt human or physical world, "to go on doing as something in him directed" (p. 419). Violet's violent attempt to stop time, to preserve her youth, to make Sebastian "carve out each day" of his life and record it in a single hand printed volume keeps him alive and functioning and sterile in his brilliant white suit. Sebastian and Violet stand apart from reality, as Violet wishes, in the classic artist's pose. (The violets that break the rocks in *Camino* are clearly not the sterile, inhibiting, decaying Violet Venable.)

However, Sebastian knew from his observations of the raucous, carnivorous birds, from his attention to insectivorous plants, and from his own life, that art is the distillate of past experience and that the process destroys that past. Art is not a synthesis but a pure expression. Death, which cleans up the debris of life, is the ultimate purification and the only monumentally significant action in life.

Tom and Val know that they must cast off and destroy the past before their search for art, truth, and themselves can begin. Val and Byron know that the search cannot take place in the physical realm, but that it must take them into the Terra Incognita, the pure supraphysical region which man normally encounters only through death. Byron and Blanche tell us "not to hang back with the brutes" although the sensual world fascinates them and nearly destroys them.

Sebastian as a young man knew even more—he knew his fate, as Violet indicates. "Poets are always clairvoyant!—And he had rheumatic fever when he was fifteen. . . . 'Violet? Mother? You're going to live longer than me, and then, when I'm gone, it will be yours, in your hands, to do whatever you please with!'—Meaning, of course, his future recognition!—That he *did* want. . . . Well, here is my son's work, Doctor, here's his life going *on!* (She lifts a thin gilt-edged volume from the patio table as if elevating the Host before the altar. . . . The old lady seems to be almost young for a moment)" (p. 353).

Elsewhere Violet says one "long ago summer" Sebastian "promised those sly Buddhist monks that he would give up the world and himself and all his worldly possessions to their mendicant order" (p. 358). Mrs. Venable's strength (sufficient to neglect a dying husband) is overpowering, however, and Sebastian's first attempt to "give himself to mendicants" fails. But Violet's power over Sebastian lies only in her youthfulness and in her ability to procure. Her aneurism destroys her dream of immortality and her power; and once the cord is broken, Sebastian can cast her aside, much as Tom leaves Amanda. Just as Violet's "heart" fails her, just as Shelley's and Kilroy's and Lawrence's hearts have failed them, just as the hearts of the Son and Daughter of Casa Blanca have betrayed them, so Sebastian's heart will betray and help destroy him.

Sebastian's emergence from the false, timeless world of his mother's mind and his resulting new freedom force him to grow older and also permit him to face the inevitability of death and indeed plan for it. He has known all along that he will die before Violet. He knows he has to die to leave her with a significant corpus, his corpse being his last poem. Furthermore, the way in which he dies is important. For the first time in his life he attempts to "correct a human situation" (p. 419)—perhaps his fatal error. He runs up the hill, away from safety, with the burden of a bad heart, to die and be devoured, to leave his blood splattered over the blazing white earth, to leave his mark on the frightening tabula rasa of the universe—an example of Williams' use of red and white. One can compare La Madrecita's red sun of blood and white moon of fear; Lawrence's hemorrhage and his black and white lap robe; Casa Rojo (sic) and Casa Blanca, or more significantly Rosalio (the son) of Casa Blanca in *Purification*; Chance's incipient mutilation and the bright white clothes of the Finley family; Flora Goforth's blood and tissue rose; Mark's canvases in *Tokyo*.

In any case Sebastian consciously seeks death and destruction. He wills and seals his fate with his action. He literally gives himself to mendicants who eat and drink his flesh and blood. Thus, the old lady, with Sebastian's blood on the steps of her altar—ego—elevates the thin volume like "the Host before the altar," and the artist is purified and transcendent.

Sebastian's recognition, which remains in his mother's hands, becomes a part of a ritual cannibalism. As he carved out the days of his life, so the urchins carve out his vital parts, cleaning up the debris of his life. As Christ destroyed the old law, so Sebastian destroys his mother's moral order. The body and the blood are taken, and as Christ permitted himself to be destroyed, subsequently transcending the physical, so does Sebastian. Williams audaciously stresses Sebastian's spiritual presence by eliminating, in the play, any trace of his physical presence. Sebastian's life goes on not as much through his poetry as through the symbolic act of raising the book like a Host, for in structuring his death Sebastian symbolically and literally structures the lives of the members of his family. Like Tom and Val, Sebastian abandons the two women, Violet and Catharine, although his posthumous control over the directions of their lives is the ultimate expression of artistic power—an ironic stance for one who "thought it unfitting to ever take any action about anything whatsoever!" (p. 419).

Suddenly Last Summer is Williams' strongest statement concerning the artist's condition; strong enough, evidently, to cause him to turn away, however slightly, from the examination of totally destructive impulses. *Suddenly* is perhaps his last positive statement on the subject if one considers the self-destructive attempt to transcend the physical as a paradoxically creative effort. In the rest of his plays the artist character is invariably an "angel of death who, nevertheless, embodies no serious self-destructive tendencies. Each is decadent in the sense that survival and endurance are more immediately important than art (see Callaghan). Each becomes or is rendered impotent in some way. Finally, each is a mysterious, drifting individual who enters the play from somewhere unknown and who departs, alone and lonely, into an equally vague future. The Gypsy in *Camino Real* describes them well when she states that "Humanity is just a work in progress" (p. 543).

Two artists appear in *Sweet Bird of Youth* (1959). Chance is a marginal artist at best, or perhaps simply a failed one, but the Princess Kosmonopolis has been, as Alexandra Del Lago, a famous actress. In the play, however, she is the aging actress, one who fears her own destruction in the passing of her youth. She has attempted a comeback but fled the premiere of her film at the sight of the first closeups of her wrinkled face. During her flight she has picked up Chance Wayne, whom she metaphorically emasculates and who uses her to return to his hometown where he will be physically castrated.

The Princess is a likable character, thanks to her cynical humor—"So . . . I'm being used. Why not? Even a dead race horse is used to make glue" (IV, 49)—and to her genuine sympathy for Chance, yet, as Williams says in a stage direction, "to indicate she is going on to further triumph would be to falsify her future" (p. 122). On the strength of the reports of the success of her film, and perhaps in part because Chance rejects her, she is able to pull herself together enough to end her flight and to return to the real world, to what little remains of her career, and to what will probably be a rather tenuous existence. Her chance encounter with Chance is enough to permit her to be a witness and accessory to his destruction. She is, in a way, his "angel of death," for ultimately her instinct for survival enables her, in her conversation with Sally Powers (an ironic name), to abandon him. Though she later asks Chance to go with her, he insists on staying. Thus both go their ways, alone.

Chance is an actor, obviously assuming various roles throughout the play—son, blackmailer, lover, young romantic with Aunt Nonnie, sophisticate in St. Cloud and at the bar, and finally Fatalist, appealing to the audience for understanding. Chance is not a competent actor, though (he forgot his lines in the high school drama competition), and he is an unsympathetic character. Nonetheless he has some qualities of the artist. He, like Val, is reaching for the sky—for Heavenly, for St. Cloud, for Kosmonopolis (the cosmic city, the New Jerusalem perhaps), for Hollywood. He exhibits self-destructive tendencies and accepts his castration, though it is likely that he is a post-*Suddenly* character who will survive. For though he attempts to hang onto his youth, he says at one point, "to change is to live" (p. 88), and his character indeed changes suddenly at the end of the play (perhaps too suddenly). Yet his attitude is that "Tonight's all that counts" (p. 54), which does not go far in reaching for the sky. Still, for Chance, as for Sebastian, "Something's got to mean something" (p. 121).

Williams' next two plays, *The Night of the Iguana* (1961) and *The Milk Train Doesn't Stop Here Anymore* (1963–64), both explore relationships similar in some ways to the one between Chance and the Princess. Weales notes that in neither *Iguana* nor *Milk Train* is the relationship physical and that "Hannah teaches Shannon to accept life" while "Chris teaches Mrs. Goforth to accept death; it is the same lesson" (p. 32). We can carry the analogy back to *Sweet Bird* (and even ahead to *The Two-Character Play*).

Chance inadvertently helps the Princess accept life: "He's doing the dreadful thing for me, asking the answer for me" (p. 115). And she teaches him to accept his mutilation and leads him to self recognition: "What else can you be? CHANCE: Nothing . . . but not part of your luggage" (p. 122). The Princess is, in a sense, the Lady of the Lake (Del Lago) who hands Chance his sword of self-recognition with one hand and who takes a sword away with the other when she renders him impotent. The bitter irony of her function is further emphasized by her first name, Alexandra, which means "defender of men." Chance and the Princess do join physically, but the encounter is incomplete and unsatisfactory. She mentions castration, and Chance replies "You did that to me this morning, here on this bed." She in turn acknowledges her own impotence: "Age does the same thing to a woman" (p. 120). "Both are faced with castration," as Williams indicates (p. 122).

Indeed the entire play is one of destruction, castration, and impotence. Boss Finley disenfranchises voters. He is responsible for the Negro's castration and is more at fault than Chance for Heavenly's sterility. Miss Lucy in turn emasculates Boss Finley, out of her frustration with her own lack of place and power, as does the heckler. Aunt Nonnie is powerless to help Chance. Dr. Scudder, an impotent chief of staff who is about to marry the woman he sterilized, can't protect Boss Finley, and so on. Williams' world view is bleak. Still, the Princess and Chance are alive at the end of the play, though alone, powerless, and futureless.

Williams continues to create futureless characters who are "angels of death." In his next play, *Iguana*, the artists are Hannah Jelkes, a painter, and her grandfather, Jonathan Coffin, who is a poet. Both enter the play from nowhere and Hannah, who stands by, at the end, as her grandfather dies, is absolutely isolated: "she looks right and left for someone to call to. There's no one" (IV, 375). She has clearly suborned her art to survival, for she does quick sketches and portraits which she sells to tourists to earn enough to get on to the next hotel. She possesses Faulknerian endurance: "Just by, just by . . . enduring" (p. 353). Hannah, as Weales has seen, is a teacher and creator, but she is impotent as far as her own situation goes. She is a forty-year-old virgin and spinster with two incidences of affection to her credit. Because she has had to care for her grandfather (who is metaphorically her coffin), she has been powerless to lead her own life.

Nonno (no-no, non-non), the grandfather, is a destructive creator in that he effectively prevents Hannah from achieving anything even resembling a normal life. He is her "angel of death" as she is his. His last, dying creative effort, his poem, is destructive in that it consigns Hannah to her fate. "And still the ripe fruit and the branch / Observe the sky begin to blanch / Without a cry, without a prayer, / With no betrayal of despair" (p. 372). Hannah must endure, stoically, not as herself but faceless and alone. Maxine says, "What are you? HANNAH: I am his granddaughter. MAXINE: Is that all you are? HANNAH: I think it's enough to be" (p. 319). Nonno dies at the end of the play with a burst of creativity, like Val and Sebastian. Nonno is more akin to the later artists, however, since his age (ninety-seven) indicates that he has obviously come to grips with reality enough to survive.

Shannon and Maxine (to say nothing of Gardner and Burton) are dramatically fascinating, but *Iguana* is Hannah's play. Maxine is the "survivor," the realist in the line of Stella and Myrtle. Shannon comes to accept life and his and Maxine's existence. He has come into the play from a very clear past (almost too clear—see the gratuitous Mother and Masturbation First Cause) and remains at the end with a relatively comfortable and predictable future. Hannah, however, is the fair, good angel (in contrast to Maxine), the wisdom of the East—"Miss Thin-Standing-Up-Female-Buddha" (p. 347)— and the moving force of the play. She is one who literally exhausts herself reaching out to others, to Shannon and Nonno particularly. She is spent and futureless, but alive at least at the end of the play, where the focus is clearly on her. She is not the first character to enter the play, but it is only with her entrance that order begins to come out of chaos; for her very presence has a calming influence on Shannon. Her name means "grace," and in the unholy trinity of the play she is the fleshless spirit. She has destroyed herself as both person and human being to save the flotsam of the world—Shannon, Nonno, Maxine, and the underwear salesman at least. She is an artist who has given herself up to the principle of survival.

Christopher Flanders, in *Milk Train*, is Hannah's counterpart. He abstains from a physical relationship with Sissy Goforth. He enters the play from a largely unknown past, except for what gave him the reputation as an "angel of death," and he will evidently retire to the oubliette at the end (V, 105), though he may move on to the elderly spinster in Taormina. He stays where he can when he can, and survives. He comes into money on one or two occasions and as easily gives it away. He too uses his art as a means to survive physically, for it is only at the end of the play, after he has hung his mobile above the dying Mrs. Goforth's bed, that she permits him to have something to eat. And then he permits her to die peacefully.

Sissy Goforth is the first in a series of Williams characters—a series which includes the gnädiges fräulein in the short play which bears her name (1965) and Myrtle in *Kingdom of Earth*. All of them may or may not be termed artists, for they have worked burlesque and the music hall. Mrs. Goforth, in addition, is working on her memoirs (see Weales, p. 19), though she does not complete them. At best they are all marginal artists, however, in that they lack sympathy and sensitivity and their deepest instincts lead them to survival at any cost. Flora Goforth marries for money three times and for love (or sex) the fourth, when it is perhaps too late. She, like Lawrence, rages "against the dying of the light." The gnädiges fräulein, blind and bleeding, fights the cocaloony birds for waste fish thrown from the dock, a trick she learned in the music hall when she had to compete with the seal for affection and thus for psychic survival. Polly and Molly rapaciously steal the fish from her, and Indian Joe in turn takes the fish from them. At the end the gnädiges fräulein simply goes out for more fish when the boat whistle blows. Somehow she survives in a "cocaloony eat cocaloony world," a competitive and cruel world of free enterprise (see Callaghan, p. 57).

Myrtle too survives. She comes with the pale, effeminate Lot, his mother's child, to the family place to function as his "angel of death." The virile, dark Chicken, however, offers her the choice of life with him or death in the flood, and Myrtle, despite her culturally conditioned reservations, chooses life, attempting, at the end of the play, to cook Chicken's supper in what is now her kitchen while Lot is dying in the crystal and velvet parlor. It is as if the angels of decadent art and of earthy vitality have struggled for her soul, though the case is not that clear cut. Chicken is not entirely black— he can almost pass for white, evidently— and Lot is not entirely fair, for he bleaches his hair (however expertly). Still, Chicken is one of the "brutes" (as his name suggests) and clearly a life force. He is associated with food and sex. He throws the cat in the flooded basement; but knows the cat will swim to the woodpile, and at the end of the scene he rescues it. The purifying floods which will destroy Lot's parlor will also, according to Chicken, "make the land richer" (V, 183) and bring it new life. And he hopes Myrtle can provide him a child. Chicken is, at the end, ascendant (presumably with Myrtle), on the roof above the flood, and heir to the property anyway by virtue of a superior constitution. Lot descends to an ironic death by water. As in *Streetcar*, those who survive in the *Kingdom of Earth* are those who are strong and brutal. Myrtle, if she is an artist (she is one of those storytellers who never comes to the point), is clearly one in Williams' later mode. Lot, were he an artist, would be one from the early period. He, like Leona's dead brother in *Confessional* (later to become *Small Craft Warnings*), or like Sebastian, is too good, too pure, too sensitive to survive. And as Jean Renoir suggests in his film *The Grand Illusion*, it is the strong, vigorous, brutal, and rising lower middle class who shall inherit the earth. Or, as Williams has it in *The Two-Character Play*, it is the gross man (Mr. Grossman) who prospers.

The message and the focus of the later plays are clear. It is survival. Myrtle, like the Princess, like Hannah, like Christopher (and Mrs. Goforth in a way), and like all the characters in *Gnädiges Fräulein*, opts for existence, even at the price of the destruction of the beautiful.

In the Bar of a Tokyo Hotel (1969–70) is a strange play, an aberration perhaps, for it is one with the usual Williams characters— Miriam, who is afraid of aging and who will refuse to age, and her husband Mark, the painter whose canvases consume him—but without Williams' usual sure sense of language (see Cohn, p. 129). The preponderance of end-stopped fragments, the non sequiturs, and the pseudoidiomatic English spoken by the Japanese barman (Williams has never been successful with any pidgin dialogue) all make the play and the relationships difficult to follow. *Tokyo Hotel* is also the only post-*Suddenly* play which fits the early pattern, wherein art and artists are totally destructive. It is an anomaly in Williams' career and probably for Williams very much like one of Mark's canvases—intimate, terrifying, uncontrollable, and deadly.

Mark is so literally wrapped up in his work that he cannot tear himself away from it, yet he is totally dependent on his wife, and he presumably dies because, among other reasons, she refuses to stay with him. She, on the other hand, professes independence, but we see her, after his death and her supposed release, with "no plans" and "nowhere to go" (*Dragon Country*, p. 53). She is evidently as dependent on him and his "circle of light," his attempt to wrench beauty from life, as he is on her, and through their interdependence they tend to destroy each other with themselves. Miriam carries a poison pill in her Regency snuff box, and though she insists that "death . . . would have to remove, wrench, tear!—the bracelets off my arms" (p. 37), "she wrenches the bracelets from her arms and flings them to her feet" (p. 53) at the end of the play. Is she death? It is not clear whether or not she poisons her husband literally— though she does metaphorically—but the possibility is there. Does she die as she wrenches off the bracelets? Her sudden conversion from a released, free spirit to one with no plans and no place to go suggests that she has metaphorically died with her husband. The circular bracelets symbolize the "circle of light" outside of which she refuses to step, but which must inevitably fade with time and despite the demise of her husband. The bracelets also suggest the circular, symbiotic, interdependent relationship between Mark and Miriam, a relationship which she has attempted to overlook.

This focus on Miriam demonstrates how widely Mark's destructive influences reach. The emphasis, however, should properly be on Mark, who is at once fighting his canvas and trying, even physically, to achieve a oneness with it. According to Miriam, he shouts at his canvas, "You bitch, it's *you* or *me!*" (p. 38). The feminine epithet suggests the similarity of his relationships to his canvas and his wife.

There is no hope for survival, however, and in this play it is Mark and his world (including Miriam) who succumb. The canvases suck the life out of him.

It is this victory of art over man, however, that separates the play from the early ones and tends to align it with the late plays. Art for Mark becomes a virtual impossibility; and while Sebastian's death is a rather clear statement, Mark's death results from his inability to make a statement. The message of the play, then, is to capitulate. Death and insanity are no longer viable solutions or meaningful statements, and Alexandra Del Lago's acceptance of the corruption, her capitulation to mortality, and her resignation to imperfection enable her to survive and enable semblances of art to exist. There is no other answer, as *The Two-Character Play* so clearly demonstrates.

The Two-Character Play is Williams' most intellectually realistic statement concerning the artist's untenable and isolated position in a modern culture. The inability of Felice and Clare (ironic names, both) to hold an audience or to communicate directly with it (they need an interpreter, V, 334), to keep a company together, to escape from the prison of the theater, or even to make a coherent artistic statement indicates the artist cannot very well communicate his ideas to anyone else. Further, he cannot play his role in society and becomes frustrated. Of course, one solution for him is to make the sort of statement no one can ignore. But Williams has come, after *Suddenly* (and perhaps with it; through Catharine's true story, which is stranger than fiction), to reject insanity and death as means of dealing with reality. In *Out Cry* especially (the 1973 version of what is renamed *The Two-Character Play*) Felice and Clare are struggling desperately against the tide of insanity. In the later version they very clearly reject suicide, for neither can come to kill the other. Their only course of action, then, is to endure their condition. However, they endure not as Hannah, in a stoic, determined, Faulknerian sense, but rather in a neverending, dreary, and pointless Beckettian fashion.

The Beckettian echoes in *The Two-Character Play* are striking. The set itself, the freezing, dimming "state theatre of a state unknown" (p. 313), the "prison, this last theatre" (p. 364), with its solitary slit of a hole in the backstage wall, is right out of *Endgame*.

Felice's description of his own play, "It's possible for a play to have no ending in the usual sense of an ending, in order to make a point about nothing really ending" (p. 360), and his statement, "With no place to return to, we have to go on" (p. 316), apply equally to *Waiting for Godot*. His concern for "the love and the—substitutions, the surrogate attachments, doomed to brief duration" (p. 310) parallels Beckett's instant gleam of light in *Godot* (p. 57b), and Beckett's contempt of his audience (pp. 10a, 10b) is not far removed from Clare's description of it as "enemy forces" (p. 317). Furthermore, Williams virtually lifts one line from *Godot*. "There's nothing to be done" (p. 366; cf. pp. 8a, 14b in *Godot*). In *Out Cry* Clare asks Felice to help her up. "He rises to help her but topples onto the cushions." She says, "Will we ever get up" (p. 63), which brings to mind Beckett's four characters, all sprawled on the floor in act two of *Godot*, unable to get up.

Felice and Clare are like Winnie and Willie, acting out their happy days as they sink into the mire, or like the character in *Act Without Words I*, from whom everything is withdrawn and who remains, at the end, lying on a bare stage looking at his hands. They are like Hamm, whose function is "to play" and to endure his misery. Like Beckett's bums, they have entered the play from an endless road trip; they attempt suicide but fail; and they have nowhere to go at the end. Their function is to pass the time, to entertain each other, to enjoy their "little canters."

Williams, to emphasize the significance of the play and the act of playing, confuses the relationship of illusion to reality. Felice and Clare perform in a play within a play, but their names and their characters' names are the same, and the play is apparently based on reality. The theater is at once their home (p. 315) and their prison. Godotlike outer worlds are associated with both the frame and the play, but Clare and Felice can function in neither outer world. They are "confined" to their roles as actors and artists, and though they play before empty houses, play they must. Thus the audience is incapable of discovering when they are in and out of character.

Williams has been more careful in the 1976 than in the 1973 version to indicate clearly the difference between the frame and the play. In *The Two-Character Play* Clare and Felice more definitely move from frame to play and back. Even so their frequent and obvious improvisation in the play indicates they are not entirely within it. Near the beginning of act three Clare says, "Have you dried up, Felice? . . . I'm afraid I have, too. FELICE: Improvise something till I— CLARE: All right. Sit down. Breathe quietly. Rest a little, Felice, I'll—" (p. 340). Elsewhere, in the frame, she says, "Sometimes you work on a play by inventing situations in life that, that—correspond to those in the play, and you're so skillfull at it that even I'm taken in . . ." (p. 365). Or, as Felice makes explicit in the frame, "the backstage phone is lifeless as the phone in *The Two-Character Play* was, finally was" (p. 362). Life, as Oscar Wilde said in *The Decay of Lying*, imitates art. Life, for the artist or actor, is one long play, a continuous creation, "a trail of days like a gallery of sculpture," to use Violet Venable's words, and the egocentric act of creation is all that matters to the artist, as the business with the revolver indicates.

The revolver exists as a prop in the play, where Felice very nervously manages to load it. "Now I remove the blank cartridges and insert the real ones . . ." (p. 356). Shortly afterward, he and Clare come out of the play, into the frame, and resolve to use the gun. But to use it they have to go back into the play where, nonetheless, they fail. The resolve, evidently, is real and the act itself unbearable, unthinkable, even in a play—or perhaps especially in a play, for what seems to keep Clare and Felice alive is the continuous activity of acting. Clare says, "Do we stop where we stopped tonight or do we look for an ending?" Felice, referring to the revolver, replies, "I think that you will find it wherever you hid it, Clare" (p. 367). The world of the play is the only one that exists for them, and the only way to end the play is to end their lives—which they seriously consider but cannot bring themselves to do.

The magic of art or the fictional world of the play which fends off the real world and "too much reality" for Felice and Clare goes back to *The Lady of Larkspur Lotion*; and the hypothetical insurance receipts in the play part of *The Two-Character Play* or the nebulous receipts, in the frame, from its production, echo the delinquent revenues from the Brazilian rubber plantation. And even on a very physical level the charade of the play keeps Clare and Felice alive, for to keep from freezing, literally, they have to reenter, at the end, the warm climate of the play within the play. Since the Williams artist is often associated with heat and light, appropriately Felice and Clare are warm only when they function as artists, in character. As real personae they freeze.

Their (and presumably Williams') commitment to art is clear in *Out Cry*. In both versions Felice insists that they perform, and Clare, though reluctant, picks up the gauntlet thrown by a hostile audience. But only in *Out Cry* Felice states, "if we're not artists, we're nothing" (p. 22), and, at the end, "Magic is the habit of our existence" (p. 72). Clare, lost in her illusory world, is oblivious to time, and she indicates that Felice is unaware of anyone around him. "Felice, there was hardly a soul in the company whose name you could remember" (p. 63). The lack of a sharp distinction, in *Out Cry*, between frame and play and between actor and character puts the focus on the play of life and on the creative act that shapes the artist's being. (In *The Two-Character Play*, Clare quite clearly moves in and out of character.)

Clare and Felice survive in *Out Cry*. Clare says, "This isn't the first time I've had to save you from self-destruction which would destroy me, too" (p. 20). They do not use the gun, but neither do they absolutely reject it, and Williams closes the play with "The lights fade, and they accept its fading, as a death, somehow transcended" (p. 72). They go on with their "magic" but it is not clear for how long.

In contrast, the commitment to life (no matter how confining) is explicit in *The Two-Character Play*. Clare picks up the gun, points it, drops it, and ends the play with, "*I can't!* . . . Can you?" (pp. 369–70). Felice wordlessly follows suit. Furthermore Williams has deleted the references, in *Out Cry*, to the old painter, "seated in *rigor mortis* before a totally blank canvas" (p. 11) and to Gwendolyn Forbes' death in a hotel fire (p. 63).

Clare is a much stronger figure in *The Two-Character Play* than in *Out Cry*. She and Felice swear at each other and argue about the script. During intermission they are at each other; "there has obviously been a physical struggle between the stars" (p. 340). Toward the end, in the frame, Felice bloodies his hands trying to claw his way out of the theater (p. 363). Throughout, their energies go more into the struggle of life than into the play or the charade of life.

Still, life is dreary and they must amuse themselves, Beckettian fashion. The play, then, is not life but the substance of life that fills the time and the void, and the artist's function is to play, even without an audience, and to create for no apparent purpose. Such is the modern condition, the reality the artist faces today. The grand gesture is passé and no more productive than mere endurance.

Clearly Felice and Clare are late-period figures, as their survival, albeit a Lady and Tiger one, indicates. They enter the nowhere of the play from nowhere and remain there. They are isolated, drifting characters rendered impotent by the world (or prison) about them. Evidently they have no control over their Company, their bookings, their theater, or even, with their latest disastrous performance, over their audience. In addition they are fearful, and the gun of the abnormality of family insanity is apparently pointed at them, rendering them powerless to leave the house, the stage, or the theater. They are also, in a way, "angels of death." In *The Two-Character Play* they indicate they have witnessed their parents' deaths. In the frame of *Out Cry* they describe the old painter's end and Gwendolyn Forbes' death. Quite possibly they may preside at each other's deaths some time in the future.

Despite their problems, however, they endure for the time of the play. They survive. They make a feeble attempt at creating art. They become, finally, as illusion and reality merge, their own "work in progress."

Clearly, that body of Williams' work which precedes and includes *Suddenly Last Summer* is, paradoxically, far more vital, in its concern with destruction, than the later work, which sacrifices any intense and clear action by an artist character for a somewhat less important ability to survive. Williams foregoes violent and meaningful death for less meaningful endurance. It is as if the "something unspoken" in the play of the same name permits characters to live in an apparent equanimity, while the spoken truth, as in *Suddenly Last Summer* (with which *Something Unspoken* ran off Broadway) tears down contrived worlds for better or, more commonly, worse. Thus the artist, who speaks out, is destructive in a very real sense for Williams (as I have tried to indicate) because his truth destroys the illusions with which man must surround himself in order to survive.

Brick knows that very well, and Eliot has expressed the idea clearly: "Humankind cannot bear very much reality."

If man cannot survive without his illusions, and if the artist discovers that fact and the truth at the same time, he in effect destroys himself along with those whose illusions he destroys.

Unfortunately for Williams, his later artists shatter the illusions of other characters without purifying themselves, without distilling their own experience into a pure statement, without transcending the physical and cleaning up the debris of their own lives. This is not to say that Williams' later artists have not come to grips with themselves. I think they have, and therefore they can live to help others toward a meaningful existence or the meaningful demise which has been so important for Williams' earlier artists. But the artist's slow, sure awakening in the later plays is not as striking dramatically as his blinding realizations, in the early plays, that death is inevitable, that life is the phoenix cycle, and that art is a destructive force.

The artist's job, then, is to salvage something from the ashes of the past and to contribute that something to the ashes of the future. Art becomes the process of turning a very real and unavoidable destruction into a positive statement. It is the mad process which keeps man free. It is the concurrent destruction and creation of man himself and whatever else he can lay his hands on. Ultimately the artist's most profound statement lies in his own destruction and resurrection. "Humanity is just a work in progress."

A Gallery of Witches

NANCY M. TISCHLER

$\bigwedge$MANDA, Blanche, Big Mama, Myrtle, Mrs. Venable, Maggie, Mrs. Stone, Alexandra del Lago—some of the many remarkable women who dominate Tennessee Williams' world. Although Tom Wingfield is the admittedly autobiographical role in *The Glass Menagerie*, any actor or director would acknowledge that Amanda is the far more challenging role to play and the far more complex character to study. Blanche, not Stanley, dominates *Streetcar*; Maggie, not Big Daddy, controls the action of *Cat on a Hot Tin Roof*. Certain male characters do approach the complexity and power of Williams' female, but by and large—for a number of reasons, both biographical and psychological—the most memorable characters created by Tennessee Williams are women.

His heroines tend to fall into two or three categories. Signi Falk separates them into southern gentlewomen, southern wenches, and southern mothers, which she catalogues and discusses briefly as types (p. 169). In light of Williams' interest in myth, the recent scholarship on the archetype of the feminine, and the changing focus of Williams' later work, this decade-old perception requires reconsideration, correction, and expansion.

That Williams is interested in myth is obvious in such titles as *Orpheus Descending* or *I Rise in Flame, Cried the Phoenix*. Further, the cast of *Camino Real* provides a ready index to Williams' private

494

and shared mythology: Mary the Mother of Christ and the perennial Virgin, the harlot Gypsy, and the superannuated Camille. The speeches of his plays are littered with symbols and images drawn from myth: for instance, Maggie compares her early days with Brick as Artemis and Apollo hunting in the woods; and her repeated cat symbolism combines with the repeated references to the Nile to associate her with ancient Egyptian myth. Even settings are usually symbolic of an archetypal human experience: *Summer and Smoke,* in its clearly bifurcated structure, mirrors the ancient perception of man's divided nature; *Orpheus Descending* and *Kingdom of Earth* both use the stairway as the archetypal ladder between the sterile and the fecund layers of his two-storied universe. Stanley emphasizes the stairs' Freudian implications by drawing Stella down them to his level of sensuality, as Maxine does Shannon as she leads him down to the sea-womb. Critics have consistently observed the symbolic structure undergirding Williams' plays, and directors have emphasized his archetypal contrasts for their inherent dramatic power.

Jungians have brought together a vast array of dream, myth, and story to outline the archetype of the Feminine. Neumann, for example, in *The Great Mother* describes four poles of development for the feminine character: the good Mother, the terrible Mother, the positive transformative character and the negative transformative character. The good mother would include the Mother aspect of Mary, of Demeter, of Isis—figures who bear and release. At the opposite pole lie the terrible Mother figures—Gorgon, Hecate, Kali— women who fix, ensnare, and even dismember their young. The other poles in his schema include the positive transformative characters—the Virgin Mary, Sophia, the Muse—sources of wisdom, vision, inspiration and ecstasy. Opposite these lie the young witches, Lilith, Circe, and Astarte, whose mysteries of drunkenness bring another pattern of ecstasy, leading to madness, impotence and stupor (p. 82).

At the conclusion of his study, Neumann insists that these universal forms he has described may be traced in modern woman as well as in ancient myth: "The stages of the self-revelation of the Feminine Self, objectivized in the world of archetypes, symbols, images, and rites, present us with a world that may be said to be both historical and eternal." He says that the realms of symbols in which the Feminine becomes visible (as Great Round, as Lady of the Plants and Animals, and finally as genetrix of the spirit, as nurturing Sophia) "correspond to stages in the self-unfolding of the feminine nature." This he calls "the Eternal Feminine, which infinitely transcends all its earthly incarnations—every woman and every individual symbol." And this "Archetypal Feminine" he insists manifests itself "in all times and all cultures," appearing "in the living reality of modern woman, in her dreams and visions, compulsions and fantasies, projections and relationships, fixations and transformations" (p. 336). Whether or not Neumann is correct in his assertions about the universal applicability of his findings, his observations appear relevant to the images in Tennessee Williams' work.

From the beginning, Williams rejected the beloved American stereotype: the good wife, good mother, loving sweetheart. One of his first plays described a woman inviting guests to dinner and then flooding the banquet hall (Tischler, *Tennessee Williams*, p. 31). Williams' mutilated people generally fall pathetically in love with the unloving or the unthinking brutes or icebergs who then ignore, abandon, or devour them. Children run from mothers or shrivel under their domination. Young men seek out old harpies who castrate them.

In a colorful article on this unAmerican, or all-too-American Williams world, Marion Magid wrote: "it is a tropical country whose vegetation is largely man-eating. . . . it has not yet been converted to Christianity, but continues to observe the myth of the annual death and resurrection of the sun-god, for which purposes it keeps on hand a constant supply of young men to sacrifice. Its young men are for the most part beautiful and fawnlike . . . ," and she continues, "The country does not observe the traditional Western sexual orientation which involves the pursuit of the female by the male; instead, its young men reluctantly allow themselves to be had on those occasions when there is no way of avoiding it. . . . They are right in general to be of two minds regarding the sexual embrace, for it is as often as not followed by the direct consequences: cannibalism, castration, burning alive, madness, surgery in various forms ranging from lobotomy to hysterectomy, depending on the nature of the offending organ" ("The Innocence of Tennessee Williams," p. 34).

Thus does Williams break the prevailing Western tradition, the standard American notions of male-female relationships, and the southern mystique of the woman. In *The Glass Menagerie*, Amanda broke the sentimental mother stereotype as well as the popular image of the southern belle. From his earliest plays he broke the southern tradition of polite evasion and chivalric gynolatry. Yet, in his very violation of American tradition, Williams has delved deeper than most of his contemporaries into the essential Feminine.

His variations in both plays and short stories of the Terrible Mother image testify to Williams' obsession with her. These variants also demonstrate the range of his talent and his method of characterization. Although some of the preliminary sketches for his fully developed character studies are cardboard and garish, he is clearly not simply an iconoclast, determined to shock and destroy. Those works in which this great hovering bird-woman is most primitive and fearful are his cartoons, not his masterpieces. A clear example of this variation on the theme would be Karen Stone, the hard-hearted harpy of Williams' solitary novel. Both Mrs. Stone and Meg Bishop, the lesbian friend, are tough older women, both career women, both verbally and psychologically aggressive. While Meg can find some satisfaction in her perversion, Karen is tragically heterosexual; she has deliberately avoided motherhood by spending her fecund years with a bunny rabbit of a husband, who has served as her surrogate baby, and whose death leaves the post-menopausal widow lusting after a lover who can also be a child. Turning to the gigolos of Rome in her furious search for the fountain of youth, the old actress finds that her hawkish manners frighten the Roman sparrows just as her predatory Juliet had overpowered her pallid Romeos.

Still cruder portrayal of the gorgon lady appears in *The Milk Train Doesn't Stop Here Anymore*. Flora Goforth has even less charm than Karen Stone, being older, more hawkish, less vulnerable. In the short story "Man Bring This Up Road," she is even more grotesque. Mistress of her sumptuous villa, she dispassionately examines her vulnerable young visitors, selecting those nubile boys most to her taste, and expelling the others from her kingdom.

A fourth appearance of this thespian witch was to become a fully developed character in Alexandra del Lago of *Sweet Bird of Youth*. Still drawing heavily on bird imagery for his aging predator, Williams again portrays the aging actress inviting the vulnerable and nubile young beach boy to her bed, where, in his fatuous egotism, he presumes to challenge the old pro to a game of King of the Mountain. Predictably, Chance Wayne, like Paolo and the poet, finds himself outmatched by the cynical old witch. He can play no Oedipus to her Sphinx, no Odysseus to her Circe. He is too gentle an antihero to take on the hazardous queen and master her. Thus, Williams encourages sympathy with her slightly balding gigolo while also creating a surprising magnificence in this great castrator.

The Princess is well past her prime, is even more dissipated by hashish and liquor than Karen Stone, but she exceeds Karen also in understanding and sympathy. Unwilling to let Chance blackmail or manipulate her to shore up the ruins of his own aborted life, she is nonetheless protective when the lynch mob threatens; she offers him the role of pet dog on a golden chain. She towers over the other characters in her rage and in her lust, sharing none of their pettiness or vengefulness. Recognizing that time is the ultimate enemy for both Chance and herself, she can acknowledge that they are both monsters, living in Beanstalk Country. She can pity Chance for being a minor monster, having neither talent nor character, and for having used up his scant store of good looks and good will so quickly and so foolishly. Although his touching faith in the Cinderella myth amuses the maternal old pro, her claws show when he tries to outwit her. Like Flora Goforth, the Princess restricts her kingdom to those who can and will pay her price. Chance insists this is the real castration, leaving him already mutilated before the lynch mob appears.

Thus does Williams pay tribute to the many heroic aging actresses he watched master his roles and their own lives—from Laurette Taylor and Helen Hayes to Tallulah Bankhead and Diana Barrymore. The Princess is no simple archetype; she incorporates the gestures and the complexity of individuals Williams came to know, respect, and admire in his long theatrical career.

The earlier older woman/mother image in Williams' work had followed more specifically autobiographical or regional paths. Williams admitted from its conception that *The Glass Menagerie* incorporated many details of the Williams/Wingfield family's painful experience in St. Louis (Tischler, *Tennessee Williams*, pp. 27 ff). Though Mrs. Williams would not admit to Laurette Taylor that she

was Amanda, both tone and style of her book *Remember Me to Tom*
justify the assumption that Amanda is based on the personality of
Edwina Dakin Williams. Williams also stated explicitly that the
play was about "mothers"—not just southern mothers. Amanda's
characterization combines the antiquated southern belle with the
image of the Terrible Mother to produce a gothic creation of enormous subtlety.

As Neumann says, the female archetype is most typically presented
from the male point of view. The man sees the woman primarily in
her elementary role as nourisher and protector. But in a pattern of
negative development, parallel to Hansel's and Gretel's discovery
that the inhabitant of the gingerbread house actually eats children,
man's image of the Good Mother often is transformed by time and
experience into the image of the Terrible Mother. This transformative development can drive the ego toward masculinization (the
fight with the dragon) or toward castration (capitulation). Tom
finally verbalizes this truth, screaming at Amanda, "You ugly . . . old
—*witch*." Though he subsequently retreats, apologizes, and finally
comes to a grudging admiration of his mother, he has nonetheless
recognized that she is the dragon he must battle if he is to pass the
threshold of manhood.

Neumann's explication of the image of the Terrible Mother reveals Amanda's universality: "it is typical for the matriarchal sphere
that the son is dominated by the Great Mother who holds him fast
even in his masculine movement and activity" (p. 48). Certainly
every part of the Wingfield apartment testifies to the matriarchal
dominance. Though Amanda also manipulates the pathetically crippled and withdrawn Laura, it is Tom who provides her with a real
challenge. She is determined to govern his work, his pleasures, his
reading, and even his eating habits. Smothering attention is, according to Neumann, characteristic of the archetype: "in the clinging,
ensnaring function of the woman we already discern a will to release
nothing from her dominion, but in the function of diminution and
devouring this will is still stronger and is seen to be aggressively
negative" (p. 69). Certainly those moments in *Menagerie* when
Amanda is triumphant after her tiny victories demonstrate her appetite for power. The wrestling of an apology from Tom and the

redecoration of their dowdy little tenement in preparation for the intended new victim should convince the audience that Tom is wise in electing the path to survival, to freedom, and to manhood.

Yet Amanda is no simple archetype any more than the Princess is. She may be frighteningly true on the mythic level, as a powerful universal image, but she also has her very human justifications for her nature. The absence of the father is perhaps symbolic—the praying mantis devours her mate when she lays her eggs, as Strindberg has so eloquently demonstrated in *The Father*. The Terrible Mother has no real need of a mate once her function has shifted from conception to nurture, for her nourishing milk flows without the male's involvement. But in *The Glass Menagerie*, the absence of the husband is no victory for Amanda. Rooted in a tradition of the genteel Southerner, she can have no social position, no financial security apart from her husband. The abandoned wife violates the code of chivalry and gynolatry; she casts suspicion on the immortality of romantic love and calls into doubt the validity of southern education of women. The woman who has no career plans outside of marriage must find her pride in her husband and her children. It is her husband who in his success adorns her with ornaments and surrounds her with comforts, and she serves as an advertisement of his power and his generosity. But Amanda, thrust unloved and unlovely into a lonely world, must construct her own symbols of comfort, hospitality and style. Thus Williams speaks of her world as "paranoia"— thereby accounting for the stridency in her voice, the faint vulgarity of her struggle for survival. She uses the D.A.R. to sell magazines, her daughter to run up grocery bills, and her son to rope in potential providers. Amanda retains her southern feminity in a grotesque ritual that has lost its meaning, a sad relic of her girlhood and her romantic marriage.

Her courage in the face of adversity makes her heroic on the human level, though threatening to her children and tiresome to her society. Williams has withdrawn from her the essentials that undergird her social being, thus forcing the audience to consider the travesty of the southern myth of woman. So much of the myth rests on the presuppositions of youth, beauty, and wealth, so little on wit, heroism, enduring love. Yet Amanda refuses to acknowledge that the myth has exploded in her face, preferring to escape into her memories of jonquil days filled with gentlemen callers. Sadly, she is more beautiful now in her strength than she could have been then in her innocence, but she ignores this new value and relishes the old, choosing the dream of voile to the reality of leather.

To this complex layering of myth and region, Williams adds yet another implication, which is often a part of both the myth and the southern treatment of it—a sexual possessiveness. Only in certain moments—the flirtation with the gentleman caller and the balcony scene with Tom—do we sense a repressed sexuality in the puritanical Amanda. It is, however, this very characteristic that Williams was to explore in Alma (of *Summer and Smoke*), Alma's mother and John's mother (in *Eccentricities of a Nightingale*), and finally and most completely in Blanche.

The heroine of *A Streetcar Named Desire* is even more complex and certainly more distraught than Amanda. Although Blanche like Amanda is an aging belle—sans youth, sans wealth, sans mate, she has less focus to her life than Amanda because she is also sans progeny. Her efforts to hover over her sister, Stella, clash with Stanley's need to dominate; her eagerness to substitute for Mitch's devouring mother crashes against his innocence and disillusionment. Blanche is at the end of a trail of such failures. Her life has become a parade of shadows that momentarily replace the lost boy of her life, her homosexual husband whom she blames herself for destroying. Each gesture of love and lust echoes her need for expiation for this guilt.

There is something of the White Goddess in Blanche. Under her white dresses—sometimes soiled white—she certainly brings sterility and destruction to the Kowalski household; she settles in as a school teacher-mother who plans to improve their minds and their manners while she peremptorily dismantles their sensual paradise. Stanley is shrewd enough to see the immediate changes in Stella and to sense the altered atmosphere of his cut-rate Elysium. Though Blanche is primarily victim in any confrontation with Stanley, she is also the "tiger"—the adversary, the threat. Elia Kazan speaks of Stanley's "spine" as being masculine pride and protection of his family. If so, then Blanche tries to break that "spine" and must at any price be cast out or destroyed.

Ironically, she has in her enough masochism that she seeks the violence he threatens. In her sick memory of her castrating attack on her young husband, she finds justification for her own rape. Enough of a Southerner to remain convinced of the propriety of clearly defined male-female roles, she seeks male dominance (e.g., Shep and Mitch, as she imagines their chivalric concern for her) so that she can relax and be truly feminine. The final poignant gesture of leaning on the doctor's arm confirms her longing to lean on a strong male.

In Blanche-Stanley, the older woman-younger man syndrome is in part a teacher-student relationship (emphasized by Blanche's profession and her attraction to young men). The teachers in *Night of the Iguana* are even more clearly harpies, attacking the exhausted Shannon, driving him out of their group. But in *Milk Train* and *Sweet Bird*, Williams abandons the pretense of the teacher role, creating instead witchlike guides into corruption. The older woman becomes the ogre-mother who initiates the perpetually virgin youth into the corruption of the human heart. In *Sweet Bird*, the Princess' education of Chance is done with combined sympathy and sternness, echoing her motherly function.

Perhaps the most extreme case of the possessive mother is Violet Venable of *Suddenly Last Summer*, whose tropical garden mirrors her sick mind. The play calls for a "jungle garden" with violent colors, a garden designed by Sebastian as an image of the world and preserved by his doting mother. "There are massive tree-flowers that suggest organs of a body, torn out, still glistening with undried blood; there are harsh cries and sibilant hissings and thrashing sounds in the garden as if it were inhabited by beasts, serpents and birds, all of a savage nature" (III, 349). The predatory female of the Williams world finds this a natural habitat: in "The Knightly Quest," the savage mother has her aviary and her castle; in *Night of the Iguana*, Maxine has her hilltop surrounded by tropical rain forest. The witch apparently requires such trappings to underscore the atavistic role she plays, which is further emphasized in *Suddenly Last Summer* by the grotesque image of the turtles. Mrs. Venable and her perverse son have come to equate this scene with God: "Over the narrow black beach of the Encantadas as the just-hatched sea turtles scrambled out of the sand pits and started their race to the sea. . . . To escape the flesh-eating birds that made the sky almost as black as the beach! . . . And the sand all alive, all alive, as the hatched sea turtles made their dash for the sea, while the birds hovered and swooped to attack. . . . They were diving down on the hatched sea turtles, turning them over to expose their soft undersides, tearing the undersides open and rending and eating their flesh. . ." (III, 356).

Mrs. Venable has made the classic mother's choice of son over husband, allowing her husband to die alone while she protects her child. Her hovering concern has a Freudian ring as she speaks of the poems the two of them took nine months to produce, poems which he could not write without her. She insists that at forty he was still celibate because she herself "was actually the only one in his life that satisfied the demands he made of people" (II, 362). And when he turns to another, younger woman, even as an alternate decoy for his boy-victims, he dies, as if she willed it to punish him for cutting the umbilical cord. Catharine, in fact, replaces Violet as a mother-image to the man, though he is older than she; but neither Violet nor Catharine can save the perverse saint from his predetermined martyrdom. Violet now turns on Catharine, whom she must destroy to preserve the purity and the reputation of the departed Sebastian. Her willingness to lobotomize her niece is testimony to her veneration of her son and to her viciousness.

The fierce Mrs. Venable is an intensification of Mrs. Buchanan (*Eccentricities of a Nightingale*) and Serafina (*The Rose Tattoo*). But mothers in Williams' world show less violence toward daughters and a more jealous concern for themselves. The Gypsy with her daughter (*Camino Real*), Mrs. Winemiller with Alma (*Eccentricities* and *Summer and Smoke*), and Serafina with Rosa remind us in some way of Amanda with Laura. The daughter is a rival to the mother, challenging her role with men, reviving her own flirtatiousness along with a certain condescending and suspect solicitousness. But this relationship is quite different as a rule from mother-son confrontations.

Of all the Williams mothers, it is Big Mama who is wisest and gentlest and best. Again, the mother hangs lovingly onto the effeminate son, apparently contributing to his affliction. But in this case, Big Daddy causes more of Brick's weakness; such fierce masculinity almost demands a contrary response in the sensitive son. So long as Big Daddy dominates the scene, his wife seems like a loving doormat. But with the revelation of his sickness and his impending death, Big Mama is transformed into a strong figure, capable of managing her family, echoing the very language of her scatological husband: "I say CRAP too, like Big Daddy! . . . *Nobody's goin' to take nothin'!*—till Big Daddy lets go of it, and maybe, just possibly, not—not even then!" (III, 156). But she does hint that she would prefer to rely on her menfolks—preferably Brick. In fact, Big Mama is an almost completely sympathetic person—perhaps because Big Daddy is the monster in the family—except in her relationship with Gooper, her firstborn. The disowning of this Esau-figure appears to be both cause and result of his unappealing personality. Her need to lavish love on the unresponsive and undependable Brick testifies to her compulsion to love those men who can hurt her most. Masochism and perverse favoritism have been perennial mysteries of mother love, apparent throughout myth and history, but uncommon in the Williams woman; this doormat woman resembles Arthur Miller's characters. Big Mama displays the Good Mother image, with barely a hint of negativism.

The harpy in this play is not the ugly old witch, but the beautiful young one. Maggie the Cat is one of Williams' most interesting and unexpected heroines. Her earlier portrait in "Three Players of a Summer Game" delineates a sterile, castrating female, seeking to dominate the weak husband. The story ends with this impressive image: "Brick's driver's license had been revoked again for some misadventure on the highway due to insufficient control of the wheel, and it was his legal wife, Margaret, who sat in the driver's seat of the Pierce-Arrow touring car. Brick did not sit beside her. He was on the back seat of the car, pitching this way and that way with the car's jolting motion, like a loosely wrapped package being delivered somewhere. Margaret Pollitt handled the car with a wonderful male assurance, her bare arms brown and muscular as a Negro field hand's, and the car's canvas top had been lowered the better to expose on its back seat the sheepishly grinning and nodding figure of Brick Pollitt." The last sentence of the story captures the impression: "It was exactly the way that some ancient conqueror, such as Caesar or Alexander the Great or Hannibal, might have led in chains through a capital city the prince of a state newly conquered" (*Hard Candy*, pp. 43–4). The play blurs this simple image with more complex motivation.

Maggie desires more than the domination of Brick; she has a lust for life, for love, for children, and for money. She is a scrappy little fighter, spitting at the enemy, purring for the master, clawing for survival. She combines the motherly attentions of Big Mama and the sexuality and aggressiveness of Big Daddy. Her youth and her determination will clearly make her the sexual victor, though it is unlikely that Brick will ever do much more than talk and drink. Her very strength will serve to replace Big Daddy's as an excuse for his diminishment. In her nurturing, protective role as mother to Brick, Maggie seeks to give Brick back his life. Her final, condescending, yet loving lines, emphasize this intent, while contrasting with the conclusion of the earlier story: "Oh, you weak, beautiful people who give up with such grace," she says to the vanquished Brick. "What you need is someone to take hold of you—gently, with love, and hand your life back to you, like something gold you let go of— and I can!" (III, 215).

The sexually aggressive female—an anathema to the Southerner— fascinates Williams. Usually her attack is on the younger male, though Maggie and Maxine are priestesses of Venus who are willing to consider males of any age. Maggie dominates Brick's friend Skip sexually and flirts with Big Daddy. Maxine (*Night of the Iguana*) moves easily from aging husband to beach boys to Shannon. She is a more highly developed and interesting version of the tough but motherly whore shown in Myrtle of the seven descents. The water imagery of *Night of the Iguana* echoes her role as womb and tomb. Her tropical retreat is the end of Shannon's world, where he can return to the earth mother, dance his final perverse, saintly dance, and die erotically in her motherly embrace. Maxine's wit makes her far more believable, colorful, and dramatic than Karen Stone as well as more motherly and warm, less hard and egocentric. Her symbols are natural ones of vegetation, water, and animal life—all indications of her archetypal function.

While Maxine, in her revealing shirt and slacks, demonstrates the amplitude of the mother, feeding her flock, offering them shelter for the night, she also demands her price. She flaunted her lusty "night-swimmers" before her dying husband, and she can tie up the iguana as she can tie up Shannon for future use. Her mothering of Shannon is both solicitous and salacious. The concluding scene, as they go down to the sea ("the cradle of life") for a night swim, is emphasized by Shannon's assertion that he can make it down the hill without her, but not back up. She insists that she can help him back up, but her comforts will not be the austere and spiritual ones that Shannon needs for renewal.

Hannah, on the other hand, the alternate mother figure in the play, is a New England spinster, who serves as a cool Oriental madonna, offering him poppy seed tea and sympathy as Shannon works through his voluptuous crucifixion. The pietà is a frequent Williams image, a combination of sexual purity, and that deep compassion that results from the blessedness of bearing and losing the child. La Madrecita de los Perdidos (*Camino Real*) is the image that haunts him, echoing the conclusion of *Glass Menagerie* (with Amanda hovering over the lost Laura), repeated in *Iguana* with Hannah cradling her dead grandfather. Ironically, this Mother Mary, who contrasts with the cruel mother of life, seems to be impotent, capable only of compassion. While Hannah would never tie up Shannon or the iguana, neither would she release them. We therefore should not expect her to travel with Shannon or to stay with him. She laughingly quips, "Spinster's loss, widow's gain," but Shannon recognizes the hovering irony of the comment.

The parallel female figures here summarize some of Williams' attitudes. Hannah-the-spinster and Maxine-the-widow are his most fully developed pair, though he uses parallel mothers in *Eccentricities of a Nightingale*, mothers and daughters in *Cat*, *Menagerie*, and *Rose Tattoo*, sisters in *Streetcar*. Hannah and Maxine are both characterized principally by their relationship to men—one having lived without sexuality, the other having reveled in it, and both now without mates. On the one hand, Hannah is proud of her virginity, wearing her purity with Athena's regality, neither ashamed nor puritanical, capable of love, of compassion, and of considerable wisdom. She has chosen her "nest" in the heart of her grandfather, with no hope of sexual satisfaction or propagation, content as Alma Winemiller could never have been.

On the other hand, Maxine has outlived one husband and proudly advertises her sexuality, planning to select a new king for her mountain, whom she will also outlive. She is no monster—any more than Maggie is a monster. She is a full-blooded woman who loved

Fred, loves Shannon, and can love again when Shannon has gone. She did not kill Fred, but she does not mourn him deeply. Like Maggie, she is no willing participant in rituals of self-destruction. And also, like Maggie, her lust for life takes brutal forms that may appear excessive. Unlike the Strindberg nightmare of Omphale's ensnaring Heracles, the binding in *Iguana* is followed by a loosing. Maxine, a "bright widow spider" (IV, 317), can endure Shannon's pain with equanimity and even contribute to it. But the action of the play disproves Shannon's assertion that "All women, whether they face it or not, want to see a man in a tied-up situation. . . . Their lives are fulfilled, they're satisfied at last, when they get a man, or as many men as they can, in the tied-up situation" (IV, 345). The play itself moderates this harsh judgment: Maxine and Hannah both see the trussing as a means to curtail Shannon's self-destructive violence. He is not quite parallel to the iguana; since he is human, his ensnarement involves choice, not simply blind force. And Maxine's enjoyment of him will not be altogether unpleasant for him.

Williams characterizes both Maxine and Hannah in depth, yet balances them as types and further exploits them as elements of Shannon's nature—his flesh and spirit, bad and good angels, id and superego. They are remarkably rich portraits of classic Williams women. Alma, Blanche, Amanda, Laura all share traits with the Yankee lady Buddha; Stella, Rosa, Maggie, Big Mama all foreshadow the earth mother of the rain forest. But they are both different from their predecessors, less tormented, more understanding of themselves and others, more content to accept their own limitations. Both are visually and verbally contrasted; both range from tragedy to comedy, but in very different modes. They share the resilience of Williams' beloved phoenix and appear to be his tribute to woman's appetite for life and capacity for survival.

If there is such a thing as development in an author, the critic must note that the movement from Amanda to Blanche to Maggie to Alexandra del Lago to Maxine/Hannah demonstrates an increasing acknowledgment of the corruption of the male victim and an expanding acceptance of therapeutic cruelty. Certainly, Amanda/Tom is modified in Maggie/Brick, which is again expanded in Alexandra/ Chance, and finally almost balanced in Maxine/Shannon. The mother-figure appears less cruel as the child grows older and more corrupt, blinder, more self-mutilating, more demonstrably wrong-headed.

It is by no means strange that Tennessee Williams should have meditated so long and with such baroque results on this mother-son syndrome. Mom and Venus are the dominant female images for America. The grotesque marriages of Venus with the spider, and the mother with the monster, appeal more to Williams—perhaps the artist's reaction against the simplistic assertions of advertisers, perhaps the Southerner's need to destroy the cloying rhetoric of gynolatry, perhaps the homosexual's observations of actual women, certainly the man's observation and confrontations in his life. Whatever the reason, his images are testimony to his versatility and his artistry. That he can play so many compelling variations on these themes demonstrates his rich sensitivity; that he must trace his redundant arabesques in so narrow a sphere suggests his compulsive and romantic mode of creativity.

The literary critic enjoys the recurrent pattern as an exciting vehicle for isolating levels of characterization: On the most universal level, he can trace the image of the Great Mother in her most terrible aspect—as primitive and frightening as the Gorgon or the dreaded Sphinx, as furious with her mate and destructive of her children as Medea, or as temptingly vicious as Circe. At this level, she is frighteningly presented as a trial to be faced by the hero—often to be fought by indirection, necessarily to be escaped if he is to survive with his manhood intact.

On the more cultural, historical level, he can trace the lineaments of the American South: the veneration of the woman, the matriarchal culture, the possessive and charming mother/belle. Under her drawl and her wit, behind her charm and vivacity is a frenzy, a desperation, a possessiveness, a clue to the more vicious archetype.

But the focus on the predatory female bird and the ensnared male iguana/turtle victim takes on an individual stress with Tennessee Williams. His signature is in the jungle imagery, the cats and birds. No other contemporary playwright has such a gallery of handsome male victims in so many stages of mutilation. The violence of Williams exceeds primitive violence because it is wrapped in the decadently lavish style of southern rhetoric. And his combinations are more subtle and more haunting than most, perhaps because they are so visual, so grotesque, so dramatic. His characters seldom live on the level of moral absolutes, though they pretend to hold to certain private ideals; victims tend to deserve their crucifixions, brutes have justification and grandeur and moments of gentleness. Witches need not be old, and youths need not be innocent. Both the hero and the Gorgon may have their recognition scene, admitting their own monstrosity, determining to accept their grim fate.

Thus, in his evaluation, the critic is bound to admit that Williams does indeed create timeless beauty and dredge haunting insights out of the hideous chaos of his memories, observations, and imagination. Although no one would select Karen Stone or Flora Goforth as memorable characters, no one should deny the brilliance of Amanda, Blanche, Maggie, Maxine, or Alexandra. Somehow, Tennessee Williams has domesticated his monsters by providing them a history, a motivation, individualism, and charm. When the Gorgon reveals that she is a former belle, now destructive, aging, and confused, when she frets about her snaky hair, and when she speaks with sardonic wit in a southern accent, we no longer fear her or approach her with mirrors. She has become one of us.

Tennessee Williams' Women: Illusion and Reality, Sexuality and Love

JEANNE M. McGLINN

THE CRITICAL LABELS commonly affixed to the women characters in the plays of Tennessee Williams are deceptively simple. Robert Jones divides the "Early Heroines" into basically two types, the gentlewoman of a genteel but mythical southern way of life and the sensual or natural woman. The gentlewoman cannot understand life in the modern world, and in her resultant alienation she seeks to recapture a way of life, the cavalier Old South, which never really existed. The sensual women are inhabitants of the New South and "seem to have been conceived by their creator, if not as representatives of a sort of salvation, then at least as attractive earth goddesses whose salvation is their own sexuality" (p. 211). Jones considers sex as either a means of escape or a sign of liberation, depending on the woman's view of her own sexuality. John von Szeliski also feels the basic dramatic action of Williams' plays is sexual (p. 67). Critics agree on reading Williams' plays as sexual dramas in which the southern gentlewoman and the natural woman represent respectively the spirit and the flesh, though the sexual is the only creative and positive form of behavior. Yet a close reading of Williams' plays reveals a complexity in the women that makes these classifications incomplete.

In seven plays written in a twenty year period, Williams uses essentially the same dramatic situation. A woman is presented at a

510

moment when frustration has led to a crisis. She has only two possible ways of acting: to face reality or to retreat into illusion. The significant question is whether she will face the crisis and choose to live in the real world, free of debilitating illusions and capable of compassion for others. Whatever value sex has for Williams, in some plays sexuality leads to illusion or is at least the result of a very self-centered view of reality. Neither situation is creative, whereas the ability to respond to the needs of another human being emerges as a higher value for Williams. The human contact may be either physical or spiritual; what matters is the attempt to love—based on a realistic understanding of both oneself and another. Between 1940 and 1960 Williams moves from the delineation of women who live in illusion and hence are unable to love to the delineation of women who accept the reality of their lives and become concerned and compassionate or at least ready for unselfish love.

In two plays of the forties, *The Glass Menagerie* and *A Streetcar Named Desire*, the women characters all act under the influence of an illusionary view of both themselves and their world and so are unloving. In *The Glass Menagerie*, both Amanda and Laura refuse to face the reality of their lives; Amanda retreats into the past, and Laura retreats into herself. Laura's withdrawal is more deadening than Amanda's, however, because she is completely self-centered. Amanda is at least trying to hold the family together, economically and spiritually. She tries to help Laura lead a normal life, first by sending her to business college then by making "plans and provisions" for a gentleman caller. These efforts for another human being, even though undermined eventually by Amanda's illusions, corroborate Williams' description of Amanda as having "dignity and tragic beauty" (I, 236).

The crisis that led to Amanda's illusion came well before the play began. Her husband's desertion of her and the family was the shock that sent her back into the golden days of her girlhood. Since Amanda cannot face the reality that she was unable to hold her husband's love, she indulges in memories of that one supreme moment of her youth, the day when she might have chosen from seventeen gentlemen callers, all rich and successful and caring for their wives. Williams describes Amanda as, "A little woman of great but confused vitality clinging frantically to another time and place," who "having failed to establish contact with reality, continues to live vitally in her illusions" (I, 129).

Removed into her past and needing to fortify an endangered sense of self-worth, Amanda assumes an archaic form of southern behavior, gentility. In the early American South a genteel code developed, giving the white southern woman homage both to safeguard her purity from the manhood of black slaves and to symbolize a civilizing influence on the decadent ways of the white landed gentry (Cash, pp. 87–9). So "gentlemen callers" represent a time when men were chivalrous and women were respected, admired, and pampered. Amanda affects the pose of superiority granted by this code to women, along with the flirtatiousness of the genteel lady who could attract and allure, giving a man hopes of reward without committing herself.

Amanda can act as the southern belle, but when she tries to force the role on Laura, the result is a complete disintegration of Laura's personality. She has precariously managed to protect herself from what she regards as a harsh and judgmental world by making her own world out of old records and tiny glass figurines. Laura's retreat from the real world is a result of her belief that since she is crippled, she is unlovely and unloveable. Feeling unattractive, Laura is frightened by a situation in which this attractiveness is directly tested, entertaining a man. Her self-consciousness and introversion thus reach a climax during her evening with Jim, the gentleman caller.

Unable to act like Amanda, Laura eventually responds to Jim's warmth. She forgets herself as they talk and even trusts him with the unicorn, a symbol for herself. But after Jim kisses her and then apologizes because he is engaged, Laura immediately retreats for protection into her inner world: "She rises unsteadily and crouches beside the Victrola to wind it up" (I, 231). Her distorted sense of reality prevents the realization that Jim's actions have nothing to do with her attractiveness. Self-centered for too long, she seems incapable of realizing that what comes into her world does not necessarily reflect on her. Given such a limited perception, Laura cannot participate in human relationships and will continue to be unhappy in the real world.

Blanche resembles both Amanda and Laura in her reactions to the harsh world. Her attempt to hold the crumbling world of the family plantation together is similar to Amanda's attempt to keep her family together. Also like Amanda, she refuses to accept the reality of her life and attempts to live under illusion. She has a false sense of gentility which is contradicted by an equally false flight to promiscuity. The conflict between these two modes of behavior means self-defeat instead of survival. At the play's end, Blanche can only retreat into an insanity that exceeds Laura's withdrawal.

Blanche's moment of crisis occurred when she discovered her husband was a homosexual and in a moment of disgust drove him to suicide. The memory recurs in vivid flashes to haunt Blanche who only wants to avoid the "blinding light." She does not want to face her rejection of her husband and the part she played in his suicide.

Criticism of Stella's sordid condition allows Blanche to forget her own unhappy life. She refuses to believe that Stella has adjusted to this new way of life which is so different from the plantation world where women were ladies. It is the "lady" that is speaking when Blanche judges Stanley, Stella's husband, as beneath them because he is not a gentleman. Blanche's attempt to maintain the image of herself as a correct and genteel lady also leads her to deny her real sexual nature. Blanche too pines for the "gentleman" who will rescue her.

Blanche's sexual nature asserts itself, however, contrary to her attempts at gentility, and this leads to her breakdown. She avoids adult sexual relationships but actively seeks affairs with adolescents. She has just been exiled from her hometown because she attempted to seduce a boy. She later admits that she has had many "one-night stands" with the young soldiers of the nearby army camp. And the stage action shows her urge to seduce a young newspaper boy. Blanche seeks relationships with boys both because she feels guilty about the death of her young husband and because she is sexually immature and inadequate. Though she does not wish for the complications of love, panic drives her to sex when her memories have made existence intolerable: "After the death of Allan—intimacies with strangers was all I seemed able to fill my empty heart with. . . . I think it was panic, just panic, that drove me from one to another, hunting for some protection . . ." (p. 386). After all, Blanche says, the opposite of death is desire.

Blanche's real motive for pursuing sexual relationships, however, seems to be the one she cannot face, her sexual inadequacy. Allan, she says, "came to me for help. I didn't know that. . . . all I knew was I'd failed him in some mysterious way . . ." (p. 354). It is this failure that Blanche is trying to exorcise by forming relationships with boys. She might be able to satisfy one of them in a way she was never able to satisfy her boyish husband Allan. This sense of inadequacy also accounts for her acute awareness of her physical attractiveness. She exercises her sexual charm to prove her allure—not for sexual gratification. Fearing that she will be unable to win a man and knowing that failure will mean she will have to face herself, Blanche pursues Mitch. But she has no wish for a mature man-woman relationship and never really views Mitch as a sexual conquest. Blanche's feelings for Mitch are totally self-centered. She sees him as "a cleft in the rock of the world that I could hide in!" (p. 387). She wants him to protect her from her persistent vision of Allan's suicide: "You've stopped that polka tune that I had caught in my head" (p. 380).

Stanley, in his ignorance and insensitivity, destroys both Blanche's hope and her illusion. He sees through her pose without understanding why she needs one. He thinks merely that she feels superior to him, and he wishes to destroy her composure to make her recognize that she is the same as he, a sexual animal. Stanley takes Blanche's teasing as a sign of real sexuality and concludes that they've "had this date with each other from the beginning!" (p. 402). The rape shatters Blanche's desperate pose for dignity and also forces on her what she is inadequate to endure, raw sexual passion. The result is insanity.

Blanche's sister, Stella, deals with reality in a basically healthy way. Rather than holding on to the old way of life at Belle Reve, she left to make her own living. Survival is always self-centered, however, as Blanche knows when she accuses Stella of deserting the family. Stella ignores the needs of others and eventually adopts her own illusion. Life with Stanley—sex with Stanley—is her highest value. Her refusal to accept Blanche's story of the rape is a commitment to self-preservation rather than love, and thus Stella contributes to Blanche's disintegration.

In *Summer and Smoke* written in 1948 Williams' characterization of women begins to change. Alma, unlike the heroines of the early plays who reject reality, develops in the course of the play from a woman who lives in the illusion of impossible aspiration and idealism into a woman who accepts reality and who actively seeks what she wants. Concurrent with this development, she grows in her capability to communicate with others. She overcomes her egocentrism and self-pity and offers kindness to someone in need.

The crisis that leads to this change in Alma is her complex feelings about herself and her life during this summer of her middle twenties. She feels that her youth is passing and knows that she is already considered an old maid. She resents the need to care for a senile and selfish mother and a self-pitying father: "I have had certain difficulties and disadvantages to cope with—which may be partly the cause of these peculiarities of mine . . ." (II, 152). Then John Buchanan, the boy whom Alma has always loved, returns and disturbs Alma with his rejection of her idealism and his insistence on the physical nature of relationships between a man and a woman.

Highly idealistic behavior has always come naturally to Alma since she is the daughter of a minister. Even as a ten-year-old child she was adultlike, dignified with a quality of spirituality, and intrigued by the idea of eternity. These characteristics have intensified with age. The playwright says, "An excessive propriety and self-consciousness is apparent in her nervous laughter . . ." (p. 135). Alma's daydreams about eternity have solidified into a philosophy of otherworldliness. The symbol of her idealism is the Gothic cathedral because "everything seems to be straining for something out of the reach of stone—or human—fingers." Life, to Alma, is "the everlasting struggle and aspiration for more than our human limits have placed in our reach." Man lives in the gutter, she believes, but "some of us are looking at the stars" (p. 197).

This idealism is illusionary, however, because Alma has been unable to translate it into positive action. Her care of her mother leads her to self-pity. She is bitter because she has not gotten anything for her sacrifice, not even recognition. Her life tied to duty, Alma has a dream about what she would do if things were different. She says to John, "Most of us have no choice but to lead useless lives! But you . . . have a chance to serve humanity. Not just to go on enduring for the sake of endurance, but to serve a noble, humanitarian cause, to relieve human suffering" (p. 154).

Alma also has an exalted notion of the role of woman as wife and mother. She thinks a woman must bring her heart and her soul to marriage, and she rejects sexuality as often no better than bestiality. She rejects John's anatomy lesson: "I reject your opinion of where love is, and the kind of truth you believe the brain to be seeking!— There is something not shown on the chart" (p. 221). Alma, of course, means the soul. John sees this ideal as another example of Alma's Gothic cathedral image of life and suggests that Alma would never be satisfied with a normal love relationship; she would be striving for the impossible. Alma admits that her attempts to establish relationships with men have all failed because of "a desert between us" (p. 198). She has never been able to care for any man: "None of them really engaged my serious feelings" (p. 200). The one man Alma loves, John, she has loved with her soul, but he rejects this love. It is, he tells her, actually what kept him away from her: "The night at the casino—I wouldn't have made love to you. . . . I'm more afraid of your soul than you're afraid of my body. You'd have been as safe as the angel of the fountain—because I wouldn't feel *decent* enough to touch you . . ." (p. 222).

With the impact of her whole situation and with John's rejection, Alma is forced to see that her idealism does not lead to positive acts in her own life. After a period of physical collapse and mental turmoil, she decides to pursue personal fulfilment. She decides that a person "can ask for the coming true of his most impossible dreams" (p. 241). Her old self is dead: "the girl who said 'no,' she doesn't exist any more" (p. 243). Though Alma realizes that she can no longer marry John, she reveals her new strength when she goes to him to declare that she loves him: "I haven't come here on any but equal terms. . . . It's no longer a secret that I love you. It never was" (p. 245). She does not indulge in self-pity. She attempts to understand what has happened to her former relationship with John and, unselfishly, hides her tears rather than detract from Nellie's happiness.

In the last scene, Alma is administering to a lonely and nervous traveling salesman. She has lost her extreme propriety; she laughs naturally and engages in light banter. Unencumbered by a false ideal of what love should be, she is ready to accept another for what he is and make the most of this human contact. This may not be a relationship "to engage her serious feelings," but it is a relationship that springs from a new genuineness and a clearer view of reality. In earlier plays women were able to find relief from emotional crises only in illusion, but in *Summer and Smoke* and the subsequent plays of the fifties except for *Orpheus Descending* Williams portrays women able to face reality and enjoy healthier relationships.

In *The Rose Tattoo*, Williams depicts Serafina, who with a "woman's heart passionately in love" (II, 270), idealizes her marriage with Rosario. To her, married sex is the ultimate experience, "a religion," and she is proud of her adherence to its values: faithfulness, chastity, and purity. But the idea that making love had consecrated her and her husband is an illusion because Rosario was not faithful, and there is no indication that he even loved Serafina. After his death, she continues to exalt his memory and maintains her idealization of their relationship. In order to do this, she cloisters herself from the real world. Putting her "heart in the marble urn with the ashes" (p. 372), she quits taking care of herself, lives in the past, and talks to the ashes.

When Serafina learns after years of homage that Rosario defiled their marriage bed, she is freed from her illusion. She does not react as Amanda does to her husband's desertion. Instead the truth frees Serafina from adoration of a memory. She is saved from despair by Alvaro to whom she turns in a relationship so practical that it cannot be idealized. He admits the economic advantages of marriage with Serafina, but at the same time he offers "Love and affection!—in a world that is lonely—and cold!" (p. 366). Serafina comes through her crisis to realize, like Alma, that life is too important to reject for a memory.

Unlike Serafina, Maggie of *Cat on a Hot Tin Roof* has no illusions at the time of the play. Instead she is clear about her two main goals: to acquire money and to overcome her estrangement from Brick. She says she wants money so she can take care of Brick, and she refuses to leave him because she loves him. It is difficult to believe her motivation is other-centered, however, because of information which indicates how selfishly she acted in her earlier days. She forced Brick to marry her; and then when she saw Skipper as a threat to her relationship with Brick, she accused him of homosexuality even though she knew it would be devastating to him. She admits she acted wrongly since she now knows Brick desires only the most ideal relationship. Her self-centeredness has caused her to act in illusion.

Maggie is motivated in part by a background of genteel poverty. Growing up, she felt inferior because her family had to struggle to maintain a respectable standard of living despite an alcoholic father. Maggie resented the rich relatives who expected her fondest gratitude in exchange for castoff possessions. Now she says she must have money to feel good in old age.

The effect of this information is to make all her actions ambiguous. When she manipulates everyone around her in her competition with Mae and Gooper for Big Daddy's estate, she may only want the money for herself. On the other hand, she may be acting out of love for Brick, as she says. No matter for what reasons, when she uses Brick's alcoholism to accomplish her ends, her actions can only appear destructive. This ambiguity is compounded because whatever Maggie does for her husband, she ultimately does for herself as well. Securing an inheritance will benefit them both. An emotionally whole Brick will be a better lover for Maggie.

Two elements of the play, Maggie's identification with Big Mama and the revised act three, indicate the author's intention and resolve our questions. Big Mama and Maggie have similar relationships with their husbands. Both love the same type of man; Big Daddy is just an older version of Brick. Williams says he "must have had something Brick has, who made himself loved so much by the 'simple expedient' of not loving enough to disturb his charming detachment, also once coupled, like Brick's, with virile beauty" (III, 138–39). And both women are misunderstood by their husbands who find it hard to believe in their love. When their wives declare their love, both men respond with the same words, "Wouldn't it be funny if that was true?" (pp. 78, 166). Big Mama's joy that Daddy will live, her anguish when she learns the truth, her refusal to let the children appropriate his power, and her hurt when she sees that Big Daddy does not know how much she loves him all demonstrate that she loves unselfishly. By identifying Maggie with Mama, Williams shows he thinks Maggie is a lover too.

The revision of the third act further explains Maggie's character. Elia Kazan influenced the changes to show a Maggie who is less ambiguous in her actions because he wanted her character to be "more clearly sympathetic to an audience." Williams accepted this suggestion "wholeheartedly" because Maggie "had become steadily more charming to me as I worked on her characterization" (p. 168). As a result, the Maggie that emerges is no longer as manipulative or destructive to others.

Maggie seems genuinely concerned about Big Mama when she calls Brick to comfort her. Whereas in the original play Maggie called Brick only at Mama's bidding, several lines of dialogue have been added to show that Maggie anticipates Big Mama's need for comfort and support against Mae and Gooper and their plans. She says to Brick, "they're going to tell Big Mama the truth now, an' she needs you!" (p. 174). Maggie even uses a threat: "I'm going to take every dam' bottle on this place an' pitch it off th' levee into th' river!" (p. 179)—to make Brick respond. In the original, when Maggie used this threat, she was manipulating a helpless man. Here Brick is strong enough that he is not threatened and hears her words as a sign of vitality and determination.

The other major change in the action grows from Brick's self-realization. In the Broadway version the change in Brick's awareness of his guilt is immediate, and so he is less defensive towards Maggie. He is able to respect her vitality and he accepts her aid. When Maggie maneuvers to defeat the ambitions of Mae and Gooper with news of her pregnancy, Brick gives her support. The revised last scene also suggests that Brick responds with love to Maggie. Encountering the thoroughness of her determination, he does not abjectly give up with nothing to say. Rather, he says, "I admire you, Maggie" (p. 214). The stage action shows his willingness to turn out the lights and begin their lovemaking. His receptiveness makes Maggie's final speech ring true: "Oh, you weak, beautiful people who give up with such grace. What you need is someone to take hold of you—gently, with love, and hand your life back to you . . . and I can! I'm determined to do it . . ." (p. 215). Maggie is a vital woman who can be misunderstood, but the weight of the play tends to move our understanding of her as a person who, if responsive to her own needs, is at least equally responsive to the needs of other persons around her.

Unlike Maggie, the women in *Orpheus Descending* are so involved in trying to survive in a hostile and violent society that they have no strength left for healthy relationships. Vee Talbot, the sheriff's wife, faces the cruelty and violence of the county jail. She sees "awful things take place" (p. 291): beatings, lynchings, runaway convicts torn to pieces by dogs. Moral corruption marks the society which spawns such violence. The women are backbiters and adulterers; the men are intolerant and sadistic.

Vee believes she has a mission to help people, to "save" them, to "build up characters!" but the townspeople scorn her religiosity. Confused by the world of light and shadow, religion and hatred, which she inhabits, Vee turns to her paintings as a method of survival. Denying the appearances of the world as misleading, she believes visions are the only way to see and so paints under their influence. Val articulates her feelings about her art best when he says, "You make some beauty out of this dark country" (p. 292). Her creativity leaves her exhausted but elevated above and purified of the gross world. Her paintings are an escape into fantasy which eventually blind her totally to the real world.

Carol, a member of an aristocratic family in the town, tried to struggle singlehandedly against its cruelty and injustice. She delivered speeches, wrote letters, and protested against the injustices done to the black people by the white minority. She says, "I thought it was wrong for pellagra and slow starvation to cut them down when the cotton crop failed from army worm or boll weevil or too much rain in summer" (p. 251). So she used her inheritance to set up free clinics. Then when a black man was electrocuted "for having improper relations with a white whore" (p. 252), she personally protested by setting off for the capital, on foot in winter, dressed in a potato sack. The reaction of the town was to hoot, jeer, spit at her, and arrest her for lewd vagrancy.

Her economic resources bankrupt and her personal sense of well-being threatened by the rejection of her family and community, Carol employs bizarre survival tactics. Having people talk about her is one way of knowing she is alive, and so she irritates the populace: "I want to be noticed, seen, heard, felt! I want them to know I'm alive!" (p. 251). Movement gives her a sense of life so her life now is the endless, restless round of "jooking," driving, drinking, dancing, and lovemaking. She uses sex, even though it is painful and potentially dangerous, just "to be not alone, even for a few moments" (p. 282). Because she sees contact with another person as a way to feel alive, Carol's idea of a relationship is holding onto another for all she's worth. She says, "What on earth can you do on this earth but catch at whatever comes near you, with both your hands, until your fingers are broken?" (p. 245). Carol is too threatened to be able to forget herself and love another for his own sake.

Lady also lives with the effects of small town hatred and intolerance. Her father was burned to death in the fire set to teach him a lesson because "he sold liquor to niggers" (p. 232). Then Lady was rejected by her lover for a woman with social status and wealth. Badly hurt, she gave up on life and "sold" herself to a loveless marriage. Yet, she believes life has some meaning. She tells Val there is more to life than corruption, because "If I thought that was the answer I'd take Jabe's pistol or his morphine tablets" (p. 273). Lady does not want to die, and so she tries to begin living again. She wants to open a replica of her father's wine garden in the confectionery of the Torrence store. In this way, she will reassert her father's presence and her own identity in the face of the town's resistance. She hopes to overcome David's rejection and regain self esteem by reviving the richness of the time when he loved her. She tells him, "don't pity me. . . . in there's the confectionery which'll reopen this spring, . . . it's going to be like—the wine garden of my father, those wine-drinking nights when you had something better than anything you've had since!" (p. 286). When Lady learns that Jabe was the leader of the Mystic Crew the night her father was burned out, the revival becomes "necessary, it's just something's got to be done to square things away. . . . *Just to be not defeated!*" (p. 329).

This single ambition to endure consumes Lady. She will use any means to obtain her end, including Val. She begs him to stay with her, not because she loves him, but because she needs him "TO LIVE. . . . TO GO ON LIVING! ! !" (p. 305). When the situation in the town threatens him and he wants to leave, Lady selfishly keeps him with her, promising that they will go after she has had her revenge. Then when she realizes she is pregnant, Lady does not need Val anymore and tells him to leave. She has life now and is self-sustaining. It seems an inconsistency when she covers Val with her body and takes her husband's bullets. This self-sacrificing behavior is out of line with her pattern of survival.

None of the women in *Orpheus Descending* achieves even the

readiness for compassionate love. A sense of acceptance of and survival in the real world must come first. Williams' characters in the fifties generally attain these qualities. This play is an exception possibly because it is a reworking of a play of 1940, *Battle of Angels*.

In *The Night of the Iguana*, Williams repeats in the character of Hannah Jelkes the basic theme that facing reality may develop compassion. Williams says, "She suggests a Gothic cathedral image of a medieval saint, but animated. . . . she is totally feminine and yet androgynous-looking—almost timeless" (IV, 266). Hannah's femininity takes the form of the comforting mother figure, as Shannon perhaps realizes when he calls her "Miss . . . Thin-Standing-Up-Female-Buddha" (p. 346). She does, in any case, immediately respond to Shannon's obvious need for compassion.

Hannah is compassionate because she has endured her own personal crisis and is able to sympathize with the confusion and panic of others. She tells Shannon: "I can help you because I've been through what you are going through now. . . . I showed [my spook] that I could endure him and I made him respect my endurance" (pp. 352–53). Hannah has saved herself from passive existence in a dream world by controlling her panic: "I never cracked up, I couldn't afford to. . . . My work, this occupational therapy that I gave myself—painting and doing quick character sketches—made me look out of myself, not in, and gradually, at the far end of the tunnel that I was struggling out of I began to see this faint, very faint grey light—the light of the world outside me—and I kept climbing toward it" (p. 355). The experience has made her feel that people need "A little understanding exchanged between them, a wanting to help each other through nights like this" (p. 352). Despite her own immediate problems with her grandfather's illness and their penury, Hannah acts on her belief that people can "see and know each other" and "if they're decent . . . help each other all that they can" (p. 324).

Hannah's kindness contrasts with the sensual egocentrism of Maxine, "a stout, swarthy woman in her middle forties—affable and rapaciously lusty" (p. 255). She demands male attention and seeks it from Shannon as well as the Mexican boys. Maxine thinks she has no illusions. She says to Shannon, "I know the difference between loving someone and just sleeping with someone—even I know about that. We've both reached a point where we've got to settle for something that works for us in our lives—even if it isn't on the highest kind of level" (p. 329). However, her willingness to substitute immediate gratification for human contact and creative love make her weaker than Hannah who always seeks the human contact. In fact, Maxine's sexual drives lead to her false assessment of the relationship between Hannah and Shannon as sexual. "I got the vibrations between you...," she says, "and there sure was a vibration between you and Shannon the moment you got here. That, just that, believe me, nothing but that has made this ... misunderstanding between us" (p. 322). As a result, Maxine wants to send Hannah and her grandfather, who is hardly able to travel, away from the hotel. Maxine's sexual drives make her selfish, deluded, and unkind.

Examination of Williams' women characters shows that oversimplified classifications are inadequate. Williams gradually characterized women to dramatize the theme that a woman must avoid illusions about both herself and others. Amanda is too involved in illusion to see her daughter's mental condition, and Laura is too involved in self to love. Blanche has failed once at love and spends the rest of her life trying to avoid it. Stella's sexuality leads her to choose illusion and life with Stanley rather than truth and love for Blanche. Later, women face reality and so acquire the capacity to be loving. Alma is saved from lovelessness by the realization that her false idealism prevents her from making real contact with others. Serafina is on the way to a healthier relationship when she realizes she has overidealized married sex and withdrawn from life. Maggie is so vital that she is not subject to illusion for long, and she eventually attains unselfish behavior.

In all these plays, sexuality has been present but not necessarily the primary ingredient in the relationships. In *The Night of the Iguana* Williams makes a clear statement that sexuality is not a necessary prerequisite to a loving relationship. Hannah is not sexual, but she is totally selfless and responsive to the needs of others. On the other hand, Maxine's sexuality makes her self-centered. Clearly, Williams indicates the independence of human compassion from human sexuality and, more importantly, the interdependence of love and understanding. The women who idealize reality retreat into an illusionary world. They use bizarre behavior because they cannot accept themselves or others. Women who face reality are in the middle ground, committed to the here and now, and vital. Their desire to live may eventually be selfish or loving. The women who are realists and who sympathize with others and their problems are the truly compassionate. Williams has called himself an old romanticist. Judging by the plays considered, by "romanticist" he must mean one who believes in the power of love; and the fullest love, as Williams shows, is compassion formed only in reality.

In Pursuit of the Lyric Quarry:
The Image of the Homosexual
in Tennessee Williams' Prose Fiction

ALFRED KAZIN has recently observed that " 'the love that dare not speak its name' (in the nineteenth century) cannot, in the twentieth century, shut up."[1] Implicit in Kazin's statement is a disturbing value judgment: even mentioning one's homosexuality, Kazin seems to imply, is tantamount to flaunting it. The problem for the confessional writer, given this reaction, should be obvious, especially when what is "confessed" is one's homosexuality. Tennessee Williams would seem to be acutely conscious of this dilemma. If, as the narrator of *Moise and the World of Reason* says, it is "sometimes hard to distinguish between a truthful report on your love life and what they call prurience" (p. 82), it may be even more difficult to evaluate the "undisguised self-revelation" (p. xviii) of the *Memoirs*, to see the work as Williams' sincere attempt to catch as firmly as possible that elusive bird of truth. In these *Memoirs* Williams, with a hatred of mendacity and hypocrisy every much as virulent as that of his own Big Daddy, completes a movement, at times a struggle toward an understanding and depiction of homosexuality that can be traced in his prose fiction from his first collection of short stories (1948) to *Moise and the World of Reason* (1975).[2]

In the *Memoirs* Williams only *seems* to warn the potential critic away from his homosexuality as an approach to his work: "an artist's

525

sexual predilections or deviations are not usually pertinent to the value of his work. Of interest, certainly. Only a homosexual could have written *Remembrance of Things Past*" (p. 142). The last sentence strongly implies an important relationship between one's personal and creative lives perhaps best described by the term "vision." In yet another context Williams has said of Proust that "no one ever used the material of his life so well. . . . [*Remembrance*] contains all the elements of a man's psychic history—his love, fear, loneliness, disgust, humor, and most important of all, his forgiving perception of the reasons for the tragicomedy of human confusion."[3] The description aptly fits Williams' own work.

In fact, Williams' homosexuality does provide the critic with an important way of understanding and perhaps of evaluating that vision so frequently labeled grotesque, decadent, and neurotic, since that vision is at many points related to homosexuality. Examples other than Williams might clarify. Certainly Proust's homosexuality made him more aware of the social masquerade and of the frequent failed commerce between the aesthetic and the moral, the role and the inner reality, which are of such importance to his social vision. Genêt's Satanic vision, with its emphasis on the perversion of divine love and of the celestial hierarchy, appears closely allied to his homosexuality, with its delight in perversion as a turning away from the normal and the licit. Yet another example might be Mishima, whose correlation of thanatos and eros, considered an integral part of his vision in works such as *Confessions of a Mask* and *Kyoko's House*, has been related to his interest in homosexual sadomasochism.[4]

Williams' so-called "decadent" vision and his preoccupation with loneliness, evasion, role-playing, wastage, sexual reluctance and sexual excess are in many instances functions of a homosexual sensibility which has been evolving steadily in the more than quarter century since the publication of *One Arm and Other Stories*. In this period Williams' treatment of homosexuality has undergone significant changes, moving from a mystical to a more social perspective, a personal, if fictional microcosm of the wider cultural demystification of homosexuality. The characteristic homosexuals of Williams' early fiction and of plays such as *Camino Real* and *Suddenly Last Summer* are lonely men, frequently vagabonds, with the aura of the demigod, saint, repentant sinner, or poète maudit. In *Moise* the homosexual is an individual with a more identifiable and "realistic" relationship to his surrounding social and historical milieus. Briefly stated, then, Williams' homosexual has moved from the mythic to the real.

In "One Arm," the title story of his first collection, Williams uses the figure of the male hustler as a vehicle for a statement on the transcendence of mundanity, alienation, and loneliness through un- conventional sexuality. Less about the homosexual sensibility or underworld than about the power of sexuality itself, a power whose object—woman, man, or self—is of relatively minor importance, the tale records the transformation of the one-armed Ollie Winemiller from hustler to pagan love god. Ollie, a blond youth of twenty evoc- ative of a "broken statue of Apollo" (p. 7), appears to be caught in forces beyond his conscious control. One of Williams' fugitive kind, Ollie, the "center of his being" (p. 9) dislocated after the loss of his arm, drifts into a life of hustling which allows him to capitalize on his broken beauty while enacting the self-destructive impulse he only half-recognizes within himself. His rootless existence is ended when he murders one of his "tricks" in an act of almost Camusian violence and finds himself on death row.

While awaiting execution, however, Ollie undergoes a strange and beautiful alteration. Because of the considerable publicity generated about this "baby-faced killer" (p. 21), many of his former contacts write him touching letters, frequently with money enclosed, describ- ing the profound influence he has had on them. Something about their fleeting contact with this hustler which transcended the physi- cal has haunted their minds ever since, and they face life as altered individuals. These men are responding not only to his beauty and grace but also to that engaging "charm of the defeated" (p. 13) that has seemed to surround him like the aura of a saint, of some remote, posturing Saint Sebastian. These letters from his disciples are in- strumental in the reestablishment of Ollie's pride; his self-conception begins to change and to unfold like an opening flower. Previously unmoved by either homosexual or heterosexual sex, in the charac- teristically self-assured manner of the hustler, Ollie now masturbates with a sense of joyless wonder, his masturbatory acts resembling the understandably selfish rites of a god. Through autoeroticism and fantasy Ollie reawakens his emotional life, but the rediscovery of his "rainbows of the flesh" (p. 19) torments as much as it enraptures him because his confinement and impending death impose obvious limits on his behavior and continued development. Ollie, now anguished by the reanimated sense of his own beauty and grace, finally suffers his death by electrocution with the letters clasped erotically between his thighs.

An episode during the terminal days of Ollie's life clarifies many of the values of the story and draws additional attention to its homosexual aspects. On a visit of charity a young Lutheran minister attempts to console Ollie. Alone with the condemned man, the minister is reminded, by Ollie's lithe, bronzed body, of the golden panther of his erotic dream life and becomes totally confused as he wipes the amber sweat from Ollie's limbs, fighting desperately against the gravity of his beauty. When Ollie, after rejecting the minister's puerile religious consolations, asks him to rub his back, dropping his shorts more seductively and confessing his loneliness and emotional frustration, the minister calls frantically for the guard to rescue him from temptation.

The minister, too fettered by concepts imposed by society and self to accept affection and love in unfamiliar guise, cannot even comprehend Ollie's fervent self-revelations. Also, the minister's latent homosexuality is not what contorts him, but rather his unwillingness to face the truth of his homosexuality, much like Brick in *Cat on a Hot Tin Roof*. The true prison is that of self, and the minister is unable to break out as Ollie is gradually learning—or relearning—to do. That the only repository of grace and perhaps of salvation in the story is a hustler is most significant. Ollie becomes a force of good in a world usually too blind or too fearful to recognize, acknowledge, or accept that good when its epiphany occurs in an unorthodox form or context. The medical students who dissect Ollie's body after death marvel at its physical beauty and feel it was "intended for some more august purpose" (p. 29), but the true, transformative mysteries of love and emotion in which Ollie has participated elude them. Although the transformation might not have been completed within Ollie, he has come closer than most to a truth of religious dimensions.

A similar situation is depicted in the Italian film *Teorema* (1967) by the homosexual director Pasolini. In this haunting film a beautiful young man appears in the lives of a bourgeois family, makes love in turn to the mother, daughter, father, and son, and then vanishes, having infused his sexual partners with a grace and an understanding of such intensity that they approach the mysterious and the inexplicable. In the end Ollie, too, appears to transcend sexual categories much as did the classical Greek and Roman gods. One critic, in fact, refers to the "mystical quality of giving which glorifies such personalities" (Falk, p. 41). Beautiful yet mutilated, guilty yet innocent, wise yet untutored, dead yet living in the memories of his former contacts, Ollie is multiple and paradoxical, the personification of a secular transcendence.

"Desire and the Black Masseur" (1948), the next of Williams' stories to deal with sexuality of an ambiguous nature, presents its own ritual of love, death, and redemption, yet in a more distorted and unrealistic manner. This tale has earned considerable notoriety because of its bizarre subject matter. Homosexual sadomasochism and cannibalism are, Edmund Fuller believes, more the province of clinical case studies than of the short story.[5] "Desire and the Black Masseur" is the account of Anthony Burns's tortured search for security. Obsessed with the desire to be swallowed and engulfed as compensation for his innate insecurity, Burns first seeks out movie houses whose film images wash over him and lull him like some therapeutic, amniotic bath. However, Burns is not long in finding the ultimate arena for his obsession, a massage parlor with much of the mystery and eroticism of Madame Irma's house of illusions in Genêt's *The Balcony*. While being pummeled by a massive black masseur, Burns discovers his own masochism as waves of pleasure, triggered by the acute pain, rush over him.

Through deft rhetorical manipulations, Burns's masochism, like Ollie's hustling or Sebastian Venable's liaisons, assumes a significance beyond the ordinary and the mundane. Burns's obsession is something greater than himself, occupying, like all desire, "a larger space than that which is afforded by the individual being" (*One Arm*, p. 84). Williams presents us with a parable similar to the one Pauline Réage was to explore later in *Story of O.*: the masochist's transcendence of his limited circumstances and his accomplishment of a religious atonement by eremitically rejecting the good things of this life and submitting to authority from a god-surrogate. Williams' conclusion, like Réage's alternative ending, implies that the logical extreme of the masochistic psychology is death, in this instance one of a particularly redemptive kind, for, in the isolated quarters of the masseur, Burns allows himself to be pummeled to death; and, in a final macabre twist, his body is ritualistically consumed by the masseur. The religious significance Williams wishes to give to his story is made clear by his counterpointing of Burns's destruction with the Easter celebration or "massive atonement" (p. 92) taking place simultaneously at a nearby church. The last vestiges of Burns in the story are his white bones, dropped into the river by the masseur, bones reminiscent of those of the Phoenician sailor in "The Waste Land," picked clean and purified beneath the waves. Burns's death, as is emphasized at the end, is a "perfection . . . slowly evolved through torture" (p. 94).

The sadomasochistic ritual merits some further comment. The chilling appropriateness of the sadomasochistic scenario, as enacted by Burns and the masseur, results from its combination of the aesthetic, the violent, and the religious. As the narrator says, art, violence, and atonement are three ways of compensating for the kind of incompletion Burns shares with alienated modern man. Atonement, described as "surrender of self to violent treatment by others" (p. 85), is motivated by the desire to absolve oneself of some dimly understood but profoundly disturbing guilt. Like O., who considers the physical, psychological, and emotional abuse of herself as "the very redemption of her sins,"[6] Burns suffers violence as a mode of self-knowledge, pleasure, and exaltation. His masochistic surrender to the masseur indicates with what intensity the Williams character shuns isolation and desires interaction with another, even if it is violent and destructive. The violence, however, is controlled and regulated in almost ludic fashion, with the interaction between Burns and the masseur suggestive of a ritual with its own lovely form and content. This is ceremonial rather than haphazard violence, as is Mishima's gladiatorial blood-theater in Confessions of a Mask in which beautiful young men are killed with much overflow of blood but "with all due ceremony."[7]

The implications of this tale for Williams' evolving theme of homosexuality are intriguing, if not heavily conclusive. Might Williams be obliquely suggesting some parallels between the erotic fascination with pain and death and the homosexual sensibility, as do Genêt and Mishima? Or perhaps he is intimating that what is fulfilment for the homosexual is actually death to this world with its restrictive social and religious standards. Possibly he is telling us that it is time for a new concept of Christ, for yet another version of the "man who died," except this time the version will be his, and not Lawrence's. Certainly in his death Burns suggests, perhaps comes close to parodying, the Christ of the Last Supper and the Passion.[8] At any rate, "Desire and the Black Masseur" is another of Williams' early stories which uses ambiguous or unconventional sexuality as a vehicle for a statement of mythic or religious import. The deaths of Ollie, Burns, and Sebastian are more like the deaths of Orpheus, Saint Sebastian, and Christ than those of more typical men.

The unusual deaths of homosexuals figure prominently in two other stories with the movie house as symbolic setting, "The Mysteries of the Joy Rio" and "Hard Candy." The stories, considered as a diptych, manifest a movement away from a heavily freighted symbolic consideration of homosexuality to a more realistic or even naturalistic treatment. In "The Mysteries of the Joy Rio" (1954) Williams' vision is planted squarely within the world of the fantastic, with the theme of loneliness, so poignantly underscored in "Hard Candy," subsidiary to the Gothic themes of exchange of personality and ghostly visitation. "The Mysteries of the Joy Rio" depicts one aspect of the homosexual life, the cruising of third-rate theaters, in a grotesque light, yet once again, as with "One Arm" and "Desire and the Black Masseur," investing the sordid with the meaningful, even with a touch of the transcendent or compensatory. Williams' bleak landscape is in part relieved by the tentative proffering of the values of companionship and compassion. The story deals with Pedro Gonzales, a forty-year-old man whose bewitching beauty has rapidly deteriorated since his youth when he began his three-year relationship with Kroger, who has been dead for almost twenty years. Now fat and ugly and looking much as did Kroger, Pedro pays furtive, daily visits to the derelict Joy Rio Theater in the waterfront section of a city that resembles New Orleans. As he cruises the theater, he silently recites, as if it were a litany, the advice of Kroger who, before he met Pedro, also made such pilgrimages to the Joy Rio. The old man gave him the benefit of his wisdom and told Pedro that no one should ever become discouraged in his search for love

and companionship but instead should continue in optimistic, relentless pursuit. Pedro's search, as was Kroger's before him, is not for
sensation but for solace, for he is driven to find that special *"one
person . . . trusted and adored"* (*Hard Candy*, p. 208) with whom
he could live in total honesty and cast off the freight of lies burden-
ing his soul. Pedro's search, although almost Sisyphean in its repetitive disappointments, provides his life with at least some structure
and the expectation of success.

One day Pedro discovers he is suffering from the same disease
that consumed Kroger, a revelation he accepts with calm resignation.
By this point it seems clear that something other than the realistic
is operative, for the similarities between the two men are more
sinister than coincidental. The climax of these correspondences occurs when, one early afternoon, Pedro, now wasted away to a wraith
of his former self, slips into the roped-off top balcony where the
ghost of Kroger lures him, with caresses, deeper into the recesses and
comforts him as he slowly dies to this life. This final tableau suggests
that true affection for the homosexual is not only hard-won, and too
often illusive and nightmarish, with the taint of the moribund, but
also perhaps narcissistic, since the dying Pedro is caressed by the
man he has come to resemble so closely in body and mind. The concluding statement of the story, however, reinforces the positive since
it emphasizes that Pedro dies having found again the trusted and
adored person he has been seeking, that he is comforted not *by* death
but before it.

Williams considerably reworked "The Mysteries of the Joy Rio"
into "Hard Candy,"[9] similar in theme and identical in setting, but
more controlled, realistic, and aesthetically effective. The story
focuses on the ugly, seventy-year-old Krupper, pursued by the eye
of the narrator from his cousin's sweetshop to the source of his mystery, once again the Joy Rio, where he goes three times a week with
his "hard candy" as bait. This theater offers not erotic films but pure
Americana, the Western. Krupper seeks his favored spot in the second balcony where, we learn as the narrator relentlessly uncovers
his unseen, unrecorded life, he entices hungry youths with his candy
and a fistful of quarters, always apprehensive that their disgust will
overcome their hunger. On this particular occasion he makes contact
with a beautiful young man who accepts his offerings. Although we

never learn what further exchange occurs between them, the ironic coda reveals that Krupper dies of a thrombosis in the second balcony of this inverse Dantesque world.

Thus, we have pursued the old man to the site of his mystery but are denied access to his last moments or to his psychology. Perhaps we are to assume he died in possession of the fleeting dream he has been trying to buy three times a week for the last thirty years, a more "real" version than Kroger's ghost. At least on this occasion, he thinks, the young man will not "go up in smoke like the dream . . . he looks" (p. 118). Instead the old man dies, but perhaps not without having first been guaranteed some few moments of companionship and pleasure. The parallel to Pedro's experience seems apt. That inevitable collapse back into loneliness and self-disgust does not occur.

So deftly does "Hard Candy" manipulate point of view and integrate theme and detail that it well deserves to be considered one of Williams' most accomplished tales. The narrative voice is effectively ironic, treating Krupper with an almost clinical detachment that poignantly underscores his situation. Two details are particularly striking. In a stairway niche stands a statuette, a female nymph with calcified flesh cold to the touch of the young man as he moves up to the balcony for his emotionless rendezvous with Krupper. Even more effective is the use of the cowboy film as the background action. The solitary, lonely heroism of the cowboy who performs his feats for the good of society only to ride off alone and womanless into the sunset provides an ironic commentary on Krupper's own actions. Krupper is denied even that male camaraderie the cowboy invariably has and which he frequently prefers to the company of women. Alone, lonely, always in quest but never in full possession of his desires, Krupper can be considered a kind of mutilé of the American dream of success and companionship. Williams drives home his point by having the old man clumsily maneuvering around the youth as the cowboy rides off, triumphant, into the archetypal sunset.

The thematic similarities between these two stories of the Joy Rio should be apparent. Both show the homosexual as a lonely individual for whom any meaningful, emotional contact is difficult to find and, when found, evanescent. Williams appears to view the homosexual in as problematic a light as Flaubert, Tolstoy, and Kate

Chopin, for instance, did their passionate women. Death, not the reformation of the constrictive society which feels itself threatened by these individuals, is the writer's solution. At this point in his treatment of homosexuality and for the remaining years of the 1950s Williams' response is clearly ambivalent and guilt-ridden. He seems more concerned with emphasizing the homosexual's plight than his position, and his homosexual characters, the Sebastians, the Charlus, the Peter Ochellos, as well as these others from his prose fiction, are in almost every instance twisted and grotesquely presented individuals. One critic of the grotesque believes the grotesque vision to be an exorcistic one which attempts to rid the artist's psyche of its fears.[10] Might this be a partial explanation for the prevalence in Williams' tales and plays of the homosexual grotesque? However, the homosexuals of these early tales, although so frequently grotesque and almost invariably lonely, are ultimately retrieved from the edge of despair by either actual event or personal illusion, emerging as perfect emblems for Williams' statement of Christian existentialism.

"Two on a Party" (1954) marks an advance toward a more realistic consideration of the cruising life than "Hard Candy," although not until twelve years later will homosexual cruising be seen in a fully positive light in "The Knightly Quest" (1966). "Two on a Party," which can stand as a definitive statement on the cruising life, is an important transition from the stories of the Joy Rio in which cruising, homosexuality, and the search for companionship are linked to the moribund. In his *Memoirs* Williams singles out this story for special praise and says he would like to see it turned into a film by Paul Morrissey whose *Flesh* and *Trash* depict the life of the Manhattan hustler as played by Joe Dallesandro. Certainly Morrissey's wasteland vision would find appropriate material in this story of the unusual ménage à deux between Billy, a thirty-five-year-old queen and male hustler, and the somewhat older prostitute Cora.

Both blasted by life, yet sensitive to its promises and beauties, they begin to pal around together, encouraging and sustaining each other as they cruise Manhattan and the key cities of the East Coast. Always in motion and frequently in flight, they strain for that brass ring which will validate their lives, not realizing it is the struggle that defines them. "The lyric quarry" (*Hard Candy*, p. 61) they believe they capture several times a week in the guise of "trade" will always remain elusive, for, like many of Williams' characters, they quest an unrealizable ideal. Perennial searchers, Grande calls them (pp. 121, 122), searchers whose motion towards the ideal reveals their humanity. As isolatoes their experience would be empty, their realization of the impossibility of their dreams a shattering awareness. Together they learn the lessons of compassion, respect, and possibly even self-respect, as all the "timid and tender values that can exist between people" (p. 61) begin to surface. Very quickly hustling becomes the pretext for their companionship.

Billy and Cora, the eternal "boy" ravaged by time and the proverbial whore with the heart of gold, both in flight from their middle-class backgrounds, form an unusual variation on those "on the road" couples of American life and literature, those Huck Finns and Nigger Jims, Sal Paradises and Dean Moriartys, Bonnies and Clydes. Cora is an ideal companion for Billy since she has "none of that desire to manage and dominate which is a typically American perversion of the female nature" (p. 57), but instead a motherly warmth and strength that never threaten him. With the sexual element in their interaction minimal, yet an inevitable source of strain, they reproduce or mimic that Whitmanian camaraderie Leslie Fiedler finds emblematic of the American experience. Like those other couples, Billy and Cora gain much of their identity and enjoyment from their "noble outlaw" status, for without that existential edge of societal disapprobation and rejection—their "never-ending contest with the squares of the world" (p. 61)—their lives would lack élan. Their interest is quickened and their camaraderie strengthened by the element of danger, by the potential thrill if "someone who looked like a Botticelli angel drew a knife, or if the law descended suddenly" (p. 53).

Several of Williams' comments in the *Memoirs* on his own life of cruising are especially pertinent to an understanding of the bond between Billy and Cora. Williams wonders "if the chief attraction [of cruising] was not our companionship, our being together" (p. 98). At another point he asks himself "how much of the cruising was for the pleasure of . . . [his] cruising partner's companionship and for the sport of pursuit" (p. 53). He recalls with nostalgia his Times Square cruising partner, Dreamy Eyes, his Calamus "buddy" for whom he felt an intense "sublimated love" (p. 98). As the narrator of *Moise and the World of Reason* expresses it, "two desperate living creatures are more often inclined, if they share a life together, to care for protectively than to abuse each other" (p. 41).

However, another attraction of the life of cruising which is actually the reverse of the ideal of companionship is that of anonymous sex. Williams believes that enjoyable sexual relationships and affectionate interaction can easily preclude each other. The narrator of "Two on a Party" says, "Sex has to be slightly selfish to have real excitement," that sex between strangers can be "like a blaze of light, but . . . between people who know each other well . . . it's likely to be self-conscious and even a little embarrassing" (p. 59). This statement also sheds some light on the psychology of the hustler, for whom the ideal sexual "trick" is the beautiful stranger who will neither disturb the hustler's own aloof stance nor require the attention the hustler narcissistically demands for himself.[11] This describes, of course, the more extreme pose of the male hustler and Billy is less a hustler than a self-designated "queen." However, his obsession with "trade," imaged as salmon leaping the falls, his continual pursuit of the "lyric quarry," promises to bring into his life a Juanesque pleasure in "numbers" more important than the economic reward. Thus Billy as well as Cora seems to manifest the Juanian pattern as defined by Camus: the attempt to find meaning through the ethic of quantity since the ethic of quality has proven impossible.[12]

However, they remain, throughout their hustlings, idealists. At story's end Billy and Cora are still questing. There is no resolution. They are "two on a party, and the rush continues" (p. 76), as they flee from one anonymous hotel to another, Cora now impossibly in love with Billy and Billy unable to face life alone.

The vision at the center of "Two on a Party," the search for love and companionship in a bleak, urban landscape, receives exaggerated, even fantastical treatment in the next of Williams' tales to deal with homosexuality in a more than cursory manner.[13] "The Knightly Quest" (1966), written during a period Williams himself describes as one of paranoia and defeat, in part caused by the death of his lover Frank Merlo,[14] has touches of Nathanael West and of the Ionesco of *The Killer*. "The Knightly Quest," however, considerably more positive than "Two on a Party," begins a more humanistic movement completed in *Moise and the World of Reason*.

It deals with the efforts of the wealthy homosexual, Gewinner Pearce, to destroy the Project, a mysterious organization working toward the discovery of the ultimate annihilatory weapon, which is polluting and terrorizing his hometown in Tennessee. Humanist values win out over those of the robot mentality. Gewinner succeeds in destroying the Project in a victory for individual freedom and identity, and then sails off in a spaceship to establish a new, rare community of love and enchantment. His elegant white scarf which doubles as a trysting sheet on his nightly quests for sexual partners is to be enshrined in a special museum, an emblem of his search for love and beauty in a disenchanted world.

Part farce, part science fiction, part satire, the story is most interesting in its parallels between Gewinner's politics and his sexuality, both imaged as chivalric endeavors. Gewinner, associated with Don Quixote, has that "alchemy of the romantic" (*Knightly Quest*, p. 84) which enables him to transform individual grievance into political action, the circumstances of his sexuality into lyrical escape. At no point does Williams associate Gewinner with the more negative aspects of the Quixote myth, with the high quotient of delusiveness and crazed ideals so frequently emphasized. Instead, Williams stresses the bond of love and companionship between Quixote and Panza, and by juxtaposition links it to the relationships between Gewinner and his sexual partners for the night. As one of the characters says, "the use of the term 'knightly quest' instead of 'nightly quest' is not just a verbal conceit but a thing of the highest significance in every part of creation, wherever a man in the prison of his body can remember his spirit" (p. 85). Thus, Gewinner's movement against the Project and his homosexuality must be seen as part of his noble attempt to liberate himself from the foul cage of corporeality, to do something finer than others are doing. To place Gewinner's homosexual cruising in as positive a light as possible, Williams also contrasts it against three negative images of sexuality, all heterosexual: Gewinner's brother's bestial coupling that sends the plaster crashing, the lechery of a small-minded agent for the Project, and the absurd attempts of Gewinner's mother to make a match between her already married son and the daughter of the President of the United States.

This Gawain of homosexuality manifests a pure, not prurient

mind, and is as simple and direct in his cruising as others are gross and devious in their flirtations and matings. In the extended description of his cruising of the football stadium, his behavior is ritualistic, culminating in his silent, tender offering of himself, completely unclothed and vulnerable, to a trembling stranger.

We are asked to accept the greater purity of Gewinner's homosexuality without explanation. His reverent attitude to himself and to others is not shown to be necessarily typical of the homosexual sensibility. In fact, not until *Moise and the World of Reason* does Williams finally make that justification so many of his early tales seem to approach, and to be minimally concerned with homosexuality as a vehicle for loneliness, alienation, and corporeal transcendence. In *Small Craft Warnings* (1972), the play that could be said to intervene thematically as well as chronologically between "The Knightly Quest" and *Moise*, Williams is as concerned with emphasizing the homosexual's humanity and normality as his loneliness and frustration. Although Quentin laments that the emotional life of the homosexual frequently becomes deadened, the younger, more balanced Billy, charged with the valuable sense of wonder at love and life, views his own homosexuality as both human and natural. Thus, "The Knightly Quest" and *Small Craft Warnings* could be said to prepare the way for *Moise*.

Moise and the World of Reason (1975), an unusual and striking, if ultimately unsuccessful work, gathers together many of the facts of Williams' life and presents them in fictional form. One could say that, along with the *Memoirs*, published in the same year, it is Williams' mature apologia pro vita sua, the first of his works to confront squarely the issue of homosexuality and to see it less in symbolic than in realistic terms. For one of the first times in his work homosexuality is clearly a donnée, something not so much imposed on the characters as generated from within, providing them with an identity and sensibility that go beyond the surface. Although *Moise* does contain a symbolic statement on homosexuality, one not easily forgotten, the novel is not as thematically dependent on a homosexual symbolism as are both "Hard Candy" and "The Knightly Quest."

The novel has three centers of interest, involving three thinly veiled versions of Williams himself at different ages and, in one instance, of a different sex, each of which contributes to the novel's thematic enunciation of the need for love and companionship and the desirability of homosexual and nonvaginal sex. There are the narrator, a "distinguished failed writer at thirty" (p. 18) who composes in Blue Jay school notebooks, an aging homosexual playwright whose latest play is being staged at the Truck and Warehouse Theater, and the obsessive woman painter Moise whose paeon to anal intercourse, with petroleum jelly as the sacramental oil, is the thematic climax of the novel.

Each of these characters inhabits a wasteland, waiting for the secular mystery of love. The narrator, during the course of the narrative, loses his current lover, Charlie, and is tortured by thoughts of his previous lover, the black ice-skater Lance, now dead. Moise feels the absence of love so strongly she wants to leave everyone and everything behind, relying only on herself. The playwright is in desperate search for a traveling companion, either male or female, with whom he can alleviate his arctic loneliness; like Doc in *Small Craft Warnings* (p. 12), he finds that "the solace of companionship" has become increasingly expensive as he has aged and the opportunities have dwindled. Moise's painting, the narrator's writing, and the dramatist's plays are their individual efforts to understand themselves and their experience better as prelude to the mystery which might never manifest itself. Each now lives "a nomadic sort of existence as if [he] were looking for something of vital importance . . . lost somewhere" (p. 47), something, it would seem, of almost Arcadian dimensions.

Rather than go in thwarted search of what has been lost, perhaps forever, Moise, who finds existence "untenable" in the "world of reason" (p. 26), decides to retreat into her "uterine" domain (p. 17) where she can nurse her wounds with gesso and oils. Yet art, even if the supplies she desperately needs arrive, will not be enough for her, or for any of the other characters either. Instead each must try to make passage to another person from the room of himself, a room more often assigned than chosen, although, like Moise who decides to imprison herself, the individual can *seem* to choose the fate that is assigned. There is, after all, some dignity in even such limited choice.

But companionship and love, not isolation and solipsism, remain the ideals and, for someone like the playwright, certainly the most desperate of the characters, ever-receding dreams. Each of them realizes, in the words of the narrator, that the "purest delight in living . . . is companionship" (p. 72). Williams' "odd couples," such pairs as Billy and Cora, Pedro and Kroger, the Princess and Chance, Elphinstone and Horne from "Happy August the Tenth," and Leona, the "faggot's moll" (p. 71) of *Small Craft Warnings*, and her current gay big brother from the bars, for example, do frequently bond together out of desperation and the need for mutual comfort. And, in the face of no one special person, they must trust in the kindness of strangers.

When the bond of companionship collapses and love dissipates, the individual can easily slip into either intense, consuming loneliness or self-protective indifference. Williams makes clear that both are to be avoided, if at all possible, and that to assume that art is created out of this kind of isolation is to make a serious error. The narrator needs human companionship to such an extent that he cannot write without some of the noise of life around him, and, when he does write, he always does so on a desk improvised out of empty crates of *Bon Ami*. Williams also suggests that one should not always throw the lifeline out to another desperately lonely person. For example, the narrator is advised by Moise to avoid the playwright whose loneliness would consume him like an open grave.

Ice, symbolic of emotionlessness and imprisonment, is probably the novel's dominant symbol. Images of ice proliferate throughout. Like Mallarmé's swan, Williams' characters risk being trapped in the iced-over lake of life, haunted by the realization of flights not made, of opportunities thwarted. The narrator, who identifies himself with the renegade Rimbaud,[15] laments that the puddle in which Rimbaud's child of "Le Bateau ivre" launches his paper boat, representative of the dreams of youth, is now ice. Even the skater Lance, the embodiment of love and compassion for the narrator, is able to dominate the world of ice only for a time until he dies in a crash in the rink.

At narrative's end, redemption intercedes in this somber landscape, not through the ministrations of art but through the "soft annealments of love" (p. 189). The narrator and Moise, in the closing scenes, are paired off with two cameramen who have come to photograph Moise's new canvas. Their sexual contact becomes metamorphosed into a liberating, redemptive, and socially significant act, not dissimilar to Gewinner's cruising. The oral and anal intercourse we can assume occurs among these characters have been celebrated bombastically only a short time before by Moise in a statement that stands as Williams' strongest, fictional justification for homosexuality: "Diminished space with increase of occupants! Incontinent spawning of more and more bellies to feed with continually less, shrinkage of rivers and seas, polluted, sea ferns, amoebic life dying . . ." (p. 182). Her solution is a "covenant for the only possible things, sucking the seed off or licensing the anus as preferable entrance . . ." (p. 183).

A pure Williams farrago of the apocalyptic, the homosexual, and the ecological that fails to convince. However, Williams could be said to be more concerned with psychological validity than verisimilitude, as is clear in not only *Moise* but also works such as *Sweet Bird of Youth, Suddenly Last Summer,* and "Desire and the Black Masseur," which wreak violence on plotting to make a thematic point. By his unusual ending and underscoring Williams suggests that the narrator and Moise may be able to avoid the future of the aging playwright who, presiding over the work like Banquo's ghost, was perhaps created by Williams out of his desire to exorcise the demon of a lonely old age. Some sort of peace and understanding have been achieved, indicated by the image of the Great Unknown One, ostensibly the force and power of love and compassion, whose footsteps are approaching the narrator's world as he prepares to have sex with the cameraman. In the face of such a nonrational, ultimately inexplicable force, art and the endeavors of the imagination are inadequate, as suggested by the last line of the work, the narrator's consummatum est: "The last Blue Jay is completed" (p. 190).

In *Moise,* as in "The Knightly Quest," Williams treats homosexuality with a reverence that at times approaches chauvinism. In fact, once again the most prurient character is a heterosexual who voyeuristically enjoys hearing of the narrator's sole heterosexual experience. *Moise* ultimately posits not a total Juanian emphasis on sensation and quantity frequently associated with the homosexual sensibility, but a Tristanian concern with quality and intensity. The narrator firmly rejects those specters of the Juanian ethic with which he is haunted: the men who attempt to molest him in their car during his childhood, the attempted seduction of his grandfather by a Hollywood producer, his unfaithful lover Charlie, and graffiti in bath houses.

Williams would seem to be guilty of misjudgment rather than insincerity in *Moise*. Perhaps he is following his sensibility rather than his intelligence, as Truman Capote feels he always does.[16] How else explain the thematic overstatement, the overzealousness? Or, for that matter, the style and organization? Williams plays with self-conscious narrative in the manner of Barth, Barthelme, and Nabokov, but his technique of parenthetical asides and uncompleted statements at most times bears as much similarity to the narrative style of "Lost in the Funhouse" or "Views of My Father Weeping" as coitus interruptus to extended and artful lovemaking. What does succeed in coming through clearly in *Moise* is what Williams accomplishes also in the *Memoirs* in a less disguised format: a revelation of himself and his values, an attempt to tell us some confidences with an infectious Whitmanian publicity.

In the *Memoirs* and *Moise* Williams' presentation of the homosexual seems to have moved from mythic figure to human being, from isolato to participant in a community of others, an indication of maturing perspective and of changing times. The current cultural situation seems to be right for Williams, since the increasing emphasis on the gay sensibility has made it more easy for him to speak more freely. It also would seem that Williams is right for the times, as the numerous recent revivals of his works indicate.

Perhaps Williams' perennial popularity is a direct function of his keen insight into man's loneliness. Man the outsider, the drifter, the fugitive kind.[17] He understands that man does not live in "Place Pig Alley any more than in Sacre Coeur de Montmartre" (p. 107), as the narrator in *Moise* says, but in the domain between, the domain of human endeavor, vulnerability, and exaltation through love, companionship, and art. Perhaps the most representative inhabitant of this domain between is Williams' homosexual, especially Billy, Gewinner, and the narrator of *Moise*. At some times more symbol than actual person, at others a homosexual in the guise of a woman, as with Moise and perhaps Cora,[18] the homosexual functions as one of Williams' most significant character-types, a fugitive kind definitely after Williams' own heart, a character not of hate, shame, or condescension, but of love and acceptance.

Notes to Edward A. Sklepowich,
"*In Pursuit of the Lyric Quarry: The Image of the Homosexual in Tennessee Williams' Prose Fiction*"

1. Alfred Kazin, "The Writer as Sexual Show-Off," *New York Magazine*, June 9, 1975, p. 38.

2. Among the best discussions is William H. Peden, "Mad Pilgrimage: The Short Stories of Tennessee Williams," *Studies in Short Fiction* 1 (1963), 243–50, which evaluates the stories on their own terms, tracing the themes of decay, abnormality, and loss through stories such as "Two on a Party" and "Desire and the Black Masseur." Luke M. Grande, "Metaphysics of Alienation in Tennessee Williams' Short Stories," *Drama Critique* 4 (1961), 118–22, focuses briefly yet sharply on metaphysical alienation and escape through sex in various of Williams' tales. A particularly interesting exploration of the collection *One Arm and Other Stories* is to be found in Signi Lenea Falk, *Tennessee Williams* (New York: Twayne Publications, 1961), pp. 38–41. John Devere, "Tennessee Williams: Naked on the Canvas," *Mandate* 1 (July 1975), 8, 53, 58, 59, 61, analyzes *Moise and the World of Reason* in considerable—and illuminating—detail, paying special attention to its homosexual theme and relating it to plays such as *Suddenly Last Summer* and *Summer and Smoke*.

3. "Prelude to a Comedy," *New York Times*, November 6, 1960, section 2, p. 3.

4. John Nathan, *Mishima* (Boston: Little, Brown and Company, 1974) and Henry Scott-Stokes, *The Life and Death of Yukio Mishima* (New York: Farrar, Straus, and Giroux, 1974) point out this aspect of Mishima's vision. Mishima's erotic fascination with the death of beautiful young men is graphically presented in *Confessions of a Mask*.

5. Edmund Fuller, *Man in Modern Fiction* (New York: Random House, 1949), p. 70.

6. Pauline Réage, *Story of O*. (New York: Grove Press, 1965), p. 93.

7. Yukio Mishima, *Confessions of a Mask*, trans. from the Japanese by Meredith Weatherby (New York: New Directions, 1958), pp. 92–3.

8. Cf. Nancy M. Tischler, *Tennessee Williams* (New York: Citadel Press, 1961), p. 259, who refers to the similarities between the action of the story and the sacrifice of the Mass but does not suggest that parody might be involved.

9. The editor's note to *Hardy Candy* verifies that "Hard Candy" is a later version of "The Mysteries of the Joy Rio."

10. Wolfgang Kayser, *The Grotesque in Literature and Art*, trans. from the German by Ulrich Weisstein (New York: McGraw-Hill, 1966), p. 188.

11. The character of Johnny Rio in John Rechy's *Numbers* (New York: Grove Press, 1967) is perhaps the clearest example of this type.

12. *The Myth of Sisyphus*, trans. from the French by Justin O'Brien (New York: Vintage Books, 1955), p. 54.

13. The focus of this essay is on those stories which manifest a significant thematic or characterological concern with homosexuality. There are, of course, other tales which deal with homosexuality, although in a rather peripheral manner, such as "The Night of the Iguana" (1948), "The Angel and the Alcove" (1948), "The Resemblance Between a Violin Case and a Coffin" (1950), "Mama's Old Stucco House" (1966), and possibly "Happy August the Tenth" (1973). These tales deal with the familiar themes of loneliness, isolation, and the appeal of anonymous sex in far less concentrated manner than the tales discussed in this essay.

14. Williams discusses this period in considerable detail in the *Memoirs*.

15. *Moise*, p. 114. Williams was interested in the myth of Rimbaud and in his

poetry. Falk suggests that at times Williams' style, with its "fragmentary bursts of rhetoric" and "disconnected sequence," reveals the influence of Rimbaud (p. 39). *Moise* is an excellent case in point.

16. Josh Greenfield, "Truman Capote, The Movie Star?" *New York Times*, December 28, 1975, section 2, p. 17.

17. Gerald Weales, *Tennessee Williams* (Minneapolis: University of Minnesota Press, 1965), p. 22.

18. Stanley Edgar Hyman, "Some Trends in the Novel," *College English* 20 (October 1958), 2 suggests that occasionally Williams, like Proust before him, creates female characters who are actually men in disguise. Hyman uses "Rubio y Morena" and *The Roman Spring of Mrs. Stone* as examples. "Two on a Party" and *Moise and the World of Reason* also seem to conform to his Albertine theory.

Sexual Roles in the Works
of Tennessee Williams

ROBERT EMMET JONES

W‌HEN TENNESSEE WILLIAMS' *Moise and the World of Reason* was published in 1975 several critics remarked that the author had finally explored a distinctly homosexual theme and had overtly created an exclusively homosexual protagonist. These observations, however, were essentially only partial truths; for elements of homosexuality and bisexuality, although often in muted or apparently disguised form, can be found in his fictional and dramatic writings since the beginning of his professional career. Despite certain archetypal characters in the Williams' canon, many of his major dramatis personae are basically sexually ambivalent and could, as the characters of most other major dramatists could not, easily have been portrayed as members of the opposite sex. Despite the conventional standards of morality that were adhered to in the theater, if not always in the fiction, of the period 1943–1963 when most of his great plays were written, Williams was a precursor, and perhaps the founder in the American theater, in the depiction of what today is known as the unisexual character, a person in whom only the organs of generation define the differences between the sexes. From a psychological point of view many of Williams' ostensibly male and female characters share a sexual ambivalence, the portrayal of which has enriched our knowledge not only of human nature but, as well, of the society that produced these types.

545

Williams is in the tradition of the Romantic writers whose works are seminally subjective. His drama and fiction are outgrowths of his own personality which, as he has stated in his *Memoirs,* is basically homosexual in orientation, but the author himself would seem, if one may judge from his characters, to be unisexual; for he identifies with both sexes and thus reveals in his works a truly Protean personality. In a recent interview with Mel Gussow Williams remarked, "No living person doesn't contain both sexes. Mine could have been either one. Truly, I have two sides to my nature" (*New York Times,* Nov. 3, 1975, p. 49). In an interview with Jim Gaines, Williams stated that his favorite character was Alma of *Summer and Smoke.* He said, "You see, Alma went through the same thing that I went through—from puritanical shackles to, well, complete profligacy." When Gaines asked him what he meant by "profligacy," Williams responded, "Freedom . . . Liberation from taboos. I don't make any kind of sex dirty except sadism" (*Saturday Review,* Apr. 29, 1972, p. 27). Alma, then, contained many of the elements of the character of Williams himself, but a Williams successfully transposed into a female.

The author of *Summer and Smoke* is perhaps the greatest contemporary exponent of the varied forms taken by sexual desire, and almost all his characters, regardless of age or sex, are prey to its whims. In his creative world his characters, no matter what their apparent sexual orientation, seek love and tenderness as a release from loneliness. But too often when these two aspirations fail to materialize the seeker looks for forgetfulness or very temporary companionship in sexual acts that are dominated by desire (a key word in Williams' vocabulary). This desire, which usually represents more a psychological than a physical need (although it usually is expressed in physical actions) has little to do with the emotion of love. Yet the quest for love, for belonging, for the ability to give love to and accept love from another might be said to be the major theme in his dramatic works and much of his fiction, but only in *The Rose Tattoo* and *Period of Adjustment* can love be found; and in the latter play its stability is somewhat precarious. The fact that love is rarely achieved in them gives to Williams' plays their pathetic and often tragic overtones because the loneliness that results from being unloved makes his characters the prey of psychological and physical desire which almost inexorably leads to their own destruction. The Judge in *The Purification* might be speaking of love when he states, "It is the lack of what he desires most keenly that twists a man out of nature" (*27 Wagons*, p. 56). Many of Williams' characters, because of their inability to love, inhabit what the playwright calls Dragon Country in a speech by the character One in *I Can't Imagine Tomorrow*: "Dragon Country, the country of pain, is an uninhabitable country which is inhabited, though. Each one crossing through that huge, barren country has his own separate track to follow across it alone. If the inhabitants, the explorers of Dragon Country, looked about them, they'd see other explorers, but in this country of endured but unendurable pain each one is so absorbed, deafened, blinded by his own journey across it, he sees, he looks for, no one else crawling across it with him. It's uphill, up mountains, the climb's very steep: takes you to the top of the bare Sierras. —I won't cross into that country where there's no choice any more" (*Dragon Country*, p. 138).

Desire and death, be the latter moral, spiritual, or physical, dominate Williams' universe, yet they are essentially synonymous. Love creates; desire destroys: Stella is fulfilled, Blanche led off to an asylum. But love, even that of Stella which has strong physical desire as its basis, is generally elusive in the works of Williams. Maggie of *Cat on a Hot Tin Roof* is unable to make Brick, her possibly homosexual husband, love her. She says, "Living with someone you love can be lonelier—than living entirely *alone!*—if the one that y' love doesn't love you" (III, 28). But love or even basic physical desire rarely has the procreative function as its object unless a question of money is involved. Maggie would undoubtedly prefer the love of Brick, but, lacking that, she will settle for a child whose birth will ensure her and Brick's inheriting Big Daddy's estate. The only children who play an important role in Williams' theater are the five "no-neck monsters" in the same play, children of Mae and Gooper, two babymaking machines scorned by everyone about them. Aside from this example, the procreative function is invariably subordinated to sexual desire for its own sake; thus, the objects of the desire may easily be, and often are, polymorphic. Only in his first major play, *The Glass Menagerie*, is the sexual proclivity of the main characters muted, and this play is the only true elegy to past hopes and to unachieved, but still desired, horizons in the Williams oeuvre; and it is undoubtedly a paean to the author's lost youth.

Ostensibly when we read or see a Williams' play we are witnessing actors and actresses who are playing carefully defined sexual roles. We see women as women and men portraying men. But we often wonder if the men are really male and the women really and exclusively female. Quite often the sexual roles of the characters are ambivalent. Even if Williams has not transposed the sexes for dramatic purposes as he undoubtedly, if unconsciously, did in the characters of Blanche and Alma, he, like Strindberg before him, sees strong elements of the female in the male and the male in the female. The conventional role of the male as the aggressor in a sexual relationship is rarely to be found in Williams' plays, the most notable exception being A Streetcar Named Desire. Men are the sex objects sought by desperate women whose interests are usually predatory. This reversal of standard sexual roles illustrates an important aspect of the sexual ambivalence of Williams' characters. Women tend to take center stage in the plays and attempt sexual dominance. In even such a trifling play as A Perfect Analysis Given by a Parrot two women in their thirties are out to prey on conventioneers in New Orleans. The Mutilated and many of the stories in Eight Mortal Ladies Possessed similarly portray women. Leona in Small Craft Warnings, one of the author's most underestimated dramas, is distinctly masculine in her aggressiveness even though Williams calls her a fully integrated woman: "the first really whole woman I have ever created and my first wholly triumphant character," he says in Saturday Review (p. 27). Leona is stronger than the many men in the play—Bill, the hustler whom she has been keeping in her trailer, Doc, Steve, Monk, or Quentin and Bobby, the two homosexuals. Bill, a passive character, is nothing more than a phallus, and his masculinity (which is questioned in the play) is only a form of narcissism. Violet, the other woman in Small Craft Warnings, is a pathetic predator. No more than Miriam of In the Bar of a Tokyo Hotel, Miss Coynte of Greene, or Woman Downtown of The Red Devil Battery Sign can she keep her hands from men's genitals; and though Violet is rather tawdry, an Alma long since gone to seed, the men, whether from boredom or because of her availability, all accept her physical advances. The two homosexuals who have just formed and are about to terminate a misalliance are essentially as passive as the other men. The young man, Quentin, seeks hetero-sexual men for sexual pleasure, and the boy, Bobby, is looking for love. In *Small Craft Warnings, Cat on a Hot Tin Roof, The Night of the Iguana, Sweet Bird of Youth*, and *In the Bar of a Tokyo Hotel* men are passive sex objects and children to be manipulated by ag-gressive mother figures, and they masochistically seem to enjoy the role.

The leading male characters remain essentially similar in Wil-liams' plays and fall into several convenient categories. Most of them are outwardly, and sometimes aggressively, masculine (Stanley Ko-walski). All seem to have or to have had a certain animal vitality that makes them attractive to women and to other men. Val of *Battle of Angels* and of the revision, *Orpheus Descending*, has "a fresh and primitive quality, a virile grace and freedom of body, and a strong physical appeal" (I, 16). Kilroy and Alvaro have the torsos of a sculpture. Brick is "still slim and firm as a boy" (III, 19). Chance is "exceptionally good-looking. His body shows no decline, yet it's the kind of a body that white silk pajamas are, or ought to be, made for" (IV, 14). The concern of Williams with the physical attributes of his males, who also include Stanley, Doctor John of *Summer and Smoke*, Shannon of *The Night of the Iguana*, Slim of *The Mutilated*, and Chris of *The Milk Train Doesn't Stop Here Anymore*, is the more remarkable since his women are rarely sex symbols. All these desirable sex objects appear ready to let themselves be victimized. Some are "the fugitive kind," like the early heroines, Blanche and Alma, in flight because society will not permit them to be what they are or what they would like to be.

Another group of male characters might be classified as the muti-lated, those who, for one reason or another, have been maimed by society either physically or psychologically (Kilroy, One Arm, Brick, Chance, Shannon, Mark of *In the Bar of a Tokyo Hotel*). They may be the objects of sexual desire, but they also have, as Maggie remarks of Brick, the charm of the defeated, which possibly explains their sexual appeal, especially to mother figures. They are passive victims both of domineering women and of the social group. Although many of the playwright's male characters are stereotypes of con-temporary ideas of masculinity—athletes, truck drivers, manual workers, studs, sailors, hustlers—they remain passive sexual objects, and other aspects of their personalities are rarely explored. They are present in the plays only to satisfy, if they can, the physical or psychological needs of women—and they are types fantasized about by homosexuals. The masculine male who is tender and who has a sense of poetry to complement his virility is desired by both men and women. Williams expresses the homoerotic longing that these men might harbor homosexual or bisexual tendencies themselves.

Williams' portraits of his male characters, fine as many of them are, contrast sharply with the beautifully nuanced characterizations of his women who, like the men, combine in their personalities both feminine and masculine traits. A subtle development occurs in the author's portrayal of women. In the early plays (*Battle of Angels, The Glass Menagerie, A Streetcar Named Desire, Summer and Smoke*) many of the heroines are aggressive, but they are defeated by not being able to resolve the conflict between their sexual proclivities and the demands of a moribund genteel code which denies them sexual fulfilment outside marriage and thus makes them unable to differentiate between illusion and reality. Williams presents Amanda, Blanche, Alma, and Marguerite of *Camino Real* as representatives of the Victorian butterfly tradition rather than as earthy females. The playwright sympathizes with them, for they, too, like many of the young men in his theater, are of "the fugitive kind," mutilated by life. Psychologically they resemble Celeste and Trinket, the two major characters in one of Williams' later plays aptly entitled *The Mutilated* (1966). Celeste, and she might be speaking for the early heroines of her creator, remarks, "Hell, I'd say, we all have our mutilations, some from birth, some from long before birth, and some from later in life, and some stay with us forever" (*Dragon Country*, p. 87). These women, along with Mrs. Stone of *The Roman Spring of Mrs. Stone*, may be mutilated victims, but they are also predators. Even in *Streetcar* the question is whether the genteel Blanche or the coarse Stanley is the predator. Both are, of course, but the one who faces up to reality, Stanley, triumphs even though his victory seems ultimately Pyrrhic. But these women are also weak and out of touch both with their surroundings and with their real selves. Many of them could have been portrayed as frustrated homosexuals.

In *The Rose Tattoo, Orpheus Descending,* and *Cat on a Hot Tin Roof* Williams portrays women with little sexual ambivalence although Maggie the Cat has some boyish qualities which might explain Brick's original attraction to her. Serafina, Myra, and Maggie are strong, loving earth mothers, who know, appreciate, and exult in their own sexuality. When an Alvaro, Val, or Brick is able to make them feel like women they become incandescent. Women of immigrant origin or representative of the New South, they are strong "modern" women who find salvation, even when it is only temporary, in their sexuality. Yet, like the later heroines, they are basically stronger than the men with whom they come into contact, and they essentially direct the action of the plays. Alvaro, despite his masculine mien, seems like an awkward adolescent in comparison to Serafina. Brick, one of the "mutilated," has become an alcoholic and has lost his sexual drive and willpower though not his masculine attractiveness. Val, one of the "fugitives," is a poet as well as a virile young stud, but Myra is more confident and therefore more powerful than he.

The women in the later plays are stronger and more dominant, if often sexless or perhaps unisexual characters. These women are invariably attempting to control the people about them, and many of them are real predators whose victims or captives are usually sensitive and/or artistic young and middle-aged men. Most of these women, from Mrs. Venable of *Suddenly Last Summer* and Flora Goforth of *The Milk Train Doesn't Stop Here Anymore* to Woman Downtown of *The Red Devil Battery Sign,* are inhabitants of Dragon Country where one goes one's way alone. They can do without others if necessary, and that is the reason they can use others. With the exception of Hannah in *The Night of the Iguana* and Leona, the women in the later plays are the hunters rather than the hunted of the earlier ones, but through fear of loss of power or fear of death they ultimately become their own victims. These women, and they could just as easily have been portrayed as men, represent certain aspects of contemporary society that reflect Williams' growing disenchantment with the predatory aspects of humanity. The irony in *Gnädiges Fräulein* is that a woman becomes an actual predator similar to the gulls spoken of in *Suddenly Last Summer.* These characters are threats to creativity, whether sexual or artistic. They are essentially sterile and would like to castrate (and often do so verbally) the male victims who appear in their orbits. Having achieved freedom of a sort—financial (by deaths of husbands or divorce) and sexual—they can indulge their whims and fantasies. Other characters, usually men but sometimes women, have become dependent on them and hence are their pawns. These females, the extreme example of whom is the caricatured Lesbian school teacher in *The Night of the Iguana,* have taken over the traditionally masculine role of dominating and leading and thus give the impression of being unfeminine. Shannon and other men in the later plays protest this domination, but their complaints are ineffectual. In these plays the traditional sexual roles appear completely inverted.

The need for opposites, sexual or not, is a dominant theme in Williams' plays. The weak seek out the strong rather than the masculine the feminine. The weak are looking for love, understanding, and usually protection. Yet we find Williams commenting in *Suddenly Last Summer* that love is using another. Thus the equality among people in Williams' works is only among victims. Even the emotionally strong Maggie is basically defeated by Brick because he won't make love to her. In general, however, Williams presents a dominant person and one less strong who either aspires to dominance or is content to be dominated as long as he/she is provided with the material things in life. When such a relationship is formed the characters are willing to go along with their chosen roles as tormentor and tormented, and their need for and possession of each other compensates temporarily for the horrors and occasional joys of their mutual existence. This relationship appears even in such minor works as "Sabbatha and Solitude" and "Happy August the Tenth." Uncertainty about a relationship is what causes the anguish that most of the characters share. Sexual boundaries are unimportant; individuals, regardless of their sex, however, *are* important, and when one does not respect another's individuality disaster ensues.

Yet Williams' work shows the value of living. The failures fail because they are more involved with themselves and with preconceived stereotypes of what their roles should be than with the concerns of others. The works are a celebration of life because many of the characters, haunted by a fear of death, decay, and sexual impotence, attempt to live with abandon and enjoy momentary pleasures even when they know they will ultimately fail to possess what they are seeking. Unfulfilled desires and their consequences and physical and psychological violence, however, dominate, or are always impending in, Williams' universe. Yet the battle for domination continues. The Princess in *Sweet Bird of Youth* says, "When monster meets monster, one monster has to give way, AND IT WILL NEVER BE ME" (IV, 43). Chance comments later: "Princess, the great difference between people in this world is not between the rich and the poor or the good and the evil, the biggest of all differences in this world is between the ones that had or have pleasure in love and those that haven't and hadn't any pleasure in love, but just watched it with envy, sick envy" (IV, 50). But love is an elusive goal. Chance had the opportunity to experience love, but because of the pressures of society, left his beloved and became a gigolo. Yet he retains the memories of young love while, we are led to believe, the Princess has never experienced this emotion. Like Blanche, Alma, and Brick, Chance can only be doomed because of his search for a lost purity and a consequently unrealizable ideal of love.

Thus the role of the poet in his dual guise as poet-saviour and poet-victim becomes all important. Because Williams' plays and stories contain, along with the tawdry refuse of quotidian life, the visionaries of both sexes such as Val, Tom, Blanche, Hannah, and Chris who do see that love and compassion are the only virtues in the modern world and that these two virtues are to be prized, the final picture presented by Williams' works is not as pessimistic as one might think at first. Without love and compassion life is meaningless even if possession of these qualities leads a person to destruction. With them life can be tolerated if not completely enjoyed. The poet recognizes this fact, but, as throughout history, the poet in Williams' works is a prophet without honor in his own country, Dragon Country, and is usually destroyed.

Perhaps the best examples of sexual ambivalence in Williams' works are to be found in *A Streetcar Named Desire* and *Summer and Smoke*. In both plays the portrayal of the leading female characters is ambivalent. Blanche is the daughter of a once genteel southern family who, surrounded by death both physical (the death of her family) and psychological (she had married a homosexual whom she loved and unwittingly caused to commit suicide), turns into a crea-

ture crazed by desire, the desire to belong, the desire to be held by
men. The men to whom she has given herself are servicemen, truck-
ers, traveling salesmen, and finally a schoolboy; she has become the
whore of the town. Alma of *Summer and Smoke* is the daughter of a
minister in a small Mississippi town. Chief member of a small literary circle, she, like Blanche, is interested in "culture." But she, as
well, is in love with the young doctor next door who likes her but
cannot return her love, and she ends up on a park bench waiting for
traveling salesmen with whom to spend the night. Williams, because he is a great dramatist, makes Blanche and Alma not only
convincing as women, but, in fact, great theatrical personae. But,
in a more recent time, he might also have made them homosexual
men. Nothing important would have been needed to change their
characterizations and, although they, as homosexuals, would probably not appeal to a wide audience, their portrayals would still ring
true. Even though we know from contemporary southern fiction
that women of good birth might well turn into whores, it seems more
logical that young homosexual men rather than young gentlewomen
would seek out the masculine types at air force bases and bus and
railroad terminals.

In *A Streetcar Named Desire* Blanche might plausibly be a man,
a homosexual who, because of the conventions of society, had married a heterosexual girl in an attempt to achieve "normalcy," and
who had then discovered his true sexual bent. Love gone, he flaunts
his sexual proclivities and eventually is asked to leave town. His
only refuge is his sister, and he takes up residence with her and her
husband. He is attracted by the brute masculinity of his brother-in-
law whom his sister has never conceived of as having homosexual
tendencies. Driven to desperation by the enticements of the brother,
the husband (Stanley) attacks him while his own wife is giving
birth to their first child and, to prove his own masculinity, rapes his
sensitive, if neurasthenic, brother-in-law. This is not Williams' play,
but it might have been, and it demonstrates the sexual ambivalence
of the characters of Blanche and Stanley. What is put in question
in the play that Williams wrote, however, is not the femininity of
Blanche but rather the masculinity of Stanley. A very homoerotic
element appears in a convincing heterosexual situation.

Homosexuality is a recurrent theme in the plays of Williams although in the drama of the forties and fifties it was understated. The whole of human sexual experience is alluded to in the plays and stories of this period although the major characters of the plays are presented as being overtly heterosexual until the appearance of the Baron de Charlus in *Camino Real* and Brick in *Cat on a Hot Tin Roof*. The Baron is an avowed homosexual and, like Roger Doremus of *Summer and Smoke*, rather effeminate. Effeminate homosexual characters, and there are not many in Williams' works, are openly ostracized or mocked by the social group. In their portrayal Williams ironically shows less compassion than he does for his other males who, even though they may be homosexual, are at least masculine in appearance and action. Brick Pollitt is accused by his wife of having had an unnatural relationship with his best friend Skipper. While expressions of their friendship were apparently confined to those of camaraderie, Skipper loved Brick and confessed this love to Brick's wife Maggie. Brick himself, if he had been sure of his heterosexuality or masculinity, would not have become an alcoholic and refused to sleep with his wife after Skipper's death. Big Daddy, a most compassionate man, recounts to Brick the story of the two men, who were lovers, for whom he worked as a young man and who left him their estate which he has made into the finest in the Delta. He looks upon their relationship with tolerance, and his sensitivity contrasts forcefully with Brick's almost painful condemnation of the two men as fairies, sissies, and queers. When Brick pronounces the word *fairies*, Williams writes in a stage direction, "In his utterance of this word, we gauge the wide and profound reach of the conventional mores he got from the world that crowned him with early laurel" (III, 120). Williams is noting here the hypocrisy and ambivalence of the moral codes of society and the effect they have on some of its more sensitive members. Brick's feeling of tenderness towards Skipper contained an element of the feminine, and therefore Brick felt it had to be destroyed because it was sexually ambivalent. Yet Brick admits that his friendship with Skipper was not normal. He says, "Normal? No!—It was too rare to be normal, any true thing between two people is too rare to be normal" (III, 121). Brick finally realizes that love between any two persons is more important than the gender of the persons involved.

Perhaps the most savage depiction of homosexuality in Williams' dramatic works is found in *Suddenly Last Summer*. Although the homosexual character Sebastian has been gruesomely murdered before the play begins, the drama is a revelation, through the confessions of his cousin Catharine, of the events leading to the murder. The young girl, who has been almost psychologically destroyed by the uses to which her cousin has put her, has been placed in a mental institution by Sebastian's mother Mrs. Venable to prevent her from recounting the story of her son's death. As Catharine recounts the story of her summer with Sebastian she reveals that Sebastian was as much a predator as his mother, for, although she attracted the young boys into her web (as Catharine unknowingly did) it was Sebastian who devoured them. In *Suddenly Last Summer* the mother figure coalesces with the predatory woman who will stop at nothing to secure pleasure for her son and thus vicariously for herself. But ironically in this play the sexual predator (Sebastian) becomes the sexual victim in a horrifying rite of cannibalism, and by extension his mother becomes a victim as well because she has lost the most important person in her life.

But until the production of *Small Craft Warnings* no major avowedly homosexual character actually appeared on Williams' stage. In this play the two homosexuals are masculine in appearance, but in the character of Bobby the unisexual aspect implicit in many of Williams' earlier plays finds its expression. Bobby says: "On the plains of Nebraska I passed a night with a group of runaway kids my age and it got cold after sunset. A lovely wild young girl invited me under a blanket with just a smile, and then a boy, me between, and both of them kept saying 'love,' one of 'em in one ear and one in the other, till I didn't know which was which 'love' in which ear or which . . . touch . . . The plain was high and the night air . . . exhilarating and the touches not heavy" (V, 264). Bobby's need for love may be satisfied by male or female, and he is unable to distinguish between the two. If society did not have its rigid codes of sexual behavior, Williams' characters might fulfill themselves without hurting others. Closeness to another and the consequent, if temporary, disappearance of loneliness are the most important goals of Williams' dramatis personae. Neither male nor female but an individual with whom one can communicate brings relief from and compensation for the horrors of modern life. The sexual boundaries are dropped in Williams' plays, and thus the sexes are often inter-changeable. The sexual character of Williams' personae is ambiv-alent but nonetheless extraordinarily human. The Carollers in *The Mutilated* (*Dragon Country*, p. 81) sing a verse that aptly sums up Williams' feelings for his suffering characters and his hopes for humanity:

> I think the mutilated will
> Be touched by hands that nearly heal,
> At night the agonized will feel
> A comfort that is nearly real.
> A miracle, a miracle!
> A comfort that is nearly real.

Tennessee Williams' Meditations on Life and Death in *Suddenly Last Summer, The Night of the Iguana* and *The Milk Train Doesn't Stop Here Anymore*

PHILIP M. ARMATO

IN TENNESSEE WILLIAMS' autobiography, the chapter dealing with his life in the sixties might well be entitled "The Inferno." His recent description of these years is chilling. Before publication of *Memoirs* he had told Rex Reed that they culminated in a "protracted death wish that lasted roughly from 1963 until my release from the psychiatric hospital [1969] where I came within a hairbreadth of death." Even before these most difficult years of spiritual and physical suffering, *death,* Williams admits in the same interview, had been an "excessively recurring theme" in his plays. His preoccupation with mortality is certainly understandable to those who are familiar with his biography. He has suffered from childhood diphtheria, numerous nervous breakdowns, two heart attacks, a tumor, prolonged bouts with alcohol/drugs and the untimely death of his personal secretary Frank Merlo from lung cancer in 1963.

Williams is the only American playwright who has regularly grappled with the problem of death. The three plays under consideration here, written during Williams' "Inferno" period, are peopled with the dying and with memories of the already dead: *Suddenly Last Summer,* 1958 (Sebastian Venable), *The Night of the Iguana,* 1961 (Frank Faulk and Jonathan Coffin called "Nonno"), *The Milk Train Doesn't Stop Here Anymore,* 1963 (Alex, Harlon Goforth,

Sally Ferguson, Madelyn's mother, an unnamed suicide and, of course, Sissy Goforth). These plays can be seen as the spiritual documents of one poet's quest for a solution to the problems created by man's awareness of the inevitability of death. It is to Williams' credit that he has not merely "survived" his years of pronounced physical and spiritual crises. During this time of most difficult circumstances, he has created plays which attempt to see death steadily and see it whole.

In *Suddenly Last Summer*, Williams presents two diametrically opposed ways of looking at death, the Christian and the existential. Sebastian Venable embodies the existential vision of death while the rival Christian view is expressed by the life of Venable's namesake, Saint Sebastian. Here, Williams uses juxtaposition to develop his first meditation on death. The life of the modern, profane man Sebastian Venable is contrasted with that of the ancient, saintly man St. Sebastian.

Sebastian Venable is despairing modern man. Mrs. Venable's description of her son's two visits to the Encantada islands reveals his grimly existential view of life. Sebastian's fascination stemmed from Melville's description of these islands as cinder heaps "looking much as the world at large might look—after a last conflagration" (III, 354–55). Sebastian, like his fellow poet Melville, sees the islands as symbols of a greater reality. For him, they come to represent the existential void, the sterility of existence. Instead of turning away from the void Sebastian, like Camus' young poet-emperor Caligula, decides to confront it. He persuades his mother to tour the Encantadas with him.

During his first tour, Sebastian discovered signs of life in the midst of the island's desertlike terrain. He saw sea turtles depositing their eggs on the beach. Surely the turtles are a hopeful sign; life can thrive in the midst of sterility. He plans to return when the eggs are ready to be hatched. On his return, Venable witnesses a savage spectacle. The newly hatched sea turtles are slaughtered by carnivorous birds as they desperately attempt to escape into the sea. Mrs. Venable says her son was fascinated by this brutal display. He spent the whole day in the ship's rigging, under the blazing tropical sun, gripped by the spectacle on the beach.

However, when Sebastian climbs down from the rigging and

announces to his startled mother that he has seen God on the beach, it becomes apparent that he is interested in the brutality only insofar as it symbolizes a larger truth. This "truth" is inextricably bound to his sarcastic reference to divinity. God, Sebastian implies, presides over a sterile, decimated world in which helpless creatures (the baby sea turtles, man) are brutalized by death (the carnivorous sea birds). That other young poet, Camus' Caligula, puts it succinctly: "Men die, and they are not happy." Venable's confrontation with the starkest facts of existence has a harrowing effect upon him. The "sickness unto death" which is caused by despair over the human condition finds its literal representation in the tropical fever-delirium that Sebastian contracts while watching the slaughter. Although he is nursed back to physical health by his mother, his continuing spiritual malaise is emphasized by his wish to enter a Buddhist monastery where meditation might cure him of despair.

"If there is no God, everything is permitted," argues Ivan Karamazov. Sebastian Venable might very well add the corollary: "If God exists but he is cruel, cruelty is the principle of order in the universe and, therefore, should not necessarily be shunned by man." Sebastian's conduct after the Encantada episode is that of a man so overwhelmed by evil/death that life and humanistic values no longer hold any ultimate meaning for him. The last days of Sebastian Venable, as sketched by his cousin and traveling companion Catharine Holly, are marked by frustration, confusion, and cruelty. Catharine reports that Sebastian was restless and moved fitfully from place to place, he could no longer concentrate on his poetry, he used Catharine to procure young boys for him, he took advantage of their poverty by paying them for performing indecencies and in moments of anger scornfully called them "beggars."

Sebastian's understanding of the Encantada episode's meaning is the force that motivates his corrupt behavior. The Encantadas taught him that existence is a cruel absurdity which cannot be improved upon, because its cruelty is a part of God's plan: "*He!—accepted!— all!—as—how!—things!—are!* . . . even though he knew that what was awful was awful, that what was wrong was wrong" (p. 419).

Surely Sebastian's polluted life finds its source in the brackish waters of his own nihilism. Also, however, Venable's brutal death results from his despairing posture. Sebastian convinced himself that man's central business on earth was to suffer and die. Because he sees himself as merely a victim in the scheme of things, he begins to act like one. As Catharine explains, Sebastian's actions are an attempt to complete "a sort of!—*image!*—he had of himself as a sort of!—*sacrifice* to a!—*terrible* sort of a— . . . God? . . . Yes, a—*cruel* one" (p. 397). The meaning of Venable's death is clear. Convinced that man can play only the role of victim on earth, he despairingly orchestrates his own murder by antagonizing the desperate and brutal beggar boys of Cabeza de Lobo. In a perverse and masochistic manner, the wish is father to the deed here. By acting upon his definition of himself as a victim, he creates the conditions of his own victimization. Because Sebastian believes death and suffering make la condition humaine absurd and cruel, his life degenerates into a cruel absurdity.

The act of meditation invites the questioning that is caused by an examination of opposing ideas. If Williams' play confined itself to only an investigation of Venable's existential despair, it could be called a *statement* but certainly not a meditation. This, however, is not the case. An alternative vision of life and death is presented, albeit cryptically, by the play's allusions to Sebastian Venable's namesake, St. Sebastian.

Using a method reminiscent of Eliot's "The Waste Land," Williams builds his complex allusion to St. Sebastian by setting up parallels between the saint's life and that of his modern counterpart, Sebastian Venable. For instance, both fall seriously ill while exercising their vocations, both are nursed back to health by women, both have many followers. And, finally, the mutilated bodies of both men are found lying in a gutter after they have been beaten to death.

The network of allusions to the life of St. Sebastian in *Suddenly Last Summer* creates a level of meaning in the play best classified by "mock-heroic." As Joyce's Leopold Bloom is mocked by the correspondence that exists between his banal, modern life and the heroic adventures of Ulysses, as Eliot's licentious secretaries suffer a diminution by comparison with their ancient counterparts, the rhine maidens, Sebastian Venable seems all the more venal when he is compared to the heroic saint. Clearly, the exemplary life of St. Sebastian demonstrates an alternative to the corruption that characterizes the life of despairing modern man.

The saint, an early martyr, is most renowned for his courage and constancy in the face of death. His legend holds numerous examples of saintly fortitude; for instance, Butler's *Lives of the Saints* (I, 130) tells of Sebastian's undaunted bearing in the "face of the clouds of arrows shot at him" and his practice of always taking the most dangerous posts. Sebastian's constancy, his refusal to despair in the face of death, is an expression of the early Christian belief in a benevolent deity. Because God was good, human existence was charged with an ultimately positive meaning—resurrection through Christ. Armed with his faith in a loving God and therefore in a meaningful universe, Sebastian prepared both himself and his fellow martyrs for death. His death at the hands of the antichristian emperor Diocletian symbolized his total devotion to Christ, his fellow Christians, and principle.

The function of the mock-heroic analogy that Williams sets up between St. Sebastian and Sebastian Venable is twofold. First, the exemplary conduct of St. Sebastian throws into relief the shameful behavior of Sebastian Venable. For instance, Venable, unlike the saint, quarrels with God's plan; he becomes totally demoralized over the fact of death. His demoralization leads to a nihilistic inability to love. Unlike St. Sebastian, Venable does not care a whit for his followers (the boys of Cabeza de Lobo), his mother, his cousin or, for that matter, himself. His death is an expression of a masochistic self-contempt. Truly, Williams' ironic pun on Sebastian's last name reveals his character. Venable is not venerable; unlike St. Sebastian, he deserves pity, not veneration. Second, the decimation of *meaning* that characterizes Venable's modern world is emphasized by the contrasting *meaningful* world of the ancient saint. The ancient view that death was a meaningful part of God's total plan facilitated a positive outlook that found its expression in lives of fortitude, charity and saintliness. The modern notion of death as the "everlasting nay" robs life of its meaning and leads, naturally enough, to acts of despair, cowardice, and corruption.

Suddenly Last Summer is clearly the most static of Williams' mature dramas. Of all his plays, it is the one that approaches closest to the condition of poetry. For instance, not only does Williams fail to develop an explicitly dramatic conflict between Venable and a foil, but he also does not present the audience with a living, breathing Venable. Moreover, although the memories of Venable's mother and his cousin give the audience a rather complete portrait of him, his counterpart, Saint Sebastian, is merely alluded to. The challenge must have been clear to Williams. If he wished effectively to dramatize an antinomy central to his time, the opposition between the absurd and the Christian views of existence, he would have to embody these opposing views in luminous dramatis personae. This is precisely Williams' greatest achievement in *The Night of the Iguana*. For here, he masterfully creates a modern, believable saintly couple (Hannah Jelkes and her grandfather Jonathan Coffin). And also he presents his audience with a most compelling portrait of "absurd man," the Reverend T. Lawrence Shannon, defrocked. Through a marvelous series of confrontations between these three characters, Williams further investigates the effect the two world views have on their adherents' spiritual health and life conduct.

Many similarities exist between Lawrence Shannon and his prototype Sebastian Venable. Their most important shared experience is witnessing an event which causes both to question the value of life and the benevolence of God. The Encantada episode propelled Venable into a period of spiritual turmoil, and a grim scene on an unnamed tropical island adds impetus to Shannon's growing despair. There he saw two old natives picking carefully through a pile of excrement in an attempt to find sustenance. The island of excrement becomes Shannon's Encantadas for it also symbolizes the harshness of human existence. Man, like the two old natives, picks his way through life in an attempt to find something of value, but he is always frustrated because life is a dungheap. This experience also convinces Shannon that God is cruel. For as Venable saw God presiding over the Encantadas' slaughtering sea birds, so Shannon sees God in the fierceness of a tropical thunderstorm, a storm described by images which recall the savage birds of the earlier play: "The storm, with its white convulsions of light, is like a giant white bird attacking the hilltop of the Costa Verde" (IV, 325).

Shannon is not, however, a mere carbon copy of Venable. Although both characters see life as an absurdity, Shannon emphasizes a different aspect of the problem. Venable was most dismayed by death's contribution to the absurdity of the human condition. Shannon, however, compulsively focuses on the harsher aspects of life and actually sees death as a benevolent liberator. Shannon's identification with the bound iguana lizard objectifies and amplifies his view of the human state. Like the iguana, tied to a post, helplessly waiting to be slaughtered by the native boys, man, helplessly tied to earth by his life, cannot evade the inevitable suffering of existence. Only death can free one from the slings and arrows of outrageous fortune. If, like Shannon, one does not have the courage to commit suicide, one's position is much like that of the tied iguana. Man's greatest hope, Shannon explains, is to get beyond the end of his rope (to death) quickly so that his inevitable suffering will be minimized: "I'll get my flashlight, I'll show you. . . . See? The iguana? At the end of its rope? Trying to go on past the end of its goddam rope? Like *you! like me!*" (pp. 367–68). Insofar as Shannon is typical of despairing modern man, we may see the nature of our spiritual turmoil in his iguana symbol. However, just as Venable's anguish was answered, albeit cryptically, by the example of St. Sebastian, so Shannon's view of life does not go unchallenged. An alternative to despair is posited by Hannah Jelkes and Jonathan Coffin. Hannah's life philosophy and Jonathan's death philosophy function as powerful rejoinders to those, like Shannon, who are hateful of life and in love with the idea of death. Williams achievement in creating an answer to Shannon that is embodied by flesh and blood characters earmarks the "special" brilliance of *The Night of the Iguana*.

Hannah Jelkes stands as an example of courage and understanding in the face of tribulation. Like Shannon and Venable, she also has experienced harrowing moments, but, unlike the two men, she has never allowed herself the luxury of despair. Her experience with the lonely, Austrian salesman effectively demonstrates the saintly response to life's trials. Certainly, Hannah's conduct during this episode serves as an example of what is finest in human nature.

While traveling in Singapore with her grandfather, Hannah accepted the salesman's invitation to join him on a boat ride. During the excursion, he asked for a piece of Hannah's underwear and performed a fetishistic act with it. Appalled by the story, Shannon immediately characterizes the event as a "sad, dirty little episode" (p.

363). It is Hannah's spirited rejoinder to this pessimistic characterization that distinguishes her exemplary approach to life. She does not become disgusted with life after this episode, nor did she envision, during the perverse act, a rancorous, cruel God enjoying her humiliation while egging the Austrian on. Instead, she calls the event a "love experience" (p. 363) and values it as such. Moreover, she does not rebel against the fact that life will often present moments of trial; instead, she wisely submits to the truism that one must "Accept whatever situation you cannot improve" (p. 363). Hannah's two-fold response of affection and endurance clearly shows the saintly virtues of charity, understanding, and courage. Surely, Williams argues through Hannah that love and courage, not hate and cowardice, are the virtues needed if one wishes to remain spiritually afloat in life's troubled waters.

Hannah's exemplary attitude toward life is supplemented by grandfather Nonno's response to the problem of death. Nonno strikes a balance between Venable's terror of death and Shannon's active death wish. The nature of Nonno's admirable thanatopsis is revealed in the lovely poem he completes just before he dies. The poem takes the form of a prayer for courage in the face of extinction. Its speaker observes that an orange tree branch remains calm and unruffled even though a violent tropical storm is approaching. The branch animistically realizes that the storm will soon destroy it, but it refuses to despair: "And still the ripe fruit and the branch/Observe the sky begin to blanch/Without a cry, without a prayer,/With no betrayal of despair" (p. 372). The speaker concludes the poem by praying for that virtue which allows the branch to face death with such equanimity: "O Courage, could you not as well/Select a second place to dwell,/Not only in that golden tree/But in the frightened heart of me?" (p. 372). The poem's lesson is clear. Life is to be valued, for it is as precious and beautiful as the orange branch; therefore, actively desiring death, as Shannon does, is perverse and wrongheaded. But, also, to turn craven in the face of the inevitable, as Venable does, is to sin against one of life's most important beautifiers, the virtue of courage. In short, man, like the orange branch, should glory in earthly existence but courageously accept death's dominion. Insofar as Nonno dies at the end of the play without any trepidation of spirit, he stands as Williams' most effective example of modern man's potential to accept death as gracefully as Socrates or St. Sebastian.

The Milk Train Doesn't Stop Here Anymore is the last of Williams' plays which presents death as a central concern. Here, Williams accepts his greatest challenge, the creation of a protagonist who is in the process of slowly dying from cancer. He portrays the special turmoil of a person in the prime of life, Sissy Goforth, who remains in love with living while slowly dying. The list of playwrights who have not grappled with this exceedingly common problem is immense. Williams' insights into the psychology of the disease-sufferer are new, fresh, and, at times, startling. This most recent dramatic statement about death distinctly follows in a logical progression from earlier positions developed in *Suddenly Last Summer* and *The Night of the Iguana*. In short, the similarities that exist between Sissy Goforth and Venable/Shannon clearly show that all three are members of the same family, despairing modern man.

Just as Shannon puzzled over the nature of existence during his sabbatical on a hilltop overlooking the Mexican coast, as Venable sought answers to overwhelming questions from his crow's nest above the ocean, Sissy Goforth ponders life's mysteries in her mountain villa perched above the Mediterranean Sea. Venable and Shannon experienced harrowing events which caused them to doubt the benevolence of God or His universe. Likewise, Sissy is spectator to a death scene which has contributed to the development of her present "fear and trembling." This scene was the panic-stricken death of her first husband, Harlon Goforth, who suffered a massive stroke while performing the act of love with Sissy. It is clear that the look of terror in Harlon's dying eyes has profoundly affected Sissy's heart and mind, for her present description of this long past event is marked by panic and trepidation of spirit: Harlon had "death in his eyes, and something worse in them, terror. . . . I move away from death, terror! . . . I go straight to the door . . . onto the terrace! . . . It's closed, I tear it open, I leave him alone with his death" (V, 58). Sissy literally ran away from Harlon's death. Like Venable's Encantadas and Shannon's isle of excrement, this grim variant of coitus interruptus aptly symbolizes man's ultimate frustration and victimization by death. Because she is afraid of death and cognizant of its dominion, Sissy lies to herself about the seriousness of her physical condition. Sissy's self-deception is a product of the despair created by the fear of death. Escape from this form of despair is possible only if Sissy learns, as Nonno learned, to accept death, to *face it* with courage.

Sissy, then, must courageously confront the reality of her own situation if she wishes to defeat Self-Deception and Despair, two of man's ogres. Like Shannon, she is lost in the wilderness, but, luckily, she also is not without a guide. Here, as in *The Night of the Iguana*, Williams creates an artist-teacher who offers wise counsel about the nature of reality to a despairing protagonist. Through this typically Williamsian figure, Christopher Flanders, the playwright makes his last (so far) major statement about the problem of death. The statement is a harsh one, for Williams was undoubtedly influenced by the slow decay of his friend Frank Merlo; it is not, however, a despairing one. For clearly, Chris as Williams teaches Sissy and us to face the grimmer aspects of existence "With no betrayal of despair."

Christopher Flanders utilizes two of his artistic creations, a mobile and a parable about suicide, as mediums through which his lesson is conveyed. Just before his final confrontation with Sissy, he hangs the mobile entitled "The Earth Is a Wheel in a Great Big Gambling Casino" from her bedroom ceiling. The mobile functions as a preamble to all that Chris will say about life and death. Its title suggests that the earth is merely a minor cogwheel in the limitless gambling casino of the universe; clearly, the title alludes to the Copernican astronomy which ushered in modern man's recognition of his unimportance in the "scheme of things." Visually, the mobile makes a second statement which logically proceeds from the first. Just as it randomly tilts and sways while being buffeted by the uncontrollable force of the wind, so helpless, diminished man is assaulted by the uncontrollable pushes and pulls of chance and fate in the gambling casino of the universe. The implications of this lesson are clear: (1) To live is to operate in a universe ruled by gambling odds. (2) Therefore, wisdom is the realization that our destinies are not controlled by ourselves, but by two lords of life, Chance and Fate. (3) Therefore, the fault, dear Brutus, does lie in our stars!

If Chris's total statement is the lesson taught by the mobile, he could certainly be accused of negativism. Luckily, for Sissy, this is not the case. Chris's second creation, the suicide parable, suggests how one might ultimately defeat the grim reality so aptly symbolized by the trepidating mobile. While walking past an ocean inlet, Chris saw an old gentleman on the beach calling for help as if he were drowning in the sand. On closer inspection, he sees the signs of a horrible disease in the old man's ravaged countenance. The old man confesses to Chris that he is no longer able to stand the extreme pain of his condition. He asks Chris to help him end it all. Obligingly, Chris carries him out into the water where the tide wafts him out "as light as a leaf." The moral of this story is clear. The diseased old man screams for help on the sandshore of life, because he finds the burden of existence unacceptable. Concomitantly, death, then, becomes his friend and liberator. The wisdom of the old man's exemplary thanatos encompasses the lesson that Chris is attempting to teach Sissy: When one's luck runs out, as the old man's has, in the casino of life, death is to be revered, not feared. By courageously embracing death we, like the old gentleman—St. Sebastian—Socrates, revolt against a tyrannical existence made up of hours of lead.

After hearing his parable, Sissy asks Chris to help her into the bedroom, just as the old man had asked Chris to carry him out to sea. Now, Sissy also desires death. She describes her new feelings about life and death in a final symbolic statement. An investigation of the statement's implications suggests that Sissy will not face death with the fear and trembling of a Harlon Goforth. Indeed, she has learned Chris's lesson well.

The preamble to Sissy's new perception of life and death is expressed in the symbolic statement which gives the play its title: The "milk train doesn't stop here anymore" (p. 117). This assertion clearly shows Sissy's realization that those aspects of life which are nutritive to the human spirit, precious, and of value, will no longer visit her, for the milk train which refuses to stop symbolizes these positive aspects of existence. Here, Sissy faces the essential absurdity of the human condition. In short, she is aware that: (1) At any given moment, the precious things in life may cease to stop at our door. (2) There seems to be no logical reason for this to happen. (3) The situation must be accepted as a fait accompli, for nothing can be done about it.

Sissy's new perception of death is a logical progression from the vision of life described above. Now she wisely realizes that when life becomes a horrible burden—when the positive aspects of existence symbolized by the milk train are no longer forthcoming, death is to be actively submitted to, not feared: "It's my turn, now, to go forth [to die]. . . . I'll do it alone. I don't want to be escorted. I want to go forth alone" (p. 117). These final lines show that Sissy, like the old gentleman, faces the harshness of reality in an absurd universe and courageously accepts death, the only antidote to a poisonous existence. By facing her situation, she casts off self-deception. By gracefully accepting death, she conquers despair. Clearly, Sissy is spiritually a victor over life's vicissitudes. For as soon as she dies, a gust of wind triumphantly whips out her flag, and a bugle in the background plays reveille in honor of her awakening, not taps.

Milk Train's most important departure from *Night of the Iguana* is in the severe asceticism of its statement. Although chaste, self-disciplined Hannah Jelkes practiced a life of denial, she and Nonno clearly reveled in the physical beauties of life. A much colder eye is cast upon earthly existence in *Milk Train,* for its message is contemptum mundi. Yet, *Milk Train* is not a retraction of the warmer regard for human life posited in *Iguana*. Both plays present important views of life. In short, *Iguana* is a play for those who still have hope; *Milk Train* is surely a play to comfort the hopeless.

In one area, however, the plays coincide in a manner that sets their protagonists apart from Sebastian Venable in *Suddenly Last Summer*. Hannah, Nonno, Shannon, Chris and Sissy see human charity as life's most precious treasure. They know that life is often like a penal colony, a hostile environment that makes creating, loving, and clear perceiving difficult. But this knowledge does not propel them into the viciousness of a Sebastian Venable. They still love, after their own manner. Even Larry Shannon warmly regards Hannah/Nonno and embraces Maxine Faulk at the end of *Iguana*. It is the later plays' preponderance of love that sets them apart from the coldness of *Suddenly Last Summer*. Although the later plays are certainly somber, they cannot be construed as defeatist, for part of their lesson is "Love thy neighbor as thyself." They show that even in a harsh universe love, charity, compassion are still possible. The despair that destroyed Sebastian Venable's humanity can be exorcised from the human spirit. Underneath the guise of southern decadence, Tennessee Williams practices the art of a decidedly Christian playwright.

Little Acts of Grace

DELMA EUGENE PRESLEY

THROUGHOUT HIS CAREER Tennessee Williams has endowed his characters with various degrees of spiritual awareness. Sometimes the vision is dim, but it is there even in the reply Stanley Kowalski makes impatiently to Blanche DuBois: "It's not my soul, it's my kidneys I'm worried about!" (I,364). A minor character can utter the words of prophecy, as does the heckler in *Sweet Bird of Youth*: "I believe that the silence of God, the absolute speechlessness of Him is a long, long and awful thing that the whole world is lost because of" (IV, 105). In some recent plays the theological statements are not so subtle: "you're a fool, Mrs. Goforth, if you don't know that finally, sooner or later, you need somebody or something to mean God to you" (V, 113), says a poet named Christopher Flanders. In his own way Williams has sought to reenact the deed performed by T. Lawrence Shannon in *The Night of the Iguana*. After Shannon cuts the rope binding a struggling iguana, Maxine Faulk asks for an explanation. Shannon replies: "So that one of God's creatures could scramble home safe and free. . . . A little act of grace, Maxine" (IV, 373).

Williams has preferred to create characters who have the kinds of problems that call for theological solutions, for little acts of grace. His characters live alone in an uncaring world, and they long for a sense of community. They acknowledge that God seems absent, and

571

572   Little Acts of Grace

they hope for a savior or his equivalent. They behold the anguish of
death, and they flinch. One of the clearest patterns in the works of
the playwright is his effort to resolve the theological problems of
isolation, God's absence, and death. At times the effort becomes a
consuming preoccupation which leads him into an ideological trap.
Hoping to rescue the creatures of his later plays, Williams strips
them of those ambiguities and perplexities that characterize humanity. His later works may be poorer precisely because of those
little acts of grace.

Tom Wingfield and Blanche DuBois, central characters in the
early plays, *The Glass Menagerie* and *A Streetcar Named Desire*,
are caught in situations which prevent any semblance of community.
The potential of understanding may exist in the Wingfield home,
but it is never fully realized. Tom understands but refuses to heed
the advice of Amanda: "In these trying times we live in, all that we
have to cling to is each other" (I, 171). His escape from responsibility is but another in a long series which began, of course, with the
father's desertion. In *Streetcar* Blanche knows what she needs when
she arrives at her sister's place in New Orleans. She tells Stella: "I
want to be *near* you, got to be *with* somebody, I *can't* be *alone!*" (I,
257). Blanche is doomed from the start not simply because it is her
fate to be overwhelmed by the bestial Stanley. She is a complex
character of conflicting emotions. She needs understanding, but
cannot really accept it. Her compassion, genuine at times, finally is
defeated by her selfishness. Her need for love is undermined by her
debauchery. Human community is not possible in *Streetcar* precisely
because the people who ought to participate in that community are
either unwilling or incapable or both.

Another cause of isolation in the early plays is the classic struggle
between the flesh and the spirit. Tom Wingfield, an avid reader of
the instinct affirming work of D. H. Lawrence, is rebuked by a religious sounding Amanda. She admonishes her son: "Don't quote
instinct to me! Instinct is something that people have got away
from! It belongs to animals! Christian adults don't want it!" (I,
174). This thematic clash again comes to the surface in a clever
dialogue in the seventh scene of *Streetcar*. Blanche's habit of spending hours in the Kowalskis' only bathroom aggravates her already

lacerated relationship with Stanley. After listening to one of his impatient remarks, she replies with a paraphrase of Jesus' words (Luke 21: 19): "Possess your soul in patience." Stanley, as noted above, immediately counters with: "It's not my soul, it's my kidneys I'm worried about!" In the context of the drama, these words are reminders that Stanley's mind is not open to the beckoning of the spirit but only to the needs of the flesh (I, 364). *Summer and Smoke*, written shortly after *Streetcar*, appears to have been conceived with the theme of the flesh versus the spirit as a problem to be solved. But pathos is the only emotion evoked in this experimental allegory which ends with the sad affirmation that the flesh (summer) cannot merge with the spirit (smoke). John (doctor of bodily ills) and Alma (Spanish for "soul") are not saved from their isolation but pathetically confirmed in it.

Another theological problem explored by Williams is the absence of God. The Wingfields, Amanda in particular, wish for a messiah in the form of a gentleman caller. Indeed, *The Glass Menagerie* is held together by the Wingfields' anticipation of Jim O'Connor and his eventual arrival. He is, as Tom points out in the opening monologue, "that long delayed but always expected something that we live for." Once Jim comes, stays briefly, and leaves, the play's action is complete. There is no one else to wait for, and Amanda's hopes for deliverance are fruitless, because Jim has made previous commitments. In *Streetcar* Blanche keeps hoping until the end that her messiah, Shep Huntleigh, will appear out of nowhere and rescue her from Stanley and his crude world. The airplane Fugitivo is the messianic symbol in *Camino Real*. It is either death at the hands of the street cleaners or escape via airplane, for the one who travels the road of reality. The tubercular woman of pleasure, Marguerite, knows the airplane is her only means of escape, but a technicality prevents her boarding this agency of salvation. Her destiny is to die in a strange land devoid of love and compassion. The most obvious reference to the absence of God in a guilt infested world comes in *Sweet Bird of Youth*. Few critics have noted the significant lines of that heckler who shouts to the crowd assembled to hear Boss Finley, the "messiah from the hills": "I don't believe it. I believe that the silence of God, the absolute speechlessness of Him is a long, long and awful thing that the whole world is lost because of. I think it's yet to be broken to any man, living or yet lived on earth—no exceptions" (IV, 105).

The human need for God poignantly reveals itself when Williams' characters encounter the reality of death. It is the very absence of divine aid which makes Big Daddy's dying so tragic in *Cat on a Hot Tin Roof*. This play confronts the viewer with a dramatic exploration of human destiny in that memorable dialogue between Brick and his father in the second act. Big Daddy stings the alcoholic Brick with the truth about his cowardly escape from life. Then the son retaliates by breaking the news that his father has cancer and will not celebrate future birthdays. There is no advice, no optimistic outlook for Big Daddy. His last words are: "CHRIST—DAMN—ALL—LYING SONS OF—LYING BITCHES! . . . Lying! Dying! Liars!" (III, 128). Life cannot continue on Brick's side of the family, for he already has willed a spiritual death. As Williams describes Brick in the text, he has "that cool air of detachment that people have who have given up the struggle" (III, 19). Life will continue for Gooper and Mae and their offspring. But as Big Daddy and Brick point out in their dialogue, the kind of existence embodied by these people is mendacious. Death is the final truth of this play.

Big Daddy's raging against the night contrasts sharply with the subdued tones of acceptance found in later works such as *The Night of the Iguana, The Milk Train Doesn't Stop Here Anymore* and *I Can't Imagine Tomorrow*. In *Iguana* the defrocked priest, Shannon, attempts to find "something like . . . God" while his teacher, Hannah Jelkes, helps prepare her father, Nonno, to face his death peacefully. In *Milk Train* a Christ substitute, Christopher Flanders, urges the dying Mrs. Goforth to find "somebody or something to mean God." A parable in *I Can't Imagine Tomorrow* suggests that death is an ultimate good much to be preferred over a life of loneliness. The small man pleads with Death to accept him, because he "can't go back down the mountain. I have no place down there. I have no one to visit in the evening, I have no one to talk to, no one to play cards with, I have no one, no one" (*Dragon Country*, p. 143). Death finally relents and makes a place for the small man.

The difference between Big Daddy and the dying mortals of the later works is that the former has tragic dimensions. The latter simply accept what they do not understand; in the process they become less than human. This, then, is what happens when Williams performs little acts of grace and offers solutions to his characters' problems. They lose their authenticity.

The threads of hopefulness in Williams' later plays are largely responsible for those erratic patterns which puzzle so many observers of his work. The wild threads appear as early as *Camino Real* (1953). In this play Williams embarked on a new course. Forsaking conventional theater's acts and scenes, he developed an allegory of timeless blocks. The title can mean both "way of reality" and "royal road." The play has many similarities to Dante's famous allegory of life as hell. The epigraph to *Camino Real* comes from canto one of *The Inferno*: "In the middle of the journey of our life, I came to myself in a dark wood where the straight way was lost." The travelers of the camino are universal figures: the eternal optimist, Don Quixote; the great lover, Casanova; the romantic in quest of an ideal, Lord Byron; the sentimental courtesan, Marguerite. The hero is that American Everyman, Kilroy; it is he who attempts to hold fast to independence, sincerity, and courage.

Kilroy travels the very real road of life which leads him to an arid fountain in the middle of a square. He discovers Don Quixote's map is right: "The spring of humanity has gone dry in this place" (II, 435). Despite Kilroy's optimism, despite his efforts to defeat the smug and cruel enemies of brotherhood, he fails. After his death, however, interns dissect him and discover that the American Everyman has a heart of gold. So the hero's idealism cannot be destroyed after all. At the end of the play, a resurrected Kilroy carries his gold heart underneath his arm as he joins a refreshed Don Quixote. They both set out to dream possible dreams. This point is underscored when Quixote exclaims: *"The violets in the mountains have broken the rocks!"* Water rushes into the once-dry fountain. Like Christ, Kilroy has become a transcendent force for good (II, 591).

Camino Real is a splendid spectacle. However, when measured by Williams' earlier standards, it is poor drama. Complex literary and historical figures such as Don Quixote, Kilroy, and Lord Byron are rendered as caricatures. Williams allows himself to become self-conscious about symbols. All at once the viewer is thrust into an incongruous system where Dante, Cervantes, T. S. Eliot, Lord Byron, Spanish folklore, and Christian sentiments intermingle without meeting. Kilroy's sudden apotheosis near the drama's end appears to be deus ex machina. The sentimental ending leaves the viewer protesting that nothing has been resolved. But the curtain falls nevertheless.

Suddenly Last Summer, produced five years after *Camino Real,* also lacks credibility. The heroine, Catharine Holly, explains that the unseen protagonist, Sebastian Venable, exemplifies what happens to people when they become obsessed with evil. Sebastian, a homosexual and an aspiring poet, was consumed by a frenzied mob of hungry street urchins. But Catharine sees Sebastian as a symbol of mankind universal. He represents the efforts of modern man to "spell God's name with the wrong alphabet blocks!" (III, 375). The play easily can be viewed as an allegory about the consequences of possessing a daemonic vision, for Sebastian sacrifices himself to his cannibalistic god. Instead of pursuing this significant point, however, the playwright turns his attention to the interrelationship of mankind. Dialogue drifts into vague generalities about the need for people to accept one another. The pious comments of Catharine and her physician fail to come to grips with the significant issues raised earlier—the nature of God and idolatry. Totally disregarding man's idolatrous nature, his making into God an image of himself, Catharine touchingly affirms a life of community in which people learn to accept the eccentricities of others. In short, the solutions provided do not really apply to the problems at hand. Subsequent plays also reveal this weakness.

In *The Night of the Iguana* Shannon and Hannah are engaged in a serious theological discussion when he explains he "cannot continue to conduct services in praise and worship of this . . . angry, petulant old man" (God) (IV, 303). So Shannon's problem later is revealed to be "the oldest one in the world—the need to believe in something or in someone," Hannah tells him.

SHANNON: Your voice sounds hopeless about it.
HANNAH: No, I'm not hopeless about it. In fact I've discovered something to believe in.
SHANNON: Something like . . . God?
HANNAH: No.
SHANNON: What?

HANNAH: Broken gates between people so they can reach each other, even if it's just for one night only.

. . . .

A little understanding exchanged between them, a wanting to help each other through nights like this (p. 352).

Hannah's point seems to be that the problem of belief will more or less take care of itself if Shannon will try to live in community with someone. But Shannon's problem is not isolation but belief (or lack of it). Hannah insists that he deal with the question of disbelief with the answer for human isolation—community. The logic is reminiscent of that used by Catharine in *Suddenly Last Summer*; she raises the question of Sebastian's demonic vision of God and then answers it with a simplistic statement about the importance of caring for other people.

While Hannah and Shannon are engaged in their discussion, a minor character, Nonno, resolves to approach death with "courage." Nonno finally completes his poem:

> O Courage, could you not as well
> Select a second place to dwell,
> Not only in that golden tree
> But in the frightened heart of me? (p. 372).

Nonno's long awaited poem came after much struggle, and one would expect Shannon to resolve his problems. Nonno struggles with success and dies, but the play is not about him. The protagonist, Shannon, eventually ignores the question of God which first was most important. Then he commits himself to a life of "community" with Maxine Faulk, one of the few persons in the play who singularly lacks empathy. Hannah's last line concludes the drama; it is intended to be a kind of benediction: "Oh God, can't we stop now? Finally? Please let us. It's so quiet here, now" (p. 375). But nothing has been resolved for Shannon.

The Milk Train Doesn't Stop Here Anymore also has an illogical resolution. Christopher's mission apparently is to prepare Mrs. Goforth for death. The epigraph from Yeats's "Sailing to Byzantium" suggests she is about to set forth into eternity. Yet it is not clear whether Williams proposes eternal life of any kind for Mrs. Goforth. If Christopher really bears Christ, such would seem to be the case. But his mission is patently selfish. He visits Mrs. Goforth, just as he has visited other dying women, not because he has a special message but because this activity saves *him* from a sense of "unreality" and "lostness." Some reviewers have claimed the drama is about a Christ figure who comes to prepare a dying aristocrat for eternal life. But such can hardly be the case in *Milk Train*. The occasion of Mrs. Goforth's death is merely a vehicle which speeds a vagrant poet toward his own psychological satisfaction.

Since Williams' turning point is *Camino Real*, it is important to notice what takes place at the time he is developing themes of hope: He also is experimenting with a theatrical structure foreign to his genius as a writer of realistic drama. The characters of *Camino Real* are stripped of their authenticity and adorned with allegorical trappings studded with gems of poetry and symbol. But the trouble with Williams' allegories is that they consistently reveal a preference for the sentimental over the authentic. Both *Camino Real* and *Suddenly Last Summer* have grace but lack truth.

The significance of Williams' experiments with technique should not be overlooked. As Mark Schorer noted in "Technique as Discovery," technique fundamentally is subject matter: "The final lesson of the modern novel is that technique is not the secondary thing it seemed to Wells, some external machination, a mechanical affair, but a deep and primary operation; not only that technique *contains* intellectual and moral implications, but that it *discovers* them" (p. 74). Williams' allegories indicate that he wants to do more than depict the loneliness and frustrations of his Tom Wingfields, Blanche DuBoises, and Chance Waynes. Most of the works appearing after *Camino Real* reveal that Williams has set out to solve some difficult problems of the heart and spirit. Commendable as his efforts might seem, he works at hope desperately and with little success.

That Williams is concerned with significant theological issues cannot be denied. Human isolation, the absence of God, and the reality of death are fundamental concerns of religion, especially of the Christian religion. Williams surely recognizes this or he would not utilize Christian sounding language and themes in many of the recent works. However, he seems not to have grasped the fundamental logic inherent in the spiritual issues. He has not found a way to portray solutions to the problems experienced by his characters, even though he employs dramatic techniques to suggest otherwise.

The great virtue of the early plays of Williams is that they are believable and do concern real people. The early hero has unmistakable dignity. Despite social and psychological pressures, he does not ignore the facts of his life. Blanche's despair is a legitimate and credible response to the nature of her existence. Tom's acute awareness of the truly disgusting aspects of his life makes him what few of the latter heroes are—truthful. As the Protestant theologian, Paul Tillich, once pointed out, the images of despair in A *Streetcar Named Desire* reveal a special kind of courage: "even comparatively positive solutions are underminded by doubt and by awareness of the ambiguity of all solutions." Williams is in "a vanguard which precedes a great change in the spiritual and social-psychological situation," Tillich wrote in *The Courage to Be* (pp. 145–46). Whether or not Williams is an existential writer, as Tillich claimed, it is clear that the frustrations and anxieties of Blanche and Tom are more real than the religious sounding clichés which fall from the tongues of Hannah Jelkes, T. Lawrence Shannon, Christopher Flanders, and others.

Lest we misunderstand or misjudge Williams, we should view his little acts of grace in perspective. Obviously, he did not have to choose hope over against despair. But at a point the playwright determined that it was necessary to move his characters out of the shadows of tragedy and into the light of comedy. It is this determination which truly distinguishes Williams as a contemporary writer. Indeed, who else has made serious efforts to explore the subjects of reconciliation and redemption? A few have tried. T. S. Eliot in his later poetry and plays charted the paths of salvation. However, as his critics so often have noted, Eliot's certainties detract from his art. Even that master of the religious imagination, Dante, is not very interesting after he leaves the Inferno and ascends toward Paradise.

Some might contend that Williams' difficulties validate the contention of those "death of God" theologians who claim that Christian thought is not relevant to a "post-Christian age." These thinkers rejoice that so many modern writers have learned to accept man's finitude. In this theological system, the joys of the flesh become the credo of a new worldly religion. Now Williams is not a stranger to such thinking. He has explored the depth and breadth of sensuality. *The Rose Tattoo* is a serious effort to emancipate captive characters through celebrations of the flesh. Indeed, Williams has considered the gospel of D. H. Lawrence—that modern man needs to experience a resurrection of the human body. But Williams has not found in Lawrence solutions to the spiritual problems which dominate so many of his characters. Thus *Kingdom of Earth* explores the potential of sex in comic proportions; yet throughout the play the apocalyptic sounds of a raging flood never cease. Neither has Williams been able to go the way of the theater of the absurd or the literature of silence. He is not content to allow his characters to wait without hope and to face nothingness by saying nothing. No, he never has attuned his poetic voice to the dissonances within the existential abyss. Always he has been a romantic who prefers to sing those sad, sweet songs which flow from the heart.

During his career Williams has improved some of his skills as a dramatist. He has refined his unique art of stage poetics, and he has become a master of theatrical effect. Nevertheless, his more recent plays fail to reach the high standards of *The Glass Menagerie* and *A Streetcar Named Desire*. In this sense his progression is from strength to weakness—from the mighty NO of Tom Wingfield and Blanche DuBois to the meek yes of Hannah Jelkes and Christopher Flanders. Desperately he has sought to redeem his fallen creatures with little acts of grace. Even though he probably would like it to be otherwise, Williams remains a dramatist of lost souls.

Williams' Power of the Keys

JOHN MacNICHOLAS

I

God, like other people, has two kinds of hands, one hand
with which to strike and another to soothe and caress with.

("Mama's Old Stucco House," *The Knightly Quest*, p. 121)

D ECLINE, NOT SEX, obsesses Tennessee Wil-
liams. *"There is a passion for declivity in this world!"* the Byron of
Camino Real declaims (II, 508), and the same may be observed in
the world of Williams' plays. Their historical macrocosms often present a world nearing collapse. The debacle of World War I frames
the action of *Summer and Smoke* and *The Eccentricities of a Nightingale,* and World War II is prominently insinuated into the temporal backgrounds of *The Glass Menagerie* and *The Night of the
Iguana.* The protagonists of these plays are likewise struggling with
problems which exhaust their personal resources. The question informing the substrata of all Williams' major work is: does personal
disintegration press merely toward insignificant inanition, or can the
soul in painful disrepair regenerate itself? Although Williams presents this question in various manners, its thematic center is the Fall,
the loss of Eden: "sooner or later, at some point in your life, the
thing that you lived for is lost or abandoned," the Princess Kosmonopolis informs Chance Wayne, "and then . . . you die, or find something else" (*Sweet Bird of Youth,* IV, 35). The interval between loss,
or more specifically *recognition* of loss, and subsequent recovery or
its impossibility, is the typical focus of most of Williams' plays. The
initiating action in Nonno's poem occurs immediately following the
zenith of the tree's life—its "second history" and onset of "mist and

581

mould." Two aspects of primal loss seem constant: the obstruction
of passion and the erosion of sincerity in either the central character
or his society, or both. The deepest despair in Williams' tragic plays
arises from the inadequacy of the "something else" to remedy disorder and especially middle-age sorrow. Williams' central characters,
then, are usually confronted with the decision of participating in
their own destruction or, by exercising an enormous act of will, altering their spiritual environment. Quite simply, he is concerned with
damnation and redemption.

The purpose of this essay will be, first, to trace the etiology of
damnation in Williams' plays and define the methods which utilize
its dramatic potential; and second, to discuss how redemption (a
much more difficult subject to dramatize) may arise out of acute
despair. The apostolic power of the keys, the binding and loosing of
spiritual life, is the dynamic which runs constant throughout the
canon.

The thematic force of Williams' vivid minor characters and their
physical worlds derives from his perception that society and the individual both are responsible for spiritual life. Binding has the effect
of excommunication, though not necessarily in the formal sense of
an ecclesiastical ostracism. Rather it is the failure of the body politic
to see in its fear of passion a separation from the only divinity which
can be certainly known on earth. If a theology were to be constructed
from Williams' plays, these tenets would be cardinal: energy is holy;
and if a God the Creator exists he is remote from our daily concerns,
an abstraction who teases his creatures out of thought. The only
deity Williams acknowledges is an untrammeled possession of the
self, a Blakean aseity: "Thou art a Man, God is no more [than
Man],/Thy own humanity learn to adore" ("Everlasting Gospel").
Williams consistently represents the dynamic of binding in terms
of an individual passion, which is usually but not always a highly
visible sexuality, opposed by a repressively centristic society. His
most unqualified dramatic sympathy falls upon victims of a truncated sexuality: Laura Wingfield, Lucretia Collins ("Portrait of a
Madonna"), Blanche DuBois, Heavenly Finley, Alma Winemiller,
Myra Torrance, Hannah Jelkes, and Violet and Quentin (*Small
Craft Warnings*). A deep fear of an enduring sexual (and hence, in

her society, a personal and familial) dispossession animates Margaret's struggle in *Cat on a Hot Tin Roof*.

Williams, like Lawrence and Blake, can conceive of no greater wasteland than that which traps and neuters individual passion. He recognizes that the real evil of prostitution is not its routine social depredations, which are in themselves terrible enough, but the spiritual dispossession which it enforces upon both parties. And so he acutely depicts the anguish arising from having no *self* to retreat into. Such dispossession (or the threat of it) may be seen in the physical and emotional entropy of Bertha in *Hello from Bertha*; in the Old Woman's desperate exploitation of her personal past in *Lord Byron's Love Letter*; in the unsuccessful breach Cornelia Scott attempts to make in Grace's privacy (*Something Unspoken*); in Vacarro's revenge upon Jake (*27 Wagons*); in the humiliating way the Princess orders Chance Wayne to her bed in the first scene of *Sweet Bird of Youth*; in Gutman's description of the ambiance of *Camino Real*, "a bazaar where the human heart is a part of the bargain" (II, 452); in the pathos of the brief interview between Myra Torrance and David Cutrere, which establishes that Myra lost once that passion which Jabe will deprive her of again: "You made whores of us both!" she tells an assenting David (*Orpheus*, III, 285); and in Sebastian Venable's pitiless exploitation of Catharine's sexuality in *Suddenly Last Summer*. The most surprising element of Williams' short story, "Two on a Party," is that Billy and Cora, whose "party" expends human resources faster than they can reasonably be replenished, have found in each other a home, a part of themselves which is private. The mystery of that privacy arrested Williams' imagination, for they are his only prostitutes who tolerate themselves. Social evil, therefore, is most keenly felt when it attempts to kill or trivialize the Orc-like energy of Val Xavier and Carol Cutrere, or Serafina Delle Rose. Blanche is most unsympathetic when she attempts to camouflage her own sexuality by degrading Stanley's, and her spiritual prototype, Amanda, is the most absurd and repressive as she removes Lawrence's novels from Tom's room and badgers him about his nocturnal activities.

A society which attacks passion or a personality which undermines it with insincerity or guilt is thus bound, cut off from vital joy.

Sweet Bird of Youth presents both forces simultaneously. No greater caricature of a meanminded social order exists in Williams' canon than Boss Finley's political machine. However, it is not Finley's wounded pride and pursuit of vengeance, but Chance Wayne's inability to atone for infecting Heavenly with syphilis that guides Wayne to his doom. The play is weakened by the fragmentation of dramatic energy inherent in the protagonist's confusion. He wants the society which is supposedly envious of his sexuality to admire him for being the wealthy young movie star that he is not. He desires from people whom he detests an acceptance of him as "local boy makes good." He wants to reclaim Heavenly, and simultaneously he desires punishment for inflicting his disease upon her. More than anything else, Wayne seeks to maneuver Finley into servicing his extraordinary masochism. The occlusion of motive from effective action here is characteristic of Williams' concept of damnation. Wayne makes his choice; however, it is hardly an informed action. In the final act he continues on his course of self-destruction, oblivious of trenchant commentary coming from the townspeople, who do not care whether he destroys himself, and from his Aunt Nonnie and the Princess, who do care for him. Defining his concept of tragedy, Williams writes: "The great and only possible dignity of man lies in his power deliberately to choose certain moral values by which to live as steadfastly as if he, too, like a character in a play, were immured against the corrupting rush of time" (II, 262). But those characters whose actions Williams seeks to invest with a tragic tone—Blanche, Val Xavier, or Chance Wayne—seem to have very little choice during their moments upon the stage. Their lives have more to do with desperation than with choice.

During the course of a tragedy, the protagonist is at times likely to be desperate—indeed, almost necessarily—but what defines his soul may not consist primarily of desperation. The self-transcendence of a tragic character is manifested at least partially in an almost kingly indifference to cost, loss, and circumstance which hitherto had made him fearful or anguished. If such indifference is predicated upon rigid self-ignorance, as Chance Wayne's is, then the dramatist to that extent forfeits the tragic tone. Aristotle, whose concept of tragedy Williams evidently respects, reserved for highest praise the tragic structure which caused the reversal to proceed immediately out of recognition. The audience is never allowed to witness Chance Wayne's recognition because it never occurs. At the end of *Sweet Bird of Youth*, he is essentially unchanged, the willing slave of a monomaniacal drive to reclaim the past with Heavenly. His character has in effect been ossified by a masochistic guilt whose very origins prevent him from carrying out his wish to be reunited with Heavenly. Even the pretense that this design is feasible obligates Chance to ignore temporal bonds. Therefore he is immunized from self-recognition, whose dramatic power always issues from a delayed and morally informed realignment of past causes and present effects. Even Blanche in the grip of psychosis comes closer than Chance Wayne in understanding the causes of her suffering. (The special nature of Blanche's recognition will be discussed in detail below.)

Not Williams' formal statements about tragedy, but the recurrent metaphors characterizing it, yield the useful insight into his drama. His favorite vehicle to convey the results of thwarted passion is disease; its reiterated expression is: the world is a hospital. His canon is filled with people whose illnesses are directly traceable to emotional causes. Willie's malapropism for the cause of her promiscuous sister's death—"lung affection" (*This Property Is Condemned, 27 Wagons*, p. 201)—precisely condenses Williams' belief that there is no greater destructive potential, even on a physical basis, than displaced eros. One thinks of the "malaria" of Amanda, Blanche, Lucretia Collins, and Alma Winemiller. In Alma especially, the effects of sexual deprivation have surfaced in physical pathology: her "heart disturbances," a pronounced physical emaciation (the stage directions of scene nine of *Summer and Smoke* describe her as though she had suffered a long illness), her stiff fingers and throat spasms, and her climactic acknowledgment of her "affliction of love." Her lover and physician, John Buchanan, compares the location of their furtive tryst to a hospital room. Carol Cutrere has survived pneumonia. Laura Wingfield's emotional pathology appears both in her glass and in her limp. Even her nickname, "Blue Roses," playfully attached to her by Jim O'Connor during their high school years, homonymically derives from her having contracted pleurosis. Myra Torrance lives in a state of "artificial respiration" (*Battle*, I, 75). Syphilis and alcoholism invade several lives in *Sweet Bird of Youth*. Violet Venable, who has had an aneurism, jokes about being kept alive by a drugstore. Her son Sebastian, who suffered from "fever," sexually debased and traumatized Catharine so that a physician who specializes in lobotomy is summoned to cut "disease" (the truth) out of Catharine's brain. Kilroy is taken out of the ring by the medics because he has "heart disease." Personal and societal decline is given an impassioned febrile description in *Auto-Da-Fé*. Elio, a prototype for Tom Wingfield, obsessively associates his slum dwelling in the Vieux Carré of New Orleans with carcinoma: "This is the primary lesion, the—focal infection, the—chancre! In medical language, it spreads by—metastasis! It creeps through the capillaries and into the main blood vessels. From there it is spread all through the surrounding tissue!" (*27 Wagons*, p. 110).

Period of Adjustment, in which the duration of the "period" is of course a lifetime, presents the metaphor in the starkest terms. The romance of George and Isabel Haverstick began in the hospital in which George attempted to recover from "the shakes" and Isabel worked as a nurse. Isabel's sexual fantasy, however, has more to do with a "youngish middle-aged doctor" than with a traumatized war veteran. The imaginary doctor's passion for her is not stinted by the leprosy which she must contract as they bravely perform missionary work side by side in an obscure tropical country. When her physician clasps her, he too becomes infected with contagion. *Period* culminates upon the same metaphor to which Thomas Mann gave definitive treatment in *The Magic Mountain*. She tells George that the world is indeed a hospital, "a big neurological ward," in which she is a student (IV, 244). This sentiment is close to Chance Wayne's description of his compulsive and dangerous return trips to see Heavenly—"like going to a hospital" (IV, 50). Now it is known that Williams himself contracted several painful and severe childhood illnesses and that during his early adult years he worked in a state hospital, but his personal experience alone cannot account for the insistency with which he represents the hospital world upon his stage. Sickness and disease are linked to a binding process, a psychomachia in which the powerfully expressive personality, such as Shannon or Blanche, will resort to visible means of self-destruction when all else fails. The more reticent personality, such as Laura Wingfield or Violet in *Small Craft Warnings*, suffers a less flamboyant but equally certain inner decay.

Every sickness seeks a physician and a victim. Williams' drama identifies these in the gentleman caller and the artist-priest respectively. The archetype for them both is the savior. The gentleman caller's function is less social than medicinal. He is a healer, and his method is to apply to the patient a benevolent rationality consonant with the assumptions of his society. He is paternal though young, kind, personally establishmentarian. He—or the expectations which inevitably gather about him—promises redemption. Tom describes the gentleman caller in openly messianic terms: "he is the long-delayed but always expected something that we live for" (I, 145). The corresponding character in *Streetcar* is Mitch. Although crudely fumbling with words and emotions, he is witheringly sincere. To a lesser extent, the pattern of *Streetcar* approximates the major theme of *Menagerie*. The seemingly plausible redemption of the frail woman by means of an eligible gentleman caller fails. Blanche's curtain line following Mitch's proposal of marriage ("Sometimes—there's God—so quickly!") confirms that she fully expects him to bear the burdens of her soul. Even after Blanche has become psychotic, the gentleman caller appears again in the form of a physician, whose firm kindness subdues her hysteria and supports the play's concluding and dignified stasis. Instead of using threats (trimming fingernails is the matron's idea of de-sexing Blanche as well as disarming her), he instructs the matron to release Blanche, whom he then leads out calmly, arm in arm—the basic gesture of all gentleman callers.

Neither cynical nor sentimental (though Tom Wingfield says otherwise), *Menagerie* and *Streetcar* are toughminded works. Each action recognizes that romantic manna may not reliably be expected to fall to earth, no matter how desperately it may be needed. The emotion aroused by these plays stems in part from Williams' technical mastery of theater, but in much larger measure from the inner structure of their action. *The Glass Menagerie* is not simply a "mood play," as it has been so often called (the term itself is unsatisfactory and vague), gingerly though brilliantly wrought upon anemic substance. Its action is a parody of one of the oldest secular fables of redemption, the sleeping beauty. The princess sleeps because her virtues are shrouded by a "sickness," but she will some day be awakened by the kiss of a prince—the gentleman caller—who correctly perceives those virtues. Jim O'Connor crudely, and not altogether inaccurately, diagnoses Laura's sickness as an inferiority complex; he is intelligent enough to respond to certain of her virtues, which he praises sincerely. He even bestows the magical kiss, which for a moment makes the dream incarnate, even though his stumbling has been revealed long before his engagement to be married is disclosed. O'Connor's fascination with money, marketable knowledge, and administrative power are far removed from mending Laura's compulsive retreat into silent glass. Correspondingly, one hardly surmises in retrospect that Mitch, whose idea of social small talk is to discuss his perspiration problems, will be a suitable man for Blanche, but her loneliness and her accurate understanding that Mitch is neither rapacious like Stanley nor callous like the poker group make the courtship with him at least credible. Blanche's repeated and desperate invocations of Shep Huntleigh, a patently impossible gentleman caller, augment the audience's belief in her romance with Mitch, whose desire and even need for her has been firmly established in scenes three and six. Huntleigh is a fantasy: Mitch is not. The pattern of the chief action in *The Glass Menagerie* is repeated with variations in *Streetcar*'s subplot; for Blanche's failure to retain Mitch's respect is the prelude to her complete disintegration.

Other gentlemen callers are, however, successful. In the second act of *The Rose Tattoo*, Serafina Delle Rose is as desperate as Blanche. She has retreated into a darkened and locked house, and she is under attack by her neighbors, her priest, and (she imagines) her daughter. Her fanatical worship of her dead husband, whom she literally enshrines, has been shattered by the strong suspicion that he had been unfaithful. Furthermore, Williams has drawn Serafina's character with a tragic tension. She has denied temporal bonds altogether, having sought in sexual passion with her husband the condition of the angels: "Each time is the first time with him. Time doesn't pass . . ." (II, 280). Her incanted strident wish—"Lady give me a sign"—conveys an urgency in her struggle whose dignity arises partly from the "Lady's" protracted silence. And indeed, her gentleman caller Alvaro appears unexpectedly; a comic gratuitousness characterizes her rescue. No questing designs were laid to make him appear. He is the dramatic cousin of Jim O'Connor and Mitch because he is "normal" and seeks his due in the world; but he differs from them in having no delusions about either Serafina herself or his own desires. So his return to her house in the final act absorbs all the tragic tension generated at the beginning. The resolution of this play dramatizes a fundamental assumption of Williams: nothing kills passion more certainly than insincerity. Serafina's and Alvaro's actions toward each other are consonant with their intentions, even when each is embarrassed to declare them, and so their relationship thrives. Jim O'Connor's kiss ironically validates the sincerity of his praise of Laura while it misrepresents his intentions toward her, and Mitch is humiliated by having believed Blanche's protestations about the reserve of a lady. He then seeks not love, only sexual revenge.

Although both Doctor Cukrowicz and John Buchanan are gentlemen callers, their functions differ considerably. Cukrowicz is an outsider whose benevolent nature is revealed when he subordinates professional fund raising to a discovery of the truth. He is an intelligent but incompletely informed eiron who milks the truth from recalcitrant, self-interested people (Catharine excepted). The structure of *Suddenly Last Summer* was drawn from Cukrowicz's perspective, for his discovery of the causes of *Catharine's* trauma is the audience's as well. His evident lack of sexual involvement with Catharine is required to make him an outsider. Quite the opposite is the relationship between Alma and John Buchanan, for both *Summer and Smoke* and *Eccentricities* (the revision) turn upon the futility of a continuing sexual relationship between them. The nature of John's involvement with Alma was a difficult matter for Williams, as a comparison of the two plays reveals. *Eccentricities* omits the subplot of Rosa Gonzales and her father, thus diminishing Buchanan's role. For in the latter play, he is no longer a hell-raising rake; and though he is restless, it is a very establishmentarian species of unrest. *Eccentricities* is more centrally organized about Alma, whereas *Summer and Smoke* is evenly divided between representing her angst and John's sexual and alcoholic excesses. Why did Williams so drastically recast Buchanan's characterization?

One response is implicit in the analysis above: the change focuses the play upon one character. The dramatist became more concerned with the destruction of Alma than with the redemption of John Buchanan. The sea-change of John Buchanan between *Summer and*

Smoke and *Eccentricities* illustrates the second kind of character mentioned above, for in the former play he is an artist-priest, in the latter a gentleman caller. Their instincts are categorically alien from each other. The artist-priest is Williams' favorite protagonist: confused, tempestuous, impatient, keenly subjective, troubled about deep and deeply felt injustices, fiercely and proudly an exile from society, his commitment is to life conducted exclusively on his own terms ("Shannon obeys only Shannon"). Val Xavier and Cassandra Whiteside are two of the earliest exemplars of this character type. They are artists in the Blakean sense of possessing an abundance of primal energy and imagination. Vee Talbot's characterization is obviously based upon that of D. H. Lawrence in the early play, *I Rise in Flame, Cried the Phoenix*. She is laughed at, considered "peculiar" (the word is used so consistently throughout the canon that it is a standard marker for Williams' outsiders), her painting is technically crude, but she *sees*. And they are priests by virtue of making their catalytic energy available to others in a quasieucharistic manner. They have passion; they know and obey its imperatives, whether mental or physical; they live without surcease in an electrified consciousness; they are intolerant of social and personal entropy; and those who do not kill themselves appear to regain their identities by means of the same supercharged volition which threatened to destroy them. A controlling dynamic characteristic of Williams' dramaturgy, then, is the polarizing energy of the Orc figure: the society which reluctantly feeds from him (or her) and envies him may reject him violently as a wanton Christ. Cassandra Whiteside, for example, proclaims, "Whoever has too much passion, we're going to be burned like witches because we know too much." When Myra asks what she is talking about, Cassandra replies: "Damnation! You see my lips have been touched by prophetic fire" (*Battle*, I, 99). Myra's deflationary retort about Cassandra's drunkenness does little to invalidate the sentiment of her words, which in fact comment upon Myra's own situation. Myra clearly expects her union with Val to save her from the barren bondage to Jabe: "I guess my heart knew that somebody must be coming to take me out of this hell! You did," she exclaims to Val in *Orpheus* (III, 333). The same desire to be saved by his passion runs throughout the last act of the earlier *Battle*; her redemption is imaged in the fig tree, which also presages the futility of her hope. Although Williams supplies a heavy handed symbolic macrocosm to both *Battle* and *Orpheus,* and to Val Xavier, the matter of "crucifixion" has little to do with Christian ideology. It has everything to do with Blake's fallen world of the devourers and the devoured, and his belief that "energy is eternal delight." Chance Wayne universalizes the Blakean division on the basis of pleasure. Those who have found pleasure in love have a sustaining meaning in their lives; those who have found no such pleasure can merely envy and look on (*Sweet Bird,* IV, 50). As Jabe Torrance's actions indicate, their envious voyeurism can have violent consequences. It provides the impetus for most of Williams' "crucifixions."

The latent cannibalism of the Eucharist, and the artist-priest who becomes an unwilling Host, are both treated dyslogistically in *Suddenly Last Summer.* When Violet Venable introduces Doctor Cukrowicz to her son's past, she holds up his book—as if to validate his function as a poet. The stage instructions indicate that she reveres it as if it were the "Host before the altar," and her gesture is punctuated with the clear note of a bird (III, 353). Similarly, as John Buchanan appears before Alma's intellectual circle, its members stare at him "with a curious sort of greediness" (*Summer and Smoke,* II, 172). When Williams revised the play, he reiterated the manner in which Buchanan arouses their envy: "How we all devoured you with our eyes," Alma tells him later, "you were like holy bread being broken among us" (*Eccentricities,* II, 79). Sexuality, which Williams regards as another secular medium for the Eucharist, is represented by an altar-bed in *Sweet Bird of Youth* and *Cat on a Hot Tin Roof.* Maggie is one of Williams' primal women who, like Serafina, want to produce "the glory." "To me," Serafina avers, "the big bed was beautiful like a religion" (II, 342). Violet's connection with "religion" is even more overt in *Small Craft Warnings.* Their drive is ruthless. Maggie decides to lock up Brick's liquor until he satisfies her sexually. Her curtain speech in the Broadway script, though softer than in the original script, does not diminish her role as initiator. Brick needs someone who can "take hold of you—gently, with love, and hand your life back to you" (III, 215). As the curtain closes, the audience can only assume that Maggie's passion establishes at last her position in the family from which she has been an exile and Brick a vegetable.

Williams identifies precisely the danger of narcosis inherent in the release of sexual passion. His characters frequently abuse sex to extinguish momentarily the demands of ego, self-consciousness, even awareness of the past. Knowing too well the terrain of "Dragon Country" and its inhospitable pain, Princess Kosmonopolis frantically seeks a narcotic oblivion. Vodka and hashish are insufficient: "I have only one way to forget these things I don't want to remember and that's through the act of love-making" (IV, 44). A shame similar to Camille's in *Camino Real*—to be an aging voluptuary who must pay rather than receive payment—is ironically one of the things the Princess wishes to forget. Various metaphors of narcosis define the self-destructive edge on which such protagonists live: the "click" which Brick Pollitt constantly drinks toward, the gambling and drinking of John Buchanan, Shannon's weakness for young girls, Chance Wayne's pills, Alma Winemiller's tranquilizer prescription, whose number she described as "the telephone number to God," the brutality of homosexuals whose act of love Quentin compares to the "jabbing of a hypodermic needle to which they're addicted but which is more and more empty of real interest and surprise" (V, 260). All paralytically stalk in vicious circles and yearn not merely for escape. They seek a prelapsarian innocence: "Now get a little sweet music on the radio," the Princess instructs Chance, "and come here to me and make me almost believe that we're a pair of young lovers without any shame" (IV, 44). An impassioned memory of the past can function narcotically, for when evoked it displaces awareness of hostile present circumstances. Retreat from consciousness varies from an undrugged abuse, such as Laura's records and glass collection (the only unthreatening repository of her girlhood), to the extreme of lobotomy which Violet Venable seeks to inflict upon Catharine. Even the mild stroke Violet has had could be considered as a quasilobotomy she has suffered to forget that her advancing age had disqualified her to be Sebastian's companion. What she has suffered, Catharine must suffer in magnified degree. All are elements of the decline which obsesses Williams; they are damning. The abdication of consciousness acquits the moral faculty from making any choice whatsoever. How can expulsion from Eden have consequential guilt if its inhabitants had no consenting part in their damnation? But when the murk of narcosis recedes, the protagonist's guilt—which was never expelled, only obscured—becomes even more insistently painful. Atonement is therefore pursued so feverishly that even when means are available they are unrecognized. Chance's urge to be punished renders him deaf to the Princess' emotionally honest offer of the only kind of relationship he can have. Tom Wingfield runs from city to city, bar to bar, in futile quest to blow out his sister's candles. Shannon, similarly wallowing in masochistic penance, perhaps hears Hannah's penetrating appraisal of his anxiety. Self-crucifixion, whether it is pursued with drugs, spooks, women, or alcohol, turns upon a self-indulgent and hence ineffective penance, which then generates fresh guilt and another round of self-abuse. Only an authentic relocation of emotion can interrupt the process. Such an action must be taken alone; but as *Night of the Iguana* implies, a basic reversal does not seem possible without the benevolent intervention of human contact.

The sadomasochistic circle of guilt and penance accounts for much of the conflict which the artist-priest experiences. The characteristic agon is defined by his search for a release from guilt by pursuing a relationship with two women, one of whom is saintly, the other whorish. But his vacillation between these two is itself a basis for sustained guilt. Thus John Buchanan moves between Alma and Rosa; Shannon between Hannah and Maxine; Chance between Heavenly and Princess; and Kilroy between Esmeralda and La Madrecita. The same dynamic is represented with homosexual overtones in *Cat*, for clearly Brick believes that his relationship with Skipper was somehow elevated above carnal desire (whether he is lying is here beside the point), whereas his connection to Maggie, or more precisely, to Maggie's flesh, disgusts him. Williams has perfectly cathected the dynamic in his characterization of Blanche, who in the course of the play appears as both saint and whore to Mitch. It is Stanley's resentment of her neurotically aggressive pretensions to a fleshless sexuality (a tenet from her cultural past's idealized concept of womanhood) that instigates his vengeful degradation of her.

The names of Williams' saintly women suggest their transcendental view of existence. The Hebrew root of "Hannah" is "grace";

"Blanche" and "La Madrecita" have obvious connotations. Alma seems proud that her name is the Spanish word for "soul." She has looked through telescopes but not microscopes; she has never been subject to youth, just as Hannah's physical appearance should seem independent of time. Heavenly needs no gloss, other than to recall that Chance, with Joycean unselfconsciousness, describes her as Venus on the half-shell. In each of these plays virtually no dramatic interplay occurs between the saintly women and their counterparts. Maxine can barely tolerate the sight of Hannah, and Blanche's mental stability is largely predicated upon repressing the Blanche known at Laurel's Flamingo Hotel. Body and psyche of the saintly women in these plays are thus schizophrenically conjoined, a discord uniquely suited to self-destruction. For obvious reasons, Williams' drama *must* keep the two types from early reconciliation, or the play risks collapse of the tension which animates their mutual exile in which the masculine protagonist stumbles to find breath. Except in *Camino Real*, Williams' dramatization of the saint-whore cathexis does not approach allegory. Yet so firmly divided are the two principles that one cannot entirely avoid the hypothesis that their characterizations are fragments of one idealized psyche. Hannah stands so utterly apart from the flesh, and Maxine is so utterly obtuse to spiritual reality, that they move like antagonistic though complementary hemispheres of one entity which may not exist except hypostatically in the artist's mind. That these personalities respond with reflexive mutual aversion holds, of course, the potential of tragedy. Williams presents their conflict as part of a triangular stalemate: Hannah understands Shannon's unfitting clerical buttons and his neck lacerations inflicted by his crucifix, but she will participate in no active part of his sexuality; Maxine, having no understanding of Shannon's spiritual torment, only a limited toleration, solicits Shannon's sexual compliance (if not obedience).

But as *Night of the Iguana* illustrates, damnation is not simply a question of excess sexuality or faulty apprehension of abstruse spirituality. Williams draws characters who mercilessly seek human contact by actions which alienate them from the people willing or able to give it. Chance spurns his Aunt Nonnie, who risks some peril to continue caring for him; Brick resists Maggie adamantly; Blanche seeks comfort and security from her sister whose husband she attacks; Violet, whom Leona befriended and nursed provisionally back into society, cannot keep her hands off Leona's man (*Small Craft*). Amanda, desperate for Tom's support, drives him further away. The family, an institution whose function is presumably to provide a mutual support system for its members, is nearly always represented in Williams' plays as a destructive trap. The enforced physical and emotional proximity within it magnifies the potential of disruption. The most anguished decision in *The Glass Menagerie*, for example, is not Jim O'Connor's—for he is ignorant of, indeed innocent of, Laura's deepest problems—but Tom's. His departure from home has generated a nearly intolerable and permanent guilt. But if he had remained, his talent and privacy would have been asphyxiated under Amanda's constant siege. Tom drunkenly discovers the emblem of his family life in the stage magician's show: how do you get out of a coffin without removing one nail? His monologues imply that he is a prodigal son who can never be reconciled with his family. Although he has bolted out of the coffin, he still feels its nails.

The prodigal may be apprehended in the roots of Brick Pollitt, John Buchanan, and Chance Wayne. By exploiting the expectation of an ultimate redemption associated with prodigals, Williams heightens the despair of these men when that possibility aborts or falls into a narcotic void. In each instance, they reject family bonds. Even in death the family offers little succor. The woman of *I Can't Imagine Tomorrow* illustrates her pain by recounting the story of an Eskimo woman who asked her family to put her on an ice floe so that she could drift away on the sea to die alone. While Big Daddy is dying, he is lied to by his family and schemed against by his elder son while his favored younger son gazes on, seemingly imperturbable in alcoholic indolence. Williams' original script of *Cat* reveals that his conception of Brick's situation did not allow for any reconciliation at all. In fact, he commented on the intractability of Brick's "moral paralysis," which Kazan wanted altered for the Broadway production: "to show a dramatic progression [in Brick's characterization] would obscure the meaning of that tragedy in him and . . . I don't believe that a conversation [Brick's with his father in act two],

however revelatory, ever effects so immediate a change in the heart
or even conduct of a person in Brick's state of spiritual disrepair"
(III, 168).

In the first scene of *Streetcar*, Blanche's account of the succession
of death in her family at Belle Reve establishes that her compulsion
to wash herself and her fear of emotional apathy are the residue of
a moribund family system which has depleted most of her resources.
Her speech about death in the last scene paradoxically links the
physical corruption resulting from eating an unwashed grape with
the timeless laving of the ocean into which she would be cast. Her
fantasy of personal salvation conferred by the mysterious astringency
of death derives great force from the intensity of image, the pathos
of her manner of departure from Stella's household, and finally
from the perspective in which she sees herself. It has not that fullness
of tragic dimension because her self-evaluation is evidently made in
madness. Self-transcendence is possible when the personality can
stand apart from itself at a little distance and perceive itself whole
and in relation to the past. It is a perspective from which the protagonist surveys his life as a completed action; hence it is necessarily
dramatic. Aristotelian recognition or disclosure brutally enforces
upon the tragic protagonist this special and terrible objectivity: "I
pray you, in your letters,/When you shall these unlucky deeds relate,/Speak of me as I am; nothing extenuate,/Nor set down aught
in malice." Blanche's images of the unwashed grape, the physician's
silver watch, and her burial in a white sack at sea sum up the forces
against which she has waged a losing battle: physical corruption in
a world headed toward death and in which she has found no effective
solace. From her speech emerges the same kind of self-evaluation
which Othello above confesses, but unlike his it comes from a psy-
chotically detached mind. Othello acknowledges full responsibility
for his actions. Lear, for example, bursts into madness rather than
make a similar acknowledgment, but Shakespeare brings Lear to
the same pass, as the aged king confesses to his daughter a true account. Blanche's fantasy does give an imaginatively true account of
her destruction, but she remains—*must* remain—unaware of it. That
Streetcar does not equal the achievement of *Lear* is hardly a deprecatory judgment. No finer picture of a lost soul appears in Williams'

canon. One must go to O'Neill's study of Mary Tyrone in *Long Day's Journey into Night* to find an equivalent in American drama.

II

He who waits to be righteous before he
enters into the Saviour's kingdom, the Divine Body, will never enter there.

Blake (*Jerusalem*, Plate 3)

In a world from which God the Creator has apparently absconded ("His oblivious majesty," as Shannon calls him), the only source of redemption lies within humanity itself. Williams' stage tableaux repeatedly suggest the pietà, for that representation, more than any other in Christian iconography, transfixes the human bond between Christ and his mother. His mutilated adult male body, father-forsaken, recumbent with death, concentrates a defeated suffering humanity into an image which powerfully animates Williams' imagination. Yet he dissociates the pietà theme from original sin. Hereditary evil springs only from the havoc caused within the soul by the uniquely human foreknowledge of physical corruption and death: "there is no way to beat the game of *being* against *nonbeing*" (II, 262). Nor is there aboriginal grace, no matter how constantly an institutionalized Christianity preaches to the contrary. No sign comes upon Serafina's impassioned supplications to the Lady, and the Blessed Mother gives Kilroy nothing but a silence. *Night of the Iguana* suggests nothing numenal to fill in the blank of Hannah's incomplete sentence. God is realized only in the actions of human beings who "play God" by responding mercifully to the suffering around them.

The plays in which Williams specifically addresses himself to redemption are, of course, comedies: *The Rose Tattoo, Camino Real, Period of Adjustment, Night of the Iguana, Kingdom of Earth,* and *Small Craft Warnings.* The tension of these plays inheres in the protagonist's reaching out for surcease from loneliness, not in the remedy itself. Two assumptions characteristic of Williams support the comic tone. As mentioned above, communication which nourishes the soul of another is sacramental. Like Portia's mercy, it is twice blessed. The redemptive quality of human communication is the basis of interaction between Hannah and Shannon, and between Ralph Bates and Isabel Haverstick in the first act of *Period of Adjustment*. And beauty itself, its creation and perception, nurtures the soul; for in the Shelleyan sense which Williams constantly ramifies, beauty is both the stimulus and the response of the religious instinct. Because the beautiful extenuates human communication, it carries the potential of redemption. It also carries liabilities. The dilemma which ensnares many of Williams' protagonists was densely formulated by Richard Rowan, the Jesuitically minded hero of Joyce's play *Exiles*: even if we are led to desire through the sense of beauty, can what we desire be called beautiful? Insofar as it generates life (Blanche says that the opposite of desire is death), Williams' characters answer Rowan's question affirmatively.

The redemptive theme in these comedies may be approached from Williams' concepts of the nature of theater, which in his view generates both beauty and intense communication. His early statement, "The History of a Play (With Parentheses)," appended to the first publication of *Battle of Angels* (*Pharos*, Spring 1945), is actually a spiritual-artistic apologia. Its tone of self-justification and wounded pride does not obscure the announcement of a dedication which, like most Romantic manifestos written since the early nineteenth century, equates artist and priest: theater offers a communion to redeem our society from its spiritual night. Before the opening of *Camino Real*, Williams wrote that his own creed as a playwright derived from Shaw's painter in *The Doctor's Dilemma*: "'I believe in Michelangelo, Velasquez and Rembrandt; in the might of design, the mystery of color, the redemption of all things by beauty everlasting and the message of art that has made these hands blessed. Amen'" (II, 423–24).

Those characters who create and respect beauty are invariably recommended to the audience's approval; conversely, the most sordid actions which Williams stages involve the willful destruction of beauty. Stanley desires to wound the best part of Blanche's soul— he rapes more than her body. Alma's response to the mystery and design of the gothic cathedral is not vague sentiment. The cathedral represents the consummation of unity and harmony which are absent from her own life. The perception of beauty is the most vital impulse of many of Williams' characters: one recalls Laura's glass and Amanda's desperate attempts to make her home attractive; Myra Torrance's thwarted desire to import her lost orchard into the confectionery, and the curtain embroidered with golden birds she places over Val's door; the small means Blanche uses to soften the environment of Stanley's apartment; the delight of Isabel and Dorothea over the negligee each wears to bed at the conclusion of *Adjustment*; Hannah's facility to put the revealing detail in a sketch, and her response to the eyes of those lying in the House of the Dying in Shanghai ("Nothing I've ever seen has seemed as beautiful to me," IV, 356); Leona's remorse over her dead brother, who was a violinist: "I'm proud that I've had something beautiful to remember as long as I live in my lifetime." Without at least one beautiful thing, she sobs, the heart inevitably corrupts: "it's all a death-time" (V, 247–8). Although Leona's aggressive remorse is a comic self-indulgence, her pain is real and her words sincere. Earning her living as a professional beautician, she is another of Williams' tempestuous artist-priests, for she has put Violet back on her feet and given her beauty treatments without charge.

Although *Camino Real* is Williams' least successful major play, it is also one of his most ambitious efforts. According to the "Foreword" published just before the Broadway premiere, the freedom of flight was the guiding principle of its composition and production stylization. *Camino Real* should present on stage "something wild and unrestricted that [runs] like water in the mountains, or clouds changing shape in a gale, or the continually dissolving and transforming images of a dream" (II, 420). Various methods were employed to stage this difficult vision. For example, a large painted silk phoenix was placed on the window behind the balcony of the Siete Mares Hotel: "this should be softly lighted now and then in the play, since resurrections are so much a part of its meaning" (p. 431). Other images of the bird are used to represent resurrection in this play. This is appropriate enough, for the bird is here, as elsewhere, Williams' dramatic vehicle for the soul: "All of us have a desperate bird in our hearts," Jacques tells Marguerite, "a memory of—some distant mother with—wings" (p. 525). When the autopsy is performed upon Kilroy, La Madrecita exhorts, "Rise, ghost! Go! Go bird!" (p. 580). But redemption is more poignantly dramatized in the struggle of Jacques and Marguerite, the romantic center of *Camino Real*. The jaundiced courtesan informs Jacques, "Caged birds accept each other but flight is what they long for" (p. 501). The Fugitivo, which promised escape by air, proved merely capricious, hence an illusory escape, unearned. Marguerite subsequently prepares to leave Jacques for the charms of a younger man with whom she hopes to forget that she missed the Fugitivo. Seeking the same futile oblivion desired by the Princess Kosmonopolis, she utterly rejects Jacques's belief in tenderness, thus providing the foundation for her return— and the play's comic movement. When the lovers clasp each other at the very end of the play, Quixote, repeating Jacques's metaphor for tenderness, declaims that the violets in the mountains have broken the rocks—even though such flowers have been fed with the droppings of carrion birds. The tone of this metaphor borrows from biblical paradox, such as Christ's assertion that faith like that of a mustard seed can move mountains. Throughout *Camino Real* the playwright's intent has been to demonstrate that the cycle of decline from wholeness and sanity to fragmented desire and barbarism can be symmetrically reversed: carrion deeds may smuggle a contraband of remorse into the human heart. The necessary pain of this reversal must be written onto the lovers' faces as the curtain closes. But the melodramatic reversal of Marguerite's emotions, whose unstaged causes must be inferred, and the platitudinous advice about self-pity which Quixote gives Kilroy are theatrically anemic compared to the ravages of the streetcleaners, omnipresent buzzards, the repeated humiliations suffered by all the principals, the indifference of time enforced by Gutman's enunciations, and the unrelenting claustrophobic atmosphere of the entire action. The pain of lost paradise, imaged in La Madrecita's adjuration to remember Kilroy in "his time of greatness, when he was not faded" (p. 578), is invested with incomparably greater dramatic energy than the renewal signaled by the violets rooting in the mountains.

In formulaic terms, the most successful of Williams' comedies are *The Rose Tattoo*, *Period of Adjustment*, and *Kingdom of Earth*, for in each of these the thwarted passion convincingly overturns the obstacles to find an appropriate locus. In *Tattoo*, for example, Williams found the image of a flying bird appropriate to portray the recovery of Serafina's passion locked in guilt and remorse. As Alvaro considers what would happen to her if the urn containing her husband's ashes should break, he imagines that he can see her heart released from a prison: then he "whistles like a bird and makes graceful winglike motions with his hands" (II, 372). This scene of their first encounter initiates the reversal of Serafina's steady decline since the beginning of the play. Williams even instructs Alvaro to make his exit by imitating with whistles a bird flying off; and so his gaiety adumbrates the fortunate direction of their relationship. *The Rose Tattoo* defines and resolves in comic terms the difficulties the protagonists have in releasing a mutually interdependent sexuality. *Kingdom of Earth* presents a similar struggle in its most doctrinaire form. Chicken, a hybrid of Stanley Kowalski and Val Xavier, lives by a stark philosophy based upon "personal satisfaction": "With human beings, the ones I known in my life, what counts most is personal satisfaction, and God knows you'll never get that by denying yourself what you want most in the world by straining and struggling for what they call salvation when it's something you're just not cut out for" (p. 105). Both the story (which opens with the same assertion slightly reworded) and the play endow the expletive "God knows" with a broad irony, for the tone of each makes it plain that Williams' God, like Blake's, *does* know that salvation and personal satisfaction are not antithetical but inseparable.

Williams constantly returns to the enduring paradox that his central characters are so often outsiders, yet they seek the warmth of the society which they scorn and become its reciprocal targets of scorn. The artist himself is the prototype for seeking such acceptance from strangers. The tone of Williams' *Pharos* essay on the opening of *Battle* strongly implies that the hostile Boston audience rejected the Eucharist. Commenting fifteen years later upon the relationship of biography and art, Williams defined lyricism as the "outcry of prisoner to prisoner from the cell in solitary where each is confined for the duration of his life" (III, 3). This metaphor recurs in Val's conversation with Myra in the second act of *Battle* and in its rewrite *Orpheus,* and also it appears in Shannon's ironic suggestion that Hannah communicate with him by wall-tapping "like convicts in separate cells" (IV, 366). Confinement within the solitary self allowed Williams, as he phrased it, to talk to the audience "as freely and intimately about what we live and die for as if I knew you better than anyone else whom you know" (III, 7). Hence the artist's self-revelatory compulsion, which Clurman has identified as the basis of Williams' Romanticism.

The "kindness of strangers," which is sought by so many of Williams' protagonists, stimulates a brief but vital osmosis among the "cells of solitary confinement." This emotional seepage, which Williams pointedly distinguishes from physical sex, reaffirms both self-hood and community; it makes possible the mutual tolerance which, in a sense, confirms the *right to live*. The cellular structures of Maxine's hotel, Alma's window which overlooks the intolerable propinquity of John Buchanan's adjacent house, the opposing hotels in *Camino Real*, the small space between the double bed and the couch in Maggie and Brick's bedroom—these mise en scènes illustrate both the need and the difficulties of vital communication among the frightened people whose living space they define. Redemption may be considered as the process of emotional osmosis enabling people to discover and accept the self and its environment. "Accept whatever situation you cannot improve" is the quintessence of Hannah's interaction with Shannon (IV, 363). Throughout *Night of the Iguana* she has constantly had to accept things entirely beyond her power to improve, yet she maintains her dignity. These words stand in direct opposition to Alma Winemiller's bitter dictum: "Ask for all, but be prepared to get nothing!" (II, 241). Alma's personal world, governed by an absolutism worthy of Antigone, must therefore fracture. Hannah's acceptance is an affirmation of life, a desire to survive intact; it is not merely a cynical submission to the world's depredations, as Shannon either mistakenly or willfully misinterprets. Her actions, her entire past, prevents her advice from being a reductive platitude.

Confession promotes Williams' societies because it speaks through cellular barriers, just as the confessional box in the Roman Church is constructed. *Small Craft Warnings*, whose original title was *Confessional*, depicts a group of outcasts who in their nexus of loneliness at Monk's bar provide a temporary home for one another. Williams does not sentimentalize this "family." Doc, Bill, Leona, and Violet treat one another roughly, and by the end of the play the fragile stability which they had been enjoying has all but completely disintegrated. Leona ejects Bill from her trailer and prepares to leave town, Bobby rejects the home Leona offers him, Quentin and Doc—both intensely self-destructive—seem likely to remain permanent outcasts. Their sorrows and despair are presented as forcefully as that which animates Williams' earlier characters, but they do not live by an all-or-nothing absolutism. They confess. Confession is, of course, the first action in the penitential sequence culminating in grace. In Williams' church, confession is the admission of human frailty which, being uttered, *claimed*, becomes a community strength: "the stories, the jokes, the confidences and confessions I've heard that night," Monk reminisces, "it makes me feel not alone" (V, 265–6). Commenting upon his receipt of a tiny legacy, the residue of remembrance from a customer absent for over five years, Monk says simply, "A thing like that is beautiful as music. These things, these people, take the place of a family in my life" (p. 265).

However briefly or inadequately, the other characters in Monk's bar have provided one another a family too. Their family is not so much a death-trap as the other families represented in Williams' canon, for escape is far simpler, but their unanchored fragile society supported by the kindness of strangers is portrayed with extraordinary sympathy. *Small Craft* closes upon an act of kindness. Monk gives Violet a temporary home which, as he realizes, is probably not so temporary. The two complementary metaphors in his curtain monologue, Violet's wornout slippers and the shower he urges her to take, respectively convey endurance in spite of human mortality, and the cleansing renewal of human contact: "I am not going up there till she's took a shower" (p. 286). Pondering his decision about Violet, he opens the doors to welcome the odor and sound of the fresh Pacific air, and then he hears the sound of her shower: "That ain't rain" (p. 287). This curtain line succinctly conveys a redemptive baptismal which is wholly integrated into the play's situational realism.

Hannah Jelkes, who is kind and equally dependent upon gratuitous kindness, defines home as "a thing that two people have between them in which each can . . . well, nest—rest—live in, emotionally speaking" (IV, 356–57). The emotional structure so built is not necessarily guided by concerns of permanence or mating, as her own history proves. And so she rejects the offer of a relationship with

Shannon, for she knows that there is no place in him in which she could rest. Yet she has benefitted from his kindness, which has been shown almost instinctively to her and Nonno, even in their first scene together. He coaxes Maxine to allow them to stay at the hotel, he prevents Nonno from falling, he brings them water to drink and urges Hannah to attend to a scratch she incurred while pushing Nonno up the hill. In the final scene he gives her his golden crucifix to pawn for travelling money. These actions form a network establishing the emotional center of the play. *Iguana* is Williams' most convincing dramatization of authentic redemption, for it is not simplistic in promoting a guiltless unselfconsciousness which characterizes the conclusion of *Kingdom of Earth*. Its resolution is neither farcical nor formulaic as those of *The Rose Tattoo* and *Period of Adjustment*. It states human separation with force and dignity and it refuses to opt for the easy solution which Shannon himself proposes. Like *Small Craft Warnings*, it celebrates the endurance, if not triumph, of lives facing rather large obstacles. For Shannon, Hannah, and Maxine will simply continue, just as Violet's slipper will still be used after the cardboard soles have been worn through, even after it is "past all repair." The rhetorical climax of Nonno's poem summons courage to live in this fallen world. The artist naturally yearns for the inviolability and timelessness of the sphere inhabited by "beings of a golden kind"—as Yeats yearned for Byzantium and Keats mused upon his unravished bride of quietness. But the imagination confers to nobody a sublunary immunity from physical corruption. Courage—which Williams characterizes as the force of spirit required to give life dignity in the onrush of time—supports man's redemptive hope, for it makes civilization possible. Otherwise, kindness, sacrifice, all artistic contemplation, would be brushed aside in a general attempt to outdistance the earth's "obscene corrupting love." That Williams assigns this poem to Nonno emphasizes the point about endurance. Redemption must occur in *this* world, not in the hypothetical next. Nonno is Williams' only character who earns the right to die; the others who die have death inflicted upon them. Considering the size of the self-destructive populace in the canon, it is remarkable that virtually none of them actively contemplates suicide. The dignity of endurance illuminates the characterizations not only of Nonno and Hannah but also of Brinda's mother in "Mama's Old Stucco House" and the generous and stoic grand-mother of "Grand."

Many lapses appear in Williams' portrayal of damnation and re-demption. Chance Wayne's frenzy and obtuse refusal to examine his motives deprive his curtain appeal of any real force. One does not think of him and his situation, "This is true"; instead, "How horrific is this spectacle!" Has not the structure of *Suddenly Last Summer* been similarly weakened by pouring Catharine's recollection neatly into the mold of a pièce bien faite? One wonders also how Shannon can be so thoroughly acquainted with sexual abuse yet repelled by Hannah's account of the underwear salesman's fetish. Is he in any better position to haul his life up the hill, even with Maxine's help, if he takes the petty revenge of urinating upon his antagonists' luggage? An indictment of unearned horror and the too facile line which sacrifice tone to an inferior end could be easily lengthened. But Williams' understanding of despair, his urgent belief in com-munity, and his celebration of endurance and human dignity are authentic. These values and the dramatic skill which inscribe them upon the stage confirm Williams' elevated position among dramatists of this century.

Prose and Poetry

John Ower finds *In the Winter of Cities,* Williams' first collection of poems, a unified volume by a versatile craftsman. The author moves immediately to an analysis of "Lady, Anemone" and shows the significance of both *erotic* and *mythology* in the essay's title. The essay reveals influences on Williams by Blake, the Romantics, and the Decadents and finds a remarkable interrelationship of themes in the volume. (A second volume of poetry is in preparation.) William Taylor briefly analyzes Williams' poetic technique.

As *Memoirs* indicates, New Orleans, where Williams owns property, seems attractive to the *man.* The question is of its attractiveness to the artist. Tom Richardson examines the realistic setting from which some of the early stories derive, some literally set in New Orleans, to get at the influence of the city on the artist. The concept of the two cities is enhanced by Williams' own use of images of light and dark and by his juxtaposition of characters from each "city."

Ren Draya finds the short stories generally well done and even suggests they are dramatically better than some of the expanded play versions. (Her comments on the variant Shannons are provocative.) She also finds a connection between the early stories and the much later *Moise and the World of Reason.* The essay also traces themes in Williams' work, especially loneliness and love.

The title of Victor Kramer's essay and the introductory paragraphs should be sufficient to lead the reader to study the following sympathetic yet objective account and analysis of *Memoirs.* This is one of several essays in this collection that deal with both the artist and the man.

607

Erotic Mythology in the Poetry
of Tennessee Williams

JOHN OWER

Tennessee Williams' collection of verse, *In the Winter of Cities*, is characterized most obviously by the "Romantic" qualities of imaginativeness, sensitivity, and passion. In more specifically historical terms, Williams is a visionary and mythmaker in the tradition of Blake and Shelley, and he also shows symptoms of the later nineteenth century "Decadence." However, the poet's Romanticism has been tempered by the opposing influence of Modernism, with its emphasis upon a discipline at once spiritual and formal. Many of his pieces display, along with the almost baroque efflorescence of his vision, the "Classical" virtues of astringency, wit, irony and a concern for the niceties of versecraft. The two poles of Williams' sensibility are manifested in his range and variety as a poet. He is equally adept with free verse in a long line and with a taut and relatively formal quatrain. He is capable of both "The Dangerous Painters," an effusion reminiscent of Allen Ginsberg's "Howl," and of such a tight "metaphysical" exercise in paradox and irony as "San Sebastiano de Sodoma." Whatever his artistic limitations, Williams is not a poet small enough to be tidily classified under a single heading.

Following in the Romantic visionary tradition, Williams uses myth and symbol, intuition and imagination, to chart the recesses of man's soul and of the universe. Like D. H. Lawrence, with whom

609

he so deeply sympathizes, Williams is aided in this venture by Freudian psychoanalysis. The influence of Freud is apparent particularly in the poet's sexual symbolism, which is fundamental to the "syntax" of repeated and modulated images that binds *In the Winter of Cities* into an artistic unity. A good example of the virtuosity with which Williams employs Freudian psychology is to be seen in "Lady, Anemone" (p. 100):

> Lady,
>> anemone,
>>> violet-soft and kissing,
>> tender scabbard with a fierce blade missing . . . .

In these lines, Williams manipulates yonic symbolism with a subtlety and wit that are worthy of Marvell. The central comparison of male and female organs to a sword and scabbard suggests that intercourse involves conflict between the sexes as much as it does their union and harmony. Thus, as an anemone *flower*, the vagina implies a feminine delicacy, innocence and tenderness, which are brutally exploited by the "fierce blade" of the phallus. On both physical and emotional levels, woman's experience of sex is equated metaphorically with a wound. However, alongside the poet's opposition of female sweetness and male barbarity, of a gentle self-surrender with savage egotism, is a symbolic reversal which indicates that the yielding vagina is a man trap in disguise. As a *sea anemone*, a woman's genital becomes a devouring stomach surrounded by grasping and paralyzing tentacles. Instead of one fierce blade, the sea anemone has a thousand deadly stings. A more powerful and ingenious variation upon the vagina dentata (devouring vagina) would be difficult to imagine.

A further dimension of complexity and force is added to Williams' conceit by the traditional associations of the anemone flower. Here the poet would, like Lawrence before him, be combining his Freudian ideas with material derived from *The Golden Bough*. In describing the festivals which accompanied the cult of Adonis, Frazer mentions the legendary associations of the anemone with the god's wounds: "Again, the scarlet anemone is said to have sprung from the blood of Adonis, or to have been stained by it; and as the anemone blooms in Syria about Easter, this may be thought to show that the festival of Adonis . . . was held in spring" (Part IV, I, 225–6). Two suggestions here are revelant to Williams' poem. The first is an ironic reversal of the idea that the "fierce blade" of male sexuality inflicts a wound upon the female. Rather, the vagina dentata threatens to fatally castrate the man. The second important hint in Frazer's discussion is conveyed by his mention of Easter, which links the death and resurrection of Adonis with that of Christ. In particular, the connection helps to explain the first line of "Lady, Anemone." "The body burned away the parting cloth" refers most obviously to the painful deflowering of a woman, but it applies equally well to the casting off of Christ's shroud at the Resurrection.

In contributing still other levels to Williams' complex treatment of the battle of the sexes, the traditional associations of the anemone help to illustrate his virtuosity as a symbolic mythmaker. At the same time, the connections of the flower with Christ and Adonis exemplify the poet's characteristic use of erotic symbolism. While Freudian psychology tends to be reductive, treating art, metaphysics and religion as veiled expressions of man's biological drives, Williams follows the opposite procedure by investing human sexuality with a broader philosophical and spiritual significance. Thus, the male figure in "Lady, Anemone" is linked not only to the divine in recalling Christ and Adonis but also to the elemental energies of nature through his associations with storm and sunrise. Similarly, the woman's sexual attraction is implicitly equated with the "tremendous impulse" of gravity. Taken together, the wider connotations of the erotic imagery of "Lady, Anemone" suggest a cosmic hierogamy of heaven and earth. This conjunction is an unstable union of opposites, in which spirit "falls" into matter, "dies" in dissipating its creative energy as "life-force," and is then "reborn" to return to its heavenly source. The final phase of the cycle is indicated by reference to Christ's Resurrection, and also by an allusion to his Ascension in the hyperbole of the departed lover having "lifted with a twist" which "put . . . [the lady] under him at least a mile!"

Although a minor piece, "Lady, Anemone" introduces many of the recurring ideas and images which, like threads in a tapestry, weave *In the Winter of Cities* into an imaginative unity. Conversely, the repetition and variation of motifs throughout Williams' collection evolves a context of meaning around each of his symbols and develops an intricate web of cross-connections among them. The unfolding of this larger matrix of significance corresponds to the "genetic" interplay of images within individual poems. In this regard, Williams "dissolves, diffuses, dissipates"[1] the normal waking consciousness, creating mythic and symbolic patterns organized according to the very different principles governing dreams and visionary states. Even when the poet makes concessions to descriptive, narrative or logical coherence, much of his meaning is carried by his syntax of images. Some of his pieces are, however, almost completely lacking in an intelligible surface, recalling the apparently free associative play in Rimbaud or in a Surrealist poet like Breton. Coherent sense cannot be made of such poems except through their patterns of symbolism. To perceive these configurations, the reader must relate images which are far removed from one another in his normal experience and which are at the same time often widely separated in the poems in which they occur.

The dominant myth which emerges from Williams' radical reordering of the empirical derives from the Neoplatonizing bent of English Romantic poetry.[2] A central issue in such thinking is the split discerned by A. O. Lovejoy between "this-worldly" and "otherworldly" tendencies in Platonist metaphysics (pp. 24–66). Corresponding to the former is the pervasive sense among the Romantics of the vital presence of spirit in material creation, an immanence which provides a basis for the deification of man, a cosmic optimism, and a symbolic sacramentalism. Such an outlook is, however, in tension with a vision of heaven and earth as conflicting and perhaps irreconcilable antinomies. From the latter point of view, immanence is a "fall," an imprisonment and corruption of the supernal essence by its opposite. Therefore man, who is compounded of flesh and a spark of divinity, is torn by a contradiction from which death is the only escape. This negative view of human existence is already implicit in Wordsworth's "Intimations" ode but, as poems like *Alastor* and *Manfred* indicate, it gains greatly in relative importance as Romanticism enters its "agony."[3] In the "Decadent" or "Aesthetic" movement, where the "agony" reaches its culmination, the tragic opposition of the physical and the spiritual is a counterpoint to the attempt to fuse the two in a symbolist art.[4] It is such late Romantic Platonism, with its rather extreme ramifications in idea and image, which underlies the symbolic mythologization of sexuality in Williams' poetry.

The crucifixion of man upon the antithesis of spirit and matter is treated in a self-consciously "decadent" fashion in "San Sebastiano de Sodoma" (p. 112). The saint's homosexual servitude, as his comparison to a desecrated chalice implies, is symbolic of the soul's defilement by a corporeal existence. In a sort of reverse transubstantiation, the divine essence is transformed by its incarnation into a "sweet, intemperate wine." The supernal becomes a Dionysian life-force, the blood which sustains the physical body and the seething emotion of sexual desire. In its fleshly existence the soul experiences the pleasures of generation, but these are accompanied by the "dolors of a concubine." Forced into a passive, feminine posture, the psyche must suffer ravishment by its opposite. In this regard, Sebastian's agony parallels the sparagmos (dismemberment) of Dionysus, which the Neoplatonic tradition interprets as an allegory of the dispersion of the spirit into the physical.[5] The saint's erotic passion is therefore also a "Passion" in the Christian sense of the term.

If the embodiment of the soul is a crucifixion, its return to heaven involves an equally painful martyrdom for the flesh. What gives "San Sebastiano de Sodoma" its characteristically "Decadent" twist is the poet's paralleling of the apparently antithetical torments of body and spirit by means of his Freudian and Catholic iconography. On a sexual level, the saint's corporeal agony is compared, through the phallic implications of the arrows which "pierced his throat and thigh," with the fellatio and sodomy by which his psyche was profaned. Similarly, Sebastian's repetition of Christ's Passion is a sign not only of the violence done to man's "divine" nature by its "incarnation," but also of the sacrifice of his "human" nature which is necessary for the spirit's "resurrection" and "ascension." Williams' superimposition of opposites creates an imaginative tension which conveys man's tragically anomalous metaphysical status. As a being who is simultaneously composed of two antithetical principles, he is caught on the horns of a cruel dilemma. Carnal pleasure is spiritual suffering, whereas the salvation of the soul involves painful physical mortification.

Although Williams makes powerful use of homosexuality in "San Sebastiano de Sodoma," he usually renders the soul's material bondage by the psychologically related image of the enveloping feminine. In "The Soft City," for instance, the mother's womb becomes a symbol of the fallen spirit's imprisonment. Through the two images of softness and melting, the poet uses the prenatal state to suggest that the incarnation of the psyche leads to a partial loss of form, which is of the very essence of its intellectual nature. Such dissolution is in turn related to the Platonic notion of the embodied soul's "amnesia"[6] by two symbolic associations. The first is Williams' connection of the uterus with the ancient conception of matter as a weaver of illusion. In spinning the "soft web" of the body around the divine essence, the mother binds it to a nature which enshrouds the "tall heaven" (p. 22) in a veil of mysteries.[7] A second and more subtle link between the concealment of the supernal from the spirit and its dissipation into material flux is Williams' implicit identification of woman as spinner with the spider. His grotesque image indicates that the womb is not a place of tender nurture, but rather a devouring stomach. Its warm amniotic fluid is really a digestive juice, and its softness therefore ironically suggests the false security of a fool's paradise.

The sinister nature of the prenatal Eden is also indicated by the way that God puts an immediate end to any discomfort by breathing "a word as soft as *morphine*," over "the panicky face upturned to entreat Him" (p. 22). Just as maternal care is a psychic cannibalism in disguise, so fatherly concern is a mask for a murderous tyranny. Here Williams' use of the narcotic drug, an obvious symbol of the embodied soul's amnesia,[8] suggests that he once again sees the parent as a demonic agent of the physical world. In this regard, the drug administered by the father is possibly connected to the parallel image of the dissolving amniotic fluid by an implicit allusion to the waters of Lethe. These are a traditional Platonic symbol of the opiate of matter which destroys the spirit's knowledge of its heavenly pre-existence.[9]

Thus, the connections of Williams' drug image link the physical and psychic compulsions of Freudian family life, whether emanating from the mother or the father, with the soul's corporeal bondage. In "The Soft City" the parental powers conspire to keep the child in a passive condition of melting "tenderness." From a Platonic viewpoint, the apparent innocence of this "tentative . . . feeling" (p.

21) is an ignorance which at once falls short of the psyche's heavenly vision and is blind to the horrors of material existence. In this regard, Williams presumably follows Blake in seeing the pain of mortal experience, starting with the birth trauma, as a blessing in disguise. Suffering shocks the spirit out of its complacency about the physical world into "Mental Fight."[10] This is in turn the beginning of the process of "recollection," by which the psyche recaptures its celestial beatitude. To sedate away "the wakeful anguish of the soul" (Keats, "Ode on Melancholy") is therefore a false mercy. As Yeats puts the matter in "Among School Children," the spirit that "Honey of generation has betrayed" must either "sleep, [or] shriek, [and] struggle to escape/As recollection or the drug decide."

The philosophical significance which is possessed by the maternal womb in "The Soft City" is connected in "Everyman" with adult sexuality. This poem turns upon a wittily grotesque travesty of the Incarnation, in which Everyman descends upon his wife in the form of a bird, creeps into her womb, and finally escapes by cleaving her in two. In ironic contrast to the lissome Mary of conventional Catholic iconography, Everyman's wife is "indolent and huge." Her bulk and inertia, along with the splitting of her body "like a stone" (p. 57), suggests Williams' characteristic equation of the feminine with dead matter. On the other hand, the name of her husband, when taken together with his bird form, implies the identification of the masculine with divine spirit. Thus, as in "Lady, Anemone," the sexual relationship metaphorically describes the soul's descent into the physical, and its subsequent escape.

In "Everyman," this Platonic cycle is linked not only to intercourse but also to gestation. As Williams emphasizes by having Everyman creep into his wife's body, the penis and the embryo enter the womb simultaneously in the generative act. After its climax, the phallus is reduced to the same state of helpless softness in the enveloping uterus as the foetus which it has implanted. However, just as the child finally fights free at birth, so the penis eventually regains its "savage" hardness. The common spiritual significance which is shared in "Everyman" by the two parallel cycles of sex and gestation is indicated by their connection with Christ's Incarnation, death and Resurrection. Thus, the "linen clothes" of Everyman's wife suggest the body that Jesus assumed through Mary, a mortal "husk" which is in turn equivalent to the winding sheet He cast aside when He arose from the dead. A second allusion to the Resurrection is implied by the way Everyman splits his wife's body "like a stone." In terms of Williams' superimposition of Catholic and Freudian symbolism, the rolling away of the rock from the mouth of Christ's tomb is equivalent to the opening of the womb at birth and to the rending phallic potency of the male. All three are symbolic of the spirit's assertion of its integrity in its escape from matter.

If the mother's physical and psychological domination of her child is a symbol of the soul's entrapment and amnesia, then a son's maturing to break away from maternal influence suggests the process of redemption through a spiritual awakening. Williams plays an autobiographical variation upon both of these themes in "Recuerdo," a piece whose title implies "recollection" in the Platonic as well as the ordinary sense of the term. In Part I of the poem, the female image of spiritual and psychosexual imprisonment is the poet's grandmother. Her symbolic function is clearly indicated by the fact that she was "accustomed to draw white curtains" (p. 78) around the little boy. The association of the grandmother with the demonic fabric, once again suggesting the soul's fleshly bondage, is reinforced by a nightmare episode in which the old lady's arthritic fingers cannot untwist the hairpin that fastens a cage of swallows. This pathetic and grotesque manifestation of physical senility works together with the image of the caged birds to convey most powerfully the death in life of the spirit's corporeal imprisonment. The same idea is also indicated by the grandmother's removal of "Spring's first almost bloodless violets" (p. 78) from her washing machine. As a symbol of Attis (Frazer, p. 267), the violets link the rebirth of nature in spring, and the renewal of phallic potency after orgasm, with the psyche's resurrection from the tomb of matter. In contrast, the old woman's isolation from the seasons in a cocoon of southern gentility, and her sexual smothering of her grandson, further identify her with the prison of the physical.

The spiritual rebellion against this entrapment which leads the little boy to place violets in his grandmother's washing machine becomes focused at puberty upon his emerging sexuality. The first and largely unsuccessful stirrings of Williams' erotic revolt are suggested by the ambiguous image of the "young witches," "indistinct beings anonymous of gender" (p. 79) which populate the poet's erotic dreams. On one level, these would seem to be Yeatsian images of the spirit world seen from an earthly perspective.[11] To the intellect still conditioned by the flesh, the supernal will appear mysterious and not a little sinister. However, the vampirelike action of the "witches" in fastening upon the poet's groin, and "drawing/the jelly out of his bones" (p. 79), implies that they have a further and purely negative significance. On a psychosexual level, just as the violet symbolizes the castration of Attis as well as his resurrection, so the "witches" in part indicate the damage done to the young Williams by his upbringing: fixation on his grandmother leads to an equation of orgasm with death and to bisexual inclinations.[12] Spiritually, this twofold ambivalence suggests that the eros of the half-awakened spirit, dazedly groping after the heavenly, can be misdirected to the physical. As the cold, corpselike quality of the boy's first ejaculations implies, matter as maya has deceived his aspirations with its alluring unrealities. The wet-dream thus becomes a symbol of the enticement of the psyche back into the waters of generation.

The notion that the celestial is fearful to the embodied intellect, already intimated by the "witches" of the first section of "Recuerdo," is basic to Parts II and III of the poem. In Part II, the theme is conveyed by the image of the violent electrical storm, which is a symbol of masculine sexual potency, and of its origin in a supernal energy. This terrible power is manifested when the poet's black nurse, who perhaps suggests the "earth-mother," is worsted by the wind in a futile "tussle" with the grandmother's awnings. A still more obvious avatar of the divinity in terms of a triumphant manhood is the telephone pole, "slippery, blanched" (p. 79), which is driven through the old lady's roof by a "Mississippi tornado" (p. 79). Williams' association of his two magnified phallic symbols with terror and destruction partly indicates that outright rebellion is necessary to free the adolescent from female dominance. However, the poet is also implying that, from the point of view of mind immersed in matter, the power of heaven which is potentially its own is not a little frightening. The awakening soul, as yet unaware of its true nature, "projects" its own innate force as the "terrible beauty" (Yeats, "Easter 1916") of a mysterious transcendence. In its confusion, it quite naturally sees its own apotheosis as a catastrophe or death.

The idea that from an earthly perspective the maturing of the soul is fearful, and its final escape a tragedy, is treated with a mixture of irony and pathos in Part III of "Recuerdo." Here, in the figure of the poet's sister, his female symbolism is reversed to suggest the Uranian Venus, the celestial beauty and truth which stimulates recollection.[13] Like Poe's Ligeia, the sister functions as an epipsyche and guide, who leads the way from material imprisonment. Thus, as a child, she is much quicker than her brother at music and mathematics, the two earthly arts which for the Platonist most perfectly reflect the heavenly harmony. With equal precocity, the girl at fifteen "plunged headlong/into . . . Love" (p. 80), running away from home and lapsing into what mundane intellects see as an "early madness" (p. 80). Williams, however, realizes that her sexual rebellion and seeming insanity were in fact divine eros and therefore signs of the ascent of her awakened spirit. The poet renders this idea with an ironic poignancy through the image of the girl's heart as a paper lantern, which is consumed in a flash by the blazing up of her soul. The complex emotional tonality of Williams' conceit suggests his ambivalent attitude towards his sister's apotheosis. More earthbound than she, his view of her apparent tragedy in part resembles that of her elders. However, as his concluding line implies, he also recognizes that the girl has been a spiritual beacon to him.

The ambiguities of the human condition which are manifested in the process of growing up are still more prominent in Williams' poems about adult sexuality. These treat passion as an ambivalent phenomenon and view the subject from several contrasting perspectives. "Across the Space" and "Her Head on the Pillow" develop the paradox that erotic love involves both the soul's aspirations and fleshly concupiscence. The former piece is based upon the idea of a physical separation between the poet and his beloved which allows a spiritual communion with each other and with a supernal reality. However, such an experience is out of keeping with man's corporeal, time-bound nature and is therefore bound to be transient. The Dionysian "riot" (p. 109) of carnal passion draws Williams to a consummation which, as a betrayal of a higher union, he compares implicitly with both the denial of Christ by Peter and His betrayal by Judas. In "Her Head on the Pillow," the same conflict between the inclinations of body and spirit is conveyed by the dichotomy, so characteristic of the Decadents, between the two contrasting images of woman as "virgin" and "harlot." Because "The heart is drawn to a thing so light/and the hand to a thing so warm . . ." the poet can simultaneously treat his beloved as an object of religious devotion, and yet take her body "by storm." The tragic antinomy in Williams' desire is rendered once more by his Christian imagery. Thus, his lady's head upon the pillow is as "bright,/as Mary's golden crown" (p. 107), while in desecrating this purity, the poet presses a "stone" to his heart. The "stone" is of course Williams' recurring image of the rock at the mouth of Christ's tomb, which is used here to emphasize that sexual love is a crucifixion upon the opposites of spirit and matter. (The myth of Sisyphus is also suggested.)

In "Death is High," consummation and not abstinence becomes the means of achieving the soul's aspirations for the heavenly. Williams sees the "breathlessness" of orgasm as a "Death" to earthly existence which exalts the mind to the supernal. This ascent is rendered in terms of a static, empty space, a pure "being" which is implicitly contrasted with the material world as a process of becoming. Once again, Williams experiences sexual love as encompassing both of these antithetical realms. His intellect, still tied to his body, is "not at ease" in the "breathless starlit air" (Yeats, "A Dialogue of Self and Soul"). The earthward inclination which the poet feels is probably meant to be opposed to the mystical desire of Dante in the "Paradiso." Inspired by his spiritual union with Beatrice, Dante soars upward against the force of gravity to the heights of Heaven. Williams on the other hand is drawn back to earth by his beloved, and crawls "against the ascending fall" of "unending torrents of light" (p. 121) in order to reach her. The poet explains his descent by his fleshly need for warmth and comfort which, through post-coital relaxation, he equates with the psychosexual desire to return to the mother's womb. Thus, the death of the body involved in the transcendence of orgasm is contrasted with the death of the spirit implicit in the sleepy torpor after intercourse. However, despite his awareness of the inevitable tension between the two sides of man's nature, Williams does not end "Death is High" upon a pessimistic note. Rather, he tenderly affirms his mundane love as a "humble star" which may to some degree reflect its counterparts in celestial space.[14]

In "The Siege" (p. 20), the relationship of flesh and spirit in sexuality is connected with the problem of the integrity of the self. The poet sees the "I" as imperiled equally by dissolution into physical flux and by the annihilation of nirvana. This dual threat can nevertheless be avoided by the fusion of body and soul in sexual passion. Against the danger of absorption into becoming, the poet builds a "tottering pillar of . . . his blood." Here the erect penis, which combines fluidity and form, represents the heavenly inclination of the poet's incarnate soul. His aspiration sets bounds to the material chaos within and around him, but it does so through a corporeal medium which protects the personality from a mystical obliteration. The same idea is conveyed by the conceit of the ejaculation as a fountain. Once more the images of liquidity and shape, of ascent and gravity, indicate by their union and tension the synthesis which protects the self against the opposing threats of spirit and matter. The successful reconciliation of contraries in erotic passion is, however, extremely fragile. Thus, the order imposed by the poet's psyche upon material flux is a mere "froth" upon its "crimson stream." Similarly, the delicate crystal "globe" of a created mundane harmony is in danger of shattering, leaving only the "timeless quality" of a pure abstract space. The love which the poet must periodically seek to secure himself against "the siege of all that is not I" (p. 20) is therefore represented as a sort of "Titanic," menaced on all sides by metaphysical icebergs.

Just as Williams attaches a complex spiritual significance to the sexual life of infancy, adolescence and maturity, so he makes powerful symbolic use of senility. In "Shadow Boxes," as in "Recuerdo," the old woman suggests the imprisonment and degradation of the soul by corporeal existence. Her spirit is so materialized by long association with the flesh that its true nature is reversed. What was once a power of vision and love is now a "shadow box," a psychic analogue of Plato's cave teeming with the spectres of selfishness and guilt. In Freudian terms, the devouring side of feminine libido becomes horrifically apparent in its decay. Williams once again conveys the hag facet of woman through the conceit of the womb as a devouring stomach. A further dimension of irony and horror is added to this metaphor by the poet's comparison of the old ladies' memories of long lost friends to "dead flies dissolving in water" (p. 61). Implicit here is an identification of the uterus with the insect-eating pitcher plant. This "metaphysical shudder" possibly renders the Platonic notion that by entering the waters of physical generation, the soul is absorbed into a "vegetated" condition.

In contrast to the images of dissolution with which Williams connects aged women, masculine senility is rendered in "Old Men with Sticks" (p. 26) by a frozen or petrified hardness. Thus, the penises of the old men are ironically transformed into "sticks clumping the iron earth of winter." Similarly, their testicles become "pearls without luster," "dim but enduring stones of hatred" which are "trafficked amongst them by stealth" (p. 26). These symbols of the inversion of libido into thanatos are reinforced by the three images of metal, winter cold, and of a frozen, empty space. Taken together, they indicate that the old men have the same significance as Blake's Urizen, the demonic sky god and winter king who represents material imprisonment masking as divine transcendence.[15] The ice, rock and iron chains which Blake associates with Urizen, like the almost identical symbolism employed by Williams, suggests the dead inertia which underlies the chaotic flux of the physical. This lifelessness is contrasted in "Old Men . . ." with images of organic vitality, and especially with the passion of youth. Williams is presumably employing the sexual here, as in "Recuerdo," to suggest the soul's awakening through a heavenly eros. However, in juxtaposing generation with degeneration, the poet may also be ironically commenting on the fate of any earthbound desire.

Thus, by employing the "four ages of man" as a symbolic framework, Williams develops into a comprehensive vision of human existence his Platonic conception of its paradoxical and fundamentally tragic nature. His complex and ingenious use of Platonic ideas and images in his verse places him in an English poetic tradition which began during the Renaissance and has persisted with great vigour into the modern period. As critics like G. M. Harper, Kathleen Raine and F. A. C. Wilson have demonstrated, Platonism exerted a very considerable influence upon English Romantic and postRomantic poetry, a situation understandable in view of the need of the artist to frame imaginative systems in the absence of a generally accepted world-picture. In particular, Platonism permeates the work of those two great mythbuilders Blake and Yeats, writers with whom Williams' own poetry suggests a sympathetic and remarkably intelligent familiarity. However, perhaps more important than any specific literary borrowing is what J. A. Notopoulos would term Williams' "natural Platonism."[16] This is a basic stance towards existence rooted in the very fibre of the personality. It conditions the mind's response to any particular influence and exists prior to any artistic or philosophical expression. Also to be taken into account in assessing Williams' debt to the past are his own considerable creative powers. These enable him to use his personal experiences poetically, to express himself in striking and subtle images of his own invention, and to frame a coherent and distinctive system of symbols as a "correlative" for his beliefs. *In the Winter of Cities* indeed furthers a great tradition, but in a manner unique to the poet's own background and sensibility.

Notes to John Ower, "Erotic Mythology in the
Poetry of Tennessee Williams"

1. Coleridge, *Biographia Literaria*, chapter 13.
2. For some useful studies in this area, which discuss many of the ideas and images mentioned in this essay, see George Mills Harper, *The Neoplatonism of William Blake* (Chapel Hill: University of North Carolina Press, 1961); Kathleen Raine, *Blake and Tradition*, 2 vols. (London: Routledge, 1969) and F. A. C. Wilson, *W. B. Yeats and Tradition* (New York: Macmillan, 1958). For the work of Thomas Taylor, a central influence in Romantic Platonism, see Kathleen Raine and George Mills Harper, eds., *Thomas Taylor the Platonist* (Princeton: Princeton University Press, 1969).
3. For a discussion of a similar vision in Keats, see Earl Wasserman, *The Finer Tone* (Baltimore: Johns Hopkins University Press, 1953).
4. See Frank Kermode, *The Romantic Image* (London: Routledge, 1957).
5. See Raine and Harper, pp. 408–9; Raine, I, 304–5; and Wilson, pp. 60–1.
6. See Raine and Harper, pp. 310–11, 382.
7. For a similar Platonic use of the image of woman as weaver, see Raine and Harper, p. 305.
8. This image is used in the same way by Yeats in l. 36 of "Among School Children."
9. Raine and Harper, pp. 310–11, 381–2; and Harper, pp. 254–5.
10. Blake, *Milton*, Plate I.
11. See Wilson, pp. 185–9.
12. Because homosexuality grows for Williams from fixation with the mother, I am assuming here that it possesses for him the same spiritual significance as the feminine.

13. For an analogous use of this image by a Romantic Platonist, see Carlos Baker, *Shelley's Major Poetry* (New York: Russell and Russell, 1961), pp. 241–2.

14. Here, Williams' imagery of "little room, warm love, humble star" recalls the Nativity, perhaps suggesting a positive value in Incarnation and the fleshly.

15. For an account of Blake's Urizen, see Northrop Frye, *Fearful Symmetry* (Princeton: Princeton University Press, 1969), pp. 34, 209–10.

16. See J. A. Notopoulos, *The Platonism of Shelley* (Durham, N. C.: Duke University Press, 1949), p. 3.

Tennessee Williams:
The Playwright as Poet

WILLIAM E. TAYLOR

PERHAPS THE SINGLE most enchanting quality of Tennessee Williams' poetry is one evident in his plays, an imagination that is liberated and daring. In the tradition of Walt Whitman and D. H. Lawrence, Williams likes to write two kinds of poems, the open, sprawling, prophetic form and the tight, delicate lyric. He shows a mastery of both techniques.

Another relationship to the plays is significant. As with any major writer, each individual play, story, novel, or poem is a piece of the total work. Thus, as one reads Williams' poems, the mind constantly flashes to characters, situations, themes, and symbols in the plays and the fiction. The poems are by no means merely footnotes to the plays, however, but impassioned flights that hover above and around the other works.

Some of the longer poems are written either in a free verse that resembles prose, or what Frost would call "loose iambic." Sometimes, too, as in the first section of "Orpheus Descending," Williams mixes iambs and anapests with nonmetrical phrases so subtly that the music and the image are inseparable:

> They say that the gold of the under kingdom weighs so
> that heads cannot lift beneath the weight of their crowns,
> hands cannot lift under jewels,
> braceleted arms do not have the strength to beckon.
> How could a girl with a wounded foot move through it?
>
> (*In the Winter of Cities*, p. 27)

624

Prose of course has prosody. Any great writer demonstrates that—Melville, Faulkner, or Williams' own plays and fiction—but these lines achieve more. The rhythms, the syntax, the images all work together—rather, are of a piece—to make a configuration that we identify with the poem as a distinct literary genre. And the configuration is made out of "lines" that, because of the rhythms and the rhetoric, are felt as units, one leading to and complementing and becoming a part of the others as they march, accumulating images that become symbols, until they reach that surprising and inevitable question: "How could a girl with a wounded foot move through it?" And there one's imagination is set aflame. One recalls Laura Wingfield and all the appalling pathos associated with her; one sees a new Eurydice, a Laura-as-Eurydice, a strange, almost absurd figure, but somehow right, limping futilely up the dim passage; and one feels the oppressive parallelism as well as the imagery.

These lines have ten anapests, seven iambs, and three amphibrachs, or "rocking feet." Normally, such a preponderance of unstressed syllables would move rapidly and, if the imagery were right, give an impression of lightness, perhaps airiness. But these lines are ponderous and move slowly. The heaviness derives from the imagery and from a grammatical parallelism emphasized by line-phrasing and line-stops. Too, the last three lines of the passage begin with heavily accented words ("hands," "braceleted," and "How"), emphasizing the stops at the ends of the preceding lines. Finally, the long pause between the fourth and fifth lines, caused by the syntactical period, the spacing, the shift from one mood to another adds deliberateness.

The problem with Williams is not that *he* does not know what he is doing. The problem is that he is doing so much, his imagination is so volatile, his symbols so rich, that the unresponsive reader is likely to be left sitting on the curb after the express has gone. Consider again the imagery of the quoted passage. It embraces both the more obvious aspect of Williams' "fugitive-philosophy" and the destructive force of materialism and parochialism that triumphs over the artistic sensibility. One thinks not only of *The Glass Menagerie* but also of Big Daddy's fortune in *Cat*, Stanley Kowalski's pragmatism in *Streetcar*, and the crude power and vicious brutality of Boss Finley in *Sweet Bird of Youth*. But on a more profound level, the symbol in these lines is an archetype that haunts all Williams' work, the archetype, in the Jungian sense, of the dead-end labyrinth, as in the alleyways outside Laura's room in *The Glass Menagerie*, and the "journeys" of the Princess and Chance Wayne in *Sweet Bird*, of Sebastian in *Suddenly Last Summer*, and of Blanche in *Streetcar*.

Sometimes Williams' imagination goes off into a zany kind of world that is neither quite absurd nor quite surrealistic, with some kind of mixture of farce and irony that suggests both but mercifully draws back from the chasm of either. The result is such a poem as "The Angels of Fructification." The situation is grotesque. The angels are robots coming off a production line. The poem contrasts the angels with the "headless men" who are producing them and a "Lieutenant"—he could be a soldier, a cop, the boss, any second-in-command—who is "troubled" because "our technological progress . . . has made the maker no longer the master" (p. 32). The last two things done to the angels are they are crudely deflowered, by hand, and they are "stamped approval . . . at the base of the spine." Then they begin to bear fruit. The imagery is sad, threatening, and funny in its syllepses. One angel, "like a serpent, hissed and dripped blue spittle." Finally, miraculously but believably in the fantastic "world" the poem has created for them, they turn into the world itself;

> The snowy plateau
> of the Andes loomed much closer;
> the burning Himalayas lunged their bellies upwards,
> longing to plunge in the cooling smother of heaven (p. 34).

This, of course, is Menippean satire, in which, however, the allegory is fantastic, absurdist, and farcical. The irony in the basic situation, the disgust engendered by the grotesque fructification of the angels of fructification, and the second irony that comes near the end of the poem,

> And still, ostensibly,
> the descent was triumphant.
> Trumpets declared the approach of the bridal party,

blend to create a scene that is a riot of emotions, from rage to disgust to, perhaps surprisingly, compassion. The factory finally becomes the Garden, and the angels, "turned out," become Nature, violated by man but achieving the best retribution possible, being fruitful, giving from "torrents of swallows" to "pink tissue paper."

Persona works differently in "The Angels of Fructification" from the way it works in "Orpheus Descending." In the latter is, first, the speaker, urbane, a little cynical, whose cynicism is, however, touched by melancholy at the inevitability of pragmatic defeat for Orpheus— "pragmatic defeat" because, ultimately, Williams' heroes are not defeated any more than Lear is. There is always the Pyrrhic victory of the spirit.

And the "you" of "Orpheus" is of course a familiar figure in Williams' work, the fugitive poet who seldom escapes and, if he does, is condemned to the role of the poète maudit. In "Orpheus Descending," this persona becomes palpable mainly through allusion. If we accept the notion that a poet's work is all *one* work (that *The Prelude* is the nave of the edifice), this technique is not only quite legitimate but highly effective. Poets are insatiable in their need for myth. It is their mackerel-crowded seas, and Williams is no exception. Just as Faulkner's Yoknapatawpha has, for example, its archetypal "maimed father," so Williams' landscape has its archetypes, and the fugitive poet is one of the most important ones.

A third persona is the Eurydice-Laura figure, discussed above. She raises the "inevitable question" of the fugitive artist, the longed-for and the unattainable, and she is where she belongs, at the center of the poem. Finally, there is the "laity," a properly vague and ambiguous persona associated with the speaker by the "we" of the poem. At the same time, however, the "we" are a little sinister because unbelieving, or because their belief is not total and uncontaminated. Consequently, not having the vision of Orpheus himself, they are at least accessories in the making of the tragedy. They represent the wall at the end of the alleyway that finally traps and destroys Orpheus. Too, "we" draws readers into the poem and implicates them in the tragedy. We too are the laity.

In "The Angels of Fructification," persona is managed as it is in Menippean or Varonian satire. That is, the fable is narrated in the third person so that the "speaker" of the poem all but disappears. He is there, as it were, only by permission, as, for example, in Dryden's "Absalom and Achitophel." The other personae, however, become vivid as allegorical personifications. As such, and in consonance with the comic absurdity in the tone of the poem, a tone similar to that of Ionesco's *The Chairs*, they are also caricatures rather than characters.

The landscape of this poem is a very strange Garden, indeed. There is the faceless creator, there are the beautiful robots with their capacity for producing not only "May birds yellow as butter" but "caps and aprons with French phrase books in their pockets," and there is that serpent, too. But again, the poem turns to a Pyrrhic victory. What, after all, is technology but man's distortion of Nature in order to control it? In the end, Nature will reclaim her own, and here she does so in abundance and beauty.

We have so far been dealing with one kind of poem from *In the Winter of Cities*, the sprawling, imaginative kind of poem where style is accommodated rapidly and easily to shifts in tone, image, and idea, where the technical strategies vary from tight rhetorical and prosodic structures to loose and open ones when the substance demands it. There are other poems in this, perhaps arbitrary, category, "The Eyes" and "The Death Embrace," for example.

A second type of poem, which Williams writes equally well, is the formal lyric. The subject matter of the lyrics—that is, the themes—is as varied as it is in the other poems, but the imagery, tone, and prosody differ. There is, for example, a poem called "Cried the Fox," dedicated to D. H. L., a fugitive poem, ending with the fox running

> across the desperate hollow,
> skirting the frantic hill,
> calling the pack to follow
> a prey that escaped them still (p. 16).

Anyone familiar with Williams' work is unsurprised that the fox seems deliberately to entice the hounds to pursue him. Williams' fugitives go out of their way to place themselves in jeopardy, as if they were determined not only to meet, but to seek out, their fates. Behind this idea somewhere is doubtless Williams' commitment to the ritual of sacrifice, particularly Christian sacrifice.

One of the strangest lyrics in this collection, "The Siege," develops a metaphysical conceit out of the persona's blood, which goes voyaging "in search of one unknown before but recognized on sight."

Before day breaks I follow back the street,
companioned, to a rocking space above.
Now do my veins in crimson cabins keep
the wild and witless passengers of love.

All is not lost, they say, all is not lost,
but with the startling knowledge of the blind
their fingers flinch to feel such flimsy walls
against the siege of all that is not I! (p. 20)

The rather heavy alliteration in "fingers flinch . . . flimsy" is attenuated as the last line powerfully closes the poem. The rather surprising situation of the poem, a narrative of a pick-up, apparently no ordinary one, uses the first four stanzas carefully to develop an atmosphere that is perilous; and the blood figure emphasizes, or better, contains, the peril. The urn that holds the blood from spilling seems almost intangible, a matter not so much of body as of will, and a desperate will, at that. Not another fugitive poem as such, this poem, through some rather daring strategies, creates a configuration for desperation itself. The blood conceit, for example, first strikes the reader as asking too much from the power of association:

I build a tottering pillar of my blood
to walk it upright on the tilting street.

One wonders, perhaps, why "pillar." But the quality of rigidity is what Williams is after, rigidity "tottering" on a "tilting" street, and with it the impression of someone who is terribly uncertain of himself, for any number of reasons. And that pillar is a kind of urn containing the life blood. Should it fall, it would certainly smash to pieces, the blood spilled to "flow downhill." Strained to the breaking point the conceit may be, but it is ultimately successful. It conveys a kind of Chaplinesque image—more grotesque than funny, however—of a body made mechanical by peril.

This imaginative violence may seem refreshing when compared with other poetry of the forties, characterized by the stifling aestheticism, similarity, and imaginative timidity of a cult of academic poets, all of whom wrote exactly alike. It is little wonder that *In the Winter of Cities* received such a poor reception in 1956–1957. For Williams the poet has another quality in common with Williams the dramatist: he is not afraid to take a chance, which is to say he trusts his imagination, wild as its flights may be.

In a way, Williams's poetry was ahead of its time. There is an audience for this kind of poetry today in the hundreds of little magazines and small presses all over the country. Were *In the Winter of Cities* to be reviewed today in, say, *Small Press Review* or *Margins*, rather than in *The Yale Review* or *The New York Times Book Review*, its chances of finding a reader receptive to it would be favorable, for Williams is interested in poems, not literature, and he is not faint-hearted about what raw material he puts into them or what he has to do to make them genuine.

The City of Day and the City of Night: New Orleans and the Exotic Unreality of Tennessee Williams

THOMAS J. RICHARDSON

THROUGHOUT ITS LONG history, the city of New Orleans has had special appeal for literary artists. W. Kenneth Holditch, Professor of English at the University of New Orleans, has mapped an unpublished list of more than fifty Vieux Carré buildings associated with prominent writers living and working in New Orleans over the past two hundred years. Among the important American writers attracted to New Orleans at various times are George W. Cable, Walt Whitman, Mark Twain, William Faulkner, Sherwood Anderson, John Dos Passos, Walker Percy and Tennessee Williams.

Yet, as Holditch himself points out, "most writers who came . . . stayed for a short time and then left."[1] One might add that practically all these artists not only left New Orleans after a brief tenure but also did their major work elsewhere—a curious fact in view of the city's immediate appeal. In a review written in 1968, Lewis P. Simpson stated that the city of New Orleans had not yet entered into the American literary idiom with any strength. The difficulty, he says, might be that "the writer assumes the literary appropriateness of New Orleans too easily." The artist's work is controlled by well-established, polarized concepts—the city that care forgot, the festival city of a perpetual Mardi Gras, a city lost in nostalgia for an irrecoverable past, or a corrupt old world city intruding in the New World. Thus, in spite of the number of American writers attracted

631

to New Orleans, the American literary imagination has persisted in defining the city's image as overwhelmingly exotic, one considerably removed from the reality of living in America. Simpson concludes that overcoming these prevailing literary notions of New Orleans may be almost impossible, but will be necessary "to bring the city into the American literary idiom with genuine force."[2]

That Whitman, Anderson, Faulkner, and the other major American writers Holditch includes on his list did their major work elsewhere lends substance to Simpson's claim that the exotic unreality of the city has not contributed significantly to American literary art. Cable, of course, unlike the rest, was a native, and his best writings, *Old Creole Days*, *The Grandissimes*, and *Madame Delphine*, do indeed focus on the New Orleans milieu. However, his enduring reputation has sprung primarily from his courageous treatment of the race issue in the South after 1865; if he had confined himself to exotic pictures of New Orleans, he would be relegated to that group of local color artists working in the South during the 1870s and 1880s, and his works would be forgotten. Even so, many critics discover a disturbing division between his social criticism and the exotic unreality of his settings.[3] The Creole community does not synthesize very well with his realistic comments on racial violence. The exotic quality of New Orleans seems to create certain difficulties even for Cable, though in all fairness he did not really inherit a prevailing literary notion of the city's image; his fiction is in large part responsible for it. As Simpson suggests, the heritage of exotic unreality places the contemporary artist under considerable pressure. He notes that Walker Percy overtly attempted to escape this heritage by using the Gentilly section of New Orleans instead of the French Quarter as a setting for *The Moviegoer*.[4]

To summarize, New Orleans has been an attractive setting for a large number of writers, yet it has failed to sustain their artistic interest, primarily because it offers either a prevailing image that is stereotyped or a world so far removed from their own experiences that no real use can be made of it. To an extent, this statement holds true for the art of Tennessee Williams. In fact, to assume a profound relationship between the city and Williams' work may be presumptuous. Not only is his present residence at 1014 Dumaine Street visited with relative infrequency, but also his actual employment of the

city as setting is equaled, even exceeded, by his use of other places—
Mississippi, St. Louis, New York, and Rome. In his recent *Memoirs*,
he speaks of Key West and New York more frequently than of New
Orleans; after *Memoirs*, one might consider Rome his favorite city.
When he first visited New Orleans during the fall and winter of
1938–1939, he was only beginning his travels. As other writers had
done, he moved on, going first to California and Mexico, then back
to St. Louis, and finally to New York. Apparently, New Orleans
failed to sustain his artistic interest.

However, I believe that Williams, unlike other American artists,
was influenced significantly by the exotic unreality of New Orleans,
so much, in fact, that the city became an informing image for his
art. In the course of his argument, Simpson says great or good literature about particular places does not just happen "because a person
of literary talent comes to a certain place, not even if he comes to it
by being born there and stays in it until he dies. Instead, the writer's
inmost self and the inner nature of his locality must come into some
kind of complex interaction."[5] Such an interaction has taken place,
I believe, between Williams and the city of New Orleans. The city
has offered Williams a deep, meaningful biographical influence, perhaps to the extent that its unreality has become reality in his artistic
vision.

One might begin with Williams' most famous use of New Orleans
as a setting in *A Streetcar Named Desire*, or cite other instances in
his major plays, such as *The Rose Tattoo* or *Summer and Smoke*,
where the city lies just beyond the horizon and gives dimension to
character and theme. However, these plays have received considerable critical attention, and the nature of the developing relationship
between Williams and New Orleans might better be defined by
focusing on his early fiction, especially that in his collection *One
Arm* (1948). For one thing, the seminal nature of Williams' fiction
is well-known; many of the stories are earlier versions of the plays.
In addition, this early fiction is closely tied to Williams' personal
experiences and can reveal important details of his relation to his
milieu. Finally, his early fiction is clearly his best work in this genre.
It has not yet received the criticism it deserves, particularly given
its role as source material. What this paper will do, therefore, is: 1)
examine Williams' personal relationship with New Orleans, focus-

634 The City of Day and the City of Night

ing on the informing image which the city offered for his art; 2) study, very briefly, the exotic unreality of the city itself, relying primarily on the WPA *City Guide*, a document prepared in 1938, about the time of Williams' first enchantment; 3) analyze the city's informing image as it appears in selections from the seminal collection *One Arm*; 4) point out, briefly, in conclusion, the impact of exotic unreality on the scope of Williams' artistic vision.

When Williams first visited New Orleans in 1938–1939, he was beginning a new era in his life, and what he saw there was partly determined by the fact that the city offered him a new freedom. Benjamin Nelson says, "for the first time he was able to give vent to his passions and desires and frustrations." Williams says himself: "I found the kind of freedom I had always needed. And the shock of it against the puritanism of my nature has given me a subject, a theme, which I have never ceased exploiting" (quoted in Nelson, p. 39). Though Williams was twenty-seven years old, had been away from home at the Universities of Missouri and Iowa, had worked a time for his father's shoe company, and had been involved in the lifestyle of an avant-garde theater group in St. Louis, the trip to New Orleans removed him from his family and introduced him to a world quite different from what he had known. Edwina Williams says, "Tom found New Orleans a complete contrast to St. Louis, a city he hated. . . . He became acquainted with a new kind of life in the French Quarter, one of wild drinking, sexual promiscuity and abnormality."[6] According to Nelson, "New Orleans became for him a kaleidoscope of drink, sex and revelry, and his companions were prostitutes, procurers, homosexuals and any other of the broken but unbowed night people who . . . were living a fringe-area life fraught with desperation and wild despair. He . . . found . . . that there was a profound difference between the city of daylight and the city of darkness. . . . And with this new knowledge and intuition came a certain sense of release" (p. 39).

Williams entered a world of unreality, I think, and that world became reality in his artistic vision. He discovered a city of night, a city defined as an undercurrent of sin, release, depravity, particularly violence and sex. Yet, as he says, his real subject was found in the shock of freedom against the puritanism of his nature. The city of night and release was a place where one could attempt escape from restrictions, inhibitions, the burdens of responsibility and time, and live only for the fulfilment of the moment. However, the city of night is always followed by the city of day, and the world of history and time can never be completely escaped. Thus, the sense of release, or freedom, is qualified not only by the division of experience—two worlds which do not readily synthesize—but also by the tensions springing from a puritan heritage of guilt. The sense of loneliness and meaninglessness which one may attempt to escape in the city of night in fact is intensified by the recognition of time and mortality. Williams' art is based, at least in part, on the tension created by the two cities of his experience—a tension which does not finally resolve in release, but rather proves that the past, both one's personal past and the broader historical past, is inescapable and the present irredeemable.

Inevitably, Williams experienced considerable identification with the city of night and its inhabitants. Edwina Williams says, "he was surrounded by the lost and lonely people about whom he later wrote" (p. 103). While part of the identification came from the sense of freedom and release, most came from the "sense of kinship with the lonely, the rootless and the outcast" (Nelson, p. 39). As Nelson states, Williams "met and gained an intimate knowledge of the strange, twisted and bizarre characters who had previously appeared only on the fringe of his consciousness and . . . he felt a relationship with them he had never felt with anyone before. . . . in New Orleans [he] recognized that loneliness and despair were not just his private griefs" (pp. 38, 39). In the face of the cruel reality of the city of day, a curious community existed among those who sought escape and meaning in the unreal world of the city of night. The community became closer, in a sense, when escape and meaning were impossible to find. Williams' characters are frequently scarred, suffering from physical and psychological wounds, and the city of night becomes the perfect image of retreat. New Orleans too has been wounded—its very age and decay are its scars—and it offers the charm of the defeated. The very frenzy of its nightlife seems to be its effort to escape its own mortality. At any rate, Williams turned in his art to the exotic unreality of the city of night, the fringe of his consciousness, and made it his reality.

At the time of Williams' initial visit to New Orleans, Lyle Saxon, author of *Fabulous New Orleans,* was head of the WPA Writer's Project, and Williams hoped to work on the Project or with the WPA Theatre. Instead, finances forced him to work as a waiter and cashier for a restaurant owned by his landlady at 722 Toulouse. He credits himself with the suggestion for opening the restaurant and for creation of the slogan, "Meals for a Quarter in the Quarter." His room apparently was ten dollars a month, and he thought the twenty-five cent meals a bargain. In a letter[7] to his mother, he says this arrangement continued until the landlady, who was upset by the Bohemian spirit of the place, poured a bucket of water over her guests and brought on a near-riot, a trial, and the closing of the restaurant. In the same letter, he says, "the process of certification for the Writer's Project will be complete the fifteenth of this month and I expect Mr. Saxon will put me on at once, as he seems very much concerned and sympathetic about my precarious situation." Apparently, this hope was not fulfilled, and early in 1939 he went west. He would return at various times during the following years, and New Orleans would continue its influence. He says, "my happiest years were there. . . . I was desperately poor . . . hocked everything but my typewriter to get by. . . . New Orleans is my favorite city of America . . . of all the world, actually."

Probably one of the most noticeable characteristics of New Orleans in 1938, as it is today, and as it has been for over two hundred years, was the sense of division between the business world dominated by the American spirit and the exotic world of the Vieux Carré. The *New Orleans City Guide,* prepared by the WPA in 1938, documents this division not only spiritually but also geographically.[8] The time-honored dividing line between the French Quarter and the American commercial and residential sectors, including the famous Garden district, is Canal Street. This street had marked the division since 1803, when the Americans came to the city in ever-increasing numbers and took commercial leadership from the Creoles, the French-Spanish aristocracy who had descended from the earliest settlers over a century earlier. Traditionally, Canal Street defines the contrasts of the American-French city which include past vs. present, Protestant vs. Catholic, age vs. youth, wealth vs. poverty, inhibitions vs. a joie de vivre, and a clearly bilingual society. The sense of two cities, a divided world, was immediately available to the young Williams. The division offered him the ready character of an informing image for his art.

Williams was primarily attracted to the Latin spirit of the Vieux Carré. He was in New Orleans during its carnival season, and the city's reputation for joys of the flesh must have had its impression. According to the *City Guide*, "the city is first of all a place in which to eat, drink, and be merry" (p. xx). In spite of his scant funds, Williams apparently found the food "amazingly inexpensive"; he wrote his mother that "the cooking was the best he had encountered away from home and he was luxuriating in raw oysters, shrimp, crabs, and lobster."[9] More important, however, as we have seen, he entered the world of revelry, the city that care forgot, and its liberal lifestyle, with some gusto. The exotic nature of the Vieux Carré makes it an appropriate symbol for the city of night. The Quarter is without question a good time town, probably paralleled only by one or two other places in the United States. Yet when Williams visited, the decadence and decay of two centuries were plainly visible in the peeling paint, rotten staircases, overgrown tropical courtyards, and buildings that seemed to be settling into the pavement. These aspects are not very obvious at night, and the Quarter appears to be a complete world, blocks of fantasy where revelry never seems to end. However, the Vieux Carré is in fact surrounded by a different city, the American New Orleans. The impact of morning sunshine, and the contrasting appearance of the city of day, reveals a world blasted by time. The comparison of values with the American mercantilism so obvious in surrounding streets raises serious questions about human values and how to live a life. At the same time, one effect of such comparison can be to send the reveller ever deeper into the city of night; he attempts to find commiseration in the unreality of the Quarter itself and in the broken spirits who are its inhabitants.

Williams published his first collection of short fiction, *One Arm and Other Stories*, in 1948, approximately a decade after his first visit to New Orleans. Three of the eleven stories, "One Arm," "The Angel in the Alcove," and "The Yellow Bird," are set in the old city, and the entire volume exhibits the influence of its image. These three stories are central to the themes and characters in the collection and can be read as touchstones, offering not only a definition of the two worlds, the city of day and the city of night, and the artistic tensions which spring from their contrast, but also the attempted escape into the city of night, identification with its lonely inhabitants, and acceptance of its unreality as the reality of experience.

In "The Angel in the Alcove," an autobiographical story, the narrator sets the action "in the old French Quarter of New Orleans when I was barely twenty" (p. 137). As noted, Williams himself was twenty-seven in 1938, but his experience in the lifestyle of New Orleans was more that of a twenty year old, and his choice of a younger first-person persona heightens the influence of the city. The narrator's room on Bourbon Street contained an alcove window in which the apparition of an angel often appeared on "those winter nights in New Orleans when slow rain is falling from a sky not clouded heavily enough to altogether separate the town from the moon" (p. 141). He says, "This lunar atmosphere of the city draws me back whenever the waves of energy which removed me to more vital towns have spent themselves and a time of recession is called for. Each time I have felt some rather profound psychic wound, a loss or a failure, I have returned to this city. At such periods I would seem to belong there and no place else in the country" (p. 142).

In such a world, the nights were comforting and offered another state of being which had no trying associations with the world. Just before sleep, the apparition of the angel appeared to assure him that "it [presumably, the pain of living] will all be gone in a moment and won't come back until morning" (p. 143). On one such night, the young writer is paid a homosexual visit by a tubercular artist who slept in the adjoining room. This sexual encounter in the city of night is marked by the appearance of the apparition, who, the narrator feels, permitted the act to occur. It is followed by the "comfort" of sleep.

The escape into the desperate comforts of the city of night is interrupted by the landlady, a representative of the materialism and cruelty of the city of day. The narrator indicates at the beginning of the story that she is the "archetype of the suspicious land-lady" (p. 137). Her suspicion affects him with an obscure sense of guilt. She often came into his room with the morning paper and read aloud some item concerning an act of crime in the Quarter. He says, "After the reading she would inspect me closely for any guilty change of countenance, and I would nearly always gratify her suspicion with a deep flush and inability to return her look" (p. 138).

However, the landlady's special wrath in this story is visited upon the tubercular artist, who invented all sorts of trivial complaints to hide from himself the knowledge that he was dying. When he complains to the landlady that bedbugs are causing the spots of blood on his pillow, she is ruthless in the reality of her judgment and becomes the brutal harbinger of time and death. She cries, "You'll die on the street, you'll cough up your lungs in the gutter! You'll go to the morgue. Nobody will claim that skinny cadaver of yours. You'll go in a box and be dumped off a barge in the river. The sooner the better is how I look at it, too" (pp. 146–47).

The narrator says this episode put an end to his story, and he escaped by way of a balcony and a pair of sheets. After this event with the artist, the comfort of the transparent angel failed to appear. Now, instead, he says, "the luminous dial of a clock and the misty grey of the alcove were all that remained for me of the visible world" (p. 149). The sense of time and mortality has invaded and overcome the comforts and release of the city of night. The old landlady had always slept in the downstairs hall, the gateway to the comforts of the angel. One could go neither in nor out without her challenge. "Her ghastly figure would spring upright on the rattling iron cot. She would utter one syllable—who?" (p. 138). The landlady's "ghastly figure" in the dark hall creates a sense of nightmare and indicates that the world of night is not finally comfortable. She seems to be a creature of fantasy, part of the world of exotic unreality, but she is a monster ruthless in her judgments and accusations. The fantastic world of the city of night is further developed in the character of an old widow named Mrs. Wayne, a wonderful raconteur of horribly morbid or salacious stories. "Whenever she smelled food cooking her door would fly open and she would dart forth with a mottled blue and white sauce pan held to her bosom coquettishly as a lace fan" (p. 139). The landlady was spellbound by the stories—"her jaws would slacken and dribble" and "A far-away mezmerized look would come into her usually pin-sharp eyes" (p. 140). Mrs. Wayne is a creature of the exotic world of the city of night and is partly responsible for its construction in the story. Yet her special talents are not able, ultimately, to remove the abiding influence of time, death, or the landlady's powers. The landlady's brutal treatment of the dying artist forces the narrator into a new awareness of the clock, and he is no longer comforted by the angel in the city of night.

As Signi Falk suggests, "The Angel in the Alcove" is not an example of Williams' best work (p. 138). However, its autobiographical, personal nature makes it significant. It defines the duality of the New Orleans which Williams experienced in 1938. New Orleans is the city of comfort and identification for a "profound psychic wound," yet its world cannot escape the invasion of time and mortality. More important, the city of night offers characters from a world of exotic unreality. Mrs. Wayne and the landlady both seem to be creatures from a nightmare, from the fringe of consciousness.

"One Arm," the title story of the volume, is set in New Orleans in the winter of 1939. It focuses on the character of Oliver Winemiller, a youth who had been a champion boxer in the navy before losing his right arm in an automobile accident. His physical mutilation brings on a profound psychic change—a sense of being lost and broken, and a sense of destruction. He travels about the country as a male hustler, doing well financially until he murders a wealthy broker on a yacht in Palm Beach. Then he is forced to travel in less conspicuous channels, and, appropriately, is in New Orleans hustling "on a certain corner of Canal Street and one of those streets that dive narrowly into the ancient part of the city" (p. 7), when he is arrested for the murder and sentenced to the electric chair.

Oliver's conviction is given wide publicity in the nation's newspapers and is seen by his hundreds of former lovers. In prison in New Orleans, he receives letters from them. "There was something about him, they wrote, not only the physical thing . . . which had made him haunt their minds since" (p. 13). This something, it seems, is "the charm of the defeated," and the letters are mostly confessions of guilt from those outside the prison, as if Oliver's death could expiate their sins.

During these last days in his isolated death cell, the broken youth is visited by a representative of the outside world, a young Lutheran minister completely unequipped to understand Oliver's life. He compares Oliver to a golden panther which he had seen in a zoo as a child and which later appeared in a "shameful" erotic dream. The minister's attempted explanation of Oliver's accident is not satisfying; and when he is invited to rub Oliver's body, he becomes nauseous and has to be carried out by the guards. The young Lutheran is torn by conflicting impulses, the restriction and inhibitions of the outside city of day and the sexual passions of the lonely city of night. As he rubs Oliver's sweaty back, "an invisible drummer had seemed to the minister to be advancing from the end of the corridor to the door of the cell and then to come through the bars and stand directly above them. It was his heartbeat. Now it was becoming irregular and his breath whistled. He dropped the towel and dug in his white shirt pocket for the box of sedatives, but when he removed it he found that the cardboard was pulpy with sweat and the tablets had oozed together in a white paste" (pp. 26–27). When the minister is taken out sick with fright, Oliver returns to his only source of comfort, the letters, and even carries them with him to his death.

In "One Arm," as in "The Angel in the Alcove," two worlds are contrasted. However, the charm of the defeated which Oliver exhibits through his physical and psychic brokenness, and the accompanying loneliness and meaninglessness, is sustained by the comforts of the letters he receives. In comparison, the Lutheran minister lives in a false, superficial world. The panther exists for the clergyman in Freudian dreams, in life's undercurrent, but its virility only causes shame in the face of his narrow inhibitions. He is unable to offer Oliver any comfort or strength and in fact retches at the "reality" of experience. Oliver's broken world, confined to death-row in New Orleans, is grotesque, but the bonds formed in it sustain its meaning and vitality.

"The Yellow Bird," the concluding story, develops the character of Alma Tutwiler, who flees from the puritanical world of her family in Arkansas to New Orleans where she becomes a prostitute and lives life to its fullest. As in "One Arm," the world of the city of night is superior to the inhibited world outside. Alma is the daughter of a minister named Increase Tutwiler, who traces his ancestry back through a long line of clergymen to the Reformation. However, his earliest American ancestor had been involved in the Salem witch trials, since the ancestor's wife had allegedly communicated with the devil through a yellow bird named Bobo. That early Tutwiler had accused his wife of witchcraft, but the satanic impulses of the yellow bird, Bobo, had nagged at the Tutwiler clan since her death. This nagging had "left the Puritan spirit fiercely aglow, from Salem, to Hobbs, Arkansas, where the Increase Tutwiler of this story was preaching" (p. 200).

Alma breaks her reputation as a very quiet and shy girl by rebelling against a long-winded sermon her father preaches. She then takes up smoking, which her father considered the "initial and, once taken, irretrievable step toward perdition" (p. 202). When her father slaps her, she not only slaps him in return, but promptly peroxides her hair and puts on lipstick. After an affair with the soda-jerk at the local drugstore, she "started going out nights as rapidly as she had taken up smoking" (p. 206). She steals the family car, picks up men on the highway, and makes the rounds of the highway drinking places until three or four in the morning. In a short time, she "had run her course in that town," and, in a second section of the story, moves on to New Orleans. Six years later, Alma had become "a character in the old French Quarter" (p. 207). Strangely, however, her life as a prostitute on Monkey-Wrench Corner does not have a dissipating effect on her. "Her face had a bright and innocent look in the mornings" (p. 207). When she is visited by a young woman, an emissary from her parents, she speaks happily of her "friends and acquaintances, strangers that pass in the night" (p. 208). Significantly, the final section of the story constructs a fantastic, unreal world. Alma has a child, "perfect," "blond and glowing," and "thoroughly bewitched" (p. 208). He obtains "fists full of gold and jewels that smelled of the sea" and Alma "grew very rich indeed" (p. 209). At the time of her death, the child's father returns and brings a horn of plenty stuffed with treasure. This fortune is left to the Home for Reckless Spenders, and the son puts up a curious monument, three figures on a leaping dolphin, inscribed with the name Bobo, "the small yellow bird that the devil and Goody Tutwiler had used as a go-between in their machinations" (p. 211).

This contrast between the world of puritan restrictions and the freedom enjoyed by one who rebels against it is a familiar Williams theme. In "The Yellow Bird," Alma is not plagued by guilt. She enters an uninhibited good time world where life can be enjoyed. Instead of punishment, she is offered riches in a world of fantasy, and supposedly satanic impulses are avenues to fulfilment. Here, the world of the city of night not only offers communion with "strangers who pass in the night," but its exotic unreality is presented as far superior to the American's long heritage of puritanism and guilt. However, the exotic unreality it provides is completely removed from the reality of American experience. Time and mortality are far away from the fantasy world of "gold and jewels that smelled of the sea." It is a complete fantasy, a dream-world, and does not really resolve the tension which "The Angel in the Alcove" defines. The attempt at escape in the city of night led the artist to construct a new world, a new reality, but it ultimately is a fairyland, a false world which is not a solution to the human predicament.

The rest of the stories in One Arm do not use New Orleans directly as a setting, but their themes and characters are influenced by its image. The most successful of the stories are those that spring from the tension between the city of day and the city of night. "The Malediction" centers on the defeat of a factory worker, Lucio, who finds comfort for a time in the city of night. Yet, in spite of the meaning he finds in a relationship with a cat named Nitchevo, his world is invaded and he is ultimately broken by the futile labors of his factory job in the city of day. He is confronted by an old man who reminds him of time and mortality by shouting the malediction: "Watch for the sun. It comes from the cemetery" (p. 51). His only escape from a lost and meaningless existence is suicide. Probably the best known of the stories in One Arm is "Desire and the Black Masseur," a complex tale of masochistic guilt and atonement. Anthony Burns, a small, timid man completely lost in the working world of a huge city, discovers release in a perverted relationship with a giant Negro masseur. "The baths were a tiny world of their own" (p. 86), a labyrinth of exotic unreality behind opaque doors and sheathings of vapor. Burns finds his fulfilment in the beatings given by the masseur; and in a grotesque conclusion, his body is devoured by the giant in the completion of a ritual of atonement. Comparably, "the earth's whole population twisted and writhed beneath the manipulations of night's black fingers and the white ones of day," and perfection "was slowly evolved through torture" (p. 94).

"Portrait of a Girl in Glass," the prelude to The Glass Menagerie, presents Laura Wingfield living in a world of "perpetual twilight."

She keeps the shades drawn on the outside world, especially on "Death Valley," an alley outside her room where a vicious chow cornered stray cats and killed them. As in the later play, Laura refuses to face the reality of experience and chooses to withdraw into her world of glass. Finally, "The Night of the Iguana," also a prelude to a major play, portrays Edith Jelkes, a "spinster of thirty," who finds comfort in her loneliness in the violent rape attempt by a fellow lodger in a hotel near Acapulco. As a captured iguana is set free, so Miss Jelkes is released from her isolation during a violent storm in the Mexican night. She glimpses something of the nature of human suffering, not only as it is symbolized by the iguana but also as it appears in the lives of her fellow guests. Significantly, Miss Jelkes represents a "historical Southern family" which had split into antithetical types, "one in which the libido was pathologically distended and another in which it would seem to be all but dried up" (p. 170). Though a proper spinster, she really represents both tendencies, since she had channeled her energies into a gift for painting. The warring types are both evident in her response to the attack made upon her, and she fights back with violent success. Yet her final sense of comfort comes from the fact that "the strangling rope of loneliness" (p. 196) had been severed; she finds new life among the broken spirits in the city of night.

Before Williams visited New Orleans in 1938, he had written early materials which treated the duality of experience and the broad themes of loneliness and meaninglessness. Yet his visit offered him an image which informed and strengthened his existing values and concerns. His "inmost self" and the "inner nature of his locality" came into complex interaction. Primarily, he found a new freedom and a lifestyle which shocked his puritanical impulses. The resulting tension, however, was considerably more profound than joie de vivre vs. inhibitions. His art is based, to some extent, on the tension defined by the two cities of his experience, the city of day and the city of night. This tension does not resolve, for it is central to Williams' view of the human predicament. In the context of time and mortality, the human condition appears inescapable and is perhaps irredeemable. Williams' best art, his early major plays *The Glass*

The Fiction of Tennessee Williams

REN DRAYA

Tennessee Williams is a good storyteller, as theater audiences have long known. The magic evoked by Laura's rendezvous with her gentleman caller or the bawdy beauty of Serafina's love scene with her clown suitor are proof of Williams' power to tell enchanting stories of enchanted lives. Unlike most playwrights who try their hands at different forms, Williams is a remarkably strong prose writer—his fiction perhaps even more consistent in quality than his drama.

Williams' first collection, *One Arm and Other Stories*, contains eleven stories. His second book, *Hard Candy*, contains nine stories; two of these, the title story and "Mysteries of the Joy Rio," are "variations on the same theme" (p. 4). *The Knightly Quest* includes the title novella and four additional stories which had appeared in magazines. The most recent collection is six stories called *Eight Mortal Ladies Possessed*. Much of Williams' fiction has appeared over the years in magazines like *Esquire*, *Mademoiselle*, and *Playboy*; and a few stories, such as "A Recluse and His Guest" (*Playboy*, January 1970), have not yet been collected. Williams has a short novel, *The Roman Spring of Mrs. Stone*, and the recent novel, *Moise and the World of Reason*.

The first collection of stories provides an interesting and characteristic sampling. "The Poet," "Chronicle of a Demise," and "The

647

Yellow Bird" are clearly the experiments of a young writer. "The Yellow Bird" has some fine comic moments, but the prose is too jerky and the ending too garbled to sustain the broad humor. The other stories in the book, however, are skillfully written: in particular, "One Arm," "Desire and the Black Masseur," and "The Night of the Iguana." The title story refers to a "broken Apollo," a gorgeous young man, once a champion boxer, who lost his arm in an accident and roams the country as a male prostitute. The physical mutilation produces a corresponding emotional loss—Oliver ceases to feel or care, and he drifts from city to city, passively accepting the favors of scores of anonymous men. He eventually is imprisoned for murder, his case attracts newspaper attention, and thousands of men who had spent nights with him write letters of love and support: "There was something about him, they wrote, not only the physical thing, important as that was, which had made him haunt their minds since.

"What they were alluding to was the charm of the defeated which Oliver possessed . . ." (p. 13). Oliver regards the letters as bills from people he owes feelings, not money; for the first time since his accident, he realizes he has a reason to live, to give, to love.

While "One Arm" succeeds as compelling narrative, it also is an early catalogue of Williams' concerns: an openly homosexual theme, the fascination with mutilation and its attendant psychic loss, the power of words (represented by the letters) to effect change, the theme of guilt and atonement, and the importance of sex both as a means of human communication and as a channel to awaken acceptance of one's existence.

Williams' fiction often serves as a drawing board for themes and characters later amplified in drama (cf. Reck). *The Milk Train Doesn't Stop Here Anymore* is an expanded version of the plot sketched out in "Man Bring This Up Road." *One Arm and Other Stories* also contains "Portrait of a Girl in Glass," the nucleus for *Glass Menagerie*. Sometimes the play and the story have only minimal connections, as in the character of Brick who appears in both *Cat on a Hot Tin Roof* and "Three Players of a Summer Game." The story is beautifully wrought—an interesting and poignant cadenza to the Brick of the familiar play. In both play and story, Brick has a wife named Margaret and a problem called alcoholism. But

Maggie in the play is a fully-developed character; and "Three Players" is essentially Brick's story—a Brick who shares some of the traits of the dramatic figure but whose story stands separately. The writing is Williams at his strongest: sure, honest dialogue, elegant and controlled description; concise diction.

Occasionally, the works are quite similar, as with the full length play and the story of the same title: *Kingdom of Earth*. Both are set against the loneliness and violence of the Mississippi Delta at flood level; the play is an expansion of the characters and images from the story. Both describe a pathetic-comic love triangle, and both use raw images of nature as backdrop to the elemental emotions.

Williams' ability to approach his material from such differing vantage points enables us to examine both his narrative and his dramatic strengths—and weaknesses. An easy judgment of quality is impossible; comparative discussions are most likely to yield interesting differences rather than deficiencies. The two versions of *The Night of the Iguana* are illustrative.

The playwright's remarks on setting and characters for the play are a more detailed account of the descriptions which open the story. The play, a full three acts, contains many more characters and thereby more conflicts and secondary motifs than the twenty-seven page story. The drama centers on Shannon: his disintegrating emotional condition, his intellectual attraction to Hannah Jelkes, his various physical lapses, and his relationship to Maxine. In the story, Maxine is called simply "the Patrona," Shannon is not presented at all, and Miss Jelkes (a painter, here called Edith) is the focal point. Perhaps because of Williams' talent in presenting sympathetic women characters—especially southern women—the story version seems the more satisfying and complete. Stripped of Baptist travelers and German patriots, the action is devoted to a tender explication of Miss Jelkes' spirit. The only additional characters are two writers staying at the resort, and, although as characters they are less developed than Shannon, their role in the story is much clearer. Williams provides just enough personal information, particularly with the older writer, to present a believable and troubled man. Unity of interest is preserved, and the story shows the author's skill in portraying a delicate yet sturdy spirit: "Miss Jelkes was outwardly such a dainty tea-pot that no one would guess that she could actually boil" (p. 171).

In both story and play, the iguana is captured, left tied up all night, and finally released. Miss Jelkes of the play requests Shannon to cut it free: he recognizes the lizard's tethering as a "parallel situation" to her elderly grandfather's "dying-out effort" (p. 370) to finish a last poem. But Williams does not include the grandfather in the story; the iguana as a metaphor therefore applies solely to Miss Jelkes. The iguana clearly represents the natural, physical instincts throttled within Miss Jelkes. Cutting the iguana free means "the strangling rope of her loneliness had also been severed" (p. 196). In confronting the demonic need within herself, her own sexuality, Miss Jelkes gains release from the fears and insecurities that have so long trapped her; although she prevents the writer from entering her body, his semen falls upon her belly, and she calmly accepts this intercourse. The story ends with a sense of resolution: Miss Jelkes has grappled with a problem and found some understanding. In contrast, the play ends on a flabby note. Dramatic tension and excitement run down, with Shannon still taking the path of least resistance. Knowledge, understanding, acceptance are absent—perhaps impossible, given Williams' portrait of the minister. At any rate, Miss Jelkes of the story seems a more unified and interesting central character than Shannon in the play. The play attempts perhaps too much. Shannon's actions and choices are those of an individual affecting an entire community; for, in abandoning his job and therein his self-respect, Shannon also abandons a group of persons who relied on his guidance. Ironically, he no longer serves as spiritual leader, but is now tour guide to the group—a pathetic comment on fallen congregations in fallen times.

Another story from the *One Arm* collection, "The Malediction," and the short lyrical play, *The Strangest Kind of Romance*, are slight variations on rather than separate treatments of a theme. Both center on a little man and his loneliness. A brazen landlady and a cat, the two inherited from a former tenant, represent the opposing demands of love—the woman is loud and sexual, the cat is gentle. Equally opposed are the two needs in the man: one, to earn a living at the harsh factory; two, to find solace for his jangled nerves. Both physically and emotionally, he is too frail for the rough demands he faces. An old man (wandering beggar in the story, father-in-law to the landlady in the play) looms as the crazed specter of truth; it is he who curses the factory for its inhuman roughness.

In the play, the little man tries to communicate the desperation of his solitude: "The body is only—a shell. It may be alive—when what's inside—is too afraid to come out! It stays locked up and alone! Single! Private!" (27 *Wagons Full of Cotton*, p. 146). This tortured message echoes through much of Williams' work. But the "body as shell" motif is left an intriguing fragment; neither play nor story is fully developed. The "Malediction" is an uneven story, but it ends with a strong sense of decision. The play is more unified but ends on a garbled and weak note. Together, however, they demonstrate Williams' skill in evoking the loneliness and terror of a vulnerable individual.

Williams' sensitivity to the lonely soul springs, in part, from his own experiences and those of his family. Often, as in "Portrait of a Girl in Glass," Williams is openly autobiographical. His troubled love for his sister Rose prompted the appealing rendering of Laura and seems also to have been the source for "The Resemblance Between a Violin Case and a Coffin" (*Hard Candy*). Both stories are written in the first person, a technique Williams also employs in two other selections from *Hard Candy*, "Three Players of a Summer Game" and "The Mattress by the Tomato Patch"; "The Kingdom of Earth" and "Grand" from *The Knightly Quest*; "Chronicle of a Demise" and "The Angel in the Alcove" from *One Arm and Other Stories*; and *Moise and the World of Reason*. Occasionally Williams invents a new persona ("Chronicle," "Three Players," "The Kingdom of Earth"), but more often "I" speaks for Williams himself. The result is a gentle blending of fiction and autobiography.

"Portrait" and "Resemblance" describe Williams' sister from puberty to about twenty-three; the latter story realistically treats the confusion and schisms caused by the onset of menstruation: "My sister had been magically suited to the wild country of childhood. . . . But between childhood and adulthood there is a broken terrain which is possibly even wilder than childhood was. The wilderness is interior" (*Hard Candy*, p. 85). The story centers around an incident when Tom's sister is about fourteen: she and a seventeen-year-old boy, Richard Miles, must prepare a piano-violin duet to present at a local recital. Tom and his sister are both obsessed by Richard, for he is their storybook hero—the golden knight of strength and beauty. For the sister, love is at first a joyous release, but Tom is filled with sad confusion. Williams brilliantly captures the unbearable agonies of an adolescent crush: "These are the intensities that one cannot live with, that he has to outgrow if he wants to survive. But who can help grieving for them? If the blood vessels could hold them, how much better to keep those early loves with us? But if we did, the veins would break and the passion explode into darkness . . ." (p. 90).

As the recital date approaches, the sister blunders more and more often, and Tom grows more and more enamoured with the grace of Richard. The concert does not go well, but Richard's brilliant playing and his sensitivity to the girl's nervousness get them through the piece. Richard died a few years later. But the author's pairing of violin case and coffin goes beyond mere physical attributes (color, shape). Williams seems to imply the fatal frailty of persons who create passionate music, or those who feel in some way the compelling need to express exquisite beauty. And so Williams' own sister cannot be adjusted to the demands of "outer" life and so Richard must die. These are interesting precursors to the later character Moise, an artist. For her, much like Rose in this early portrait, "things became more and more untenable" (p. 26). Moise wishes to leave the world of reason—the world antithetical to the interior wilderness—and retire to her own world, her own room, much as Rose and Laura retreat from the demands of society.

Similarly, Williams' own grandmother was the kind of person who retreated from the world of movement and change; she "formed quiet but deeply emotional attachments to places and people and would have been happy to stay forever in one rectory. . . ." These words open "Grand" (*The Knightly Quest*, p. 169), a simple tale of remembrance and love. Yet despite its gentle tone, the story is remarkable in creating a crescendo of tension and anguish. Williams writes honestly of the pain of Grand's death and of his own sense of loss.

In drawing upon his own experiences, Williams frequently makes use of the places in which he has lived and wandered—New Orleans, the California coast, various sleepy Delta towns, seedy Manhattan streets, grim midwestern industrial cities. New Orleans, for example, is the setting for several of his plays (*Auto-Da-Fé, Lord Byron's Love Letter, The Mutilated,* and *Suddenly Last Summer*) and for three of the early stories ("One Arm" and "The Angel in the Alcove" from the first collection and "The Coming of Something to the Widow Holly" in *Hard Candy*). "The Angel" is taken directly from Williams' own lean apprentice years. The story is especially interesting because the author is both narrator and outside character—it is he who lived in a rundown rooming house, finally leaving "by way of a balcony and a pair of sheets" (*One Arm,* p. 137). It is also he who served as model for the young tuberculin homosexual artist (Rex Reed, "Tennessee Williams Turns Sixty," p. 220).

Clearly, Williams' plays and stories are not drastically separate artistic efforts, but subtle variations of the same voice: character, style, theme are similar. Characterization by types provides a telling illustration of the unity in Williams' work. One favorite Williams figure, the earthy middle-aged woman, appears variously in the drama as Maxine (*Iguana*), the landlady in *The Lady of Larkspur Lotion,* (short play from *27 Wagons Full of Cotton*); Myrtle (*Kingdom of Earth*), Leona (*Small Craft Warnings*); Celeste (*The Mutilated*); Miriam (*In the Bar of a Tokyo Hotel*). In the fiction she is represented by Olga ("The Mattress by the Tomato Patch"), Myrtle ("Kingdom of Earth"), Cora ("Two on a Party"), Mrs. Hutcheson ("The Malediction"). Another recurring character is the handsome (often dark) young man, sensual and compelling: Stanley (*A Streetcar Named Desire*), Silva Vicarro (*27 Wagons Full of Cotton*), Chicken (*Kingdom of Earth*), and Val (*Orpheus Descending*) have their fictional counterparts in Paolo (*Roman Spring of Mrs. Stone*), Giovanni ("Sabbatha and Solitude"), Oliver ("One Arm") and Chicken ("Kingdom of Earth"). In contrast to these sexual beings, Williams often portrays a person (a woman, usually) repressed and fearful; examples are Mrs. Collins ("Portrait of a Madonna"), Blanche (*A Streetcar Named Desire*), Alma (*Summer and Smoke*), Isabel (*Period of Adjustment*), Hannah Jelkes (*The Night of the Iguana*), Laura (*Glass Menagerie*), and Eloi (*Auto-Da-Fé*); in the fiction they appear as Karen Stone (*The Roman Spring of Mrs. Stone*), Edith Jelkes ("The Night of the Iguana"), and Laura ("Portrait of a Girl in Glass").

The qualities of repression and fear are parts of the dominant Williams motif of the outcast: the emotional or physical cripple who suffers intense loneliness and hunger for love and acceptance. Both the 1967 "slapstick tragedy," *The Mutilated,* and the early story "One Arm" explicitly label physical deformities. Laura in "Portrait" is shy and secretive, but in the play Williams adds a visible deformity (lame foot) to emphasize the girl's estrangement from society. Many Williams characters are set off from society by their looks or manners; for example, Flora in "The Important Thing" has a homely face, a strange way of smiling and blinking, a fast and shrill voice. "She belonged nowhere . . . , she was a fugitive with no place to run to" (*One Arm,* p. 133). But her honest individuality and her keen intellect are traits far superior to superficial prettiness or conformity. And John, the rather more ordinary young man who is drawn to Flora, learns to accept the girl as she is. Flora's masculine counterpart is Homer Stallcup in "The Field of Blue Children": "Nobody in Myra's social *milieu* knew him or paid him any attention" (*One Arm,* p. 157).

Sometimes Williams' outcast is aged: Mr. Krupper is "a man of gross and unattractive appearance and with no family connections" (*Hard Candy,* p. 103). Or he may simply go unnoticed, like the cuckolded Ernie in "The Mattress by the Tomato Patch" or the timorous Anthony Burns in "Desire and the Black Masseur": "Everything absorbed him and swallowed him up, and still he did not feel secure" (*One Arm,* p. 83). Similarly, Miss Rosemary McCool is "an odd-looking girl, very pale and gangling, . . . determined and destined to slip through the world as an all but unseen and unheard being" (*Eight Mortal Ladies Possessed,* pp. 81–3). Rosemary's awkwardness and fear of speaking are compounded by an unfortunate "sexual malfunction": although she is nearly twenty years old, she has not yet experienced her first menstruation. The unhappy girl writes for English class: "I HAVE NO PURPOSE IN LIFE EXCEP COMPLETE IT QUIK AS POSIBLE FOR ALL CONSERNED IF ANY BESIDE MY ANT ELLA" (p. 83).

Lack of purpose in life is the sad corollary to lack of identity. Williams knows that we all seek "someone or something"; ultimately, we seek love—it is the something that gives life purpose. And love, of course, is Williams' primary concern. As in the plays, Williams' fictional explorations range from the bawdy to the beautiful to the bizarre. More exactly, he is concerned with the need for love and with the various relationships possible between love and sex. Both "The Important Thing" and "The Field of Blue Children" examine the relationship between sexual knowledge and the elusive sense of fulfilment. In contrast to these rather abstract seekers, Chicken— one of Williams' most natural, earthy male figures—describes the sexual act: "Good, good, good. The best thing in the world, that burning sensation and then the running over, the sweet relaxing and letting all of it go, shot off inside her, leaving you weak and satisfied completely and ready for sleep. Yes, there was nothing like it in all the world, nothing able to compare with it even. Just that thing and nothing more is perfect" (*The Knightly Quest*, p. 154). For Chicken, a simple man with simple and direct needs, life's problems are solved by sex.

But most of Williams' characters, realistically, are more complex, and the search for love is more tortured. Love must include communication and sharing; the married couple in Williams' short story "The Vine" realize this need in much the same way as do the two couples in his "serious comedy," *Period of Adjustment*. But straight man/woman marriages are not Williams' chief interest. More often he describes nonconventional love relationships: two women ("Happy August Tenth"); a young man and an older woman (*Sweet Bird of Youth, Roman Spring of Mrs. Stone*, "Sabbatha and Solitude"); two men (*Moise and the World of Reason*); or any number of interracial combinations ("Rubio y Morena," *Kingdom of Earth* and the short story so named, as well as *Moise and the World of Reason*).

In a short story from *Eight Mortal Ladies Possessed*, "Miss Coynte of Greene," Williams presents the epitome of joyous sex between a white woman and a black man—indeed, black men. The black lovers of Miss Coynte (the name probably a pun) like the part-black Chicken, respond naturally to sex. Similarly, the dark lover Amada ("loved") in "Rubio y Morena" is a simple earth figure; she appears from nowhere, makes love, stays on with no questions asked.

But whites and blacks do not always integrate successfully. In the early "Desire and the Black Masseur," Williams demonstrates his awareness of the subtle balance between love and hate as well as the power of black pride. The black man "hated white-skinned bodies because they abused his pride. He loved to have their white skin prone beneath him, to bring his fist or the palm of his hand down hard on its passive surface. He had barely been able to hold this love in restraint, to control the wish that he felt to pound more fiercely and use the full of his power" (*One Arm*, p. 90). The timid hero, Burns, is the perfect victim; for in knowing so little about himself and in having virtually no contact with society, he drifts into a situation of masochism—culminating, Christlike, in his own death. Williams offers a chilling rationale for the outcast who willfully sacrifices himself.

Self-sacrifice is one option in the face of basic questions of survival: "I think the thing to fuss over is not competitive philosophies of art or even political ideas, which are curiously outside our introverted orbit, but simply this: a method of survival!" (Williams' preface to "The Summer Belevedere," in *Five Young American Poets*). "How do you live?" "How do you get along?" are questions Williams has never stopped asking. His answers assume that we will, and must, suffer. In "Desire and the Black Masseur" he notes: "For the sins of the world are really only its partialities, its incompletions, and these are what suffering must atone for. . . . The nature of man is full of such make-shift arrangements, devised by himself to cover his incompletion. . . . The use of imagination, resorting to dreams or the loftier purpose of art, is a mask he devises to cover his incompletion. . . . Then there is still another compensation. This one is found in the principle of atonement, the surrender of self to violent treatment by others with the idea of thereby clearing one's self of his guilt. This last way was the one that Anthony Burns unconsciously had elected" (*One Arm*, p. 85). Many of Williams' major plays delineate various workings and worrying of this guilt; in the preface to *Sweet Bird of Youth*, the playwright discusses his preoccupation: "Guilt is universal . . . . If there exists any area in which a man can rise above his moral condition, imposed upon him at birth, by the nature of the breed, then I think it is only a willingness to know it, to face its existence in him, and I think that at least below the conscious level we all face it" (IV, 6). For Williams, "the nature of the breed" has remained fairly constant over the years. Characters and situations, from the early stories to the recent plays and fiction, are the artistic rendering of his mea culpa. Since Williams posits guilt as universal, the audience (or reader) thus joins him in a communion of collective guilt and in a tacit quest for small moments of "completion" in an incomplete world. "Desire and the Black Masseur" unites the themes of guilt and atonement; the story is one of Williams' most carefully crafted and succeeds as serious, startling fiction.

Age differences mark some of the love relationships in Williams' work. *The Roman Spring of Mrs. Stone* and "Sabbatha and Solitude" provide an interesting comparison; Sabbatha is more eccentric, more bizarre, more aged than Karen Stone, but the theme of old artist and young Italian lover is the same. Williams in the 1970s seems to find more potential for "happy" endings, or at least for resolutions which emphasize acceptance and mutual recognition of dependencies. Karen is scared and scarred. Her early fear of sex is more accurately a fear of pregnancy; thus menopause, which marks so frighteningly the decay of her beauty, also frees her to enjoy lovemaking. Sabbatha, ribald and raucous, rails at the world which rejects her. She believes, stubbornly, in her own worth as a poet and in her own sexuality; yet, she knows that she can live, and even die, alone. Her strength releases her from the narrow bond of social approval that defines Karen's abilities to cope with her life. Without seeking, Sabbatha receives her lover back. But Karen turns in despair to a new, more depraved substitute for the beautiful Paolo.

Roman Spring is Williams' first extended work of fiction, but in some ways it is more a play than a novel. The opening paragraph, which describes place and lighting, seems much like Williams' introductory remarks to *Camino Real* or *Sweet Bird of Youth*—the effect is visual and prepares an audience for a scene with actors. The Roman street with its derelict horde is similar to the clamoring background crowd in *Suddenly Last Summer* or *Camino Real*. Mrs. Stone enters the scene in the second chapter; but unity of place is preserved, and it is easy to visualize this sequence as stage action. Williams uses no quotation marks—dialogue is simply set out on the page, a device used often in his fiction. The technique adds a fluid quality to the prose; *Roman Spring* seems breathless, sometimes appropriately hysterical—qualities which suit the character of Mrs. Stone. The style also allows for easy inclusion of past material, in a touch of quasi-stream of consciousness. For example, hints of an abortive lesbian incident in the past are interwoven with the narrative. But lacking the dramatic tension which marks so much of Williams' work, this novel seems diffuse and only erratically charged. A screen play atmosphere prevails; minor characters appear like cameo spots.

The "star," like so many Williams characters, is unhappy and isolated. Lines from an early Williams poem, "One and Two," present a stark picture of isolation:

ONE: (slowly and gravely)
        All your confessions are made to yourself.
        You never conveniently drop your private journal on the stairs.
        How can another person ever get near you?
TWO: (dully)
        Why should another person want to get near me?
ONE: (looking out the window)
        Loneliness.
TWO: (flicking an ash from a Russian cigarette)
        One of my earliest discoveries about life was the usual lack
            of very much satisfaction among the living. . .
        You don't seem to understand how anyone, having to choose
            between something and nothing, might choose nothing
            because he wanted something. . . .
                                        (*Five Young American Poets*, pp. 141–2)

Choosing nothing may be a safer course for many people, for choosing something requires the risk of loss. In "A Recluse and His Guest," the recluse rejects warmth and companionship, too fearful of possible pain and the complexities of relating to another person. He chooses boarded-up solitude because he is unable to trust his own ability to return love. Karen Stone—despite her wealth and career and acquaintances—is similarly a lonely recluse. She is a victim of "the usual lack of satisfaction among the living." In choosing between something and nothing, she marries an impotent man and thus avoids copulation. Because she wants so much to experience deep passion, but so fears facing the pain of real life, she substitutes the ephemeral "nothing" of the stage. At age fifty she tries to play Juliet, but the white satin dress cannot conceal the marks of age or diminish her inability to "get near" another person. Since she cannot trust herself, she will never trust others; yet she cannot bear to be alone. Mrs. Stone is a credible and sympathetic character, yet the novel creates less impact than many of Williams' shorter pieces of fiction. The reader knows Mrs. Stone well but is not apt to care deeply about her. A similar problem marks Williams' recent novel, *Moise and the World of Reason.*

Moise and the World of Reason is Williams' longest piece of fiction to date. The novel both succeeds and fails. Many parts are dull, the characters often unbelievable or simply uninteresting. Readers will invariably identify the writer-narrator as Tennessee Williams himself; further, an old derelict playwright—whom Moise recognizes as the writer grown old—is associated with the Truck and Warehouse (TW) Theater and thus is a blunt projection of the most seedy and unattractive aspects of Williams himself.

Moise's chief success is its evocation of mood—seeking, scared, bitter-sweet—and place. Manhattan streets at night, rundown lofts, abandoned warehouses are all strongly drawn and serve as appropriate setting for this tale of loss and love. Moise's apartment seems a sanctuary, not unlike the café in *Small Craft Warnings* which Williams describes as a "place of refuge for vulnerable vessels." In *Moise* Williams uses a particularly urban phrase, "the sudden subway," as metaphor for the disastrous inadvertencies against which the creative individual is helpless and almost hopeless. The "almost" is important, for Williams' dark night of the soul is a strangely sad tale, but not pessimistic or self-pitying. The protagonist calls himself distinguished and failed, yet he continues to write and to look for love. Just as writing was early a refuge for Williams, so this present-day character calls his writing desk "Bon Ami"—it is a packing crate for the product of that name, and the actual act of writing is thus a cleansing occupation. All through this novel various comments about writing (and playwrighting and painting) serve as a whimsical detour from the theme of the search for love. For example, Moise accuses writers of substituting "words and phrases, slogans, shibboleths and so forth for the simplicities of true feeling" (pp. 160–61). The target is not really the narrator, for Williams has always understood the symbolic value of language and the power of words to express emotion. "Words are a net to catch beauty," declares a would-be poet in "The Field of Blue Children" (*One Arm*, p. 156). And the judge in Williams' early verse play, *The Purification*, advises, "Speak out the broken language of your hearts and we'll supply the sense where it seems to be needed" (*27 Wagons*, p. 33).

Perhaps Williams sees "broken language" as the most honest attempt for "simplicities of feelings" and thus employs the choppy, awkward style of *Moise.* The novel does not flow with the lyrical grace so often characteristic of Williams' prose; rather, the new work is especially marked by fragments, abrupt changes, unfinished sentences. These devices have appeared in earlier works such as *Iguana, Camino, In the Bar of a Tokyo Hotel,* and *I Can't Imagine Tomorrow,* but have not before become dominant, or disruptive, techniques. Williams is engaging in the popular sport of mocking the act of writing, punning, poking self-consciously at words and sentences and their attempts to describe emotions. Suspended thought, absence of resolution are marks of Moise's indecisions and fears as well as symptoms of the narrator's inability to accept a finality. But the technique is overly conscious and seemingly contrived; it is repeated in the novel too many times to remain effective and fresh. Although *Moise* has a "happy" ending, it is a tale throughout of unhappiness and anguish. Unfortunately, reading the novel is an equally anguishing experience. Unlike the bulk of Williams' fiction, which is marked by a compassionate and delicate delineation of pain, *Moise* is marred by an awkward, tedious style. Frequently the prose is pretentiously solemn or irritatingly vapid; the characterizations are clumsy and uneven.

In theme, *Moise* is a longer treatment of a problem Williams called the oldest in the world—"the need to believe in something or someone." Just as Hannah Jelkes can believe in "broken gates between people so they reach each other, even if it's just for one night only" (*Iguana,* IV, 352), so the nameless narrator of *Moise* searches in the one night of the novel for the broken gates available to him. One of his most cherished memories is of a night with Moise, not a night of sex, but one of communication: two persons lying side by side with locked fingers, two persons who know for this short time they are not alone (a version of the incident with Brick and the widow in "Three Players"). Hannah too was aware of the basic need for these nights in which two persons can exchange a little understanding, can share a little portion of comfort against the cruel forces of the outer world. That world—Moise's term is the "world of reason"—is variously represented in the novel by the narrator's family, by the police, by any rigid and conforming member of "proper" society. Williams often compares gays and straights, for the characters of this novel are outcasts by dint of their sexuality as well as their artistry.

Christopher Lehmann-Haupt, in the *New York Times* review (May 15, 1975) of *Moise*, praises the novel for its open treatment of homosexuality and states that this is the first time Williams "has dealt at length, overtly and even graphically with the subject of homosexuality." Williams' drama has surely contained more than covert "hints" of homosexuality—for example, direct allusions to Brick and Skipper in *Cat on a Hot Tin Roof*; and Williams' fiction has always contained a number of clear, open characterizations of gay men and women. Gewinner Pierce ("Gay-winner"), the prince-like jaded hero of "The Knightly Quest," is explicitly gay. For him, "night is a quest." The novella is seriously flawed, however; its blend of fantasy and satire contains amusing portions, but as a whole it is a confused work, and the matter of Gewinner's sexuality seems particularly irrelevant.

Williams refers over and over to the "queen world" in "Two on a Party" as he summarizes the bitter-sweet relationship of a "lush and a fairy." The story is a truthful portrait of people who must hustle for a living. Other stories that explicitly focus on homosexuals are "One Arm," "The Angel in the Alcove," "Hard Candy," "Mysteries of the Joy Rio," and "Happy August the Tenth." It may be simply that Williams' fiction has not been widely enough read (or appreciated) for this homosexual, and often bisexual, bias to have been noted. At any rate, *Moise* is openly, humorously, courageously homosexual. From the start, the narrator talks of his first great love, Lance, "the living nigger on ice." Williams takes a sure and proud stand— "deviation being the course of my life" (p. 63), even to the point of commitment to organized gay liberation (p. 139).

In addition to the homosexual theme, the novel, like so much of Williams' work, is marked by an awareness of the passage of time. Big Mama in *Cat* says, "Time goes by so fast. Nothin' can outrun it. Death commences too early—almost before you're half acquainted with life—you meet with the other . . ." (III, 152). "The Timeless World of a Play," preface to *The Rose Tattoo*, contains a summary of Williams' attitude toward the world of time: "It is this continual rush of time, so violent that it appears to be screaming, that deprives our actual lives of so much dignity and meaning, and it is, perhaps more than anything else, the *arrest of time* which has taken place in a completed work of art that gives to certain plays their feeling of depth and significance. . . . The great and only possible dignity of man lies in his power deliberately to choose certain moral values by which to live as steadfastly as if he, too, like a character in a play were immured against the corrupting rush of time." And so the narrator of *Moise* is aware of time: "Clock-beat, heartbeat: you don't want to hear either, but you always trust their going on with you, for otherwise you'd stop, too" (p. 143). Almost thirty years ago, Williams wrote "time . . . is short and it doesn't return again. It is slipping away while I write this and while you read it, and the monosyllable of the clock is Loss, Loss, Loss, unless you devote your heart to its opposition" (Introduction to Signet edition of *A Streetcar Named Desire*). For Moise, opposition takes the form of her painting. For the narrator, as for Williams, writing is the great magic trick.

At the novel's end, the narrator returns to Moise's room—i.e., her world, the world of self that opposes the limited world of reason and clocktime. Moise delivers a tirade against overpopulation, pollution, the arms race—but these concerns are not her element. Essentially she is a painter; the pigments and the canvas are her milieu, "not the words and the impossible letting of things" (p. 185). Her world thus becomes untenable when she runs out of art supplies. At the end of the tale, a great package of supplies is delivered ("an act of divine Providence") so that Moise can continue her work. She is thereby protected from the ravages of the outside world. Williams had remarked in the introduction to *A Streetcar Named Desire*, "It is only in his work that an artist can find reality and satisfaction." And Moise and the narrator also find love: two photographers enter, and Moise whispers, "I do believe we all belong in this room." That room is the world of love and creativity; it is for these that Tennessee Williams lives. *Moise* is not representative of Williams' talent as a fiction writer. The large output of short stories, along with his verse and drama, stand as personal testimony to that world of love and artistry.

Memoirs of Self-Indictment:
The Solitude of Tennessee Williams

S OME WILL SAY a book like Williams' *Memoirs* might well not be published; it seems so calculated to be honest that in its attempt to be brutally truthful it finally stands as a self-indictment, yet it is precisely as self-indictment that his unusual book has its value. Williams knew, as he wrote his volume of memories, just as Hemingway knew when he wrote the quiet lamentations of *A Moveable Feast*, that many would be shocked by a book such as this one. Yet now we see that Hemingway's reflective sketches are, in a sense, the coda to much of his fiction, writing which grew out of a troubled life, and it also appears that Williams' *Memoirs* has a similar value. Through this often disjointed book we can better understand the major theme of the author's writing, in his words, "the affliction of loneliness that follows me like my shadow, a very ponderous shadow too heavy to drag after me all of my days and nights ..." (p. 99). That loneliness, and the happiness which sometimes relieved it, a severe loneliness which gave birth to some of the most memorable plays of the last three decades, is recalled in these pages which trace the progression of his life as he wandered from Missouri to California to Key West and to Rome.

Williams' life might be described as a solitary quest for meaning which can be viewed as either a personal disaster or as the basis for much of his art. It is in fact both, and *Memoirs* provides informa-

663

tion about both personal loneliness and the distillation of that lone-liness into art. Many readers *must* find a book such as this disturbing; but it is ironic that readers should object to Williams' attempts to be honest. Williams realizes that it is the combination of many circumstances which have contributed to his life and art. In addition, he is intrigued with the fact that much of anyone's life can never be communicated to others; yet he seems convinced that if he confronts this difficulty he may be able at least to suggest the mystery of what it has meant for him to be an artist.

Williams' odyssey has been a progression into and through mad-ness, and we suspect that parts of his story are distorted because of the pain which must come with the retelling, but to read this honest account of loneliness produces a therapeutic effect upon the reader. We feel purged because Williams is willing to attempt honesty; and in seeing such an attempt to document *his* truth, to invent nothing, we are able to apprehend more clearly what it means to be an artist in modern America. In William Carlos Williams' *In the American Grain,* Poe is described as not an aberration, but the clear and logical product of his American society; and while many readers may not want to admit such a surprising fact, Williams is similarly the result of his contemporary America.[1] If, therefore, we read these *Memoirs* as the product of free associations, not wishing that its author had written a more finished book, it takes on a poignant significance. Above all, the *Memoirs* emphasizes Williams' separation from so much of what we imagine is American, yet simultaneously reminds us that such separation is the essence of being an artist in America. Further, in his isolation, perhaps better than those who do not realize they are alone, Williams sees and articulates what many must feel.

At the core of *Memoirs* is Williams' awareness of the disjunction between the public person (artist, lover, family member) and the private person. What Williams implies is that all use of language can only hint at the reality of living. As an artist who uses words he feels a responsibility to get as close to the truth as possible. This has to be a variety of the truth which is, to some degree, distorted in the remembrance and retelling. Williams' implication is that other printed records of his life, opinions, and public performances are also distorted; for such reasons he opens this book with an episode about a weekend he spent "at one of the last great country houses in

England." He explains that during the weekend he found a book entitled "*International Who's Who* or something of this sort," and he reports he was at first amused at the inaccuracy of the "considerable data upon that non-existent personage who bears . . . [his] professional name," but he continues, "the data contained a number of harmless inaccuracies but one of those inaccuracies was distinctly unfortunate in its effect upon my humor." He then notes how the facts listed in *Who's Who* indicated that during one of the years before the success of *The Glass Menagerie* he had been given a thousand dollar grant from the National Institute of Arts and Letters, while in fact that was a period when no grants were forthcoming. That was a time, he muses, when he had to hock "literally everything." Williams remembers: "it was the year when I was bounced from lodging to lodging for nonpayment of rent . . . when I had to go out on the street to bum a cigarette, that absolutely essential cigarette that a living and smoking writer must have to start work in the morning." Williams also notes that he has journals which prove the specifics of his recollections, and he ironically adds that he is now even "a tolerated member" of the very institute which theoretically had given him the grant (pp. 1–2). What Williams wants his reader to appreciate is that his life is finally quite different from any "facts" printed as a public record. In the memoirs, which are admittedly egocentric, Williams provides additional data to help set some of the record straight. Clearly, he would be willing to admit that a part of his motivation is a variety of egomania, but such self-centeredness is justified if we assume, as Williams does, that there are many varieties of truth.

The plays are Williams' legacy from his generation, but this volume of memoirs was composed in seriousness, and it too merits our attention. At times, the memoirs seem to be a dialogue of the writer with himself; and more often than not, questions are raised instead of answers found. Three types of readers might be drawn to the book: specialists seeking particular access to the plays; general readers who want basic information about Williams in relation to the dramas; and, lastly, those who may be interested in this document as a variety of revelation about what it means to be an artist, like Williams, in modern America. The specialist will probably find scattered specialized items that will allow him to fill in gaps; the general readers will, more than anything else, be puzzled by the remembrances here; expectations will hardly be fulfilled for either of these varieties of readers since Williams provides so little specific information either about his craft or about his own judgments concerning the plays. Such information is, of course, already much more clearly available through interviews and critical writing. For those who see this recollection as a document which clarifies aspects of what it means to be a poet today, the book (while sometimes frightening, and even poorly written) has a clear value because it reveals how Williams thinks about himself; and while such thoughts may in retrospect be distorted, the general pattern revealed is significant.

Much Williams recalls about his life emphasizes the loneliness basic to the frustrations of living and the impossibility of ever communicating such loneliness. Driven in his life, and in these memoirs, to a variety of exhibitionism which can be shocking, Williams' recollections simultaneously possess a quality of honesty which we have to admire. We must assume through the evidence of frequent use of ellipses marks in the text, as well as through press notices, that the complete manuscript for this book (edited for publication) would be even more revealing. Williams has blamed the "seeming preoccupation" in the memoirs on his publisher "for deleting other material and distorting the book's balance."[2]

What the criteria are for the editorial omissions in Williams' manuscript cannot be determined until the complete manuscript is available. But in over fifty places in the book ellipses mar the text. Some of the ellipses marks may be for stylistic effect, but since Williams definitely feels all his experience is one web, we must conclude that his complete text could be more informative and (perhaps) even more entertaining. Possibly the publisher has often insisted on omissions as a matter of taste or out of fear of libel; but the amount of cutting when Williams recalls details about his family (see pp. 39, 147, 241) or his philosophy of art (see pp. 99, 173, 243) suggests he may have had more to say but that an editorial decision ruled out some details. It is true that Williams is no systematic philosopher, and he has few answers to the enigma of his life and art; but it is also true that his readers are not well served by a book which has been cut frequently. If it was necessary to omit many of Williams' personal comments about friends and associates who have fallen into his disfavor (or the reverse), in a book built on free associations all unnecessary omissions make the total picture cloudier than it might be otherwise.

As noted, the method of the memoirs is a therapeutic one, for Williams notes: the "book is written by something like the process of 'free association,' which I learned to practice during my several periods of psychoanalysis." He admits the facts he deals with include matters both trivial and significant, but he stresses that all have taken on importance for him. He also notes that in the process of composition, his manuscript took on a significance which had not before existed within merely the realm of the potential. Williams admits he began the book "for mercenary reasons," but adds that once he got into the writing of the book he "forgot the financial angle and became more and more pleasurably involved in this [for him] new form, undisguised self-revelation" (p. xviii). The resulting book is one organized around personal, not professional, concerns. The title is colorless, yet collectively these memories reveal much of what Williams has suffered. He mentions his friend José Quintero's volume of memoirs, and notes he was so enchanted by the title *If You Don't Dance They Beat You* that he considered changing the title of his own book to suggest the same idea (p. 202). Precisely in such minor revelations the book has its cumulative effect. And cumulatively Williams implies throughout these recollections that he realizes how his career forced him to keep producing and competing. Such competition is wrong, he feels, and in the long run destructive. Williams' life is, by many American standards, a success, but to be that successful he drove himself into poor health and insanity. Such is the life of the artist in America. The observation sounds like a cliché, but we would do well to listen.

One fact that emerges from this recollection is that much of Williams' career has been spent isolated from others—not that he did not have encouraging fellow artists and friends, especially as he remembers his earliest days; but finally what he has accomplished as an artist was done alone. Williams insists that when he was first infatuated with the theater he "knew and associated" with many other young artists, but while he insists that during those years there was a community, his choice of metaphor betrays his basic method of thinking: he remembers friends, but also remembers how each disregarded "the small craft warnings in the face of which we were continually sailing . . . each with his crew of one, himself that crew and its captain . . . in our separate small crafts but . . . in sight of each other and sometimes in touch. I mean like huddling in the same inlet of the rock, storm-ridden shoreline, and this gave us a warm sense of community" (p. 2). Such "community" may have existed during the earliest parts of Williams' career, yet it is not clear exactly how it existed; and when we read his recollections of those earliest years, what seems most memorable is that what he learned best to do as artist was accomplished apart from others, and especially in isolation from other artists.

Apparently his life had to become his most basic material. The artistic shaping came with solitude. Still another significant fact about Williams' literary career supported by the *Memoirs* is that with just a few striking exceptions his drama cannot easily be assigned clear influences. Williams is not a writer who easily assimilates other writers. He mentions contemporaries with whom he has rubbed elbows; but he seldom mentions books he has read. He acknowledges his admiration of writers such as Chekhov, Lawrence, Jane Bowles, and Carson McCullers; yet apparently it is only with Lawrence that we can clearly trace "influence." Williams' personal life is, it seems, to an almost extreme degree the raw material for his dramas, and it is because of this that the memoirs are of definite value. They document the difficulty of maintaining one's artistic integrity when by circumstance (of family and culture, of personalities and society) one chooses to write while one has also been separated from so many traditional forms of community.

Some of the actions of Williams recounted in this book, so publicly atrocious and embarrassingly frank, seem, almost unconsciously, to have been calculated to guarantee his insularity from much of America, and much of even the theatergoing public. Williams certainly understands this, and as he retrospectively looks at his life and the dilemma of, as his old friend Gore Vidal once put it, "too much bad personal exposure for anything to help . . . much anymore," he admits "In a way, it does seem that I have almost asked for it." He admits overtly and through the incidents he includes in the memoirs that he desires the "understanding" and "empathy" of a favorable critical response, but he also realizes he is "quite through with the kind of play that established my early and popular reputation." He also stresses that his artistic aim has always been "my world and my experience of it in whatever form seems suitable to the material" (p. xvii). As a writer, he says, he has no other choice. Yet he also believes the circumstances of his life, especially since writing *The Night of the Iguana*, have demanded a less traditional style of writing. Such a conviction accounts for the "rather unusual structure" of what Williams finally comes to call "this 'thing,'" his memoir, a memoir which sometimes seems like a confession.

The cumulative contents of Williams' "thing" emphasize his awareness of the simple fact that the reality of his life will never be communicated to others. Some parts of the life have been distilled into stories, poems, and the plays, but much remains only in memory. Williams chooses to reveal many of the particular circumstances of his life, not that he hopes to set the record completely straight (he is much too tolerant for that) but so that he can suggest how inaccurate any record is. The contents of the memoir are, occasionally, frightening, but the violence represented there does have definite justification. Above all, Williams seems to say, "See my mistakes, and do otherwise." We are reminded of the earlier "Preface" to *Sweet Bird of Youth*, where he speculated that "if there is any truth in the Aristotelian idea that violence is purged by its poetic representation on a stage, then it may be that my cycle of violent plays have had a moral justification. . . . I know that I have felt it. I have always felt a release from the sense of meaninglessness and death when a work of tragic intention has seemed to me to have achieved that intention" (IV, 7). What he implies in the *Memoirs* is that he understands man must struggle and that it is the duty of the artist to reflect that constant struggle. *Memoirs* therefore reflects the writer's personal struggle, especially during the last many years when "the circumstances of my life have demanded . . . a continually less traditional style of dramatic writing" (p. xviii).

Parts of this book seem to function like a journal, or letter written to intimates; other parts are like a cry in a crowd, or an obscene gesture in a room full of people. Williams insists his life has been "a life full of rented rooms" (p. 139), but he also emphasizes his conviction that "one should not refer to one's life as a sad hotel when it has often been a merry tavern," and he adds, "it is quite dishonest to pretend one is eager to vacate it" (p. 202). We should accept such statements at face value because like the plays this recollection of episodes from the life is instruction, a lesson in how difficult it is to "make it" in the theater, especially when one is continually expected to go beyond oneself. Strangely, but not surprisingly, a basic emphasis throughout *Memoirs* is upon how Williams has continued to write even while his goal as writer was not always completely clear. He began to write at age eleven or twelve, just about the time, he recalls, when he and his sister were introduced to "The malign exercise of snobbery in 'middle American' life," an introduction provided (in his opinion) by the snobbery of his own mother. He suggests that his early story telling "was a compensation, perhaps . . ." (Williams' ellipsis, p. 14).

For some years, until he was twenty-four, Williams did dull work for a wholesale shoe company; but his health was already bad, and when he had a heart attack he quickly made the transition to serious writer. His account of his 1934 *Cairo, Shanghai, Bombay!* manifests his attitude about much of that early writing and his subsequent career, a marriage: he and the theater "found each other for better and for worse" (p. 42). Similarly, an account of a hotel party in 1937, after the critics had attacked his *Fugitive Kind*, suggests an intensity which had developed with his devotion to writing. This episode is also an example of the type of remembrance which may be distorted in the retelling, but the essence of Williams' often disturbing life is reflected in this prose: *Fugitive Kind* "was a much better and more promising play than the first long play, *Candles to the Sun*, but the critics put it down. Afterward there was a desperately drunk party in someone's downtown hotel room. I made a sudden dash for a window but was tackled and cannot say reliably whether or not it was my intention to jump.

The point is that I already knew that writing was my life, and its failure would be my death . . ." (p. 44).

The general progression of Williams' life and writing is marked by a continuation of a similar desperate yearning for success or, if not that, oblivion. Thus, his wanderings (in the sense Gertrude Stein used the word to describe Melanctha) and his loves, writing, and frustrations, his sanity and his madness are recalled here as of one fabric. He even notes explicitly: "What is my profession but living and putting it all down in stories and plays and now in this book?" (p. 161). (This attempt to "put down" one's living may account for the type of materials in *Memoirs*, materials sometimes, without a doubt, in poor taste. It might well be argued that not only has Williams' editor encouraged distortion through omissions, but that still other problems have been introduced because of the often repetitive recapitulation of sexual escapades, even if such details do help us understand Williams' fears and needs.) One thing is, above all, clear to him: without the persons who in so many ways sustained him throughout his life he could not have written anything, and surely not the plays.

Like most artists Williams seems to have been driven to his writing partly as an escape from a private world. This is certainly the way he began his writing career in the 1930s. The memoirs stress his realization of how for him life and art blend. He recalls an essay which accompanies some editions of *Cat on a Hot Tin Roof*, where he elaborates his goal in writing: "Somehow to capture the constantly evanescent quality of existence" (p. 84). Yet throughout this volume of memoirs Williams insists that in his art he was seldom able to accomplish such a goal, to bring about a successful blending. Critics have pointed out that Williams' best work can be conceived of as imagistic in method, moments caught which suggest the essence of living.[3] What should be noticed is that apparently many of the incidents recalled in *Memoirs* are also such fleeting images. Although he must apologize for many of the remembrances as recollections of trivia and "amatory activities" (p. 87), the author views all these fleeting moments and relations as finally crucial parts of the life, a life which made his art possible.

The same might be said of the facts of madness and hospitalization, experiences which have made it nearly impossible to produce successful art. Yet even the time in "Friggins Division of Barnacle Hospital in the City of St. Pollution" (p. 220), the embarrassment of remembering what one did there, helps Williams to realize he did have the strength to survive. He comments: "However dreadful they were at the time of their occurrence, there are incidents and characters whom you recall, at a safe distance, with a shocked amusement," as he recalls a "great, monolithic black woman" whom he would see in the dayroom of the hospital. She would compliment him, "'You're so sweet. . . .'" But then one day she took a swing at him "that would have flattened me on the floor had she not swung off target" (p. 225). This incident was later incorporated in *Stopped Rocking*, a television special which Williams did, and what he suggests by recalling the episode outlined in *Memoirs* is that all survive as best they can. It is appropriate that this particular episode is also surrounded by other remembrances about his immediate family who cared for him during the period of hospitalization. He is both embarrassed and angered when he recalls how he lashed out at his mother and his brother, but such verbal striking out was also a form of survival.

Williams' depression and mental collapse were, he notes, directly related to his loss of Frank Merlo. Succinctly, Williams insists: "As long as Frank was well, I was happy. He had a gift for creating a life and, when he ceased to be alive, I couldn't create a life for myself. So I went into a seven-year depression" (p. 194). Such revelation is surprising, but it is honest, and finally moving as well. In fact, one of the most moving aspects of this work is Williams' honest admission of his love for Frank Merlo. Merlo was one of the most important single influences in Williams' life, and it is certain, as Williams puts it, that Frankie "sustained . . . [his] life" (p. 195). The loss of Merlo was, Williams realizes, the loss of his greatest support. When he says he cannot now bear to look at the "enlarged passport photo which stares at me from the back of the writing desk," and adds he turns it "face down among the pages of my poem 'Old Men Go Mad at Night'" (p. 227), we are forced to respect the inclusion of such trivia to reveal the important basic patterns of his life.[4] The same might be said for the references to his family, most especially his mother, "Miss Edwina," and his sister Rose. By no accident the book ends with an extended recollection of his relationship with his sister, long a patient in a mental institution. He too has been there.

A general pattern about the life revealed here includes Williams' realization and admission of his self-destructive tendencies, a self-destructiveness which has literally ruined his health, as well as many relationships with others. Yet what he also implies, although he does not approve of the reactions of some friends and family members, is that he realizes he still needs love. Perhaps for such reasons he often writes so fondly of his grandfather.

One could make a catalogue of the bizarre things Williams records in *Memoirs* (or make a list of all the drugs he has taken), but all such surface events, items of his disintegration, are only "trivia" "to be set down in the record of one's life."[5] Much more significant is what is implied; an expression of the need for others seems to be the crucial underlying theme.

The real value of this strange document exists in what is implied in it as a record of an artist's struggle to achieve form from a life which has been largely chaotic. For example, when he recalls his love for his sister we can better appreciate the process of creating fiction from the facts of their lives, facts transformed to make both "Portrait of a Girl in Glass" and *Menagerie*. Through art, mysteries become clearer; to write of his sister is to write of a complexity which can be observed but not understood; but it is also to find "release" (see pp. 55, 58, 59 for other examples of how Williams' life provided material for the art). One lives the inexplicable; then writes of it. Williams is haunted by remembrances of his sister, Rose, but he finally must state to his reader: "you don't know Miss Rose and you never will unless you come to know her through this 'thing,' for Laura of *Menagerie* was like Miss Rose only in her inescapable 'difference,' which that old female bobcat Amanda would not believe existed" (p. 125). What he implies is that even a person who is closest to him is never understood. Such mystery can only be hinted.

When Williams' own life fell apart in the sixties, his "stoned age," it was, he says, like "a slow-motion photo of a building being demolished by dynamite: it occurred in protracted stages, but the protraction gave it no comfort" (p. 203). What we finally have in this "thing" is the writer's realization that he must now continue living without many of the things and, more important, persons that had earlier sustained him. In this respect it has to be a very sad book, and one could wish that Williams had not insisted on spelling out so much; but he gives us a clear view of facets of American life, and such facts of life, not always pretty, make it possible for any artist to write at all. Williams wants to give his readers as direct and complete a picture of the life as possible. He cannot be concerned that the result of the *Memoirs* is to provide a variety of self-indictment. Related to this kind of revelation, and still another significant aspect of the volume, is its collection of one hundred and forty-four photographs, many with captions apparently written by Williams. The

photos of family and friends function like the varied isolated remembrances and recollections, for they give us additional access to moments of significance and Williams' memory of those earlier years.
These too are only fragments, but together with the words spun out
by Williams they reflect facets of the complexity of his life, which
became the basis for some of the most significant drama written in
the twentieth century. Williams' lonely recollections are ultimately
not just a self-indictment but also an indictment of the culture as a
whole. His story is but an extreme version of many.

Memoirs can profitably be compared to the school of poetry which
Robert Lowell helped establish in modern America, that of the confessional poets. While many readers of conventional poetry are
startled at the change of emphasis in Lowell's poetry, or the lack of
reticence in a poet like Anne Sexton, a growing body of opinion
reflects the conviction that if such poetry is painful in its treatment
of a writer's sense of a loss or awareness of a vacuum within modern
life, such poems also have great value because they do honestly confront the emptiness of modern life. If good is to come of the suffering
reflected in so much of modern literature, logically rebirth can come
about only when the culture is willing to admit its losses. Out of the
dislocation which has affected so many, lessons can be learned.

At one point Williams recalls that his friend Jane Bowles told
him he was "never much of a conversationalist," and then he relates
that her statement, which was in answer to a confession of his that
he found it difficult to speak, made him laugh. Her answer, he recalls,
to his "anguished confession" "was a relief for a while" (p. 187).
This incident helps us to focus on all of *Memoirs;* throughout the
book Williams admits his deficiencies and acknowledges his needs
with a sense of humor. Such confrontation with the truth is what
makes art possible. Williams tells us, by the way, that the summer
in Tangier which occasioned this remark by his friend has been
described in the poem "The Speechless Summer" (p. 187).

Williams cannot use theological language when he describes his
own life and drifting, and in the light of what he does say within his
recollections it would be incorrect to impute theological meaning to
the losses he reports. But clearly implied throughout his "thing" is
both the sense of a loss of contact with a community of believers and
an intense respect for life and the duties of the artist who mirrors

that life. Thus, the book Williams gives us as *Memoirs* laments his personal losses but, in its sometimes abundant detail, documents a continued quest for ways to bring about wholeness.

Notes to Victor Kramer,
"Memoirs of Self-Indictment:
The Solitude of Tennessee Williams"

1. William Carlos Williams begins his essay with the statement: "Poe was not a 'fault of nature,' 'a find for French eyes,' ripe but unaccountable . . . but a genius intimately shaped by his locality and time. It is to save our faces that we've given him a crazy reputation, a writer from whose classic accuracies we have not known how else to escape." The complete essay is of value in an appraisal of Tennessee Williams; significantly the essay includes the following sentences near its conclusion: "Had he lived in a world where love throve, his poems might have grown differently. But living where he did, surrounded as he was by that world of unreality, a formless 'population' —terror possessed him." *In the American Grain* (New York: New Directions, 1956), pp. 216, 233.

2. *The Atlanta Constitution*, 11 February, 1976, p. 8-B.

3. Esther Merle Jackson provides a good defense of Williams' method in *The Broken World of Tennessee Williams* (Madison: The University of Wisconsin Press, 1966). See especially, pp. 26–42, "Williams and the Lyric Movement."

4. Cf. "Old Men Are Fond," *In the Winter of Cities*, p. 122.

5. The fact that this book is full of names and references is enhanced by a detailed index that runs to twelve full pages. While so much of the book is anecdotal, the cross-references connect themes which range from alcohol to family, from mental health to relationships with his literary agents.

Techniques

Judith Thompson uses Williams' concept of symbols to study the technique and the purpose of some of his plays. The author explains the multileveled use of myth as a design to reenact in the play the basic story of the play, in a sense a doubled use of the same myth. But Williams' technique is complex as well as ironic, she feels, and an amazing number of allusions is implied in the symbolism—ranging from classical myth to comic-book characters. By a process of what the author calls mythicization, characters gradually take on a great many symbols of which a part of the action and purpose of the play is to divest them, leaving them as mere disillusioned and ordinary creatures facing reality. David Matthew approaches this theory in his discussion of *Battle* and *Orpheus* (in PLAYS) as does Diane Turner in discussing *Camino Real* in the same section.

Gerald Berkowitz examines Williams' use of the old fictional technique of setting the action in a foreign land, creating a setting that makes the strange acceptable because it happens "elsewhere." The technique is particularly important for Williams (and effective, in the author's opinion) because the playwright thereby encourages audiences and readers to accept the numerous oddities of character and action in the plays. The discussion leads to a reconsideration of *A Streetcar Named Desire*.

Charles Brooks some years ago outlined the comic aspects of *The Rose Tattoo*, *Cat on a Hot Tin Roof*, and *A Streetcar Named Desire*, to conclude that Williams' comic vitality was marred by sentimentalism (see bibliography). This new essay examines the various facets of Williams' comedy, the satire and the use of traditional comic types, and shows the complexity of characterization that derives from a mixture of comic elements with other characteristics.

Leonard Casper discerns a technique "constructed of triangles," as he says, that Williams uses in his plays. The idea here is used,

677

among other purposes, to interpret *Kingdom of Earth* and *The Milk Train Doesn't Stop Here Anymore*. In Williams, the technique serves in varied ways for various purposes.

James Hafley feels that Williams' language is one of his main contributions to *theater*. The author's examples, references to performances and learned comparisons with other outstanding playwrights help substantiate his claim. A discussion of some of the words Williams repeatedly uses leads toward a discussion of themes.

William Scheick finds that numerous references to talking and touching as means of physical communication indicate critics have oversimplified Williams' view on the relationship of flesh and spirit. His analysis of Nonno's poem leads the author to trace his theme through numerous plays and to study Williams' use of mirrors.

Albert Kalson's unusual essay begins with a discussion of the many references to movies and moviegoing, both of which Williams uses for various purposes. The author moves on to a study of the influence of specific movies in several plays and to a discussion of Williams' use of literal motion picture techniques. Well-chosen examples and perceptive comments make the essay much more than a study of a limited and specialized topic.

Norman Fedder's unassuming title heads an essay that severely assesses Williams as a working playwright. But the author also gives Williams credit for what he has done in creating dialogue and generally adding to the repertory of American theater. The author is himself in theater, and his is another essay that studies matters beyond the range of his topic.

Symbol, Myth, and Ritual in
The Glass Menagerie, The Rose Tattoo,
and *Orpheus Descending*

JUDITH J. THOMPSON

IN "FOREWORD" TO *Camino Real,* Tennessee Williams says "symbols are nothing but the natural speech of drama" (II, 421). According to C. G. Jung, a symbol is "a term, a name, or even a picture that may be familiar in daily life, yet that possesses specific connotations in addition to its conventional and obvious meaning. . . . It has a wider 'unconscious" aspect that is never precisely defined or fully explained" (*Man and his Symbols,* pp. 3–4). Williams' belief in the evocative value of symbols closely resembles Jung's theories of the "collective unconscious," that second psychic system of a "collective, universal, and impersonal nature which is identical in all individuals" (*Portable Jung,* p. 60). As Williams notes, "We all have in our conscious and unconscious minds a great vocabulary of images, and I think all human communication is based on these images as are our dreams" (II, 421). Based on familiar religious, mythical, and literary associations, Williams' symbols tap the emotional depths of the collective unconscious with its store of "archetypes," those "mental forms . . . which seem to be aboriginal, innate, and inherited shapes of the human mind" (*Man and his Symbols,* p. 57).

Williams' dramatic use of universally evocative symbols derives from his concept of and concern with the interrelationship of the

679

playwright, the audience, and the play. He characterizes himself as one of those playwrights "permitted only to feel" (II, 423). Creative motivation, he believes, has its source in "the particular and sometimes peculiar concerns of the artist himself" (III, 3). Williams is keenly aware, however, that the unique nature of individual consciousness both defines the ego and serves as a barrier separating the self from the other, to the extent that "We're all of us sentenced to solitary confinement inside our own skins" (III, 3). Thus, in his *Playboy* interview, Williams identifies "loneliness" as his major and recurrent theme (p. 76). Not content simply to dramatize this fundamental condition of human existence, Williams offers his theater as a kind of corrective for it. He attests to "a highly personal, even intimate relationship with people who go to see plays" (III, 5), and conceives of his plays as vehicles through which he works toward an embrace with the audience. Describing his dramatic mode as "personal lyricism," he seeks to elicit from an audience that "outcry of prisoner to prisoner from the cell in solitary where each is confined for the duration of his life" (III, 3): a cri de coeur intended to purge the individual of personal loneliness by his recognition of and participation in the suffering of his fellow isolato.

The fundamental theatrical concern of Williams, then, is to transform his personal emotions, as they are embodied in the particular and sometimes peculiar maladies, neuroses, and illusions of his characters, into recognizably universal feelings. He would rise "above the singular to the plural concern, from personal to general import" (III, 4). Through the communal associations provided by mythical symbols and ritual patterns, Williams attempts to create in his audience an empathetic response to his characterizations of the lonely, the neurotic, the alienated, and persecuted, thereby evoking that shock of recognition by which the audience acknowledges as familiar the characters' psychic conflicts. As Williams describes the experience, "Our hearts are wrung by recognition and pity, so that the dusky shell of the auditorium where we are gathered anonymously together is flooded with an almost liquid warmth of unchecked human sympathies, relieved of self-consciousness, allowed to function . . ." (II, 262). A major function of Williams' symbols, then, is to form an emotional bridge with the audience, to create a drama so emotionally charged with the concrete universals of archetypal images that their realization breaks down the psychological walls of our separate selves, making the particular general, the strange familiar, and even the grotesque recognizable as but another dimension of the human condition.

Two types of symbols, concrete and transcendent, are used by Williams to evoke this communal response. Concrete symbols embody the psychic reality of the characters in substantial sensory forms, which appeal to the emotions through the physical senses, visual and aural. The subjective world of the characters is thus displayed on stage by the constructs or props of the set, by the significant gestures and movements of the actors, by the sounds of music, often the lyrical, staccato, or antiphonal rhythms of speech itself, and by the effects of light and color. They constitute what T. S. Eliot has defined as the "objective correlatives" of states of mind or feeling, that "set of objects, a situation, a chain of events which shall be the formula of that particular emotion; such that when the external facts . . . are given, the emotion is immediately evoked" (pp. 124–5). Thus, the objective correlatives of a character's wounded psyche may reside in the furniture of the stage set: Laura Wingfield's arrested development in the old-fashioned knick-knack case filled with tiny glass animals, Serafina Delle Rose's repressed sexuality in an urn set in front of a small shrine, Alma Winemiller's frigidity in the form of a massive stone angel, or Shannon's infantile regression in a centrally placed canvas hammock. The emotions of nostalgia or memories of lost innocence may be evoked through music or by the uninhibited voices of children at play; the recurrent bleating of the unleashed goat in The Rose Tattoo reminds us of the necessity of fulfilling the physical present, while the "constant, dry, scuffling sound" of a lizard tied under a porch in The Night of the Iguana evokes the frustrations of unfulfilled desires. A character's futile attempt to recapture the past may be embodied in his costume: in Amanda's yellowed dress and her bouquet of jonquils, in Brick Pollitt's bathrobe and crutch, in Serafina's outgrown girdle, or in the defrocked Shannon's clerical collar that will not stay buttoned. Finally, a character's consciousness may be indicated by nuances of lighting, the rose-colored or shuttered light of dusk and very early daybreak embodying his dreams or fixation with the past, while brief moments of radiance may symbolize his confrontation with the present. These techniques, often used simultaneously, create an atmosphere in which the objective correlatives of the psychic wounds of the characters continuously bombard the senses and stimulate an intensely sympathetic response.

The symbols of transcendence are allusive rather than sensory; they are drawn from religious, mythical, and literary sources rather than from the phenomena of objective reality. Most significant, their function is not to anchor the psychic reality of the character in corresponding sensory forms, but to enlarge and expand our consciousness of his subjective world beyond the time and space of the particular dramatic situation of the play. The nature and pattern of these symbols and their significance to *The Glass Menagerie*, *The Rose Tattoo*, and *Orpheus Descending* are the main concerns of this essay.

One of the most significant functions of these symbols is to give a mythic dimension or stature to the characters. Williams has said, "All my *great* characters are larger than life, not realistic" (*Playboy*, p. 80). One purpose for making his characters larger than life is to universalize the particular and the peculiar, to find those analogues or archetypes in myth, legend, or fairy tale that will tap the collective unconscious and give archetypal meaning to personal plight. Williams rarely makes a one-to-one identification of a character with a mythical archetype, however, for his purpose is not narrowly allegorical but allusive. His characters are made larger than life through a method of multiple images (see Jackson, *Broken World*, pp. 83–5). Each is a composite figure drawn from fragments of pagan and Christian prototypes and their diminutive forms in fairy tale and comic strips. By using both romantic and ironic modes in characterization, Williams stresses the illusory nature of the character's mythic or godlike stature. Thus, Rosario in *The Rose Tattoo* is a composite of the Dionysian god, the popular film star Valentino, and the lecherous goat. Maggie in *Cat on a Hot Tin Roof* is both Diana, goddess of the hunt, the moon, and nature, and "a cat in heat." The diverse images surrounding Chance Wayne in *Sweet Bird of Youth* include those of Adonis, the god of fertility (see Hays, pp. 255–258), Jack and the Beanstalk, a Christ figure, and an aging romance knight. Thus, even as Williams symbolizes the illusions, delusions, and romantic aspirations of his characters to transcend their human limitations, he continually invokes their instinctual animal nature and the flesh-and-blood needs which keep them earthbound.

The method by which Williams invests his characters with mythic dimensions is the story or recollection of the past, told usually by the protagonist about himself, at the beginning of each of these three plays. This story is often an elevated or exaggerated memory of an event or a relationship, invested with idyllic, romantic, or religious overtones. It is because of this memory, usually a vision of intense beauty, that the protagonists are often frozen or transfixed in the posture or attitude of looking backward, their emotional growth arrested, and their human dimensions inflated with romantic illusions of a once perfect condition.

Furthermore, the story itself is retold or dramatized in the course of the play. In essence, the dramatic events of the second half of each play are a reenactment of the story told at its beginning. Thus, Amanda's story of the seventeen gentlemen callers is reenacted by Laura and Jim in *The Glass Menagerie*; Serafina's idealized account of her transcendent relationship with her husband Rosario is reenacted by Serafina and Alvaro in *The Rose Tattoo*; the story of idyllic love and fertility in the wine garden between Lady Torrance and David Cutrere is reenacted by Lady with Val Xavier in *Orpheus Descending*. The recurrent structure of a story told, then reenacted in a second version, is in itself an analogue of myth and ritual. The personal story assumes the dimensions of myth, its reenactment a ritual which parallels the events of the myth. However, unlike the ancient myths and rituals of initiation, fertility, and rebirth or resurrection which these stories suggest, the second version of the original story in Williams' plays rarely culminates in the celebration of fulfilled or realized aspirations.

The diminished myth or unsuccessful ritual which is reenacted reveals as ironic the relationship of mythic symbolism to character, theme, and structure in these plays. In short, Williams invests his characters with mythic stature only to divest them of it in the process of the play. The climax of each play, then, rests in an event of demythicization: that moment when the character is divested of his mythic or godlike dimensions, stripped of his illusions and delusions, and forced to recognize his human limitations, his animal instincts, and his inherently antiheroic nature. Furthermore, the symbolic moment of divestment is generally dramatized through the gesture of breaking, rending, or shattering the concrete symbol which has been identified as the objective correlative of the character's psychic reality. Thus, Jim's breaking of Laura's unicorn in *The Glass Menagerie*, Serafina's shattering the urn of Rosario in *The Rose Tattoo*, Mitch's tearing Blanche's paper lantern from the naked light bulb in *A Streetcar Named Desire*, Shannon's freeing the iguana in *The Night of the Iguana*, Maggie's disposal of Brick's crutch and liquor bottles in *Cat on a Hot Tin Roof*, the crash of the suitcase filled with Casanova's mementos and the literal stripping away of Marguerite's clothes in *Camino Real* are all symbolic acts which divest the characters of their mythic dimensions, deflate their romantic illusions, and force them to confront a diminished or impoverished reality. Paradoxically, it is this moment which generally affords the character the opportunity to assume a new, more fully human, stature, in the expression of love, sympathy, or compassion with another. But for those who cannot or will not accept their self-limitations or the compromise of their mythic world, their lost Eden, the result is destruction or withdrawal.

Williams' plays do not simply recall the old mythic images and religious rituals; they transform them in their reenactment. Many of his plays are based on myths of dying gods, but, unlike the original myth, they culminate in neither rebirth nor resurrection. His drama is structured as ritual, but as a ritual of the divestment of illusion, or as a parody of the romantic quest, whose ironic destination is what Northrop Frye calls the *tour abolie*, archetypal image of "the goal of the quest that isn't there" (p. 239). Thus, Williams constructs from the old myths and rituals new meanings relevant to an age and culture bereft of a commonly shared mythology. Seeking to restore symbolic meaning to the life of modern man, Williams offers a theatrical experience intended to encourage our investing symbolic significance and value in merely human relationships, however limited and compensatory they might seem. In its sympathetic portrayal of our yearnings for transcendence, its realistic depiction of our inherent limitations, and its utter insistence on the necessity of imbuing with religious significance the rare and transient communion of man with his fellow, Williams' drama is a myth for our time.

The Glass Menagerie is one of Williams' most symbolically informed plays. The symbols—concrete, allusive, and evocative—are so structured as to define a world which is at once existentially constrictive and metaphorically expansive. Even as the physical constructs of time and circumstance identify the characters by their human limitations, the metaphors through which their aspirations are expressed enlarge their individual dimensions to those of archetypal stature and elevate their personal plight to universal significance.

The principal symbol in the play is, as the title suggests, the glass menagerie. It is specifically Laura's symbol, the objective correlative of her fragile, other-worldly beauty. Its stylized animal forms image her own immobilized animal or sexual nature, her arrested emotional development, and her inability to cope with the demands of a flesh-and-blood world. Given broader implications, the separate pieces of the glass collection reflect the fixed attitudes of all the members of the Wingfield family as well as their isolation from one another. Presented as crystallized forms in Tom's memory, each character is shown to be psychologically encased in a world of his own. Seeking escape, refuge, or rebirth, each imagines different versions of a transcendent reality, themselves a collection of isolatos condemned to individual fragmentation and mutual misunderstanding. Finally, in its quintessential form, the glass menagerie is symbolic of stasis, that temporal mode central to the play's internal structure. The underlying structure of *The Glass Menagerie* is formed by a tension between the illusion of moving forward and the reality of moving backward, between dream and destiny, the two so perfectly balanced that the effect is the arrest of time. Within this frozen moment, however, resides the significant action of the play: a cyclical motion of repetition and recurrence, the acting out again and again of a single futile pattern.

The dynamic symbol of that recurrent pattern is Amanda's story of the courtship ritual, herein an ironic process of anticipation, momentary fulfilment, and subsequent loss, desolation, and disillusionment. As symbol, the story of Amanda and her seventeen gentlemen callers forms a paradigm of experience which underlies the structure of the entire play. Life is envisioned as a series of losses, beginning with innocent expectations of its infinite possibilities and ending in confrontation with its inherent limitations. It is, indeed, this story told by Amanda at the beginning of the play which is re-enacted in its second half by Laura and Jim. Furthermore, every other event in the play repeats the process. A similar pattern of great expectations and subsequent despair informs the story of Tom, the aspiring poet whose dreams of life as a meaningful voyage end only in aimless drifting. Although Jim's ability to compromise with a diminished reality differentiates him from the other characters, the pattern also informs his story, for he is the high school hero—"The Pirate of Penzance"—who is reduced to a clerk in a warehouse, his romantic libretto exchanged for a paean to capitalistic enterprise. The pattern of anticipation, brief fulfilment, and subsequent loss is capsulized at the very beginning of the play in the message contained in the father's picture postcard: "Hello—Goodbye!" (I, 145), a microcosmic summary of the play's symbolic structure.

A symbolic embodiment of the last of the gentlemen callers, the father is present throughout the play in the image of a larger-than-life-size photograph which lights up whenever Amanda recalls him, thereby reminding the audience of the entire pattern of her story, from its inflated beginnings to its prosaic end. The inevitability of the pattern is reinforced by implied analogies among the three male figures. As the suitor with the winning smile, the father is linked with Jim, the reincarnated gentleman caller, who shares his charm and grin. As the deserting husband, he is linked with Tom, the prodigal son, who shares his escapist impulse. All three embody the romantic concept of war as heroic adventure in their respective roles of World War I doughboy, make-believe pirate, and merchant seaman. Moreover, Jim's romantic stage role as the Pirate of Penzance in Gilbert and Sullivan's comic opera both foreshadows and mocks Tom's dream of playing a similarly romantic role by joining the Merchant Marines. Thus, Jim's stage symbol, the image of "a sailing vessel with Jolly Roger" (pp. 173, 200)—the black flag of the pirate ship—is flashed on the screen whenever *Tom* dreams of his maritime adventure, a subliminal undermining of Tom's transcendent aspirations. Even in their family name, juxtaposing *wing* with *field*, the symbols of transcendence are fused with the constructs of mundane reality, relentlessly suggesting the painful disparity between aspiration and actuality, or between what the characters would be and what they must be.

The tension between the ideal and the real is also exemplified in the religious imagery which ironically links both the members of this fragmented household and the romanticized Jim to the Christian Holy Family. The incongruity of superimposing the images of Christian archetypes of love and sacrifice onto pathetically inadequate representatives painfully emphasizes modern man's loss of that original mythic union between heaven and earth, the divine and the human, spirit and flesh. At the same time, it poignantly reveals a continued yearning for redemption from a world devoid of spiritually transcendent values. Thus, the intensity of Amanda's disappointment with Laura's failure to fulfill her expectations at Rubicam's Business College suggests her analogy to "the picture of Jesus' mother in the museum" (p. 155), the mater dolorosa of Christian art, image of martyred maternity. Laura herself evokes the image of saint, nun, or child of God whose relics, the profane collection of her father's phonograph records, assume the miraculous function of creating a harmonious sanctuary in which her crippled psyche is momentarily healed of the wounds incurred in a discordant reality. The All-American Jim is elevated to a Christ figure or savior, the news of his coming to dinner referred to as an "annunciation" (p. 181), the promise of birth. Tom suggests an ironic inversion of the archetypal Son, a "bastard son of a bastard" (p. 202), a dispossessed heir who "followed . . . in my father's footsteps" (p. 237) by his liberation from and repudiation of inherited responsibilities. The father himself, "a telephone man—who fell in love with long distance" (p. 204), is thus symbolic of the absent and incommunicado God of the modern world (cf. Fritscher, p. 215).

The play's symbols are not derived exclusively from Christian myth, however. Each character is invested with a matrix of multiple images, drawn from sources both sacred and secular, Christian and pagan. Amanda's character and monologues are infused with a nostalgia which taps an emotional memory far beyond her "*Gone With the Wind*" account of her southern girlhood. In her first monologue of the seventeen gentlemen callers, the very exaggeration of the number of suitors recalls fairy tale and the legends of romance in which the princess is beleaguered by suitors until the perfect knight or prince appears. The pastoral implications of suitors who are "planters and sons of planters" (p. 148) recall both the Edenic garden and ancient myths of gods and goddesses of fertility. Amanda is an Aphrodite called on by multiple analogues of Adonis. Her story always begins the same, on a Sunday morning in Blue Mountain, combining the Christian religious day with overtones of Olympus, the archetypal point of epiphany. It always ends at Moon Lake, evoking the experience of a fall, from chastity or innocence. At Moon Lake, the pastoral scene disintegrates into a graveyard, the uprooted or unweeded garden, Amanda's admirers having "turned up their toes to the daisies" (p. 149) after meeting violent ends. Success or survival depends on transplantation, the exchange of those genteel values of the fertile Delta of Greene County for those of the cold North, where at least one of her former suitors is transformed from beauty and youth to a lone "Wolf of Wall Street" (p. 149), a modern Midas whose touch turns all sustenance to unregenerative gold. The significance of the allusive imagery and fatalistic pattern of Amanda's story extends beyond that of a paradigm for the historical collapse of the Plantation South in civil strife, beyond the corruption of the New World through mercenary exploitation. It evokes the myth of the Fall itself: humankind's expulsion from Eden, the subsequent violence of brother against brother, and the perversion by man's inherently defective nature of all attempts to cultivate "a paradise within."

In anticipation of a new gentleman caller, Amanda recounts a still earlier memory of spring and courtship, set in a kind of Dionysian meadow where the sexual and the spiritual were once reconciled: fever and flowers, the heat of passion and the sympathetic sensuousness of nature. Amanda's description of that momentous spring when she met her husband is perhaps one of the most lyrical passages in Williams' plays. At a breathless pace, Amanda more nearly sings than speaks her story, repeating the word *jonquils* until its sensuous and lyrical syllables assume incantatory power, invoking a flood of memories of rebirth and rejuvenation. Amanda is endowed with the archetypal attributes of May Queen, the spirit of vegetation and fertility crowned with flowers, who, amidst gaiety and dancing, enacts the ritual of spring, the mating rite. Because the boy she meets is also the husband who abandons her to the dark tenement in an impoverished reality, the story of Amanda also recalls the myth of Persephone, goddess of spring whom Pluto snatched from her flower-gathering to his dark underworld. Like Persephone, Amanda has lost her eternal spring and bitterly mourns the transitory nature of youth, love, and beauty. Her experience has taught her that beauty and charm may be enticements of seduction and love itself an instrument of exploitation. Thus, the youthful Amanda who triggers collective images of Aphrodite, May Queen, Persephone, and Princess also reveals the darker side of the feminine archetype, of woman as entrapment and danger. To Laura she speaks as femme fatale: "All pretty girls are a trap" (p. 192). To Tom, she is the Terrible Mother, the womb of the earth become the devouring maw of the underworld, to which the fairy-tale analogue is the "ugly—babbling old—witch" (p. 164), as Tom calls her. The anticipation of a gentleman caller, however, not only permits Amanda to take on the attributes of May Queen again for a brief time but also allows her to assume the benevolent role of fairy godmother, attempting to transform the crippled Laura into a Cinderella, as she urges her to wish on a "little silver slipper of a moon" (p. 189).

The symbolism associated with Laura is composed largely of religious and ascetic images connoting the innocent other-worldiness of the saint, the cloistered nun, and the chaste virgin. In "Production Notes," Williams says that the light upon Laura should have "a peculiar pristine clarity such as light used in early religious portraits of female saints or madonnas" (pp. 133–34). Appropriately, candlelight, the halo of illumination set before shrines, is her milieu. Jim's attentions light "her inwardly with altar candles" (p. 219), the warmth of religious devotion, while her final disappointment is revealed as if "the holy candles on the altar of Laura's face have been snuffed out" (p. 230), the loss of faith. In reinforcement of her saintly aspect, Amanda, Jim, and Tom call her "Sister," the traditional address for a nun, and she calls herself "an old maid" (p. 150), the eternal virgin. Her favorite animal in the glass menagerie is the mythical unicorn, "emblem of chastity and the lover of virgins" (Frye, p. 152). The recurrent music of "The Glass Menagerie," which may be imagined as the distant sound of a calliope on a merry-go-round, evokes all the other images which characterize Laura's inner world: the tiny stationary glass animals, her childlike nature, and her uniqueness—in circus terms called freakishness; in religious terms, miraculous; in temporal terms, anachronistic. Her symbolic name of "Blue Roses" emphasizes her unnatural or extraterrestrial nature, as does her favorite retreat, "the Jewel Box, that big glass house where they raise the tropical flowers" (p. 155), a metaphor for Laura's inner world, herself the rara avis or exotic flower that cannot survive transplantation to the outside world. Finally, Laura's name resembles *laurel*, the name of the flowering tree into which the mythic Daphne was transformed after evading the sexual pursuit of Apollo, thereby refusing the call to sexual maturity (see Campbell, pp. 60–62).

Images of modern existential man dominate Tom's symbolic characterization: the demonic images of fragmentation, suffocation, and alienation. He identifies both the urban tenement and the warehouse as modern analogues of hell, himself sealed in a coffin, an ironic "*czar* of the *underworld*" (p. 164), his deepest aspirations smoldering in frustration. Driven by the oppressive and repressive circumstances of his life and seduced by the illusory images of the movie screen to believe in a rainbow at the end of the journey, Tom attempts the sea voyage which is not only his personal quest for self-realization, but also represents the attempt of twentieth century man to restore to wholeness the fragmented self, threatened by dehumanization and disintegration. Tom's struggle to integrate the primal instincts of "a lover, a hunter, a fighter" (p. 174) with the creative impulse of the poet suggests the attempt of modern man to heal that deep split between body and soul, the senses and the spirit, which characterizes the modern malaise. Liberated from Hades, however, Tom finds himself an aimless drifter in its modern equivalent, the Wasteland, self-exiled among the ruins of a nihilistic landscape. All the symbols of hope through which the characters have expressed their private visions of transcendence—Amanda's colorful jonquils, Laura's iridescent glass figures, Tom's flickering screen images, and the large glass sphere in the Paradise Dance Hall—are ultimately revealed as fragments of broken dreams, as "bits of a shattered rainbow" (p. 237). Haunted by his abandonment of the others in his futile quest for self, Tom joins the ranks of other guilt-haunted wanderers—Cain, the Wandering Jew, the Flying Dutchman, the Ancient Mariner—representatives of archetypal alienation. Tom becomes the poète maudit, cursed with existential knowledge of the human condition and compelled to retell his story, a modern fable of the failure of love and of man's inability to transcend his solitude in a world devoid of transcendent goals.

Jim O'Connor is at once the most symbolic character in the play and the most realistic. Accordingly, the allusive imagery from which he is constructed is multiple and paradoxical, romantic and ironic. As a reincarnation of the gentleman caller, he evokes both the infinite possibilities suggested by all seventeen suitors and the limited reality defined by the last caller, the father who abandoned wife and family. Thus, Jim represents both that "long-delayed but always expected something that we live for" (p. 145) and, ironically, "a nice, ordinary, young man" (p. 129), both the ideal and the real. "Like some archetype of the universal unconscious" (p. 159), Jim is invested with multiple heroic images. As the reborn gentleman caller, he may be identified with a fertility god, the regenerative planter; his annunciation signals the rebirth or second coming of Christ as the savior; Amanda's wish upon "the little silver slipper of a moon" casts Jim in the role of Prince Charming to Laura's Cinderella and her Sleeping Beauty. He is the singing Pirate who will charm the Lady, and he is Superman (p. 210) who never fails to rescue Lois Lane. All of these symbols of expectation are invested in a character who is the epitome of the All-American boy—extroverted, dynamic, and optimistic—thoroughly acculturated to the popular version of happiness achieved through technological progress, status, and material success.

The enlargement of the characters through allusive imagery in the first part of the play is designed to heighten the emotional intensity of its climactic scene, the meeting between Laura and Jim. The mythicization of the characters combined with the symbolic value invested in the concrete props of the scene—Laura's physical transformation, the suggestion of rain, the circle of candlelight from the miraculously fire-salvaged candelabrum, and the glass of dandelion wine—all elevate the significance of their meeting beyond mere social ceremony to suggest the pagan ritual of fertility or initiation, the Christian rite of Holy Communion, and the romantic ideal of courtship. In this instance, however, symbol is divorced from substance, the mythical distinguished from the actual, and the bubbles of subjective reality in which the characters have insulated themselves are broken. At the same time, the infusion of symbolic meaning into ordinary human experience evokes an emotional response appropriate to an event of momentous import, thereby deepening the significance of the failure of union between Laura and Jim.

The process of demythicization begins with Jim's breaking of the unicorn, medieval emblem of chastity and innocence, which signals the beginning of Laura's healthy sexual and emotional development and the diminishment of her symbolic dimensions as virgin, saint, and child. As the unicorn divested of its horn is now "just like all the other horses" (p. 226), so Laura no longer feels freakish and estranged from vital human experience. Her emergence into Jim's world of dynamic optimism is dramatically expressed by her cavalier reaction to the broken unicorn, her private world of imaginary animals having become less important than the real one of human relationships. Thus, her use of popular slang parallels Jim's own idiomatic diction: "It's no tragedy, Freckles. Glass breaks so easily" (p. 226). While Laura's sexuality is awakened by Jim's natural exuberance, his deeper sensibilities are aroused by her vulnerability and virginal beauty. Thus, for the brief moment of their kiss, the symbolic fusion of experience and innocence, body and soul, sense and spirit, or reality and dream is achieved. Jim's subsequent revelation of his engagement to another girl and the finality of his departure not only abandon Laura to her shattered dreams but also deflate the entire matrix of mythical, romantic, and religious symbols. Mocked by their symbols of transcendence, the characters are identified starkly as "a mother deserted, an unmarried sister who's crippled" and a son who's a "selfish dreamer" (p. 236). The end of all the images and symbols developed in the play is to evoke an overwhelming sense of loss. The failure of Jim to save Laura is also the failure of the fertility god to complete the initiation rite, the failure of Christ's second coming, the failures of Prince Charming, the Pirate, and Superman to rescue the maiden in distress. Because Williams has so extended the symbolic meaning of Jim, the loss becomes one of "infinite desolation" (p. 230). It is the loss of all heroes, the death of all gods. Thus, through a profusion of symbolic references and a recurrent pattern of anticipation, momentary fulfilment, and ultimate despair, the meaning of the play is enlarged. It is not simply the story of one shy crippled girl, a neurotic mother, and a dreamer of a son, not the story of just one more broken family, but an analogue of modern man's alienation from God and isolation from his fellow man.

The Glass Menagerie embodies Williams' vision of the fundamental human situation as one of solitude in a universe indifferent to our fate. By the infusion of symbol, myth, and ritual into a naturalistic drama, Williams evokes a painful awareness of the central paradox of modern existence, that the transcendent imagination remains undiminished in a world empty of transcendent value. Thus, only by the divestment of deceptive illusions and romantic hopes of transcending the human condition is the communication of self with other possible. However, human love itself is shown as inadequate compensation for our epiphanic desires. Fleeting, incomplete, and too easily betrayed, human love too often leads only to mutual recognition of despair.

The play ends, then, in an ironic family portrait. No longer sealed within private visions of transcendence, the members of the Wingfield family are united in their mutual understanding of their inherent isolation. The ironic embrace is achieved aesthetically by simultaneous views of Amanda, Laura, and the departed Tom. In mime, Amanda makes a gesture of compassion toward Laura, as Laura smiles with new understanding at Amanda, and Tom relates his bitter discovery of an unredemptive reality, threatened by holocaust and ruled by forces inimical to innocence, beauty, or spiritual values. Paradoxically, the symbolic tableau itself transcends for a moment the literal meaning of despair, but only for a moment. The play closes in darkness, all three characters confined to the prisons of self once more in a reality unrelieved by dreams of deliverance.

The structural images of The Rose Tattoo are more cohesive, though, than those of The Glass Menagerie, for The Rose Tattoo is concerned with union and reconciliation rather than disintegration and alienation. Appropriately, the rose tattoo, the central concrete symbol of the play, is itself an emblem of the union of spirit with flesh. The rose, by itself, evokes a flood of images, both secular and spiritual. It is the conventional symbol of human love, female sexuality, and natural beauty. In its spiritual aspect, the rose is the concrete universal of communion (Frye, p. 144). In its literal form, it reflects the shape of the play's internal structure, a circle, the archetype of wholeness or unity. Most significant to this play, which dramatizes the struggle of its protagonist to reconcile the traditions of Catholic morality with the fulfilment of her own sexual nature, the rose is Dante's symbol for Mary, the miraculous vehicle through whom divinity is humanized: "Here is the Rose, wherein the Word of God/Made itself flesh" (*Portable Dante*, p. 488). The other half of the symbol, the tattoo, also suggests both mundane and mystical meanings. Associated with the sailor and other wanderers and adventurers, the tattoo appears to be an indication of both male virility and sentimentality. Religious connotations derive from its approximation to both the stigmata, those sympathetic scars resembling the wounds of the crucified Christ, and the brand of Cain, marks of infamy and disgrace.

Throughout the play, the symbol reflects the unfolding awareness of life's ambiguities in the mind of Serafina. The religious significance imparted to the image of the rose, which is actually etched on the chest of Rosario, reflects Serafina's own need to create a reality suffused with transcendent meanings. The alleged duplication of the rose tattoo on Serafina's breast as an emblem prophetic of conception represents her inflation of the sexual relations between herself and her husband to the religious experience of mystical union. Accordingly, Serafina's description of the sensations accompanying the mysterious appearance of the rose on her breast suggests not only the process of tattooing but also the ecstatic suffering associated with stigmata: "That night I woke up with a burning pain on me, here, on my left breast! A pain like a needle, quick, quick, hot little stitches" (II, 277). However, even as Serafina imbues her experience with miraculous import, elevating her husband to a Christ figure, herself to a devoted saint, and their sexual union to the level of religious ecstasy, her language derives from her mundane role as a lowly seamstress, who creates fabrications from the raw material of experience. Serafina's analogy between the religious experience and her familiar occupation of sewing suggests that stigmata appear not only to the religiously ecstatic but also to the hysterically neurotic. The sensation of stitches as from a needle which pricks Serafina ironically reveals the image of the rose to be psychosomatically self-inflicted.

Throughout the play, the reduplication of the rose tattoo parallels Serafina's struggle to acknowledge that the glory with which she has exalted Rosario and sanctified herself represents only gross invention. The symbol is corrupted to represent infidelity and adultery when found on Estelle, Rosario's mistress. It is compromised for Serafina when reproduced on the chest of Alvaro, Rosario's clownish double. It reappears on the breast of Serafina as an emblem of birth and re-birth only after she has fully accepted all its meanings and has her-self transcended the need for ego inflation.

While fragmented myths reflect the disintegration of a tran-scendent mythos for Western civilization in *The Glass Menagerie*, in *The Rose Tattoo* a pagan nature myth is offered in its entirety as a viable substitute for religious romanticism. The myth of Dionysus, the Greek seasonal demigod of wine, fertility, and passionate inspira-tion informs characterization, structure, and atmosphere. Like the symbolic rose tattoo, the myth represents a fusion of the sensual and the spiritual. Its structural aspect is the cyclical pattern of a god who dies and is reborn. Rosario embodies the play's initial representation of the archetypal Dionysian spirit. As Dionysus was known as the vegetation or "fruitful" god (Frazer, pp. 351–52), so Rosario repre-sents the apotheosis of sexual prowess and fertility, reflected in his job as the driver of a ten-ton truck of bananas. As Dionysus was often represented as a floral god (Frazer, p. 352), so Rosario is for Serafina "my rose of the world" (p. 345). Finally, like Dionysus, Rosario is to Serafina the god of love who suffers a violent death. He is idealized sexually as "the *first* best, the *only* best" (p. 311), and pictured as an eternally youthful god: "I remember my husband with a body like a young boy and hair on his head as thick and black as mine is and skin on him smooth and sweet as a yellow rose petal" (p. 311). Unable to acknowledge an unalloyed sexuality in human nature, however, Serafina attempts to imbue the Dionysian spirit with Christian symbol in her religious elevation of Rosario. Thus, Serafina makes her sexual union with Rosario seem like an ecstatic ritual: "To me the big bed was beautiful like a religion (p. 342). . . . Each night for twelve years. Four thousand-three hundred-and eighty" (p. 312). The idealized Rosario is to Serafina what the romanticized gentleman caller is to Amanda. Both women must mythicize, romanticize, or civilize the expression of natural instincts to fulfill their longings for transcendent experience.

The Dionysian spirit, however, embodies not only the inspired passion of religious ecstasy to which Serafina would restrict it but also sexuality at its most libidinous and indiscriminate. Serafina attempts to confine the orgiastic impulse of the Dionysian spirit to the monogamous relationship of the marriage vow. The raw sexuality of Rosario is revealed through the discovery of his adulterous relationship with Estelle Hohengarten, who describes him as "wild like a Gypsy" (p. 283). Characteristically, Serafina refuses to acknowledge Rosario's betrayal: "I don't know nothing about wild men and wild women" (p. 283). Appropriately, it is the Strega's goat of which Serafina is most afraid, for Dionysus was often believed reincarnated in the form of a goat and worshipped in ritual as "the one of the Black Goatskin" (Frazer, p. 355). As the objective correlative of the Dionysian spirit of unleashed lust, the black goat also symbolizes Serafina's own unconscious desires, her fear of it deriving from the repression of her own sexuality in its instinctual and unelevated form.

At the death of Rosario, Serafina (like Amanda) is transfixed in the posture of looking backward to a state of idealized and illusory perfection. Attempting to immortalize her elevated image of Rosario while denying his true nature, she puts his ashes into a funeral urn and worships them before the shrine of the Madonna. To so Christianize the Dionysian spirit is to asceticize natural passion and attempt to fix its cyclical nature in an image of heavenly ascension. Serafina attempts to deny the Dionysian impulse in herself, to enshrine her own body by refusing to participate in the regenerative process of life. As Alvaro tells her, "You have put your heart in the marble urn with the ashes" (p. 372).

Like *The Glass Menagerie*, *The Rose Tattoo* is a story told then reenacted in a diminished version. Serafina's idealized version of her relationship with Rosario is reenacted in a fully human version between herself and Alvaro. Similarly, the wild or illicit relationship of natural passion between Estelle and Rosario is reenacted in an inherently innocent version between Rosario's daughter, "a twig off the old rosebush" (p. 281) and Jack Hunter, the sailor. In each case, the second version of these parallel stories ends more happily than the first. Rosa's defiance of moral conventions points the way to Serafina's own liberation from false idols and to her realization that human love needs no other consecration than its own expression.

The play turns from its tragic potential to its ultimate comic fulfilment with the appearance of Alvaro, an obvious parody of the exalted Rosario: *"My husband's body,* with the head of a *clown!"* (p. 354). Accordingly, his social status is not that of the figurehead Baron but that of "the grandson of the village idiot" (p. 366). A compromise of Rosario's idealized virility, Alvaro drives only an eight-ton truck of bananas. Whereas implications of mystery surround Rosario—"On top of the truck is bananas! But underneath— something else!" (p. 279)—nothing is mystifying about Alvaro. His identification with the unelevated sexuality of Dionysus is dramatized by his own resemblance to the goat, which he appropriately catches for Serafina. When the drunken Alvaro spies the sleeping Rosa, his cries of "Che bella" are echoed by the antiphonal responses of the goat's bleating "Baaa" outside, a love song to natural beauty inspired by natural passion. Finally, Alvaro's last name, Mangiacavallo, which means "Eat-a-horse" (p. 356), is a pun on the ritual custom of endowing a pagan god with a similar epithet in recognition of his animal reincarnation. Thus, Dionysus, who was believed reincarnated in one form as a bull, was known as "eater-of-bulls" (Frazer, p. 356). The name is here demythicized to the popular hyperbole, to be so hungry one could "eat a horse." Obviously, the ritual custom need not be known nor consciously grasped to elicit humor. The animal epithet appears instantly ludicrous by contrast to the other names invested with religious and mystical connotations: Rosario Delle Rose—the rosary of the rose; Serafina Delle Rose—the seraph or archangel of the rose; and Rosa Delle Rose—the rose of the rose.

Alvaro, then, is characterized not as half-mortal, half-divine, but as a fully humanized animal, his humanity elevating him from mindless bestiality even as his animal instincts lead him to offer "Love and affection!—in a world that is lonely—and cold!" (p. 366). Combining masculine strength with feminine tenderness, Alvaro's androgynous nature is presented as so sympathetic, sensitive, and passionate that it makes up for the loss of a god.

The divestment of Serafina's illusions is dramatized in this play too through an act of breakage: Serafina shatters the urn filled with Rosario's ashes and realizes the Madonna icon is only "a poor little doll with the paint peeling off" (p. 396). Her deflated view of both Rosario and herself is a prelude to the liberation of her Dionysian spirit from all the restraints imposed by her adherence to social conventions, moral strictures, and sexual taboos. The moment of disillusionment is followed not only by the necessary confrontation with human limitations but also by an embrace of the diminished reality. The divestment of her mythical dimensions as Madonna releases her repressed sexual spirit, and her illicit act of passion with Alvaro frees her from the social proprieties and sexually constrictive role of Widow, represented throughout the play by an inanimate and faceless dummy. Similarly, the relinquishment of her exalted social status as Baronessa restores her to the community of Sicilian women. Finally, Rosa's exposure of the hypocritical disparity between Serafina's public image and her private desires, between her moral affectations and her sexual needs, not only frees Serafina from social pretense but also leads her to self-integration and self-acceptance. Thus mitigated by Alvaro's love and sanctioned by Rosa's example, the divestment of Serafina's self-generated mythos and mysticism results neither in the existential loneliness of the Wingfield family nor in the psychic withdrawal of Blanche DuBois. Instead, Serafina's embrace of reality leads to the blossoming of natural experience, itself so full and rich that its expression simultaneously fulfills the imagination and the flesh. She is led to understand the capricious sexual vitality of Rosario in the acceptance of her own animal nature and in her realization of life as a process of fulfilling instinctual and all-too-human needs and desires. As fervently as she had previously attempted to arrest time, she is now able to follow Rosa's example and surrender to its flow. As Williams himself remarked in "The Rose Tattoo," Serafina learns that the spirit of Dionysus "can not be confined to memory nor an urn, nor the conventions and proprieties of a plump little seamstress who wanted to fortify her happiness with the respect of the community," but that "the blood of the wild young daughter was better, as a memorial, than ashes kept in a crematory urn" (*Vogue*, p. 96).

The play ends in a crescendo of color, motion, and music. Serafina's embrace of inclusive experience permits the symbols of corruption, mortality, and death to transcend their meanings in the assumption of the regenerative values of reunion and rebirth. The apocalyptic finality of Christian ontology has been exchanged for the regenerative cycle of the Dionysian spirit. The rose tattoo reproduced on Alvaro reappears on the breast of Serafina, once more as a symbol of conception and of her own passionate rebirth, but also as the imprint of flesh against flesh. The rose silk shirt, symbol of Rosario's infidelity, is invested with Serafina's renewed faith in life as it becomes her gift of love to Alvaro. The wind, symbol of life's transience as well as its vitality, assumes major metaphorical significance. Scattering the ashes of Rosario, it releases the impregnating power of the Dionysian spirit and carries the child's red kite, symbol of Serafina's uninhibited freedom. Finally, it is the windlike motion of the Sicilian women that propels the rose-colored shirt "like a streak of flame shooting up a dry hill" (p. 413), uniting Serafina with Alvaro, with the community, and with her own passionate nature. The shirt is a banner joyfully spread in celebration of the dynamic process of life in all its human complexity and a testimony to the intrinsically transcendent function of passionate human communion. In this play, the annual rebirth of the Dionysian spirit is a ritual successfully reenacted in a fully human version.

In *Orpheus Descending*, the symbolic structure of a story told, then reenacted in a diminished version, is multiplied. Not one, but several stories structure the major events of this play. Furthermore, one of the major stories dramatized by the play is not told by a protagonist in the play but has its reference in the title: the Greek myth of Orpheus and Eurydice. The other major story, which is organic to the human drama, is recounted at the beginning of the play by Dolly and Beulah about Lady Torrance, and is later retold by Lady herself before it is reenacted. Unlike the contrast between inflated myths and circumscribed reality developed in *The Glass Menagerie*, or the fusion of myth with experience achieved in *The Rose Tattoo*, in this play the myth of Orpheus emerges as a separate story with its own protagonist. As a result, the myth too often seems superimposed onto the human conflicts integral to the play. Attempts to fuse these two stories create confusion, for each story vies with the other to assume clarity and focus. (see Nelson, pp. 228–231).

The myth of Orpheus and Eurydice not only informs structure and characterization in the play but is itself reenacted in a modern existential version. In the original myth, Orpheus descends into the underworld in an attempt to rescue Eurydice after she has been bitten by a snake and abducted by Pluto. His music so charms the guardians of Hades that Eurydice's return is promised him on the condition that he not look back at her as she follows him out of the underworld. But Orpheus disobeys and by looking back loses Eurydice to the underworld forever.

Val Xavier has the mythical attributes of Orpheus, while Lady Torrance is his Eurydice; and Jabe Torrance, Lady's dying husband, is Pluto's equivalent. Like Orpheus, Val is a wandering minstrel, his guitar correlative to the Orphic lyre, although his charm resides more in his inherent sexuality than in his music. Nevertheless, his ideal is to attain the Orphic qualities of asceticism, peace, and civilized behavior. The underworld of the provincial southern town into which this Orpheus descends combines the demonic atmosphere of the Christian Hell with a savage and brutal pagan upper world inhabited by the Dionysian Maenads, those female embodiments of passion gone mad who tore the mythic Orpheus to pieces. In this subterranean world, Val finds not only a Eurydice in Lady Torrance but also a Cassandra in Carol Cutrere and a Christian fanatic in Vee Talbot. All three are sexually repressed or frustrated women who either tacitly or verbally implore Val to "Take me out of this hell!" (III, 333). Val fails, as Orpheus did. But Williams' attempt to parallel Val's failure to rescue Lady with the Orphic act of looking back lends confusion to the conclusion of the play. Val tells Lady that he is leaving but that he loves her and indicates that she is to follow him: "I'll wait for you out of this country" (p. 331). However, a series of frenzied indecisions prevent Lady from following Val out of her underworld. Her refusal to leave derives from complications in her own story—in particular, her discovery of her husband's part in the destruction of her father, which motivates her to intentions of revenge: "Death has got to die before we can go" (p. 333). At Lady's insistence, then, Val returns to the underworld and by so looking back loses Lady forever to the play's Pluto, her husband who kills her. Val's act not only causes Lady's destruction but also leads to his own violent analogue of Orphic dismemberment: immolation by blowtorch, administered by the male counterparts to the Mae- nads, the savage and mad "Dawgs" of this infernal southern town.

In the Orphic myth, the rebirth of the demigod is symbolized by the Muses' salvaging of his severed head, which continues, even after his death, to sing, testifying to the irrepressibility of the transcendent spirit. Not Val's head but his snakeskin jacket is saved (by the Con- jure Man) and passed on to Carol Cutrere, the town's promiscuous pariah. As a symbol, the snakeskin evokes multiple associations. Mythically, it brings to mind the snake whose bite kills Eurydice. It also suggests the serpentine guise of Satan whose seduction of Eve brings about the loss of Eden and the fall from innocence. Its stun- ning appearance evokes the ambivalence with which fallen man regards his sexual nature: his simultaneous attraction to it and re- pulsion from it. Finally, although the shedding of the snakeskin in nature also seems to connote transformation, in fact its divestment simply heralds the growth of another similar covering. While all of these allusions identify Val (himself called "Snakeskin") as an embodiment of man's inherently fallen nature, his affinity to the mythical bird of Paradise, which spends its life in empyrean purity, reveals his Orphic yearnings to transcend his corporeal and earth- bound condition. His story of the bird who never lands on earth is commemorated by Coleridge in "The Eolian Harp," which com- pares the ethereal music of the harp to "Melodies . . . Footless and wild, like birds of Paradise,/Nor pause, nor perch, hovering on un- tam'd wing!" (11. 23–5). The failure of Val's efforts to reconcile spirit and flesh—to become, as it were, a winged serpent, mediator between heaven and earth—reveals only how tightly wrapped around him is the snakeskin, concrete symbol of his own earthly nature of tainted sexuality. It is Val who says, "We're all of us sentenced to solitary confinement inside our own skins, for life!" (p. 271). At- tempting to mitigate Lady's loneliness, Val becomes a victim of his own intrinsic sexuality and of the world's inherent corruption. Un- like the head of Orpheus, then, the snakeskin jacket does not sym- bolize the rebirth of man's transcendent spirit or spiritual nature. Its reappearance after Val's death represents only a futile and unregenerative martyrdom, the sacrificial death of its wearer a testimony to man's inability to rise above his own flawed nature, to escape his own skin. Assumed by Carol Cutrere, embittered liberal reformer, the snakeskin is the emblem of "the fugitive kind" (p. 341), idealistic purveyors of love, freedom, and brotherhood, who would deliver humankind from lives filled with frustration, alienation, and oppression, but who are continually persecuted by the forces of hatred, bigotry, and violence, or betrayed by their own carnal needs.

In the course of the play, the symbols elevating Val proliferate, their religious connotations tempered by reminders of his innately profane nature. Valentine Xavier, his very name suggestive of love and salvation, assumes the composite dimensions of a jaded Dionysus, a world-weary Orpheus, and an ironic Christ. Attempting to redeem himself from his Dionysian past, Val not only repudiates his former life of corrupt sensuality but also attempts to deny his inherent sexuality. He becomes the Orphic figure who yearns for a life of ascetic purity. The ballad of "Heavenly Grass" which Val plays refers to a Williams' poem (*In the Winter of Cities*, p. 101) whose lyrics not only express a desire for transcendence from earthly life but also suggest nostalgia for a Wordsworthian preexistence from which humankind is painfully exiled at birth:

> My feet took a walk in heavenly grass.
> All day while the sky shone clear as glass.
> My feet took a walk in heavenly grass,
>
> . . . .
>
> Then my feet come down to walk on earth,
> And my mother cried when she give me birth.
> Now my feet walk far and my feet walk fast,
> But they still got an itch for heavenly grass.

Finally, Val is envisioned through Vee Talbot's eyes as the Christ figure who embodies her desire for both sexual and spiritual fulfilment, sent to redeem her from the corruption and violent reprisals she has witnessed in this world. Interestingly enough, this triadic image of Val and its evolution in his personal history have a basis in the historical progression of the Greco-Roman and Christian religions. According to Joseph L. Henderson in "Ancient Myths and Modern Man," as the rites of Dionysus became too wildly orgiastic, they "lost their emotive religious power. There emerged an almost oriental longing for liberation from their exclusive preoccupation with the purely natural symbols of life and love. . . . These [more ascetic souls] came to experience their religious ecstasies inwardly, in the worship of Orpheus" (*Man and his Symbols*, p. 135). Just as the religion of Dionysus gave way to that of Orpheus, so too "the early Christian church saw in Orpheus the prototype of Christ." Thus, the Dionysian process of seasonal rebirth and the Christian hope of a final and ultimate resurrection "somehow fuse in the figure of Orpheus, the god who remembers Dionysus but looks forward to Christ" (*Man and his Symbols*, p. 140).

Like Orpheus, both Dionysus and Christ make a descent into the underworld: Dionysus to save his mother Semele and Christ to liberate the preChristian faithful. Christian doctrine places the time of Christ's descent into Hell on Holy Saturday, the day which falls between his Crucifixion on Good Friday and his Resurrection on Easter Sunday. Appropriately, the destruction of Val takes place on "the Saturday before Easter" (p. 306). But Val descends into death's underworld and remains there. No resurrection occurs. In a poem entitled "Orpheus Descending" Williams attests to the unredemptive condition of twentieth century man and to the futility of Val's transcendent vision:

> And you must learn, even you, what we have learned,
> the passion there is for declivity in this world,
> the impulse to fall that follows a rising fountain.
>
> Now Orpheus, crawl, O shamefaced fugitive, crawl
> back under the crumbling broken wall of yourself,
> for you are not stars, sky-set in the shape of a lyre,
> but the dust of those who have been dismembered by Furies!
> (*In the Winter of Cities*, p. 28)

The conflict dramatized both within Val and between him and the native inhabitants of the small southern town represents the psychic and societal battle between the anarchic energy of the Dionysian spirit and the Orphic impulse to civilize, reform, and redirect that energy toward compassionate and humane ends. In this play, the forces of darkness win.

The second major story told and reenacted in the play is a human

drama whose protagonist is Lady Torrance. Its theme is the youthful love affair between Lady and David Cutrere, recalled as an idyllic moment of passionate fulfilment in the wine garden built by
Lady's immigrant father in the orchard on Moon Lake, Williams'
recurrent analogue for the fallen world. In the midst of this fallen
world, Papa Romero attempts to create an earthly paradise; its
"grapevines and fruit trees" (p. 231), its white latticed arbors and
couples making love evoke the combined image of Adam and Eve's
Edenic bower and the Dionysian wine grove. Both the inspirational
and savage aspects of the Dionysian spirit inform this story. The
ecstatic passion of David and Lady bears fruit in Lady's conceiving,
while the savage side of the Dionysian spirit is embodied in the
Mystic Crew, who burn up the wine garden because Papa Romero
"sold liquor to niggers" (p. 232). Thus, Papa Romero represents one
of "the fugitive kind," who is burned alive by those envious of his
attempt to realize an Edenic unity. The result is both a moral and
a psychic Wasteland: Lady has an abortion, David is bought by a
rich society girl, and, in despair, Lady sells herself to Jabe Torrance,
unaware that he is one of the men who burned the wine garden, her
father, and her dreams.

Lady Torrance, like Amanda and Serafina, is one of Williams'
transfixed or frozen characters; her emotional life is arrested by the
memory of her youthful love with David Cutrere and the idyllic
vision of the wine garden, her lost Eden. She dreams of recreating
the wine garden in the confectionery of her store, but "looking
backward" is to be her destruction as well as Val's. Val's arrival not
only concurs with her reconstruction of the wine garden but also
brings about the reenactment of her entire story, from its passionate
beginning to its tragic end. The love affair between Lady and David
in the orchard is reenacted between herself and Val in the store behind a faded Oriental curtain with the design of "a gold tree with
scarlet fruit and fantastic birds" (p. 227), the mere façade of the
former earthly paradise. Their passion also leads to fertility and conception, but ends in the permanent sterility of their deaths. Although
professing love to Lady, Val indicates that he, like David Cutrere,
is leaving with "a rich society girl." The girl is, ironically, David's
sister, Carol. At the discovery of Lady's pregnancy, Jabe fulfills his
role as Pluto, once again imprisoning the play's Eurydice, this time

forever, by murdering Lady as she attempts to protect Val. As a final parallel to the original story, Val, like Papa Romero, is burned alive.

In this version of the story, the attempt to restore fertility and love to the underworld is undermined not only by the savagery and brutality of mob action but also by an individual betrayal of love. Lady Torrance, in her loneliness and despair, exploits Val as a means to her own rejuvenation and rebirth, even as her heart remains with David and his with her. She seduces the passive and idealistic Val in the surrogate orchard, thereby corrupting his Orphic attempts to rise above his sexual appetites. She betrays the love he professes for her by dismissing him after he has rendered his sexual service of impregnating her: "You gotta go now. . . . You've done what you came here to do. . . . You've given me life, you can go!" (p. 337). The mythic dimensions of Val as Orpheus, Dionysus, and Christ the Redeemer are reduced to the status of "Male at Stud" (p. 258). It is this story of loneliness, passion, betrayal, and revenge which is organic to the play, but which is obscured and confused by a welter of frenzied actions, multiple allusions, and symbolic attempts to integrate it with the Orphic myth, the Dionysian duality, and an ironic Christ.

The frenzied see-saw of anticipation and loss, of expectation and disappointment, of hope and ultimate despair which characterizes the action is exacerbated in the final act by the introduction of two other stories, both told by Lady Torrance and quickly reenacted. Lady's story of the barren fig tree in her father's garden which miraculously bears fruit and which she adorns with Christmas ornaments as a symbol of her own rebirth invests Lady with the Christian symbolism already surrounding Val. Her story is a kind of apocryphal conclusion to the New Testament parable of the fig tree, wherein the possibility of rebirth is tentative at best. In the gospel, the story is told of the landowner who, consulted about the fate of a barren fig tree, orders it cut down. But his gardener counsels him otherwise: "Let it alone, sir, this year also, till I dig about it and put on manure. And if it bears fruit next year, well and good; but if not, you can cut it down" (Luke 13: 6–9). However, in another version of the parable, the barren fig tree receives no second chance, but instead is given Christ's curse: "In the morning . . . he was hungry. And seeing a fig tree . . . he went to it, and found nothing on it but leaves only. And he said to it, 'May no fruit ever come from you again!' And the fig tree withered at once" (Matthew 21: 18–22). Lady, identified with the fig tree, is first blessed with a second chance for fertility then cursed with total and everlasting sterility.

The other story is also introduced in the last act and is reenacted almost immediately. It is, perhaps, the real story of the play; its theme is the divestment of illusion, the futility of rejuvenation, and the finality of death. The story is told by Lady about a monkey sold to her father by a man who claimed it was young, "but he was a liar, it was a very old monkey, it was on its last legs, ha, ha, ha!" (p. 325). The monkey was dressed up in a "green velvet suit and a little red cap that it tipped and a tambourine that it passed around for money" (p. 325), as the organ grinder played and the monkey danced in the sun. The image of the monkey and the organ grinder reminds us of Lady Torrance herself and her father in the wine garden, where "The Wop and his daughter would sing and play Dago songs" (p. 232). But, as Lady says, "One day, the monkey danced too much in the sun and it was a very old monkey and it dropped dead. . . . My Papa, he turned to the people, he made them a bow and he said, 'The show is over, the monkey is dead.' Ha, ha!" (p. 325). Like the monkey, Lady is an aging woman who attempts to revitalize her youthful passion and restore her fertility. She too attempts rejuvenation by going to the beauty parlor and getting all dressed up on the night of her opening of the recreated wine garden. But it is all artifice, only the illusion of restoration: an "Electric moon, cutout silver-paper stars and artificial vines" (p. 324). She too attempts to "dance in the sun," to infuse life and vitality into her sterile existence. But her final frenzied and grotesque dance in celebration of her fertility and freedom becomes a danse macabre as Jabe descends the stairs and kills her. Thus, Lady's last words, echoing the grim punch line of her father's story, are an admission of ultimate despair, confirming the futility of dreams, the sterility of life, and the finality of death without redemption: "The show is over. The monkey is dead" (p. 339).

Beneath the mythic stories of Orpheus, Dionysus, and Christ, and beyond the human story of loneliness, love, and betrayal lies Williams' darkest tale of humankind's fundamental nature: the story of a monkey and a stud. It is the vision of man as an animal, bought and sold, a slave to his own base instincts and abused by those more brutal than he. As Benjamin Nelson has remarked, "In *Orpheus Descending*, there is the strong sense of disgust with reality. Whatever is human, whatever is of the earth, is prey to corruption" (p. 238). Neither the aesthetic reconciliation which concludes the naturalistic drama in *The Glass Menagerie* nor the essential faith in human instincts expressed in *The Rose Tattoo* redeems Williams' vision in *Orpheus* of the inevitable corruption inherent in human nature. Human sexuality, which Williams has elsewhere suggested is man's only salvation from psychic and metaphysical loneliness, is herein revealed as his original sin. Val and Lady are martyred victims of their own inescapable fallen natures.

In an attempt to reenact several stories in this play rather than just one, Williams sacrifices the clarity achieved by the evocation of a single emotion. The play seems to be an attempt to fuse a tragic vision, an epic consciousness, and an existential or absurdist attitude. The result is not the *"arrest of time . . .* that gives to certain plays their feeling of depth and significance," but an approximation of the "continual rush of time, so violent that it appears to be screaming, that deprives our actual lives of so much dignity and meaning" (II, 259). Furthermore, in this play, Williams does not so much tap the collective unconscious or trigger emotional memory as he tests our knowledge of myth, Christian doctrine, and biblical parable. Because many of his symbols or symbolic references are not evocative but intellectual and often obscure, they can be apprehended only as puzzling or extraneous. Analysis of the profusion of symbols and allusions indicates not that Williams thought too little about his nihilistic theme but that during seventeen years of revising *Battle of Angels*, the play's original version, perhaps he thought too much. Despite its intellectual symbolism and its multiplicity of stories, the central statement of the play emerges clearly from its frenzied action and perhaps justifies its histrionics: it is the single dark vision of life as "a tale/Told by an idiot, full of sound and fury,/Signifying nothing."

The Glass Menagerie, The Rose Tattoo, and *Orpheus Descending* are ostensibly completely different dramatic expressions of life and human nature, evoking respectively a tragic sense of life, a comic celebration of human nature, and a violent dramatization of the brutality and savagery that divest life of dignity and meaning. All three, however, have at their core the same fundamental structure of recurrence, of a story first told then reenacted. All three dramatize the plight of a protagonist who is transfixed by an idyllic memory that must be acted out again to liberate her from her illusions. All three dramatize a ritual of divestment, of old myths and of old gods, and attempt to invest new, human, and sometimes shocking meaning into those rites de passage which have become conventional and lost their emotive power: the rites of initiation, of marriage, and of sacrificial atonement.

In his "Foreword" to *Camino Real*, Williams describes that play in terms which may be applied to all his plays and characters as a drama that is "nothing more nor less than my conception of the time and world that I live in, and its people are mostly archetypes of certain basic attitudes and qualities with those mutations that would occur if they had continued along the road to this hypothetical terminal point in it" (II, 419). Williams' genre, then, may be described as that of ironic myth, defined by Northrop Frye as "a parody of romance: the application of romantic mythical forms to a more realistic content which fits them in unexpected ways" (p. 223). The characters in all of his plays are but the "shadow-images" (Jackson, p. 74) of mythical, legendary, and archetypal heroes who once provided exempla of humankind's potential for courage, honor, gentility, and love, but who have since been diminished and demythicized by time, history, and circumstance (see Jackson, pp. 68–74).

That central myth of which the characters are divested in Williams' plays is one that is fundamental to the human psyche. It is the myth of an original wholeness to humankind and of a unified cosmos without dichotomies of heaven and earth, God and man, spirit and flesh. According to Jungian psychology, we emerge from the womb with this inflated sense of totality or at-one-ness with the universe: "This is the original state of unconscious wholeness and perfection which is responsible for the nostalgia we all have toward our origins, both personal and historical" (Edinger, p. 7). This oceanic sense is experienced by the infant or young child before his realization of himself as an individuated ego, differentiated from the world about him. It survives in the collective memory in various forms: in Christian theology, it gives rise to that depiction of harmony and unity between man, nature, and God before man's fall from that Edenic

Paradise; in mythology, it appears in the Platonic belief in an immortal preexistent state of wholeness which man tries throughout
his entire earthly existence to regain; its romantic literary expression
culminates, perhaps, in Wordsworth's "Ode: Intimations of Immortality," in which the poet-persona nostalgically laments his loss
of an intuitive spiritual communion with a deified nature even as he
philosophically accepts the compensations offered by an embodied
mortal existence: "Though nothing can bring back the hour/Of
splendor in the grass, of glory in the flower;/We will grieve not,
rather find/Strength in what remains behind" (X, 177–180). Just
as Jung insists upon the relinquishing of the inflated infantile ego
in the process of healthy self-individuation, so Williams divests his
transfixed characters of their dreams of regaining that idyllic state
by confrontation with the existential reality of the human condition,
marked by its impermanence, its incompleteness, and its intrinsic
alienation. In "Desire and the Black Masseur" (*One Arm and Other
Stories*), Williams articulates the attitude implicit in his dramatizations of the mythopoeic mind in confrontation with an amoral and
naturalistic universe: "For the sins of the world are really only its
partialities, its incompletions. . . . The nature of man is full of . . .
makeshift arrangements, devised by himself to cover his incompletion. . . . The use of imagination, resorting to dreams or the loftier
purpose of art, is a mask he devises to cover his incompletion. . . .
Then there is still another compensation. This one is found in the
principle of atonement, the surrender of self to violent treatment by
others with the idea of thereby cleansing one's self of his guilt"
(p. 85).

It is this struggle to reconcile the romantic and the existential
views of life that informs all of Williams' work: the conflict between
his empirical knowledge of humankind's isolation and alienation
from a unified cosmos and his romantic empathy for humankind's
yearning for transcendence and for reconciliation with self, other,
and a God. Those characters haunted or transfixed by a vision of
transcendental wholeness or by a desire for reconcilation between
their spiritual aspirations and their sexual needs include not only
the Wingfields, Serafina Delle Rose, Lady Torrance and Val Xavier.
In *A Streetcar Named Desire* it is Blanche DuBois who attempts to
personify the belle reve of an idealized Old South of chivalric love

and gentility in order to deny its decadent reality and her own human needs, weaknesses, and guilt. The story Blanche tells is of the idyllic love she held for her husband, destroyed by her discovery and repulsion of his homosexuality, resulting in his suicide. In its reenactment, it is Blanche whose desperate grasp for Mitch's love is thwarted by Stanley's exposure of her own sexual promiscuity, driving her to psychic suicide. In *Cat on a Hot Tin Roof*, the idyllic memory of Platonic love between Brick Pollitt and Skipper immobilizes Brick in alcoholic impotence, preventing a healthy heterosexual relationship between himself and Maggie. In this case, it is the retelling of the story and its revaluation by Big Daddy that forces Brick to confront his own betrayal of Skipper's love and so purge himself of both his illusions and his guilt. In *Sweet Bird of Youth*, it is the remembered vision of virginal love between Chance Wayne and Heavenly Finley which Chance returns to reclaim, only to discover that he had himself desecrated that dream on his previous return and this time is himself divested of the means ever to realize it. In *Summer and Smoke*, the chaste and idealistic Alma Winemiller exchanges her romantic view of life for the naturalistic one held by John Buchanan just as he ironically embraces her spirituality. Thus, the story Alma tells of Mrs. Ewell, the merry widow of Glorious Hill who waits at the train station to seduce the traveling salesmen, *foretells* her own fate. In *The Night of the Iguana*, both Hannah Jelkes' example and her narration of her personal history free the defrocked Shannon from his illusions of transcending his inherent sexuality and enable him to accept its value as a compensation from an existential loneliness. Finally, in *Camino Real*, the romantic characters—Jacques Casanova, Marguerite Gautier (Camille), Lord Byron, Kilroy, and Don Quixote—must be divested of their fictive and inflated self-images in order to embrace in mutual compassion and sympathy and to continue their quest for love in a diminished reality. The demonic obsession of Sebastian Venable in *Suddenly Last Summer* to be reunited with the "savage face" of God revealed to him by the cannibalistic relationship between the carnivorous birds and the newly-hatched turtles on the Galapagos Islands is, in a sense, only the other side of the romantic vision of Edenic reunion which afflicts Williams' other protagonists. Both the romantic vision of self-transcendence and the demonic vision of self-annihilation by surrender to primal violence represent futile attempts to attain atonement (at-one-ment) or ultimate reconciliation with a universal order. The fundamental story of cannibalism is retold and reenacted multiple times. Melville's dark vision of life on the Galapagos Islands is first retold through Sebastian's witnessing there an elementary voracity in nature subsequently realized through his own dismemberment by the starving natives of Cabeza de Lobo. Even as Catharine narrates these events, she is herself threatened by their reenactment, as the victim of Violet Venable who would force her to undergo a prefrontal lobotomy in an effort to discredit Catharine's realization that Sebastian's horrible vision of an instinctively ruthless nature is but "a true story of our time and the world we live in" (III, 382).

Williams offers no solutions for metaphysical loneliness, except for that rare and transient embrace with our fellow man. His is a carpe diem philosophy elevated to a belief in the inherent potential of man to be God to his fellow, to reach not epiphany but empathy through compassion and understanding. Williams has declared his artistic ethos in similar terms: "Every artist has a basic premise pervading his whole life, . . . and that premise can provide the impulse to everything he creates. For me the dominating premise has been the need for understanding and tenderness and fortitude among individuals trapped by circumstance" (Barnett, *Life*, p. 116). As compensation for the loss of a transcendent myth and of a primordial unity, Williams offers a theater of atonement, whereby the purgation of self-pity and existential loneliness is made possible: by the recognition of our own transgressions in those of his protagonists, by our compassionate assumption of their sufferings and guilt, and by forgiveness of our mutual deficiencies and inherent limitations. His symbolic representations of violent emotions and tortured psyches are intended to fulfill for us, as for himself, a communal cathartic function, "a release from the sense of meaninglessness and death" (IV, 7). Through the dramatization of modern man's existential angst as ritual, evoking archetypal and mythic images, Williams attempts to create a theatrical experience of such emotional intensity that we his audience will be compelled to "see it feelingly," and so become participants in his own artistic quest to invest a "broken world" (Jackson) with viable meaning.

Williams' "Other Places"—A Theatrical Metaphor in the Plays

GERALD M. BERKOWITZ

SOME AXIOMS TO begin with—they're nice, safe generalizations, and shouldn't be difficult to accept. In contrast to Arthur Miller, whose archetypal hero is the Common Man, Williams writes about uncommon people—outcasts, misfits, even freaks. And while Miller's aim is to illuminate the heroic potential of the most ordinary mortals, Williams leads us to understand, sympathize with, and ultimately identify with his freaks, by showing us that they are driven by the same needs and haunted by the same demons as us normal folk. Miller's art is vertical, saluting the heights man can achieve; Williams' is horizontal, celebrating the breadth and diversity of humanity and the common bonds that overshadow surface dissimilarities.

If this is indeed Williams' aim, his primary obligation is to inspire sympathy and identification with his characters. For the plays to work at all, we must overcome our original alienation, and even repugnance, and come to accept these misfits as our brothers and sisters. Moreover, since the dramatic effectiveness of the reversal depends on its being a radical one, such figures as Amanda, Stanley, Brick and Shannon are all first presented in ways that accent their extraordinariness. In each case, then, Williams must lead us or trick us out of one prejudice and into another; he must make us like those

712

that he made us dislike, embrace (or at least respect) those that we recoiled from.

One means Williams employs to reverse our attitudes toward his characters is a simple but subtle geographical metaphor that recurs throughout his work, but which has been insufficiently analysed or even noticed. *The Glass Menagerie, A Streetcar Named Desire, Cat on a Hot Tin Roof, The Night of the Iguana* and several other plays all take place in physical settings that are defined, theatrically or symbolically, as being *someplace else,* a spot cut off from the rest of the universe. These settings—an apartment reached only through a back alley and a fire escape, a mountaintop in Mexico, a private island in the Mediterranean—allow Williams to play with our perspective and jog us out of our conventional responses. Finding ourselves in another world, we are forced to accept its natives as norms, while we (and the plays' representatives of our world) are the outsiders and misfits. We discover that character traits that struck us as freakish become acceptable and perhaps even appropriate in this new terrain and that—allowing for the differing context—the misfits actually function in ways that are not as foreign from ours as we thought. We are led to respect this alternative world as a benign haven for those who are out of place in our world and to realize that "out of place" is more a matter of perspective than of essence. By the end of each play the "normal" characters—Jim, Gooper, Miss Fellowes and perhaps even Blanche—are the misfits and the invaders. And by the end of each play we have realized that to some extent we all try to create our own reality around us as a life-support system and that the proper response when encountering someone who has such a haven is to salute and celebrate his good fortune.

This device, this creation of a second reality that we are led into and made to view our own world from, is most openly employed in *The Glass Menagerie,* whose narrator speaks of a distance further than that to the moon and of "a world of reality that we were somehow set apart from" (I, 145). I have dealt with this play at more length elsewhere (*Players*), but a brief sketch of Williams' use of his technique here will be a useful introduction to the analysis of its use in other plays. The isolation and separateness of the Wingfield apartment is repeatedly underlined: it is literally on the far side of Paradise; the electric power from outside is cut off; Amanda's telephone customers hang up on her; and the symbolic fire escape frustrates entrance and exit, swallowing Tom's key and tripping Laura when she goes out. Its inhabitants are unable to function successfully in the outside world. Amanda lives in memories and fantasies; Laura stays at home or seeks the protection of a botanical hothouse; and Tom neglects his job to write poetry on shoeboxes, fails to pay bills, and escapes into the magic worlds of movies and escapable coffins.

But it is not the purpose of *The Glass Menagerie* to alienate us from the Wingfields or to emphasize their peculiarities. Except for Tom's frame scenes, we see the Wingfields only within their world, and as the play progresses they come to seem more and more normal in this setting. As Tom points out, one hardly notices Laura's lameness when she's at home, and even her shyness disappears when she talks about her animals. It is Jim, the "emissary from a world of reality," who is clumsy and destructive here; it is Jim whose dreams of getting in on the ground floor in television sound more unreal than Amanda's memories of her youth; and it is Jim, ultimately, who is the play's greatest failure, since he isn't even the gentleman caller he is supposed to be.

Thus, when Laura banishes her "less freakish" ex-unicorn and retires to her glass world, we accept this as proper rather than psychotic action. When we realize the truth in Amanda's fear that "all we have to cling to is—each other" (I, 171), she becomes heroic, even "tragic," rather than foolish. And when we see that Tom's repeated insistence that the world of Guernica and Berchtesgaden is the only reality simply isn't true, we understand why he will always be haunted by his memories as he wanders through our world as a perpetual alien. We come away from the play pitying Tom, not Laura, because she has a home and he doesn't; and, because we recognize that need in ourselves, we acknowledge the humanity we share with the Wingfields.

The geography of *Cat on a Hot Tin Roof* also plays a major role in determining our attitude toward the major characters. If we had no other reason for identifying with Brick and Maggie, the simple fact that the entire play is set in their bedroom would establish a sense of intimacy. Moreover, virtually by definition every other character is an outsider in this setting, and that impression must affect our sympathies. In the most limited sense Brick belongs in this place and Gooper doesn't; and if Gooper and the others thus become *them* in our eyes, then Brick and Maggie must become *us*, if only by default. But *Cat* goes beyond *Menagerie* in using this device not merely to control our sympathies but also to make basic thematic points. Certainly one of the play's major statements is that in some larger sense Brick does belong here more than Gooper, and it is the geography, as much as anything that is said, that leads us to this realization.

Williams takes pains to inform us that this is no ordinary room; "it is gently and poetically haunted by a relationship that must have involved a tenderness which was uncommon" (III, 15). In addition, it is the master bedroom of the big house on a plantation that is itself repeatedly set apart from the rest of the world by the play's language, and thus is something of an inner temple, a holy of holies. And the fact that Brick rather than his brother, or even his father, occupies this room establishes his legitimacy as an heir even before the plot gets underway.

Even more important, the fact that Gooper, the normal, functioning brother, is the outsider leads us to a major readjustment of the values by which we make our judgments in this play. If we sense that Brick "belongs" in spite of his weakness and childlessness, and that Gooper doesn't belong in spite of his success and his wife's fertility, then we have implicitly decided those are not the significant factors in judging, and we are ready to accept Williams' replacements. We are not convinced by any arguments Williams offers in support of the "correct" values; indeed, the play contains no such arguments. By controlling our perspective Williams has made us *feel* that Brick and Maggie belong and that Gooper and Mae are the misfits, and we will accept any explanation he offers to justify that induced prejudice after the fact. And when the explanation turns out to involve an identification of Brick with Big Daddy and the statement that he is his parents' "only son," it is again merely a reinforcement of an impression that the setting had inspired from the beginning.

Cat's setting also affects our response to the play's other concern, the marriage of Brick and Maggie. Here the fact that the room is not actually as isolated as it is symbolically becomes important. Other people are constantly entering this room, invited or not, and interrupting Brick's and Maggie's private life. Such interruptions are inevitably offensive, be they by a vindictive child or a loving mother, and their effect is not only to make us see the intruders as outsiders and invaders but also to increase our respect for and interest in the conversations and attempts at intimacy they are frustrating. One major reason we come to believe that Maggie's attempt to save her marriage is important is that the whole outside world seems determined to get in her way; and one major reason we come to hope she will succeed is that she carries on in spite of these external obstacles. And if we do want her to succeed, if at the end of the play we hope or believe that she does have life in her and that she can "take hold of" Brick, then it is for the same reason that we believe they deserve to inherit the estate—as much a matter of *where* the events of the play took place as of the events themselves.

With the pattern thus established, it is easy to see that Williams is also employing this device in *The Night of the Iguana*, though once more he has expanded its utility and significance. Maxine's mountaintop is established as the end of the world, the last stop before the "long swim," a place at the edge of the "cradle of life" that is also a house of death. Entering this other world alters the perspective by which we view our own reality; the repressed Miss Fellowes and the grotesque German tourists, the representatives of the outside world, are the play's true freaks and misfits, not Maxine and Shannon. (In passing, one might note that the only real reason for setting the play in 1940 is to allow for the inclusion of the Germans and their radio broadcasts from the outside world.)

Thus once again our original impression is reversed; we not only come to sympathize with Shannon and Maxine rather than being repelled by them, but we also reject the values and assumptions that would lead us to disapprove of them and are prepared to embrace the alternate values Williams offers us. Failure in the outside world's terms, and being "bigger than life and twice as unnatural" (IV, 270), as seen from the conventional moral perspective, become irrelevant factors. Then and only then can we see what we were blind to before: that Maxine's open acceptance of her sexuality is not out of place in her private world, and in fact is one of the major supports of her spiritual survival; and that Shannon is not being destroyed by his sins, but by the values of a world that is not his, which label as sins those natural qualities which will be his salvation when he realizes that they are acceptable here.

In many ways Shannon is an extension of Tom Wingfield. Like Tom he is unable to cope with the outside world and unable to understand why. He even shares Tom's symbolic homelessness; both the merchant seaman and the tour guide are perpetual foreigners, and Shannon has literally been locked out of the place where he wrongly thinks he belongs. Just as Tom kept insisting that Guernica and the Depression were the only reality, Shannon is almost broken by the guilt that he believes to be the only true response to his failures. And just as Tom begs Laura to blow out her candles, tragically turning his back on the only light that could guide him to a peaceful haven, Shannon insists on wearing a clerical collar that will not fit and a crucifix chain that bites into his flesh. But the difference between the two is that Shannon learns to take off the crucifix; he is tied down and forced to learn he is not alone in his pain; and he discovers that the alternative world offered to him will not only be an escape from his suffering, but a place where he can grow and fill a useful role, supporting Maxine as she supports him. Once again the geography of the play has led us to an identification with the misfits, and that identification leads to an awareness of our shared experience. At the play's end Hannah envies Shannon because he has found a place to "stop" and rest, and we too must recognize and celebrate his good fortune.

One could easily expand this list of isolated "other places" in Williams' plays; the Mediterranean island of *Milk Train* and the flood-threatened home of *Kingdom of Earth* come immediately to mind. But I would like to consider only one more play, because I think recognition that Williams is following a familiar pattern may be the key to the central problem in interpreting A *Streetcar Named Desire*: the question of whom we are meant to sympathize with and just whose play it is. Most critics and audiences sense that Williams himself identified most strongly with Blanche and that he has consciously or unconsciously encouraged sympathy with her. But while some go as far as saying that *Streetcar* is her play, and that it is about the difficulty or impossibility of survival for the weak and friendless, the geographical imagery of the play clearly contradicts this reading. *Streetcar* is set in a special reality as sharply distinguished as the others I have discussed, and it is Stanley and Stella who are its native inhabitants, with Blanche falling into a schematic role analogous to those of Jim, Gooper and Miss Fellowes. And that fact implies a decidedly different interpretation of the play.

That the setting of *Streetcar* is a separate reality is clearly established from the beginning of the play. The Elysian Fields, literally beyond the Cemeteries, cut off on either side by a river and a railroad track, is a place of muted colors and soft music. It is repeatedly contrasted to Belle Reve, the only piece of the outside world we are given any view of, in terms which leave little ambiguity about which we are to prefer: a place of pregnancy and birth, as opposed to the headquarters of the Grim Reaper; colored lights rather than white columns; sexuality in place of repression; Capricorn instead of Virgo; and Desire, the opposite of Death. And whatever Stella's background may have been, she and Stanley belong here and flourish here. He took her down from the white columns and started the colored lights in her life, and she says, "I'm not in anything I want to get out of" (I, 314). She is fulfilled with him and he with her; she can't stand it when he's away, and he cries out for her when she leaves him. Whatever this household may look like to Blanche, it is presented to us as the Wingfield apartment and Maxine's mountaintop are—a hospitable and supportive environment for those who are a "different species" from the inhabitants of the outside world.

But "the Kowalskis and the DuBoises have different notions" (I, 275), and Blanche enters this world as an outsider and a misfit. From her first entrance "her appearance is incongruous to this setting" (I, 245), and if she sees it as a landscape out of Edgar Allan Poe, it is her vision that is faulty and to be rejected. There is, however, an important difference between Blanche and the other real-world emissaries I have discussed. Jim O'Connor was merely foolish and inadequate in the foreign territory, Gooper and Mae were clearly interlopers to be rejected, Miss Fellowes and Jake Latta were annoyances to be shaken off. But Blanche is a real threat to this world and to the survival of Stanley and Stella. She brings neurasthenic sterility and repression into this world of sexuality and life; she tries to make Stella feel guilty for hanging back with the beasts and not sharing her values; and her simple presence interferes with their uninhibited enjoyment of the "colored lights" and the "things that happen between a man and a woman in the dark—that sort of make everything else seem—unimportant" (I, 321).

Thus, when Stanley conspires to eject her, it is not out of malice but in an attempt to protect the life and reality he needs. When Stella acquiesces in the ejection, it is not because she really thinks Blanche is insane, but because she agrees with Eunice that "Life has got to go on," and she knows that she "couldn't believe her story and go on living with Stanley" (I, 405). And though we may regret that Blanche must be destroyed at the end of the play, we do not object. By attempting to impose the outside world on the Kowalski home she was threatening its existence, stealing from Stanley and Stella the island of security that Williams takes such pains to give to the "misfits" in his other plays.

I suggest, therefore, that the geographical metaphor that is at the center of *Streetcar* places it firmly within the pattern of the other plays I have discussed and that we are intended to reject Blanche and the world she represents as well as celebrate the good fortune of Stanley and Stella in finding each other and a world that allows them to flourish. We can grieve for Blanche and see that she is as homeless and tormented as Tom Wingfield, but when she poses a threat to the survival of others we must allow her to be destroyed and rejoice in the narrow escape. In the preface to *Cat on a Hot Tin Roof*, Williams speaks of "the cell in solitary where each is confined for the duration of his life . . . , because my world is different from yours, as different as every man's world is from the world of others" (III, 3-4). Our ultimate discovery in all the plays is that the Kowalskis, the Wingfields, the Pollits and the Shannons are not as alien as they may first have seemed, but merely striking and dramatic examples of that solitary confinement that we all have in common.

Williams' Comedy

CHARLES B. BROOKS

SEVERAL OF THE most significant serious playwrights of the modern era have possessed fine comic gifts which
enhance their plays, including Chekhov, O'Casey, Giraudoux,
Anouilh, Beckett, and Pinter. Tennessee Williams belongs in this
group. Although his vision of the world is not primarily comic, comedy contributes to his success.

A few of his plays he labels comedies: *You Touched Me!* is "A
Romantic Comedy," *27 Wagons Full of Cotton* is "A Mississippi
Delta Comedy," and *Period of Adjustment* is "A Serious Comedy."
The term "serious comedy," like "slapstick tragedy" (for *The Muti-
lated* and *The Gnädiges Fräulein* in New York in 1966), indicates
how intimately his comic vision is woven into his serious outlook.

It is not chiefly a matter of verbal wit or gags, although there are
some of these: a character wonders about the whereabouts of a girl
who was stood up at her wedding, and another remarks, "Some people say she went crazy an' some people say she went to Cincinnati
to study voice" (*Battle of Angels*, I, 40); when Tom tells his mother
the gentleman caller's name is James Delancy O'Connor, Amanda
exclaims, "Irish on *both* sides! *Gracious!* And doesn't drink?" (*The
Glass Menagerie*, I, 185); when, to Stanley's complaint that Blanche
is taking too long in the bathroom, she tells him to "Possess your
soul in patience!" his answer is "It's not my soul, it's my kidneys I'm

720

worried about!" (*A Streetcar Named Desire*, I, 363–64); in *Period of Adjustment* Isabel's comment on her husband's car is that "It ought to be retired with an old-age pension" (IV, 133), and Ralph complains that, because of her buck teeth, kissing his wife "was like kissing a rock pile" (p. 145); in *The Night of the Iguana*, when Shannon tells Maxine he has been guiding a tour of eleven old maids, she calls them "a football squad" and he comes back with "Yeah, and I'm the football" (IV, 258); in *In the Bar of a Tokyo Hotel*, when Leonard describes the oddities of some of the painters who exhibit in his gallery and mentions that one paints with his penis, Miriam queries, "Erect or soft?" (*Dragon Country*, pp. 40–41).

There are several slapstick gags in *The Gnädiges Fräulein*. As Indian Joe and the Cocaloony bird are sparring and exchanging sounds of "awk" and "ugh," Polly says, "Reminds me of the Lincoln-Douglas debates" (*Dragon Country*, p. 239). When Joe announces, "I feel like a bull," Polly goes "MOOOO! MOOOOO!" and follows him into the house (pp. 250–51).

One exchange in that play goes like this:

POLLY: HOW.
INDIAN JOE: POW.
MOLLY: WOW. (He jerks the screen door open and enters the interior.)
POLLY: Strong character! (p. 240).

This is something more than mere gagging—it caricatures cliché Indian-dialogue, "how" and "pow wow," along with the slang exclamation "wow," just as Joe is a take-off on cliché attitudes towards Indians. Much of Williams' verbal humor has such appropriateness. In *Battle of Angels* after Val, having unexpectedly been promised a job, stammers, "God, I—! Lady, you—!" Myra's comeback points up the vanity which is his weakness, at the same time showing a certain self-awareness of her own weakness—"God you an' lady me, huh. I think you are kind of exaggerating a little in both cases" (I, 33). In *Cat on a Hot Tin Roof*, Maggie suddenly turns on the hi-fi, loud, and Big Daddy, anxious to be the center of attention, shouts to turn it off; just as she complies, Big Mama runs in, and he tells Maggie to turn it back on. Though ostensibly a joke, his words reveal the dislike of her that he expresses clearly later on, and it harmonizes with the portrait of Big Mama as silly and possessive and disliked or ignored by her children and in-laws in spite of the outward fuss they make over her, a portrait that contributes to the play's exposure of the hollowness of many American attitudes. Later Gooper and Mae get in a good dig at Brick—Gooper having asked whether he made his famous run in the Sugar Bowl or the Rose Bowl, Mae shouts that it was the punch bowl—but it's as much another exposure of their malice, closely tied to their jealousy and greed, as it is of Brick's alcoholism. Similarly in *Sweet Bird of Youth* Boss Finley exposes his deep southern prejudice while being consciously and cleverly sarcastic when he suggests that the question of whether a criminal degenerate is sane or insane should be taken to the Supreme Court: "They'll tell you a handsome young criminal degenerate like Chance Wayne is the mental and moral equal of any white man in the country" (IV, 60–61). Shannon's dig in *The Night of the Iguana* at Judith Fellowes is cruel and prejudiced ("Hey, Jake, did you know they had Lesbians in Texas—without the dikes the plains of Texas would be engulfed by the Gulf" [IV, 334]) but at least partly deserved because she has acted so self-righteously and obnoxiously.

Many of the verbal witticisms are thus appropriate to characterization or theme. Wit, however, is not Williams' chief comic technique. More verbal humor is in the styles of speech that so fit characters who unconsciously reveal their follies or weaknesses—Amanda's affected reminiscing about seventeen gentleman callers and her futile attempts on the telephone to praise a trashy magazine serial (*The Glass Menagerie*); Stanley's stilted syntax and frequent repetition, showing brutishness and insensitivity rather than the shrewdness and virility he prides himself on, as he probes Blanche's past and her handling of the estate ("I got an acquaintance" is a characteristic statement of his—a version of the comic stereotype "I got a friend—") (*A Streetcar Named Desire*); Gypsy's New York turns of expression as she gleefully fleeces anyone she can (*Camino Real*); the deliberately vulgar, backwoodsy, bragging speech, full of racial slurs, of Big Daddy (*Cat on a Hot Tin Roof*) and Boss Finley (*Sweet Bird of Youth*); the assertive, accusing, threatening language of Judith Fellowes with her repetitiousness of "It says in the brochure" (*The

Night of the Iguana). Individuality of speech contributes to the exposure of shortcomings in these characterizations.

As with verbal gags, comic incidents enliven many of the plays without being plentiful, and they relate to character or theme rather than being gratuitous. Tom's love of the vicarious thrills he gets from movies is underscored when he returns, drunk, after the violent quarrel with his mother and while searching for his key brings out "a shower of movie ticket stubs" (*The Glass Menagerie*, I, 166). A funny scene in *You Touched Me!* in which the prudish Emmie and the Reverend are moving toward an agreement to contract a platonic marriage while the maid is trying to keep the drunken Captain quiet in the next room reaches a climax in which at the key moment the Captain bursts forth in pursuit of the maid and the Reverend beats a hasty retreat. In *A Streetcar Named Desire*, Blanche silences Stanley's demand to know how she lost the plantation by pouring out before him an envelope full of papers; when Blanche plays a radio in spite of Stanley's protest, he stalks into the room, snatches it up, and tosses it out a window; and when asked to help clear the table after dinner, he throws dishes to the floor. In *Small Craft Warnings*, after Monk has assured Doc the toilet in the men's room has been repaired and Doc has gone in, he returns, in the midst of a violent altercation, with wet pants cuffs and the rueful announcement that the toilet still overflows.

The most fanciful of the plays, *Camino Real* and *The Gnädiges Fräulein*, are also the ones fullest of activity. *Camino Real* generates comic energy with the running about that occurs, especially the frantic shoving, smuggling, bribing, arresting, inspecting baggage, shouting, and whistling accompanying the departure of the plane El Fugitivo and the "serio-comic, grotesque lyric" Fiesta (II, 533). *The Gnädiges Fräulein* has the Fräulein periodically rushing off to meet an incoming fishing boat so she can fight the birds for cast-off fish; Molly and Polly rocking in their chairs for sexual thrills; Indian Joe going in and out; and the cocaloony bird. The presence of this bird as well as the other fanciful activity is similar to what happens in O'Casey's *Cock-a-Doodle-Dandy*; but O'Casey's cock is a joyful bird while the cocaloony is a mean degenerate of a once self-reliant creature. The comic energy of the wild action competes for effect with the pathos of the Fräulein's situation and the suggestiveness of the rest of the setting, this southernmost point of the United States (or "Disunited Mistakes" [*Dragon Country*, p. 219]) being as degenerate as the cocaloony bird. Similarly, the town portrayed in *Camino Real* is the end of the road; Casanova, the great lover, becomes King of Cuckolds, and Kilroy pawns his golden gloves and loses his heart of gold as big as the head of a baby.

Occasional energetic action occurs in other plays, notably *Cat on a Hot Tin Roof*, where the no-neck monsters are romping about; *The Night of the Iguana*, where Shannon struggles to keep the women from escaping in the bus; and *The Rose Tattoo*, where Serafina periodically struggles with neighbors, a goat that gets into the yard, and her daughter Rosa. A violent serio-comic altercation between Leona and a night watchman takes place off-stage in *Small Craft Warnings* while various conversations are going on in the bar, including Doc's sad story of the deaths of the woman and newborn child he has just illegally treated.

A more important aspect of Williams' comedy than the verbal and the active is characterization. Among his great array of vividly depicted characters are a number of caricatures of American types. The Sheriff, his deputy Pee Wee, and their friends in *Battle of Angels* are thoroughly prejudiced, tough-acting, insensitive southern lawmen—"Pack 'em all off togethuh," one of the men says, "Jews, and radicals, and niggers! Ship 'em all back to *Rooshuh!*" (I, 69). A related, more developed portrait is Boss Finley of *Sweet Bird of Youth*, the redneck who came down barefoot from the clay hills as a boy and with his God-given mission to shield sacred white blood from pollution has built a powerful political empire. He is vulgar, brutal, vain of his power, ruthless in applying it, a demagogue playing on the bigotry of others, a hypocrite who mouths morality but keeps an expensive mistress. He brags of having taken his wife a $15,000 clip so she would think she wasn't going to die yet and is oblivous of his daughter's sarcasm when she points out that, since he got his money back, it cost him nothing to be so generous and thoughtful. Boss Finley and the Sheriff are satiric exposures of a type of southern politician.

Dolly, Beulah, and the Temple sisters in *Battle of Angels* and *Orpheus Descending* are satiric portraits of prying, narrowminded, self-centered, gossipy, hypocritically moral, middle-aged southern women. In *Battle of Angels*, these four along with the Sheriff and Pee Wee and a group of giggling high school girls are present enough throughout to provide a social backdrop, a sort of chorus of townspeople, who contrast with the flawed, tormented, doomed, but more admirably passionate and individual Sandra, Myra, and Val. This aspect of the play is not so present in *Orpheus Descending*, where the Sheriff, Pee Wee, and the Temple sisters are less developed. Dolly and Beulah are the same shallow busybodies, but they don't seem to be meant to suggest society in general. Meanwhile Vee (the Sheriff's wife) is presented in a more clearly comic light as a quite different type—a religious hypocrite who has visions and lusts. The sharpest criticism, in *Orpheus Descending*, of society as an enemy to individual aspiration comes in the first scene, when Vee scolds Beulah and Dolly for their drinking parties and Sunday card gatherings; Beulah and Dolly retort by attacking her as a gossipmonger, killjoy, and hypocrite; and then, when they have left, the Temple sisters attack them for being common.

Similar to Beulah and Dolly are Bessie and Flora of *The Rose Tattoo* and the one-act *A Perfect Analysis Given by a Parrot*. Williams introduces them in *The Rose Tattoo* as middle-aged clowns. They look down on the "Wop" Serafina, but they are shallow, mean, and interested only in having what they consider to be fun with the Legionnaires on convention. As Lady's depth and dignity are enhanced by contrast with Beulah and Dolly in *Orpheus Descending*, so Serafina's are by contrast with Bessie and Flora. Reappearing in *A Perfect Analysis Given by a Parrot*, they are attending a convention in St. Louis of the Sons of Mars. While drinking at a bar, they bicker and criticize each other until a couple of Sons of Mars show up, leap-frog over each other to the table, and sing "Mademoiselle from Armentieres" (a song the Legionnaires also sing in *The Rose Tattoo*). This play is a comic exposure of two shallow women and a satiric attack on some conventional American attitudes; the girls think the Sons of Mars are hilarious for doing such things as dropping waterbags out of hotel windows—but also call them a serious organization without which the country would be in a terrible fix. Williams makes fun of the juvenile idea of fun which so many Americans have.

All of these characters and most of Williams' other satiric caricatures are quite southern in their speech, but except for Boss Finley and the Sheriff and Pee Wee, they represent types with prejudices and characteristics common to all of America, not just the South. There is the smooth-talking novelty salesman who crowds Alvaro off the highway in *The Rose Tattoo*, calls him foul names, and in their brief fight takes advantage of his integrity to deliver a dirty blow. In *Period of Adjustment* there are the McGillicuddys, self-centered, vulgar, materialistic, domineering, who sweep through the house in the third act grabbing everything their daughter might possibly have a claim to. George protects the silver tableware from them by sitting on it, getting stuck by the forks in a bit of comic action. They represent a wealthy American couple that has made money in business. They are bossy and self-satisfied, and McGillicuddy takes pleasure in sarcastically calling Ralph "war hero." But their whole system of values is monetary, their possessiveness has practically ruined their daughter psychologically, and they show little respect for each other. The scene in which they appear is rowdy, fast-moving, and vigorous, and through them Williams ridicules the materialistic upper middle class American family. Similarly he ridicules suburban living by setting the play in a house in a development called High Point built over a cavern into which the houses are steadily slipping, a house so similar to all its neighbors that Isabel can't find her way back when she goes for a walk.

Another possessive and snobblish mother is Mrs. Buchanan in *The Eccentricities of a Nightingale*, who does all she can to keep her son from becoming involved with the minister's daughter she is sure is not worthy of him. She is unaware that her son laughs at her pretentions.

A marital relationship similar to that of the McGillicuddys exists between Big Daddy and Big Mama in *Cat on a Hot Tin Roof*. Big Daddy makes no secret to Brick that he can't stand the woman he has lived with all these years. Big Mama is the chief caricature in this play, making a considerable display of affection for her husband and children, but always cutting a silly figure and inspiring contempt in them in spite of their pretense of respect. Child worship is ridiculed by the presentation of the cooing mother, who is actually greedy, selfish, and spiteful, and her five screaming monsters whom she considers darling no matter how they annoy other people. In addition there is the sibling jealousy of Gooper. During this family reunion in celebration of the patriarch's birthday, we have a devastating display of jealousy, cattiness, social climbing, false worship of virility, and hollow marital relationships based on lust or greed.

A minor character in *Cat on a Hot Tin Roof* is the Reverend Tooker, who has a penchant for saying the wrong thing and whose chief interest is in the memorial gift for Big Daddy which the family may present to the church—the foolish clergyman, a typical comic character.

In *A Streetcar Named Desire* there are Steve and Eunice, who are constantly fighting, sometimes quite violently, but have an essentially healthy attachment to each other. After one battle Eunice runs to get the police—and instead stops at a bar for a drink. Going after her, Steve, in a conventional comic moment, peeks timidly around the corner to make sure she is not in sight before boldly chasing her. Steve and Eunice are a reflection in comic caricature of Stanley and Stella.

In *The Night of the Iguana* an effective caricature is Judith Fellowes, the tough masculine leader of the busload of women teachers. She hounds Shannon to stick exactly to the itinerary in the printed brochure. But it is made clear that her hostility to him is principally the result of jealousy because he has seduced the young music pupil she would like for herself. The presentation of Judith and of the busload of women teachers ridicules American tourists. They complain about anything that slightly deviates from the promises of the brochure, no matter what good reason the guide has for the deviation, yet they have taken the cheapest possible tour. A great tour it sounds —Miss Fellowes organizes community sings on the bus, and after supper the math instructor carefully checks the bill. The climax of Shannon's struggle with the ladies occurs after he has been fired. He runs down the hill and urinates on the ladies' luggage, an incident narrated rather than shown but a fitting comic sendoff for this obnoxious busload of tourists.

There is also the German family, the puffed up tank manufacturer who always has a portable radio at his ear playing news broadcasts of Nazi victories or speeches by Hitler, his fat wife, their simpleminded daughter, and her new Wagnerian-tenor bridegroom. From time to time these Germans march haughtily by on their way to or from the beach. They have no doubt that they are a superior race destined to conquer the world. And they insensitively snub the tender, artistic Hannah and her poet grandfather.

There are some fuller comic characterizations. Gypsy in *Camino Real* is a tough, cynical gal who is never at a loss in her quest for money; her forceful style of operation lifts her from the ranks of a stereotype. Mitch in *A Streetcar Named Desire* is a little like Archie, the obtuse, self-satisfied husband of *27 Wagons Full of Cotton* who so deserves his cuckolding. Mitch rationalizes his weight problem; he has vanity and lack of self-awareness. He is taken in completely by Blanche's coquetry. Knowing that he can't understand French, she makes fun of him by asking in French if he wants to go to bed with her. When, having been told the truth about Blanche, he demands that she make love to him, she makes a fool of him by yelling "Fire," sending him on precipitous flight. But Mitch is pathetic as well as comic. His greatest mistake is not that he is blind to Blanche's blandishments, but that he fails to realize that in spite of her past and her trickery she could rescue him from loneliness. It is a bleak and loveless future he flees to.

Mitch is a bridge between the essentially comic caricatures of Steve and Eunice on the one hand and the portrait of Blanche on the other. Blanche's pretentiousness is constantly exposed by Stanley; she is frequently made to look foolish. But she has outgrown self-delusion. She is aware of her failings, creating her illusions deliberately in a desperate struggle to salvage something of her life. She finally invites sympathy and pathos rather than laughter. Similarly she exposes Stanley's crudeness on many occasions, but he too is presented sympathetically because there is joyous passion in his relationship with Stella.

Alvaro Mangiacavallo in *The Rose Tattoo* frequently manages to look foolish, beginning with his defeat by the vulgar salesman. He has a comical name, is the grandson of a village idiot, has a household of useless relatives to support. Hearing of Serafina's husband's rose tattoo, he has a rose tattooed on his own chest. After a "grotesquely violent and comic chase" (II, 386), he is stopped by Serafina's threat to slam his box of chocolates in his face, and he drops to the floor, sobbing that everything he does turns to this kind of failure. On the morning after his night with Serafina, he clumsily awakens Rosa, revealing to her the truth about her mother. But he is basically honest and loving; his clownishness becomes part of his charm. Serafina has illusions about her former husband; she is laughed at by the neighbors who know the truth; she cuts a ridiculous figure wandering about her house sloppily in a slip, keeping her husband's ashes in an urn to be worshiped, trying to deny her daughter the passion that she herself has found so important. But she is so vigorous, so emotionally alive that she is triumphant rather than foolish. The people who try to ridicule or hurt her are so shallow by comparison to her that she is the victorious one.

In *The Glass Menagerie*, Jim is the most clearly comic character. He is outgoing, anxious to please—when Amanda tells a rather bad joke (when the lights went out, Moses was in the dark), he is quick to laugh (I, 207); when the lights fail, he indicates that he prefers candlelight; he plunges into conversation with anyone, and it is this quality that enables him to draw Laura out of her usually debilitating shyness. But this is part of his egotistic self-confidence. It is himself he is full of. He is taking public speaking in night school, sure he can learn how to influence people. He brags of his psychological insight and proceeds to demonstrate it by saying what is perfectly obvious about Laura. While he is supposedly trying to stir self-confidence in her, he is mainly talking about himself—noticing how big the candlelight makes his shadow, glancing at himself in the mirror. His high school girl friend was a "kraut-head" who invented rumors about his wanting to marry her. He is a gum-chewing optimist who becomes starry-eyed as he dreams of the great future he will have when television gets going—"*Knowledge*—Zzzzzp! *Money*—Zzzzzzp! —*Power!*" His vanity is nearly limitless, but he claims to have had an inferiority complex, and "I guess you think I think a lot of myself!" (p. 222) is a vast understatement. In spite of his vanity and optimism, he is merely a shipping clerk in a warehouse.

Tom is foolish on a number of occasions—in his obsession with the movies, in his illusion that he is a great poet (writing poems on shoeboxes), in his bumbling of the attempt to find a gentleman caller for Laura, in his belief that flight (joining the merchant marine) is a solution to his problem. His explanation of how he became drunk at the movies—volunteering to drink the whisky which the stage magician made out of water—is amusing. But Tom also has flashes of awareness (perhaps developed later in his life) when he explains America's infatuation with movies, liquor, dance halls, and other forms of escapism. He is partly comic, but as a dreamer trapped in a life he hates he develops sympathy.

In spite of her ridiculous inability to cope, Laura is too pathetic and too genuinely tender and sensitive to be comic. Amanda, though, is a rich comic creation, full of folly and yet strong enough to inspire admiration. She seems ridiculous whenever she reminisces about what a beautiful, delicate girl she was, wooed by the most eligible men, especially when she tries to re-create the role for Jim's benefit, draping her sturdy figure with a frilly dress and adopting coquettish airs. Tom makes fun of her with his story of going to opium dens after she has expressed doubt that he spends all his time in the movies. Angry with Tom, and yet having to continue to direct the household, she rather childishly speaks to him only indirectly through Laura; then when he finally apologizes, she becomes sentimental and oversolicitous—but is soon nagging as she always did. When Tom announces that he has invited a visitor, her mind races forward, marrying Laura off before she has even met the visitor. But Amanda does manage to keep the family going; and unselfconscious and mistaken though she may be, she gives the impression of being indestructible no matter how dreadful her situation. Amanda deserves admiration as well as laughter.

One other group of comic characters needs to be mentioned, Alma's "intellectual" group in *Summer and Smoke* and *The Eccentricities of a Nightingale*—the pseudo-poet Vernon, awkward Rosemary, bossy and gossipy Mrs. Bassett, and effeminate Roger. The most humorous scene in *Summer and Smoke* is the club meeting. They bicker about hearing a verse play or a paper on Blake, Mrs. Bassett shows her ignorance of Blake, and they frequently make catty remarks to each other. The individuals and their club are quite foolish. This scene is expanded in *The Eccentricities of a Nightingale*, and Mrs. Buchanan cuttingly describes the group as the "freaks" of the town, people who don't fit in with others, who imagine they have talents, and who band together to bolster each other's illusion that he is unwanted because he is superior. Further humor is provided in these two plays by the imbecilic Mrs. Winemiller, with her love of ice cream cones and her penchant for speaking out at the wrong time, especially revealing truths about her husband and her daughter that they want to hide. Mrs. Winemiller is not herself funny but pathetic, except that at times she gets a malicious pleasure out of embarrassing the other two; there is method in her madness. But her exposures of the pretenses of the others makes her a vehicle for comedy. She is also a reminder that the club members are not altogether to be laughed at; they are "freaks," misfits, people who don't quite fit in and are struggling as best they are able against loneliness and isolation. Mrs. Buchanan's description is vicious, and the possessive Mrs. Buchanan is hardly one whose opinions are to be admired.

Mrs. Winemiller's insanity and the freakish club members help to place Alma, a woman with considerable potential talent, intelligence, and passion but without adequate outlet for them. With her affectations she would be as ridiculous as the other club members if she were not presented with a richer context that suggests what has made her that way and arouses sympathy for her plight. *The Eccentricities of a Nightingale* gives the name for Alma and the others —they are eccentric, different, and therefore usually doomed to disappointment. It is the eccentricities of people that Williams is most concerned with, and he invites understanding of and sympathy with these people to such an extent that the comic and the pathetic vie in the audience's reaction. "Tender irony," he says in "Notes After the Second Invited Audience," is the keynote to the success of *Small Craft Warnings* (V, 289), where the helpless Violet and the tough Leona, the drunken Doc, the vain Bill, the homosexual Quentin are psychologically sick in their different ways and, throughout, more to be pitied than laughed at. In *Kingdom of Earth* a character comments, "I think everything's funny. In this world. I even think it's funny I'm going to die" (V, 167). Here "funny" is much closer to "strange" than to "laughable." When the oddities of people are pretty much beyond their control and drive or expose them to failure, they become tragic or pathetic. The recluse brother and sister of the play-within-a-play in *The Two-Character Play* are frequently ridiculous as they unsuccessfully try to talk themselves into doing something to escape their plight. When the insurance company refused to pay on their father's policy on the "legal technicality" that it was forfeited in case of suicide, they appealed in the interests of humanity, fully expecting to be taken seriously. In the earlier version of this play, *Out Cry*, Williams suggested about one action that it should "have a touch of pathos but not be ludicrous" (p. 51). The line between the pathetic and the ludicrous is thin, as it is in many of his plays.

"The freaks of the cosmic circus are men" ("Carrousel Tune," *In the Winter of Cities*, p. 91)—sometimes to be laughed at, sometimes to be despised, but perhaps most often to be pitied, and sometimes even to be admired.

Characterization is the strongest comic element of Williams' plays. Some of them also have a message that might be called a new romanticism. As in traditional romantic comedy young lovers overcome obstacles and finally enjoy the fruition of their mutual attachment, so Williams sometimes shows sexual satisfaction as a triumph over the miseries or ignominies or lonelinesses of life. I call this "new" romanticism because it is related to the glorification of sexual intercourse that has become prominent in our culture in the last couple of decades. *You Touched Me!* has a conventional ending as Matilda flees with Hadrian. *The Rose Tattoo* ends with Rosa running off with her boy and Serafina waiting for the return of her new lover, both affairs apparently to end in marriage but inspired by strong sexual longing. *Cat on a Hot Tin Roof* ends triumphantly for Maggie when she finally gets Brick to return to her bed. In *A Streetcar Named Desire*, Stella may live a life of hard work in a grim slum, but she is sexually content. Alma in *Summer and Smoke* and even more clearly in *The Eccentricities of a Nightingale* is released from disabling frustrations when she submits to (or achieves) sexual intercourse. *Period of Adjustment* ends with some hope that the two marriages will work out; "The world is a big hospital," Isabel tells George, "and I am a nurse in it" (IV, 244), expressing the idea that sexual satisfaction is a possible solution for an otherwise sick existence.

In *Kingdom of Earth* the earthy Chicken triumphs over his effete half-brother Lot when he seduces Myrtle, at the same time giving her some chance of a future more satisfying than her unfortunate past. Toward the end of the play Chicken expresses this romantic philosophy in a long speech. Nothing in life—property, success—compares with "what's able to happen between a man and a woman." A thoroughly, mutually satisfying sexual relationship compensates even for great poverty (V, 211), and Chicken is thinking physically, not spiritually. There is the new romanticism in a nutshell. *Small Craft Warnings*, after its presentation of the various frustrations and sorrows of the characters, ends on a wistful note as Monk hears Violet bathing and goes upstairs to join her in bed.

Not all the plays present sexuality in this romantic light, as not all the plays are comic. A fruitless search for sexual fulfilment is part of the torment Sandra feels in *Battle of Angels* and her counterpart Carol feels in *Orpheus Descending*. Val in both plays is finally brought to his destruction by the sexual desires he arouses in women, while he himself, proclaiming that he searches for a relationship more fulfilling than the merely physical, tries to flee from any lasting involvement. Chance Wayne in *Sweet Bird of Youth* is similar; he lives by serving rich older women, but he has brought disaster to his true love (partly the fault of her father) and finally expiates that crime by refusing to flee though he will be castrated. In *Suddenly Last Summer*, Sebastian's unusual sexual proclivities eventually devour him. In *Camino Real*, the great lover Casanova is crowned King of Cuckolds and can only escape the ignominy of living in the Ritz Men Only by courting the aging Marguerite (Camille), who in turn has been reduced to paying for men's favors; Kilroy wants to be true to his beloved wife but is chosen to lift the veil of Esmeralda (the booby prize, as Gypsy puts it) and, because of his weak heart, is brought by this action to the dissection table; sexual drives, in this play, are partly what makes living a disaster.

The plot of *The Night of the Iguana* is the opposite of sexual union as a romantic triumph. His sexual drives have contributed to Larry Shannon's downfall, and the play shows his desperate struggle to escape becoming merely Maxine Faulk's lover. He tries to remain independent but fails when he loses his busload of women tourists. His degradation accompanies the death of the ninety-seven-year-old poet just after the poet completes the final poem he has been working on for a long time, a poem about the decay and death of an orange tree, a golden and green kind of being not meant for earth's obscene, corrupting love. Meanwhile the encounter of Hannah and Shannon, though sexless, is a love experience. They manage to comfort each other during this day between the months of suffering that have preceded it and those that will follow.

Love and sex thus vary in their effects. They can contribute to the tragedy or poignancy of life, or they can be joyful experiences. When presented as the latter, they are one of the comic aspects, along with verbal humor, amusing incidents, satire, and characterization, that give Williams' plays such variety.

In his serious fiction, Williams seldom introduces comic moments. An exception is a humorous argument, in the otherwise bleak *The Roman Spring of Mrs. Stone*, between the vain dandy Paolo and his greedy sponsor the Contessa, ending when she hits him in a spot which will put him out of business for the night. Williams has written a few satiric stories. "The Yellow Bird," on which *Summer and Smoke* is loosely based, presents a satiric portrait of a long-winded preacher and his daughter's finally triumphant rebellion. "The Inventory at Fontana Bella" ridicules the hangers-on surrounding an ancient wealthy Principessa. It includes a grotesquely delightful moment when the Principessa wakes up in her deserted palace, thinks she is being dressed, wanders naked to the terrace, and squats on an imaginary pot to relieve herself. "Miss Coynte of Greene" exaggerates nymphomania to the point of being parody. It, too, contains a moment of effective comic surprise and delight, the first rebellion of Miss Coynte. Williams has sympathetically described her plight as the poor relative who has to care for a nasty, demanding, incontinent old lady. One day when the old lady demands a bowl of sherbet, Miss Coynte shocks her to death with a filthy reply.

After that moment, "Miss Coynte of Greene" turns into fantasy. So does the last part of "The Yellow Bird," after Alma goes to New Orleans. "The Coming of Something to the Widow Holly" is a comic fantasy about some impossible roomers in a French Quarter house; two old ladies, constantly battling, tear off the fixtures to throw at each other. The Widow finally triumphs with the help of a metaphysician named Christopher D. Cosmos. In his fiction, fantasy is Williams' chief way of being comic.

Similarly Williams' longest satiric work, *The Knightly Quest*, ends with the hero and his friends escaping in a space ship. Before that Williams has painted some devastating portraits of greed, ambition, lust, and prejudice, chiefly of Braden Pierce, owner of The Project, the ultimate in industrial development, well on the way to taking over the world and destroying all individuality, spirit, and natural beauty. Braden's chief drive is to eliminate color—to get rid of the yellows, blacks, and reds, to make the world white, uniform, mechanical. The churches, represented by a Catholic priest and a Methodist minister, are shown to be thoroughly in the service of this representative of the Establishment. Children are represented by a bratty girl whose mother, after one look at her, bought a diaphragm. In one comic scene Braden is engaged in sexual gymnastics with his wife while in the room below his brother takes advantage of the embarrassment of his mother and her friends to fleece them at bridge. Braden's brother Gewinner, the protagonist, represents the romantic spirit, the essentially gentle, generous, sensitive, beauty-loving knight in eternal struggle against the vulgar, deceitful, selfish materialists. In this particular fantasy, as in *Camino Real*, the romantic is finally triumphant, though one is not supposed to feel too hopeful that it can be that way in actual life. The triumph is achieved by flight from the world.

Nevertheless, Don Quixote is still abroad, according to Tennessee Williams. The knightly quest has not yet ceased; the nightly one is sometimes rewarding. Despair may be the dominant tone in Williams as in most modern literature, but comic delight sometimes leavens it and livens the works.

Triangles of Transaction
in Tennessee Williams

LEONARD CASPER

Writing in "Poetry and Drama" (1951) of the writer's dilemma in trying to decide whether to emphasize the music of poetic drama or its stagecraft, T. S. Eliot counseled seeing each as intensifier of the other. Just such a postmodern solution-by-nonexclusion seems natural to the temperament of Tennessee Williams, for whom theatrics and dramatics are intentional allies, not antagonists; for whom dialogue and progressive action cycle through planes both realistic and figurative; and for whom, philosophically, nothing is repellent but *un-kindness*, denial of human resemblance. Such openness makes the playwright subject, on one hand, to charges of slothful overwriting and even self-indulgent amorality; but, on the other, to respectful reconsideration as a precursor of the New Uncertainty.

Williams has often been declared a Romantic because of his reliance on the symbolic imagination, for the heightened speech and gesture of his plays as well as the visionary dimensioning of so many characters. But if Romanticism implies unqualified faith in heroic individualism, or equates personal will with irreversible destiny, or gives equal weight to all claims of mystic insight: then Williams is as antiromantic as he is antinaturalistic. His plays have consistently admitted the darkness of human conditioning. Only then do they—sometimes—make the postmodern "leap of doubt," in a negation of

736

nihilism. Skepticism turns on itself, after realization that where there is doubt, there is possibility. Postmodern uncertainty sees beyond apparent entropy or absurdity, into paradox regained, preferring even the terror of insoluble mystery to that of an utter void.

In Williams' characters, resilience is earned and cautionary; rather than predetermined and illustrative only. Person after person tends to be self-enclosed, without being permitted self-satisfaction. Their only hope of justifying their existence to themselves is through "intimacy with strangers," in a trial community. Honoring southern values (as well, perhaps, as longing to compensate for personal deficiencies declared in his Memoirs, 1975), Williams proclaims the strength of diverse weaknesses unified, while acknowledging how often the effort ends in divisiveness. The struggle for personal emergence, through convergence with others equally imperfect, multiplies grotesque effects. Yet Williams implicitly argues (as Flannery O'Connor does explicitly, in her introduction to A Memoir of Mary Ann, 1961) that grotesque appearances may prove only that "in us the good is something under construction."

The circulatory, matchmaking quality of Williams' imagination has already received extensive recognition: in comments, for example, on the dense image-cluster of omnivorousness in Suddenly Last Summer—Venus flytrap, birds of prey off the Encantadas, narcissistic incest, homosexuality, cannibalism, prospective lobotomy, and the like; or the harmonics of character names in The Night of the Iguana—Shannon, Hannah, Nonno; or the symmetry of reverse roles in Summer and Smoke, body and spirit never quite intersecting. In addition, there often has been a special geometry constructed of triangles; not necessarily visible in the staging but, however subliminal, organic to the shape of the play's complications.

Sometimes they function as triangles of opposition, where the two base angles exert such counterforce against one another that they threaten to collapse the apex hovering above and between them. Suddenly Last Summer, for example, although presented in four scenes, has a two-part dramatic division. Dr. Cukrowicz is required to judge between contrasting versions of the lifestyle and death of Sebastian: that of his mother, Mrs. Venable, and that of his cousin Catharine. The arguments by the "plaintiff" and by the "defense" are presented in a controlled sequence seemingly as justly proportioned as the placement of counterweights on a balance arm. Yet, perhaps because Dr. Cukrowicz has had his own integrity suborned by Mrs. Venable in advance, he refuses the lobotomy which will silence the ring of truth in Catharine's voice, when he decides, "I think we ought at least to consider the possibility that the girl's story could be true . . ." (III, 423). The triangle is dissolved by the joining of two angles against the other. (The "possibility" seen by Dr. Cukrowicz thus becomes a dramatic probability, distinct from such postmodern enigmas as the multiplex of motives one can assign Sebastian's participation in his own death.)

An equally spectacular triangle of opposition underframes the eleven scenes of A *Streetcar Named Desire*. Stella is the apex figure being pulled down, and apart, by her sister Blanche and her husband Stanley, usually described as diametrically opposed figures: either the fragile dreamer versus the natural brute; or, conversely, the dangerous fantasist versus the defensive realist. However, the fact that Stella finds it impossible to decide between Blanche's and Stanley's demands may be a clue to more than her preoccupation with pregnancy or any escapist entrancement in her personal history. It may well be that the play's greatest irony lies in the mutual mirroring of Blanche and Stanley; its greatest delusion in the effort each makes to smash that mirror and its reflected truth. Blanche's capacity for compassion is demonstrated by persistent remembrance of how her rejection of her homosexual husband incited him to suicide. Yet the very erosion of identity and self-esteem which had made her so dependent on him for definition has reached such extremes, by now, that Blanche is more than ever sensitive to her own needs only. She mistakes Stanley's aggressiveness for strength, rather than perceives it to be a defense mechanism much like her own dreams of importance. Each figure lunges against the other as projection of the inner self with which neither can cope directly. Stella cannot hold the triangle together because both Blanche and Stanley, while making familial claims, resist the fullness of a family sense. The release of tensions with Blanche's removal at the end is deliberately deceptive. Williams knows that the newborn child is Stanley's next rival and that the triangle of opposition will merely have its corners recast.

Where a playform is basically one of confrontation, the expected effect is polarization; and the outcome, annihilation of one antagonist by the other. However, Williams' triangles of opposition, at their best, resist reliance on customary "either-or" differences and incline instead towards "both-and" inclusiveness: for example, by letting the identity of assumed opponents converge, as in *Streetcar*. Where the cause of confrontation is not finally exposed as just such lack of comprehension, he has sometimes reacted with guilty restlessness and an urge to reconsider. Only dissatisfaction of this sort can explain the *radical, if gradual, conversion* of *27 Wagons Full of Cotton* into *Kingdom of Earth*, over a period of twenty years.

The earlier play has the spareness of motives and movement proper to a folk classic. Flora Meighan is the helpless victim of Silva Vicarro's revenge against her husband Jake's violence. Jake has burned out the Syndicate Plantation's gin mill, in order that some share of the business will return to him. Flora virtually admits as much, under cross-examination from Silva, the Plantation supervisor. She is a pliant earth-mother figure, not used to human wiles. Silva proceeds to cuckold Jake, in primitive satisfaction of justice: "tit for tat," a travesty of the "good neighbor policy" (*Baby Doll*, pp. 169; 159–60, 187). Jake is too beguiled by the prospect of regularly ginning Plantation cotton to notice his wife's abuse. The play depends on broad, coarse humor (the witless outwitted; the deflowering of Flora), rather than on any deep sympathy with her ravishment by the two men, or on perception of a possible rapport between her and Silva as victims of Jake's self-involvement.

Somewhat more concern, and even admiration, are provided Aunt Rose in *The Long Stay Cut Short, or: The Unsatisfactory Supper*. She evolves rapidly from the pathetic old relative about to be discarded by Archie Lee Bowman and his wife Baby Doll to a figure of durable strength beyond their comprehension or control. True, she "resembles a delicate white-headed monkey" (p. 194); she forgets to light a fire under their greens; the Bowmans are afraid she will break a hip and become a permanent burden to them (she is eighty-five years old). Still she is the only one to stand sturdily against the twister threatening at the end of the play. Nevertheless, in its disposition of the three characters, *The Unsatisfactory Supper* is even more simplified than *27 Wagons Full of Cotton*.

Aunt Rose is caught in the crosscut of Bowman meanness, as the stage directions strongly suggest: "The evenly cadenced lines of the dialogue between BABY DOLL and ARCHIE LEE may be given a singsong reading" and "passages may be divided as strophe and antistrophe" (p. 192) according to Baby Doll's movements across the porch. The cleavage is severe and is maintained.

Writing the screenplay for *Baby Doll*, ten years later, Williams was able to preserve the ribaldry of these originals and at the same time complicate the characters and their intertwining. Archie Lee (Meighan now) is as obtuse as ever, but more brutal because of frustrated lust. He cannot touch his wife until tomorrow, her twentieth birthday. Baby Doll herself has changed significantly: she is younger, prettier, virginal—twice the prize that Flora was—and "Suddenly grown up" (p. 122). Neither passive nor pathetic, she backtalks Archie Lee, invites seduction after a playful romp with Silva (now Vacarro), rocks him gently in her crib, and allies herself with him against her husband. She considers her marriage contract annulled by Archie Lee's failure to retain their five rooms of furniture. (Some of these strengths seem to have been borrowed from her Aunt Rose Comfort, whose role is reduced to helpless victim of Archie Lee.) Silva, whatever his early impulse towards vindictiveness, is softened by Baby Doll's innocence. Their frolic is supposed to resemble the games "of two shy children trying to strike up a friendship" (p. 106). They defend Aunt Rose together, Silva offering her a place as cook in his household. As the screenplay ends, these three begin to form a new triangle—of sensitives outside the gross world of Archie Lee. Silva speaks for all of them (the fugitive kind), when he asks rhetorically, "Does anyone know where to go, or what to do?" (p. 139). Several times he has referred to himself defensively as a "foreign wop"; and in the eye of the blind, Baby Doll and her aunt are also grotesques. Ultimately their difference from others is both their bond and their good fortune.

Many of these character insights along with their supportive devices reappear, ripened by a dozen years, in *Kingdom of Earth* (*The Seven Descents of Myrtle*). Again, a woman (Myrtle) is manipulated by two men (half-brothers Chicken and Lot) in their struggle against each other. Again, stage business depends on natural disaster (where there was whirlwind or conflagration before, now there are a hurricane and a flood); on a literal/figurative ascent (to the Meighan attic, where Baby Doll's sense of life is heightened; to the Ravenstock rooftree, where Myrtle hopes to rise above the killing flood); as well as on a document dictated to the woman (Baby Doll's affidavit incriminating her husband; Myrtle's agreement not to inherit Ravenstock when Lot dies). There is even a resemblance between Aunt Rose's failure to heat her greens; and Myrtle's, to peel her potatoes before frying them: a comic index, in each case, to the degree of serious distraction and inner disturbance. But the familiar devices are given added dimension through a re-conception of character. At first it seems as if Williams has playfully reversed the earlier Meighan-Vicarro types. Chicken, identifiable with the vulgarity of Archie Lee, is now also the dark outcast (his mother presumably was negroid; and he is illegitimate). Lot, his younger half-brother, is as civilized as Silva—but impotent and fatally consumptive; he is outwitted and outmaneuvered by Chicken. However, what seems like casual reshuffling of types turns out to be acute recognition of human complexity.

Chicken emerges as a figure of more than carnivorous vitality. Though some evidence has been retracted in the 1975 revisions, Williams seems yet to maintain an open mind about his character's worth. If Chicken is so minuscule a Big Daddy or so crude a Laurentian totem as to be questionable and confusing, still he is never so clearly disclaimed as is Gooper or Meighan. His brutishness is the mask he must wear as the unwanted. Beneath his seeming indifference is a passion for generativeness, completion of some putative potential in himself through another, and extension of that self through identification with what he calls "the kingdom of earth" (V, 211). His language, naturally limited, still parallels rather than parodies Quentin's poetic elaboration of that same kingdom in *Small Craft Warnings* (V, 261). For both, being alive is feeling the fullness of that being. What is fearsome to Quentin (and presumably to Chicken) is not some final annihilation of self circumvented by dreams of an afterlife, but nonbeing now, loss of the capacity to wonder, weightless incompletion.

Myrtle also may be less roundly humanized than Leona in *Small*

Craft Warnings. Still her instincts, though expressed typically in terms of survival, seem to have sources in this same rapport with creation, the dynamics of surprise, the gift of growth. In each of the seven scenes she descends from the bedroom above where Lot is dying to the earthiness of Chicken; and those sanative encounters make possible the final ascension, to the roof top where rescue into a new life may occur. She has nursed Lot unselfishly, even after realizing that he has wed her only to keep the family property from passing on to his half-brother. She is dismayed only by the revelation that he is dying. (In the 1968 version she already had mothered five children but lost them through adoption.) Where can she hang her heart? It is not enough to be the last of the "Hot Shots from Mobile"; she must give life and receive it in return.

Nevertheless, however much more complicated Chicken and Myrtle are than Silva and Baby Doll, the format of *Kingdom of Earth* would not be critically different from that of *Baby Doll* unless the figure of Lot were adjusted too. *27 Wagons Full of Cotton, The Unsatisfactory Supper,* and *Baby Doll* all present variations of two characters ranged against one. Basically, *Kingdom of Earth* also pits Lot and Myrtle against Chicken, then Chicken and Myrtle against Lot. But its inclination to be generous tolerates, and even pities, Lot's identification with his dead mother (a woman of elegant dreams long inhibited by her "hawg" husband). His transvestiture, "both bizarre and beautiful" (pp. 211–12), is described with respect as a transfiguration. There is even something of Aunt Rose Comfort's courage in the way he hangs on to Charlotte's garden hat "as if a wind might blow it away" (p. 212). In the original, Chicken himself conveyed Lot's lifeless body "almost tenderly" (p. 108) to the sofa in his mother's parlor. Perhaps it is only death which, circumventing some symbolic ménage à trois, converts it into a pathetic game of odd-man-out. Essentially each of the three has been seeking self-possession—a sign of acceptance, a sense of home—in the Ravenstock property; and surely Myrtle speaks for them all, at their best, when she assures Lot early in the play that not all desperate people think only of themselves. However, Lot does die; and just as the Silva-Baby Doll-Aunt Rose triad is left incomplete, at the end of the screenplay, so in *Kingdom of Earth* Williams stops short of the metamorphosis of counterforces into counterparts.

In addition to such prototypes of conflict, in which third parties represent either witnesses-in-judgment or the prizes contested, some of Williams' most subtle psychological plays have depended on *triangles not of uncompromising opposition but of compassionate apposition.* Chronologically, this other pattern (appealing to the playwright's impulse towards conciliation rather than closure) is evident as early as *The Glass Menagerie.* At the level of action, Tom and his mother Amanda battle over crippled Laura with all the intense resentment natural to their own roles as poets manqué or displaced persons, among the tenements of St. Louis. Yet their seeming incompatibility is only a surface tension. Even after Tom has "escaped" to the merchant marine and seen the world, his mind like a homing device returns to celebrate his earlier and only life. What the three Wingfields had in common, more important than alienation from their surroundings, was a permanent affection for one another.

It is ironic that their private diversions—Amanda's memorialization of a courtly past; Laura's fixation in her transparent present; Tom's growing obsession with flight to some future "other"—should ever divide them. For these images of belonging are variations on the same larger dream, of individual worth within some familiar/familial array. Loneliness is a birth defect; love and loyalty, its ritual compensations (called imagination, the impulse to transcend the self, in "Desire and the Black Masseur" where alternatives include those more desperate ones of violence and justification through atonement). As memory play, *The Glass Menagerie* offers simultaneously a sense of coffinlike confinement and the comfort of togetherness, of like clinging to like with "dignity and tragic beauty" (I, 236), as Williams describes Amanda's final gesture towards her daughter. Self may be preserved by flight, but never fulfilled. We cannot know how Tom's runaway father feels about his family; but Tom himself is forever inseparable from them. It is only the distances which are imaginary.

In *Cat on a Hot Tin Roof* the three-cornered opposition also proves to be an appearance only. Skipper is as much an offstage presence, if not quite so awesome in his ambiguity, as Sebastian in *Suddenly Last Summer.* Nevertheless, the triangle which Skipper completes recedes drastically in importance, as a parallelogram of forces develops in its stead. Maggie's insecurity, masked as jealousy, requires that she interpret her husband Brick's closeness to Skipper as latent homosexuality. Skipper's impotency with her, during a subsequent trial of his maleness, leaves that possibility still open. Brick's identical fear prevents him from reassuring Skipper and thus forestalling his friend's suicide. The first two acts of the play are filled with the violence needed to pry loose, from Brick, admission of those bone-deep doubts which have caused a series of deaths: Skipper's, the union of Brick and Maggie, and Big Daddy's dream of family continuity as personal transcendence. It is finally Maggie's ability to identify with Big Daddy's mystique of the land as life-force which frees her from the endless turnabout of the Skipper-ridden triangle. When she asserts falsely that she is pregnant, she rejects the past conceived as completion and entrapment, but acknowledges the past as continuum and everpresent promise. Hers is a "true lie," an act of the will to believe, a commitment which may in fact occasion a child but which, in the interim, has at least regenerated Brick's faith in himself and Big Daddy's hope for an heir to his dreams. The third act bonds together two couples, capable of these imaginative leaps into a created future: Maggie and Brick, Big Daddy and Big Mama; contrasted with the breeders of objects, the dull dog-brains: Gooper, Mae, and their brood. Mortality and all other human weaknesses are overwhelmed in that communal enlargement.

The geometry of the true family, planting rows of possibility in its common ground, is officially rare in Williams. Indeed, the theme of the brother's keeper is more often travestied, in figures of buyers and sellers of their own flesh, such as Catharine Holly's relatives, as well as Mrs. Venable or Gooper (and even, intermittently, Amanda Wingfield). Yet the model remains constantly in the corner of Tennessee Williams' eye, if only to measure the deficiency or failure of persons directly in front of him. The achieved parallelogram of *Cat on a Hot Tin Roof* (a double triangle, with Brick-Big Daddy as the common hypotenuse) becomes at least an idealized extension of a whole second order of human systems, conciliatory rather than competitive. Typically, their membership depends more on the "kindness of strangers" than on blood ties or joint real estate; so that they must represent a vision of possibility larger than even the extended family or regional customs of hospitality.

In *Orpheus Descending*, for example, the principal role of Carol Cutrere seems to be that of the hovering witness. A once-committed, considerate person driven to society's periphery by its indifference, her purpose is restored when she sees Val Xavier restore life to Lady, in the innermost circle of death's realm. Lady's husband Jabe once burned down her father's winery, destroying him along with it; then bought Lady, who thought marriage to death appropriate after David Cutrere deserted her and she aborted their child. But the old joy-in-life still stirs in her. She plans a confectionery adjacent to Jabe's drygoods store, and she is encouraged in her feelings by the arrival of Valentine Xavier, dreamer of a legless bird which would die if it ever alighted. Yet, although Val is an orphic figure in so many ways (he carries a guitar autographed by Leadbelly, Bessie Smith, and other passional singers, and wears a snakeskin jacket), Val has wasted his youth and is now in search of seclusion. He is himself rescued from this deadly stasis, as surely as he rescues Lady, by impregnating her. Together they assert a life-affirmation which Jabe's murderous vengeance against them and their unborn child cannot mute. Lady and Val exist in a creative tension, as mutually supportive as Blanche and Stanley in *Streetcar* are destructive. They survive in the rebirth of Carol, whose transformation from spiritual voyeur to renewed voyager is reinforced by her apposition, in turn, with the Conjure Man (whose wild Choctaw cry professes freedom) and Vee, the dull-witted sheriff's visionary wife. In *Suddenly Last Summer* the decisive testimony must come from the intensity of Catharine's vision authenticating itself, while she remains disoriented medium only: a great burden, in antiheroic times. In *Orpheus Descending* any one of the bearers of "the dream," considered singly, might reasonably be ridiculed; but their choric voice can only be disputed, not denied.

In *Sweet Bird of Youth* the two-act division helps establish the polarization between a triangle of apposition (Chance, Princess, Heavenly) and one of opposition (Boss Finley, Tom Jr., Heavenly); between the kindness of strangers and mutilation by kinsmen. Heavenly is the common apex, a figure torn between life-and-death forces.

Initially, Chance and Princess (Alexandra Del Lago) savage one another, in futile misdirected anger against the ravishments of time which both have suffered. Their saving grace is their shame; and the first act ends with an alliance struck, between former scapegoats, to rescue Heavenly from servitude to her father. Erotic escapism and sexual extortion are transformed into a love-kiss of true concern. Although Chance's needs are the more immediate and Princess therefore has the more magnanimous role, she seems to speak for the good will in both when she says, "Believe me, not everybody wants to hurt everybody" (IV, 52).

This early transformation and its declaration are necessary because the second act, with its violent ending, is principally under the control of forces that travesty the claim of one human being on another, and Williams will not risk their confounding the whole-play's nearly classic expression of tragic faith. Similarly, because Princess, Chance, and Boss Finley are all "dreamers," Williams has either to treat them all alike or offer some measure for differentiating the imaginative dreamer from the imaginary. The degree of their capacity for outreach comes to stand for that measure. Occasionally in Boss Finley appears a flicker of genuine feeling for Heavenly. But essentially he is self-infatuated, invoking divine authority for his own ends; and if God can be bent to Boss Finley's will, why not his own children? His messianic frenzies, therefore, are clearly a self-delusion. He is neither generator nor sharer of life (as Big Daddy is) but an inverted kind of Cronos perversely trying to extend his life by devouring his future. By contrast, Chance manages to mature beyond the pathetic role of pure victim assigned him by his earlier words: "all my vices were caught from other people" (p. 37). When he realizes how he infected his lover and robbed her of the power of self-renewal through children, he condemns himself and welcomes castration by Boss Finley's troopers as punishment proper. At the end, he establishes the measure of the play one final time: by foregoing self-pity or justification by contrast; and by soliciting, from whatever strangers constitute the "innocent" bystanders, only recognition of their collective identity, their kind-ness, their part in human imperfection.

The curtain speech does not explicate the play so much as the play offers a reading between lines which otherwise seem quietly despairing, acquiescent to the triumph of time as attrition and certainly to the Cronos figure of Finley. Here the role of Heavenly, for all her remoteness and cryptic silences, becomes more crucially integrative in its play than is Carol Cutrere's in *Orpheus Descending*. At first it may seem as if she has come to symbolize the rot, the void, in all post-paradise experience. Yet just as she once offered her virginity as consolation prize to Chance, and seems to have sent him from St. Cloud originally in order to protect him from her father's fury (although her words are angry, she waves goodbye from a mist of rainbows); so also, having defied Boss Finley by refusing to be an accessory to his politicized Youth movement, nevertheless she appears with him so that Chance will not end up on a garbage scow in the Gulf. In spite of her self-description as "Dry, cold, empty" (p. 71), clearly she is none of these. Her capacity to love has survived the loss of both her virginity and her fertility. That her judgment of Chance and Boss Finley has been remarkably accurate, always, is established by the testimony of Aunt Nonnie and Miss Lucy, proxies in her absence (and parts of an ancillary triangle). To perceive her affirmative role, then, is to consider the possibility that a "comeback" can occur; that the Easter culmination for the action is not sardonic; that by confessing his fault and by accepting his penance, Chance warrants absolution—a superior innocence, after the fall: and if this is a persuasive argument at all for Williams to make, then since innocence and youth have been equated throughout, and regeneration is now conceivable, time as inevitable deterioration does not triumph after all.

Princess returns in the second act; and though she and Chance speak morosely of mutual castration, she serves as other self and companion as far as she can go. But Heavenly, in her own quietly generous way, travels even farther with Chance, farther than he ever knows. Williams clearly is declaring (as Brick did, of Maggie), "This girl has life in her body" (III, 212).

In *The Night of the Iguana*, the triangle of transaction has the peculiarity of seeming to shift its apex figure subtly during the play. On the level of sheer sound compatibility, Shannon and Hannah (reinforced by Nonno, who blesses the world's attunement) unquestionably are mated; and the play divisions confirm this harmony. Act one ends with Shannon (the defrocked minister who just previously has exclaimed on his own behalf: "Don't! Break! *Human! Pride!*" IV, 276) successfully pleading with Maxine, his old friend and protectress, to shelter both the 97-years-young poet, Jonathan Coffin, and his granddaughter/fellow pilgrim and artist, Hannah Jelkes. In act two, having chided Shannon for deserting his congregation, regardless of their differences, and having tried to protect him from Maxine's persistent offers of alcohol, Hannah assures him that "people have wanted to help you, the little they can" (p. 324), despite his self-engrossment. In turn, he "shepherds" (p. 325) Nonno to the back of the verandah, as the tropical rainfall starts. And in the final act, the central event involves Hannah's rescue of Shannon from his sense of worthlessness, by tying him in a hammock all during his darkest night. One might think that such convergences would create a momentum which could be satisfied only by the (at least symbolic) marriage of Shannon and Hannah at the end, especially since Nonno has died and she may therefore suffer "blue devils" of her own again.

However, Nonno's poem, climaxing a long lifetime of thoughtful experience, describes life as cycling through realms of fruiting, falling, decomposition, and refertilization. Hannah's prayer is for stasis and quiet, which she confuses with peace. Her whole life she has been conditioned to a heightened, but largely withheld, sensitivity. She longs for a simplicity too abstract for this world (although it is not to be equated with the Nazis' singlemindedness, excessive to the point of being antihuman, if only because, as her kabuki robe signifies, Hannah's inclination toward minimal embodiment makes her physically incapable of doing harm).

It is Maxine—her name marred by that grating interference with vowels and liquid consonants—who comes closer to the image offered, of life in all its prolific contradictions. Her knowledge of her own ambivalence ("I know the difference between loving someone and just sleeping with someone," p. 329), her mixed feelings about her dead husband Fred, even her distance from the special spiritual problems of Shannon: these ambiguities resemble the iguana's concealment of delicate meat under hideous armor; the dungheap to which Shannon takes tourists, so they can see how even offal supports life, the life of scavengers; and indeed, Nonno's own words about the transfiguration of death.

Shannon saw God not as a "senile delinquent" (p. 303), but as thunder and lightning, because he yearned to be punished for his fornication and heresy. Since both of these sins, however, seem to have originated in the loneliness of masturbation, poor substitute for a mother's close attendance, his defiance of God is a spiteful provocation, a circuitous prayer that incries be answered and suffering be purposeful. His foreseeable years with Maxine will be equally tempestuous, confused, but above all passionate: affirmative not of etherealization, but of life as a variegated process of human endurance, unsure evolution, and obscure discovery.

The most effective plays of apposition seem to generate a field between two major, matched characters, which animates a third, in turn. When that basic balance is upset, as in *The Milk Train Doesn't Stop Here Anymore*, the ingathering design seems more superimposed than organic. Sissy Goforth is without peer in the play, Chris Flanders serving at best as custodian of the deathwatch. He helps gentle her departure; but it is her rage, her refusal to be less than she was or ever to cease, which keeps the play alive and counterpoints the rhythmic boom-doom! of the waves below. By insisting, with her last breath, "Be here, when I wake up" (V, 118), she offers Chris a chance to be an angel attendant on resurrection, not just the Angel of Death. He has already initiated that ritual of hope himself, having placed the rings "Under her pillow like a Pharaoh's breakfast waiting for the Pharaoh to wake up hungry" (p. 120). Still he reports afterwards to her secretary Blackie that there's no sign of her fierce vitality anywhere, anymore. (Such behavior goes far towards disestablishing him as mystic, and undercutting the prospect of his being a crypto-Christopher, unwitting bearer of Christ.) His agnosticism may well represent Williams' yea-saying undergoing self-restraint (the sea "says 'Boom' and that's what it means. No translation . . ." (p. 120); the voice of God, as in *Sweet Bird of Youth*, is silent, and man must look to the kingdom of the earth). But the effect is a distinct dampening of dramatic spirits.

Blackie, a compassionate and intelligent woman, would be companion enough for Sissy Goforth, did the latter not require at least the facsimile of greater intimacy with life in the flesh. Her memoirs are an effort to restore what seemed only momentary, especially the wondrous presence of her last husband Alex. The one attraction that

Chris has for her, despite all his deficiencies, is his resemblance to Alex: both are poets garbed in lederhosen. But Chris, even in his own eyes, is more apparitional than real. He watches over the dying, hoping to relieve his terror at the present, not prospective, experience of his own nonbeing. The calm he contributes is difficult to distinguish from coldness. Ethereal as Hannah is in *The Night of the Iguana*, she manages to project her presence; by contrast, Chris is an abstract figure. What ought to be rich ambiguity in his conduct becomes diffuseness. His mobile, "The Earth Is a Wheel in a Great Big Gambling Casino," means to be reminiscent of Pascal's famous wager: we have nothing to lose by a leap of faith. But it cannot be Pascalian if its operation is passive rather than self-propelled. Where Sissy is life-enacting, Chris is merely life-asserting—as are the kabuki attendants who realize their superfluity even as they proclaim, at the end, that the muted bugle is blowing reveille for Sissy, not taps.

As a result of the great disproportion between Sissy and her two companions, the triad of solidarity becomes more token than fact. The real death deplored in this play is loneliness, reinforced only by Sissy's literal dying. But if we live in each other or not at all, can a solitary voice be sufficient sign of life triumphant? The metaphysical dimensions of that seeming contradiction are enormous; the dramatic dimensions, perhaps insuperable.

In an earlier model for this play, *I Rise in Flame, Cried the Phoenix*, Williams' intention is far less uncertain. It too concentrates on the last living fraction of a person (D. H. Lawrence) dying of tuberculosis (Sissy has lung cancer), on a sea cliff overlooking the Mediterranean (the Riviera, as against the Divina Costiera), with the banner of a phoenix at his back (Sissy's heraldic device is the griffin: half lion, half eagle). Lawrence, like Sissy, is determined to outstare the sun. With him are his Valkyrian wife Frieda (though her role as the Angel of Death remains latent) and their virginal friend Bertha. Yet despite the closeness which their conversations show they share, for Lawrence woman is the dark night that would permanently sheathe his maleness. He intends to be whole again, and to be whole is to be solitary, self-sustaining. "I want to do it alone" (*Dragon Country*, p. 75), he says of his death. He collapses as the sun sets, having prophesied his own rearising. Even with its overtones of confused love and hate, essentially *I Rise in Flame, Cried the Phoe-*

nix is about the pride and pleasure of being one person, alone and intact. Strategies of both opposition and apposition are presented but kept minimal, even negligible. Lawrence is a blazing fire that throws two transparent shadows. Even the consolation of transcendence offered him at the moment of death, although it connects him with the cosmos, is empowered by his own imperious imagination. The play is a monument to Lorenzo the Magnificent.

In the Laurentian drama, profound ambivalence is not present; nor would it be appropriate. In *The Milk Train Doesn't Stop Here Anymore*, it is present; but its propriety is unclear. Is the dominant sound of this play a shattering outcry, one voice protesting the inevitability of aloneness? Does its eloquence lie in the tenacity with which Sissy holds past life present in her emotions, without the natural confidence of Lawrence (who *is* the life force) and therefore his articulate control? Does the play inscribe a visionary shape of apposition as a ceremony of self-ascendancy, while still conceding the very real loneliness of dying (and of living)? Or is it, plainly, a defective shape: a one-legged woman clutching two sawed-off crutches? Does it fail those transactional conventions which Williams himself has helped evolve; or are such conventions simply not adequate to the admission he proposed to express?

In his *Memoirs*, Williams indicates that his work since *The Night of the Iguana* has become more experimental—whether in stagecraft or fable, he does not specify. *Milk Train* may indeed be as exploratory a piece as he reports Boston critic Elliot Norton once conjectured. Perhaps its asymmetry is deliberate; its simultaneous yea-nays more postmodern, more antiromantic than usual. In the same autobiography Williams intimates that the final version of *Milk Train* remains to be written; consequently, final judgment may have to be suspended. Or can there ever be a final word about the nonfinality of knowledge?

Revision, which can prevent hardening of a speculative mode into self-imitation, has often been part of the history of a Williams play (or story). In addition, Williams has avoided relying exclusively on triangulation for his Q. E. D.'s. (What is the geometry, for example, of *Camino Real*; or of *Small Craft Warnings*; or of *Out Cry*?) Still the extensive use, intended or not, of triangles of transaction may be enough to sour certain critical tastes. It can be interpreted as a sign of excessive reinforcement, caused by the playwright's lack of confidence or loss of artistic control. Particularly is this a likely response to appositional *assistance* (since *resistance* may be assumed requisite to dramatic conflict). Or one might conclude from the preoccupation with design that, for all his seeming compassion, Williams is essentially an abstractionist whose geometric orders are no more man-centered than, say, the data-processing fiction of a Robbe-Grillet.

Nevertheless, the greatest likelihood lies in such third-party configurations being, for Williams, visual/subliminal metaphors of compensation for human fallibility (probationary proofs, . · .) but especially for human incompletion (earthly trinities). Each person has fullest access to himself through others. That would be impossible, were there not some common human condition, some kind-ness. In that realization of coinheritance is the beginning of coinherence. And to the extent that coinherence is achieved and sustained, there is justification for affirming purpose to life, in spite of individual defect or apparent defeat. The triangles may simply represent the cellular structure of a proper community: composed of diverse elements (apposition), but without divisiveness (opposition). In that prospectus, all men are intermediaries to one another's missions; as they are media for engaging their interim mysteries.

Abstraction and Order in the Language
of Tennessee Williams

JAMES HAFLEY

T|HE AMERICAN THEATER—the theater of the United
States, at least—has impressive traditions of stagecraft and even of
acting, but has next to no literary tradition whatsoever: it has no
Sophocles or Webster, no Racine or Yeats; and lacking even solitary
poets, it is of course lacking in anything like a community of theme.
In a drama in which *The Cocktail Party* is looked upon as theatrical
literature by critical and careless alike, one need not hope to find any
established sense of language itself taken seriously as art, as dramatic
art. Indeed, the worst thing a drama critic can say of a play is that
this or that in it is "literary"; and "theatrical" is a corresponding
insult whenever an English professor uses it.

It is perhaps for this reason that so much depends upon, but so
little comes of, our continual references to the "poetic style" of Tennessee Williams: the one style, the only sustained style, in our
theater that clearly isn't "prosy" and that is hence a sort of vindica-
tion for literary and theater people alike; but nonetheless a style
whose poeticism is generally illustrated (never demonstrated) by
instances of trope or local usage, for all the world as though nothing
else *could* be meant by "poetic style." Thus, we expect Williams
somehow alone to absolve our theater of the sin of language intensely
boring in itself (yes—the language of O'Neill off stage, which sags
till propped up by a production), and at the same time we neglect

753

to investigate beyond our most superficial sense of the singular importance of his language not just to his own art but to that of our entire theater, which Williams' style is expected to fructify like a linguistic TVA. We ask almost everything, and yet we make scant effort to understand how very much he gives us.

It seems to me that Williams' style—by which I mean no more nor less than his care for our language—is precisely not a natural resource but a burgeoning in the desert that makes it perhaps the chief single technical glory of our theater to date. If I cannot begin to explore that thesis in the scope of one brief essay, that is all right; what I want to do is only suggest a way or so in which it can be justified by anyone interested in literary excellence. And it is because so often, too often, Williams' "poetic" quality is located in concretes—in simile and metaphor, in symbol—that I choose to point out some instances of how even the mere vocabulary of abstraction he employs can be studied to rich advantage. I do not think I shall call upon a single regionalism of word or syntax here, and I shall cite concretes only in their relation to abstractions. Further, though I can't resist some generalization about the language, I don't want to emphasize how it works in the plays (a subject for at least a book) but mostly to cite examples from the poems. Yet everything I say should be applicable most valuably to the plays, and apprehensible at its most complex there. When O'Neill wants "poetry" at the end of *Long Day's Journey* he injects extended passages from Swinburne into his text; when Williams wants such intense effects he doesn't have to import them. The last speech of Blanche is generated out of the play's own poetic matrix.

II

Williams' abstractions invariably relate to absolutes, about which he is disarmingly ambivalent: he at once celebrates and shies from transcendence. Thus, the white blackbird and black blackbird of his epigraph to *Moise* exist in a Neoplatonic pattern which is familiar enough; but a tension between conventional longing for the absolute (named by a world of abstract nouns) and individual preference for the spatial/temporal even at its most perilously transitory—this is what is characteristic of Williams. In Williams is neither a sacrificing of real for ideal, nor (as in some Keats or Whitman, say) a total discovery of the ideal in the real; there is dualism and the pull of spirit against flesh, abstraction against concretion, but at the same time a grudge against the very idea of the absolute. His is a world longing for otherness and yet sad or spiteful that such a concept even exists to disturb location in the self; yet self-consciousness defines but also damns by delimitation the identity that it defines.

This ambivalent attitude towards the idea of the ideal is everywhere apparent in Williams' language, where it is dramatized at least as thoroughly as in event. A title like *A Streetcar Named Desire* is apt demonstration. The abstraction "desire"—ranging in its meanings from longing for the absolute to a contradictory lust—is evoked only to be ridiculed as naming a mechanical contrivance, a vulgar corruption of some such conveyance as the ship of life. At the same time, in double irony, the vehicle seems poignantly in need of a magnitude beyond it, like a mailman trying to perform one of the labors of Hercules, or a tenement child named for a king. But the ultimate revelation is of Desire itself as merely a place name, no more in stature or consolation than the streetcar that literally goes there. In the play, Blanche says desire is the opposite of death: it is her conviction prompted by her encounter with the Mexican woman offering flowers for the dead. But she is wrong, and these two grand abstractions, "death" and "desire" ("desire" in Blanche's sense of longing for transcendence) are the same; Stanley's "desire," lust, is the true opponent of death, and the life he gives, like the home he gives, is both pitifully sordid and absolutely necessary to sanity. In this play about homes, Blanche's sublimation of earthy desire that has been denied her leads her from a lost Paradise to a rest home: from innocence to innocence. Stanley's desire and Stella's keep them soundly, vitally located in the experience of time present, in the slum that is the very nutrient of life lived. The situation is not unlike that in Shelley's *Alastor*: humankind can be grateful to the poet, to Blanche, for reaching out to saving ideals; but though the ideal is a model for the salvation of humankind, it is just as surely an illusive alternate to the reality of experienced life. Shelley's speaker, at the end of his account of the idealist poet, cries "O, that the dream . . . were the true law/Of this so lovely world!" In Williams' play, Stella, pulled between the unreal beauty of Blanche's "home" and "desire" and the naked realities of Stanley's, opts for the latter, for law instead of dream—indeed for the legal kinship of her bond to him rather than for her past familial kindness to Blanche. Blanche must rely upon strangers in seeking her kind: sisterhood is a kindness far too real to sustain her elevated sense of home and family, impossibly ideal, impossibly lost. Williams' epigraph from Hart Crane's "The Broken Tower" points to this theme, to "the visionary company" that is a "kindness of strangers," versus the civic family that is a cruelty of kin. *Desire, lost, home*—these words recur tellingly among the play's abstractions. Belle Reve is prelapsarian; the real Elysian Fields is to be found between the L & N tracks and the river.

But major throughout the play are words of relationship (familiarity): *species, type, attachment, kind* and *kindness, companionship,* developing up to Blanche's last speech and giving it its astonishing poetic power and control. In the battle between love and sex, desire and desire, Stanley's crude but real strength, relying on kidneys and not souls, is like the gross earth that alone can nourish belief, imagination, the reaching for the moon which the play defines as "lunacy" in the literal sense of the term. Life is redeemed only by lunatic aspiration, yet it must violate the ideal if only to sustain its desperate knowledge that the L & N tracks are after all not the woodland of Weir. Blanche's name may mean *white*, but her legal name, her married name, is Grey. And all the wonderfully exciting conflicts of this play are first and last conflicts among words, just as the network of conflict I have noticed here is one of battle between concrete and abstract words handled with full awareness of their self-defeating contradictions.

III

Williams' favorite abstracts seem to be *light* (regularly "fading" or "dimming"), *love, reverence, blue* and the constantly recurring *youth. Light* is most often related to imagery of glass, from Laura's animals to a profusion of mirrors to the ice of *Moise.* Glass exhibits the favored ambivalence: it can reveal, or seem to, what is beyond, or it can reflect what is only before it; it can tell truth, but is the most fragile of substances; like smoke it hovers as image between the concrete and the abstract: next to invisible, yet with a visibility that must ultimately damn it into mortality. For in Williams' world knowledge has only negative value when pitted against the lunatic falsehood of justifying fancy. The light as it dims, as it fades, proves the glass to be literal glass only.

Light can be either a concrete or an abstract noun; even more so *youth*, which as word and image (object) is central in this art. *Youth* is at once the most attractive abstract and the most transitory concrete: what's soonest lost but most needs finding, soonest faded but most deserves perduration. The poem "Testa Dell' Effebo"—"Testa" both real and simulated—is a convenient example of the paradox of youth as both lost and saved: as real in life but ideal in art. The sculpture of that poem is analogous to the word *youth* (art) as opposed to the condition of youth (life). The sculpture, the word, are at once involved with life and safe from it: art is a solution infinitely preferable to lunacy. Art allows comedy as lunacy demands tragedy (here mortality). In this poem the language dramatizes the word become Word (compare Hart Crane's *Voyages*). The real youth after his youth has ended, dimmed, must have become lunatic; the youth in art remains youth to time present—"this" time—and indeed prompts the language of life in this speech of praise. He has progressed from Flora to copper, but the speech reenacts his past most comfortably, and the copper cast exhibits, eternalizes, the "luster" and "repose" (the only two abstract words in the poem), hence realizing the ideal as it idealizes the real in a turning of change to permanence. Indeed, the last line suggests both that the sculpture has immortalized the youth and that he has shed his mortality, cast it off in pure ideality. The ancillary imagery here of eyes, glasses, birds, typically marks the youth's turning from seeming to genuine permanence. Like the marvelous children of "In Jack-O'-Lantern's Weather" he exists "north of time": located beyond location.

But art itself is subject to decay, as the mere thought of *The Glass Menagerie* insists. If a zoo of Kowalskis can be tamed into glass, its fixity is transparent in both senses. And if the obligingly mediating glass can not only idealize the real but also realize the ideal, the unicorn, that realization is almost certainly a betrayal into the merely ordinary, the horse. Glass is for Williams a grand correlative for abstraction as ideal: a meeting ground where the miracle occurs but, occurring, subjects itself to time and hence to destruction. As the copper of "Testa" permitted the comic *ars longa* (art endures), so, and much oftener, the glass announces *vita brevis ars brevisque* (both life and art soon perish). Like Laura's unicorn the abstractions of *Menagerie* are shattered by the concretes, just as time present in that play is mere illusion, and time past (the same thing) only a memory.

However, despite his distrust of airy realms (or suspicious admiration of them)—which is of course rendered provocative because of a concomitant disdain for the essential earthy—Williams effects relationships between abstract and concrete in many satisfying ways other than by invoking the fusing miracle of art. And his verbal strategies remind me of none more than of Wordsworth's when he affirms the possibility of a peace or at least a truce between real and ideal.

"Mornings on Bourbon Street" is in its modest way Williams' "Tintern Abbey." In Wordsworth's poem language again and again not only describes but enacts, dramatizes, the union of real and ideal. One instance will suffice to illustrate that: "these steep and lofty cliffs,/That on a wild secluded scene impress/Thoughts of more deep seclusion; and connect/The landscape with the quiet of the sky." I am interested here not so much in how cliffs impress thoughts, or in how a secluded scene is productive of seclusion itself, as in how cliffs connect landscape with quiet—concrete cliffs impress abstract thoughts and thereby connect concretion (landscape) and abstraction (quiet). It is purely a verbal maneuver and as such it is stunning: a painter might pictorialize cliffs connecting landscape and sky, but never landscape and quiet: that is a relationship possible only as language.

Now the situation in "Mornings on Bourbon Street" is amazingly similar to that in "Tintern Abbey": will time present and future vindicate a conviction of time past? Williams' poem does not answer the question but only shows how truly it is a question; Wordsworth's poem may seem to answer, but in fact concludes in such tentativeness of diction and syntax as to provide no more than the wishful thinking of Williams. (Aside: Surely it is not a question we want answered: reassurance is a cheap commodity.) But more remarkable than the similarity of situation is that of language between these two poems, as if Williams has, not remembered Wordsworth, but worked out the same linguistic solution to the same psychic problem. The vocabulary of epistemology and of abstraction doesn't require underscoring. Nor does the conflict between knowing and believing, saying and believing (because saying is not believing, any more than seeing is). What does demand attention is the relationship between concretion and abstraction, absorbed together into a texture of affirmation that both justifies the speaker's problem and suggests the salvific importance of a positive answer to his question. A line like "faint mumble of benediction with faint surprise" demonstrates this perfectly: the concrete (or sensuous) "mumble" joined through syntactical balancing with the abstract (or metaphysical) "surprise," each qualified with the emotive "faint" and each given new meaning through the spiritual "benediction." The amalgam of sensuous/emotive/conceptual/spiritual here is every bit as impressive as in Wordsworth; this is indeed poetic style dependent upon effects that are achieved only through a most rigorous technique, a most intense concentration of and upon language, for the line that I have isolated is characteristic of a linguistic enactment continuous in the whole poem and in Williams' art almost everywhere.

Incidentally, if this poem is Williams' "Tintern Abbey," surely "Heavenly Grass" is his little "Immortality Ode." Can anyone have failed to notice that? And the title itself plays upon the same tragicomic paradox so dear to Williams. The impulse to ballad everywhere in Williams' verse is surely related to the motive to drama; enactment, whether as language or event, is his passion, and *Moise* can be read as not least a dramatization of the act of writing itself. At the end of "In Jack-O'-Lantern's Weather" there are "geometry problems whose Q. E. D./is surely speechless wonder," and *Moise* more than any other work by Williams inverts that to translate speechless wonder into Q. E. D.

"A Separate Poem," the last of *In the Winter of Cities*, most clearly of all the poems handles concretes and abstracts to dramatize what I might call Williams' stoic hedonism—the two birds in the bush undeniably better than one in the hand, but after all not to be hoped for whereas the one is surely someday to be despaired of. This poem more or less glosses that strange utterance from "The Dangerous Painters," "It was not good, it was God,/and I could not endure it. I had to go away." There is the center of Williams' Angst. God is better than good, but good is as much as one can endure in a condition of mutability that seems positively unalterable save in death and in that version of art which is also beyond the framework of life lived. "A Separate Poem" settles for the tarnished image that lasts awhile, rather than reaching for the sweet bird already on the wing. It predicates an end of error, but that is clearly less satisfying than an ending truth: "lies die, but truth doesn't live except in the truth of our island/which is a truth that wanders." And the last three lines of the poem find out that transience even in art, even of the intransigent, had better be accepted ruefully than let go of for any suprahuman stability. One is reminded, as so often, of the great looking-glass scene in *Sweet Bird,* and Alexandra's victory over Chance. For however close to the Romantics Williams may approach, he can't, even for the moon, let go of his earthly wisdom, the world of reason.

IV

I have been trying to think what are my expectations as I sit in a theater waiting for a Tennessee Williams play, new or in new production—new to me or known from its first production and on through many others. What exactly am I expecting, and how is it special, how is it different from my expectation before a performance of, say, O'Neill or Albee? What would, in a new play, most surprise me were it not there? What missing item would I wait for and grow restless at not having?

These are difficult questions for me. Easiest to start with O'Neill. I expect information. In some instances—*A Touch of the Poet*—I am overwhelmed by so much more than I expected that I want to complain there won't be time to do anything with so much. But in other instances—*Long Day's Journey*—I see that a long speech of information (about the speaker now, the speech as act, as well as about what he tells of, to be sure) is beginning and I lean forward to the excitement of it; then there is reaction (my own but most significantly that of the other players), and that builds toward another moment of information: the Monumental Informative. I think that in O'Neill almost every other thing—revelation or concealment—comes as information.

And in Albee I expect surprise. Well, that is what one expects always from every play, I suppose: anticipated surprise, the paradox of art. But in Albee I expect the unanticipated more than elsewhere. Surprise in stage properties (*Tiny Alice* so filled with phrenological specimen and caged cardinal and dollhouse-Hell that one could enjoy the empty stage a long while for all of its surprises) and in talking fish and in Agnes' complex, unfinished sentence in *A Delicate Balance* that is surprisingly and simply finished much later on. Surprise in the absurdly pleasant surprises of *The American Dream* and horrible ones of *Zoo Story*, and in even the unsurprising as surprising: the announcement at the end of *All Over* that it's all over.

In Tennessee Williams I may receive both information and surprise (but there is very little of either, if you compare), but what I expect, what I am awaiting is the excitement of speech itself. This may be called poetic style, or language as gesture, or drama as literature, or—more properly—literature as theater, but it is speech itself. I listen and the language builds and develops itself into structures that both are and lead to the gloriously inevitable. With Williams, the more I know the more my expectation is rewarded. I have cited Blanche's last speech to suggest how this phenomenon occurs, how her last line is great because it depends on the kindness of all the language that has preceded it. I can cite Amanda's last line in *Glass Menagerie* just as well, as another particularly evident example of the thousands in these plays. She will say "Go, then! Then go to the moon—you selfish dreamer!" The language of the play has made this last speech, these particular last words, of hers all but inevitable, just as Tom's smashing the glass on the floor right afterwards is all but inevitable in the directions. (Yet a production is perfectly sensible without that event; it would be unthinkable without Amanda's line.) Her speech puts all but the last few pieces into an almost completed pattern of enacted language.

And it is this inevitability of speech itself that makes each production of a known play brand new to me. I have heard descriptions of how the legendary Laurette Taylor said that line, and I can try to imagine it and wish I'd been able to hear it, to remember it myself; I can remember how many Amandas said it (most thrillingly for me Helen Hayes as if using up the very last breath of her life to get it said), and at a recent new production I could hear the superb Maureen Stapleton say it. I have not a central memory of Amandas in appearance, gesture, "personality"—in fact Katharine Hepburn's tremor distracted me precisely by making me think how appropriate it was—but of Amandas in speech, and of course in all of their speeches, and of all the plays as speech itself enacting and enacted. I understand through Williams alone in American theater the joy Racine's audiences can have comparing versions of his great central speeches. The same joy I have in opera thinking of Albanese's Violetta or Pons's or Sutherland's. And the comparison with opera is perhaps most suiting of any: the theater of Williams is a drama of language itself as art, as fine art.

"An Intercourse Not Well Designed": Talk and Touch in the Plays of Tennessee Williams

WILLIAM J. SCHEICK

B Y OVEREMPHASIZING the influence of D. H. Lawrence and August Strindberg on Tennessee Williams' concern with the dichotomy of flesh and spirit, critics have underrated his treatment of the theme.[1] Williams actually perceives no *real* conflict between the spirit and the flesh. Quite consistently throughout his plays both forces constitute the human self, and both inherently incline toward defining that self. In *Summer and Smoke*, for instance, Alma Winemiller eventually realizes that she indeed has a doppelgänger; besides the spiritual force suggested by her name she has also a physical force, "another person inside me, another self" (II, 241). When, earlier in the play, Alma explains to John Buchanan, who is oriented toward the body, that she thinks he is as confused as she is "but in a different way" (p. 196), she intuits not a hierarchical superiority of one component of the self over the other but a common bond of inadequacy or failure between the spirit and the flesh. In *The Milk Train Doesn't Stop Here Anymore* Christopher Flanders states this relationship more positively: "the spirit has to live in the body, and so you have to keep the body in a state of repair because it's the home of the—spirit" (V, 74–75). The spirit and the flesh share an impulse to eradicate confusion by achieving definition or wholeness of self; but, for reasons unknown to man,

763

their qualitative differences prevent them from adequately reinforcing each other in this endeavor.

This failure to interact sometimes leads Williams' characters to repudiate one or the other of the two forces, as if the negation of one would augment the chances of the other for satisfying the self's need for definition. Frequently Williams' characters will desperately vacillate in an extreme manner from one force to the other at different moments. A disproportionate restraint of either force "grows and grows until it gets to be something enormous. Then finally there is so much of it, it explodes inside them—and they go to pieces" (*You Touched Me!*, p. 65). Nevertheless, the antagonism between the flesh and the spirit is only apparent, only a felt or subjective reality. Actually they are mutually aligned in an attempt to secure permanent definition or wholeness for the self, of which they are the essential components.

Williams dramatizes this intrinsic attempt at uniting flesh and spirit principally through the two basic vehicles of human communication, talk and touch. In *You Touched Me!*, for example, Captain Rockley says "the talk is the touch" and his adopted son Hadrian replies, "the touch is the talk" (p. 85). In *Cat on a Hot Tin Roof* Williams refers to words functioning as soft caresses (III, 24), and his prefatory remarks imply a correlation: "we talk to each other, write and wire each other, call each other short and long distance across land and sea, clasp hands with each other at meeting and at parting" in our "always somewhat thwarted effort to break through walls to each other" (III, 3). In *27 Wagons Full of Cotton* Flora Meighan refers, with unwitting irony, to her sexual liaison with Silva Vicarro as "a nice conversation" (p. 26). And in *Orpheus Descending* Lady Torrance tells Val Xavier that she is touched by his talk (III, 303). When Tom Wingfield, in *A Glass Menagerie*, says that he tried "to find in motion what was lost in space" (I, 237; cf. I, 190) —by which he means, among other things, that his birdlike spirit sought escape from the physical law of gravity—he seems to emphasize the disparity between the flesh and the spirit; but his attempt to escape proves unsuccessful because motion occurs in space, and space is defined by motion. In short, space and motion, like the flesh and the spirit, are interrelated features of human experience.

Talking and touching participate in a circular dynamic. Both attempt to communicate the self outwardly to another so that the recipient, through his response, will reflect this communication to the source, thereby developing consciousness and deepening identity. From Williams' point of view, however, a bitter irony lies in this process: the resultant, tentative self-awareness tends to be hard to bear and never satisfies the compulsion behind the search for identity. The circular dynamic of talk and touch, consequently, is usually painful and vexing for Williams' characters. Introspection constrictingly encircles, preventing any penetration to the crucial ontological questions that need answering if the self is to attain wholeness or full identity. This restricting circumscription cautions us, I think, against an unqualified acceptance of such assertions (as Arthur Ganz makes in "The Desperate Morality of the Plays of Tennessee Williams") that Williams advocates a neo-Lawrentian trust in the absolute goodness of the natural instincts. The natural or temporal reality within the circumference of communicative acts always remains ambiguous for Williams' characters and always proves insufficient to pacify the compulsion underlying the search for completeness through talk and touch.

Near the conclusion of *The Night of the Iguana*, Jonathan Coffin (Nonno) finishes a poem that contains the central notions underlying Williams' use of the motif of talk and touch. The first four stanzas of the poem read:

> How calmly does the orange branch
> Observe the sky begin to blanch
> Without a cry, without a prayer,
> With no betrayal of despair.
>
> Sometime while night obscures the tree
> The zenith of its life will be
> Gone past forever, and from thence
> A second history will commence.
>
> A chronicle no longer gold,
> A bargaining with mist and mould,
> And finally the broken stem
> The plummeting to earth; and then
>
> An intercourse not well designed
> For beings of a golden kind

> Whose native green must arch above
> The earth's obscene, corrupting love (IV, 371).

As Ferdinand Leon suggests in an essay not entirely convincing ("Time, Fantasy, and Reality in *Night of the Iguana*," pp. 94–5), Nonno's poem provides a nexus for several motifs in *Iguana*, but it also epitomizes Williams' portrayal, throughout his plays, of the postlapsarian human condition. Man is depicted as a branch of the tree of life, an offshoot once paradisiacally young (innocent) and capable of producing golden fruit (oranges), which however at some obscure period in its existence (night) will be broken away from the supporting and defining trunk. The point of transition remains a mystery, though *chronicle* and *history* suggest Williams' characteristic emphasis on time as the chief inimical factor in this change. In its fallen condition the branch cannot grow upward toward the sun, the source of life as golden as the orange fruit once borne by the branch; it must now reconcile its earthly orientation with an inherent impulse for aerial ascendancy. For the trunk, from which the branch derived, earth and sky presumably are not antagonistic; they constitute two features of reality readily integrated by the tree, the roots of which find sustenance from the ground so the branch may bear golden fruit in the air. The fallen branch, however, cannot unite these two extremes, though it retains an inclination to do so.

The pivotal fourth stanza of Nonno's poem especially focuses on this deficiency. Here the broken branch, the isolated self, ceaselessly and unsuccessfully attempts to integrate the two forces defining its nature. This failure produces in the fallen branch an experience of an apparent conflict between its earthward orientation and its aerial inclination. The truncated self, symbolized by the branch, is racked between the impulse of its "native green" to maintain ascendancy in the sky, the realm of light and birds (IV, 357), recurring images for the spirit in Williams' plays, and an inevitable predisposition toward the earth, the realm of mist and mold. After the "obscure" event, the compulsion to integrate these two forces, as the self engages in "An intercourse not well designed/For beings of a golden kind," results in interminable frustration.

In this stanza the latent reference to Christ recalls Williams' use of the Christ figure to suggest the attempt to combine the skyward impulse of the spirit and the earthward orientation of the flesh. Inability to unite the two results in crucifixion; and indeed Nonno's observation that the "native green must arch above/The earth's obscene, corrupting love" suggests an image of someone crucified between earth and sky forces. In this context *intercourse* intimates that man should be, like Christ, the Word made flesh; that is, the intimated Christ imagery in the stanza ironically accentuates the human failure to integrate spirit and flesh in spite of their essential affinity. *Intercourse* refers both to conversation (talk) and to the sex act (touch), expressive modes of the spirit and the flesh which not only should be mutually reinforcing but also should provide an excellent means for interaction with others and for achieving identity. In spite of their mutual objective, however, the flesh and the spirit do not unite in man because he lacks the ability to integrate their qualitative differences; and this is why their expressive modes of talk and touch also fail to unite people. The ultimate irony in Williams' plays is that man is compelled by a sense of incompleteness to engage in the intercourse of talking and touching yet always fails to satisfy that urgency because he is unable to unite the forces of the flesh and the spirit. Consequently he feels crucified by their apparent antagonism.

Williams' characters persist in this sacrificial self-expression because the alternative is death. As Blanche DuBois remarks in *A Streetcar Named Desire*, one's choice is between desire and death (I, 388–89). By desire she means the human need to communicate through talking and touching. Indeed, Blanche, who once was tender (touch) as well as trusting (talk) and who cannot bear to be alone (pp. 257, 376), is a compulsive talker in spite of her doubts about the successfulness of direct speech (pp. 253, 318). That she is also given periodically to an uncontrollable urge to touch is evident when she kisses the young newsboy on the mouth (pp. 338–39), the organ used for both talking and touching. In this action she symbolically integrates the spirit and the flesh within herself and also combines talk and touch as reciprocal modes of interaction with others. And when Blanche earlier grasps her sister's hand and presses it to her lips, she says, "*believe* I feel things more than I *tell* you" (p. 333), a remark which, like the action it follows, implies the essential alignment of talk (telling) and touch (feeling) but also explicitly indicates the inability to integrate them as a determinant feature of Blanche's problems.

Desire, as manifest through talking and touching, characterizes life in Williams' plays, and it is life that Brick Pollitt wishes to escape in *Cat*. Brick not only avoids being touched by Maggie, by his mother and by his father but also withdraws from all physical contact (III, 156). Moreover Maggie is driven to lecture him about his silence (p. 31) because he detests talking as much as he does touching. Since speaking is painful for him, Brick prefers an alcohol-induced "click" which occurs, he says, only when he is alone and not conversing (p. 99). The deathlike internal silence provided by this "click" suppresses Brick's impulse to talk and to touch, temporarily arresting his search for identity. In other words, Brick wants to die, as Big Daddy perceives in his observation that his son's wish for "perfect unbroken quiet" will be amply fulfilled in the grave (pp. 89–90). That no one can live and simultaneously escape the quest for identity through talking and touching is as evident at the conclusion of *Cat* as it is in an earlier one-act play entitled *Portrait of a Madonna*, in which Miss Lucretia Collins has withdrawn into a gravelike room but still compulsively engages in conversations with her deceased mother and in sexual activity with an imaginary rapist.

In many of Williams' plays the prevalence of mirrors, or of imagery or actions suggesting mirrorlike characteristics, symbolizes the basic circularity of the search for definition. As a traditional symbol for consciousness, the mirror objectifies in Williams' plays an individual's attempt to achieve self-reflection through his intercourse with others. Whereas Brick prefers to avoid speech because in evading self-awareness he unconsciously wishes to annihilate selfhood, Maggie craves identity. Maggie's desire for completion is overtly dramatized in her effort to share in the security of Big Daddy's bequest; it is also subtly implied by her use of mirrors. Early in the action Maggie adjusts a mirror to straighten an eyelash (p. 20); very shortly thereafter she again stops before a mirror and still later in the same act asks her reflection in a mirror, "Who are you?" (pp. 25, 48). Seeing herself in a mirror understandably makes her think about her image as reflected in human responses to her (p. 49); for human intercourse is, in Williams' plays, essentially reflexive. Because he avoids talking and touching, Brick does not fulfill Maggie's need for self-reflection; however, Big Daddy and Maggie both serve as mirrors for Brick, eventually leading him to perceive his failure to function as a mirror for Skipper (pp. 124–25). Brick's apt remark to Big Daddy, "You told *me!* I told *you!*" (p. 128), refers not merely to the truth each has revealed to the other but also to the fundamental circularity or reflexiveness of all genuine human intercourse.

In the penultimate scene of *Streetcar* Blanche holds a mirror in her hand (I, 391). However different in other respects, she is similar to Maggie in her need for an identity achieved through the circular process of human intercourse. Time and again Blanche solicits comments about her appearance (I, 278, 289), and her proclivity toward exhibitionism (I, 293–94) dramatizes her compulsion to see her reflection in others. In *Orpheus* exhibitionism serves the same purpose for Carol Cutrere, who asserts, "*I'm an exhibitionist!* I want to be noticed, seen, heard, felt!" (III, 250). To be heard and felt, to talk and touch, are Carol's means for acquiring identity; and she uses Val, who is "a peculiar talker" (p. 264), as her mirror (e.g., pp. 281–82), even as Alex in *Milk Train* apparently used Mrs. Goforth's "eyes for his mirrors" (V, 47). In *Menagerie* Laura, albeit no exhibitionist, desperately seeks a reflection of herself in Jim O'Connor's eyes in lieu of her nonreflecting, transparent and lifeless glass figurines. In *Suddenly Last Summer* Mrs. Venable suggests that she had functioned as a mirror for her son: "I'd reach across a table and touch his hands and say not a word, just look, and touch his hands with my hand until his hands stopped shaking and his eyes looked out, not in" (III, 408). Unable to find anyone who will believe her and thereby complete the circuit of human intercourse for her, Catharine Holly in the same play suffers from a diminishing sense of personal identity; it is not surprising that she begins to write her journal entries in the third person (p. 398).

In *Sweet Bird of Youth* the Princess Kosmonopolis has seen herself all too clearly on the movie screen, which she speaks of as a mirror (IV, 34); yet she is still compelled to look into mirrors (p. 46). Through her intercourse, both sexual and conversational, with Chance Wayne she tries to perceive a more youthful reflection of herself (p. 97). At the end of the play Chance forces her to look into a mirror and asks her what she sees (p. 119), implying, among other things, that he has been her mirror and an intimate part of her identity. Chance's final request for "your recognition of me in you" (p. 124) expresses the essential mirrorlike circular process defining human identity. Likewise in *Iguana* Hannah Jelkes provides Shannon with an image of himself through her sketches and her conversation: "I'm just attempting to give you a character sketch of yourself, in words instead of pastel crayons or charcoal" (p. 344). Near the conclusion of the play she accuses him of talking to himself, but he replies that he has been speaking to her (pp. 369–70); actually both are correct, for Shannon speaks to Hannah and, as a result of her mirrorlike function, addresses himself as well.

Williams' characters find increased self-awareness painful and vexing, though in his later plays some begin to adjust. Reflections of themselves are not only hard to bear; they are also always insufficient to satisfy the yearning for identity. In fact every reflection only intensifies the compulsion for wholeness. Failure to harmonize spirit and flesh prevents successful interaction with others through the two primary modes of expression. As Nonno's poem indicates, the human self engages in "An intercourse not well designed/For beings of a golden kind." In *The Purification* a character remarks that "words are too loosely woven to catch" truth (*27 Wagons*, p. 40); nor can touch guarantee completion, as Val Xavier has learned (III, 270). The Princess Kosmonopolis in *Sweet Bird* unsuccessfully tries, through talk and touch, to "hold" (IV, 104) Chance back from destruction; and similarly Catharine in *Suddenly* is unable to "take hold" (III, 406) of Sebastian and save him. The trouble is that whereas talk proves to be too indirect, as Blanche knows (I, 318), and as Big Daddy discovers (III, 111), touch tends to be too direct. Though both are mutually aligned in the objective of defining the self, talk and touch mysteriously differ qualitatively.

In *Talk to Me Like the Rain and Let Me Listen . . .*, an early one-act play in *27 Wagons Full of Cotton*, Williams presents a very condensed, stark presentation of the failed dynamic of talk and touch. The play concerns the act of intercourse, in both senses, between a man and a woman, neither of whom is named. Images of abortive efforts to communicate abound in the work. The woman complains that she was unable to read the note left by the man and that when she dialed the telephone number scribbled on the note she could not hear what was said on the other end of the line.

Similarly the man complains of his inability to get answers over the telephone and, evoking an image of a misused vehicle of communication, laments that he has been "passed around like a dirty *post*card among people" (p. 214). Throughout the brief play he asks the woman to talk to him, and the first time he makes this request he also touches her. The combined contact of talking and touching helps him initiate the process of limited self-awareness; for although he is speaking ostensibly to the woman, she does not seem to hear him and ultimately he is talking to himself. Likewise, when the woman expresses her frustrations, she uses the man as a mirror for self-reflection. In narrating her fantasy about attaining innocence through an ideal solitary confinement leading to death, she mentions that she will read the books of dead poets and that she "won't have to touch them or answer their questions" (p. 217). Like Brick, she prefers death rather than interaction through talk and touch. She too refers to a mirror, but instead of gaining self-awareness she fantasizes that her hair turns white and her body grows thin, "almost transparent" (p. 217), until she does not "have any body at all" (p. 218). This act of intimate verbal intercourse, however, provides her with no relief from her internal vexation. Negligibly affected, the man presses his mouth to her throat (symbolizing the fundamental unity of talk and touch) and asks her to come back to bed with him, a request she makes to him a few seconds later. Everything in the play suggests that their sexual communication has been and will continue to be as frustratingly unfulfilling as their verbal intercourse.

This play both emphasizes the essential circularity of all human communication and shows that talking and touching never really satisfy the desire for completeness. Nothing has changed in this play, which begins and ends with a bed scene. The man and the woman have participated in a static ritual. Williams says there is an impression "that the present scene between them is the repetition of one that has been repeated so often that its plausible emotional contents, such as reproach and contrition, have been completely worn out and there is nothing left but acceptance of something hopelessly inalterable between them" (p. 211). The circular pattern of talk and touch as well as the unfulfilled mutual longing of the spirit and the flesh remain inalterable. Touching and talking are the chief defining movements one has in space (to return to Tom

Wingfield's images); but finally they are merely motions in space, always unable to surpass their limitations in time and never attaining that "mystical" moment or that "touch" of something transcendent which would complete the self. The self remains unfulfilled; or, as Benjamin Nelson says in *Tennessee Williams*, "The sins of the earth are its incompletions, Williams tells us; the universe is fragmented and man born into it is born into incompletion" (p. 290).

Although Williams does not assert that something transcendent in fact exists beyond the phenomenological circularity of the self's communicative actions, he does indicate the ceaseless ache for an experience of such an ultimate reality.[2] Sometimes Williams resorts to religious imagery to convey the desire for this elusive fulfilment. In *Streetcar* Blanche momentarily and elliptically expresses the underlying impulse of the self when, as a result of Mitch's kiss on her lips (the symbolic act joining talk and touch), she gasps, "Sometimes—there's God—so quickly!" (I, 356). In *Milk Train* Chris refers to everyone's need for "somebody or something to mean God" (V, 113), and *Suddenly* recounts Sebastian's failure to find some transcendent meaning beyond the temporal. According to Maggie, in *Cat*, she and Brick "hit heaven together ev'ry time that we loved" (III, 58); understandably, then, in the heat of an argument she refers to Brick as a "godlike being" (p. 56), for it is through him that she has come closest to fulfilling the yearning for completion. Through Brick, Maggie, whom Williams introduces as a sort of priestess (p. 17), almost transcends the limitations of the circular temporal reality of all intercourse between persons.

When, in *Iguana*, Hannah equates communication among people to traditional belief in God (IV, 352) and when Mrs. Goforth, in *Milk Train*, thinks that "Devils can be driven out of the heart by the touch of a hand on a hand, or a mouth on a mouth" (V, 85), they express Williams' notion of the religious, even sacramental nature of talk and touch. But, however sacramental, neither mode can transubstantiate the temporal limits of human communication into something transcendent or eternal. Thomas P. Adler, in "The Search for God in the Plays of Tennessee Williams," is correct in arguing that Williams seems to say "we must be like God to the other, and the other must be like God to us" (p. 56); but in fact no one is God and so no one succeeds in the sacramental actions of talk and touch. For Williams' characters the quest for identity, for wholeness, results only in a perennially unanswered knock in the heart (*Orpheus*, III, 250), in incomplete sentences (*Iguana*, IV, 369), and in unfulfilled physical desires. Man should be the Word made flesh, but ironically he is unable to interact effectively with others through words and feelings. He fails in part because words and feelings differ qualitatively but primarily because he is unable to integrate spirit and body. Consequently his impulse for internal harmony and wholeness of self crucifies him between the aerial and earthly extremities, between the spiritual and fleshly forces constituting his identity. In this unchanging, painful condition the victim is "like a blind man climbing a staircase that goes to nowhere" (*Iguana*, IV, 346). Man's crucifixion between the polarities of his identity lacks redemptive power or even discernible purpose; yet the climb, the absurd sacrifice, continues because it is the fate of humanity to use the sacramental modes of talk and touch in an endlessly frustrated attempt to detect some trace of transcendence which will fulfill the self and integrate the spirit and the flesh. Confronted by an incomplete self circularly trying to define itself, Williams' characters engage in "An intercourse not well designed" and find themselves, as Val Xavier states, endlessly "waiting for something like if you ask a question you wait for someone to answer, but you ask the wrong question or you ask the wrong person and the answer don't come" (*Orpheus*, III, 271). Such is life as Williams portrays it; the alternative to this flawed dynamic of human intercourse, to the failure of talk and touch, is the silence and the insensitivity of unredeeming death.

Notes to William J. Scheick,
"An Intercourse Not Well Designed"

1. The influence of D. H. Lawrence is best documented in Norman J. Fedder's otherwise disappointing *The Influence of D. H. Lawrence on Tennessee Williams*; and William Sharp overstresses Williams' view of the comforts of sex in "An Unfashionable View of Tennessee Williams." Among others, two comparisons between Strindberg and Williams appear in Richard B. Vowles' "Tennessee Williams and Strindberg" and Nancy Tischler's *Tennessee Williams: Rebellious Puritan*.

2. In *The Broken World of Tennessee Williams* Esther Merle Jackson makes some pertinent observations about this theme of transcendence, though she is inclined at times to presuppose Williams' belief in God; other noteworthy religious dimensions are indicated by John J. Fritscher, "Some Attitudes and a Posture: Religious Metaphor and Ritual in Tennessee Williams' Query of the American God" and by Donald P. Costello, "Tennessee Williams' Fugitive Kind."

Tennessee Williams
at the Delta Brilliant

ALBERT E. KALSON

I

IN A MOMENT of ecstatic happiness in *Battle of Angels*, Myra exclaims to Val, "Greta Garbo is at the Delta Brilliant" (I, 79). In the third act of his first full-length play, Tennessee Williams alludes to the movies to suggest the possibility of the merging of illusion and reality, of celluloid world and harsh existence. In *The Eccentricities of a Nightingale* John takes Alma to the Delta Brilliant to see a Mary Pickford film as prelude to a night of love. Life as Hollywood dream, however, fades quickly for Myra and Alma—one is murdered by her husband, and the other loses her lover. For other Williams characters, however, what is playing at the Delta Brilliant emphasizes the gulf between unattainable dream and empty life. Sitting in the white section of the Delta Brilliant, Chicken in *Kingdom of Earth* is aroused by the actresses on the screen but shunned by the women around him because of his Negro blood (p. 101). Willie, the young girl in *This Property Is Condemned*, has been to the Delta Brilliant to see Garbo die beautifully of consumption with "Violins playing. And loads and loads of white flowers" (*27 Wagons*, p. 202). Tuberculosis was not so pretty, however, when her sister Alva, who looked like a movie star and was "The Main Attraction" for the local railroad men, died of the same wasting disease.

774

For many Williams characters, Hollywood is what life never is—but ought to be. Kilroy in *Camino Real* remembers his wife as "a platinum blonde the same as Jean Harlow," but it is the film star, not the wife, about whom he dreams: "Wouldn't it be wonderful if you could sprinkle them ashes over the ground like seeds, and out of each would spring another Jean Harlow? And when spring comes you could just walk out and pick them off the bush!" (II, 551). He is about to pay dearly for the lesser charms of Esmeralda, the Gypsy's daughter, who spends her time between customers reading *Screen Secrets*, and dreaming, as Kilroy suggests, of seeing herself in Paramount Pictures (p. 558).

For other Williams characters, to make it in the movies is life's ultimate goal, and one must at least dress the part while waiting. Sometime-stripper Myrtle of *Kingdom of Earth*, whose "appearance suggests an imitation of a Hollywood glamor girl which doesn't succeed as a good imitation" (V, 127), tells Chicken, "like every girl in show business, and many out of it, too, Hollywood was my dream" (p. 149). If the dream will never come true for Myrtle, she can still attempt to provide Lot's farmhouse parlor with a gaudy splendor: she will wash the crystal pendants "and make them shine like the chandelier in *Loew's State* on Main Street in Memphis!" (p. 134). In *Sweet Bird of Youth*, Chance Wayne resorts to blackmail in an attempt to break into films. In his younger days as barman of the Royal Palms Hotel, he had copied his uniform "from an outfit Vic Mature wore in a Foreign Legion picture, and I looked better in it than he did," he says (IV, 78). In the surreal *Gnädiges Fräulein*, blond Indian Joe is dressed like a Hollywood Indian, for, as the author reveals in his production notes, "he doesn't have to be anything but an erotic fantasy in appearance" (*Dragon Country*, p. 218).

A few Williams characters even attempt to turn erotic fantasy into reality under the cover of darkness in motion picture palaces. After being bored by Roger's blurred magic lantern stills in *Eccentricities*, Alma is stimulated by the moving pictures at the Delta Brilliant to the point where she dares to apply pressure to John's knee. She tells him later that she had once rushed out of the theater when she had felt the pressure of a stranger's knee. She now wonders if she would have sprung from her seat had the stranger even faintly resembled John, "a dangerous speculation for a minister's daughter!" (II, 93). In *The Night of the Iguana* Hannah tells Shannon about one of the few encounters in her life that she considers a love experience: at sixteen, she was at the Saturday matinee at the Nantucket movie theater when a young man pushed his knee against hers; she had screamed, and he had been arrested for molesting a minor. Later, she got him off by telling the police she was just overexcited by the Clara Bow picture (IV, 361). In the short stories "Hard Candy" and "The Mysteries of the Joy Rio," two men ignore the images on the screen as they seek sexual gratification in the dark recesses of the balcony of the Joy Rio. For both, the search ends in death.

Filmgoing for the rest of Williams' characters is less dangerous. In fact for most, the movies offer a refuge, a temporary haven, a place of protection if not always a place to dream. Laura in *The Glass Menagerie* takes shelter there from the rigors of secretarial school. Stella in *Streetcar* uses the movies to keep Blanche from Stanley's squalid poker night; and to cheer up her despairing friend Trinket, Celeste in *The Mutilated* suggests "an afternoon at the movies with a large size Hershey" (*Dragon Country*, p. 126).

For at least one Williams character who does not aspire to stardom, the movies provide an idealized goal. Isabel Haverstick in *Period of Adjustment* has become a nurse, she tells Ralph Bates, because she thought she had a vocation. She saw herself "as a Florence Nightingale. . . . Establishin' clinics in the—upper Amazon country . . . working side by side with a . . . doctor . . . administering to the plague victims in the jungle, exposing myself to contagion." Blemishes would appear on her hands and progress to the wrists and forearms. Discovering she has contracted the plague, "the *youngish middle-aged* doctor" would seize her in his arms—thus exposing himself. "And love is stronger than death," Isabel continues. "You get the picture?" "Yep, I've seen the picture," Ralph responds as they both laugh (IV, 152–54). Inspired by the likes of Garbo in *The Painted Veil*, Bette Davis in *Jezebel* and Greer Garson in *Madame Curie*, Nurse Isabel has actually had no great demands exacted from her, has made no romantic sacrifice. Instead she has become involved with a neurotic young man suffering with the shakes, and she has married him.

In a conversation with Ralph later in the play, Isabel's husband George prepares the way for one of Williams' most telling statements concerning the necessary function of the movies in American life. By 1960, the time of *Period of Adjustment*, technological progress has made it possible for man to pursue his dreams at home. He no longer needs to go out to the Delta Brilliant; he merely flicks a switch:

> GEORGE: Turn on your TV any late afternoon or early evenin' and what do you get—beside the commercials, I mean? A goddam Western, on film. Y'know what I see, outside the camera range? A big painted sign that says: "Haverstick-Bates Ranch." . . . "The Last Stand of the Texas Longhorn, a Dignified Beast! We breed cattle for TV Westerns." We breed us some buffalo, too. The buffalo is also a dignified beast, almost extinct, only thirty thousand head of the buffalo left in this land. . . . Hell, we could double that number befo' we—
>
> RALPH: Hang up our boots an' saddles under the—dignified sky of West Texas?
>
> GEORGE (with feeling): There *is* dignity in that sky! There's dignity in the agrarian, the pastoral—way of—existence! A dignity too long lost out of the—American dream—(IV, 197).

As luck—and Williams—would have it, they turn the set on in time to watch a cowboy comfort his sweetheart and start a cattle stampede:

> GEORGE: Will you look at that? A Western on Christmas Eve, even! It's a goddam NATIONAL OBSESSIONAL.
>
> RALPH: Yep, a national homesickness in the American heart for the old wild frontiers with the yelping redskins and the covered wagons on fire . . . (IV, 205).

There are no worlds to be conquered, no frontiers to be tamed. Romance and adventure have gone out of American life. Yet twentieth-century man still yearns for something more daring than the life of factory hand, bank teller, or sales clerk. But only vicarious experience—the film experience—can assuage the pain of the uneventful present for the two veterans of the Korean conflict.

For Tom Wingfield in *The Glass Menagerie*, the movies become the impetus for his desertion of the drab hell of home and factory for the more stimulating hell of a world at war. Written near the end of World War II, sixteen years before *Period of Adjustment*, *Menagerie* provides a portrait of the budding artist for which Williams himself served as model. Tom typifies a generation stultified by the Depression, anticipating the coming war as a means of escape into a world of adventure. "I'm going to the *movies!*" is his plaintive leitmotif, his repeated response to every crisis at home. When his mother accuses him of lying—after all no normal young man goes nightly to the movies—Tom turns on her: "I'm going to opium dens! . . . I'm a hired assassin, I carry a tommy gun in a violin case! . . . They call me Killer, Killer Wingfield, I'm leading a double-life, a simple, honest warehouse worker by day, by night a dynamic *czar* of the *underworld, Mother.* I go to gambling casinos. . . . sometimes I put on green whiskers. On those occasions they call me—*El Diablo!* . . . My enemies plan to dynamite this place. They're going to blow us all sky-high some night! . . . You'll go up, up on a broomstick, over Blue Mountain with seventeen gentlemen callers! You ugly—babbling old—*witch* . . ." (I, 164).

His vehement response is an obvious giveaway, for only the movies could have provided the shy young warehouse hand with such a fantasized impression of underworld life. Tom seems to have been to a double bill of *Scarface* and *The Wizard of Oz*! When he comes home a little drunk one night and fishes in his pockets for his key, the "shower of movie ticket stubs" that appears unmistakably reveals that Tom has not been lying to Amanda. Nor does he lie to Laura when he explains why he is so late: "There was a very long program. There was a Garbo picture and a Mickey Mouse and a travelogue and a newsreel and a preview of coming attractions. And there was an organ solo and a collection for the Milk Fund—simultaneously—which ended up in a terrible fight between a fat lady and an usher!" (pp. 166–67).

Every moviegoer of the thirties and forties has shared Tom's experience. And every moviegoer has at one time or another shared his eventual exasperation for falling under the spell of an illusionary world on film. "I'm tired of the movies," he tells his friend Jim. As "the incandescent marquees and signs of the first-run movie houses light his face from across the alley," Tom continues his anguished outburst: "All of those glamorous people—having adventures—hogging it all, gobbling the whole thing up! You know what happens?

People go to the *movies* instead of *moving!* Hollywood characters are supposed to have all the adventures for everybody in America, while everybody in America sits in a dark room and watches them have them! Yes, until there's a war. That's when adventure becomes available to the masses! . . . It's our turn now, to go to the South Sea Island . . . to be exotic, far-off! But I'm not patient. I don't want to wait till then. I'm tired of the *movies* and I am *about* to *move!*" (pp. 200–201).

At the end of *Menagerie*, however, Williams reveals that even as a merchant seaman far from his St. Louis home, Tom still must rely on the movies as a means of escape. At home he dreamt of adventure; out in the world he is haunted by the memory of the sister he deserted. The memory brings too much pain; it must be obliterated, and there is a way: "I reach for a cigarette, I cross the street, I run into the movies . . ." (p. 237).

II

Like Tom Wingfield, Tennessee Williams is an inveterate moviegoer—and for the same reasons. The young Williams found the movies his only escape from the reality of an unhappy home until he took further solace in writing. While still a teenager, he wrote a review of the silent film version of *Stella Dallas* which won him ten dollars in a contest sponsored by the Loew's State Theatre in St. Louis. Movies were at times so intensely exciting for him that he recalls an attack of heart palpitations on his way home from one— *The Scarlet Pimpernel*.

His first work for the motion pictures was as an usher in a Broadway movie house when he was down on his luck in New York in 1943. By then he had suffered the closing of his first play in Boston, *Battle of Angels*, and written a fantasy containing a flashback dream sequence, *Stairs to the Roof*, for both stage and screen, which he could not sell. For a time the job as usher seemed the closest he would get to the film industry, until his remarkable agent Audrey Wood landed him a six-month contract as scriptwriter at Metro-Goldwyn-Mayer. He went to Hollywood, but stayed with MGM for only a month. First assigned to adapt *The Sun Is My Undoing* to the screen, he was transferred briefly to a Lana Turner vehicle, *Marriage Is a Private Affair*, only to part company with his employers after a difference of opinion concerning a script for child star Margaret O'Brien. Shortly afterwards he sent MGM a script entitled *The Gentleman Caller*, which he claimed would "run twice as long as *Gone With the Wind*." When the script was rejected, he revised it as a play. *The Gentleman Caller* became *The Glass Menagerie*, and Williams' career as a successful dramatist was launched. Since then he has returned to Hollywood from time to time, as sole author of the films *Baby Doll* (1956), an amalgamation of some shorter works, and *Boom!* (1968), based on *The Milk Train Doesn't Stop Here Anymore*, and as collaborator on the film versions of several of his plays—*The Glass Menagerie* (1950), *A Streetcar Named Desire* (1951), *The Rose Tattoo* (1955), *Suddenly Last Summer* (1959), and *The Fugitive Kind* (1960).

In the light of Williams' varied film career, that some of his plays contain transfigured moments from Hollywood movies is hardly surprising. Although Maria Ley-Piscator claims in *The Piscator Experiment* that *Menagerie* owes a debt to her husband's epic theater, surely the screen device and captions for that play are to some extent the writer's homage to the silent screen which nurtured him in his younger days.[1] Piscator and Brecht might well have applauded such a caption as "The Crust of Humility" (I, 155), but they would not have tolerated the sentiment of "The accent of a coming foot" (p. 191), "A pretty trap" (p. 192), "This is my sister: Celebrate her with strings!" (p. 193), "Terror!" "The Opening of a Door!" (p. 196), "A souvenir" (p. 228) and "And so goodbye . . ." (p. 236). D. W. Griffith, on the other hand, might have written them himself!

Films of the sound era influenced him too. The effect toward which Williams and his collaborator Donald Windham are striving at the entrance of the hero in *You Touched Me!*, produced on Broadway after *Menagerie* although written before it, is a calculated gamble which probably cannot be brought off on stage: "There is the sound of a train pulling in and the clanging of iron bells. After a little while, the front door is pushed open and HADRIAN enters quietly. At this moment the sun emerges. The smoke from the engine which is directly across the road puffs into the open door about his figure and the mist has a yellowish glow" (p. 12). There is no further reference to the train which pulls up remarkably close to the residence in which the play is set; it exists to provide that one puff of smoke.

A face materializing through the billowing smoke of an arriving train had worked wondrously on screen when the face was Garbo's at her first appearance in *Anna Karenina* (1935). It proved an unforgettable moment—at least for Williams and Windham.

That Williams' first play, *Battle of Angels*, is set within a flashback frame, a convention traditional to the screen but alien to the stage, further emphasizes the influence of the movies on Williams' techniques. *Battle of Angels* offers more convincing proof that certain films have imbedded themselves somewhere in the Williams subconscious: Jabe's climactic first entrance late in the play is described in terms which bring to mind the most chilling moments of the horror films of the thirties: "The door slams open on the landing. At this instant a flickering match light appears on the stairs and spills down them and across the floor. Heavy dragging footsteps and hoarse breathing are heard." "Christ in Heaven, what's that?" Myra whispers as the suspenseful build-up to Jabe's entrance continues: "The ghastly, phantomlike effect of this entrance is dramatically underlined. JABE's shadow precedes him down the stairs and his approach has the slow, clumping fatality of the traditional spook's. He is a living symbol of death. . . . He wears a purple bathrobe which hangs shroudlike about his figure and his face is a virtual death mask. Just as he appears in full view of the stairwell, the match which he holds under his face flickers out and disappears from view, swallowed in darkness like a vanished apparition." Myra's unloved husband is as frightening as Frankenstein's monster, as sinister as Count Dracula:

MYRA (horrified, incredulous): Jabe.
JABE (hoarsely): Yes, it's me! (He strikes another match and this time his face wears a grotesque, grinning expression.) (I, 111).

Realizing that the lurid horror-film effect was overdone, Williams gives Jabe in the play's revision, *Orpheus Descending*, a brief scene in the first act, and considerably tones down his second entrance.

Whereas *You Touched Me!* and *Battle of Angels* indicate isolated borrowings from films, at least one play reveals genuine indebtedness to Hollywood. Describing the setting of *Camino Real*, the 1953 revision of a shorter play of the early forties first published in *American Blues* in 1948, the dramatist writes in the prologue: "[The plaza] belongs to a tropical seaport that bears a confusing, but somehow harmonious, resemblance to such widely scattered ports as Tangiers, Havana, Vera Cruz, Casablanca, Shanghai, New Orleans" (II, 431). The fourth-named city, Casablanca, provides more than an ambiance for Williams' play. The general atmosphere, several of the characters, even a major incident in *Camino Real* have been filtered through Williams' perhaps unconscious memory of Warner Brothers' 1943 Academy-Award-winning film *Casablanca*, directed by Michael Curtiz from a script by Julius J. and Philip G. Epstein and Howard Koch.

The film *Casablanca* concerns Ingrid Bergman's desperate attempt to secure a flight for herself and her screen husband Paul Henreid from Casablanca, a no-man's-land where the permanent residents are outnumbered by the transients stranded by World War II. All are eager to obtain exit visas to continue by plane to Lisbon, point of embarkation for the United States and freedom. Flight is the film's motif, and flight was the motivating word for Williams and director Elia Kazan as they prepared the Broadway production of *Camino Real*. Williams states in his foreword, "We have kept saying the word 'flight' to each other as if the play were merely an abstraction of the impulse to fly" (II, 420).

World War II Casablanca becomes in *Camino Real* a de Chirico landscape, a universal Everywhere for each frustrated human being who has lost direction, hope and love, facing the fact that time is running out while he frequents, in the play as well as the film, hotels, bars, pawn shops and gambling dens. The scene in the play most reminiscent of the film is Block Nine, one added to the revised version, in which Marguerite Gautier hears a noise in the sky and learns that the Fugitivo, an unscheduled plane, is landing and will soon take off again. (*Casablanca* opens with all eyes watching a descending plane which each character hopes soon to board.) Marguerite tries every means to get on the flight, but her francs are unacceptable, and her lover Jacques Casanova will not surrender her identity papers to her. He himself must remain, waiting for the remittance checks which will never arrive. He does not want to lose the little warmth which Marguerite's love has provided him. The scene indeed inverts the most famous, most widely imitated scene of any Hollywood 'forties film: in *Casablanca*'s final scene Bogart as Rick pretends to be leaving on the plane with Bergman, but demonstrates at the last moment that he has retained what all of Williams' characters have lost—a sense of honor. In a quixotic gesture, he gives up his two letters of transit to Bergman and Henreid (unlike Marguerite, Bergman would have given up her place to secure passage for Henreid) and walks off into the night with Claude Rains in search of a better world where honorable men can lead honorable lives. In *Camino Real*, Marguerite would leave the man she supposedly loves, is frustrated in the attempt, and finally remains only to be unfaithful to him.

Despite the inverted Fugitivo scene, *Camino Real* ends as *Casablanca* does. Don Quixote, who has lost his Sancho Panza early in the play, finds a new companion in Kilroy, a down-and-out fighter, and goes off with him into Terra Incognita, a desert wasteland. Before joining forces with Rains, the prefect of police, Rick-Bogart had restlessly roamed the world with his own Sancho Panza, Sam, the black piano player who sings a song whose title suggests the themes of mutability and mortality which run through Williams' *Camino Real* and much of his later work—"As Time Goes By." ("Time goes by so fast," says Big Mama in *Cat on a Hot Tin Roof*, III, 157). Rick has arranged for Sam to remain in Casablanca in the employ of Signor Ferrari, who runs a seedy bar which is actually the front for the black market. The role is played by Warner Brothers' archetypal fat man, Sidney Greenstreet, who also finds his way into *Camino Real* as Gutman, sinister proprietor of the Siete Mares Hotel. It is surely no coincidence that Greenstreet's most famous screen characterization was that of Kasper Gutman, archvillain of *The Maltese Falcon* (1941), a film of desperate characters seeking the cure to their frustrations in a supposedly priceless figurine which turns out to be worthless lead.

In *Camino Real* Gutman carries on his wrist a white cockatoo named Aurora. In a flashback in *Casablanca* the bar which serves as meeting place for Bergman and Bogart is the Belle Aurore. Ferrari's bar in the film is called the Blue Parrot. In the play a character names the town's hotspots as "the Pink Flamingo, the Yellow Pelican, the Blue Heron, and the Prothonotary Warbler! They call it the Bird Circuit" (II, 469). And Greenstreet also has a white cockatoo in MGM's *Malaya* (1950), in which he plays a barkeeper named the Dutchman, who, despite the war in the Pacific, can manage deals with Americans and Japanese alike. Clearly Greenstreet has been an obsession with Williams—his one-act play *The Last of My Solid Gold Watches* is dedicated to the monumental actor (*27 Wagons*, p. 73); and the dramatist may even have had the actor in mind as he conceived *Cat*'s Big Daddy.

Still other echoes of *Casablanca* find their way into *Camino Real*. When Henreid leads the others in the singing of the "Marseillaise" to drown out the singing of "Wacht am Rhein," the German major orders the closing of Rick's cafe. In Williams' play, the Dreamer shouts the forbidden word—"*Hermano!*" and "The cry is repeated like springing fire and a loud murmur sweeps the crowd." Gutman says, "The word has disturbed the people and made it necessary to invoke martial law!" (II, 450–52). A monocled English gentleman has his wallet stolen in the film as he sits at an outdoor cafe with his wife; in the play, which contains the minor stereotyped characters of Lord and Lady Mulligan, a pickpocket lifts Kilroy's wallet (II, 459). Just as gendarmes seize Peter Lorre, who in the film breaks from them to plead for help from Rick, officers in the play press in on Kilroy, who gets away temporarily to dash into the theater, beseeching the audience to help him (II, 479–83). *Casablanca*'s gendarmes, who round up suspects throughout the film, become, surrealistically, *Camino Real*'s omnipresent Streetcleaners, waiting for the moment of death to pounce on their prey and cart them away.

Another Warner Brothers' film of the period, *Hold Back the Dawn* (1941), based on a Ketti Frings story with a screenplay by Charles Brackett and Billy Wilder, may also have contributed atmosphere and character to *Camino Real*. Within a flashback frame, *Hold Back the Dawn* tells the story of yet another European refugee waiting in still another limbo, a Mexican border town. Iscovescu, played by Charles Boyer, a former dancer, now a gigolo, manages to get a room at the seedy Esperanza Hotel, run by Flores, like Gutman a rotund proprietor in a white linen suit; the actor this time is Nestor Paiva, not Greenstreet. The room becomes available suddenly when its former occupant, another refugee waiting for entry into the United States, hangs himself. In Block Six of *Camino Real*, when Kilroy asks the proprietor of the rundown Ritz Men Only for a room, a voice is heard above: "*Stiff in number seven! Call the Streetclean-*

ers!" "Number seven is vacant," the proprietor tells Kilroy, "with absolutely no change in face or voice" (II, 476–77). Iscovescu, irresistible to women, exploits a naive schoolteacher played by Olivia de Havilland and marries her to gain access to the United States and freedom. *Camino Real's* Iscovescu-like Casanova, however, in a further plot inversion is himself exploited by Marguerite Gautier. During an auto trip through the rain in *Hold Back the Dawn*, de Havilland listens to the sounds of the windshield wipers, which she likens to breathing, as she watches them arc away from each other to return again and again. Over and over she repeats the word "together." In *Camino Real* a defeated Marguerite returns to Casanova, and he comforts her: "and we are together, breathing quietly together, leaning together, quietly, quietly together, completely, sweetly together, not frightened, now, not alone, but completely quietly together" (II, 524–25).

While Williams has never publicly acknowledged a debt to either *Hold Back the Dawn* or *Casablanca*, he has himself conveniently supplied evidence that he has seen the latter—over and over again. Describing the early years of his career in a *Playboy* interview (April 1973, p. 80), Williams said, "In 1943, I was ushering at Broadway's Strand Theater for $17 a week. The attraction was *Casablanca* and for several months I was able to catch Dooley Wilson singing *As Time Goes By*." Memory plays curious tricks: *Casablanca* played the Strand for only five weeks, but that was long enough for the film to insinuate itself into the writer's unconscious. Williams' memory may even have tricked him into forgetting his own sleight of hand in transforming *Casablanca* into *Camino Real*.

III

More significant in Williams' development than his sometimes occasional, sometimes extensive borrowings, intentional or otherwise, from specific films is the studied use throughout his career of film techniques adapted to the stage. The production notes for *The Glass Menagerie* contain Williams' manifesto "for a new, plastic theatre which must take the place of the exhausted theatre of realistic conventions if the theatre is to resume vitality as a part of our culture" (I, 131). "When a play employs unconventional techniques," Williams writes, "it is not, or certainly shouldn't be, trying to escape its responsibility of dealing with reality, or interpreting experience, but is actually or should be attempting to find a closer approach, a more penetrating and vivid expression of things as they are." Such unconventional elements as the screen device, the music and the lighting techniques which Williams calls for in *Menagerie* are all borrowed from films past and present which provide a fluidity often lacking in the conventional fourth-wall realism of the modern theater.

While the screen device was rejected by *Menagerie*'s first director, Eddie Dowling, and Williams has not attempted to employ it again, music plays a consistently important role in all the plays, establishing atmosphere as well as providing leitmotifs for various characters. At times the music has a realistic source; at times it is simply there, serving as background, as it does in most films. In *Menagerie*, for example, music comes from both the victrola which Laura plays and the bars and cafes in the vicinity of the Wingfield tenement. Essential to the play, however, is the single recurrent theme which has no obvious source, but weaves in and out of the scenes like distant circus music which "serves as a thread of connection and allusion between the narrator with his separate point in time and space and the subject of the story" (I, 133). Generally associated with Laura, the music provides, as does the background music of nearly every film of the first two decades following the introduction of sound, an "emotional emphasis to suitable passages."

In *A Streetcar Named Desire* music comes from the radio and from the bars of the French Quarter, but the recurring "Varsouviana" polka suggests Blanche's loosening hold on reality and is heard by her alone—and the audience (I, 376, 411, 414). The music in *Battle of Angels* has a realistic basis—a character plays a guitar, a juke box is heard. Even the religious chant which swells in exultation as the play ends, reminiscent of the many choirs of heavenly angels at the close of Hollywood films, comes from the church across the fields (I, 122). In *Orpheus Descending*, however, mandolin music fades in and out as Lady recalls her father's wine garden. Occasionally a "phrase of primitive music or percussion" is indicated (III, 239). A band of carollers provides an a cappella commentary on

The Mutilated (Dragon Country, p. 79) and sings of miracles as the play ends. One basic musical theme recurs in *Summer and Smoke* (II, 121), while *Suddenly Last Summer* employs music suggestive of the Encantadas (III, 367); and thematic music which Williams refers to as "The Lament" underscores *Sweet Bird of Youth* (IV, 9).

Some of the plays use unlocalized sounds in addition to background music. Echoing voices and jungle noises are also heard in *Suddenly Last Summer* along with harsh bird cries that come "in rhythmic waves like a savage chant" (III, 356). *The Milk Train Doesn't Stop Here Anymore* uses amplified heart beats to indicate Mrs. Goforth's agitation (V, 13), and wind chimes sound throughout *In the Bar of a Tokyo Hotel (Dragon Country*, p. 7).

While music and sound emanate from behind the scenes, the lighting of a play controls what the audience sees on the stage. The basic unit of a Williams play, like that of a film, is the scene rather than the act. The structures of *Menagerie, Streetcar, Summer and Smoke, The Rose Tattoo, Camino Real, Orpheus Descending, Milk Train* and *Kingdom of Earth* all depend on the juxtaposition and progressive effect of relatively short scenes. Of the unconventional techniques discussed in his *Menagerie* notes, the most significant in the structuring of his plays is the lighting, through which Williams achieves tension and its release. It is the adaptation to the stage of film transitions through lighting effects which provides the Williams play with its fluidity and cohesion.

A Williams play generally presents a set designer with an extraordinary challenge. All of the above named plays require settings which reveal at once more than one locale. Exteriors and interiors, at times on different levels, must all be on stage simultaneously. Occasionally the audience sees the full set; at times only one area remains in view. Williams, however, has nearly solved the designer's problem for him by indicating throughout how lighting controls the play's focus, just as the film camera controls what the eye may see. And he does so by borrowing from the movies such transitional devices as the iris, the fade in and fade out, the lap dissolve and the crosscut.

Effectively, albeit infrequently, Williams calls for a pinpoint of light to open or close a scene, just as Griffith used the iris in (the "gradual appearance of the scene through an expanding circle")[2] and the iris out (the "gradual disappearance of the scene through a contracting circle"). Williams directs the eye, as Griffith did, to a particular object or to a person—even a part of a human being. The dramatist's most telling iris in opens *You Touched Me!*, a play about a young girl's awakening, which inverts the Sleeping Beauty myth in the crucial scene in which Matilda touches Hadrian's forehead as he pretends to sleep. Williams prepares for the moment from the beginning of the play: "Before the full stage lights come up, a pin spot of light appears on a large piece of heavy silver and the hands of MATILDA moving dreamily over its surface with a polishing cloth. The light blooms gradually from this" (pp. 4–5).

Summer and Smoke, the play with the most elaborate lighting design, makes more extensive use of the iris effect. In scene four, for example, when John is drawn toward Alma—the soul—but embraces Rosa—the body—in front of the anatomy chart, "the light lingers on the chart as the interior dims out" (II, 187). After Rosa's father shoots Dr. Buchanan in scene seven, "everything dims out but a spot of light on Rosa standing against the chart . . . and light disappears from everything but the wings of the stone angel" (II, 216–17). Other scenes begin or end with a circle of light on either Alma or the angel representing eternity. *The Night of the Iguana* makes a single use of the iris out at the emotional peak which ends the second act: "A pure white flash of lightning reveals HANNAH and NONNO against the wall, behind SHANNON, and the electric globe suspended from the roof goes out, the power extinguished by the storm. A clear shaft of light stays on SHANNON's reaching-out hands till the stage curtain has fallen, slowly" (IV, 326). *Small Craft Warnings* also ends an act with the effect: "A pin-spot of light picks up Violet's tear-stained and tranced face at the otherwise dark table" as the curtain falls (V, 266).

A more usual transition in films—and also in Williams' plays—is a fade in or fade out. It is Williams' practice in all of his plays to separate individual scenes with lights dimming gradually, then coming up again. The curtain is used only to mark the ends of acts. Scene four of the second act of *Orpheus Descending* fades out with a backlighting effect before the curtain falls. As Lady goes to Val, she closes the curtain over the entrance to the alcove: "Its bizarre design . . . is softly translucent with the bulb lighted behind it" (III, 305).

Occasionally a fade in is accompanied and immediately preceded by a sound transition as in scene three of *Menagerie*: "Before the lights come up again, the violent voices of Tom and Amanda are heard" (I, 160). The technique, which suggests the sound-overlap of the movies, is repeated in *Summer and Smoke*: "Before the light comes up a soprano voice is heard singing . . ." (II, 188).

The opening of *Menagerie* seems a development of the establishing shot which begins nearly every film. The audience learns where it is before subsequent scenes can be further localized. The Wingfield apartment is shown flanked by St. Louis alleys. Tom speaks to the audience as the alleys and the tenement wall fade away, and light comes up within the apartment. By means of a scrim, a lap dissolve—in film terms—is effected. The same technique opens *The Rose Tattoo*. Serafina's frame cottage is located within an environmental setting representing a Gulf Coast community. Scenes dissolve from exterior to interior as the play progresses.[3]

One side of the stage in *Summer and Smoke* represents the rectory, the realm of Alma and soul, a spiritual world; the other side of the stage is the doctor's office, the realm of John and body, a material world. Between them is a neutral area dominated by the statue of Eternity. The movement between the extremes is effected and their interrelationship revealed by the lighting transitions within and between the scenes. The lap dissolve repeatedly allows the light to diminish in one area as it increases in another. At times a light comes up on Alma in the rectory as John and Rosa play a scene in the already lit office. The structure of the play is a logical adaptation of D. W. Griffith's technique of crosscutting, which enables the audience to follow simultaneous action in two or more locales.

That the authors of *You Touched Me!*, written before *Summer and Smoke*, are aware of the possibilities of stage crosscutting is revealed in the second act when "a dual scene" is indicated with the Captain and Hadrian in one room and Emmie and Matilda overhearing them and reacting in another (p. 65). After *Summer and Smoke* Williams again effects crosscutting by the manipulation of lighting. The last scene of *Period of Adjustment* alternates between living room and bedroom. Ralph and Dorothea prepare for bed in the one room while Isabel and George prepare for bed in the other. The opening and closing of the bathroom door directs the focus of attention as light enters the bedroom and is shut off again. The alternating action in the two rooms is obviously to be considered a simultaneous occurrence.

On two occasions in *Menagerie*, Amanda, alone on stage, telephones subscribers to women's magazines (I, 160, 177). As she speaks, a spotlight brings her face sharply into focus in scenes which are otherwise static. Williams uses lighting to blot out the rest of the playing area as Amanda is seen in the equivalent of the film close-up. Williams calls for the close-up again and again in quiet moments of little or no action in a number of his plays. If the amber follow-spots on the two players in *I Can't Imagine Tomorrow* (*Dragon Country*, p. 133) suggest the lighting of the opera, the ballet, or the outmoded stage of another era, Williams intends their use as did O'Neill in *Welded* to help an audience focus on faces and words, for the play is void of action. Gutman calls for a "follow-spot on the face of the ancient knight" at the end of *Camino Real* as Don Quixote takes out a pocket mirror and grooms his beard and moustache in preparation for a final journey into the unknown (II, 589). The static *In the Bar of a Tokyo Hotel* is played in a small area of intense light, and the sun brings the face of the dying D. H. Lawrence into close-up in *I Rise in Flame, Cried the Phoenix* (*Dragon Country*, pp. 3, 59). Throughout *Small Craft Warnings* as each character disengages himself from the others to speak to himself, "the light in the bar should dim, and a special spot should illuminate" him (V, 225). The latter part of the final scene in *Suddenly Last Summer* is virtually a monologue in which Catharine relates the horror of Sebastian's death. As her story progresses, the surrounding area dims out "and a hot white spot is focused on" her (III, 414). Catharine's revelation ends in a riveting close-up.

Lighting enables Williams to employ yet another film technique— the reaction shot, a variation of the close-up, which shows "the effect, on one or more characters, of something seen, heard, or otherwise realized" (Fulton, p. 310). Although he relies on it in several plays, the technique is most fully explained in *Menagerie*'s notes: "Shafts of light are focused on selected areas or actors, sometimes in contradistinction to what is the apparent center. For instance, in the quarrel scene between Tom and Amanda, in which Laura has no active part, the clearest pool of light is on her figure. This is also true of the supper scene, when her silent figure on the sofa should remain the visual center" (I, 133). Even the absent father has an opportunity to react in *Menagerie* as his photo lights up (I, 168). Throughout his plays lights come up and lights fade away as Williams views all his subjects through the eye of a camera.

IV

In addition to the various projections which, together with the captions, punctuate the action of *Menagerie*, Williams suggests the use of scenic projections in the form of stars, clouds, sea, palm trees and sunflowers on a cyclorama in *Summer and Smoke, Sweet Bird of Youth* and *Out Cry*. Of all his plays, however, only *Sweet Bird* calls for the actual projection of film onto the stage. In the entire Williams canon *Sweet Bird* is unique in one other respect—it is the only play in which Williams considers the possibility of films as works of art.

At the end of the second act of *Sweet Bird*, southern demagogue Boss Finley arrives at the Royal Palms Hotel for his nationally televised speech at a "Youth for Tom Finley" rally in the hotel ballroom. Although the setting for the scene is the adjacent cocktail lounge, "there suddenly appears on the big TV screen, which is the whole back wall of the stage, the image of BOSS FINLEY" (IV, 106), as Williams uses film to enlarge the scope of the stage. While Finley is pictured building toward the climax of his oft-repeated "Voice of God" speech, the voice of the heckler is heard, as the TV camera pans to reveal him at the back of the hall. The picture cuts to a reaction shot of Heavenly registering horror, then back again to the monstrous head of her politician father, as Finley quells the disturbance by reminding his audience that it is Easter and likening himself to the risen Christ. But Finley as savior is merely illusion on a flickering screen. In front of his image, counterpointing it, a gruesome scene is enacted. The heckler has been removed from the hall and is silently and systematically beaten by Finley's thugs, as Chance in a "tight intense follow spot beam" reacts to what he sees—the illusion of film, the reality of life (IV, 108).

While film was startlingly employed in *Sweet Bird*'s Broadway production in 1959, it is possible to perform the scene—less effectively certainly—without film. The film portion was omitted in the Kennedy Center revival of the play for the American Bicentennial Theatre Series in 1975; only Finley's voice was heard, as the lighting suggested the rally taking place offstage.

What cannot be omitted from *Sweet Bird*, however, is the character of Alexandra del Lago as the soul of art—suffering, devouring, enduring, perhaps even triumphant. Alexandra, or the Princess Kosmonopolis as she calls herself while traveling incognito, is literary kin to the protagonist of Williams' 1950 novella *The Roman Spring of Mrs. Stone*. Mrs. Stone, a stage actress, finds solace in retirement in the arms of the beautiful Italian boy she buys. Friends urge her to attempt a comeback, but the actress knows it is, for her, too late. She had always been a presence, a personality, rather than an artist. Her career has faded with her beauty. By the time Williams' aging actress reappears in *Sweet Bird*, she has acquired the stylized grotesquerie of Norma Desmond, the has-been film goddess played by one-time film goddess Gloria Swanson in Charles Brackett and Billy Wilder's bizarre and compelling Paramount film *Sunset Boulevard* (1950). Desmond, determined to make a comeback, hires a failed script writer to polish the creaking vehicle she has fashioned for her return to the screen. Naively thinking he has the upper hand in their relationship, the writer, William Holden, is eventually destroyed as the actress succumbs to madness.

In another plot inversion, Williams' Alexandra del Lago, a conquering lady of the lake, has fled from the screening of her comeback film, which she thinks is a fiasco, into a sordid round of sex, drugs and drink. She is accompanied on her journey into oblivion by Chance Wayne, a no-longer-young young man, who has retained the only commodity he can offer the world, an incredible beauty that is fading. As Chance uses Alexandra to gain access to the glamorous world of Hollywood, she exploits him in turn—for art is a voracious mistress. Before Finley's men can literally castrate Chance, Alexandra has figuratively beaten them to it. For Alexandra is a survivor, and she goes off to enjoy a temporary triumph. Her comeback is no disaster; the "picture has broken box-office records. In New York and L.A.!" (IV, 118). Although she knows in her heart that her latest triumph may be her last, she at least has the strength to carry on. She is finally touched by Chance's plight; she has compassion for him and would rescue him if she could. But there is no hope,

Alexandra realizes, for Chance. His youth has gone; her art endures.

"The screen's a very clear mirror," Alexandra tells Chance early in the play as she speaks of her career: "There's a thing called a close-up. The camera advances and you stand still and your head, your face, is caught in the frame of the picture with a light blazing on it and all your terrible history screams while you smile" (p. 34). Late in the play Williams demonstrates that the stage too can reflect the truth of life: "The PRINCESS moves out onto forestage; surrounding areas dim till nothing is clear behind her but the Palm Garden" (p. 115). By manipulating Alexandra into the stage equivalent of a screen close-up, Williams reveals conclusively that stage truth can be achieved through the adaptation of screen technique. In close-up, Alexandra, film star, recognizes herself as artist: "I seem to be standing in light with everything else dimmed out. He's in the dimmed-out background as if he'd never left the obscurity he was born in. I've taken the light again as a crown on my head to which I am suited by something in the cells of my blood and body from the time of my birth. It's mine, I was born to it" (pp. 115–16). When word comes that her comeback is successful, the artist accepts it, understands it: "Out of the passion and torment of my existence I have created a thing that I can unveil, a sculpture, almost heroic, that I can unveil, which is true" (p. 120). Significantly, the medium of her art is the movies.

In *Sweet Bird of Youth* a dramatist embraces the movies and proclaims them a valid form of art. There may be differences of opinion on the subject, but there can be no difference of opinion finally on the validity of Williams as artist. And Williams enhanced his art—at the Delta Brilliant.

Notes to Albert E. Kalson, "Tennessee Williams at the Delta Brilliant"

1. Maria Ley-Piscator, *The Piscator Experiment: The Political Theatre* (New York: James H. Heineman, Inc., 1967), p. 236. Gerald Weales, *Tennessee Williams* (Minneapolis: University of Minnesota Press, 1965), p. 33, and Edward Murray, *The Cinematic Imagination* (New York: Frederick Ungar Publishing Co., 1972), pp. 49–50 note the relationships between the screen device, silent films and epic theater, as does George Brandt in an excellent seminal study, "Cinematic Structure in the Work of Tennessee Williams," *American Theatre*, ed. John Russell Brown and Bernard Harris (London: Edward Arnold Ltd., 1967), pp. 184–185.

2. Film terms are here defined as in "Glossary of Motion-Picture Terms," A. R.

Fulton, *Motion Pictures: The Development of an Art from Silent Films to the Age of Television* (Norman: University of Oklahoma Press, 1960), pp. 307–11.

3. Brandt, "Cinematic Structure," p. 169 points out that O'Neill, before Williams, "achieved a kind of cinematic flow" in the movement from exterior to interior and back again in *Desire Under the Elms*, and Travis Bogard, *Contour in Time* (New York: Oxford University Press, 1972), p. 344 suggests that the special curtain which shows the house as seen from the street at the opening of each part of O'Neill's trilogy, *Mourning Becomes Electra*, "is in cinematic terms a long shot, giving a perspective on the close-ups to follow."

Tennessee Williams' Dramatic Technique

NORMAN J. FEDDER

"THE QUESTION NOW for Tennessee Williams," wrote Benjamin Nelson in 1961, "is what happens next? Has he come to the end of something and is he ready to set off in a new direction, or will he continue to explore his image of the universe which has hardened not only into a philosophical but an artistic commitment? His art is often so good that we find ourselves asking him for greater mastery, and deploring his loss of control. We tend to think less of what he has accomplished than what he could accomplish. We continually wonder if his art is great enough not only to sustain itself, but to develop further" (p. 294).

That statement seems sadly appropriate, looking back on it from the vantage point of the mid-seventies. For it was in 1961 that *The Night of the Iguana* opened in New York and became the last Williams work to date to "sustain itself" with the public and the critics. Since then, one play after another has either been kindly lamented or angrily deplored. We tend now to think on "what he has accomplished" and have given up on "what he could accomplish." Revival productions of his earlier works are received with rave notices, and he is again and again hailed as "America's greatest living playwright." But the hope of his sustaining himself in new plays, not to speak of "developing further," seems futile.

This may well be a foolishly premature judgment. Similar state-

795

ments had been made about O'Neill while he was at work on his greatest achievements. At the moment, however, we confront a playwright who seems, in the words of a current reviewer, "a flickering shadow of his former self" (from review of *The Red Devil Battery Sign* production, *Boston Globe*, quoted in *Time*, July 7, 1975, p. 29).

Has he perhaps "set off in a new direction"? This is Williams' view of the matter. "I am quite through with the kind of play that established my early and popular reputation," he explains in *Memoirs* (quotations from pp. xvii, xviii except as noted). "Since *The Night of the Iguana*, the circumstances of my life have demanded of me a continually less traditional style of dramatic writing." Yet, his life account provides nothing new, apart from its biographical candor, with respect to the playwright's basic premises: "many of the things which concerned me in the past continue to preoccupy me today." *Memoirs*, like the plays, focuses on his pervasive central theme "the need for understanding and tenderness and fortitude among individuals trapped by circumstance" (Barnett, p. 113). His beloved "freaks of the cosmic circus" (*Winter of Cities*, p. 91) frolic through its pages, and there is still the obsessive Williams emphasis on "That sensual music."

Has his *technique*, then, changed so radically? What the critics have deplored in his later writing has been evident enough in the earlier: discursive plotmaking, excessive theatricality, verbal superfluity. What has happened, I think, is not a change in style, but in emphasis—a bringing to stage center of that "loss of control" which has often marred his major plays and continually doomed his most recent.

To support this viewpoint I propose to examine Tennessee Williams' dramatic technique as it functions, in general, in his major plays through *The Night of the Iguana*—and as it alters, in particular, in each play since then. Technique is defined as the way in which a playwright employs *plot*, *theatricality* and *language* to establish tone, create character and express theme.

PLOT

The freakish vs. the conventional or normal; the delicate vs. the brutal or virile; the vital vs. the sterile or mechanical—Tom and Laura vs. Amanda and Jim; Blanche vs. Stanley; Maggie and Big

Daddy vs. Brick and Gooper. These are the essential dramatic confrontations in Williams' plays. The sharpness of the contrasts and the consequent intensity of the struggles make for consistent tonal power, but not always for successful character creation and thematic statement.

For one thing the contrast may be made too simplistic or stark or overlaid with more symbolic significance than is credible. Both *Battle of Angels* and *Orpheus Descending* portray a hero who is presumably a prototype of sexual and spiritual liberation—a fleshly Christ who will redeem through self-sacrifice all womankind. Yet, his major accomplishments seem to be the ability to "hold my breath three minutes without passing out," go "all day without passing water," and "burn down" "any two-footed woman" (III, 264). In *You Touched Me!* Hadrian not only effects Matilda's sexual liberation but also her international self-consciousness. Williams imperfectly attempts "to unite a personal and cosmic hero"—"to unite phallic worship and a new league of nations" (Joseph Wood Krutch, review, *Nation*, October 6, 1945).

On the other hand, the contrast can be lost in an attempt to avoid oversimplification. Williams responded to the criticisms of *Summer and Smoke* by rewriting it as *The Eccentricities of a Nightingale*. The conflict between John and Alma has been so scaled down and subtlized that it is hardly a conflict at all, with the spirit vs. flesh polarity a peripheral matter. The play has become distinctly undramatic in comparison with its predecessor, however more credible its plot.

Or the conflict can be dissipated in episodic or free associative plotmaking. Williams has been criticized for being more a *scene* wright than a playwright—of often losing his command of the central dramatic action by introducing tangential or repetitive situations (Falk, p. 175). *Battle of Angels—Orpheus Descending* and *Camino Real* are overwhelmed with superfluous characters and conflicts. The focus of *The Glass Menagerie* wanders episodically among Amanda, Tom, and Laura. The second-act confrontation between Brick and Big Daddy is probably the finest scene in all Williams, but no version of act three of *Cat on a Hot Tin Roof* adequately resolves Brick's encounter with "mendacity." (Williams wrote a third version of the act for a production in New England.) Although culminating in the eloquent interchange between Shannon and Hannah, *The Night of the Iguana* is rather loosely structured around the former's nervous breakdown. That *A Streetcar Named Desire* is his greatest play is due in no small measure to his unswerving focus on Blanche's disintegration—making each scene contribute in rising tension to the climactic insanity. Blanche battles to the very end to maintain her values against an equally bellicose antagonist. The conflict is unified and progressive.

But often in Williams, as in the case of Shannon, the protagonist seems defeated before he even starts, or struggles half-heartedly, or faces opposition of minimal challenge. The most effective central characters in Williams, as in all plays, must earn their right to their dramatic destiny through unified and developing conflict with worthy antagonists. Otherwise, the plays go nowhere dramatically—and the consequent tone, characterization, and theme diminish in credibility, power, and magnitude.

Williams has written, for the most part, in the realistic mode, but always on the borderline of the fantastic—and, occasionally, right in the thick of it. The quality of Williams' plots—their essentially larger-than-life tonality— points readily beyond realism, leading him often to highly symbolic situations such as the Easter analogies in a number of plays or to outright Expressionism as in *Camino Real*.

This method easily spills over into comedy which thrives on incongruity and exaggeration. Much is comic in Amanda's idiosyncrasies, Stanley's mannerisms, Big Daddy's obscenities, Shannon's fantasies. *Camino Real* abounds in the farcical. *The Rose Tattoo* and *Period of Adjustment* are fully comic in tone. (Not to mention the early *You Touched Me!*)

Williams' comic technique helps to minimize the melodrama inherent in his grotesque situations, and have us laugh *with* him, not at him. It is rarely light comedy since it always derives from an essentially morbid situation which is never far from reach—the "American black comedy" which he claims to have invented (*Memoirs*, p. 212). And one wonders whether it isn't less successful in his comedies than in his tragedies—for the "happy endings" of the "light" plays seem to have been forced upon Williams by the genre.

Since his typical plot involves the defeat or destruction of a highly pitiable protagonist, the theme of compassion is omnipresent.

Often the antagonist is equally pathetic—Val and Lady, Amanda and Laura, Chance and the Princess, Shannon and Hannah. And the so-called strong men—Jim, Stanley, John—get their share of sympathy. Here Williams indulges in sentimentality—in demanding our compassion for aberrant characters who have not at all earned it in the action of the play. When, for example, Chance implores the audience for "recognition of me in you," we have a right to reply, "Says you, buddy; keep your sick head to yourself!" What compels Chance's fall from stud to castrato is a mess of *his* making—and hardly "the enemy, time, in us all" (IV, 124).

THEATRICALITY

"... a symbol in a play has only one legitimate purpose which is to say a thing more directly and simply and beautifully than it could be said in words. ... the incontinent blaze of a live theatre, a theatre meant for seeing and for feeling ... the vulgarity of performance ... The color, the grace and levitation, the structural pattern in motion, the quick interplay of live beings, suspended like fitful lightning in a cloud, these things are the play, not words on paper" (II, 421, 423).

Williams' employment of theatrical symbolism is a major aspect of his dramatic technique. Setting, lighting, sound, costumes, props, and movement are everywhere expressive of tone, character, and theme. His sets always symbolize the values of the play. From the start he cautioned designers against photographic likeness. He was writing for "a new, plastic theatre which must take the place of the exhausted theatre of realistic conventions" (I, 131): The drab mercantile store which becomes transformed into the attractive casino in *Battle of Angels*; the rectory and the angel opposite the dispensary and anatomy chart in *Summer and Smoke*; the jungle garden in *Suddenly Last Summer*; the verandah with its separate cubicles in *The Night of the Iguana*.

Some of the most effective aspects of a Williams production derive from his theatricality: The theme of illusion vs. reality defined through the breaking of a tiny glass animal or the shading of a light bulb; characterization through old gowns and letters; the recurrent counterpoint of off-stage sounds to enhance a world of moods and meanings.

But frequently his love for the theatrical runs riot. *Orpheus*

Descending is overloaded with symbolic theatrics. Val Xavier, for example, plays music like Orpheus, wears a D. H. Lawrence snakeskin, and resembles J. Christ in portraiture and martyrdom. This symbolism works considerably against his credibility and evokes an unintended tone of ludicrousness. *Camino Real* is a forest of symbols for which one cannot see the trees! Archetypically costumed characters rush about a metaphorical set wielding prototypal props and shouting mythic verities. If and when the trees are discernible, they remain just such—wooden, not human. Excessive theatricalism overwhelms both *The Rose Tattoo* and *Sweet Bird of Youth*—in myriad roses and mammoth television images. As Signi Falk observes: "Williams often is more concerned with what is theatrical than with truth" (p. 175).

LANGUAGE

Williams' language has been unequaled in the American theater in its ability to be both conversationally idiomatic and poetically vivid—true to both the surface appearance and the inner truth. Williams has brought poetry back to the theater to a more significant degree than T. S. Eliot, Christopher Fry, and Maxwell Anderson, by hardly seeming to do so. Our perception of his vivid characters derives in great measure from their manner of expression:

The elaborate imagery of his delicate ladies—Blanche: "I shall die of eating an unwashed grape one day out on the ocean. . . . And I'll be buried at sea sewn up in a clean white sack and dropped overboard—at noon—in the blaze of summer—and into an ocean as blue as . . . my first lover's eyes!" (I, 410).

The earthy exuberance of his virile males—Big Daddy: "They say you got just so many and each one is numbered. Well, I got a few left in me, a few, and I'm going to pick me a good one to spend 'em on! I'm going to pick me a choice one, I don't care how much she costs, I'll smother her in—minks! Ha ha! I'll strip her naked and smother her in minks and choke her with diamonds! Ha ha! I'll strip her naked and choke her with diamonds and smother her with minks and hump her from hell to breakfast. *Ha aha ha ha ha!*" (III, 96).

The morbid eloquence of his decadent artists—The Princess: "There's nowhere else to retire to when you retire from an art, because, believe it or not, I really was once an artist. So I retired to the moon, but the atmosphere of the moon doesn't have any oxygen in it. I began to feel breathless, in that withered, withering country, of time coming after time not meant to come after" (IV, 33).

The graphic clichés of his solid burghers—Jim: "I believe in the future of television! . . . I wish to be ready to go right along with it. Therefore I'm planning to get in on the ground floor. In fact I've already made the right connections and all that remains is for industry itself to get under way! Full steam . . . *Knowledge*—Zzzzzp! *Money*—Zzzzzzp!—*Power!* That's the cycle democracy is built on!" (I, 222).

The right word, the right image, the right turn of phrase—to convey the sense of their uniqueness.

Williams has written some of the most memorable dialogues in all theater literature—building from encounter to confrontation to revelation to explosion. But he has also made use of the extended monologue and the choral interlude—with varying success. Tom's narrative comments are effective to a point, but they tend to inflation. Chance's lengthy apostrophes are purely hot air. The "cast of orators" in *Camino Real* compete in tedium. On the other hand, Catharine's mounting narrative of Sebastian's demise is dramatically perfect. The literary ladies in *Summer and Smoke* and *The Rose Tattoo* townsfolk are chorally relevant. The flower vendor belongs at Blanche's grave. The "no-neck monsters" interweave Brick's evasions in telling comic relief and contrast. However, who needs the "*Heil*-eluyah Chorus" of *The Night of the Iguana*?

Finally, Williams' words sound his favorite themes:

Psychological:

The liberating and humanizing qualities of uninhibited sexuality—Chance: "the great difference between people in this world is not between the rich and the poor or the good and the evil, the biggest of all differences in this world is between the ones that had or have pleasure in love and those that haven't and hadn't any pleasure in love, but just watched it with envy, sick envy" (IV, 50).

Romantic illusion as preferable to gross reality—Blanche: "I don't want realism. I want magic! . . . Yes, yes, magic! I try to give that to people. I misrepresent things to them. I don't tell truth, I tell what *ought* to be truth" (I, 385).

The need for compassion for the psychically maimed—Hannah: "Nothing human disgusts me unless it's unkind, violent" (IV, 363–4).

Social:

The lamentable decay of the old southern aristocracy—Amanda: "Well, in the South we had so many servants. Gone, gone, gone. All vestige of gracious living! Gone completely! I wasn't prepared for what the future brought me" (I, 204).

The dehumanizing qualities of industrial civilization—Serafina: "They make the life without glory. Instead of the heart they got the deep-freeze in the house" (II, 342).

The Romantic rebel as superhero confronting the enemy time— Byron: "lately, I've found myself listening to hired musicians behind a row of artificial palm trees—instead of the single
—pure-stringed instrument of my heart . . .
Well, then, it's time to leave here!
—There's a time for departure even when there's no certain place to go!
. . . .
Make voyages!—Attempt them!—there's nothing else . . ." (II, 508).

Theological:

God viewed as a brutal predator in the classic Darwinian framework —Shannon: "the gospel of God as Lightning and Thunder . . . stray dogs vivisected" (IV, 305).

The depraved artist as sacrificial Christ figure—Frieda: "You can't stand Jesus Christ because he beat you to it. Oh, how you would have loved to suffer the *original* crucifixion! (*Dragon Country*, p. 62).

The essential loneliness of the human condition—Val: "We're all . . . sentenced to solitary confinement inside our own skins" (III, 271).

When these themes arise naturally from the plays as inferences derived from the behavior of the characters, they are convincing and persuasive. But too often they remain simplistically in the mouths of their spokesmen as gratuitous outbursts unrelated to the action. This "besetting sin"—as Eric Bentley puts it—of "fake philosophizing," "straining after big statements" (*What Is Theatre?* p. 63) is particularly obtrusive in the rhetoric of Val, Chance, and Shannon— and of nearly everybody in *Camino Real*.

Such is the essence of Williams' technique in the "traditional style of dramatic writing" (*Memoirs*, xviii) which he left behind with *The Night of the Iguana*—but only in degree, not kind. The plays which follow differ in technique only in the enlargement of these earlier tendencies. "Free associative in style," "undisguised in self-revelation," they anticipate the *Memoirs* (p. xviii) to come. Like his heroine in the first of these efforts, Williams now lets it all harangue out—if only for an audience of tape recorders.

The Milk Train Doesn't Stop Here Anymore (1963)

The play has a plot of sorts. Mrs. Goforth is in conflict with a number of characters—chiefly the Christlike Christopher Flanders whose presumed attempt to minister to her last hours constitutes the main line of action. But Chris is a negligible antagonist against the egomaniacal heroine who does him in at every turn, as she vanquishes all others in her way—and almost immediately. The result is hardly any sense of developing tension—and the structure of the play becomes not much more than an endless monologue as the dying old nympho records for posterity her every orgasm.

The plot recalls Val's awakening of the death-bound Lady in *Orpheus Descending* and its comic counterpart in Mangiacavallo's rejuvenation of the eternally mourning Serafina in *The Rose Tattoo*. And even more closely—the misalliance of the not-so-young-anymore would-be actor Chance with the aging not-so-famous-anymore movie actress The Princess in *Sweet Bird of Youth*. The retrospective structural method parallels the plot of *Suddenly Last Summer* where the heart of the play is the narrative revelation of the death of Sebastian by Catharine Holly. Yet, each of these plays has considerably more dramatic tension and power than this tedious version of them. Equally matched combatants appear in the earlier plays, and the conflicts build and develop in the course of the action. The sense of fait accompli comes only with the final curtain. Even in *Suddenly*, Catharine's story is told in defiance of hostile auditors who would cut out a piece of her brain to silence her. Her story is not simply a narrative but an invasion of the resistant illusions of Mrs. Venable. Goforth's tale, in contrast, is recorded—not resisted—goes nowhere dramatically—is merely boring.

The setting is replete with screens which two kabuki-style stage assistants move about to "gracefully" reveal and mask the various scenes. Instead, these and the numerous other theatrical elements— exotic costumes and settings, microphones connected to tape recorders, a mobile named "The Earth is a Wheel in a Great Big Gambling Casino"—do just the opposite: garishly reveal the structural aimlessness and mask the thematic integrity of the play. The excessive theatrics serve to call to attention the insubstantial meaning.

This meaning is largely conveyed through the speeches of Mrs. Goforth and Christopher rather than through the action. Thus, although her ribald ramblings and his messianic mumblings are true enough to type, they are hardly tenable as the universal truths the playwright speaks through them.

Slapstick Tragedy (1966)

The Mutilated

For the most part, this play is a series of cat fights between two floozies interacting with assorted types of equally mutilated humanity in no particular dramatic order and culminating in a wholly unmotivated tableau of Christian togetherness and a vision of "Our Lady." A chorus of carollers wanders in and out singing of pity for "the strange, the crazed, the queer" (*Dragon Country*, p. 81). This is, of course, the old Williams message—so admirably rendered in the fables of the mutilated Laura, Alma, Blanche. But *rendered*, through the valiant struggles of these blighted ladies against overwhelming dramatic odds—not merely *talked about* in the lengthy monologues which have, unfortunately, become Williams' chief method of character portrayal.

The set is to be "as delicate as Japanese line drawings"—"so spidery . . . that the audience will accept the nonrealistic style of the play"

(p. 80). Yet not the style is unacceptable but the substance—which is not enhanced in its credibility by an excess of visual and sound effects such as The Bird Girl and her glued-on chicken feathers, Jack In Black and the carollers, and the garishly costumed ladies. Such effects in themselves need not be distracting—as indeed they are not in A Streetcar Named Desire, where they everywhere contribute to the developing dramatic action rather than call attention to themselves. Finally, the bosom talk which defines Trinket and Celeste well enough serves only to enlarge their essential flatness—their mutilations of body and spirit reduced to a singletoned language of lust: Celeste's hooker argot, Trinket's whine of "LOVE!"

The Gnädiges Fräulein

There is a unified and developing action in the Fräulein's tragi-comic struggle to outcatch the cocaloony birds as they tear away her costume, her eyes, her hair, her flesh—a struggle at which she continues to persist as the curtain falls. However, much of the plot is the accompanying commentary of the callous Polly and Molly, effective to a point as exposition and contrast, but entirely too long.

Is this Williams' black comic comment on his own career: determined to persist in creative endeavor—however transformed in talent or circumstance, however hostile the public and critics, however self-destructive the means? The quixotic struggle of the fantastic Fräulein is indeed evocative of such overtones. And it has been admired in a number of quarters in this regard. William Inge thought the "personal humor" "just marvelous" (Steen, p. 120). Williams calls it "my best work of the sixties" (Memoirs, Illustration 141).

More than in any play since Camino Real, the playwright has indulged his love for elaborate sights and sounds: a frame cottage as if Picasso had designed it—the pelican-hued Polly and Molly contrasted with the wild-colored Fräulein—the giant cocaloonies—a blond-bewigged Indian dancer—the singing heroine rushing off and on in successive states of undress and mutilation, until she is "transfigured as a saint under torture" (Dragon Country, p. 245). Much of this is integral to the theatrical conception, but one can't help feeling Williams could have spent more time in developing the character of the Fräulein and less on concocting all those fanciful fireworks. For the Gnädiges Fräulein is too one-dimensional to embody meanings much beyond her strange self, defined as she is through the words of others. Her inarticulateness reduces her complexity. The play is too much the discursive squawk of the pelican ladies rather than the compelling cry of the indomitable songbird.

Kingdom of Earth (1968)

Estelle Parsons (Myrtle in the Broadway production) speaks favorably of a critic's comment that "the play and Tennessee's later works had now a vertical quality where it wasn't so much the story line, but it was characters. The exploration of characters more than a story line" (Steen, p. 272). This remark well explains Williams' current structural approach. Again and again characters are depicted not by developing dramatic action but by loosely connected monologues and incidents. Yet, as Walter Kerr has observed, character divorced from situation is lifeless. Situation stirs the fires of creative characterization. Character is heightened by story because there is a correlation between "the range of a play's activity and the size of its characterization. . . . It takes a certain number of psychological responses to enable a man to stir a cup of tea. It takes a good many more to enable him to kill his father" (*How Not to Write a Play*, pp. 120–23).

And it is ironic that Miss Parsons should cite *Kingdom of Earth* as primarily a play of character. It has more of a story line than any of the later plays: the developing struggle of Chicken against Lot for the possession of their ancestral home through the allegiance of Myrtle. If we find these characters as "fascinating" as Miss Parsons does, it will be through our involvement with this story line.

But in fact these characters are less attractive than ever in a Williams fable—mindless, gross, abhorrent. Of course, this is nothing new in criticism of the playwright's subject matter. A score of critics condemn him for his "sewer mentality"—his "evil or disagreeable or deplorable characters" (Donahue, pp. 230–31).

Williams has answered them effectively. Morbidity in drama is not *his* invention. Evil appears in Shakespeare and Brecht. A writer must express the world as *he* sees it—however disreputable that world may be. "The magnitude . . . does not exist in the matter but in the manner" (Donahue, pp. 232–4). But it is in this respect that *Kingdom of Earth* is artistically wanting. The manner of the work diminishes the matter. Chicken, Lot, and Myrtle are considerably less compelling than Stanley, Blanche, and Stella.

It is a technical, not a thematic, question. The clash of the delicate and depraved (Lot) with the virile and depraved (Chicken and Myrtle), resulting in the destruction of the former and the union of the two latter, reminds us strongly of Blanche's tragic encounter with Stanley and Stella. But *Kingdom of Earth* seems to be a parody of *A Streetcar Named Desire,* largely because of the *manner* of writing: the *reduction* of the characters' sensibilities in the plot, theatricality, and language.

Too much of the plot is centered on the simplistic and contrived business of appropriating pieces of paper—the deed, the marriage license. The crotch-stroking Chicken, the bellowing Myrtle, the transvestite Lot are theatrically repellent. And the set of elegant bedroom over primitive kitchen for metaphorical ascending and descending is especially gauche. The characters speak low-level stuff—of barnyards and show biz and beauty parlors—when from nowhere Chicken wheels on the old "Big Bed Ex-Machina": "There's nothing in the world, in the whole kingdom of earth, that can compare with one thing . . . on the bed . . . a woman waiting" (V, 211) and wanting it. Chicken's kingdom of earth, like the play which promotes it, never gets off the ground.

In the Bar of a Tokyo Hotel (1969)

Structurally, the play consists of a sequence of two character scenes—mostly between Miriam and the barman—in which Miriam holds forth on her pathetic relationship with her artist husband and grabs for the barman's genitals. The husband is really the focus of the play. And he takes his place in Williams' gallery of neurasthenic artist-heroes—a male Gnädiges Fräulein in his last stages of dissolution: falling down without will, crawling naked over his canvases, convinced he has invented color—his dying breath a torrent of paranoid invective. But, again, we see more of the relatively bland wife and the barman than of the dynamic husband. And what we see of him is so highly sensational and one-dimensional as to render him abhorrent.

The theatrical environment is starkly realistic. It serves as both a frame for the coldness of encounter between wife and barman and as a contrast with the flamboyance of the artist's monologues. But despite the climactic costume and complexion change, the play's theatricality lies essentially in its language. The dialogue is consciously spare and strange. Williams has his characters follow the barman's unidiomatic English by clipping their sentences:

BARMAN: My instruction is. (*Dragon Country*, p. 5)
MIRIAM: The important idioms can be learned very. (p. 6)
MARK: I covered the floor with several sheets
of newspaper before I. (p. 14)

This effect of incompletion perhaps relates to the central image of faded brightness: "the circle of light is the approving look of God" (p. 53). Mark "thought that he could create his own circle of light" (p. 53). It is certainly expressive of this shadowy play, which falls far short of illuminating its fascinating subject.

Nothing is essentially wrong with the technique of making one character live through the language of another. The character, in fact, may become more vivid than if he were physically present. This is certainly the case in the brilliant evocation of the character of Sebastian in *Suddenly Last Summer*. But it is vital then that the one through whom we learn of that character be equally vivid and that description be given the proper focus and fullness in the body of the play. But Miriam—like Molly and Polly before her—is considerably less eloquent than Catharine in rendering the tragedy of her artist—and the artist is diminished accordingly.

Small Craft Warnings (1972)

The short play *Confessional* was expanded into this longer version. And "confessional" is an apt description of both its dramatic structure and its artistic failings. The plot consists of the assorted squabbles of a variety of barroom denizens: the raucous beautician Leona letting loose her ire against the phallic defection of her lover Bill with her friend Violet; the malpractice of a drunken, unlicensed doctor; the wornout homosexual Quentin warding off the tendered affection of the idealistic young Bobby. All this is presided over by Williams' alter ego, the bartender Monk, who speaks for the author in his sincere compassion for these blighted creatures. And each character is given the spotlight at one point to "confess" his raison d'etre.

The play seems closest of all Williams' work to the structural practice of the Chekhov whom he considers his major literary influence. Yet, the play lacks the through line of action which permeates even the most variegated of the Russian's dramas: Irena's and Masha's developing relationships with Tusenbach and Vershinin (*The Three Sisters*); Lopahin's growing struggle with Madame Ranevski (*The Cherry Orchard*). Moreover, the various subplots in Chekhov reinforce the main one in theme and tone; and the whole is of sufficient magnitude to have impact on an audience.

Any central conflict in *Small Craft Warnings* is Leona's. But she has already more or less decided to leave Bill. Rather than a dramatic encounter between the two, we have an endless stream of invective against Bill. Just at what point Leona will storm out for the curtain is anybody's guess. The central conflict lacks dramatic contour. Such is equally true of the sporadic actions of the other characters, attenuating the impact of the play. It is difficult to maintain much interest in the random behavior of a variety of screwballs, unless you're getting fifty dollars an hour.

The setting is adequate to the play, but invites comparison with the more successful barroom dramas, *The Time of Your Life* and *The Iceman Cometh*, which gather up their forgotten souls into a framework we long remember. There is a symbolic sailfish to which Quentin refers and a confessional spotlight. But this is the least theatrical Williams play, and closest to the photographic realism he deplores.

It is upon his characters' confessional eloquence that Williams depends in lieu of plot and theatricality. As Walter Kerr discerns: "Mr. Williams' gift for knowing how people think, feel, and speak reasserts itself at least enough to keep us fully attentive." Well, at least until intermission time. "*Small Craft Warnings* has no need at all of another act. . . . it grows heart-heavy with repetition, our own capacity for surprise wanes. The people have long since told us all we need to know, perhaps all there is to know, about them" (*New York Times*, April 16, 1972).

The play recalls Masters' poetic graveyard: a *Small Craft Anthology* of posthumous lives. But from this point of view these vessels were well warned. The one-act *Confessional* was the measure of their size. They are out of their depths in the longer version.

Out Cry (1973)

"... about the play," Clare says in one version, "I wonder sometimes if it isn't a little too personal, too special, for most audiences.
... it's more like an exercise in performance by two star performers,
than like a play, a real play" (p. 62). Clare's perception of the structural quality of *Out Cry* is concurred with by her creator in his
Memoirs. The play will not "hold," he writes, without "stars" playing Felice and Clare. And he accounted for the Broadway failure in
just these terms—the lack of "name" and "stage presence" of Cara
Duff-MacCormick (p. 233). But can a play so discursive in structure
and private in content hold any audience except big name fans and
advanced acting students? For Williams is more determined than
ever to "confess all"—this time through the mouths of a sibling
duo intent on performing their *Two-Character Play* of psychotic
self-revelation.

Nothing is inherently esoteric or uninteresting about their story:
their deranged father killing their mother and then himself—their
increasingly frenetic and hopeless attempts to live down the tragedy
against the derision and ostracism of the community—their loss of
economic security—their ultimate mental breakdown.

Much recommends the dramatic method of telling that story
through a Pirandelloesque structure of "two actors in search of an
audience." Yet, rather than employ the highly suspenseful approach
of increasingly more intense dramatic revelation—as in Catharine's
story or Blanche's confessions—Williams resorts again to a free associative style, to the play's detriment.

The essential plot is the drive of Felice and Clare to render their
story as actors in a theater. Ironically and ultimately they realize
they are doomed forever to reenact that story in a theater they can
never leave. The problems inherent in turning life into theater are
fascinating, and Williams touches on them throughout the play—
but he has made them only peripheral to his desire to reveal the
rambling thoughts and moods of the two characters.

Yet, early in the play we know almost everything we need to know
about them. All they do later is spin out verbal variations on their
problems. Why return for act two? Moreover, although Felice is
perhaps a little more aggressive than Clare, he is so much like her

that there is relatively little dramatic contrast. They do conflict with one another even to the point of violence; but too often they merely exchange bon mots on their common mental states. Consequently, one gets the sense of having eavesdropped on a conversation between a couple of wonderfully articulate lunatics, which proves interesting for a while, but ultimately tedious.

The version of 1973 describes a "fragmentary set" in the "vault of a foreign theater"—"a huge, dark statue upstage, a work of great power and darkly subjective meaning . . . of things anguished and perverse"—"mechanical sounds suggesting an inhuman quality"—"Images . . . projected on the stage backdrop" of "a subjective quality, changing subtly with the mood of the play" (pp. 6–7). The theatrical environment is appropriate for this theatrical play—although the dark statue seems a pretentious addition, as do a number of seemingly gratuitous theatrical moments—the card under the door, the bubble blowing, the pillow smothering. They obtrude on, rather than derive from, the dialogue—having been apparently added to compensate for the talkiness. (In the revision for volume five of *The Theatre*, 1976, reentitled *The Two-Character Play*, Williams does manage to decrease the obtrusiveness of his statue.)

The talk is, nevertheless, the best part of the play. Interchangeable as are the speeches—in a sense a monologue broken up between two voices—these voices ring true in theme, character, and tone. They cry out brilliantly for as long as we can bear—not too long.

"There is nothing slap-dash about Williams' work. Although it often gives the appearance of having been done at breakneck speed, it is always the product of alterations and careful revisions. It is a mistake to view Williams as a literary anarchist although he often seems to abandon himself to impulse and emotion" (Nelson, pp. 181–2). Again Nelson's statement in 1961 is no less descriptive of Williams' current practice. As much as his *Memoirs* extol revolution, his approach to his art has not radically changed. Each of these later plays has developed from shorter versions through numerous drafts and try-out productions. His impulse to excess inheres in his vision, not his craft.

Williams well knows what his public wants—a technique in plot, theatricality, and language of control and balance—that "taut alliance" between release and restraint of the plays which made him famous (Nelson, pp. 291–2). But while wanting the approval and understanding of audiences, he insists on writing in keeping with *his* needs: "I have always written for deeper necessities than the term 'professional' implies, and I think this has sometimes been to the detriment of my career but more of the time to its advantage." (*Memoirs*, pp. xviii–xix). In light of the "detriment" of the last fifteen years, one might question the "advantage" of a dramatic technique which prefers self-indulgence to professionalism.

Assessment

This section contains three special essays on Tennessee Williams. Their diverse approaches and their content reflect the continuing disagreement about both the man and the artist, a discussion that Williams himself apparently persists in motivating. Yet, perhaps the disagreement itself is one of the most complimentary tributes to Williams. He extends his famous struggle for survival as a man and refuses to end his career as an artist.

William Free examines the shortcomings of *Small Craft Warnings* and *Out Cry*, in making an assessment of Williams' accomplishment in his last *published* plays. (Sy Kahn in PLAYS writes on the unpublished *Red Devil Battery Sign*.) A note at the end of the essay comments on the most recent published revision of *Out Cry* (renamed *The Two-Character Play*).

Donald Pease examines the relationship between Williams as man and Williams as artist. The opening paragraph succinctly presents the complexities of the relationships. A discussion of the forewords to the published editions of the plays and of major Williams characters gradually elucidates both title and subtitle of this unusual essay. Recent publication of *Memoirs* (1975), with its intermixture of art and autobiography, makes the essay especially pertinent.

One of Williams' most appreciative critics has the last word in this collection. Alan Chesler's essay is an informative study of Williams' achievement or, as the author says, "an attempt to define and evaluate Williams' literary reputation in the United States." (Regretably, as noted elsewhere, this collection contains no essay on Williams' wide reputation abroad.) The author maintains that *The Glass Menagerie, A Streetcar Named Desire, Cat on a Hot Tin Roof* and *The Night of the Iguana* will survive as the major plays. But to this list he adds *Suddenly Last Summer*, an addition he explains both by a survey of the criticism and by an interpretation. Interpretations of all the plays chosen add a dimension that makes this essay far more than a perceptive survey of criticism.

813

Williams in the Seventies:
Directions and Discontents

WILLIAM J. FREE

CRITICAL DISSATISFACTION over Tennessee
Williams' plays of the seventies has been almost unanimous. Of
the reviewers of *Out Cry* and *Small Craft Warnings*, only Clive
Barnes found much virtue in either play, and his likings seemed more
vague than directed. On the other hand, discontent with the plays
was specifically directed and uniform. Harold Clurman's reviews in
The Nation are fairly representative. Of *Small Craft Warnings*: "an
old play . . . old in the sense that it repeats the mood and mode of
much earlier work. Williams has been there before—and so have
we" (24 April 1972, p. 540). Of *Out Cry*: "it is too limited in its
symbolic imagery and construction . . . to hold us. . . . Williams has
always held to the romantic idea of art as self-revelation, but in this
instance the mask of an objective dramatic argument is so thin that
there is hardly a separation between the mask and the face" (19
March 1973, p. 380).

Clurman's remarks typify two general themes in Williams criticism: the charge that Williams repeats himself by going over and
over the same territory and the charge that his plays, for better or
worse, are autobiographical. The latter theme has especially prevailed in academic criticism, which has always tended to read Williams allegorically. The fact that he has repeatedly, and as recently

815

as a *New York Times* interview in December 1975, branded such attempts "ludicrous" has of course failed to deter anyone.

Both charges against Williams do his plays an injustice by failing to take them on their own terms. Deflection of our interest from an author's work to his life, particularly in Williams' case, too often reflects a taste for lurid sexual detail rather than for art. Furthermore, the artist's work relates not to the outer details of his life but to the inner world of his imagination, so to jump from an account of Williams' sexual preferences to an allegorization of his plays is to ignore an important middle step, as the publication of his *Memoirs* should clearly establish. Few artists of our century have been more delighted to detail their private lives or more reluctant to reveal the working of their imaginations as Williams. Even the few mentions of people from his life in relationship to his plays deny that any individual is the direct model for any character or that any situation from life relates directly to any dramatic event. Williams tells us in the *Memoirs* that the imagination is the only place in which the artist can live, but he continues to live there privately and secretly. Thus the temptations to identify Williams' emotional crack-up of the sixties too directly with the confinement and emotional hysteria of the brother and sister in *Out Cry*, and either to allegorize Doc in *Small Craft Warnings* (the role Williams himself played on stage and with which he says he most identifies in the play) as a description of Williams' sense of his own alienation from the contemporary theater or to consider Quentin's relationship with Bobby in the same play as simply a dramatization of the playwright's own middle-aged homosexuality, are too easy to have much value.

The charge of repeating himself, on the other hand, is perhaps more relevant if viewed in its proper context. True, the variety as well as the depth of an artist's imagination is a factor in his ultimate worth. On the other hand, even the writer who repeats himself, if by that we mean that each of his works is an analogue to the same narrow imaginative content, can be of great value provided each work makes us genuinely experience that content anew and delight in the experience. The real charge to be brought against *Out Cry* and *Small Craft Warnings* is not that they repeat Williams' earlier plays. Both plays, I believe, move into territory which Williams has not fully revealed to us in his earlier plays. But neither play succeeds

completely in revealing that territory. They are failures of dramatization rather than failures of theme. Their problem is not that they
are autobiographical or that they specifically repeat Williams' other
work but that they are inadequate expressions of whatever is in the
playwright's imagination.

Small Craft Warnings seems to me torn between two impulses,
neither of which gets fully realized. One is a theme relatively new
to Williams. The other is a stylistic device, the lyrical confession,
which isn't new, but which here neither becomes integrated with the
dramatization of theme nor works itself out fully.

In his most revealing comment about *Small Craft Warnings*, Williams says: "I have suddenly undertaken to correct what I've gradually come to recognize as the principal structural flaw in *Small Craft
Warnings*, the long monologue of the bartender Monk coming directly after the monologue of Quentin, the homosexual film-scripter,
which is much the most effective piece of writing in the play, and
since the play's values are so largely verbal, Quentin's speech is obviously the climax, at least of Act One" (*Memoirs*, p. 234). Quentin's speech is the source of the play's values, but the key to those
values perhaps comes less in the monologue than in the lines which
immediately precede it and which give it its meaningful context:

> QUENTIN: What is the thing that you mustn't lose in this world
> before you're ready to leave it? The one thing you mustn't lose ever?
> LEONA: . . . Love?
> (Quentin laughs.)
> BOBBY: Interest?
> QUENTIN: That's closer, much closer. Yes, that's almost it. The word
> that I had in mind is surprise, though. The capacity for being surprised.
> I've lost the capacity for being surprised, so completely lost it, that if
> I woke up in my bedroom late some night and saw that fantastic fish
> swimming right over my head, I wouldn't be really surprised.
>
> (V, 259–60)

Quentin goes on to relate his loss of surprise to his being a homosexual, too facilely perhaps. For what Quentin is describing is not
simply a homosexual experience but a world-weariness which comes
from realizing a lack of variety in essential human relationships. The
monologue functions to remove the theme from a narrow sexual
context to that of quasi-philosophical questioning:

I've asked all the questions, shouted them at deaf heaven, till I was hoarse in the voice box and blue in the face, and gotten no answer, not the whisper of one, nothing at all, you see, but the sun coming up each morning and going down that night, and the galaxies of the night sky trooping onstage like chorines, robot chorines: one, two, three, kick, one, two, three, kick . . . Repeat any question too often and what do you get, what's given? . . . A big carved rock by the desert, a . . . monumental symbol of wornout passion and bewilderment in you, a stupid stone paralyzed sphinx that knows no answers that you don't but comes on like the oracle of all time, waiting on her belly to give out some outcries of universal wisdom, and if she woke up some midnight at the edge of the desert and saw that fantastic fish swimming over her head . . . y'know what she'd say, too? She'd say: "Oh, well" . . . and go back to sleep for another five thousands years (V, 261).

The idea is not new, either in Williams or in Western culture. The universe has remained enigmatically silent to man for well over a century. Nor, unfortunately, are the metaphors particularly fresh, nor the philosophical musing particularly related to its dramatic context. The source of Quentin's mal d'esprit is not the world's refusal to answer the "big questions" but the dulling effect of the narrow repetitiousness of life's common experiences, a dilemma to which the homosexual has no special access, for it is universal.

The intensity of the boredom, however, is a new tone in Williams' work. This theme of dulling repetition provides a matrix within which we can understand his characters. Leona rages against it. Bill is too stupid and too centered on his penis to know it exists; Bobby too young to have experienced it yet. Doc can still wonder at the mystery of birth and death and can still see them through "this cloud of . . . irreverent . . . paraphernalia" (V, 250) thrown up by society and medical science. For Monk, providing a refuge for wanderers is enough to give life meaning. For Violet, only refuge itself matters. All are running from the loneliness and confinement of life. In one sense, the source of Quentin's values lies in all Williams' life and work. As he describes in his *Memoirs*, his life has always been a tentative bohemian existence characterized, as are practically all his plays, by the most fragile human contacts. Describing his early days in New Orleans, he expresses this obsession of his life in the metaphor which gives this play its title: "I knew and associated closely with a good many other young writers and/

or artists and all of us were disregarding the small craft warnings in the face of which we were continually sailing our small crafts, each with his crew of one, himself that crew and its captain. We were sailing along in our separate small crafts but we were in sight of each other and sometimes in touch, I mean like huddling in the same inlet of the rocky, storm-ridden shoreline, and this gave us a warm sense of community" (p. 2).

The need for, and the temporariness of, that inlet thematically pervades Williams' plays to the degree that the reader can find in all of them characters to whom the description applies: Laura, Blanche, Alma Winemiller, Brick, Chance Wayne, Shannon: everyone can supply his own list. The newness in *Small Craft Warnings* is the note of boredom and weariness with life, or, more accurately, a delicate tonal quality to that weariness seldom encountered before. Quentin is not, like Blanche, for example, destroyed by the callous indifference or downright brutality of others; he is simply deadened by the repetitiousness of the act of love and by his recognition of the essential sameness of life. Blanche and most of Williams' other characters long for the inlet and the sense of community; to Quentin, the sailing isn't worth it any more. And, however much the other characters in *Small Craft Warnings* may resist that sense of futility, it surrounds them all.

The central problem with *Small Craft Warnings* is that Williams does not find an adequate dramatic expression for the matrix within which his characters exist. Several reviewers have compared the play to O'Neill's *Iceman*. But the comparison is, I think, somewhat superficial. In *Iceman*, Hickey provides a dramatic center which sets the static lives of the other characters in motion; and although most of the residents of Harry Hope's Tavern return to their starting places, at least Hickey has sent them out into the street. O'Neill makes us see the simultaneous need for and futility of pipe dreams by the dramatic interaction of his characters and lets us observe and realize the ironic results. Williams' characters in *Small Craft Warnings*, on the other hand, are at their worst when they interact. The conflicts among them seem both trivial and irrelevant to the play's main theme. The sense of life in the play comes about instead in the monologues in which they reveal themselves and their positions within the thematic matrix Williams sets up. Each has his turn, and each plots his position. This side of the play is essentially lyrical rather than dramatic, and it exists almost separately from the parts of the play in which the characters interact.

A much more fruitful contrast for the play, I believe, is to Robert Patrick's *Kennedy's Children*. In a bar of similar social standing as Monk's, six characters reveal their involvement in and disillusionment with the sixties in a series of monologues, never speaking directly to one another or recognizing another's presence. The effect is that of a series of confessionals with the audience acting as priest. *Kennedy's Children* is not totally successful; perhaps no play completely devoid of dramatic interaction can be. But it is of a piece. Patrick has the courage to sustain his monologues. Williams loses his nerve and retreats into the familiar territory of Tennessee Williams' particular brand of romantic naturalism. It is in these retreats that we sense a traversing of familiar ground and feel that the other times over the terrain were much more interesting. The result is a division of focus in the play from which it cannot recover.

The comparison to *Kennedy's Children* reveals a further weakness in the style of Williams' monologues, a weakness in the poetry of his language. The problem becomes apparent when we compare Quentin's monologue with a speech of similar philosophical ennui, one of Clara's monologues from *Kennedy's Children*. Clara has set out to become the new Marilyn Monroe only to discover that no one wants a new Marilyn Monroe. "Weren't all the disguises and masks supposed to have been dropped? I mean, when Raquel Welch and a bunch of drag-queens are the current sex symbols—isn't there something wrong? What made them hate women? And men, what made them hate men? Is it just because there are so many people, and media and all have made them so much alike? Is that why everything keeps harking back to another era? Any other era? Any freak, any monster, anything different? Why don't we want anything beautiful? Why don't we want anything beautiful to be, to exist, to live? Is it overpopulation or what? Are we just instinctually avoiding reproduction? Stimulation, involvement, reproduction? Everybody's drunk, everybody's drugged, everybody's making TV commercials—where are the stars! What's wrong with them? What's wrong with me?" (in *Plays and Players*, 22, p. 48).

Although Patrick's language lacks the phonetic gracefulness of

Williams', Clara's monologue has something that Quentin's lacks. It reverberates against a solid sense of reality and history. Quentin's imagery never leaves the hot-house world of literary symbolism. It is a free-floating imagery assembled in the writer's imagination but lacking in substantial context. Its symbolism—the fish, the chorines, the sphinx—reaches toward abstractions which are not located in time and space, not even, as I indicated above, fully in Quentin's own experience. Clara's imagery, though poorer as pure imagery, is so situated. Its reverberations evoke the structure of our own experience with the sixties in a substantial context. This difference, the abstractness of Williams' symbolism, contributes strongly to the sense of repetition because the level of abstraction relates the words to the entire modernist movement and leaves it essentially without concrete location.

Out Cry is a more complex play than Small Craft Warnings and in the long run a better play. But some of the same problems of unity exist in it, too, and some of the same misunderstandings about its basic nature exist in the criticism of it. Mel Gussow, writing in the New York Times, contended that Out Cry is basically a monologue: "the two characters are too similar, not conflicting halves of a personality as much as one person talking to himself, a feeling that is intensified by the fact that each often finishes sentences for the other" (11 March 1973, II, 1). The implication here, and in other critics, is that the person doing the talking is really Tennessee Williams. Such an interpretation, I believe, badly misunderstands the play.

Structurally, Williams organizes Out Cry by enclosing its earlier version, The Two-Character Play, in a play-within-a-play device. Felice and Clare, brother and sister, are the surviving members of a traveling theatrical company on tour in an unspecified foreign country. After establishing their theatrical context, they perform one of the familiar pieces in their repertory, The Two-Character Play. As the play develops, the theater becomes a metaphor for their loneliness and confinement and The Two-Character Play doubles their situation by locating it in a fictional context in the southern Gothic tradition familiar to all who know Williams. Their father, a mystic of questionable sanity, has murdered their mother and committed suicide. The psychological effect on them is to confine them in their house, trapped by their fear of the outside world and by an unspecified morbidity at the core of their characters. The hint of dual suicide as a solution functions on both the levels of the outer structure and the play-within-a-play. But at the end, Clare and Felice find themselves locked in the theater, the cold and darkness closing in on them, and choose to continue the *Two-Character Play* to its end.

Critics of *Out Cry* have complained specifically about the overwhelming triteness of the dialogue and the personal subjectivity of the dramatic images. Clare herself wonders about their *Two-Character Play*, "if it isn't a little too personal, too special, for most audiences" (p. 62). Williams has acknowledged the play's thematic closeness to his own experience: "Confinement has always been the greatest dread of my life: that can be seen in my play *Out Cry*." (*Memoirs*, p. 233) Confinement is a legitimate fear and the playwright's subjective response a legitimate subject for drama. But here, Williams neither completely focuses his material nor makes it totally convincing.

The problem is not that the play is thinly veiled autobiography nor that the characters are merely superficial masks for the playwright. To assert, as does Gussow, that Felice and Clare are really the same personality is to ignore the rather considerable effort Williams goes to, particularly at the beginning of act one, to distinguish them. The *actors* Clare and Felice do not think alike and do not complete each other's lines. Their identities draw together only when they are portraying the *characters* Clare and Felice in the *Two-Character Play*. We are dealing not with a pair of static masks, but with a shifting pair of dynamic characters whose identities begin to merge as they perform their play. Williams' device of having them complete each other's lines does not indicate that their lines are really part of a monologue but that they are giving each other needed support in an emotionally difficult situation and that they are so familiar with their play that they are rushing toward its conclusion.

The true weakness of *Out Cry* lies in the relationship between the symbolism of the play-within-a-play device and the content of the *Two-Character Play*. Williams' theatrical symbolism is, of course, derivative from Pirandello and the playwrights of the absurd, perhaps too directly so to be effective. Clare and Felice are at the end of their rope. Only continuing the tour continues life; if the tour stops, they cease to exist. Furthermore, what Clare calls their "unexpected and—*unalterable—circumstance*" (p. 11) continues to narrow their possibilities until they are reduced to repeating the *Two-Character Play*.

The *Two-Character Play* forces on them a new level of confinement. The trauma of their father's act has stopped time. Clare is afraid to leave her house: "Suppose I came home alone, and in front of the house there was a collection of people around an ambulance or police car or both? We've had that happen before" (p. 34). Does her statement indicate that her life has morbidly stopped at a moment in her past and that she is doomed to live always suspended at that point, or does it indicate her fear that she might return to find that her brother has followed in his father's steps? Their circumstance has so confined them that their only alternatives seem to be death or separation and isolation in State Haven. Felice has apparently already experienced the latter alternative, as had their father, and both he and Clare find it unacceptable. Only in the safe harbor of their home can each find the human closeness necessary to sustain life. Thus, at least superficially, their confinement in their New Bethesda mansion seems equivalent to the confinement of the actors Clare and Felice in their theater and in the necessity of continuing their tour.

But only superficially. The theater metaphor draws upon the teatro del mundo tradition and, presumably, attempts to represent the total human condition. We, like they, have to continue our tours, even though "unexpected and unalterable circumstance" narrows our possibilities and confines us to smaller and smaller circumferences. The symbolism is shopworn and obvious, but clear. But we have much more difficulty accepting the characters in *Two-Character Play* as representative of the human condition. Rather, they are representative of neurotic, perhaps even psychotic, behavior. We see them not as images of ourselves but as psychopathic case histories observed from a distance.

The really telling difficulty is the existence of a world outside their mansion: the world of Grossman's market, the "Citizen's Relief" organization, the Reverend Wiley, whom Clare impulsively telephones. This world is hostile and confining only in their imaginations. Grossman even comes across as a somewhat patient man. Their confinement is not, then, representative of the human condition, as it is in the theater motif, but is a projection of their own warped imaginations, warped by an unusual circumstance in their lives rather than by the fundamental limitations of being human. Thus the relationship between the two levels of the play is not concentric but excentric, and our interest in the characters as case histories overpowers our ability to accept them as reflections of ourselves.

The use of theatrical symbolism is similarly unfocused. The burning rose in the carpet, the twin-headed sunflowers, and the statue which dominates the stage, "a work of great power and darkly subjective meaning" (p. 7), are either too obvious or too "darkly subjective" to exercise any controlling force over our responses. How subjective we can realize by comparing the statue in *Out Cry* to the stone angel which dominates the set of *Summer and Smoke*. In the earlier play, the angel provides us an unchanging frame of reference against which to see the progressive decline and narrowing of Alma Winemiller's life. As Alma undergoes her own unexpected and unalterable circumstances, the angel assumes a richer and richer meaning and somehow manages at the end to encapsule the pathos of her life. But the statue in *Out Cry* never gets charged with meaning. Whatever "anguished and perverse" (p. 7) things it supposedly represents never emerge from the play and attach themselves to it. It remains subjective in the worst sense of the word.

In both *Out Cry* and *Small Craft Warnings*, Williams' failure is neither self-repetition nor self-dramatization. It is an inability to fuse the disparate elements of his imagination into an effective whole. Too many times our interest is led outward on wild goose chases after a scattering of dramatic motifs which never really lead us back into the play. To cite only two examples: Doc's bungling complicity in the deaths of the mother and her infant and the question of Felice and Clare's father's religious mysticism. In a sense, perhaps, Doc's failure is an ironic bungling of his sense of the mystery of birth and death; but the triteness and melodrama of the drunken physician stereotype weaken its effectiveness as a characterizing device. The event stands out as an attempt to shock for the sake of shock. Similarly, the father's insane mysticism may be simply a motivational device to explain his actions and, perhaps, to suggest a hereditary morbidity in his children; but, if the former, it arouses interest disproportionate to its function and, if the latter, it simply further removes Clare and Felice from the universal human condition into psychopathological peculiarity. All these are missteps that the younger Williams did not commit.

Furthermore, I believe the dissatisfaction we feel with these plays comes at least in part from our subsconsciously placing them in the context of the theater of the sixties. Williams, having for all practical effect lost the decade of the sixties from his life, seems to be trying to create "Theatre of the Absurd" without knowing it has already been done. Others before him, particularly Samuel Beckett, have etched the experience of confinement so deeply into our sensibilities and have done so with such control of their dramatic medium that Williams' plays seem old hat in comparison. For example, I think the repetitious indecision about whether to go out to Grossman's Market must echo Hamm's and Clov's similar indecision in *Endgame*. But the differences in the two situations are startling. To Hamm and Clov the alternative to confinement is nothingness. Their confinement is absolute; so is their dependence on each other. There is nothing but mutual confinement, just as there are no more pap, pain killer, coffins, and nature. Even "what we call making an exit" (as Clov says) is a perpetual remaining on stage. True, Clare and Felice will also remain perpetually on stage, but because someone has locked the doors, not because the stage is all there is.

The experience of his crack-up and the encroachments of middle age have given Williams new insights into life and new thematic directions to his imagination. But if he is to make the richness of his imagination available to us again, he must find and control the means of dramatic expression better than he has done thus far in the seventies. Otherwise we will continue to feel (with sadness) the same discontents.

Since I completed the above article Williams has published, in *The Theatre of Tennessee Williams*, volume five, a considerably revised version of *Out Cry*, returning to his previous title, *The Two-Character Play*. The revision indicates not only that the play is of high personal value to Williams but, more importantly, that he is aware of its flaws and is in sufficient control of his talent to make headway in correcting them. Although the revised play may not stand as one of Williams' grander achievements, it demonstrates a surer grasp of dramatic technique than anything he has done in the seventies, and it deserves a new and impartial production.

The new *Two-Character Play* keeps the play-within-the-play relatively intact, but the scenes which enclose it have a tightness and energy lacking in *Out Cry*. In particular, the characters lose most of the rhetorical, introspective quality which so weakened them and which perhaps caused the impression that they were but mouthpieces for the author. Secondly, the excessive theatrical symbolism to which I objected above is largely gone.

Perhaps the single most noticeable improvement is in the toughness of Clare. Her first appearance suffices as illustration. In *Out Cry* Clare enters "falteringly, blindly" and encounters, fearfully, the statue which in that version dominates the stage. She quickly goes into a disjointed and somewhat insane (and symbol ridden) speech: "I forget—*unalterable circumstance*, but—Remember the time that destitute old—painter—invited us to tea on the—Viale—something—somewhere and when we arrived—the concierge said, suspiciously, 'Oh, him, huh, five flights up, not worth it!'—Five flights up, not worth it!—No, not exactly worth it, the old, old painter was seated in *rigor mortis* before a totally blank canvas, teakettle boiled dry on the—burner—under a skylight—that sort of light through a dirty winter skylight is—*unalterable—circumstance*—but there is no skylight here, I haven't noticed a window—Is this theater under the ground? Is this the subterranean— pleasure-dome of—Kabla—Kubla —Koon? . . .—Sacred river must be—frozen over—(She collides with something: a startled cry.) *Felice!*" (p. 11).

The speech illustrates one of the great problems with *Out Cry*: the characters are so drugged or so on the edge of hysteria that they are unable to follow the train of their own thought and speak in phrases punctuated by pauses, yet they are able to construct elaborate and somewhat coherent patterns of poetic symbolism. To produce such a speech at the beginning of the play gives away too much by connecting the theater, death, and their circumstances before the mood of the *Two-Character Play* has a chance to work on the audience.

In the revised version, Clare is somewhat nervous, but far from the outer edge of self control. Her "fear" is of her own shadow, not the "monstrous aberration" (p. 9) of the previous version, and she can talk rather playfully about it. She enters, not to protest that she can't go on, but to encounter a press reception, and her reaction to learning that it has been cancelled reveals a different Clare from the character in *Out Cry*: "No press reception? Artists' Management guaranteed, Magnus personally promised, no opening without maximum press coverage on this fucking junket into the boondocks.— Jesus, you know I'm wonderful with the press . . ." (V, 312). The Clare of *Out Cry* would never have been "wonderful with the press."

The hardening of Clare's character improves the play in two important ways. First, it etches more sharply the individuality of the characters of the brother and sister, further obviating the contention that they are a single character. Felice becomes the softer and more sensitive of the two and Clare the more businesslike and direct. Their outlines are distinct and the conflicts between them more believable. Secondly, by causing Clare to be less neurotic, Williams strengthens the possibility of our accepting her condition as normal rather than exceptional. She comes across not as an embodiment of vague poetry but as an actress on a two-bit tour and somewhat at the end of her rope. This improvement does not completely eliminate the discrepancy between the two layers of the drama, but it makes a major stride in that direction.

Perhaps the most striking improvement in the play is the reduction of the dramatic symbolism. The grotesque statue which Williams wanted to dominate *Out Cry* has practically disappeared as a motive for dialogue and, more importantly, has lost all its sinister and mysterious connotations to become merely a papier-mâché giant. Although the sunflower symbolism remains, it seems less obtrusive because it no longer has to compete with the emotionally charged set. The set as Williams now describes it is obviously a theater, not the demonic figment of someone's imagination described in *Out Cry*.

Williams' revisions of *The Two-Character Play* may not reverse the verdict against *Out Cry*, but they do reopen the case. More importantly, they do demonstrate a recapturing both of dramatic control and of objectivity in Williams' work. Perhaps the unburdening of himself in the *Memoirs* will enable Williams to escape the obsessions which have plagued his imagination during the last decade and enable him, in his twilight years, to regain his position as our most eminent living dramatist.

Reflections on Moon Lake:
The Presences of the Playwright

DONALD PEASE

T ENNESSEE WILLIAMS' recent publication of his autobiography has resulted in an increased concern over the relationship
between his art and his life. Williams uses his art as an organizing
principle for his life, but it remains unclear whether he sees his plays
as pretexts for his self-revelations or his life as merely a context for
his art. The central figure in the *Memoirs* is neither Williams the
man nor Williams the playwright but Williams the actor who plays
a part in an Off Broadway production of one of Williams' own plays.
While acting in the play, Williams remembers the past as a series of
disconnected incidents that cannot be integrated into his role within
the play.

An analysis of the *Memoirs* would obviously merit a paper in itself, but even these surface observations make it clear that the autobiography emphasizes the complicated relationship between the life
and the work. In so doing, the *Memoirs* only continues a familiar
Williams concern. In a sense the *Memoirs* can be described as extended forewords, for in the New Directions edition of his plays Williams wrote forewords that present the disparity between the world
of his plays and his personal life. Since the forewords appear *before*
the plays, the reader must begin Williams' dramatic enterprise with
a rendition of the personal difficulties that necessitated the creation
of the plays. On occasion these difficulties shadow rather than intro-

duce the drama, for while Williams continually asserts the successful transformation of his being into the acts of the play, he does so
in a way that suggests the impossibility of the conversion: "It is
amazing and frightening how completely one's whole being becomes absorbed in the making of a play. It is almost as if you were
frantically constructing another world while the world that you live
in dissolves beneath your feet, and that your survival depends on
completing this construction at least one second before the old
habitation collapses" (II, 419).

It seems that Williams placed these forewords at the beginning of
the plays so that his plays might be seen not only to originate in and
transform but also to replace his individual life. In the forewords he
provides personal background not to clarify his plays but to dramatize his life. He constructs his forewords out of the worldly struggles
of Tennessee Williams the man, so that this man might become an
actor in the *"world without time"* (II, 260) of his plays. Once Williams can be seen as frightened of his mortality, the timeless world
of the play can likewise be seen to emanate from and displace this
fear.

The forewords prepare the reader to view the plays as the conversion of the frustration of Williams' life into the immortal struggles
of the plays. Williams even implies that, after juxtaposing his life
and his art, his act of writing itself constitutes a moral code that he
cannot help casting in dramatic terms: "The great and only possible
dignity of man lies in his power deliberately to choose certain moral
values by which to live as steadfastly as if he, too, like a character in
a play, were immured against the corrupting rush of time" (II, 262).

However, the very description of this project reveals the impossibility of success. What is the reader left with after reading the forewords but the memory of a life that needs to be transformed but
cannot be? The very separation of the play and the forewords into
two discrete forms implies that while the life can be dramatically
narrated it cannot be fully dramatized. The narration can dramatize,
but only as narration not as drama. The forewords reveal that behind
the playwright who finds his great subject in unfulfillable desire
stands a man who is tragically unable to fulfill his own desire to turn
his life into drama. Williams is condemned to write forewords that

expose a wish that can never come true. In this light, the overdramatized outbursts in the forewords seem the shadowy, unassimilable, unregenerate origins of the plays. Almost all the forewords record the tragic separation of the man from his plays, and they reveal the plays to be the projection and elaboration of this alienation.

Yet the forewords are not limited to the narration of failures. While Williams cannot be transformed into the world of the play, the reader sees that his need to be can turn him into a playwright. The same Williams who cannot be turned into a figure in the play can be absorbed into the act of making plays. And when Williams acts as a playwright he exists between the mortal world measured by time and the timeless world of the play. From this perspective the forewords constitute a narrative interlude wherein Williams is inspired by the threat of his own mortality. According to the time logic implicit in the forewords, Williams as playwright exists between the world of time and the world without time; as playwright he dwells in a world undefined by time.

Through the forewords the reader begins Williams' plays by witnessing the unfulfillable desire that leads to the making of the playwright. Moreover the forewords invite the reader to consider the inevitable loss implicit in Williams' motive for becoming a playwright: unless Williams can remain a perpetual playwright, he must once again confront his mortality. As soon as he finishes a play, he must once again become a man limited by time.

All these implications suggest that Williams cannot see himself as a successful playwright until he can find a play wherein he can abide as playwright. If most of the finished plays separate him from his desire to be the eternal playwright, one of his plays manages to unite him with this desire. In the foreword and notes to *Cat on a Hot Tin Roof*, Williams the man is completely absorbed into the role of Williams the playwright. In failing to have the play produced in the version he wished, the playwright himself succeeds in becoming a Tennessee Williams hero.

Before Williams can be seen as a hero still another foreword is necessary. Some preliminary survey of what constitutes a Tennessee Williams hero must precede any discussion of Williams as hero. But this discussion of the forewords is not meant to be merely introductory, for a discussion of Williams' early plays in terms of the forewords can be illuminating. Indeed many of these plays seem to reenact the struggle narrated in the forewords.

Just as Williams begins his plays with forewords that dramatize the writer's wish to become part of his play, so Williams the writer actually began his dramatic career with the invention of the writer as his hero. Nor is it surprising that in his first full-length play written for Broadway production, *Battle of Angels*, the hero should become a writer in order to express his inability to fulfill his desire. Valentine Xavier becomes a writer on the day he discovers that making love cannot fulfill his wish or answer his questions of the universe. He wants to know the answer to the "why" of this world. Lovemaking only causes the question to disappear momentarily. He becomes a writer in order to let the secrets of the world abide within him. Williams, who fears the world outside the play, invents as his first "real" character a writer whose motivating impulse is to bring the world within himself. Valentine Xavier hopes to make his consciousness expansive enough to hold within it the creative center of the universe. But he discovers that creative center to be a reflection of his own nature, for in becoming a writer Val discovers the secret for the continuation of the universe to be frustrated desire. When Val writes he becomes the means whereby desire can reenact the conditions of its own frustration.

The orphan Valentine was dispossessed of the land. As a result he was free to roam the world with an awareness as expansive as the globe's. As a wanderer, he temporalizes the desire to know the secret impulses of the world. He can express his desire only as the flight of longing, for flight is the eternal expression of unfulfillable desire. When he rests on his journey he awakens the desire of those he meets. Valentine Xavier becomes an angel of light who awakens the world into freedom by putting it back in touch with its desires. "Valentine" loves and "Xavier" cures through an erotic touch, for the erotic is the universal expression of desire. However, each character Val awakens comes to the perception that he or she is trapped. Valentine remains free only because he stands outside the world as a man dispossessed who wishes to hold within himself the secret creative impulses of the world. Moreover, his freedom becomes the stage upon which the characters act out their lack of freedom. When Val touches these characters he invariably reminds them of some world of innocence and fulfilled desire that they lost. Ironically the angel of light calls forth an angel of darkness who becomes violent in his inability to get what he wants.

For example, when Val embraces Vee Talbott while he fits her for shoes, he liberates her erotic instinct and thereby enables her to fulfill her lifelong goal to paint the savior. When she paints the savior, he turns out to be an image of Valentine Xavier. Xavier's *painted* eyes accuse her with the look of a desire she must keep suppressed to remain a respectable member of the community. Her art becomes the revelation of her alienated desire. Her embodiment of that desire as Val confirms Val in the role of displaced or dispossessed desire. Valentine is the incarnation of society's repressed desire. In this role Valentine polarizes individuals and the society as a whole.

If Vee Talbott sees Valentine as the simultaneous release and accusation of desire, Myra Torrance sees him as both an angel of light and an angel of darkness. For Myra, Val seems the replication of her lost love David Anderson, who loved her at Moon Lake but left her to marry a wealthy planter's daughter. As such Val represents both fulfilled and unfulfilled desire.

After David abandoned her for the planter's daughter, Myra conceived of herself as a barren piece of land; so she sold herself to the merchant Jabe Torrance. Yet all the time she lived with Jabe, she remained engaged to David Anderson in her dream life. Jabe gave her the social standing that would make her David's social equal, but he also forced her to see barrenness as the cost of that equality. When Valentine arrives he frees her from the barren land to return her to her dream world at Moon Lake. Val's search for life's meaning reminds Myra of her love for David. Val becomes a reincarnation of David who motivates her to separate herself from the waste land incorporated in the "mercantile store" and attach herself to the idyllic world of Moon Lake, which she recreates in her decorations of the confectionery store. But almost as soon as Myra regains her dream world through Val and the confectionery store, she is condemned to lose it again. When Val arrived, Myra had tried to turn him into David. She did not see Val as Val, but as her lost love, David, reincarnated. She treats Val as the vehicle for a lost memory; he is not valuable in himself but only for what he represents. Likewise, the confectionery store is not Moon Lake, but only an attempt at a restoration of Moon Lake—the confectionery store can only signify loss; it cannot regain for Myra what she lost. Myra has not rediscovered love; she has only merchandised it. She has treated Valentine just as she feels Jabe has treated her, for she has tried to trap him within the confines of her world. She has attempted to enclose him within the skin of her secret world. Val cannot inaugurate her reunion with David, but after she traps Val he can repeat her loss of David by running away. By the end of the play Myra realizes that even the child she conceived with Val reproduces the death and not the regeneration of the Moon Lake world. Myra wanted to destroy Jabe's world, for she felt it was destroying her. Instead Jabe's world did destroy *her*; destructive impulses caused her to become an agent of the world she wished to destroy. Myra became a replica of the woman from Waco, Texas, who accused Val of rape because he could not be bought.

Once Val releases the frustrated desires of Vee and Myra, he becomes the symbolic expression for the town of everything it must destroy to survive. Valentine Xavier's primitive, elemental passion mirrors the interior the townspeople had to alienate once they became orderly and ordinary citizens. He is burned to death with a blowtorch on Good Friday as the expression of the town's internal conflagration. The people could not choose a more fitting instrument for the immolation of the passion they wish to alienate than a blowtorch, which itself represents an exteriorization of repressed emotion. Immediately after the deaths of the major characters, the townspeople convert the mercantile store into a museum where they can view the remnants of a world they had to destroy.

But, as with all worlds that come to an end on Good Friday, this one rises again as the play *Battle of Angels*. If Val the writer wished that the secrets of the world could take life within him, the play fulfills his wish, for his snakeskin literally becomes the curtain for the world of the play which exposes the creative secret of the world to be perpetual loss. Of course Val's wish reflects Williams' desires to convert the real world into his interior, created world. Poetry only partially fulfills that desire, for Williams' poetry only lyricizes the individual interior world. "Personal lyricism is the outcry of prisoner to prisoner from the cell in solitary where each is confined for the duration of his life" (III, 3). Personal lyricism must master "its necessary trick of rising above the singular to the plural concern, from personal to general import" (III, 4), and the way to this mastery involves the metamorphosis of lyric poetry into drama. Only drama can satisfy a writer who thinks "of writing as something more organic than words, something closer to being and action" (III, 5). Usually when a lyric poet writes in a more public setting, he devises a setting that coincides with his lyrical vision of the world—the setting becomes an idyllic world where every character and every object fulfills the longing of the lyricist. Tennessee Williams' settings do not satisfy the desires of the lyric poet so much as they repeat them. Whereas the lyrical world always reminds the poet of his separation from a world that cannot fulfill him, it also always deludes him into trying to be lyrical. Tennessee Williams invents a dramatic world that publicizes his private one. His dramatic world is not a place of fulfilled desire, but one which dramatizes and immortalizes the impossibility of ever fulfilling desire. Williams overcomes personal loneliness by inventing a dramatic world that becomes the dream space for every man's loneliness. Like Val he converts his interior world into the world's interior. When he does so, his plays themselves become mankind's expression of the separation between desire and act, wish and reality. Perversely, Williams fulfills the dream of the lyric poet by inventing a dramatic world in which desire cannot be fulfilled.

Once such a world is invented, the wish becomes one of reunion with a real world. A world orginating in frustration is bound to be prone to catastrophe. Such catastrophes coincide with the disasters Williams' life is heir to. In fact Williams conceives of his plays as his disasters, and when the world rejects them as disasters the actual world replicates the invented world. After Boston enthusiastically rejected *Battle of Angels*, Williams re-formed the incident into a dramatic event where he becomes Val and Boston becomes the incensed town of his play: "As we crossed the Common there was a series of loud reports like gunfire from the street that we were approaching, and one of us said, 'My God, they're shooting at us!'" (III, 219). However, while the dramatic rendering embodies Williams' wish to unite the two worlds, his humor exposes their irreconcilable separation.

These two worlds did not remain separated indefinitely. The public accepted *The Glass Menagerie* with almost as much ardor as it exercised in rejecting *Battle of Angels*. In *The Glass Menagerie* the writer Valentine Xavier, who was a fugitive, becomes the writer Tom Wingfield, who dreams of running away from the imprisoning world ruled by his mother, where he must replace his fugitive father as the family's means of support. Tom lives for the future, while everyone else in the house dwells in the past. Once the present fails to satisfy longing, the past projects itself into the memory as a tempting idyllic world of contentment, but such a world is always an evasion of the present—a wish not to be. In *The Glass Menagerie*, Myra's memories of David at Moon Lake become the lost world of the Old South peopled by Amanda Wingfield's gentlemen callers. Both Myra's and Amanda's worlds are tombs masquerading as pastoral settings, for both worlds are attempts to forget the betrayals that destroyed Myra and Amanda. Laura Wingfield conflates the idyll and the museum into a glass menagerie that houses glass animals whose substance consists of Laura's sympathy and compassion. Since Laura is crippled, she cannot temporalize her longing through flight; so she memorializes it in her glass animals.

These memorabilia expose and shatter Amanda's self-deceiving memories when she attempts to relive her past through her daughter. When Tom invites Jim O'Connor as a guest for dinner, he invites a man who is a living piece of memorabilia, for he is a relic from Laura's past. In high school, Jim was a great success, but since then he lost his status. Success for him would inhere in recapturing his former status. While Jim seems only a ghost of his former self he embodies the deepest wish of every member of the Wingfield house. As the substitute father, he would allow Tom to escape by replacing him; as the gentleman caller, he would return Amanda to the glories of the South; as her dream lover come true, he would turn Laura's glass menagerie back into the real world. In fact Jim does momentarily change the Wingfield apartment into a heavenly paradise when he seems truly to love Laura. However, he leaves it a haunted house peopled by shattered dreams after it becomes clear that he has only used Laura as a proving ground for his powers of persuasion. When he talks with Laura, his dream of success collides with her dream of love. When his dream of success takes him back in memory to his past success in high school, both dreams combine to make the present reality seem ghostly. Jim reinstates Laura in her glass menagerie world by replacing her dream of love with the image of his dream girl. Hence the gentleman caller reenacts the original crisis of each character. When he abandons them, he becomes Laura's father and Amanda's husband. Far from replacing Tom as family provider, he previews Tom's following in his father's footsteps.

Battle of Angels used violence to unveil Val's interior; *The Glass Menagerie* reveals Tom's interior world to be one inhabited by two women confined to live with their dreams of escape. Unable to run away, Laura must stabilize her escape within the glass menagerie. Through this world Laura can recall the impossibility of ever realizing her dream. While Amanda tries to suppress the beastly instincts of the members of her household, Laura knows that each person is a transparent beast whose interior can be filled only with the light of a shared longing. Laura's failure with Jim strangely reunites her with her mother, for Laura has duplicated Amanda's loss of her gentleman caller. They now share a common experience of loss. When we last see Amanda, she bends over Laura and treats her with the sympathy Laura reserves for her glass animals. Moreover, Laura's failure constitutes the substance of Tom's quest. When he flees home to see the world, Tom sees it through Laura's eyes. The entire world becomes a glass menagerie made transparent through the intensity of longing. Laura's glass menagerie has become the essence not merely of Tom's world, but of the entire world, and Laura abides in Tom as his soul. All his efforts to flee from home result in his understanding that all the world suffers from the same disease as his home. Paradoxically, whereas Tom could not accept his home as his world, on leaving home he sees all the world's frustrations in terms of his home. The world seems only an expanded version of his home. When Tom writes, the world of his play becomes the living record of the world he would escape. By extension, the actual world's essence is revealed as its desire to escape from itself.

The Glass Menagerie domesticates the violent world of *Battle of Angels*. Tom Wingfield writes a play that illuminates two significant elements in Williams' dramatic world. Tom writes a play that instead of becoming an escape from his family becomes an expression of his family's and all America's need to escape from a world of unfulfilled desire. The play displaces the individual desire to run away by universalizing that desire. Moreover, Tom's narration of this play about unfulfilled desire reflects Williams' narration of his own unfulfillable desire in forewords.

Was the success of *The Glass Menagerie* the world's revenge on Tennessee Williams? Financial success made it possible for Williams to get everything he wanted out of the world—but that was precisely what Williams did not want. Worldly success separated him from the source of his poetic creation. It threatened to strip him of the need for his dream by offering him the opportunity to live the American myth of success. Success put Williams in possession of everything that his dramatic world proscribed. As a result the world threatened to dispossess him of his need to create. Williams responded by seeing the success of *The Glass Menagerie* as a catastrophe. His preface to the New Directions edition of *The Glass Menagerie* was originally entitled "The Catastrophe of Success." In this essay Williams pits his former way of life against the effete existence success threatened to provide: "The sort of life that I had had previous to this popular success was one that required endurance, a life of clawing and scratching along a sheer surface and holding on tight with raw fingers to every inch of rock higher than the one caught hold of before, but it was a good life because it was the sort of life for which the human organism is created" (I, 136). External success causes him to feel part of this world, but such a feeling dislocates him from the spiritual world of his creation. To defend himself from this sense of spiritual dismemberment, he develops a feeling of enmity for his play and so hears all praise of it as a manifestation of hypocrisy. That play threatened to be his last because it returned him to a world from which he had to feel displaced in order to create. Williams finally developed a saving strategy. He entered the hospital to have his fourth eye operation. Once his eye was operated on, he did not have to *see* this world, but his world would have to see him as disabled. People once again sounded sincere. Williams cannot hear compliments—they are all evasions for him, because they imply that a man works out of self-possession; but he does hear concern and worry, for they are expressions of loss. In essence, Williams cures himself of the disease of success by abandoning his public self with all of its "vanities and conceits and laxities" (I, 140) and exchanging it for "the only somebody worth being . . . the solitary and unseen you that existed from your first breath and which is the sum of your actions and so is constantly in a state of becoming under your own violation" (I, 140). Yet as we have seen, Williams can realize this "solitary and unseen" personality only through the act of writing a play, and the play world replaces the public ego with the world of a play; for it "is only in his work that an artist can find reality and satisfaction, for the actual world is less intense than the world of his invention and consequently his life, without resource to violent disorder, does not seem very substantial" (I, 138). Predictably, as a final act of spiritual restoration, Tennessee Williams overcomes success by writing a play also destined to be successful, A *Streetcar Named Desire*.

In *Battle of Angels*, the writer was the savior who became the symbol of everyone's lost love; in *The Glass Menagerie*, the writer mediated between the lost world and everyday reality; but in A *Streetcar Named Desire*, the writer himself embodied the lost world. As Allan Grey, he is not the substitute but the actual beloved who was betrayed. Love letters and poems secreted at the bottom of Blanche's suitcase are all that remains of Allan. These writings beg Blanche to help Allan regain hold on the world. Blanche was to be Allan's center of being in the world; she was to be his hold on reality. But Blanche betrayed her mission when she discovered that she could not be Allan's sole object of desire. Finding Allan alone in a room with an older man, she goes with him to the place where all dreams begin and are shattered in Williams' plays, Moon Lake, and there she tells Allan that his actions disgusted her. After Allan shoots himself out of shame, Blanche leads her life as an effort to regain Allan. When she becomes the prostitute for all the soldiers, she becomes the desired object she was not for Allan. If Blanche can satisfy the soldiers' desires as Allan's, perhaps she can remake Allan after the image of a soldier. Likewise, she seduces the seventeen year old boy both to regain Allan through him and to fashion for herself a reputation as bad as Allan's.

Interestingly, Allan Grey signals a turning point in Williams' conception of the character of the writer, for Allan Grey is not the primitive become writer but the writer become the polar opposite of the primitive. Stanley Kowalski possesses all the brutal instincts that Allan Grey lacked. Whereas the writer now appears as a figure whose desire could neither fulfill nor be fulfilled, Stanley Kowalski manages to live in a world where his dream can flourish. It is revealing that such a disjunction in Williams' characters should appear *after* the success of *The Glass Menagerie*. In fact the doubling of the role of writer/primitive into a dead writer and a flourishing primitive seems an appropriate response from a playwright who feels that the writer was almost destroyed by the vanity and insincerity that appeared with success. The changed level of Kowalski's desire and his capacity for insensitivity and brutality mirror Williams' reactions after the success of *The Glass Menagerie*. Stanley Kowalski lives in a world uninformed by the transforming power of art, and this world became Tennessee Williams' spectral reality after the writer in him was almost destroyed through the creation of a successful play.

When Tennessee Williams flees to the elemental world of Mexico, he writes a play in which the world he flees not only reappears but prevails. *A Streetcar Named Desire* makes it clear that for Williams the act of fleeing always becomes the act of re-living the past. Flight forces the presence of the past on his characters as the presence of what they attempt to flee. Flight only intensifies the presence of the past. When Blanche DuBois runs away from Laurel and Belle Reve, she does not leave that world behind but instead transports it to the Elysian Fields of Stanley Kowalski. Blanche flies from the world of her past to begin a new life, but Stanley forces her to re-enact the scene in her past that she attempts to flee, her destruction of her love, Allan. Stanley becomes her nemesis, for he responds to her with the same brutal frankness she directed at Allan on the night he destroyed himself. Conversely, Blanche exposes Stanley's apparently idyllic world as a museum of the spirit. Long before Blanche, Stella abandoned the world of Belle Reve in exchange for a dream world of sexual fulfilment with Stanley. When she stepped down from her mansion Stella gave Stanley's world its power and its magic, for his world needs Stella's acquiescence to remain a reality. Stanley can maintain the illusion of kingship in his world only by repeatedly pillaging Stella's mansion. After Blanche arrives, Stanley's world is threatened because Blanche can see it as a dream. She can see through his dream because she is conscious of her own need to invent a false world.

To Stanley, Blanche's dream represents the tenuous unreality of his life. Blanche has tried to return his wife to the world of Belle Reve, so Stanley must repossess his dream world by ravaging Blanche's. Stanley causes the world to see Blanche's dream for a lie and his own dream for the truth. His world depends on the destruction of everything Blanche's world represents. By revealing her reputation as a prostitute, he forces Blanche back into her past. As we have seen, Blanche's promiscuity was an expression of her loss. When Stanley labels her a whore, he turns this expression of her loss of love into her essence.

However, Stanley does not take her as he would a whore; he rapes her as an embodiment of Belle Reve. Through Blanche he re-enacts his initial triumph with Stella. By raping Blanche, Stanley once again pillages Belle Reve. Stanley must ravage Blanche, for he can regain the supremacy of his illusion only after he has reduced Belle Reve to ruins. After he rapes Blanche, her dream changes from the vision of a new life to the reverie of dying at sea. At play's end Blanche's desire has become one with its opposite—death.

This brief discussion of Williams' early plays indicates that the central action for his artistic work is transformation. If Myra sees Val as the metamorphosis of David, and Amanda discovers Jim O'Connor to be her gentleman callers returned, Blanche DuBois recovers her lost love in Mitch. Once she learns that Mitch has remained devoted to a girl who died, she can easily convert him into a representative of her lost love. The image that emphasizes this action is the moth or bird that leaves behind the abandoned cocoon or the broken shell to fly in a nighttime world. Since such metamorphoses involve an element of conflict, it is not surprising that Williams sets many of his transformation scenes against an open sky that itself turns cloudy or stormy as a projection of the inward sky of the characters. Williams' sets are the exteriorizations of the dream worlds envisioned by his characters, and they change *as* his characters change mood. All these transformations find their origin in the characters' need to evade some past event. In *Battle of Angels* and *The Glass Menagerie*, it was the loss of love; in *Streetcar Named*

Desire it was the brutalization of love. Are these past events within the plays themselves shadowy images of Williams' need to transform his "public self" (I, 138) into the world of a play? Is the loss that Williams sees his life to be the original loss that all his plays look back to? Are not his forewords the residue, the broken shell of a life that has failed to be transformed? These forewords express Williams' life somehow as a betrayal of his dream. They shadow the plays with such renditions of Williams' mortality as: "Whether or not we admit it to ourselves, we are all haunted by a truly awful sense of impermanence. I have always had a particularly keen sense of this at New York cocktail parties, and perhaps that is why I drink the martinis almost as fast as I can snatch them from the tray" (II, 261). The plays overshadow this fear by dramatizing Williams' fear of mortality, and once the mortality is dramatized it is immortalized in the world of the play in which time is arrested: "The diminishing influence of life's destroyer, time, must be somehow worked into the context of his play. . . . almost surely, unless he contrives in some way to relate the dimensions of his tragedy to the dimensions of a world in which time is *included*—he will be left among his magnificent debris on a dark stage, muttering to himself, 'Those fools'" (II, 264). Whereas time reduces Williams' life to debris, the plays use that debris as the setting for the timeless world of the play. In this play world, Williams wishes to bring all the members of the audience within the unifying warmth of a re-created shell, the transformed remnants of the shell of the world formerly shattered. Williams can feel at home only within his theater: "Our hearts are wrung by recognition and pity, so that the dusky shell of the auditorium where we are gathered anonymously together is flooded with an almost liquid warmth of unchecked human sympathies, relieved of self-consciousness, allowed to function . . ." (II, 262).

The forewords reveal the distance between Williams' art and a life that cannot be rendered into art but can only be the precondition for such a rendering. Even the accounts of incidents from his life remain merely forgettable incidents and not the events which become immortal once charged with the remarkable tensions in his drama. Only in *Cat on a Hot Tin Roof* does Williams manage to bridge the chasm between the world of his forewords and that of his plays.

In the New Directions edition, *Williams'* version of the play becomes a foreword to the performed version of it. Williams wrote two versions of *Cat on a Hot Tin Roof*. He preferred his first version but rewrote it because the director, Elia Kazan, felt a rewritten version of the second and third acts would make better dramatic sense. Williams had to rewrite the entire third act of this play because he was afraid to lose his director, Elia Kazan. To satisfy the demands of his director, Williams compromised his own vision of the play. It was Kazan's version and not Williams' which won the Pulitzer Prize and the New York Drama Critics' award, and the success of Kazan's play meant the failure of Williams' art. Whereas in his previous plays, the disaster of Williams' life was the necessary precedent for the creation of a play, now the failure of his art became an event in his life—an event which he could transcribe as part of his printed edition of the play. When a director reads this edition, he must choose between Williams and Kazan. As a result Williams has translated himself from an abandoned cocoon into an *act* of choice. Moreover, this act makes it clear that once one chooses Williams or Kazan, one chooses Williams *transformed into* the third act of his play. If his previous play turned Williams' life into art, *Cat on a Hot Tin Roof* turned his art into an event in his life and then enabled that event to be seen as the failure of his art.

In the foreword to this play, "Person-to-Person," Williams outlines the boundaries of this failure. After noticing that an artist's plays invariably find themselves rooted in the deeply personal, emotional life of the artist, he asserts that his own plays constitute his effort to break through the lonely walls of himself to reach out and embrace another. Williams lays bare the personal dimension of his play and the desperate attempt at communication to let the reader see its failure to communicate as a personal failure. In this play, which focuses on the difference between truth and reality, Williams is forced to lie just as is his central character Maggie.

Like Myra, Amanda and Blanche, Maggie the cat finds herself backed into a trap and she must claw her way out. Unlike Myra and Amanda, but like Blanche, Maggie married her dream lover, Brick. And like Blanche, she discovered that her lover did not love her as much as he did another. Brick devised a way of coping with the problem of human mortality that mirrored Williams' own. He tried to remain eternally young by playing the game of his youth with his youthful companion as long as he could. While Brick played football, he remained in a play world outside the parameters of human history. He and Skipper could maintain the illusion of youth by the authority of the illusory world of games.

Complications resulted when Maggie tried to get as close to Brick as Skipper was. Unable to achieve such intimacy in the bedroom, she tried to love Brick through the man to whom he was devoted. She tried to attract Brick's desire by forcing Skipper to confess to Brick that he was a homosexual and in love with Brick. Brick did not want to enter human time. He attempted to remain outside time through a game that was his idealization of the world. Skipper's phoned admission of his homosexuality distorted and profaned that ideal world and so made it part of the historical world. Brick could not accept the truth of that statement and remain Skipper's friend; so Brick answered Skipper's confession with silence. Just as Blanche's disgust led to Allan's suicide, Brick's disgust with Skipper ended in Skipper's death. If Blanche tried to atone for Allan's death by becoming the object of desire for every soldier in Laurel, Brick makes amends to Skipper by trying to drink himself into Skipper's grave. Alcoholism replaces football as the idealized form of their atemporal relationship. Brick drinks until he hears the "click" of the telephone receiver he slammed on Skipper's confession just as Blanche drinks until she hears Allan fire the gun at the Moon Lake Casino.

Brick lives as Skipper's principle of death. Not a rebirth but a second death, Brick lives his life as a form of Skipper's dying. Ironically Brick's father, who is afraid he is about to die, sees in Brick the emblem of his own life. When Big Daddy tries to reform Brick's life, he does so because he sees Brick as the objectification of the life he is about to lose. In their second-act confrontation scene, Big Daddy forces Brick to confess that it was his own mendacity, his inability to face his disgust for Skipper's desire that led to Skipper's death. Whereas Big Daddy had hoped that such a recognition of the truth would lead to Brick's reformation, Brick takes the scene as a revelation of the mortality and degeneracy of human existence. Big Daddy began this scene with Brick because he needed to talk with someone. He has just been told he did not have the cancer he feared. All the animal screams of terror he had suppressed when he struggled with his fear of death, he turned into a *conversion* sermon when he talked with Brick. Brick is the younger version of himself. Since Big Daddy had just conquered death within himself, he wished to conquer death in the exterior version of himself. However, Brick reconverts the scene when he tells the father the truth of his condition. Big Daddy had compelled Brick to face the truth of his mendacity. Now Brick forces his father to confront the truth of his own mortality when he tells him the doctor lied. Brick speaks as Big Daddy's own fear that diagnoses his disease to be terminal intestinal cancer.

In the second act both Big Daddy and Brick have attempted to evade the truth. Brick used alcohol, while his father tried a more subtle form of self-deception. Big Daddy tried to escape from his knowledge that man is the beast who must die, by resolving to live his newly recovered life *as if* he were starting life again. That is why he must reject Big Mama. She represents his past life which now has revealed itself to be mortal. He must replace her with some fantasized woman even though Big Mama remains as faithful to him as his rich Delta plantation.

While the second act reveals the truth that life is death for both Brick and Big Daddy, the first and third acts suggest that Maggie's lie can come true. Maggie tries to regain Brick in the first act by offering him a part in her game of love, but after he rejects this ploy, she regains him as her loss in the third act. After Mae and Gooper tell Big Mama that Big Daddy will die of cancer, she tries to evade this truth by begging Brick to father a child and thereby a second Big Daddy. She hopes to remember Big Daddy through Brick. Although Brick ignores her plea, Maggie tries desperately to remain in the game by announcing that she and Brick will have a child. Brick neither agrees nor disagrees, for by this time he listens only to the "click" that will give him the peace of Skipper's death. Williams' version of the third act climaxes in a remarkable tour de force wherein Maggie literally draws life from death. Unlike David Anderson, Jim O'Connor, or Allan Grey, Brick is the living memory of lost love, and what is more he is the abiding image of a dead man. Not a substitute but the dying version of the man Maggie loves, Brick haunts Maggie with the presence of a past love. Refusing to be defeated by the death that haunts Big Daddy and Brick, Maggie takes this man in her arms and literally conceives a child out of Brick's death. She makes love to Brick as she probably made love to Skipper, and when she whispers her devotion to Brick they resonate as words she might have originally whispered to Brick that night when she made love to him as Skipper. Now that Brick has become the alcoholic and dying version of Skipper, Maggie can repeat those words, "Oh, you weak people, you weak, beautiful people!—who give up.—What you want is someone to—take hold of you.—Gently, gently, with love! And—I *do* love you, Brick, I *do*" (III, 165–6). While Maggie remarries her husband as death, Brick does not begin to reform himself, but begins to perfect his slow ritual of dying. Big Daddy's second act dissertation on man as the beast who must die, which itself was a sublimation of his fear of death, now reverts to the beastly howl of the beast who knows he faces death. In the third act Big Daddy is transformed into the animal howl he earlier repressed.

In the performed version of the play, Brick tries to reform himself, and Big Daddy actually reappears on the stage. These two events belong together because Williams has secretly converted Kazan's directorial imperatives into another of Big Daddy's orders. Once Tennessee Williams presents a reformed Brick, he compromises Brick's fidelity to the death of his friend, but he affirms Brick's obedience to Big Daddy's second act command to reform himself. Brick lies to his own truth and acts as if Big Daddy's *wish* for immortality concealed in his attempt at Brick's rehabilitation could come true. Big Daddy also lies, for he now sees Maggie as the dream woman he fantasized as a promise of immortality. After Maggie announces that she will have a child, he picks her up off the floor and agrees that she does indeed have life in her. However, he feels this life as the erotic life he desires. In helping to make Maggie's lie seem true, Brick and Big Daddy betray the truths they discovered in the second act and seem compromised victims of self-deception. In Williams' version Brick's decision to remain an alcoholic seemed the decision of a man who remained strong in his devotion to a dead friend. Alcoholism was his prayer of devotion. That strength gave Maggie's final action a certain stature. But in the performed version Maggie does not conceive life with death but only manages a hysterical union with a weak man.

Not the characters but Tennessee Williams himself emerges as the real victim in this play, for he exists in this third act as a betrayed presence. His printed version of the play dramatizes Williams' victimization by a director whose drive for success has made a catastrophe out of one of Williams' most intimate plays. The performed version of the play was a success, but the price of this success was the destruction of Williams' version. *Cat on a Hot Tin Roof* marks the high point in Williams' career for it not only enables him to see the success of his play as a personal disaster but it enables his reader to see it as well. The printed version of this play itself becomes a dramatic representation of the author's central dramatic metaphor, for it dramatizes the destruction of Williams' personal vision and its resurrection by the world as a distorted image of the original. When the reader looks at the order of the printed version of *Cat*, he can see the successful version as an unsuccessful replica, as the loss of the vision Williams had earlier attained. When the reader can see this he can see that this work represents the play as itself a repetition of the eternal loss that always haunts and motivates Tennessee Williams.

Williams' play world has come full circle and duplicated his original reason for writing plays. He could see his version of the play as the world of Moon Lake betrayed and distorted by a Jabe Torrance figure who tried to merchandise and take possession of this dream world. The play has descended into reality, for the successful version performs the absence and not the presence of Williams' vision. Yet this failure in the midst of success extirpates and focuses Williams' need to be a playwright.

Tennessee Williams:
Reassessment and Assessment

S. ALAN CHESLER

Tennessee Williams' career gained great momentum with the New York production of *The Glass Menagerie* in 1945. Five years earlier, however, the fiasco of *Battle of Angels* in Boston had almost ended his professional dramatic career at its outset. The audience hissed, booed, and even left before the final curtain, some enveloped in smoke from faulty technical work backstage. Nevertheless, five years later the playwright's first New York production was an immediate popular and critical success. *The Glass Menagerie* ran for 563 performances and won the New York Drama Critics' Award as the best American play of the season.

Menagerie brought Tennessee Williams' name to the forefront of the American stage scene. And the stunning success of his next play, *A Streetcar Named Desire*, in 1947, confirmed the initial critical reaction to this new American playwright. In fact, many critics felt that *Streetcar* was a better play than *Menagerie*. Williams' second Broadway play earned not only a second New York Drama Critics' Award but a Pulitzer Prize as well.

The forties also saw the unsuccessful Broadway production of *Summer and Smoke* (1948), a play more satisfactorily staged off Broadway eleven years later in José Quintero's Circle in the Square production. Williams considered his revision of this imperfect work a better play; but the revised version, *Eccentricities of a Nightingale*,

848

has never received the Broadway production for which the playwright had hoped. Brooks Atkinson considered *Summer and Smoke* to be a great work, but most critics and scholars agree that it shows more promise than fulfilment of greatness.

Williams ventured into other dramatic modes in the 1950s. *The Rose Tattoo* (1951) was an earthy, lyrical comedy about Sicilians living along the Gulf Coast near New Orleans. Although this play was not highly regarded by most critics, it enjoyed a successful run on Broadway. After completing *The Rose Tattoo*, Williams once more experimented with a new form in the writing of *Camino Real*, which opened in 1953. Though not commercially successful, it was the most controversial and stimulating theatrical event of the season. In this work Williams employed Absurdist and Surrealist techniques in a highly stylized representation of the horrors of twentieth-century life. Few felt that *Camino Real* was an artistic triumph, but most agreed that it was a gigantic attempt and that seeing it was a fascinating, albeit uneven, theatrical experience.

Orpheus Descending (1957) represented seventeen years of periodic revision on Williams' ill-fated first play, *Battle of Angels*. Like *Summer and Smoke*, *Orpheus* contained examples of Williams' unique playwriting talent, especially dialogue of poetic intensity; on the other hand, also like *Summer and Smoke*, it illustrated to an even greater extent the playwright's characteristic weaknesses: heavy-handed symbolism, obtrusive theatricality and violence, and excessive and incongruous moralizing.

During this middle phase of his career, Williams also again wrote successful naturalistic dramas, *Cat on a Hot Tin Roof* (1955) and *Sweet Bird of Youth* (1959). Although both achieved popular success, the latter was not considered as fine an achievement as Williams' major works had been. *Cat*, however, offered some of Williams' most compelling characterizations as well as perhaps the highest degree of dramatic intensity the playwright has ever accomplished. Despite valid criticism of the ending, *Cat* won a third New York Drama Critics' Award and remains a major achievement in Williams' career.

In 1958 Williams demonstrated another aspect of his playwriting versatility. *Suddenly Last Summer* is a short, symbolic play in which every element works both to build its tension and to move it toward its inevitable climax. In this work Williams exercises the control of his craft, especially in the use of symbolism, that was lacking in his less successful efforts and even in some of his major plays.

The 1960s saw only one major Williams play, *The Night of the Iguana* (1961), which won a fourth New York Drama Critics' Award and which was also a popular success. *Period of Adjustment* (1960), *The Milk Train Doesn't Stop Here Anymore* (1964), *Slapstick Tragedy* (1966), *Kingdom of Earth* (*The Seven Descents of Myrtle*, 1968), and *In the Bar of a Tokyo Hotel* (1969) all deservedly received mixed or negative reaction from both critics and audiences, as did the Williams plays of the seventies: *Small Craft Warnings* (1972) and *Out Cry* (1973).

Critics generally agree that Tennessee Williams has increased the flexibility of modern American drama with his utilization of expressionistic and impressionistic techniques within a realistic dramatic framework. John Gassner and Edward Quinn (*The Reader's Encyclopedia of World Drama*, 1969), for example, call Williams' imposition of nonrealistic devices upon realistic plays one of the major accomplishments in the U.S. theater since the middle of this century (p. 291). Williams' reputation, however, has not been firmly established beyond this effort to place him in an historical perspective. Furthermore, since the subjects of many Williams plays broke through sexual and moral barriers, initial popular and critical response often was heatedly beside the point. For instance, *Streetcar*, *Cat*, and *Suddenly* at first offended theatergoers and critics alike. Now these plays not only are performed in local little theater groups around the country but also have found their way into drama anthologies for classroom study. Consequently, the purpose of this essay is to survey a selected body of criticism in an attempt to define and evaluate Williams' literary reputation in the United States. I concentrate on the five plays that will most likely form the basis of the playwright's lasting reputation: *The Glass Menagerie*, *A Streetcar Named Desire*, *Cat on a Hot Tin Roof*, and *The Night of the Iguana*, because they are the Williams works most generally praised and most often performed; and *Suddenly Last Summer*, still misunderstood and therefore not fully appreciated, which I feel will be ranked eventually with the other four plays as Williams' finest achievements.

The Glass Menagerie became an immediate success to both the

New York theatergoing public and the critics. The audience gave the opening-night performance a standing ovation and repeatedly called for the author until he finally made an appearance. The critics, with few exceptions, were just as enthusiastic as the public. There was excitement in the air, the excitement of experiencing the work of a new talent and very likely a landmark in the history of American drama. This opening performance of Williams' first Broadway play on March 31, 1945 began a production so successful that it continued for 563 performances. *The Glass Menagerie* won the *Billboard*-sponsored Donaldson Award (voted upon by 2,000 people in show business), the Sidney Howard Memorial Award (presented by the Playwright's Company), and the fourth annual award of the Catholic monthly, *The Sign*. The most significant acclaim accorded *The Glass Menagerie* was its selection by the New York Drama Critics as the best American play of the 1944–45 season.

Eleven years after its 1945 premiere in New York, *Menagerie* was revived at the New York City Center. The critical response, again, was very favorable. And on May 4, 1965, twenty years after the play's Broadway opening, another New York revival was booked for a two-month engagement. The critical and box office reaction was so favorable, however, that the producers extended the run until October 2. This production of *Menagerie* enjoyed the longest Broadway run of any American play revival during the preceding twenty-five years. The test of time had conclusively demonstrated that not Laurette Taylor's legendary performance as Amanda but Tennessee Williams' craftsmanship had been chiefly responsible for the astounding success of the drama in 1945.

Clearly, the New York theater reviewers from 1945 to 1965 deemed *Menagerie* an outstanding play, one that already had established itself as an American drama classic. Scholars of modern American drama corroborate this assessment. John Gassner (*Treasury of the Theatre*, 1950) and Benjamin Nelson (*Tennessee Williams: His Life and Work*, 1961) commended Williams' objectivity in handling the material of *Menagerie*. Nelson, in a perceptive analysis of the play, sees Amanda Wingfield as its crucial character. Citing the playwright's own words from an interview shortly after the opening of *Menagerie*, that "the most magnificent thing in human nature is valor—and endurance," Nelson points out that precisely these qualities elevate Amanda above the role as foolish, nagging mother to the stature of a "truly valiant woman." Williams' objectivity is responsible for her being among "the most compelling and honest" characters he has created (pp. 104–105). Gassner too lauds Williams' objectivity, which he feels informs the play with strength of characterization. Although the playwright sympathizes with his characters, he also shows clearly that their approach to life is not only an ineffectual one but also an attitude emanating from weakness, not strength (p. 1033).

John Von Dornum ("The Major Plays of Tennessee Williams, 1940–1960," 1962) attributes the vitality of the characters to the playwright's skill in recreating the rhythms and patterns of ordinary speech and adds that perhaps this ability to augment the "illusion of reality" through the speech of his characters is one of Williams' major contributions to modern American dramatic literature (p. 52). What is especially worth noting about the dialogue in *Menagerie*, Von Dornum continues, is the playwright's dramatic use of poetic language fluently integrated into the movement of the play (pp. 46–49).

Roger Stein ("*Glass Menagerie* Revisited: Catastrophe without Violence," 1964) contends that *Menagerie* is Williams' finest work. Stein, like many other scholars, praises Williams' two-level writing: On the dramatic level the author builds up a credible family situation revolving around the desire for a gentleman caller, while simultaneously he weaves through this plot the level of allusion that significantly extends, through symbolism, the play's meaning. It is on the second level that Williams' play transcends the poignant, personal drama of the Wingfields, highlighted and exacerbated by a society confronting economic and international crises, and reaches to the universal plight of "man abandoned in the universe" (p. 143).

Williams' blending of the imaginary and the realistic, his representation of past and present concurrently, and his actualization in word and act of internal states of consciousness, have led scholars to debate whether *Menagerie* is expressionistic, realistic or a combination of the two. Williams (*The Theatre of Tennessee Williams*, 1971) himself provides the framework for these analyses in the production notes, in which he propounds his theory of expressionism.

Everyone should know nowadays the unimportance of the photographic in art: that truth, life, or reality is an organic thing which the poetic imagination can represent or suggest, in essence, only through changing into other forms than those which were merely present in appearance.

These remarks are not meant as a preface only to this particular play. They have to do with a conception of a new, plastic theatre which must take the place of the exhausted theatre of realistic conventions if the theatre is to resume vitality as a part of our culture (I, 131).

Directors, beginning with Eddie Dowling's premier production of the play, have wisely omitted the screen device for the projection of images and titles. But set, music, and lighting usually have followed Williams' descriptions; and these, Frederick Shroyer and Louis Gardemal (*Types of Drama*, 1970) contend, help to establish mood and symbols that heighten a realistic portrayal of the four characters' situations. All four persons find themselves "in the Zolaesque sense, quite trapped—trapped by heredity and the accident of the world, but more so by an airless, crushing environment" (pp. 513–514).

Gassner, referring to Williams' expressionistic stage directions calling for images and phrases to be projected onstage during highly emotional moments in the play, claims that the dramatist failed to control his materials in an apparent attempt to depart from the restrictions of photographic realism in the theater. Nevertheless, his "acute dramatic sensibility" led him to find the right form for his dramatic intentions (*Treasury of the Theatre*, p. 1033). Williams' uniting of expressionistic and realistic elements produces what Nancy Tischler (*Tennessee Williams: Rebellious Puritan*, 1961) considers the playwright's most intensely poetic work. In a similar vein, Esther Jackson (*The Broken World of Tennessee Williams*, 1965) discerningly views this combination of dramaturgical methods as attempting a poetic aim, of endeavoring "to interpret obscure realities in a universal language." Although this attempt had been made by other American playwrights, such as Wilder, Odets, and Saroyan, Williams, like O'Neill, had more "comprehensive motives" than these three dramatists. He sought to bring to "popular theatre an ancient purpose: the exposure of human suffering" (p. xii).

Williams, as his narrator-son Tom Wingfield explains in his first speech, tries to show poetic truth, presented in a form which may appear to be illusion: "Yes, I have tricks in my pocket, I have things up my sleeve. But I am the opposite of a stage magician. He gives you illusion that has the appearance of truth. I give you truth in the pleasant disguise of illusion" (I, 144). For this purpose, Williams utilized nonrealistic theatrical devices. Gassner and Quinn feel this use of nonrealistic elements in the "essentially realistic American theatre" was one of the outstanding contributions to American drama after World War II (p. 921).

Whether the critics labeled *Menagerie* realistic, expressionistic, or something in between, the consensus ever since 1945 has been that the play is a major American work. Furthermore, for many scholars it has assumed the position of a landmark in modern theater history. Jackson claims the opening of *Menagerie* in 1945 commenced a new era in the annals of Western theater, an era in which Williams succeeded O'Neill "as the chief architect of form in the American drama" (p. vii).

The public, as well as the critics, has recognized *Menagerie* as a classic of the American theater. Like Wilder's *Our Town*, it has become one of the American plays most often revived in community, college, and high school productions, whose audiences respond enthusiastically to both its personal and its universal appeals.

After the opening of *The Glass Menagerie*, Williams traveled to Chapala, Mexico, a remote spot suitable to the rigorous daily writing schedule he has always set for himself. The result of this Mexican stay was his third Broadway play, *A Streetcar Named Desire*. (*You Touched Me!*, an unsuccessful joint effort by Williams and Donald Windham, opened for a short run on Broadway in late 1945.) *Streetcar* premiered in New York in December 1947, and continued for 855 performances—the longest run for any Williams play. His second Broadway success won Williams not only a second Donaldson Award and a second Drama Critics' Award but his first Pulitzer Prize as well. As Laurette Taylor had done before in a Williams leading lady role, Jessica Tandy won the Antoinette Perry award as the best actress of the season for her portrayal of Blanche DuBois.

Theatergoers loved *Streetcar*, packing the Barrymore Theatre for over two seasons. The New York theater critics reacted as favorably, but for one notable exception. George Jean Nathan, the only substantially negative reviewer, insisted that Williams' play was merely a "shocker." Many critics, as was to be expected, compared *Streetcar* to *The Glass Menagerie*. Most attested that in his new play Williams more than equaled the achievement of his first Broadway success: in *Streetcar*, they felt, he displayed greater maturity and defter craftsmanship than in *Menagerie*. The New York reviewers considered *Streetcar* an outstanding drama for its shockingly honest depiction of moral decay, the explosive power of the production, and the fascinating characterizations.

In 1973, the twenty-fifth anniversary of its New York opening, major productions of the drama were mounted in cities across the United States. This is an unusual phenomenon in the American theater, but one has only to examine scholarly reaction to *Streetcar* during the past twenty-five years to acknowledge that it has already become established as a classic American play.

Scholarly evaluation has, for the most part, concentrated on the two leading characters, Blanche DuBois and Stanley Kowalski and the relationship between them. A fascinating quality of the play has been its tendency to evoke varying interpretations of Blanche and Stanley—including some that are the very antitheses of others. For instance, Von Dornum sees Kowalski as a negative figure, a symbol of modern man's animal brutality. On the other hand, Signi Falk (*Tennessee Williams*, 1961), an adherent of the psychologically oriented "method" approach to acting, views him as a natural man: honest, straightforward, and masculine. Most assessors of *Streetcar*, however, find Stanley to be a composite of what both of these schools represent. Eric Bentley (*The Dramatic Event*, 1956) offers one of the soundest and most interesting discussions of Stanley's complex nature: "Kowalski is an impure phenomenon: if he is the fullblooded husband that every woman craves, he is also destructive and evil. In fact he is the cunning mixture of good and evil, health and sickness, that, for millions of spectators, has proved a fascination." Robert Brustein "America's New Cultural Hero," 1958) offers another perceptive explanation of Kowalski's intriguing duality. Stanley, according to Brustein, is "a highly complex and ambiguous character, one who can be taken either as hero or as villain. As a social or cultural figure, Stanley is a villain, in mindless opposition to civilization and culture—the "new man" of the modern world whom Williams seems to find responsible for the present-day decline in art, language, decorum, and culture. As a psychological or sexual figure, however, Stanley exists on a somewhat more heroic moral plane. He is akin to those silent, sullen game-keepers and grooms of D. H. Lawrence . . . whose sexuality, though violent, is unmental, unspiritual, and, therefore, in some way free from taint. The conflict between Blanche and Stanley allegorizes the struggle between effeminate culture and masculine libido" (p. 124). Bentley and Brustein have hit upon one reason for *Streetcar*'s enormous audience appeal: the ability of its central characters to elicit *both sympathy and antipathy toward themselves*—as do people in real life.

Although critics vary considerably in their interpretations of Stanley, one point is clear: his portrayal by Marlon Brando had a significant impact on the American theater. As R. L. Dillard ("The Tennessee Williams Hero," 1965) states, Stanley Kowalski, as created by Brando in both the Broadway play and the motion picture, became "the prototype of a style of acting which . . . characterized the American theater for over a decade." Kowalski's mumbled speech, crude manners, simian movements and careless appearance became associated with the method school of acting which dominated the American theater after World War II (p. 191).

Blanche DuBois, the principal figure in *Streetcar*, has undergone even more critical scrutiny than Stanley. If *Streetcar* as a whole is to be judged an artistic success, Blanche's conflicts must be plausible not only as those of a single human being but also as representative of universal human problems—so that the drama's meaning extends beyond the domestic confines of the Kowalski household to the world at large.

One interesting point of contention regarding the characterization of Blanche has resulted from the claim of some scholars that Blanche's troubled existence seems more like a unique psychological case history than the dramatic representation of a universal human struggle, and, therefore, that the play's significance is diminished considerably. John Gassner (*Dramatic Soundings*, 1968) asserts that if a playwright shows "that normal people try to evade reality and are punished by failure," he is making a statement of universal application and importance. "When [he] also associate[s] specific class habits and limitations with them," he is making a valid statement about a social class and their style of life. However, Gassner continues, when an abnormal person like Blanche is the vehicle for this type of statement, such universality is lost (p. 311).

Tischler, who calls Blanche "Williams' finest creation," disputes such interpretations as Gassner's. She persuasively maintains that Williams presents through the struggles of Blanche the universal plight of womanhood. Blanche manifests this universality in her dependence upon men, her realization of her fading beauty, and her terror of the aging process. Tischler regards Blanche as the representative of "tradition and idealism, seeing herself as she would like to be, denying what she is, trying to appear special and different" (p. 138). Elia Kazan (*Directors on Directing*, 1963) concurs with this interpretation of Blanche. He calls her "a heightened version, an artistic intensification of all women. That is what makes the play universal" (p. 370). Marya Mannes ("The Morbid Magic of Tennessee Williams," 1955) carries this interpretation even further. She sees Blanche's conflicts as being representative of not only what every woman encounters but every man as well; and this identification, Mannes feels, is largely responsible for the play's emotional impact upon audiences. "Her progressive insanity is only an extension of that gap in all of us between what we think we are and what we are." Mannes lauds Williams' successful creation of both Blanches at the same time as an especially noteworthy achievement (p. 42).

Of those critics who discern the universality and symbolic ramifications of Blanche's desperate struggle, perhaps Leonard Quirino ("The Darkest Celebrations of Tennessee Williams," 1946) offers the most philosophic and most significant analysis. Quirino's perceptive interpretation sees Williams' characterization of Blanche as being metaphorical. He considers her inability to find satisfaction—not to mention fulfilment—in either Belle Reve or Elysian Fields the playwright's representation of the universally human struggle between the soul and the body which possesses it. Neither the artificial, romantic world of Belle Reve nor the animalistic "death-in-life of Elysian Fields" can provide salvation for Blanche, because only death can resolve her conflict (pp. 67–69).

The greatest source of controversy regarding *Streetcar* has been the contention by some scholars that Williams failed to make clear the position he took toward his material, specifically toward his characters; the result, they claim, is an ambiguous, unsatisfactory denouement. Gassner (*Theatre in Our Times*, 1954), although he maintains respect for Williams' drama, criticizes the playwright for what he regards as an ambivalent attitude toward both Blanche and Stanley. Obviously, "Williams loves Blanche's overrefinement as much as he exposes it. The brute masculinity of Stanley Kowalski also unduly fascinates Williams at the same time that he deplores it. . . ." This ambivalence on the part of the playwright, Gassner contends, causes audiences to fluctuate between understanding and outrage toward Stanley when he rapes his sister-in-law while his wife is in the hospital giving birth to his child. Williams' ambivalence "produces a provocative, but also damaging, ambiguity in the play; damaging to the point of preventing *Streetcar* from attaining tragic magnificence" (p. 350).

Quirino, on the other hand, argues that it is "simpleminded" both to label as ambivalent Williams' portrayal of the positive and negative aspects of the two very different life styles and further to remark that such ambiguity mars *Streetcar*. Quirino claims that Williams pits "the sterility of Belle Reve against the fertility of Elysian Fields, the weakness of Blanche against the insensitive stolidity of Stanley . . . to dramatize the inevitable succumbing of the former to the greater power of the latter" (p. 72).

Nelson too disputes convincingly the claim that Williams' alleged ambivalence weakens *Streetcar*. The playwright's objectivity in handling his characters should not, Nelson asserts, be mistaken for ambiguity. However, Nelson continues, much of the play's "beauty and power" results from Williams' sympathy for Blanche, whose "plight is that she is in some way on the side of what is civilized and refined in a time when both a civilization in which to live and a tradition to which to pledge loyalty are both denied the human being." All the same, Blanche, like Myra Torrance (*Battle of Angels*) and Amanda Wingfield (*The Glass Menagerie*) before her, possesses many faults, a fact indicative of the objectivity with which Williams draws his female portraits. All three women, Nelson notes, "are cloying, often foolish, they put on airs, live in illusions, cannot make adjustments." Nevertheless, Nelson sees these fading ladies, who are trapped by the effects of an anachronistic tradition, as the characters who come closest to expressing the playwright's own feelings (p. 149).

John Golden (*The Death of Tinkerbell*, 1967) offers a recent and perhaps the most cogent discussion of the question of ambiguity in Williams' plays. Golden labels the framework of Williams' outlook "a double dilemma." "On the one hand, the puritan instinct in conflict with human corruption; on the other, a fragmented and chaotic universe in conflict with the intuition and skill of an orderly dramatist. Williams not only has found the means to reconcile the moral and aesthetic division in both art and life, but has been able to convert the psychic tensions these divisions produce into a source of uncommonly high dramatic energy" (p. 125). At this point in his analysis, Golden makes an important critical judgment—that Williams' ability to effect this reconciliation has made him the most gifted American dramatist. Williams' first conflict, the sensualist against the puritan, is the more interesting. "In the true spirit of the allegorist, Williams forces his character to travel over an eerie landscape, a moral obstacle course full of the spiritual traps and fleshly aberrations that reveal the profound divisions in human nature." Golden adds that in virtually all his plays Williams deals with basic conflicts within human beings: "the primitive struggle between light and dark, between God and the Devil, between love and death, between innocence and corruption, and between illusion and reality." This internal conflict, this ambivalence, is a yearning for a paradise lost, one that "promises the kind of fulfillment, total engagement with the full range of sensual experiences that life promises but never seems to deliver" (p. 125).

Scholars do not agree about a precise meaning, a single idea that informs the thematic framework of *Streetcar*. They do, nevertheless, see the play as dramatizing basic human conflicts—struggles not peculiar to twentieth-century man, but common to all humanity. Gassner feels that if there is one overriding conviction in Williams' works, "it is the belief in the power of libido to both animate and destroy a human being" (*Theatre in Our Times*, p. 349). Von Dornum's interpretation of *Streetcar* is similar. He sees the major concern in the play to be with the frustrations that result "from a destructive conflict between the natural mode of life and the artificial, between flesh and spirit" (p. 63). Charles Brooks and Esther Jackson also consider this theme to be basic to an understanding of Williams' drama. Brooks ("The Comic Tennessee Williams," 1958) sees Williams as showing that neither Stanley's brutal manliness nor Blanche's pretentious refinement offers a healthy, viable approach to civilized living (pp. 279–80). Jackson proposes that "Perhaps the crux of the moral dilemma . . . is that neither of these protagonists represents an even remotely acceptable moral choice" (p. 137).

Most critics consider *Streetcar* to be a finer play than *The Glass Menagerie*. Tischler offers sound reasons for this opinion: the lyrical lines are more relevant because they belong to the mannered Blanche, and the method of presentation is less theatrical. The play as a whole, therefore, becomes "more coherent, more lucid," and contains "no loose ends" (p. 143). Williams' skillful use of language in *Streetcar* received almost unanimous acclaim from drama scholars. Typical commendation accorded the playwright's handling of language in this play is Gassner's remark that a part of the reason for the drama's "compelling power" is "the variety and magic of the dialogue" (*Theatre in Our Times*, p. 363). Von Dornum points out that one of the earlier weaknesses of Williams does not mar the dialogue of *Streetcar*: "the set piece that is not well integrated— disappears" in this drama. By having Blanche, whose heritage and overrefined personality "enable her to use high-flown language congruously," articulate the poetic, philosophic ideas of *Streetcar*, Williams avoids the incongruous and obtrusive authorial passages that weaken his earlier works. Blanche's lyrical outpourings are both characteristic of her and integrated smoothly into the play's structure (pp. 62–63).

Streetcar's reputation has not diminished over the years. Since its opening in 1947, it has proved to be the greatest artistic and commercial success of any Williams play. Von Dornum attributes this fact mainly to the playwright's artistic control: "The elements of the drama—construction, language, characterization—are handled with a mature skill that indicates that the playwright had finally achieved a mastery over his dramatic methods. The play is an intricate structure of balances: form with content, pathos with humor, objective reality with illusion" (p. 67). Martin Gottfried (*A Theater Divided*, 1967) feels that *Streetcar*'s greatness stems to a large extent from its dramatic power, its beautiful handling of language, and its skillful construction; nevertheless, he continues, it is "the play's central concept—its story, its mood and its lavish characters" that produce such a magnificent piece of dramatic art. Gottfried believes that in American theater history, Stanley and Blanche are "two of the finest character creations . . . perhaps matched only by O'Neill's Hickey in *The Iceman Cometh*" (p. 252). Gottfried's assessment of *Streetcar* speaks for the majority of theatergoers, theater critics, and drama scholars. He regards it as Williams' most significant drama, a play that "ranks with *Death of a Salesman* as one of the two American masterpieces of the postwar years. While the Williams [play] does not aim for the philosophical grandiose, it *is* art and its art will endure. For it is an exquisite play—perhaps the most romantic, poetic and sensitive play ever written for the American theater" (p. 250).

In 1955 Williams again won both the Pulitzer Prize and the New York Drama Critics' Award, this time for the most controversial play of the 1954–55 season, *Cat on a Hot Tin Roof*. *Cat*, one of Williams' most successful dramas, ran for 694 performances over a period of approximately eighteen months. Writing in 1966, Abe Laufe (*Anatomy of a Hit*) points out that of the five plays receiving both the Pulitzer Prize and the Drama Critics' Award since 1950, *Cat* was certainly the "most controversial" (p. 309). At the time of *Cat*'s New York opening, there were two reasons for the controversy: the play's crude language and its treatment of homosexuality. Although theatergoers and critics anticipated that *Cat* would earn the Critics' Award, they also predicted that the Pulitzer Committee would object to the play's handling of homosexuality, as it apparently had in 1935 when Lillian Hellman's *The Children's Hour* failed to win the award.

The majority of the New York theater critics felt that in *Cat* Williams generated his greatest dramatic intensity. Even those reviewers who had reservations about the drama agreed that it possessed an extraordinary power that resulted largely from the playwright's brutally honest characterizations. Critics also had much praise for Williams' incisive examination of human mendacity.

Drama scholars, unlike New York theatergoers and theater critics, who saw the play performed with what has become known as the

"Broadway third act," have a more complex task in attempting to evaluate *Cat*. Before the play opened in New York, the author rewrote its third act to please the director, Elia Kazan. After reading the original version of act three, Kazan, according to Williams, had three reservations: "One, he felt that Big Daddy was too vivid and important a character to disappear from the play except as an off-stage cry after the second act curtain; two, he felt that the character of Brick should undergo some apparent mutation as a result of the virtual vivisection that he undergoes in his interview with his father in Act Two. Three, he felt that the character of Margaret, while he understood that I sympathized with her and liked her myself, should be, if possible, more clearly sympathetic to an audience" (III, 167–68). Williams, because he wanted Kazan to direct his play and because he feared the director might decline to work on *Cat* if the script were not reexamined with his suggestions in mind, rewrote the third act. As a result, the Broadway production included the second version of act three. The three marked changes in this version are Big Daddy's return onstage (which serves no dramatic purpose other than to bring back the play's most fascinating character); Brick's support of Maggie's lie about her being pregnant (which indicates he has undergone some change of character, especially regarding his marital relationship); and a more sympathetic portrayal of Maggie.

Drama scholars had the opportunity to read both versions, since the play was published later in 1955 with the original version first and the Broadway version after it. The playwright also indicated in a "Note of Explanation," inserted between the two third acts, that he concurred with only one of Kazan's reasons for having the act rewritten. Williams could agree only with the final suggestion since he had become more and more attached to Maggie as he worked on her characterization. But he had serious reservations about the first two criticisms. He did not want Big Daddy to reappear after the second act, and he felt even more strongly that Brick would not experience a change in character as a result of the climactic scene with Big Daddy.

Drama scholars almost unanimously disapprove of the Broadway production's third act. Even those who agree with Kazan's suggestions feel that Williams' revision does not satisfactorily achieve the goals delineated in the director's recommendations. Nelson feels, as do most other scholars, that the absence of Big Daddy in the last act is sensed strongly by an audience because he dominates the drama by his appearances before this point. Nevertheless, the token appearance that Williams provides for Big Daddy in the revised version of act three, "is a rather anemic return for the most vital, extraordinary character in the play" (p. 222). Tischler (pp. 207–08) and Von Dornum (p. 111) agree that Big Daddy's return serves no significant purpose.

Leonard Quirino's cogent analysis sums up scholarly opinion about the two third acts. Quirino shows that neither ending of *Cat* satisfactorily concludes the play. Although the first version maintains the "tone and outlook" established in the first two acts, it suffers dramatically by not allowing the drama's most dominant and intriguing figure to reappear onstage. On the other hand, the revision does benefit theatrically from the return of Big Daddy, but weakens the play's impact by mitigating the second act's forceful dramatization of one of the play's themes—the inability of human beings to communicate satisfactorily (pp. 114–15).

The scholars who respect *Cat* most seem to be those who understand the playwright's intention in writing this drama and who see the relationship between this aim and the realization of it as depicted in the finished play. Whether or not Brick's sexual inclinations are somewhat homosexual is unimportant. Nor should the absence of a neat resolution of Brick's and Maggie's marital problems cause dissatisfaction. As Williams explains in the stage directions, "The bird that I hope to catch in the net of this play is not the solution of one man's psychological problem." Rather, he continues, it deals with "the true quality of experience in a group of people, that cloudy, flickering, evanescent—fiercely charged!—interplay of live human beings in the thundercloud of a common crisis" (III, 114).

Scholars who understand Williams' intention have found, as Quirino explains, that in *Cat* the playwright deals with three basic themes: man's awareness of his mortality, his mendacity, and his seemingly unreachable goals of knowing himself and those around him. Rather than being a study of Brick Pollitt's psychosexual problems, *Cat*, as Williams indicates, is a group drama. Falk defines the theme as the terrible difficulty of communication among members of the Pollitt clan (p. 103); and Quirino adds that because man cannot communicate satisfactorily with other human beings, Williams has him rely upon various mechanisms to attempt temporary escape from the loneliness of existence (p. 114).

Kenneth Tynan (*Curtains*, 1961) sees Williams as dealing, like O'Neill, with the theme of truth versus illusion; but, Tynan adds, whereas the earlier playwright feels that man's illusions are necessary to him, Williams condemns them under the generic heading of mendacity (p. 204). Von Dornum carries this interpretation further when he suggests that, although Williams condemns these illusions, he shows that mendacity is an inevitable escape device in human relationships (p. 123). Similarly, Jackson feels Williams demonstrates through the conflicts of the Pollitt family that truth and meaningful communication cannot exist for human beings (p. 141).

Despite claims by some critics that *Cat* is unduly concerned with sex, violence, and abnormality, the most astute and most convincing analyses regard *Cat* as dealing with pervasive moral problems and with the affirmation of human values. Quirino assesses *Cat*'s meaning to be similar to that of *Camino Real*, which was produced two years earlier in 1953. In both plays Williams shows that life brings frustration and pain but that it is still preferable to the frightening alternatives of both Terra Incognita (the terrifying wasteland in *Camino Real*, from which no person has ever returned) and death. Quirino's interpretation receives sound substantiation from Big Daddy's lines during his second-act confrontation with Brick—the scene which most scholars feel forms the thematic core of the drama: "*I've* lived with mendacity!—Why can't *you* live with it? Hell, you *got* to live with it, there's nothing *else* to *live* with except mendacity, is there?" (III, 109).

Nelson, who also finds *Cat* "extremely moral," insists that despite the hypocrisy, scheming, and greed that permeate the drama, Williams' pervading declaration is that human existence can have meaning—if one vitally engages life. Detachment from life, such as Brick's, offers neither consolation nor satisfaction (pp. 212–13). In response to Robert Hatch's claim (reviewing in *The Nation*, 1955) that Williams' investigation of human nature goes beyond the point where humanity exists, that "without love and hope, discussion of vice and virtue becomes academic" (pp. 314–15), Nelson insists that more than any Williams' play written before it, *Cat* affirms man's moral potential. For notwithstanding the traces of deceit and cupidity to a lesser or greater extent in almost every character, some of these same people also exhibit "nobility and dignity and tenderness and love, and courage" (pp. 212–13).

Von Dornum asserts that *Cat*'s theme is not only more affirmative but also more profound than those of earlier Williams plays. He explains that although Williams admires Brick's absolute morality, Brick's desire for purity, however admirable it may be, makes his existence sterile. His realization that absolute purity in life is unattainable causes him to withdraw from life, and Williams emphasizes through the characters of Big Daddy and Maggie that only through direct, active involvement in life, whatever its flaws, can man survive (pp. 123–24). Von Dornum and Nelson recognize that, despite his respect for idealistic inclinations, Williams demonstrates through the characterization of Brick, and through Maggie's and Big Daddy's speeches, the dangers inherent in a classically idealistic approach to life. Analyses of *Cat* such as those of Quirino, Nelson, and Von Dornum show that allegations of *Cat*'s surface immorality—when larger, vital questions of human values are at stake—are of little, if any, consequence.

If scholars agree about any one aspect of *Cat*, it is that the drama derives most of its dramatic intensity from its extraordinary characterizations, especially those of Big Daddy and Maggie. Although Brick maintains the focal position in the play, his passive attitude toward both people and life serves mainly as stark contrast to the ebullient, dynamic personalities of his father and his wife. Drama scholars, like audiences and theater critics, express enthusiastic admiration for the credibility and the vitality of these two characters.

Of all the reasons proffered to explain *Cat*'s power, one of the most important is the play's universality. As several scholars indicate, in this drama Williams does not confine his interest to a fading southern belle or a defeated idealistic male; he presents fascinating, dynamic figures—both male and female—as well as a portrait of an idealist clinging to his dreams of purity. The contrast and conflict between Big Daddy and Brick dramatizes what Durant Da Ponte ("Tennessee's Tennessee Williams," 1956) calls the mythic theme "of the alienated son and the dying father" (p. 13), and what Jackson considers a "modern myth" in which the playwright parallels the "Greek horror of crime against life" (p. 63).

The most penetrating interpretations of *Cat* do not fail to recognize some of Williams' characteristic weaknesses; but, at the same time, they do not fail to appreciate the play's powerful rendering of universal human conflicts. As Quirino maintains, despite its flaws, *Cat on a Hot Tin Roof* is among the playwright's "greatest achievements." (p. 119).

The Night of the Iguana was first produced at the third annual Festival of Two Worlds at Spoleto, Italy, in 1959. Williams revised the play steadily before it reached Broadway; in fact, he was busy rewriting while the play was being tried out in its pre-Broadway run. *Iguana* opened in New York in December 1961 and became the recipient of the Drama Critics' Award for the 1961–62 season.

The majority of the New York reviewers responded favorably to *Iguana*. Many happily acknowledged Williams' movement away from shocking materials and violence toward a more lyrical examination of human existence. Although their reviews were on the whole positive, some critics alleged that the play lacked sufficient dramatic action (Watts, *New York Post*), a clear point of view (Coleman, *New York Mirror*), and dramatic purpose for its minor characters (Kerr, *New York Herald Tribune*). Despite its shortcomings, *Iguana* was a critical and popular success. With this drama Williams had shown that his talents as a playwright were not limited to the sensational and violent expression of the themes that have always haunted him. *Iguana* treated these themes in a new, modulated tone which proved to be just as effective as the more characteristic Williams approach.

Generally, scholars view *Iguana* as Williams' finest drama since *Cat on a Hot Tin Roof*. Richard Gilman (*Common and Uncommon Modes*, 1971, pp. 141–42) and Allan Lewis (*American Plays and Playwrights of the Contemporary Theatre*, 1965, pp. 58–60) were among the few critics to claim that the inclusion of the German tourists is a superimposition of symbolic characterization which is never integrated into the play and which is too obvious an attempt to intensify the drama's theme. Their criticism is one with which the makers of the film adaptation apparently concurred, since the German family was omitted.

Roger Stein's assessment of *Iguana* typifies those which found similarities between this play and *Menagerie*. Both works, Stein observes, create a "muffled and elegiac" mood (p. 142). But Williams' concern with questions regarding man's lonely, painful existence and man's relationship with God link *Iguana*—despite its lack of violence —much closer to *Suddenly* than to *Menagerie*.

The main theme of *Iguana*, according to Dillard, is an affirmation of life through acceptance, despite the frightening passing of time and the concomitant process of decay. Williams underscores this theme through Nonno's struggle to complete his poem before he dies—a poem celebrating courage even in light of one's imminent mortality (p. 175). Ferdinand Leon's reading ("Time, Fantasy, and Reality in *Night of the Iguana*," 1968) of Nonno's poem supports Dillard but infers wider and more significant ramifications. The poem's main theme, and therefore the play's as well, in Leon's view, is that man must "imitate . . . nature's reconciliation of extremes." Leon indicates that the poem not only reflects Nonno's and Hannah's philosophic approach to life; it also reverberates Shannon's dichotomous struggle with reality. Eventually, the courage and compassion of Hannah enable Shannon to reestablish a desire to live (pp. 94–96).

Jackson makes an important observation related to the resolution of Shannon's conflicts: Williams' earlier plays concentrate on transgression; *Iguana* deals mainly with redemption. The dramatist of *Iguana* views man as a sinful being who can find valuation only through compassion or love (p. 87).

Although Shannon doubtlessly is Williams' protagonist in *Iguana*, critics agree that Hannah Jelkes is the most effective and important characterization in the play. Jackson concisely sums up Hannah's crucial role: she serves the drama's two main progressions, that of the dying Nonno toward completion of his poem and of the tortured Shannon toward redemption. In addition, Hannah stands out among the gallery of Williams' female portraits. As Jackson points out, she is not only highly moral; she also possesses self-respect (p. 153). D. J. Mraz ("The Changing Image of Female Characters in the Works of Tennessee Williams," 1967) makes the interesting observation that in Williams' later plays his heroines display greater intelligence and strength than their predecessors do. He thinks Hannah is Williams' finest female portrait since Blanche DuBois. In Hannah, Williams blends the romantic nature of Blanche with the pragmatic strength of Maggie the cat so that she not only well serves Williams' dramatic purposes, she also remains at all times believable (p. 119).

Iguana proved to be Williams' greatest popular and critical success since *Cat*, produced six years earlier. The new drama won a fourth New York Drama Critics' Award for its author and is highly regarded by the majority of drama scholars. Although some criticize the play for its lack of coherence, deficiency of dramatic action, and strained symbolic devices, the consensus maintains that *Iguana*'s merits far outweigh these weaknesses. Scholars accord much praise to Williams' credible and engrossing characters, especially Hannah Jelkes, whom some consider one of the playwright's most compelling female figures. *Iguana* is also highly esteemed for its poetic, yet natural dialogue, its sustained lyrical mood, and its affirmation of human dignity. In this work, critics agree, Williams again manifests his keen insight into human nature, his mastery of dialogue and his extraordinary theater sense. In this case, however, his talents utilize little trace of the violence and sensationalism that had characterized most of his earlier dramatic efforts.

While he underwent psychoanalysis during the summer and fall of 1957, Williams wrote a short play entitled *Suddenly Last Summer*. Realizing this drama would not be long enough for a standard theater evening's entertainment, he prefaced it with a shorter play, *Something Unspoken*, which he had written years earlier, and the two works were given the collective title, *Garden District*, referring to the section of New Orleans which serves as the setting for both plays.

Garden District opened off Broadway on January 7, 1958, and once again (like *Cat* in 1955), a Tennessee Williams drama became a season's most controversial play. *Suddenly*, which brought together both homosexuality and cannibalism, shocked critics and theatergoers alike. Nevertheless, five of the six New York drama reviewers wrote affirmative appraisals of the play. They lauded Williams' craftsmanship, especially as manifested in his dialogue, his theatrical sense and his imagery—all of which serve to build the drama's tension, which they felt was very gripping. Although the critics' concentration on the shocking elements of *Suddenly* did not prevent them from appreciating the play's theatrical effectiveness, it, unfortunately, did prevent them from realizing the drama's complexity, its depth, and its significance.

Drama scholars, with few exceptions, unfortunately show little more understanding of *Suddenly* than theater reviewers did. For the most part they too concern themselves mainly with the shocking elements of Williams' play and fail to see them as integral to a coherent, aesthetically satisfying work of art. Whether they praised or disparaged *Suddenly*, their criticism generally indicated a failure to understand the symbolic nature and the multilayered dimensions.

Except for four perceptive students of *Suddenly*, theater scholars fall into three categories: those who do not even attempt to analyze the work, those whose attempt to understand the play never delves beneath the surface level of its meaning, and those who flagrantly misinterpret the work. Francis Donahue (*The Dramatic World of Tennessee Williams*, 1964) is one who offers no analysis of *Suddenly Last Summer* whatsoever, but who remarks that Williams' one-act play is "a tightly written drama, with a strange, almost repulsive fascination about it" (p. 105). R. H. Gardner (*The Splintered Stage*, 1965), like Donahue, does not interpret *Suddenly* at all. Instead, he labels Williams a masterful "dealer in horror" and regrets "that the morbid outlook and fascination for the gutter prevent his putting his fertile imagination, poetic vision and superb sense of the theater to better use" (p. 121).

Tischler and Gassner fall into the second category. They appreciate *Suddenly* but offer only vague, incomplete interpretations of the drama. Tischler calls *Suddenly* a morality play in which the playwright "points up the degradation and horror of using other people in violation of their human dignity" (p. 262). Although this point is undeniably emphasized in *Suddenly*, it hardly represents the total thematic concerns. Tischler considers the drama inferior to Williams' other successes because of deficiencies in characterization and dialogue, sources of Williams' greater power. Yet, she claims that in no other play has the dramatist "created so much by words alone" (p. 256).

Gassner (*Theatre at the Crossroads*, 1960) describes *Suddenly* as "a work of perversely overwhelming power," despite Williams' "morbid pessimism" and nihilism. As he had noted in discussing earlier Williams works, Gassner points to the playwright's "objectivity of characterization" as the key to his creative achievement. Gassner then makes an obvious point, but one that some critics apparently do not see: "taking note of evil is not the same thing as accepting it at the expense of judgment" (pp. 227–28).

Unfortunately, Gassner's openmindedness is not coupled with a deep understanding of the play. Although he admires *Suddenly* for dialogue that has "intensity of feeling and vividness of imagery" and feels that Williams has seldom achieved this level of excellence, he regrets that Williams' "genius" is not brought once again to the writing of as simple and lovely a play as *Menagerie*. Gassner indicates that Williams displays greater maturity of craftsmanship in *Suddenly* than he did in *Menagerie* (p. 228), but he fails to see the greater scope and depth of meaning in the later work.

Among the third group of scholars is Falk, who, like many other critics of *Suddenly*, apparently allows her affronted sensibilities to interfere with an objective critical evaluation of the play. She dismisses *Suddenly* as representing "another private and very sick view of the world." She adds that the piling on of horror upon horror indicates how far Williams will go for shock effects, which tend to weaken the play's intended meaning. Falk's failure to understand Williams' intentions—and the significance of these intentions—is evidenced in her statement that "Williams has carried his private symbolism to incredible extremes when he would make a decadent artist and aging homosexual, a sybarite who never took a stand for either right or wrong . . . a symbol to represent all men of our times" (pp. 154–55). Falk attempts to substantiate her opinion with Catharine's line, "I know it's a hideous story but it's a true story of our time and the world we live in and what did truly happen to Cousin Sebastian in Cabeza de Lobo" (III, 382). However, nowhere in this speech or elsewhere in the play does Williams indicate that Sebastian's decadence and perversity represent "all men of our times."

Though *Suddenly* portrays Sebastian as a decadent, inhumane pervert, three scholars view him as a modern-day martyr. Tynan claims that Williams sees all aesthetes, including Sebastian, as being "sacred" and that audiences find it difficult "to see in his death (as Mr. Williams clearly wants us to) a modern re-enactment of the martyrdoms of St. Sebastian" (p. 279). Similarly, J. G. Weightman

("Varieties of Decomposition," 1958) sees the characterization of Sebastian as an unsuccessful abstraction of the martyred poet (pp. 461–63). Von Dornum mistakenly sees Sebastian as a symbol of the innocent artist, whose purity "must inevitably be destroyed in a hideous world dedicated to the persecution of beauty." Although Von Dornum admits that Williams presents Sebastian not only as a "dedicated artist who strives to give meaning to existence" but also as "a super esthete, a pampered dandy, a pervert who uses his mother and his cousin to procure for him," he claims that the playwright wished audiences to concentrate on Sebastian the dedicated artist and forget the corrupt dandy. In a weak attempt to support this untenable statement, Von Dornum states vaguely that "this play as well as earlier ones suggests that esthetes, regardless of their behavior, are sacred." Von Dornum is forced to admit that *Suddenly* presents Sebastian's corruption much more forcefully than his innocence and that unfortunately this fact diminishes "the significance of Sebastian's exemplary role as purity martyred in an evil world" (p. 144).

William E. Taylor ("Tennessee Williams: Academia on Broadway," 1963) has the strangest interpretation of all. He claims that Sebastian is the hero of *Suddenly*: "He is the poet, in whom the way of the world is transformed, misunderstood, and destroyed." Taylor goes so far as to add that "Even Mrs. Venable is in a sense justified; bizarre as she is, she is nevertheless on the side of the saints in a world of merely wolfish mediocrity" (p. 96).

Of all the studies of *Suddenly*, only four probe beneath the surface layer of sexual symbolism to understand and appreciate Williams' artistic intentions and achievement. Nelson begins his analysis of the play by rebuking those critics who discount its worth because the material seems repugnant to them. He thereby emphasizes an important point: that the basis for any sound criticism should not be an affront to a critic's sensibilities but whether or not the author's point of view, however disquieting, remains consistent throughout the work. Although one may not accept Williams' outlook in *Suddenly*, Nelson says, the undeniable fact remains that the play "adheres faithfully and almost flawlessly" to Williams' point of view and is "Williams' artistic triumph." Because Williams' play is "so brilliantly wrought," even viewers who were offended by its content, were haunted by its impact: "Every word and every symbol are controlled and executed by the playwright to shape his image. His universe is presented on three organic levels and almost every interaction in it manifests the destructive, devouring element." Every aspect of the play, Nelson adds, builds toward its climax, which is the "ritualistic, sacrificial act." Finally, Nelson claims that, throughout this building process, the play maintains a consistent point of view "with an almost infernal beauty and directness" (p. 259).

Nelson sees *Suddenly* as a tale that is mainly about "cannibalism— the cannibalism that the author envisions as inherent in human relationships. The destruction of Sebastian symbolizes the destructive quality in the relationships of all the other characters which in turn symbolizes the voraciousness in mankind." Nelson explains that from Williams' point of view man manifests this voracity even through love and hate (p. 253). As Catharine expresses this outlook in the play, "We all use each other and that's what we think of as love, and not being able to use each other is what's—hate . . ." (III, 396).

This is the point at which Gassner and Tischler end their analyses of *Suddenly*. Nelson, on the other hand, carries his interpretation further—to the crucial aspects of Williams' dramatic genius. Nelson sees in this play, as well as in all of the dramatist's work, an attempt "to transcend a universe which is inimical to man, a universe which embodies the original sin of fragmentation and forces man into transgression through his spiritual if not physical mutilation." Most often man's sinning is sexual, and the retribution for it is usually harsher than the transgression. Nelson points out that Williams explains in his story, "Desire and the Black Masseur," that man is an incomplete being in an incomplete universe. He is subject to "corruption from birth, and the punishment for the acts which evolve out of this corruption. Williams' characters are fighting a losing battle against the universe in a vain attempt to transcend it." In this vain attempt, the playwright acknowledges "their courage, beauty, and gallantry, but never the possibility of triumph" (pp. 248–49). Nelson sees a remarkable achievement in *Suddenly*, one that few other scholars recognize: in this work Williams does not try either to transcend or remove himself from the universe, but "faces it unflinchingly by fashioning the destructive element itself into the central protagonist" (p. 249).

James R. Hurt's fine article ("*Suddenly Last Summer*: Williams and Melville," 1961) appeared in the same year as Nelson's book. Hurt's interpretation of Williams' drama begins with the playwright's allusion to Melville in the first scene and goes on to investigate its ramifications through the rest of the play. Hurt feels that in *Suddenly* Williams primarily concerns himself with "the very Melvillian problem of the nature of the universe, in this case, the universe of sex" (p. 396). He demonstrates, with constant substantiation from the play, that Sebastian, like Melville's Ahab, believes that he has seen the face of God and "fails to see that this 'God' (the cruelty of the universe) is uncaring. Both protagonists attribute 'inscrutable malignity' to this God, and both, because of his error, are themselves destroyed by this malignity" (p. 399).

Hurt explains that Williams' symbolic use of whiteness enables him to dramatize man's attribution of both "beneficence and malevolence" to an ambivalent color, "which is, in fact, completely neutral." He ends his article by summarizing thematically Williams' "true story of our time and the world we live in. . . ." The story is of two men, Sebastian and Dr. Cukrowicz, the former who saw in "the neutral whiteness of nature" only evil and the latter who hopes to regain for Catharine "the peaceful blueness of a summer sky." *Suddenly* dramatizes the conflict in Catharine between these opposite views of the universe. The truth about Sebastian's "final walk into that terrible whiteness brings purgation, resolution and sanity" (p. 400).

In "*Suddenly Last Summer* as a Morality Play," 1966, Paul Hurley asserts that *Suddenly* has been misinterpreted not only by those who find it repugnant but even by those who uphold an artist's right to choose any material he deems suitable to his purpose. One common reason for critics' misreading the drama is their viewing Sebastian as the hero rather than the villain. The result of this error, Hurley correctly comments, is their misunderstanding *Suddenly*'s meaning and their accusing its playwright of views that his play does not substantiate.

Hurley's reading of *Suddenly* is very close to Hurt's. He sees Williams as showing "that recognition of evil, if carried to the point of a consuming obsession, may be the worst form of evil. To look about oneself for manifestations of sinfulness and to become so overwhelmed by the viciousness of humanity that one begins to see cruelty and vulgarity as the only truths about human nature is, for Williams, . . . a fearful sin. A daemonic vision of human nature may irredeemably corrupt the one who possesses that vision." Hurley points out that critics have mistakenly dwelt on the literal incidents in the play and have not discerned their symbolic purpose. In order to understand Williams' rendering of his theme, one must realize that he employs homosexuality and cannibalism as metaphors: they dramatize his conviction "that man may be destroyed by ignoring, rather than succumbing to, the need for participation in society. Turning in upon oneself and away from the concerns of one's fellow man represents a sort of self-cannibalism; man may be consumed by his own inversion" (p. 393).

Sebastian's image of God, Hurley explains, reflected his own view of man and nature, which was dominated by cruelty and ugliness. In the light of this truth, Sebastian felt that man could do nothing but resign himself to life's horrors; the will of God cannot be changed by man. Hurley shows that Sebastian's vision of the universe is the distorted concept "of a personality which has turned in upon himself. Sebastian's isolation from society is symbolized by his homosexuality; his inversion is literal *and* metaphorical" (p. 396).

A crucial point Hurley makes is that Sebastian's concentration on himself and rejection of all except those who are useful to him leads to his inversion which "with its suggestions of refusal to accept the responsibilities of a mature sexual relationship becomes a symbol of a refusal to face moral responsibilities." Hurley remarks that this situation is similar to Williams' treatment of sexuality in *Cat*. Williams concerns himself mainly with "the problem of individual moral responsibility, not sexual orientation." *Cat*'s central concern lies not in whether Brick possesses homosexual inclinations but in the fact that social pressures force Brick to show himself to be morally weak when his best friend needs strength from him (p. 394).

Hurley then discusses another level of *Suddenly*'s multilayered meaning: Williams' concern with Sebastian as an artist. One of Sebastian's obvious failings is his inability to love, a weakness which

Williams feels would prevent him from fulfilling his function as an artist. To substantiate this claim, Hurley cites an interview in which Williams describes his conception of the artist's relationship to his audience. "I think of writing as something more organic than words, something closer to being and action. I want to work more and more with a more plastic theatre than the one I have before. I have never for one moment doubted that there are people—millions!—to say things to. We come to each other, gradually, but with love. It is the short reach of my arms that hinders, not the length and multiplicity of theirs. With love and with honesty, the embrace is inevitable" (III, 5). Sebastian's homosexuality, Hurley explains, symbolically suggests this artist's removal from his fellow man's concerns. "Sebastian's greatest failure as an artist and as a human being was not that he failed to reach his audience but that he refused, absolutely" the embrace that Williams felt was necessary between the artist and his fellow men (p. 399).

Critics agree that the narration of Sebastian's death marks the climactic point. Hurley explains that Sebastian's perverse attitude toward life brought about his own death. Williams indicates this fact on the literal level by having Sebastian attacked by the young boys whose sexual favors he had purchased; in addition, he associates the horrible death of Sebastian at the hands of this swarm of bird-like creatures with the devouring of the Galapagos sea turtles by carnivorous birds—a sight which represented in Sebastian's distorted view a vision of God. Hurley shows that Sebastian's undoing was caused not by a cruel God but by Sebastian's "selfish concern for himself and his own sense of corruption" (p. 401).

Quirino, who offers the most comprehensive analysis of *Suddenly*, feels that it is Williams' "most richly textured, most misunderstood and most maligned" play. He proceeds, step by step, to explain how every part of the drama, from the first visual and sound effects to the last words, cohere tightly to the playwright's tight design. Quirino demonstrates that "In *Suddenly Last Summer* Williams has cut the fabric of his vision from the timeless cloth of myth and, through the use of metaphor and symbol, has fashioned it to clothe what a character in the play whom he has given little reason to disbelieve calls 'a true story of our time and the world we live in.'" Quirino shows, with substantiation from Frazer's *The Golden Bough*, the striking similarities between the Sebastian-Violet relationship and its mythical prototype, the Attis-Cybele relationship. Furthermore, without losing sight of Williams' text for the sake of proving a point, Quirino presents the psychological (Freudian, Jungian) and the religious (Christian, pagan) dimensions of Williams' drama. Quirino's interpretation indicates that of all Williams' plays, *Suddenly* remains the most carefully crafted and the most aesthetically satisfying—despite its shocking content (p. 125).

Almost every critic of the play mentioned the effectiveness of *Suddenly*'s set design and quoted from Williams' descriptions which describe Sebastian's garden-jungle: "The set may be as unrealistic as the decor of a dramatic ballet. It represents part of a mansion of Victorian Gothic style in the Garden District of New Orleans on a late afternoon, between late summer and early fall. The interior is blended with a fantastic garden which is more like a tropical jungle, or forest, in the prehistoric age of giant fern-forests when living creatures had flippers turning to limbs and scales to skin. The colors of this jungle-garden are violent, especially since it is steaming with heat after rain. There are massive tree-flowers that suggest organs of a body, torn out, still glistening with undried blood; there are harsh cries and sibilant hissings and thrashing sounds in the garden as if it were inhabited by beasts, serpents and birds, all of savage nature . . ." (III, 349). But few take the playwright at his word, once they get past the setting to the content. As Quirino comments, with the opening description of the setting, "Williams suggests that the mode of the play is to be abstract and ceremonial rather than naturalistic and the action that will unfold abstractly expressionistic rather than merely literal" (p. 130).

Quirino's statement that Williams "fuses the human and vegetable realms as part of one cosmically destructive scheme" is supported by Nelson's recognition that Williams' characters "all have names symbolic of organic life as if they too were intimately related to the jungle which lurks around them—Mrs. Venable's name is Violet; her attendant is named Miss Foxhill; Catharine, George and their mother are the Hollys, and R. Cukrowicz explains that his name in Polish means sugar."

Although many critics of the play complained that little action takes place on stage, Quirino perceives a cannibalism in the behavior of every character onstage except Catharine Holly and Dr. Cuk-rowicz. The greedy characters onstage indulge in "horrors of rapac-ity," though they live in a civilized society. Catharine's story of Sebastian represents the universality of such rapacity in its "primi-tive, mythic, archetypal form" (p. 155).

Quirino, Hurley, Hurt, and Nelson were the first to appreciate fully the universality and artistic worth of *Suddenly*. Now that the shock value of the play has diminished with the passing of time, other scholars may restudy the work and objectively reassess this neglected masterpiece. One hopeful sign is that Leonard Lief and James F. Light chose to include Williams' play in their literature anthology (*The Modern Age*, 1969), which they designed for fresh-man English and introductory literature courses. Certainly this fact indicates that *Suddenly Last Summer* has begun to be recognized as a work of art rather than merely as a theatrically shocking, if effective, play.

Critics agree that Tennessee Williams is one of the few outstand-ing playwrights in modern American theater history. Like his prede-cessor and compeer, Eugene O'Neill, who all but dominated the realm of American playwriting during the first thirty years of this century, Williams, along with Arthur Miller, has all but dominated the theater since World War II.

Williams has been an extremely prolific playwright. Bulk of out-put alone does not assure a dramatist a major position in theater history. Williams, however, has not only written a great number of plays; he has also enjoyed an extraordinary record of successful pro-ductions. Of the plays produced in New York, only his most recent were not successful. *Summer and Smoke, Camino Real*, and *Orpheus Descending* had also had less than successful runs when they opened on Broadway, but all three were later revived off Broadway where they were better received by critics and the public alike. Of the re-maining ten plays, four won New York Drama Critics' Awards: *The Glass Menagerie, A Streetcar Named Desire, Cat on a Hot Tin Roof*, and *The Night of the Iguana*; and two also won Pulitzer Prizes: *Streetcar* and *Cat*.

Critics note that Williams has been America's most popular mod-ern dramatist. One reason for this enormous popularity has been the adaptation of many of his plays into motion pictures. Williams' concern with visual and auditory images has made his plays very suitable to cinematic adaptation. Twelve of his full-length plays have already been made into film: *The Glass Menagerie, A Streetcar Named Desire, The Rose Tattoo, Suddenly Last Summer, Summer and Smoke, Sweet Bird of Youth, Period of Adjustment, The Night of the Iguana, The Milk Train Doesn't Stop Here Anymore* and *The Seven Descents of Myrtle (Kingdom of Earth).*

Another reason for Williams' popularity is his plays' direct appeal to basic human emotions. This appeal results from both Williams' concentrated treatment of man's purely emotional response to his environment and the original, often symbolistic, means he employs to dramatize this concern. In communicating his conception of modern man's existential problems, Williams has utilized a wide range of theatrical and literary techniques which convey underlying human feelings that traditional, realistic drama could not present.

The majority of scholars agree that Williams' most significant contribution to the American theater has been this utilization of various theatrical techniques to universalize what on the surface seemed to be uniquely individual situations. By combining impressionistic and expressionistic staging devices with the naturalist's keen observations and the realist's objectivity in handling his materials, Williams has created a new poetic drama in the United States. From the opening of *The Glass Menagerie* in 1945 until the present, Williams has demonstrated his commitment to dramatic experimentation. His innovative "plastic theatre" has involved a more flexible and complete theatrical communication than is conveyed by dialogue alone. Williams has employed visual and auditory effects to previously unattempted extents by emphasizing color, music and scenic devices to increase the flexibility of the theater presentation of ideas and images, especially those representing human feelings.

The versatility of Williams' dramatic talents has been surpassed in America only by Eugene O'Neill. On merely the basis of having written his two greatest critical and popular successes, *The Glass Menagerie* and *A Streetcar Named Desire*, Williams must be considered an outstanding American playwright. Both plays have already established themselves as classics of the American theater. Remarkably, these two dramas, though produced only two years apart, show the wide range of Williams' extraordinary sense of the theater. At almost the same time in his career when he wrote *Menagerie*, a fragile mood piece loosely held together by various impressionistic and poetic techniques, Williams also created *Streetcar*, a tightly-knit naturalistic drama of brutal power and intensity. Whereas *Menagerie* is a series of almost actionless vignettes introduced, linked together, and commented upon by a narrator, *Streetcar* relies almost completely upon a naturalistic unfolding of plot line which develops more directly and more dynamically. But, despite their differences in form, the two plays have important similarities—which are characteristic of Williams' greatest gifts as a dramatist. In both works, Williams' characterization excels. He renders fascinating individuals who at the same time have abstract, representational values. Amanda Wingfield and Blanche DuBois are among the roles in American theater annals that entice, challenge, and satisfy our greatest actresses. Furthermore, although Williams does not directly comment on social problems in these dramas of personal struggles, the plays nonetheless reverberate with the economic, political, and social problems from which the personal conflicts emerge. The enduring appeal of *Menagerie* and *Streetcar* is largely derived from Williams' ability to base Amanda's and Blanche's conflicts in environments that are at the same time both specific and general.

Critics point out that when Williams was not in sufficient control of his craft, his attempts to broaden his plays' meanings resulted in stereotyped characterizations (*Camino Real, Sweet Bird of Youth, Orpheus Descending, The Rose Tattoo, The Seven Descents of Myrtle*), heavy-handed symbolism (*Summer and Smoke, Camino Real, Orpheus Descending, The Milk Train Doesn't Stop Here Anymore, Slapstick Tragedy, In the Bar of a Tokyo Hotel, Out Cry*), obtrusive moralizing (*Orpheus Descending, Camino Real, Sweet Bird of Youth, In the Bar of a Tokyo Hotel, Small Craft Warnings*), and unsuccessful experimentation (*Slapstick Tragedy, Small Craft Warnings, Out Cry*). But in his best plays, *Cat on a Hot Tin Roof, Suddenly Last Summer* and *The Night of the Iguana*, as well as *Menagerie* and *Streetcar*, his unique sense of the theater's enormous flexibility is usually combined with the necessary artistic control.

Another of Williams' dramatic gifts that critics praise is his command of dialogue. While functioning organically to further plot line, Williams' poetic dialogue fulfills esthetic purposes as well. In his finest dramas (*Menagerie, Streetcar, Cat, Suddenly,* and *Iguana*), the playwright's dialogue simultaneously serves the functions of plot progression, revelation of character, and thematic and symbolic patterns. Although they are functional, the lines of Williams' dialogue sound natural and appropriate to the characters who deliver them— a fact which testifies to the playwright's careful attention to nuances of speech.

Williams' attempts by means of symbolic and nonrealistic dramatic techniques to shock people into recognition and understanding has often been mistakenly criticized by those critics who view his plays as traditional realistic dramas. However, the passing of time has already abated the shock value of Williams' sexual and violent symbolism so that during the past fifteen years several critics and scholars have begun to reassess with greater objectivity and insight such once shocking works as *Cat on a Hot Tin Roof* and *Suddenly Last Summer.*

Williams made another contribution to the American theater by dealing with subjects that had before his time been carefully avoided. Through his handling of sexuality and violence, Williams served as a harbinger for the new generation of playwrights who followed him— writers like William Inge, Edward Albee, Jack Richardson, and LeRoi Jones. The general favorable critical and popular reception of their bold treatment of sex and their hard-hitting dialogue is doubtlessly to some degree the result of Williams' having broken ground for them in these areas.

Critics agree that Williams' creation of a new poetic drama in the United States is the foundation upon which his permanent literary reputation is most likely to rest. Nevertheless, since Williams is still writing plays and since critics continue to revaluate his dramatic works, his position in American theater history will doubtlessly be modified with time. At present, the increasing respect accorded to *Cat on a Hot Tin Roof, The Night of the Iguana,* and *Suddenly Last Summer* during the past fifteen years, along with the fact that *The Glass Menagerie* and *A Streetcar Named Desire* have not diminished in stature during the twenty-five years since they were first produced, indicates that Williams, his failures notwithstanding, has already established himself not only as a crucial figure in the history of the American theater but also as a playwright of the first rank.

Selected Bibliography

The primary sources, in Part I, are those from which quotations are taken for this volume. Other bibliographical data appear in the acknowledgments. Students of Williams know that bibliographical information is very complex because of revisions, title changes and unpublished manuscripts. For example, *Kingdom of Earth* is listed separately in Part I because it is sometimes quoted in the text, while a revision appearing in *The Theatre of Tennessee Williams* is also quoted.

The following list of both primary and secondary materials is intended only for the convenience of the reader in locating citations and the publisher in providing necessary information. Items identified in the text or the notes may not appear in the list of secondary materials.

Books on Williams contain bibliographical information. Many of Williams' own essays on his work are reprinted in *The Theatre*. Interviews cited in the text are listed in the bibliography under the name of the interviewer. Sundry volumes of *New York Theatre Critics' Reviews* reprint essays on various plays. *Vogue*, March 15, 1951 contains an essay by Williams on *The Rose Tattoo*.

Readers may be interested to learn of an item that has been very helpful in the preparation of this volume: Delma E. Presley, "Tennessee Williams: 25 Years of Criticism," *Bulletin of Bibliography and Magazine Notes* 30: 1 (January–March 1973), 21–29.

PART I

Works of Tennessee Williams

American Blues: Five Short Plays. New York: Dramatists Play Service, 1948. (Includes *Moony's Kid Don't Cry, The Long Stay Cut Short, or, The Unsatisfactory Supper, The Case of the Crushed Petunias, Ten Blocks on the Camino Real, The Dark Room.*)
Baby Doll. New York: New Directions, 1956.
Dragon Country. New York: New Directions paperbook, 1970.
Eight Mortal Ladies Possessed. New York: New Directions paperbook, 1974.
Five Young American Poets. Norfolk, Conn.: New Directions, 1944.
Hard Candy: A Book of Stories. New York: New Directions paperbook, 1967.
I Rise in Flame, Cried the Phoenix. Norfolk, Conn.: [New Directions], 1951.
In the Winter of Cities. New York: New Directions paperbook, 1964.

Kingdom of Earth. New York: New Directions, 1967.
Knightly Quest ,The: A Novella and Four Short Stories. New York: New Directions, 1966.
Memoirs. New York. Doubleday and Co., 1975.
Milk Train Doesn't Stop Here Anymore, The. Norfolk, Conn.: New Directions, 1964.
Moise and the World of Reason. New York: Simon and Schuster, 1975.
One Arm and Other Stories. New York: New Directions paperbook, 1967.
Out Cry. New York: New Directions paperbook, 1973.
Roman Spring of Mrs. Stone, The. New York: New Directions paperbook, 1950.
Small Craft Warnings. New York: New Directions paperbook, 1972.
Theatre of Tennessee Williams, The. Five volumes. New York: New Directions, 1971–1976.
27 Wagons Full of Cotton and other One-Act Plays. New York: New Directions paperbook, 1966.
Two-Character Play, The. New York: New Directions, 1969.
You Touched Me! (with Donald Windham). New York: Samuel French, 1947.

PART II

SECONDARY MATERIAL

Adler, Jacob H. "*Night of the Iguana,* a new Tennessee Williams?" *Ramparts* 1 (November 1962), 59–68.
Adler, Thomas P. "The Search for God in the Plays of Tennessee Williams." *Renascence* 26 (Autumn 1973), 48–56.
Atkinson, Brooks. "Theatre: Rural Orpheus." *The New York Times,* March 22, 1957; reprinted in *New York Theatre Critics' Reviews* 18 (1957), 310.
Auden, W. H. "The Christian Tragic Hero." *The New York Times Book Review* (December 16, 1945). Reprinted in Corrigan, Robert W. Ed. *Tragedy: Vision and Form.* San Francisco: Chandler Publishing Company, 1965.
Auerbach, Erich. *Mimesis (The Representation of Reality in Western Literature).* Trans. Willard Trask. Garden City: Doubleday, Anchor Books, 1957.
Barnett, Lincoln. "Tennessee Williams." *Life* 24 (February 16, 1948), 113–14.
Barrett, William. *Irrational Man: A Study in Existential Philosophy.* New York: Doubleday, Anchor Books, 1958.
Bachelard, Gaston. *The Poetics of Space.* Trans. from the French by Maria Jolas. Boston: Beacon Press, 1969.
Bauland, Peter. *The Hooded Eagle: Modern German Drama on the New York Stage.* Syracuse: Syracuse University Press, 1968.
Beckerman, Bernard. *Dynamics of Drama.* New York: Alfred A. Knopf, 1970.
Beckett, Samuel. *Waiting for Godot.* New York: Grove Press, 1954.
Beer, Otto F. "Sein Faust? Tennessee Williams versucht in Wien ein Comeback." *Süddeutsche Zeitung,* January 7, 1976 (review of *The Red Devil Battery Sign*).

Bentley, Eric. *The Dramatic Event.* Boston: Beacon Press, 1956.
————. *In Search of Theatre.* New York: Alfred A. Knopf, 1953.
————. *The Life of the Drama.* New York: Atheneum Publishers, 1964.
————. *What Is Theatre?* Boston: Beacon Press, 1956.
Berkman, Leonard. "The Tragic Downfall of Blanche DuBois." *Modern Drama* 10: 3 (December 1967), 249–257.
Berkowitz, Gerald. "The 'Other World' of *The Glass Menagerie.*" *Players* 48: 4 (1973), 150–153.
Berne, Eric. *Games People Play.* New York: Grove Press, 1964.
Brooks, Charles. "The Comic Tennessee Williams." *The Quarterly Journal of Speech* 44: 3 (October 1958), 275–284.
Broussard, Louis. *American Drama: Contemporary Allegory from Eugene O'Neill to Tennessee Williams.* Norman: University of Oklahoma Press, 1962.
Brustein, Robert. "America's New Cultural Hero." *Commentary* 25 (February 1958), 123–128.
————. *The Theatre of Revolt (An Approach to the Modern Drama).* Boston: Little, Brown & Co., Atlantic Monthly Press Book, 1964.
Callaghan, Barry. "Tennessee Williams and the Cocaloony Birds." *Tamarack Review* (Toronto) 39 (1966), 52–58.
Campbell, Joseph. *The Hero with a Thousand Faces.* New York: Meridian Books, 1956.
Cargill, Oscar, et al. *O'Neill and His Plays: Four Decades of Criticism.* New York: New York University Press, 1961.
Cash, W. J. *The Mind of the South.* New York: Random House, Vintage, 1941.
Clurman, Harold. *The Divine Pastime.* New York: Macmillan, 1974.
————. *Lies Like Truth.* New York: Macmillan, 1958.
Cohn, Ruby. *Dialogue in American Drama.* Bloomington: Indiana University Press, 1971.
Da Ponte, Durant. "Tennessee's Tennessee Williams." *Tennessee Studies in Literature* 1 (1956), 12–13.
Davis, Joseph K. "The South of History and Metahistory: The Mind of W. J. Cash." *The Poetry of Community: Essays on the Southern Sensibility of History and Literature.* Ed. Lewis P. Simpson (Atlanta: Georgia State University Press, 1972), pp. 11–24.
Dillard, R. L. "The Tennessee Williams Hero: An Analytic Survey." Ph. D. Dissertation, University of Missouri, 1965.
Donahue, Francis. *The Dramatic World of Tennessee Williams.* New York: Unger Publishing Co., 1964.
Edinger, Edward F. *Ego and Archetype: Individuation and the Religious Function of the Psyche.* Baltimore: Penguin Books, 1973.
Eliade, Mircea. *Myth and Reality.* Trans. Willard R. Trask. New York: Harper and Row, 1963.
Eliot, T. S. "Hamlet." *Selected Essays.* Harcourt, Brace and Co., 1950.
Esslin, Martin. *The Theatre of the Absurd.* Revised edition. New York: Doubleday, Anchor Books, 1969.
Falk, Signi. *Tennessee Williams.* New Haven: College and University Press, 1961.

Fedder, Norman J. *The Influence of D. H. Lawrence on Tennessee Williams.* The Hague: Mouton and Company, 1966.

Frazer, Sir James G. *The New Golden Bough.* Ed. Theodor H. Gaster. New York: Criterion Books, 1959.

Fritscher, John J. "Some Attitudes and a Posture: Religious Metaphor and Ritual in Tennessee Williams' Query of the American God." *Modern Drama* 13 (September 1970), 201–215.

Frye, Northrop. *Anatomy of Criticism: Four Essays.* Princeton: Princeton University Press, 1971.

———. *Fables of Identity: Studies in Poetic Mythology.* New York: Harcourt, Brace, and World, 1963.

Funke, Lewis and Booth, John E. "Williams on Williams." *Theatre Arts* 46 (January 1962), 17–19, 72–73.

Gaines, Jim. "A Talk about Life and Style with Tennessee Williams." *Saturday Review,* April 29, 1972, pp. 25–29.

Ganz, Arthur. "The Desperate Morality of the Plays of Tennessee Williams." *American Scholar* 31 (Spring 1962), 278–294.

Gardner, R. H. *The Splintered Stage: The Decline of the American Theatre.* New York: Macmillan, 1965.

Gassner, John. "Broadway in Review." *Educational Theatre Journal* 11 (May 1959), 122–124.

———. *Directions in Modern Theatre and Drama.* New York: Holt, Rinehart and Winston, 1965.

———. *Dramatic Soundings.* New York: Crown Publishers, 1968.

———. *Form and Idea in Modern Theatre.* New York: Dryden Press, 1956.

———. *Theatre at the Crossroads.* New York: Holt, Rinehart and Winston, 1960.

———. *The Theatre in Our Times.* New York: Crown Publishers, 1954.

———. *Treasury of the Theatre.* New York: Simon and Schuster, 1950.

Gassner, John and Quinn, Edward. *The Reader's Encyclopedia of World Drama.* New York: Thomas Y. Crowell, 1969.

Gilman, Richard. *Common and Uncommon Modes: Workings on the Theatre—1961–1970.* New York: Random House, 1971.

Golden, Joseph. *The Death of Tinkerbell.* Syracuse: Syracuse University Press, 1967.

Gottfried, Martin. *A Theatre Divided.* Boston: Little, Brown and Co., 1967.

Guthke, Karl S. *Modern Tragicomedy.* New York: Random House, 1966.

Hays, Peter L. "Tennessee Williams' Use of Myth in *Sweet Bird of Youth*." *Educational Theatre Journal* 18 (1966), 255–258.

Heilman, Robert. "Tennessee Williams: Approach to Tragedy." *Southern Review* (n. s.) 1 (Autumn 1965), 770–790.

———. *Tragedy and Melodrama: Versions of Experience.* Seattle: University of Washington Press, 1968.

Henderson, Joseph L. "Ancient Myths and Modern Man." *Man and His Symbols.* Ed. Carl G. Jung. Garden City: Doubleday and Co., 1964.

Hewes, Henry. "The Boundaries of Tennessee." *Saturday Review,* December 29, 1956, pp. 23–24.

———. "Broadway Postscript: Tennessee Williams—Last of our Solid Gold Bohemians." *Saturday Review,* March 28, 1955, pp. 25–27.

Hilfer, Anthony C. and Ramsey, R. Vance. *"Baby Doll*: A Study in Comedy and Critical Awareness." *Ohio University Review* 20 (1969), 75–88.

Huizinga, Johan. *Homo Ludens: A Study of the Play Element in Culture.* Boston: Beacon Press, 1955.

Hurley, Paul J. *"Suddenly Last Summer* as a Morality Play." *Modern Drama* 8 (February 1966), 392–402.

Hurrell, John D., ed. *Two Modern American Tragedies; Reviews and Criticism of "Death of a Salesman" and "A Streetcar Named Desire."* New York: Charles Scribner's Sons, 1961.

Hurt, James R. *"Suddenly Last Summer*: Williams and Melville." *Modern Drama* 3 (1961), 396–400.

Jackson, Esther Merle. *The Broken World of Tennessee Williams.* Madison: University of Wisconsin Press, 1965.

Jaspers, Karl. *The Origin and Goal of History.* Trans. Michael Bullock. New Haven: Yale University Press, 1953.

Jennings, Robert. "Tennessee Williams: A Candid Conversation with the Brilliant, Anguished Playwright." *Playboy,* April 1973, pp. 69–84.

Jones, Robert Emmet. "Tennessee Williams' Early Heroines." *Modern Drama* 2 (1959), 211–219.

Jung, Carl Gustav. *The Basic Writings of Carl Gustav Jung.* Trans. and ed. Violet Staub De Laszlo. New York: Random House, 1959.

————. "Approaching the Unconscious." *Man and His Symbols.* Ed. Carl G. Jung. New York: Dell Publishing Co., 1973.

————. "The Concept of the Collective Unconscious." *The Portable Jung.* Ed. Joseph Campbell. New York: The Viking Press, 1971.

————. *Symbols of Transformation: An Analysis of the Prelude to a Case of Schizophrenia.* Trans. R. F. C. Hull. New York: Pantheon Books, 1956.

Kazan, Elia. "Notebook for *A Streetcar Named Desire." Directors on Directing.* Ed. Toby Cole and Helen Krich Chinoy. New York: Bobbs-Merrill Co., 1963.

Kerr, Walter. *God on the Gymnasium Floor and Other Theatrical Adventures.* New York: Simon and Schuster, 1969.

————. *How Not to Write a Play.* New York: Simon and Schuster, 1955.

King, Thomas L. "Irony and Distance in *The Glass Menagerie." Educational Theatre Journal* 25 (May 1973), 207–214.

Krutch, Joseph Wood. *"Modernism" in Modern Drama.* Ithaca: Cornell University Press, 1953.

Langer, Susanne. *Feeling and Form.* New York: Charles Scribner's Sons, 1953.

Laufe, Abe. *Anatomy of a Hit.* New York: Hawthorn Books, 1966.

Leon, Ferdinand. "Time, Fantasy, and Reality in *The Night of the Iguana." Modern Drama* 11 (1968), 87–96.

Lewis, Allan. *American Plays and Playwrights of the Contemporary Theatre.* New York: Crown Publishers, 1965.

Lewis, R. C. "Man Named Tennessee." *Newsweek,* April 1, 1957, p. 81.

————. "A Playwright Named Tennessee." *The New York Times Magazine,* May 19, 1947, pp. 19 ff.

Lewisohn, Ludwig. *Expression in America.* New York: Harper and Brothers, 1932.

Ley-Piscator, Maria. *The Piscator Experiment: The Political Theatre.* New York: James H. Heineman, 1967.

Lief, Leonard and Light, James F. *The Modern Age.* New York: Holt, Rinehart and Winston, 1969.

Lovejoy, A. O. *The Great Chain of Being.* Cambridge: Harvard University Press, 1942.

Lumley, Frederick. *New Trends in 20th Century Drama: A Survey Since Ibsen and Shaw.* Fourth new edition. New York: Oxford University Press, 1972.

McCarthy, Mary Therese. "A Streetcar Called Success." *Sights and Spectacles.* New York: Farrar, Straus and Cudahy, 1956.

Magid, Marion. "The Innocence of Tennessee Williams." *Commentary* 25 (January 1963), 34–43.

Mann, Otto and Friedmann, Hermann. *Expressionismus.* Heidelberg: Wolfgang Rothe Verlag, 1956.

Mannes, Marya. "The Morbid Magic of Tennessee Williams." *The Reporter* 12 (May 19, 1955), 41–44.

Miller, Jordan Y., ed., *Twentieth Century Interpretations of A Streetcar Named Desire.* Englewood Cliffs: Prentice-Hall, 1971.

Milton, John R. "The Esthetic Fault of Strindberg's 'Dream Plays.'" *Tulane Drama Review* 4 (1960), 108–116.

Myers, Bernard S. *The German Expressionists.* New York: McGraw-Hill, 1957.

Mraz, D. J. "The Changing Image of the Female Characters in the Works of Tennessee Williams." Ph. D. Dissertation, University of Southern California, Los Angeles, 1967.

Nelson, Benjamin. *Tennessee Williams: His Life and Work.* New York: Ivan Obolensky, 1961.

Neumann, Erich. *The Great Mother.* New York: Pantheon Books, 1955.

O'Neill, Eugene. *Nine Plays.* New York: Random House, Modern Library, 1932.

Otto, Rudolf. *The Idea of the Holy.* Second edition. Trans. John W. Harvey. New York: Oxford University Press, Galaxy Books, 1958.

Patrick, Robert. *Kennedy's Children. Plays and Players* 22: 6 (March 1975), 43–49.

Pearce, Richard. *Stages of the Clown.* Carbondale: Southern Illinois University Press, 1970.

Peden, William H. "Broken Apollos and Blasted Dreams." *Saturday Review,* January 8, 1955, pp. 11–12.

———. "Mad Pilgrimage: The Short Stories of Tennessee Williams." *Studies in Short Fiction* 1 (1963), 243–250.

Popkin, Henry. "The Plays of Tennessee Williams." *Tulane Drama Review* 4: 3 (1960), 45–64.

Quirino, Leonard Salvator. "The Darkest Celebrations of Tennessee Williams." Ph. D. Dissertation, Brown University, 1964.

Reck, Tom S. "The Short Stories of Tennessee Williams: Nucleus for His Drama." *Tennessee Studies in Literature* 16 (1971), 141–154.

Reed, Rex. "Tennessee Williams Turns Sixty." *Esquire* 76 (September 1971), 105–108, 216–223.

Rice, Elmer. *The Living Theatre.* New York: Harper and Row, 1959.

Rice, Robert. "A Man Named Tennessee." *New York Post*, April 29, 1958.

Roberts, Vera. *On Stage*. New York: Harper and Row, 1962.

Sachs, Hans. *The Creative Unconscious: Studies in the Psychoanalysis of Art*. Second edition. Trans. Dr. A. A. Roback. Cambridge, Mass.: Sci-Art Publishers, 1951.

Sacksteder, William. "The Three Cats: A Study in Dramatic Structure." *Drama Survey* 5: 252–266.

Sagar, K. M. "What Mr. Williams has Made of D. H. Lawrence." *Twentieth Century* 168 (August 1960), 143–153.

Schorer, Mark. "Technique as Discovery." *The Modern Critical Spectrum*. Ed. Gerald J. and Nancy M. Goldberg. Englewood Cliffs: Prentice-Hall, 1962.

Scott, Nathan A. Jr. *The Broken Center: Studies in the Theological Horizon of Modern Literature*. New Haven: Yale University Press, 1966.

Seward, Barbara. *The Symbolic Rose*. New York: Columbia University Press, 1960.

Sharp, William. "An Unfashionable View of Tennessee Williams." *Tulane Drama Review* 6: 3 (1962), 160–171.

Shroyer, Frederick and Gardemal, Louis. *Types of Drama*. Glenview: Scott, Foresman and Co., 1970.

Skloot, Robert. "Submitting Self to Flame: The Artist's Quest in Tennessee Williams, 1935–1954." *Educational Theatre Journal* 25 (May 1973), 199–206.

Sokel, Walter. Introduction to *An Anthology of German Expressionist Drama*. Ed. Walter Sokel. Garden City: Doubleday, Anchor, 1963.

————. *The Writer in Extremis: Expressionism in Twentieth Century German Literature*. Stanford: Stanford University Press, 1959.

Sprinchorn, Evert. "The Logic of *A Dream Play*." *Modern Drama* 5 (December 1962), 352–365.

Starnes, Leland. "The Grotesque Children of *The Rose Tattoo*." *Modern Drama* 12 (February 1970), 357–369.

States, Bert O. *Irony and Drama*. Ithaca: Cornell University Press, 1971.

Steen, Mike. *A Look at Tennessee Williams*. New York: Hawthorn Books, 1969.

Stein, Roger B. "*Glass Menagerie* Revisited: Catastrophe Without Violence." *Western Humanities Review* 18 (1964), 141–153.

Strindberg, August. *Eight Expressionistic Plays*. Trans. Arvid Paulson. New York: New York University Press, 1965.

Styan, John. *The Dark Comedy*. Cambridge: Cambridge University Press, 1968.

————. *Drama, Stage and Audience*. New York: Cambridge University Press, 1975.

Sypher, Wylie. *Comedy*. Garden City: Doubleday, Anchor, 1956.

Taylor, William E. "Tennessee Williams: Academia on Broadway." *Essays in Modern American Literature*. Ed. Richard E. Langford. Deland, Florida: Stetson University Press, 1963.

Tillich, Paul. *The Courage to Be*. New Haven: Yale University Press, 1952.

Tischler, Nancy. *Tennessee Williams: Rebellious Puritan*. New York: Citadel Press, 1961.

Tynan, Kenneth. *Curtains*. New York: Atheneum, 1961.

Valgemae, Mardi. *Accelerated Grimace: Expressionism in the American Drama of the 1920's*. Carbondale: Southern Illinois University Press, 1972.

Von Dornum, John Howard. "The Major Plays of Tennessee Williams, 1940–1960." Ph. D. Dissertation, University of Southern California, Los Angeles, 1962.

Von Szeliski, John L. "Tennessee Williams and the Tragedy of Sensitivity." *Twentieth Century Interpretations of A Streetcar Named Desire*. Ed. Jordan Y. Miller. Englewood Cliffs: Prentice-Hall, 1971. Reprinted from *Western Humanities Review* 20 (1966), 203–211.

Vowles, Richard B. "Tennessee Williams and Strindberg." *Modern Drama* 1 (December 1958), 166–171.

Weales, Gerald C. *Tennessee Williams*. Minneapolis: University of Minnesota Press, 1965.

Weightman, J. G. "Varieties of Decomposition." *Twentieth Century* 164 (November 1958), 461–463.

Wigman, Mary. *The Language of Dance*. Trans. Walter Sorrell. Middletown, Conn.: Wesleyan University Press, 1968.

Contributors

Jacob H. Adler is head of the department and professor of English at Purdue University, West Lafayette, Indiana.

Philip M. Armato is assistant professor at Northern Illinois University, De Kalb, Illinois.

Beate Hein Bennett is teaching associate at the department of English, University of South Carolina, Columbia, South Carolina.

Gerald M. Berkowitz is assistant professor of English at Northern Illinois University, DeKalb, Illinois.

Normand Berlin is professor of English at the University of Massachusetts, Amherst.

Charles B. Brooks is professor of English at California State University at Long Beach.

Bert Cardullo is dramaturge at Cornell University Theatre, Ithaca, New York.

Leonard Casper is professor of English at Boston College, Boston, Massachusetts.

S. Alan Chesler is assistant professor of English at Northern Illinois University, DeKalb, Illinois.

James Coakley is associate professor of dramatic production at Northwestern University, department of theatre, Evanston, Illinois.

Mary Ann Corrigan is lecturer at Northern Virginia Community College, Annandale, Virginia.

Joseph K. Davis is associate professor of English at the University of Southern Mississippi, Hattiesburg, Mississippi.

Vivienne Dickson is working on an M. L. S. at Louisiana State University, Baton Rouge, Louisiana.

Ren Draya is instructor at the University of Colorado, Boulder, Colorado.

Alan Ehrlich is teaching assistant at the University of New Mexico, Albuquerque, New Mexico.

Glenn Embrey is lecturer in the English department at the University of California, Los Angeles.

Norman J. Fedder is associate professor of theatre and director of the playwright's workshop in the speech department at Kansas State University, Manhattan, Kansas.

William J. Free is associate professor of English at the University of Georgia, Athens, Georgia.

Alvin Goldfarb is an adjunct-lecturer at Hunter College (department of theater) and City College (department of speech), Bronx, New York.

James Hafley is professor of English and American language and literature at St. John's University, Jamaica, New York.

Britton J. Harwood is associate professor of English at Miami University, Oxford, Ohio.

889

Esther M. Jackson is professor of theatre and drama at the University of Wisconsin, Madison.

Robert Emmett Jones is professor of French and humanities at the Massachusetts Institute of Technology, Cambridge, Massachusetts.

Sy Kahn is chairman of the drama department and professor of English and drama at the University of the Pacific, Stockton, California.

Albert E. Kalson is associate professor of English at Purdue University, Lafayette, Indiana.

Philip C. Kolin is assistant professor of English at the University of Southern Mississippi, Hattiesburg, Mississippi.

Victor A. Kramer is associate professor of English at Georgia State University, Atlanta, Georgia.

June Bennett Larsen is lecturer at Queens College of the City University of New York.

John MacNicholas is assistant professor of English at the University of South Carolina, Columbia, South Carolina.

Mary McBride is assistant professor of English at Texas Tech University, Lubbock, Texas.

Jeanne M. McGlinn is at University of Kansas, Lawrence, Kansas.

David C. C. Matthew is a lecturer at City College of the City University of New York.

Charles E. May is associate professor of English at California State University, Long Beach.

Charles Moorman is professor of English and vice president for academic affairs at the University of Southern Mississippi, Hattiesburg, Mississippi.

George Niesen teaches English courses for Hartnell College at Soledad prison.

John Ower is assistant professor of English at the University of South Carolina, Columbia, South Carolina.

Donald Pease is assistant professor at Dartmouth College, Hanover, New Hampshire.

Jerrold A. Phillips is assistant professor of drama at Northeastern University, Boston, Massachusetts.

Peggy W. Prenshaw is Honors Associate Professor of English at the University of Southern Mississippi, Hattiesburg, Mississippi.

Delma Eugene Presley is associate professor of English at Georgia Southern College, Statesboro, Georgia.

Leonard Quirino is professor of English at Western Connecticut State College, Danbury, Connecticut.

Thomas J. Richardson is assistant professor of English at the University of Southern Mississippi, Hattiesburg, Mississippi.

John M. Roderick is assistant professor of English at Rhode Island College, Providence, Rhode Island.

William J. Scheick is associate professor of English at the University of Texas at Austin.

Thomas E. Scheye is associate professor of English at Loyola College, Baltimore, Maryland.

Edward A. Sklepowich is assistant professor of English at the State University of New York at Albany.

Rexford Stamper is associate professor of English at the University of Southern Mississippi, Hattiesburg, Mississippi.

William E. Taylor is chairman of the department and professor of English at Stetson University, Deland, Florida.

Judith J. Thompson is an assistant instructor at the University of Kansas, Lawrence, Kansas.

Nancy M. Tischler is professor of English and humanities at the Capital Campus, Pennsylvania State University, University Park, Pennsylvania.

Diane E. Turner is instructor in English at Frederick Community College, Frederick, Maryland.

Morris Philip Wolf is formerly professor of business communications, University of Houston, and formerly professor of English and speech at Augusta College, university system of Georgia.

Index

Note: Because of the volume and complexity of material, this index is divided as follows: Characters, Symbols, Techniques, Themes, and Works.

CHARACTERS

Alexandra del Lago (Princess Kosmonopolis): *Sweet Bird of Youth*, 22, 24, 46, 497, 553, 746, 792

Alma Winemiller: *Summer and Smoke*, *Eccentricities of a Nightingale*, 13–29 passim, 30 ff., 227, 255, 259, 393, 399, 452, 475, 501, 506, 514, 546, 548, 554

Alvaro: *The Rose Tattoo*, 217–31 passim

Amanda: *The Glass Menagerie*, 198 ff., 259, 341–42, 399, 500, 511, 687–89, 729

Baby Doll, 292–309 passim

Big Daddy: *Cat on a Hot Tin Roof*, 16–29 passim, 337

Big Mama, 504, 518

Blanche: *A Streetcar Named Desire*, 15–29 passim, 30, 41, 49, 77–171 passim, 110 ff., 122 ff., 131 ff., 258, 259, 313, 341–2, 366, 393, 399, 400, 452, 475, 501, 513, 548, 798

Brick: *Cat on a Hot Tin Roof*, 261, 265, 277–91 passim, 312, 341–42, 390, 476, 518

Byron: *Camino Real*, 25, 399, 473 ff., 575

Chance Wayne: *Sweet Bird of Youth*, 22, 390, 746

Chicken: *Kingdom of Earth*, 349–53 passim

Chris (Christopher Flanders): *The Milk Train Doesn't Stop Here Anymore*, 343–48 passim, 567–69 passim, 577–80 passim, 749

Don Quixote: *Camino Real*, 232–76 passim, 397–412, 421 ff., 575

Hannah Jelkes: *The Night of the Iguana*, 18–29 passim, 49 ff., 326–40 passim, 332, 452–55, 483, 506, 522–24

Jim O'Connor: *The Glass Menagerie*,

691–92, 729. *See also* Symbols: gentleman caller

Kilroy: *Camino Real*, 238–51 passim, 252–76 passim, 264, 397–412, 401 ff., 424 ff., 474

Laura: *The Glass Menagerie*, 192–213 passim, 227, 452, 468, 511, 689–90. *See also* "Portrait of a Girl in Glass"

Lot: *Kingdom of Earth*, 349–53 passim. *See also* "The Kingdom of Earth"; techniques: triangles of opposition

Maggie: *Cat on a Hot Tin Roof*, 16–29 passim, 504, 517

Maxine: *The Night of the Iguana*, 333–40 passim, 484, 505, 522–24, 748

Moise: *Moise and the World of Reason*, 15, 428

Myrtle: *Kingdom of Earth*, 349–53 passim, 485, 505. *See also* women; "The Kingdom of Earth"; techniques: triangles of transaction

Nonno: *The Night of the Iguana*, 323, 326–40 passim, 455, 484

Sebastian Venable: *Suddenly Last Summer*, 22–3, 417 ff., 477–81

Serafina: *The Rose Tattoo*, 21–29 passim, 43, 214–31 passim, 503, 694 ff.

Shannon: *The Night of the Iguana*, 21, 326–40 passim, 484, 506

Sissy Goforth: *The Milk Train Doesn't Stop Here Anymore*, 22, 341–48 passim, 485, 497

Stanley Kowalski: *A Streetcar Named Desire*, 77–171 passim, 131 ff., 264

Stone, Mrs. (Karen): *The Roman Spring of Mrs. Stone*, 259, 497

Tom: *The Glass Menagerie*, 192–206 passim, 207–13 passim, 255, 312, 390, 455, 690–91, 729

Vacarro (Vicarro): *Baby Doll* (*The Long Stay Cut Short* and *27 Wagons Full of Cotton*), 21, 292–309 passim

893

Val: *Battle of Angels, Orpheus Descending*, 172–91 passim, 463, 469
Violet Venable, 390, 478, 502–03
Woman Downtown: *The Red Devil Battery Sign*, 364–71 passim

SYMBOLS

Birds, 403–04, 497, 599, 757, 766
Camino, 232–76 passim
Christmas, 314
Colors, 269 ff., 480
Dreamer, 311
Examples of; 427, 681 ff.
Fire, 272
Gentleman caller, 194, 209–13 passim, 305, 306, 311, 312, 392, 467, 587, 588, 590, 647, 686; as messiah, 573. *See also* Jim O'Connor
Heart, 404–12 passim, 480
Ice, 440 ff., 540, 756
Iguana, 318–40 passim, 322, 323, 331, 507, 571, 748
Light, 269 ff.
Mirrors, 438 ff., 756, 768–70
Moon Lake, 187, 704, 829–47 passim
Rose, 43; in *Out Cry*, 359
Stairway, 269, 495
Sunflowers, 356–61 passim
Water, 505. *See also Kingdom of Earth*

TECHNIQUES

Comic, 214–31 passim, 292–309 passim, 310–17 passim, 597, 720–35; slapstick, 419, 720. *See also Camino Real; The Rose Tattoo*
Dramatic, 252–76, 375–96, 795–812, opposition triangles, 737 ff., apposition triangles, 743 ff.
Film, 774–94 passim; influence of *Casablanca*, 782–85; silent film, 409
Language, 753–62, 800–03
Mythology, 679–711. *See also* Themes: Mythology
Poetic, 624, 630. *See also In the Winter of Cities*
Symbolist, 413–28 passim
Symbols: defined, illustrated, 681 ff.

THEMES

Absurd (as concept), 422–59 passim
Aesthetics, 53–72 passim, 283–91 passim, 287, 433 ff., 493; of Symbolists, 413–

28 passim; 598, 601, 830. *See also* Art—artist
Art—artist, 11 ff., 24 ff., 172–91 passim; "angel of death," 354–58 passim, 481 ff.; artist, 355 ff., 463–93; artist and society, 429–59 passim, 463 ff.; artist-priest, 487, 590
Baby, 136, 153
Body-spirit, 30 ff., 388, 473, 516, 594, 613, 620, 763. *See also* Alma; *Summer and Smoke*; Blanche; *Suddenly Last Summer*
Culture and power, 5–29 passim, 30–52 passim
Death, 77–171 passim, 341–48 passim, 414–28 passim, 488, 492, 534, 558–70 passim, 572. *See also* Blanche; *A Streetcar Named Desire*
Decadence—decadent, 51, 308, 413, 512, 526, 609, 612, 613. *See also* Symbolists
Decline—declivity, 581 ff. *See also Camino Real*; Byron; Desire (and destruction); Death
Desire, 77–171, passim, 98–100; sex, 11 ff., 277–91 passim, 510–24 passim, 525–44, 582 ff., 733; sex and power, 37, 46; death, destruction, 126–36 passim, 175–91 passim, 325–40 passim, 547, 617, 619; sex and love, 369, 655; unisexual figure, 545–57; sex and male characters, 549–50; sex and disease, 585 ff.; sex and religion, 591
Expressionism, 27, 375–412 passim
Illusion, 341–48 passim, 510–24
Infernalism, 430 ff.
Light, 100 ff., 756, 766. *See also* Symbols—light
Love, 339, 353, 369, 546, 552; and sex 510–24 passim, 756. *See also* Desire
Mendacity, 277–91 passim
Mythology: use of, 172–91 passim; Orpheus, 195 ff.; rebirth, 237–51 passim; mythmaking, 444–59; Jungian, 494 ff.
New Orleans: as setting, 631–46, 653
Quest: theme of, 172–91 passim
Religion, theology, God, 63–69 passim, 175, 327–40 passim, 350–53, 418, 571–80 passim, 581–606 passim, 582 ff., 597, 674
Sex. *See* Desire
Symbolists, 413–28 passim
Time, 5–29 passim, 193–207 passim, 229 ff., 232–36 passim, 237 ff., 240, 430–59 passim